# CASES AND MATERIALS ON
# EMPLOYMENT DISCRIMINATION

# CASES AND MATERIALS ON EMPLOYMENT DISCRIMINATION

## Sixth Edition

**MICHAEL J. ZIMMER**
**Professor of Law**
**Seton Hall University**

**CHARLES A. SULLIVAN**
**Professor of Law**
**Seton Hall University**

**REBECCA HANNER WHITE**
**J. Alton Hosch Professor of Law**
**University of Georgia**

1185 Avenue of the Americas, New York, NY 10036
www.aspenpublishers.com

Permissions
Aspen Publishers
1185 Avenue of the Americas
New York, NY 10036

Printed in the United States of America.

1  2  3  4  5  6  7  8  9  0

ISBN 0-7355-3648-1

**Library of Congress Cataloging-in-Publication Data**

Cases and materials on employment discrimination /
Michael J. Zimmer . . . [et al.]. — 6th ed.
     p.       cm.
  Includes bibliographical references.
  ISBN 0-7355-3648-1
  1. Discrimination in employment — Law and legislation — United States — Cases. I.
Zimmer, Michael J., 1942-

KF3464.A7Z55 2003
344.7301'133 — dc21

2002043950

# About Aspen Publishers

Aspen Publishers, headquartered in New York City, is a leading information provider for attorneys, business professionals, and law students. Written by preeminent authorities, our products consist of analytical and practical information covering both U.S. and international topics. We publish in the full range of formats, including updated manuals, books, periodicals, CDs, and online products.

Our proprietary content is complemented by 2,500 legal databases, containing over 11 million documents, available through our Loislaw division. Aspen Publishers also offers a wide range of topical legal and business databases linked to Loislaw's primary material. Our mission is to provide accurate, timely, and authoritative content in easily accessible formats, supported by unmatched customer care.

To order any Aspen Publishers title, go to *www.aspenpublishers.com* or call 1-800-638-8437.

To reinstate your manual update service, call 1-800-638-8437.

For more information on Loislaw products, go to *www.loislaw.com* or call 1-800-364-2512.

For Customer Care issues, e-mail CustomerCare@aspenpublishers.com; call 1-800-234-1660; or fax 1-800-901-9075.

**Aspen Publishers**
**A Wolters Kluwer Company**

To Margaret, Michael, and Lanier
M.J.Z.

To Leila, Meghan, Moira, the Marks,
and especially Jessica Leigh
C.A.S.

To Dan, Brendan, and Maren
R.H.W.

# SUMMARY OF CONTENTS

# CONTENTS

## Chapter 2

## PART II

## THE CONCEPT OF DISCRIMINATION UNDER TITLE VII, THE AGE DISCRIMINATION IN EMPLOYMENT ACT, AND SECTION 1981

## Chapter 3

# Chapter 4

## Systemic Disparate Treatment Discrimination                    199

# Chapter 5

# Chapter 6

## Chapter 7

## Special Problems in Applying Title VII, Section 1981, and the ADEA          461

# PART III

## ALTERNATIVE APPROACHES TO DISCRIMINATION          673

## Chapter 8

### Disability Discrimination          675

# PART IV

## PROCEDURES AND REMEDIES                                    831

### Chapter 9

### Chapter 10

# PREFACE

For the authors, this Sixth Edition marks a bittersweet moment. Our heartfelt gratitude goes out to departing authors Richard F. Richards and Deborah A. Calloway. Dick was one of the original authors, and his mark continues to reverberate throughout this work. He is the master of remedies, blazed the trail when the ADA was first passed, and tried (often unsuccessfully) to control his co-authors' idiosyncracies. Deborah joined the team for the Third, Fourth and Fifth Editions. She brought new energy and insights that still profoundly influence core portions of this effort. We give both our heartfelt thanks. Joining this casebook for the first time with the Sixth Edition is Rebecca Hanner White, our collaborator on EMPLOYMENT DISCRIMINATION LAW & PRACTICE (Aspen 2002), in many ways a companion volume to this work. Rebecca brings a wide-ranging scholarly vision to this effort, a vision which is manifested throughout this Edition.

Since the Fifth Edition, we have also established a website to support the teaching mission of the casebook. Our aim, which has been achieved within normal limits of scholarly procrastination, is to reflect recent developments no more than a month after they occur. We do not attempt to track every judicial, legislative, or administrative change since there are services that do that far better than we can. Rather, our goal is to identify the more important developments and key them to the casebook while providing a resource that faculty and student can both use in a variety of ways. The page, for example, tried to keep track of faculty websites, reproduce professors' past examinations, suggest teaching ideas and provide links to a variety of other resources. Please visit the website at **http://law.shu.edu/discrimination/**. The site contains a "contact" button, but we can also be reached at:

Michael J. Zimmer: zimmermi@shu.edu

Charles A. Sullivan: sullivch@shu.edu

Rebecca Hanner White: rhwhite@arches.uga.edu

The Sixth Edition continues our effort to integrate continuing changes in the field, ranging from dramatic developments in the disability area to less heralded, but perhaps equally important, changes in the procedural landscape, especially with respect to the increasing role of arbitration in resolving discrimination disputes. As with the Fifth Edition, we have made a conscious effort to keep the size of this book manageable. We have, however, provided substantial space to the ramifications of important decisions like *Reeves v. Sanderson Plumbing Products* and *Boy Scouts of America v.*

*Dale.* Once again, judicial resculpting of the Americans with Disabilities Act landscape has led us to rewrite the ADA chapter.

The basic structure remains identical to the Fifth Edition. We begin with two short chapters aimed at enhancing students' appreciation of the complexities of the subjects they will explore. Thus, in order to provide students with the context in which employment discrimination law operates, Chapter 1 introduces other kinds of legal regulation of the employment relationship. Chapter 2 then offers professors an opportunity to explore, in a nondogmatic and nondoctrinal way, the theoretic bases for prohibiting discrimination in employment. It uses a "Devil's Advocate" approach, focusing on extracts from Richard A. Epstein's frontal assault on the wisdom of antidiscrimination legislation in Forbidden Grounds: The Case Against Employment Discrimination Laws (1992). This chapter reflects a host of counterattacks that Epstein's work has triggered, reaffirming and clarifying the values of our discipline. Some teachers may prefer to delay assigning this chapter until the end of the semester or at least reconsider it in light of what the students have learned during the rest of the course.

We have retained the core of the prior editions' chapters, treating each of the three basic theories of discrimination — individual disparate treatment, systemic disparate treatment, and disparate impact (Chapters 3, 4, 5), followed by a chapter on the interrelation of those theories (Chapter 6) and one on "special problems" (Chapter 7). In these chapters, this edition continues the prior editions' merger of the treatment of the Age Discrimination in Employment Act and the Reconstruction Civil Rights Acts, primarily 42 U.S.C.S. § 1981 (2003), into the Title VII discussion. Pedagogically, the casebook now reflects the increasing statutory and common law unification of discrimination analysis under all three statutes. Remaining differences are noted in the relevant chapters or collected in Chapter 7 on "special problems."

However, those who used the Fifth Edition will find changes in these core chapters. Perhaps most obvious is our efforts to both capture and assess the implications of *Reeves v. Sanderson Plumbing Products* on the *McDonnell Douglas-Hicks* structure. Prior users will find the ADA treatment dramatically different since Chapter 8 has been reconceptualized to reflect the dramatic developments in the area, not only with the rash of Supreme Court decisions over the last three years but also a large number of influential circuit court cases.

Some professors who use this book have asked about coverage. No two of the authors take the same approach, and some of us vary depending on the semester. We all teach three credit courses. While none of us tries to cover the entire book, all teach the four chapters that make up its core — Chapters 3 through 6. We also all teach most of "Special Problems" and believe that the Gender and Retaliation materials are essential to a comprehensive course in Employment Discrimination. Most of us also teach the rest of Chapter 7. We have all come increasingly to believe that Chapter 8, the ADA, must be taught, although some of us omit more esoteric material in that chapter.

The choice of the remaining material is a matter of individual instructor preference. Chapter 1 is, obviously, dispensable, since it provides background information, but it can easily be treated as assigned reading without class discussion. Chapter 2 could be taught at the beginning or the end of the course, or simply omitted on the theory that the themes there will emerge (if in a less structured fashion) from the course in any event. We have individual preferences as to Chapter 9, Procedures, and Chapter 10, Remedies, and at different times, teach one or the other.

A final word about our editing of excerpted material is appropriate. All omissions are indicated by ellipses or brackets, except that footnotes, internal cross-references, parallel citations, and repetitive citations are deleted with no indication. Footnotes in extract retain their original numbers, while those added by us are indicated by asterisks and daggers.

*Michael J. Zimmer*
*Charles A. Sullivan*
*Rebecca Hanner White*

March 2003

# ACKNOWLEDGMENTS

We would like to acknowledge the insights of the many teachers who have used the earlier editions of this work and have shared their thoughts with us. As indicated in the Preface, our former co-authors, Dick Richards and Deborah Calloway, have left their imprint on this Sixth Edition. Our colleagues have also provided useful insights. We thank especially Jake Barnes and Calvin Sharpe for reviewing portions of this book in order to steer us closer to the correct path. The hard questions of our students have also guided us in keeping this work accessible even as the field of employment discrimination becomes increasingly complex and sophisticated. At Aspen (formerly Little, Brown), Carol McGeehan (who copyedited the First Edition) has gently nudged us through subsequent editions in her present position as Associate Publisher, and Elsie Starbecker has kept pace with our constant updates during the production process.

Our research assistants have kept us honest and this book accurate, not to mention making the professors' lives easier in innumerable other ways. At Seton Hall Law, we thank:

- Stefania DiTrolio, Sonia Middlebrooks, Mara Timourian, Dawn Woodruff, and Megan Jordan, Class of 2004;
- Jenny Kramer and Amanda Dowd, Class of 2001;
- Jonathan Green, Richard Kielbania, Chantal Kopp, and Shannon Philpott, Class of 2000;
- Tara Schillari, Class of 1999;
- Kim Essaf, Jessica Lerner, Michael MacManus, Jason Marx, and Colleen Walsh, Class of 1998;
- Victoria Melillo, Class of 1997;
- Jessica Stein and Thomas Crino, Class of 1996;
- Dena Epstein, Wendy Whitbeck, Claudine Leone, and Thomas Sarno, Class of 1995;
- Susan Farrell, Class of 1989;
- Rosanne Maraziti, Linda Biancardi, Nancy Johnson, and Julie Murray, Class of 1988;
- Laurie Fierro and Lorrie Van de Castle, Class of 1983.

To these must be added the dedication the support staff at Seton Hall has provided, especially Jo Ann Hipolito, Gwen Davis, and Silvia Cardoso. Finally, we thank Moira Sullivan for dedicated proofreading.

At the University of Georgia, we thank Laura Wheaton, Class of 2002, and Coby Nixon and Rebecca Wasserman, Class of 2003, for excellent and timely research assistance.

We gratefully acknowledge the permissions granted to reproduce the following materials:

Mary E. Becker, The Law and Economics of Racial Discrimination in Employment Needed in the Nineties: Improved Individual and Structural Remedies for Racial and Sexual Disadvantages in Employment, 79 Geo. L.J. 1659 (1991). Reprinted with the permission of the publisher, copyright © 1991, The Georgetown Law Journal Association and Georgetown University.

Deborah A. Calloway, *St. Mary's Honor Center v. Hicks:* Questioning the Basic Assumption, 26 Conn. L. Rev. 997 (1995). Copyright © 1995 by the University of Connecticut Law Review. Reprinted by permission.

Walter B. Connolly, Jr., David W. Peterson, and Michael J. Connolly, Use of Statistics in Equal Employment Opportunity Litigation § 10.05 (1985). Reprinted with permission. Published and copyright by Law Journal Seminars-Press, 111 Eighth Avenue, New York, New York 10011. All rights reserved.

Richard Delgado, Words That Wound: A Tort Action for Racial Insults, Epithets, and Name Calling, 17 Harvard C.R.-C.L. L. Rev. 133, 136-140 (1982). Permission granted by the Harvard Civil Rights-Civil Liberties Law Review. Copyright © 1982 by the President and Fellows of Harvard College.

John J. Donohue III, Advocacy Versus Analysis in Assessing Employment Discrimination Law, 44 Stan. L. Rev. 1583 (1992). Copyright © 1992 by the Board of Trustees of the Leland Stanford Junior University. Reprinted by permission of Stanford Law Review and Fred B. Rothman and Company.

Nancy E. Dowd, Liberty v. Equality: In Defense of Privileged White Males, 34 Wm. & Mary L. Rev. 429 (1993). Copyright © 1993 by William & Mary Law Review. Reprinted with permission.

Richard A. Epstein, Forbidden Grounds: The Case Against Employment Discrimination Laws 20-77 (1992). Reprinted by permission of the publishers from Forbidden Grounds: The Case Against Employment Discrimination Laws by Richard A. Epstein, Cambridge Mass.: Harvard University Press. Copyright © 1992 by the President and Fellows of Harvard College.

Owen Fiss, A Theory of Fair Employment Laws, 38 U. Chi. L. Rev. 235, 237-240 (1971). Copyright © 1971 by the University of Chicago: 38 U. Chi. L. Rev. 235, 237-240 (1971).

Alan D. Freeman, Antidiscrimination Law: The View from 1989, in The Politics of Law: A Progressive Critique 121 (David Kairys ed., rev. ed. 1990). Copyright © 1990 by Alan D. Freeman. Reprinted by permission of Pantheon Books, a division of Random House, Inc.

Michael C. Harper, Age-Based Exit Incentives, Coercion, and the Prospective Waiver of ADEA Rights: The Failure of the Older Workers Benefit Protection Act, 79 Va. L. Rev. 1271 (1993). Copyright © 1993. Reprinted with permission of Virginia Law Review Association and Fred B. Rothman and Company.

Samuel Issacharoff, Contractual Liberties in Discriminatory Markets, 70 Tex. L. Rev. 1219 (1992). Published originally in 70 Texas Law Review 1219, 1225, 1241 (1992). Copyright © 1992 by the Texas Law Review Association. Reprinted by permission.

Doreen Kimura, Sex Differences in the Brain, Scientific American, September 1992, pp. 119 to 125. From Sex Differences in the Brain, Doreen Kimura. Copyright © 1992 by Scientific American, Inc. All rights reserved.

Charles R. Lawrence III, The Id, the Ego, and Equal Protection: Reckoning with Unconscious Racism, 39 Stan. L. Rev. 317, 321-323 (1987). Copyright © 1987 by the

Board of Trustees of Leland Stanford Junior University. Reprinted by permission of Stanford Law Review and Fred B. Rothman and Company.

Douglas A. Laycock, Statistical Proof and Theories of Discrimination, 49 Law & Contemp. Probs. 97, 98-99 (Autumn 1986). Copyright © 1986, Duke University School of Law.

Deborah C. Malamud, The Last Minuet: Disparate Treatment After *Hicks*, 93 Mich. L. Rev. 2229 (1995). Copyright © 1995 by the University of Michigan Law Review. Reprinted by permission.

Note, The Civil Rights Act of 1991: The Business Necessity Standard, 106 Harv. L. Rev. 896 (1993). Copyright © 1993 by the Harvard Law Review Association.

David Benjamin Oppenheimer, Understanding Affirmative Action, 23 Hastings Const. L.Q. 921, 965-968 (1996). Copyright © 1996 by Hastings College of the Law. Reprinted by permission.

Richard Posner, Economic Analysis of Law § 27.1 (2d ed. 1977). Reprinted by permission.

George Rutherglen, Abolition in a Different Voice, 78 Va. L. Rev. 1463, 1469 (1992). Copyright © 1992. Reprinted by permission of Virginia Law Review Association and Fred B. Rothman and Company.

George Schatzki, *United Steelworkers of America v. Weber*: An Exercise in Understandable Indecision, 56 Wash. L. Rev. 51, 56-57 (1980). Reprinted by permission of the author and the Washington Law Review Association.

Elaine Shoben, Differential Pass-Fail Rates in Employment Testing, 91 Harv. L. Rev. 793 (1978). Copyright © 1978 by the Harvard Law Review Association. Reprinted by permission.

Nadine Taub, Keeping Women in Their Place: Stereotyping Per Se as a Form of Discrimination, 21 B.C. L. Rev. 345, 353-354 (1980). Reprinted with permission of the copyright owner, Boston College Law School.

L. Thurow, The Zero Sum Society: Distribution and Possibilities for Economic Change 184-187 (1980). Copyright © 1980 by Basic Books, Inc. Reprinted by permission of Basic Books, a division of Harper Collins Publishers, Inc.

Margery Austin Turner, Michael Fix & Raymond J. Struyk, Opportunities Denied, Opportunities Diminished: Discrimination in Hiring 11-12 (1991). Copyright © 1991. Reprinted by permission.

J. Hoult Verkerke, Free to Search, 105 Harv. L. Rev. 2080 (1992). Copyright © 1992 by the Harvard Law Review Association.

Judith Vladeck and Margaret Young (Moses), Sex Discrimination in Higher Education: It's Not Academic, 4 Women's Rights L. Rep. 59, 74-75 (1978). Reprinted by permission.

Patricia J. Williams, The Alchemy of Race and Rights 44-49 (1991). Reprinted by permission of the publishers from The Alchemy of Race and Rights by Patricia J. Williams, Cambridge, Mass.: Harvard University Press. Copyright © 1991 by the President and Fellows of Harvard College.

# CASES AND MATERIALS ON
# EMPLOYMENT DISCRIMINATION

# PART I

---

## THE EMPLOYMENT RELATION AND THE PROBLEM OF DISCRIMINATION

# Chapter 1

# Legal Approaches to the
# Employment Relation

## A.  HISTORY

This book is devoted to employment discrimination, one of the most important areas of legal regulation of the rights and responsibilities of employers and employees. This course is concerned with the question of "discrimination" in employment and is, therefore, limited to legal doctrines that fall within the definition of that term. Indeed, much of this book is devoted to the twin questions of how "discrimination" should be defined and how it is proven in the litigation context. As you will see, employment discrimination, on both the social and the legal levels, is a complex and controversial problem, affecting the rights of millions of workers.

But however important the topic of employment discrimination, it is only a subset of the more general problem of legal regulation of the employment relationship. As you will learn, the term "employment discrimination" is usually limited to discrimination against employees on the basis of statutorily defined characteristics. These characteristics may be immutable — such as race, gender, age, or national origin — or subject to change — such as religion, alienage, or marital status— or of either kind — such as disability discrimination, which includes mental and physical disabilities without regard to their causes.

While these categories are the traditional domain of the law of employment discrimination, employers routinely "discriminate" (perhaps we should use the word "differentiate") among employees or applicants in ways that have nothing to do with race, gender, age, or any of the other reasons prohibited by discrimination statutes. Further, employers may base their actions on rational reasons (hiring the best-qualified applicant); questionable reasons (promoting the daughter of an important customer over a better worker who lacks such "connections"); reasons that are eccentric but not necessarily legally wrong (choosing employees on the basis of astrological sign); or socially and morally unacceptable reasons (firing a "whistleblower" whose conduct had saved human lives).

The ultimate question, of course, is what, if any, limitations the law should place on the employer's power to deal with employees. This topic is typically taken up more comprehensively in courses on employment law or individual employee rights. See generally, Mark A. Rothstein, Charles B. Craver, Elinor P. Schroeder & Elaine W. Shoben, Employment Law (2d ed. 1999). While employment discrimination is itself a distinct area of study, the student of employment discrimination should have some sense of the law's treatment of other aspects of the employment relation for at least two reasons. First, practitioners of employment law have traditionally specialized in one of the many varieties of employment regulation. But overspecialization is not always in the best interest of the employment lawyer's client. For example, an attorney who focuses only on discrimination may ignore more easily established contract, tort, or labor law claims implicated by a particular discharge. Second, an introduction to other forms of regulation of the employment relation is helpful in understanding the policy implications of regulating employment through the application of the antidiscrimination laws. Accordingly, this chapter provides a broad overview of the field.

Inherent in the question of what limitations the law should place on an employer's ability to deal with its employees is an underlying assumption: employers have power over their employees that may be abused in ways requiring legal control. While perhaps most would agree that this is an accurate description of reality, it is fair to say that the law historically did not recognize that reality.

Any discussion of the legal history of the employment relationship risks getting mired in addressing definitional problems as well as in deciding where to start. For example, if we begin with the feudal system, it might be fair to describe the entire structure as a complex legal regulation of the employment relationship, with the workers (serfs) at the bottom of the ladder. As Western society emerged from feudalism, English law evolved legal institutions reminiscent of the prior system. The Statute of Laborers [1350], 25 Edw. III, st. 1, was enacted to restrict "employee" mobility after the Black Death had decimated the population of England and, therefore, had increased the demand for workers. Under the apprentice system, the father of the apprentice negotiated training in a craft for his son in return for long-term service. Finally, indentured servants worked for long terms in return for room, board, training in a craft, and, in the United States, transportation from Europe.

Both apprenticeship and indentured servitude were transplanted to the colonies. And, overshadowing much of our history, another legal system emerged regulating a large segment of the working force in this country — slavery. To a great extent, the law of employment discrimination deals with the consequences of that system and its abolition. Similarly, the historical treatment of women as inferior legal beings and the end of that unequal treatment provide the backdrop for much of what is discussed in employment discrimination courses.

After the abolition of slavery as a legal institution, the law purported to treat the employment relation as it treated other business relationships. By the last quarter of the nineteenth century, before the emergence of pervasive social legislation, the law's twin pillars were contract law and tort law. From a contract perspective, the law in theory approached employment as it would any other business relationship. "Freedom of contract" was the governing principle, which meant that courts claimed to limit their role to ascertaining and enforcing the agreement of the parties. In employment, as in other areas of contract law, policing the fairness of bargains was the exception, rather than the rule. Contract law purported to implement this approach to employment by adopting a general rule that prevailed in the United States for nearly a century: absent an express written contract for a term of years, the relationship between an employer and its employees was "at will." One court explained the rule and its rationale:

> Generally speaking, a contract for permanent employment, for life employment, or for other terms purporting permanent employment, where the employee furnishes no consideration additional to the services incident to the employment, amounts to an indefinite general hiring terminable at the will of either party, and a discharge without cause does not constitute a breach of such contract justifying recovery of damages. The same is true where the contract of hiring specifies no term of duration but fixes compensation at a certain amount per day, week, or month. Although not absolute, the above stated rule appears to be in the nature of a strong presumption in favor of a contract terminable at will unless the terms of the contract or other circumstances clearly manifest the parties' intent to bind each other. The presumption is grounded on a policy that it would otherwise be unreasonable for a man to bind himself permanently to a position, thus eliminating the possibility of later improving that position.

Forrer v. Sears, Roebuck & Co., 153 N.W.2d 587, 589 (Wis. 1967). The employment at-will rule is neutral in the sense that either party can terminate the relationship without liability to the other. Indeed, *Forrer* justified the rule as enabling *employees* to improve their positions. Nevertheless, the at-will doctrine in practice meant that the employer could discharge an employee for good reason, bad reason, or no reason at all.

From a tort viewpoint, the employment relation was more complicated. One question was whether an employer was liable for the torts committed by its employees (or, as it would have more typically been phrased, whether a master was liable for the torts of his servants). The answer to this question at common law was found in the law of agency and depended on whether the tortfeasor was a servant (or employee) as opposed to an "independent contractor." If the principal had sufficient "control" over the work of the agent, it was liable for the agent's torts. The principal was then called a master or an employer, and the agent became a servant or an employee. If the degree of control was insufficient, the agent was labelled an "independent contractor," and the principal was not liable for his torts. This regime, which evolved mainly to determine the rights of parties outside the employment relation, came to have implications for the rights of workers against their employers. As we will see, much social legislation is directed at "employment," thus placing other kinds of business relationships beyond its purview. For example, a plaintiff will be outside the protection of employment discrimination statutes if the court views her as an independent contractor.

Even before such legislation, a central tort question in the nineteenth century was the liability of the employer for injuries the employee sustained. Theoretically, tort law treated the parties to the employment relation as it would anyone else: it was as much an assault for a master to strike a servant as for a servant to strike a master. But, even in the area of intentional torts, some rules tended to favor employers. For example, an employer was "privileged" to treat an employee in ways that he might not have been allowed to treat third parties. This included a qualified privilege to defame an employee, as when the employer provided a job reference to another employer.

More important, the common law developed doctrines, including the fellow servant rule, assumption of risk, and contributory negligence, the confluence of which strongly tended to immunize employers from tort suits by their workers. Contributory negligence prevented employees from suing if they were responsible for their own harm to any degree at all, regardless of the employer's negligence. Similarly, the assumption of risk doctrine amounted to waiver of an employee's right to sue for an employer's negligence. Finally, the fellow servant rule created an exception to the normal principle of respondeat superior, barring suit against the employer when the harm was caused by the negligence of a co-worker.

Contract and tort law approaches often combined to leave employees at the mercy of their employers. While some exceptionally valuable employees were able to negotiate contractual protections for themselves, most workers were economically fungible; that is, they lacked the bargaining power to obtain more than the very narrow rights accorded by the law. To a large extent, the history of the law governing the employment relation over the last century has consisted of the efforts of Congress, state legislatures, administrative agencies, and the courts to address perceived evils resulting from the economic dominance of employers vis-à-vis employees and the failure of the common law to limit employer misuse of this power. Those efforts have resulted in a variety of approaches to regulation of the employment relation.

## 1. Employee Safety

By the end of the nineteenth century, tort law theoretically applied to workplace injuries, but, in fact, employees seeking compensation for negligence were often frustrated by the three doctrines just mentioned: contributory negligence, assumption of risk, and the fellow servant rule. Rather than abolishing these restrictive doctrines, populist reformers advanced workers' compensation laws as a major reform. The system, which won universal acceptance, was a compromise between full compensation for employees and the extant hit-or-miss cause of action for negligence. See generally Arthur Larson, Larson's Workers' Compensation Law (1997); Price Fishback & Shawn Everett Kantor, The Adoption of Worker's Compensation in the United States, 1900-30, 41 J.L. & Econ. 305 (1998).

Workers' compensation laws replaced the common law tort of negligence with an administrative system of strict liability for work-related injuries and diseases providing more certain recovery but restricting the amount of compensation. Thus, workers' compensation provides substantially lower recoveries as compared to those for prevailing plaintiffs in tort suits for comparable injuries. While medical expenses are completely covered, lost wages are not. It has been estimated that employees recover between one-half and two-thirds of lost wages. Theodore F. Haas, On Reintegrating Workers' Compensation and Employers' Liability, 21 Ga. L. Rev. 843, 847 n.20 (1987). Workers' compensation also excludes pain and suffering damages.

The trade-off of lower amounts for more certain recovery requires that workers' compensation be the exclusive remedy against the employer for physical injuries to employees in accidents arising out of their employment. With the emergence of compensation statutes, the use of tort law to redress employee injuries went into eclipse for compensable injuries. Ironically, employees originally preferred to be within workers' compensation regimes because of the hostility of the tort system, but, a century later, employees often seek higher damages by claiming that their injuries are not covered by workers' compensation, while employers now frequently seek to defeat tort suits by arguing workers' compensation exclusivity. See generally Ruth C. Vance, Workers' Compensation and Sexual Harassment in the Workplace: A Remedy for Employees, Or a Shield for Employers?, 11 Hofstra Lab. L.J. 141 (1993); Jean Love, Actions for Nonphysical Harm: The Relationship Between the Tort System and No-Fault Compensation (With an Emphasis on Workers' Compensation), 73 Cal. L. Rev. 857 (1985).

Employers face substantial costs under workers' compensation, either directly as self-insurers or more commonly in terms of their compensation insurance premiums, which will reflect, at least to some extent, a company's claim history. The annual total cost of the system for employers rose from $1 billion in 1950 to $35 billion in 1986. 1 American Law Institute, Enterprise Liability and Personal Injury 106 (1991). It has continued to increase to the point where there is talk of a compensation crisis. See generally Martha T. McCluskey, Insurer Moral Hazard in the Worker's Compensation Crisis: Reforming Cost Inflation, Not Rate Supression, 5 Emp. Rts. & Employ. Pol'y J. 55 (2001); Martha T. McCluskey, The Illusion of Efficiency in Workers' Compensation "Reform," 50 Rutgers L. Rev. 657 (1998).

Such costs can create real incentives to reduce safety hazards. See Michael J. Moore & W. Kip Viscusi, Compensation Mechanisms for Job Risks: Wages, Workers' Compensation, and Product Liability 151-178 (1990). However, limitations on employer liability reduce the incentives to eliminate workplace hazards below the point a tort system would set and perhaps below what is acceptable from a societal perspective. Haas, supra at 849-50; see generally Emily A. Spieler, Perpetuating Risk? Workers' Compensation and the Persistence of Occupational Injuries, 31 Hous. L. Rev. 119 (1994). The most direct attack on the problem of workplace safety came in 1970 when Congress enacted the federal Occupational Safety and Health Act (OSHA), 29 U.S.C.S. §§ 651 et seq. (2003), which, together with its state counterparts, sought to prevent, instead of merely compensate, workplace injuries. See generally Mark Rothstein, Occupational Safety and Health Law (4th ed. 1998). The effectiveness of OSHA is, however, questionable. E.g., David Barstow & Lowell Bergman, At a Texas Foundry, an Indifference to Life, N.Y. Times, Jan. 8, 2003, at 1A. See generally James A. Gross, The Broken Promises of the National Labor Relations Act and the Occupational Safety and Health Act: Conflicting Values and Conceptions of Rights and Justice, 73 Chi.-Kent L. Rev. 351 (1998); Office of Technology Assessment, Preventing Illness and Injury in the Workplace (1985); Sidney A. Shapiro & Thomas O. McGarity, Reorienting OSHA: Regulatory Alternatives and Legislative Reform, 6 Yale J. on Reg. 1 (1989); W. Kip Viscusi, The Structure and Enforcement of Job Safety Regulation, 49 J.L. & Contemp. Probs. 127 (1986).

## 2. Unionization

The origins of the union movement reach back well before the nineteenth century. However, as the industrialization of the United States picked up momentum after the Civil War, the union movement became increasingly important. The law was at first hostile to unions. Union leaders were the target of conspiracy prosecutions as early as the eighteenth century. Ironically, the passage of the Sherman Antitrust Act, 15 U.S.C.S. §§ 1 et seq. (2003), in 1890, which was designed to limit abuses of economic power by business entities, triggered a renewal of antiunion attacks. See Edward Berman, Labor and Sherman Act (1969).

In the twentieth century, however, unionism became increasingly respectable, especially because the union movement was viewed as preferable to the more radical socialist and communist movements, which also appealed to workers who felt abused by their employers. During the Depression, the federal government adopted what is now known as the National Labor Relations Act (NLRA), 29 U.S.C.S. §§ 151 et seq. (2003). That statute encourages unions by declaring it an unfair labor practice for employers to discriminate against workers seeking to unionize and by requiring the employer to bargain with unions that succeed in organizing that employer's work-force. The NLRA also protects workers who engage in "concerted activity for the purpose of mutual aid or protection." The statute established the National Labor Re-lations Board (NLRB) to enforce its dictates. See generally Patrick Hardin ed., The Developing Labor Law: The Board, the Courts, and the National Labor Relations Act (4th ed. 2002); Florian Bartosic & Roger C. Hartley, Labor Relations Law in the Private Sector (2d ed. 1986). Theoretically, unions prevent employers' abuse of their economic power over their workers by creating a source of countervailing power — the collective strength of labor. To reduce economic warfare between the two sides, with its concomitant economic and social costs, employers are required to bargain in good faith with recognized labor organizations.

Where this process is a success, a collective bargaining agreement emerges, which not only specifies wages and hours but also typically regulates many other terms and conditions of employment. In addition to elevating wages and improving working conditions, such agreements provide millions of American workers with two kinds of job security. First, they specify the method of dismissing workers in the event of a de-cline in business. Usually, such layoffs are by seniority: last in, first out. Recall rights also turn on seniority. Second, when an employer wishes to discipline or discharge an individual employee, the collective bargaining agreement typically permits such ac-tion only when the employer has "just cause." To ensure that discipline is based on just cause, the collective bargaining agreement normally includes a grievance proced-ure that culminates in binding arbitration, thus subjecting an employer's discharge of a worker to review by an outside decision-maker.

This legal regime, however, scarcely proved a panacea. While many unions suc-ceeded in raising wages, improving working conditions, and providing increased job security for those they represented, large segments of the American workforce re-mained unorganized. By the beginning of the 1990s, the proportion of the organized workforce had shrunk to less than that when the NLRA was passed, reaching about 12 percent of the private workforce. Robert J. Lalonde & Bernard D. Meltzer, Hard Times for Unions: Another Look at the Significance of Employer Illegalities, 58 U. Chi. L. Rev. 953, 953 n.1 (1991). There is considerable debate about whether this de-cline is attributable to employer resistance, economic realities (including increased foreign competition caused by globalization), or deficiencies within the legal struc-ture. See generally Paul Weiler, Governing the Workplace: The Future of Labor and Employment Law (1990). Further, there are recurrent criticisms that even the suc-cesses of unions come at the expense of other, unorganized workers. In addition, it is sometimes charged that unions and employers have joined in an unholy alliance to benefit each other unreasonably at the expense of consumers by using collective bar-gaining agreements to suppress competition.

A recurrent problem has been maintaining a fair balance of power between man-agement and labor in their conflicts. For example, two of labor's most effective techniques — the slowdown and the secondary boycott — were declared invalid in Elk Lumber Co., 91 N.L.R.B. 333 (1950), and the 1947 Taft-Hartley amendments to the NLRA. On the other side, management's use of tactics such as the lockout and multiemployer bargaining has been questioned. Over the years, the legal system has frequently tinkered with the balance of power between the two sides, often leaving neither satisfied.

Finally, creating labor organizations as countervailing power centers has generated its own problems of misuse of power vis-à-vis union members. For example, the courts created the duty of fair representation to ensure a union's responsiveness to the workers it represents. E.g., Electrical Workers IBEW v. Foust, 442 U.S. 42 (1979); Steele v. Louisville & Nashville R.R. Co., 323 U.S. 192 (1944). See generally Michael Harper & Ira C. Lupu, Fair Representation as Equal Protection, 98 Harv. L. Rev. 1211 (1985); Mayer Freed, Daniel D. Polsby & Matthew L. Spitzer, Unions, Fairness and the Conundrums of Collective Choice, 56 S. Cal. L. Rev. 461 (1983).

## 3.   *Direct Control of Wages and Other Compensation*

Even before the adoption of a federal labor policy favoring collective bargaining, there were attempts to directly regulate perceived abuses by employers. Some of the earliest efforts were state laws restricting child labor. Although a number of jurisdictions also passed statutes controlling the hours of employment of adults, the most far-reaching were frequently struck down by the Supreme Court in the days of substantive due process. E.g., Lochner v. New York, 198 U.S. 45 (1905). One major exception occurred with respect to women. The famous Brandeis Brief provided the Supreme Court in Muller v. Oregon, 208 U.S. 412 (1908), with a basis for upholding legislation protecting women while similar statutes applied to men were being struck down.

With the demise of substantive due process, e.g., Opp Cotton Mills v. Administrator of Wage & Hour Div., 312 U.S. 126 (1941); West Coast Hotel Co. v. Parrish, 300 U.S. 379 (1937), statutes directly controlling hours worked and wages paid became the norm in the United States. At the federal level, the Fair Labor Standards Act (FLSA), 29 U.S.C.S. §§ 201 et seq. (2003), is the primary mechanism for dealing with perceived abuses. But, like the union movement, this approach has its critics. Some claim that establishing a minimum wage above that which would be set by the market results in artificially reducing the demand for labor; accordingly, those fortunate enough to secure work do so at a better wage, but only at the expense of others denied employment entirely. See J. Kreps, P. Martin, R. Perlman & G. Somers, Contemporary Labor Economics and Labor Relations (1980). See also Harry Hutchinson, Toward a Critical Race Reformist Conception of Minimum Wage Regimes: Exploding the Power of Myth, Fantasy, and Hierarchy, 34 Harv. J. on Legis. 93, 93 (1997) ("Despite the widely held belief that minimum wage regimes are a progressive program aimed at helping the disadvantaged . . . a Critical Race reformist perspective [reveals] that minimum wage regimes are in fact an abuse of power.") The issue is debated cyclically in Congress when efforts are made to increase the FLSA minimum wage. See William P. Quigley, A Fair Day's Pay for a Fair Day's Work: Time to Raise and Index the Minimum Wage, 27 St. Mary's L.J. 513 (1996).

In the 1970s, concerns about abuses by employer retirement programs led to increased federal regulation of retirement plans and other fringe benefits. The Employee Retirement Income Security Act (ERISA), 29 U.S.C.S §§ 1002 et seq. (2003), may be more successful than other enactments dealing with employee compensation because it provides not merely sanctions but also incentives. Unlike the earlier legislation such as the FLSA, which was largely prohibitory, ERISA combines its restrictions on employer benefit plans with tax incentives that effectively reduce the cost of such plans to employers. See generally Ronald J. Cooke, ERISA Practice and Procedure (1989); Betty Linn Krikorian, Fiduciary Standards in Pension and Trust Fund Management (1989). In the last several years, the declining stock market, the collapse of 401(K) plans heavily invested in employer stock, and new methods of computing pensions have raised questions about the effectiveness of ERISA.

## 4. Protections for Special Groups of Employees

Particular groups of employees have sought, and sometimes attained, legal protections denied the majority of the workforce. Two of the broadest schemes of job security protection in the United States (in terms of the number of employees affected) are civil service systems and tenure in educational institutions.

Civil service systems, whether at the federal, state, or local level, generally are committed in theory to employment on the basis of the merit of the individual workers. They implement this goal by basing selection on merit (typically, using an exam for initial hiring or promotion) and by ensuring workers continued employment "during good behavior." To achieve this last goal, civil service systems usually announce a substantive standard of protection for "permanent" workers, that is, employees who have been retained after completing a "probationary" period. During the probationary period, the worker is not yet fully protected by the civil service system. But once recognized as a permanent employee, the worker can be discharged or disciplined only for certain reasons. Further, the systems establish procedures to determine whether permanent workers have fallen short of the substantive standard. Civil service systems are, of course, limited to public employment and are established by statute or ordinance. See Isadore Silver, Public Employee Discharge and Discipline (1989); Robert G. Vaughan, Merit Systems Protection Board: Rights and Remedies (1984).

Academic tenure is similar to the civil service systems. The core concept is that certain employees can, after a probationary period, be awarded job security. The "tenure" they receive provides two forms of protection against discharge. First, like civil service systems, academic tenure accords employees procedural rights to a hearing before they are terminated. Second, and again like civil service systems, academic tenure provides substantive protections: tenured employees can be discharged only for "just cause" relating to their individual performance — e.g., Riggin v. Board of Trustees of Ball State Univ., 489 N.E.2d 616 (Ind. App. 1986) (teaching incompetence), In re Kozy, 371 S.E.2d 778 (N.C. App. 1988) (sexual harassment) — or because of "financial exigency" affecting the institution for which they work. Gwen Seaquist & Eileen Kelly, Faculty Dismissed Because of Enrollment Declines, 28 J.L. & Educ. 193 (1999).

While tenure owes its origins to the notion of academic freedom most strongly found in our universities, see J. Peter Byrne, Academic Freedom: A "Special Concern of the First Amendment," 99 Yale L.J. 251 (1989), it is much broader in practice. In public educational institutions, whether at the elementary or the high school level or in state colleges and universities, state statutes typically provide that continued employment by the institution after a period of years in probationary service (generally, three to seven) confers tenure on a teacher. In private institutions, especially those in higher education, tenure is not a matter of statutory grant, but the result of a contract between the employer and its employees. And while the substantive protections of tenure as well as procedural rights are frequently spelled out in state statutes for public institutions, the content of the tenure right is a matter of contract interpretation in private colleges. See American Assn. of Univ. Professors v. Bloomfield College, 346 A.2d 615 (N.J. Super. 1975). Academic tenure has been criticized for decades in American higher education, but remains intact at most educational institutions. See Matthew Finkin, The Case for Tenure (1996); James J. Fishman, Tenure and Its Discontents: The Worst Form of Employment Relationship Save All of the Others, 21 Pace L. Rev. 159 (2000).

## 5.  *Constitutional Protections*

In public-sector employment, a public employee who has the requisite property interest in his or her job, see Roth v. Board of Regents, 408 U.S. 564 (1972); Perry v. Sindermann, 408 U.S. 598 (1972), may not be discharged without being provided due process of law (typically, a pretermination hearing). This protection reaches beyond formal civil service systems and may provide more meaningful protections because the Constitution determines the level of procedural protection required. Cleveland Board of Education v. Loudermill, 470 U.S. 532 (1985). Further, substantive due process may limit the reasons a public employer can rely on to terminate an employee. See Harrah Indep. Sch. Dist. v. Martin, 440 U.S. 194 (1979).

Only public employees are eligible for this protection, which is further limited by the requirement that the employee have a property interest in the job in question. Although a formal civil service system or the formal award of tenure is not required, the employee must be able to point to some basis beyond her own unilateral hopes — a statutory right or an employment contract — before the due process clause applies.

Beyond due process, the most important form of constitutional protection lies in the First Amendment's guarantee of freedom of speech and association. These rights reach beyond those employees with property interests to embrace all employees of governmental bodies. The landmark case, Pickering v. Board of Education, 391 U.S. 563 (1968), invalidated a school board's discharge of a teacher who wrote a letter to a local newspaper challenging a school bond proposal. Although *Pickering* itself recognized limitations on the First Amendment rights of public employees, later cases cut back substantially on the protection provided. In Connick v. Myers, 461 U.S. 138 (1983), the Court stressed that, to be protected, employee speech must address a matter of "public concern," although the speech itself may be a private conversation. Givhan v. Western Line Consol. Sch. Dist., 439 U.S. 410 (1979). Even when the speech in question qualifies, however, decisions have tended to defer to employer justifications for disciplining employees for their expression. Connick v. Myers, supra. But see Rankin v. McPherson, 483 U.S. 378 (1987) (overturning discharge of clerical employee in constable's office for remarking, after hearing of an attempt on President Reagan's life, "If they go for him again, I hope they get him."). See generally Michael Wells, Section 1983, The First Amendment, and Public Employee Speech: Shaping the Right to Fit the Remedy (and Vice Versa), 35 Ga. L. Rev. 939 (2001); Alexander Gruber & Barbara Kritchevsky, The Uneasy Coexistence of Equal Protection and Free Speech Claims in the Public Employment Context, 31 U. Mem. L. Rev. 559 (2001); Rodric B. Schoen, *Pickering* Plus Thirty Years: Public Employees and Free Speech, 30 Tex. Tech L. Rev. 5 (1999); Lawrence Rosenthal, Permissable Content Discrimination Under the First Amendment: The Strange Case of the Public Employee, 25 Hastings Const. L.Q. 529 (1998); Cynthia L. Estlund, Free Speech and Due Process in the Workplace, 71 Ind. L.J. 601 (1995); Stephen Allred, From *Connick* to Confusion: The Struggle to Define Speech on Matters of Public Concern, 64 Ind. L.J. 43 (1988); Toni M. Massaro, Significant Silences: Freedom of Speech in the Public Sector Workplace, 61 S. Cal. L. Rev. 1 (1987).

More recently, the Supreme Court has further weakened the First Amendment protection of public employees by holding that an employer's reaction need only be reasonable — not necessarily correct — when it discharges a worker for fear of disruption. Waters v. Churchill, 511 U.S. 661 (1994). See generally Charles W. Hemingway, A Closer Look at *Waters v. Churchill* and *United States v. National Treasury Employees Union*: Constitutional Tensions Between the Government as Employer and the Citizen as Federal Employee, 44 Am. U. L. Rev. 2231 (1995).

The Court has also addressed First Amendment concerns in the context of public employee unions (e.g., Perry Educ. Assn. v. Perry Local Educators' Assn., 460 U.S. 37 (1983); City of Madison Joint Sch. Dist. No. 8 v. Wisconsin Empl. Relations Commn., 429 U.S. 167 (1976); see generally Terry Nicole Steinberg, Rival Union Access to Public Employees: A New First Amendment Balancing Test, 2 Geo. Mason Ind. L. Rev. 36 (1994); Robert C. Post, Between Governance and Management: The History and Theory of the Public Forum, 34 UCLA L. Rev. 1713 (1987); Deborah A. Schmedemann, Of Meetings and Mailboxes: The First Amendment and Exclusive Representation in Public Sector Labor Relations, 72 Va. L. Rev. 91 (1986)), in connection with restrictions on public employee political activity (United States Civil Service Commn. v. National Assn. of Letter Carriers, 413 U.S. 548 (1973); Broadrick v. Oklahoma, 413 U.S. 601 (1973); United Public Workers v. Mitchell, 330 U.S. 75 (1947)), and in the use of political party affiliation as a basis for public employment (Elrod v. Burns, 427 U.S. 347 (1976); Branti v. Finkel, 445 U.S. 507 (1980)).

## 6. *Social Security and Insurance*

Another response to the problems of workers has been to provide government-controlled benefit and insurance plans. Workers' compensation, discussed earlier, was the earliest effort, but the Depression led to the enactment of the federal Social Security scheme. Financed largely (but not exclusively) from employer and employee contributions, Social Security is the broadest "safety net" for workers' disability and retirement. Also important is unemployment compensation, a kind of insurance that provides benefits for workers who lose their employment. But this is not the only governmental response to the risks employees face. California, for example, requires a scheme of compensation for disabilities. One common thread running through all these arrangements is the perception that employers will not provide the requisite benefits unless compelled by the government; a second common feature is the requirement that both employers and employees contribute to the costs of the plan.

## 7. *Privacy*

As more individuals spend the better part of their day at work, the distinction between the private and the professional has become blurred. Private possessions are often taken to work, and private conversations via telephone, e-mail, or fax often occur in the workplace. Consequently, the conflict between employee privacy rights and employer choice has escalated. Modern technology enables employers to keep even closer tabs on their employees. Through drug testing, monitoring telephone conversations and messages, supervising computer use and e-mail, searching employee offices and workspaces, and polygraph testing, employers now have unprecedented access to private information about their employees. Employers believe that such access will lead to higher levels of productivity and fewer instances of carelessness or criminal activity. Knowing of a drug use problem or of a particular medical condition before hiring can limit the employer's tort liability. Despite, or perhaps because of, these arguments, privacy in the workplace is a growing concern to the public and its lawmakers.

Privacy protections depend in large part on the status of the employer. Only government workers are protected by the Constitution, but a patchwork of statutes and common law doctrines provides erratic protection to both private and public sector employees. Contract and tort remedies can also sometimes be invoked.

In the employment context, drug tests have been attempted in a variety of situations: testing of all prospective employees; testing only those who exhibit some signs of drug use; random testing of all current employees or of employees in safety-sensitive positions; testing of employees involved in accidents; and testing as part of an annual physical examination. See generally John B. Wefing, Employer Drug Testing: Disparate Judicial and Legislative Responses, 63 Alb. L. Rev. 799 (2000). These drug testing programs are not designed to trigger criminal proceedings, but instead to deter drug use among employees. While drug testing is a significant "interference with individual privacy," National Treasury Employees Union v. Von Raab, 489 U.S. 656 (1989), and therefore subject to constitutional restrictions when the government is doing the testing, it is frequently allowed. *Von Raab* upheld drug tests to prevent the promotion of drug users to United States Customs positions that required the carrying of a firearm. The Court reasoned that employees in such positions had a diminished expectation of privacy, and that interest was clearly outweighed by the government's compelling interests in the protection of our borders. In Chandler v. Miller, 520 U.S. 305 (1997), on the other hand, the Court invalidated a Georgia statute requiring all candidates for public office to take a drug test because a "special" need for such testing was not established; instead the need was merely "symbolic." Id. at 322.

The Federal Wiretap Act, 18 U.S.C.S. §2511 (2003), which applies to both government officials and private parties, restricts audio monitoring but is subject to three exceptions: first, the law does not apply when one party to a communication gives consent to the interception; second, the carriers of wire or electronic communications are exempt from the restrictions; third, the law does not apply when an employer uses the intercepting devices "in the ordinary course of business." See generally Daniel J. Solove, Information Privacy Law 664-85 (2003). In Watkins v. L. M. Berry & Co., 704 F.2d 577 (11th Cir. 1983), the company routinely monitored sales calls as part of its regular training program. Employees were allowed to make personal calls, but the court held such calls may be intercepted "in the ordinary course of business" only to the extent necessary to guard against unauthorized use of the telephone or to determine whether a call is personal. Similarly, having a legitimate business reason for listening in (suspecting an employee of burglary) is not enough to justify broad interception. Deal v. Spears, 980 F.2d 1153 (8th Cir. 1992).

As e-mail has rapidly become the preferred method for both personal and professional communication, e-mail privacy has been much debated. An e-mail travels through several systems before reaching its destination, thus making it easier to intercept. Further, employees often use their employer's e-mail systems and are typically sending and receiving messages from company computers during working hours. In this context, what is the reasonable expectation of privacy? In Smyth v. Pillsbury Co., 914 F. Supp. 97 (E.D. Pa. 1996), the court found that, once an employee voluntarily communicated over an e-mail system provided by and used by the company, any reasonable expectation of privacy is lost. Moreover, the company's interest in preventing unprofessional comments over the company system outweighed the employee's privacy interest in exchanging such comments. Id. at 101. Another court held that, if the employer has a policy clearly stating that employees are subject to Internet/e-mail monitoring, they are put on notice and therefore cannot reasonably expect their activity to be private. United States v. Simons, 206 F.3d 392 (4th Cir. 2000).

There is also an issue as to privacy of offices and personal property brought into the workplace. As a constitutional matter, "not everything that passes through the confines of the business address can be considered part of the workplace context" O'Connor v. Ortega, 480 U.S. 709 (1987). A closed handbag still receives an expectation of privacy, whereas an item or space whose contents relate to work may not. In *Ortega* the Court found that a public employee's expectations of privacy may be diminished by virtue of actual office practices, such as frequently accessed offices or file cabinets. Such "operational realities" may make some intrusions by supervisors exempt from Fourth Amendment protection. In *Simons*, the court found that Simons possessed a legitimate expectation of privacy in his office and therefore a search pursuant to an investigation of work-related misconduct would be constitutional only if "reasonable in its inception and scope." 206 F.3d at 400. Because the employer had a "reasonable grounds for suspecting" that office would yield evidence and the search was "reasonably related to the objective," the search was permissible. Id. at 401.

Employers sometimes utilize polygraphs to detect physiological responses to questions and so conclude that employees are lying. In 1988 Congress passed the Employee Polygraph Protection Act, 29 U.S.C.S. § 2002 (2003), applying only to private-sector employees. While the Act limits the use of polygraphs in the employment context, it has several exceptions. Thus, polygraphs are permitted when the employer has a reasonable suspicion that the employee was involved in an incident under investigation or when the test is given in relation to an investigation of economic loss to the employer. 29 U.S.C.S. § 2002 (2003). However, even when polygraph tests are used under these exceptions, the test cannot be the sole reason for negative employment action. Daniel J. Solove, Information Privacy Law 657-62 (2003).

Finally, tort law provides some protection for employee privacy. See page 24.

### 8.   *Common Law Protection*

To a large extent, the circle has begun to close. Although the unresponsiveness of the common law to employee concerns triggered the search for alternative legal mechanisms for protecting employees, the development of other protections has in turn contributed to an ongoing and radical reassessment of basic common law doctrines.

## B.   THE REASSESSMENT OF CONTRACT LAW

The origins of the at-will rule in the United States are usually traced to Horace Gay Wood, who, in his treatise on master-servant relations published in 1877, wrote:

> With us the rule is inflexible, that a general or indefinite hiring is prima facie a hiring at-will, and if the servant seeks to make it a yearly hiring, the burden is upon him to establish it by proof. A hiring at so much a day, week, month or year, no time being specified, is an indefinite hiring, and no presumption attaches that it was for a day even, but only at the rate fixed for whatever time the party may serve.

H. Wood, A Treatise on the Law of Master and Servant 272 (1877). Wood's principle is generally viewed as not only a marked departure from the law in England but also ill-founded in the American cases he cited. Jay A. Feinman, The Development of the Employment at Will Rule, 20 Am. J. Leg. Hist. 118 (1976). But see Mayer Freed & Daniel D. Polsby, The Doubtful Provenance of "Wood's Rule" Revisited, 22 Ariz. St. L. Rev. 551 (1990). Professor Feinman responded in The Development of the Employment at Will Rule Revisited, 23 Ariz. St. L. Rev. 733 (1990). See also Andrew P. Morriss, Developing a Framework for Empirical Research on the Common Law: General Principles and Case Studies of the Decline of Employment-At-Will, 45 Case W. Res. L. Rev. 999 (1995). In any event, Wood's formulation was almost immediately accepted by courts and became the "American" rule. Indeed, Wood's principle so suited the demands of the times that the courts soon went beyond his pronouncement. Wood's formulation did not purport to establish employment at will as a rule of substantive law. It did not effect an agreement for a definite time, and, even as to "a general or indefinite hiring," it was phrased merely as an aid to construction. "Prima facie" such employment is at will, but the "servant" can establish a hiring for some period by appropriate proof. Nevertheless, the courts quickly came to apply the at-will employment doctrine as a rule of substantive law.

The process proceeded so far that in Fisher v. Jackson, 118 A.2d 316 (Conn. 1955), for example, plaintiff was held to be an at-will employee even though he had been promised employment for life with specified yearly salary increases. As a result, the courts, with no apparent embarrassment, found promises of "permanent" employment to nevertheless be at will. Only in the face of the clearest proof — typically, a formal, written contract for a specified term of years — would the courts hold the employment relationship not to be at will. In those instances, an employee could be discharged before the expiration of the contract only if she failed to substantially perform her duties, thus breaching her own obligation. Compare Central Alaska Broadcasting, Inc. v. Bracale, 637 P.2d 711 (Alaska 1981) with Rudman v. Cowles Communications, Inc., 280 N.E.2d 867 (N.Y. 1972).

As our survey of other approaches indicates, the at-will rule was never as pervasive as many have assumed. And, in the last decade, the courts have done a significant about-face, recognizing that the at-will rule as it has evolved in the United States is less a manifestation of freedom of contract than a denial of it. The presumption of an at-will relationship frequently operates to defy the intent of the parties to the arrangement, rather than implement it. Accordingly, courts increasingly recognize that statements or assurances by employers about job security may create reasonable expectations that the employment is not purely at will. Further, the courts, by looking to personnel policy manuals and other employment rules, have discerned the intent of the parties as to the terms of their relationship.

At its height, the at-will doctrine had several strands that raised barriers to finding a meaningful employment contract. The first strand was the presumption that the parties intend employment to be at will. The courts usually treated the presumption as almost irrebuttable. More recent decisions, while not entirely abandoning the presumption of at-will employment, take a much more hospitable approach to evidence that shows the actual intent of the parties. For example, substantial reliance by the employee, as by quitting another job, may be a basis for concluding that the parties did not intend merely an at-will relation. See, e.g., Collins v. Parsons College, 203 N.W.2d 594 (Iowa 1973).

The second strand is the use of consideration doctrine: courts sometimes refused to enforce agreements plainly contemplating long-term employment by invoking the doctrine of "mutuality of obligation." Because employees were typically free to quit work at any time, the employer should not be bound. This reasoning, however, is at odds with normal contract principles. While it is hornbook consideration law that a contract does not exist unless each party is bound to do something, it is equally elementary that the obligations of the parties need not be even roughly comparable. There is normally no inquiry into the adequacy of consideration. In the last two decades, the courts have increasingly rejected a mutuality requirement in employment contracts, as they have in other contractual arrangements. See, e.g., Eales v. Tanana Valley Medical Surgical Group, 663 P.2d 958 (Alaska 1983); Pine River State Bank v. Mettille, 333 N.W.2d 622 (Minn. 1983).

A third strand, a variation on the consideration theme, is the requirement that, to enforce a promise for lifetime or permanent employment, the employee must provide the employer with independent consideration, that is, consideration in addition to merely performing his employment duties. Many commentators have demonstrated that this requirement is fundamentally inconsistent with contract law's general approach to the adequacy of consideration. The courts are coming to accept this view. At most, the presence or absence of independent consideration serves an evidentiary function in helping to ascertain the parties' intent.

With most of the barriers to contract analysis presented by the employment at will doctrine swept away, the application of traditional contract approaches to the employment relation has proceeded along four main lines. First, courts have recognized that oral employment contracts may provide some rights against unjust discharge. Second, employer statements of policy, frequently found in employee handbooks or personnel manuals, may have a binding effect. Third, the doctrine of promissory estoppel has played an increasing role. Finally, a few courts have limited employers' discretion by enforcing the "good faith" clause implicit in all contracts.

## 1.  *Oral Contracts*

In the last two decades courts have given legal effect to oral assurances of job security. E.g., Larson v. Kreiser's Inc., 472 N.W.2d 761 (S.D. 1991) (promise of future promotion in return for work may give rise to just cause protection); Romack v. Public Service Co., 511 N.E.2d 1024 (Ind. 1987) (police officer stated claim by alleging that, when he was recruited by a private firm for a security position, he received assurances of security comparable to that he enjoyed as a police officer). A promise of permanent employment, for example, is likely to be viewed as employment until retirement, death, or disability. See Hodge v. Evans Fin. Corp., 823 F.2d 559 (D.C. Cir. 1987) (2-1). Contra Meredith v. Rockwell Intl. Corp., 826 F.2d 463 (6th Cir. 1987). At the extreme, courts have recognized implied promises of job security in long-standing employment relationships. E.g., Foley v. Interactive Data Corp., 765 P.2d 373 (Cal. 1988). When a promise should be implied and what degree of job security is impliedly promised are, of course, serious issues. See Karen McMahon, The Employment-At-Will Doctrine: Can Oral Assurances of Job Security Overcome the At-Will Presumption?, 23 Wm. Mitchell L. Rev. 465 (1997). Even when an express oral promise is alleged, however, a number of questions arise. Aside from the factual issue of what, if anything, was promised, there are legal questions concerning the authority of the promisor to bind the employer, see generally Mark A. Rothstein, Charles B. Craver, Elinor P. Schroeder & Elaine W. Shoben, Employment Law § 8.4 (2d ed. 1999), and the application of the statute of frauds, e.g., Finley v. Aetna Life &

Cas. Co., 520 A.2d 208 (Conn. 1987) (contract of indefinite duration not within statute of frauds).

## 2.   *Employer Policies*

Another development is the trend among courts to recognize that formal employer policies may be enforceable under traditional contract analysis. A good example is Woolley v. Hoffman La Roche, Inc., 491 A.2d 1257 (N.J. 1985), which treated a personnel policy manual as a general agreement covering all employees. In sharp contrast to earlier cases in that state, the court said, "There is no reason to treat such a document with hostility." Id. at 1264. Further, the court concluded that when an employer of a substantial number of employees circulates a manual that, when fairly read, provides that certain benefits are an incident of the employment (including, especially, job security provisions), the judiciary, instead of "grudgingly" conceding the enforceability of those provisions, should construe them in accordance with the reasonable expectations of the employees. Id. As the court concluded, "Whatever Hoffmann La Roche may have intended, that which was read by its employees was a promise not to fire them except for cause." Id. at 1266.

While several courts have rejected this analysis, e.g., Heideck v. Kent Gen. Hosp., 446 A.2d 1095 (Del. 1982); Gates v. Life of Montana Ins. Co., 638 P.2d 1063 (Mont. 1982), most decisions in the last two decades have concluded that employer policies may constitute enforceable promises when they give rise to reasonable expectations on the part of employees. See, e.g., O'Brien v. New England Telephone & Telegraph Co., 664 N.E. 2d. 843 (Mass. 1996); Leikvold v. Valley View Community Hosp., 688 P.2d 170 (Ariz. 1984); Pine River State Bank v. Mettille, 333 N.W.2d 622 (Minn. 1983); see generally Paul Berks, Social Change and Judicial Response: The Handbook Exception to Employment-at-Will, 4 Emp. Rts. & Employ. Pol'y J. 231 (2000); Carlotta McCarthy, Employers Beware: Employee's "Reasonable Reliance" on Promises Contained in Employee Handbooks May Create Contractual Rights, 31 Suffolk U. L. Rev. 227 (1997); Deborah A. Schmedemann & Judi McLean Parks, Contract Formation and Employee Handbooks: Legal, Psychological, and Empirical Analyses, 29 Wake Forest L. Rev. 647 (1994); Richard J. Pratt, Unilateral Modification of Employment Handbooks: Further Encroachments on the Employment-At-Will Doctrine, 139 U. Pa. L. Rev. 197 (1990). This result is usually reached by applying unilateral contract theory, that is, viewing a policy manual or employee handbook as an offer by the employer that is accepted by the continued work of the employees. The agreement is thus reached, and the continued work by the employee is the consideration supporting enforcement of the contract. See generally E. Allan Farnsworth, Contracts § 3.24 (3d ed. 1998).

Even states that adopt this theory, however, recognize an exception to it. *Woolley* noted that, consistent with the contract basis of the theory, the parties could agree otherwise. As a result, employers have been placing disclaimers of contractual liability in their handbooks and manuals, and courts have given effect to them, e.g., Workman v. UPS 234 F.3d 998 (7th Cir. 2000); Dell v. Montgomery Ward & Co., 811 F.2d 970 (6th Cir. 1987); Lincoln v. Wackenhut Corp., 687 P.2d 701 (Wyo. 1994); or to acknowledgments of at-will employment on job applications or other forms, e.g., Scholz v. Montgomery Ward & Co., Inc., 468 N.W.2d 845 (Mich. 1991). Disclaimers, however, are not necessarily effective. Their validity is likely to depend on their conspicuousness, McDonald v. Mobil Coal Producing, Inc., 820 P.2d 986

(Wyo. 1991), and whether they are phrased clearly. Even assuming clear and conspicuous disclaimers, some courts have held that contractual obligations may still exist. See Zaccardi v. Zale Corp., 856 F.2d 1473 (10th Cir. 1988) (2-1) (disclaimer did not warrant summary judgment for the company because it must be read in terms of the parties' expectations, which could have been affected because parts of the manual were phrased in mandatory language); Jones v. Central Peninsula Gen. Hosp., 779 P.2d 783 (Alaska 1989) (one-sentence disclaimer ineffective in light of 85 pages of detailed provisions, many of which purport to grant rights). Finally, assuming that a disclaimer would be effective as to new employees, there is a serious question as to whether it binds workers who already obtained job security by virtue of a policy manual. See In re Certified Question, 443 N.W.2d 112 (Mich. 1989) (new manual may extinguish rights created by old manual even when original manual did not reserve right to modify).

## 3.  *Promissory Estoppel*

Section 90(1) of the Restatement (Second) of Contracts states the general principle of promissory estoppel:

> A promise which the promissor should reasonably expect to induce action or forbearance on the part of the promisee or a third person and which does induce such action or forbearance is binding if injustice can be avoided only by enforcement of the promise.

While utilizing promissory estoppel to bind an employer to perform promises for benefits such as pensions is traditional, the use of promissory estoppel to enforce promises for job security is a new development. In Gorham v. Benson Optical, 539 N.W.2d 798 (Minn. App. 1995), a store manager resigned one job in reliance on the promise of employment from the defendant. The court invoked promissory estoppel to award the plaintiff his reliance interest.

The underlying basis of promissory estoppel is that employees must rely on a promise. An employee may rely by relocating to a job, Hackett v. Foodmaker, Inc., 245 N.W.2d 140 (Mich. App. 1976); turning down other employment; or merely continuing to work. The more difficult issue is what the employer promised. If the promise is merely employment, the traditional view is that the promise is only for at-will employment. In order for promissory estoppel to provide any greater rights in this situation, the court must find an implied promise to employ permanently, during good performance, or at least for a reasonable period. If that promise is found, however, the employee's work will provide the consideration, so it is not apparent why there is any need to rely on promissory estoppel.

## 4.  *Good Faith*

A final "contract" theory of enforcement of employee rights looks not to express promises for its basis, but to an implied covenant of good faith that is read into all contracts by the law. See generally Note, Protecting At Will Employees Against Wrongful Discharge: The Duty to Terminate Only in Good Faith, 93 Harv. L. Rev. 1816 (1980). Although this theory shares some characteristics of tort law because the duty is imposed by law and is nondisclaimable, good faith has achieved general acceptance in contract law. As with all such principles, however, the duty of good faith is easier to approve than to define. See Foley v. Interactive Data Corp., 765 P.2d 373 (Cal. 1988).

The usual invocation of the good faith principle occurs when one party performs an act that is not expressly barred by the contract in question but is contrary to the reasonable expectations of the other party. In the employment context, the classic case is Fortune v. National Cash Register, 364 N.E.2d 1251 (Mass. 1977), in which plaintiff claimed that he was discharged the day after securing for his employer a $5 million contract that would have yielded him substantial commissions under the compensation system in effect. The court found that the employment relation contained an implied covenant of good faith that prevented the employer from firing an employee merely to deprive him of the fruits of his labors. Accord Wakefield v. Northern Telecom, 769 F.2d 109 (2d Cir. 1985); contra Willis v. Champlain Cable Corp., 748 P.2d 621 (Wash. 1988).

Although the principle that an employer cannot deprive an employee of an earned benefit — whether it be salary, commissions, or fringe benefits — is scarcely innovative, *Fortune* may go beyond that normal rule. The essential question is whether the good faith basis for this rule can be extended to provide some form of job security. The broadest extension of the good faith principle would require an employer to have good cause to discharge an employee. No court has yet adopted such an interpretation, and a number of decisions have either totally rejected the implied covenant in the employment context or at least held that the covenant cannot be used as a basis for recognizing job security rights in what would otherwise be an at-will relationship. E.g., Vanlente v. University of Wyoming Research Corp., 975 P.2d 594 (Wyo. 1999); Morriss v. Coleman Co., 738 P.2d 841 (Kan. 1987); Hunt v. IBM Mid Am. Fed. Credit Union, 384 N.W.2d 853 (Minn. 1986).

But narrower formulations are also possible. "Good faith" may be viewed as simply excluding certain reasons as legitimate bases for the employer's conduct, while leaving large areas to the employer's discretion. E.g., ARCO Alaska v. Akers, 753 P.2d 1150 (Alaska 1988) (proof that employee was discharged for personal animosity and not for work-related reasons sufficient for duty of good faith suit); Stark v. Circle K Corp., 751 P.2d 162 (Mont. 1988) (despite at-will status acknowledged on employment application, employee had a cause of action when he was terminated for insubordination for refusing to sign a report he believed to be erroneous). Indeed, the narrowest formulation of good faith will look to the subjective connotation of the term and argue that a discharge is permissible if the employer, however unreasonably, is sincere in its belief that the interests of the business require discharge.

## 5.   *Varieties of Job Security*

The duty of good faith suggests the range of promises that may be implied. This is also true where the promise must be implied in fact from the employer's practices. For instance, does an employer who publishes a list of reasons for discharge impliedly promise that other reasons are not a sufficient basis? Compare Watson v. Idaho Falls Consolidated Hosp., 720 P.2d 632 (Idaho 1986) with Bauer v. American Freight Sys., Inc., 422 N.W.2d 435 (S.D. 1988). But even when an employer has made an express promise, its implications must be ascertained. For example, where an employer assures its workers certain procedural protections, does this promise suggest a substantive standard that the procedure is designed to determine? Callcon v. Miyagi, 876 P.2d 1278 (Haw. 1994).

Even express promises may take many forms. A company may assure a worker that it will employ her for as long as certain objective conditions are met — say, as long as at least 100 units a month are sold. Or it could promise more generally to employ unless there is "just cause" for discharge, the kind of protection provided in collective bargaining agreements and civil service systems.

Under those regimes, just cause protection has two different forms. The first is cause related to the individual in question and focuses on such factors as inadequate job performance, disloyalty, and misconduct or violence. See Roger Abrams & Dennis Nolan, Toward a Theory of "Just Cause" in Employee Discharge Cases, 1985 Duke L.J. 594. Adequate job performance includes regular attendance, a reasonable quantity and quality of work, and obedience to rules, at least reasonable ones, for work performance. But the question is not necessarily "fault." An employee who is repeatedly sick might be subject to discharge no matter how authentic her illness.

The second form of just cause focuses on systemic causes related to the business, typically involving a large-scale termination of employees in the context of a reorganization or a reduction in force during an economic downturn, including, at the extreme, shutting down entire departments or even plants. In Woolley v. Hoffmann La Roche, Inc., 491 A.2d 1257, 1257 n.8 (N.J. 1985), the court described this form of "just cause" for termination. Instead of a promise of good cause protection, an employer could promise "lifetime" employment. In Woolley, the New Jersey Supreme Court distinguished a promise of lifetime employment from just cause protection: "The essential difference is that the 'lifetime' contract purports to protect the employment against any termination; the contract arising from the manual [in question] protects the employment only from arbitrary termination." Id. Is protecting an employee from "arbitrary termination" the same as requiring the employer to have just cause for termination?

Still another form of job security is an employer's promise not to discharge an employee as long as her performance is "satisfactory." The standard hypothetical contract for "satisfactory" performance is a promise to pay a painter for a portrait if it is "satisfactory" to the promisor. If payment is wholly discretionary, there is no consideration for the contract: the promise to pay is illusory because the promisor is as free after the promise as she was before it. However, if the promise is construed, as it normally will be, to require at least "honest satisfaction," there is consideration: the promisor is still free to reject the portrait if she is truly dissatisfied with it, but is not free to do so for other reasons. As Judge Learned Hand suggested, the promise is enforceable if the promisor is satisfied with the performance even if she has come to regret the bargain on other grounds, such as the price she has promised. Thompson Starrett Co. v. La Belle Iron Works, 17 F.2d 536, 541 (2d Cir. 1927).

More restrictive than "honest" satisfaction is "reasonable" satisfaction. As the adjective suggests, the focus here is objective, rather than subjective. If the promise is construed to be of this kind, the promisor's sincere dissatisfaction is irrelevant if a "reasonable" person in her position would be satisfied with the portrait. While promises may be phrased so clearly as to indicate what kind of satisfaction is required, courts generally look to the circumstances of the transaction, most notably whether the performance is personal or commercial, to decide the content of the promise. See Morrin Building Prods. Co. v. Baystone Constr., 717 F.2d 413 (7th Cir. 1983). See generally E. Allan Farnsworth, Contracts § 8.4 (3d ed. 1998). Obviously, then, the significance of a promise of work during satisfactory performance depends on whether an objective or a subjective standard is used.

## C.   THE REASSESSMENT OF TORT LAW

As contract law has undergone a transformation in the employment context, so also has tort law. A threshold question in tort cases is whether the action is within the exclusive jurisdiction of the workers' compensation law. However, that law is typically exclusive only for accidental injury, leaving employees free to sue for intentional torts. E.g., Ford v. Revlon, Inc., 734 P.2d 580 (Ariz. 1987) (sexual harassment tort suit permitted). Contra Haddon v. Metropolitan Life Ins. Co., 389 S.E.2d 712 (Va. 1990) (workers' compensation the exclusive remedy for sexual harassment). Accordingly, suits may be possible under such theories as intentional infliction of emotional distress, intentional interference with contractual relations, deceit, defamation, and invasion of privacy. See generally Joseph H. King, The Exclusiveness of an Employee's Workers' Compensation Remedy Against His Employer, 55 Tenn. L. Rev. 405 (1988). Assuming that workers' compensation laws are no barrier, tort law has a wide arsenal of theories that may be utilized in the employment setting. Some of the more important ones follow.

### 1.   *Intentional Infliction of Emotional Distress*

Intentional infliction of emotional or mental distress has tended to distill into a single question: the outrageousness of defendant's conduct. See § 46 of the Restatement (Second) of Torts. "Liability has been found only where the conduct has been so outrageous in character, and so extreme in degree, as to go beyond all possible bounds of decency, and to be regarded as atrocious, and utterly intolerable in a civilized community." § 46, comment d (1965). An important factor in judging the outrageousness of the conduct is whether the defendant is abusing a position of power over the plaintiff. Id. at comment e. But, as a counterbalance, the "actor is never liable . . . where he has done no more than to insist upon his legal rights in a permissible way, even though he is well aware that such insistence is certain to cause emotional distress." Id. at comment g.

In the employment setting, the landmark outrage case is Agis v. Howard Johnson Co., 355 N.E.2d 315 (Mass. 1976), where the employer dealt with theft in a restaurant by announcing that waitresses would be discharged in alphabetical order until the person responsible for the theft was discovered. Plaintiff was first on the list and thus was fired even though defendant had no reason to suspect that she was the thief. The court recognized a cause of action for outrage. This tort has also been used by victims of racist slurs, Woods v. Graphic Communications, 925 F.2d 1195 (9th Cir. 1991); by workers interrogated as to supposed misconduct, Tandy Corp. v. Bone, 678 S.W.2d 312 (Ark. 1984); by a worker who was framed by a supervisor who placed checks in her purse to make it appear as if she were a thief, Dean v. Ford Motor Credit Co., 885 F.2d 300 (5th Cir. 1989); and by a worker who was fired by his supervisors who came to his home to do so while he was in bed recovering from a heart attack, Archer v. Farmer Bros. Co., 2002 Colo. App. LEXIS 718. See generally Dennis P. Duffy, Intentional Infliction of Emotional Distress and Employment at Will: The Case Against "Tortification" of Labor and Employment Law, 74 B.U. L. Rev. 382 (1994); Regina Austin, Employer Abuse, Worker Resistance, and the Tort of Intentional Infliction of Emotional Distress, 41 Stan. L. Rev. 1 (1988).

## 2.   *Fraud*

Another potentially applicable tort when an employee is discharged is fraud. See
§ 525 of the Restatement (Second) of Torts. A good example of misrepresentation
in the employment setting is Bondi v. Jewels by Edwar, Ltd., 73 Cal. Rptr. 494 (Ct.
App. 1968), in which plaintiff was induced to close his shop and go to work for a competitor. He was found to have stated a cause of action in fraud against his new employer when he was discharged from his at-will job after only two weeks. Proving
fraudulent misrepresentation, however, is quite difficult. Plaintiff must show that defendant knew when he made his representations that they would not be carried out.
E.g., Shebar v. Sanyo Business Sys., 526 A.2d 1144 (N.J. App. Div. 1987), *aff'd*, 544
A.2d 377 (N.J. 1988) (intent not to perform promise of lifetime employment to
employee made in order to keep him from going to a competitor was established
by testimony of executive recruiter that Sanyo sought a replacement for plaintiff immediately after the promise was made). Further, not only must detrimental reliance
be established, but also the reliance must be shown to be reasonable. See, e.g.,
Shelby v. Zayre Corp., 474 So. 2d 1069 (Ala. 1985) (reliance on promise of permanent employment unreasonable in face of signed application form that employment
was at will).

## 3.   *Defamation*

A cause of action for defamation arises when statements are made in writing (libel) or
orally (slander) that tend "to harm the reputation of another so as to lower him in the
estimation of the community or to deter third persons from association or dealing
with him." Restatement (Second) of Torts § 558 (1977). The elements of a defamation action are (1) a defamatory statement (2) made about the plaintiff (3) that is published to a third party.
    In the employment context, defamatory statements often occur. Words that impute
to an employee fraud, dishonesty, misconduct, incapacity, or unfitness are defamatory. The test is how the words would be understood using the reasonable person standard. For example, in Falls v. Sporting News Publishing Co., 834 F.2d 611 (6th Cir.
1987), the court found a defamation claim stated when, in response to a reader's inquiries about a newspaper's decision to discontinue plaintiff's column, one editor
wrote: "I know Joe brightened a lot of hearts with his column through the years but
we felt it was time to make a change, with more energetic columnists who attend
more events and are closer to today's sports scene." Id. at 614.
    Given the breadth of the concept of defamation, one commentator has noted,
"Any discharge for cause, negative evaluation, or unfavorable reference of a former
employee gives rise to a potential cause of action for defamation, whether or not an
employee has sustained actual economic harm." Freeman, Employee Discharge:
Defamation Through the Form of Termination, 39 N.Y.U. Conf. on Labor § 17.01, at
634 (1986). Indeed, a "statement" is not always necessary. See Tyler v. Macks Stores
of N.C. Inc., 272 S.E.2d 633 (S.C. 1980) (where an employee was fired soon after
being required to take a polygraph, the court recognized that "a defamatory insinua-
tion may be made by actions or conduct as well as by word"). Further, the common
law presumed injury flowing from disparagement of a person in his business or
calling. See also Litman v. Massachusetts Mut. Life Ins. Co., 739 F.2d 1549 (11th
Cir. 1984).

Nor is "publication" often a problem in the employment setting. In most jurisdictions, the publication requirement can be satisfied even when the defamatory communication remains within the employer's organization. E.g., Stukuls v. State, 366 N.E.2d 829 (N.Y. 1977); Restatement (Second) of Torts § 577, comment e. Some courts have even found the defendant responsible when the plaintiff himself republishes the defamation under the "compulsory self-publication" doctrine. E.g., Lewis v. Equitable Life Assurance Socy., 389 N.W.2d 876 (Minn. 1986).

On the other side of the ledger, however, truth is an absolute defense, and only the "gist" or "sting" of the statement need be true. Perhaps as important, most defamation in the employment context is subject to a privilege. For example, while internal communications among agents of the corporate employer satisfy the publication requirement in most jurisdictions, such communications will frequently be qualifiedly privileged. Similarly, a qualified privilege exists when a prior employer gives a reference to a new or prospective employer. E.g., Turner v. Halliburton Co., 722 P.2d 1106 (Kan. 1986). See generally Restatement (Second) of Torts §§ 600 et seq. The scope of the privilege, however, is exceeded if the communication is published beyond those people who have an interest in the matter. A qualified privilege is also lost when the statement is made with malice or ill will toward the plaintiff, or when the employer acts recklessly, without regard to whether the statements are true.

## 4.   *Intentional Interference with Contract*

Tort law also protects parties to a contract from intentional interference with their relationship by third parties. See generally Alex Long, The Disconnect Between At-Will Employment and Tortious Interference with Business Relations: Rethinking Tortious Interference Claims in the Employment Context. 33 Ariz. St. L.J. 491 (2001); Mark P. Gergen, Tortious Interference: How It Is Engulfing Commercial Law, Why This Is Not Entirely Bad, and a Prudential Response, 38 Ariz. L. Rev. 1175 (1996); Restatement (Second) of Torts §§ 766, 767 (1979). This tort applies to employment contracts, including at-will employment. See, e.g., Zippertubing Co. v. Teleflex, Inc., 757 F.2d 1401 (3d Cir. 1985); Sterner v. Marathon Oil Co., 767 S.W.2d 686 (Tex. 1989).

Intentional interference with contract requires (1) the existence of a contract between an employer and an employee; (2) knowledge of that relationship by the third party; (3) interference with that relationship by, for example, seeking the employee's discharge; (4) lack of justification; and (5) proximately caused damages. William Holloway & Michael Leech, Employment Termination: Rights and Remedies 194 (1992).

A problem with applying this tort in the typical discharge situation is that there must be someone who counts as a third party to the contract who can be charged with interference. While there are some precedents requiring that the third party be someone other than an agent of the employer, e.g., Bowman v. State Bank of Keysville, 331 S.E.2d 797 (Va. 1985), most authority treats an employee's co-workers as third parties chargeable with interference with the employment contract between the employee and the employer, e.g., Cappiello v. Ragen Precision Indus., 471 A.2d 432 (N.J. App. Div. 1984); Ramsey v. Greenwald, 414 N.E.2d 1226 (Ill. App. 1980).

This does not mean, however, that the tort of intentional interference is committed every time a supervisor fires an employee on behalf of a corporation. Justification (sometimes called privilege) is at the core of the contractual interference tort and consists of showing that the defendant acted reasonably in pursuit of interests that are entitled to equal or greater protection than the plaintiff's interest in the job. Some interests have been held not legitimate. E.g., Sides v. Duke Hospital, 328 S.E.2d 818 (N.C. App. 1985) (doctors who induced a hospital to discharge plaintiff, a nurse, because her deposition in a malpractice suit was damaging to them, were acting for improper or strictly personal motives), Hatten v. Union Oil Co., 778 P.2d 1150 (Alaska 1989) (no privilege if personal reasons were predominant motive).

On the other hand, an employee is justified in procuring the discharge of another employee when he acts in accordance with his job duties and in the best interests of the employer. Smith v. Ford Motor Co., 221 S.E.2d 282 (N.C. 1976). As a result, the reporting of wrongful conduct by another employee on the job may be privileged. E.g., Davenport v. Epperly, 744 P.2d 1110 (Wyo. 1987) (reporting a co-worker who was out hunting while supposedly disabled was not sufficient to impose liability absent a bad motive).

## 5.  Privacy

"Privacy" as a tort, is a multifaceted cause of action. Tort law recognizes a legally protected interest in privacy in four basic situations: (1) intrusion on seclusion, (2) appropriation of name or likeness, (3) publicity given to private life, and (4) publicity placing a person in false light. Restatement (Second) of Torts §§ 652B, 652C, 652D, and 652E (1977). While all four varieties may arise in employment situations, perhaps the most likely application of the tort is intrusion on seclusion. For example, in K-Mart Corp. v. Trotti, 677 S.W.2d 632 (Tx. App. 1984), the employer provided employees with lockers for optional storage of personal items during their shifts. There was no individual assignment of lockers and the employees were to provide their own lock. The court held that opening and searching such a locker was in clear disregard of the employees' legitimate expectations of privacy; an "intrusion upon seclusion." Id. at 638. Further, public disclosure of the contents of a personnel file, for example, might give rise to a privacy action when publicity is given to the private life of a person even if it does not put the person in a false light. Henry Perritt, Employee Dismissal Law and Practice § 7.47 (4th ed. 1998). See also Saldana v. Kelsey-Hayes Co., 443 N.W.2d 382 (Mich. App. 1989) (off-workplace surveillance of employee who claimed to be injured to determine if he was malingering).

## 6.  The Public Policy Exception

The most important recent addition to the arsenal of tort causes of action applicable to employment is the "public policy exception" to the at-will doctrine, which, as usually formulated, limits an employer's power to discharge when the employee has engaged in conduct protected by an important public policy. The public policy exception is frequently attributed to the New Hampshire Supreme Court's decision in Monge v. Beebe Rubber Co., 316 A.2d 549 (N.H. 1974), which held that the discharge of an employee for her refusal to accede to a supervisor's sexual advances is actionable as a breach of contract. Its origins, however, can be traced back to a California case, Petermann v. International Bhd. of Teamsters Local 396, 344 P.2d 25 (Cal. App.

1959), in which the court held it impermissible to discharge an employee for refusing to commit perjury.

While some modern decisions have rejected the public policy exception entirely, e.g., Murphy v. American Home Prods., 448 N.E.2d 86 (N.Y. 1983), the majority of courts considering the question over the last 25 years have recognized a cause of action for at least some public policy discharges. For example, courts applying this principle have upheld causes of action when employees were discharged for refusing to violate laws relating to the public health O'Sullivan v. Mallon, 390 A.2d 149 (N.J. Super. 1973); for complying with a court-issued subpoena, e.g., Hummer v. Evans, 923 P.2d 981 (Idaho 1996); for complaining about the shipping of defective parts, Green v. Ralee Engineering Co., 960 P.2d 1046 (Cal. 1998); for violating a company rule when the motivation was attempting to assist another who was in danger of serious physical injury or death, Gardner v. Loomis Armored Inc., 913 P.2d 377 (Wash. 1996); for filing charges of assault and battery arising from workplace sexual harassment, Watson v. Peoples Sec. Life Ins. Co., 588 A.2d 760 (Md. 1991); for filing a workers' compensation claim, e.g., Hansen v. Harrah's, 675 P.2d 394 (Nev. 1984); for serving on a jury, e.g., Nees v. Hock, 536 P.2d 512 (Or. 1975); for cooperating with public investigations, e.g., Palmateer v. International Harvester Co., 421 N.E.2d 876 (Ill. 1981); for acting in accordance with professional responsibilities, e.g., Pierce v. Ortho Pharmaceutical Corp., 417 A.2d 505 (N.J. 1980); and for refusing to assist in illegal acts, e.g., Tameny v. Atlantic Richfield Co., 610 P.2d 1330 (Cal. 1980).

In Foley v. Interactive Data Corp., 765 P.2d 373 (Cal. 1988), the California Supreme Court articulated a test for determining the scope of the public policy exception to the at-will doctrine. Plaintiff, citing the duty of an employee to report relevant business information to his employer, claimed a violation of public policy when his employer discharged him for informing management that his supervisor was under federal investigation for embezzling funds from a prior employer. The court found plaintiff's claim outside the protection of public policy because any duty to report ran to his employer, not to the public. Under this approach, the employer can discharge an employee because he failed to provide relevant business information and because he did provide that information. The result may not seem fair, but it is the essence of the at-will doctrine.

In approaching the public policy exception, the basic problem is defining what constitutes a sufficient public policy basis on which to predicate a right to be free of retaliatory discharge. In order to limit the theory, some courts have required that the policy be traced to some specific statute or constitutional provision. See, e.g., Brockmeyer v. Dun & Bradstreet, 335 N.W.2d 834 (Wis. 1983). But see Winkelman v. Beloit Memorial Hosp., 483 N.W.2d 211 (Wis. 1992). Others, while not limiting the source of the policy, insist that the employer's action must violate a "clear mandate." Pierce v. Ortho Pharmaceutical Corp., supra. Still others are beginning to recognize the existence of conflicting public policies that limit the application of the tort. This problem has emerged most starkly in the area of discharge of attorneys. Jacobson v. Knepper & Moga, P.C., 706 N.E.2d 491 (Ill. 1998), found no cause of action for an attorney discharged for reporting the firm's illegal practices to a partner. Accord Nordling v. Northern States Power Co., 465 N.W.2d 141 (Minn. App. 1991). See also General Dynamics Corp. v. Superior Court, 876 P.2d 487 (Cal. 1994); Mourad v. Automobile Club Ins. Assn., 465 N.W.2d 395 (Mich. App. 1991). See generally Cathryn C. Dakin, Protecting Attorneys Against Wrongful Discharge: Extension of the Public Policy Exception, 44 Case W. Res. L. Rev. 1343 (1995); Justine Thompson, Who Is Right About Responsibility: An Application of Rights Talk to

*Balla v. Gambro, Inc.* and *General Dynamics Corp. v. Rose*, 44 Duke L.J. 1020 (1995). Similar issues can arise with other professionals.

In addition to restricting the sources of public policy, some courts seem willing to extend the cause of action only to cases in which the employer required the employee to violate the law or constitution. There are many public policies whose vindication would not fall within this limitation on the cause of action. Other decisions go further and bar discharge for conduct that public policy encourages but does not require. For example, although failure to report a criminal violation to public authorities is rarely illegal, public policy clearly encourages "whistleblowing." E.g., Garibaldi v. Lucky Food Stores, Inc., 726 F.2d 1366 (9th Cir. 1984) (adulterated milk); Palmer v. Brown, 752 P.2d 685 (Kan. 1988) (Medicaid fraud); Shriner v. Megginnis Ford Co., 421 N.W.2d 755 (Neb. 1988) (odometer falsification).

Still other courts protect employees who are said to be exercising a public right. Into this classification can be placed the many decisions recognizing a cause of action when an employee is discharged for filing a workers' compensation claim. E.g., Springer v. Weeks & Leo Co., 429 N.W.2d 558 (Iowa 1988). Decisions related to polygraphs fall in this group. E.g., Ambroz v. Cornhusker Sq. Ltd., 416 N.W.2d 510 (Neb. 1987). On the other hand, much conduct that is in some sense socially desirable is not protected by public policy in the sense the courts require. And the notion of "public right" may be of limited usefulness because employers have been permitted to fire workers for doing that which they had an abstract "right" to do. See Beam v. IPCO, 838 F.2d 242 (7th Cir. 1988) (hiring an attorney not protected); Miller v. Sevamp, Inc., 362 S.E.2d 915 (Va. 1987) (testifying at grievance hearing not protected by public policy); Scroghan v. Kraftco Corp., 551 S.W.2d 811 (Ky. App. 1977) (allowing discharge of an employee for attending law school).

Another issue arises when the statutory scheme that is the basis of the public policy provides for private enforcement. For example, as we will see, it is against public policy to fire a worker because she has become pregnant. But the statutes that establish that policy — Title VII and its state analogs — typically establish an enforcement scheme that has its own procedural and remedial provisions. May an employee escape the limitations of those laws by simply bringing a "public policy" tort action? The courts tend to answer in the negative. Makovi v. Sherwin Williams Co., 561 A.2d 179 (Md. 1989) (pregnancy discrimination); Sands Regent v. Valgardson, 777 P.2d 898 (Nev. 1989) (age discrimination); Webb v. Puget Sound Broad. Co., 1998 Wash. App. LEXIS 1795 (sexual orientation). But see Collins v. Elkay Mining Co., 371 S.E.2d 46 (W. Va. 1988) (tort action allowed for discharge for refusal to falsify mine safety reports because administrative remedies were inadequate and the statutes did not specify that their remedies were exclusive). See generally Mark D. Greenebaum, Toward a Common Law of Employment Discrimination, 58 Temple L.Q. 65 (1985).

In the wake of the public policy cases, some jurisdictions have enacted "whistleblower" statutes. See, e.g., Conn. Gen. Stat. Ann. § 31-51m (West Supp. 1992); Me. Rev. Stat. Ann. tit. 26, § 833 (West 1995); Mich. Comp. Laws Ann. §§ 15.361 to 15.368 (West 1991); Minn. Stat. § 181.932 (1996); Montana Wrongful Discharge from Employment Act, Mont. Code Ann. §§ 39-2-501 et seq. (1987); N.J. Conscientious Employee Protection Act, N.J. Stat. Ann. §§ 34:191 et seq. (West 1986); N.Y. Lab. Law § 740 (McKinney 1988); Tenn. Code Ann. § 50-1-304 (2001). These laws are themselves sources of employee rights, and they are not necessarily coextensive with the public policy exception as recognized by the courts in these jurisdictions. The relationship between the common law tort and the statutory cause of action is sometimes dealt with in the whistleblower law, but sometimes not.

## D.   THE FUTURE OF EMPLOYMENT LAW

The foregoing discussion, of course, omits still another area of employment law: the antidiscrimination statutes that will be examined in this book. Nevertheless, it should be clear that employment law, as it currently stands, is basically a collection of pigeonholes. To the extent that a problem fits into the nooks and crannies the law recognizes, employees have rights against their employers. To the extent that it does not, employees can be discharged at the will of their employers.

As an employment lawyer, it is important for you to understand that an employment case may fit into more than one of the law's pigeonholes. Learning to recognize and analyze the issues and arguments available on behalf of employees and employers in discrimination cases is an important first step to adequately representing their interests. You must, however, be cognizant of the alternative rights and remedies available to your clients.

From a policy perspective, it is also important to recognize that there are employment problems that fit none of the predetermined categories. It is true that in the last several decades the number of pigeonholes has multiplied. But, while providing more protection to increasing numbers of workers, this expansion has in some ways merely underscored the incoherence of the underlying legal structures.

The ultimate policy question is whether the law of employment security can or should be rationalized. There are efforts in that direction. For example, the Montana Wrongful Discharge from Employment Act, Mont. Code Ann. §§ 39-2-501 et seq. (1987), attempts to reduce that state's law of job security to a single statute. See Marc Jarsulic, Protecting Workers From Wrongful Discharge: Montana's Experience with Tort and Statutory Regimes, 3 Emp. Rts. & Employ. Pol'y J. 105 (1999). A uniform state solution has also been proposed, but not yet adopted in any state. Uniform Employment Termination Act of the National Conference of Commissioners on Uniform State Law. These initiatives involve complex questions of substantive rights, procedures, and remedies concerning the underlying policy justifications for regulating the employment relation. See generally Kenneth A. Sprang, Beware the Toothless Tiger: A Critique of the Model Employment Termination Act, 43 Am. U. L. Rev. 849 (1994); Theodore J. St. Antoine, Employment-At-Will — Is the Model Act the Answer?, 23 Stetson L. Rev. 179 (1993).

State law reforms, however, even if they approach general just-cause job security, will not eliminate the need for federal antidiscrimination laws, which are the subject of this book. First, federal antidiscrimination legislation cannot be supplanted by state regulation. Second, antidiscrimination laws do not provide general job security or mandate terms and conditions of employment. Rather, antidiscrimination statutes focus on prohibiting employers from making employment decisions based on membership in statutorily protected groups. This approach is both broader and narrower than the other approaches we have surveyed.

## E.   THE ORGANIZATION OF THIS BOOK

Antidiscrimination statutes have spawned complex legal theories defining discrimination and the methods used to prove it. Although the basic prohibitions enjoy broad support, the development of theories of proof and the enactment of statutory reforms expanding employer duties have generated considerable social controversy. Affirmative action, sexual harassment, discrimination on the basis of sexual orientation, comparable worth, and disparate impact liability are just a few of the issues that have tested the limits of discrimination theory. Before we embark on a study of antidiscrimination law, therefore, we explore the underlying policy justifications for the statutes in Chapter 2.

The remainder of this casebook undertakes a complete consideration of the federal antidiscrimination laws. The enactment of Title VII as part of the Civil Rights Act of 1964 marked a legal watershed. Although the statute had precursors, they had proved insufficient to deal with the problem of employment discrimination. State laws against discrimination were often inadequately enforced, and many states where discrimination was most pronounced did not have such laws. Other federal efforts were very limited (e.g., the Equal Pay Act, which guarantees women equal pay, but only for "equal work"), addressed discrimination issues obliquely (e.g., the National Labor Relations Act, which imposes on unions a duty to fairly represent all employees), or reached a relatively few employers (e.g., executive orders prohibiting discrimination by government contractors). Title VII, then, marked the first comprehensive national attack on the problem of employment discrimination.

In the wake of Title VII, a number of developments expanded the federal courts' involvement with employment problems. First, Congress passed additional statutes, most notably the Age Discrimination in Employment Act of 1967, prohibiting discrimination against older workers, and the Americans with Disabilities Act of 1990, barring discrimination against individuals with disabilities. Second, the Supreme Court resuscitated civil rights statutes passed during the Reconstruction era following the Civil War. Sections 1981 and 1983 of Title 42 of the United States Code were among the laws passed to protect the newly freed slaves in the South by implementing the Thirteenth, Fourteenth, and Fifteenth Amendments. Although these statutes had been eviscerated by the Supreme Court in the years shortly after their enactment, the Warren Court revived the early statutes, creating a wide range of statutory tools to deal with employment discrimination. While the Burger and Rehnquist Courts have restricted both the modern civil rights laws and their Reconstruction era predecessors, Congress has reacted strongly on a number of occasions to restore the effectiveness of the antidiscrimination statutes. Most notably, the Pregnancy Discrimination Act in 1978 defined pregnancy discrimination as sex discrimination after the Supreme Court had held the contrary, and the Civil Rights Act of 1991 reversed or substantially modified a number of Supreme Court decisions limiting the effectiveness of Title VII and § 1981.

This book considers all these legislative and judicial efforts to address discrimination in employment. Part II, which focuses on Title VII, the Age Discrimination in Employment Act (ADEA), and 42 U.S.C.S. § 1981 (2003), begins with the foundation problem — defining discrimination in terms of the three theories of liability the courts have evolved. Chapter 3 takes up the most basic concept, intentional discrimination against particular applicants or employees — individual disparate treatment discrimination. Chapter 4 then extends the intentional discrimination concept to broader patterns of such practices — systemic disparate treatment. Chapter 5 considers an alternative test of discrimination, disparate impact. Then Chapter 6 attempts to synthesize the approaches previously developed into a coherent theory of discrimination. Chapter 7 takes up special problems that arise when antidiscrimination law is applied to such issues as pregnancy, sexual harassment, sexual orientation, religion, national origin, age, and retaliation.

Part III then turns to a statute that approaches the question of discrimination somewhat differently. Chapter 8 treats the Americans with Disabilities Act (ADA), which borrows discrimination concepts from the earlier statutes, but applies them in unique ways to a form of discrimination that is itself very different from that studied previously.

Finally, Part IV considers the procedures and the remedial questions that have arisen under the antidiscrimination statutes. Thus, Chapter 9 considers procedures, focusing primarily on Title VII, which is the procedural paradigm for both the ADEA and the ADA. Chapter 10 analyzes the remedies available to redress violations of all the statutes addressed in this book.

# Chapter 2

# The Policy Bases for Antidiscrimination Law

## A. INTRODUCTION

At the beginning of the twenty-first century, federal laws bar discrimination by employers on a number of grounds: race, sex, religion, national origin, age, and disability. In addition, many state laws extend the list of prohibited grounds to marital status, political affiliation, and, increasingly, sexual orientation. What is so bad about discrimination? Employers "discriminate" all the time in the sense that they differentiate between employees for all sorts of reasons. But some bases of differentiation — race, sex, religion, national origin, age, disability — are impermissible, while other bases are perfectly legal. Still other bases, such as sexual orientation, are illegal in a minority of states. Antidiscrimination laws generally prohibit employers from basing their employment decisions on protected group membership, rather than on an employee's qualifications or some other neutral factor. But reliance on neutral factors that disadvantage protected groups is sometimes prohibited as discrimination unless the neutral factor is job related.

The choice to prohibit discrimination emerges from two considerations. Most obviously, discrimination on the basis of certain characteristics, especially race and sex, is usually viewed as unfair because such characteristics are immutable and, therefore, beyond an individual's control. Because discrimination imposes costs on the victim, which he or she in no sense deserves, it is also often viewed as immoral. This rationale, however, has uncertain application to sexual orientation and does not explain the prohibition against discrimination on the basis of religion. Similarly, discrimination on the basis of mutable characteristics, such as political affiliation and marital status, is often viewed as wrongful because of deep-rooted concerns about human autonomy and the inalienability of fundamental rights. From this perspective, then, discrimination is wrongful because it damages the dignity of its victims.

Second, there is an economic thrust to antidiscrimination laws. This emerges most clearly with respect to the Age Discrimination in Employment Act (ADEA), 29 U.S.C.S. §§ 621 et seq. (2003), and the Americans with Disabilities Act (ADA), 42 U.S.C.S. §§ 12101 et seq. (2003), where Congress stressed the waste of human resources caused by discrimination against older workers and workers with disabilities: employer action results not only in individual harm but also in the loss to society of the contributions of those whose abilities are not fully utilized. Although subordinate to dignity values, a concern for the economic consequences of discrimination was also prominent in the enactment of Title VII.* Under this view, reliance on an immutable characteristic or the exercise of a fundamental right to deny employment is objectionable because such factors are unrelated to the individual's ability to work for his own support and that of society. The results can be devastating to the individual victims and to the groups to which they belong.

From this perspective, antidiscrimination statutes are united by two simple premises: first, the groups to be protected by the statute are disadvantaged economically; second, the discriminatory and unfair conduct of employers causes, or at least contributes to, that disadvantage. Approached this way, the statutes seek to end discrimination in order to improve the economic condition of members of protected groups by allowing them to compete freely for jobs on the basis of their qualifications.

Although equal employment opportunity has received almost unanimous support among all racial groups as an abstract principle, the antidiscrimination laws have proved to be controversial in their application. The basic prohibition against express intentional racial discrimination is generally accepted, but a number of discrimination issues, including affirmative action, pregnancy discrimination, sexual harassment, disparate impact, and discrimination on the basis of sexual orientation, have generated intense national debate. Questions have also been raised about the effectiveness of antidiscrimination laws in raising the standard of living of protected groups.

Not everyone, however, agrees that discrimination should be prohibited. Some even question the basic prohibition against express intentional discrimination on account of race. From the beginning, there were those who defended the morality of discrimination or at least questioned the morality of legislating nondiscrimination. The debates over Title VII were filled with arguments by opponents of the statute that it is wrong, even immoral, to force individuals to work with people with whom, for whatever reason, they do not wish to associate. More recently, the argument has been made that discrimination may be rational and efficient. Still another view is that, even if discrimination is wrongful, antidiscrimination laws are unnecessary either

---

* The culmination of the massive civil rights movement of the 1960s was Congress's enactment of the Civil Rights Act of 1964. That statute had a number of important provisions. The centerpiece of the Civil Rights Act of 1964, however, was undoubtedly Title VII, whose focus was unabashedly economic. Because the primary basis of wealth in modern-day America is employment, Congress sought to improve the economic plight of African Americans by opening up employment opportunities to them. The congressional debates on Title VII are replete with references to the economic condition of blacks. Although the emphasis on the economic impact of the legislation was, in part, designed to establish congressional authority for enacting the statute under the commerce clause, Congress clearly hoped to facilitate full participation by African Americans in the U.S. economy.

because market forces will eliminate discrimination without government interference or because discrimination no longer exists as a significant social problem.

This chapter will proceed in section B to consider the claim that prohibiting discrimination is unnecessary because market forces will suffice: they will eradicate all discrimination or at least discrimination that is not "rational." Section C then turns to the harms caused by discrimination. Finally, section D considers the benefits and costs of regulating discrimination.

Most of the discussion in this chapter concerns race discrimination. That is appropriate historically because federal antidiscrimination policy has its roots in the African-American civil rights movement. Further, there is no doubt that race relations remain a critical problem for the United States. As you read, however, consider whether the policy issues addressed in the context of race discrimination are equally applicable to other forms of discrimination.

## B.  ARE ANTIDISCRIMINATION LAWS NECESSARY TO ELIMINATE DISCRIMINATION?

Discrimination, like other real-world phenomena, has posed serious problems for economic theoreticians. Most fundamentally, it is not clear how discrimination can long exist in a free market. An employer that discriminates, after all, must pay a price: artificially contracting the supply of available labor tends to raise the price of the labor purchased. If many employers discriminate, the price (wages) of their workforce will climb. Competitors will be free to exploit the pool of excluded black workers at lower wages, thus gaining a competitive advantage. As more employers seek lower-cost black workers, their value will rise. Thus, discrimination will be corrected by the market, without the need for legal intervention.

While no one believes the competitive model precisely reflects the real world, a number of noted economists have argued that the unregulated market will actually eliminate discrimination. Professor John J. Donohue III, in Advocacy Versus Analysis in Assessing Employment Discrimination Law, 44 Stan. L. Rev. 1583, 1591 (1992), recounts Chicago School opposition to Title VII's passage:

> Thirty years ago, powerful intellectual voices at the University of Chicago registered their strong opposition to the passage of federal civil rights legislation on theoretical grounds. For example, in 1962, Milton Friedman [in Capitalism and Freedom] emphasized that fair employment practice laws were unnecessary because the existing free markets were generating great progress for blacks: "The maintenance of the general rules of private property and of capitalism have [sic] been a major source of opportunity for Negroes and have [sic] permitted them to make greater progress than they otherwise could have made."
>
> Friedman's view became the established orthodoxy for many within the Chicago School tradition who believed that antidiscrimination laws were both unnecessary and unsuccessful at providing economic benefits for blacks. . . .

Implicit in this view is the suggestion that (at least absent government compulsion, as in the pre-1964 South) discrimination does not exist; the poor economic status of statutorily protected groups must, therefore, result from their own choices or their lack of the qualifications necessary to compete.

The market forces argument reappeared more recently in a book by Professor Richard A. Epstein, which added to the economic argument a strong libertarian thrust averse to government intervention. As its title indicates, Forbidden Grounds: The Case Against Employment Discrimination Laws (1992) is an assault on the whole concept of antidiscrimination statutes. While it is hard to know how seriously to take this work in terms of practical politics, the book, and the strong responses to it, help define many of the issues we will encounter in this casebook.

In reading the excerpts in this section and the following one, however, you should be aware of several points. First, these excerpts are a much-abridged version of a considerably longer work and thus risk blurring some of Professor Epstein's argument. Second, Epstein's attack on antidiscrimination laws is consistent with his overall libertarian focus, reflected in Takings: Private Property and the Power of Eminent Domain (1985), and with his prior attacks both on labor law, A Common Law for Labor Relations: A Critique of the New Deal Labor Legislation, 92 Yale L.J. 1357 (1983), and on legal inroads into the at-will rule, In Defense of the Contract At Will, 51 U. Chi. L. Rev. 947 (1984).

## RICHARD A. EPSTEIN, FORBIDDEN GROUNDS: THE CASE AGAINST EMPLOYMENT DISCRIMINATION LAWS
### 20-58 (1992)

The standard autonomy hypothesis has as its major function ruling slavery out of bounds by making self-ownership the natural or inalienable right from which all other rights flow. Other persons cannot simply take people and make them slaves. . . .

It is instructive to recall that the major premise of Locke's theory of property was that each person is the exclusive owner of his own labor: "Though the Earth, and all inferior Creatures be common to all Men, yet every Man has a Property in his own Person. This no Body has any Right to but himself. The Labour of his Body; and the Work of his Hands, we may say, are properly his."[10] Although that notion of ownership did not mean that every person could do exactly what he wanted, it did mean that no person could commandeer the labor of another for his own private use. The ability to use the talents of other persons depended not on coercion but rather on consent — including consent that was purchased in voluntary transactions. . . .

The simplicity of the Lockean position of self-ownership works, as a rough approximation, to the advantage of everyone. In making this claim one finds it possible to tie the arguments for autonomy with the modern economic definitions of social welfare (the test of Pareto superiority), which state that system A is better than system B if no one in A is worse off than in B and at least one person is better off in A than in B. Indeed, we can go one step better than that. The system of self-ownership of labor and talents seems to give major advantages to all persons simultaneously. This advantage explains why the modern attacks on the self-ownership principle, including the antidiscrimination laws, have conceded its basic soundness and have then sought to limit its scope with exceptions and qualifications.

---

10. John Locke, The Second Treatise of Civil Government, ch. 5, 1127 (1690).

## FREEDOM OF CONTRACT AND THE ANTIDISCRIMINATION LAWS

The self-ownership of individual labor forms the cornerstone for freedom of contract in labor markets, with immediate political relevance to the antidiscrimination laws. . . . [T]he autonomy system has one cardinal virtue: it leads to widely decentralized control of labor and property. All individuals own their own labor, and hence can act as both producers and consumers in a relatively competitive labor market. The distinct natural inclinations of separate individuals thus lead toward a system with many centers of property, and many centers of power. The common law, like the Lockean philosopher, knows only a single rule of individual ownership of labor. But it is a rule that permits all labor to be assigned to some unique owner, without incurring the enormous costs of coordination from the center — or from the top. . . .

Setting out the initial entitlement rules for both labor and material resources has important implications for the structure of employment markets in a world devoid of antidiscrimination laws. The basic assumption of markets is that each person is the best judge of what he or she wants and is willing to pay for it. The thing received may be property or a job. The thing surrendered may be cash or labor. But in either case the exchange is one over which each person has veto power. Once initial entitlements are secure, a system of voluntary exchange has no natural stopping point. Endowments of labor or capital are never frozen into their present condition by operation of law. As long as there is a willing buyer and a willing seller, any good can be exchanged between them, even if the rest of the world is indifferent to the exchange or opposed to it.

Similarly, the administrative demands imposed on such a legal system are relatively low [because the exchange need be monitored only to ensure against force, fraud, and incompetence]. When those minimum conditions are satisfied, then the consent of both parties guarantees that the transaction works to their common benefit will surrender only as much as he is willing to give in order to obtain in exchange something he values more. There is no need to plumb the subjective valuations each party attaches to the goods or services that are obtained or transferred. It is enough to know that each party has its own reasons to be satisfied. If consent can be observed, the benefit can be inferred, even if we do not understand the reasons for the transaction ourselves. The task of external validation is far easier than the business judgment of whether or not to make an agreement.

The gains from voluntary exchange are normally not confined to the parties to the transaction, for strangers to the transaction, taken as a class and over the long haul, benefit as well. The greater post-transaction wealth of the contracting parties presents an increased opportunity for exchange that other parties can then exploit by making bargains of their own. . . . In the aggregate (virtually) no one is left worse off under this system than under a system in which all trade is prohibited, and all gains from trade are thereby extinguished. . . .

The antidiscrimination laws should be understood as an assault on the completeness of these common law rules and the intellectual foundations on which they rest. . . .

## VICTIMS OF FORCE AND VICTIMS OF DISCRIMINATION

The rules of self-ownership ensure that there is always a large number of independent suppliers of labor in the general market — and, incidentally, a large number of potential purchasers for that labor. Indeed, it is impossible to organize a labor market in a way that will improve on the world in which each person has the exclusive right to sell his or her own labor. Similarly, the rule of first possession, coupled with the right to resell property acquired by voluntary exchange, ensures large numbers of independent suppliers of goods and property. Satisfying these twin conditions makes it highly likely that competitive markets will emerge. The gains that each person can obtain in transacting with another will be limited not by any barriers created by the legal system, but only by the prospect that potential trading partners can always go elsewhere if the price exceeds what the market will bear. Free entry thus becomes the cardinal feature of the emergent system.

Within this framework it becomes possible to analyze the effect that private discrimination has both on the operation of the market as a whole and on the victims of discrimination. The standard modern accounts of the antidiscrimination laws in effect treat the refusal to deal on grounds of race, sex, or age as a legal wrong, that is, a wrong wholly separate from a breach of contract, and thus (at least by analogy) as some form of common law tort involving harm to strangers. One way to assess the soundness of the equation is to compare the legal prohibition against discrimination (including a refusal to deal) with the tort law's prohibition against the use of force and fraud. Just as there are victims of force, so too there are victims of discrimination, each in his own way an appealing claimant for redress. The parallel between force and discrimination has an apparent verbal seductiveness, but the differences [are profound].

[I]n dealing with force, each of us has to be concerned about the person who bears us the most ill will. That is why we lock our house even when 99 percent of our neighbors are friendly. And even if our worst enemy is bought off or placated, peace is not at hand, for another enemy virtually indistinguishable from the first may rise up to threaten us. The case for public force to constrain aggression thus becomes overpowering because it promises . . . some release from what otherwise would be an endless set of violent interactions with people that each of us would rather avoid. . . .

Markets offer a radical contrast, for (with force and fraud out of bounds) each person now need look only to the other tail of the distribution — the people who make the best offers. The person who wishes to discriminate against another for any reason has it in her power only to refuse to do business with him, not to use force against him. The victim of discrimination, unlike the victim of force, keeps his initial set of entitlements — life, limb, and possession — even if he does not realize the gains from trade with a particular person.

[T]he counterstrategies for the victim of discrimination are clear. No resources need be devoted to self-defense because aggression is already prohibited. Instead, the victim can unilaterally . . . seek out those persons who wish to make the most favorable transactions with him. Thus, in a world in which 90 percent of the people are opposed to doing business with me, I shall concentrate my attention on doing business with the other 10 percent, secure in the knowledge that as long as the tort law (with its prohibitions against the forceful interference with contract or prospective trading advantage) is in place, my enemies are powerless to block our mutually beneficial transactions by their use of force. The universe of potential trading partners is surely smaller . . . [but] the critical question for my welfare is not which opportunities are lost but which are retained. Even for persons who find themselves in relatively isolated minorities, the opportunities retained will not be trivial as the number of persons in society increases from the tens to the hundreds, thousands, and millions. Viable trading economies have thrived in much smaller populations. . . .

In a world of free access to open markets, systematic discrimination, even by a large majority, offers little peril to the isolated minority. Unconstrained by external force, members of minority groups are free to search for jobs with those firms that do want to hire them.

[As for employers, they will tend to have different views about the characteristics of various groups of workers. Even if all employers believe that members of one group (say, whites), on average, tend to be more qualified than members of another group (say, African Americans), there may not be any problem. While such a belief would lead employers to choose less-qualified whites over better-qualified blacks, it would occur only when the employers could obtain no information about individual abilities. In such a case, if the employers' beliefs are based on accurate data, the discrimination will be rational from any individual employer's perspective, but inefficient. More realistically, however, employers will be able to obtain at least some information about the members of each group and will attempt to obtain the best-qualified members from each.]

[O]nce the market environment allows an employer to conduct an interview, ask for a reference, or require the employee to take an aptitude, skill, or psychological test, reliance on general statistical information will diminish because of the ever greater ability to individuate employees.

[Under these conditions, an employer should not concentrate its hiring efforts exclusively on the higher-talent pool because that pool would deteriorate in average quality as employers hire from it. They will no longer hire at random. Rather,] given the variation in the quality of individuals within the pool, each firm will seek to skim off the cream of the workers available at any set wage. . . . When the quality of the workers in the less desired pool exceeds the average quality of the remaining workers in the more desirable pool, then hiring will migrate toward the second pool, notwithstanding the original desire to remain with the preferred talent pool only. . . .

[This argument works even if most firms are not rational], provided there is one firm that understands that it is in its interest to seek gold in a new mine after the old mine has been worked out.

[Further, even if all workers in the first pool are regarded by all employers as superior to any of the workers in the second pool, employers will still look to second pool workers if they can hire them at lower wages.] The workers in the less desired pool can seek to offset their perceived disadvantages by engaging in price cutting. They can provide the same services for less, so the net return to an employer from hiring these workers is the same regardless of the hiring pool. . . .

## Natural Limits on Discrimination

[B]oth employers and employees have strong, if imperfect, incentives to beat the statistical averages by engaging in search. A decision not to trade with a given person cannot be made lightly. As Gary Becker has pointed out,[14] people who decide that they do not want to trade with or hire certain people because of race, sex, or age are making a decision that has more than just external costs. They bear a large part of the costs themselves, for their decision will surely limit their own opportunities for advancement and success, even as it leaves others free to pursue alternate opportunities. The greater the class of persons who are regarded as off-limits, and the more irrational

---

14. See Gary S. Becker, The Economics of Discrimination, ch. 3 (2d ed., 1971). The first edition of the book dates from 1957.

the preferences, the more the decision will hurt the people who make it, and the more numerous the options it will open to rival traders.

[Freedom of contract allows bargains to be made for good reason, bad reason, or no reason at all, but the system works well because people, in the pursuit of their own interests, are sensitive to changes in costs and benefits. "There are natural curbs against irrational contracting behavior even in a system that makes no formal condemnation of practices that others think, perhaps rightly, to be irrational."]

The point is important to an understanding of the weaknesses in some defenses of the antidiscrimination law. When Kenneth Arrow, for example, seeks to give demand-side explanations for the perpetuation of discrimination in employment markets, he writes as though all employers had the same utility function that seeks to maximize a mix of monetary profit and minimize contact with black workers, whom they dislike:

> If we assume away productivity differences between black and white employees, the simplest explanation of the existence of wage differences is the taste of the employer. Formally, we might suppose that the employer acts so as to maximize a utility function that depends not only on profits but also on the numbers of white and black employees. Presumably, other variables being held constant, the employer has a negative marginal utility for black labor. A specific version of this hypothesis would be that the employer's utility depends only on the ratio of black to white workers and is independent of the scale of operations of the firm.[16]

Although that profile may be true of some employers, it surely is not true of all. . . . And as long as there is any difference, those employers who do not dislike dealing with blacks will have a comparative advantage over those who do. Nor is there any reason to assume that all employers are white males, especially in an open market where women and blacks and other minority individuals may become employers, and have in fact increasingly assumed hiring and personnel functions in mainstream corporations. . . .

The same conclusion holds when we deal with the preferences of employees. [Arrow's argument is derived from Becker's. Both posit asymmetrical preferences — blacks uniformly prefer to be with whites, but whites prefer not to be with blacks.] Empirically, however, the premise itself seems false, relative to a more realistic set of assumptions, parallel to those made about employer preferences, which yields very different conclusions. If we assume that some blacks prefer to work with blacks and some whites prefer to work with whites, we should see some firms that voluntarily segregate their work forces and others that do not. . . .

[O]ne can explain why voluntary market segregation will occur as long as there is some fraction of the population that prefers (irrationally or not) to work with persons of like kind, whether defined along racial, ethnic, religious, sexual, or age lines. Yet, by the same token, it is possible that this market is in equilibrium, because the sorting that has taken place is efficient and therefore may generate higher incomes than are otherwise obtainable with work forces integrated under legal mandate. Each firm will make an efficient deployment of its labor resources, and so members of each group should have a wage equal to their marginal product whether they choose to work in a firm that observes voluntary segregation or one that is mixed with respect to race.

16. Kenneth J. Arrow, "Models of Job Discrimination," in Racial Discrimination in Economic Life 83, 86 (Anthony H. Pascal ed. 1972). Arrow previously noted that supplyside explanations (e.g., differentials in human capital) could not account, according to the existing evidence, for more than about 50 or 60 percent of the wage differential. Id. at 84–85.

In theory, then, the persistence of voluntary segregated markets with free entry is not odious. . . .

## SOME EMPIRICAL EVIDENCE

The arguments just advanced are all of a distinct theoretical cast. The question naturally arises as to the state of the empirical evidence in unregulated markets. That evidence is of course difficult if not impossible to find in labor markets today, given the pervasive presence of Title VII. Defenders of the antidiscrimination law therefore have sought to find evidence of persistent market discrimination based on the preferences of white employers, workers, or consumers, which could account for wage differentials that are unrelated to differences in output. In principle, as long as the alternative of voluntary sorting is available, overall wage effects of this sort should be small. Nonetheless, . . . recent studies have sought to show that the effects of discrimination are larger than one might have supposed. . . . [One] study, on the level of dealer markups on staged car purchase transactions, was undertaken by Ian Ayres.[25] [Another], by the Urban Institute, deals with the effects of discrimination in two selected employment markets.[26]

[Ayres's study sent student-testers into automobile showrooms with detailed instructions on how to negotiate the purchase price of certain models. As described by Epstein, the average markup for white males was lower than the markups for white women, black women, and black males. The difference from top to bottom was about 10 percent of retail price and a much larger percentage of the retail markups.]

[I]t is possible, as Ayres acknowledges, that cost-based differentials could account for some portion of the difference. As I have noted, sales personnel pressed financing issues even though the testers all announced that they could pay cash. If the sellers thought that their potential buyers needed financing, they would have believed there was more of a chance that the deal would fall through, and acted accordingly. The greater risk arguably associated with black and female customers could induce sales personnel to charge higher prices to cover their own costs. Similarly, if any additional services had to be provided to customers to sell the car, say, because of differential customer knowledge, these too would be reflected in the bids elicited. No attempt to standardize testers along these different dimensions could be completely successful, for the shrewd car seller will take into account not only what individual customers say but whatever reliable background information he or she possesses about the relevant groups. Some portion of the observed differential may be cost driven. . . .

[In 1991, the Urban Institute used matched pairs of black and white testers to study entry-level positions in the retail and service trades advertised in Washington, D.C., and Chicago newspapers. The study found discrimination against young black job seekers. Epstein's criticisms include noting that, in most cases, neither of the testers received an offer or both did. But in the cases where only one received an offer, 15 percent of the overall cases had the white tester successful, compared to 5 percent of the cases with a successful black tester. Stating these results most strongly, Epstein agrees that 28 percent of the white testers received offers, compared to only 18 percent of the black testers, "a significant difference of over 50 percent in hiring rates."

25. Ian Ayres, "Fair Driving: Gender and Race Discrimination in Retail Car Negotiations," 104 Harv. L. Rev. 817 (1991).
26. Margery Austin Turner, Michael Fix, and Raymond J. Struyk, Opportunities Denied, Opportunities Diminished: Discrimination in Hiring (1991).

But he goes on to raise "serious methodological difficulties" with the study. Covering only a small segment of the job market, and limiting the study to jobs advertised in newspapers, "destroys any possibility of randomization." He stressed that "[t]he public sector is excluded from the entire sample, as are a disproportionate percentage of private firms with affirmative action programs." Second, he questions the assumption that differential hiring rates establish discrimination because it is impossible to be sure that the only difference between the black and white members of each pair was race.]

The Institute also was unable to hold constant the relative cost to the firm of the two applicants. The point manifests itself in two ways. First, . . . an important concern for a firm is how a given worker fits in. The ability to maintain cohesion within the firm and with a customer base may depend in part on the race of an employee. If these costs are higher in some settings for workers of one race than another, then we should expect to see some difference in hiring patterns. The differences need not all cut in the same direction, as is evident by the preferences that some black testers received in the Institute's own study. To hold, as the Institute does, that the reasons for the discrimination are wholly irrelevant is to say that some costs are irrelevant as well.

Second, all the employers who were tested operated not in an unregulated market but in a Title VII environment. If they perceived that it would be more difficult to fire blacks once hired, then the cost of taking a black worker would be higher than that of taking a white worker. Again, that difference in cost could easily be translated into a lower level of offers for black workers. The matter is complicated because under Title VII the cost of turning down a black applicant may also be higher, given the risk of suit. But the two effects need not be equal in magnitude in all cases. . . .

*NOTES*

1. Professor Epstein's starting point is the right of every human to own his or her own labor. He undoubtedly shares this common ground with his many critics. Earlier in the book, however, Epstein writes:

> There remains a very hard question of whether contracts to create slavery should be allowed. On the one side it seems consistent with the autonomy principle to permit this to happen. But the issue is surely more complicated. One difficulty is with externalities: are the children of slaves to be slaves as well? Another is with the intrinsic imbalance of the exchange. If the prohibition against selling selves into slavery were lifted, how many contracts of this sort would be observed? And if there were only a few, could we say that there are good reasons to believe that most of these would be tainted with incompetence, fraud, and duress, themselves inferable from the intrinsic inequality of the terms of the exchange, just as when one sells a share of stock worth $100 for $1 in cash?

Richard A. Epstein, Forbidden Grounds 20 n.6 (1992). Is it possible to take seriously a political theory that would find slavery "a very hard question"? Alternatively, if Epstein would reject such contracts because of externalities or because most "would be tainted with incompetence, fraud, and duress," is his libertarian proscription as simple as it seems?

2. Like Milton Friedman, Epstein suggests that the market should eliminate most discrimination. But if this is so, how did race and gender segregation exist so pervasively in our country before 1964? For economists, one explanation for continuing discrimination is simply that the free market is hamstrung by government regulation.

In an extended discussion in a part of his book not reproduced, Professor Epstein attributes discrimination in the South prior to the Civil Rights Act of 1964 to regulation by state and local governments and their condoning of private violence to keep the black population "in its place." As Professor Gregory S. Crespi, Market Magic: Can the Invisible Hand Strangle Bigotry?, 72 B.U. L. Rev. 991, 1002 (1992), summarized:

> In [Epstein's] opinion, the pre-1964 South cannot be fairly characterized as a market system, but was instead a totalitarian system in which discriminatory attitudes were strongly reinforced by a pervasive system of both governmental and extralegal sanctions imposed upon anyone who opposed the racist consensus. Any firm that contemplated hiring black workers for positions traditionally held by whites had to consider not only the likely reactions of its current workers, owners, suppliers, and customers — which to Epstein are altogether legitimate considerations in a market system — but also the very real possibility of state and local governmental harassment, as well as the possibility of extralegal actions such as vandalism and threats of violence from local racists.

Because of this, Professor Donohue notes that, despite philosophical similarities to Friedman, "Epstein departs from the Chicago School orthodoxy by acknowledging the initial economic gains for blacks that [Title VII] generated." John J. Donohue III, Advocacy Versus Analysis in Assessing Employment Discrimination Law, 44 Stan. L. Rev. 1583, 1593 (1992). For Epstein, Title VII is no longer necessary as long as state and local governments do not return to the days of de jure segregation and toleration of private violence.

3. While no one denies the evils of formal racial segregation and repression reflected in Jim Crow laws, other commentators strongly disagree that Southern discrimination prior to 1964 was merely the result of such laws. Almost no statutes required private employers to discriminate against black workers. Professor J. Hoult Verkerke, Free to Search, 105 Harv. L. Rev. 2080, 2080 (1992), rebuts Epstein's contention that "the history of slavery and racial discrimination in the Jim Crow South shows that state government coercion and private violence were necessary to maintain discrimination."

> The available evidence does not support Epstein's claims. First, the historical record fails to show that state government coercion was necessary to maintain the segregated system. With the exception of the South Carolina textile employment segregation law, all of the statutes to which Epstein refers involved areas of economic and social life other than labor markets. The best explanation for these statutes is that they were enacted to patch holes in the preexisting system of segregation and subordination, which was itself sufficiently ingrained that it required no state coercion to maintain. Contrary to Epstein's hypothesis, the absence of discriminatory statutes mandating employment segregation suggests strongly that there was no hole to be patched in that area. In the labor market, at least, other forces sufficiently enforced the segregationist norm. The role of private violence in enforcing the segregationist norm was undoubtedly greater than that of state law. . . . Nonetheless, a widely shared belief in the inferiority of blacks, coupled with the powerful cultural norms establishing white economic, social, and political dominance were other important forces that maintained segregation. We can only speculate about whether social norms and economic pressure alone could have sustained the subordination of blacks.
> . . . Although Epstein champions freedom in social and contractual relations, he fails to acknowledge the powerful influence that a concerted refusal to deal, coupled with social ostracism, could have on someone who failed to conform to the segregation-

ist norm. Social pressures and economic boycotts or other forms of retaliation against nonconforming white employers all fall outside the reach of Epstein's libertarian prohibition against force and fraud. Thus, these sanctions would be protected from legal prohibition just as Epstein would protect the discriminatory refusal to deal. Yet such pressures might easily have been sufficient to maintain much of the segregationist system.

Professor Verkerke then criticized Epstein for offering no meaningful explanation for segregation and discrimination in the North. Professor John J. Donohue III, supra note 2, at 1594, also addresses Epstein's focus on the 1915 South Carolina statute: "Heckman and Payner document that the exclusion of blacks in the industry was complete from 1910-15 (prior to the passage of the law)." He asks, "Where was the vaunted power of the market to break down discriminatory exclusions?" See also Norman C. Amaker, Quittin' Time?: The Antidiscrimination Principle of Title VII vs. the Free Market, 60 U. Chi. L. Rev. 757, 767-69 (1993).

4. How would Epstein account for the pervasive occupational sex segregation that existed prior to the Civil Rights Act of 1964? Relatively few occupations were legally closed to women, and there were no analogs to lynching to deter occupational gender desegregation.

5. Even if race discrimination persisted despite free markets prior to the Civil Rights Act, it could be argued that discrimination has been successfully eliminated and that continued application of the antidiscrimination laws is, therefore, unnecessary. While Professor Epstein questions the validity of studies showing current discrimination, is he doubting the existence of discrimination or merely denying that discrimination has a detrimental economic impact? Concerning the existence of discrimination, David Benjamin Oppenheimer, in Negligent Discrimination, 141 U. Pa. L. Rev. 899 (1993), concludes that racial attitudes persist. Although he posits that these attitudes largely reflect "unconscious racism," most of the data he cites could equally support more conscious views. In national opinion polls, while whites almost unanimously support equal employment opportunity in the abstract, there is considerably less support on more concrete issues, and on particular questions, strong evidence of racial attitudes exists. For example, 62 percent of the subjects rated blacks as less hard-working than whites. Id. at 908-09. Similarly, "unobtrusive studies" of white racial attitudes, such as the willingness to voluntarily help people facing everyday difficulties, demonstrate a tendency of whites to assist whites more than blacks. See also Donohue, supra note 2, at 1583.

6. The Urban Institute study was criticized by Epstein for its methodological difficulties. It found strong evidence of continued discrimination in hiring even in a world in which many believe that affirmative action has provided hiring advantages to racial minorities. The researchers randomly selected newspaper advertisements for job vacancies. Matched pairs of black and white "auditors" then applied for the jobs:

> The hiring audits were conducted by ten pairs of full-time, paid auditors, five pairs in each of the two audit sites. Careful recruitment, matching and training of auditors was integral to the success of the study. The auditors, one black and one white, were carefully matched to control for all "job relevant" characteristics. Specifically, these were experience, education, age, and physical strength and size. Audit partners were made identical in a defined set of job qualifications and trained so that other attributes — demeanor, openness, articulateness, and energy level — were as similar as possible. Race was the only important difference between the two members of each audit team.

Margery Austin Turner, Michael Fix & Raymond J. Struyk, Opportunities Denied, Opportunities Diminished: Discrimination in Hiring 11-12 (1991). The study summarized the results:

> A total of 576 hiring audits were conducted in the metropolitan areas of Washington D.C. and Chicago during the summer of 1990. In one out of five audits, the white applicant was able to advance farther through the hiring process than his equally qualified black counterpart. In other words, the white was able to either submit an application, receive a formal interview, or the white was offered a job when the black was not. Overall, in one out of eight or 15 percent of the audits, the white was offered a job although his equally qualified black partner was not.
>
> By way of contrast, black auditors advanced farther than their white counterparts on only 7 percent of the audits and the black auditors received job offers where their white partners did not in 5 percent of the audits. In sum, if equally qualified black and white candidates are in competition for a job, when differential treatment occurs, it is three times more likely to favor the white applicant than to favor the black.

Id. at 31-32. The report notes that "[a]ll statistical results presented in this summary are significant at the 99 percent confidence level." Id. at 32 n.33. It suggests that the results are realistic, if not underrepresentative, of the level of discrimination in hiring in part because the researchers studied public advertisements rather than hiring done through word of mouth or employment agencies, where there are even more opportunities for discrimination. See also Fair Employment Council of Greater Washington, Inc., Measuring Employment Discrimination Through Controlled Experiments (1991) (similar study reaching similar results).

7. The Urban Institute study noted other surveys supporting the continued pervasiveness of discriminatory attitudes. The Institute had conducted an earlier audit of discrimination against Hispanics in Chicago and San Diego. "[I]n 31 percent of the Hispanic-Anglo audits, the majority applicant advanced farther through the hiring process, compared to 20 percent of the black-white audits." Turner, Fix & Struyk, supra note 6, at 32.

8. A recent study concluded that, while some progress had been made, women and minorities still have significant problems with employment discrimination. Professors Alfred W. Blumrosen and Ruth G. Blumrosen drew on EEOC data for some 200,000 large and midsize employers and concluded that about two million workers were affected by intentional discrimination in 1999. "Roughly a third of the employers studied appeared to have discriminated against women or minorities in at least one job category. . . ." Reed Abelson, Study Finds Bias on the Job Is Still Common, N.Y. Times, July 24, 2002, at C2. "About 22,000 employers were identified as 'hard core' discriminators. These companies employed below-average numbers of women and minorities for 10 years and their hiring of women or minorities was so far below the averages that there was only one chance in a hundred that the discrimination occurred randomly." The study is available at www.eeo1.com (last visited on Dec. 6, 2002). The use of statistical analysis to establish discrimination is explored further at pages 236-251.

9. The groups protected by antidiscrimination laws all suffer from some degree of economic disadvantage. See section D. Does this persistent disadvantage suggest discriminatory conduct on the part of employers, or are there alternative explanations? For example, some feminists emphasize that women view the world differently than men. See, e.g., Carol Gilligan, In a Different Voice (1982). Employers have seized on this notion to argue that the segregation of the employment market along gender

lines and the paucity of females in certain positions are the result of female choices, rather than intentional gender discrimination by employers. Arguments like this have been used to defeat employment discrimination suits on behalf of women. See EEOC v. Sears, Roebuck & Co. (reproduced at page 253). See generally Vicki Schultz, Telling Stories About Women and Work: Judicial Interpretations of Sex Segregation in the Workplace in Title VII Cases Raising the Lack of Interest Argument, 103 Harv. L. Rev. 1749 (1990); Lucinda Finley, Choice and Freedom: Elusive Issues in the Search for Gender Justice, 96 Yale L.J. 914 (1987); Joan Williams, Deconstructing Gender, 87 Mich. L. Rev. 797 (1989).

10. If significant discrimination persists, how can economic theory explain its continuance despite free markets? Epstein refers to the theory, articulated by Gary Becker in The Economics of Discrimination (2d ed. 1971), that employers have a "taste for discrimination." The basic idea was expressed in Richard A. Posner, Economic Analysis of Law § 27.1, at 525-26 (2d ed. 1977):

Many people would prefer not to associate with the members of particular racial, religious, or ethnic groups different from their own and would pay a price to indulge their taste. Thus, although there are pecuniary gains to trade between blacks and whites — to blacks working for whites (or vice versa), whites selling houses to blacks, and so forth — . . . by increasing the contact between members of the two races such trade imposes nonpecuniary, but real, costs on those members of either race who dislike association with members of the other race. . . .

What is the impact of reduced exchange on the wealth of the groups involved? Assume that whites do not like to associate with blacks but that blacks are indifferent to the racial identity of those with whom they associate. The incomes of many whites will be lower than they would be if they did not have such a taste. They forgo advantageous exchanges: for example, they may refuse to sell their houses to blacks who are willing to pay higher prices than white purchasers. The racial preference of the whites will also reduce the incomes of the blacks, by preventing them from making advantageous exchanges with whites, and the reduction in the blacks' incomes will be proportionately greater than the reduction in the whites' income. Because blacks are only a small part of the economy, the number of advantageous exchanges that blacks can make with whites is greater than the number of advantageous transactions that whites can make with blacks. The white sector is so large as to be virtually self-sufficient; the black sector is much smaller and more dependent on trade with the white.

[Discrimination is consistent with competition, but in a competitive market,] there are economic forces working to minimize discrimination that are blunted in a market either monopolized or controlled by government. In a market of many sellers one can expect the intensity of the prejudice against blacks to vary considerably. Some sellers will have only a mild prejudice against them. These sellers will not forgo as many advantageous transactions with blacks as their more prejudiced competitors. Their costs will therefore be lower and this will enable them to increase their share of the market. The least prejudiced sellers will come to dominate the market in much the same way as people who are least afraid of heights come to dominate occupations that require working at heights: they demand a smaller premium for working at such a job.

Professor David A. Strauss, in The Law and Economics of Racial Discrimination in Employment: The Case for Numerical Standards, 79 Geo. L.J. 1619 (1991), notes that the "taste" may be that of the employer itself or of someone the employer has to consider — other employees or customers. Depending on the strength of the taste, a black may not be employed at all or may be employed at a wage that is low enough to compensate for the "distaste" of employing her. Strauss explores different models depending on whether discrimination results from animus by employers, coworkers, or customers. See also David Charny & G. Mitu Gulati, Efficiency — Wages, Tournaments, and Discrimination: A Theory of Employment Discrimination Law for High-Level Jobs, 33 Harv. C.R.-C.L. L. Rev. 57, 68 (1998) (arguing that in high-level jobs, "difficulties in monitoring (or, equivalently, discretion by managers in evaluating workers) create powerful opportunities for discriminatory hiring and promotion").

11. Professor Epstein cites Gary Becker's work, but seems unimpressed by it because differences in employer tastes should work to eliminate discrimination. He does concede, however, that "voluntary market segregation" might occur, although "it is possible that this market is in equilibrium, because the sorting that has taken place is efficient and therefore may generate higher incomes than are otherwise obtainable with work forces integrated under legal mandate." Is his point that all-white firms will be matched by all-black firms? If so, does this confirm or refute Becker's point?

12. Both the "taste for discrimination" theory and Epstein's "voluntary market segregation" acknowledge that, in a free market system, some employment decisions are made on the basis of race. This is, of course, the essence of discrimination. Market forces may reduce discrimination, but they will not eliminate it. Whether government regulation prohibiting discrimination is necessary, therefore, cannot rest solely on the argument that discrimination does not exist in a free market system. Given that market economists acknowledge that discrimination — employment decisions based on membership in a statutorily protected group — exists even when the market is unregulated, the issue becomes the extent to which discrimination is harmful. Even if discrimination is wrong, government prohibition might not be the appropriate solution, but government regulation certainly makes no sense unless discrimination causes meaningful harm.

## C.  WHY PROHIBIT DISCRIMINATION?

Opponents of the Civil Rights Act argued that prohibiting discrimination infringes on the freedom to associate. In this view, discrimination is not wrongful because it is merely a form of the right to associate with whomever one pleases. Echoes of this debate were heard in connection with the 1987 nomination of Judge Robert Bork as a Justice of the United States Supreme Court. In 1963, Judge Bork had written an article attacking proposed civil rights legislation:

> Of the ugliness of racial discrimination there need be no argument (though there may be some presumption in identifying one's own hotly controverted aims with the objective of the nation). But it is one thing when stubborn people express their racial antipathies in laws which prevent individuals, whether white or Negro, from dealing with those who are willing to deal with them, and quite another to tell them that even as individuals they may not act on their racial preferences in particular areas of life. The principle of such legislation is that if I find your behavior ugly by my standards, law or aesthetic, and if you prove stubborn about adopting my view of the situation, I am justified in having the state coerce you into more righteous paths. That is itself a principle of unsurpassed ugliness.

Robert Bork, Civil Rights — A Challenge, The New Republic, Aug. 31, 1963, at 22. While Bork's position contributed to the defeat of his nomination in 1987, the notions that discrimination is not necessarily wrongful and that prohibiting it is bad policy have reappeared in a different form in Professor Epstein's book.

## RICHARD A. EPSTEIN, FORBIDDEN GROUNDS: THE CASE AGAINST EMPLOYMENT DISCRIMINATION LAWS
### 59-77 (1992)

[F]ree entry and multiple employers provide ample protection for all workers, even those faced with policies of overt and hostile discrimination by some employers. Where markets do not have formal barriers to entry, the victims of discrimination have effective strategies of self-protection and powerful allies whose own self-interest will operate on their behalf. Imperfections in employment markets, however, are not limited to imperfect information about employee quality. Other frictions must be taken into account as well. [Search costs and governance costs] help explain why certain forms of discrimination may be rational from the point of view of both the firm and the larger society. In a nutshell, discrimination in some contexts is a rational response to the frictions that necessarily arise out of long-term employment contracts.

The traditional conclusion, often repeated in the economic literature, starting with Becker, that competitive markets will drive out all forms of discrimination should hold in a world in which transaction costs do not matter. But once the analysis turns to the world of positive transaction costs, identified with Ronald Coase,[1] that conclusion is no longer valid. It is now possible that some forms of discrimination could improve the ability of certain firms to compete. If so, then we should not expect to see all forms of discrimination driven out in unregulated markets. The arguments . . . indicate why all groups have some rational incentives to discriminate on the very grounds — race, creed, sex, age, religion — that Title VII prohibits. And if these cases of rational discrimination are the ones likely to persist, then the hidden costs of Title VII are higher than is ordinarily supposed. . . .

### COLLECTIVE CHOICE WITHIN GROUPS . . .

The group that can minimize differences in tastes will sometimes be ahead of the game, relative to one that has to rely on sophisticated decision rules to resolve deepseated divisions of opinion. To see why, assume for the moment that all workers have identical preferences on all matters relevant to the employment relation. If the question is whether or not they wish to have music piped into a common work area, they all want music. If the question is what kind of music they wish to hear, the answer is classical — indeed, mostly Mozart. If the question is how loud, the agreement is perfect down to the exact decibel. In this employment utopia, decisions of collective governance are easy to make. The employer who satisfies preferences of any single worker knows that he or she has satisfied the preferences of the entire work force. It takes little effort and little money to achieve the highest level of group satisfaction. The nonwage terms of collective importance can be set in ways that unambiguously promote firm harmony.

---

1. Ronald Coase, "The Problem of Social Cost," 3 J.L. & Econ. 1 (1960).

The situation is quite different once it is assumed that there is no employee homo-geneity in taste within the workplace. . . . The general proposition is clear: as the tastes within the group start to diverge, it becomes harder to reach a decision that works for the common good. If half the workers crave classical music but loathe rock, and half like rock but disdain classical music, it is very difficult to decide whether mu-sic shall be played in the workplace at all, and if so what kind. The wider the variation in taste, the more troublesome these collective decisions are. . . . If the level of dissat-isfaction increases exponentially as the gap between private choice and collective de-cision increases, then the people at either tail of the distribution have additional in-centives to leave the group when the decision goes against them.

[One way to cut costs is to reduce variances in tastes among group members.] Henry Hansmann has noted the reluctance of many law firms to take women in as part-time partners.[5] In addition to offering the conventional explanations that part-time attorneys are not at the beck and call of clients, and may not hone their legal skills, he identifies governance cost as a possible source of concern by noting:

> It appears likely that such inequalities among members of the firm are also resisted at least in part because they tend to destabilize the governance structure. A simple rule, under which everyone does essentially the same amount and kind of work, and receives the same pay, is by far the easiest to agree upon and to enforce, and these advantages are evidently often sufficient to outweigh the costs such a simple rule engenders in the form of inflexibility, poor incentives, and lack of diversification among the workforce.

In a sense Hansmann's point is overstated, because it is evident that the relevant trade-offs will not be made in such stark terms. Some variation in work or pay may well be worth the additional strain it places on governance costs. But even when that correc-tion is taken into account, the relation between firm composition and governance cost persists. . . .

The identical set of concerns carries over to employment situations. The increase in the harmony of tastes and preferences thus works in the long-run interest of all mem-bers. To the extent, therefore, that individual tastes are grouped by race, by sex, by age, by national origin — and to some extent they are — then there is a necessary conflict between the commands of any antidiscrimination law and the smooth operation of the firm. Firms whose members have diverse and clashing views may well find it more difficult to make collective decisions than firms with a closer agreement over tastes.

Again, the point here does not lead to the prediction that all voluntary firms will organize along lines that are regarded as illegal under the antidiscrimination laws. . . . First, as Hansmann notes, the firms that are reluctant to accept part-time women partners routinely make arrangements to take part-time associates, including perma-nent associates. As long as associates are not directly involved in firm governance, their continued participation in the firm may work to everyone's advantage. Second, an employer may be concerned that having a perfectly homogeneous work force exposes the firm to the threat of unionization or other concerted employee action that could reduce its effectiveness. It may well be that some differentiation is de-sirable where this threat is large, but not in instances where it is not. The ultimate question is an empirical one, but provided there are some cases in which the gains from homogenization outweigh the costs, then we should see firms (or perhaps only

5. Henry Hansmann, "When Does Worker Ownership Work? ESOPs, Law Firms, Codetermination, and Economic Democracy," 99 Yale L.J. 1749, 1787-88 (1990).

departments within firms) concerned about the interactive effects of workers and the composition of their work force.

Thus far it has been shown only that voluntary sorting can reduce the costs of making and enforcing group decisions. It remains to be noted that this sorting often takes place on racial, ethnic, religious, or sexual lines. The missing premise is that persons who are "the same" in some fundamental way are more likely to bring similar preferences to the workplace. In some cases the explanations are relatively benign. Workers may prefer to sort themselves out by language. It is easier and cheaper for everyone if Spanish-speaking workers work with Spanish-speaking workers and Polish-speaking workers with Polish-speaking workers, all other things held constant. Indeed, it seems quite possible that there are variations within the English language that make communication easier between blacks and other blacks than between blacks and whites.[6] These language differences tend to lead to a prediction of voluntary segregation within the workplace, the intensity of which varies as a function of the level of separation between the languages.

The commonality of preferences may extend beyond language to other features of collective life: the music played in the workplace, the food that is brought in for lunch, the holidays on which the business is closed down, the banter around the coffeepot, the places chosen for firm outings, and a thousand other small details that contribute to the efficiency of the firm. "Like attracts like" is not a universal or a necessary truth; but as long as it is an empirical and a partial one, it helps explain why in unregulated markets some firms are organized along specialized lines while others are not. . . .

In certain cases it may be that the preferences for voluntary segregation are based on ill will or other uglier sentiments. Nonetheless, the advantages of voluntary sorting cannot be ignored here either. If all persons who have a rabid hatred for members of different racial, ethnic, or other groups are concentrated within a small number of firms, then it makes governance questions easier for the remaining firms, as they do not have to contend constantly with dissidents and troublemakers. It follows, therefore, that voluntary sorting should (other skills being held constant) raise the level of satisfaction for all workers in the workplace. Not only are market segregation and market discrimination (that is, income differentials) distinct concepts, as Becker noted, but they are also variables that may be negatively correlated: real income will tend to rise for all as the level of voluntary sorting increases. . . .

There are, however, two sides to this question. Still to be considered are the benefits of diversity. . . . If all employees are exactly alike, then the firm may find it more difficult to establish bonds with some classes of potential customers. Diversity in a sales force may provide a benefit that offsets the costs of internal divisions on collective tastes. But the opposite conclusion may hold if the firm caters to a single class of customers. The problem for the firm is to find a way to maximize its profits, taking into account its total costs, including organizational costs. In some cases the gains from diversity will be rejected as too costly. But in others, firms will choose to maintain some degree of diversity and some degree of homogeneity, and expend resources (on retreats, picnics, intramural athletics, personnel departments) to foster a spirit of cooperation. In this type of environment, moreover, workers who are content to go along with most decisions offer a valuable asset their more eccentric colleagues lack: at the very least, they do not make waves, and they may help foster a communal spirit within the firm. As organizations grow and seek to serve broad national or international

6. See Kevin Lang, "A Language Theory of Discrimination," 101 Quart. J. Econ. 363 (1986).

markets, it is highly doubtful that the firm itself could employ only members of one race, sex, or ethnic background. But it is quite possible even for large firms to maintain segregated divisions of workers in its various subdepartments or plants. . . .

### EXPANDING EMPLOYMENT OPPORTUNITIES

The actual dynamics internal to the firm are thus quite complex. There are good reasons why diversity is a strength, and others why it is a weakness. The basic complexity is difficult to measure, and perilous to regulate, from the outside. All that can be said with confidence is that the forces that tug in opposite directions need not be of the same strength across different firms, or even within different divisions of the same firm. Within voluntary markets we should expect to see, even in the long run, a wide divergence in the level of voluntary discrimination, but not, as it has sometimes been supposed, the total elimination of discrimination by competitive forces.[12] Some firms will practice it widely; others will find it of little value.

These natural differences in firm profile count as a strong argument against the view, so common in modern legal and political thinking, that any deviation between the composition of the firm and the larger work force should be met with hostility and suspicion. In fact, quite the opposite is true. A perfect correspondence between the firm and the market demonstrates that the gains from trade available through specialization have not been realized; the identical structure and composition of all firms is a clear sign of underdeveloped markets, and of the dangerous effects of regulation. . . .

[Further, the costs of government intervention are not inconsiderable.] First, it is a mistake to assume that the number of opportunities available to workers is constant regardless of the external legal rules that govern the operation of the firm. The antidiscrimination provision places powerful limitations on firm structure, and should, like any tax, be expected to reduce the number of firms that enter the marketplace, and hence the number of employment opportunities. Some firms at the margin will not survive in an environment in which their costs are increased by regulation. . . .

Second, the antidiscrimination policy, as I have noted, makes the problem of internal governance more difficult than would otherwise be the case. If workers who have strong preferences against any particular group are allowed to break off and form their own firms, it improves the value of the opportunities that other individuals enjoy in the firms that remain. If all the bigots and troublemakers are isolated in a small number of firms, other workers have a more attractive array of firms to choose from than they would if bigoted workers were distributed randomly across all firms. Thus, although the number of opportunities may go down, the value of the opportunities that do remain should increase.

Third, the argument for equal access presupposes some powerful notion of "legitimate" preferences that allows us to rule out of bounds the preferences of workers who do not have accepted or correct views on workplace arrangements. [Theoretically,] there is no obvious reason why the preferences of any individuals should be excluded in determining the desirability of public regulation. Certainly there is no standard measure of social welfare that says the preferences of some persons are to be counted while the preferences of others are to be systematically ignored.

This basic point is valid across the board, and extends to the core cases of illegal conduct. The standard prohibition against force and fraud does not depend on a simple assertion that killing or murder is just illegitimate. Rather, it rests on the

---

12. As postulated in John J. Donohue, "Is Title VII Efficient?" 134 U. Pa. L. Rev. 1411 (1986).

powerful, albeit empirical, judgment that all people value their right to be free from coercion far more than they value their right to coerce others in a Hobbesian war of all against all. . . . But there are no similar universal gains from a rule that says people who have distinct and distasteful preferences cannot go their own way by working and associating only with people of similar views. We may find their tastes offensive, just as they find our tastes offensive and our actions meddlesome. But we do not have to determine the relative intensity of clashing preferences in order to make powerful social judgments. . . . [T]here is good evidence that the preferences are so strong on both sides that no mutually acceptable gains are to be made from long-term forced amalgamation. The fallback position when the antidiscrimination norm is eliminated is not violence and anarchy; it is voluntary separation and competition. The uneasy truce between private voluntary groups can continue over the long run, for it is always possible to have spot trades between individuals who are loath to form permanent associations with one another. . . .

### IS TITLE VII EFFICIENT?

The point of the foregoing arguments is to demonstrate the good reasons for expecting rational discrimination to persist in private markets. My position is at variance with some of the standard economic literature, which says that many forms of discrimination cannot survive in competitive markets. That conclusion would surely be true if we could say about race, sex, or religious discrimination that it were arbitrary, in the sense that it imposes costs on the firm without any offsetting benefits. Under those circumstances, as Gary Becker has shown, the inefficient firms would be at a systematic disadvantage relative to rival firms that did not labor under similar inhibitions. But once we recognize that firms are loose and imperfect networks of contracts, we can no longer treat firms as identical atoms at work in the same external market. The looseness in the internal structure of the firm is often better contained by informal than by formal sanctions, for discrimination has survival value which is apt to be missed if firm behavior is modeled on the more traditional, pre-Coasean pattern of homogeneous actors in a world of zero transaction costs. It follows that discrimination has benefits as well as costs and will be the low-cost solution in some circumstances but not in others. We should not, therefore, expect that in some long-run equilibrium there will be no private-market discrimination.

Ignoring the rational grounds for discrimination has, I believe, sent John J. Donohue astray in his efforts to show on traditional neoclassical assumptions (assumptions that seek to take into account all preferences, including those of employers and workers who prefer discrimination) that Title VII is nonetheless efficient, at least in the case of race. The basis of Donohue's argument is that in the long run the efficient firms will all be free of discrimination because [the inability of discriminatory firms to compete means that they will eventually be driven from the market. Title VII can thus speed up a process that would otherwise take place, albeit more slowly]. The trade-off involved in Donohue's view is whether the costs of expediting a nondiscriminatory workplace are justified by the benefits obtained. . . .

### NOTES

1. One argument that seeks to explain the persistence of discrimination in free markets is that some types of discrimination are "rational" because race (or sex or

some other prohibited ground) is correlated with ability. This theory is sometimes called "statistical discrimination":

> A rational employer will discriminate, even if no relevant actor has any discriminatory animus, if the employer concludes that race is a useful proxy for job qualifications.
>
> Discrimination of this form occurs because information about an employee's qualifications is often costly to obtain. An employee's race, however, is cheaply ascertained. Therefore, if a firm concludes that an employee's race correlates with his or her qualifications, and if better information about the qualifications is too costly to discover, it will be rational, profit-maximizing behavior for the firm to offer lower wages to a minority employee than it would offer to a nonminority employee.
>
> A firm might rationally discriminate in this way even if, so far as the firm has determined, the two employees are identical except for race. In a world of cost-free information, the employer could ascertain each employee's qualifications perfectly. If two employees were found to be identical in every relevant respect, it would not be rational to offer them different wages. In the real world, however, information is costly, and the employer will therefore stop trying to ascertain qualifications at some point. At that point, it may be rational for the employer to rely on a surrogate that it knows to be imperfect but that is cheaply ascertained.

David A. Strauss, The Law and Economics of Racial Discrimination in Employment: The Case for Numerical Standards, 79 Geo. L.J. 1619, 1622 (1991). See also Ruth Blumrosen, Wage Discrimination, Job Segregation, and Title VII of the Civil Rights Act of 1964, 12 U. Mich. J.L. Ref. 399, 447-48 (1978).

The logic of statistical discrimination does not require any assertion that racial or gender differences are inherent — the correlation between race or gender and productivity could be the result of factors such as past societal discrimination. The term "statistical discrimination" does not, however, mean that the employer acts only on the basis of scientifically ascertained differences. Indeed, such discrimination will be more or less "rational" depending on the relationship between the stereotype used and statistical reality. Professor Strauss concludes that, if racial generalizations reflect actual differences between groups, they are more likely to persist than if they do not: "If an employer is using an inaccurate generalization about minority employees in making employment decisions, it has an incentive to correct its assumptions. If it does not, there is an opportunity for an employer who is not using such a generalization to seize a competitive advantage." Strauss, supra at 1640.

2. Is statistical discrimination objectionable even if it is accurate in group terms? Rational or not, relying on generalizations (perhaps better called stereotypes) excludes entire groups without any assessment of individual abilities. This is particularly problematic if the generalization is itself rooted in prior discrimination. Professor Mary Becker, in The Law and Economics of Racial Discrimination in Employment: Needed in the Nineties: Improved Individual and Structural Remedies for Racial and Sexual Disadvantages in Employment, 79 Geo. L.J. 1659, 1664 (1991), writes:

> [A]s a historical matter, current preferences are in part the result of past forms of regulation which are not exogenous to the legal system. Slavery and Jim Crow are closely connected to the refusal of many whites today to interact with African Americans as equals. Past legal limitations on women's ability to function as autonomous human beings are closely connected to the refusal of many men today to interact with women as equals.

Professor Becker uses "exogenous" to mean preferences arising outside the legal system. See also Cass R. Sunstein, Legal Interference with Private Preferences, 53 U.

Chi. L. Rev. 1129 (1986). A number of scholars, most notably those writing from a feminist perspective, have argued that racial and gender differences are "socially constructed" in part by the legal system, but also by other powerful societal forces. Professor Nancy E. Dowd, in Liberty vs. Equality: In Defense of Privileged White Males, 34 Wm. & Mary L. Rev. 429 (1993), criticizes Epstein for ignoring the rich literature on the social construction of gender differences, citing, among others, Martha A. Fineman, The Illusion of Equality (1991); Martha Minow, Making All the Difference (1990); Deborah L. Rhode, Justice and Gender: Sex Discrimination and the Law (1989); and Catharine A. Mackinnon, Feminism Unmodified (1987). Dowd also criticizes Epstein for ignoring Critical Race scholars, e.g., Derrick Bell, Faces at the Bottom of the Well: The Permanence of Racism (1992); Derrick Bell, And We Are Not Saved (1987). If Epstein were to agree about social construction of gender, would it affect his argument?

3. Even if the perceived productivity differences are real, is it necessarily efficient for an employer to rely on them? Professor Samuel Issacharoff, in Contractual Liberties in Discriminatory Markets, 70 Tex. L. Rev. 1219, 1222 (1992), criticizes Epstein's "fundamental assumption that each individual is delivered to the labor market as a more or less intact bundle of skills and abilities." This is "a shockingly static view" of what is, in fact, a dynamic process. Indeed, it is the very "disincentives for optimal acquisition of human capital" brought about by discrimination that justify intervention in the market. See also Strauss, supra note 1; Cass Sunstein, Why Markets Don't Stop Discrimination, in Reassessing Civil Rights 23 (Ellen F. Paul et al. eds., 1991). But see John J. Donohue III & James J. Heckman, The Law and Economics of Racial Discrimination in Employment: Re-Evaluating Federal Civil Rights Policy, 79 Geo. L.J. 1713, 1725 (1991) ("Since 1980, however, young blacks (those with less than sixteen years of labor market experience) have actually earned somewhat greater returns than their white counterparts from each additional year of schooling.").

4. What does Professor Epstein say about statistical discrimination? At some points, he seems to reject that possibility because there will always be employers who exploit any untapped pool of workers. In other places, Epstein recognizes the existence of discrimination, but argues that the kind of discrimination that persists is not harmful.

5. When discussing Ayers's auto sales study, Epstein seems to argue that drawing distinctions on the basis of race is not discriminatory if the difference in price is cost based: "The greater risk arguably associated with black and female customers could induce sales personnel to charge higher prices to cover their own costs." Isn't he admitting that dealers discriminate, but justifying the discrimination as rational? The same point seems to be made with respect to the Urban Institute study: "The ability to maintain cohesion within the firm and with a customer base may depend in part on the race of an employee. If these costs are higher in some settings for workers of one race than another, then we should expect to see some difference in hiring patterns." Are his explanations examples of "statistical discrimination"? From the victim's perspective, if he must pay more for a car or she must look longer for a job, does it matter that the discrimination was rational?

6. This "explanation" may simply presage Epstein's basic point that "voluntary sorting" on race and gender grounds is not invidious because workers with common interests and backgrounds work well together. It is this assertion that has drawn the most fire from various reviewers.

7. Professor Nancy E. Dowd, supra note 2, at 429, views Epstein as a relatively frank apologist for racism and sexism. She quotes Epstein to the effect that individual

tastes are grouped to some extent by race and sex and that these tastes necessarily conflict with the smooth operation of at least some firms:

> These are outrageous statements, filled with stereotypes and race and gender essential-ism reduced to implicit biological "natural" preference, amounting to an outright justification for skin and gender privilege. Epstein is saying that the costs of diversity make discrimination reasonable and logical. He assumes that the characteristics he names are related to differences that affect governing the workplace with no other au-thority than his own perception that "[i]t is harder to do business as social distance be-tween persons increases." What we also know, and what Epstein ignores, is that in most firms of any size women and minorities are present, but in positions of inferiority. That evidence suggests that it is not that privileged white males do not like to associate with women or minorities; rather, they like to associate with them, but only as long as it is in unequal ways. Group stereotyping replaces individual characteristics in Epstein's scheme. Furthermore, group-identified differences (stereotypes with a basis in fact, he would call these) are presumed to have employment consequences. There is little con-sideration of the possibility that other characteristics — such as education, class back-ground, socioeconomic status, marital or parental status — may be more predictive of workplace-related governance costs than those he cites. There also is little examination of whether diversity has any benefits — after all, aren't we looking at both costs and benefits?

Id. at 442. See also Andrew Koppelman, Feminism & Libertarianism: A Response to Richard Epstein, 1999 U. Chi. Legal F. 115 (1999); Marion Crain, Rationalizing In-equality: An Antifeminist Defense of the "Free" Market, 61 Geo. Wash. L. Rev. 556 (1993); Kathryn Abrams, Social Construction, Roving Biologism, and Reasonable Women: A Response to Professor Epstein, 41 DePaul L. Rev. 1021 (1992). For Dowd, not only is Epstein's result flawed, but his methodology is also defective: "[T]his book is not an intellectual argument; it is political polemic with little intellectual credibil-ity. The book is riddled with statements of fact that have no visible means of support other than the unsubstantiated and uninformed views of the author." Dowd, supra at 432. In her view, "Epstein's biggest failure is his refusal to confront and analyze schol-arly work that undermines or challenges the fundamental basis of his position. Op-posing positions are dismissed with a sentence or simply ignored." Id.

8. In more temperate language, Professor J. Hoult Verkerke, in Free to Search, 105 Harv. L. Rev. 2080, 2088 (1992), doubts "the usefulness of racial and ethnic affilia-tions as a proxy for job-related preferences of workers. The potential for intragroup heterogeneity of preferences seems to me every bit as great as the potential for dis-agreement between members of different racial or ethnic groups."

9. In Professor Epstein's view, free market forces strongly discourage discrimin-ation, and any remaining discrimination is not wrongful or harmful because it is efficient. In the first excerpt, Epstein acknowledged the need for government regula-tion to protect citizens against force and fraud, but distinguished antidiscrimination regulation. While noting the "apparent verbal seductiveness" of "the parallel be-tween force and discrimination," he dismissed the analogy.

10. Professor Mary Becker, supra note 2, at 1659, criticizes economic models for the human dimensions they ignore. She begins by stressing that much discrimination is not rational. Indeed, "discrimination" is a poorly chosen word because it also means the ability to make fine distinctions.

> Racism and misogyny — the belief that people of color and women are less than fully human — are not "discrimination" in this sense. One does not believe that African

Americans and women are less than fully human because of an analytically rigorous delineation of subtle differences between them and white men. To the contrary, racism
and misogyny are deeply irrational emotions, based on hatred or a lack of empathy for
"the other," often accompanied by the need to establish one's own importance by denying others' humanity. . . .

The failure to include the desire to subordinate is a major gap in [the taste for discrimination and the statistical discrimination] economic models of discrimination.
Some people discriminate, not because of a desire to work with those like themselves,
but because they desire to dominate certain people from other groups.

Another form of discrimination not addressed by the economic models is a lessened
ability to empathize and identify with women and people of color and to put oneself in
their shoes, incorporating their hurts and needs into one's perceptions. We all empathize best with those most like ourselves, but we live in a society in which white men
disproportionately hold positions of power. . . .

Again, the economic models fail to describe this form of discrimination. It is based
neither on an aversion to contact with members of certain groups nor on a perception
that groups differ with respect to productivity, the two forms of discrimination encompassed by the economic models. If lessened ability to empathize with women and
people of color is widespread, the market will not drive out this unconscious emotional
failing. It certainly has not eliminated it yet. . . .

Id. at 1664. While Professor Becker's argument is designed to identify forms of discrimination that are not accounted for by economic analysis, doesn't her approach
also suggest that, whether or not discrimination is efficient, it causes psychic harms
that the government has an interest in preventing? Doesn't Professor Epstein's complete dismissal of the analogy between force and discrimination demonstrate his inability "to empathize and identify with women and people of color?" See Verkerke,
supra note 9, at 2086 (Epstein's "account ignores the denigration, frustration and
anger that the victim of discrimination experiences").

## PATRICIA J. WILLIAMS, THE ALCHEMY
## OF RACE AND RIGHTS
### 44-49 (1991)

Buzzers are big in New York City. Favored particularly by smaller stores and bou-
tiques, merchants throughout the city have installed them as screening devices to reduce the incidence of robbery: if the face at the door looks desirable, the buzzer is
pressed and the door is unlocked. If the face is that of an undesirable, the door stays
locked. Predictably, the issue of undesirability has revealed itself to be a racial determination. While controversial enough at first, even civil-rights organizations backed
down eventually in the face of arguments that the buzzer system is a "necessary evil,"
that it is a "mere inconvenience" in comparison to the risks of being murdered, that
suffering discrimination is not as bad as being assaulted, and that in any event it is not
all blacks who are barred, just "17-year-old black males wearing running shoes and
hooded sweatshirts."

The installation of these buzzers happened swiftly in New York; stores that had always had their doors wide open suddenly became exclusive or received people by appointment only. I discovered them and their meaning on a Saturday in 1986. I was
shopping in Soho and saw in a store window a sweater that I wanted to buy for my
mother. I pressed my round brown face to the window and my finger to the buzzer,

seeking admittance. A narrow-eyed, white teenager wearing running shoes and feasting on bubble gum glared out, evaluating me for signs that would pit me against the limits of his social understanding. After about five seconds, he mouthed "We're closed," and blew pink rubber at me. It was two Saturdays before Christmas, at one o'clock in the afternoon; there were several white people in the store who appeared to be shopping for things for their mothers.

I was enraged. At that moment I literally wanted to break all the windows of the store and take lots of sweaters for my mother. In the flicker of his judgmental gray eyes, that saleschild had transformed my brightly sentimental, joy-to-the-world, pre-Christmas spree to a shambles. He snuffed my sense of humanitarian catholicity, and there was nothing I could do to snuff his, without making a spectacle of myself.

I am still struck by the structure of power that drove me into such a blizzard of rage. There was almost nothing I could do, short of physically intruding upon him, that would humiliate him the way he humiliated me. No words, no gestures, no prejudices of my own would make a bit of difference to him; his refusal to let me into the store — it was Benetton's, whose colorfully punnish ad campaign is premised on wrapping every one of the world's peoples in its cottons and woolens — was an outward manifestation of his never having let someone like me into the realm of his reality. He had no compassion, no remorse, no reference to me; and no desire to acknowledge me even at the estranged level of arm's-length transactor. He saw me only as one who would take his money and therefore could not conceive that I was there to give him money.

In this weird ontological imbalance, I realized that buying something in that store was like bestowing a gift, the gift of my commerce, the lucre of my patronage. In the wake of my outrage, I wanted to take back the gift of appreciation that my peering in the window must have appeared to be. I wanted to take it back in the form of unappreciation, disrespect, defilement. I wanted to work so hard at wishing he could feel what I felt that he would never again mistake my hatred for some sort of plaintive wish to be included. I was quite willing to disenfranchise myself, in the heat of my need to revoke the flattery of my purchasing power. I was willing to boycott Benetton's, random white-owned businesses, and anyone who ever blew bubble gum in my face again.

My rage was admittedly diffuse, even self-destructive, but it was symmetrical. The perhaps loose-ended but utter propriety of that rage is no doubt lost not just to the young man who actually barred me, but to those who would appreciate my being barred only as an abstract precaution, who approve of those who would bar even as they deny that they would bar me.

The violence of my desire to burst into Benetton's is probably quite apparent. I often wonder if the violence, the exclusionary hatred, is equally apparent in the repeated public urgings that blacks understand the buzzer system by putting themselves in the shoes of white storeowners — that, in effect, blacks look into the mirror of frightened white faces for the reality of their undesirability; and that then blacks would "just as surely conclude that [they] would not let [themselves] in under similar circumstances." (That some blacks might agree merely shows that some of us have learned too well the lessons of privatized intimacies of self-hatred and rationalized away the fullness of our public, participatory selves.)

On the same day I was barred from Benetton's, I went home and wrote the above impassioned account in my journal. On the day after that, I found I was still brooding, so I turned to a form of catharsis I have always found healing. I typed up as much of the story as I have just told, made a big poster of it, put a nice colorful border around it, and, after Benetton's was truly closed, stuck it to their big sweater-filled window. I exercised my first-amendment right to place my business with them right out in the street.

So that was the first telling of this story. The second telling came a few months later, for a symposium on Excluded Voices sponsored by a law review. I wrote an essay summing up my feelings about being excluded from Benetton's and analyzing "how the rhetoric of increased privatization, in response to racial issues, functions as the rationalizing agent of public unaccountability and, ultimately, irresponsibility." Weeks later, I received the first edit. From the first page to the last, my fury had been carefully cut out. My rushing, run-on-rage had been reduced to simple declarative sentences. The active personal had been inverted in favor of the passive impersonal. My words were different; they spoke to me upside down. I was afraid to read too much of it at a time — meanings rose up at me oddly, stolen and strange.

A week and a half later, I received the second edit. All reference to Benetton's had been deleted because, according to the editors and the faculty adviser, it was defamatory; they feared harassment and liability; they said printing it would be irresponsible. I called them and offered to supply a footnote attesting to this as my personal experience at one particular location and of a buzzer system not limited to Benetton's; the editors told me that they were not in the habit of publishing things that were unverifiable. I could not but wonder, in this refusal even to let me file an affidavit, what it would take to make my experience verifiable. The testimony of an independent white bystander? (a requirement in fact imposed in the U.S. Supreme Court holdings through the first part of the century).

Two days after the piece was sent to press, I received copies of the final page proofs. All reference to my race had been eliminated because it was against "editorial policy" to permit descriptions of "physiognomy." . . .

Ultimately I did convince the editors that mention of my race was central to the whole sense of the subsequent text; that my story became one of extreme paranoia without the information that I am black; or that it became one in which the reader had to fill in the gap by assumption, presumption, prejudgment, or prejudice. What was most interesting to me in this experience was how the blind application of principles of neutrality, through the device of omission, acted either to make me look crazy or to make the reader participate in old habits of cultural bias.

That was the second telling of my story. The third telling came last April, when I was invited to participate in a law-school conference on equality and difference. . . . I opined:

> Law and legal writing aspire to formalized color-blind, liberal ideals. Neutrality is the standard for assuring these ideals; yet the adherence to it is often determined by reference to an aesthetic of uniformity, in which difference is simply omitted. For example, when segregation was eradicated from the American lexicon, its omission led many to actually believe that racism therefore no longer existed. Race-neutrality in law has become the presumed antidote for race bias in real life. With the entrenchment of the notion of race-neutrality came attacks on the concept of affirmative action and the rise of reverse discrimination suits. Blacks for so many generations deprived of jobs based on the color of our skin, are now told that we ought to find it demeaning to be hired, based on the color of our skin. Such is the silliness of simplistic either-or inversions as remedies to complex problems.
> What is truly demeaning in this era of double-speak-no-evil is going to interviews and not getting hired because someone doesn't think we'll be comfortable. It is demeaning not to get promoted because we're judged "too weak," then putting in a lot of energy the

next time and getting fired because we're "too strong." It is demeaning to be told what we find demeaning. It is very demeaning to stand on street corners unemployed and begging. It is downright demeaning to have to explain why we haven't been employed for months and then watch the job go to someone who is "more experienced." It is outrageously demeaning that none of this can be called racism, even if it happens only to, or to large numbers of, black people; as long as it's done with a smile, a handshake and a shrug; as long as the phantom-word "race" is never used.

*NOTES*

1. A similar story is told about Condoleezza Rice, although with a considerably different ending. As recounted in the New Yorker of Oct. 14, 2002, p. 164, Dr. Rice is shopping at a store and the clerk tries to show her costume jewelry. There follows an exchange of words capped by Dr. Rice saying, "Let's get one thing straight. You're behind the counter because you have to work for six dollars an hour. I'm on this side asking to see the good jewelry because I make considerably more."

2. Professor Williams's intense reaction to perceived discrimination is not unique to her. In 1968, two black psychiatrists, Dr. William H. Grier and Dr. Price M. Cobbs, first described what they termed "The Black Norm" in Black Rage 177-78 (1992 ed.):

> We submit that it is necessary for a black man in America to develop a profound distrust of his white fellow citizens and of the nation. He must be on guard to protect himself against physical hurt. He must cushion himself against cheating, slander, humiliation, and outright mistreatment by the official representatives of society. If he does not so protect himself, he will live a life of such pain and shock as to find life itself unbearable. For his own survival, then, he must develop a cultural paranoia in which every white man is a potential enemy unless proved otherwise and every social system is set against him unless he personally finds out differently.

3. Professor Richard Delgado reviewed the psychological literature on the impact of prejudice and discrimination in Words That Wound: A Tort Action for Racial Insults, Epithets, and Name-Calling, 17 Harv. C.R.-C.L. L. Rev. 133, 136-40 (1982):

> The psychological harms caused by racial stigmatization are often much more severe than those created by other stereotyping actions. Unlike many characteristics upon which stigmatization may be based, membership in a racial minority can be considered neither self-induced, like alcoholism or prostitution, nor alterable. Race-based stigmatization is, therefore, "one of the most fruitful causes of human misery. Poverty can be eliminated — but skin color cannot." . . .
>     . . . Kenneth Clark has observed, "Human beings . . . whose daily experience tells them that almost nowhere in society are they respected and granted the ordinary dignity and courtesy accorded to others will, as a matter of course, begin to doubt their own worth." Minorities may come to believe the frequent accusations that they are lazy, ignorant, dirty, and superstitious. "The accumulation of negative images . . . present[s] them with one massive and destructive choice: either to hate one's self, as culture so systematically demand[s], or to have no self at all, to be nothing."
>     The psychological responses to such stigmatization consist of feelings of humiliation, isolation, and self-hatred. Consequently, it is neither unusual nor abnormal for stigmatized individuals to feel ambivalent about their self-worth and identity. This ambivalence arises from the stigmatized individual's awareness that others perceive him or her as falling short of societal standards, standards which the individual has adopted. Stig-

matized individuals thus often are hypersensitive and anticipate pain at the prospect of contact with "normals." . . .

The psychological effects of racism may also result in mental illness and psychosomatic disease. The affected person may react by seeking escape through alcohol, drugs, or other kinds of antisocial behavior. The rates of narcotic use and admission to public psychiatric hospitals are much higher in minority communities than in society as a whole.

The achievement of high socioeconomic status does not diminish the psychological harms caused by prejudice. The effort to achieve success in business and managerial careers exacts a psychological toll even among exceptionally ambitious and upwardly mobile members of minority groups. . . . As a result, the incidence of severe psychological impairment caused by the environmental stress of prejudice and discrimination is not lower among minority group members of high socioeconomic status. . . .

In addition to such emotional and physical consequences, racial stigmatization may damage a victim's pecuniary interests. The psychological injuries severely handicap the victim's pursuit of a career. The person who is timid, withdrawn, bitter, hypertense, or psychotic will almost certainly fare poorly in employment settings. An experiment in which blacks and whites of similar aptitudes and capacities were put into a competitive situation found that the blacks exhibited defeatism, halfhearted competitiveness, and "high expectancies of failures." . . .

4. Should the harm described by Professors Williams and Delgado be a matter of legal concern? Professor Williams resorted to self-help, hanging a damning sign in the window of the offending shop and publishing books and articles exposing her unfair treatment. She also contemplated an economic attack — boycotting Benetton or perhaps all white-owned businesses. Why aren't these responses sufficient to control discrimination? Is legal regulation more effective? Is law capable of changing deeply ingrained social attitudes?

5. While not in the employment context, "racial profiling" has been much in the news recently. In 1998, after New Jersey state troopers shot and seriously wounded three unarmed men who were driving on the New Jersey Turnpike, the use of racial profiling by state troopers drew national attention. David Kocieniewski, New Jersey Argues That the U.S. Wrote the Book on Racial Profiling, N.Y. Times, Nov. 29, 2000, at A1; David Kocieniewski, New Jersey Senate Asks Whitman's Staff to Turn Over Documents on Racial Profiling, N.Y. Times, Nov. 21, 2000, at B5. By 2000, racial profiling became an incendiary issue in New Jersey and in other parts of the country. Prior to September 11, 2001, the use of racial profiling by law enforcement was almost unanimously condemned. However, in the wake of September 11, many now defend racial profiling as a means of increasing national security. "I am aware of the increased racial profiling of Arabs, Muslims, and even those who may look Muslim, including me and members of my family. However, if it helps in controlling terrorism — even though some innocent people may be inconvenienced — it is justified for our safety." Priya Rai, Commentary, I Once Believed in Diversity; But Then Came September 11, The Hartford Courant, June 9, 2002, at C1. Another author wrote in response to increased security in the entry and departure of immigrants that "the ethnic and racial profiling involved is troubling, but not troubling enough to derail needed efforts to lessen American vulnerability to attacks like those carried on September 11, 2001 by terrorists who relocated here to carry out their own form of cultural profiling in targeting Americans." A Matter of Survival, The Buffalo News, June 7, 2002, at C10.

While there has been a greater public acceptance of ethnic or religious profiling by law enforcement officers dealing with potential terrorists in the wake of September 11, many still oppose the use of race or ethnicity without regard to possible justifications: "Civil rights violations against Muslims in the U.S. have noticeably increased since September 11 . . . we seek to bring to light such issues like racial profiling, detentions and hate crimes." Kausalya Mohan Babu, Muslim Advocates See a Need to Lobby, The Washington Times, June 28, 2002, at A18. See generally, Samuel R. Gross & Debra Livingston, Racial Profiling Under Attack, 102 Colum. L. Rev. 1413 (2002).

6. Consider Professor John J. Donohue III's criticism in Advocacy Versus Analysis in Assessing Employment Discrimination Law, 44 Stan. L. Rev. 1583, 1587 (1992), faulting the simplistic nature of Epstein's economic analysis:

> To support his contention that governmental efforts to inhibit discrimination in labor markets are misguided, Epstein enlists the standard microeconomic argument that wealth will be maximized if competitive markets can operate without restraint. This conclusion only follows, however, if either all costs are internalized or the transaction costs of the affected parties are low. For example, free markets do not maximize wealth in settings where pollution costs and bargaining costs are high. Because of free rider problems and other transaction costs, the victims of widespread pollution will generally be unable to induce the polluters to stop polluting, even when the social benefits from such a contract would exceed the social costs. Once it is recognized that discrimination in labor markets imposes external costs that are quite analogous to the costs of pollution, the case for laissez-faire evaporates at a theoretical level and can only be sustained through a proper assessment of the costs and benefits of an antidiscrimination regime. Private discrimination is a form of psychological pollution that corrodes the well-being of both victims and [those who have not personally suffered discrimination but are morally offended by it], and excluding these costs from the social calculus — as Epstein does — would be as illogical as excluding the costs of chemical pollution in assessing environmental programs.

7. Professor J. Hoult Verkerke has suggested that, even from Epstein's libertarian perspective, the psychic harm associated with discrimination is relevant because it creates inefficiencies in the market:

> Once black workers learn that they will experience discrimination in the labor market, this dignitary harm operates as a tax on their efforts to search for employment opportunities.[18] Blacks would react rationally to this tax by decreasing their search efforts. [This reduction in search activity is an economic inefficiency of discrimination and if it produces] inefficiencies that private transactions cannot remedy, regulatory intervention would be justified even in Epstein's libertarian regime.

Free to Search, 105 Harv. L. Rev. 2080, 2086 (1992).

8. Whether the psychic harm associated with discrimination is weighed into the balance as an economic factor or weighed against efficiency as a matter of fairness, the question remains whether laws prohibiting discrimination create more benefits than costs.

---

18. Epstein appears to discount the possibility that discriminatory decisions will produce dignitary harms. However, by rejecting the analogy between discrimination and force or fraud, Epstein essentially asks blacks to ignore any dignitary harm that might be produced by discriminatory decisions. This approach is an unwelcome application to private conduct of Justice Brown's argument that state-imposed racial classifications are only harmful and stigmatizing if blacks choose to view them as such. See Plessy v. Ferguson, 163 U.S. 537, 551 (1896).

## D.   THE COSTS AND BENEFITS OF PROHIBITING DISCRIMINATION

Prohibiting discrimination clearly has costs for society. Epstein identifies possible losses in efficiency. But even without considering the theoretical losses that might be associated with regulating the free market, prohibiting discrimination imposes administrative costs on society. You will be able to fully assess these only after you have completed this book and understand the mechanisms Congress has created to deal with different types of discrimination. But before addressing these issues, it is important to understand the economic dimensions of the problems faced by the groups protected by antidiscrimination statutes and the impact of antidiscrimination laws on the economic condition of protected groups.

## 1.   *Weighing Economic Costs and Benefits*

In a book published in 1980, The Zero Sum Society, Professor Lester C. Thurow wrote:

> The essence of any minority group's position can be captured with the answer to three questions: (1) Relative to the majority group, what is the probability of the minority's finding employment? (2) For those who are employed, what are the earnings opportunities relative to the majority? (3) Are minority group members making a breakthrough into the high-income jobs of the economy?

Id. at 184. He reported some sobering facts, including persistent heavy black unemployment (twice the rate of whites). Id. at 185. Similarly, "Using the top 5 percent of all jobs (based on earnings) as the definition of a 'good job,' blacks hold 2 percent of these jobs while whites hold 98 percent. Since blacks constitute 12 percent of the labor force they are obviously underrepresented in this category." Id. at 186. Hispanics were doing slightly better than African Americans, although various subgroups showed differing success. Native Americans were the poorest ethnic/racial group. As for women, in 1980 Thurow wrote: "Female workers hold the dubious distinction of having made the least progress in the labor market. In 1939 full-time, full-year women earned 61 percent of what men earned. In 1977 they earned 57 percent as much." Id. at 187. Female unemployment also rose relative to male unemployment, and this group held only 4 percent of the top jobs in the country.

Professor Thurow drew many of his statistics from the 1970 census, and even his most recent figures were from 1979. Have the economic conditions of protected groups improved over time? In discussing whether there was a continuing need for affirmative action, a recent commentator reexamined group economic success.

## DAVID BENJAMIN OPPENHEIMER, UNDERSTANDING AFFIRMATIVE ACTION
### 23 Hastings Const. L.Q. 921, 965-968 (1996)

Blacks, Hispanics and Asian Americans earn substantially less than do whites, and in some respects things are getting worse. In 1980, the average black male worker earned $751 for every $1,000 earned by a white male worker.[267] By 1990 it had dropped to $731. Higher education helps, but not much. In 1990 the average black male college graduate earned $798 for every $1,000 earned by a white male college graduate. Those who attended at least one year of graduate school dropped to $771. In 1979, Chinese American men with college degrees earned approximately $862 for every $1,000 earned by comparably educated white men.[271] For Japanese American men with college degrees, the comparable figure was approximately $944. In 1990, Hispanic men earned $810 for every $1,000 earned by similarly educated white men.[273]

Women of all races continue to earn substantially less than men. In the 1960s women earned 60% of what men earned on average; by 1993, it had risen only to 72%. The average woman with a masters degree earns the same amount as the average man with an associate (junior college) degree. Hispanic women earn less than 65% of the wages earned by white men at the same education level. An Hispanic woman with a college degree earns, on average, less than a white man with only a high school degree. As of 1995, black women earn 10% less than white women and 36% less than white men, while Hispanic women earn 24% less than white women and 46% less than white men.[278] Almost two thirds of all working women earn less than $20,000 annually — over one third earn less than $10,000.[279]

Although white men make up only 43% of the workforce,[280] they constitute 97% of the top executives (vice-presidents and above) at the 1,500 largest American corporations.[281] Black women with professional degrees who do attain top management positions earn 60% of what white men in similar positions earn. Among physicians, women earn less than 60% as much as men.[282] A recent study revealed that women graduates of the University of Michigan Law School earned just 61% of what male graduates earned after fifteen years of practice, and that after controlling for grades, career choice, experience, work hours and family responsibilities, there remained an unexplained gap of 13%.

Black employment remains concentrated in the least respected, most undesirable job categories. Although blacks constitute 12% of the population and 10% of the workforce, they fill over 30% of the nursing aide and orderly jobs and almost 25% of the domestic servant jobs, but only 3% of the jobs for lawyers and doctors. In 1993, black and Hispanic men were only half as likely as white men to be managers or professionals. Similarly, women are disproportionately steered into service jobs — although there are nearly as many women as men in the workforce, under 25% of all doctors and lawyers are women.[287] Women comprise over 90% of all dental hygienists, but only 10.5% of the dentists.

267. [Andrew Hacker, Two Nations: Black and White, Separate, Hostile, Unequal (1993)] at 101.
271. Min Zhou & Yoshinori Kamo, An Analysis of Earnings Patterns for Chinese, Japanese, and Non-Hispanic Caucasian Males in the United States, 35 Soc. Q. 581, 591 tbl. 2 (1994).
273. Affirmative Action Review[: Report to the President (1995)] at 14.
278. Hearings on Affirmative Action in Employment: Hearings on H.R. 2128 Before the Subcomm. on Employee-Employer Relations of the House Comm. on Economic and Educational Opportunities, 104th Cong., 1st Sess. 268 (1995) (statement of Marcia D. Greenberger, Co-President, Natl. Women's Law Ctr.).
279. See Economics and Statistics Admin., Bureau of the Census, Ser. P60, No. 184, Money Income of Households, Families, and Persons in the United States: 1992, at 150 tbl. 31 (1993).
280. Federal Glass Ceiling Commn., Good For Business: Making Full Use of the Nation's Human Capital 10-11 (1995).
281. Affirmative Action Review, supra note [273], at 23. The "glass ceiling" issue has been a subject of particular interest to Asian-Americans, as well as women of all races. See U.S. Commn. on Civil Rights, Civil Rights Issues Facing Asian Americans in the 1990s, at 130 (1992).
282. Women's Bureau, U.S. Department of Labor, Women Workers: Trends and Issues 35 (1993).
287. Economics and Statistics Admin., Bureau of the Census, Statistical Abstract of the United States: 1994, at 407-409 (1994).

In the area of unemployment, the situation is getting worse, not better, for blacks. During the 1970s the average unemployment rate for blacks was twice as high as it was for whites. By 1990, the black unemployment rate was 2.76 times higher than the white rate.

As dramatic as these differentials are, they give us only part of the picture. Many unemployed workers are not counted by the Bureau of Labor Statistics because they have stopped actively looking for work — if we count these "hidden unemployed," the first quarter 1992 black unemployment rate was 25.5%.[291] For black teenagers, the official unemployment rate was 38%; adding the hidden unemployed raised the true figure to almost 60%. Moreover, unemployed blacks took longer to find new jobs than unemployed whites, and were only half as likely to qualify for unemployment insurance.

## NOTES

1. While others have noted similar statistics, see, e.g., Nancy E. Dowd, Liberty vs. Equality: In Defense of Privileged White Males, 34 Wm. & Mary L. Rev. 429, 476 (1993), there are more hopeful indicators. Data reporting the economic status of the black population as a whole mask significant changes that have occurred in the economic status of subgroups of this population. For example, the percentage of black families with a family income exceeding $50,000 quadrupled since 1967 and doubled during the 1980s; the earnings of college-graduated black couples between the ages of 25 and 44 are approximately 93 percent of the earnings of similarly described white families. However, the persistence of high unemployment and the increase of single-parent families with large numbers of children and headed by black females have held down the median family income of blacks in the United States. The percentage of black families living below the poverty line has remained at approximately 30 percent from the 1960s until the present. See Gap Grows Between Black Middle Class and Those Mired in Poverty, L.A. Times, Aug. 9, 1991, at A27. Similarly, with respect to women, Professor Dowd reports that the labor participation rate for women is now about 60 percent. She goes on:

> The rate of participation increases to 70% for divorced and separated women; single women are close behind with a 65% participation rate; the average rate for married women is 56%; and 65% of women with minor children are in the workforce. The most dramatic growth in labor force participation in the past decade has been among women with children of school age. The dominant workforce pattern for women is now very similar to that of men.

34 Wm. & Mary L. Rev. at 476 (citing Bureau of Labor Statistics, Handbook of Labor Statistics 12 (1989)). Furthermore, for full-time, full-year workers, the male/female earnings ratio increased to 68 percent in 1989,* and to an all-time high of 72 percent in 1990. Although the ratio dropped back to 71 percent in 1991, researchers believe this is a temporary setback associated with the recession. Women's Progress Stalled? Just Not So, N.Y. Times, Oct. 18, 1992, at 3-1.† Studies of younger workers indicate

291. National Urban League, Perils of Neglect: Black Unemployment in the Nineties 1 (1992).
* U.S. Bureau of the Census, Household Income, Family Income, Earnings of Year-Round Full-Time Workers, Per Capita Income (Nov. 5, 1990).
† The information in this article was derived from Claudia Goldin, Understanding the Gender Gap, An Economic History of American Women (1990); Francine Blau & Marianne Ferber, The Economics of Women, Men and Work (1986); and studies by June O'Neill, an economist at Baruch College in New York City.

that the economic status of females in the workplace is improving more rapidly than total female population statistics suggest. For example, in 1990, women between 24 and 35 years old earned "80 cents for every dollar earned by men of the same age group, up from 69 cents in 1980." Id.

2. The excerpt from Professor Oppenheimer does not address the economic disadvantage of the elderly. This is, in fact, a complicated question because older Americans are wealthier than the average American, but many subgroups — particularly minority women — are among the poorest in our society. Their participation in the workforce drops off relatively early. Thus, the labor force participation for men aged 55 to 64 fell to 67.2 percent in 1989 from 83 percent in 1970. Nearly half of all male workers and almost 60 percent of females begin receiving Social Security at age 62. Employee Benefit Research Institute, Trends and Issues in Early Retirement, 103 EBRI Issue Brief 1, 1 (June 1990), cited in Larry Polivka, In Florida the Future Is Now: Aging Issues and Policies in the 1990's, 18 Fla. St. U. L. Rev. 401, 423 (1991). To a large extent, this results from voluntary retirements, often in response to employer incentive programs with adequate income and medical benefits. However, there are also many older workers whose "retirement" or acceptance of Social Security is involuntary and for whom there are inadequate benefits to maintain even minimally decent living standards. Similarly, while older workers who remain employed are often very well paid, those who lose their positions frequently find themselves unable to obtain comparable employment.

3. Recent scholarship has considered whether the differences between age discrimination and race/gender discrimination require reconsidering the rules governing age discrimination. Professor George Rutherglen, From Race to Age: The Expanding Scope of Employment Discrimination Laws, 24 J. Leg. Stud. 491 (1995), questioned the underlying basis of the ADEA. Taking up this theme, Samuel Issacharoff and Erica Worth Harris, Is Age Discrimination Really Age Discrimination?: The ADEA's Unnatural Solution, 72 N.Y.U. L. Rev. 780 (1997), argued that the elderly do not fit into the usual antidiscrimination model because "far from being discrete and insular, the elderly represent the normal unfolding of life's processes for all persons. As a group, older Americans do not suffer from poverty or face the disabling social stigma characteristically borne by black Americans. . . ." Id. at 781. Their article does not recommend repeal of the statute but rather proposes modifying the law to recognize that "the dramatic shift in wealth towards older Americans and the diminished job prospects of the young provoke grave concern that a misguided antidiscrimination model has allowed a concerted and politically powerful group of Americans to engage in a textbook example of what economists would term 'rent-seeking.'" Id. at 783.

Professor Christine Jolls, Hands-Tying and the Age Discrimination in Employment Act, 74 Tex. L. Rev. 1813 (1996), agrees that the traditional justifications for antidiscrimination legislation may not apply to the ADEA. However, she argues that the statute may prevent employer opportunism. The empirical observation that older workers are often paid more for doing the same work as younger employees may simply reflect a preference by both workers and employers for wages to rise over time. Such a preference, however, can only be achieved if employers can tie their own hands, that is, avoid the temptations of opportunistically replacing expensive, older workers with cheaper, younger ones. The ADEA, by providing legal protection for older workers, provides this "hands-tying." This analysis may justify the application of disparate impact to age cases.

4. Another group not discussed by Professor Oppenheimer consists of individuals with disabilities. While we will see that the statutory definition of disability is

complex and that it probably makes more sense to speak of subgroups of individuals with disabilities, by any definition such persons are economically disadvantaged. Bonnie P. Tucker, in The Americans with Disabilities Act: An Overview, 1989 U. Ill. L. Rev. 923, 926, summarizes a 1989 Census Bureau report, Study on Disabled and Jobs Finds Work and Good Pay Are Scarce, N.Y. Times, Aug. 16, 1989, at A22, as showing:

> (1) In 1988, only 23.4% of disabled men worked full-time (down from 29.8% in 1981); (2) in 1988, only 13.1% of disabled women worked full-time (up from 11.4% in 1981); (3) the earnings of disabled men fell from 77% of what all workers made in 1981 to 64% of what all workers made in 1988; and (4) the earnings of disabled women fell from 69% of what all workers made in 1981 to 62% of what all workers made in 1988.

See generally U.S. Commission on Civil Rights, Accommodating the Spectrum of Individual Abilities ch. 2 (1983).

5. The economic data, of course, raise a critical question for this course and our society: to what extent is discrimination by employers responsible for the economic problems of these groups? The excerpt from Professor Oppenheimer's article is largely descriptive, but in other sections he claims that a substantial explanation for these data is discrimination against women and minority group members. However, even if discrimination is largely responsible, the perpetrators may frequently not be employers: Professor Oppenheimer documents other barriers to minority advancement, including education and housing. Nevertheless, he claims that discrimination in employment against women and minorities is "pervasive," id. at 969, and recurrent manifestations such as that involving Texaco, see page 168, lend weight to this view. However, others disagree, and the degree to which these problems are the result of continuing discrimination by employers is, to a large extent, the subject of this entire book.

6. An illustration of the complexity of the problem may be drawn from the statistical discrepancy between male and female wages. Factors other than intentional discrimination are clearly at work. Some part of the "gender gap" is undoubtedly due to lower female education rates and less sustained participation in the labor market by women as a group. However, there is no question that a large part of this gap is due to occupational segregation. Vicki Schultz, in Telling Stories About Women and Work: Judicial Interpretations of Sex Segregation in the Workplace in Title VII Cases Raising the Lack of Interest Argument, 103 Harv. L. Rev. 1749, 1749 n.1 (1990), reports that "[a]s recently as 1985, over two-thirds of working women were employed in occupations in which at least 70% of the workers were female." She cites Jerry Jacobs, Revolving Doors: Sex Segregation and Women's Careers 20 (1989); Jerry Jacobs, Long-Term Trends in Occupational Segregation by Sex, 95 Am. J. Soc. 160 (1989). See also Barbara R. Bergmann, The Economic Emergence of Women (1986); Paula England & George Farkas, Households, Employment, and Gender: A Social, Economic, and Demographic View 121-96 (1986); Women's Work, Men's Work: Sex Segregation on the Job (Barbara F. Reskin & Heidi I. Hartmann eds., 1986). This, however, does not resolve the question. Although the origins of most occupational segregation can be traced to societal and employer discrimination in earlier times, the extent to which it is perpetuated, or at least capitalized on, by current employer practices is much debated. Such practices can range from blatantly discriminatory assignments to channeling of workers through unthinking stereotyping to neutral practices that tend to maintain the earlier segregated occupations.

7. No one believes that the sole cause of disadvantage of various groups is present-day discrimination by employers or, more generally, by today's society at large. The economic condition of African Americans, for example, can be traced in large part to slavery and its legacy. For example, Professor Owen Fiss, in A Theory of Fair Employment Laws, 38 U. Chi. L. Rev. 235, 238-39 (1971), wrote:

> Persistent inequalities in job distribution may be attributable to factors unrelated to particular employment decisions (that is, the conduct regulated by fair employment laws). For example, at any one point in time, unemployment rates differ from industry to industry, from region to region, and from employer to employer; and disproportionate unemployment of blacks may be due to a heavy concentration of blacks in the industry, region, or business enterprise that has at any one moment the greatest unemployment. This unequal distribution may be due to custom, individual preference, or actual or imagined discrimination in areas other than employment, such as housing. It may simply be due to the fact that for blacks the starting point in the labor market was in the South and in agriculture. The concentration of blacks in nongrowth industries and regions, or business enterprises, may be corrected over time as the unemployed relocate themselves; but that takes time, and whites will also be relocating.
>
> Inequalities in the actual distribution of jobs between the races might also be due to the decisions of individual employers — the subject regulated by fair employment laws. One need not resurrect any notions of "innate inferiority" to explain this possibility. One need only be realistic about the historical legacy of blacks in America — one century of slavery and another of Jim Crowism. This legacy may result in inequalities in the actual distribution of jobs in several ways.
>
> First, even if race is not used by an employer, his decisions may be based on criteria that do not seem conducive to productivity and that because of the legacy, give whites an edge. In an industrial system where whites have a preexisting edge, rules that prefer relatives of the existing work force (nepotism) or those who started working for the firm at an earlier point in time (seniority) are examples of such criteria. The color-blind version of fair employment laws emphasizes the negative proposition that race is not a permissible basis for allocating jobs, but it does not purport affirmatively to catalog the permissible criteria, requiring that they all be conducive to productivity.

An approach to discrimination that merely requires employment decisions to be color-blind, then, would not resolve the problem. While a broader approach focusing on the use of such criteria as seniority and nepotism might be more effective, there are limitations even to this. For example, there is the possibility that centuries of discrimination have left their victims with handicaps:

> One disability might be motivational. Conceivably, this legacy of slavery and discrimination has been responsible for the lessening of motivation of the class, making its members less willing to compete aggressively for the opportunities that are open or less willing to submit to industrial discipline. The legacy may have also made it more difficult for Negroes to acquire the references necessary to evaluate future promise. Finally, the legacy may have left the class without the qualities, abilities, skills or experience that efficiency-oriented employment criteria demand. This impact of the legacy need not be confined to the older members of the class. For younger blacks, not directly exposed to slavery or Jim Crowism, the disabilities might be "inheritable." The disabilities may have affected family structure, which in turn has an impact on a child's aspirations and on the guidance available. The disabilities also may have affected family wealth, which has an impact on the child's ability to acquire the training or credentials necessary to compete more successfully.

Id. at 239. Similar observations can be made about women. Centuries of pigeon-holing women into primary roles as wives and mothers, with employment limited to strictly defined kinds of "women's work," are reflected in today's persistent occupational segregation.

8. Nevertheless, there are some positive trends in the economic conditions of various groups, and there is some evidence that antidiscrimination legislation has played an important role in improving the economic status of protected groups. Even Epstein clearly believes blacks have benefitted from Title VII, and there is no doubt about African-American progress (whatever its causes) since 1965. E.g., John J. Donohue III & James J. Heckman, The Law and Economics of Racial Discrimination in Employment: Re-Evaluating Federal Civil Rights Policy, 79 Geo. L.J. 1713 (1991); John J. Donohue III & James Heckman, Continuous Versus Episodic Change: The Impact of Civil Rights Policy on the Economic Status of Blacks, 29 J. Econ. Literature 1603 (1991); James J. Heckman & J. Hoult Verkerke, Responses to Epstein, 8 Yale L. & Poly. Rev. 320 (1990).

9. With respect to women, see Andrea H. Beller, The Effects of Title VII of the Civil Rights Act of 1964 on Women's Entry into Nontraditional Occupations: An Economic Analysis, 1 Law & Ineq. J. 73, 75 (1983). Again, the results are mixed: the wage gap and job segregation have persisted, see Chapter 7, pages 573-582. But younger, educated women have made spectacular gains, which some attribute directly to the 1964 Civil Rights Act. See Women's Progress Stalled? Just Not So, N.Y. Times, Oct. 18, 1992, at 3-6. But see Tamar Lewin, Women Losing Ground to Men in Widening Income Difference, N.Y. Times, Sept. 15, 1997, at A1 (While the wage gap narrowed from 1979 to 1993, increasing the median of full-time working women from 62 to 77% of the male median, the female median has since dropped back to 75%.).

10. Even if Title VII creates economic gains for the groups subject to its protection, are these gains outweighed by losses of efficiency that negatively impact on the economic welfare of society as a whole? This debate can be analyzed in economically oriented terms by considering the application of two different types of "efficiency" — Pareto optimality and Kaldor-Hicks efficiency. A reallocation of resources is Pareto-optimal when someone is better off and no one is worse off. Antidiscrimination laws are not Pareto-optimal because, while blacks, women, and others may be better off, others (employers, employee competitors, and white racists) are worse off.

11. The competing test for efficiency is "the broader, more controversial Kaldor-Hicks wealth-maximization criterion — which endorses all measures whose total benefits exceed their total costs, as measured by willingness-to-pay, without regard to the incidence of costs and benefits across the affected population." Gregory S. Crespi, Market Magic: Can the Invisible Hand Strangle Bigotry?, 72 B.U. L. Rev. 991, 994 (1992). Put otherwise, Kaldor-Hicks "requires only that government action produce sufficient gains for its beneficiaries to allow them hypothetically to compensate those who are injured by the regulation, not that those who are injured in fact are compensated." J. Hoult Verkerke, Free to Search, 105 Harv. L. Rev. 2080, 2088 (1992). The antidiscrimination laws have been defended as efficient in the Kaldor-Hicks sense of increasing total societal output. The basic argument is that these laws bring about a more efficient economy by encouraging more efficient use of human resources. Discrimination can underutilize millions of disfavored individuals. In other words, endemic discrimination against certain groups not only prevents members of those groups from fully developing their opportunities but also deprives society of the fruits of that development. By eliminating discrimination, all individuals, not merely the immediate victims, will be better off. Subjecting this belief to a

cost-benefit analysis can, however, be daunting. See John J. Donohue III, Is Title VII Efficient?, 134 U. Pa. L. Rev. 1411 (1986), who argues that Title VII may produce allocative benefits by accelerating the processes by which discriminatory employers will be driven out of the market. On page 50, Epstein contends that Donohue is wrong. Is he persuasive?

12. For Epstein, some of this benefit is legitimate because it resulted from market adjustments after ending Southern repression. Other parts of it are questionable for him because they may be at the expense of others. Indeed, at various points, Epstein suggests that there are costs to blacks from antidiscrimination laws, including employers' unwillingness to hire African Americans because the antidiscrimination laws make it more difficult to fire them. But Epstein also argues that the antidiscrimination laws have benefitted middle-class blacks at the expense of poorer blacks. Professor Samuel Issacharoff, in Contractual Liberties in Discriminatory Markets, 70 Tex. L. Rev. 1219, 1241 (1992), responds:

> Epstein takes as his premise numerous observations, including those of sociologist William Julius Wilson, that Title VII has been a tremendous boon to skilled blacks, particularly in the professions, but has produced no discernible improvement in the life station of the increasing black underclass. Epstein attempts to argue that just as the minimum wage is thought to raise the cost of marginal labor and actually decrease opportunity for teenage and other marginal laborers, so too must Title VII be responsible for shutting out the low-skilled layers of the black work force: "The chief effect of Title VII is to make highly skilled black labor more desirable relative to low-skilled black labor. As with the minimum wage, Title VII works a redistribution from worse-off to better-off blacks, which is surely far from what its principled supporters intended."
>
> The logic here is startling. Epstein's best evidence to support his thesis is that the black lower classes have grown more desperate, more atomized, and more forlorn since the 1960s, when Title VII went into effect. . . . None of this evidence leads to the causation analysis that Epstein reaches for. It is nothing less than stunning that there is no mention in this section of the beginning of the deindustrialization of the United States during the period in question and the long cyclical decline in manufacturing and other industrial jobs that had long provided the primary avenue of advancement for ethnic groups arriving into the work force.

Issacharoff goes on to ask why opening up advancement to the black middle class should not "stand as a real, though partial, gain[.] Epstein argues that whatever gains blacks accomplished under Title VII must have been at the expense of the lower layers of the black community. The evidence for this is tenuous and unpersuasive." Id. at 1243.

13. Consider whether employment rules, including employment discrimination law, may be counterproductive in terms of its intended beneficiaries:

> Legal requirements that employers provide specified benefits to their workers, such as workers' compensation and family leave, are virtually omnipresent in modern employment law. Some mandates are directed to workers as a whole, and many of these date back to the early part of the twentieth century (workers' compensation, for instance). But other, newer mandates are directed to discrete, identifiable groups of workers, such as the disabled. These mandates are intended to accommodate the unique needs of those workers.
> . . . In broad terms, my framework predicts that accommodation mandates targeted to disabled workers will increase or leave unchanged the wages of these workers relative to the wages of nondisabled workers while simultaneously reducing disabled workers'

relative employment levels; the framework also predicts that accommodation mandates targeted to female workers will reduce the relative wages of these workers (contrary to the case of disabled workers) and will have ambiguous effects on their relative employment levels. . . .

Christine Jolls, Accommodation Mandates, 53 Stan. L. Rev. 223, 225-30 (2000).
    14. John J. Donohue III, Understanding the Reasons for and Impact of Legislatively Mandated Benefits for Selected Workers, 53 Stan. L. Rev. 897, 897-98, 901-04 (2001), addresses Professor Joll's article and the general question of measures that

"seek to provide specific additional benefits to certain identifiable demographic groups: blacks and other minorities, women, those over forty, and the disabled." In her richly nuanced and impressively comprehensive article, Accommodation Mandates, Christine Jolls [Accommodation Mandates, 53 Stan. L. Rev. 223 (2000)] develops the theoretical framework needed to analyze the effect of this class of laws mandating employers to provide benefits to particular, presumably "disadvantaged," groups of workers. Specifically, Jolls enriches the existing economic model of universal mandates in order to analyze the impact on wages and employment of these targeted labor-market interventions. One can easily go on at great length about the virtues of this paper . . . Specifically, Jolls shows that when antidiscrimination law works as it is supposed to — that is, when protected workers do not suffer wage or employment disadvantages — and when the targeted benefit is worth more to the worker than it costs the employer, then the impact of the accommodation mandate is exactly what its supporters would hope: The wages and employment level of the accommodated group will rise. Moreover, Jolls argues that the typical Chicago school response — arguing that the value of the mandate must be less than its costs or the employer already would have supplied it — is not fatal to her optimistic conclusion that accommodation mandates can benefit disadvantaged workers even when the cost of the mandate exceeds its value to workers. The requirement for the optimistic conclusion to go through, however, is that antidiscrimination law is fully effective in protecting the wage and employment levels of the disadvantaged workers who will receive the accommodation mandates. Without the protection of fully effective antidiscrimination law, accommodation mandates will always lower the wages or the employment levels of the disadvantaged workers, or both. Put differently, when antidiscrimination law works in only a partially effective way (by restraining wage discrimination or employment discrimination but not both) or is completely ineffective, accommodation mandates hurt their intended beneficiaries. Since the evidence suggests that antidiscrimination law is not fully effective, it is conceivable that Jolls' analysis will be used to marshal a case against enacting most accommodating mandates. . . .
    One might think of the rules prohibiting sex harassment as a type of accommodation mandate in that employers must take special steps to protect primarily female employees from harassing behavior by supervisors or fellow workers. . . .
    It is certainly plausible that the value to the female employees [of protection] is greater [than the cost to the employer], so we can begin with this case. Here the prediction is that the wages of women will fall but their level of employment will rise. Indeed, once we assume that the restrictions on wage differentials are not binding, the Jolls framework predicts that female wages will fall regardless of the relationship between the value of this accommodation and its cost. If the value of the accommodation is less than its cost, then not only will the wage fall but the employment of women will fall as well. Therefore, the Jolls framework indicates that women will pay for the anti-sex harassment mandate with lower wages. Uncertainty remains, however, as to whether the lower relative wages of women are offset by increases in the employment of women (which would be my hunch, as this would be consistent with the observed large increases in female

labor force participation in the United States), or whether women suffer the double whammy of lower wages and lower employment (in this case where they value the mandate less than its cost of provision). The notion that sex harassment law has imposed any costs on women is something that is probably not well recognized.

You should reconsider this argument when we meet sexual harassment in Chapter 7.

15. Cass R. Sunstein, Human Behavior and the Law of Work , 87 Va. L. Rev. 205, 206-08 (2001), takes a somewhat different approach, creating rights but allowing them to be waived.

> . . . I offer two general claims. The first is that waivable workers' rights represent a promising approach for the future, partly because waivable rights lack the rigidity of nonwaivable ones, and partly because they ensure that employers will provide key information to workers. The second claim is that traditional understandings of employee behavior and employment law make many blunders, because they are based on an inadequate sense of workers' actual values and behavior. Contrary to the conventional wisdom:
>
> Workers are especially averse to losses, and not as much concerned with obtaining gains; Workers often do not know about legal rules, including key rules denying them rights; Workers may well suffer from excessive optimism; Workers care a great deal about being treated fairly, and are willing to punish employers who have treated them unfairly, even at the workers' own expense; Workers often prefer increasing wage profiles; Many workers greatly discount the future, sometimes treating it as irrelevant; and Workers often care more about their relative economic position, or how their income compares with others, than about their absolute economic position, or how many dollars they are making in the abstract.
>
> In short, workers are like most people. They behave like homo sapiens, not like homo economicus. . . .
>
> . . . I suggest that in many situations, the law should confer certain entitlements on employees rather than employers, but allow those entitlements to be waived, either at a market price (an "unconstrained waiver") or subject to governmentally determined floors, whether procedural or substantive (a "constrained waiver"). The principal purpose of this approach is to ensure that employers fully disclose contractual terms to employees and allow employees to waive only when waiver is thought to be worthwhile, without producing the rigidity, inefficiency, and potential harm to workers and consumers alike that are created by systems of nonwaivable, "one-size-fits-all" terms.

Should discrimination be a waivable or non-waivable right? Given Professor Donohue's point about women bearing the costs of anti-sexual harassment policies, should women be able to waive their protection? Does such a waiver make any sense? As long as one woman would not waive her rights, wouldn't the employer have to bear most if not all of the costs of an anti-harassment policy?

## 2.   Weighing Noneconomic Costs and Benefits

Whether or not antidiscrimination laws improve the economic condition of protected groups and whether or not they improve or impair the efficiency of the economy in general, antidiscrimination laws provide protected groups with a remedy for the loss of dignity and associated psychic harm caused by discrimination. Epstein ignores psychic harm and seems to argue that eliminating Title VII would have little adverse economic effect on African Americans or other groups. While there would be discrimination, it would tend to even out: some would discriminate against blacks, some in favor of them. He refers to the process as "voluntary sorting." Consider the similarities between Epstein's viewpoint and the following extract from Plessy v. Ferguson, 163 U.S. 537, 550-52 (1896), the case that held segregation by the "separate but equal" standard did not violate the Fourteenth Amendment's equal protection clause:

> [W]e cannot say that a law which authorizes or even requires the separation of the two races in public conveyances [violates] the fourteenth amendment. . . .
>
> We consider the underlying fallacy of the plaintiff's argument to consist in the assumption that the enforced separation of the two races stamps the colored race with a badge of inferiority. If this be so, it is not by reason of anything found in the act, but solely because the colored race chooses to put that construction upon it. The argument necessarily assumes that if, as has been more than once the case, and is not unlikely to be so again, the colored race should become the dominant power in the state legislature, and should enact a law in precisely similar terms, it would thereby relegate the white race to an inferior position. We imagine that the white race, at least, would not acquiesce in this assumption. The argument also assumes that social prejudices may be overcome by legislation, and that equal rights cannot be secured to the negro except by an enforced commingling of the two races. We cannot accept this proposition. If the two races are to meet upon terms of social equality, it must be the result of natural affinities, a mutual appreciation of each other's merits and a voluntary consent of individuals. As was said by the Court of Appeals of New York in People v. Gallagher, 93 N.Y. 438, 448, "this end can neither be accomplished nor promoted by laws which conflict with the general sentiment of the community upon whom they are designed to operate. When the government, therefore, has secured to each of its citizens equal rights before the law and equal opportunities for improvement and progress, it has accomplished the end for which it was organized and performed all of the functions respecting social advantages with which it is endowed." Legislation is powerless to eradicate racial instincts or to abolish distinctions based upon physical differences, and the attempt to do so can only result in accentuating the difficulties of the present situation. If the civil and political rights of both races be equal one cannot be inferior to the other civilly or politically. If one race be inferior to the other socially, the Constitution of the United States cannot put them upon the same plane.

Professor George Schatzki, in *United Steelworkers of America v. Weber: An Exercise in Understandable Indecision*, 56 Wash. L. Rev. 51, 56-57 (1980), recognized the advantages of voluntary separation, but nonetheless reached a very different conclusion than Professor Epstein or the Supreme Court in *Plessy:*

> It is not clear we would want to outlaw racial employment discrimination, however irrational we believed it to be, if all persons were sometimes the discriminators and sometimes the discriminatees; if all ethnic groups had equal, statistical access to jobs; if all ethnic groups were equally affluent, prestigious, and influential. At least I am not sure we should want to outlaw a pluralism that allowed random ethnic discrimination. Although, on balance, I might prefer the "melting pot," or I might prefer some integration as well as some identifiable pluralism, it is not clear to me that we, as a society, desire to destroy ethnic pride, consciousness, and behavior. Destruction of that pluralistic attitude and behavior would be difficult; quick destruction might be possible, but only with involvement of the law.
>
> [Since pluralism is desired by large segments of our society, the passage of Title VII must be explained in part by the fact that] in the United States, the burden of discrimination (in employment and elsewhere) has fallen on the members of certain ethnic groups.

Racial discrimination is not random. Most of us do not suffer the burdens and barbs of ethnic discrimination; more importantly, whether or not we do suffer this irrationality sometimes, most of us have been treated most of the time by dominant persons or institutions without our race being a handicap. Saying that about blacks or chicanos, for example, would be an outright lie. These are people in our society — as a whole — who suffer in a vastly disproportionate way because of their ethnicity. The degrees of suffering and disparity are probably immeasurable, but few — if any — would deny their existence.

Is the benefit of providing a remedy for the "tort" of discrimination outweighed by the economic and social costs of antidiscrimination laws? Are there other benefits associated with antidiscrimination laws? Professor John J. Donohue III, in Advocacy Versus Analysis in Assessing Employment Discrimination Law, 44 Stan. L. Rev. 1583, 1606 (1992), sounds a chilling note:

> In considering the value of antidiscrimination law, one should at least consider that the repeal of Title VII holds the remote possibility of cataclysmic racial conflict. The lessons of slavery, Jim Crow, and Nazi Germany all serve to remind us that racial prejudice can be a dangerous force. Just as efforts to push affirmative action too forcefully may ignite dangerous passions, the injustices of private sector employment discrimination, at a time when black incomes and wealth are far below those of whites, also has a potential for explosive consequences. While I certainly do not purport to speak with authority on the mechanism through which prejudice reverberates throughout a community, it is plausible that a certain amount of bigotry can exist in a society without catastrophic result, but that beyond some threshold, the prejudice could spiral out of control. . . . [T]hrough conscientious efforts to eradicate private discrimination, we [may] limit the likelihood of racial antagonism growing to the point where the demand for malicious or mean-spirited governmental action is difficult to check. Therefore, society may tolerate a law that seems socially costly, based on a purely contemporary assessment of costs and benefits, in order to diminish the (albeit small) likelihood that the repeal of Title VII would breach the bigotry threshold and lead to catastrophic social costs.[113] [S]ociety may not be willing to gamble with the risk of suffering a near infinite burden — such as the holocaust in Nazi Germany — even if the chance of such a burden is minuscule.

In addition to providing a remedy for offenses against dignity and preventing violent uprising, antidiscrimination laws could be viewed as beneficial because they seek to remedy the historic wrongs inflicted on blacks in this country. Professor George Rutherglen, in Abolition in a Different Voice, 78 Va. L. Rev. 1463, 1469 (1992), brings together Epstein's theme in Takings: Private Property and the Power of Eminent Domain (1985) that government appropriations of property should be compensated with his theme in Forbidden Grounds that each individual owns his or her own labor and criticizes Epstein for taking inconsistent positions in the two books:

> Slavery, of course, was a notorious violation of this principle and would therefore require some form of rectification, such as payment of reparations to the descendants of the slaves or various forms of affirmative action. This is a claim — indeed, the best possible claim — of a taking without just compensation to which libertarians like Epstein should be especially sympathetic. Yet in this book he dismisses all questions of rectification at the outset with the assertion that "there is no adequate remedy" for such historical injustices.

113. This argument is quite similar to those frequently offered by economists in support of the need to restrain inflation. Even if the social costs of restraining inflation at any point in time outweigh the social benefits, the small risk of hyperinflation, with its potential for causing an economic collapse that could ultimately threaten our democracy, justifies the costly vigilance.

J. Hoult Verkerke, in Free to Search, 105 Harv. L. Rev. 2080, 2085 (1992), agrees that, even assuming a libertarian perspective, antidiscrimination laws are:

> justified as necessary to remedy an unjust distribution of resources. As Epstein himself recognizes, the legitimacy of the libertarian common law system of private property and free contract ultimately depends on a libertarian principle of distributive justice. Thus, a given distribution is just if it is the result of voluntary exchanges starting from an initial just distribution, conditions that are not met in the case of black workers. However just the initial distribution may have been, the legacy of slavery and institutional discrimination is decidedly one of involuntary appropriation of labor and wealth from African Americans. Corrective justice demands that society attempt to remedy these wrongful appropriations.

Whatever the benefits antidiscrimination laws provide for protected groups, the argument remains that these benefits may be outweighed by their negative impact on society as a whole. Professor Samuel Issacharoff, in Contractual Liberties in Discriminatory Markets, 70 Tex. L. Rev. 1219, 1225 (1992), perceives Epstein's work as driven by a "bedrock faith in the principle of aggregate social utility. . . . Thus Epstein repeatedly measures the utility of antidiscrimination laws by asking whether 'from the social point of view, when [individuals] take this action, will it lead to an increase or a decrease in overall levels of social satisfaction, subjectively measured for all persons?'" But Issacharoff goes on to question utilitarianism:

> [T]he central question arises: even assuming the capacity to devise a utility function that can accurately measure subjective levels of satisfaction, what is the normative basis for assuming that "overall levels of social satisfaction" are the appropriate benchmarks for proper or improper societal interventions into employment markets? It is entirely conceivable that if a ninety-five percent majority of the population benefitted from the near enslavement of the remaining five percent, an equilibrium could be achieved in which any improvement of the status of the minority population would decrease the "overall levels of social satisfaction" — as measured primarily by the ninety-five percent majority. To my mind, this neither justifies the initial oppression nor invalidates the moral force of efforts to eradicate the vestiges of the oppression of the minority.

Id.

Considering the general social good, however, can it be argued that antidiscrimination laws have beneficial noneconomic effects beyond the benefits provided to members of protected groups? Professor J. Hoult Verkerke, supra at 2084, writes:

> [M]any readers will simply reject the libertarian premise on which his case against employment discrimination laws rests, adopting instead a political philosophy that supports more extensive regulation of private conduct. For example, many communitarians, who view law as part of the social framework within which values are formed,[10] might contend that public endorsement and enforcement of the antidiscrimination principle are essential to forming a good community. Modern liberals similarly endorse the antidiscrimination principle as part of their conception of social justice. John Rawls [A Theory of Justice 302 (1971)], for instance, derives his second principle of justice — that all positions should be open to all persons under conditions of "fair equality of opportunity" — from the exercise of personal autonomy behind the veil of ignorance.

10. See Stephen A. Gardbaum, Law, Politics, and the Claims of Community, 90 Mich. L. Rev. 685, 705-19 (1992) (analyzing the "metaethical communitarianism" implicit in the work of Richard Rorty, Michael Walzer, and Jurgen Habermas).

Assuming that some kinds of discrimination are to be prohibited, what kinds and in what situations? Professor Alan Freeman, in his essay Antidiscrimination Law: The View from 1989, in The Politics of Law: A Progressive Critique 121, 124-126 (David Kairys ed., rev. ed. 1990), distinguishes two perspectives for judging antidiscrimination law — the victim perspective and the perpetrator perspective.

> The first view, the one rooted in social reality, may be characterized as the "victim" perspective. Central to the victim perspective is an insistence on concrete historical experience rather than timeless abstract norm. For black Americans, that experience has been one of harsh oppression, exclusion, compulsory reduced status, and of being perceived not as a person but as a derogatory cultural stereotype. Years of oppression have left their mark in the form of identifiable consequences of racism: residential segregation, inadequate education, overrepresentation in lowest-status jobs, disproportionately low political power, and a disproportionate share in the least and worst of everything valued most in our materialistic society. From the victim perspective, when antidiscrimination law announces that racial discrimination has become illegal, the law's promise will be tested by the only relevant measure of success — results.
>
> The victim perspective focuses on the persistence of conditions traditionally associated with racist practice. . . . If [racist practices] exist in virtually identical form after antidiscrimination laws have prohibited racial discrimination, the law has not yet done its job. Those conditions are presumptive violations.
>
> The other view, which is the dominant one in American legal culture, may be termed the "perpetrator" perspective. Its concern is with rooting out the behaviors of individual bad actors who have engaged in "prejudicial" discriminatory practices. From the perpetrator perspective, the goal of antidiscrimination law is to apply timeless and abstract norms, unsullied by history or social reality. Its job is to isolate and punish racial discrimination viewed as an instance of individual badness in an otherwise nondiscriminatory social realm. Thus, we cannot find violations of antidiscrimination in objective social conditions, but only in the actions of identifiable perpetrators who have purposely and intentionally caused harm to identifiable victims who will be offered a compensatory remedy.
>
> Central to the perpetrator perspective is the principle of individual (or sometimes institutional) fault. All we need do is identify and catch the villains; having done so, we can, with confidence, place responsibility where it belongs. A corollary of this fault principle is that those who, under applicable legal doctrines, are not labeled perpetrators have every reason to believe in their own innocence and noninvolvement in the problem. One who is not a perpetrator can say "It's not my fault; I'm just an innocent societal bystander." Why should the mere bystander be called to account or implicated at all in the business of eradicating the past? This emphasis on fault provides the psychic structure of the "reverse discrimination" issue.
>
> The perpetrator perspective also denies historical reality — in particular, the fact that we would never have fashioned antidiscrimination law had it not been for the specific historical oppression of particular races. Denial leads all too quickly to the startling claim of "ethnic fungibility" — the notion that each of us bears an "ethnicity" with an equivalent legal significance, and with identical claim to protection against "discrimination," despite the grossly disproportionate experience that generated the legal intervention in the first place. Thus, discrimination on the basis of "whiteness" gains the same disreputable status as discrimination against blacks, and efforts to improve conditions for historic victims of discrimination are struck down on grounds of "principle." The key principle is that of "color blindness," which would be the appropriate rule in a future society that had totally eliminated racial discrimination, or, more likely, had never had such a problem at all.

As you proceed through this book, keep in mind the extent to which these perspectives influence various views, whether legislative, administrative, or judicial.

# PART II

---

## THE CONCEPT OF DISCRIMINATION UNDER TITLE VII, THE AGE DISCRIMINATION IN EMPLOYMENT ACT, AND SECTION 1981

# Chapter 3

## Individual Disparate Treatment Discrimination

### A. INTRODUCTION

In order to address the pervasive problems of employment discrimination, Congress enacted a series of statutes that deal with various aspects of the phenomenon. These laws include Title VII of the Civil Rights Act of 1964; the Civil War Reconstruction statutes, especially 42 U.S.C.S. § 1981 (2003); the Age Discrimination in Employment Act of 1967 (ADEA); the Rehabilitation Act of 1973; and the Americans with Disabilities Act of 1990 (ADA).

The avenues of relief under the statutes differ from each other in important ways, but all are concerned with discrimination in employment. It is "discrimination" that provides the unifying theme for this casebook. That concept, however, has been developed by the courts in ways that are not always intuitively obvious. Indeed, "discrimination" is now a term of art that embraces several different definitions, each with its own distinctive theory and methods of proof.

In broad terms, three statutes adopt a unitary definition of what has been called "disparate treatment" discrimination. The term originated in cases decided under Title VII of the Civil Rights Act of 1964 and has been applied essentially unchanged in both ADEA cases and suits brought under § 1981. Disparate treatment, however, has developed in two distinct ways. Individual disparate treatment is the focus of this chapter, while systemic disparate treatment is taken up in Chapter 4. In addition, Title VII jurisprudence has developed the theory of disparate impact discrimination.

That theory is not available under § 1981, but may or may not apply to suits under the ADEA.

Title VII of the Civil Rights Act of 1964, 42 U.S.C.S. §§ 2000e to 2000e-17 (2003), which embraces almost all employers of 15 or more employees, broadly proscribes discrimination in employment on the basis of race, color, religion, sex, or national origin. Section 703(a), 42 U.S.C.S. § 2000e-2(a) (2003), states the basic substantive standard:

It shall be an unlawful employment practice for an employer —

(1) to fail or refuse to hire or to discharge any individual, or otherwise to discriminate against any individual with respect to his compensation, terms, conditions, or privileges of employment, because of such individual's race, color, religion, sex, or national origin; or

(2) to limit, segregate, or classify his employees or applicants for employment in any way which would deprive or tend to deprive any individual of employment opportunities or otherwise adversely affect his status as an employee, because of such individual's race, color, religion, sex, or national origin.

The ADEA, 29 U.S.C.S. §§ 631-634 (2003), applies to employers with 20 or more workers. It tracks Title VII's language but ends each clause with "because of such individual's age." 29 U.S.C.S. § 623(a) (2003). The ADEA, however, defines "age" to include only those at least 40 years of age. 29 U.S.C.S. § 631(a) (2003).

Finally, in its present form, 42 U.S.C.S. § 1981 (2003), provides:

(a) All persons within the jurisdiction of the United States shall have the same right in every State and Territory to make and enforce contracts, to sue, be parties, give evidence, and to the full and equal benefit of all laws and proceedings for the security of persons and property as is enjoyed by white citizens, and shall be subject to like punishments, pains, penalties, taxes, licenses, and exactions of every kind, and to no other.

(b) For purposes of this section, the term "make and enforce contracts" includes the making, performance, modification, and termination of contracts, and the enjoyment of all benefits, privileges, terms, and conditions of the contractual relationship.

(c) The rights protected by this section are protected against impairment by nongovernmental discrimination and impairment under color of State law.

Section 1981 originated in the post-Civil War Reconstruction era as one of several statutes intended to protect former slaves. Its success, however, in promoting racial equality was limited for a century because of doubts whether it barred private discrimination and, if so, whether it was constitutional. See Civil Rights Cases, 109 U.S. 3 (1883). These doubts ended in 1975 with Johnson v. Railway Express Agency, Inc., 421 U.S. 454, 459-60 (1975), where the Court wrote: "[I]t is well settled among the Federal Courts of Appeals — and we now join them — that § 1981 affords a federal remedy against discrimination in private employment on the basis of race." In the years following, § 1981 became an important weapon against race discrimination until 1989, when Patterson v. McLean Credit Union, 491 U.S. 164, 176 (1989), cut it back radically by strictly reading the language of paragraph (a) to "extend only to the formation of a contract, but not to problems that may arise later from the conditions of continuing employment." In the Civil Rights Act of 1991, Congress amended § 1981, adding what are now paragraphs (b) and (c), to ensure that § 1981 continues to play an important role in employment discrimination law. As amended, § 1981 reaches the conduct that Title VII governs under the "terms and conditions of employment" language of § 703.

## B.   THE MEANING OF DISCRIMINATORY INTENT

### SLACK v. HAVENS
**7 FEP 885 (S.D. Cal. 1973),** *aff'd as modified,*
**522 F.2d 1091 (9th Cir. 1975)**

THOMPSON, J.: This action is brought by the plaintiffs, four black women, who allege they were discriminatorily discharged, due to their race, in violation of the Civil Rights Act of 1964, specifically 42 U.S.C. § 2000e-2(a)(1). . . .

4. On January 31, 1968, plaintiffs Berrel Matthews, Emily Hampton and Isabell Slack were working in the bonding and coating department of defendant Industries' plant, engaged in preparing and assembling certain tubing components for defendant's product. A white co-worker, Sharon Murphy, was also assigned to the bonding and coating department on that day and was performing the same general work as the three plaintiffs mentioned above. The fourth plaintiff, Kathleen Hale, was working in another department on January 31st.

Near the end of the working day, plaintiffs Matthews, Hampton and Slack were called together by their immediate supervisor, Ray Pohasky, and informed that the following morning, upon reporting to work, they would suspend regular production and engage in a general cleanup of the bonding and coating department. The cleanup was to consist of washing walls and windows whose sills were approximately 12 to 15 feet above the floor, cleaning light fixtures, and scraping the floor which was caked with deposits of hardened resin. Plaintiffs Matthews, Hampton and Slack protested the assigned work, arguing that it was not within their job description, which included only light cleanup in their immediate work areas, and that it was too hard and dangerous. Mr. Pohasky agreed that it was hard work and said that he would check to see if they had to do it.

5. On the following work day, February 1, 1968, plaintiffs Matthews, Hampton, and Slack reported to the bonding and coating department along with Sharon Murphy, their white co-worker. However, Mr. Pohasky excused Sharon Murphy to another department for the day, calling in plaintiff Kathleen Hale from the winding department where she had been on loan from the bonding and coating department for about a week. Mr. Pohasky then repeated his announcement that the heavy cleaning would have to be done. The four plaintiffs joined in protest against the heavy cleanup work. They pointed out that they had not been hired to do janitorial type work, and one of the plaintiffs inquired as to why Sharon Murphy had been excused from the cleanup detail even though she had very little seniority among the ladies in the bonding and coating department. In reply, they were told by Mr. Pohasky that they would do the work, "or else." There was uncontradicted testimony that at sometime during their conversation Pohasky injected the statement that "Colored people should stay in their places," or words to that effect. Some further discussion took place between plaintiffs and Pohasky and then with Gary Helming, plaintiffs' general supervisor, but eventually each of the plaintiffs was taken to the office of Mr. Helming where she was given her final paycheck and fired. Plaintiff Matthews testified without

contradiction that on the way to Mr. Helming's office Mr. Pohasky made the comment that "Colored folks are hired to clean because they clean better."

6. The general cleanup work was later performed by newly-hired male employees. Sharon Murphy was never asked to participate in this cleanup before or after the plaintiffs' termination.

7. The day following the plaintiffs' firing a conference was held between plaintiffs and defendant Glenn G. Havens, together with Mr. Helming, Mr. Pohasky and other company officials, but the dispute was not resolved as to the work plaintiffs were expected to do. Apparently, the plaintiffs were offered reinstatement if they would now agree to do the same cleanup work. They refused. . . .

B. Having concluded that defendant Industries is an "employer" under Title VII of the Civil Rights Act for the purposes of this action, we must next consider whether plaintiffs' termination amounted to unlawful discrimination against them because of their race. Defendants deny that the facts support such a conclusion, contending that plaintiffs' case amounts to nothing more than a dispute as to their job classification.

Admittedly, the majority of the discussion between plaintiffs and Industries' management on January 31 and February 1, 1968 centered around the nature of the duties which plaintiffs were ordered to perform. Plaintiffs pointed out that they had not been hired with the understanding that they would be expected to perform more than light cleanup work immediately adjacent to their work stations. They were met with an ultimatum that they do the work — or else. Additionally, no explanation was offered as to why Sharon Murphy, a white co-worker, had been transferred out of the bonding and coating department the morning that the heavy cleaning was to begin there, while plaintiff Hale was called back from the winding department, where she had been working, to the bonding and coating area, specifically for participation in the general cleanup. It is not disputed that Sharon Murphy had less seniority than all of the plaintiffs except plaintiff Hale (having been hired 8 days prior to plaintiff Hale) and no evidence of a bona fide business reason was ever educed by defendants as to why Sharon Murphy was excused from assisting the plaintiffs in the proposed cleaning project.

The only evidence that did surface at the trial regarding the motives for the decisions of the management of defendant Industries consisted of certain statements by supervisor Pohasky, who commented to plaintiff Matthews that "colored folks were hired to clean because they clean better," and "colored folks should stay in their place," or words to that effect. Defendants attempt to disown these statements with the argument that Pohasky's state of mind and arguably discriminatory conduct was immaterial and not causative of the plaintiffs' discharge.

But defendants cannot be allowed to divorce Mr. Pohasky's conduct from that of Industries so easily. First of all, 42 U.S.C. § 2000e(b) expressly includes "any agent" of an employer within the definition of "employer." Secondly, there was a definite causal relation between Pohasky's apparently discriminatory conduct and the firings. Had Pohasky not discriminated against the plaintiffs by demanding they perform work he would not require of a white female employee, they would not have been faced with the unreasonable choice of having to choose between obeying his discriminatory work order and the loss of their employment. Finally, by backing up Pohasky's ultimatum the top level management of Industries ratified his discriminatory conduct and must be held liable for the consequences thereof. . . .

From all the evidence before it, this Court is compelled to find that defendant Industries, through its managers and supervisor, Mr. Pohasky, meant to require the plaintiffs to perform the admittedly heavy and possibly dangerous work of cleaning the bonding and coating department, when they would not require the same work from plaintiffs' white fellow employee. Furthermore, it meant to enforce that decision by firing the plaintiffs when they refused to perform that work. The consequence of the above was racial discrimination whatever the motivation of the management of defendant Industries may have been. Therefore, the totality of Industries' conduct amounted, in the Court's opinion, to an unlawful employment practice prohibited by the Civil Rights Act, specifically, 42 U.S.C. § 2000e-2(a)(1).

*NOTES*

1. The traditional common law rule of employment contracts is that any contract not for a definite time is terminable at will by either party — for any reason or for no reason, for good reason or for bad reason. Slack v. Havens clearly changes this. How would you state the rule in cases to which Title VII and other antidiscrimination statutes apply?

2. In *Slack*, there was apparently no union involved. Had there been, the plaintiffs would probably not have been at-will employees because most collective bargaining agreements protect workers from discharge unless there is just cause. Nevertheless, because insubordination generally is considered just cause, an employee may be discharged for refusing to obey a supervisor's order even if the work ordered was not part of the employee's job description. There is a general arbitration rule that an employee must "obey now, grieve later." The illegality exception to the rule states that no employee will be punished for disobeying an order that is illegal, unethical, or immoral, or that would endanger the employee or others. See Pan Am Corp. v. Air Line Pilots Assoc., Intl., 206 F. Supp. 2d 12 (D.D.C. 2002); see generally Frank Elkouri & Edna Elkouri, How Arbitration Works 154-59 (5th ed. 1997). Does *Slack* change this? Cf. Smith v. Texas Dept. of Water Resources, 799 F.2d 1026 (5th Cir. 1986), where plaintiff was discharged from her position as engineering aide because she refused to act as a relief secretary. The court reversed a finding that the discharge for insubordination was not sex discrimination. Is the law that insubordination justifies discharge unless the employee is right that the job assignment she refuses is discriminatory?

3. Title VII also prohibits retaliation against employees who oppose discrimination. Suppose Slack and the co-worker contended they were fired not because they were black but because they opposed what they reasonably and in good faith believed to be discriminatory job assignment. Would they have won on that theory? Did they win on that theory? Retaliation is discussed in Chapter 7.

4. Would there be sufficient evidence in the case without the statements of Pohasky — that "colored folks are hired to clean because they clean better" — to support a fact finding that the cleaning assignment was made to plaintiffs because they were African Americans? What evidence supports the conclusion of race discrimination? Is there any evidence that the assignment was not made because of plaintiffs' race?

5. Suppose you represented the defendant in *Slack*. What defenses might you consider when faced with this fact situation? What information would you look for with respect to Sharon Murphy?

6. Why do Pohasky's statements show his intent to discriminate? Other examples of statements indicating different kinds of discriminatory intent follow.

(a) In a race discrimination case, a statement of a witness that the mayor had said "'that he wasn't gonna let no Federal government make him hire no god-dam nigger.'" Wilson v. City of Aliceville, 779 F.2d 631, 633 (11th Cir. 1986).

(b) In a sex discrimination case, Suggs v. ServiceMaster Educ. Food Management, 72 F.3d 1228, 1231 (6th Cir. 1996), a manager told a male replacement that it was "time to show a man could run the operation better." See also EEOC v. Farmer Bros. Co., 31 F.3d 891, 896 (9th Cir. 1994) (company president announced he "would spend every last dime" to keep women employees from coming back).

(c) In a religious discrimination case, after the employee was involved in an accident, he was told, "If you are a man of God why don't you just ask God to fix your neck." Further, when the employee was having problems with his work, "You are supposed to be a man of God, why don't you get God to do it for you or get it for you." Abraham v. Diagnostic Center Hosp. Corp. of Texas, 138 F. Supp. 2d 809 (S.D. Tex. 2001).

(d) In ADEA age discrimination cases, referring to older workers as "contaminated" and "Bad Apples," Abdu-Brisson v. Delta Airlines, Inc., 239 F.3d 456, 468 (2d Cir. 2000) (New York law); or statements that "'old dogs don't know how to hunt.'" Siegel v. Alpha Wire Corp., 894 F.2d 50, 52 (3d Cir. 1990).

(e) In a national origin discrimination case, statements calling plaintiff a "camel jockey" and "rug peddler" and telling him to "'go back to Syria and fight the Israeli Army and kill the Jews.'" Boutros v. Canton Regional Transit Auth., 997 F.2d 198, 201 (6th Cir. 1993).

7. Pohasky apparently assigned plaintiffs to the cleaning work in question because he believed them to be better cleaners. Is this pejorative? If so, is it pejorative because it suggests that blacks can only do menial jobs like cleaning?

8. Pohasky's comments suggest he was lumping all blacks together precisely because of their race. This phenomenon is called stereotyping and is not limited to Pohasky. For example, Al Campanis, vice-president of the Dodgers, was interviewed on a Nightline show dealing with the 40th anniversary of Jackie Robinson's breaking of baseball's color barrier. Asked why the major leagues had no black managers, general managers, or owners, Campanis denied there was prejudice. "I truly believe that they may not have some of the necessities to be, let's say, a field manager or perhaps a general manager." Asked if he really believed that, he said, "Well, I don't say that all of them, but they certainly are short. How many quarterbacks do you have, how many pitchers do you have, that are black? Why are black men or black people not good swimmers? Because they don't have the buoyancy." N.Y. Times, April 9, 1987, at B13.

9. These statements reflect the phenomenon of stereotyping individual members of a group because of the characteristics (or the perceived characteristics) of the group as a whole. Even the Supreme Court is not free of the phenomenon of stereotyping if one source discussing Phillips v. Martin Marietta Corp., 400 U.S. 542 (1971), is to be believed:

> Later that term, in a sex discrimination case . . . Burger wanted to rule in favor of a company that refused to hire women with preschool-age children. He strongly supported the company's policy. "I will never hire a woman clerk," Burger told his clerks. A woman would have to leave work at 6 P.M. to go home and cook dinner for her husband. His first clerk back in 1956 at the Court of Appeals had been a woman, he told them. It had not worked out well at all. As far as he was concerned, an employer could fire whomever he wanted and for whatever reason. That was the boss's prerogative.
>
> When it was suggested that his position amounted to a declaration that part of the Civil Rights Act was unconstitutional, Burger angrily shut off the discussion. He didn't want to argue legal niceties. His experience showed him that women with young children just didn't work out as well as men in the same jobs. The employer was within his rights.
>
> At conference, however, the majority voted the other way. Burger returned to his

chambers and announced that he wanted a per curiam (unsigned opinion) drafted, ruling that unless the company could show that conflicting family obligations were somehow more relevant to job performance for women than for men, the company would have to lose. "It was the best I could do," Burger told his amazed clerks. The decision became another liberal opinion for the Burger Court.

Scott Armstrong & Bob Woodward, The Brethren 123 (1979).

10. Obviously, stereotyping is a key problem in the employment area because much discrimination stems from employer perceptions about the abilities of various groups (racial, ethnic, or gender) in society. Part of the danger of stereotypes is that these beliefs may well be held without the employer being aware of them.

Attitudinal factors affect the employment opportunities available to women in a number of ways. The phenomenon of statistical discrimination, for example, involves the deliberate substitution of generalizations often embodying stereotypes and preconceptions about groups for individualized judgments of productivity. It is engaged in by employers who wish to minimize both their information costs, and the risks of uncertainty. In other instances, even where the employer does make some individual inquiry, group stereotypes may cause the employer to discount or reinterpret the objective data produced by the inquiry.

Social psychologists have documented extensively similar effects in the perception and evaluation of individual competence. The same professional article, for example, has been rated higher when attributed to a male, rather than a female, author.[38] Male artistic endeavors were judged, in the absence of authoritative criteria, superior to those attributed to a female. Male success is attributed to skill, while female success is seen more often as a matter of luck. Other studies show that for a highly competent female to gain recognition for her work, her accomplishments must be regarded as demonstrably exceptional. Not only must a woman be seen as succeeding in a realm outside traditional women's roles within a context requiring unusual drive and dedication, but her worth must be supported by the positive evaluation of an authoritative source.[40] These findings would seem to account for the phenomenon reported by sociologists of competent women simply "not being heard."[41]

Studies focusing specifically on employment decisions also show the impact of sex-based biases on perception. In simulated hiring situations, male applicants for managerial positions are rated higher and accepted more frequently than equally qualified females, particularly for more demanding positions.[42] On the other hand, when performance in low-level, unskilled tasks such as stocking store shelves is scored, there is a tendency to inflate female performance.[43] Some research suggests that it is the interaction between the applicant's sex and the sex-orientation of the position that influences hiring decisions.[44]

38. Goldberg, Are Women Prejudiced Against Women, 5 Transaction 28 (1968); Bem & Bem, Case Study of a Non-conscious Ideology: Training the Woman to Know Her Place, [in] Beliefs, Attitudes and Human Affairs (D. J. Bem, ed. 1970).
40. O'Leary, Some Attitudinal Barriers to Occupational Aspirations in Women, 81 Psych. Bull. 809, 812 (1974), citing findings of Taynor & Deuz, When Women Are More Deserving than Men: Equity, Attribution and Perceived Sex Differences, 28 J. Pers. & Soc. Psych. 360-67 (1973).
41. Epstein, What Keeps Women Out of the Executive Suite, [in] Bringing Women into Management (F. Gordon & M. Strober, eds., 1975).
42. Rosen & Jerdee, Effects of Applicant's Sex and Difficulty of Job Evaluation of Candidates for Managerial Positions, 59 J. App. Psych. 511 (1974).
43. Hamner, Kin, Baird & Bigoness, Race and Sex as Determinants of Ratings by Potential Employers in a Simulated Work-Sampling Task, 59 J. App. Psych. 705 (1974).
44. Cohen & Bunker, Subtle Effects of Sex Role Stereotypes on Recruiters' Hiring Decisions, 60 J. App. Psych. 566 (1975) (hiring for male-oriented position of personnel technician and female-oriented position of editorial assistant).

Similar biases have been observed in simulations of post-hiring decisions. An equally qualified woman is less likely to be promoted, to be offered training opportunities, and to have her personnel assessments accepted than her male counterpart.[45] Stereotypic role expectations are particularly evident in findings that married women are less likely to be promoted to positions involving travel than comparably situated males. Similarly, where equally qualified male and female applicants indicate that their families come first, the woman is less likely to be promoted.[46] Consistent with such employer attitudes toward male and female family responsibilities, men are less likely to be granted leaves for child care. Similarly, less effort is deemed appropriate to attempt to retain a female employee who has been offered a job elsewhere.

Nadine Taub, Keeping Women in Their Place: Stereotyping Per Se as a Form of Discrimination, 21 B.C. L. Rev. 345, 353-54 (1980). See also Charles R. Lawrence III, The Id, the Ego, and Equal Protection: Reckoning with Unconscious Racism, 39 Stan. L. Rev. 317 (1987); Deborah L. Rhode, The "No-Problem" Problem: Feminist Challenges and Cultural Change, 100 Yale L.J. 1731 (1991); Mary F. Radford, Sex Stereotyping and the Promotion of Women to Positions of Power, 41 Hastings L.J. 471 (1990); David Benjamin Oppenheimer, Negligent Discrimination, 141 U. Pa. L. Rev. 899 (1993). Cf. Barbara Flagg, "Was Blind, But Now I See": White Race Consciousness and the Requirement of Discriminatory Intent, 91 Mich. L. Rev. 953 (1993).

11. Professor Linda Hamilton Krieger, The Content of Our Categories: A Cognitive Bias Approach to Discrimination and Equal Employment Opportunity, 47 Stan. L. Rev. 1161 (1995), used the insights provided by cognitive psychology to conclude that stereotyping by race and gender is an "unintended consequence" of the necessity for humans to categorize their sensory perceptions in order to make any sense of the world:

[The] central premise of social cognition theory [is] that cognitive structures and processes involved in categorization and information processing can in and of themselves result in stereotyping and other forms of biased intergroup judgment previously attributed to motivational processes. The social cognition approach to discrimination comprises three claims relevant to our present inquiry. The first is that stereotyping . . . is nothing special. It is simply a form of categorization [of our sensory perceptions], similar in structure and function to the categorization of natural objects. According to this view, stereotypes, like other categorical structures, are cognitive mechanisms that all people, not just "prejudiced" ones, use to simplify the task of perceiving, processing, and retaining information about people in memory. They are central, and indeed essential to normal cognitive functioning.

The second claim posited in social cognition theory is that, once in place, stereotypes bias intergroup judgment and decisionmaking. . . . [T]hey function as implicit theories, biasing in predictable ways the perception, interpretation, encoding, retention, and recall of information about other people. These biases are cognitive rather than motivational. They operate absent intent to favor or disfavor members of a particular social group. And, perhaps most significant for present purposes, they bias a decisionmaker's judgment long before the "moment of decision" [when the employment decision in question is made], as a decisionmaker attends to relevant data and interprets, encodes, stores, and retrieves it from memory. These biases "sneak up on" the decisionmaker, distorting bit by bit the data upon which his decision is eventually based.

45. Rosen & Jerdee, Influence of Sex Role Stereotypes on Personnel Decisions, 59 J. App. Psych. 9 (1974) (bank managers as subjects).
46. Rosen, Jerdee & Prestwich, Dual-Career Marital Adjustment: Potential Effects of Discriminatory Managerial Attitudes, 37 J. Marr. & Fam. 565 (1975) (national sample of managers and executives).

The third claim follows from the second. Stereotypes, when they function as implicit prototypes or schemas [by which we evaluate each other], operate beyond the reach of decisionmaker self-awareness. Empirical evidence indicates that people's access to their own cognitive processes is in fact poor. Accordingly, cognitive bias may well be both unintentional and unconscious.

Id. at 1187-88. If acting on stereotyping is unintentional and unconscious, should acting based on stereotypes constitute individual disparate treatment discrimination? It is treating people differently based on their race or gender, but is that what antidiscrimination law proscribes? Or does intentional discrimination require a conscious intent to discriminate?

12. Professor Amy Wax, in Discrimination as Accident, 74 Ind. L.J. 1129 (1999), agrees with Krieger that much discrimination may be unconscious disparate treatment, which she describes as a kind of industrial accident. She then both questions whether current law reaches this phenomenon and whether it should. Because, by definition, such discrimination is not conscious, employer efforts to reduce it will likely be unavailing, according to Wax. She "predicts that liability for unconscious discrimination will be inefficient and will fail to compensate victims accurately." Id. at 1226. While stopping short of calling for an amendment to Title VII to establish that only conscious bias violates the statute, she clearly is opposed to any of the more dramatic efforts to expand Title VII liability in order to reach "discrimination as accident." Professor Michael Selmi provides a spirited response in Discrimination as Accident: Old Whine, New Bottle, 74 Ind. L.J. 1234 (1999). One of his themes is that the psychological literature is neither as clear as Professor Wax claims, nor does it view unconscious bias as beyond control.

13. Christine Jolls similarly suggests that hiring situations are not as resistant to efforts to eliminate bias as Professor Wax argues. Is there a Glass Ceiling?, 25 Harv. Women's L.J. 1, 3-4 (2002), describes a study by Claudia Goldin & Cecilia Rouse, Orchestrating Impartiality: The Impact of "Blind" Auditions on Female Musicians, 90 Am. Econ. Rev. 715 (2000), on the effect of blind selection of musicians by symphony orchestras: most now have auditions behind a screen. According to the study, "blind auditions substantially increased the likelihood that a female candidate would advance out of the preliminary round in an orchestra's selection process. The move to blind auditions also had a substantial effect on the ultimate likelihood that a female candidate would be selected for an orchestra position." Although Jolls notes that Goldin and Rouse's sample was too small to yield statistical significance, "the overall weight of the evidence they present — which stems from a significant range of sources and is studied a wide variety of ways — points convincingly to a substantial effect on the sex composition of new orchestra hires of changing from non-blind to blind audition procedures." 25 Harv. Women's L.J. at 4. She goes on:

The labor market discrimination suggested by Goldin and Rouse's findings could perhaps be rational (in the sense of maximizing orchestras' returns or profits); it is possible, for instance, that existing players might have better morale, and thus play better as a group, if they were with "like" (male) individuals, and it is also possible that long-time patrons of a traditionally male orchestra such as the Vienna Philharmonic might be unsupportive of hiring female musicians. In such circumstances, the orchestras' behavior would be rational, but nonetheless it would clearly be unlawful.

Reluctance to hire female musicians might also be rational for orchestras if, as a player for the Vienna Philharmonic once contended, female musicians would often take leave time because of pregnancy or have shorter tenures than their male counterparts, so that these musicians would typically impose greater costs on orchestras than the average male musician However, Goldin and Rouse's data show that in the period studied male and female musicians took statistically indistinguishable numbers of medical and other leaves and did not appear to differ in their tenures, at least in the direction posited by the account here. Thus, cost differentials of this sort cannot explain the treatment the female musicians received.

Id. at 4-5. See also Alan B. Krueger, Sticks and Stones Can Break Bones, But a Wrong Name Can Make a Job Hard to Find, N.Y. Times, Dec. 12, 2002, at C2 (reporting a study in which job applicants "with white-sounding names were 50 percent more likely to be called for interviews than were those with black-sounding names."). Is this discrimination conscious or unconscious?

14. Does intentional discrimination require a conscious intent to discriminate, or is it enough to find the plaintiff's protected class status caused the decision to occur? If a supervisor honestly believed he was acting for a nondiscriminatory reason, even if his unconscious biases in fact influenced his decision, will liability be imposed? How would a plaintiff prove that, despite the supervisor's "honest belief," racial bias caused the decision?

15. A distinctive contribution to the literature on stereotyping is Trina Jones, Shades of Brown: The Law of Skin Color, 49 Duke L. J. 1487 (2000), which deals with "colorism," that is, "discrimination within racial classifications on the basis of skin color." Such discrimination, Professor Jones argues, occurs in both the white and black communities, and she predicts that this form of discrimination will assume increasing significance in the future.

16. Accepting that discriminatory bias creeps into everyday decisions in the workplace, Professor Tristin Green, in Discrimination in Workplace Dynamics: Toward a Structural Account of Disparate Treatment Theory, 38 Harv. C.R.-C.L. L. Rev. 91, 128 (2003), argues for a legal theory that focuses on the ways in which organizational structures and institutional practices enable discriminatory bias in individuals. As she explains:

> An independent conceptualization of a form of discrimination in terms of workplace dynamics tells a certain and important causal story about how discrimination continues to operate in the modern workplace. Significantly, it recognizes the role that discriminatory bias, even in individuals who subscribe to an egalitarian ideal, continues to play in the allocation of opportunity and perpetuation of stratification. This story tells individual employees that they do not stand as innocent bystanders to inequity and discrimination simply because they believe that all employees should be judged equally on merit rather than race- or sex-based characteristics. But it also recognizes that discrimination today rarely operates in isolated states of mind; rather, it is often influenced, enabled, even encouraged by the structures, practices, and opportunities of the organizations within which groups and individuals work.

17. Some scholars argue that the effects of stereotyping are even more subtle, if more pervasive, than might first appear. By focusing on the reactions of members of groups who may be subject to such stereotyping, Devon W. Carbado and Mitu Gulati develop some further insights into the workplace. In Working Identity, 85 Cornell L. Rev. 1259, 1262 (2000), they contend:

> [B]ecause members of these groups are often likely to perceive themselves as subject to negative stereotypes, they are also likely to feel the need to do significant amounts of

"extra" identity work to counter those stereotypes. Depending on the context, that extra work may not only result in significant opportunity costs, but may also entail a high level of risk. . . .

18. *Slack* was both an early decision in the history of Title VII and in some ways an easy case: the employer's conduct was suspicious, and the employer's agent made statements to the plaintiffs that confirmed the motivations that they inferred from his conduct. Later decisions have come to characterize cases depending on proof of discriminatory motivation as "disparate treatment" cases. Further, both suspicious conduct and "direct evidence" of discrimination have generated their own complexities in terms of proof structures for disparate treatment cases. While we will encounter these shortly, it is useful to first focus more closely on precisely what the plaintiff is seeking to prove in a disparate treatment case: intent to discriminate.

## HAZEN PAPER CO. v. BIGGINS
### 507 U.S. 604 (1993)

Justice O'CONNOR delivered the opinion of the Court.

[Hazen Paper Company manufactures coated, laminated, and printed paper and paperboard. It is owned and operated by two cousins, petitioners Robert Hazen and Thomas N. Hazen. Walter F. Biggins was hired as technical director in 1977. He was fired in 1986, when he was 62 years old. Biggins sued, claiming to have been discharged in violation of both the Age Discrimination in Employment Act and the Employee Retirement Income Security Act of 1974 (ERISA), 29 U.S.C. § 1140. The company claimed that he had been fired for doing business with competitors. The case was tried to a jury, which rendered a verdict for Biggins on his ADEA claim and also found a violation of ERISA. The district court denied defendant's motion for a judgment n.o.v., and the court of appeals affirmed.]

In affirming the judgments of liability, the Court of Appeals relied heavily on the evidence that petitioners had fired respondent in order to prevent his pension benefits from vesting. That evidence, as construed most favorably to respondent by the court, showed that the Hazen Paper pension plan had a 10-year vesting period and that respondent would have reached the 10-year mark had he worked "a few more weeks" after being fired. There was also testimony that petitioners had offered to retain respondent as a consultant to Hazen Paper, in which capacity he would not have been entitled to receive pension benefits. The Court of Appeals found this evidence of pension interference to be sufficient for ERISA liability, and also gave it considerable emphasis in upholding ADEA liability. After summarizing all the testimony tending to show age discrimination, the court stated:

> Based on the foregoing evidence, the jury could reasonably have found that Thomas Hazen decided to fire [respondent] before his pension rights vested and used the confidentiality agreement [that petitioners had asked respondent to sign] as a means to that end. The jury could also have reasonably found that age was inextricably intertwined with the decision to fire [respondent]. If it were not for [his] age, sixty-two, his pension rights would not have been within a hairbreadth of vesting. [Respondent] was fifty-two years old when he was hired; his pension rights vested in ten years.

. . . The courts of appeals repeatedly have faced the question whether an employer violates the ADEA by acting on the basis of a factor, such as an employee's pension status or seniority, that is empirically correlated with age. We now clarify that there is no disparate treatment under the ADEA when the factor motivating the employer is some feature other than the employee's age. We long have distinguished between "disparate treatment" and "disparate impact" theories of employment discrimination.

> "Disparate treatment" . . . is the most easily understood type of discrimination. The employer simply treats some people less favorably than others because of their race, color, religion [or other protected characteristics]. Proof of discriminatory motive is critical, although it can in some situations be inferred from the mere fact of differences in treatment. . . . Claims that stress "disparate impact" [by contrast] involve employment practices that are facially neutral in their treatment of different groups but that in fact fall more harshly on one group than another and cannot be justified by business necessity. Proof of discriminatory motive . . . is not required under a disparate-impact theory.

Teamsters v. United States, 431 U.S. 324, 335, n.15 (1977) (construing Title VII of Civil Rights Act of 1964). The disparate treatment theory is of course available under the ADEA, as the language of that statute makes clear. "It shall be unlawful for an employer . . . to fail or refuse to hire or to discharge any individual or otherwise discriminate against any individual with respect to his compensation, terms, conditions, or privileges of employment, *because of such individual's age*." 29 U.S.C. § 623(a)(1) (emphasis added). By contrast, we have never decided whether a disparate impact theory of liability is available under the ADEA, see Markham v. Geller, 451 U.S. 945 (1981) (Rehnquist, J., dissenting from denial of certiorari), and we need not do so here. Respondent claims only that he received disparate treatment.

In a disparate treatment case, liability depends on whether the protected trait (under the ADEA, age) actually motivated the employer's decision. The employer may have relied upon a formal, facially discriminatory policy requiring adverse treatment of employees with that trait. Or the employer may have been motivated by the protected trait on an ad hoc, informal basis. Whatever the employer's decisionmaking process, a disparate treatment claim cannot succeed unless the employee's protected trait actually played a role in that process and had a determinative influence on the outcome.

Disparate treatment, thus defined, captures the essence of what Congress sought to prohibit in the ADEA. It is the very essence of age discrimination for an older employee to be fired because the employer believes that productivity and competence decline with old age. As we explained in EEOC v. Wyoming, 460 U.S. 226 (1983), Congress' promulgation of the ADEA was prompted by its concern that older workers were being deprived of employment on the basis of inaccurate and stigmatizing stereotypes.

> Although age discrimination rarely was based on the sort of animus motivating some other forms of discrimination, it was based in large part on stereotypes unsupported by objective fact. . . . Moreover, the available empirical evidence demonstrated that arbitrary age lines were in fact generally unfounded and that, as an overall matter, the performance of older workers was at least as good as that of younger workers.

Thus the ADEA commands that "employers are to evaluate [older] employees . . . on their merits and not their age." Western Air Lines, Inc. v. Criswell, 472 U.S. 400 (1985). The employer cannot rely on age as a proxy for an employee's remaining characteristics, such as productivity, but must instead focus on those factors directly.

When the employer's decision is wholly motivated by factors other than age, the problem of inaccurate and stigmatizing stereotypes disappears. This is true even if the motivating factor is correlated with age, as pension status typically is. Pension plans typically provide that an employee's accrued benefits will become nonforfeitable, or "vested," once the employee completes a certain number of years of service with the employer. See 1 J. Mamorsky, Employee Benefits Law § 5.03 (1992). On average, an older employee has had more years in the work force than a younger employee, and thus may well have accumulated more years of service with a particular employer. Yet an employee's age is analytically distinct from his years of service. An employee who is younger than 40, and therefore outside the class of older workers as defined by the ADEA, may have worked for a particular employer his entire career, while an older worker may have been newly hired. Because age and years of service are analytically distinct, an employer can take account of one while ignoring the other, and thus it is incorrect to say that a decision based on years of service is necessarily "age-based."

The instant case is illustrative. Under the Hazen Paper pension plan, as construed by the Court of Appeals, an employee's pension benefits vest after the employee completes 10 years of service with the company. Perhaps it is true that older employees of Hazen Paper are more likely to be "close to vesting" than younger employees. Yet a decision by the company to fire an older employee solely because he has nine-plus years of service and therefore is "close to vesting" would not constitute discriminatory treatment on the basis of age. The prohibited stereotype ("Older employees are likely to be ___") would not have figured in this decision, and the attendant stigma would not ensue. The decision would not be the result of an inaccurate and denigrating generalization about age, but would rather represent an accurate judgment about the employee — that he indeed is "close to vesting."

We do not mean to suggest that an employer lawfully could fire an employee in order to prevent his pension benefits from vesting. Such conduct is actionable under § 510 of ERISA, as the Court of Appeals rightly found in affirming judgment for respondent under that statute. But it would not, without more, violate the ADEA. That law requires the employer to ignore an employee's age (absent a statutory exemption or defense); it does not specify further characteristics that an employer must also ignore. Although some language in our prior decisions might be read to mean that an employer violates the ADEA whenever its reason for firing an employee is improper in any respect, see McDonnell Douglas Corp. v. Green, 411 U.S. 792 (1973) (creating proof framework applicable to ADEA; employer must have "legitimate, nondiscriminatory reason" for action against employee), this reading is obviously incorrect. For example, it cannot be true that an employer who fires an older black worker because the worker is black thereby violates the ADEA. The employee's race is an improper reason, but it is improper under Title VII, not the ADEA.

We do not preclude the possibility that an employer who targets employees with a particular pension status on the assumption that these employees are likely to be older thereby engages in age discrimination. Pension status may be a proxy for age, not in the sense that the ADEA makes the two factors equivalent, cf. Metz [v. Transit Mix Co., 828 F.2d 1202, 1208 (7th Cir. 1987)] (using "proxy" to mean statutory equivalence), but in the sense that the employer may suppose a correlation between the two factors and act accordingly. Nor do we rule out the possibility of dual liability under ERISA and the ADEA where the decision to fire the employee was motivated both by the employee's age and by his pension status. Finally, we do not consider the special case where an employee is about to vest in pension benefits as a result of his age, rather than years of service, see 1 Mamorsky, supra, at § 5.02[2], and the employer fires the employee in order to prevent vesting. That case is not presented here.

Our holding is simply that an employer does not violate the ADEA just by interfering with an older employee's pension benefits that would have vested by virtue of the employee's years of service.

Besides the evidence of pension interference, the Court of Appeals cited some additional evidentiary support for ADEA liability. Although there was no direct evidence of petitioners' motivation, except for two isolated comments by the Hazens, the Court of Appeals did note the following indirect evidence: Respondent was asked to sign a confidentiality agreement, even though no other employee had been required to do so, and his replacement was a younger man who was given a less onerous agreement. In the ordinary ADEA case, indirect evidence of this kind may well suffice to support liability if the plaintiff also shows that the employer's explanation for its decision — here, that respondent had been disloyal to Hazen Paper by doing business with its competitors — is "'unworthy of credence.'" But inferring age-motivation from the implausibility of the employer's explanation may be problematic in cases where other unsavory motives, such as pension interference, were present. . . . We therefore remand the case for the Court of Appeals to reconsider whether the jury had sufficient evidence to find an ADEA violation. . . .

## NOTES

1. *Biggins* makes clear that "intent to discriminate" is critical to what it calls a "disparate treatment" violation. The Court cites two kinds of disparate treatment cases: (1) the employer may have "a formal, facially discriminatory policy requiring adverse treatment of employees with a protected trait"; or (2) the employer "may have been motivated by a protected trait on an ad hoc, informal basis." The use of "protected trait" is apparently an attempt to include the various prohibited grounds of discrimination within Title VII and the ADEA. Most of the cases cited by the Court involved race or sex discrimination, not age discrimination. It is clear, therefore, that the Court intends a unified analysis of both statutes.

2. For the Court, this was not a case involving "direct evidence" of individual disparate treatment. There were only two "isolated comments" by the Hazens related to age. Rather, it was an inferential case based on circumstantial evidence: is age discrimination the best explanation for a particular course of conduct? Although we will soon examine the structure of proof of such cases, the Court in *Biggins* was concerned with the inferences that could be drawn from the evidence presented, not with the order of proof. The only issue was whether the jury verdict was supportable: should judgment as a matter of law (formerly called judgment n.o.v.) have been granted on the ADEA claim because no reasonable jury could have inferred age discrimination in light of the proof offered? As a civil case, the jury verdict need be supportable only by a preponderance of the evidence. That is, the jury does not have to be certain or even reasonably certain; it need only conclude that it is more likely than not that age motivated the employer's decision to discharge Biggins.

3. Whether the jury properly found age discrimination depends on what the jury was supposed to have been looking for. The Court found the answer easy: "It is the very essence of age discrimination for an older employee to be fired because the employer believes that productivity and competence decline with old age." Does that mean that the jury must believe that the Hazens fired Biggins because his increasing age led them to (incorrectly) conclude that his competence was declining? Surely

that cannot be the only kind of discriminatory intent within the statute: what if the jury found that Biggins was fired because the Hazens thought customers would not like working with older people? Older people are also often seen as "stuck in their ways," resistant to new ideas. If Hazen Paper viewed Biggins as not being sufficiently innovative, might that also indicate age stereotyping?

4. How likely is it that the Hazens incorrectly believed Biggins's competence declined? Aren't employers more likely to act on "inaccurate and stigmatizing stereotypes" regarding competence in refusing to hire older workers than in firing them? While in the past mandatory retirement rules have, in effect, presumed incompetence after age 65 or 70, such rules have long been illegal under the ADEA. They are, in fact, the kind of formal policy subject to the systemic disparate treatment theory. In this case, however, the Hazens had the opportunity to watch plaintiff perform over almost a decade. If they fired him because they believed his competence was diminishing, how could that be the result of a stereotype? Or does Professor Krieger's article explain this? To prevail, would Biggins have had to show (a) that they incorrectly evaluated his competence and (b) that they attributed his perceived loss of competence to his age? What if they correctly believed Biggins's competence was dropping, but also attributed it to his age?

5. Suppose an employer asks an older worker about her plans for retirement. Does this suggest age discrimination? See Cox v. Dubuque Bank & Trust Co., 163 F.3d 492 (8th Cir. 1998) (in ADEA action, employer was entitled to jury instruction that it had a right to make reasonable inquiries into employee's retirement plans). Montgomery v. John Deere & Co., Inc., 169 F.3d 556 (8th Cir. 1999) (plaintiff's being repeatedly asked whether he was going to take retirement not sufficient to show age discrimination).

6. Some circuit courts have considered cases in which the plaintiff was denied a position because he was "overqualified." E.g., Taggart v. Time Inc., 924 F.2d 43 (2d Cir. 1991). While the *Taggart* court's opinion is unclear as to whether "overqualification" is a proxy for age discrimination or a pure pretext, see generally Julia Lamber, Overqualified, Unqualified, or Just About Right: Thinking About Age Discrimination and *Taggart v. Time*, 58 Brook. L. Rev. 347 (1992), can *Taggart* survive *Biggins*? If Time really believed Taggart was overqualified, it could scarcely have thought his competence had diminished. But perhaps Time acted on other stereotypes: older workers have a hard time adjusting to new positions, or older workers feel resentful if they feel the work they are given is beneath them. But couldn't both these principles apply to persons of any age? How would the *Biggins* Court address the "overqualified" question? In EEOC v. Board of Regents of the University of Wisconsin, 288 F.3d 296, 303 (7th Cir. 2002), the court upheld a finding of age discrimination where defendants had prepared a "justification" for laying off plaintiffs in a reduction in force: "A reasonable jury could believe that the 'justification' uses code words which reflect an age bias. It refers to Evenson as having skills suited to the 'pre-electronic' era and that he would have to be brought 'up to speed' on 'new trends of advertising with electronic means.'"

7. Unlike race or sex, age stretches out along a continuum. The ADEA treats everyone who is 40 or older the same, in the sense that all are protected from age discrimination. But 40 is obviously an arbitrary line. Most professional athletes in major sports have finished their careers long before 40. Even today, some employers have age limits that are effective as to those below 40, but not effective for those 40 and older. Doyle v. Suffolk County, 786 F.2d 523 (2d Cir. 1986). While discrimination can start at any age, it is more likely in most kinds of employment at advanced ages, probably

because stereotypes become stronger as age increases. While the ADEA does not bar discrimination against individuals for being too young, some state antidiscrimination laws do. E.g., Bergen Commercial Bank v. Sisler, 723 A.2d 944 (N.J. 1999).

8. Some commentators have warned of "opportunistic" conduct by employers. In Governing the Workplace: The Future of Labor and Employment Law 64-65 (1988), Professor Paul Weiler argues that workers tend to be paid less than they are worth when first hired and more than they are worth in the later stages of their careers. Compensation tends to be linked to seniority in the firm, and workers with greater seniority receive more than their increased productivity would justify. This structure tends to keep employees loyal to the firm throughout their working lives but also creates a potential for "opportunistic" employer behavior, that is, taking advantage of the situation by replacing senior employees with younger, lower-paid workers. Older discharged workers rarely will be able to command the same compensation from another employer because their skills tend to be firm-specific. This reality has been proffered as a justification for modifying the at-will rule, Note, Employer Opportunism and the Need for a Just Cause Standard, 103 Harv. L. Rev. 510 (1989), but has obvious implications for the ADEA. Thus, Professor John J. Donohue III, in Advocacy Versus Analysis in Assessing Employment Discrimination Law, 44 Stan. L. Rev. 1583, 1586 n.14 (1992), states:

> One of the major theoretical arguments favoring age discrimination statutes [is] that such laws protect against the violation of implicit contracts between workers and firms. Conceivably, in order to increase productivity and reduce monitoring costs, firms may promise workers the carrot of considerable deferred compensation in return for many years of work at wages that are low in relation to the workers' marginal product. Once the workers have performed their part of the deal, management [has] an incentive to fire all the older workers, depriving them of their anticipated compensation.

Does *Biggins* reject this analysis of the ADEA? Professor Donohue notes that "the ADEA does not limit its protection to long-tenured workers, as this theory might suggest it should." Id. While mandatory retirement remains generally illegal under the ADEA, has *Biggins* freed employers to make productivity-based judgments? If so, does it resurrect the problem of opportunistic behavior?

9. One commentator has argued that the *Biggins* Court failed to take into account the provision of the ADEA permitting employers to differentiate "based on reasonable factors other than age." 29 U.S.C.S. § 623(f)(1) (2003). According to Professor Judith Johnson, in Semantic Cover for Age Discrimination: Twilight of the ADEA, 42 Wayne L. Rev. 1 (1995), this provision means that factors that correlate strongly with age (but are not age-based) can be used by an employer only if they are "reasonable." We will meet this provision again (see page 658), but was *Biggins* wrong in not considering it in determining what constitutes age discrimination?

10. Biggins may have been discharged to prevent his pension from vesting. While that reason is illegal under ERISA, doesn't the existence of a strong non-age reason effectively prevent the jury from finding an age motivation? The Court recognizes the possibility that both age discrimination and pension discrimination might coexist, but how could a jury find both without direct evidence? Is that what the Court means by saying that "inferring age-motivation from the implausibility of the employer's explanation may be problematic in cases where other unsavory motives, such as pension interference, were present"? See also Broaddus v. Florida Power Corp., 145 F.3d 1283 (11th Cir. 1998) (granting new trial because jury might have been confused that evidence relevant only to ERISA violation was also probative as to ADEA claim). We

will consider the defendant's burden to articulate a legitimate, nondiscriminatory reason in section C.2 infra. What if the decision is motivated by both age discrimination and other factors? We will study this "mixed motive" problem in connection with Price Waterhouse v. Hopkins (reproduced at page 152).

11. Suppose a 38-year-old woman is discharged, and she thinks it was because of her gender and her age. Because the ADEA's protection from age discrimination applies only after age 40, she does not have a federal claim of age discrimination. If she sues only on the basis of sex discrimination, the employer can rebut that claim by admitting it acted because of her age. While such an admission is neither legitimate nor nondiscriminatory, would the *Biggins* Court find the employer's rebuttal sufficient? *Biggins* pressures plaintiffs to sue on every possible basis to avoid the employer defeating the lawsuit by "admitting" it acted on some ground the plaintiffs failed to assert. On the other hand, if a sex discrimination plaintiff adds a count of age discrimination to avoid the trap set by the first part of *Biggins,* she faces the risk of dilution established by the second part of *Biggins* — the power of an inference drawn from circumstantial evidence to support any one claim of discrimination diminishes as the range of claims expands.

12. Under Title VII both race and sex discrimination are prohibited. An employer could not escape liability for race discrimination by admitting sex discrimination. But is there a hybrid — race and sex — claim that is different from either a race or a sex discrimination claim? In her essay A Black Feminist Critique of Antidiscrimination Law and Politics, in The Politics of Law: A Progressive Critique 193, 200-01 (David Kairys ed., rev. ed. 1990), Professor Kimberle Crenshaw puts the problem this way:

> I am suggesting that Black women can experience discrimination in ways that are both similar to and different from those experienced by white women and Black men. Black women sometimes experience discrimination in ways similar to white women's experience; sometimes they share very similar experiences with Black men. Yet often they experience double discrimination — the combined effects of practices which discriminate on the basis of race, and on the basis of sex. And sometimes, they experience discrimination as Black women — not the sum of race and sex discrimination, but as Black women.

This theory of "intersectionality," then, posits that discrimination can occur at the intersection of two or more traditional protected characteristics. As Professor Crenshaw suggests, an individual may be subject to discrimination not just because she is African-American and not just because she is a woman, but because she is both and by virtue of race and gender is situated within two systems of subordination: racism and sexism. They may also experience discrimination against a black woman, based on stereotypes different from those about white women or about black men (interactive discrimination). See also Floyd D. Weatherspoon, Remedying Employment Discrimination Against African-American Males: Stereotypical Biases Engender a Case of Race Plus Sex Discrimination, 36 Washburn L.J. 23 (1996) (arguing that African-American males are victims of race and sex discrimination that should be recognized as separate from either race or sex discrimination claims); Tanya Kateri Hernandez, "Multiracial" Discourse: Racial Classification in an Era of Color-Blind Jurisprudence, 57 Md. L. Rev. 97 (1998) (arguing that mixed-race census count will reinforce current judicial negation of the experiences of racial discrimination against persons of color and therefore maintain a system of race-based privilege); But see e. christi cunningham, The Rise of Identity Politics I: The Myth of the Protected Class in Title VII Disparate Treatment Cases, 30 Conn. L. Rev. 441 (1998) (arguing that using protected-class analysis restricts scope of Title VII by compartmentalizing the identity of individuals); Devon W. Carbado & Mitu Gulati, The Fifth Black Woman, 11 J. Contemp. Leg. Issues 701 (2001) (intersectionality theory does not capture discrimination based on how individuals "perform" their identity in the workplace).

To date, the courts tend to focus separately on the issues of race discrimination and gender discrimination. A few decisions are sympathetic to intersectionality claims. In Lam v. University of Hawaii, 40 F.3d 1551, 1562 (9th Cir. 1994), the court acknowledged that a claim brought by an Asian woman might be based upon multiple factors: "rather than aiding the decisional process, the attempt to bisect a person's identity at the intersection of race and gender will often distort or ignore the particular nature of the plaintiff's experiences." See also Hafford v. Seidner, 183 F.3d 506 (6th Cir. 1999) (district court should consider at trial whether harassment was based on race and religion, because plaintiff was a black Muslim).

13. According to the *Biggins* Court, the essence of age discrimination is adverse action taken because an employer "believes that productivity and competence decline with old age." Don't productivity and competence, in fact, decline with increasing age, at least in many jobs and at some age? Is this an example of a stereotype that is "true"? The ADEA, through the bona fide occupational qualification (bfoq) defense, see page 265, permits age discrimination when the employer can factually demonstrate an age-linked decline (just as Title VII has a bfoq allowing sex, religion, and national origin discrimination). The employer, however, has the burden of proof as to the bfoq. See pages 266-267. The point of the ADEA, as *Biggins* sees it, is that employers should not presume any decline in abilities and, even where declines occur, the employer should not act on those changes unless they are relevant to the job in question. Although Biggins may no longer be able to play basketball, that does not mean he is unable to be a technical director.

14. Recall the study of male and female musicians cited on page 85. Suppose that female musicians as a group *did* miss more work than male musicians as a group? In such a case, it may be rational for an employer to avoid hiring female musicians, but it would also be illegal. Why?

15. *Biggins* makes it more difficult to challenge employment decisions that use criteria that are highly, but not perfectly, correlated with age. Thus, an employer could fire everyone with 20 years' seniority and not necessarily violate the ADEA's proscription against intentional age discrimination: "Because age and years of service are analytically distinct, an employer can take account of one while ignoring the other, and thus it is incorrect to say that a decision based on years of service is necessarily 'age-based.'" Of course, seniority may be a pretext for age discrimination in the sense that the employer uses it to hide the true age basis for its decision. It may also "be a proxy for age, not in the sense that the ADEA makes the two factors equivalent, . . . but in the sense that the employer may suppose a correlation between the two factors and act accordingly." If the jury finds either to be true, the employer will be liable. But see EEOC v. McDonnell Douglas Corp., 191 F.3d 948 (8th Cir. 1999). In that case, summary judgment was granted to the employer even though the EEOC proffered admissions by managers that "retirement eligibility" was a factor in deciding who to lay off; under *Biggins*, this did not constitute age discrimination. Such evidence — even coupled with statistical evidence that older workers were laid off at twice the rate of younger workers and evidence that some managers manipulated performance evaluations to favor younger workers — did not prove a pattern or practice of age discrimination. See also Frank v. United Airlines, Inc., 216 F.3d 845 (9th Cir. 2000) (airline's weight policy for flight attendants did not violate ADEA even if weight is corre-

lated with age); Dilla v. West, 179 F.3d 1348 (11th Cir. 1999) ("reliance on factors correlated with age does not by itself constitute age discrimination"); Sack v. Bentsen, 51 F.3d 264 (1st Cir. 1995) (policy preferring recent law school graduation to more remote graduation did not discriminate on the basis of age). See generally Robert J. Gregory, There Is Life in That Old (I Mean, More "Senior") Dog Yet: The Age-Proxy Theory After *Hazen Paper Co. v. Biggins*, 11 Hofstra Lab. L.J. 391 (1994) (proxy theory can still be used as a tool for inferring intent to discriminate).

16. Professor Gary Minda in Opportunistic Downsizing of Aging Workers: The 1990s' Version of Age and Pension Discrimination in Employment, 48 Hastings L.J. 511 (1997), argues that opportunistic downsizing is a unique form of disparate treatment based on age that conflicts with the congressional purpose underlying both ADEA and ERISA because older workers are particularly vulnerable. Id. at 513. Such actions violate the ADEA when the employer's decision to downsize older, late-career workers is motivated by the higher salaries and benefits such workers earn due to seniority. Id. at 513-14. Taking issue with Michael J. Zimmer, The Emerging Uniform Structure of Disparate Treatment Discrimination Litigation, 30 Ga. L. Rev. 563, 573 (1996), Professor Minda writes:

> According to [one] view, *Biggins* rules out the possibility of using salary and pension as a "proxy" for proving age discrimination. A prime advocate of this view is Michael Zimmer, who has recently argued that *Biggins* creates two serious impediments to age discrimination claims. First, it makes it easier for employers to defend against a claim at the rebuttal stage. Instead of producing evidence that they had "legitimate, nondiscriminatory reasons" for their actions, employers can now satisfy their burden by producing evidence of any reason so long as the reason is not age. . . . The second impediment established by *Biggins*, according to Zimmer, is that the decision has restricted the "range of circumstantial evidence upon which a factfinder can draw the inference of discrimination." In refusing to allow the *Biggins* plaintiff to prove age discrimination on the basis of the employer's pension interference, the Court seemingly ruled out the possibility of proving unlawful motive through circumstantial evidence based on an accumulation of years of service. . . . If Zimmer's interpretation of *Biggins* is followed, then ADEA would be of little help to older workers who lose their jobs whenever their employer has any other non-age reasons of terminating employment. Pension status or length of service could not be used as proxies for age, even though there might be a positive correlation between pension status or length of service and age. In restricting the range of circumstantial evidence, *Biggins* has potentially opened the door for employers to escape ADEA liability by using length of service, pension status, and salary level as nondiscriminatory proxies for firing older workers.

Id. at 536-37. Professor Minda proffers an alternative reading of *Biggins*, one that is more optimistic about establishing age discrimination claims on the basis of salary and pension status. Focusing on one sentence in the case — "Pension status may be a proxy for age, not in the sense that ADEA makes the two factors equivalent, but in the sense that the employer may suppose a correlation between the two factors and act accordingly" — Professor Minda argues that the ADEA protects older workers who are fired because their salary is higher than their productivity. See also Judith D. Fischer, Public Policy and the Tyranny of the Bottom Line in the Termination of Older Workers, 53 S.C. L. Rev. 21 (2002); Stewart Schwab, Life-Cycle Justice: Accommodating Just Cause and Employment At Will, 92 Mich. L. Rev. 8 (1993). Professor Minda does note that the Seventh Circuit has interpreted *Biggins* to support Zimmer's conclusion. EEOC v. Francis W. Parker Sch., 41 F.3d 1073, 1076 (7th Cir. 1994). Has

Zimmer overstated the effect of *Biggins*? Or do the post-*Biggins* cases cited in Note 15 suggest that it is Professor Minda who was too optimistic?

17. Remember that Biggins challenged his employer's conduct solely on disparate treatment grounds. Under Title VII, a criterion that is highly correlated with a protected classification, such as race, may be challenged on the ground that its use has a disparate impact on protected group members. Using a criterion with a disparate impact violates Title VII unless it is job related and consistent with business necessity. The *Biggins* Court specifically reserved the question whether disparate impact is available under the ADEA. Should it be? Disparate impact is considered in Chapter 5.

18. After *Biggins*, can reliance on a factor that is highly correlated with a protected classification ever be the basis of a disparate treatment claim? What about physical features, such as wrinkles (age) or blue eyes (race) or breasts (gender)? Can a characteristic be so highly correlated with protected-group membership that it becomes a proxy for membership in that group? In Odima v. Westin Tucson Hotel, 53 F.3d 1484 (9th Cir. 1995), the court found the defendant's reason for not promoting the Nigerian-born plaintiff was a pretext for discrimination based on race and national origin. The defendant explained it had denied the plaintiff's requests for transfer because the plaintiff's accent would interfere with his communications with the public. Is this proxy or pretext? See also Hollins v. Atlantic Co., 188 F.3d 652 (6th Cir. 1999) (a company's regulation of a black female employee's hairstyle was actionable, at least where there was evidence that white workers with identical styles were not regulated). But see Scott v. Parkview Mem. Hosp., 175 F.3d 523 (7th Cir. 1999) (interview questions seeking to determine whether candidate had nurturing and caring attitudes did not establish gender discrimination against male).

19. The *Biggins* Court obviously does not believe that most age discrimination is motivated by animus or hostility toward older individuals. Rather, it springs from overbroad generalizations about declining productivity. Stereotypes may also operate with respect to race (e.g., blacks are shiftless and good athletes), sex (e.g., women are bad drivers and good cooks), religion (e.g., Jews are pushy and smart), or national origin (e.g., Irish are alcoholics and poetic). Some of these beliefs may not be hostile to the group involved, but certainly others reflect animus or hostility. Must discrimination be motivated by animus in order to be prohibited? Was Pohasky insulting blacks when he said they cleaned better? Or was he insulting whites? Does it matter? Suppose an employer refused to hire women to work a higher-paid night shift because it wished to protect them from the hazards of being out at night. Would good intentions pave the way to a Title VII violation?

20. In Parson v. Kaiser Aluminum & Chemical Corp., 727 F.2d 473, 477 (5th Cir. 1984), plaintiff proved that his employer's failure to promote him was based on the "not necessarily misplaced fear that Parson's promotion would trigger a violent and prolonged (and, thus expensive) reaction on the part of certain white, racially-motivated employees." The Fifth Circuit found intentional discrimination. Was that because the white workers' racial animus was imputed to the employer? Or because, whatever the reason, the employer intentionally used a different standard for promoting blacks?

21. While animus may not be necessary to a discrimination case under Title VII or the ADEA, hatred and hostility frequently exist. *Biggins* views discrimination in a bloodless way: employers, for reasons of convenience or out of ignorance, make stereotyped assumptions about older workers. But discrimination cases are frequently much more emotionally charged. Members of traditionally excluded groups often are resented when they arrive. Discrimination may also be motivated by a desire to subordinate. Consider the following:

Some people discriminate, not because of a desire to work with those like themselves, but because they desire to dominate certain people from other groups. . . . Some whites might, for example, prefer to employ blacks as domestic or menial workers because this would be consistent with their notions of the appropriate roles for whites and blacks. Part of one's identity can be superiority to members of other groups, and appropriate interactions can be ego enhancing.

This desire for subordination, rather than aversion, may be a greater part of discrimination against women than against racial minorities. Sexist men do not, as a general rule, try to avoid all contact with women. On the contrary, they desire contact in certain subordinating forms, such as having women as secretaries and dependent wives. In contrast, many whites would prefer to avoid all contact with African Americans, although other whites . . . enjoy subordinating relationships with people of color.

Mary Becker, The Law and Economics of Racial Discrimination in Employment: Needed in the Nineties: Improved Individual and Structural Remedies for Racial and Sexual Disadvantages in Employment, 79 Geo. L.J. 1659, 1667 (1991). What do you think of this argument? Does it apply to age discrimination?

22. Neither *Slack* nor *Biggins* focuses on burdens of proof, but it has become clear that, under the disparate treatment theory, the plaintiff has the burden of establishing discriminatory intent. This raises two distinct problems. *Slack* primarily involved "direct" evidence of intent: Pohasky's statements indicating why he acted as he did. In contrast, *Biggins* involved circumstantial, or inferential, methods of proof. The next section considers the structure of an inferential case of individual disparate treatment. Even where direct evidence of bias is present, the defendant may try to claim that the discriminatory intent, although present, did not cause the actual treatment of the employee. We will discuss the direct evidence approach in the succeeding section in connection with Price Waterhouse v. Hopkins (reproduced at page 152).

## C. CIRCUMSTANTIAL EVIDENCE OF DISCRIMINATORY INTENT

### 1. The Plaintiff's Prima Facie Case

#### McDONNELL DOUGLAS CORP. v. GREEN
#### 411 U.S. 792 (1973)

Justice POWELL delivered the opinion of the Court.

. . . Petitioner, McDonnell Douglas Corp., is an aerospace and aircraft manufacturer headquartered in St. Louis, Missouri, where it employs over 30,000 people. Respondent, a black citizen of St. Louis, worked for petitioner as a mechanic and laboratory technician from 1956 until August 28, 1964 when he was laid off in the course of a general reduction in petitioner's work force.

Respondent, a long-time activist in the civil rights movement, protested vigorously that his discharge and the general hiring practices of petitioner were racially motivated. As part of this protest, respondent and other members of the Congress on Racial Equality illegally stalled their cars on the main roads leading to petitioner's plant for the purpose of blocking access to it at the time of the morning shift change. The District Judge described the plan for, and respondent's participation in, the "stall-in" as follows:

[F]ive teams, each consisting of four cars would "tie up" five main access roads into McDonnell at the time of the morning rush hour. The drivers of the cars were instructed to line up next to each other completely blocking the intersections or roads. The drivers were also instructed to stop their cars, turn off the engines, pull the emergency brake, raise all windows, lock the doors, and remain in their cars until the police arrived. The plan was to have the cars remain in position for one hour.

Acting under the "stall in" plan, plaintiff [respondent in the present action] drove his car onto Brown Road, a McDonnell access road, at approximately 7:00 a.m., at the start of the morning rush hour. Plaintiff was aware of the traffic problem that would result. He stopped his car with the intent to block traffic. The police arrived shortly and requested plaintiff to move his car. He refused to move his car voluntarily. Plaintiff's car was towed away by the police, and he was arrested for obstructing traffic. Plaintiff pleaded guilty to the charge of obstructing traffic and was fined.

[O]n July 25, 1965, petitioner publicly advertised for qualified mechanics, respondent's trade, and respondent promptly applied for re-employment. Petitioner turned down respondent, basing its rejection on respondent's participation in the "stall-in." . . . Shortly thereafter, respondent filed a formal complaint with the Equal Employment Opportunity Commission, claiming that petitioner had refused to rehire him because of his race and persistent involvement in the civil rights movement, in violation of §§ 703(a)(1) and 704(a) of the Civil Rights Act of 1964. The former section generally prohibits racial discrimination in any employment decision while the latter forbids discrimination against applicants or employees for attempting to protest or correct allegedly discriminatory conditions of employment.

. . . The District Court also found that petitioner's refusal to rehire respondent was based solely on his participation in the illegal demonstrations and not on his legitimate civil rights activities. The court concluded that nothing in Title VII or § 704 protected "such activity as employed by the plaintiff in the 'stall in' and 'lock in' demonstrations."

On appeal, the Eighth Circuit affirmed that unlawful protests were not protected activities under § 704(a),[6] but reversed the dismissal of respondent's § 703(a)(1) claim relating to racially discriminatory hiring practices. . . .

## II

The critical issue before us concerns the order and allocation of proof in a private, non-class action challenging employment discrimination. The language of Title VII makes plain the purpose of Congress to assure equality of employment opportunities and to eliminate those discriminatory practices and devices which have fostered racially stratified job environments to the disadvantage of minority citizens. Griggs v. Duke Power Co., 401 U.S. 424, 429 (1971) [reproduced at page 322]. As noted in Griggs, "Congress did not intend by Title VII, however, to guarantee a job to every person regardless of qualifications. In short, the Act does not command that any person be hired simply because he was formerly the subject of discrimination, or because he is a member of a minority group. Discriminatory preference for any group, minority or majority, is precisely and only what Congress has proscribed. What is required by Congress is the removal of artificial, arbitrary, and unnecessary barriers to employment when the barriers operate invidiously to discriminate on the basis of racial or other impermissible classification."

There are societal as well as personal interests on both sides of this equation. The

6. Respondent has not sought review of this issue.

broad, overriding interest, shared by employer, employee, and consumer, is efficient and trustworthy workmanship assured through fair and racially neutral employment and personnel decisions. In the implementation of such decisions, it is abundantly clear that Title VII tolerates no racial discrimination, subtle or otherwise. In this case, respondent, the complainant below, charges that he was denied employment "because of his involvement in civil rights activities" and "because of his race and color." Petitioner denied discrimination of any kind, asserting that its failure to re-employ respondent was based upon and justified by his participation in the unlawful conduct against it. Thus, the issue at the trial on remand is framed by those opposing factual contentions. . . .

The complainant in a Title VII trial must carry the initial burden under the statute of establishing a prima facie case of racial discrimination. This may be done by showing (i) that he belongs to a racial minority; (ii) that he applied and was qualified for a job for which the employer was seeking applicants; (iii) that, despite his qualifications, he was rejected; and (iv) that, after his rejection, the position remained open and the employer continued to seek applicants from persons of complainant's qualifications.[13] In the instant case, we agree with the Court of Appeals that respondent proved a prima facie case. Petitioner sought mechanics, respondent's trade, and continued to do so after respondent's rejection. Petitioner, moreover, does not dispute respondent's qualifications[14] and acknowledges that his past work performance in petitioner's employ was "satisfactory."

The burden then must shift to the employer to articulate some legitimate, nondiscriminatory reason for the employee's rejection. We need not attempt in the instant case to detail every matter which fairly could be recognized as a reasonable basis for a refusal to hire. Here petitioner has assigned respondent's participation in unlawful conduct against it as the cause for his rejection. We think that this suffices to discharge petitioner's burden of proof at this stage and to meet respondent's prima facie case of discrimination.

The Court of Appeals intimated, however, that petitioner's stated reason for refusing to rehire respondent was a "subjective" rather than objective criterion which "carr[ies] little weight in rebutting charges of discrimination." This was among the statements which caused the dissenting judge to read the opinion as taking "the position that such unlawful acts as Green committed against McDonnell would not legally entitle McDonnell to refuse to hire him, even though no racial motivation was involved. . . ." Regardless of whether this was the intended import of the opinion, we think the court below seriously underestimated the rebuttal weight to which petitioner's reasons were entitled. Respondent admittedly had taken part in a carefully planned "stall-in," designed to tie up access to and egress from petitioner's plant at a peak traffic hour.[16] Nothing in Title VII compels an employer to absolve and rehire one who has engaged in such deliberate, unlawful activity against it.[17] In upholding,

13. The facts necessarily will vary in Title VII cases, and the specification above of the prima facie proof required from respondent is not necessarily applicable in every respect to differing factual situations.

14. We note that the issue of what may properly be used to test qualifications for employment is not present in this case. Where employees have instituted employment tests and qualifications with an exclusionary effect on minority applicants, such requirements must be "shown to bear a demonstrable relationship to successful performance of the jobs" for which they were used, Griggs v. Duke Power Co.

16. The trial judge noted that no personal injury or property damage resulted from the "stall-in" due "solely to the fact that law enforcement officials had obtained notice in advance of plaintiff's . . . demonstration and were at the scene to remove plaintiff's car from the highway."

17. The unlawful activity in this case was directed specifically against petitioner. We need not consider or decide here whether, or under what circumstances, unlawful activity not directed against the particular employer may be a legitimate justification for refusing to hire.

under the National Labor Relations Act, the discharge of employees who had seized and forcibly retained an employer's factory buildings in an illegal sit-down strike, the Court noted pertinently: "We are unable to conclude that Congress intended to compel employers to retain persons in their employ regardless of their unlawful conduct, — to invest those who go on strike with an immunity from discharge for acts of trespass or violence against the employer's property. . . . Apart from the question of the constitutional validity of an enactment of that sort, it is enough to say that such a legislative intention should be found in some definite and unmistakable expression." NLRB v. Fansteel Corp., 306 U.S. 240, 255 (1939).

Petitioner's reason for rejection thus suffices to meet the prima facie case, but the inquiry must not end here. While Title VII does not, without more, compel rehiring of respondent, neither does it permit petitioner to use respondent's conduct as a pretext for the sort of discrimination prohibited by § 703(a)(1). On remand, respondent must, as the Court of Appeals recognized, be afforded a fair opportunity to show that petitioner's stated reason for respondent's rejection was in fact pretext. Especially relevant to such a showing would be evidence that white employees involved in acts against petitioner of comparable seriousness to the "stall-in" were nevertheless retained or rehired. Petitioner may justifiably refuse to rehire one who was engaged in unlawful, disruptive acts against it, but only if this criterion is applied alike to members of all races.

Other evidence that may be relevant to any showing of pretext includes facts as to the petitioner's treatment of respondent during his prior term of employment; petitioner's reaction, if any, to respondent's legitimate civil rights activities; and petitioner's general policy and practice with respect to minority employment. On the latter point, statistics as to petitioner's employment policy and practice may be helpful to a determination of whether petitioner's refusal to rehire respondent in this case conformed to a general pattern of discrimination against blacks. Jones v. Lee Way Motor Freight, Inc., 431 F.2d 245 (C.A. 10 1970); Blumrosen, Strangers in Paradise: *Griggs v. Duke Power Co.*, and the Concept of Employment Discrimination, 71 Mich. L. Rev. 59, 91-94 (1972).[19] In short, on the retrial respondent must be given a full and fair opportunity to demonstrate by competent evidence that the presumptively valid reasons for his rejection were in fact a coverup for a racially discriminatory decision.

The court below appeared to rely upon Griggs v. Duke Power Co., in which the Court stated: "If an employment practice which operates to exclude Negroes cannot be shown to be related to job performance, the practice is prohibited." But *Griggs* differs from the instant case in important respects. It dealt with standardized testing devices which, however neutral on their face, operated to exclude many blacks who were capable of performing effectively in the desired positions. *Griggs* was rightly concerned that childhood deficiencies in the education and background of minority citizens, resulting from forces beyond their control, not be allowed to work a cumulative and invidious burden on such citizens for the remainder of their lives. Respondent, however, appears in different clothing. He had engaged in a seriously disruptive act against the very one from whom he now seeks employment. And petitioner does not seek his exclusion on the basis of a testing device which overstates what is necessary for competent performance, or through some sweeping disqualification of all those with any past record of unlawful behavior, however remote, insubstantial, or

---

19. The District Court may, for example, determine, after reasonable discovery that "the [racial] composition of defendant's labor force is itself reflective of restrictive or exclusionary practices." See Blumrosen, supra, at 92. We caution that such general determinations, while helpful, may not be in and of themselves controlling as to an individualized hiring decision, particularly in the presence of an otherwise justifiable reason for refusing to rehire. See generally Blumrosen, supra, n.19, at 93.

unrelated to applicant's personal qualifications as an employee. Petitioner assertedly rejected respondent for unlawful conduct against it and in the absence of proof or pretext or discriminatory application of such a reason, this cannot be thought the kind of "artificial, arbitrary, and unnecessary barriers to employment" which the Court found to be the intention of Congress to remove.[21]

## III

In sum, respondent should have been allowed to pursue his claim under § 703(a)(1). If the evidence on retrial is substantially in accord with that before us in this case, we think that respondent carried his burden of establishing a prima facie case of racial discrimination and that petitioner successfully rebutted that case. But this does not end the matter. On retrial, respondent must be afforded a fair opportunity to demonstrate that petitioner's assigned reason for refusing to re-employ was a pretext or discriminatory in its application. . . .

### NOTES

1. As in *Biggins*, the *McDonnell Douglas* theory of liability was "disparate treatment," relying on proof of intent to discriminate. *McDonnell Douglas* established the structure for litigating cases of individual disparate treatment based on circumstantial evidence. The first step, the prima facie case, appeared to be framed in terms of the four elements. It is obvious, however, that these elements do not fit every fact situation. In Teamsters v. United States, 431 U.S. 324, 358 n.44 (1977), the Court described the rationale for the prima facie case:

> The *McDonnell Douglas* case involved an individual complainant seeking to prove one instance of unlawful discrimination. An employer's isolated decision to reject an applicant who belongs to a racial minority does not show that the rejection was racially based. Although the *McDonnell Douglas* formula does not require direct proof of discrimination, it does demand that the alleged discriminatee demonstrate at least that his rejection did not result from the two most common legitimate reasons on which an employer might rely to reject a job applicant: an absolute or relative lack of qualifications or the absence of a vacancy in the job sought. Elimination of these reasons for the refusal to hire is sufficient, absent other explanation, to create an inference that the decision was a discriminatory one.

In Texas Department of Community Affairs v. Burdine, 450 U.S. 248 (1981), the Court described the consequences of proof of a prima facie case:

> Establishment of the prima facie case in effect creates a presumption that the employer unlawfully discriminated against the employee. If the trier of fact believes the plaintiff's evidence, and if the employer is silent in the face of the presumption, the court must enter judgment for the plaintiff because no issue of fact remains in the case.

21. It is, of course, a predictive evaluation, resistant to empirical proof, whether "an applicant's past participation in unlawful conduct directed at his prospective employer might indicate the applicant's lack of a responsible attitude toward performing work for that employer." But, in this case, given the seriousness and harmful potential of respondent's participation in the "stall-in" and the accompanying inconvenience to other employees, it cannot be said that petitioner's refusal to employ lacked a rational and neutral business justification. As the Court has noted elsewhere: "Past conduct may well relate to present fitness; past loyalty may have a reasonable relationship to present and future trust." Garner v. Los Angeles Board, 341 U.S. 716, 720 (1951).

In accompanying footnote 7, *Burdine* said its use of the term "prima facie case" in *McDonnell Douglas* denoted "the establishment of a legally mandatory, rebuttable presumption," not as a description of "the plaintiff's burden of producing enough evidence to permit the trier of fact to infer the fact at issue." Presumably, the point of the distinction is that a plaintiff's proof of a prima facie case is not necessarily sufficient to create a jury question.

2. *McDonnell Douglas/Burdine* makes it relatively easy to establish a prima facie case. But *McDonnell Douglas* is highly focused on the failure-to-rehire context. Suppose, however, that Green had never worked for the defendant. If you represented him, how would you prove the "qualification" aspect of element (ii)? What if Green had had no prior experience in the industry and the employer required experience? Would Green not have a prima facie case?

3. What if the job Green sought had not remained open because the employer hired a white worker over Green? This would bar application of the fourth prong as *McDonnell Douglas* formulated it. How could Green then make out a prima facie case? By proving that the white was less qualified? See, e.g., Suggs v. ServiceMaster Educ. Food Management, 72 F.3d 1228 (6th Cir. 1996). *McDonnell Douglas* involved the easiest kind of case: the plaintiff was not hired, but the job remained open. Because the plaintiff had the basic qualifications, that was suspicious. In *Burdine*, the job similarly remained open for several months. But suppose an African American and a white apply for a job. Even if the black applicant has the minimum qualifications, does selecting the white applicant create a prima facie case? Must the plaintiff also prove superior qualifications, or at least equal qualifications, before a prima facie case is made out? In *Teamsters*, the Court spoke of plaintiff disproving "the two most common reasons on which an employer might rely to reject a job applicant: an absolute or *relative* lack of qualifications. . . ." 431 U.S. 324, 358 n.44 (emphasis added). But see Walker v. Morthan, 158 F.3d 1177 (11th Cir. 1998) (en banc) (plaintiff need not prove he was equally or better qualified than those he compares himself to for purposes of the prima facie case). See Elizabeth Bartholet, Proof of Discriminatory Intent Under Title VII: *United States Postal Service Board of Governors v. Aikens*, 70 Cal. L. Rev. 1201 (1982).

4. In O'Connor v. Consolidated Coin Caterers Corp., 517 U.S. 308, 311-12 (1996), the lower court had found that a 56-year-old plaintiff had not made out a prima facie case of age discrimination under *McDonnell Douglas/Burdine* because the person who replaced plaintiff was over age 40 and thus in the same protected group as plaintiff. The Supreme Court rejected this approach:

> As the very name "prima facie case" suggests, there must be at least a logical connection between each element of the prima facie case and the illegal discrimination for which it establishes a "legally mandatory, rebuttable presumption." The element of replacement by someone under 40 fails this requirement. The discrimination prohibited by the ADEA is discrimination "because of [an] individual's age," though the prohibition is "limited to individuals who are at least 40 years of age." This language does not ban discrimination because they are aged 40 or over; it bans discrimination against employees because of their age, but limits the protected class to those who are 40 or older. The fact that one person in the protected class has lost out to another person in the protected class is thus irrelevant, so long as he has lost out because of his age. Or to put the point more concretely, there can be no greater inference of age discrimination (as opposed to "40 or over" discrimination) when a 40 year-old is replaced by a 39 year-old than when a 56 year-old is replaced by a 40 year-old.

Why is it irrelevant that O'Connor's replacement was over age 40? Or is it just irrelevant to the prima facie case? At the same time O'Connor was fired, another manager, age 57, was demoted and replaced by someone age 37. Is the inference of age discrimination equally powerful in both cases?

5. The Court in *O'Connor* went on to deal with the hypothetical situations of a 68-year-old replaced by a 65-year-old and a 40-year-old replaced by a 39-year-old and indicated that it would not be proper to draw an inference of discrimination in either case. An inference of age discrimination "can not be drawn from the replacement of one worker with another worker insignificantly younger. Because the ADEA prohibits discrimination on the basis of age and not class membership, the fact that a replacement is substantially younger than the plaintiff is a far more reliable indicator of age discrimination than is the fact that the plaintiff was replaced by someone outside the protected class." 517 U.S. at 313. In Barber v. CSX Distribution Servs., 68 F.3d 694, 699 (3d Cir. 1995), the court, acknowledging there "is no magical formula to measure a particular age gap and determine if it is sufficiently wide to give rise to an inference of discrimination," found that an eight-year difference between the plaintiff and the beneficiary of the discrimination could support a finding that the beneficiary was "sufficiently younger" than the plaintiff to permit an inference of age discrimination. In contrast, in the absence of other evidence, a seven-year age difference was not enough to establish a prima facie case in Richter v. Hook-SupeRx, Inc., 142 F.3d 1024 (7th Cir. 1998). Cf. Showalter v. University of Pittsburgh Med. Ctr., 190 F.3d 231 (3d Cir. 1999) (employer's retention of over-40 employees in a reduction in force does not prevent a 61-year-old worker from establishing a prima facie case when the retained workers were 52 and 45, and therefore sufficiently younger than plaintiff to raise an inference of discrimination). While the Seventh Circuit generally requires that plaintiff be replaced by persons at least 10 years younger, that rule is "not so bright as to exclude cases where the gap is smaller but evidence nevertheless reveals the employer's decision to be motivated by plaintiff's age." EEOC v. Board of Regents of the University of Wisconsin System, 288 F.3d 296, 302 (7th Cir. 2002). In contrast, in Kadas v. MCI Systemhouse Corp., 255 F.3d 359, 361, 362 (7th Cir. 2001), the court held that "it is eminently reasonable to doubt that, as in this case, a worker hired at an age well beyond that at which the protections of the age discrimination law click in and terminated *within months*, that is, before appreciably older, was a victim of age discrimination. . . . A company that didn't want 54-year-olds on its payroll would be unlikely to hire one rather than to hire one and promptly fire him. . . ."

6. Greene v. Safeway Stores, Inc., 98 F.3d 55 (10th Cir. 1996), applied *O'Connor* to permit a plaintiff to proceed even when he was replaced by an *older* worker. Does this push *O'Connor* too far? In Carson v. Bethlehem Steel Corp., 82 F.3d 157 (7th Cir. 1996), the court held that the replacement of a white worker with another white worker did not prevent the establishment of a prima facie case of race discrimination under Title VII. Indeed, seven of eight federal courts of appeals have held that, in a termination case, the plaintiff need not prove as part of the prima facie case that she was replaced by someone outside the relevant class. See Pivirotto v. Innovative Systems, Inc., 191 F.3d 344 (3d Cir. 1999) (collecting cases); Abdu-Brisson v. Delta Airlines, Inc., 239 F.3d 456, 468 (2d Cir. 2001); Kendricks v. Penske Transp. Serv., 220 F.3d 1220, 1229 (10th Cir. 2000). One court requires a plaintiff in a sex discrimination case to prove she was replaced by a man. Brown v. McLean, 159 F.3d 898, 905 (4th Cir. 1998). The *Pivirotto* court explained:

> An employer's failure to hire someone of a different class from the plaintiff, after the plaintiff's discharge, could be explained in many ways. . . . [A]n employer may treat women less favorably than men, but still be willing to hire a woman to fill a position left vacant by the firing of a discriminated-against woman. Or an employer may act on

gender-based stereotypes, firing women it perceives as not feminine enough (or as too feminine), or discharging women who are too aggressive while not doing the same to male employees. Such an employer would not necessarily replace a discriminated-against female employee with a man. Indeed, some employers, anticipating litigation, may hire a woman solely to attempt to defeat a sex discrimination claim.

If a plaintiff cannot show that she was replaced with a man, what proof is sufficient to make out a prima facie case?

What if the defendant hires or promotes a member of the same protected group as the plaintiff? If another African American had been awarded the position Green wanted, could he make out a prima facie case of discrimination? Cf. O'Connor v. Consolidated Coin Caterers Corp., 517 U.S. 308 (1996) (fact that replacement is in group protected against age discrimination does not destroy prima facie case of age discrimination). Or would it be relevant only to the defendant's "nondiscriminatory" reason? In Walker v. St. Anthony's Med. Ctr., 881 F.2d 554, 558 (8th Cir. 1989), the court said:

> Although the elements of a prima facie case . . . lend support to the district court's belief that Walker was required to show that she was replaced by an individual from outside the protected class in question . . . , no per se requirement has traditionally been imposed in cases brought under Title VII. . . . Certainly, if a woman alleging sex discrimination is replaced by a female, this fact is relevant in evaluating the employer's motive. Nevertheless, it is entirely conceivable that a woman discharged and eventually replaced by another woman may be able to establish that she was the object of impermissible discrimination related to her gender.

Do you agree?

7. "Disparate" treatment, as the phrase suggests, requires ultimately proving that the plaintiff was treated differently than a person of a different race or sex would have been treated. See Foster v. Arthur Andersen, LLP, 168 F.3d 1029 (7th Cir. 1999). Thus, many disparate treatment cases turn on whether the plaintiff can identify "comparators" who are similarly situated to her except for her race, sex, etc., but were treated differently. To the extent courts require comparators to be identical to plaintiff in characteristics other than, say, sex, for purposes of the prima facie case, the antidiscrimination statutes will have limited effect. To the extent they are more permissive in what constitutes similarly situated comparators, discrimination will be more easily established. See Lynn v. Deaconess Med. Ctr., 160 F.3d 484 (8th Cir. 1998) (plaintiff need not compare himself with those who committed the same offense; he could use those whose violations were of comparable seriousness).

8. Refusing to hire (as in *McDonnell Douglas*) or discharge (as in *O'Connor*) are obviously sufficient to justify relief if wrongfully motivated. But not all differences in treatment because of race, sex, religion, or age have been viewed as actionable. Some courts, often relying on the notion that the antidiscrimination statutes reach only "terms and conditions" of employment, hold that minor effects do not give rise to a claim. They require *material adverse* effects for a suit to go forward. E.g., Bruno v. City of Crown Point, 950 F.2d 355 (7th Cir. 1991) (evidence that family-oriented questions are asked only of female job applicant not sufficient to support a finding of intentional sex discrimination); Primes v. Reno, 190 F.3d 765 (6th Cir. 1999) (mid-range evaluation not actionable); Williams v. Bristol-Myers Squibb Co., 85 F.3d 270 (7th Cir. 1996) (lateral transfer not actionable when any diminution in pay was "indirect and minor") (ADEA); Enowmbitang v. Seagate Tech., 148 F.3d 970, 973 (8th

Cir. 1998) (employer's failure to provide plaintiff with a computer "does not rise above a 'mere inconvenience' and therefore does not constitute adverse employment action[;] . . . whether Seagate wishes to give its technicians specific pieces of equipment is a business decision that is not susceptible to judicial oversight"); Ledergerber v. Strangler, 122 F.3d 1142 (8th Cir. 1997) (replacement of personal staff and placing employer's standard antidiscrimination statement in personnel file did not constitute adverse employment since employee's position was not affected). Davis v. Town of Lake Park, Fla., 245 F.3d 1232, 1242-1243 (11th Cir. 2001) ("A negative evaluation that otherwise would not be actionable will rarely, if ever, become actionable merely because the employee comes forward with evidence that his future prospects have been or will be hindered as a result."). Cf. Russell v. Principi, 257 F.3d 815, 819 (D.C. Cir. 2001) ("the logic of an action that is 'adverse in an absolute sense' fits poorly with employment decisions involving bonuses. The denial of a bonus, or the award of a lesser bonus for discriminatory reasons, could never be considered 'adverse in an absolute sense.' A performance evaluation can drop below an average, but a bonus cannot be negative.").

What is a material adverse effect on the terms and conditions of employment? If an employer will not permit the women to work at night and the pay and responsibilities are the same for day and night workers, is this a material adverse effect? What if a woman has child care responsibilities that make night work more convenient? Isn't this discrimination just because it is *different* treatment? Title VII speaks of discrimination "against" employees and talks about classifying employees in ways that adversely affect their employment opportunities. These words may support the limited approach, but is it consistent with legislative intent to permit the employer to, for example, assign offices on the basis of race even if the offices are, from an objective point of view, substantially equal? What about the dignitary thrust of the statute, especially after the addition of general damages recovery for Title VII in the Civil Rights Act of 1991?

Professor Rebecca Hanner White in De Minimis Discrimination, 47 Emory L.J. 1121, 1148, 1151 (1998), criticizes these kinds of restrictions:

> "Ultimate employment decisions," "materially adverse employment actions," or "adverse employment actions" are not terms found in the plain language of the statute. . . . Those courts that view Title VII as encompassing only employment decisions that are ultimate or materially adverse have focused in part on Section 703(a)(1)'s reference to the "compensation, terms, conditions, or privileges" of employment. They conclude that discrimination must materially harm the employee in one of these respects to be actionable. . . .
>
>     But this is not the only, nor even the best, reading of the statute. Congress's use of the phrase "compensation, terms, conditions, or privileges of employment" emphasizes the employment-related nature of the prohibited discrimination. The phrase is better read as making clear that an employer who discriminates against an employee in a non-job-related context would not run afoul of Title VII, rather than as sheltering employment discrimination that does not significantly disadvantage an employee.

See also Tristin K. Green, Discrimination in Workplace Dynamics: Toward a Structural Account of Disparate Treatment Theory, 38 Harv. C.R.-C.L. L. Rev. 98, 102 (2002) ("As hierarchies flatten, movement between institutions increases, and the employment relationship is redefined in terms of individual achievement over hierarchical advancement, employees will find it more difficult to satisfy [a material adverse action] requirement."); Ernest F. Lidge III, The Meaning of Discrimination: Why

Courts Have Erred in Requiring Employment Discrimination Plaintiffs to Prove that the Employer's Action Was Materially Adverse or Ultimate, 47 U. Kan. L. Rev. 333 (1999); Theresa M. Beiner, Do Reindeer Games Count as Terms, Conditions or Privileges of Employment Under Title VII?, 37 B.C. L. Rev. 643 (1996) (arguing that "reindeer games," benefits such as golf games and lunches accorded to male employees but not to females, are terms and conditions of employment; denying access to such benefits to women should be treated similarly to a hostile work environment).

9. In her article, "De Minimis Discrimination," Professor White distinguishes between requiring a materially adverse employment action before discrimination will be actionable, which she concludes is an incorrect reading of the statute, and requiring an adverse action as an element of a *McDonnell Douglas* prima facie case which she finds is appropriate:

> [I]n determining whether an employer's treatment of an employee raises an inference that the treatment was a product of unlawful motive, courts are correct to look for an adverse action. . . . Before finding an inference of unlawful motive — one that will pass the burden of producing evidence to the defendant, that will entitle the plaintiff to judgment as a matter of law if the defendant remains silent, and that will make a trial far more likely than not, — there should be circumstances that suggest that discriminatory motive indeed is operating. But insistence on this adverse action is only proper in determining whether a prima facie case has been presented. Adversity, whether or not material, is not an element of a discrimination claim, only of a prima facie case based on inferential evidence. If why the employer is taking action is known, then no inference of discrimination is necessary, and thus a search for an action adverse enough to create the inference of unlawful intent need not occur.
>
> Although often phrased in terms of whether a prima facie case has been presented, some courts appear to have equated the elements of prima facie case with the elements of a claim. Recognizing that an adverse action is needed to create an inference of unlawful motive, they have concluded an adverse action is necessary for a Title VII claim. While the former is a correct application of disparate treatment theory, the latter is not.

47 Emory L.J. at 1180-81.

10. Defendant may rebut a prima facie case by "articulat[ing] some legitimate, nondiscriminatory reason" for its action. *McDonnell Douglas* established that disloyalty is such a reason. Suppose the court finds as a fact that Green was not rehired because he was a vegetarian. Is this a "legitimate, nondiscriminatory reason"? If so, what does "legitimate" mean? See *Biggins*. See also Panis v. Mission Hills Bank, 60 F.3d 1486 (10th Cir. 1995) (plaintiff failed to establish that defendant's reason for terminating her was a pretext when it claimed that she was discharged for fear of losing its customers' confidence because her husband was indicted for defrauding customers of another bank). We will return to this problem in the next section.

11. In *Burdine*, the Court described the consequences of the defendant carrying its rebuttal burden:

> The burden that shifts to the defendant, therefore, is to rebut the presumption of discrimination by producing evidence that the plaintiff was rejected, or someone else was preferred, for a legitimate, nondiscriminatory reason. The defendant need not persuade the court that it was actually motivated by the proffered reasons. It is sufficient if the defendant's evidence raises a genuine issue of fact as to whether it discriminated against the plaintiff. To accomplish this, the defendant must clearly set forth, through the introduction of admissible evidence, the reasons for the plaintiff's rejection. The explanation

provided must be legally sufficient to justify a judgment for the defendant. If the defendant carries this burden of production, the presumption raised by the prima facie case is rebutted, and the factual inquiry proceeds to a new level of specificity.

450 U.S. at 254-55. In accompanying footnote 8, the Court described the purpose of the shifting burdens: "In a Title VII case, the allocation of burdens and the creation of a presumption by the establishment of a prima facie case is intended progressively to sharpen the inquiry into the elusive factual question of intentional discrimination."

12. To achieve this progressive sharpening, it is critical that the courts keep the various stages of litigation distinct. In Cline v. Catholic Diocese of Toledo, 206 F.3d 651 (6th Cir. 2000), the Sixth Circuit reversed summary judgment for the defendant where plaintiff claimed that defendant refused to renew her teaching contract because of her pregnancy; defendant claimed that it so acted because her obvious pregnancy revealed that she had engaged in premarital sex, which violated her contract commitment to "reflect the values of the Catholic Church" by her "word and example." Id. at 656. In rejecting the plaintiff's prima facie case, the district court erred by relying on the defendant's rebuttal explanation to grant summary judgment: "[W]hen assessing whether a plaintiff has met her employer's legitimate expectations at the prima facie stage of a termination case, a court must examine [the] plaintiff's evidence independent of the nondiscriminatory reason 'produced' by the defense as its reason for terminating [the] plaintiff." Id. at 660-61. In Slattery v. Swiss Reinsurance America Corp., 248 F.3d 87, 92 (11th Cir. 2001), the court stressed that: "The qualification prong must not, however, be interpreted in such a way as to shift onto the plaintiff an obligation to anticipate and disprove, in his *prima facie* case, the employer's proffer of a legitimate, non-discriminatory basis for its decision."

13. What role does "pretext" play? In *Burdine*, the Court, in emphasizing that the "ultimate burden of persuading the trier of fact that the defendant intentionally discriminated against the plaintiff remains at all times with the plaintiff," described the pretext stage:

> The plaintiff retains the burden of persuasion. She now must have the opportunity to demonstrate that the proffered reason was not the true reason for the employment decision. This burden now merges with the ultimate burden of persuading the court that she has been the victim of intentional discrimination. She may succeed in this either directly by persuading the court that a discriminatory reason more likely motivated the employer or indirectly by showing that the employer's proffered explanation is unworthy of credence.

450 U.S. at 256.

14. Applying *McDonnell Douglas/Burdine* to the procedural steps in litigation:

(a) In response to plaintiff's complaint, defendant may move under Rule 12(b)(6) of the Federal Rules of Civil Procedure to dismiss for "failure to state a claim upon which relief can be granted." In Swierkiewicz v. Sorenma N.A, 534 U.S. 506 (2002), a unanimous Supreme Court held that the notice pleading standard of Rule 8(a) of the Federal Rules of Civil Procedure applies to the pleadings in employment discrimination cases. Thus, it reversed a lower court decision that dismissed plaintiff's complaint for failing to plead the specific facts establishing the four prongs of a prima facie case under *McDonnell Douglas*: "the prima facie case relates to the employee's burden of presenting evidence that raises an inference of discrimination" and does not "apply to the pleading standard that plaintiffs must satisfy in order to survive a motion to dismiss." Id. at 511. Plaintiff satisfied Rule 8(a)(2)'s requirement that a complaint must include only "a short and plain statement of the claim showing that the pleader is entitled to relief." Petitioner alleged that he had been terminated on account of his national origin in violation of Title VII and on account of his age in violation of the ADEA. His complaint detailed the events leading to his termination, provided relevant dates, and included the ages and nationalities of at least some of the relevant persons involved with his termination. These allegations give respondent fair notice of petitioner's claims and the grounds upon which they rest. In addition, they state claims upon which relief could be granted under Title VII and the ADEA. Notice pleading makes it difficult for an employer to win a Rule 12(b)(6) motion. See also Gavura v. Pennsylvania State House of Representatives, 2002 U.S. App. LEXIS 27345 (3d Cir. Oct. 29, 2002) (pro se complaint, while inartful, gave sufficient notice of sex discrimination claim for head-of-household pay policy). Thus, defendants will be forced to file and answer as the responsive pleading to a compliant.

(b) Under Rule 56(b) of the Federal Rules, the defendant can, after discovery, move for summary judgment. Liberalized Supreme Court standards allow summary judgment much more freely than in the past. Matsushita Elec. Indus. Corp. v. Zenith Radio Corp., 475 U.S. 574 (1986); Anderson v. Liberty Lobby, 477 U.S. 242 (1986); Celotex Corp. v. Catrett, 477 U.S. 317 (1986). Summary judgment may be granted either because plaintiff is not able to create at least an issue of fact as to each element of his prima facie case or because he is unable to establish at least an issue of fact that defendant's nondiscriminatory reason was a pretext. Because many discrimination cases depend on drawing inferences, courts often award summary judgment against plaintiffs on the ground that a reasonable jury could not infer discrimination from the facts that plaintiff is able to put into evidence. See generally Ann C. McGinley, Credulous Courts and the Tortured Trilogy: The Improper Use of Summary Judgment in Title VII and ADEA Cases, 34 B.C. L. Rev. 203 (1993).

Deborah C. Malamud, The Last Minuet: Disparate Treatment After *Hicks*, 93 Mich. L. Rev. 2229, 2237 (1995), reviewed district courts' use of *McDonnell Douglas/Burdine* at the pretrial stage:

> A review of district court summary judgment cases demonstrates that to accord legal significance to the plaintiff's satisfaction of the "requirements" of the prima facie "stage" and the pretext "stage" of *McDonnell Douglas-Burdine* is to engage in an act of misplaced concreteness. The world of practice under *McDonnell Douglas-Burdine* remains a disorderly one, in which the assignment of categories of facts to "stages" is unstable. Furthermore, to the extent that *McDonnell Douglas-Burdine* does constrain fact finding, it tends to discourage the kind of holistic fact finding that is most likely to reveal the truth about discrimination in the workplace.

See also Kenneth R. Davis, The Stumbling: Three-Step Burden Shifting Approach in Employment Discrimination Cases, 61 Brook. L. Rev. 703, 753 (1995) (courts have applied *McDonnell Douglas/Burdine* too formalistically; requiring plaintiffs to satisfy the prima facie case "has doomed otherwise valid discriminating claims").

(c) If the defendant's motion for summary judgment is denied, the case proceeds to trial. At the close of plaintiff's case in chief, the defendant may, pursuant to Rule 50(a) of the Federal Rules, move for judgment as a matter of law if "there is no legally sufficient evidentiary basis for a reasonable jury to find for" the plaintiff. Presumably, *McDonnell Douglas/Burdine* means that evidence sufficient to support each of the four elements of a prima facie case would sustain plaintiff's action against defendant's motion for judgment as a matter of law.

(d) If the defendant loses on its motion for judgment as a matter of law and proceeds to introduce its own case, the issue of plaintiff's proof of a prima facie case can no longer be raised.

> [W]hen the defendant fails to persuade the district court to dismiss the action for lack of a prima facie case, and responds to plaintiff's proof by offering evidence of the reason for the plaintiff's rejection, the factfinder must then decide whether the rejection was discriminatory within the meaning of Title VII. . . . Where the defendant has done everything that would be required of him if the plaintiff had properly made out a prima facie case, whether he did so is no longer relevant. The district court has before it all the evidence it needs to decide whether "the defendant intentionally discriminated against the plaintiff."

United States Postal Service Bd. of Governors v. Aikens, 460 U.S. 711, 715 (1983).

(e) At the close of all the evidence, another motion for a judgment as a matter of law is appropriate. Reconsider Hazen Paper Co. v. Biggins. Should the court on remand issue a judgment as a matter of law on the ADEA claim? In retrospect, should the ADEA claim have been allowed to go to the jury at all? If the judge denies a motion for judgment as a matter of law at the close of the case, the case is submitted to the factfinder.

(f) In a bench trial, the district judge is the finder of fact. Under the federal rules, her determinations are entitled to great deference. In Anderson v. City of Bessemer City, 470 U.S. 564 (1985), the trial court found that plaintiff had been denied an appointment because of her gender, but the Fourth Circuit reversed. Under Rule 52 of the Federal Rules of Civil Procedure, an appellate court may reverse on factual grounds only if the district judge's findings are "clearly erroneous." The Supreme Court found that the appellate court had overstepped its bounds:

> In detecting clear error in the District Court's finding that petitioner was better qualified than Mr. Kincaid [the male who was offered the job], the Fourth Circuit improperly conducted what amounted to a de novo weighing of the evidence in the record. . . .
> Based on our own reading of the record, we cannot say that either interpretation of the facts is illogical or implausible. Each has support in inferences that may be drawn from the facts in the record; and if either interpretation had been drawn by a district court on the record before us, we would not be inclined to find it clearly erroneous. The question we must answer, however, is not whether the Fourth Circuit's interpretation of the facts was clearly erroneous, but whether the District Court's finding was clearly erroneous. . . .

470 U.S. at 577. Even greater deference should be given to findings of fact based on credibility determinations: "[W]hen a trial judge's finding is based on his decision to credit the testimony of one of two or more witnesses, each of whom has told a coherent and facially plausible story that is not contradicted by extrinsic evidence, that finding, if not internally inconsistent, can virtually never be clear error." Id. at 575. See Michael J. Zimmer & Charles A. Sullivan, The Structure of Title VII Individual Disparate Treatment Litigation: *Anderson v. City of Bessemer City*, Inferences of Discrimination and Burdens of Proof, 9 Harv. Women's L.J. 25 (1986). Despite *Anderson*, courts of appeals still have difficulty applying the clearly erroneous rule. See Ezold v. Wolf, Block, Schorr & Solis-Cohen, 983 F.2d 509 (3d Cir. 1992) (overturning finding of discrimination in partnership decision on clearly erroneous grounds); Cronin v. Aetna Life Ins. Co., 46 F.3d 196 (2d Cir. 1995).

(g) While Title VII bench trials will continue when the parties so agree, the 1991

Civil Rights Act for the first time made jury trials available under Title VII. Jury trials were already available under § 1981 and the ADEA. Therefore, the purpose of allocating burdens under all three statutes will also help the judge determine whether the litigants have created an issue of fact to be decided by the jury. Presumably, the judge will grant a directed verdict if a reasonable jury could not infer discrimination from the plaintiff's proof. A similar question arises when a defendant seeks a judgment as a matter of law after the plaintiff prevails. At this stage, however, the question is whether, in light of all the evidence, a reasonable jury could have found discrimination.

15. Jury trials create a new issue for Title VII cases: is the jury to be instructed in terms of the *McDonnell Douglas/Burdine* allocation of burdens, or need it merely be told to determine the ultimate fact of discrimination? In Smith v. Borough of Wilkinsburg, 147 F.3d 272 (3d Cir. 1998), a jury verdict for defendant was reversed because of error in instructions:

> [T]he jury must be given the legal context in which it is to find and apply the facts. . . . [T]he jurors must be instructed that they are entitled to infer, but need not, that the plaintiff's ultimate burden of demonstrating intentional discrimination by a preponderance of the evidence can be met if they find that the facts needed to make up the prima facie case have been established and they disbelieve the employer's explanation for its decision.

Id. at 279. In the accompanying footnote 4, the court added that "this does not mean that the instruction should include the technical aspects of the *McDonnell Douglas* burden shifting, a charge reviewed as unduly confusing and irrelevant for a jury." Id. See also Anchor v. Riverside Golf Club, 117 F.3d 339 (7th Cir. 1997) (jury instructions that failed to allocate the burdens are not fatal to a jury verdict as long as the jury understood that its task was to decide who told the truth about what happened).

16. In Schaffner v. Glencoe Park Dist., 256 F.3d 616, 621 (8th Cir. 2001) the defendant had previously hired an applicant who did not possess the required degree; therefore, the plaintiff argued that the degree was not really a job qualification. The court disagreed: "The fact that the Park District hired an unqualified person for a job when there were no qualified candidates available does not mean that Schaffner herself is qualified for the position." Doesn't holding plaintiff to a requirement not imposed on others raise a question as to why defendant acted the way it did?

17. In a hiring case, *McDonnell Douglas* requires plaintiff to show that, "despite his qualifications, [plaintiff] was rejected." Formal rejection will, of course, suffice as would filling the position with another candidate, but failure to act on an application for an unreasonable length of time should be deemed the equivalent of rejection, at least for purposes of plaintiff's prima facie case. In cases of employment termination, the analogous issue is whether the employee voluntarily quit or was discharged. Scott v. Goodyear Tire & Rubber Co., 160 F.3d 1121 (6th Cir. 1998). The doctrine of constructive discharge, see Chapter 10, deals with situations where an apparent quit is viewed as a discharge.

18. What are the other elements of a prima facie case in a discharge case? Most ADEA cases involve discharges, and the lower courts have had to formulate the elements for this context. Indeed, two alternative formulations of *McDonnell Douglas* have emerged — one for individual discharges and the other for discharges in the course of reductions in force (rifs). In individual discharge cases involving a single employee who is fired, courts have tended to require him to show that he was doing

apparently satisfactory work in order to carry his prima facie case burden. E.g., Hong v. Children's Memorial Hosp., 993 F.2d 1257 (7th Cir. 1993); Johnson v. Group Health Plan, 994 F.2d 543 (8th Cir. 1993). Being replaced by a younger person is at least helpful. Tuck v. Henkel Corp., 973 F.2d 371 (4th Cir. 1992); Douglas v. Anderson, 656 F.2d 528 (9th Cir. 1981).

19. In reductions in force, that is, situations where a number of employees are terminated simultaneously, the "legitimate, nondiscriminatory reason" — the need to reduce expenses — is apparent on its face. Because "positions" are being eliminated, the power of proof that the plaintiff is doing an apparently satisfactory job diminishes. Barnes v. Gencorp, Inc., 896 F.2d 1457 (6th Cir. 1990). Courts have, therefore, tended to require a plaintiff to produce other evidence, such as identifying younger workers who were retained when she was discharged. Montana v. First Federal Sav. & Loan Assn. of Rochester, 869 F.2d 100 (2d Cir. 1989); Oxman v. WLS-TV, 846 F.2d 448 (7th Cir. 1988). See generally Mack Player, Proof of Disparate Treatment Under the Age Discrimination in Employment Act: Variations on a Title VII Theme, 17 Ga. L. Rev. 569 (1983). An age pattern of terminations may help, although this proof may be more properly viewed as systemic disparate treatment. See Chapter 4.

20. Many ADEA reduction-in-force cases involve employees who choose "early" retirement; when that choice is truly voluntary, there can be no age discrimination against the retiree, who is merely offered an additional benefit. See Ackerman v. Diamond Shamrock Corp., 670 F.2d 66 (6th Cir. 1982). But in some situations, the option of early retirement is merely the lesser of two evils because the employer threatens — expressly or implicitly — discharge, demotion, or transfer as the alternative. Where the employee has formally sought early retirement, establishing this prong of the prima facie case requires proof that he did so under pressure. As Judge Easterbrook phrased it, is the employer's conduct equivalent to "Don Corleone's 'Make him an offer he can't refuse'"? Henn v. National Geographic Socy., 819 F.2d 824, 826 (7th Cir. 1987); but see Paolillo v. Dresser Indus., Inc., 884 F.2d 707 (2d Cir. 1989). See generally Michael C. Harper, Age-Based Exit Incentives, Coercion, and the Prospective Waiver of ADEA Rights: The Failure of the Older Workers Benefit Protection Act, 79 Va. L. Rev. 1271 (1993); Judith A. McMorrow, Retirement and Worker Choice: Incentives to Retire and the Age Discrimination in Employment Act, 29 B.C. L. Rev. 347 (1988). This issue is entwined with the question of when an employee can waive statutory rights; see page 666.

21. Although *McDonnell Douglas* focuses on § 703(a), the Court also notes that plaintiff asserted a cause of action under § 704(a), Title VII's antiretaliation provision. Didn't the defendant admit discriminating against Green on the basis of his "opposition" conduct? We will examine that provision in Chapter 7.

### McDONALD v. SANTA FE TRAIL
### TRANSPORTATION CO.
**427 U.S. 273 (1976)**

Justice MARSHALL delivered the opinion of the Court.

. . . On September 26, 1970, petitioners, both white, and Charles Jackson, a Negro employee of Santa Fe, were jointly and severally charged with misappropriating 60 one-gallon cans of antifreeze which was part of a shipment Santa Fe was carrying for one of its customers. Six days later, petitioners were fired by Santa Fe, while Jackson was retained. . . .

[The plaintiffs sued their employer under both Title VII and § 1981 for discrimination in the discharge and their union for discrimination in not properly pursuing their grievances. The district court dismissed the complaint because "the dismissal of white employees charged with misappropriating company property while not dismissing a similarly charged Negro employee" violated neither Title VII nor § 1981.]

## II

Title VII of the Civil Rights Act of 1964 prohibits the discharge of "any individual" because of "such individual's race." Its terms are not limited to discrimination against members of any particular race. Thus, although we were not there confronted with racial discrimination against whites, we described the Act in Griggs v. Duke Power Co., as prohibiting "[d]iscriminatory preference for *any* [racial] group, *minority* or *majority*" (emphasis added).[6] Similarly the Equal Employment Opportunity Commission (EEOC), whose interpretations are entitled to great deference, has consistently interpreted Title VII to proscribe racial discrimination in private employment against whites on the same terms as racial discrimination against nonwhites. . . . EEOC Decision No. 74-31, 7 FEP 1326, 1328, CCH EEOC Decisions ¶6404, p. 4084 (1973). This conclusion is in accord with uncontradicted legislative history to the effect that Title VII was intended to "cover white men and white women and all Americans," 110 Cong. Rec. 2578 (1964) (remarks of Rep. Celler), and create an "obligation not to discriminate against whites," id., at 7218 (memorandum of Sen. Clark); id., at 8912 (remarks of Sen. Williams). We therefore hold today that Title VII prohibits racial discrimination against the white petitioners in this case upon the same standards as would be applicable were they Negroes and Jackson white. . . .[8]

Respondents contend that, even though generally applicable to white persons, Title VII affords petitioners no protection in this case, because their dismissal was based upon their commission of a serious criminal offense against their employer. We think this argument is foreclosed by our decision in McDonnell Douglas Corp. v. Green. [The Court quoted that case and elaborated on the "pretext" phrasing:

The use of the term "pretext" in this context does not mean, of course, that the Title VII plaintiff must show that he would have in any event been rejected or discharged solely on the basis of his race, without regard to the alleged deficiencies; . . . no more is required to be shown than that race was a "but for" cause.]

We find this case indistinguishable from *McDonnell Douglas*. Fairly read, the complaint asserted that petitioners were discharged for their alleged participation in a misappropriation of cargo entrusted to Santa Fe, but that a fellow employee, likewise implicated, was not so disciplined, and that the reason for the discrepancy in disci-

6. Our discussion in McDonnell Douglas Corp. v. Green of the means by which a Title VII litigant might make out a prima facie case of racial discrimination is not contrary. . . . As we particularly noted, however, this "specification . . . of the prima facie proof required . . . is not necessarily applicable in every respect to differing factual situations." Requirement (i) of this sample pattern of proof was set out only to demonstrate how the racial character of the discrimination could be established in the most common sort of case, and not as an indication of any substantive limitation of Title VII's prohibition of racial discrimination.

8. . . . Santa Fe disclaims that the actions challenged here were any part of an affirmative action program, and we emphasize that we do not consider here the permissibility of such a program, whether judicially required or otherwise prompted.

pline was that the favored employee is Negro while petitioners are white.[11] While Santa Fe may decide that participation in a theft of cargo may render an employee unqualified for employment, this criterion must be "applied, alike to members of all races," and Title VII is violated if, as petitioners alleged, it was not.

We cannot accept respondents' argument that the principles of *McDonnell Douglas* are inapplicable where the discharge was based, as petitioners' complaint admitted, on participation in serious misconduct or crime directed against the employer. The Act prohibits all racial discrimination in employment, without exception for any group of particular employees, and while crime or other misconduct may be a legitimate basis for discharge, it is hardly one for racial discrimination. Indeed, the Title VII plaintiff in *McDonnell Douglas* had been convicted for a nontrivial offense against his former employer. It may be that theft of property entrusted to an employer for carriage is a more compelling basis for discharge than obstruction of an employer's traffic arteries, but this does not diminish the illogic in retaining guilty employees of one color while discharging those of another color. . . .

### III

. . . We have previously held, where discrimination against Negroes was in question, that § 1981 affords a federal remedy against discrimination in private employment on the basis of race, and respondents do not contend otherwise. Johnson v. Railway Express Agency, 421 U.S. 454 (1975). The question here is whether § 1981 prohibits racial discrimination in private employment against whites as well as non-whites.

While neither of the courts below elaborated its reasons for not applying § 1981 to racial discrimination against white persons, respondents suggest two lines of argument to support that judgment. First, they argue that by operation of the phrase "as is enjoyed by white citizens," § 1981 unambiguously limits itself to the protection of nonwhite persons against racial discrimination. Second, they contend that such a reading is consistent with the legislative history of the provision, which derives its operative language from § 1 of the Civil Rights Act of 1866. The 1866 statute, they assert, was concerned predominantly with assuring specified civil rights to the former Negro slaves freed by virtue of the Thirteenth Amendment, and not at all with protecting the corresponding civil rights of white persons.

We find neither argument persuasive. Rather, our examination of the language and history of § 1981 convinces us that § 1981 is applicable to racial discrimination in private employment against white persons.

First, we cannot accept the view that the terms of § 1981 exclude its application to racial discrimination against white persons. On the contrary, the statute explicitly applies to "*all* persons" (emphasis added), including white persons. While a mechanical reading of the phrase "as is enjoyed by white citizens" would seem to lend support to respondents' reading of the statute, we have previously described this phrase simply as emphasizing "the racial character of the rights being protected." Georgia v.

---

11. Santa Fe contends that petitioners were required to plead with "particularity" the degree of similarity between their culpability in the alleged theft and the involvement of the favored coemployee, Jackson. [But] precise equivalence in culpability between employees is not the ultimate question: as we indicated in *McDonnell Douglas,* an allegation that other "employees involved in acts against [the employer] of *comparable seriousness* . . . were nevertheless retained . . ." is adequate to plead an inferential case that the employer's reliance on his discharged employee's misconduct as grounds for terminating him was merely a pretext (emphasis added).

Rachel, 384 U.S. 780, 791 (1966). In any event, whatever ambiguity there may be in the language of § 1981 is clarified by an examination of the legislative history of § 1981's language as it was originally forged in the Civil Rights Act of 1866. It is to this subject that we now turn.

The bill ultimately enacted as the Civil Rights Act of 1866 was introduced by Senator Trumbull of Illinois as a "bill . . . to protect *all* persons in the United States in their civil rights . . ." (emphasis added), and was initially described by him as applying to "every race and color." Cong. Globe, 39th Cong., 1st Sess., 211 (1866) (hereinafter Cong. Globe). Consistent with the views of its draftsmen, and the prevailing view in the Congress as to the reach of its powers under the enforcement section of the Thirteenth Amendment, the terms of the bill prohibited any racial discrimination in the making and enforcement of contracts against whites as well as nonwhites. . . .

While it is, of course, true that the immediate impetus for the bill was the necessity for further relief of the constitutionally emancipated former Negro slaves, the general discussion of the scope of the bill did not circumscribe its broad language to that limited goal. On the contrary, the bill was routinely viewed, by its opponents and supporters alike, as applying to the civil rights of whites as well as nonwhites. . . .

It is clear, thus, that the bill, as it passed the Senate, was not limited in scope to discrimination against nonwhites. Accordingly, respondents pitch their legislative history argument largely upon the House's amendment of the Senate bill to add the "as is enjoyed by white citizens" phrase. But the statutory history is equally clear that that phrase was not intended to have the effect of eliminating from the bill the prohibition of racial discrimination against whites. . . .

This cumulative evidence of congressional intent makes clear, we think, that the 1866 statute, designed to protect the "same right . . . to make and enforce contracts" of "citizens of every race and color" was not understood or intended to be reduced by Representative Wilson's amendment, or any other provision, to the protection solely of nonwhites. Rather, the Act was meant, by its broad terms, to proscribe discrimination in the making or enforcement of contracts against, or in favor of, any race. Unlikely as it might have appeared in 1866 that white citizens would encounter substantial racial discrimination of the sort proscribed under the Act, the statutory structure and legislative history persuade us that the 39th Congress was intent upon establishing in the federal law a broader principle than would have been necessary simply to meet the particular and immediate plight of the newly freed Negro slaves. And while the statutory language has been somewhat streamlined in re-enactment and codification, there is no indication that § 1981 is intended to provide any less than the Congress enacted in 1866 regarding racial discrimination against white persons. Thus, we conclude that the District Court erred in dismissing petitioners' claims under § 1981 on the ground that the protections of that provision are unavailable to white persons.

## NOTES

1. *Santa Fe* introduces us in more detail to 42 U.S.C.S. § 1981 (2003). Johnson v. Railway Express Agency, 421 U.S. 454 (1975), held that private race discrimination against blacks is prohibited by the statute, and *Santa Fe* confirms that, despite the "as

is enjoyed by white citizens" language, whites are also protected from racial discrimination. Thus, § 1981 is at once both broader and narrower than Title VII. While coverage questions are discussed in more detail in Chapter 7, § 1981 is broader insofar as it covers all employment contracts, even those of small employers, and it reaches beyond employment to all contracts. It is narrower in that it is limited to race (and probably alienage discrimination, see page 631) discrimination, while Title VII includes sex, religion, and national origin.

2. Does § 1981 require mere racial motivation or actual racial animus? A number of Supreme Court cases, e.g., Saint Francis College v. Al-Khazraji, 481 U.S. 604 (1987), have used the latter term, while others, such as *Santa Fe*, seem to focus on the racial nature of the motivation. See also General Building Contractors Assn. v. Pennsylvania, 458 U.S. 375 (1982) (using "racial animus" interchangeably with "purposeful discrimination" and "racially motivated" discrimination).

3. The plaintiffs in *Santa Fe* sued not only their employer, but also their union, Local 988. While the prohibitions of § 703(a) are limited to "employers," there are parallel prohibitions for unions (§ 703(c)) and employment agencies (§ 703(b)). But what about § 1981? Is the union's relationship with the individuals it represents "contractual"? As for union members, the answer is certainly yes. NLRB v. Boeing Co., 412 U.S. 67, 74-8 (1973). But what of non-members who are represented by virtue of the National Labor Relations Act (NLRA)? Does it matter that discrimination by unions (racial and otherwise) is also barred by the duty of fair representation under the NLRA? See page 636.

4. After *Santa Fe*, it is clear that whites are protected against race discrimination under both Title VII and § 1981. It is equally clear that men are protected against sex discrimination in employment under Title VII. Does *Santa Fe* create a "just cause" standard for all employees that supersedes the common law standard that contracts of employment are terminable at will? See Garcia v. Gloor, 618 F.2d 264, 269 (5th Cir. 1980) (Title VII "does not prohibit all arbitrary employment practices. It does not forbid employers to hire only persons born under a certain sign of the Zodiac."). The point of *Slack*, *McDonnell Douglas/Burdine*, and *Santa Fe* is that racial or gender motivation taints an employment decision, just as age motivation was critical in *Biggins*.

5. While subsequent cases have made clear that the employer need not have a good reason to discharge as long as its reason is not a prohibited one (e.g., race, sex, or age), the enactment of antidiscrimination statutes tends toward a just cause rule: with African Americans, Caucasians, women, men, older workers, individuals with disabilities, etc., all free to challenge adverse decisions as discriminatory, employers are well advised to have just cause for their actions. But see Ann C. McGinley, The Emerging Cronyism Defense and Affirmative Action: A Critical Perspective on the Distinction Between Color-Blind and Race Conscious Decision Making Under Title VII, 39 Ariz. L. Rev. 1003 (1997) (arguing that recent Supreme Court cases have unreasonably narrowed the intent requirement in Title VII law, permitting the emergence of the cronyism defense; the cronyism defense exalts the employer's liberty interest over an employee's right to equality in hiring); see also Ann C. McGinley, Rethinking Civil Rights and Employment at Will, 57 Ohio St. L.J. 1443 (1996).

6. In Deffenbaugh-Williams v. Wal-Mart Stores, Inc., 156 F.3d 581, 589 (5th Cir. 1998), the employer argued that a white plaintiff, claiming discrimination because of her interracial relationship, failed to show that she was a member of a class protected by Title VII. Finding that Title VII prohibits discrimination premised on an interracial

relationship, the court rejected Wal-Mart's argument. "[A] reasonable juror could find that Deffenbaugh was discriminated against because of her race (white), if that discrimination was premised on the fact that she, a white person, had a relationship with a black person."

7. *Santa Fe* makes clear that "reverse" discrimination is cognizable under both Title VII and § 1981, although the affirmative action plan question, reserved in footnote 8 in *Santa Fe*, was resolved in favor of the voluntary use of racial and gender preferences. See Johnson v. Transportation Agency of Santa Clara County (reproduced at page 283). Thus, some racial preferences are permissible and some are not under those statutes.

8. How does a white or male plaintiff make out a prima facie case? Suppose that the employer is Harlem Enterprises, Inc., a black-owned and -operated business. See Lincoln v. Board of Regents, 697 F.2d 928 (11th Cir. 1983), affirming judgment against a predominately black university in an action brought by a white faculty member. Might one also expect that employers will discriminate against males when they attempt to perform traditionally female jobs? See Martinez v. El Paso County, 710 F.2d 1102 (5th Cir. 1983), affirming a finding of sex discrimination against a male secretary.

9. In these cases, the plaintiffs were "minorities" in the institution or occupation where they sought work. *McDonnell Douglas* applies with little adjustment. But when a predominately white institution discharges a white worker, how will he establish a prima facie case? In *Santa Fe*, did the plaintiffs make out a prima facie case by showing that they were whites who were fired, while a black was not, although he engaged in the same conduct? Clearly, an African-American plaintiff would make out a prima facie case by proving that white workers were favored in such a situation. Does that mean that whites can also?

10. In Iadimarco v. Runyon, 190 F.3d 151, 158 (3d Cir. 1999), the Third Circuit disagreed with the holdings of three other circuits that, to establish a prima facie case, a "reverse" discrimination plaintiff must establish "background circumstances that support an inference that the defendant employer is 'the unusual employer who discriminates against the majority'" (quoting Parker v. Baltimore & Ohio R.R. Co., 652 F.2d 1012, 1017 (D.C. Cir. 1981)). That could be done by proof that the particular employer had "some reason or inclination to discriminate invidiously against whites" or that there was something "fishy" about the facts of the case that raised an inference of discrimination. Id. Finding that the "concept of 'background circumstances' is irremediably vague and ill-defined," id. at 161, *Iadimarco* held that a prima facie case in the context of 'reverse' discrimination requires merely that the plaintiff present sufficient evidence to allow a fact finder to conclude that the employer is treating some people less favorably than others based upon a trait that is protected under Title VII. But the court then held that this test was not satisfied by showing that the managers who made the decision plaintiff challenged were African American. Other circumstances, however, were sufficient to raise "material issues of fact as to whether the proffered explanation for not hiring him was a pretext for illegal discrimination." Id. at 167. Even in the Third Circuit, is it still harder for a white plaintiff than for an African American to make out a prima facie case?

11. Does the existence of an affirmative action plan make it easier for a white or a male plaintiff to establish discrimination, even if the employer may be able to justify it? In Bass v. Board of County Commissioners, 256 F.3d 1095 (11th Cir. 2001), plaintiff, a white male, challenged his layoff when the fire department was reorganized. He claimed that he was not appointed to a newly created position because of his race.

Defendant claimed that he was not chosen because he had not scored as well on his interview as the other candidates selected for the position. While there was an affirmative action plan in place, the defendant did not rely on it; instead, plaintiff claimed the defendant had relied on the plan, which, he argued, was invalid.

> In a typical Title VII case involving an affirmative action plan, an employer asserts in response to a plaintiff's prima facie showing of discrimination that its employment decision was made pursuant to an affirmative action plan and that its compliance with such a plan was a legitimate, nondiscriminatory reason for its action. . . . In this case, the County has sought no cover from its affirmative action plans . . . and it is Bass who relies on the County's affirmative action plans in support of his claims. . . .
>
> The first step in ascertaining whether the County can be held liable for discrimination as a result of its affirmative action plans is a determination of whether there is sufficient evidence that it acted pursuant to those plans. . . . [Second], the existence of an affirmative action plan, when combined with evidence that the plan was followed in an employment decision, is sufficient to constitute direct evidence of unlawful discrimination unless the plan is valid.

Id. at 1009-10. The court concluded: "[W]e hold that where there is an invalid affirmative action plan in effect relating to the employer's allegedly discriminatory actions, that plan constitutes direct evidence of discrimination if there is sufficient circumstantial evidence to permit a jury reasonably to conclude the employer acted pursuant to the plan when it took the employment actions in question." Id. at 1111.

12. Because discrimination must be "racial" to fall within § 1981, gender discrimination obviously is not covered. E.g., Bobo v. ITT, Continental Banking Co., 662 F.2d 340 (5th Cir. 1981). See also Runyon v. McCrary, 427 U.S. 160, 167 (1976). But other kinds of discrimination are less clear. For example, is anti-Semitism racial or religious bias? Is discrimination against Puerto Ricans based on their race or their national origin?

13. Under Title VII, such questions are rarely important because the statute bars race, religion, and national origin discrimination (although religion and national origin discrimination can both be justified by a bona fide occupational qualification, while race discrimination cannot). Under § 1981, however, recovery depends on the charged conduct being race-based. Recall *Biggins*. Suppose an employer discharges plaintiff, calling her a "wetback." See Ugalde v. W. A. McKenzie Asphalt Co., 990 F.2d 239 (5th Cir. 1993) (Title VII). Does the reference suggest bias against Mexicans? If so, are Mexicans a "racial" group? We will see in Chapter 7 that § 1981 may also prohibit alienage discrimination, so that bias against "wetbacks" might be barred on that ground.

14. While "race" seems intuitive, "race" as a legal concept is more complicated. The Supreme Court addressed this question in Saint Francis College v. Al-Khazraji, 481 U.S. 604 (1987), a suit by a United States citizen who had been born in Iraq and claimed that he was denied tenure at the college based on his Arab ancestry. The district court rejected his § 1981 claim because Arabs are generally considered Caucasians. The Supreme Court disagreed, noting modern debates over the meaning of "race":

> There is a common popular understanding that there are three major human races — Caucasoid, Mongoloid, and Negroid. Many modern biologists and anthropologists, however, criticize racial classifications as arbitrary and of little use in understanding the

variability of human beings. It is said that genetically homogeneous populations do not exist and traits are not discontinuous between populations; therefore, a population can only be described in terms of relative frequencies of various traits. Clear-cut categories do not exist. The particular traits which have generally been chosen to characterize races have been criticized as having little biological significance. It has been found that differences between individuals of the same race are often greater than the differences between the "average" individuals of different races. These observations and others led some, but not all, scientists to conclude that racial classifications are for the most part sociopolitical, rather than biological, in nature. S. Molnar, Human Variation (2d ed. 1983); S. Gould, The Mismeasure of Man (1981); M. Banton & J. Harwood, The Race Concept (1975); A. Montagu, Man's Most Dangerous Myth (1974); A. Montagu, Statement on Race (1972); Science and the Concept of Race (M. Mead, T. Dobzhansky, E. Tobach, & R. Light eds. 1968); A. Montagu, The Concept of Race (1964); R. Benedict, Race and Racism (1942); Littlefield, Lieberman, & Reynolds, Redefining Race: The Potential Demise of a Concept in Physical Anthropology, 23 Current Anthropology 641 (1982); Biological Aspects of Race, 17 Intl. S. Sci. J. 71 (1965); Washburn, The Study of Race, 65 American Anthropologist 521 (1963).

Id. at 610 n.4. Current scientific thinking on race, however, was ultimately irrelevant to the Court. Even if Arabs are now considered Caucasians, that was not the understanding in the nineteenth century when § 1981 was enacted:

In the middle years of the 19th century, dictionaries commonly referred to race as a "continued series of descendants from a parent who is called the *stock*," N. Webster, An American Dictionary of the English Language 666 (New York 1830) (emphasis in original), "[t]he lineage of a family," N. Webster, 2 A Dictionary of the English Language 411 (New Haven 1841), or "descendants of a common ancestor," J. Donald, Chambers's Etymological Dictionary of the English Language 415 (London 1871). The 1887 edition of Webster's expanded the definition somewhat: "The descendants of a common ancestor; a family, tribe, people or nation, believed or presumed to belong to the same stock." N. Webster, Dictionary of the English Language (W. Wheeler ed. 1887). It was not until the 20th century that dictionaries began referring to the Caucasian, Mongolian and Negro races, 8 The Century Dictionary and Cyclopedia 4926 (1911), or to race as involving divisions of mankind based upon different physical characteristics. Webster's Collegiate Dictionary 794 (1916). Even so, modern dictionaries still include among the definitions of race as being "a family, tribe, people, or nation belonging to the same stock." Webster's Third New International Dictionary 1870 (1971); Webster's Ninth New Collegiate Dictionary 969 (Springfield, Mass. 1986).

Encyclopedias of the 19th century also described race in terms of ethnic groups, which is a narrower concept of race than petitioners urge. Encyclopedia Americana in 1858, for example, referred in 1854 to various races such as Finns, gypsies, Basques, and Hebrews. The 1863 version of the New American Cyclopaedia divided the Arabs into a number of subsidiary races; represented the Hebrews as of the Semitic race, and identified numerous other groups as constituting races, including Swedes, Norwegians, Germans, Greeks, Finns, Italians (referring to mixture of different races), Spanish, Mongolians, Russians, and the like. The Ninth edition of the Encyclopedia Britannica also referred to Arabs, Jews, and other ethnic groups such as Germans, Hungarians, and Greeks, as separate races.

These dictionary and encyclopedic sources are somewhat diverse, but it is clear that they do not support the claim that for the purposes of § 1981, Arabs, Englishmen, Germans, and certain other ethnic groups are to be considered a single race. We would expect the legislative history of § 1981, which the Court held in Runyon v. McCrary had its source in the Civil Rights Act of 1866, as well as the Voting Rights Acts of 1870, to reflect this common understanding, which it surely does.

Id. at 611-12. The Court noted references to "race" for Scandinavians, Chinese, Spanish, Anglo-Saxons, blacks, Mongolians, and gypsies. In this light, it concluded:

Congress intended to protect from discrimination identifiable classes of persons who are subjected to intentional discrimination solely because of their ancestry or ethnic characteristics. Such discrimination is racial discrimination that Congress intended §1981 to forbid, whether or not it would be classified as racial in terms of modern scientific theory. The Court of Appeals was thus quite right in holding that §1981, "at a minimum," reaches discrimination against an individual "because he or she is genetically part of an ethnically and physiognomically distinctive sub-grouping of homo sapiens." It is clear from our holding, however, that a distinctive physiognomy is not essential to qualify for §1981 protection. If respondent on remand can prove that he was subjected to intentional discrimination based on the fact that he was born an Arab, rather than solely on the place or nation of his origin, or his religion, he will have made out a case under §1981.

Id. at 613. See also Shaare Tefila Congregation v. Cobb, 481 U.S. 615, 617 (1987) (§ 1982 suit by a synagogue for defacement of its walls with anti-Semitic slogans permissible because, when § 1982 was adopted, "Jews and Arabs were among the people then considered to be distinct races and hence within the protection of the statute").

15. Title VII was enacted nearly one hundred years after § 1981. By 1964, "race" had acquired its present meaning. Does that mean that discrimination against Arabs is not actionable under Title VII as race discrimination? If discrimination against Arabs is not racial discrimination, is it national origin discrimination? Does it matter that Arabs do not come from one political entity, but rather from a number of states in the Mideast? Similarly, with respect to Jews, is anti-Semitism actionable as race, religion, or national origin discrimination under Title VII? Before you answer that question too quickly, remember that much anti-Semitism, including the ultimate discrimination manifested in the Holocaust, made no distinctions between religious and non-religious Jews, but rather defined its victims in terms of race-like characteristics. See Sinai v. New England Telephone & Telegraph Co., 3 F.3d 471, 474 (1st Cir. 1993) (derogatory comments about Israel, plaintiff's birthplace, could be the basis for inferring race discrimination).

16. Some commentators believe that the distinctions drawn in Saint Francis College and Shaare Tefila Congregation are of more academic interest than practical significance. Suppose a person from the Philippines is denied a promotion. The denial does not violate under § 1981 if based on the employee's national origin, but is impermissible if based on her race. In the typical case, however, the defendant will deny either motivation, asserting instead that it acted for a "legitimate, nondiscriminatory reason." If the trier of fact concludes that this reason is a pretext, is it likely to go further and decide whether the employer acted on the basis of race or national origin? How can the trier of fact sort out motive when the victim of discrimination was a member of several protected groups? She is a Filipina and, therefore, probably an "Asian" and possibly "Hispanic" in extraction. Reconsider this question after you have read St. Mary's Honor Center v. Hicks (reproduced at page 130). Does Biggins suggest that defendant could defeat a § 1981 claim by picking a ground not covered by

§ 1981 and admitting to having discriminated on that basis? Even under Title VII, race is not subject to a bona fide occupational qualification defense, but national origin is. See Chapter 7.

## NOTE COMPARING SECTION 1981 AND TITLE VII

Unlike modern civil rights legislation, § 1981 is devoid of express procedural provisions governing the enforcement of its substantive proscription against racial discrimination in private employment. Indeed, this is one important advantage of choosing § 1981 instead of Title VII when both are available to attack employment discrimination. See Chapter 9. Section 1981 remedies also are somewhat broader than those available under Title VII due to the absence of a statutory cap on damages. See Chapter 10. A third advantage of § 1981 is that, unlike Title VII, its coverage is not expressly limited to employment. See Chapter 7. For example, discrimination in partnership decisions is fully actionable. A fourth advantage is the generally longer statutes of limitations governing § 1981. See Chapter 9.

The Supreme Court has made clear that both statutes may be invoked. In Johnson v. Railway Express Agency, Inc., 421 U.S. 454, 461 (1975), the Supreme Court wrote: "We generally conclude, therefore, that the remedies available under Title VII and under § 1981, although related, and although directed to most of the same ends, are separate, distinct, and independent." Thus, § 1981 may be pursued without reference to Title VII. E.g., Taylor v. Safeway Stores, Inc., 524 F.2d 263 (10th Cir. 1975); Gresham v. Chambers, 501 F.2d 687 (2d Cir. 1974).

Independent of Title VII, however, it has been argued that the federal courts should as a matter of judicial policy require exhaustion of state remedies as a precondition to § 1981 suits. This argument was rejected by the Supreme Court in a § 1983 case, Patsy v. Board of Regents, 457 U.S. 496 (1982), based in large part on an analysis of the legislative history of § 1983. Because § 1981, like § 1983, springs from the Civil Rights Act of 1871, *Patsy* should govern.

Of course, a plaintiff may wish to bring a Title VII suit and a § 1981 action concurrently. While this is common, the plaintiff must meet the requirements of each statute as a precondition to suit. This may pose some problems of coordination because filing with the EEOC does not toll the § 1981 statute of limitations. Johnson v. Railway Express Agency, Inc., supra. Accordingly, a plaintiff must be careful not to let that cause of action expire while waiting for the jurisdictional prerequisites for Title VII suit to be met.

## NOTE ON "REVERSE" AGE DISCRIMINATION

"Reverse discrimination" is a somewhat different concept under the Age Discrimination in Employment Act than under Title VII or § 1981. Because the protected "age" is defined as at least 40, discrimination against workers who are younger than 40 simply is not illegal under the statute. E.g., Doyle v. Suffolk County, 786 F.2d 523 (2d Cir. 1986); Thomas v. United States Postal Inspection Serv., 647 F.2d 1035 (10th Cir. 1981). Nevertheless, the *Santa Fe* question arises with respect to discrimination within the protected group, for example, hiring someone 55 years old in preference to a 43-year-old. This question has two facets. First, given the wide range of ages covered by the ADEA and the undoubted fact that discrimination increases as workers grow older, it must be impermissible to discriminate against older protected workers in favor of younger, but still protected, workers. Can it be argued, however, that favoring older workers within the protected group is legal?

If age discrimination becomes more frequent and harmful as workers get older, preferences for older workers are not necessarily inconsistent with the statute's purposes. Such an argument would draw on Title VII cases that hold that certain racial preferences favoring blacks and gender preferences favoring women are permitted despite the apparently plain language of the statute barring discrimination on account of race or gender. The contrary view is simply that the ADEA prohibits age discrimination against a class of persons, and it would be anomalous to allow some members of that class to be preferred over others. Under this view, the Title VII authority is inapposite because those cases do not involve the subordination of the rights of some victims of discrimination to those of other victims of that same kind of discrimination.

The EEOC's Interpretive Rules, 29 C.F.R. §§ 1625.1 et seq. (2002), generally bar any kind of intragroup discrimination, but also recognize that greater benefits to older workers within the protected group may be permissible. 29 C.F.R. § 1625.2(b). Taken literally, the rules recognize only a very narrow exception to the prohibition of intragroup discrimination: while severance pay may "counteract problems related to age discrimination" in searching for a new job, other benefits, for example, an exemption from compulsory overtime for older workers, would not seem to be permissible under the interpretations. However, the legislative history of the 1978 amendments to the ADEA suggests that "special jobs, part-time employment, retraining and transfer to less physically demanding jobs" are permissible for older workers, though not required of the employer. H.R. Rep. No. 527, 95th Cong., 2d Sess. 12 (July 25, 1977). Does this mean, at least, that basic hiring and firing decisions cannot discriminate between older and younger members of the class even if it remains to be seen whether some ancillary benefits can be adjusted to favor older workers?

The two appellate cases to address this question have split. Hamilton v. Caterpillar Inc., 966 F.2d 1226 (7th Cir. 1992), involved a challenge to a special early retirement program for plant closings, which extended early retirement benefits to workers 50 or older who had at least ten years of service. The plaintiffs all had ten years of service, and they were between the ages of 40 and 50. Although within the ADEA protected group, they were too young to qualify for early retirement benefits. Without reaching the validity of the plan under the "bona fide employee benefit plan" provision of § 4(f)(2) of the ADEA, see page 659, the court found that reverse discrimination was simply not within the statute. The court rejected the EEOC regulation, 29 C.F.R. § 1625.2(a) (1999), to the extent it was contrary:

> There is no evidence in the legislative history that Congress had any concern for the plight of workers arbitrarily denied opportunities and benefits because they are too young. Age discrimination is thus somewhat like handicap discrimination: Congress was concerned that older people were being cast aside on the basis of inaccurate stereotypes about their abilities. The young, like the non-handicapped, cannot argue that they are similarly victimized.

966 F.2d at 1288.

In Cline v. General Dynamics Land Sys., 246 F.3d 466 (6th Cir. 2002), the plaintiffs were all between the ages of 40 and 49 when the collective bargaining agreement went into effect, and claimed that they were discriminated against under the terms of the new agreement. It provided health benefits upon retirement to employees over the age of 50, but did not provide health benefits upon retirement to those in the plaintiffs' age bracket. The court held that the clear and unambiguous language of the ADEA provided that the employer could not discriminate against any individual age 40 or older on the basis of age. Because the employees were covered by the plain language of the statute, they were entitled to bring an action, even if the group that was being treated more favorably was a group of older, as opposed to younger, workers.

## 2.   *Defendant's Rebuttal and Plaintiff's Proof of Pretext*

### PATTERSON v. McLEAN CREDIT UNION
#### 491 U.S. 164 (1989)

Justice KENNEDY delivered the opinion of the Court. . . .

### I

[Brenda Patterson, a black woman, was employed by McLean Credit Union as a teller and a file coordinator from 1972 until 1982, when she was laid off. She sued, claiming that McLean had violated § 1981 by harassing her, failing to promote her to an intermediate accounting clerk position, and then discharging her because of her race. The jury found for defendant on the claims for discharge and the failure to promote. In a portion of the opinion since overturned by the Civil Rights Act of 1991, the Supreme Court held that § 1981 did not reach racial harassment. The new statute also overruled the portion of the Court's opinion limiting promotion claims under § 1981 to those in which "the nature of the change in position was such that it involved the opportunity to enter into a new contract with the employer." These portions of the opinion are not reproduced below. Plaintiff also challenged the district court's instructions to the jury that, in order to prevail as to her promotion, she had to show that she was better qualified than her successful white competitor. Because defendant had not argued that the promotion claim was outside of § 1981, the Court had to decide whether the instruction to the jury on proving pretext was correct.]

This brings us to the question of the District Court's jury instructions on petitioner's promotion claim. We think the District Court erred when it instructed the jury that petitioner had to prove that she was better qualified than the white employee who allegedly received the promotion. In order to prevail under § 1981, a plaintiff must prove purposeful discrimination. General Building Contractors Assn., Inc. v. Pennsylvania, 458 U.S. 375, 391 (1982). We have developed, in analogous areas of civil rights law, a carefully designed framework of proof to determine, in the context of disparate treatment, the ultimate issue whether the defendant intentionally discriminated against the plaintiff. See Texas Dept. of Community Affairs v. Burdine; McDonnell Douglas Corp. v. Green. We agree with the Court of Appeals that this scheme of proof, structured as a "sensible, orderly way to evaluate the evidence in light of common experience as it bears on the critical question of discrimination," should apply to claims of racial discrimination under § 1981.

Although the Court of Appeals recognized that the *McDonnell Douglas/Burdine* scheme of proof should apply in § 1981 cases such as this one, it erred in describing petitioner's burden. Under our well-established framework, the plaintiff has the initial burden of proving, by a preponderance of the evidence, a prima facie case of discrimination. *Burdine*. The burden is not onerous. Here, petitioner need only prove by a preponderance of the evidence that she applied for and was qualified for an available position, that she was rejected, and that after she was rejected respondent either continued to seek applicants for the position, or, as is alleged here, filled the position with a white employee. *McDonnell Douglas*.[7]

Once the plaintiff establishes a prima facie case, an inference of discrimination arises. See *Burdine*. In order to rebut this inference, the employer must present evidence that the plaintiff was rejected, or the other applicant was chosen, for a legitimate nondiscriminatory reason. Here, respondent presented evidence that it gave the job to the white applicant because she was better qualified for the position, and therefore rebutted any presumption of discrimination that petitioner may have established. At this point, as our prior cases make clear, petitioner retains the final burden of persuading the jury of intentional discrimination.

Although petitioner retains the ultimate burden of persuasion, our cases make clear that she must also have the opportunity to demonstrate that respondent's proffered reasons for its decision were not its true reasons. In doing so, petitioner is not limited to presenting evidence of a certain type. This is where the District Court erred. The evidence which petitioner can present in an attempt to establish that respondent's stated reasons are pretextual may take a variety of forms. *McDonnell Douglas*. Indeed, she might seek to demonstrate that respondent's claim to have promoted a better qualified applicant was pretextual by showing that she was in fact better qualified than the person chosen for the position. The District Court erred, however, in instructing the jury that in order to succeed petitioner was required to make such a showing. There are certainly other ways in which petitioner could seek to prove that respondent's reasons were pretextual. Thus, for example, petitioner could seek to persuade the jury that respondent had not offered the true reason for its promotion decision by presenting evidence of respondent's past treatment of petitioner, including the instances of the racial harassment which she alleges and respondent's failure to train her for an accounting position. While we do not intend to say this evidence necessarily would be sufficient to carry the day, it cannot be denied that it is one of the various ways in which petitioner might seek to prove intentional discrimination on the part of respondent. She may not be forced to pursue any particular means of demonstrating that respondent's stated reasons are pretextual. It was, therefore, error for the District Court to instruct the jury that petitioner could carry her burden of persuasion only by showing that she was in fact better qualified than the white applicant who got the job.

## NOTES

1. *McLean* formally adopts the *McDonnell Douglas/Burdine* litigation structure for § 1981 cases. Together with *Biggins*, these cases adopt a unified approach to cases of individual disparate treatment under Title VII, § 1981, and the ADEA.

7. Here, respondent argues that petitioner cannot make out a prima facie case on her promotion claim because she did not prove either that respondent was seeking applicants for the intermediate accounting clerk position or that the white employee named to fill that position in fact received a "promotion" from her prior job. Although we express no opinion on the merits of these claims, we do emphasize that in order to prove that she was denied the same right to make and enforce contracts as white citizens, petitioner must show, inter alia, that she was in fact denied an available position.

2. We earlier raised the question whether, when plaintiff is passed over in favor of another, she must prove her qualifications were equal or superior to those of the successful competitor. It is obvious that defendant can put into evidence the superior qualifications of the person promoted in its rebuttal case, but it will not need to do so if plaintiff must prove her qualifications are equal or superior in order to establish a prima facie case. Does *McLean* answer the question? The Court takes a minimalist approach: "[P]etitioner need only prove by a preponderance of the evidence that she applied for and was qualified for an available position, that she was rejected, and that after she was rejected respondent either continued to seek applicants for the position, or, as is alleged here, filled the position with a white employee." Thus, to carry her initial burden, plaintiff need not demonstrate that she was even as well qualified as her white competitor. The partial dissent of Justices Brennan and Stevens agreed on this point. At the prima facie stage, "[w]e have required . . . proof only that a plaintiff was qualified for the position she sought, not proof that she was better qualified than other applicants."

3. "Qualification" is a word susceptible of different meanings. The lower courts have disagreed about what "qualifications" fall within plaintiff's prima facie case as opposed to defendant's rebuttal, a question often phrased in terms of absolute versus relative qualifications, objective versus subjective qualifications, or minimal versus comparative qualifications. For example, Ang v. Procter & Gamble Co., 932 F.2d 540 (6th Cir. 1991), upheld dismissal because plaintiff had not established his qualifications for the job even though he had successfully performed it for 14 years. Plaintiff "was not qualified for his position because he failed to meet his employer's expectations." Id. at 548. See also Menard v. First Sec. Servs. Corp., 848 F.2d 281 (1st Cir. 1988). *Ang* was decided after *Patterson*. Isn't it clearly wrong? Other authorities require plaintiff to show only minimal or objective qualifications, postponing any real focus on alleged deficiencies until the employer's rebuttal. E.g., Slattery v. Swiss Reinsurance America Corp., 2001 U.S. App. LEXIS 15,058 (11th Cir. June 6, 2001); MacDonald v. Eastern Wyo. Mental Health Ctr., 941 F.2d 1115 (10th Cir. 1991); Siegel v. Alpha Wire Corp., 894 F.2d 50 (3d Cir. 1990). Aren't these decisions clearly correct? But see Millbrook v. IBP, Inc., 280 F.3d 1169 (7th Cir. 2002); Lee v. GTE Fla., Inc., 226 F.3d 1249, 1255 (11th Cir. 2000); Dienes v. Texas Dept. of Protective & Reg. Serv., 164 F.3d 277, 279 (5th Cir. 1999), holding that plaintiff must show she was substantially more qualified than the person defendant selected. See also Simms v. Oklahoma, 165 F.3d 1321, 1330 (10th Cir. 1999) (employer may select between candidates unless plaintiff is "clearly better qualified"). See generally Anne Lawton, The Meritocracy Myth and the Illusion of Equal Employment Opportunity, 85 Minn. L. Rev. 587, 645 (2000): "The problem with this [clearly better qualified] requirement is that it is very difficult for plaintiffs to demonstrate that they are more qualified than the candidate selected by the employer. Employers normally hire and promote on the basis of multiple criteria. As a result, an employer can always point to at least one criterion, which it claims is critical to the position, on which the plaintiff is weaker than the candidate selected."

4. In Cook v. CSX Transportation Co., 988 F.2d 507 (4th Cir. 1993), the plaintiff sought to establish a prima facie case by evidence that he was disciplined differently from a similarly situated white worker. The court found no prima facie case because plaintiff did not account for other instances of discipline that negated the racial inference. Is the court correct as to the prima facie case? Aren't the other instances part of defendant's rebuttal? Suppose the plaintiff simply put the single instance before the

jury at trial: how would the court even know about the other instances until the defendant put them in evidence? See also Grant v. News Group Boston, Inc., 55 F.3d 1 (1st Cir. 1994).

5. What is the effect of the employer's breach of its own policies or practices? Is it relevant to the prima facie case, or to pretext, or to both? In Carter v. Three Springs Res. Treatment, 132 F.3d 635 (11th Cir. 1998), the court reversed summary judgment for the employer in a failure-to-promote case. "Carter proved that Three Springs had a policy of posting job vacancies, not adhered to in this case. We have held that the failure to promulgate hiring and promotion policies can be circumstantial evidence of discrimination. . . . Certainly, it is even more suspicious where it is alleged that established rules were bent or broken to give a non-minority applicant an edge in the hiring process." Id. at 644. See also Lyoch v. Anheuser-Busch Cos., 139 F.3d 612 (8th Cir. 1998).

6. Courts have declined to infer a discriminatory intent when the person who hired an older worker also discharged him within a relatively short period of time. The rationale is that, had the employer held stereotypical views, he would not have hired the plaintiff in the first place. Brown v. CSC Logic, Inc. 82 F.3d 651 (5th Cir. 1996); Romd v. C.F. Indus. Inc., 42 F.3d 1139 (7th Cir. 1994); Lowe v. J. B. Hunt Transport, Inc., 963 F.2d 173 (8th Cir. 1992) (two years); Proud v. Stone, 945 F.2d 796 (4th Cir. 1991) (six months) (citing John J. Donahue & Peter Siegelman, The Changing Nature of Employment Discrimination Litigation, 43 Stan. L. Rev. 983 (1991)). Several circuits have applied this inference to discrimination cases outside the ADEA. See, e.g., Jaques v. Clean-Up Group, Inc., 96 F.3d 506 (1st Cir. 1996) (disability discrimination); Jiminez v. Mary Washington College, 57 F.3d 369 (4th Cir. 1995) (race and national origin discrimination); Bradley v. Harcourt, Brace & Co., 104 F.3d 267 (9th Cir. 1996) (sex discrimination).

The conditions for the "same actor" defense are restrictive: obviously, the same supervisor must make both decisions, and the decisions must be in tension with one another. For example, a decision to discharge may be different from a decision to deny promotion. A person who hires an older worker or a woman for one position might be expected not to discriminate in discharging that person, but could easily hold stereotypic views about the limitations of such persons with respect to higher-level jobs. The strength of the inference will also vary depending on the circumstances, including the length of time between the hiring and the adverse action, although at least one circuit has held that a relatively brief period is not an absolute requirement. See Buhrmaster v. Overnite Transp. Co., 61 F.3d 461 (6th Cir. 1995) (upholding a jury instruction on the same actor inference: "time weakens the same actor inference, it does not destroy it[;] . . . a short period of time is not an essential element where plaintiff's class does not change.").

Even within these limitations, the precise role of the "same actor" defense is not clear. It has sometimes been labelled a "presumption," but seems better described as an inference arising from judicial perceptions about how human beings normally act. See Williams v. Vitro Services, Inc., 144 F.3d 1438, 1443 (11th Cir. 1998) ("we decline to accord this 'same actor' factual circumstance a *presumption* that discrimination was necessarily absent . . . [but] believe these facts give rise to a *permissible inference* that no discriminatory animus" motivated the discharge); Waldron v. SL Industries, Inc., 56 F.3d 491 (3d Cir. 1995) (that hirer and firer are the same and discharge occurred shortly after hiring is simply evidence like any other and should not be accorded any presumptive value); Madel v. FCI Mktg., Inc., 116 F.3d 1247 (8th Cir. 1997) (any presumption inappropriate where evidence of overt discrimination exists). See generally

Anna Laurie Bryant & Richard A. Bales, Using the Same Actor "Inference" in Employment Discrimination Cases, 1999 Utah L. Rev. 225; Julie S. Northrop, The Same Actor Inference in Employment Discrimination, 73 Wash. L. Rev. 193 (1998).

One decision, Johnson v. Zema Systems Corp., 170 F.3d 734, 745 (7th Cir. 1999), concluded that the inference was unlikely to make a difference in many cases:

> The psychological assumption underlying the same-actor inference [that it hardly makes sense to hire workers from a group one dislikes] may not hold true on the facts of the particular case. For example, a manager might hire a person of a certain race expecting them not to rise to a position in the company where daily contact with the manager would be necessary. Or an employer might hire an employee of a certain gender expecting that person to act, or dress, or talk in a way that employer deems acceptable for that gender and then fire that employee if she fails to comply with the employer's gender stereotypes. Similarly, if an employee were the first African-American hired, an employer might be unaware of his own stereotypical views of African-Americans at the time of hiring.

In *Johnson* itself, there was sufficient evidence that the employer hired Johnson, expecting him to comply with the race-segregated structure of the sales department. "The evidence suggests that when Johnson failed to comply with these limitations, he was fired." Id. The Seventh Circuit has also rejected the "same-actor" defense where the supervisor who laid the plaintiff off was even older than the plaintiff: "For it is altogether common and natural for older people, first, to exempt themselves from what they believe to be the characteristic decline of energy and ability with age; second, to want to surround themselves with younger people; third, to want to protect their jobs by making sure the workforce is not too old, which might, if 'ageist' prejudice is rampant, lead to RIF's of which they themselves might be the victim; and fourth, to be oblivious to the prejudices they hold, especially perhaps prejudices against the group to which they belong." Radas v. MCI Systemhouse Corp., 255 F.3d 359, 361 (7th Cir. 2001). Assuming that a person who is age biased is unlikely to hire an older worker in the first place, is this fact relevant to the plaintiff's prima facie case or the defendant's rebuttal?

7. Although plaintiff's prima facie case is easily established, so is defendant's rebuttal. In *Patterson*, the employer claimed that it chose a white applicant "because she was better qualified for the position." If this reason were put into evidence, it would carry defendant's burden of production. Presumably, the decision-maker would testify as to why the successful white was better qualified and compare the plaintiff's qualifications with those of the successful competitor.

8. With respect to defendant's rebuttal, *Burdine* did not directly address what non-racial or non-gender motivations are "legitimate." Justice Powell's opinion uses the words "legitimate" and "lawful" interchangeably to describe the "reasons" that will rebut a prima facie case. *Biggins* expands "legitimate" to include "unlawful": a reason that is unlawful, but nondiscriminatory under the antidiscrimination statute in question, rebuts the prima facie case. A reason that violates the Employee Retirement Income Security Act (ERISA) or Title VII may demonstrate that the employer did not violate the ADEA.

9. In Purkett v. Elem, 514 U.S. 765 (1995), a case dealing with peremptory challenges to jurors, the prosecutor tried to explain its exclusion of several blacks because of their hair length and facial hair and not their race. The Supreme Court relied on Title VII analysis to indicate that even nonsensical explanations — "implausible," "silly," "fantastic," or "superstitious" — satisfied defendant's burden of production.

10. Assuming the defendant's testimony has carried its burden of production, the

plaintiff "retains the final burden of persuading the jury of intentional discrimination." The *Patterson* Court was clear that, in demonstrating pretext, the plaintiff "is not limited to presenting evidence of a certain type." Her proof "may take a variety of forms." The Court agreed with the lower court that the plaintiff might try to show "that she was in fact better qualified than the person chosen for the position," but she could not be limited to such proof.

11. The central problem is the meaning of "pretext." Perhaps the defendant's reason is objectively false. Suppose the plaintiff proves she has a college degree, while the defendant claims it did not promote her because she did not have a degree. See Golumb v. Prudential Ins. Co. of Am., 688 F.2d 547 (7th Cir. 1982). Although the reason is not objectively true, the employer may have believed it to be true and acted on it, rather than on the basis of the employee's age. E.g., Grohs v. Gold Bond Bldg. Prods., 859 F.2d 1283 (7th Cir. 1988); Bienkowski v. American Airlines, Inc., 851 F.2d 1503 (5th Cir. 1988). Alternatively, the reason might be true, but fail to explain the decision. For example, if the employer claims the employee was discharged for tardiness, the female plaintiff might admit that she was frequently late, but claim that men were late and were not fired. By proving that males were treated more favorably in regard to the asserted reason, the plaintiff undercuts the defendant's explanation. Anderson v. Savage Lab., Inc., 675 F.2d 1221 (11th Cir. 1982). But even here such a showing may not be definitive because the employer might have been unaware of the violations by others. Mechnig v. Sears, Roebuck & Co., 864 F.2d 1359 (7th Cir. 1988).

12. In Beaird v. Seagate Technology, 145 F.3d 1159, 1168 (10th Cir. 1998), a rif case, the court wrote that a plaintiff can demonstrate pretext in three ways:

> First, she can argue that her own termination does not accord with the RIF criteria supposedly employed. . . .
>
> Second, a plaintiff can adduce evidence that her evaluation under the defendant's RIF criteria was deliberately falsified or manipulated so as to effect her termination or otherwise adversely alter her employment status. . . . One method of demonstrating manipulation or falsification of evaluation is to produce evidence that a supervisor responsible for assessing her performance displayed ageist animus.
>
> Third, a plaintiff can adduce evidence that the RIF is more generally pretextual. For instance, a plaintiff may establish that an employer actively sought to replace a number of RIF-terminated employees with new hires. . . . Statistical evidence may, in certain circumstances, be relevant to this purpose. . . . Contrary to defendant's argument, however, statistical evidence cannot defeat the pretext claim of an individual plaintiff where the plaintiff's case rests on non-statistical evidence.

13. In McDaniel v. Wal-Mart Stores, Inc., 2002 U.S. App. LEXIS 6200, at *13 (6th Cir. Mar. 29, 2002), the court defined pretext as a showing either "(1) that the proffered reasons had no basis in fact, (2) that the proffered reasons did not actually motivate his discharge, or (3) that they were insufficient to motivate discharge." In the case, the nondiscriminatory reason defendant advanced to justify plaintiff's discharge was that plaintiff had violated a company rule by engaging in a high speed vehicle chase of shoplifting suspects off the store's property. Plaintiff admitted the chase, but claimed that it was insufficient to explain his discharge because a white worker who had also engaged in the chase had not been disciplined. In upholding summary judgment for defendant, the court held that plaintiff and his comparator must be similar in "all of the relevant aspects." Id. at *15. While the white co-worker, Jester, initially drove the Wal-Mart vehicle off store property chasing the suspects, he did it because plaintiff was in the back of the suspects' pickup, wrestling with one of them. After the

suspects' pickup stopped and plaintiff got off, plaintiff took the wheel of the Wal-Mart vehicle, with Jester as a passenger, and the chase commenced again. McDaniel admitted he "drove at speed from 35 to 55 miles per hour, collided with the suspects' truck twice, caused the suspects to drive in a highly reckless manner which in turn forced an innocent motorist off the road, drove through a traffic light that was 'turning red,' and continued the vehicle chase through a residential subdivision." The court found that plaintiff and his white comparator were not similar in all relevant aspects:

> We note that there is a significant difference between controlling a vehicle in a dangerous manner and riding along as a passenger. The decision to run through a red light and to ram another vehicle was made by McDaniel the driver, not Jester the passenger. We recognize, however, that this fact alone may not be enough to distinguish Jester. If it were shown, for example, that Jester offered his assistance in order to encourage McDaniel to give chase to the suspects, we think Jester could be considered partly culpable for the hazardous pursuit that ensued.

Id. at *19. The court, nevertheless, upheld the dismissal of plaintiff's complaint because Wal-Mart asserted that it believed Jester's decision to accompany McDaniel was "motivated solely by Jester's concern for McDaniel's safety, not his own enthusiasm for the chase." Id.

14. *Patterson* allows plaintiff to challenge defendant's claimed reason indirectly, as "by presenting evidence of respondent's past treatment of petitioner, including the instances of the racial harassment which she alleges and respondent's failure to train her for an accounting position." The partial dissent of Justices Brennan and Stevens argued that the jury instruction below was

> much too restrictive, cutting off other methods of proving pretext plainly recognized in our cases. We suggested in *McDonnell Douglas*, for example, that a black plaintiff might be able to prove pretext by showing that the employer has promoted white employees who lack the qualifications the employer relies upon, or by proving the employer's "general policy and practice with respect to minority employment." And, of particular relevance given petitioner's evidence of racial harassment and her allegation that respondent failed to train her for an accounting position because of her race, we suggested that evidence of the employer's past treatment of the plaintiff would be relevant to a showing that the employer's proffered legitimate reason was not its true reason.

Id. at 217. What is the point of this proof?

(a) Proving that the employer promoted whites without the asserted qualifications tends to show that the qualifications are unnecessary, even in the employer's own view.

(b) Showing the employer's "general policy and practice with respect to minority employment" suggests that, if the employer generally discriminates, it is more likely it discriminated as to the particular plaintiff.

(c) What about evidence of racial harassment? We will see that harassment itself, if sufficiently severe, violates Title VII, see Chapter 7, but the point here is different: a company that conducts or condones racial harassment is more likely to be discriminatory in promotions. Is this true? Does it depend on the decision-maker's knowledge of the harassment?

(d) As for defendant's failure to train plaintiff, and its general past treatment of her, this may be probative unless the reason for adverse treatment was peculiar to plaintiff and unrelated to her race.

Will plaintiff at least get to the jury if she adduces evidence sufficient to raise a material issue of fact on one of these claims?

15. Proving pretext often requires inquiry into the state of mind of decision-makers, but often does so by looking at how the employer treated co-workers who were similarly situated to the plaintiff. This, in turn, requires discovery of the employment histories of co-workers. Defendants sometimes have argued that such inquiries are foreclosed or limited. For example, it was argued that, in institutions of higher education, there is an "academic freedom" privilege not to reveal information concerning personnel decisions. The Supreme Court, however, unanimously held that a university enjoys no special privilege, grounded either in common law or in academic freedom protected by the First Amendment, against disclosing faculty peer review materials to the EEOC for use in the investigation into claimed discrimination in a tenure decision. University of Pennsylvania v. EEOC, 493 U.S. 182 (1990). Arguments framed in terms of the privacy interests of co-workers have been no more successful, see CNA Financial Corp. v. Donovan, 830 F.2d 1132 (D.C. Cir. 1987), although protective orders frequently are entered that limit disclosure to plaintiff and her counsel, EEOC v. University of New Mexico, 504 F.2d 1296 (10th Cir. 1974).

16. While formal discovery is often effective, it also can be costly. Can a plaintiff's attorney simply contact her client's co-workers in order to develop her case, either in place of or in addition to formal depositions? Although this kind of fact investigation is permitted in most civil litigation, employers sometimes accuse plaintiffs' attorneys who contact employees of unethical conduct or seek a protective order against such contacts. The basis of this argument is Rule 4.2 of the Model Rules of Professional Conduct, which provides that, "[i]n representing a client, a lawyer shall not communicate about the subject of the representation with a party the lawyer knows to be represented by another lawyer in the matter, unless the lawyer has the consent of the other lawyer or is authorized by law to do so." See also DR 7-104(A)(1) of the Model Code of Professional Responsibility. Defendants have argued that their employees are clients of the defendants' attorneys within the meaning of this rule. The Official Comment explains:

> In the case of an organization, this Rule prohibits communications by a lawyer for one party concerning the matter in representation with persons having a managerial responsibility on behalf of the organization, and with any other person whose act or omission in connection with that matter may be imputed to the organization for purposes of civil or criminal liability or whose statement may constitute an admission on the part of the organization.

Most courts interpreting Rule 4.2 have held that an outright prohibition on contact is inappropriate. Rather, in determining whether informal interviews may be conducted, the courts balance the needs of the party seeking informal contacts against the interests of the corporation or organization. E.g., N.A.A.C.P. v. Florida, 122 F. Supp. 2d 1335 (M.D. Fla. 2000); Suggs v. Capital Cities/ABC, Inc., 1990 U.S. Dist. LEXIS 4774 (S.D.N.Y. Apr. 24, 1990). See generally Susan J. Becker, Conducting Informal Discovery of a Party's Former Employees: Legal and Ethical Concerns and Constraints, 51 Md. L. Rev. 239 (1992). The employer's legitimate interests are said to include avoiding statements by employees that could bind the corporation as admissions, see Fed. R. Evid. 801(d)(2)(D), and preventing disclosure of privileged information, such as attorney-client communications, see Upjohn Co. v. United

States, 449 U.S. 383 (1981). The plaintiff's interests include reducing litigation costs and obtaining information that co-workers may be hesitant to provide if their employer knows of their participation. However, the interests that are not necessarily reflected in this calculus are those of the co-workers themselves. Title VII and the ADEA ensure each employee a right to participate in proceedings against discrimination, see Chapter 7, and it is by no means clear that the attorneys for defendant employers who claim the protection of Rule 4.2 have so advised the "clients" they claim to represent. See Patriarca v. Center for Living & Working, Inc., 778 N.E.2d 877 (Mass. 2002) (vacating protective order as overbroad to the extent of limited contact with employees without an employee-specific analysis of whether the defense counsel actually represented the individual or contact was otherwise inappropriate). Obviously, this area is fraught with the potential for conflicts of interest for defense counsel.

17. While plaintiff's attorneys are trying to ferret out evidence of discriminatory motives, the prospects of exposure for discrimination and other employment litigation have led to increasing efforts to "bulletproof" employment decisions. Management attorneys have increasingly trained and counseled employers about discharging or disciplining workers in a manner that limits liability. Are such programs effective ways to achieve compliance with the statute, or ways to immunize discriminatory decisions, or perhaps both? See generally Susan Bisom-Rapp, Bullet-Proofing the Workplace: Symbol and Substance in Employment Discrimination Law Practice, 26 Fla. St. U. L. Rev. 959 (1999) (while litigation prevention strategies developed by defense firms for employers "may prompt managers to identify and remedy certain biased actions, it is equally possible that preventive practices mask rather than eliminate some discriminatory decisions").

18. *Patterson* held it error to limit the jury's consideration of pretext. Is it error not to instruct the jury that the employer has the right to make business judgments that are free of discrimination? Walker v. AT&T Technologies, 995 F.2d 846 (8th Cir. 1993) (yes). But see Kelley v. Airborne Freight Corp., 140 F.3d 335 (1st Cir. 1998).

## ST. MARY'S HONOR CENTER v. HICKS
### 509 U.S. 502 (1993)

Justice SCALIA delivered the opinion of the Court. . . .

## I

Petitioner St. Mary's Honor Center (St. Mary's) is a halfway house operated by the Missouri Department of Corrections and Human Resources (MDCHR). Respondent Melvin Hicks, a black man, was hired as a correctional officer at St. Mary's in August 1978 and was promoted to shift commander, one of six supervisory positions, in February 1980.

In 1983 MDCHR conducted an investigation of the administration of St. Mary's, which resulted in extensive supervisory changes in January 1984. Respondent retained his position, but John Powell became the new chief of custody (respondent's immediate supervisor) and petitioner Steve Long the new superintendent. Prior to these personnel changes respondent had enjoyed a satisfactory employment record, but soon thereafter became the subject of repeated, and increasingly severe, disciplinary actions. He was suspended for five days for violations of institutional rules by his subordinates on March 3, 1984. He received a letter of reprimand for alleged

failure to conduct an adequate investigation of a brawl between inmates that occurred during his shift on March 21. He was later demoted from shift commander to
correctional officer for his failure to ensure that his subordinates entered their use of
a St. Mary's vehicle into the official log book on March 19, 1984. Finally, on June 7,
1984, he was discharged for threatening Powell during an exchange of heated words
on April 19. . . .

## II . . .

With the goal of "progressively . . . sharpening the inquiry into the elusive factual question of intentional discrimination," Texas Dept. of Community Affairs v.
Burdine, our opinion in McDonnell Douglas Corp. v. Green established an allocation of the burden of production and an order for the presentation of proof in Title
VII discriminatory-treatment cases. The plaintiff in such a case, we said, must first establish, by a preponderance of the evidence, a "prima facie" case of racial discrimination. Burdine. Petitioners do not challenge the District Court's finding that respondent satisfied the minimal requirements of such a prima facie case by proving (1) that
he is black, (2) that he was qualified for the position of shift commander, (3) that he
was demoted from that position and ultimately discharged, and (4) that the position
remained open and was ultimately filled by a white man.

Under the McDonnell Douglas scheme, "establishment of the prima facie case
in effect creates a presumption that the employer unlawfully discriminated against
the employee." Burdine. To establish a "presumption" is to say that a finding of
the predicate fact (here, the prima facie case) produces "a required conclusion in
the absence of explanation" (here, the finding of unlawful discrimination). 1 D. Louisell & C. Mueller, Federal Evidence § 67, p. 536 (1977). Thus, the McDonnell Douglas presumption places upon the defendant the burden of producing an explanation to rebut the prima facie case — i.e., the burden of "producing evidence" that
the adverse employment actions were taken "for a legitimate, nondiscriminatory
reason." Burdine. "The defendant must clearly set forth, through the introduction
of admissible evidence," reasons for its actions which, if believed by the trier of
fact, would support a finding that unlawful discrimination was not the cause of
the employment action. It is important to note, however, that although the Mc-
Donnell Douglas presumption shifts the burden of production to the defendant, "the
ultimate burden of persuading the trier of fact that the defendant intentionally discriminated against the plaintiff remains at all times with the plaintiff." In this
regard it operates like all presumptions, as described in Rule 301 of the Federal Rules
of Evidence:

> In all civil actions and proceedings not otherwise provided for by Act of Congress or by
> these rules, a presumption imposes on the party against whom it is directed the burden
> of going forward with evidence to rebut or meet the presumption, but does not shift to
> such party the burden of proof in the sense of the risk of nonpersuasion, which remains
> throughout the trial upon the party on whom it was originally cast.

Respondent does not challenge the District Court's finding that petitioners sustained
their burden of production by introducing evidence of two legitimate, nondiscriminatory reasons for their actions: the severity and the accumulation of rules violations
committed by respondent. Our cases make clear that at that point the shifted burden
of production became irrelevant: "If the defendant carries this burden of production,
the presumption raised by the prima facie case is rebutted," Burdine, and "drops from

the case." The plaintiff then has "the full and fair opportunity to demonstrate," through presentation of his own case and through cross-examination of the defendant's witnesses, "that the proffered reason was not the true reason for the employment decision," and that race was. He retains that "ultimate burden of persuading the [trier of fact] that [he] has been the victim of intentional discrimination."

The District Court, acting as trier of fact in this bench trial, found that the reasons petitioners gave were not the real reasons for respondent's demotion and discharge. It found that respondent was the only supervisor disciplined for violations committed by his subordinates; that similar and even more serious violations committed by respondent's coworkers were either disregarded or treated more leniently; and that Powell manufactured the final verbal confrontation in order to provoke respondent into threatening him. It nonetheless held that respondent had failed to carry his ultimate burden of proving that his race was the determining factor in petitioners' decision first to demote and then to dismiss him.[2] In short, the District Court concluded that "although [respondent] has proven the existence of a crusade to terminate him, he has not proven that the crusade was racially rather than personally motivated." The Court of Appeals set this determination aside on the ground that "once [respondent] proved all of [petitioners'] proffered reasons for the adverse employment actions to be pretextual, [respondent] was entitled to judgment as a matter of law." The Court of Appeals reasoned:

> Because all of defendants' proffered reasons were discredited, defendants were in a position of having offered no legitimate reason for their actions. In other words, defendants were in no better position than if they had remained silent, offering no rebuttal to an established inference that they had unlawfully discriminated against plaintiff on the basis of his race.

That is not so. By producing evidence (whether ultimately persuasive or not) of nondiscriminatory reasons, petitioners sustained their burden of production, and thus placed themselves in a "better position than if they had remained silent."

In the nature of things, the determination that a defendant has met its burden of production (and has thus rebutted any legal presumption of intentional discrimination) can involve no credibility assessment. For the burden-of-production determination necessarily precedes the credibility-assessment stage. At the close of the defendant's case, the court is asked to decide whether an issue of fact remains for the trier of fact to determine. None does if, on the evidence presented, (1) any rational person would have to find the existence of facts constituting a prima facie case, and (2) the defendant has failed to meet its burden of production — i.e., has failed to introduce evidence which, taken as true, would permit the conclusion that there was a nondiscriminatory reason for the adverse action. In that event, the court must award judgment to the plaintiff as a matter of law under Federal Rule of Civil Procedure 50(a)(1) (in the case of jury trials) or Federal Rule of Civil Procedure 52(c) (in the case of bench trials). See F. James & G. Hazard, Civil Procedure § 7.9, p. 327 (3d ed. 1985); 1 Louisell & Mueller, Federal Evidence § 70, at 568. If the defendant has failed to sustain its burden but reasonable minds could differ as to whether a preponderance of the evidence establishes the facts of a prima facie case, then a question of fact does remain, which the

2. Various considerations led it to this conclusion, including the fact that two blacks sat on the disciplinary review board that recommended disciplining respondent, that respondent's black subordinates who actually committed the violations were not disciplined, and that "the number of black employees at St. Mary's remained constant."

trier of fact will be called upon to answer.[3] If, on the other hand, the defendant has suc-ceeded in carrying its burden of production, the *McDonnell Douglas* framework — with its presumptions and burdens — is no longer relevant. To resurrect it later, after the trier of fact has determined that what was "produced" to meet the burden of pro-duction is not credible, flies in the face of our holding in *Burdine* that to rebut the pre-sumption "the defendant need not persuade the court that it was actually motivated by the proffered reasons." The presumption, having fulfilled its role of forcing the defen-dant to come forward with some response, simply drops out of the picture. The defen-dant's "production" (whatever its persuasive effect) having been made, the trier of fact proceeds to decide the ultimate question: whether plaintiff has proven "that the defen-dant intention-ally discriminated against [him]" because of his race. The factfinder's disbelief of the reasons put forward by the defendant (particularly if disbelief is accom-panied by a suspicion of mendacity) may, together with the elements of the prima facie case, suffice to show intentional discrimination. Thus, rejection of the defendant's proffered reasons, will permit the trier of fact to infer the ultimate fact of intentional discrimination,[4] and the Court of Appeals was correct when it noted that, upon such rejection, "no additional proof of discrimination is *required*," (emphasis added). But the Court of Appeals' holding that rejection of the defendant's proffered reasons compels judgment for the plaintiff disregards the fundamental principle of Rule 301 that a presumption does not shift the burden of proof, and ignores our repeated admonition that the Title VII plaintiff at all times bears the "ultimate burden of persuasion." . . .

## IV

We turn, finally, to the dire practical consequences that the respondents and the dissent claim our decision today will produce. What appears to trouble the dissent more than anything is that, in its view, our rule is adopted "for the benefit of employ-ers who have been found to have given false evidence in a court of law," whom we "favor" by "exempting them from responsibility for lies." As we shall explain, our rule in no way gives special favor to those employers whose evidence is disbelieved. But initially we must point out that there is no justification for assuming (as the dissent

---

3. If the finder of fact answers affirmatively — if it finds that the prima facie case is supported by a sup-ported by a preponderance of the evidence — it must find the existence of the presumed fact of unlawful discrimination and must, therefore, render a verdict for the plaintiff. See Texas Dept. of Community Affairs v. Burdine; F. James & G. Hazard, Civil Procedure § 7.9, p. 327 (3d ed. 1985); 1 D. Louisell & C. Mueller, Federal Evidence § 70, pp. 568-569 (1977). Thus, the effect of failing to produce evidence to rebut the McDonnell Douglas Corp. v. Green presumption is not felt until the prima facie case has been established, either as a matter of law (because the plaintiff's facts are uncontested) or by the fact finder's determination that the plaintiff's facts are supported by a preponderance of the evidence. . . . As a practi-cal matter, however, and in the real-life sequence of a trial, the defendant feels the "burden" not when the plaintiff's prima facie case is proved, but as soon as evidence of it is introduced. The defendant then knows that its failure to introduce evidence of a nondiscriminatory reason will cause judgment to go against it unless the plaintiff's prima facie case is held to be inadequate in law or fails to convince the factfinder. It is this practical coercion which causes the *McDonnell Douglas* presumption to function as a means of "arranging the presentation of evidence," Watson v. Fort Worth Bank & Trust, 487 U.S. 977 (1988).

4. Contrary to the dissent's confusion-producing analysis, there is nothing whatever inconsistent be-tween this statement and our later statements that (1) the plaintiff must show "both that the reason was false, and that discrimination was the real reason," and (2) "it is not enough . . . to disbelieve the em-ployer." Even though (as we say here) rejection of the defendant's proffered reasons is enough at law to sustain a finding of discrimination, there must be a finding of discrimination.

repeatedly does) that those employers whose evidence is disbelieved are perjurers and liars. . . . Even if these were typically cases in which an individual defendant's sworn assertion regarding a physical occurrence was pitted against an individual plaintiff's sworn assertion regarding the same physical occurrence, surely it would be imprudent to call the party whose assertion is (by a mere preponderance of the evidence) disbelieved, a perjurer and a liar. And in these Title VII cases, the defendant is ordinarily not an individual but a company, which must rely upon the statement of an employee — often a relatively low-level employee — as to the central fact; and that central fact is not a physical occurrence, but rather that employee's state of mind. To say that the company which in good faith introduces such testimony, or even the testifying employee himself, becomes a liar and a perjurer when the testimony is not believed, is nothing short of absurd.

Undoubtedly some employers (or at least their employees) will be lying. But even if we could readily identify these perjurers, what an extraordinary notion, that we "exempt them from responsibility for their lies" unless we enter Title VII judgments for the plaintiffs! Title VII is not a cause of action for perjury; we have other civil and criminal remedies for that. . . .

The respondent's argument based upon the employer's supposed lying is a more modest one: "A defendant which unsuccessfully offers a 'phony reason' logically cannot be in a better legal position [i.e., the position of having overcome the presumption from the plaintiff's prima facie case] than a defendant who remains silent, and offers no reasons at all for its conduct." But there is no anomaly in that, once one recognizes that the *McDonnell Douglas* presumption is a procedural device, designed only to establish an order of proof and production. The books are full of procedural rules that place the perjurer (initially, at least) in a better position than the truthful litigant who makes no response at all. A defendant who fails to answer a complaint will, on motion, suffer a default judgment that a deceitful response could have avoided. Fed. Rule Civ. Proc. 55(a). A defendant whose answer fails to contest critical averments in the complaint will, on motion, suffer a judgment on the pleadings that untruthful denials could have avoided. Rule 12(c). And a defendant who fails to submit affidavits creating a genuine issue of fact in response to a motion for summary judgment will suffer a dismissal that false affidavits could have avoided. Rule 56(e). In all of those cases, as under the *McDonnell Douglas* framework, perjury may purchase the defendant a chance at the factfinder — though there, as here, it also carries substantial risks, see Rules 11 and 56(g); 18 U.S.C. § 1621. . . .

The dissent repeatedly raises a procedural objection that is impressive only to one who mistakes the basic nature of the *McDonnell Douglas* procedure. It asserts that "the Court now holds that the further enquiry [i.e., the inquiry that follows the employer's response to the prima facie case] is wide open, not limited at all by the scope of the employer's proffered explanation." The plaintiff . . . should not "be saddled with the tremendous disadvantage of having to confront, not the defined task of proving the employer's stated reasons to be false, but the amorphous requirement of disproving all possible nondiscriminatory reasons that a factfinder might find lurking in the record." . . . These statements imply that the employer's "proffered explanation," his "stated reasons," his "articulated reasons," somehow exist apart from the record — in some pleading, or perhaps in some formal, nontestimonial statement made on behalf of the defendant to the factfinder. ("Your honor, pursuant to *McDonnell Douglas* the defendant hereby formally asserts, as its reason for the dismissal at issue here, incompetence of the employee.") Of course it does not work like that. The reasons the defendant sets forth are set forth "through the introduction of admissible evidence."

*Burdine.* In other words, the defendant's "articulated reasons" themselves are to be found "lurking in the record." . . .

Justice SOUTER, with whom Justice WHITE, Justice BLACKMUN, and Justice STEVENS join, dissenting.

[T]he Court holds that, once a Title VII plaintiff succeeds in showing at trial that the defendant has come forward with pretextual reasons for its actions in response to a prima facie showing of discrimination, the factfinder still may proceed to roam the record, searching for some nondiscriminatory explanation that the defendant has not raised and that the plaintiff has had no fair opportunity to disprove. Because the majority departs from settled precedent in substituting a scheme of proof for disparate-treatment actions that promises to be unfair and unworkable, I respectfully dissent. . . .

[Everyone conceded that Melvin Hicks established a prima facie case under *McDonnell Douglas/ Burdine.*] Proof of a prima facie case not only raises an inference of discrimination; in the absence of further evidence, it also creates a mandatory presumption in favor of the plaintiff. Although the employer bears no trial burden at all until the plaintiff proves his prima facie case, once the plaintiff does so the employer must either respond or lose. As we made clear in *Burdine,* "If the employer is silent in the face of the presumption, the court must enter judgment for the plaintiff." Thus, if the employer remains silent because it acted for a reason it is too embarrassed to reveal, or for a reason it fails to discover, the plaintiff is entitled to judgment under *Burdine.*

Obviously, it would be unfair to bar an employer from coming forward at this stage with a nondiscriminatory explanation for its actions, since the lack of an open position and the plaintiff's lack of qualifications do not exhaust the set of nondiscriminatory reasons that might explain an adverse personnel decision. If the trier of fact could not consider other explanations, employers' autonomy would be curtailed far beyond what is needed to rectify the discrimination identified by Congress. On the other hand, it would be equally unfair and utterly impractical to saddle the victims of discrimination with the burden of either producing direct evidence of discriminatory intent or eliminating the entire universe of possible nondiscriminatory reasons for a personnel decision. The Court in *McDonnell Douglas* reconciled these competing interests in a very sensible way by requiring the employer to "articulate," through the introduction of admissible evidence, one or more "legitimate, nondiscriminatory reasons" for its actions. Proof of a prima facie case thus serves as a catalyst obligating the employer to step forward with an explanation for its actions. St. Mary's, in this case, used this opportunity to provide two reasons for its treatment of Hicks: the severity and accumulation of rule infractions he had allegedly committed.

The Court emphasizes that the employer's obligation at this stage is only a burden of production, and that, if the employer meets the burden, the presumption entitling the plaintiff to judgment "drops from the case." This much is certainly true, but the obligation also serves an important function neglected by the majority, in requiring the employer "to frame the factual issue with sufficient clarity so that the plaintiff will have a full and fair opportunity to demonstrate pretext." The employer, in other words, has a "burden of production" that gives it the right to choose the scope of the factual issues to be resolved by the factfinder. But investing the employer with this choice has no point unless the scope it chooses binds the employer as well as the plaintiff. Nor does it make sense to tell the employer, as this Court has done, that its explanation of legitimate reasons "must be clear and reasonably specific," if the factfinder can rely on a reason not clearly articulated, or on one not articulated at all, to rule in favor of the employer.[3]

Once the employer chooses the battleground in this manner, "the factual inquiry proceeds to a new level of specificity." During this final, more specific enquiry, the employer has no burden to prove that its proffered reasons are true; rather, the plaintiff must prove by a preponderance of the evidence that the proffered reasons are pretextual. *McDonnell Douglas* makes it clear that if the plaintiff fails to show "pretext," the challenged employment action "must stand." If, on the other hand, the plaintiff carries his burden of showing "pretext," the court "must order a prompt and appropriate remedy." Or, as we said in *Burdine:* "[The plaintiff] now must have the opportunity to demonstrate that the proffered reason was not the true reason for the employment decision. This burden now merges with the ultimate burden of persuading the court that [the plaintiff] has been the victim of intentional discrimination." *Burdine* drives home the point that the case has proceeded to "a new level of specificity" by explaining that the plaintiff can meet his burden of persuasion in either of two ways: "either directly by persuading the court that a discriminatory reason more likely motivated the employer or indirectly by showing that the employer's proffered explanation is unworthy of credence." That the plaintiff can succeed simply by showing that "the employer's proffered explanation is unworthy of credence" indicates that the case has been narrowed to the question whether the employer's proffered reasons are pretextual. Thus, because Hicks carried his burden of persuasion by showing that St. Mary's proffered reasons were "unworthy of credence," the Court of Appeals properly concluded that he was entitled to judgment.[9] . . .

## REEVES v. SANDERSON PLUMBING PRODUCTS, INC.
### 530 U.S. 133 (2000)

Justice O'CONNOR delivered the opinion of the Court.

This case concerns the kind and amount of evidence necessary to sustain a jury's verdict that an employer unlawfully discriminated on the basis of age. Specifically, we must resolve whether a defendant is entitled to judgment as a matter of law when the plaintiff's case consists exclusively of a prima facie case of discrimination and sufficient evidence for the trier of fact to disbelieve the defendant's legitimate, nondiscriminatory explanation for its action. We must also decide whether the employer was entitled to judgment as a matter of law under the particular circumstances presented here.

---

3. The majority is simply wrong when it suggests that my reading of *McDonnell Douglas* and *Burdine* proceeds on the assumption that the employer's reasons must be stated "apart from the record." (emphasis omitted). As I mentioned above, and I repeat here, such reasons must be set forth "through the introduction of admissible evidence." Such reasons cannot simply be found "lurking in the record," as the Court suggests, for *Burdine* requires the employer to articulate its reasons through testimony or other admissible evidence that is "clear and reasonably specific." . . .

9. The foregoing analysis of burdens describes who wins on various combinations of evidence and proof. It may or may not also describe the actual sequence of events at trial. In a bench trial, for example, the parties may be limited in their presentation of evidence until the court has decided whether the plaintiff has made his prima facie showing. But the court also may allow in all the evidence at once. In such a situation, under our decision in *Aikens*, the defendant will have to choose whether it wishes simply to attack the prima facie case or whether it wants to present nondiscriminatory reasons for its actions. If the defendant chooses the former approach, the factfinder will decide at the end of the trial whether the plaintiff has proven his prima facie case. If the defendant takes the latter approach, the only question for the factfinder will be the issue of pretext.

I

In October 1995, petitioner Roger Reeves was 57 years old and had spent 40 years in the employ of respondent, Sanderson Plumbing Products, Inc., a manufacturer of toilet seats and covers. Petitioner worked in a department known as the "Hinge Room," where he supervised the "regular line." Joe Oswalt, in his mid-thirties, supervised the Hinge Room's "special line," and Russell Caldwell, the manager of the Hinge Room and age 45, supervised both petitioner and Oswalt. Petitioner's responsibilities included recording the attendance and hours of those under his supervision, and reviewing a weekly report that listed the hours worked by each employee.

In the summer of 1995, Caldwell informed Powe Chesnut, the director of manufacturing and the husband of company president Sandra Sanderson, that "production was down" in the Hinge Room because employees were often absent and were "coming in late and leaving early." Because the monthly attendance reports did not indicate a problem, Chesnut ordered an audit of the Hinge Room's timesheets for July, August, and September of that year. According to Chesnut's testimony, that investigation revealed "numerous timekeeping errors and misrepresentations on the part of Caldwell, Reeves, and Oswalt." Following the audit, Chesnut, along with Dana Jester, vice president of human resources, and Tom Whitaker, vice president of operations, recommended to company president Sanderson that petitioner and Caldwell be fired. In October 1995, Sanderson followed the recommendation and discharged both petitioner and Caldwell.

At trial, respondent contended that it had fired petitioner due to his failure to maintain accurate attendance records, while petitioner attempted to demonstrate that respondent's explanation was pretext for age discrimination. Petitioner introduced evidence that he had accurately recorded the attendance and hours of the employees under his supervision, and that Chesnut, whom Oswalt described as wielding "absolute power" within the company had demonstrated age-based animus in his dealings with petitioner.

[The jury returned a verdict in favor of petitioner of $35,000 in compensatory damages, which the judge doubled as liquidated damages pursuant to the jury's finding that the employer's age discrimination was "willful." The judge also awarded plaintiff $28,490.80 in front pay for two years' lost income.]

The Court of Appeals for the Fifth Circuit reversed, holding that petitioner had not introduced sufficient evidence to sustain the jury's finding of unlawful discrimination. After noting respondent's proffered justification for petitioner's discharge, the court acknowledged that petitioner "very well may" have offered sufficient evidence for "a reasonable jury [to] have found that [respondent's] explanation for its employment decision was pretextual." The court explained, however, that this was "not dispositive" of the ultimate issue — namely, "whether Reeves presented sufficient evidence that his age motivated [respondent's] employment decision." Addressing this question, the court weighed petitioner's additional evidence of discrimination against other circumstances surrounding his discharge. Specifically, the court noted that Chesnut's age-based comments "were not made in the direct context of Reeves's termination"; there was no allegation that the two other individuals who had recommended that petitioner be fired (Jester and Whitaker) were motivated by age; two of the decision makers involved in petitioner's discharge (Jester and Sanderson) were over the age of 50; all three of the Hinge Room supervisors were accused of inaccurate record keeping; and several of respondent's management positions were filled by persons over age 50 when petitioner was fired. On this basis, the court concluded that petitioner had not introduced sufficient evidence for a rational jury to conclude that he had been discharged because of his age. . . .

## II

Under the ADEA, it is "unlawful for an employer . . . to fail or refuse to hire or to discharge any individual or otherwise discriminate against any individual with respect to his compensation, terms, conditions, or privileges of employment, because of such individual's age." When a plaintiff alleges disparate treatment, "liability depends on whether the protected trait (under the ADEA, age) actually motivated the employer's decision." *Hazen Paper Co. v. Biggins.* That is, the plaintiff's age must have "actually played a role in [the employer's decision making] process and had a determinative influence on the outcome." Recognizing that "the question facing triers of fact in discrimination cases is both sensitive and difficult," and that "there will seldom be 'eyewitness' testimony as to the employer's mental processes," *Postal Service Bd. of Governors v. Aikens,* the Courts of Appeals, including the Fifth Circuit in this case, have employed some variant of the framework articulated in *McDonnell Douglas* to analyze ADEA claims that are based principally on circumstantial evidence. . . . This Court has not squarely addressed whether the *McDonnell Douglas* framework, developed to assess claims brought under § 703(a)(1) of Title VII of the Civil Rights Act of 1964, also applies to ADEA actions. Because the parties do not dispute the issue, we shall assume, arguendo, that the *McDonnell Douglas* framework is fully applicable here.

[Under this framework, petitioner established a prima facie case and respondent rebutted it.] Although intermediate evidentiary burdens shift back and forth under this framework, "the ultimate burden of persuading the trier of fact that the defendant intentionally discriminated against the plaintiff remains at all times with the plaintiff." And in attempting to satisfy this burden, the plaintiff — once the employer produces sufficient evidence to support a nondiscriminatory explanation for its decision — must be afforded the "opportunity to prove by a preponderance of the evidence that the legitimate reasons offered by the defendant were not its true reasons, but were a pretext for discrimination." That is, the plaintiff may attempt to establish that he was the victim of intentional discrimination "by showing that the employer's proffered explanation is unworthy of credence." Moreover, although the presumption of discrimination "drops out of the picture" once the defendant meets its burden of production, the trier of fact may still consider the evidence establishing the plaintiff's prima facie case "and inferences properly drawn therefrom . . . on the issue of whether the defendant's explanation is pretextual."

In this case, the evidence supporting respondent's explanation for petitioner's discharge consisted primarily of testimony by Chesnut and Sanderson and documentation of petitioner's alleged "shoddy record keeping." Chesnut testified that a 1993 audit of Hinge Room operations revealed "a very lax assembly line" where employees were not adhering to general work rules. As a result of that audit, petitioner was placed on 90 days' probation for unsatisfactory performance. In 1995, Chesnut ordered another investigation of the Hinge Room, which, according to his testimony, revealed that petitioner was not correctly recording the absences and hours of employees. Respondent introduced summaries of that investigation documenting several attendance violations by 12 employees under petitioner's supervision, and noting that each should have been disciplined in some manner. Chesnut testified that this failure to discipline absent and late employees is "extremely important when you are dealing with a union" because uneven enforcement across departments would keep the company "in grievance and arbitration cases, which are costly, all the time." He and Sanderson also stated that petitioner's errors, by failing to adjust for hours not worked, cost the company overpaid wages. Sanderson testified that she accepted the recommendation to discharge petitioner because he had "intentionally falsified company pay records."

Petitioner, however, made a substantial showing that respondent's explanation was false. First, petitioner offered evidence that he had properly maintained the attendance records. Most of the timekeeping errors cited by respondent involved employees who were not marked late but who were recorded as having arrived at the plant at 7 A.M. for the 7 A.M. shift. Respondent contended that employees arriving at 7 A.M. could not have been at their workstations by 7 A.M., and therefore must have been late. But both petitioner and Oswalt testified that the company's automated timeclock often failed to scan employees' timecards, so that the timesheets would not record any time of arrival. On these occasions, petitioner and Oswalt would visually check the workstations and record whether the employees were present at the start of the shift. They stated that if an employee arrived promptly but the timesheet contained no time of arrival, they would reconcile the two by marking "7 A.M." as the employee's arrival time, even if the employee actually arrived at the plant earlier. On cross-examination, Chesnut acknowledged that the timeclock sometimes malfunctioned, and that if "people were there at their work stations" at the start of the shift, the supervisor "would write in seven o'clock." Petitioner also testified that when employees arrived before or stayed after their shifts, he would assign them additional work so they would not be overpaid.

Petitioner similarly cast doubt on whether he was responsible for any failure to discipline late and absent employees. Petitioner testified that his job only included reviewing the daily and weekly attendance reports, and that disciplinary write-ups were based on the monthly reports, which were reviewed by Caldwell. Sanderson admitted that Caldwell, and not petitioner, was responsible for citing employees for violations of the company's attendance policy. Further, Chesnut conceded that there had never been a union grievance or employee complaint arising from petitioner's record keeping, and that the company had never calculated the amount of overpayments allegedly attributable to petitioner's errors. Petitioner also testified that, on the day he was fired, Chesnut said that his discharge was due to his failure to report as absent one employee, Gina Mae Coley, on two days in September 1995. But petitioner explained that he had spent those days in the hospital, and that Caldwell was therefore responsible for any overpayment of Coley. Finally, petitioner stated that on previous occasions that employees were paid for hours they had not worked, the company had simply adjusted those employees' next paychecks to correct the errors.

Based on this evidence, the Court of Appeals concluded that petitioner "very well may be correct" that "a reasonable jury could have found that [respondent's] explanation for its employment decision was pretextual." Nonetheless, the court held that this showing, standing alone, was insufficient to sustain the jury's finding of liability: "We must, as an essential final step, determine whether Reeves presented sufficient evidence that his age motivated [respondent's] employment decision." And in making this determination, the Court of Appeals ignored the evidence supporting petitioner's prima facie case and challenging respondent's explanation for its decision. The court confined its review of evidence favoring petitioner to that evidence showing that Chesnut had directed derogatory, age-based comments at petitioner, and that Chesnut had singled out petitioner for harsher treatment than younger employees.

It is therefore apparent that the court believed that only this additional evidence of discrimination was relevant to whether the jury's verdict should stand. That is, the Court of Appeals proceeded from the assumption that a prima facie case of discrimination, combined with sufficient evidence for the trier of fact to disbelieve the defendant's legitimate, nondiscriminatory reason for its decision, is insufficient as a matter of law to sustain a jury's finding of intentional discrimination.

In so reasoning, the Court of Appeals misconceived the evidentiary burden borne by plaintiffs who attempt to prove intentional discrimination through indirect evidence. This much is evident from our decision in *St. Mary's Honor Center*. There we held that the factfinder's rejection of the employer's legitimate, nondiscriminatory reason for its action does not compel judgment for the plaintiff. The ultimate question is whether the employer intentionally discriminated, and proof that "the employer's proffered reason is unpersuasive, or even obviously contrived, does not necessarily establish that the plaintiff's proffered reason . . . is correct." In other words, "it is not enough . . . to disbelieve the employer; the factfinder must believe the plaintiff's explanation of intentional discrimination."

In reaching this conclusion, however, we reasoned that it is permissible for the trier of fact to infer the ultimate fact of discrimination from the falsity of the employer's explanation. Specifically, we stated:

> The factfinder's disbelief of the reasons put forward by the defendant (particularly if disbelief is accompanied by a suspicion of mendacity) may, together with the elements of the prima facie case, suffice to show intentional discrimination. Thus, rejection of the defendant's proffered reasons will permit the trier of fact to infer the ultimate fact of intentional discrimination.

Proof that the defendant's explanation is unworthy of credence is simply one form of circumstantial evidence that is probative of intentional discrimination, and it may be quite persuasive. [*St. Mary's Honor Center.*] ("Proving the employer's reason false becomes part of (and often considerably assists) the greater enterprise of proving that the real reason was intentional discrimination"). In appropriate circumstances, the trier of fact can reasonably infer from the falsity of the explanation that the employer is dissembling to cover up a discriminatory purpose. Such an inference is consistent with the general principle of evidence law that the factfinder is entitled to consider a party's dishonesty about a material fact as "affirmative evidence of guilt." Wright v. West, 505 U.S. 277 (1992); 2 J. Wigmore, Evidence §278(2), p. 133 (J. Chadbourn rev. ed. 1979). Moreover, once the employer's justification has been eliminated, discrimination may well be the most likely alternative explanation, especially since the employer is in the best position to put forth the actual reason for its decision. Cf. Furnco Constr. Corp. v. Waters, 438 U.S. 567, 577 (1978) ("When all legitimate reasons for rejecting an applicant have been eliminated as possible reasons for the employer's actions, it is more likely than not the employer, who we generally assume acts with some reason, based his decision on an impermissible consideration"). Thus, a plaintiff's prima facie case, combined with sufficient evidence to find that the employer's asserted justification is false, may permit the trier of fact to conclude that the employer unlawfully discriminated.

This is not to say that such a showing by the plaintiff will always be adequate to sustain a jury's finding of liability. Certainly there will be instances where, although the plaintiff has established a prima facie case and set forth sufficient evidence to reject the defendant's explanation, no rational factfinder could conclude that the action was discriminatory. For instance, an employer would be entitled to judgment as a matter of law if the record conclusively revealed some other, nondiscriminatory reason for the employer's decision, or if the plaintiff created only a weak issue of fact as to whether the employer's reason was untrue and there was abundant and uncontroverted independent evidence that no discrimination had occurred. See Fisher v. Vassar College, 114 F.3d 1332, 1338 (2d Cir. 1997) ("If the circumstances show that the defendant gave the false explanation to conceal something other than discrimination, the inference of discrimination will be weak or nonexistent"). To hold otherwise would be effectively to insulate an entire category of employment discrimination cases from review under Rule 50, and we have reiterated that trial courts should not "'treat discrimination differently from other ultimate questions of fact.'" *St. Mary's Honor Center.*

Whether judgment as a matter of law is appropriate in any particular case will depend on a number of factors. Those include the strength of the plaintiff's prima facie case, the probative value of the proof that the employer's explanation is false, and any other evidence that supports the employer's case and that properly may be considered on a motion for judgment as a matter of law. For purposes of this case, we need not — and could not — resolve all of the circumstances in which such factors would entitle an employer to judgment as a matter of law. It suffices to say that, because a prima facie case and sufficient evidence to reject the employer's explanation may permit a finding of liability, the Court of Appeals erred in proceeding from the premise that a plaintiff must always introduce additional, independent evidence of discrimination.

## III

### A

The remaining question is whether, despite the Court of Appeals' misconception of petitioner's evidentiary burden, respondent was nonetheless entitled to judgment as a matter of law. Under Rule 50, a court should render judgment as a matter of law when "a party has been fully heard on an issue and there is no legally sufficient evidentiary basis for a reasonable jury to find for that party on that issue." . . .

[I]n entertaining a motion for judgment as a matter of law, the court should review all of the evidence in the record.] In doing so, however, the court must draw all reasonable inferences in favor of the nonmoving party, and it may not make credibility determinations or weigh the evidence. Lytle v. Household Mfg., Inc., 494 U.S. 545, 554-55 (1990). "Credibility determinations, the weighing of the evidence, and the drawing of legitimate inferences from the facts are jury functions, not those of a judge." [Anderson v. Liberty Lobby, 477 U.S. 242 (1986).] Thus, although the court should review the record as a whole, it must disregard all evidence favorable to the moving party that the jury is not required to believe. See Wright & Miller 299. That is, the court should give credence to the evidence favoring the nonmovant as well as that "evidence supporting the moving party that is uncontradicted and unimpeached, at least to the extent that that evidence comes from disinterested witnesses."

### B

Applying this standard here, it is apparent that respondent was not entitled to judgment as a matter of law. In this case, in addition to establishing a prima facie case of discrimination and creating a jury issue as to the falsity of the employer's explanation, petitioner introduced additional evidence that Chesnut was motivated by age-based animus and was principally responsible for petitioner's firing. Petitioner testified that Chesnut had told him that he "was so old [he] must have come over on the Mayflower" and, on one occasion when petitioner was having difficulty starting a machine, that he "was too damn old to do [his] job." According to petitioner, Chesnut would regularly "cuss at me and shake his finger in my face." Oswalt, roughly 24 years younger than petitioner, corroborated that there was an "obvious difference" in how Chesnut treated them. He stated that, although he and Chesnut "had [their] differences," "it was nothing compared to the way [Chesnut] treated Roger." Oswalt explained that Chesnut "tolerated quite a bit" from him even though he "defied" Chesnut "quite often," but that Chesnut treated petitioner "in a manner, as you would . . . treat . . . a child when . . . you're angry with [him]." Petitioner also demonstrated that, according to company records, he and Oswalt had nearly identical rates of productivity in 1993. Yet respondent conducted an efficiency study of only the regular line, supervised by petitioner, and placed only petitioner on probation. Chesnut conducted that efficiency study and, after having testified to the contrary on direct examination, acknowledged on cross-examination that he had recommended that petitioner be placed on probation following the study.

Further, petitioner introduced evidence that Chesnut was the actual decision-maker behind his firing. Chesnut was married to Sanderson, who made the formal decision to discharge petitioner. Although Sanderson testified that she fired petitioner because he had "intentionally falsified company pay records," respondent only introduced evidence concerning the inaccuracy of the records, not their falsification. A 1994 letter authored by Chesnut indicated that he berated other company directors, who were supposedly his co-equals, about how to do their jobs. Moreover, Oswalt testified that all of respondent's employees feared Chesnut, and that Chesnut had exercised "absolute power" within the company for "as long as [he] can remember."

In holding that the record contained insufficient evidence to sustain the jury's verdict, the Court of Appeals misapplied the standard of review dictated by Rule 50. Again, the court disregarded critical evidence favorable to petitioner — namely, the evidence supporting petitioner's prima facie case and undermining respondent's nondiscriminatory explanation. The court also failed to draw all reasonable inferences in favor of petitioner. For instance, while acknowledging "the potentially damning nature" of Chesnut's age-related comments, the court discounted them on the ground that they "were not made in the direct context of Reeves's termination." And the court discredited petitioner's evidence that Chesnut was the actual decision maker by giving weight to the fact that there was "no evidence to suggest that any of the other decision makers were motivated by age." Moreover, the other evidence on which the court relied — that Caldwell and Oswalt were also cited for poor record keeping, and that respondent employed many managers over age 50 — although relevant, is certainly not dispositive. In concluding that these circumstances so overwhelmed the evidence favoring petitioner that no rational trier of fact could have found that petitioner was fired because of his age, the Court of Appeals impermissibly substituted its judgment concerning the weight of the evidence for the jury's.

The ultimate question in every employment discrimination case involving a claim of disparate treatment is whether the plaintiff was the victim of intentional discrimination. Given the evidence in the record supporting petitioner, we see no reason to subject the parties to an additional round of litigation before the Court of Appeals rather than to resolve the matter here. The District Court plainly informed the jury that petitioner was required to show "by a preponderance of the evidence that his age was a determining and motivating factor in the decision of [respondent] to terminate him." The court instructed the jury that, to show that respondent's explanation was a pretext for discrimination, petitioner had to demonstrate "1, that the stated reasons were not the real reasons for [petitioner's] discharge; and 2, that age discrimination was the real reason for [petitioner's] discharge." Given that petitioner established a prima facie case of discrimination, introduced enough evidence for the jury to reject respondent's explanation, and produced additional evidence of age-based animus, there was sufficient evidence for the jury to find that respondent had intentionally discriminated. The District Court was therefore correct to submit the case to the jury, and the Court of Appeals erred in overturning its verdict.

Justice GINSBURG, concurring.

The Court today holds that an employment discrimination plaintiff may survive judgment as a matter of law by submitting two categories of evidence: first, evidence establishing a "prima facie case," as that term is used in McDonnell Douglas Corp. v. Green, and second, evidence from which a rational factfinder could conclude that the employer's proffered explanation for its actions was false. Because the Court of Appeals in this case plainly, and erroneously, required the plaintiff to offer some evidence beyond those two categories, no broader holding is necessary to support reversal.

I write separately to note that it may be incumbent on the Court, in an appropriate case, to define more precisely the circumstances in which plaintiffs will be required to submit evidence beyond these two categories in order to survive a motion for judgment as a matter of law. I anticipate that such circumstances will be uncommon. As the Court notes, it is a principle of evidence law that the jury is entitled to treat a party's dishonesty about a material fact as evidence of culpability. Under this commonsense principle, evidence suggesting that a defendant accused of illegal discrimination has chosen to give a false explanation for its actions gives rise to a rational inference that the defendant could be masking its actual, illegal motivation. Whether the defendant was in fact motivated by discrimination is of course for the finder of fact to decide; that is the lesson of St. Mary's Honor Center v. Hicks. But the inference remains — unless it is conclusively demonstrated, by evidence the district court is required to credit on a motion for judgment as a matter of law, that discrimination could not have been the defendant's true motivation. If such conclusive demonstrations are (as I suspect) atypical, it follows that the ultimate question of liability ordinarily should not be taken from the jury once the plaintiff has introduced the two categories of evidence described above. Because the Court's opinion leaves room for such further elaboration in an appropriate case, I join it in full.

*NOTES*

1. Adversarial litigation is often said to be a search for truth. Nevertheless, our legal system inevitably gives great effect to the parties' strategic decisions, usually requiring them to live with the consequences of those decisions. These two ideas are generally consistent when the dialectic process of contending claims, and claimants, works to produce a complete record of all the relevant evidence for the factfinder to find the truth. But these two views of an adversarial system came sharply into conflict in *Hicks*. According to the dissent, when the factfinder finds the defendant's proffered nondiscriminatory reason not to be the true explanation for why Hicks was fired, the defendant must lose because that is the consequence of its decision to place in evidence the reason that it did. The majority in *Hicks*, however, believes that point of the

whole exercise to be the search for discriminatory intent. Thus, unless the trier of fact believes that there was such intent, the plaintiff must lose.

2. In *Hicks*, the only evidence regarding personal animosity between the plaintiff and his supervisor was the testimony of the supervisor denying that it existed. Thus, the factfinder could not have found that the supervisor's personal animosity was the reason for the plaintiff's discharge. Is the response simply that the factfinder need not determine that personal animosity was the reason for the employer's action? Instead, it must decide only whether unlawful discrimination was the actual reason for the challenged action. Because the plaintiff bears the burden of persuasion, she will lose if, based on the evidence in the record, the factfinder fails to conclude that the employer's intent to discriminate motivated the adverse action plaintiff challenges. On remand, what should the Court of Appeals do? Since defendant denied its reason was personal animus between Hicks and his supervisor, but the trial court thought that was why Hicks was fired, should a new trial be granted to give Hicks a chance to introduce evidence on that issue? What evidence would be relevant? Evidence that personal animosity was tinged with racism or racial stereotyping?

3. After *Hicks*, what is the significance of establishing a prima facie case? Justice Souter's dissent describes it as "not only rais[ing] an inference of discrimination; in the absence of further evidence, it also creates a mandatory presumption in favor of the plaintiff." Does Justice Scalia agree that a prima facie case creates a mandatory presumption? Isn't the point of the majority that the presumption is mandatory while it lasts, but that it disappears as soon as the defendant carries its burden of production? This explains both *Burdine* ("if the employer is silent in the face of the presumption, the court must enter judgment for the plaintiff," 450 U.S. at 254) and *Aikens* (once defendant produces evidence of a nondiscriminatory explanation, the presumption drops from the case). But what is the effect of the proof that established the prima face case?

4. After *Hicks*, how important is it that the employer's rebuttal narrow and sharpen the factual inquiry? Judge Denny Chin and Jodi Golinsky in Employment Discrimination: Beyond McDonnell Douglas: A Simplified Method for Assessing Evidence in Discrimination Cases, 64 Brook. L. Rev. 659, 666 (1998), conclude that "there is not a single reported case in which a plaintiff prevails at the second step in a discrimination lawsuit because a defendant employer is unwilling or unable to articulate a legitimate, nondiscriminatory reason for its employment action."

5. While plaintiffs have an incentive to focus on discriminatory, rather than nondiscriminatory, explanations for decisions, defendants have an incentive to bring forward every nondiscriminatory reason for the challenged action. Why would an employer not advance the true reason for its action if it were not discriminatory? One possibility goes back to *Biggins*: the true reason might violate another law — for example, another federal statute, such as ERISA, or some state cause of action, such as the public policy tort. See Chapter 1. Doesn't *Biggins* mean that a court should not find a violation of Title VII or the ADEA when the employer's real reason violates some other source of right? Alternatively, the *Hicks* Court seemed to envision true reasons that, while not illegal, are embarrassing. In Bell v. AT&T, 946 F.2d 1507 (10th Cir. 1991), plaintiff identified a person more vulnerable to layoff than she was. Although the employer said this comparator had been spared the layoff because of an impending transfer, the trial judge instead found that the comparator was the beneficiary of nepotism by a higher-up in the organization. Under *Hicks*, isn't it clear there would be no violation if that were true?

6. David N. Rosen & Jonathan M. Freiman, Remodeling McDonnell Douglas: *Fisher v. Vassar College* and Structure of Employment Discrimination Law, 17 Quinnipiac L. Rev. 725, 775 (1998), propose that more structured trial preparation can diminish the problem posed by *Hicks*:

> [p]laintiffs should ask defendants in depositions and interrogatories to identify all the reasons that may have played any part in the adverse employment decision at issue. Those discovery requests should be followed with requests for admission [pursuant to Federal Rule 36] asking the defendant to admit that there are no reasons for its actions other than those that have been identified. A trial memorandum of the kind widely in use in the district courts can further specify and limit the potential explanations for a defendant's decision that a jury is entitle to consider. . . . A diligent plaintiff may then be in a position to proceed by way of elimination by disproving all the alternative explanations.

Would this prevent the trier of fact from finding a denied reason actually motivated the decision? Even if so, would it prevent the factfinder from finding that discrimination did not motivate the decision?

7. Is *Hicks* consistent with *McDonnell Douglas/ Burdine*, and *Aikens*? Or is the decision a change? If so, how do you articulate the change? An excellent discussion of the entire problem, although preceding *Hicks*, is cited by the dissent. Catherine J. Lanctot, the Defendant Lies and the Plaintiff Loses: The Fallacy of "Pretext-Plus" Rule in Employment Discrimination Cases, 43 Hastings L.J. 59 (1991).

Professor Deborah C. Malamud, The Last Minuet: Disparate Treatment After *Hicks*, 93 Mich. L. Rev. 2229 (1995), argues that *Hicks* is correctly decided, given that the Court's earlier decisions avoided dealing with the hard issues.

> [I analyze] the Court's prior disparate treatment decisions and conclude that the Supreme Court never succeeded in setting the prima facie case threshold high enough to permit the proven prima facie case to support a sufficiently strong inference of discrimination to mandate judgment for the plaintiff when combined only with disbelief of the employer's stated justification. . . . I conclude that the major thrust of the Court's disparate treatment jurisprudence is the attempt to insulate disparate treatment cases from the radical innovations of the disparate impact standard. There is a marked conservative overtone to the *McDonnell Douglas/Burdine* line of cases — and against its background, the nostalgic critique of *Hicks* is unacceptable.

Id. at 2236-37.

8. *Hicks* has been severely criticized. Mark S. Brodin, The Demise of Circumstantial Proof in Employment Discrimination Litigation: *St. Mary's Honor Center v. Hicks*, Pretext, and the "Personality" Excuse, 18 Berkeley J. Emp. & Lab. L. 183 (1997), attacks *Hicks* for violating "two of the most basic tenets of American procedure . . . first, that court is a passive tribunal, not an active player in the construction of arguments and theories, and second, that cases are to be decided solely on the basis of the evidence presented, not the conjecture of the factfinder." Id. at 209-10. More broadly, he concludes that *Hicks* "stands as a veritable guide for avoiding liability. Title VII should not become the vehicle for legitimating the very conduct it is directed towards prohibiting." Id. at 239. See also William R. Corbett, Of Babies, Bathwater, and Throwing Out Proof Structures: It is Not Time to Jettison *McDonnell Douglas*, 2 Emp. Rts. & Employ. Pol'y J. 361 (1998); Ruth Gana Okediji, Status Rules: Doctrine as Discrimination in a Post-*Hicks* Environment, 26 Fla. St. L. Rev. 49 (1998); Stephen Plass, Truth: The Last Virtue in Title VII Litigation,

29 Seton Hall L. Rev. 599 (1998) (pointing out that, contrary to Justice Scalia's claim that even perjury does not warrant a verdict, employee lies in litigation are often out-come-determinative, including dismissal of their cases); Sherie L. Coons, Proving Disparate Treatment After St. Mary's Honor Center v. Hicks, 19 J. Corp. L. 379 (1994); Robert Brookings, Hicks, Lies, and Ideology: The Wages of Sin Is Now Ex-culpation, 28 Creighton L. Rev. 939, 994 (1995) criticizing Hicks because "Title VII's rules must help plaintiffs pierce corporate and governmental veils of secrecy and subjectivity, probe the nooks and crannies of decision-making arenas, and, ultimately, scrape away concreted discriminatory sediment"); Melissa A. Essary, The Disman-tling of McDonnell Douglas v. Green: The High Court Muddies the Evidentiary Wa-ters in Discrimination Cases, 21 Pepp. L. Rev. 385 (1994).

Professor Henry L. Chambers, Jr., Discrimination, Plain and Simple, 36 Tulsa L.J. 557, 573 (2001), argues:

> The Hicks Court also leaves the McDonnell Douglas structure in a somewhat confused state. By undervaluing the McDonnell Douglas structure and its implications, the Hicks Court suggests that courts view evidence of pretext more skeptically than they should. Proving that an employer's LNRs [legitimate nondiscriminatory reasons] are untrue is not easy. Given that LNRs are provided by the employer presumably to fit the contours of its case and are vigorously defended by its counsel, convincing a factfinder that the LNRs are untrue or not credible is difficult and should be treated as powerful evidence of discrimination when it occurs. A plaintiff's showing of pretext should always be sufficient to avoid a directed verdict against a plaintiff and should generally yield a ver-dict for the plaintiff.

Does Reeves satisfy Professor Chambers' critique?

9. Professor Deborah A. Calloway, in St. Mary's Honor Center v. Hicks: Question-ing the Basic Assumption, 26 Conn. L. Rev. 997 (1995), argues that the Supreme Court has revised its underlying assumption about the pervasiveness of the discrimi-nation, which is the real significance of Hicks:

> Hicks is significant, not for its narrow legal holding, but for the attitude underlying that holding. The majority and dissent argue about parsing precedent and legal niceties such as the meaning of a rebuttable presumption and allocating burdens of proof. But this case is not about who bears the burden of proof. Instead, this case is about what evi-dence is sufficient to meet the plaintiff's burden of persuasion on discriminatory intent. What evidence makes it "more likely than not" that the defendant discriminated? The answer to this question depends on one's beliefs about the prevalence of discrimination. Whether a reasonable person (or judge) will be convinced that discrimination has been shown depends on whether he believes that discrimination is a logical inference in the absence of some other explanation for adverse conduct. The district court and the ma-jority of the Supreme Court in Hicks reached their result, not because it was required by any formal legal rules, but rather because they just plain do not believe in that basic assumption.

Id. at 1008-09.

10. Following Hicks, most circuits adopted a "pretext-only" rule. E.g., Shaw v. HCA Health Servs. of Midwest, Inc., 79 F.3d 99 (8th Cir. 1996); Barbour v. Merrill, 48 F.3d 1270, 1277 (D.C. Cir. 1995). Some adopted a "pretext-plus" rule, which required plaintiff to introduce additional evidence of discrimination, even if she had established a prima facie case and shown that defendant's reason was not true. See generally David Culp, Age Discrimination in Employment Act; Life After St. Mary's Honor Center v. Hicks — Rolling the Dice Against a Stacked Deck, 36 Duq. L. Rev. 795 (1998).

What basis is there in *Hicks* to support the "pretext-plus" rule? *Hicks* was a contentious 5-4 decision but *Reeves*, in rejecting the "pretext-plus" rule, was unanimous. Why the difference? How do the decisions compare? In *Hicks*, the Court rejected the lower court's rule that plaintiff always wins by establishing a prima facie case and proving defendant's reason was untrue. *Reeves* rejected the lower court's rule that plaintiff always loses if that is all she can prove. Is the result of the two decisions that a factfinder always gets to decide the case where plaintiff proves a prima facie case and creates a jury question whether the defendant's reason is true?

11. Professor Catherine J. Lanctot, Secrets and Lies: The Need for a Definitive Rule of Law in Pretext Cases, 61 La. L. Rev. 539 (2001), views *Reeves* as a simple replay of *Hicks*, and, before *Hicks*, of *Burdine*. For her, the fundamental flaw of all of these decisions is the failure of the Supreme Court to lay down a rule of law that would foreclose the lower courts from using discretion "to limit or expand the scope of pretext cases at will." "[C]ourts will exploit any loopholes provided by the Supreme Court to dismiss what they consider to be unmeritorious discrimination suits." Id. at 546. The loopholes in the Supreme Court decisions work to the disadvantage of plaintiffs. "The antipathy of the lower courts to circumstantial proof of disparate treatment claims may be explained by many factors, including the ideological disposition of many lower court judges, the societal changes in perception of the prevalence of discrimination, and a desire to control the burgeoning dockets of the federal courts." Id. What seems "to haunt so many federal judges [is] the specter of an undeserving plaintiff prevailing in an employment discrimination case by showing pretext when the real reason being concealed by the employer was not discrimination, but something else." Id. at 548-49.

Professor Lanctot proposes that the Court adopt a true rule of law to address this problem. Her rule, which she calls a "pretext always" rule, would require that plaintiff, in addition to proving a prima facie case and proving that the reason offered by the defendant was not the real reason for the decision, must prove a third element to establish liability and be entitled to a judgment as a matter of law. Plaintiff must show "that any other reason that reasonably may be inferred from the evidence was not the real reason for the employment action." Id. at 547–48. The new, third part of the rule, is designed to address the hypothetical concealed but non-discriminatory reason that Professor Lanctot thinks has led to the creation of the loopholes under the present scheme. How would *Hicks* be decided under this "pretext always" rule? Since there was no evidence that plaintiff's supervisor harbored personal animosity against Hicks, would that mean that Hicks would be entitled to judgment as a matter of law upon proof of a prima facie case and that the reason defendant offered was not the real reason for the employment action?

12. Professor Michael Zimmer, Leading by Example: An Holistic Approach to Individual Disparate Treatment Law, 11 Kan. J. of L. & Pub. Pol'y 177, 187 (2001), criticizes the "pretext always" rule if it extends to inferences that could be drawn from evidence in the record:

> Plaintiff would seem to be required to imagine every reason that could be inferred from the evidence, even if there is no evidence in the record as to those reasons, and then prove that none of these reasons explained defendant's decision. . . . The problem under Professor Lanctot's proposed rule is that [Hicks] would be expected to imagine and then disprove that the real reason was this personality conflict despite the fact that the only evidence in the record about that was the denial by the supervisor that he had such a conflict with plaintiff. Instructing a jury about how this works would be challenging.

Was *Reeves* itself rightly decided under Professor Lanctot's approach?

13. Professor Michael Selmi, Why Are Employment Discrimination Cases So Hard to Win?, 61 La. L. Rev. 555 (2001), compares the disposition in federal court of employment discrimination cases and insurance cases, concluding that insurance defendants fare much worse than employers as defendants under any measure. The reason for this difference, in Professor Selmi's opinion, is the same unconscious bias on the part of judges that has been demonstrated more generally through the use of cognitive psychology. Professor Selmi proposes that plaintiffs try to counter this judicial bias by presenting evidence trying "to explain the nature of the discrimination at issue, and in presenting the evidence should generally assume the court is hostile to the claim. This may necessitate expert testimony on the nature of unconscious or subtle discrimination, which currently is used only rarely but which can be quite influential as a means of providing the necessary causation to establish a claim. . . ." Id. at 573. How could the plaintiff's attorney in *Hicks* have proven that there was a racial element in the personal animosity the supervisor felt toward the plaintiff? Professor Selmi also cautions plaintiffs' lawyers to take only strong cases to trial. Do you think plaintiffs' lawyers take cases they know to be weak forward to trial? Put yourself in the shoes of Hicks's or Reeves's lawyer. Were these weak cases?

14. Professor Michael Zimmer, Slicing & Dicing of Individual Disparate Treatment Law, 61 La. L. Rev. 577 (2001), views *Reeves* as broader than merely rejecting the lower court's "pretext-plus" rule. He argues that the Court rejected the underpinning for that rule, which was that the probative value of the evidence supporting plaintiff's prima facie case "drops out of the picture" once defendant introduces evidence of its non-discriminatory reason for its action.

> These [pretext-plus] courts extended this "drops out of the picture" language [from *Hicks*] beyond dropping the presumption of discrimination created by the prima facie case to go further and drop out the probative value of the evidence supporting the prima facie case. With that evidence gone, more evidence was necessary before plaintiff would be able to prove discrimination. Justice O'Connor rejected that extension stating, "although the presumption of discrimination 'drops out of the picture' once the defendant meets its burden of production [*Hicks*] . . . the trier of fact may still consider the evidence establishing the plaintiff's prima facie case and inferences properly drawn therefrom . . . on the issue of whether the defendant's explanation is pretextual."

Id. at 587-88. *Reeves* also made clear that all the circumstantial evidence in the record needs to be reviewed in deciding motions for summary judgment or judgment as a matter of law.

> For *Reeves* to be a truly significant case . . . it is necessary to look at the underlying and unifying rationale of both parts of the opinion. That rationale is that, despite the intricacies of the *McDonnell Douglas* analysis and its procedural operation to develop a record, it is necessary to consider all the evidence that is produced as a result of those procedures being followed. That evidence includes evidence supporting the prima facie case, evidence tending to prove the defendant's proffered reason to be false, and all other circumstantial evidence such as age-related comments of decision makers that supports plaintiff's case. Slicing and dicing away of plaintiff's evidence to leave only evidence supporting defendant's case is inconsistent with the true nature of the *McDonnell Douglas* method of analyzing individual disparate treatment cases. . . . It is a mistake to throw out most of plaintiff's evidence before reviewing the record for a motion for judgment as a matter of law. All the evidence in the record supporting plaintiff's case and every inference based on that evidence must be viewed in favor of the nonmoving plaintiff. The most significant lesson of the Supreme Court in *Reeves* is the necessity to

include all the probative evidence in the record, without regard to which part of the *McDonnell Douglas* analysis it might be relevant, before deciding motions for summary judgment and judgment as a matter of law.

Id. at 591-92.

15. The response of the lower courts to *Reeves* to date is mixed. The Fifth Circuit, which was reversed in *Reeves,* now accepts the Supreme Court approach. Ratliff v. City of Gainesville, Tex., 256 F.3d 355, 361 (5th Cir. 2001) ("The 'pretext plus' strand of analysis requires a plaintiff not only to disprove an employer's proffered reasons for the discrimination, but also to introduce additional evidence of discrimination. In contrast, the 'permissive pretext only' standard is a more lenient approach, and if the plaintiff establishes that the defendant's reasons are pretextual, the trier of fact is permitted, but not required, to enter judgment for the plaintiff . . . this Court has unequivocally stated that it no longer adheres to its pretext-plus requirement in light of the Supreme Court's decision in *Reeves.*"). See also EEOC v. Sears Roebuck & Co., 243 F.3d 846, 854 (4th Cir. 2001); Ross v. Campbell Soup Co., 237 F.3d 701,709 (6th Cir. 2001); Chuang v. University of California-Davis, 225 F.3d 1115, 1130 (9th Cir. 2000); Hinson v. Clinch County, Ga. Bd. of Educ., 231 F.3d 821, 831-32 (11th Cir. 2000).

16. While most circuits appear to be following *Reeves* by focusing on the evidence in the record and the inferences that can be drawn from that evidence in deciding motions for summary judgment and judgment as a matter of law, several circuits appear to be going their own way. At one extreme, the Seventh Circuit has reincarnated the pretext-plus rule in terms of pretext-is-a-lie. In Kulumani v. Blue Cross Blue Shield Assn., 224 F.3d 681 (7th Cir. 2000), the court defined pretext as a showing more than that defendant's asserted reason is not the real reason but also requiring a showing that the employer was deceitful in asserting the reason. In Millbrook v. IBP, Inc., 280 F.3d 1169 (7th Cir. 2002), the court, with one dissenter, reemphasized *Kulumani:*

> Pretext means a lie, specifically a phony reason for some action. The question is not whether the employer properly evaluated the competing applicants, but whether the employer's reason for choosing one candidate over the other was honest. Pretext for discrimination means more than an unusual act; it means something worse than a business error; pretext means deceit used to cover one's tracks. Thus, even if IBP's reason for selecting Harris over Millbrook were mistaken, ill considered or foolish, so long as [the employer] honestly believed those reasons, pretext has not been shown.

Id. at 1175 (internal quotes and citations omitted).

17. The Second Circuit continues to grant motions for summary judgment and judgments as a matter of law in a pattern that suggests *Reeves* has had little impact. In Zimmerman v. Associates First Capital Corp., 252 F.3d 376, 382 (2d Cir. 2001), the court emphasized the loophole in the *Reeves* opinion. "[W]e have simply ruled in several cases that a record that included a prima facie case and . . . pretext did not suffice" noting that the Supreme Court had said "such occasions exist." Id. In Schnabel v. Abramson, 232 F.3d 83, 88 n.3 (2d Cir. 2000), the court held that plaintiff had introduced enough evidence to allow a jury to "conclude that the stated reasons for discharging the plaintiff were a pretext" but nevertheless affirmed summary judgment for the employer since plaintiff had "not demonstrated that the asserted pretextual reasons were intended to mask age discrimination." See David J. Turek, Comment Affirming Ambiguity: *Reeves v. Sanderson Plumbing Products, Inc.* and the Burden-Shifting Framework of Disparate Treatment Cases, 85 Marq. L. Rev. 283 (2001).

18. Despite the holding in United States Postal Service Bd. of Governors v. Aikens, 460 U.S. 711, 715 (1983), that, once a case goes to trial, the issue of whether plaintiff proved a prima facie case can no longer be raised, several courts may be getting around *Reeves* by scrutinizing the record to determine whether plaintiff made out a prima facie case. In Millbook v. IBP, Inc., 280 F.3d 1169, 1178 (7th Cir. 2002), the court reversed the district court's denial of the employer's motion for judgment as a matter of law:

> What we have here then are two qualified applicants with varying credentials, and different views as to which candidate is best for the job. Millbrook argues that when an employer asserts that it chose another applicant over the plaintiff because the selected candidate was more qualified, the jury may return a verdict of discrimination if, after reviewing the applicant's relative qualifications, it simply does not believe the employer's assertion [that it picked the most qualified candidate].

The court rejected that approach unless plaintiff introduced additional evidence of discrimination: "[A]bsent such additional evidence of discrimination, this court has held that a jury verdict for the employee cannot stand if the jury is simply disagreeing with the company as to who is best qualified." Id. While that is true, the real question is whether, based on the evidence in the record, the jury could draw the inference that the company did not pick the best qualified employee because of an intent to discriminate. In EEOC v. Board of Regents of the University of Wisconsin, 288 F.3d 296, 301-02 (7th Cir. 2002), the court justified looking at the elements of a prima facie case in deciding a motion for judgment as a matter of law because the Supreme Court in *Reeves* "spent a good deal of time evaluating whether the evidence met the *McDonnell Douglas* criteria." That is not inconsistent with *Aikens*, because "what we are looking for is proof of intentional discrimination based on an examination of all the evidence in the record viewed in the light favorable to the nonmoving party." See also Gray v. Toshiba America Consumer Products, Inc., 263 F.3d 595, 600 (6th Cir. 2001) ("[I]n light of *Reeves* . . . whether the plaintiff has in fact presented evidence supporting each element of her prima facie case is material to the determination of whether she has demonstrated that the employer's articulated reason for the discharge is not credible"), Contra, Dennis v. Columbia Colleton Medical Center, Inc., 290 F.3d 639, 648 n.4 (4th Cir. 2002), in deciding motions for judgment as a matter of law, the court should not review the record to determine whether plaintiff proved that she was better qualified than the person selected by the employer: "*Reeves* plainly instructs us to apply a contrary approach by affirming that it is permissible for the trier of fact to infer the ultimate fact of discrimination from the falsity of the employer's explanation."

19. Consistent with *Reeves*, the circuits appear to be finding that "stray comment" evidence that fails to satisfy the circuit's test for direct evidence of discrimination is, nevertheless, circumstantial evidence that the factfinder may consider in deciding whether the employer acted with an intent to discriminate. Dominguez-Cruz v. Suttle Caribe, Inc., 202 F.3d 424, 433 (1st Cir. 2000); Santiago-Ramos v. Centiennial P.R. Wireless Corp., 217 F.3d 46, 55 (1st Cir. 2000); Russell v. McKinney Hosp. Venture, Inc., 235 F.3d 219, 225-26 (5th Cir. 2000); Gorence v. Eagle Food Ctrs., Inc., 242 F.3d 759, 763 (7th Cir. 2001) ("evidence of inappropriate remarks not shown to be directly related to the employment decision may not support a direct-method-of-proof case, but, in connection with other evidence, might support a case under *McDonnell Douglas*"); Fisher v. Pharmacia & Upjohn, 225 F.3d 915, 922 (8th Cir.

2000) ("Stray remarks therefore constitute circumstantial evidence of age discrimination."). But see Stone v. Autoliv Asp., Inc., 210 F.3d 1132, 1136 (10th Cir. 2000) ("Age-related comments referring directly to the plaintiff can support an inference of age discrimination, but 'isolated or ambiguous comments' may be, as here, too abstract to support such an inference."). Laina Rose Reinsmith, Note, Proving an Employer's Intent: Disparate Treatment Discrimination and the Stray Remarks Doctrine After *Reeves v. Sanderson Plumbing Products*, 55 Vand. L. Rev. 219, 255 (2002) (stray remarks evidence should be treated the same as other circumstantial evidence).

20. In his Slicing & Dicing article, Note 14 supra, Professor Zimmer suggests two reasons why lower courts may not feel compelled to follow *Reeves* closely. First, *Reeves* "did not really focus on the Fifth Circuit's slicing and dicing approach to reviewing the record. . . . Instead, the focus was on the wrong application of the facts of the particular case to the rule that all the evidence is to be reviewed in deciding motions for judgment as a matter of law. . . . The application phase of any Supreme Court opinion may not be viewed as significant beyond its resolution of the particular case." 61 La. L. Rev. at 591. Second, *Reeves* may illustrate the limited power that the Supreme Court actually has to shape federal statutory law as enforced in the lower federal courts. Given the few cases the Court decides every year (around 75) and the wide array of constitutional and statutory issues before the Court, it is not surprising that, "since the Rehnquist Court set what it saw as the structure of individual disparate treatment law with . . . *Hicks* and *Hazen Paper* in 1993, the Court has only revisited this area of the law in O'Connor v. Consolidated Coin Caterers Corp. in 1996 and *Reeves* in 2000. Both of these decisions reined in lower courts that were narrowing the *McDonnell Douglas* wing of individual disparate treatment law even further than the Court had in *Hicks* and *Hazen*. It may be too much to expect that the Supreme Court has the capacity to make sure that its deeper vision of individual disparate treatment law will be fully implemented by the lower courts." Id. at 602-03. Nevertheless, more individual disparate treatment cases will probably go to juries because of *Reeves*. Charles F. Thompson, Jr., Juries Will Decide More Discrimination Cases: An Examination of *Reeves v. Sanderson Plumbing Products, Inc.*, 26 Vt. L. Rev. 1 (2001) (includes history leading up to *Reeves*). See also Leland Ware, Inferring Intent from Proof of Pretext: Resolving the Summary Judgment Confusion in Employment Discrimination Cases Alleging Disparate Treatment, 4 Emp. Rts. & Employ. Pol'y J. 37 (2000), for an excellent discussion of the relation of general summary judgment jurisprudence and how disparate treatment cases work in that system.

21. Recall our hypothetical about *Patterson*: defendant claims that plaintiff was not promoted because she was less educated than the successful whites, and plaintiff establishes that she has a college degree, while her successful competitors did not. *Hicks* and *Reeves* clearly permit the defendant to prevail if the trier of fact believes that defendant had made an honest mistake. Even if *Hicks* and *Reeves* had not been decided as they were, could it be argued that the issue was not whether plaintiff was, in fact, more qualified than the successful competitor, but rather whether the defendant truly believed she was? See Waggoner v. Garland, 987 F.2d 1160 (5th Cir. 1993) (irrelevant whether plaintiff was innocent of sexual harassment charges; employer could not be guilty of age discrimination if it in good faith believed the charges were true). Proving that the reason is incorrect does not necessarily establish that it was not the real reason. See Kralman v. Illinois Dept. of Veteran' Affairs, 23 F.3d 150 (7th Cir. 1994) (defendant mistakenly believed it had to give priority in rehiring to a disabled veteran over the plaintiff).

## D.  DIRECT EVIDENCE OF DISCRIMINATORY INTENT

### PRICE WATERHOUSE v. HOPKINS
#### 490 U.S. 228 (1989)

Justice BRENNAN announced the judgment of the Court and delivered an opinion, in which Justice MARSHALL, Justice BLACKMUN, and Justice STEVENS join. . . .

. . . At Price Waterhouse, a nationwide professional accounting partnership, a senior manager becomes a candidate for partnership when the partners in her local office submit her name as a candidate. All of the other partners in the firm are then invited to submit written comments on each candidate — either on a "long" or a "short" form, depending on the partner's degree of exposure to the candidate. Not every partner in the firm submits comments on every candidate. After reviewing the comments and interviewing the partners who submitted them, the firm's Admissions Committee makes a recommendation to the Policy Board. This recommendation will be either that the firm accept the candidate for partnership, put her application on "hold," or deny her the promotion outright. The Policy Board then decides whether to submit the candidate's name to the entire partnership for a vote, to "hold" her candidacy, or to reject her. The recommendation of the Admissions Committee, and the decision of the Policy Board, are not controlled by fixed guidelines: a certain number of positive comments from partners will not guarantee a candidate's admission to the partnership, nor will a specific quantity of negative comments necessarily defeat her application. Price Waterhouse places no limit on the number of persons whom it will admit to the partnership in any given year.

Ann Hopkins had worked at Price Waterhouse's Office of Government Services in Washington, D.C., for five years when the partners in that office proposed her as a candidate for partnership. Of the 662 partners at the firm at that time, 7 were women. Of the 88 persons proposed for partnership that year, only 1 — Hopkins — was a woman. Forty-seven of these candidates were admitted to the partnership, 21 were rejected, and 20 — including Hopkins — were "held" for reconsideration the following year. Thirteen of the 32 partners who had submitted comments on Hopkins supported her bid for partnership. Three partners recommended that her candidacy be placed on hold, eight stated that they did not have an informed opinion about her, and eight recommended that she be denied partnership.

In a jointly prepared statement supporting her candidacy, the partners in Hopkins' office showcased her successful 2-year effort to secure a $25 million contract with the Department of State, labeling it "an outstanding performance" and one that Hopkins carried out "virtually at the partner level." Despite Price Waterhouse's attempt at trial to minimize her contribution to this project, Judge Gesell specifically found that Hopkins had "played a key role in Price Waterhouse's successful effort to win a multimillion dollar contract with the Department of State." Indeed, he went on, "[n]one of the other partnership candidates at Price Waterhouse that year had a comparable record in terms of successfully securing major contracts for the partnership."

The partners in Hopkins' office praised her character as well as her accomplishments, describing her in their joint statement as "an outstanding professional" who had a "deft touch," a "strong character, independence and integrity." Clients appear to have agreed with these assessments. At trial, one official from the State Department described her as "extremely competent, intelligent," "strong and forthright, very productive, energetic and creative." Another high-ranking official praised Hopkins' decisiveness, broadmindedness, and "intellectual clarity"; she was, in his words, "a stimulating conversationalist." Evaluations such as these led Judge Gesell to conclude that Hopkins "had no difficulty dealing with clients and her clients appear to have been very pleased with her work" and that she "was generally viewed as a highly competent project leader who worked long hours, pushed vigorously to meet deadlines and demanded much from the multidisciplinary staffs with which she worked."

On too many occasions, however, Hopkins' aggressiveness apparently spilled over into abrasiveness. Staff members seem to have borne the brunt of Hopkins' brusqueness. Long before her bid for partnership, partners evaluating her work had counseled her to improve her relations with staff members. Although later evaluations indicate an improvement, Hopkins' perceived shortcomings in this important area eventually doomed her bid for partnership. Virtually all of the partners' negative remarks about Hopkins — even those of partners supporting her — had to do with her "interpersonal skills." Both "[s]upporters and opponents of her candidacy," stressed Judge Gesell, "indicated that she was sometimes overly aggressive, unduly harsh, difficult to work with and impatient with staff."

There were clear signs, though, that some of the partners reacted negatively to Hopkins' personality because she was a woman. One partner described her as "macho"; another suggested that she "overcompensated for being a woman"; a third advised her to take "a course at charm school." Several partners criticized her use of profanity; in response, one partner suggested that those partners objected to her swearing only "because it[']s a lady using foul language." Another supporter explained that Hopkins "ha[d] matured from a tough-talking somewhat masculine hard-nosed mgr to an authoritative, formidable, but much more appealing lady ptr candidate." But it was the man who, as Judge Gesell found, bore responsibility for explaining to Hopkins the reasons for the Policy Board's decision to place her candidacy on hold who delivered the coup de grace: in order to improve her chances for partnership, Thomas Beyer advised, Hopkins should "walk more femininely, talk more femininely, dress more femininely, wear make-up, have her hair styled, and wear jewelry."

Dr. Susan Fiske, a social psychologist and Associate Professor of Psychology at Carnegie-Mellon University, testified at trial that the partnership selection process at Price Waterhouse was likely influenced by sex stereotyping. Her testimony focused not only on the overtly sex-based comments of partners but also on gender-neutral remarks, made by partners who knew Hopkins only slightly, that were intensely critical of her. One partner, for example, baldly stated that Hopkins was "universally disliked" by staff, and another described her as "consistently annoying and irritating"; yet these were people who had had very little contact with Hopkins. According to Fiske, Hopkins' uniqueness (as the only woman in the pool of candidates) and the subjectivity of the evaluations made it likely that sharply critical remarks such as these were the product of sex stereotyping — although Fiske admitted that she could not say with certainty whether any particular comment was the result of stereotyping. Fiske based her opinion on a review of the submitted comments, explaining that it was commonly accepted practice for social psychologists to reach this kind of conclusion without having met any of the people involved in the decisionmaking process.

In previous years, other female candidates for partnership also had been evaluated in sex-based terms. As a general matter, Judge Gesell concluded, "[c]andidates were viewed favorably if partners believed they maintained their femin[in]ity while becoming effective professional managers"; in this environment, "[t]o be identified as a 'women's lib[b]er' was regarded as [a] negative comment." In fact, the judge found that in previous years "[o]ne partner repeatedly commented that he could not consider any woman seriously as a partnership candidate and believed that women were not even capable of functioning as senior managers — yet the firm took no action to discourage his comments and recorded his vote in the overall summary of the evaluations."

Judge Gesell found that Price Waterhouse legitimately emphasized interpersonal skills in its partnership decisions, and also found that the firm had not fabricated its complaints about Hopkins' interpersonal skills as a pretext for discrimination. Moreover, he concluded, the firm did not give decisive emphasis to such traits only because Hopkins was a woman; although there were male candidates who lacked these skills but who were admitted to partnership, the judge found that these candidates possessed other, positive traits that Hopkins lacked.

The judge went on to decide, however, that some of the partners' remarks about Hopkins stemmed from an impermissibly cabined view of the proper behavior of women, and that Price Waterhouse had done nothing to disavow reliance on such comments. He held that Price Waterhouse had unlawfully discriminated against Hopkins on the basis of sex by consciously giving credence and effect to partners' comments that resulted from sex stereotyping. Noting that Price Waterhouse could avoid equitable relief by proving by clear and convincing evidence that it would have placed Hopkins' candidacy on hold even absent this discrimination, the judge decided that the firm had not carried this heavy burden. . . .

II . . .

In passing Title VII, Congress made the simple but momentous announcement that sex, race, religion, and national origin are not relevant to the selection, evaluation, or compensation of employees.[4] Yet, the statute does not purport to limit the other qualities and characteristics that employers may take into account in making employment decisions. The converse, therefore, of "for cause" legislation, Title VII eliminates certain bases for distinguishing among employees while otherwise preserving employers' freedom of choice. This balance between employee rights and employer prerogatives turns out to be decisive in the case before us.

Congress' intent to forbid employers to take gender into account in making employment decisions appears on the face of the statute. In now-familiar language, the statute forbids an employer to "[discriminate] *because of* such individual's . . . sex." (emphasis added). We take these words to mean that gender must be irrelevant to employment decisions. To construe the words "because of" as colloquial shorthand for "but-for causation," as does Price Waterhouse, is to misunderstand them.

But-for causation is a hypothetical construct. In determining whether a particular factor was a but-for cause of a given event, we begin by assuming that that factor was present at the time of the event, and then ask whether, even if that factor had been absent, the event nevertheless would have transpired in the same way. The present, active tense of the operative verbs of § 703(a)(1) ("to fail or refuse"), in contrast, turns our attention to the actual moment of the event in question, the adverse employment decision. The critical inquiry, the one commanded by the words of § 703(a)(1), is whether gender was a factor in the employment decision *at the moment it was made*. Moreover, since we know that the words "because of" do not mean "solely because of," [8] we also know that Title VII meant to condemn even those decisions based on a

----

4. We disregard, for purposes of this discussion, the special context of affirmative action.

8. Congress specifically rejected an amendment that would have placed the word "solely" in front of the words "because of." 110 Cong. Rec. 2728, 13837 (1964).

mixture of legitimate and illegitimate considerations. When, therefore, an employer considers both gender and legitimate factors at the time of making a decision, that decision was "because of" sex and the other, legitimate considerations — even if we may say later, in the context of litigation, that the decision would have been the same if gender had not been taken into account.

To attribute this meaning to the words "because of" does not, as the dissent asserts, divest them of causal significance. A simple example illustrates the point. Suppose two physical forces act upon and move an object, and suppose that either force acting alone would have moved the object. As the dissent would have it, neither physical force was a "cause" of the motion unless we can show that but for one or both of them, the object would not have moved; to use the dissent's terminology, both forces were simply "in the air" unless we can identify at least one of them as a but-for cause of the object's movement. Events that are causally overdetermined, in other words, may not have any "cause" at all. This cannot be so.

[Congress did not intend to require a plaintiff "to identify the precise causal role played by legitimate and illegitimate motivations"; it meant only to require her "to prove that the employer relied upon sex-based considerations" in its decision.]

To say that an employer may not take gender into account is not, however, the end of the matter, for that describes only one aspect of Title VII. The other important aspect of the statute is its preservation of an employer's remaining freedom of choice. We conclude that the preservation of this freedom means that an employer shall not be liable if it can prove that, even if it had not taken gender into account, it would have come to the same decision regarding a particular person. The statute's maintenance of employer prerogatives is evident from the statute itself and from its history, both in Congress and in this Court. . . .

The central point is this: while an employer may not take gender into account in making an employment decision . . ., it is free to decide against a woman for other reasons. We think these principles require that, once a plaintiff in a Title VII case shows that gender played a motivating part in an employment decision, the defendant may avoid a finding of liability only by proving that it would have made the same decision even if it had not allowed gender to play such a role. This balance of burdens is the direct result of Title VII's balance of rights.

Our holding casts no shadow on *Burdine,* in which we decided that, even after a plaintiff has made out a prima facie case of discrimination under Title VII, the burden of persuasion does not shift to the employer to show that its stated legitimate reason for the employment decision was the true reason. We stress, first, that neither court below shifted the burden of persuasion to Price Waterhouse on this question, and in fact, the District Court found that Hopkins had not shown that the firm's stated reason for its decision was pretextual. Moreover, since we hold that the plaintiff retains the burden of persuasion on the issue whether gender played a part in the employment decision, the situation before us is not the one of "shifting burdens" that we addressed in *Burdine.* Instead, the employer's burden is most appropriately deemed an affirmative defense: the plaintiff must persuade the factfinder on one point, and then the employer, if it wishes to prevail, must persuade it on another. See NLRB v. Transportation Management Corp., 462 U.S. 393 (1983).[12]

12. [Contrary to the dissent, it is] perfectly consistent to say both that gender was a factor in a particular decision when it was made and that, when the situation is viewed hypothetically and after the fact, the same decision would have been made even in the absence of discrimination. . . . [W]here liability is imposed because an employer is unable to prove that it would have made the same decision even if it had not discriminated, this is not an imposition of liability "where sex made no difference to the outcome."

Price Waterhouse's claim that the employer does not bear any burden of proof (if it bears one at all) until the plaintiff has shown "substantial evidence that Price Waterhouse's explanation for failing to promote Hopkins was not the 'true reason' for its action" merely restates its argument that the plaintiff in a mixed-motives case must squeeze her proof into *Burdine*'s framework. Where a decision was the product of a mixture of legitimate and illegitimate motives, however, it simply makes no sense to ask whether the legitimate reason was "the 'true reason'" for the decision — which is the question asked by *Burdine*.[13] . . .

## B

We have reached a similar conclusion in other contexts where the law announces that a certain characteristic is irrelevant to the allocation of burdens and benefits. In Mt. Healthy City School Dist. Board of Education v. Doyle, 429 U.S. 274 (1977), the plaintiff claimed that he had been discharged as a public school teacher for exercising his free-speech rights under the First Amendment. Because we did not wish to "place an employee in a better position as a result of the exercise of constitutionally protected conduct than he would have occupied had he done nothing," we concluded that such an employee "ought not to be able, by engaging in such conduct, to prevent his employer from assessing his performance record and reaching a decision not to rehire on the basis of that record." We therefore held that once the plaintiff had shown that his constitutionally protected speech was a "substantial" or "motivating" factor in the adverse treatment of him by his employer, the employer was obligated to prove "by a preponderance of the evidence that it would have reached the same decision as to [the plaintiff] even in the absence of the protected conduct." A court that finds for a plaintiff under this standard has effectively concluded that an illegitimate motive was a "but-for" cause of the employment decision. See Givhan v. Western Line Consolidated School District, 439 U.S. 410, 417 (1979). . . .

We have, in short, been here before. Each time, we have concluded that the plaintiff who shows that an impermissible motive played a motivating part in an adverse employment decision has thereby placed upon the defendant the burden to show that it would have made the same decision in the absence of the unlawful motive. Our decision today treads this well-worn path.

## C

In saying that gender played a motivating part in an employment decision, we mean that, if we asked the employer at the moment of the decision what its reasons were and if we received a truthful response, one of those reasons would be that the

---

In our adversary system, where a party has the burden of proving a particular assertion and where that party is unable to meet its burden, we assume that that assertion is inaccurate. Thus, where an employer is unable to prove its claim that it would have made the same decision in the absence of discrimination, we are entitled to conclude that gender did make a difference to the outcome.

13. [A case need not be labelled either a "pretext" case or a "mixed motives" case from the beginning; plaintiffs often will allege both. At some point, however, the district court must decide whether mixed motives are involved.] If the plaintiff fails to satisfy the factfinder that it is more likely than not that a forbidden characteristic played a part in the employment decision, then she may prevail only if she proves, following *Burdine*, that the employer's stated reason for its decision is pretextual. The dissent need not worry that this evidentiary scheme, if used during a jury trial, will be so impossibly confused and complex as it imagines. Juries long have decided cases in which defendants raise affirmative defenses. . . .

applicant or employee was a woman. In the specific context of sex stereotyping, an employer who acts on the basis of a belief that a woman cannot be aggressive, or that she must not be, has acted on the basis of gender.

. . . As to the existence of sex stereotyping in this case, we are not inclined to quarrel with the District Court's conclusion that a number of the partners' comments showed sex stereotyping at work. As for the legal relevance of sex stereotyping, we are beyond the day when an employer could evaluate employees by assuming or insisting that they matched the stereotype associated with their group. . . . An employer who objects to aggressiveness in women but whose positions require this trait places women in an intolerable and impermissible Catch-22: out of a job if they behave aggressively and out of a job if they don't. Title VII lifts women out of this bind.

Remarks at work that are based on sex stereotypes do not inevitably prove that gender played a part in a particular employment decision. The plaintiff must show that the employer actually relied on her gender in making its decision. In making this showing, stereotyped remarks can certainly be evidence that gender played a part. In any event, the stereotyping in this case did not simply consist of stray remarks. On the contrary, Hopkins proved that Price Waterhouse invited partners to submit comments; that some of the comments stemmed from sex stereotypes; that an important part of the Policy Board's decision on Hopkins was an assessment of the submitted comments; and that Price Waterhouse in no way disclaimed reliance on the sex-linked evaluations. This is not, as Price Waterhouse suggests, "discrimination in the air"; rather, it is, as Hopkins puts it, "discrimination brought to ground and visited upon" an employee. By focusing on Hopkins' specific proof, however, we do not suggest a limitation on the possible ways of proving that stereotyping played a motivating role in an employment decision, and we refrain from deciding here which specific facts, "standing alone," would or would not establish a plaintiff's case, since such a decision is unnecessary in this case. But see [O'Connor, J., at page 159, concurring in the judgment].

As to the employer's proof, in most cases, the employer should be able to present some objective evidence as to its probable decision in the absence of an impermissible motive.[15] Moreover, proving "that the same decision would have been justified . . . is not the same as proving that the same decision would have been made." An employer may not, in other words, prevail in a mixed-motives case by offering a legitimate and sufficient reason for its decision if that reason did not motivate it at the time of the decision. Finally, an employer may not meet its burden in such a case by merely showing that at the time of the decision it was motivated only in part by a legitimate reason. The very premise of a mixed-motives case is that a legitimate reason was present, and indeed, in this case, Price Waterhouse already has made this showing by convincing Judge Gesell that Hopkins' interpersonal problems were a legitimate concern. The employer instead must show that its legitimate reason, standing alone, would have induced it to make the same decision.

## III

The courts below held that an employer who has allowed a discriminatory impulse to play a motivating part in an employment decision must prove by clear and

15. Justice White's suggestion that the employer's own testimony as to the probable decision in the absence of discrimination is due special credence where the court has, contrary to the employer's testimony, found that an illegitimate factor played a part in the decision, is baffling.

convincing evidence that it would have made the same decision in the absence of discrimination. We are persuaded that the better rule is that the employer must make this showing by a preponderance of the evidence. . . .

## IV

[Price Waterhouse challenges as clearly erroneous the district court's findings both that stereotyping occurred and that it played any part in the decision to place Hopkins' candidacy on hold. The plurality disagreed.]

In finding that some of the partners' comments reflected sex stereotyping, the District Court relied in part on Dr. Fiske's expert testimony. Without directly impugning Dr. Fiske's credentials or qualifications, Price Waterhouse insinuates that a social psychologist is unable to identify sex stereotyping in evaluations without investigating whether those evaluations have a basis in reality. This argument comes too late. At trial, counsel for Price Waterhouse twice assured the court that he did not question Dr. Fiske's expertise and failed to challenge the legitimacy of her discipline. Without contradiction from Price Waterhouse, Fiske testified that she discerned sex stereotyping in the partners' evaluations of Hopkins and she further explained that it was part of her business to identify stereotyping in written documents. We are not inclined to accept petitioner's belated and unsubstantiated characterization of Dr. Fiske's testimony as "gossamer evidence" based only on "intuitive hunches" and of her detection of sex stereotyping as "intuitively divined." Nor are we disposed to adopt the dissent's dismissive attitude toward Dr. Fiske's field of study and toward her own professional integrity.

Indeed, we are tempted to say that Dr. Fiske's expert testimony was merely icing on Hopkins' cake. It takes no special training to discern sex stereotyping in a description of an aggressive female employee as requiring "a course at charm school." Nor, turning to Thomas Beyer's memorable advice to Hopkins, does it require expertise in psychology to know that, if an employee's flawed "interpersonal skills" can be corrected by a soft-hued suit or a new shade of lipstick, perhaps it is the employee's sex and not her interpersonal skills that has drawn the criticism.

Price Waterhouse also charges that Hopkins produced no evidence that sex stereotyping played a role in the decision to place her candidacy on hold. As we have stressed, however, Hopkins showed that the partnership solicited evaluations from all of the firm's partners; that it generally relied very heavily on such evaluations in making its decision; that some of the partners' comments were the product of stereotyping; and that the firm in no way disclaimed reliance on those particular comments, either in Hopkins' case or in the past. Certainly a plausible — and, one might say, inevitable — conclusion to draw from this set of circumstances is that the Policy Board in making its decision did in fact take into account all of the partners' comments, including the comments that were motivated by stereotypical notions about women's proper deportment. . . .

Nor is the finding that sex stereotyping played a part in the Policy Board's decision undermined by the fact that many of the suspect comments were made by supporters rather than detractors of Hopkins. A negative comment, even when made in the context of a generally favorable review, nevertheless may influence the decisionmaker to think less highly of the candidate. . . . The additional suggestion that the comments were made by "persons outside the decisionmaking chain" — and therefore could not have harmed Hopkins — simply ignores the critical role that partners' comments played in the Policy Board's partnership decisions.

Price Waterhouse appears to think that we cannot affirm the factual findings of the trial court without deciding that, instead of being overbearing and aggressive and curt, Hopkins is in fact kind and considerate and patient. If this is indeed its impression, petitioner misunderstands the theory on which Hopkins prevailed. The District Judge acknowledged that Hopkins' conduct justified complaints about her behavior as a senior manager. But he also concluded that the reactions of at least some of the partners were reactions to her as a woman manager. Where an evaluation is based on a subjective assessment of a person's strengths and weaknesses, it is simply not true that each evaluator will focus on, or even mention, the same weaknesses. Thus, even if we knew that Hopkins had "personality problems," this would not tell us that the partners who cast their evaluations of Hopkins in sex-based terms would have criticized her as sharply (or criticized her at all) if she had been a man. It is not our job to review the evidence and decide that the negative reactions to Hopkins were based on reality; our perception of Hopkins' character is irrelevant. We sit not to determine whether Ms. Hopkins is nice, but to decide whether the partners reacted negatively to her personality because she is a woman.

V

We hold that when a plaintiff in a Title VII case proves that her gender played a motivating part in an employment decision, the defendant may avoid a finding of liability only by proving by a preponderance of the evidence that it would have made the same decision even if it had not taken the plaintiff's gender into account. . . .

Justice WHITE, concurring in the judgment.

In my view, to determine the proper approach to causation in this case, we need look only to the Court's opinion in Mt. Healthy City School District Board of Education v. Doyle. . . .

It is not necessary to get into semantic discussions on whether the *Mt. Healthy* approach is "but for" causation in another guise or creates an affirmative defense on the part of the employer to see its clear application to the issues before us in this case. As in *Mt. Healthy*, the District Court found that the employer was motivated by both legitimate and illegitimate factors. And here, as in *Mt. Healthy*, and as the Court now holds, Hopkins was not required to prove that the illegitimate factor was the only, principal, or true reason for the petitioner's action. Rather, as Justice O'Connor states, her burden was to show that the unlawful motive was a substantial factor in the adverse employment action. . . .

[As for the employer's burden,] the plurality seems to require, at least in most cases, that the employer submit objective evidence that the same result would have occurred absent the unlawful motivation. In my view, however, there is no special requirement that the employer carry its burden by objective evidence. In a mixed motive case, where the legitimate motive found would have been ample grounds for the action taken, and the employer credibly testifies that the action would have been taken for the legitimate reasons alone, this should be ample proof. This would even more plainly be the case where the employer denies any illegitimate motive in the first place but the court finds that illegitimate, as well as legitimate, factors motivated the adverse action.

Justice O'CONNOR, concurring in the judgment.

I agree with the plurality that on the facts presented in this case, the burden of persuasion should shift to the employer to demonstrate by a preponderance of the evidence that it would have reached the same decision concerning Ann Hopkins' candidacy absent consideration of her gender. I further agree that this burden shift is properly part of the liability phase of the litigation. I thus concur in the judgment of the Court. My disagreement stems from the plurality's conclusions concerning the substantive requirement of causation under the statute and its broad statements regarding the applicability of the allocation of the burden of proof applied in this case. . . .

## I

. . . The legislative history of Title VII bears out what its plain language suggests: a substantive violation of the statute only occurs when consideration of an illegitimate criterion is the "but-for" cause of an adverse employment action. The legislative history makes it clear that Congress was attempting to eradicate discriminatory actions in the employment setting, not mere discriminatory thoughts. Critics of the bill that became Title VII labeled it a "thought control bill," and argued that it created a "punishable crime that does not require an illegal external act as a basis for judgment." Senator Case . . . responded:

> The man must do or fail to do something in regard to employment. There must be some specific external act, more than a mental act. Only if he does the act because of the grounds stated in the bill would there be any legal consequences.

Thus, I disagree with the plurality's dictum that the words "because of" do not mean "but-for" causation; manifestly they do. We should not, and need not, deviate from that policy today. . . .

The evidence of congressional intent as to which party should bear the burden of proof on the issue of causation is considerably less clear. . . . [In the area of tort liability,] the law has long recognized that in certain "civil cases" leaving the burden of persuasion on the plaintiff to prove "but-for" causation would be both unfair and destructive of the deterrent purposes embodied in the concept of duty of care. Thus, in multiple causation cases, where a breach of duty has been established, the common law of torts has long shifted the burden of proof to multiple defendants to prove that their negligent actions were not the "but-for" cause of the plaintiff's injury. See, e.g., Summers v. Tice, 33 Cal. 2d 80, 199 P.2d 1 (1948). The same rule has been applied where the effect of a defendant's tortious conduct combines with a force of unknown or innocent origin to produce the harm to the plaintiff. See Kingston v. Chicago & N.W.R. Co., 191 Wis. 610, 616, 211 N.W. 913, 915 (1927). . . . See also 2 J. Wigmore, Select Cases on the Law of Torts, § 153, p. 865 (1912). . . .

[At times, however, the but-for] "test demands the impossible. It challenges the imagination of the trier to probe into a purely fanciful and unknowable state of affairs. He is invited to make an estimate concerning facts that concededly never existed. The very uncertainty as to what might have happened opens the door wide for conjecture. But when conjecture is demanded it can be given a direction that is consistent with the policy considerations that underlie the controversy."

. . . There is no doubt that Congress considered reliance on gender or race in making employment decisions an evil in itself. . . . Reliance on such factors is exactly what the threat of Title VII liability was meant to deter. While the main concern of the statute was with employment opportunity, Congress was certainly not blind to the stigmatic harm which comes from being evaluated by a process which treats one as an inferior by reason of one's race or sex. . . . At the same time, Congress clearly conditioned legal liability on a determination that the consideration of an illegitimate factor caused a tangible employment injury of some kind.

Where an individual disparate treatment plaintiff has shown by a preponderance of the evidence that an illegitimate criterion was a *substantial* factor in an adverse employment decision, the deterrent purpose of the statute has clearly been triggered. More importantly, as an evidentiary matter, a reasonable factfinder could conclude that absent further explanation, the employer's discriminatory motivation "caused" the employment decision. The employer has not yet been shown to be a violator, but neither is it entitled to the same presumption of good faith concerning its employment decisions which is accorded employers facing only circumstantial evidence of discrimination. Both the policies behind the statute, and the evidentiary principles developed in the analogous area of causation in the law of torts, suggest that at this point the employer may be required to convince the factfinder that, despite the smoke, there is no fire. . . .

## II

. . . *McDonnell Douglas* and *Burdine* assumed that the plaintiff would bear the burden of persuasion as to both these attacks, and we clearly depart from that framework today. Such a departure requires justification, and its outlines should be carefully drawn.

First, *McDonnell Douglas* itself dealt with a situation where the plaintiff presented no direct evidence that the employer had relied on a forbidden factor under Title VII in making an employment decision. . . . I do not think that the employer is entitled to the same presumption of good faith where there is direct evidence that it has placed substantial reliance on factors whose consideration is forbidden by Title VII. . . .

[T]he entire purpose of the *McDonnell Douglas* prima facie case is to compensate for the fact that direct evidence of intentional discrimination is hard to come by. That the employer's burden in rebutting such an inferential case of discrimination is only one of production does not mean that the scales should be weighted in the same manner where there is direct evidence of intentional discrimination. . . .

Second, the facts of this case, and a growing number like it decided by the Courts of Appeals, convince me that the evidentiary standard I propose is necessary to make real the promise of *McDonnell Douglas*. . . . As the Court of Appeals characterized it, Ann Hopkins proved that Price Waterhouse "permitt[ed] stereotypical attitudes towards women to play a significant, though unquantifiable, role in its decision not to invite her to become a partner."

At this point Ann Hopkins had taken her proof as far as it could go. She had proved discriminatory input into the decisional process, and had proved that participants in the process considered her failure to conform to the stereotypes credited by a number of the decisionmakers had been a substantial factor in the decision. It is as if Ann Hopkins were sitting in the hall outside the room where partnership decisions were being made. As the partners filed in to consider her candidacy, she heard several of them make sexist remarks in discussing her suitability for partnership. As the decisionmakers exited the room, she was told by one of those privy to the decisionmaking process that her gender was a major reason for the rejection of her partnership bid. [If "presumptions] shifting the burden of proof are often created to reflect judicial evaluations of probabilities and to conform with a party's superior access to the proof," one would be hard pressed to think of a situation where it would be more appropriate to require the defendant to show that its decision would have been justified by wholly legitimate concerns. . . .

[The plurality, however, goes too far by holding that the burden shifts when "a decisional process is 'tainted' by awareness of sex or race in any way."]

In my view, in order to justify shifting the burden on the issue of causation to the defendant, a disparate treatment plaintiff must show by direct evidence that an illegitimate criterion was a substantial factor in the decision. . . . Requiring that the plaintiff demonstrate that an illegitimate factor played a substantial role in the employment decision identifies those employment situations where the deterrent purpose of Title VII is most clearly implicated. As an evidentiary matter, where a plaintiff has made this type of strong showing of illicit motivation, the factfinder is entitled to presume that the employer's discriminatory animus made a difference to the outcome, absent proof to the contrary from the employer. Where a disparate treatment plaintiff has made such a showing, the burden then rests with the employer to convince the trier of fact that it is more likely than not that the decision would have been the same absent consideration of the illegitimate factor. The employer need not isolate the sole cause for the decision; rather it must demonstrate that with the illegitimate factor removed from the calculus, sufficient business reasons would have induced it to take the same employment action. This evidentiary scheme essentially requires the employer to place the employee in the same position he or she would have occupied absent discrimination. Cf. Mt. Healthy Board of Education v. Doyle. If the employer fails to carry this burden, the factfinder is justified in concluding that the decision was made "because of" consideration of the illegitimate factor and the substantive standard for liability under the statute is satisfied.

Thus, stray remarks in the workplace, while perhaps probative of sexual harassment, see Meritor Savings Bank v. Vinson, 477 U.S. 57 (1986), cannot justify requiring the employer to prove that its hiring or promotion decisions were based on legitimate criteria. Nor can statements by nondecisionmakers, or statements by decisionmakers unrelated to the decisional process itself suffice to satisfy the plaintiff's burden in this regard. In addition, in my view testimony such as Dr. Fiske's in this case, standing alone, would not justify shifting the burden of persuasion to the employer. Race and gender always "play a role" in an employment decision in the benign sense that these are human characteristics of which decisionmakers are aware and may comment on in a perfectly neutral and nondiscriminatory fashion. For example, in the context of this case, a mere reference to "a lady candidate" might show that gender "played a role" in the decision, but by no means could support a rational factfinder's inference that the decision was made "because of" sex. What is required is what Ann Hopkins showed here: direct evidence that decisionmakers placed substantial negative reliance on an illegitimate criterion in reaching their decision.

It should be obvious that the threshold standard I would adopt for shifting the burden of persuasion to the defendant differs substantially from that proposed by the plurality, the plurality's suggestion to the contrary notwithstanding. . . . Under my approach, the plaintiff must produce evidence sufficient to show that an illegitimate criterion was a substantial factor in the particular employment decision such that a reasonable factfinder could draw an inference that the decision was made "because of" the plaintiff's protected status. Only then would the burden of proof shift to the defendant to prove that the decision would have been justified by other, wholly legitimate considerations. See also [White, J., at page 159, concurring in the judgment].

In sum, . . . I would retain but supplement the framework we established in *McDonnell Douglas* and subsequent cases. The structure of the presentation of evidence in an individual treatment case should conform to the general outlines we established in *McDonnell Douglas* and *Burdine*. First, the plaintiff must establish the *McDonnell Douglas* prima facie case by showing membership in a protected group, qualification for the job, rejection for the position, and that after rejection the employer continued to seek applicants of complainant's general qualifications. The plaintiff should also present any direct evidence of discriminatory animus in the decisional process. The defendant should then present its case, including its evidence as to legitimate, nondiscriminatory reasons for the employment decision. . . . Once all the evidence has been received, the court should determine whether the *McDonnell Douglas* or *Price Waterhouse* framework properly applies to the evidence before it. If the plaintiff has failed to satisfy the *Price Waterhouse* threshold, the case should be decided under the principles enunciated in *McDonnell Douglas* and *Burdine*, with the plaintiff bearing the burden of persuasion on the ultimate issue whether the employment action was taken because of discrimination. . . .

I agree with the dissent, that the evidentiary framework I propose should be available to all disparate treatment plaintiffs where an illegitimate consideration played a substantial role in an adverse employment decision. The Court's allocation of the burden of proof in Johnson v. Transportation Agency, 480 U.S. 616 (1987), rested squarely on "the analytical framework set forth in *McDonnell Douglas*," which we alter today. It would be odd to say the least if the evidentiary rules applicable to Title VII actions were themselves dependent on the gender or the skin color of the litigants. . . .

[Justice KENNEDY, joined by Chief Justice REHNQUIST and Justice SCALIA, dissented. The dissent viewed the plurality, despite its rhetoric, as adopting a but-for standard. "Labels aside, the import of today's decision is not that Title VII liability can arise without but-for causation, but that in certain cases it is not the plaintiff who must prove the presence of causation, but the defendant who must prove its absence."

The dissent was particularly critical of Dr. Fiske: she "purported to discern stereotyping in comments that were gender neutral — e.g., 'overbearing and abrasive' — without any knowledge of the comments' basis in reality and without having met the speaker or subject." It quoted a judge below to the effect that, "[t]o an expert of Dr. Fiske's qualifications, it seems plain that no woman could be overbearing, arrogant, or abrasive: any observations to that effect would necessarily be discounted as the product of stereotyping. If analysis like this is to prevail in federal courts, no employer can base any adverse action as to a woman on such attributes."]

*NOTES*

1. Are *Price Waterhouse* and *McDonnell Douglas/Burdine* separate theories of individual disparate treatment discrimination or merely parts of a unitary theory? The *Price Waterhouse* plurality describes the "same decision" issue as an affirmative defense, which would support the idea of a unitary theory. If they are simply parts in a unitary theory of individual disparate treatment discrimination, however, how do you account for the use by the plurality of the term "pretext" to describe one case and "mixed motive" to describe the other? The answer is complicated because Justice Brennan speaks only for a plurality; the holding of the case is determined by joining either Justice O'Connor's or Justice White's opinion to the plurality to form a majority.

2. Justice O'Connor stresses the need for "direct" evidence of intent to discriminate. Neither Justice White nor the plurality focuses on this. Is "direct evidence" necessary for a *Price Waterhouse* case, or do five justices permit such a case even in the absence of direct evidence?

3. What is "direct evidence" anyway? If the term means anything, it refers to evidence that, if believed, would establish a fact at issue without the need to draw any inferences. In disparate treatment cases, the fact at issue is discriminatory intent. An evidence purist would say that there can be no direct evidence of the state of mind of a person because intent is internal and cannot be directly observed. See generally Charles A. Sullivan, Accounting for *Price Waterhouse:* Proving Disparate Treatment Under Title VII, 56 Brook. L. Rev. 1107 (1991). As used by Justice O'Connor, "direct evidence" would seem to require a statement by the decision-maker that showed he was motivated by illegitimate considerations with respect to the at-issue decision.

4. Analytically, this raises at least three questions. First, what did the decision-maker actually say? The decision-maker may, of course, testify as to his reasons. But testimony of out-of-court statements will be allowed even if the party allegedly making the statement now denies that he did so. In such case, the factfinder must first decide if the admission was actually made. See EEOC v. Alton Packaging Corp., 901 F.2d 920 (11th Cir. 1990).

5. Second, does the comment reflect illegitimate considerations? As Justice O'Connor noted, some statements may refer to a candidate purely descriptively: "the candidate is a woman who. . . ." In the ADEA context, see Montgomery v. John Deere & Co., 169 F.3d 556 (8th Cir. 1999) (plaintiff's being continually referred to as an "old fart" and being repeatedly asked whether he was going to take retirement not sufficient to create a direct evidence case); Thomas v. Sears, Roebuck & Co., 144 F.3d 31, 34 (1st Cir. 1998) ("Plaintiff in fact agreed that at least part of the motivation to select him for layoff was his disagreement with the company's change in business philosophy. Under such circumstances, a criticism that someone is unable to change is not a coded allusion cloaking age discrimination."). Other remarks may be complimentary. Still other comments may be pejorative, but lack a connection to a prohibited ground. For example, a manager who said that he did not like plaintiff's "type" might have been referring to plaintiff's race, but the remark was found too ambiguous on its face to have much value. Smith v. Firestone Tire & Rubber Co., 875 F.2d 1325 (7th Cir. 1989). Suppose an employer asks a female candidate questions about her family obligations that he does not ask of her male competitor. If he gets the position, does she have a *Price Waterhouse* case? Heather K. Gerken, Note, Understanding Mixed Motive Claims Under the Civil Rights Act of 1991: An Analysis of Intentional Discrimination Claims Based on Sex-Stereotyped Interview Questions, 91 Mich. L. Rev. 1824 (1993).

What about a comment that is taken as racial, but not intended as such? Debate broke out several years ago after Washington, D.C.'s ombudsman, David Howard, used the word "niggardly" in a budget discussion. The word, which means miserly or stingy, has Scandinavian origins, with no racial overtones or linguistic link to the racial slur it sounds like. Howard's use of the word, however, offended a black colleague, causing him to storm out of the room before an explanation of the word's meaning could be given. Mr. Howard immediately resigned from his position. Some criticized the mayor's hasty acceptance of Mr. Howard's resignation, viewing it as censorship of language based on other people's lack of understanding. But others applauded the mayor's decision, urging heightened sensitivity in race relations. Melinda Henneberger, Race Mix-Up Raises Havoc for Capital, N.Y. Times, Jan. 29, 1999, at

A10. Ultimately, the mayor asked Mr. Howard to return to his job; Howard accepted the offer to return, but requested a different assignment. Michael Janofsky, In a Word, Return, N.Y. Times, Feb. 7, 1999, http://nytimes.com. Mr. Howard reported that he learned the word "niggardly" studying for his S.A.T. test during high school.

As this incident illustrates, words can cause offense, regardless of the speaker's intent or the technical meaning of the word. Could the mere use of such a word be evidence of discriminatory intent under *Price Waterhouse?* Of course, the defendant would have an opportunity to explain what it meant, and presumably would escape any liability under *Price Waterhouse* if the factfinder concluded that the speaker did not have a racial meaning in mind. Or is the use of a word that might cause offense objectionable, regardless of the speaker's intent? Some have argued that, because "niggardly" sounds too much like the racial slur "nigger," it should not be used, regardless of its literal correctness. In practice, this would require a heightened sensitivity to word usage and possible unintended racial connotations. It might also mean inferring discriminatory intent from knowing use of words others find offensive, whether or not they were "reasonable" in taking offense. Others respond that "heightened sensitivity" is just another term for censorship. If some people's "hyper-sensitivity" forces others to change their speech, conversation will be impeded, and communication will be impaired. If this occurs only with a handful of phrases, the problems are minor; but many other phrases and terms were raised during the Howard debate as possibly causing offense to African Americans or other ethnic groups, including "spade" (as in, "to call a spade a spade"), "tarbaby," "denigrate," "spic and span," and "blackmail." The same argument applies to words with gender or sexual orientation connotations. "Fairy," "queen," "fag," and "queer" all connote both sexual orientation and far different meanings. As for gender itself, there are a myriad of words which could cause offense, depending on the meaning intended by the speaker or heard by the listener. See generally Randall Kennedy, Nigger: The Strange Career of a Troublesome Word 119-23 (2002).

6. Whether words have a particular meaning merges with the third issue of whether the speaker meant what he said. The fact that a statement is made is not determinative: the speaker might have been joking or have misspoken himself. An example comes from Scott Turow's Presumed Innocent. When the protagonist, Rusty Savitch, is confronted with a charge of murder, he replies sarcastically, "Yeah, you're right. I did it." Putting aside aspects peculiar to criminal cases, this evidence would be admissible, but would scarcely be determinative of Savitch's guilt. The jury would still have to decide whether Savitch meant what he said.

Lest one think that fiction is stranger than truth, a bizarre Title VII case illustrates the point that a speaker may not mean what he says. In Gray v. University of Arkansas, 883 F.2d 1394 (8th Cir. 1989), the plaintiff introduced tape recordings of conversations with her supervisor, Dr. Farrell, who told her that the coach of the Razorback football team wanted to replace her with a man: "He wanted somebody to go up there [the athletes' dormitory] and jack em [the players] out of bed and that's all he ever said." Id. at 1399. The district court gave little weight to what was said by Farrell because he was suffering under a mental illness at the time, ultimately committing suicide.

7. In Lim v. Trustees of Indiana Univ., 297 F.3d 575, 579 (7th Cir. 2002), the University president wrote a letter to the Director of the Office for Women of IU, stating, "Your point, for example, of the tenure decision of Soo-Siang Li [sic] Anatomy, as an instance of continued unfairness in the treatment of women in the Medical School is well taken . . . the problems are so entrenched in the culture of the University, and

especially in such disciplines of Medicine, change proved difficult to effect." Up-holding summary judgment for the University, the Seventh Circuit found the letter not to be direct evidence of discrimination. "One possible interpretation of these comments [as an admission of discriminatory intent] is not enough to transform them into direct evidence of discrimination." Id. at 580. Direct evidence, said the court, must prove the fact without inference or interpretation.

8. The circuits have a range of definitions of what constitutes "direct evidence." Some lower courts have purported to follow Justice O'Connor's view, but have given the term "direct evidence" a broader reading than Justice O'Connor might desire. Other courts have explicitly applied *Price Waterhouse* to situations involving admit-tedly circumstantial evidence. In Ostrowski v. Atlantic Mutual Insurance Cos., 968 F.2d 171, 182 (2d Cir. 1992), the court found that either "direct" or "circumstantial" evidence could be used in a *Price Waterhouse* case, but not all evidence admissible in a *McDonnell Douglas/Burdine* case would suffice:

> We would emphasize here that though sufficient proof that the forbidden factor played a "motivating role" to entitle the plaintiff to a burden-shifting instruction may be fur-nished through circumstantial evidence, that circumstantial evidence must be tied directly to the alleged discriminatory animus. For example, purely statistical evidence would not warrant such a charge; nor would evidence merely of the plaintiff's quali-fication for and the availability of a given position; nor would "stray" remarks in the work-place by persons who are not involved in the pertinent decision-making process. Those categories of evidence, though they may suffice to present a prima facie case under the framework set forth in *McDonnell Douglas/Burdine* and may indeed persuade the fact-finder that the plaintiff has carried his or her ultimate burden of persuasion, see gener-ally *Price Waterhouse* [footnote 12 of the plurality opinion], would not suffice, even if credited, to warrant a *Price Waterhouse* charge. If, however, the plaintiff's nonstatistical evidence is directly tied to the forbidden animus, for example policy documents or state-ments of a person involved in the decision-making process that reflect a discriminatory or retaliatory animus of the type complained of in the suit, that plaintiff is entitled to a burden-shifting instruction.

Accord, Griffiths v. CIGNA Corp., 988 F.2d 457, 470 (3d Cir. 1993).

Is this test better described as "direct or very good circumstantial evidence"? Deneen v. Northwest Airlines, 132 F.3d 431, 436 (8th Cir. 1998), affirmed a jury ver-dict that defendant had engaged in pregnancy discrimination. The court found that plaintiff "presented direct evidence of discrimination" when she showed that her su-pervisor refused to allow her to return to work from layoff status without a note from her physician because of her pregnancy-related condition, even though the supervi-sor never referred explicitly to plaintiff's pregnancy. In Thomas v. National Football League Players Assn., 131 F.3d 198, 204 (D.C. Cir. 1997), the court described Justice O'Connor's use of the term "direct" evidence as including circumstantial evidence:

> In our view, Justice O'Connor's invocation of "direct" evidence is not intended to dis-qualify circumstantial evidence nor to require that the evidence signify without infer-ence. In context, the notion of "direct" evidence in Justice O'Connor's concurrence means only that the evidence marshaled in support of the substantiality of the discrimi-natory motive must actually relate to the question of discrimination in the particular employment decision, not to the mere existence of other, potentially unrelated, forms of discrimination in the workplace.

See generally Robert Belton, Mixed-Motive Cases in Employment Discrimination Law Revisited: A Brief Updated View of the Swamp, 51 Mercer L. Rev. 651 (2000).

9. Other cases have tended to read *Price Waterhouse* as applying only when "direct evidence," in the classic evidentiary sense of the term, that the evidence proves the fact at issue without need to draw any inferences, e.g., Randle v. La Salle Telecommunications, Inc., 876 F.2d 563 (7th Cir. 1989); Holland v. Jefferson National Life Ins. Co., 883 F.2d 1307 (7th Cir. 1989); Fuller v. Phipps, 67 F.3d 1137 (4th Cir. 1995), and have demanded a very close connection between the evidence and the alleged discriminatory decision. A startling example is Indurante v. Local 705, International Brotherhood of Teamsters, 160 F.3d 364 (7th Cir. 1998), where plaintiff claimed national origin discrimination in his discharge from a union job. The defendant argued that Indurante was discharged because he was part of the "Ligurotis reign" and had to be removed to rid the union of corruption. Plaintiff submitted affidavits from former business agents that a newly appointed business agent, McCormick, had earlier said that "all Italians were going to be fired . . . that all the Italians were nothing but mobsters and gangsters." The affidavit of another former business agent said, "In June, 1993, Trustee Burke told me that the plans were 'to get rid of all the Italians.'" Both McCormick and Burke played a role in Indurante's subsequent dismissal. Another former union organizer filed an affidavit that Trustee Zero, who made the decision to fire Indurante, had told him shortly afterwards that "the days of the goombahs are over." In nevertheless affirming summary judgment for defendant, the court described two approaches to determining what was direct evidence:

> The phrase "related to the employment decision in question" may simply mean that the comments should refer, first of all, to an employment decision, and second, to the same type of employment decision as the plaintiff is challenging. So comments about discrimination in hiring may not suffice if the case involves a discharge. But language in other cases goes further, suggesting that the comments should refer to the individual plaintiff's employment decision. . . . To the extent that the remarks ought to refer to Indurante's termination, that would pose a problem for Indurante's case: the remarks of Burke, McCormick and Zero were not made to Indurante and do not mention Indurante or his termination at all. In addition, the statements of Burke and McCormick are not contemporaneous with Indurante's firing: they come about 16 months earlier. . . . While Zero's purported remark — "the days of the goombahs are over" — does come fewer than five months after Indurante's firing, it was not even made to employees of the Local and does not expressly refer to employment.

Id. at 367. Judge Rovner dissented:

> When two decisionmakers reveal that there is a plan in the works to get rid of the Italian-Americans, the omission to mention the plaintiff or his discharge in particular would seem to be a minor point — there is no dispute, after all, that Indurante is Italian-American, was perceived as such, and that he was indeed terminated. That McCormick and Burke uttered these remarks sixteen months before Zero fired Indurante is a more salient observation, but one addressed to the ultimate weight of this evidence rather than to whether it is stray or on point. The fact is, some plans take a good while to carry out.

Id. at 368. Even more shocking, Shorter v. ICG Holdings, Inc., 188 F.3d 1204 (10th Cir. 1999), held that defendant's manager referring to plaintiff as an "incompetent nigger" within a day or two of having fired her was not direct evidence of discriminatory intent. The statement was merely a matter of personal opinion. Similarly restrictive is Harris v. Shelby County Board of Education, 99 F.3d 1078, 1080 (11th Cir. 1996), where the court defined direct evidence as "evidence, which if believed, proves the existence of fact in issue without inference or presumption." It then ruled that a statement by the school district superintendent — "we did not need to employ a black [as principal] at Thompson High School" — was *not* direct evidence that the school district did not pick plaintiff as principal because he was an African American. The statement, the court said, was not direct evidence since it "could by inference have more than one possible meaning." Finally, Carter v. Three Springs Res. Treatment, 132 F.3d 635, 642 (11th Cir. 1998), rejected as direct evidence an affidavit of a former worker that related a conversation with Ms. Cook, the manager who decided not to promote plaintiff, in which she said that she "identified [in herself] a bias against blacks and she found that they were difficult for her to trust or get along with":

> [T]he statement does not amount to direct evidence. First, the statement is susceptible to more than one interpretation. Cook, in explaining her bias to a black colleague, could have been expressing a desire to get past prior prejudices. We have held that statements that are open to more than one interpretation do not constitute direct evidence of racial discrimination. . . . Second, the statement does not relate directly to the decision to promote Carter to the position of Program Director. To say that Cook "identified a bias" to Allen is not the same as saying that Cook exercised that bias in the case of Carter's promotion. Direct evidence, by definition, is evidence that does not require such an inferential leap between fact and conclusion.

In the ADEA context, some courts have been equally reluctant to find direct evidence. Statements made by a supervisor to the plaintiff, saying that at plaintiff's "age, it would be difficult to train for another position" and "difficult to find a new job," were held to be expressions of personal opinion and not direct evidence of age discrimination. Stone v. Autoliv Asp., Inc., 210 F.3d 1132, 1136 (10th Cir. 2000). Finally, remember that in *Reeves,* Justice O'Connor appeared to accept the lower court's determination that statements about plaintiff made by one of the decision-makers several months before plaintiff was discharged that he was "so old he must have come over on the Mayflower" and that he "was too damn old to do the job" were not direct evidence of age discrimination. Cf. Lee v. American Intl. Group, Inc., 2002 U.S. App. LEXIS 5975 (2d Cir. 2002), in which summary judgment for the employer was reversed on an age discrimination claim because of direct evidence of the company vice president discouraging plaintiff from applying for a position because competing applicants for the position "were younger and more sophisticated."

10. In some cases, proving racial animus is likely to be dispositive, even if it cannot be linked to a particular decision. In 1996, the upper management of Texaco was virtually all white. Not a single black employee had ever held a job in the highest pay grade of the company. Of the 873 executives who made more than $106,000 annually, only 6 were black. N.Y. Times, Nov. 10, 1996, at A-1. In responding to a lawsuit charging Texaco with discrimination, a group of white male senior executives allegedly met in August 1994 to plan the destruction of company documents demanded by plaintiffs in discovery. One of those present carried a tape recorder. In 1996, after that executive had been let go by Texaco, the tape of the meeting was provided to the plaintiffs in the lawsuit.

On Monday, November 4, 1996, the New York Times published a story, Kurt Eichenwald, Texaco Executives, on Tape, Discussed Impeding a Bias Suit, at A1, about the contents of the tapes that allegedly included racial epithets. By the following Monday, Texaco released the findings of an independent investigator it had hired. Based on enhanced digital processing techniques, the investigator concluded that the transcript of the tape made by the plaintiffs was in error. Plaintiffs' transcript indicated that one executive said, "I'm still having trouble with Hanukkah. Now we have Kwanzaa. . . . Fucking niggers they shitted all over us with this." The independent investigator's version says, "I'm still struggling with Hanukkah and now we have Kwanzaa, I mean I lost Christmas, poor St. Nicholas, they shitted all over his beard." Both transcriptions agree that the tape then included the following discussion. One executive said, "This diversity thing. You know how black jelly beans agree. . . ." Another person responded, "That's funny. All the black jelly beans seem to be glued to the bottom of the bag." The independent investigator said that the reference to jelly beans came from a diversity training session that Texaco had sponsored, which was run by Dr. R. Roosevelt Thomas, Jr., the former president of the American Institute for Managing Diversity at Morehouse College. See Texaco Releases Findings of Independent Investigation Related to Racial Epithets (Texaco Inc., White Plains, N.Y., Nov. 11, 1996).

Facing a nationwide consumer boycott and a substantial drop in its stock price, on November 15, 1996, Texaco agreed with the plaintiffs, subject to court approval, to settle the case for the largest award ever paid in a race discrimination suit. Texaco promised to pay $115 million to approximately 1,400 class members, to give $26.1 million in raises over the next five years to minority workers, and to allocate $35 million to fund a task force to implement changes in the company's human resources program for a five-year period. Texaco agreed to implement all changes proposed by the task force unless it files with the court an objection that the proposal involves "the application of unsound business judgment or is technically not feasible." See courttv.com/library/business/texaco/ settlement.html. The final report of the task force can be found at http://www.texaco.com/archive/diversity/.

11. Are you convinced by the *Price Waterhouse* plurality that its approach is not but-for causation? Suppose a job requires an applicant to be 18 years old and a resident of the state. A 17-year-old nonresident applies and is rejected. Is it sensible to say that being underage "caused" the applicant to be turned down? Would your answer change if the employer testified that, when he reviewed the application, he noted that the first line indicated that the applicant was under 18? He then rejected the applicant without looking further and never knew that the applicant was also a nonresident.

12. Ironically, the one point on which all nine justices agreed in *Price Waterhouse* — that there had to be a finding that discrimination caused harm before Title VII liability attached — was soon legislatively modified. The Civil Rights Act of 1991 added a new § 703(m), 42 U.S.C.S. § 2000e-2(m) (2003), providing that "an unlawful employment practice is established when the complaining party demonstrates that race, color, religion, sex, or national origin was a motivating factor for any employment practice, even though other factors also motivated the practice." Thus, the "a motivating factor" test of the *Price Waterhouse* plurality is accepted, as is the corollary of "mixed-motive" violations. But the amendment also modifies *Price Waterhouse* by establishing that the plaintiff's proof of an illegitimate "motivating factor" does not merely shift the burden of proving no causation to the defendant, but actually establishes a violation, without regard to what the defendant can prove on rebuttal.

The new statute, however, produces an opportunity for defendants to limit plaintiff's remedies even if a violation has been established. A new paragraph was added to § 706(g), 42 U.S.C.S. § 2000e-5(g) (2003), which provides that, in § 703(m) cases, if a respondent can "demonstrate" that it "would have taken the same action in the absence of the impermissible motivating factor," plaintiff's remedies are limited. Thus, a court

> (i) may grant declaratory relief, injunctive relief (except as provided in clause (ii)), and attorney's fees and costs demonstrated to be directly attributable only to the pursuit of a claim under section 703(m); and (ii) shall not award damages or issue an order requiring any admission, reinstatement, hiring, promotion, or payment. . . .

13. Suppose an employer places a sign outside its personnel office, saying, "No blacks need apply." Is that a violation of Title VII? Surprisingly, the plurality opinion suggests that the answer is "not necessarily" because the sign might not be a causative factor in any particular decision. Reread footnote 10. What is the law now that § 703(m) and (g) have been added? Wouldn't plaintiff still need to prove that race was a motivating factor as to denying her a job in order to establish a violation? Note that § 704(b) of Title VII prohibits notices or advertisements indicating a preference or limitation on one of the prohibited grounds. Does § 704(b) cast any light on whether actual adverse effects on an individual are necessary for a § 703(a)(1) or § 703(m) violation? Or does it merely pretermit the need to establish a violation under those sections?

14. Some have defended a causation requirement (of some kind) as being necessary to avoid First Amendment problems of "thought control," a concern reflected in Justice O'Connor's opinion. See Robert Belton, Causation in Employment Discrimination Law, 34 Wayne L. Rev. 1235 (1988). What do you think of this argument? The enactment of § 703(m) may clarify congressional intent, but what about the First Amendment? Congress could not constitutionally bar either the thought or the expression of the thought that certain races or one sex is inferior or unsuited to a particular job. See generally Kingsley R. Browne, Title VII as Censorship: Hostile Environment Harassment and the First Amendment, 52 Ohio St. L.J. 481 (1991); Nadine Strossen, Regulating Racist Speech: A Modest Proposal?, 1990 Duke L.J. 484. But see Mari Matsuda, Public Response to Racist Speech: Considering the Victim's Story, 87 Mich. L. Rev. 2320 (1989); Richard Delgado, Campus Antiracism Rules: Constitutional Narratives in Collision, 85 Nw. U. L. Rev. 343 (1991); Charles Lawrence, If He Hollers, Let Him Go: Regulating Racist Speech on Campus, 1990 Duke L.J. 431.

The core of the "thought control" position is the distinction between "prejudice" and "discrimination." Prejudice, and even the expression of prejudice, is constitutionally protected; discrimination, which is "prejudice in action," is not. Regulation of discriminatory advertising has been upheld against constitutional attack. Pittsburgh Press Co. v. Pittsburgh Commn. on Human Relations, 413 U.S. 376 (1973). Consider a variation on the sign example: "This company does not believe blacks should be given equal opportunity, but this company knows that it is required by law to do so and, therefore, will accord blacks equality of job opportunity here." Objectionable as this sign may be, it is probably constitutionally protected — that is, the mere posting of the sign could not, constitutionally, be made a violation. Of course, the sign presents the employer with other problems: a court considering an individual employment decision may find the expressed prejudice probative. Does § 703(m) appropriately distinguish between expression and action? See Note on the First Amendment Implications of Sexual Harassment Liability in Chapter 7, at page 537.

15. Are the different tests of causation a sliding scale? How would you articulate the differences among "sole cause," "but-for cause," "determinative influence," "a substantial factor cause," and "a motivating factor cause"? How small a part can the discriminatory motivation play and still establish intent to discriminate? Is a factor motivating if it plays any part at all in the decision? Is intent to discriminate established where an employer discharges an African American for poor work performance but is happy to do so because the employer dislikes African Americans?

16. In his concurring opinion in Miller v. CIGNA Corp., 47 F.3d 586 (3d Cir. 1995) (en banc), Judge Greenberg argued that all individual disparate treatment cases could involve mixed motives.

[U]nder the language of Biggins, a plaintiff could succeed under Burdine without proving that the employer's reasons are wholly pretextual. And, if the reasons are not wholly pretextual, some of them must be true. Further still, if some of the employer's reasons are true, pretext cases sometimes involve mixed motives.

17. In Ostrowski v. Atlantic Mutual Insurance Cos., 968 F.2d 171, 181 (2d Cir. 1992), the court reversed a judgment for the employer in an age discrimination case where the trial judge instructed the jury under *McDonnell Douglas/Burdine*, but refused to give plaintiff's requested *Price Waterhouse* instruction:

> The *Price Waterhouse* principle often leads to the paradoxical situation, as it did in the present case, of a plaintiff asking for a mixed-motive instruction. The *Price Waterhouse* issue does not arise for the trier of fact until the plaintiff has carried the burden of persuading the trier that the forbidden animus was a motivating factor in the employment decision but has failed to persuade the trier that non-discriminatory reasons proffered by the employer were pretexts and not also motivating factors. Once the presentation of evidence is sufficient to create the possibility, the employer has the option of defending on the *Price Waterhouse* ground that it would have made the same decision even in the absence of a discriminatory motive. *Price Waterhouse* is thus a defense. However, for tactical reasons, it is often only the plaintiff who asks for a *Price Waterhouse* instruction, for when requests to charge are submitted, the employer may well choose to avoid the burden-shifting language in the *Price Waterhouse* charge, hoping that the jury either will not find a forbidden animus or will believe the burden is on the plaintiff in the case of a mixed motive. We thus believe that the plaintiff will be entitled to a burden-shifting instruction on the *Price Waterhouse* defense where the evidence is sufficient to allow a trier to find both forbidden and permissible motives. In such circumstances, the failure to give such an instruction would create a risk that the jury, having agreed with the plaintiff's evidence that a forbidden animus played a motivating part in the employment decision but not with the plaintiff's contention that the employer's proffered explanations were pretextual, would mistakenly believe that the plaintiff had the burden of showing that the same employment decision would not have occurred in the absence of the forbidden motive.

Is this correct? If so, doesn't it apply to Title VII jury trials? The court cautioned, however, that "the jury must be told that the mixed-motive issue does not arise unless it first determines that the plaintiff has carried the burden of proving a forbidden motive but has failed to prove that the employer's explanations were pretextual." Id.

18. Do new §703(m) and amended §703(g) apply in a *McDonnell Douglas/Burdine* case? Section 703(m) states that a Title VII violation is established when the plaintiff demonstrates that race or sex "was a motivating factor for any employment practice, even though other factors also motivated the practice." Especially after *Hicks* and *Reeves*, isn't it clear that a plaintiff may win an inferential case only by convincing the finder of fact that it was discrimination that motivated the defendant's treatment of her? See Tyler v. Bethlehem Steel Co., 958 F.2d 1176 (2d Cir. 1992). See generally Charles A. Sullivan, Accounting for *Price Waterhouse:* Proving Disparate Treatment Under Title VII, 56 Brook. L. Rev. 1107 (1991). Does it make a difference? In an inferential case, must not the factfinder draw the inference of motivation from the difference in treatment?

19. In Ezold v. Wolf, Black, Schorr & Solis-Cohen, 983 F.2d 509 (3d Cir. 1992), plaintiff claimed she was denied partnership in a law firm because of her sex. She won at trial, but the judgment was reversed on appeal. Treating the case as a *McDonnell Douglas/Burdine* "pretext" case and not a *Price Waterhouse* "mixed-motive" case, the Third Circuit purported to apply the "clearly erroneous" standard to the district court's pretext finding. Defendant's articulated reason was the Wolf firm's "belief,

based on a subtle and subjective consensus among the partners, that [Ezold] did not possess sufficient legal analytical ability to handle complex litigation." Id. at 526. The district court was clearly erroneous in finding pretext because plaintiff could not "point to an objectively quantifiable factor by which Wolf compared her qualifications against those of the male associates considered for partnership." Id. at 530. The Third Circuit explained:

> Were the factors Wolf considered in deciding which associates should be admitted to the partnership objective, as opposed to subjective, the conflicts in various partners' views about Ezold's legal analytical ability that this record shows might amount to no more than a conflict in the evidence that the district court as fact-finder had full power to resolve. The principles governing valid comparisons between members of a protected minority and those fortunate enough to be part of a favored majority reveal an obvious difficulty plaintiffs must face in an unlawful discrimination case involving promotions that are dependent on an employer's balanced evaluation of various subjective criteria. This difficulty is the lack of an objective qualification or factor that a plaintiff can use as a yardstick to compare herself with similarly situated employees.

Id. at 529. Is this consistent with *McDonnell Douglas/Burdine?* If it is, does this mean that individual disparate treatment cases involving subjective factors can be won only under *Price Waterhouse?*

Why was *Ezold* not a *Price Waterhouse* mixed-motive case? When Ezold was hired, she was told that "it would not be easy for her at Wolf, Black because she did not fit the Wolf, Black mold since she was a woman, had not attended an Ivy League law school, and had not been on law review." 751 F. Supp. 1175, 1177 (1990). Part of Ezold's negative appraisals resulted from her "perceived concern about women's issues, such as the Firm's treatment of paralegals, who were virtually all female and the Firm's treatment of part-time attorneys who were all female." Id. at 1178. Further,

> [t]he plaintiff was criticized for being very demanding and was expected by some members of the Firm to be nonassertive and acquiescent to the predominately male partnership. Her failure to accept this role was a factor which resulted in her not being promoted to partner. However, several male associates who had been evaluated negatively for lacking sufficient assertiveness in their demeanor were made partners.

Id. at 1189. Is this sufficient direct evidence to make out a *Price Waterhouse* case? While concern with Ezold's analytical ability might have been legitimate, gender may also have motivated the decision not to make her a partner.

20. In Wilkerson v. Columbus Separate School District, 985 F.2d 815 (5th Cir. 1993), the plaintiff, a white high school head coach who had been nonrenewed for inadequate supervision of players, claimed that the action was racial. There was testimony that a black coach had been nonrenewed recently and that black members of the school board had said, "'You got the black, now you are going to get the white'" and "'what is fair for the goose is fair for the gander.'" Id. at 818. The Fifth Circuit found a *Price Waterhouse* issue. How should the case be decided? Does it matter that plaintiff claimed that his misconduct was less egregious than the conduct of the black coach?

21. When *A* testifies to his own motivations, there is no hearsay problem. When, however, *B* testifies as to what *A* said about *A*'s motivations, the testimony is technically hearsay if it is introduced for its truth, that is, that *A* had such motivations.

An example from *Price Waterhouse* is the partner who stated that no woman should ever be promoted to partner. If this statement was introduced for its truth, that is, that the speaker thought as he spoke, it is hearsay. (If it were introduced merely for its effects on other partners, its truth would be irrelevant, and it would not be hearsay.) The law of evidence admits such statements only pursuant to some exception to the hearsay rule. The most common hearsay exception in Title VII cases is admissions of a party opponent. See Edward W. Cleary, McCormick on Evidence, § 262, at 777 (3d ed. 1984). To the extent that the speaker was commenting about matters within the scope of his or her employment at the time of the statement, such comments would generally be admissible under that rubric. Is a *Price Waterhouse* case dependent on employer "admissions"? Is that the distinction between this case and a *Burdine* case?

22. Can expert testimony be used to prove that ambiguous comments reflect bias? What were the various views in *Price Waterhouse* about Dr. Susan Fiske? Justice Kennedy wrote that "Fiske purported to discern stereotyping in comments that were gender neutral — e.g., 'overbearing and abrasive' — without any knowledge of the comments' basis in reality and without having met the speaker or subject." Is this criticism valid? May not certain statements be susceptible of varying meanings, with expert testimony helping the factfinder in deciding whether the statements are likely to reflect stereotyping? See generally Theodore Y. Blumoff & Harold Lewis, The Reagan Court and Title VII: A Common Law Outlook on a Statutory Task, 69 N.C. L. Rev. 1 (1990); Martha Chamallas, Listening to Dr. Fiske: The Easy Case of *Price Waterhouse v. Hopkins*, 15 Vt. L. Rev. 1989 (1991).

23. In Galdieri-Ambrosini v. National Realty & Dev. Corp., 136 F.3d 276, 290 (2d Cir. 1998), the plaintiff, a secretary, claimed that she had been fired because she had been forced to do personal work for her boss, tasks which were stereotypical women's work. The court rejected the claim that being compelled to do "quintessential" secretarial work including "typing her employer's personal letters or making appointments for him with the cable installer, in the absence of evidence that could permit an inference that gender played a role in those work assignments."

24. Brown v. Trustees of Boston University, 891 F.2d 337 (1st Cir. 1989), upheld the award of tenure to a female professor. Although the university's decision-making process was complex, one thrust of plaintiff's proof was the attitudes of the president of the university, John Silber, who was quoted by a witness as saying, "'I don't see what a good woman in your department is worried about. The place is a damned matriarchy.'" Id. at 349. Is this direct evidence? Even putting aside the pejorative denotation of "damned" and the pejorative connotation of "matriarchy," the remark plainly indicated the belief that women dominated the department. Might this be merely a statement of fact? But doesn't it indicate hostility to women? How would your assessment be influenced by proof that, at the time, the department in question, although chaired by a woman, had only 7 women out of 26 tenured faculty members? Might an expert on stereotyping, such as Dr. Fiske, play a role here?

25. Suppose the defendant does have a burden of persuasion. Justice White objects to any requirement that the employer submit objective evidence to support its affirmative defense. Further, he notes that "where the legitimate motive found would have been ample grounds for the action taken, and the employer credibly testifies that the action would have been taken for the legitimate reason alone, this should be ample proof." Is this true? What about his further statement: "This would even more plainly be the case where the employer denies any illegitimate motive in the first

place but the court finds that illegitimate, as well as legitimate, factors motivated the adverse action." The plurality characterized as "baffling" the position of Justice White in giving any special credence to the testimony of an employer who has been found to have relied on an illegal reason in its decision-making. Do you agree? Does it matter, given that the plurality and Justice O'Connor form a majority apparently rejecting this view?

26. How can an employer shoulder its burden under amended § 706(g)? Justice White's opinion to the contrary notwithstanding, testimony by a person found to have discriminated is of dubious credibility. The employer could try to extract from the pattern of its other decisions a kind of template of requirements for advancement. The employer might introduce expert testimony of the factors that operated in its decision-making and how they would have netted out in the plaintiff's case. Another method would be a "customs of the trade" approach, again employing expert testimony, but this time to establish how a "reasonable" employer would have evaluated the candidate. In the abstract, this evidence is less probative than proof of how the employer treated favored workers because the issue is what the defendant, not a hypothetical employer, would have done absent bias. After all, the defendant might be more strict or more liberal than others in the industry and is entitled to be so. But trade practice is nevertheless relevant because it seems appropriate to assume that a particular employer conforms to industry standards or general practice until it is shown otherwise.

27. The plurality in *Price Waterhouse* notes that at "some point in the proceedings . . . the District Court must decide whether a particular case involves mixed motives." At what point in the trial does this decision take place? Now that Title VII cases include jury trials, how would you prepare jury instructions on *McDonnell Douglas/Burdine* and *Price Waterhouse?* If the instructions accurately stated the law, would jurors be likely to understand them? See Donovan v. Milk Mktg. Inc., 243 F.3d 584, 585-86 (2d Cir. 2001) ("When a plaintiff claiming employment discrimination presents credible evidence that illegal discrimination was a factor in his dismissal and his employer responds with credible evidence of valid, non-discriminatory reasons, it is quite possible that a jury will credit both sets of motives, finding that both the prohibited motivation and a lawful one were involved in the adverse action taken by the employer; . . . when the jury might reasonably conclude on the evidence that both illegal discrimination and legitimate non-discriminatory reasons were present in an employer's decisionmaking process, the court may charge the jury on mixed-motivation in accordance with *Price Waterhouse.*").

28. The Civil Rights Act of 1991 did not amend either § 1981 or the ADEA. Does that mean that those statutes continue to be governed by the *Price Waterhouse* analysis? See Howard Eglit, The Age Discrimination in Employment Act, Title VII, and the Civil Rights Act of 1991: Three Acts and a Dog That Didn't Bark, 39 Wayne L. Rev. 1096 (1993). In O'Connor v. Consolidated Coin Caterers Corp., 517 U.S. 308, 311 (1996), Justice Scalia planted a seed of doubt whether the uniform structure of individual disparate treatment law that had developed without regard to the statutory source of a particular cause of action would continue. "In assessing claims of age discrimination brought under the ADEA, the Fourth Circuit, like others, has applied some variant of the basic evidentiary framework set forth in *McDonnell Douglas.* We have never had occasion to decide whether that application of the Title VII rule to the ADEA context is correct, but since the parties do not contest that point, we shall assume it." In *Reeves,* the Court again assumed arguendo a unified structure.

29. Contrast *Price Waterhouse* with McKennon v. Nashville Banner Publishing Co., 513 U.S. 352 (1995), dealing with evidence of plaintiff's wrongdoing acquired after a discrimination claim was filed. In a deposition of plaintiff concerning her age discrimination claim, she admitted that she had taken copies of some employer documents home and shared them with her husband. The Court found that an employee discharged because of discrimination is not barred from all relief when, after her discharge, her employer discovers wrongdoing that would have led to her termination on lawful and legitimate grounds had the employer known of it at the time of the discharge. This is consistent with *Price Waterhouse* since the employer did not base its decision to discharge the plaintiff on the after-acquired evidence. For an interesting article linking *McKennon* with *Hicks* and critiquing both, see William R. Corbett, The Fall of *Summers*, the Rise of "Pretext Plus," and the Escalating Subordination of Federal Employment Discrimination Laws to Employment at Will: Lessons From *McKennon* and *Hicks*, 30 Ga. L. Rev. 305 (1996). Remedial questions concerning after-acquired evidence are explored in more detail in Chapter 10.

## NOTE ON THE INTENT OF MULTIPLE DECISION-MAKERS

While disparate treatment is often discussed in terms of the intent of the "employer," employers frequently are corporations or partnerships, sometimes involved in complicated relationships. One issue that arises is when the intent of one person or entity should be imputed to another. In General Building Contractors Association v. Pennsylvania, 458 U.S. 375 (1982), the plaintiffs claimed discrimination in the operation of a union hiring hall. They sued not only the union, but also the employer association that bargained with the union and the employers who were bound by the resultant collective bargaining agreement to hire exclusively through the union's hiring hall. While there was discriminatory intent on the part of the union, the Court found no intent to discriminate by the employer association or the individual contractors. Accordingly, to recover from these defendants under § 1981, the purposeful discrimination by the union in the operation of its hiring hall had to be imputed to the defendants who had not purposely discriminated. The Court rejected two possible ways to do this. On the narrow issue of vicarious liability for the union's intentional discrimination, the doctrine of respondeat superior, was held inapplicable to the relationships between the union and the three defendants. There was no fiduciary relationship, and neither the employer association nor the contractors had any control over the union. The Court also rejected the concept of a "nondelegable duty" under § 1981 that would impose a kind of strict liability on employers when their hiring methods result in the exclusion of blacks.

While *General Building Contractors* involved a number of distinct juridical entities, the problem of imputed intent also exists within a single corporation or partnership. Where business associations are concerned, the intent that matters is that of the actual decision-maker. But many decisions involve not a single decision-maker, but multiple deciders, in a collegial, a hierarchical structure, or some combination of the two. Multiple decision-makers will be found where the decision is made collegially (as by a board or a committee) and where it is made by a hierarchical process (A recommends to B who recommends to C who "decides").

The collegial body obviously does not "think" at all; its human members have whatever motivations may be relevant for Title VII purposes. But the motivations of individuals may be attributed to the body in appropriate circumstances — most obviously, when a majority of the members have such thoughts. It should not be necessary, however, that even a majority of members share a particular thought: one or more members may be so influential that they can effectively determine the result. If such "opinion leaders" act from prohibited motives, it may be fair to conclude that the decision of the body is tainted. This can be true even where the "followers" do not know of the prohibited considerations. Another variation occurs when some members of the body cast untainted votes, but the votes of those influenced by prohibited considerations decide the outcome.

If the fact-finder finds that one member acted with intent to discriminate, does that establish that discrimination was a "motivating factor" under § 703(m) or must more be shown to establish liability? In Barbano v. Madison County, 922 F.2d 139 (2d Cir. 1990), plaintiff was interviewed by a committee, one of whose members openly objected to hiring her because she was a woman and might become pregnant. Although the committee found all interviewees qualified, it ranked them and recommended a male to the board. The court upheld a finding that the committee's tolerance of its member's discriminatory conduct, and the refusal of the other members to ask any questions not focusing on plaintiff's gender, warranted a finding that the committee as a whole discriminated. The board's subsequent decision was, therefore, also tainted by discrimination, especially because the board had been appraised of the misconduct, but did nothing about it. In contrast Mason v. Village of El Portal, 240 F.3d 1337, 1339 (11th Cir. 2001) considered "whether the alleged racially discriminatory motive of only one member of a three-member majority of a five-member council can give rise to municipal liability." The court held that no liability could extend to the municipality in this instance."

Barbano involved both the collegial and the hierarchical models. Note that, in the latter situation, if A has the requisite thoughts, his "recommendation" to B may be influenced by those thoughts. At this point, however, B may be able to filter out any of A's mistakes; indeed, that is the only reason, organizationally, that B exists in the chain of command — to review the actions of A. But B may instead "rubber-stamp" A's recommendations for a variety of reasons, ranging from being too busy to consider the matter thoroughly to being influenced by friendship to maintaining organizational loyalty. And, even if B faithfully reviews A's recommendations, A may be able to skew B's decision by the way in which he presents or fails to present data. This may range from simply putting the preferred "spin" on the recommendation to fabricating negative statements concerning the candidate. See Jiles v. Ingram, 944 F.2d 409 (8th Cir. 1991) (finding of no intent to discriminate by decision-makers not inconsistent with disparate treatment violation when a lower-level supervisor had contrived an incident of "insubordination" to avoid working with a black); Simpson v. Diversitech Gen., Inc., 945 F.2d 156 (6th Cir. 1991) (if race played a role in supervisor's decision to initiate disciplinary proceedings, the fact that an unprejudiced person "pulled the trigger" did not matter). But see Cesaro v. Lakeville Community Sch. Dist., 953 F.2d 252 (6th Cir. 1992), an extremely questionable decision holding that there was no discrimination by the school board, the ultimate decision-maker, even if, but for the superintendent's discriminatory motivation, the district would not have conducted an external search and the plaintiff would, therefore, have been chosen as the best of the internal candidates.

One case allowed the employer to avoid liability, despite the demonstrated racism of lower supervisors. The decision-maker asked the employee to prove that she had been "set up" by one of those supervisors, but the employee failed to do so. Willis v.

Marion County Auditor's Office, 118 F.3d 542 (7th Cir. 1997), upheld setting aside of a verdict for plaintiff:

> [T]here can be situations in which the forbidden motive of a subordinate employee can be imputed to the employer because, under the circumstances of the case, the employer simply acted as the "cat's paw" of the subordinate. . . . However, it is clear that, when the causal relationship between the subordinate's illicit motive and the employer's ultimate decision is broken, and the ultimate decision is clearly made on the independent and a legally permissive basis, the bias of the subordinate is not relevant.

Id. at 546. Such a view does not mean that such evidence is not admissible, only that it is not necessarily sufficient. See also Nichols v. Loral Vought Sys. Corp., 81 F.3d 38, 41-42 (5th Cir. 1996) In Griffin v. Washington Convention Ctr., 142 F.3d 1308, 1310 (D.C. Cir. 1998) ("Evidence of a subordinate's bias is relevant where, as here, the ultimate decisionmaker is not insulated from the subordinate's influence"); Russell v. McKinney Hospital Venture, Inc., 235 F.3d 219, 226 (5th Cir. 2000) ("[I]f the employee can demonstrate that others had influence or leverage over the official decision maker, and thus were not ordinary coworkers, it is proper to impute their discriminatory attitudes to the formal decision maker."); Hill v. Lockheed Martin Logistics Mgt., Inc., 2003 U.S. App. LEXIS 146 (4th Cir. Jan. 7, 2003).

In another case, Fisher v. Vassar College, 114 F.3d 1332 (2d Cir. 1997), the court commented that a system of multiple decision-makers can easily produce evidence of reasons for a decision that differ from the reason the employer claims to be the basis for the challenged decision. "Because there are numerous participants in the decision-making process [of granting tenure in a college], each potentially having individual reasons for rejecting a plaintiff, there is a greater likelihood that some of those reasons will differ from the reason officially given by the institution." Id. at 1338. In accompanying footnote 4, the court further commented: "The involvement of multiple decision-makers increases the likelihood that the institution's stated reason may differ from the true reasons held by some of the decision-makers — without increasing the likelihood that discrimination played any role in their decision." Id.

Rebecca Hanner White & Linda Hamilton Krieger, Whose Motive Matters?: Discrimination in Multi-Actor Employment Decision Making, 61 La. L. Rev. 495, 534 (2001), combines doctrinal analysis with insights from cognitive psychology to advocate a causation-driven approach to intent. Rather than asking whether the ultimate decision-maker consciously intended to discriminate, the question is whether there exists an unbroken chain of causation between the victim's race or sex and the decision being challenged. If so, then a disparate treatment claim should be recognized, so long as the causal link may be attributed to the employer, either directly or vicariously. The article notes that lower courts generally are following this approach in cases involving multiple decision-makers but have been less willing to embrace a causation driven approach in cases involving individual decision-makers. The article analogizes decisions that involve multiple decision-makers, who may be unaware of the biases of others in the decision-making chain, to decisions by individuals who are unaware of their own biases. "Exploring the various ways in which discrimination can occur when multiple agents play a role in the decision making process, and examining the parallels between group and individual decision making, helps clarify that the question of intent in employment discrimination cases must, at bottom, be approached as a question of causation." Id. at 500.

*Price Waterhouse* involved multiple decision-makers in both a hierarchical and a collegial sense. How did the Court decide whose intent counted?

## NOTE ON SECTION 1983

While § 1981 is the most important of the Reconstruction-era civil rights statutes for purposes of employment discrimination, another enactment from that period should be noted. 42 U.S.C.S. § 1983 (2003) provides:

> Every person who, under color of any statute, ordinance, regulation, custom, or usage, of any State or Territory or the District of Columbia, subjects, or causes to be subjected, any citizen of the United States or other person . . . to the deprivation of any rights, privileges, or immunities secured by the Constitution and laws, shall be liable to the party injured in an action at law, [or] suit in equity. . . .

Section 1983, derived from the Ku Klux Klan Act of 1871, creates no substantive rights, but merely provides a remedy for violation of "rights, privileges, or immunities secured by the Constitution and laws." For employment discrimination purposes, the central right invoked in § 1983 suits is denial of equal protection under the Fourteenth Amendment. Because, however, that amendment applies only to state action, § 1983 can be used only against state actors.

Despite its simple formulation, § 1983 is an enormously complicated statute. In part for that reason, plaintiffs have preferred to rely on Title VII since that statute was extended in 1972 to cover state and local employees. Many of § 1983's former remedial advantages also have been eliminated by the Civil Rights Act of 1991, which enhanced Title VII remedies.

Nevertheless, § 1983 is sometimes a valuable additional avenue of recourse, having advantages over Title VII in substance, remedies, and procedures. As to substance, Title VII is limited to the prescribed grounds under the statute. Section 1983, however, can be used to redress any constitutional violation. For example, discrimination on grounds such as sexual orientation, which is outside Title VII, has been attacked under § 1983. See Chapter 7.

Nevertheless, constitutional doctrine itself tends to confine equal protection suits to the grounds prohibited by Title VII: race discrimination is subject to strict scrutiny, sex discrimination to intermediate scrutiny, and most other classifications to "rational basis" review, which generally results in upholding them. Where disparate treatment is at issue, the same litigation structure applies to § 1983 suits as to Title VII disparate treatment actions. E.g., Stewart v. Rutgers, State Univ., 120 F.3d 426 (3d Cir. 1997); Maull v. Division of State Police, 2002 U.S. App. LEXIS 13879 (3d Cir. 2002). Disparate impact is not an available theory under the Fourteenth Amendment and, therefore, may not be pursued in a § 1983 suit. See Washington v. Davis, 426 U.S. 229 (1976); Personnel Administrator v. Feeney (reproduced at page 000).

As for procedures and remedies, § 1983 continues to have some advantages over Title VII, including no requirement that plaintiffs resort to administrative remedies or state remedies, Patsy v. Board of Regents, 457 U.S. 496 (1982); longer time limits, see Chapter 9; and the absence of a statutory cap on damages, see Chapter 10.

*Relationship of Title VII and §1983.*    There has been some debate about the relationship between §1983 and Title VII. For example, some have questioned whether both statutes may be used to attack the same conduct, arguing that §1983 is inapplicable to employment discrimination cases simply because Title VII now protects public employees. Cf. Great American Federal Savings & Loan Assn. v. Novotny, 442 U.S. 366 (1979) (§1985(3)). Looking to Title VII's legislative history, the circuit courts generally have concluded that Congress did not intend Title VII to supplant §1983. Johnson v. City of Fort Lauderdale, 148 F.3d 1228 (11th Cir. 1998) (Civil Rights Act of 1991 did not implicitly render Title VII and §1981 the exclusive remedies for employment discrimination by municipality and its employees, thereby displacing parallel constitutional remedies under §1983). Trigg v. Fort Wayne Community Sch., 766 F.2d 299 (7th Cir. 1985); see also Beardsley v. Webb, 30 F.3d 524 (4th Cir. 1994).

*Relationship of §1981 and §1983.* Section 1981 is broader than §1983 insofar as it reaches all contracts, not merely ones that involve state actors. But it is narrower than §1983 in most other respects because it is limited to racial (and alienage) discrimination in the enforcement of contracts, while §1983 may be used to enforce any constitutional (and many statutory) guarantees where there is state action. Where the two overlap—race discrimination in contractual dealings by state or local governments—a question arose as to the relationship of the two laws. In Jett v. Dallas Independent School District, 491 U.S. 701 (1989), the Supreme Court sought to harmonize the two by holding that "the express 'action at law' provided by §1983 . . . provides the exclusive damage remedy for violation of the rights guaranteed by §1981 when the claim is pressed against a state actor." *Jett* effectively nullified the utility of §1981 as a means of avoiding some of the technical doctrines that have sprung up around §1983. Further, during the same term in which *Jett* was decided, the Court decided Will v. Michigan Department of State Police, 491 U.S. 58 (1989), holding that §1983 does not permit suit against state officials acting in their official capacities even when the suit is pressed in state court. Such defendants are not "persons" within the meaning of §1983. Another effect of *Jett*, then, was to bar §1981 suits against state officials in their official capacities.

The Civil Rights Act of 1991 may or may not have altered the effect of these decisions. That Act added a new paragraph (c) to § 1981, providing that "[t]he rights protected by this section are protected against impairment by nongovernmental discrimination and impairment under color of State law." This makes clear that § 1981 applies to discrimination by state or local entities and apparently frees the statute from any subordinate role to § 1983. While the amendment does not expressly provide that a § 1981 suit may be pressed even when a § 1983 suit would not lie, Federation of African American Contractors v. City of Oakland, 96 F.3d 1204 (9th Cir. 1996), held that § 1981(c) created a private right of action against state officials. Other circuits have disagreed. See Oden v. Oktibbeha County, 246 F.3d 458 (5th Cir. 2001); Butts v. County of Volusia, 222 F.3d 891 (11th Cir. 2000); Dennis v. County of Fairfax, 55 F.3d 151 (4th Cir. 1995). There are, however, Eleventh Amendment concerns with such an extension. See page 000.

*Limitations on §1983.* Section 1983 is limited to state actors, both natural persons and local governments. Monell v. Department of Social Services, 436 U.S. 658 (1978), held that municipalities are liable only for their acts as entities. *Monell* distinguished the case before it, a challenge to an officially promulgated maternity leave policy, from cases in which a municipality is sued merely because of the conduct of one of its employees. Vicarious liability will not extend to an employer solely on the basis of an employment relationship with a tortfeasor. See also Federation of African American Contractors v. City of Oakland, 96 F.3d 1204 (9th Cir. 1996) (§1981(c), added by the Civil Rights Act of 1991, did not authorize suit against municipalities on the basis of respondeat superior).

In contrast to municipalities, states have been protected from suit in federal court under § 1983. One obstacle is the Eleventh Amendment. While this immunity can be nullified by express and valid exercises of congressional power under the Fourteenth Amendment, the Court has held that § 1983 does not override state immunity. Quern v. Jordan, 440 U.S. 332 (1979). Although § 1983 suits can normally be brought in state court, Will v. Michigan Dept. of State Police, 491 U.S. 58 (1989), held that § 1983 does not authorize suits for damages in state court against the state government or against state officials acting in their official capacities because such defendants were not "persons" within the meaning of the statute. See also Alden v. Maine, 527 U.S. 706 (1999). There are, of course, questions concerning what governmental entities constitute the "state," e.g., Miccosukee Tribe of Indians v. Florida State Ath. Commn., 226 F.3d 1226 (11th Cir. 2000).

Where government officials are individual defendants in § 1983 actions, courts have erected barriers and defenses to liability that are phrased in terms of the doctrine of immunity. See generally Alan K. Chen, The Burdens of Qualified Immunity: Summary Judgment and the Role of Facts in Constitutional Tort Law, 47 Am. U. L. Rev. 1 (1997); Kit Kinports, Qualified Immunity in Section 1983 Cases: The Unanswered Questions, 23 Ga. L. Rev. 597 (1989). Such immunity is of two kinds, absolute and qualified. State legislators have been held to be absolutely immune from § 1983 actions when engaged in legitimate legislative activity. Tenney v. Brandhove, 341 U.S. 367 (1951). The Court also extended absolute immunity to a state judge acting in his judicial role. Stump v. Sparkman, 435 U.S. 349 (1978). Cf. Forrester v. White, 484 U.S. 219 (1988) (decision of a judge to discharge a probation officer not a judicial act).

More common is qualified immunity. Scheuer v. Rhodes, 416 U.S. 232, 247-48 (1974), recognized immunity depending on the "scope of discretion and responsibilities of the office and all the circumstances as they reasonably appeared at the time of the action on which liability is sought to be based." See also Wood v. Strickland, 420 U.S. 308, 322 (1975). According to Davis v. Scherer, 468 U.S. 183, 197 (1984), qualified immunity can be overcome "only by showing that those rights were clearly established at the time of the conduct in issue." Because this is an entirely objective standard, the official's subjective state of mind is irrelevant. In Anderson v. Creighton, 483 U.S. 635 (1987), the Court strengthened this immunity by holding that it is not sufficient for a defendant to know that constitutional rights are implicated; "[t]he contours of the right must be sufficiently clear that a reasonable official would understand that what he is doing violates that right." Id. at 640.

Nevertheless, the focus on the objective, reasonable official, rather than on the subjective state of mind of the actual defendant invoking immunity, does not always render intent irrelevant. In many cases, the constitutional right being vindicated is precisely (and only) a right against wrongly motivated conduct. The paradigmatic race discrimination case — a refusal to hire because of race — challenges a decision that, but for the intent of the decision-maker, would not be subject to attack because there is no general right to government employment; rather, there is a right not to be denied employment because of one's race. For such claims, a decision on qualified immunity necessarily entails an inquiry into the defendant's mental state. The inquiry has been phrased as limited to factors bearing on intent, but not extending to the defendant's knowledge of the state of the law. E.g., Poe v. Haydon, 853 F.2d 418 (6th Cir. 1988).

Most of these limitations of § 1983 apply to damage actions, not ones seeking injunctive relief. Where equitable remedies are sought, different principles often apply. E.g., Kentucky v. Graham, 473 U.S. 159 (1985); Pulliam v. Allen, 466 U.S. 522 (1984).

# E.   THE PRESENT AND FUTURE OF INDIVIDUAL DISPARATE TREATMENT LAW

## COSTA v. DESERT PALACE, INC.
### 299 F.3d 838 (9th Cir. 2002) (en banc), *cert. granted,* 71 U.S.L.W. 3470 (U.S. Jan. 10, 2003)

McKEOWN, Circuit Judge:

We agreed to hear this case en banc primarily to examine the legal standard for proof of a violation of Title VII. . . . In this classic instance of what has been termed a "mixed-motive" case, the employer, Caesars Palace Hotel and Casino ("Caesars"), terminated Catharina Costa, the only woman in her bargaining unit, citing disciplinary problems. Costa argued, and the jury agreed, that sex was "a motivating factor" in her termination. 42 U.S.C. § 2000e-2(m). Because Caesars failed to establish that she would have been terminated without consideration of her sex, the jury awarded back pay and compensatory damages. . . . Caesars argues that Costa should have been held to a special, higher standard of "direct evidence," a threshold it claims she did not meet. We disagree. Title VII imposes no special or heightened evidentiary burden on a plaintiff in a so-called "mixed-motive" case. . . .

### BACKGROUND

Catharina Costa is a trailblazer. She has worked most of her life in a male-dominated environment, driving trucks and operating heavy equipment. At Caesars, a well known casino in Las Vegas, she worked in a warehouse and, along with members of her bargaining unit, Teamsters Local 995, operated the forklifts and pallet jacks to retrieve food and beverage orders. Costa was the only woman in this job.

Costa's work was characterized as "excellent" and "good." As her supervisor explained: "We knew when she was out there the job would get done." Nonetheless, she experienced a number of problems with management and her co-workers. At first, she responded by simply focusing on doing her job well. Slowly, Costa began to notice that she was being singled out because she was a woman. Her concerns not only fell on deaf ears — "my word meant nothing" — but resulted in her being treated as an "outcast."

In a series of escalating events that included informal rebukes, denial of privileges accorded her male co-workers, suspension, and finally discharge, Costa's efforts to resolve problems were thwarted along the way. The situation deteriorated so significantly that she finally complained to the human resources department, which declined to intervene.

There were "so many" incidents, it was difficult for her to recount them all. Nonetheless, her testimony at trial on this point was detailed and extensive. For example, when men came in late, they were often given overtime to make up the lost time; when Costa came in late, in one case, one minute late, she was issued a written reprimand, known as a record of counseling. When men missed work for medical reasons, they were given overtime to make up the lost time; when Costa missed work for medical reasons, she was disciplined. On one occasion, a warehouse supervisor actually suspended her because she had missed work while undergoing surgery to remove a tumor; only the intervention of the director of human resources voided this action.

In another episode, corroborated at trial by a fellow employee who was an eyewitness, a number of workers were in the office eating soup on a cold day. A supervisor walked in, looked directly at Costa, and said, "Don't you have work to do?" He did not reprimand any of her colleagues — all men. Another supervisor began to follow her around the warehouse. Although several other Teamsters complained about this supervisor's scrutiny, three witnesses, in addition to Costa, testified that she was singled out for particularly intense "stalking."

Costa presented extensive evidence that she received harsher discipline than the men. For instance, she was frequently warned and even suspended for allegedly hazardous use of equipment and for use of profanity, yet other Teamsters engaged in this conduct with impunity. In at least one instance, such a charge against Costa was found to have been fabricated and the suspension voided. Supervisors began to "stack" her disciplinary record. In one case, a supervisor issued multiple warnings on a single day, including docking her for an absence that dated back over eight months and for absences that occurred when Costa was under a doctor's care. Another warehouse manager steered a co-worker who had a dispute with Costa to security instead of handling the matter himself because the manager wanted to bring "this problem with Costa to a 'head.'"

[Costa was also treated less favorably than her male colleagues in the assignment of overtime. For although she wanted more overtime, she was denied it and was offered it only at the last minute, when it was impractical for her to accept.] The situation became more blatant when Costa asked her supervisors point blank about the differential treatment of another Teamster who was favored with overtime assignments. The response: He "has a family to support."

Costa also presented evidence that she was penalized for her failure to conform to sexual stereotypes. Although her fellow Teamsters frequently lost their tempers, swore at fellow employees, and sometimes had physical altercations, it was Costa, identified in one report as "the lady Teamster," who was called a "bitch," and told "you got more balls than the guys." Even at trial, and despite testimony that she "got along with most people" and had "few arguments," Caesars' managers continued to characterize her as "strong willed," "opinionated," and "confrontational," leading counsel to call her "bossy" in closing argument. Supervisor Karen Hallett, who later signed Costa's termination order, expressly declared her intent to "get rid of that bitch," referring to Costa.

Supervisors frequently used or tolerated verbal slurs that were sex-based or tinged with sexual overtones. Most memorably, one co-worker called her a "fucking cunt." When she wrote a letter to management expressing her concern with this epithet, which stood out from the ordinary rough-and-tumble banter, she received a three-day suspension in response. Although the other employee admitted using the epithet, Costa was faulted for "engaging in verbal confrontation with co-worker in the warehouse resulting in use of profane and vulgar language by other employee."

These events culminated in Caesars' termination of Costa. The purported basis for termination was a physical altercation in the warehouse elevator with another Teamster, Herb Gerber. This incident began, as Gerber admitted, when he went looking for Costa, upset about a report that he believed she had made about his unauthorized lunch breaks. Gerber trapped Costa in an elevator and shoved her against the wall, bruising her arm. Costa gave a detailed account of the altercation. Right away she told supervisor Hallett. Reassured that Hallett would investigate, Costa returned to work, only to have Gerber seek her out and "come at" her a second time. Costa's account was also corroborated by her immediate reports to union officials, by photographs of the bruises, and by a witness who had seen Gerber blocking the elevator door. In contrast, Gerber did not immediately report the incident, had no physical corroboration, and provided few details. He first denied that the altercation was physical, but then changed his story to state that Costa had, in fact, hit him.

Nonetheless, Caesars did not believe Costa. Caesars reasoned that the facts were in dispute, so it disciplined both employees — Gerber with a five-day suspension and Costa with termination.

At trial, Caesars maintained that Costa was terminated because of her disciplinary history and her altercation with Gerber. Costa did not suggest that she was a model employee, but rather that her sex was a motivating factor in her termination. After hearing Costa's testimony, Judge Hagen, the trial judge, admonished counsel: "This is a case that should have settled." He denied Caesars' motion for judgment as a matter of law at the close of Costa's case, which was renewed at the close of the evidence. The jury returned a verdict in favor of Costa for $64,377.74 back pay, [and] $200,000 compensatory damages. . . . When Judge Hagen denied defense motions for judgment as a matter of law notwithstanding the verdict, and for a new trial, he elaborated as follows: "At trial, the evidence showed a pattern of disparate treatment favoring male co-workers over plaintiff in the application of disciplinary standards, allowance of overtime, and in her termination. From this evidence reasonable minds could infer that plaintiff's gender played a motivating part in Caesars's conduct towards plaintiff . . ." He did, however, grant remittitur, and Costa agreed to reduce compensatory damages to $100,000.

## DISCUSSION

Title VII itself provides the benchmark for resolving the primary question in this case. Although the road from Title VII to resolution of Costa's case rests ultimately on a straightforward examination of the statute, it is helpful to examine the statute's structure and the history of the 1991 amendments to the statute. After analyzing the import of the passing reference to "direct evidence" in Justice O'Connor's concurring opinion in Price Waterhouse v. Hopkins, and the framework for Title VII cases, we address the evidence in Costa's case, including the claim that evidence of an arbitration award was erroneously excluded, and the propriety of giving a "mixed-motive" jury instruction. . . .

## I.   TITLE VII STATUTORY FRAMEWORK AND DEVELOPMENT

Title VII prohibits discrimination "because of" a protected characteristic, such as race or sex [quoting § 703 (a)]. . . . The 1991 Act added § 2000e-2(m), which provides that "an unlawful employment practice is established" when a protected characteristic is "a motivating factor" in an employment action [quoting § 703 (m)]. . . . The 1991 Act also provided an affirmative defense that limits the remedies if an employer demonstrates that it would have nonetheless made the "same decision" [quoting § 706 (g)(2)(B)]. . . .

We think this text is crystal clear: an employee makes out a Title VII violation by showing discrimination "because of" race, sex, or another protected factor. Such discrimination is characterized by the statute as "an unlawful employment practice."

More specifically, "an unlawful employment practice" encompasses any situation in which a protected characteristic was "a motivating factor" in an employment action, even if there were other motives. In such a case — sometimes labeled with the "mixed-motive" moniker — if the employee succeeds in proving only that a protected characteristic was one of several factors motivating the employment action, an employer cannot avoid liability altogether, but instead may assert an affirmative defense to bar certain types of relief by showing the absence of "but for" causation.

The amendments to the statute have done nothing to change the plaintiff's long-standing burden: "The ultimate burden of persuading the trier of fact that the defendant intentionally discriminated against the plaintiff remains at all times with the plaintiff." *Burdine*; accord *Reeves*. Nor can we discover anything in this statute that warrants imposing a special evidentiary rule on or hurdle for victims of discrimination to prove their case.

> The burden of showing something by a "preponderance of the evidence," the most common standard in the civil law, "simply requires the trier of fact 'to believe that the existence of a fact is more probable than its nonexistence before [it] may find in favor of the party who has the burden to persuade the [jury] of the fact's existence.'"

The inquiry is simply that of any civil case: whether the plaintiff's evidence is sufficient for a rational factfinder to conclude by a preponderance of the evidence that the employer violated the statute — that "race, color, religion, sex, or national origin was a motivating factor for any employment practice."

## A.   PRICE WATERHOUSE

Although Title VII imposes no special burden of proof on discrimination plaintiffs, some courts have fashioned a heightened burden based not on the statute but on the case that prompted its amendment, Price Waterhouse v. Hopkins. We turn to that case. There, the Supreme Court confronted a problem not previously encountered in the statute's twenty-five year history: causation. The issue presented was whether there should be liability where an adverse employment decision was the result of mixed motives. More specifically, the trial court found that the failure to select Ann Hopkins for partner at an accounting firm was motivated both by legitimate concerns about her interpersonal skills and by "an impermissibly cabined view of the proper behavior of women."

All nine justices essentially agreed that liability was inappropriate where the employer would have made the same decision absent sex discrimination — in other words, the illegitimate factor was not a "but for" cause — but they divided over the nuances of the burden of proof. Four justices agreed that "when a plaintiff in a Title VII case proves that her gender played a motivating part in an employment decision, the defendant may avoid a finding of liability only by proving by a preponderance of the evidence that it would have made the same decision even if it had not taken the plaintiff's gender into account." These justices made clear that when "an employer considers both gender and legitimate factors at the time of making a decision, that decision was 'because of' sex." But, the employer could escape liability through the "same decision" affirmative defense. The dissent criticized the plurality for "its shift to the defendant of the burden of proof," and argued that the plaintiff should have to prove, by a preponderance of the evidence, that discrimination was the "but for" cause of the challenged action. In response, the plurality emphasized that it offered the defendant an affirmative defense to liability only *after* the plaintiff established that discriminatory animus played a role in the challenged employment action. . . . Regardless of nomenclature, the plurality agreed that if the employer showed a lack of "but for" causation, then that showing precluded liability.

Justice O'Connor had . . . gatekeeping concerns about when what she considered to be a special "burden shift" might be invoked, thus permitting the plaintiff to make less than the full showing necessary for a statutory violation:

> I believe there are significant differences between shifting the burden of persuasion to the employer in a case resting purely on statistical proof as in the disparate impact setting and shifting the burden of persuasion in a case like this one, where an employee has demonstrated by direct evidence that an illegitimate factor played a substantial role in a particular employment decision.

It was in this context that she discussed a need for "direct evidence" to show that the employer's "decisional process has been substantially infected by discrimination" before the special burden shift would be triggered. Because it was arguably the "narrowest ground" for the decision, Justice O'Connor's one-justice concurring opinion was considered by some to be the controlling analysis. Fernandes v. Costa Bros. Masonry, 199 F.3d 572, 580 (1st Cir. 1999).

### B.  1991 CIVIL RIGHTS ACT AMENDMENTS TO TITLE VII

Congress quickly responded to *Price Waterhouse* and a handful of other Supreme Court employment discrimination decisions with the introduction of the Civil Rights Act of 1990, which targeted "the Supreme Court's recent decisions by restoring the civil rights protections that were dramatically limited by those decisions." H.R. Cong. Rep. No. 101-856, at 1 (1990). Although the 1990 legislation ultimately floundered, an amended version, with much of the text intact, became the Civil Rights Act of 1991, which expressly overruled the basic premise that an employer could avoid all liability under Title VII by establishing the absence of "but for" causation.

Now, under Title VII, the use of a prohibited characteristic (race, color, religion, sex, or national origin) as simply "a motivating factor" in an employment action is unlawful. Congress did, however, add one safety valve: an employer can escape damages and orders of reinstatement, hiring, promotion and the like — but not attorney's fees or declaratory or injunctive relief — by proving the absence of "but for" causation as an affirmative defense. To the extent that there was confusion after *Price Waterhouse* — semantic or otherwise — with respect to burden shifting, the amendment clarified (1) that a Title VII violation is established through proof that a protected characteristic was "a motivating factor" in the employment action and (2) that the employer's "same decision" evidence serves as an affirmative defense with respect to the scope of remedies, not as a defense to liability.

The legislative history evinces a clear intent to overrule *Price Waterhouse*. In a subsection titled "The Need to Overturn *Price Waterhouse*," the report accompanying the 1991 Civil Rights Act reflects congressional concern that the "inevitable effect of the *Price Waterhouse* decision [was] to permit prohibited employment discrimination to escape sanction under Title VII." H.R. Rep. No. 102-40(I), at 46 (1991), *reprinted in* 1991 U.S.C.C.A.N. 549, 584. The report elaborates:

> When Congress enacted the Civil Rights Act of 1964, it precluded all invidious consideration of a person's race, color, religion, sex or national origin in employment. The ef-

fectiveness of Title VII's ban on discrimination on the basis of race, color, religion, sex or national origin has been severely undercut by the recent Supreme Court decision in Price Waterhouse v. Hopkins.

We do not disagree with those courts that have noted that the legislative history does not address Justice O'Connor's "direct evidence" comment. See, e.g., Watson v. Southeastern Pa. Transp. Auth., 207 F.3d 207, 218-19 (3d Cir. 2000).[2] What the history does show beyond doubt, however, is that the premise for Justice O'Connor's comment is wholly abrogated: No longer may "employers' discriminatory conduct escape[] liability," H.R. Rep. 40(I) at 47, simply by showing other sufficient causes. Consequently, there is no longer a basis for any special "evidentiary scheme" or heightened standard of proof to determine "but for" causation.

### C.   "DIRECT EVIDENCE"

Following Price Waterhouse and the Civil Rights Act of 1991, much has been made of Justice O'Connor's passing reference to "direct evidence." Indeed, the reference has spawned a virtual cottage industry of litigation over the effect and meaning of the phrase. It is unnecessary, however, to get mired in the debate over whether Justice O'Connor's opinion was controlling or not because the resolution to this conundrum lies in the 1991 amendments.

Justice O'Connor's reference must be interpreted in light of the Court's understanding at the time of Price Waterhouse, namely, that "but for" causation was factored into proof of a Title VII violation, either as an affirmative defense (plurality) or as part of the plaintiff's proof (dissent). Justice O'Connor wrote separately in part to "express [her] views as to when and how the strong medicine of requiring the employer to bear the burden of persuasion on the issue of causation should be administered." Her reference to "direct evidence" was intertwined with her concern about a scheme that shifted the burden on the question of liability from the employee to employer, albeit through an affirmative defense. The 1991 Act eliminated any confusion about burden-shifting and the proof necessary for a Title VII violation, so it is not surprising that courts have had trouble converting Justice O'Connor's reference into a legal standard under the new statutory provision.

The resulting jurisprudence has been a quagmire that defies characterization despite the valiant efforts of various courts and commentators. Within circuits, and often within opinions, different approaches are conflated, mixing burden of persuasion with evidentiary standards, confusing burden of ultimate persuasion with the burden to establish an affirmative defense, and declining to acknowledge the role of circumstantial evidence. We see no need to get bogged down in this debate. Rather, based on the language of the statute — which requires proof of only "a motivating factor" and does not set out any special proof burdens — we conclude that Congress did not impose a special or heightened evidentiary burden on the plaintiff in a Title VII case in which discriminatory animus may have constituted one of two or more reasons for the employer's challenged actions. 42 U.S.C. § 2000e-2(m).

This approach is consistent with recent Supreme Court cases underscoring that no special pleading or proof hurdles may be imposed on Title VII plaintiffs. For example, in Swierkiewicz v. Sorema N.A., 534 U.S. 506 (2002), the Court struck down

---

2. For a thorough analysis concluding that the legislative history is unhelpful on the "direct evidence" requirement, see Benjamin C. Mizer, Note, Toward a Motivating Factor Test for Individual Disparate Treatment Claims, 100 Mich. L. Rev. 234, 256-60 (2001).

judicially imposed heightened pleading standards. Just two years earlier, in *Reeves*, it declined to require independent evidence of discrimination in addition to prima facie evidence and sufficient evidence to rebut pretext. Instead, the Court emphasized that the jury determines the ultimate question of liability.

To understand why we should stick to the statute rather than divine a new standard of proof, it is instructive to look at the state of circuit law in this area. Judge Selya has made an attempt to categorize the circuits' approaches in a framework that provides a useful overview. Fernandes v. Costa Bros. Masonry, Inc., 199 F.3d at 582 (1st Cir. 1999). He first discusses the "classic" position, an approach that takes the definition of "direct evidence" from the dictionary: "'evidence, which if believed, proves existence of fact in issue *without inference or presumption*.'" Judge Selya notes that "only the Fifth and Tenth Circuits cling consistently to this view, [but] other tribunals have embraced it periodically."

Next is the "animus plus" position, which basically requires that the plaintiff prove a particularly strong case — more than ordinarily would be required for an inference of discrimination to be permissible. Our review indicates that a majority of courts that impose a "direct evidence" requirement adhere to this view, either explicitly or implicitly. See, e.g., Thomas [v. NFL Players Assn., 131 F.3d 198, 204 (D.D.C. 1997)] (defining direct evidence as "a relationship between proof and incidents"); Fernandes (explaining the function of direct evidence as restricting the mixed-motive analysis "to those infrequent cases in which a plaintiff can demonstrate [discrimination] with a high degree of assurance"); Fuller v. Phipps, 67 F.3d 1137, 1143 (4th Cir. 1995) (holding that the determination "hinges on the strength of the evidence"); Bass v. Bd. of County Comm'rs, 256 F.3d 1095, 1105 (11th Cir. 2001) (requiring, under the rhetoric of banning circumstantial evidence, "only the most blatant remarks") (citation omitted). Judge Selya places the Fourth, D.C., Ninth, and Third circuits in this camp, not without hesitation, and indicates that other circuits indicate "occasional approval" of this approach. *Fernandes.*

Finally, there is the "animus" position, which simply requires evidence that bears on the alleged discriminatory animus or, put even more simply, evidence of discrimination. Judge Selya places the Second Circuit, the Eighth Circuit "intermittently," and other stray cases, in this camp.

Other courts and commentators have had even more difficulty articulating an order to the chaos. See, e.g., *Thomas* (citing Fifth, Tenth, and Eleventh Circuits as taking "direct evidence" to mean non-inferential); Christopher Y. Chen, Note, Rethinking the Direct Evidence Requirement: A Suggested Approach in Analyzing Mixed-Motives Discrimination Claims, 86 Cornell L. Rev. 899, 908-15 (2001); Robert Belton, Mixed-Motive Cases in Employment Discrimination Law Revisited: A Brief Updated View of the Swamp, 51 Mercer L. Rev. 651, 663 (2000) ("The line between *McDonnell Douglas* and *Price Waterhouse* is very murky.").

Indeed, within circuits, cases sometimes take different approaches. See Wright v. Southland Corp., 187 F.3d 1287, 1294 (11th Cir. 1999) (recognizing intra-circuit splits). For example, the First Circuit first embraced the animus plus approach in *Fernandes*, but recently implied in Weston-Smith v. Cooley Dickinson Hospital, 282 F.3d 60, 64 (1st Cir. 2002), that it took the classic approach. The Eleventh Circuit first allowed "broad statements" of discriminatory attitude, Burrell v. Bd. of Trustees of Ga. Military Coll., 125 F.3d 1390, 1394 n.7 (11th Cir. 1997), but later concluded that only statements related to the decisionmaking process were sufficient to overcome the special "direct evidence" hurdle, *Bass*.

In a carefully considered decision issued shortly after the Civil Rights Act of 1991, the Second Circuit held that direct evidence simply meant evidence sufficient to permit the trier of fact to conclude that an illegitimate characteristic was a motivating factor in the challenged decision under Title VII. Tyler [v. Bethlehem Steel, 958 F.2d 1183, 1185 (2d Cir. 1992)]. However, a few months later, a different panel held that discrimination victims face the special hurdle of presenting "evidence of conduct or statements by persons involved in the decisionmaking process that may be viewed as directly reflecting the alleged discriminatory attitude." Ostrowski v. Atlantic Mut. Ins. Cos., 968 F.2d 171, 182 (2d Cir. 1992). Although *Ostrowski* squarely rejected a definition of "direct evidence" as non-circumstantial evidence, some cases quote it as though it supported the noncircumstantial requirement. See, e.g., Cronquist v. City of Minneapolis, 237 F.3d 920, 925 (8th Cir. 2001). *Ostrowski* was an age discrimination case, but has been widely applied in the Title VII context, apparently without analysis of the difference in the statutes. See, e.g., Lightfoot v. Union Carbide Corp., 110 F.3d 898, 913 (2d Cir. 1997).

In the Tenth Circuit, the court initially declined to impose a heightened "direct evidence" requirement, only to be ignored by a panel ruling six months later. Compare Medlock v. Ortho Biotech, Inc., 164 F.3d 545, 553 (10th Cir. 1999) ("A mixed motive instruction is . . . appropriate in any case where the evidence is sufficient to allow a trier to find both forbidden and permissible motives." (citation and internal quotation marks omitted)) with Shorter v. ICG Holdings, Inc., 188 F.3d 1204, 1207 (10th Cir. 1999) (imposing a "direct evidence" requirement as classically defined, and excluding "statements of personal opinion, even when reflecting a personal bias").

We believe that the best way out of this morass is a return to the language of the statute, which imposes no special requirement and does not reference "direct evidence." To the extent that courts are using "direct evidence" as a veiled excuse to substitute their own judgment for that of the jury, we reject that approach. In so doing, we follow the Second Circuit's *Tyler* case, the Eleventh Circuit's *Wright* case, the Tenth Circuit's approach in *Medlock*, and the Eighth Circuit in Schleiniger v. Des Moines Water Works, 925 F.2d 1100 (8th Cir. 1991). We also agree with other courts to the extent that they hold that non-circumstantial evidence is not the magical threshold for Title VII liability. See, e.g., *Thomas* (collecting cases).

Put simply, the plaintiff in any Title VII case may establish a violation through a preponderance of evidence (whether direct or circumstantial)[4] that a protected characteristic played "a motivating factor." Like the Supreme Court, "we think it generally undesirable, where holdings of the Court are not at issue, to dissect the sentences of the United States Reports as though they were the United States Code." St. Mary's Honor Ctr. v. Hicks. The "direct evidence" quagmire results from just such a misdirected inquiry, and we decline to be drawn in.

### D.   THE FRAMEWORK FOR PROVING A TITLE VII VIOLATION

In addition to the confusion over "direct evidence," there has been considerable misunderstanding regarding the relationship among the *McDonnell Douglas* burden-shifting analysis (sometimes referred to as "pretext" analysis), which primarily applies to summary judgment proceedings, and the terms single-motive and mixed-motive, which primarily refer to the theory or theories by which the defendant opposes the

---

4. The general rule bears repeating: in proving a case, circumstantial evidence "is weighed on the same scale and laid before the jury in the same manner as direct evidence." In other words, "circumstantial evidence is not inherently less probative than direct evidence." United States v. Cruz, 536 F.2d 1264, 1266 (9th Cir. 1976) (citation and internal quotation marks omitted).

plaintiff's claim of discrimination. The short answer is that all of these concepts coexist without conflict.

Caesars' argument in favor of a higher evidentiary burden is emblematic of the confusion. Caesars maintains that without special proof, "any plaintiff who is able to establish a prima facie showing in a pretext case would qualify for a mixed-motive instruction, conflating the two categories of cases." This argument mistakenly juxtaposes the pretrial *McDonnell Douglas* legal framework and the "mixed-motive" characterization.

To place *McDonnell Douglas* in perspective, it must be remembered that the current form of Title VII is the result of twenty-seven years of dynamic exchange between the Supreme Court and Congress, working toward a framework that provides a remedy for barriers of discrimination and inequality in the workplace. . . . *McDonnell Douglas* was the first in a series of cases dealing with the difficulties of proving intent to discriminate in a disparate treatment context. The Supreme Court detailed circumstances sufficient to support an inference of discrimination, the now-eponymous [four-factor] *McDonnell Douglas* "prima facie case and burden-shifting paradigm." The Court recently reaffirmed that "the precise requirements of a prima facie case can vary depending on the context and were 'never intended to be rigid, mechanized, or ritualistic.'" *Swierkiewicz* (quoting Furnco Constr. Corp. v. Waters, 438 U.S. 567, 577 (1978)). This legal proof structure is a tool to assist plaintiffs at the summary judgment stage so that they may reach trial.

As the Supreme Court elaborated a few years after *McDonnell Douglas*, the prima facie case "eliminates the most common nondiscriminatory reasons for the plaintiff's rejection." *Burdine*. Therefore, "we presume these acts, if otherwise unexplained, are more likely than not based on the consideration of impermissible factors." *Burdine* clarified, however, that the plaintiff need not rely on this presumption: "She may succeed . . . either directly by persuading the court that a discriminatory reason more likely motivated the employer or indirectly by showing that the employer's proffered explanation is unworthy of credence."

Throughout these cases and those that followed, the court reaffirmed the canons of proof: the plaintiff retains the "ultimate burden of persuading the court that she has been the victim of intentional discrimination," the question comes down to whether she has made her case. See also *Hicks; Reeves*.

The plaintiff may make out a prima facie case — which may, admittedly, be a weak showing — that entitles her to a commensurately small benefit, a transitory presumption of discrimination: the burden of *production* only shifts briefly to the employer to explain why it took the challenged action, if not based on the protected characteristic. In practice, employers quickly rebut the presumption and it "drops from the case." *Burdine*. The burden of production then shifts back to the plaintiff to introduce evidence from which the factfinder could conclude that the employer's proffered reason was pretextual. The burden of *persuasion* always remains with the employee to prove the ultimate Title VII violation — unlawful discrimination.

It is important to emphasize, however, that nothing compels the parties to invoke the *McDonnell Douglas* presumption. United States Postal Serv. Bd. v. Aikens. Evidence can be in the form of the *McDonnell Douglas* prima facie case, or other sufficient evidence — direct or circumstantial — of discriminatory intent. Thus, although *McDonnell Douglas* may be used where a single motive is at issue, this proof scheme is not the exclusive means of proof in such a case. Indeed, it also might be invoked in cases in which the defendant asserts a "same decision" defense to certain remedies, a circumstance in which mixed motives are at issue.

Regardless of the method chosen to arrive at trial, it is not normally appropriate to introduce the *McDonnell Douglas* burden-shifting framework to the jury.[6] At that stage, the framework "unnecessarily evades the ultimate question of discrimination *vel non.*" *Aikens.*

Once at the trial stage, the plaintiff is required to put forward evidence of discrimination "because of" a protected characteristic.[7] After hearing both parties' evidence, the district court must decide what legal conclusions the evidence could reasonably support and instruct the jury accordingly. This determination is distinct from the question of whether to invoke the *McDonnell Douglas* presumption, which occurs at a separate, earlier stage of proceedings, involves summary judgment rather than jury instructions, and is unrelated to the number of possible motives for the challenged action. Instead, the choice of jury instructions depends simply on a determination of whether the evidence supports a finding that just one — or more than one — factor actually motivated the challenged decision. Justice White, in his concurring opinion in *Price Waterhouse*, succinctly described how the type of evidence presented affects the question facing the jury:

> In [single-motive] cases, "the issue is whether either illegal or legal motives, but not both, were the 'true' motives behind the decision." In mixed-motive cases, however, there is no one "true" motive behind the decision. Instead, the decision is a result of multiple factors, at least one of which is legitimate.

*Price Waterhouse* (White, J., concurring in the judgment).[8] Following the 1991 amendments, characterizing the evidence as mixed-motive instead of single-motive results only in the availability of a different defense, a difference which derives directly from the statutory text, not from judicially created proof structures.

As a practical matter, the question of how many motives the evidence reasonably supports affects the jury instructions as follows:

If, based on the evidence, the trial court determines that the only reasonable conclusion a jury could reach is that discriminatory animus is the *sole* cause for the challenged employment action or that discrimination played *no* role at all in the employer's decisionmaking, then the jury should be instructed to determine whether the challenged action was taken "because of" the prohibited reason. 42 U.S.C. § 2000e-2(a). If the jury determines that the employer acted because of discriminatory intent, the employee prevails and may receive the full remedies available under Title VII; if not, the employer prevails. In such cases the employer does not benefit from the "same decision" defense, which, if successful, significantly limits the employee's remedies.

In contrast, in cases in which the evidence could support a finding that discrimination is one of two or more reasons for the challenged decision, at least one of which may be legitimate, the jury should be instructed to determine first whether the

---

6. The presumption is thus what has been termed a "bursting bubble" presumption. In one limited circumstance, the presumption retains vitality at trial: where there is no rebuttal by the employer, but the plaintiff's prima facie case is in factual dispute. The jury then determines whether the prima facie case is established. If it is, the jury must find discrimination. *Hicks.*

7. As the Supreme Court has observed, a case need not be characterized or labeled at the outset. Rather, the shape will often emerge after discovery or even at trial. Similarly, the complaint itself need not contain more than the allegation that the adverse employment action was taken because of a protected characteristic. See *Price Waterhouse* (plurality opinion).

8. Although Justice White used the term "pretext cases" in the first sentence of this passage, it is clear from the context that he was referring to single-motive cases, including those involving pretext. Id. at 260.

discriminatory reason was "a motivating factor" in the challenged action. If the jury's answer to this question is in the affirmative, then the employer has violated Title VII. However, if the jury then finds that the employer has proved the "same decision" affirmative defense by a preponderance of the evidence the employer will escape the imposition of damages and any order of reinstatement, hiring, promotion, and the like, and is liable solely for attorney's fees, declaratory relief, and an order prohibiting future discriminatory actions.

Regardless of what kind of instructions are given, we emphasize that there are not two fundamentally different types of Title VII cases. In some cases, the employer may be entitled to the "same decision" affirmative defense instruction. In others, it may not. The employee's ultimate burden of proof in all cases remains the same: to show by a preponderance of the evidence that the challenged employment decision was "because of" discrimination.

Finally, we turn to the question of where the concept of pretext fits in this frame-work. Although cases in which the *McDonnell Douglas* framework is applied are sometimes referred to as "pretext cases," and we have no wish to change a quarter century of usage, it should be noted that questions of pretext may arise in any Title VII case, regardless of whether it is analyzed under *McDonnell Douglas*. Cases in which the dispute is only over whether or not the employer possessed the discriminatory motive alleged need not involve pretext, although they often do. For example, if the plaintiff chooses not to invoke the *McDonnell Douglas* framework, the employer need not proffer any explanation for the challenged action, but may simply require the plaintiff to prove her case of discrimination. Nor is the concept of pretext alien to cases in which an employer asserts a "same decision" or "but for" defense. For example, one of the employer's purportedly legitimate reasons may be pretextual. On the other hand, another may not. As Justice O'Connor recently explained in writing for the Court: "Proof that the defendant's explanation is unworthy of credence is simply one form of circumstantial evidence that is probative of intentional discrimination. . . ." *Reeves*.

To summarize: *McDonnell Douglas* and "mixed-motive" are not two opposing types of cases. Rather, they are separate inquiries that occur at separate stages of the litigation. Nor are "single-motive" and "mixed-motive" cases fundamentally different categories of cases. Both require the employee to prove discrimination; they simply reflect the type of evidence offered. Where the employer asserts that, even if the factfinder determines that a discriminatory motive exists, the employer would in any event have taken the adverse employment action for other reasons, it may take advantage of the "same decision" affirmative defense. The remedies will differ if the employer prevails on that defense. With this framework in mind, we turn to the evidence in Costa's case.

## II.   MIXED-MOTIVE INSTRUCTION AND SUFFICIENCY OF THE EVIDENCE

Although Caesars invokes the *McDonnell Douglas* analysis, that framework is not instructive at this stage of the case. See *Aikens*. Rather, we are asked to review the district court's decision to give a mixed-motive instruction and the sufficiency of the evidence to support the jury's verdict, as challenged in a motion for judgment as a matter of law made at the close of the evidence.

### A.   THE MIXED-MOTIVE JURY INSTRUCTION

We must first determine the applicable standard of review. The standards are well known and often stated: we generally review the formulation of instructions for abuse of discretion, but whether an instruction misstates the law is a legal issue reviewed de novo. At issue here is whether the evidence can be characterized as establishing multiple motives, and thus warranting the affirmative defense. Because this evaluation is, at bottom, an evaluation of the evidence, an abuse of discretion standard is appropriate.

The district court submitted both claims — the termination and the conditions of employment — to the jury. It first instructed the jury that:

> The plaintiff has the burden of proving each of the following by a preponderance of the evidence:
>
> 1. Costa suffered adverse work conditions, and
> 2. Costa's gender was a motivating factor in any such work conditions imposed upon her. Gender refers to the quality of being male or female.
>
> If you find that each of these things has been proved against a defendant, your verdict should be for the plaintiff and against the defendant. On the other hand, if any of these things has not been proved against a defendant, your verdict should be for the defendant.

The jury was next given the following mixed-motive instruction, which is central to this appeal:

> You have heard evidence that the defendant's treatment of the plaintiff was motivated by the plaintiff's sex and also by other lawful reasons. If you find that the plaintiff's sex was a motivating factor in the defendant's treatment of the plaintiff, the plaintiff is entitled to your verdict, even if you find that the defendant's conduct was also motivated by a lawful reason. However, if you find that the defendant's treatment of the plaintiff was motivated by both gender and lawful reasons, you must decide whether the plaintiff is entitled to damages. The plaintiff is entitled to damages unless the defendant proves by a preponderance of the evidence that the defendant would have treated plaintiff similarly even if the plaintiff's gender had played no role in the employment decision.

Caesars first intimates that the wording of the mixed motive instruction was invalid because it inappropriately implied a judicial determination that sex was in fact a motivation for the challenged treatment. Caesars, however, waived any objection to the form of the instruction by conceding at trial that it was "a reasonable statement of the mixed motive instruction." Fed. R. Civ. P. 51.

As for Caesars' main contention, we are not persuaded that the district court erred in giving a mixed-motive instruction. In many respects, Costa's case presents a typical Title VII case in which a plaintiff alleges that she was discharged or disciplined for a discriminatory reason and the employer counters that the reason for its action was entirely different. The evidence did not require the jury to believe that discrimination was the only motive, nor that Caesars' stated reasons were all bogus or pretextual. For example, there was evidence that Hallett, Stewart, and other decisionmakers were legitimately concerned about Costa's behavior and altercations with co-workers, but there was likewise significant evidence that they would not have taken such drastic disciplinary measures against a man. Similarly, the jury could reasonably have concluded that the overtime assignment system was in a state of disarray that allowed favoritism and that one element of that favoritism was preferential treatment for male workers. The fact is that Caesars may have had legitimate reasons to terminate Costa. Indeed, unlike in many Title VII cases, Costa does not dispute many of the events that took place. Nor does she wholly discount that these events may have been part of the basis for her discipline and termination. Nonetheless, the wide array of discriminatory treatment is sufficient to support a conclusion that sex was also a motivating factor in the decision-making process. Thus, the district court did not abuse its discretion in giving a mixed-motive instruction.

### B.   SUFFICIENCY OF THE EVIDENCE

We review de novo Caesars' challenge to the district court's denial of its Rule 50(b) motion for judgment as a matter of law. At the outset, we note that the standard that Caesars must meet is very high. We can overturn the jury's verdict and grant such a motion only if "'there is no legally sufficient basis for a reasonable jury to find for that party on that issue.'" *Reeves* (quoting Fed. R. Civ. P. 50(a)). Because we "may not substitute [our] view of the evidence for that of the jury," we neither make credibility determinations nor weigh the evidence and we must draw all inferences in favor of Costa, *Reeves*. The Supreme Court cautions us to "disregard all evidence favorable to the moving party that the jury is not required to believe." This high hurdle recognizes that credibility, inferences, and factfinding are the province of the jury, not this court.

### 1.   Liability Determination

Applying the analysis outlined above, we begin, not surprisingly, with the text of the statute, asking whether a reasonable jury could conclude that sex was "a motivating factor" in the challenged actions. The discriminatory treatment ran the gamut from disparate discipline and "stacking" Costa's personnel file to stalking her, singling her out for different treatment in the workplace, and discriminating against her in the assignment of overtime. In the final analysis, the jury heard testimony from Costa and fifteen other witnesses. Testimony included the chronology of escalating discipline and targeting of Costa, co-workers who identified discrimination because of sex, and multiple examples of disparate treatment purposefully directed at Costa because of her sex. Lending credence to the claim that sex was a motivating factor in her treatment, Costa also offered evidence of sexual stereotyping and sexual epithets. Viewing the evidence from her perspective and drawing all inferences in her favor, we cannot conclude that "there is no legally sufficient evidentiary basis for a reasonable jury," *Reeves*, to find that intentional discrimination on the basis of sex was "a motivating factor" in subjecting Costa to a number of adverse employment actions, and culminating in her termination.

Costa presents overwhelming evidence that she was more harshly treated than her male coworkers. Because she was the only woman in an otherwise all-male unit, linking the differential treatment to her sex was not a difficult leap. The jury could easily infer that sex was one of the reasons Costa was singled out for negative treatment. Indeed, the evidence is sufficiently strong that for many of the incidents the jury might have concluded that sex was the only reason for the adverse action. "Proof of discriminatory motive . . . can in some situations be inferred from the mere fact of differences in treatment." Int'l Bhd. of Teamsters v. United States. Mindful of the Supreme Court's admonishment to "draw all reasonable inferences in favor of" the prevailing party, *Reeves*, we conclude that the jury was entitled to view the differential treatment here as evidence of discrimination. . . .

The most prominent example of this differential treatment was Caesars' decision to terminate Costa for an incident that netted her male co-worker only a five-day suspension. Costa's claim that she was shoved against an elevator wall and sustained bruises from the altercation is not one to be taken lightly. The excuse that the management could not figure out whom to believe — Costa or Gerber — is questionable given the strong corroboration of Costa's story and the inconsistencies in Gerber's account. The explanation offered by Caesars was lacking in several respects, and the jury was certainly not required to believe it. The jury was entitled instead to infer that Costa was fired, while Gerber was only suspended, because Costa was a woman. This is precisely the circumstance in which we credit the inference in Costa's favor.

Finally, the jury could easily have believed that Costa's record was itself largely a result of discrimination because of repeated incidents of unfair discipline that accumulated over time. For example, her supervisor's decision to backfill the records with prior alleged misconduct supports such a conclusion.

Caesars presents us with alternate rationales for the termination, and asks us to hold as a matter of law that Costa's conduct was the only element motivating its decision. We decline this invitation. Perhaps the disparities in how Costa was treated were in part because supervisor Hallett disliked her as a person and not as a woman. Perhaps they were in part because Costa had a history of "not getting along" with her co-workers, although there was contrary testimony. What the jury implicitly concluded, however, was that the disparities were also in part because she was a woman. In so finding, the jury did not necessarily reject all of Caesars' legitimate complaints about Costa. But even if it credited certain of these explanations, in following the jury instructions, it reasonably found that sex was "a motivating factor" in the termination. The evidence of differential treatment was so persuasive and long-standing that the judgment may be upheld on this ground alone. . . .

We turn next to Costa's evidence that she was chastised for failing to conform to the role stereotypically assigned to women. The jury heard remarks that could reasonably be viewed to "stem[] from an impermissibly cabined view of the proper behavior of women." *Price Waterhouse*. She was told that she did not deserve overtime because she did not have a family to support. In her view, the implication was that she was not *a man* with a family to support. The jury could interpret this as a comment directed to her as a woman, indicating that the discriminatory action, a failure to assign overtime, was based on her not being a male breadwinner. The Seventh Circuit held similar facts to be evidence of sex stereotyping. See Bruno v. City of Crown Point, 950 F.2d 355, 362 (7th Cir. 1991) (holding that jury could believe employer held sexual stereotypes when female paramedic applicant was the only one asked about family responsibilities).

She was also disciplined in circumstances that the jury could reasonably infer amounted to telling her to "walk more femininely, talk more femininely." *Price Waterhouse*. For example, Costa was told "you got more balls than the guys." And yet, arguably when she acted tough like the guys, she received harsher discipline rather than an "atta boy" reinforcement. At trial, Caesars' consistent objection to Costa as an employee was that she was "strong-willed" and "opinionated," a view that the jury could have reasonably interpreted as gender stereotyping. As was clear from her testimony, Costa sought no special treatment, only equal treatment.

Finally, reinforcing the inference that her gender motivated the adverse view of her character, Costa presented evidence of sexual language and epithets directed to her. Specifically, Costa presented evidence that Hallett, the very supervisor who signed her discharge, had declared an intention on several occasions to "get rid of that bitch." Whether this term is part of the everyday give-and-take of a warehouse environment or is inherently offensive is not for us to say. Instead, we simply conclude that the jury could interpret it here to be one piece of evidence among many, a derogatory term indicating sex-based hostility.[9] In addition, managers encouraged sex-based epithets directed at Costa by disciplining her for failing to tolerate the slurs silently. Admittedly, Costa worked in a rough and tumble and often vulgar environment. But the prevalence of race or sex-based slurs does not excuse them. See Swinton v. Potomac Corp., 270 F.3d 794, 807 (9th Cir. 2001).

As we explained in Steiner v. Showboat Operating Co., 25 F.3d 1459, 1463-64 (9th Cir. 1994), when abuse directed at women "centers on the fact that they [are] females," a jury may infer discrimination. In Steiner, a hostile environment case, a supervisor "was indeed abusive to men, but . . . his abuse of women was different. It relied on sexual epithets, offensive, explicit references to women's bodies and sexual conduct." Similarly here, the evidence supports the inference that the abuse directed toward Costa was different in nature and degree.

In the context of this case, we need not decide whether this sexual language is dispositive of discrimination. Rather, this language was simply one more factor for the jury to consider in the face of repeated differential treatment by Hallett and others at Caesars. Viewing the evidence in Costa's favor, the jury could have easily inferred that the use of highly charged and offensive sexual language was simply another means of singling Costa out because she was a woman.

Finally, we detour briefly to address the suggestion that Hallett was somehow incapable of discriminating against Costa because Hallett was herself a woman. This argument was resoundingly rejected by a unanimous Supreme Court in Oncale. In a society where historically discriminatory attitudes about women are "firmly rooted in our national consciousness," Frontiero v. Richardson, 411 U.S. 677, 684, (1973) (plurality opinion), we cannot discount that the jury perceived Hallett, a former Army officer now placed in a supervisory position in a virtually male-only world, as demonstrating hostility toward Costa as a woman as a means of showing that she was "one of the boys." Life was not necessarily easy for Hallett, but that was no excuse for visiting harsh discipline on Costa.

## 2.  Affirmative Defense — "Same Decision"

Once the jury found liability on the part of Caesars, it was asked to decide whether the "defendant proved by a preponderance of the evidence that the defendant would have made the same decisions if the plaintiff's gender had played no role in the employment decision." The jury checked the "NO" box. This question on the special verdict form reflects the "same decision" affirmative defense provided in 42 U.S.C. 2000e-5(g)(2)(B).

Caesars, not Costa, has the burden on this question, and we must still filter the evidence in the light most favorable to Costa. Under this lens, much of the evidence of differential treatment removes this question from the realm of the hypothetical and shows what, in fact, Caesars did do when men violated its policies. Costa's

---

9. See Galloway v. Gen'l Motors Serv. Parts Operations, 78 F.3d 1164, 1168 (7th Cir. 1996) (holding that the legal meaning of the word "bitch" is context-specific; "The word 'bitch' is sometimes used as a label for women who possess such 'woman faults' as 'ill-temper . . .,' and latterly as a label for women considered by some men to be too aggressive or careerist." (citation omitted)), overruled in part on other grounds by AMTRAK v. Morgan, 122 S. Ct. 2061 (2002); Kriss v. Sprint Communications Co., 58 F.3d 1276, 1281 (8th Cir. 1995) (noting that use of the word "bitch" might be evidence of discrimination in some contexts); Neuren v. Adduci, Mastriani, Meeks & Schill, 43 F.3d 1507, 1513 (D.C. Cir. 1995) ("This pejorative term may support an inference that an employment decision is discriminatory under different circumstances. . . .").

infractions may have played a role in her termination. But the evidence also under-scores how the documentation of her infractions and discipline stemmed in part from sex discrimination. Based on the extensive testimony, the jury simply did not believe that Caesars would have made the same decision "but for" Costa's sex. There was a substantial basis for the jury to conclude that Caesars did not meet its burden in demonstrating that it would have made the same decision absent consideration of sex.

GOULD, Circuit Judge, with whom KOZINSKI, FERNANDEZ, and KLEINFELD, Circuit Judges, join, dissenting:

I respectfully dissent because the majority does not follow the Supreme Court's holding in *Price Waterhouse* in Title VII mixed motives cases. The majority's analysis is not persuasive and should be corrected because it disregards the holding of *Hopkins* that is reflected in Justice O'Connor's concurring opinion. . . .

Justice O'Connor would allow a plaintiff to use a mixed motive test only in narrow circumstances. In concurrence, Justice O'Connor held that she would require a Title VII plaintiff in a mixed motive case to produce "direct evidence" showing that "decisionmakers placed substantial negative reliance on [the] illegitimate criterion."

I do not point to Justice O'Connor's concurring opinion merely to admire its common sense, though that is admirable. Rather, we must heed the direct evidence rule of *Hopkins* as controlling, and we may not diminish it, in the majority's terms, as a "passing reference." Justice O'Connor's concurring opinion in *Hopkins*, which in considered language required the use of direct evidence to prove a mixed motive case, must be viewed as the holding of the Court, under the rule of Marks v. United States, 430 U.S. 188, 193, (1977) ("When a fragmented Court decides a case and no single rationale explaining the result enjoys the assent of five Justices, the holding of the Court may be viewed as that position taken by those Members who concurred in the judgments on the narrowest grounds").

Because Justice O'Connor would permit the use of the mixed motives test only when direct evidence is present, Justice O'Connor "concurred in the judgment on the narrowest grounds," and her concurrence is to be considered the holding of *Hopkins* under the rule described in *Marks*. The view that Justice O'Connor's opinion is the holding in *Hopkins* is supported by Congress' actions in amending Title VII in 1991, by the holdings of other circuits on the issue, and by sound policy.

The 1991 amendments to Title VII did not modify the Supreme Court's prior holding on the need for direct evidence. Subsection (m) of 42 U.S.C. § 2000e-2, which incorporates the premise of *Hopkins* that discrimination can be shown in a mixed motive case so long as it is one factor, was enacted two years after *Hopkins*. . . . Though Congress responded to other aspects of the Court's holding in *Hopkins*, specifically the holding that an employer could completely avoid liability if it could show that it would have made the same decision absent the discriminatory motive, see 42 U.S.C. § 2000e-5(g)(2), Congress, in amending Title VII, did not respond at all to Justice O'Connor's direct evidence requirement, which had already been adopted by several circuit courts. Instead, the statutory amendments are silent as to that subject, neither praising nor condemning, neither adopting nor rejecting, and clearly not modifying Justice O'Connor's test, which is properly viewed as the holding of *Hopkins*. This silence indicates that Congress left undisturbed Justice O'Connor's holding and the prior circuit decisions that adhered to it. As we remain bound by the Supreme Court's precedent, we must follow the direct evidence rule as explained in Justice O'Connor's concurrence.

By vitiating Justice O'Connor's direct evidence requirement, the majority's hold-ing puts our circuit in conflict with almost all others. See Jackson v. Harvard Univ., 900 F.2d 464, 467 (1st Cir. 1990); Ostrowski v. Atl. Mut. Ins. Cos., 968 F.2d 171, 182 (2d Cir. 1992); Starceski v. Westinghouse Elec. Corp., 54 F.3d 1089, 1096 (3d Cir. 1995); Fuller v. Phipps, 67 F.3d 1137, 1142 (4th Cir. 1995); Brown v. E. Miss. Elec. Power Ass'n, 989 F.2d 858, 861 (5th Cir. 1993); Wilson v. Firestone Tire & Rubber Co., 932 F.2d 510, 514 (6th Cir. 1991); Plair v. E.J. Brach & Sons, Inc., 105 F.3d 343, 347 (7th Cir. 1997); Schleiniger v. Des Moines Water Works, 925 F.2d 1100, 1101 (8th Cir. 1991); Heim v. Utah, 8 F.3d 1541, 1547 (10th Cir. 1993); E.E.O.C. v. Alton Packaging Corp., 901 F.2d 920, 923 (11th Cir. 1990). As suggested in the decision of the three-judge panel in *Costa*, and as reflected in the cases cited above, these circuits have correctly viewed Justice O'Connor's opinion in *Hopkins* as the holding of the Court and have followed it on that basis. I agree with the other circuits and with the reasoning of the prior opinion of the three-judge panel in *Costa*, which I adopt be-cause it is faithful to precedent.[1] We should not rush to join a decision that turns its back on our colleagues' wisdom and engages our circuit in a fanciful frolic of its own.

Finally, apart from our duty to abide by precedent, policy concerns favor adher-ing to Justice O'Connor's view of mixed motives analysis. Mixed motives analysis is a departure from the well-established *McDonnell Douglas* framework. Whereas *McDonnell Douglas* requires the plaintiff to make a pretext showing once an em-ployer puts forth evidence of legitimate nondiscriminatory reasons for the challenged employment practice, mixed motive analysis allows a plaintiff to prevail even when she cannot prove pretext.

To keep the mixed motive framework from overriding in all cases the *McDonnell Douglas* rule and the pretext requirement, which it clearly was not meant to do, mixed motive analysis properly is available only in a special subset of cases. Justice O'Connor's direct evidence requirement meets this need: It requires the plaintiff to produce highly probative, direct evidence, before she may utilize the more lenient, mixed mo-tives test. As a practical matter, without this or some similar constraint on when a plaintiff may invoke the mixed motives test, any plaintiff would opt for the *Hopkins* framework to avoid having to show pretext. The Supreme Court's seminal opinion in *McDonnell Douglas* would be effectively overruled by an incorrect interpretation of *Hopkins* that jettisons the direct evidence requirement, an effect that could not have been intended in *Hopkins* and an effect that will create uncertainty in our settled law.

Taken with the idea that plaintiff, an unsatisfactory employee, is a "trailblazer," the majority departs from the path of precedent and blazes its own trail beyond the fron-tiers of settled law into regions of error. I respectfully dissent.

*NOTES*

1. The majority opinion of this 7 to 4 en banc decision traces the considerable con-fusion and disarray among and within the circuits concerning the dividing line be-

---

1. The three-judge panel held that: Costa's case comes down to the fact that she was the only woman in her workplace and that in some instances she was treated less favorably than her male coworkers. But she has failed to produce evidence that she was treated differently *because* she was a woman — "direct and substantial evidence of discriminatory animus." Accordingly, the district court erred in giving the jury a mixed-motive instruction. Because the court's instructions shifted the burden of proof to Caesars, the error was not harmless. Caesars was prejudiced, moreover, by the court's instruction that the jury had "heard evidence that the defendant's treatment of the plaintiff was motivated by the plaintiff's sex," a state-ment not supported by the record. Accordingly, the judgment must be vacated.

tween *Price Waterhouse* and *McDonnell Douglas* cases. How does the majority resolve that conflict?

2. According to the majority, both *Price Waterhouse* and *McDonnell Douglas* survive its decision. What function does *McDonnell Douglas* now play? At the pre-trial level, *McDonnell Douglas* is available as a presumption to aid finding a prima facie case sufficient to resist a motion for summary judgment. But the majority recognizes that plaintiff does not always need the help where her case is strong. The majority says *McDonnell Douglas* still survives at trial if the evidence supports the possibility that the decision plaintiff challenges was either only for the reason defendant asserts or the reason was only a pretext for discrimination. Won't this be the exceptional case? If plaintiff simply denies it discriminates, without stating a nondiscriminatory reason, won't plaintiff be entitled to judgment as a matter of law?

3. Historically, most individual disparate treatment cases have been analyzed as *McDonnell Douglas* cases because of the lack of "direct" evidence of intent to discriminate no matter what definition of "direct" was used. Will that still be true applying *Costa*? Won't most cases involve the possibility that both discrimination as well as some other, nondiscriminatory reason might be involved in the decision plaintiff challenges? After all, there are few perfect employees and few perfectly bad employees.

4. Justice O'Connor's concurrence in *Price Waterhouse* is key to the prevailing distinction between "direct" evidence and "circumstantial" evidence cases. She is also the author of *Reeves*. Given the Supreme Court's grant of certiorari in *Costa*, she will have the opportunity to clarify her position. Will she go along with the majority or the dissent in *Costa*? How will the Civil Rights Act of 1991 affect her vote?

5. Is there now a unified theory of individual disparate treatment law? See generally John Valery White, The Irrational Turn in Employment Discrimination Law: Slouching Toward a Unified Approach to Civil Rights Law, 53 Mercer L. Rev. 709 (2002).

## PROBLEM 3.1

In response to a help-wanted ad, Jane Armstrong, a 38-year-old woman, applies for a job as a cab driver at the Hacker Cab Company. She has a valid driver's license and has driven extensively, but not for pay, for 20 years. She is a vegetarian and a Capricorn. After a brief interview, at which all these facts emerge, she is rejected by "Tip" O'Neill, Hacker's president. Armstrong comes to you for legal counsel. You do some investigation. The first call you make is to O'Neill, who admits that the job is still open, but explains that he rejected Armstrong because "Capricorns make lousy drivers; besides she's too old to adjust to the rigors of cab driving, especially since she doesn't eat meat." When asked whether Armstrong's gender played a part in the decision, O'Neill replied, "Hell no. Some of my best friends are women. I don't care if my brother marries one. Har, har." A "windshield survey" of the Hacker Cab Company at shift-changing times reveals an almost total absence of women drivers. It is common knowledge that there is a heavy turnover in the cab-driving business.

How would you analyze this case based on *Price Waterhouse*, *McDonnell Douglas*, and Costa v. Desert Place?

# Chapter 4

## Systemic Disparate Treatment Discrimination

## A.  INTRODUCTION

In Chapter 3, individuals challenged adverse employment decisions, requiring the courts to focus on how plaintiffs had been individually treated by defendants. Plaintiffs also can challenge employment policies that sweep more broadly. Thus, an employer's policy to hire only men, to fire older workers, or to separate employees by race, gender, or age raises systemic issues. This chapter will develop systemic disparate treatment, one of the two concepts of systemic discrimination presently governing Title VII actions. 42 U.S.C.S. §§ 2000e to 2000e-17 (2003). This theory is also available under the Age Discrimination in Employment Act ("ADEA"), 29 U.S.C.S. §§ 631-634 (2003), and under 42 U.S.C.S. § 1981 (2003), Anderson v. Fulton County, Ga., 207 F.3d 1303 (11th Cir. 2000). The other systemic concept, disparate impact, is available under Title VII and perhaps the ADEA but is not available under § 1981. Disparate impact will be considered in Chapter 5.

Systemic disparate treatment can be proven in two ways. First, the plaintiff may simply demonstrate that the employer has an announced, formal policy of discrimination. Second, the plaintiff who fails to prove a formal policy may nevertheless establish that the employer's pattern of employment decisions reveals that a policy of disparate treatment operates. Although these two methods parallel the direct and inferential proof of individual disparate treatment examined in Chapter 3, there are significant differences between the theories.

199

## B.  FORMAL POLICIES OF DISCRIMINATION

The employer in Slack v. Havens (reproduced at page 79) violated Title VII by
requiring three employees to perform a cleaning job because they were black. If
such a requirement is part of a policy that regularly segregates black workers into
unfavorable jobs, a systemic claim of discrimination could be established. Historically, formal systems excluding women and minority group members or segregating
them into inferior jobs were common. An example was the sign that appeared in
a Boston window in the nineteenth century, "Irish need not apply." During much
of the twentieth century, many employers, particularly in the South, segregated jobs
by race, with blacks typically consigned to lower-paying, less attractive jobs. Most
employers also segregated many jobs by gender, again with lower-level jobs assigned
to female workers. With the passage of Title VII in 1964, most formal discriminatory
policies of race or sex discrimination ended. Similarly, prior to the passage of the
Age Discrimination in Employment Act, employers frequently had formal policies
explicitly discriminating on account of age. For example, policies mandating retirement at age 65 were common. The ADEA generally bars discrimination on account of age for those over 40, and most such formal discriminatory policies have
disappeared. Nevertheless, not all formal policies were rescinded without court
intervention.

### LOS ANGELES DEPARTMENT OF WATER
### & POWER v. MANHART
#### 435 U.S. 702 (1978)

Justice STEVENS delivered the opinion of the Court.
As a class, women live longer than men. For this reason, the Los Angeles Department of Water and Power required its female employees to make larger contributions
to its pension fund than its male employees. We granted certiorari to decide whether
this practice discriminated against individual female employees because of their sex
in violation of § 703(a)(1) of the Civil Rights Act of 1964, as amended.
For many years the Department had administered retirement, disability, and
death-benefit programs for its employees. Upon retirement each employee is eligible
for a monthly retirement benefit computed as a fraction of his or her salary multiplied by years of service. The monthly benefits of men and women of the same age,
seniority and salary are equal. Benefits are funded entirely by contributions from the
employees and the Department, augmented by the income earned on those contributions. No private insurance company is involved in the administration or payment
of benefits.
Based on a study of mortality tables and its own experience, the Department determined that its 2,000 female employees, on the average, will live a few years longer
than its 10,000 male employees. The cost of a pension for the average retired female
is greater than for the average male retiree because more monthly payments must be
made to the average woman. The Department therefore required female employees
to make monthly contributions to the fund which were 14.84% higher than the contributions required of comparable male employees. Because employee contributions

were withheld from paychecks, a female employee took home less pay than a male employee earning the same salary.[5] . . .

## I

There are both real and fictional differences between women and men. It is true that the average man is taller than the average woman; it is not true that the average woman driver is more accident prone than the average man. Before the Civil Rights Act of 1964 was enacted, an employer could fashion his personnel policies on the basis of assumptions about the differences between men and women, whether or not the assumptions were valid.

It is now well recognized that employment decisions cannot be predicated on mere "stereotyped" impressions about the characteristics of males or females. Myths and purely habitual assumptions about a woman's inability to perform certain kinds of work are no longer acceptable reasons for refusing to employ qualified individuals, or for paying them less. This case does not, however, involve a fictional difference between men and women. It involves a generalization that the parties accept as unquestionably true: Women, as a class, do live longer than men. The Department treated its women employees differently from its men employees because the two classes are in fact different. It is equally true, however, that all individuals in the respective classes do not share the characteristic that differentiates the average class representatives. Many women do not live as long as the average man and many men outlive the average woman. The question, therefore, is whether the existence or nonexistence of "discrimination" is to be determined by comparison of class characteristics or individual characteristics. A "stereotyped" answer to that question may not be the same as the answer that the language and purpose of the statute command.

The statute makes it unlawful "to discriminate against any *individual* with respect to his compensation, terms, conditions, or privileges of employment, because of such *individual's* race, color, religion, sex, or national origin (emphasis added). The statute's focus on the individual is unambiguous. It precludes treatment of individuals as simply components of a racial, religious, sexual, or national class. If height is required for a job, a tall woman may not be refused employment merely because, on the average, women are too short. Even a true generalization about the class is an insufficient reason for disqualifying an individual to whom the generalization does not apply.

That proposition is of critical importance in this case because there is no assurance that any individual woman working for the Department will actually fit the generalization on which the Department's policy is based. Many of those individuals will not live as long as the average man. While they were working, those individuals received smaller paychecks because of their sex, but they will receive no compensating advantage when they retire.

It is true, of course, that while contributions are being collected from the employees, the Department cannot know which individuals will predecease the average woman. Therefore, unless women as a class are assessed an extra charge, they will be

---

5. The significance of the disparity is illustrated by the record of one woman whose contributions to the fund (including interest on the amount withheld each month) amounted to $18,171.40; a similarly situated male would have contributed only $12,843.53.

subsidized, to some extent, by the class of male employees.[14] It follows, according to the Department, that fairness to its class of male employees justifies the extra assessment against all of its female employees.

But the question of fairness to various classes affected by the statute is essentially a matter of policy for the legislature to address. Congress has decided that classifications based on sex, like those based on national origin or race, are unlawful. Actuarial studies could unquestionably identify differences in life expectancy based on race or national origin, as well as sex.[15] But a statute that was designed to make race irrelevant in the employment market could not reasonably be construed to permit a take-home-pay differential based on a racial classification.

Even if the statutory language were less clear, the basic policy of the statute requires that we focus on fairness to individuals rather than fairness to classes. Practices that classify employees in terms of religion, race, or sex tend to preserve traditional assumptions about groups rather than thoughtful scrutiny of individuals. The generalization involved in this case illustrates the point. Separate mortality tables are easily interpreted as reflecting innate differences between the sexes; but a significant part of the longevity differential may be explained by the social fact that men are heavier smokers than women.

Finally, there is no reason to believe that Congress intended a special definition of discrimination in the context of employee group insurance coverage. It is true that insurance is concerned with events that are individually unpredictable, but that is characteristic of many employment decisions. Individual risks, like individual performance, may not be predicted by resort to classifications proscribed by Title VII. Indeed, the fact that this case involves a group insurance program highlights a basic flaw in the Department's fairness argument. For when insurance risks are grouped, the better risks always subsidize the poorer risks. Healthy persons subsidize medical benefits for the less healthy; unmarried workers subsidize the pensions of married workers;[18] persons who eat, drink, or smoke to excess may subsidize pension benefits for persons whose habits are more temperate. Treating different classes of risks as though they were the same for purposes of group insurance is a common practice that has never been considered inherently unfair. To insure the flabby and the fit as though they were equivalent risks may be more common than treating men and women alike;[19] but nothing more than habit makes one "subsidy" seem less fair than the other.[20]

14. The size of the subsidy involved in this case is open to doubt, because the Department's plan provides for survivor's benefits. Since female spouses of male employees are likely to have greater life expectancies than the male spouses of female employees, whatever benefits men lose in "primary" coverage for themselves, they may regain in "secondary" coverage for their wives.

15. For example, the life expectancy of a white baby in 1973 was 72.2 years; a nonwhite baby could expect to live 65.9 years, a difference of 6.3 years. See Public Health Service, IIA Vital Statistics of the United States 1973, Table 5-3.

18. A study of life expectancy in the United States for 1949-1951 showed that 20-year-old men could expect to live to 60.6 years of age if they were divorced. If married, they could expect to reach 70.9 years of age, a difference of more than 10 years. Id., at 93.

19. The record indicates, however, that the Department has funded its death-benefit plan by equal contributions from male and female employees. A death benefit — unlike a pension benefit — has less value for persons with longer life expectancies. Under the Department's concept of fairness, then, this neutral funding of death benefits is unfair to women as a class.

20. A variation on the Department's fairness theme is the suggestion that a gender-neutral pension plan would itself violate Title VII because of its disproportionately heavy impact on male employees. Cf. Griggs v. Duke Power Co. This suggestion has no force in the sex discrimination context because each retiree's total pension benefits are ultimately determined by his actual life span; any differential in benefits paid to men and women in the aggregate is thus "based on [a] factor other than sex," and consequently immune from challenge under the Equal Pay Act, 29 U.S.C. § 206(d). Even under Title VII itself — assuming disparate-impact analysis applies to fringe benefits, cf. Nashville Gas Co. v. Satty, 434 U.S. 136,

An employment practice that requires 2,000 individuals to contribute more money into a fund than 10,000 other employees simply because each of them is a woman, rather than a man, is in direct conflict with both the language and the policy of the Act. Such a practice does not pass the simple test of whether the evidence shows "treatment of a person in a manner which but for that person's sex would be different." It constitutes discrimination and is unlawful unless exempted by the Equal Pay Act of 1963 or some other affirmative justification.

III . . .

[T]he Department argues that the absence of a discriminatory effect on women as a class justifies an employment practice which, on its face, discriminated against individual employees because of their sex. But even if the Department's actuarial evidence is sufficient to prevent plaintiffs from establishing a prima facie case on the theory that the effect of the practice on women as a class was discriminatory, that evidence does not defeat the claim that the practice, on its face, discriminated against every individual woman employed by the Department.[30]

In essence, the Department is arguing that the prima facie showing of discrimination based on evidence of different contributions for the respective sexes is rebutted by its demonstration that there is a like difference in the cost of providing benefits for the respective classes. That argument might prevail if Title VII contained a cost-justification defense comparable to the affirmative defense available in a price discrimination suit. But neither Congress nor the courts have recognized such a defense under Title VII.

Although we conclude that the Department's practice violated Title VII, we do not suggest that the statute was intended to revolutionize the insurance and pension industries. All that is at issue today is a requirement that men and women make unequal contributions to an employer-operated pension fund. Nothing in our holding implies that it would be unlawful for an employer to set aside equal retirement contributions for each employee and let each retiree purchase the largest benefit which his or her accumulated contributions could command in the open market.[33] Nor does it call into question the insurance industry practice of considering the composition of an employer's work force in determining the probable cost of a retirement or

---

144-145 — the male employees would not prevail. Even a completely neutral practice will inevitably have some disproportionate impact on one group or another. *Griggs* does not imply, and this Court has never held, that discrimination must always be inferred from such consequences.

30. Some amici suggest that the Department's discrimination is justified by business necessity. They argue that, if no gender distinction is drawn, many male employees will withdraw from the plan, or even the Department, because they can get a better pension plan in the private market. But the Department has long required equal contributions to its death-benefit plan, and since 1975 it has required equal contributions to its pension plan. Yet the Department points to no "adverse selection" by the affected employees, presumably because an employee who wants to leave the plan must also leave his job, and few workers will quit because one of their fringe benefits could theoretically be obtained at a marginally lower price on the open market. In short, there has been no showing that sex distinctions are reasonably necessary to the normal operation of the Department's retirement plan.

33. Title VII and the Equal Pay Act primarily govern relations between employees and their employer, not between employees and third parties. We do not suggest, of course, that an employer can avoid its responsibilities by delegating discriminatory programs to corporate shells. Title VII applies to "any agent" of a covered employer, 42 U.S.C. § 2000e(b), and the Equal Pay Act applies to "any person acting directly or indirectly in the interest of an employer in relation to an employee." 29 U.S.C. § 206(d). In this case, for example, the Department could not deny that the administrative board was its agent after it successfully argued that the two were so inseparable that both shared the city's immunity from suit under 42 U.S.C. § 1983.

death benefit plan.[34] Finally, we recognize that in a case of this kind it may be necessary to take special care in fashioning appropriate relief. . . .

## NOTES

1. Why would the city adopt a facially discriminatory plan? The city may have believed that, although the plan technically discriminated on gender grounds, no court would find it to be sex discrimination. Second, whether or not it is sex discrimination, the city may have believed that it fit within a statutory exception. Third, the plan may predate Title VII and the city may have never reviewed it once Title VII became effective.

2. The first possibility is not as far-fetched as one might think. Sex distinctions in employer dress and grooming codes generally have been held not to constitute illegal sex discrimination under Title VII when they treat male and female employees separately, but equally. See page 541. We also will encounter racial and gender preferences that sometimes are permissible under Title VII as part of valid affirmative action plans. See page 282.

3. Why might the city have thought that the gender distinction would not be viewed as discriminatory? While it seems unfair to women that they all receive less take-home pay than men paid the same salary, women, as a group, will receive more months of retirement pay because, as a group, they live longer than men. In group terms, lower monthly salary is offset by more months of coverage.

4. But an individual female may get the short end of the stick: if she does not live as long as predicted, she will receive less each month but will not be compensated by more months of coverage. While insurance risks are, individually, unpredictable, this woman's disadvantage results solely from her sex.

5. Does using gender as a formal classification have the same evidentiary effect here as the direct evidence in the individual disparate treatment cases, such as *Price Waterhouse*, that is, eliminating any employer response except for statutory defenses?

6. Perhaps the city thought it could not be guilty of sex discrimination because it was motivated neither by animus nor by a desire to disadvantage women. The city merely used gender as a proxy for longevity. If so, is that disparate treatment? See *Biggins*.

7. But perhaps the city did intend to disadvantage women. The city did not use sex-segregated life expectancy tables to set contribution levels for life insurance. Because women live longer than men, sex-based tables would have resulted in lower premiums for women. If it truly wanted to treat the sexes equally, why wasn't the employer consistent? Perhaps the city focused only on its male employees, both for pensions and life insurance.

8. Even if an employer discriminates on the basis of gender, there may be a statutory defense. The most obvious one is the bona fide occupational qualification ("bfoq"). Because the employer concededly used gender to classify pension contributions, why couldn't it claim a bfoq defense? See page 265.

9. Title VII is not the only federal statute dealing with sex discrimination in employment. A much narrower enactment, the Equal Pay Act of 1963, 29 U.S.C.S.

---

34. Title VII bans discrimination against an "individual" because of "such individual's" sex, 42 U.S.C. § 2000e-2(a)(1). The Equal Pay Act prohibits discrimination "within any establishment," and discrimination is defined as "paying wages to employees . . . at a rate less than the rate at which [the employer] pays wages to employees of the opposite sex" for equal work. 29 U.S.C. § 206(d)(1). Neither of these provisions makes it unlawful to determine the funding requirements for an establishment's benefit plan by considering the composition of the entire force.

§ 206(d) (2003), bars discrimination in pay on account of sex where members of each gen-der are doing "equal work." See pages 573-582. The Bennett Amendment to Title VII makes discrimination authorized by the Equal Pay Act legal under Title VII. The city might have hoped to bring its plan within the EPA provision allowing differentials based on a factor "other than sex." How can something that is sex discrimination under Title VII be "other than sex" within the EPA?

10. The city might also have hoped to establish what the Court termed a "cost justification" defense. While such a defense is not written into the statute, is it so unlikely that the courts would recognize one judicially, at least in extreme cases? Should the courts recognize a cost justification defense? We will see that, where age is concerned, the ADEA has a kind of cost justification for fringe benefits. See page 658.

11. The city might also have hoped to convince the courts that its conduct was not discriminatory by arguing that it was damned if it did and damned if it didn't: (a) by requiring females to make larger contributions than males, disparate treatment discrimination is established; (b) if equal contributions were collected from all employees, retired women as a group would collect more than retired men as a class, thereby creating an adverse impact on males. How did the Court avoid this dilemma? Does footnote 20 help? See page 202.

12. *Manhart* established that gender-explicit classifications in pension contributions violate Title VII. Some of the questions left unanswered by *Manhart* were resolved in Arizona Governing Committee v. Norris, 463 U.S. 1073 (1983), holding that Title VII was violated by offering women lower monthly retirement benefits than men who contributed the same amount. The *Norris* Court first applied *Manhart*: "We conclude that it is just as much discrimination 'because of . . . sex' to pay a woman lower benefits when she has made the same contributions as a man as it is to make her pay larger contributions to obtain the same benefits." Id. at 1086. A different majority decided that all retirement benefits derived from contributions made after the date of the decision must be calculated without regard to the gender of the beneficiary.

13. A twist in *Norris* was the defendant's argument that it was not responsible for the discrimination: the employer collected employee contributions, but the plan was administered and all benefits paid by private insurance companies. The employer argued that it was within the language in *Manhart* suggesting that an employer would not be liable if it set aside contributions and paid them in a lump sum upon retirement. The defendant also stressed that all available annuities used sex-segregated life expectancy tables. The Court rejected those arguments:

> Under these circumstances there can be no serious question that petitioners are legally responsible for the discriminatory terms on which annuities are offered by the companies chosen to participate in the plan. Having created a plan whereby employees can obtain the advantages of using deferred compensation to purchase an annuity only if they invest in one of the companies specifically selected by the State, the State cannot disclaim responsibility for the discriminatory features of the insurers' options.

463 U.S. at 1088-89.

14. Are insurance companies now forbidden to offer annuities based on sex-segregated mortality tables? The majority in *Norris* rejected the argument that the McCarran-Ferguson Act, 15 U.S.C.S. §§ 1011 et seq. (2003), which restricts federal statutory preemption of state laws regulating "the business of insurance," exempted the

conduct in question. It concluded that, because the attack at issue was on an employment practice, Title VII simply did not purport to reach "the business of insurance."

15. *Manhart* involved a "defined benefit" pension plan. Few such plans continue to exist — most are defined contribution plans or 401(k)s. Will women seeking to buy an annuity with their accumulated contributions face sex-segregated mortality labels?

## TRANS WORLD AIRLINES, INC. v. THURSTON
### 469 U.S. 111 (1985)

Justice POWELL delivered the opinion of the Court.

Trans World Airlines, Inc. (TWA), a commercial airline, permits captains disqualified from serving in that capacity for reasons other than age to transfer automatically to the position of flight engineer. In this case, we must decide whether the Age Discrimination in Employment Act of 1967 requires the airline to afford this same "privilege of employment" to those captains disqualified by their age. . . .

### I

#### A

TWA has approximately 3,000 employees who fill the three cockpit positions on most of its flights. The "captain" is the pilot and controls the aircraft. He is responsible for all phases of its operation. The "first officer" is the copilot and assists the captain. The "flight engineer" usually monitors a side-facing instrument panel. He does not operate the flight controls unless the captain and the first officer become incapacitated.

In 1977, TWA and the Air Line Pilots Association (ALPA) entered into a collective-bargaining agreement, under which every employee in a cockpit position was required to retire when he reached the age of 60. This provision for mandatory retirement was lawful under the ADEA [until April 6, 1978, when] the Act was amended to prohibit the mandatory retirement of a protected individual because of his age. TWA officials became concerned that the company's retirement policy, at least as it applied to flight engineers, violated the amended ADEA.[3]

[After discussions with ALPA, which contended that the collective bargaining agreement prohibited employing flight engineers after age 60, TWA adopted a plan providing that] any employee in "flight engineer status" at age 60 is entitled to continue working in that capacity. The new plan . . . does not give 60-year-old captains the right automatically to begin training as flight engineers. Instead, a captain may remain with the airline only if he has been able to obtain "flight engineer status" through the bidding procedures outlined in the collective-bargaining agreement. These procedures require a captain, prior to his 60th birthday, to submit a "standing bid" for the position of flight engineer. When a vacancy occurs, it is assigned to the most senior captain with a standing bid. If no vacancy occurs prior to his 60th birthday, or if he lacks sufficient seniority to bid successfully for those vacancies that do occur, the captain is retired.

---

3. A regulation promulgated by the Federal Aviation Administration prohibits anyone from serving after age 60 as a pilot on a commercial carrier. 14 C.F.R. § 121.383(c) (1984). Captains and first officers are considered "pilots" subject to this regulation; flight engineers are not. Therefore, TWA officials were concerned primarily with the effect that the 1978 amendments had on the company's policy of mandatory retirement of flight engineers.

Under the collective-bargaining agreement, a captain displaced for any reason besides age need not resort to the bidding procedures. For example, a captain unable to maintain the requisite first-class medical certificate, see 14 C.F.R. § 67.13 (1984), may displace automatically, or "bump," a less senior flight engineer. The medically disabled captain's ability to bump does not depend upon the availability of a vacancy. Similarly, a captain whose position is eliminated due to reduced manpower needs can "bump" a less senior flight engineer. Even if a captain is found to be incompetent to serve in that capacity, he is not discharged, but is allowed to transfer to a position as flight engineer without resort to the bidding procedures.

Respondents Harold Thurston, Christopher J. Clark, and Clifton A. Parkhill, former captains for TWA, were retired upon reaching the age of 60. Each was denied an opportunity to "bump" a less senior flight engineer. . . .

## II

### A

The ADEA "broadly prohibits arbitrary discrimination in the workplace based on age." Lorillard v. Pons, 434 U.S. 575, 577 (1978). Section 4(a)(1) of the Act proscribes differential treatment of older workers "with respect to . . . [a] privileg[e] of employment." 29 U.S.C. § 623(a). Under TWA's transfer policy, 60-year-old captains are denied a "privilege of employment" on the basis of age. Captains who become disqualified from serving in that position for reasons other than age automatically are able to displace less senior flight engineers. Captains disqualified because of age are not afforded this same "bumping" privilege. Instead, they are forced to resort to the bidding procedures set forth in the collective-bargaining agreement. If there is no vacancy prior to a bidding captain's 60th birthday, he must retire.[15]

The Act does not require TWA to grant transfer privileges to disqualified captains. Nevertheless, if TWA does grant some disqualified captains the "privilege" of "bumping" less senior flight engineers, it may not deny this opportunity to others because of their age. In Hishon v. King & Spalding, 467 U.S. 69 (1984), we held that "[a] benefit that is part and parcel of the employment relationship may not be doled out in a discriminatory fashion, even if the employer would be free . . . not to provide the benefit at all." This interpretation of Title VII of the Civil Rights Act of 1964 applies with equal force in the context of age discrimination, for the substantive provisions of the ADEA "were derived in *haec verba* from Title VII." Lorillard v. Pons.

TWA contends that the respondents failed to make out a prima facie case of age discrimination under McDonnell Douglas v. Green because at the time they were retired, no flight engineer vacancies existed. This argument fails, for the *McDonnell Douglas* test is inapplicable where the plaintiff presents direct evidence of discrimination. The shifting burdens of proof set forth in *McDonnell Douglas* are designed to assure that the "plaintiff [has] his day in court despite the unavailability of direct evidence." Loeb v. Textron, Inc., 600 F.2d 1003, 1014 (CA1 1979). In this case there is direct evidence that the method of transfer available to a disqualified captain depends upon his age. Since it allows captains who become disqualified for any reason other than age to "bump" less senior flight engineers, TWA's transfer policy is discriminatory on its face. Cf. Los Angeles Dept. of Water & Power v. Manhart.

---

15. The discriminatory transfer policy may violate the Act even though 83% of the 60-year-old captains were able to obtain positions as flight engineers through the bidding procedures. See Phillips v. Martin Marietta Corp., 400 U.S. 542 (1971) (per curiam). . . .

B

Although we find that TWA's transfer policy discriminates against disqualified captains on the basis of age, our inquiry cannot end here. Petitioners contend that the age-based transfer policy is justified by two of the ADEA's five affirmative defenses. Petitioners first argue that the discharge of respondents was lawful because age is a "bona fide occupational qualification" (BFOQ) for the position of captain. 29 U.S.C. § 623(f)(1). Furthermore, TWA claims that its retirement policy is part of a "bona fide seniority system," and thus exempt from the Act's coverage. 29 U.S.C. § 623(f)(2).

Section 4(f)(1) of the ADEA provides that an employer may take "any action otherwise prohibited" where age is a "bona fide occupational qualification." In order to be permissible under § 4(f)(1), however, the age-based discrimination must relate to a "particular business." Every court to consider the issue has assumed that the "particular business" to which the statute refers is the job from which the protected individual is excluded. . . .

TWA's discriminatory transfer policy is not permissible under § 4(f)(1) because age is not a BFOQ for the "particular" position of flight engineer. It is necessary to recognize that the airline has two age-based policies: (i) captains are not allowed to serve in that capacity after reaching the age of 60; and (ii) age-disqualified captains are not given the transfer privileges afforded captains disqualified for other reasons. The first policy, which precludes individuals from serving as captains, is not challenged by respondents.[17] The second practice does not operate to exclude protected individuals from the position of captain; rather it prevents qualified 60-year-olds from working as flight engineers. Thus, it is the "particular" job of flight engineer from which the respondents were excluded by the discriminatory transfer policy. Because age under 60 is not a BFOQ for the position of flight engineer,[18] the age-based discrimination at issue in this case cannot be justified by § 4(f)(1).

TWA nevertheless contends that its BFOQ argument is supported by the legislative history of the amendments to the ADEA. [The Court cited sources indicating that, in the 1978 amendments to the ADEA, which generally barred mandatory retirement, § 4(f)(2), 29 U.S.C. § 623(f)(2), Congress intended to permit such policies where they were justified as a bfoq. This] history shows only that the ADEA does not prohibit TWA from retiring all disqualified captains, including those who are incapacitated because of age. This does not mean, however, that TWA can make dependent upon the age of the individual the availability of a transfer to a position for which age is not a BFOQ. Nothing in the legislative history cited by petitioners indicates a congressional intention to allow an employer to discriminate against an older worker seeking to transfer to another position, on the ground that age was a BFOQ for his *former* job.

TWA also contends that its discriminatory transfer policy is lawful under the Act because it is part of a "bona fide seniority system." 29 U.S.C. § 623(f)(2). The Court of Appeals held that the airline's retirement policy is not mandated by the negotiated seniority plan. We need not address this finding; any seniority system that includes the challenged practice is not "bona fide" under the statute. The Act provides that a seniority system may not "require or permit" the involuntary retirement of a

---

17. In this litigation, the respondents have not challenged TWA's claim that the FAA regulation establishes a BFOQ for the position of captain. The EEOC guidelines, however, do not list the FAA's age-60 rule as an example of a BFOQ because the EEOC wishes to avoid any appearance that it endorses the rule. 46 Fed. Reg. 47724, 47725 (1981).

18. The petitioners do not contend that age is a BFOQ for the position of flight engineer. Indeed, the airline has employed at least 148 flight engineers who are over 60 years old.

protected individual because of his age. Although the FAA "age 60 rule" may have caused respondents' retirement, TWA's seniority plan certainly "permitted" it within the meaning of the ADEA. Moreover, because captains disqualified for reasons other than age are allowed to "bump" less senior flight engineers, the mandatory retirement was age-based. Therefore, the "bona fide seniority system" defense is unavailable to the petitioners.

In summary, TWA's transfer policy discriminates against protected individuals on the basis of age, and thereby violates the Act. The two statutory defenses raised by petitioners do not support the argument that this discrimination is justified. . . .

## NOTES

1. Why would TWA promulgate a policy that was so clearly age discrimination? As in *Manhart*, the employer may have believed that, given the FAA rule and the ALPA collective bargaining agreement, the courts would not treat the plan as age discriminatory even though it differentiated on the basis of age. Alternatively, perhaps TWA believed that the plan was discriminatory, but nevertheless legal because it fell within a statutory defense.

2. As for facial discrimination, the Court viewed the airline as dividing employees into two categories: those disqualified to be captains by age and those disqualified by any other reason. Because the former group was given fewer "bumping" rights than the latter, this constituted a formal policy of systemic disparate treatment age discrimination. See also EEOC v. Commonwealth of Massachusetts, 987 F.2d 64 (1st Cir. 1993) (state statute requiring state and local employees over age 70 to take an annual medical examination violated the ADEA).

3. Footnote 15 states that 83 percent of captains disqualified by age obtained engineer positions. Why is this fact not relevant to the threshold question of age discrimination? If there were no proof of an explicit policy that takes age into account in structuring transfers, would it be possible to prove that the employer discriminated?

4. Why is the *McDonnell Douglas* method of inferring discrimination inappropriate in this case? Is it because a facial age distinction necessarily reveals an intent to discriminate? Presumably, even an employer using a facially discriminatory criterion could escape liability for damages by using the "same decision anyway" defense of *Price Waterhouse*.

5. Suppose all persons disqualified as captains were denied bumping rights. Is that age discrimination if most disqualified employees are disqualified by age? There would then be no facially discriminatory policy. There might be a disparate impact case if impact theory is available under the ADEA. See Chapter 5. Could a plaintiff win by proving that a facially neutral rule was, in fact, motivated by a desire to exclude older workers? Does *Biggins* help? What about *McDonnell Douglas*?

6. As for statutory defenses, we will examine the bona fide occupational qualification (bfoq) defense in some detail later in this chapter. In this case, the possibility that being under age 60 is a bfoq for the flight engineer position is given short shrift by the Court, mostly because many persons over age 60 continue to work as flight engineers for TWA. The airline's own practices defeated its argument.

7. *Thurston* also raises the bona fide seniority system defense. Again, the Court deals briefly with this defense because a system is not bona fide if it requires mandatory retirement. But suppose the airline were to negotiate a new collective bargaining agreement with the union that provided for "departmental seniority," that is, different

seniority ladders for captains and flight engineers. Would that be legal under the ADEA? Would it depend on the purpose? The question of seniority systems is taken up at page 415.

8. *Manhart* and *Thurston* involved formal policies of discrimination that facially treated men/women and older/younger workers differently. There was no need, therefore, to search further for intent to discriminate. But the systemic disparate treatment theory goes beyond formal policies to reach pervasive practices rooted in intentional discrimination.

# C.  PATTERNS AND PRACTICES OF DISCRIMINATION

## TEAMSTERS v. UNITED STATES
### 431 U.S. 324 (1977)

Justice STEWART delivered the opinion of the Court.

This litigation brings here several important questions under Title VII. The issues grow out of alleged unlawful employment practices engaged in by an employer and a union. The employer is a common carrier of motor freight with nationwide operations, and the union represents a large group of its employees. The District Court and the Court of Appeals held that the employer had violated Title VII by engaging in a pattern and practice of employment discrimination against Negroes and Spanish-surnamed Americans and that the union had violated the Act by agreeing with the employer to create and maintain a seniority system that perpetuated the effects of past racial and ethnic discrimination. . . .

I

[The United States brought two actions, which were consolidated for trial. The first was against T.I.M.E.-D.C., charging discriminatory hiring, assignment, and promotion policies against Negroes at its Nashville terminal in violation of § 707(a). The second action against the company charged a pattern and practice of employment discrimination against Negroes and Spanish-surnamed persons throughout the company's transportation system. The International Brotherhood of Teamsters union was named a defendant.]

The central claim in both lawsuits was that the company had engaged in a pattern or practice of discriminating against minorities in hiring so-called line drivers. Those Negroes and Spanish-surnamed persons who had been hired, the Government alleged, were given lower paying, less desirable jobs as servicemen or local city drivers, and were thereafter discriminated against with respect to promotions and transfers.[3] . . .

---

3. Line drivers, also known as over-the-road drivers, engage in long-distance hauling between company terminals. They compose a separate bargaining unit at the company. Other distinct bargaining units include servicemen, who service trucks, unhook tractors and trailers, and perform similar tasks; and city operations, composed of dockmen, hostlers, and city drivers who pick up and deliver freight within the immediate area of a particular terminal. All of these employees were represented by the petitioner union.

## II

In this Court the company and the union contend that their conduct did not violate Title VII in any respect, asserting first that the evidence introduced at trial was insufficient to show that the company engaged in a "pattern or practice" of employment discrimination. . . .

### A

Consideration of the question whether the company engaged in a pattern or practice of discriminatory hiring practices involves controlling legal principles that are relatively clear. The Government's theory of discrimination was simply that the company, in violation of § 703(a) of Title VII, regularly and purposefully treated Negroes and Spanish-surnamed Americans less favorably than white persons. The disparity in treatment allegedly involved the refusal to recruit, hire, transfer, or promote minority group members on an equal basis with white people, particularly with respect to line-driving positions. The ultimate factual issues are thus simply whether there was a pattern or practice of such disparate treatment and, if so, whether the differences were "racially premised." McDonnell Douglas Corp. v. Green.[15]

As the plaintiff, the Government bore the initial burden of making out a prima facie case of discrimination. Albermarle Paper Co. v. Moody, 422 U.S. 405, 425; McDonnell Douglas Corp. v. Green. And, because it alleged a systemwide pattern or practice of resistance to the full enjoyment of Title VII rights, the Government ultimately had to prove more than the mere occurrence of isolated or "accidental" or sporadic discriminatory acts. It had to establish by a preponderance of the evidence that racial discrimination was the Company's standard operating procedure — the regular rather than the unusual practice.[16]

We agree with the District Court and the Court of Appeals that the Government carried its burden of proof. As of March 31, 1971, shortly after the Government filed its complaint alleging systemwide discrimination, the company had 6,472 employees. Of these, 314 (5%) were Negroes and 257 (4%) were Spanish-surnamed Americans. Of the 1,828 line drivers, however, there were only 8 (0.4%) Negroes and 5 (0.3%) Spanish-surnamed persons, and all of the Negroes had been hired after the litigation had commenced. With one exception — a man who worked as a line driver at

---

15. "Disparate treatment" such as is alleged in the present case is the most easily understood type of discrimination. The employer simply treats some people less favorably than others because of their race, color, religion, sex, or national origin. Proof of discriminatory motive is critical, although it can in some situations be inferred from the mere fact of differences in treatment. See, e.g., Arlington Heights v. Metropolitan Housing Dev. Corp., 429 U.S. 252, 265-266. Undoubtedly disparate treatment was the most obvious evil Congress had in mind when it enacted Title VII. See, e.g., 110 Cong. Rec. 13088 (1964) (remarks of Sen. Humphrey) ("What the bill does . . . is simply to make it an illegal practice to use race as a factor in denying employment. It provides that men and women shall be employed on the basis of their qualifications, not as Catholic citizens, not as Protestant citizens, not as Jewish citizens, not as colored citizens, but as citizens of the United States.").

Claims of disparate treatment may be distinguished from claims that stress "disparate impact." The latter involve employment practices that are facially neutral in their treatment of different groups but that in fact fall more harshly on one group than another and cannot be justified by business necessity. Proof of discriminatory motive, we have held, is not required under a disparate-impact theory. Compare, e.g., Griggs v. Duke Power Co., with McDonnell Douglas Corp. v. Green. See generally B. Schlei & P. Grossman, Employment Discrimination Law 1-12 (1976); Blumrosen, Strangers in Paradise: Griggs v. Duke Power Co. and the Concept of Employment Discrimination, 71 Mich. L. Rev. 59 (1972). Either theory may, of course, be applied to a particular set of facts.

16. The "pattern or practice" language in § 707(a) of Title VII was not intended as a term of art, and the words reflect only their usual meaning. . . .

the Chicago terminal from 1950 to 1959 — the company and its predecessors did not employ a Negro on a regular basis as a line driver until 1969. And, as the Government showed, even in 1971 there were terminals in areas of substantial Negro population where all of the Company's line drivers were white.[17] A great majority of the Negroes (83%) and Spanish-surnamed Americans (78%) who did work for the company held the lower paying city operations and serviceman jobs,[18] whereas only 39% of the non-minority employees held jobs in those categories.

The Government bolstered its statistical evidence with the testimony of individuals who recounted over 40 specific instances of discrimination. Upon the basis of his testimony the District Court found that "[n]umerous qualified black and Spanish-surnamed American applicants who sought line driving jobs at the company over the years had either their requests ignored, were given false or misleading information about requirements, opportunities, and application procedures, or were not considered and hired on the same basis that whites were considered and hired." Minority employees who wanted to transfer to line-driver jobs met with similar difficulties.[19]

The company's principal response to this evidence is that statistics can never in and of themselves prove the existence of a pattern or practice of discrimination, or even establish a prima facie case shifting to the employer the burden of rebutting the inference raised by the figures. But, as even our brief summary of the evidence shows, this was not a case in which the Government relied on "statistics alone." The individuals who testified about their personal experiences with the company brought the cold numbers convincingly to life.

In any event, our cases make it unmistakably clear that "[s]tatistical analyses have served and will continue to serve an important role" in cases in which the existence of discrimination is a disputed issue. Mayor of Philadelphia v. Educational Equality League, 415 U.S. 605, 620. See also McDonnell Douglas Corp. v. Green. Cf. Washington v. Davis, 426 U.S. 229, 241-242. We have repeatedly approved the use of statistical proof, where it reached proportions comparable to those in this case, to establish a prima facie case of racial discrimination in jury selection cases, see, e.g., Turner v. Fouche, 396 U.S. 346; Hernandez v. Texas, 347 U.S. 475; Norris v. Alabama, 294 U.S. 587. Statistics are equally competent in proving employment discrimination.[20]

17. In Atlanta, for instance, Negroes composed 22.35% of the population in the surrounding metropolitan area and 51.3% of the population in the city proper. The company's Atlanta terminal employed 57 line drivers. All were white. In Los Angeles, 10.84% of the greater metropolitan population and 17.88% of the city population were Negro. But at the company's two Los Angeles terminals there was not a single Negro among the 374 line drivers. The proof showed similar disparities in San Francisco, Denver, Nashville, Chicago, Dallas, and at several other terminals.

18. Although line-driver jobs pay more than other jobs, and the District Court found them to be "considered the most desirable of the driving jobs," it is by no means clear that all employees, even driver employees, would prefer to be line drivers. Of course, Title VII provides for equal opportunity to compete for any job, whether it is thought better or worse than another.

19. Two examples are illustrative: George Taylor, a Negro, worked for the company as a city driver in Los Angeles, beginning late in 1966. In 1968, after hearing that a white city driver had transferred to a line-driver job, he told the terminal manager that he also would like to consider line driving. The manager replied that there would be "a lot of problems on the road . . . with different people, Caucasian, et cetera," and stated: "I don't feel that the company is ready for this right now. . . . Give us a little time. It will come around, you know." Mr. Taylor made similar requests some months later and got similar responses. He was never offered a line-driving job or an application. Feliberto Trujillo worked as a dockman at the company's Denver terminal. When he applied for a line-driver job in 1967, he was told by a personnel officer that he had one strike against him. He asked what that was and was told: "You're a Chicano, and as far as we know, there isn't a Chicano driver in the system."

20. Petitioners argue that statistics, at least those comparing the racial composition of an employer's work force to the composition of the population at large, should never be given decisive weight in a Title VII case because to do so would conflict with § 703(j) of the Act. That section provides: "Nothing contained

We caution only that statistics are not irrefutable; they come in infinite variety and, like any other kind of evidence, they may be rebutted. In short, their usefulness depends on all of the surrounding facts and circumstances.

In addition to its general protest against the use of statistics in Title VII cases, the company claims that in this case the statistics revealing racial imbalance are misleading because they fail to take into account the company's particular business situation as of the effective date of Title VII. The company concedes that its line drivers were virtually all white in July 1965, but it claims that thereafter business conditions were such that its work force dropped. Its argument is that low personnel turnover, rather than post-Act discrimination, accounts for more recent statistical disparities. It points to substantial minority hiring in later years, especially after 1971, as showing that any pre-Act patterns of discrimination were broken.

The argument would be a forceful one if this were an employer who, at the time of suit, had done virtually no new hiring since the effective date of Title VII. But it is not. Although the company's total number of employees apparently dropped somewhat during the late 1960s, the record shows that many line drivers continued to be hired throughout this period, and that almost all of them were white.[21] To be sure, there were improvements in the company's hiring practices. The Court of Appeals commented that "T.I.M.E.-D.C.'s recent minority hiring progress stands as a laudable good faith effort to eradicate the effects of past discrimination in the area of hiring and initial assignment."[22]

But the District Court and the Court of Appeals found upon substantial evidence that the Company had engaged in a course of discrimination that continued well after the effective date of Title VII. The company's later changes in its hiring and promotion policies could be of little comfort to the victims of the earlier post-Act

---

in this subchapter shall be interpreted to require any employer . . . to grant preferential treatment to any individual or to any group because of the race . . . or national origin of such individual or group on account of an imbalance which may exist with respect to the total number or percentage of persons of any race . . . or national origin employed by any employer . . . in comparison with the total number or percentage of persons of such race . . . or national origin in any community, State, section, or other area, or in the available work force in any community, State, section, or other area."

The argument fails in this case because the statistical evidence was not offered or used to support an erroneous theory that Title VII requires an employer's work force to be racially balanced. Statistics showing racial or ethnic imbalance are probative in a case such as this one only because such imbalance is often a telltale sign of purposeful discrimination; absent explanation, it is ordinarily to be expected that nondiscriminatory hiring practices will in time result in a work force more or less representative of the racial and ethnic composition of the population in the community from which employees are hired. Evidence of longlasting and gross disparity between the composition of a work force and that of the general population thus may be significant even though § 703(j) makes clear that Title VII imposes no requirement that a work force mirror the general population. See, e.g., United States v. Sheet Metal Workers Local 36, 416 F.2d 123, 127 n.7 (C.A. 8). Considerations such as small sample size may, of course, detract from the value of such evidence, see, e.g., Mayor of Philadelphia v. Educational Equality League, 415 U.S. 605, 620-621, and evidence showing that the figures for the general population might not accurately reflect that pool of qualified job applicants would also be relevant. Ibid. See generally Schlei & Grossman, supra, n.15, at 1161-1193.

"Since the passage of the Civil Rights Act of 1964, the courts have frequently relied upon statistical evidence to prove a violation. . . . In many cases the only available avenue of proof is the use of racial statistics to uncover clandestine and covert discrimination by the employer or union involved." United States v. Ironworkers Local 86, 443 F.2d, at 551.

21. Between July 2, 1965, and January 1, 1969, hundreds of line drivers were hired systemwide, either from the outside or from the ranks of employees filling other jobs within the company. None was a Negro.

22. For example, in 1971 the company hired 116 new line drivers, of whom 16% were Negro or Spanish-surnamed Americans. Minority employees composed 7.1% of the company's systemwide work force in 1967 and 10.5% in 1972. Minority hiring increased greatly in 1972 and 1973, presumably due at least in part to the existence of the consent decree.

discrimination, and could not erase its previous illegal conduct or its obligation to afford relief to those who suffered because of it.[23]

The District Court and the Court of Appeals, on the basis of substantial evidence, held that the Government had proved a prima facie case of systematic and purposeful employment discrimination, continuing well beyond the effective date of Title VII. The company's attempts to rebut that conclusion were held to be inadequate.[24] For the reasons we have summarized, there is no warrant for this Court to disturb the findings of the District Court and the Court of Appeals on this basic issue. . . .

### NOTES

1. *Teamsters* was a government "pattern and practice" case. The Equal Employment Opportunity Commission (EEOC) now brings such actions instead of the Attorney General. See Chapter 9, at page 915. Private plaintiffs may also bring the functional equivalent of such suits by filing class actions. See Chapter 9, at pages 904-915.

2. We have seen the Court's definition of "disparate treatment" before: it has become the standard expression of the underlying theory. But this case is very different from either the individual disparate treatment cases studied in Chapter 3 or the instances of facially discriminatory policies seen earlier in this chapter.

3. Would it be fair to say that the plaintiff proves systemic disparate treatment by showing that the employer's practices have the cumulative effect of excluding a particular group, such as African Americans, Latinos, or women? But does such an effect, or result, necessarily show the intent that *Teamsters* clearly required?

4. In Washington v. Davis, 426 U.S. 229 (1976), plaintiffs mounted an equal protection attack on a test used for selecting recruits for police training in Washington, D.C., before Title VII was extended to government employment. The Court, rejecting the use of the disparate impact theory in an equal protection case, required that

---

23. The company's narrower attacks upon the statistical evidence — that there was no precise delineation of the areas referred to in the general population statistics, that the Government did not demonstrate that minority populations were located closer to terminals or that transportation was available, that the statistics failed to show what portion of the minority population was suited by age, health, or other qualifications to hold trucking jobs, etc — are equally lacking in force. At best, these attacks go only to the accuracy of the comparison between the composition of the company's work force at various terminals and the general population of the surrounding communities. They detract little from the Government's further showing that Negroes and Spanish-surnamed Americans who were hired were overwhelmingly excluded from line-driver jobs. Such employees were willing to work, had access to the terminal, were healthy and of working age, and often were at least sufficiently qualified to hold city-driver jobs. Yet they became line drivers with far less frequency than whites. (Of 2,919 whites who held driving jobs in 1971, 1,802 (62%) were line drivers and 1,117 (38%) were city drivers; of 180 Negroes and Spanish-surnamed Americans who held driving jobs, 13 (7%) were line drivers and 167 (93%) were city drivers.) In any event, fine tuning of the statistics could not have obscured the glaring absence of minority line drivers. As the Court of Appeals remarked, the company's inability to rebut the inference of discrimination came not from a misuse of statistics but from "the inexorable zero."

24. The company's evidence, apart from the showing of recent changes in hiring and promotion policies, consisted mainly of general statements that it hired only the best qualified applicants. But "affirmations of good faith in making individual selections are insufficient to dispel a prima facie case of systematic exclusion." Alexander v. Louisiana, 405 U.S. 625, 632.

The company also attempted to show that all of the witnesses who testified to specific instances of discrimination either were not discriminated against or suffered no injury. The Court of Appeals correctly ruled that the trial judge was not bound to accept this testimony and that it committed no error by relying instead on the other overpowering evidence in the case. The Court of Appeals was also correct in the view that individual proof concerning each class member's specific injury was appropriately left to proceedings to determine individual relief. In a suit brought by the Government under § 707(a) of the Act, the District Court's initial concern is in deciding whether the Government has proved that the defendant has engaged in a pattern or practice of discriminatory conduct.

intent to discriminate be shown. Liability under the equal protection clause, therefore, depends on proving what would, in Title VII terms, be called disparate treatment. But this does not mean that the effect or impact of an employer's actions is irrelevant to a disparate treatment case.

> This is not to say that the necessary discriminatory racial purpose must be express or appear on the face of the statute or that a law's disproportionate impact is irrelevant in cases involving Constitution-based claims of racial discrimination. A statute, otherwise neutral on its face, must not be applied so as invidiously to discriminate on the basis of race. . . .
>
> Necessarily, an invidious discriminatory purpose may often be inferred from the totality of the relevant facts, including the fact, if it is true, that the law bears more heavily on one race than another. It is also not infrequently true that the discriminatory impact . . . may for all practical purposes demonstrate unconstitutionality because in various circumstances the discrimination is very difficult to explain on nonracial grounds. . . . Disproportionate impact is not irrelevant, but it is not the sole touchstone of an invidious racial discrimination forbidden by the Constitution.

426 U.S. at 241-42.

5. *Teamsters* teaches that the effect of an employer's practices can be evidence of an underlying intent to discriminate under Title VII, as is true under the equal protection clause. This is not to suggest, however, that statutory and constitutional challenges are identical. As a practical matter, the governmental decision-making process may be different from that of typical private employers, less hierarchical and more participatory, at least in some settings. See Village of Arlington Heights v. Metropolitan Hous. Dev. Corp., 429 U.S. 252, 266-68 (1977). Second, there are judicial concerns about deference to other branches of government that may lead to more hesitation to find a discriminatory motivation than there would be in the case of private employers. "[J]udicial inquiries into legislative or executive motivation represent a substantial intrusion into the workings of other branches of government." *Arlington Heights*, 429 U.S. at 268 n.18.

6. In a concurring opinion in Washington v. Davis, Justice Stevens described a rationale for using impact data to show intent to discriminate:

> Frequently the most probative evidence of intent will be objective evidence of what actually happened rather than evidence describing the subjective state of mind of the actor. For normally the actor is presumed to have intended the natural consequences of his deeds. This is particularly true in the case of governmental action which is frequently the product of compromise, of collective decision-making, and of mixed motivation. It is unrealistic, on the one hand, to require the victim of alleged discrimination to uncover the actual subjective intent of the decision-maker or, conversely, to invalidate otherwise legitimate action simply because an improper motive affected the deliberation of a participant in the decisional process. A law conscripting clerics should not be invalidated because an atheist voted for it.

429 U.S. at 253.

7. Professor Charles Lawrence, in The Id, the Ego, and Equal Protection: Reckoning with Unconscious Racism, 39 Stan. L. Rev. 317, 321-24 (1987), criticizes the intent to discriminate element established in Washington v. Davis in a passage that also has implications for disparate treatment analysis under Title VII.

> Americans share a common historical and cultural heritage in which racism has played and still plays a dominant role. Because of this shared experience, we also inevitably

share many ideas, attitudes, and beliefs that attach significance to an individual's race and induce negative feelings and opinions about nonwhites. To the extent that this cultural belief system has influenced all of us, we are all racists. At the same time, most of us are unaware of our racism. We do not recognize the ways in which our cultural experience has influenced our beliefs about race or the occasions on which those beliefs affect our actions. In other words, a large part of the behavior that produces racial discrimination is influenced by unconscious racial motivation.

There are two explanations for the unconscious nature of our racially discriminatory beliefs and ideas. First, Freudian theory states that the human mind defends itself against the discomfort of guilt by denying or refusing to recognize those ideas, wishes, and beliefs that conflict with what the individual has learned is good or right. While our historical experience has made racism an integral part of our culture, our society has more recently embraced an ideal that rejects racism as immoral. When an individual experiences conflict between racist ideas and the societal ethic that condemns those ideas, the mind excludes this racism from consciousness.

Second, the theory of cognitive psychology states that the culture — including, for example, the media and an individual's parents, peers, and authority figures — transmits certain beliefs and preferences. Because these beliefs are so much a part of the culture, they are not experienced as explicit lessons. Instead, they seem part of the individual's rational ordering of her perceptions of the world. The individual is unaware, for example, that the ubiquitous presence of a cultural stereotype has influenced her perception that blacks are lazy or unintelligent. Because racism is so deeply ingrained in our culture, it is likely to be transmitted by tacit understandings: Even if a child is not told that blacks are inferior, he learns that lesson by observing the behavior of others. These tacit understandings, because they have never been articulated, are less likely to be experienced at a conscious level.

In short, requiring proof of conscious or intentional motivation as a prerequisite to constitutional recognition that a decision is race-dependent ignores much of what we understand about how the human mind works. It also disregards both the irrationality of racism and the profound effect that the history of American race relations has had on the individual and collective unconscious. . . .

Professor Linda Hamilton Krieger, in Content of Our Categories: A Cognitive Bias Approach to Discrimination and Equal Employment Opportunity, 47 Stan. L. Rev. 1161, 1188 (1995), expanded on Professor Lawrence's study of cognitive psychology and concluded that "stereotypes, like other categorical structures, are cognitive mechanisms that all people, not just 'prejudiced' ones, use to simplify the task of perceiving, processing, and retaining information about people in memory. They are central, and indeed essential to normal cognitive functioning. . . . [O]nce in place, stereotypes bias intergroup judgment and decisionmaking. . . . They operate absent intent to favor or disfavor members of a particular social group. . . . Stereotypes . . . operate beyond the reach of decisionmaker self-awareness." See also Ann C. McGinley, ¡Viva La Evolucion!: Recognizing Unconscious Motive in Title VII, 9 Cornell J.L. & Pub. Pol'y 415, 426-27 (2000) (summarizing social science research showing that "While consciously holding egalitarian values, whites simultaneously harbor unconscious negative feelings towards blacks as a result of cognitive and motivational biases combined with socialization into a racist culture.").

Is that why systemic disparate treatment is such a powerful tool — precisely because it focuses on the one aspect of racist decision-making that cannot be ignored — the cumulative outcome of individual racist decisions? Is it possible, however, that racism is so ingrained that we will not recognize a discriminatory outcome when we see it? See Barbara Flagg, "Was Blind, But Now I See": White Race Consciousness and the Requirement of Discriminatory Intent, 91 Mich. L. Rev. 953 (1993).

8. Assuming racism is as pervasive as Professor Lawrence claims, what about other grounds for discrimination? Feminist legal scholars have written much about the social construction of gender. E.g., Ruth Frankenberg, White Women, Race Matters: The Social Construction of Gender (1993); Carol C. Gould, Gender: Key Concepts in Critical Theory (1997); Marie Withers Osmond & Barrie Thorne, Feminist Theories: The Social Construction of Gender (1993); Robin J. Ely, The Power in Demography: Women's Social Constructions of Gender Identity at Work, Academy of Management Journal 38(3) (1995); Mary Joe Frug, A Postmodern Feminist Legal Manifesto, 105 Harv. L. Rev. 1045 (1992); Dennis Patterson, Postmodernism/Feminism/Law, 77 Cornell L. Rev. 254 (1992); Joan C. Williams, Dissolving the Sameness/Difference Debate: A Post-Modern Path Beyond Essentialism in Feminist and Critical Race Theory, 1991 Duke L.J. 296; Katharine T. Bartlett, Feminist Legal Methods, 103 Harv. L. Rev. 829 (1990); Martha L. Fineman, Challenging Law, Establishing Differences: The Future of Feminist Legal Scholarship, 42 Fla. L. Rev. 25 (1990); Robin West, Feminism, Critical Social Theory and Law, 1989 U. Chi. Legal F. 59; Joan C. Williams, Deconstructing Gender, 87 Mich. L. Rev. 797 (1989); Robin West, Jurisprudence and Gender, 55 U. Chi. L. Rev. 1 (1988).

9. What about religious or national origin discrimination? And are we all "ageists," even as we grow old? In Kadas v. MCI Systemhouse Corp., 255 F.3d 359, 361 (11th Cir. 2001), Judge Posner suggested that older people might be "oblivious to the prejudices they hold especially perhaps prejudices against the group to which they belong."

10. *Teamsters* differs from *Manhart* in not requiring proof of a facially discriminatory policy. Is *Teamsters* to *McDonnell Douglas* as *Manhart* is to *Price Waterhouse*? *Teamsters* did rely on some "direct evidence" of discrimination. See footnote 19. Would the Taylor and Trujillo incidents have made out a *Price Waterhouse* case for those individuals? Even if so, a few such incidents would not be enough to establish a companywide practice. The core of the *Teamsters* case really is the statistical evidence from which the Court infers discriminatory intent. But is statistical evidence alone sufficient to establish a prima facie case? Is some direct evidence of the defendant's discriminatory state of mind necessary, or at least some *McDonnell Douglas* inferential evidence of individual cases?

11. What is the rationale for using statistical evidence to show disparate treatment? Does Title VII require an employer's workforce to be racially balanced? Is the defendant bound by the showing of the "inexorable zero" because that result demonstrates a purpose to discriminate? What level of representation above "zero" can still make out a disparate treatment case?

12. *Teamsters* and *McDonnell Douglas* are both "disparate treatment" cases. See footnote 15. But *Teamsters*, as a *systemic* disparate treatment case, differs in significant ways from the *individual* disparate treatment cases we have studied.

(a) *Proof of the prima facie case.* In *Teamsters*, the Court noted many instances of individual discrimination. But it also intimated that a statistical showing alone would suffice. Thus, it may be possible to make out a violation with no proof of any specific instance of disparate treatment. See Hazelwood Sch. Dist. v. United States, page 218.

(b) *Rebutting the prima facie case.* The *Teamsters* Court in footnote 24 rejected two rebuttal efforts by the defendants. First, the defendants' general claims of good faith — that they merely hired the best-qualified applicants — were not adequate. Would such claims at least satisfy defendants' burden of coming forward with a nondiscriminatory reason under *McDonnell Douglas*? Cf. *Burdine*. Second, the Court upheld rejection of the defendants' proof directed to individual instances of discrimination. Was this proof inadmissible or merely not persuasive? Clearly, such proof is appropriate in a *McDonnell Douglas* case. And it also is appropriate at the remedy stage of systemic disparate treatment cases but only to avoid liability to individual members of the class of discriminatees. See Chapter 10. Does this suggest that an employer would not be permitted to justify each of its post-Act employment decisions? Would such a result be sensible, at least if the statistical evidence were less overwhelming than in *Teamsters?*

13. What justification is there for treating systemic cases more permissively than individual ones? Is it that we are more confident of our conclusions as to the existence of discriminatory intent when a cluster of employment decisions is involved? Put simply, one might with greater reason suspect the fairness of a coin that yielded 60 "heads" in 100 tosses than one that comes up "heads" 6 times out of 10. But perhaps even with larger numbers, the inference of intentional discrimination is not always as strong as may first appear.

14. Extended treatment of remedies problems is deferred until Chapter 10, but what remedies would seem appropriate in *Teamsters* to eradicate the systemic violation? In *McDonnell Douglas*, finding a violation obviously would have justified an order to hire Green and make him whole by awarding backpay. In a systemic disparate treatment case, granting an injunction against further discrimination is mandatory. In addition, establishing systemic liability creates a rebuttable presumption of individual relief for all members of the affected class of employees or applicants. Does this mirror the burden shifting approved for mixed-motive individual disparate treatment cases in *Price Waterhouse?* Justice O'Connor, in her *Price Waterhouse* concurrence, apparantly thought so. See 490 U.S. at 266-67.

15. The question of discriminatory intent under Title VII is one of fact and, therefore, subject to the "clearly erroneous" standard of appellate review. This is true not only in cases of individual disparate treatment, Anderson v. City of Bessemer City, 470 U.S. 564 (1985), but also with respect to systemic disparate treatment, *Pullman-Standard, Inc. v. Swint*, 456 U.S. 273 (1982). See generally Charles R. Calleros, Title VII and Rule 52(a): Standards of Appellate Review in Disparate Treatment Cases — Limiting the Reach of *Pullman-Standard v. Swint*, 58 Tul. L. Rev. 403 (1983).

16. *Teamsters* presented a relatively easy statistical case of discrimination. Virtually no minority group members were assigned line-driver positions. What must a plaintiff do to establish a statistical case of systemic disparate treatment discrimination when the numbers are not so stark?

## HAZELWOOD SCHOOL DISTRICT v. UNITED STATES
### 433 U.S. 299 (1977)

Justice STEWART delivered the opinion of the Court.

[Hazelwood School District is in the northern part of St. Louis County, Missouri. The Attorney General sued Hazelwood, alleging a "pattern or practice" of employment discrimination in violation of Title VII.]

Hazelwood was formed from 13 rural school districts between 1949 and 1951 by a process of annexation. By the 1967-1968 school year, 17,550 students were enrolled in the district, of whom only 59 were Negro; the number of Negro pupils increased to 576 of 25,166 in 1972-1973, a total of just over 2%.

From the beginning, Hazelwood followed relatively unstructured procedures in hiring its teachers. Every person requesting an application for a teaching position was sent one, and completed applications were submitted to a central personnel office, where they were kept on file. During the early 1960s the personnel office notified all applicants whenever a teaching position became available, but as the number of applications on file increased in the late 1960s and early 1970s, this practice was no longer considered feasible. The personnel office thus began the practice of selecting anywhere from 3 to 10 applicants for interviews at the school where the vacancy existed. The personnel office did not substantively screen the applicants in determining which of them to send for interviews, other than to ascertain that each applicant, if selected, would be eligible for state certification by the time he began the job. Generally, those who had most recently submitted applications were most likely to be chosen for interviews.

Interviews were conducted by a department chairman, program coordinator, or the principal at the school where the teaching vacancy existed. Although those conducting the interviews did fill out forms rating the applicants in a number of respects, it is undisputed that each school principal possessed virtually unlimited discretion in hiring teachers for his school. The only general guidance given to the principals was to hire the "most competent" person available, and such intangibles as "personality, disposition, appearance, poise, voice, articulation, and ability to deal with people" counted heavily. The principal's choice was routinely honored by Hazelwood's Superintendent and the Board of Education.

In the early 1960s Hazelwood found it necessary to recruit new teachers, and for that purpose members of its staff visited a number of colleges and universities in Missouri and bordering States. All the institutions visited were predominantly white, and Hazelwood did not seriously recruit at either of the two predominantly Negro four-year colleges in Missouri. As a buyer's market began to develop for public school teachers, Hazelwood curtailed its recruiting efforts. For the 1971-1972 school year, 3,127 persons applied for only 234 teaching vacancies; for the 1972-1973 school year, there were 2,373 applications for 282 vacancies. A number of the applicants who were not hired were Negroes.

Hazelwood hired its first Negro teacher in 1969. The number of Negro faculty members gradually increased in successive years: 6 of 957 in the 1970 school year; 16 of 1,107 by the end of the 1972 school year; 22 of 1,231 in the 1973 school year. By comparison, according to 1970 census figures, of more than 19,000 teachers employed in that year in the St. Louis area, 15.4% were Negro. That percentage figure included the St. Louis City School District, which in recent years has followed a policy of attempting to maintain a 50% Negro teaching staff. Apart from that school district, 5.7% of the teachers in the county were Negro in 1970.

Drawing upon these historic facts, the Government mounted its "pattern or practice" attack in the District Court upon four different fronts. It adduced evidence of (1) a history of alleged racially discriminatory practices, (2) statistical disparities in hiring, (3) the standardless and largely subjective hiring procedures, and (4) specific instances of alleged discrimination against 55 unsuccessful Negro applicants for teaching jobs. Hazelwood offered virtually no additional evidence in response, relying instead on evidence introduced by the Government, perceived deficiencies in the Government's case, and its own officially promulgated policy "to hire all teachers on the basis of training, preparation and recommendations, regardless of race, color or creed."

The District Court ruled that the Government had failed to establish a pattern or practice of discrimination. The court was unpersuaded by the alleged history of discrimination, noting that no dual school system had ever existed in Hazelwood. The statistics showing that relatively small numbers of Negroes were employed as teachers were found nonprobative, on the ground that the percentage of Negro pupils in Hazelwood was similarly small. The court found nothing illegal or suspect in the teacher-hiring procedures that Hazelwood had followed. Finally, the court reviewed the evidence in the 55 cases of alleged individual discrimination, and after stating that the burden of proving intentional discrimination was on the Government, it found that this burden had not been sustained in a single instance. Hence, the court entered judgment for the defendants.

The Court of Appeals for the Eighth Circuit reversed. After suggesting that the District Court had assigned inadequate weight to evidence of discriminatory conduct on the part of Hazelwood before [March 24, 1972] the effective date of Title VII [for public employment], the Court of Appeals rejected the trial court's analysis of the statistical data as resting on an irrelevant comparison of Negro teachers to Negro pupils in Hazelwood. The proper comparison, in the appellate court's view, was one between Negro teachers in Hazelwood and Negro teachers in the relevant labor market area. Selecting St. Louis County and St. Louis City as the relevant area,[8] the Court of Appeals compared the 1970 census figures, showing that 15.4% of teachers in that area were Negro, to the racial composition of Hazelwood's teaching staff. In the 1972-1973 and 1973-1974 school years, only 1.4% and 1.8%, respectively, of Hazelwood's teachers were Negroes. This statistical disparity, particularly when viewed against the background of the teacher-hiring procedures that Hazelwood had followed, was held to constitute a prima facie case of a pattern or practice of racial discrimination.

In addition, the Court of Appeals reasoned that the trial court had erred in failing to measure the 55 instances in which Negro applicants were denied jobs against the four-part standard for establishing a prima facie case of individual discrimination set out in this Court's opinion in McDonnell Douglas Corp. v. Green. Applying that standard, the appellate court found 16 cases of individual discrimination, which "buttressed" the statistical proof. Because Hazelwood had not rebutted the Government's prima facie case of a pattern or practice of racial discrimination, the Court of Appeals directed judgment for the Government. . . .

The petitioners primarily attack the judgment of the Court of Appeals for its reliance on "undifferentiated work force statistics to find an unrebutted prima facie case of employment discrimination." The question they raise, in short, is whether a basic component in the Court of Appeals' finding of a pattern or practice of discrimination — the comparatively small percentage of Negro employees on Hazelwood's teaching staff — was lacking in probative force.

This Court's recent consideration in Teamsters v. United States of the role of statistics in pattern-or-practice suits under Title VII provides substantial guidance in evaluating the arguments advanced by the petitioners. In that case we stated that it is the Government's burden to "establish by a preponderance of the evidence that racial discrimination was the [employer's] standard operating procedure — the regular rather than the unusual practice." We also noted that statistics can be an important source of proof in employment discrimination cases, since "absent explanation, it is ordinarily to be expected that nondiscriminatory hiring practices will in time result in a work force more or less representative of the racial and ethnic composition of the population in the community from which employees are hired. Evidence of long lasting and gross disparity between the composition of a work force and that of the general

8. The city of St. Louis is surrounded by, but not included in, St. Louis County.

population thus may be significant even though §703(j) makes clear that Title VII imposes no requirement that a work force mirror the general population." See also Arlington Heights v. Metropolitan Housing Dev. Corp., 429 U.S. 252, 266; Washington v. Davis. Where gross statistical disparities can be shown, they alone may in a proper case constitute prima facie proof of a pattern or practice of discrimination. *Teamsters*.

There can be no doubt, in light of the *Teamsters* case, that the District Court's comparison of Hazelwood's teacher work force to its student population fundamentally misconceived the role of statistics in employment discrimination cases. The Court of Appeals was correct in the view that a proper comparison was between the racial composition of Hazelwood's teaching staff and the racial composition of the qualified public school teacher population in the relevant labor market.[13] See *Teamsters*. The percentage of Negroes on Hazelwood's teaching staff in 1972-1973 was 1.4%, and in 1973-1974 it was 1.8%. By contrast, the percentage of qualified Negro teachers in the area was, according to the 1970 census, at least 5.7%.[14] Although these differences were on their face substantial, the Court of Appeals erred in substituting its judgment for that of the District Court and holding that the Government had conclusively proved its "pattern or practice" lawsuit.

The Court of Appeals totally disregarded the possibility that this prima facie statistical proof in the record might at the trial court level be rebutted by statistics dealing with Hazelwood's hiring after it became subject to Title VII. Racial discrimination by public employers was not made illegal under Title VII until March 24, 1972. A public employer who from that date forward made all its employment decisions in a wholly nondiscriminatory way would not violate Title VII even if it had formerly maintained an all-white work force by purposefully excluding Negroes.[15] For this

13. In *Teamsters*, the comparison between the percentage of Negroes on the employer's work force and the percentage in the general areawide population was highly probative, because the job skill there involved — the ability to drive a truck — is one that many persons possess or can fairly readily acquire. When special qualifications are required to fill particular jobs, comparisons to the general population (rather than to the smaller group of individuals who possess the necessary qualifications) may have little probative value. The comparative statistics introduced by the Government in the District Court, however, were properly limited to public school teachers, and therefore this is not a case like Mayor v. Educational Equality League, 415 U.S. 605, in which the racial-composition comparisons failed to take into account special qualifications for the position in question.

Although the petitioners concede as a general matter the probative force of the comparative work-force statistics, they object to the Court of Appeals' heavy reliance on these data on the ground that applicant-flow data, showing the actual percentage of white and Negro applicants for teaching positions at Hazelwood, would be firmer proof. . . . [T]here was no clear evidence of such statistics. We leave it to the District Court on remand to determine whether competent proof of those data can be adduced. If so, it would, of course, be very relevant. Cf. Dothard v. Rawlinson [reproduced at page 358].

14. As is discussed below, the Government contends that a comparative figure of 15.4%, rather than 5.7%, is the appropriate one. But even assuming, arguendo, that the 5.7% figure urged by the petitioners is correct, the disparity between that figure and the percentage of Negroes on Hazelwood's teaching staff would be more than fourfold for the 1972-1973 school year, and threefold for the 1973-1974 school year. A precise method of measuring the significance of such statistical disparities was explained in Castaneda v. Partida, 430 U.S. 482, 496-497, n.17. It involves calculation of the "standard deviation" as a measure of predicted fluctuations from the expected value of a sample. Using the 5.7% figure as the basis for calculating the expected value, the expected number of Negroes on the Hazelwood teaching staff would be roughly 63 in 1972-1973 and 70 in 1973-1974. The observed number in those years was 16 and 22, respectively. The difference between the observed and expected values was more than six standard deviations in 1972-1973 and more than five standard deviations in 1973-1974. The Court in *Castaneda* noted that "[a]s a general rule for such large samples, if the difference between the expected value and the observed number is greater than two or three standard deviations," then the hypothesis that teachers were hired without regard to race would be suspect. 430 U.S., at 497 n.17.

15. This is not to say that evidence of pre-Act discrimination can never have any probative force. Proof that an employer engaged in racial discrimination prior to the effective date of Title VII might in some

reason, the Court cautioned in the *Teamsters* opinion that once a prima facie case has been established by statistical work force disparities, the employer must be given an opportunity to show that "the claimed discriminatory pattern is a product of pre-Act hiring rather than unlawful post-Act discriminations."

The record in this case showed that for the 1972-1973 school year, Hazelwood hired 282 new teachers, 10 of whom (3.5%) were Negroes; for the following school year it hired 123 new teachers, 5 of whom (4.1%) were Negroes. Over the two-year period, Negroes constituted a total of 15 of the 405 new teachers hired (3.7%). Although the Court of Appeals briefly mentioned these data in reciting the facts, it wholly ignored them in discussing whether the Government had shown a pattern or practice of discrimination. And it gave no consideration at all to the possibility that post-Act data as to the number of Negroes hired compared to the total number of Negro applicants might tell a totally different story.

What the hiring figures prove obviously depends upon the figures to which they are compared. The Court of Appeals accepted the Government's argument that the relevant comparison was to the labor market area of St. Louis County and the city of St. Louis, in which, according to the 1970 census, 15.4% of all teachers were Negro. The propriety of that comparison was vigorously disputed by the petitioners, who urged that because the city of St. Louis has made special attempts to maintain a 50% Negro teaching staff, inclusion of that school district in the relevant market area distorts the comparison. Were that argument accepted, the percentage of Negro teachers in the relevant labor market area (St. Louis County alone) as shown in the 1970 census would be 5.7% rather than 15.4%.

The difference between these figures may well be important; the disparity between 3.7% (the percentage of Negro teachers hired by Hazelwood in 1972-1973 and 1973-1974) and 5.7% may be sufficiently small to weaken the Government's other proof, while the disparity between 3.7% and 15.4% may be sufficiently large to reinforce it.[17] In determining which of the two figures — or, very possibly, what

---

circumstances support the inference that such discrimination continued, particularly where relevant aspects of the decisionmaking process had undergone little change. Cf. Fed. Rule Evid. 406; Arlington Heights v. Metropolitan Housing Dev. Corp., 429 U.S. 252, 267; 1 J. Wigmore, Evidence 92 (3d ed. 1940); 2 id., 302-305, 371, 375. And, of course, a public employer even before the extension of Title VII in 1972 was subject to the command of the Fourteenth Amendment not to engage in purposeful racial discrimination.

17. Indeed, under the statistical methodology explained in Castaneda v. Partida, supra, at 496-497, n.17, involving the calculation of the standard deviation as a measure of predicted fluctuations, the difference between using 15.4% and 5.7% as the areawide figure would be significant. If the 15.4% figure is taken as the basis for comparison, the expected number of Negro teachers hired by Hazelwood in 1972-1973 would be 43 (rather than the actual figure of 10) of a total of 282, a difference of more than five standard deviations; the expected number in 1973-1974 would be 19 (rather than the actual figure 5) of a total of 123, a difference of more than three standard deviations. For the two years combined, the difference between the observed number of 15 Negro teachers hired (of a total of 405) would vary from the expected number of 62 by more than six standard deviations. Because a fluctuation of more than two or three standard deviations would undercut the hypothesis that decisions were being made randomly with respect to race, 430 U.S., at 497 n.17, each of these statistical comparisons would reinforce rather than rebut the Government's other proof. If, however, the 5.7% areawide figure is used, the expected number of Negro teachers hired in 1972-1973 would be roughly 16, less than two standard deviations from the observed number of 10; for 1973-1974, the expected value would be roughly seven, less than one standard deviation from the observed value of 5; and for the two years combined, the expected value of 23 would be less than two standard deviations from the observed total of 15. A more precise method of analyzing these statistics confirms the results of the standard deviation analysis. See F. Mosteller, R. Rourke, & G. Thomas, Probability with Statistical Applications 494 (2d ed. 1970).

These observations are not intended to suggest that precise calculations of statistical significance are necessary in employing statistical proof, but merely to highlight the importance of the choice of the relevant labor market area.

intermediate figure — provides the most accurate basis for comparison to the hiring figures at Hazelwood, it will be necessary to evaluate such considerations as (i) whether the racially based hiring policies of the St. Louis City School District were in effect as far back as 1970, the year in which the census figures were taken; (ii) to what extent those policies have changed the racial composition of that district's teaching staff from what it would otherwise have been; (iii) to what extent St. Louis' recruitment policies have diverted to the city, teachers who might otherwise have applied to Hazelwood; (iv) to what extent Negro teachers employed by the city would prefer employment in other districts such as Hazelwood; and (v) what the experience in other school districts in St. Louis County indicates about the validity of excluding the City School District from the relevant labor market. . . .

We hold, therefore, that the Court of Appeals erred in disregarding the post-Act hiring statistics in the record, and that it should have remanded the case to the District Court for further findings as to the relevant labor market area and for an ultimate determination of whether Hazelwood engaged in a pattern or practice of employment discrimination after March 24, 1972.[21] . . .

Justice WHITE, concurring.

I join the Court's opinion . . . but with reservations with respect to the relative neglect of applicant pool data in finding a prima facie case of employment discrimination and heavy reliance on the disparity between the areawide percentage of black public school teachers and the percentage of blacks on Hazelwood's teaching staff. Since the issue is whether Hazelwood discriminated against blacks in hiring after Title VII became applicable to it in 1972, perhaps the Government should have looked initially to Hazelwood's hiring practices in the 1972-1973 and 1973-1974 academic years with respect to the applicant pool, rather than to history and to comparative work-force statistics from other school districts. [A]rguably the United States should have been required to adduce evidence as to the applicant pool before it was entitled to its prima facie presumption. At least it might have been required to present some defensible ground for believing that the racial composition of Hazelwood's applicant pool was roughly the same as that for the school districts in the general area, before relying on comparative work-force data to establish its prima facie case. . . .

Justice STEVENS, dissenting. . . .

I

The first question [whether the government established a prima facie case], is clearly answered by the Government's statistical evidence, its historical evidence, and its evidence relating to specific acts of discrimination.

One-third of the teachers hired by Hazelwood resided in the city of St. Louis at the time of their initial employment. As Mr. Justice Clark explained in his opinion for the Court of Appeals, it was therefore appropriate to treat the city, as well as the county, as part of the relevant labor market. In that market, 15% of the teachers were black. In the Hazelwood District at the time of trial less than 2% of the teachers were

21. It will also be open to the District Court on remand to determine whether sufficiently reliable applicant-flow data are available to permit consideration of the petitioner's argument that those data may undercut a statistical analysis dependent upon hirings alone.

black. An even more telling statistic is that after Title VII became applicable to it, only 3.7% of the new teachers hired by Hazelwood were black. Proof of these gross disparities was in itself sufficient to make out a prima facie case of discrimination. See Teamsters v. United States; Castaneda v. Partida.

As a matter of history, Hazelwood employed no black teachers until 1969. Both before and after the 1972 amendment making the statute applicable to public school districts, Hazelwood used a standardless and largely subjective hiring procedure. Since "relevant aspects of the decisionmaking process had undergone little change," it is proper to infer that the pre-Act policy of preferring white teachers continued to influence Hazelwood's hiring practices.

The inference of discrimination was corroborated by post-Act evidence that Hazelwood had refused to hire 16 qualified black applicants for racial reasons. Taking the Government's evidence as a whole, there can be no doubt about the sufficiency of its prima facie case.

## II

Hazelwood "offered virtually no additional evidence in response." It challenges the Government's statistical analysis by claiming that the city of St. Louis should be excluded from the relevant market and pointing out that only 5.7% of the teachers in the county (excluding the city) were black. It further argues that the city's policy of trying to maintain a 50% black teaching staff diverted teachers from the county to the city. There are two separate reasons why these arguments are insufficient: they are not supported by the evidence; even if true, they do not overcome the Government's case.

The petitioners offered no evidence concerning wage differentials, commuting problems, or the relative advantages of teaching in an inner-city school as opposed to a suburban school. Without any such evidence in the record, it is difficult to understand why the simple fact that the city was the source of a third of Hazelwood's faculty should not be sufficient to demonstrate that it is a part of the relevant market. The city's policy of attempting to maintain a 50/50 ratio clearly does not undermine that conclusion, particularly when the record reveals no shortage of qualified black applicants in either Hazelwood or other suburban school districts. Surely not all of the 2,000 black teachers employed by the city were unavailable for employment in Hazelwood at the time of their initial hire.

But even if it were proper to exclude the city of St. Louis from the market, the statistical evidence would still tend to prove discrimination. With the city excluded, 5.7% of the teachers in the remaining market were black. On the basis of a random selection, one would therefore expect 5.7% of the 405 teachers hired by Hazelwood in the 1972-1973 and 1973-1974 school years to have been black. But instead of 23 black teachers, Hazelwood hired only 15, less than two-thirds of the expected number. Without the benefit of expert testimony, I would hesitate to infer that the disparity between 23 and 15 is great enough, in itself, to prove discrimination.[5] It is perfectly clear, however, that whatever probative force this disparity has, it tends to prove

---

5. After I had drafted this opinion, one of my law clerks advised me that, given the size of the two-year sample, there is only about a 5% likelihood that a disparity this large would be produced by a random selection from the labor pool. If his calculation (which was made using the method described in H. Blalock, Social Statistics 151-173 (1972)) is correct, it is easy to understand why Hazelwood offered no expert testimony.

discrimination and does absolutely nothing in the way of carrying Hazelwood's burden of overcoming the Government's prima facie case.

Absolute precision in the analysis of market data is too much to expect. We may fairly assume that a nondiscriminatory selection process would have resulted in the hiring of somewhere between the 15% suggested by the Government and the 5.7% suggested by petitioners, or perhaps 30 or 40 black teachers, instead of the 15 actually hired.[6] On that assumption, the Court of Appeals' determination that there were 16 individual cases of discriminatory refusal to hire black applicants in the post-1972 period seems remarkably accurate.

In sum, the Government is entitled to prevail on the present record. It proved a prima facie case, which Hazelwood failed to rebut. Why, then, should we burden a busy federal court with another trial? . . .

## NOTES

1. *Hazelwood* confirms the statistical approach in *Teamsters* but refines it. Without the "inexorable zero," plaintiff had to compare the representation of African Americans in the employer's workforce with the percentage of African Americans available to the employer. Do you understand why the district court was wrong in comparing the ratio of black teachers to the ratio of black students in the school district?

2. *Hazelwood* requires that this comparison be appropriate in three dimensions — time, space, and skill. From a time perspective, the passage of Title VII required comparing Hazelwood's hiring of blacks since 1972, not the overall percentage of blacks in the school system. Where plaintiff uses a "snapshot" of the employer's workforce composition on any particular day as the basis for comparison with the relevant labor pool, defendant may rebut by showing whether the claimed discriminatory pattern is a product of pre-Act hiring, rather than unlawful post-Act discrimination. Thus, "flow" statistics, or movements in and out of jobs over time, are relevant to show whether the snapshot statistics incorporate pre-Act conduct. Because it has been decades since the last major expansion of Title VII coverage, it is unlikely that the temporal dimension of defining the labor market will often be of consequence. Defining the labor market geographically and by skills, however, will continue to be critical.

3. Population data can be deceptive. Suppose an employer's typing pool is 99 percent female or a mining company's complement of miners is 99 percent male. Is it appropriate to draw an inference of intent to discriminate in these cases? See EEOC v. Sears, Roebuck & Co. (reproduced at page 253). What is the relevance of applicant flow data — that is, the gender composition of those who apply?

4. Looking only at actual applicants for the job in question eliminates many problems: it is unlikely that persons lacking minimal skills will apply, and, by definition, those who apply are interested in the work and willing to consider the location. Justice White is surely correct when he suggests that applicant flow data are usually the best data for a comparison. But employers such as Hazelwood do not always keep applications, and Hazelwood's haphazard method of dealing with applications might make such data suspect. Further, what if the employer keeps all application forms but has no record of the race or gender of any of the applicants? Gender is usually ascertainable by first name, but race is not.

6. Some of the other school districts in the county have a 10% ratio of blacks on their faculties.

5. In EEOC v. Joe's Stone Crab, Inc., 220 F.3d 1263 (11th Cir. 2000), reproduced at page 438, the at-issue jobs were wait staff positions at a popular Miami Beach restaurant. Rather than using the 44.1 percent representation of women among food servers in Miami Beach, the district court "refined" the relevant labor pool to include food "servers who lived or worked in Miami Beach and earned between $25,000 and $50,000 . . . thereby using past earnings as a proxy for experience, and by extension, experience as a proxy for qualification." Id. at 1272. The resulting pool was 31.1 percent female, which the court concluded resulted in a disparity that "bordered on statistical significance" and did support a prima facie case. Why discount the pool by income? Wouldn't lower income food servers be exactly the people you would expect to apply for higher paying jobs, such as at Joe's Stone Crab? Should experience and qualifications matter for determining the appropriate labor pool? See Kevin Gilmartin, Identifying Similarly Situated Employees in Employment Discrimination Cases, 31 Jurimetrics J. 429 (1991), for discussion of statistical approaches to constructing comparison pools.

6. What if the job in question is completely unskilled? For purposes of comparison, can plaintiff argue for the use of the pool of unskilled laborers, rather than general population figures, because the pool of unskilled workers has a higher minority or female component than the general population?

7. Defining the geographic labor market was more difficult. Should the city of St. Louis be included? Isn't Justice Stevens clearly right that the high number of actual Hazelwood teachers who reside in the city mandates the inclusion of teachers there? The defendant, however, claimed that St. Louis City hired to meet a goal of 50 percent black teachers. What is the significance of such a hiring pattern? Two possibilities might be raised:

(a) St. Louis pays more; therefore, Hazelwood cannot attract St. Louis teachers into its system. Factually, one would have expected Hazelwood to have made this argument the first time if it had been true. Analytically, is it a reason to exclude the whole St. Louis pool or merely to discount it somewhat? Might not some teachers prefer teaching jobs in the suburbs, even at lower pay?

(b) St. Louis hires unqualified persons for affirmative action purposes. In that case, the pool of qualified teachers may not be as large as it first appears. But is it true? Second, even if some less-qualified persons were hired, should the St. Louis pool be discounted, or eliminated?

8. How should the geographic area of the labor pool be established? Is it the geographic area from which the employer recruits employees? In most areas of the United States, substantial housing segregation exists. See NAACP v. Town of Harrison, 940 F.2d 792 (3d Cir. 1991) (resident-only hiring rule of town struck down as disparate impact discrimination because of housing segregation). Was the Hazelwood school district attempting to take advantage of segregated housing patterns by excluding the city of St. Louis from the relevant labor pool? How would you state a fair standard for establishing the geographic area? In Abron v. Black & Decker Mfg. Co., 439 F. Supp. 1095, 1105 (D. Md. 1977), rev'd on other grounds, 654 F.3d 951 (4th Cir. 1981), the court found that "the appropriate labor force is that which is encompassed in the area within which an employer can reasonably expect people to commute." See Louis J. Braun, Statistics and the Law: Hypothesis Testing and Its Application to Title VII Cases, 32 Hastings L.J. 59 (1980).

9. Professors Alfred W. Blumrosen and Ruth G. Blumrosen, in The Reality of Intentional Discrimination in Metropolitan America — 1999 (2002) (available at www.eeo1.com), have undertaken a major study of the data employers with over 50

employees are required to submit annually to the EEOC on the EEO-1 Form. Looking at the data from 1975 through 1999, the authors found some good and some bad news. First, the good news is that minorities and women have made significant gains in employment since 1975. While the whole work force grew during this period, the proportion of women and minority men in the workforce increased:

> The bottom line . . . is that minorities increased their proportion of the EEO-1 Labor Force between 1975 and 1999 by more than 4.6 million workers. These Minorities were 57% Black, 27% Hispanic, 9% Asian and .2% Native American. The net inflow of minorities in the EEO-1 Labor Force was an additional seven million workers, nearly doubling the minority labor force of 1975.
>
> Women increased their proportion of the EEO-1 Labor Force by nearly 3.8 million workers. The net inflow of women was an additional 9 million women, more than doubling the female labor force of 1975. The women workers were 69% White, 17% Black, 9% Hispanic, 5% Asian and 1% Native American.

Id. at 26. "More important, all groups increased their share of 'better jobs' as officials, managers, professional, technical and sales workers." Id. at xvi.

The bad news is that one third of the employers who were legally obligated to file EEO-1 Forms failed to do so. For those employers who did file, the authors looked at the establishments of employers within common metropolitan areas and compared the representation of women and minority men holding jobs in common occupational areas using the binomial distribution technique approved in *Hazelwood*.

> For 1999, we analyzed the 160,297 reports filed by establishments with 50 or more employees that operate in Metropolitan Statistical Areas (MSA). The MSA's are defined by the Census Bureau as "a core area containing a large population nucleus, together with adjacent communities that have a high degree of social and economic integration." We treat each MSA as a labor market because of this social and economic integration. . . .
>
> We compared only establishments in MSA's that employ at least 50 workers to ensure reliability of the data. We required that an establishment have at least 20 employees in the occupational category examined; that there be two other establishments with at least 20 employees in that occupation; that there be at least 120 employees in the occupation in the MSA; and that no establishment have more than 80% of the employees in order to have sufficient employment to assure that there was a labor market for such workers, and that no single establishment dominated the market. This data set is identified as the EEO-1 Labor Force. Within the EEO-1 Labor Force, we examine each industry separately, because different industries have different technologies and different employment needs. Each establishment describes its principal product or activity on its EEO-1 form. Establishments are then classified by industry in accordance with the 1987 *Standard Industrial Classification (SIC) Manual*, Office of Management and Budget.

Id. at 30. As a result of these exclusions, the study covers many fewer than half of all employees. But, based on the comparison of individual, though unidentified, employers, against their peers in the same industry and metropolitan area, the study found that there was considerable discrimination:

> For 1999, 75,793 — or 37% — of establishments discriminated against Minorities in at least one occupational category. This discrimination affected 1,361,083 Minorities who were qualified and available to work in the labor markets, industries and occupations of

those who discriminated. These Minorities were 57% Black, 27% Hispanic, 9% Asian and .2% Native American.

For 1999, 60,425 — or 29% — of establishments discriminated against Women in at least one occupational category. This discrimination affected 952,130 Women who were qualified and available to work in the labor markets, industries and occupations of those who discriminated. Women were 69% White, 17% Black, 9% Hispanic, 5% Asian and 1% Native American.

A "hard core" of 22,369 establishments appear to have discriminated over a nine-year period against Minorities, and 13,173 establishments appear to have done so against Women. This "hard core" is responsible for roughly half of the intentional discrimination we have identified.

Id. at 74. Hard core discriminators were "so far below average in an occupation that there is only one in one hundred chances that the result occurred by accident (2.5 standard deviations [versus the 2 standard deviation or 5% chance standard used in *Hazelwood*]) in at least two years between 1991 and 1999, and was not above average between 1991 and 1999." Id. at 95.

The authors make recommendations including having the government disclose to employers the results of this type of study in the expectation that many of them at risk will do something about it. They do not recommend that the EEOC use this information as the basis of lawsuits. Why not? Why not start with enforcement actions against the many employers who simply fail to file EEO-1 Forms? Aren't these employers likely to be among the worst offenders? After that, why not start going after the "hard core" discriminators? Would these statistical studies hold up to prove discrimination? The authors concede that the use of Metropolitan Statistical Areas as one parameter of the EEO-1 Labor Force can raise problems since some MSAs are huge and hetrogeneous while some establishments with as few as 50 employees have much smaller employee recruitment areas. Assuming that is true, wouldn't it be good policy for the EEOC to start with the largest establishments that are deemed "hard core" discriminators?

10. Systemic disparate treatment cases can also be litigated under the ADEA. In Adams v. Ameritech Servs., Inc., 231 F.3d 414 (7th Cir. 2000), the employer substantially reduced its personnel, eliminating some 2500 of 21,000 management employees "either by persuasion or by force." Plaintiffs' evidence of age discrimination included statistical analysis of the outcomes, the manner of the layoffs, the use of combination of age and pension status in the employer's plans "which the plaintiffs assert created a strong financial incentive to terminate people below the chronological age thresholds set by the Plan," and certain statements allegedly showing age bias. The Seventh Circuit reversed the district court's grant of summary judgment to the defendant. It reaffirmed the admissibility of statistical evidence in systemic discrimination cases, found the statistical evidence plaintiffs had proffered admissible, and held that this evidence, together with plaintiffs' other evidence, precluded summary judgment. The defendants' incentive program encouraged voluntary attrition, after which individuals were chosen for layoff. The court summarized the evidence against one of the defendants:

> In the end, ASI let go 1,320 managers (19.72%). Of those, 591 volunteered, with 200 of the "volunteers" deciding to do so only after they found out they had been selected for termination. Of the 1,320, 894 (67.73%) were 40 or older. Looking for the moment at its managerial ranks as a whole, . . . . ASI selected for termination 12.63% of those aged 40-44, 16.71% of those aged 45-49, 24.58% of those aged 50-54, and 29.19% of those aged 55 and older.

231 F.3d at 419-20. Plaintiff's statistician analyzed this data, including the termination rate of each 10-year age cohort, comparing the share of terminations of those 40 and over with their share of the pretermination workforce. The age differences were found statistically significant. The Seventh Circuit held erroneous the district court's determination that these analyses were inadmissible. This data, together with other evidence, precluded summary judgment to the defendant. *Adams* thus clearly illustrates how a large-scale reduction in force can become a textbook exercise in the application of statistical analysis to prove a correlation between age and layoff in order to make out a prima facie case of systemic disparate treatment. See also Mistretta v. Sandia Corp., 649 F.2d 1383 (10th Cir. 1981), *aff'g* EEOC v. Sandia Corp., 1977 U.S. Dist. LEXIS 13368 (D.N.M. 1977).

11. By contrast, in EEOC v. McDonnell Douglas Corp., 191 F.3d 948 (8th Cir. 1999), the court found that a statistical showing that employees 55 years of age or older were more than twice as likely to be laid off as younger workers was not sufficient to preclude summary judgment for defendant; the court noted that individuals aged 55 or older comprised 13.6 percent of the workforce after the layoffs and only 14.7 percent before. Why is this not probative of age discrimination? Summary judgment was granted even though the EEOC proffered admissions by managers that "retirement eligibility" was a factor in deciding who to lay off. Under *Biggins*, this did not constitute age discrimination. Such evidence, even coupled with evidence that some managers manipulated performance evaluations to favor younger workers, was held insufficient to create a question whether there was a pattern or practice of age discrimination.

12. Should systemic cases of age discrimination be viewed more skeptically by the courts than systemic cases based on other prohibited reasons? Laugesen v. Anaconda Co., 510 F.2d 307 (6th Cir. 1975), stated:

> The progression of age is a universal human process. In the very nature of the problem, it is apparent that in the usual case, absent any discriminatory intent, discharged employees will more often than not be replaced by those younger than they, for older employees are constantly moving out of the labor market, while younger ones move in.

Id. at 313 n.4. Should a court be hesitant to find a systemic age case from a pattern of conduct? Wouldn't this concern be satisfied by the choice of statistics to use? Those who exit the firm because of death, disability, or truly voluntary retirement should be factored out of the analysis.

13. In discussing what would satisfy plaintiff's burden in a systemic disparate treatment case, Segar v. Smith, 738 F.2d 1249 (D.C. Cir. 1984), differentiated between two situations. "[W]hen a plaintiff's statistical methodology focuses on the appropriate labor pool and generates evidence of discrimination at a statistically significant level, no sound policy reason exists for subjecting the plaintiff to the additional requirement of either providing anecdotal evidence or showing gross disparities." Id. at 1278. In contrast, when a plaintiff uses population statistics as a basis of comparison with the employer's workforce statistics, a higher standard of proof would apply.

> Thus, if the court [in *Hazelwood*] intended any specific rule by the "gross disparity" language, the Court meant that rule to apply when a plaintiff relies on general population/ workforce comparisons and lacks anecdotal evidence. Such a requirement might be appropriate because a population/workforce comparison will usually yield only rough evidence of discrimination; the method is not finely tuned to the population of those eligible for and interested in the positions at issue. Absent anecdotal evidence, an inference of discrimination is less secure when such statistics show only slight disparities.

Id. If the underlying question is the state of mind of the employer, should the standard of proof differ depending on the type of evidence relied on? Should the standard be the same, but the level of impact (and whatever buttressing can be found in anecdotes of discrimination) more substantial when there is some doubt that the pool used for comparison with the employer's workforce includes only those with qualifications necessary for the at-issue jobs? In Winbush v. State of Iowa by Glenwood State Hospital, 66 F.3d 1471 (8th Cir. 1995), the court upheld a systemic disparate treatment claim as to promotions. The evidence established that the defendant used various pre-selection devices to avoid using a merit system of the civil service system in order to "fill open positions with friends and other favored individuals," which process "99% of the time" did not include African Americans. Id. at 1480 n.14. In response to the argument that African-American employees did not apply for promotions, the court upheld the lower court's finding that "application was futile due to the defendants' discriminatory practices." Id. at 1481.

14. Bringing job qualifications to bear leaves much room for manipulation. See Judith P. Vladeck & Margaret M. Young (Moses), Sex Discrimination in Higher Education: It's Not Academic, 4 Women's Rights L. Rep. 59, 74–75 (1978).

As for job qualifications consider a School of Arts and Sciences at X University which is structured as follows:

| Department | Number of Faculty Members |
|---|---|
| English | 50 |
| Psychology | 20 |
| History | 20 |
| Philosophy | 10 |
| | 100 |

Assume also that X University requires all of its faculty members to have a doctoral degree. In order to determine how many women one would expect to find in this school absent discrimination, one should look at the percentage of doctorates earned nationally by women in each of these fields. The national statistics are as follows:

| English | 27.6% |
|---|---|
| Psychology | 21.4% |
| History | 13.2% |
| Philosophy | 9.7% |

Applying the EEOC's 11% to 14% figure of all doctorates earned nationally by women, we would expect that 11 to 14 of the 100 faculty members in Arts and Sciences of X University would be women. An average of doctorates earned by women in English, psychology, philosophy and history, however, would produce a mean of 18%, or an expectancy that 18 members of the School of Arts and Sciences would be women. If we also include a weight factor based on the size of each department, we would get a still higher figure. Taking each department separately, and determining what percentage of the department should be women, then adding these numbers, we find that absent discrimination, one would expect approximately 22 members, or 22% of the School of Arts and Sciences to be women.

English:                                          27.6% × 50 faculty members = 13.88
Psychology:                                     21.4% × 20 faculty members =   4.28
History:                                           13.2% × 20 faculty members =   2.64
Philosophy:                                       9.7% × 10 faculty members =    .97
       Total approximately = 21.69
                 or 22.00

The expected female representation exceeds the mean percentage of women doctorates in these fields, which was 18%, because of the greater number of faculty positions in areas with high concentrations of women doctorates, here English and psychology. Using a weight factor may also, of course, create an expectancy of fewer women in areas of high concentration of male doctorates, but in the interest of fairness the only way a reasonable analysis can be made is to consider the size of a particular department as a factor in computing the expected female representation in a school or division. This requires a department by department analysis.

15. In Hill v. Ross, 183 F.3d 586 (7th Cir. 1999), the court looked skeptically on a university's attempt to defend its rejection of a male candidate because of supposed discrimination against females. Dean Ross had justified rejecting the male plaintiff for a position in the psychology department. He had suggested a target of 61.8 percent females in the department, presumably because that was the proportion of doctorates in clinical psychology held by women from 1980 forward. Judge Easterbrook responded:

Suppose the University hired blindly from a pool that is 62% women? How likely is it that *exactly* seven of twelve [members of the department] would be women? What the University appears to have in mind is a world in which the absence of discrimination would mean that *every* department would *exactly* mirror the population from which its members are hired. But that is statistical nonsense. Suppose a university has 64 departments or faculties, each with five persons; that half of all persons meeting its standards for appointment are women; and that the university makes appointments by drawing blindly from an urn containing infinitely many balls, each one representing a candidate. Then the most likely outcome is that two of the 64 departments would be all male ($2^5 = 32$) and two would be all female. Ten of the 64 departments would be 80% male, and another ten would be 80% female. The remaining forty would have three men and two women, or three women and two men. The existence of this hypothetical university of 24 departments that were composed of 80% or more of one sex would do nothing at all to imply discrimination or a need for corrective action; such a distribution is simply the result of chance.

Id. at 591 (emphasis in original). The gender composition of the university's psychology department (ten professors at the time when Hill's appointment was blocked, four of whom were women), was very likely to occur by chance. Easterbrook did recognize that statistical techniques could assess whether any given distribution is the result of chance. "Suppose a given university turned out to have six or eight [unbalanced] departments. Fairly simple statistical inquiries can reveal the probability that a circumstance less wholesome than chance was to blame." Id. But the university had provided no data as to other departments.

## BAZEMORE v. FRIDAY
### 478 U.S. 385 (1986)

[The Court announced its decision by per curiam opinion, indicating that, for reasons stated by Justice Brennan for a unanimous Court, the court of appeals had erred in a number of ways, including finding statistical studies of salary discrimination to be irrelevant.]

The case concerned North Carolina's agricultural extension program, which, before passage of the Civil Rights Act of 1964, operated racially segregated branches. With passage of the Act, the "white branch" and the "Negro branch" were merged, but salary disparities between employees in the two branches were not entirely eliminated. In part I of his opinion, Justice Brennan found that "[t]he Court of Appeals plainly erred in holding that the pre-Act discriminatory difference in salaries did not have to be eliminated." He then turned to proof of systemic disparate treatment by means of multiple regression analysis.]

## B

We now turn to the issue of whether the Court of Appeals erred in upholding the District Court's refusal to accept the petitioners' expert statistical evidence as proof of discrimination by a preponderance of the evidence. In a case alleging that a defendant has engaged in a pattern and practice of discrimination under § 707(a) plaintiffs must "establish by a preponderance of the evidence that racial discrimination was the company's standard operating procedure — the regular rather than the unusual practice." Teamsters v. United States. Further, our decision in United Postal Service Board of Governors v. Aikens, 460 U.S. 711, although not decided in the context of a pattern and practice case, makes clear that if the defendants have not succeeded in having a case dismissed on the ground that plaintiffs have failed to establish a prima facie case, and have responded to the plaintiffs' proof by offering evidence of their own, the factfinder then must decide whether the plaintiffs have demonstrated a pattern or practice of discrimination by a preponderance of the evidence. This is because the only issue to be decided at that point is whether the plaintiffs have actually proved discrimination. This determination is subject to the clearly erroneous standard on appellate review.

At trial, petitioners relied heavily on multiple regression analyses designed to demonstrate that blacks were paid less than similarly situated whites. The United States' expert prepared multiple regression analyses relating to salaries for the years 1974, 1975, and 1981. Certain of these regressions used four independent variables — race, education, tenure, and job title. Petitioners selected these variables based on discovery testimony by an Extension Service official that four factors were determinative of salary: education, tenure, job title, and job performance. In addition, regressions done by the Extension Service itself for 1971 included the variables race, sex, education, and experience; and another in 1974 used the variables race, education, and tenure to check for disparities between the salaries of blacks and whites.

The regressions purported to demonstrate that in 1974 the average black employee earned $331 less per year than a white employee with the same job title, education, and tenure; and that in 1975 the disparity was $395.[9] The regression for 1981 showed a smaller disparity which lacked statistical significance.

The Court of Appeals stated that the

> district court refused to accept plaintiffs' expert testimony as proof of discrimination by a preponderance of the evidence because the plaintiffs' expert had not included a number of variable factors the court considered relevant, among them being the across the board and percentage pay increases which varied from county to county. The district court was, of course, correct in this analysis.

---

9. Petitioners' expert testified that both of these disparities were statistically significant.

The Court of Appeals thought the District Court correct for essentially two reasons: First, the Court of Appeals rejected petitioners' regression analysis because it "contained salary figures which reflect the effect of pre-Act discrimination, a consideration not actionable under Title VII. . . ." Second, the court believed that "[a]n appropriate regression analysis of salary should . . . include all measurable variables thought to have an effect on salary level." In particular, the court found that the failure to consider county to county differences in salary increases was significant. It concluded, noting that "both experts omitted from their respective analysis variables which ought to be reasonably viewed as determinants of salary. As a result, the regression analysis presented here must be considered unacceptable as evidence of discrimination." The Court of Appeals' treatment of the statistical evidence in this case was erroneous in important respects.

I

The Court of Appeals erred in stating that petitioners' regression analyses were "unacceptable as evidence of discrimination," because they did not include "all measurable variables thought to have an effect on salary level." The court's view of the evidentiary value of the regression analyses was plainly incorrect. While the omission of variables from a regression analysis may render the analysis less probative than it otherwise might be, it can hardly be said, absent some other infirmity, that an analysis which accounts for the major factors "must be considered unacceptable as evidence of discrimination." Normally, failure to include variables will affect the analysis' probativeness, not its admissibility.[10]

Importantly, it is clear that a regression analysis that includes less than "all measurable variables" may serve to prove a plaintiff's case. A plaintiff in a Title VII suit need not prove discrimination with scientific certainty; rather, his or her burden is to prove discrimination by a preponderance of the evidence. Whether, in fact, such a regression analysis does carry the plaintiffs' ultimate burden will depend in a given case on the factual context of each case in light of all the evidence presented by both the plaintiff and the defendant. However, as long as the court may fairly conclude, in light of all the evidence, that it is more likely than not that impermissible discrimination exists, the plaintiff is entitled to prevail.

2

In this case the Court of Appeals failed utterly to examine the regression analyses in light of all the evidence in the record. Looked at in its entirety, the petitioners offered an impressive array of evidence to support their contention that the Extension Service engaged in a pattern or practice of discrimination with respect to salaries. In addition to their own regression analyses described above, petitioners offered regressions done by the Extension Service for 1971 and 1974 that showed results similar to those revealed by petitioners' regressions. Petitioners also claim support from multiple regressions presented by respondents at trial for the year 1975. Using the same model that the petitioners had used, and similar variables, respondents' expert obtained substantially the same result for 1975, a statistically significant racial effect of $384. Indeed, respondents also included in their analysis, "quartile rank" as an independent variable, and this increased the racial effect to $475.

---

10. There may, of course, be some regressions so incomplete as to be inadmissible as irrelevant; but such was clearly not the case here.

Petitioners also presented evidence of pre-Act salary discrimination, and of respondents' ineffectual attempts to eradicate it. . . . As we made clear in Hazelwood School District v. United States, "[p]roof that an employer engaged in racial discrimination prior to the effective date of Title VII might in some circumstances support the inference that such discrimination continued, particularly where relevant aspects of the decisionmaking process had undergone little change."

Further, petitioners presented evidence to rebut respondents' contention that county to county variations in contributions to salary explain the established disparity between black and white salaries. The United States presented evidence, which it claims respondents did not rebut, establishing that black employees were not located disproportionately in the counties that contributed only a small amount to Extension Service salaries. Absent a disproportionate concentration of blacks in such counties, it is difficult, if not impossible, to understand how the fact that some counties contribute less to salaries than others could explain disparities between black and white salaries. In addition, the United States presented an exhibit based on 1973 data for 23 counties showing 29 black employees who were earning less than whites in the same county who had comparable or lower positions and tenure.

Finally, and there was some overlap here with evidence used to discredit the county to county variation theory, the petitioners presented evidence consisting of individual comparisons between salaries of blacks and whites similarly situated. Witness testimony, claimed by petitioners to be unrebutted, also confirmed the continued existence of such disparities.

Setting out the range of persuasive evidence offered by the petitioners demonstrates the error of the Court of Appeals in focusing solely on the characteristics of the regression analysis. Although we think that consideration of the evidence makes a strong case for finding the District Court's conclusion clearly erroneous,[14] we leave that task to the Court of Appeals on remand which must make such a determination based on the "entire evidence" in the record.[15]

## NOTES

1. What is required to establish a prima facie case by statistical evidence? *Bazemore* held that statistical evidence was admissible, but does that decision mean that the

14. There was very little evidence to show that there was in fact no disparity in salaries between blacks and whites, or to demonstrate that any disparities that existed were the product of chance. The District Court did point to cases of individual differences that it found to be successfully rebutted by respondents. . . . The District Court also pointed to "scattergrams" or graphs based on the data in respondents' regressions, concluding that these graphs displayed the salaries of blacks and whites "in a completely random distribution." Yet, as pointed out by the United States in its brief below, the very purpose of a regression analysis is to organize and explain data that may appear to be random. See Fisher, Multiple Regression in Legal Proceedings, 80 Colum. L. Rev. 702, 705-707 (1980). Thus, it is simply wrong to give weight to a scattergram while ignoring the underlying regression analysis. Respondents' strategy at trial was to declare simply that many factors go into making up an individual employee's salary; they made no attempt that we are aware of — statistical or otherwise — to demonstrate that when these factors were properly organized and accounted for there was no significant disparity between the salaries of blacks and whites.

15. We do note, however, that certain conclusions of the District Court are inexplicable in light of the record. . . . [T]he district court complained about the inclusion of the County Chairmen in the petitioners' regression analysis, fearing that the fact that they were disproportionately white would skew the salary statistics to show whites earning more than blacks. Yet, because the regressions controlled for job title, adding County Chairman as a variable in the regression would simply mean that the salaries of white County Chairmen would be compared with those of nonwhite County Chairmen. In any event, respondents' own regression at trial excluded County Chairmen and revealed a differential between black and white salaries.

testimony of a qualified expert that a statistically significant relationship exists between race and the challenged employment practice is always sufficient to get to the finder of fact?

2. What may the employer do to rebut plaintiff's prima facie case? Merely pointing out additional variables that might be relevant may not suffice. Must the employer produce proof that including these variables would destroy the statistical evidence of plaintiff's study? Presumably, this would require the employer to perform its own regressions. How does that comport with keeping the burden of persuasion on plaintiff?

3. In Smith v. Virginia Commonwealth University, 84 F.3d 672 (4th Cir. 1996) (en banc), plaintiffs were male professors who challenged pay raises that Virginia Commonwealth University gave its female faculty in response to a salary equity study showing that women faculty members had been underpaid. The pay equity study was a multiple regression that controlled for such differences as doctoral degree, academic rank, tenure statue, number of years of VCU experience, and number of years of prior academic experience. Any difference in salary after controlling for these factors was attributed to sex. The difference attributed to sex ranged from $1,354 to $1,982. The male plaintiffs, however, contended that salary was based on merit, with merit determined by an annual review of teaching load, teaching quality, quantity and quality of publications, and service to the community. Plaintiffs introduced expert testimony that the inclusion of the performance factors was possible and necessary to ensure accurate statistical data. Plaintiffs' experts, however, did not conduct their own pay study.

Applying the standards applicable to attacks to affirmative action plans, see page 282, the court reversed the summary judgment for VCU. "Given the number of important variables omitted from the multiple regression analysis, and the evidence presented by the [plaintiffs] that these variables are crucial, a dispute of material fact remains as to the validity of the study." Id. at 677. One judge dissented. "[Plaintiff's] expert totally failed to back up his opinion with facts or data showing that any allegedly omitted factor was a major one, that is, one that would be "statistically significant," in showing that gender had no effects on salaries." Id. See also Maitland v. Univ. of Minn., 155 F.3d 1013 (8th Cir. 1998).

4. In Hemmings v. Tidyman's Inc., 285 F.3d 1174 (9th Cir. 2002), plaintiffs claimed the defendant discriminated against them because of their sex by failing to pay them wages and compensation equal to their male counterparts and by failing to promote them. Based on the information defendant provided in discovery, plaintiff's statistician provided evidence of discrimination.

Women in management at Tidyman's earn an average of $12,000 less than men in management. The mean starting salary for women in management at Tidyman's was $26,400, while the mean starting salary for men was $38,400. Dr. Polissar also testified that he analyzed the progression of wages of women and men over time as a method of controlling for factors other than gender — such as experience — that might explain the initial wage differential. Dr. Polissar used regression analysis to control for differences in experience, and reached the same conclusion — that gender predicted a statistically significant wage differential. Dr. Polissar also performed a "step analysis," which compared the number of women to the number of men within each rank of Tidyman's' management hierarchy. Dr. Polissar explained that some of the step levels had no women employees, which made comparison impossible for those levels. Where comparisons were possible, Dr. Polissar testified that the step analysis revealed wage differentials between men and women for most of the ranks. For example, at the "step four" level, the average salary for female workers was $29,400, while the average salary for male workers was $40,800.

Finally, Dr. Polissar analyzed the distribution of men and women in different job categories at Tidyman's and concluded that the distribution reflected a pattern of segregation
of men and women that was unlikely to be due to chance. He also testified that the percentage of women in hourly positions was higher than the percentage of women in salary.

Id. at 1183-84. The court rejected defendant's attack on this statistical evidence. First,
defendant argued that including the lower management positions in the labor pool
was error, but the court found that such use was appropriate. "Tidyman's fills higher
management by internal promotions. Therefore, the potential applicant pool — and
thus the appropriate comparison pool — for promotions to upper and middle management jobs at Tidyman's is comprised of the current employees in lower management positions. The analysis of Tidyman's management data base included the
qualified individuals under consideration for promotions." Id. at 1185-86. Second,
the defendants argued that including store management in with corporate management positions was error because plaintiffs were not qualified to be store managers.
The court rejected that argument since "Tidyman's does not dispute that store management may be a career path to corporate management for some employees." Id. at
1186. "Even assuming the individual plaintiffs were unqualified for store management positions, the inclusion of the store management employees in the management data set was proper given the fluid movement of employees between the store
and corporate management." Id. at 1187, n.15. Finally, based on *Bazemore*, the court
rejected defendant's argument that the statistical analysis should have been excluded
because it did not eliminate all possible legitimate, nondiscriminatory factors, including the employee's qualifications, level of education, and preferences. "[T]he law
does not require the near-impossible standard of eliminating all possible nondiscriminatory factors. . . . Vigorous cross-examination of a study's inadequacies allows the
jury to appropriately weigh the alleged defects and reduces the possibility of prejudice." Id. at 1188. Further, if "the defendant believed information about the employees' educational background, for example, would have explained the differences in
promotions and compensation between male and female upper level employees,
Tidyman's should have provided information about educational level to the plaintiffs
[to be used by their expert], or at a minimum, introduced testimony that education
was a central factor in promotions." Id. at 1188-89.

5. The developing systemic disparate treatment cases, from *Teamsters* to *Hazelwood*
to *Bazemore*, reveal a progressively greater reliance on sophisticated statistical techniques to establish plaintiff's case. It has become clear that at least an elementary grasp
of statistical methodology is necessary for the employment discrimination practitioner.

## NOTE ON SOPHISTICATED STATISTICAL TECHNIQUES*

***Application of Statistical Analysis to Discrimination Litigation.***   The basis for
the use of statistical evidence in employment discrimination litigation is, as the
Court said in *Teamsters*, probability theory.

> [A]bsent explanation, it is ordinarily to be expected that non-discriminatory hiring
> practices will in time result in a work force more or less representative of the racial and
> ethnic composition of the population in the community from which employees are hired.

* For a general study on the use of statistics in litigation, see David W. Barnes, Statistics as Proof: Fundamentals of Quantitative Evidence (1983). Professor Barnes has also been kind enough to review this
section, and make some suggestions for improvement.

The converse of this is that a substantial departure from what is to be expected, absent discrimination, is so improbable that the trier of fact should conclude, at least prima facie, that discrimination explains the disparity.

This assumption has been controverted. Professor Kingsley R. Browne, in Statistical Proof of Discrimination: Beyond "Damned Lies," 68 Wash. L. Rev. 477 (1993), questions what he calls the "Central Assumption" of statistical proof in employment discrimination: that different racial and ethnic groups and both genders have the same interests and abilities. It follows from that assumption that it is "to be expected" that a particular employer's workforce will be "more or less representative" of the population in the community. Browne argues that this is at odds with the real world and inconsistent with the conceptual underpinnings of disparate impact theory, which assumes people have different interests and abilities related to ethnic, racial, and gender differences. Professor Browne does recognize that, to some extent, these differences are taken into account in formulating the relevant labor market: the percentage of African-American teachers in the labor market in *Hazelwood* was undoubtedly less than the percentage of African Americans in the general population. The comparison, therefore, filtered out — at least in gross terms — those whose abilities and interests were very different. But Browne doubts that abilities and interests are randomly distributed by race or sex even within the relevant labor market.* Professor Browne also recognizes that the Central Assumption is only a tool for the plaintiff's prima facie case and that the defendant can, theoretically at least, rebut the inference of discrimination by showing factors other than the employer's discriminatory selection process that produce the nonrepresentative result. He believes, however, that the Central Assumption imposes an unfair burden on employers, a burden that is heightened by the tendency of some courts to require a strong rebuttal showing to defeat a systemic case. Reconsider this argument after you have read EEOC v. Sears, Roebuck & Co., 839 F.2d 302 (7th Cir. 1988) (reproduced at page 253). The Supreme Court has, however, endorsed the Central Assumption, and the courts have refined it by looking increasingly to sophisticated statistical proofs.

Probability is the basis of the science of statistics. As reflected in employment discrimination cases, probability theory starts with a comparison between the "observed" racial (or gender) distribution in the employer's workforce and the "expected," that is, the racial distribution one would anticipate if race were not a factor in the selection of employees. To use probability theory to prove discrimination, a statistician would construct an assumption, called the null hypothesis, which would then be tested and either accepted or rejected. The null hypothesis is based on two assumptions: first, that there is no difference between the observed and the expected, that is, that the difference is null; second, that if there is any difference between the observed (the sample we are examining) and the expected, that difference is the result of chance. The classic example is determining whether a coin is fair. A statistician would start with an assumption, the null hypothesis, that flipping a coin would result in no difference between the number of heads and the number of tails, and that, if there is a difference, it is due to chance.

---

* Some of Professor Browne's objections can be met by the defendant's introduction of its own statistical proof. For example, Browne criticizes the approach of defining the relevant labor market in terms of those with minimal qualifications. If, however, the employer hires only (or disproportionately) persons with higher qualifications, a statistical study could show that it is qualifications, not race, that explain the makeup of the workforce. Similarly, the defendant can proffer studies using other variables not reflected in plaintiff's analysis. It is true, however, that some factors — "subjective or otherwise unquantifiable" — will be hard to account for in this way.

In the employment context, this means that the assumption is that the employer does not discriminate, so that there will be no difference between the observed number of minorities employed and the expected number if hiring continued in the present way indefinitely. Second, if there is a difference between the observed sample we are looking at (the employer's workforce) and the expected, that difference is due to chance. The plaintiff obviously wants to rule out the null hypothesis — that is, to show that the difference is unlikely to be due to chance. The employer would prefer to confirm the null hypothesis — that is, to show that any difference is due to chance. The statistician's job is to determine the probability that chance explains the difference.

With a coin, the statistician could test the null hypothesis by experimenting with coin flips and counting up the number of "heads" and "tails" when the coin is flipped. Suppose the statistician flips the coin 100 times, resulting in 49 heads and 51 tails. That outcome would be so close to what would be expected if the coin were fair (50 percent "heads," 50 percent "tails") that the statistician could accept the null hypothesis. Based on reason and logic, but not statistics, the statistician would take the next step and conclude that, because it cannot be shown that the coin is unfair, it may be concluded that the coin is fair.

An example more attuned to the discrimination context is that of the selection of marbles from a fishbowl. Suppose the statistician knows the racial composition of the relevant universe, that is, the percentages of white marbles and black marbles in the fishbowl — say, 80 percent white and 20 percent black. She can then make some probability judgments about the "fairness" of a drawing of a sample from the fishbowl that obtains 100 white marbles and no black ones.

Indeed, it should be apparent that the *Teamsters* decision is simply a commonsense conclusion that the employer's draw of a sample (i.e., its workforce of line drivers) from the fishbowl (i.e., the relevant labor market of city drivers) is so obviously unfair as to at least require an explanation. Further, the *Hazelwood* use of standard deviation analysis is merely a way of quantifying the commonsense judgment by stating how unlikely it is that the draw of 100 white marbles could occur if being white were totally unconnected with the selection.

In short, a statistician can inform the court how probable it is that a certain pattern of selections would have occurred if color were not somehow influencing the selection decision.

***When One Should Reject the Null Hypothesis.***   Accepting or rejecting a null hypothesis, like making any decision, always entails a risk of being mistaken:

> Two possible errors may result from a decision based on sample information: a party who should not be found liable may be found liable (a "false inculpation"), and a party who should be found liable may be found not liable (a "false exculpation"). Statisticians have labeled false inculpations as "Type I error" and false exculpations as "Type II error."

Neil B. Cohen, Confidence in Probability: Burdens of Persuasion in a World of Imperfect Knowledge, 60 N.Y.U. L. Rev. 385, 410 (1985). In law, a jury that finds a defendant guilty of a crime when he is innocent commits what statisticians would call a Type I error, false inculpation. Juries in criminal cases are instructed to test the evidence under the "beyond a reasonable doubt" standard. Thus, unless the jury is convinced of the defendant's guilt beyond all reasonable doubt, the jury must acquit. This reflects the legal policy decision that it is much worse to convict an innocent person, a Type I false inculpation error, than it is to commit a Type II false exculpation error by letting a guilty person go free. In terms of probability theory, the criminal law sets the test of proof so that, if error is made, it is more likely to be a Type II error than a Type I error. This is a deliberate policy decision that Type I errors are worse than Type II errors: many guilty people should go free, rather than one innocent person be convicted.

Statisticians address the probability of error in rejecting a null hypothesis based on a particular observation in terms of "significance level" or "p-value," which are used interchangeably. The threshold or critical significance level specifies the degree of risk of error the decision-maker is willing to accept. The higher the p-value, therefore, the greater the risk of error. Once the level of significance is set, the null hypothesis will be rejected only if the calculated significance level (or p-value) is less than the threshold level.

By setting the level of confidence before a probability estimate is accepted, statisticians are directly deciding the risk of Type I error. The level is set by hundredths from zero to one. If it is very important to avoid Type I errors, that is, to avoid incorrectly finding employers guilty of discrimination, statisticians would set the level of statistical significance very high. Setting the level of significance at 0.05 means that a Type I error is made in only 5 percent of the cases, that is, 5 in 100 times.*

In Statistical Proof of Discrimination: Beyond "Damned Lies," 68 Wash. L. Rev. 477 (1993), Professor Kingsley R. Browne argues that courts and commentators have erred by confusing one particular employer's workforce statistics with the overall probabilities. Professor Browne uses as an example an experiment in which each of 100 persons flips a coin 100 times. Prior to the coin toss, one would predict that, even if the coin is fair, five of the subjects would obtain a split of 60/40 or greater. Thus, with respect to any one subject chosen at random, there is a prior probability of 5 percent of obtaining such a split. What is the likelihood that a particular subject who got a 60/40 split when flipping a coin used a fair coin? Those who equate the significance level with the likelihood of a random result would conclude that there is only a 5 percent chance that the subject obtained that result by chance and therefore a 95 percent chance that there was a nonrandom cause. However, in reaching that conclusion they confuse the probability of a particular result given the null hypothesis with the probability of the null hypothesis given the observed result.

This analysis can be applied to the employment setting. By hypothesis, one knows that 1 out of 20 employers will have a statistically significant disparity, so in an economy with, say, 200,000 nondiscriminating employers, there will be 10,000 employers who in fact do not discriminate but whose workforce statistics will suggest that they did discriminate. This is the thrust of Professor Browne's claim. However, without knowing how many discriminating employers there actually are, it is not possible to estimate the likelihood that a given statistical imbalance was caused by chance, by discrimination, or by some other nonrandom factor. For example, suppose the background rate of systemic discrimination is 1 percent. Then, based on statistical

---

*The risk to innocent defendants is actually somewhat higher than 5 percent. Statistics only suggest a connection between race and employment decisions. They do not determine whether that connection is intentional discrimination. Statistical significance set at .05 means that in 5 percent of the cases statistics will find a correlation between race and employment decisions when there is, in fact, no relationship (e.g., the defendant is innocent). Even if there is a relationship, however, that relationship could result from some reason other than intentional discrimination. Thus, some defendants will be innocent even though statistics have accurately identified a relationship. In order to simplify the discussion of Type I and Type II errors, however, we will assume that, whenever there is a relationship between race and employment decisions, this relationship results from intentional discrimination.

evidence, 6 out of 100 employers will be found liable, but only 1 of those 6 employers will actually be guilty of discrimination. Therefore, the likelihood that the employer discriminated is less than 17 percent. According to Professor Browne, this flawed statistical logic leads courts faced with a statistically significant disparity to reason, "I'm faced with a disparity that is very unlikely to have occured by chance; this rare result is suspicious, and the employer ought to explain it," when it should be thinking, "The plaintiff has described statistics that would be true for thousands of nondiscriminating employers; if the plaintiff wants me to suspect discrimination, he'd better give me a lot more than that." Id. at 490.

The problem is a "base rate" one, and the standard illustration of base rate is testing for diseases. Suppose a test is developed which is 99 percent accurate in testing positive, that is, 99 percent of the positive test results correctly identify the presence of the disease and only 1 percent of the tests yield a Type I false positive, that is, incorrectly indicate the presence of a disease that the patient does not have. While the test is in some sense highly accurate, its use could result in far more false positives than true positives if the base rate of the disease is very low. The population of the United States is about 250 million, so that a disease so rare that only one person in a million suffers from it, would result in the number of afflicted persons in the United States being 250. But if the test is to be administered to the entire population of this country, its 99 percent accuracy rate would result in about 2,500,000 positives, of which all but 250 would be false.

Professor Browne argues that a similar problem exists with the use of the 5 percent level in employment discrimination. While he is theoretically correct, Professor Browne fails to demonstrate why the legal system should conclude that base rate discrimination is especially rare. If 10 percent of employers discriminate, two true positives will be reported for every false positive. If 20 percent discriminate, there will be four true positives for every Type I false inculpation. Does the Blumrosens study (see pages 226-228) suggest that the base rate is much higher than Professor Browne believes? Further, Professor Browne's analysis does not take sufficiently into account the role of the statistical proof in discrimination litigation. Such proof never does more than establish plaintiff's case, leaving defendant the opportunity to rebut by offering proof that it does not discriminate. Sufficiently strong testimony might convince the jury that it was chance that explained the disparity.

Although the risks of Type I and Type II errors are inversely related (increasing one decreases the other), they are not simple complements. John M. Dawson, in Investigation of Fact — The Role of the Statistician, 11 Forum 896, 907-08 (1976), has created a model for an employment discrimination case by setting the risk of Type I error at 5 percent. With the confidence level at 95 percent, he estimates the risk of Type II error to be approximately 50 percent, or .5. That means that there is a 5 percent risk that an innocent defendant will be found liable, while the risk that a guilty defendant will be exonerated is about 50 percent. Does this answer the question posed by Professor Browne?

While this outcome may be appropriate in criminal law, where the primary value is not to convict the innocent, there is no similar policy in civil litigation, such as employment discrimination cases. The standard of proof for civil litigation is the preponderance of evidence test, which means that there is no important social value difference between finding an innocent defendant liable, a Type I error, and finding a guilty defendant not liable, a Type II error. In probability terms, the preponderance of evidence test is 0.501, rather than the 0.05 level used by scientists.

Perhaps taking this into account, the Supreme Court has recognized that, in relying on statistical evidence, courts are not bound by scientific tests of significance. In *Bazemore*, the Court said, "A plaintiff in a Title VII suit need not prove discrimination with scientific certainty; rather, his or her burden is to prove discrimination by a preponderance of evidence." 478 U.S. 385, 400 (1985). However, the District of Columbia Circuit, in a case decided after *Bazemore*, stated that "statistical evidence must meet the 5% significance level . . . for it alone to establish a prima facie case under Title VII." Palmer v. Shultz (Kissinger), 815 F.2d 84 (D.C. Cir. 1987). In contrast, in Kadas v. MCI Systemhouse Corp., the court said, "The 5 percent test is arbitrary . . . [T]he question whether a study is responsible and therefore admissible under the *Daubert* standard is different from the weight to be accorded to the significance of a particular correlation found by the study. It is for the judge to say, on the basis of the evidence of a trained statistician, whether a particular significance level, in the context of a particular study in a particular case, is too low to make the study worth the consideration of judge or jury." 255 F.3d 359, 362-63 (7th Cir. 2001). The reference was to Daubert v. Merrell Dow Pharmaceuticals, Inc., 509 U.S. 579 (1993), dealing with the standards for admissibility of scientific evidence.

In sum, probability theory suggests a basis for the use of statistical evidence in disparate treatment discrimination cases. Within probability theory, there are numerous statistical techniques available to analyze whether a null hypothesis should be accepted or rejected. When any one of these techniques is used to conclude that the null hypothesis (that discrimination is not involved because there is no difference between the observed and the expected or that any difference is the result of chance) should be rejected, the next step, based on reason and logic, should be to reach the legal conclusion that systemic disparate treatment has occurred. While the employer will have an opportunity to rebut that conclusion, the prima facie case will be established.

***Using the Two- or Three-Standard Deviations Test.*** The Supreme Court decided two cases in 1977 that used binomial distribution. The first, Castaneda v. Partida, 430 U.S. 482, 496 n.17 (1977), involved the exclusion of Mexican Americans from juries. The null hypothesis was that the juries are randomly drawn, without regard to whether a person picked was Mexican American. The probability, or expected outcome given random selection, was based on the percentage of Mexican Americans in the population, which was 79.1 percent. Among the 870 persons picked for juries over an 11-year period, on average 79.1 percent, or 688, are expected to be Mexican American. Over that period, only 339 of the persons selected were Mexican Americans. While in a random selection process it is unlikely that each jury panel drawn would approximate 79.1 percent Mexican Americans, the probability assumption is that the observed outcomes should be bunched close to that expected figure. Figure 4.1 shows the expected outcome.

Each X plots the Mexican American representation in one jury panel. As the percentage of Mexican American representation in the panels departs from the expected outcome of 79.1 percent, fewer panels are represented. The "range" of the distribution is the spread of observed outcomes from highest to lowest. If samples are randomly drawn, some values will be higher and some lower than the expected value, so the range will include the expected value. In this example of an expected outcome, the range is between 66 and 92 percent, but in some other sample of jury panel selections, the range could be greater or smaller. For example, some juries may have no Mexican Americans, and others would be 100 percent Mexican American. In such a sample, the range would be from zero to 100 percent. To use the coin-flipping example, in some experimental runs the results will be bunched closer together than in

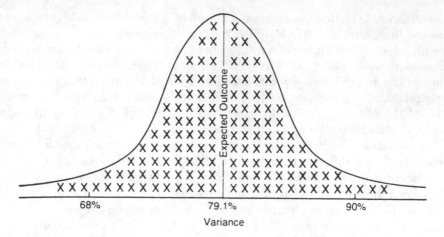

Figure 4.1

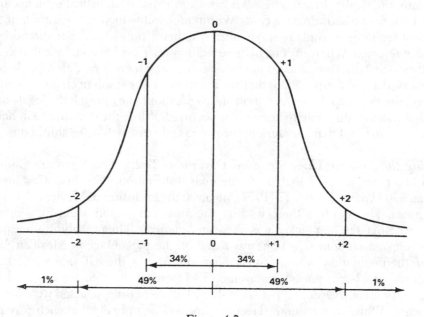

Figure 4.2

other samples. In one sample, few, if any, outcomes of 100 flips will be more than 3 or 4 percent apart — say, 48 to 52 percent "heads" — while, in others, the variance might be much greater; some sample flips will be, say, 40 "heads" to 60 "tails."

Statisticians need some way of determining what kind of deviations from the expected value are possible, and how much deviation from the expected value can be viewed as due to chance. It is here that the concept of "standard deviation" is used. Standard deviation may be thought of as "normal" or "typical" or "average" deviation. Without regard to the exact variance along any baseline, 68 percent of all outcomes will fall between 1 and 2 "standard deviations" of the expected outcome. Only 2 percent of the outcomes will fall beyond 1 and 2 standard deviations from the expected outcome. Figure 4.2 illustrates this use of the standard deviation.

By characterizing data in terms of the number of standard deviations, it is possible to

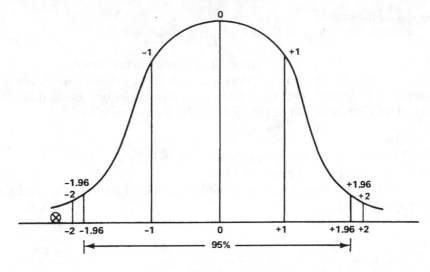

Figure 4.3

use standard deviation as a way of deciding whether to reject the null hypothesis. The test normally used is to reject the null hypothesis when an outcome falls more than 2 standard deviations from the expected value. The reason for rejecting the null hypothesis in this situation is based on probability. The outcome is not likely to be the result of chance: when a result is more than 2 standard deviations from the norm, there are only 4 chances in 100 that the result is consistent with the null hypothesis, that the differences are the result of chance. There is a general statistical convention that the null hypothesis should be rejected when there is less than a 5 percent chance that the result could occur without there being a relationship between the two variables. In terms of standard deviation analysis, the 5 percent (or .05) level occurs when an outcome falls outside plus or minus 1.96 standard deviations. This .05 level of statistical significance as a basis for rejecting the null hypothesis is shown in Figure 4.3.

The outcome X casts doubt on the null hypothesis because that outcome could be consistent with the hypothesis less than 5 percent of the time if chance were the explanation. Rejecting the null hypothesis means that it is much more likely than not (though not certain) that the null hypothesis is incorrect. In the coin-flipping example, an outcome so far from the expected, as X is in Figure 4.3, is so unlikely if the coin is fair that it is a better judgment to reject the idea that the coin is fair.

So far, standard deviation has been described verbally and graphically, but it can also be performed mathematically. To calculate the probability of a Type I error in cases like *Castaneda*, statisticians start by calculating a "Z score." A Z score is simply the number of standard deviations between the observed and the expected. In mathematical terms, the Z score is

$$Z = \frac{O - NP}{\sqrt{NP(1 - P)}}$$

where

Z = number of standard deviations
O = observed number of minority group members in the sample

N = size of the sample
P = minority percentage of the underlying population.

N × P, therefore, is the expected number of minorities in the sample.

In this formula, the top (or numerator) is the difference between the observed and the expected. The bottom (or denominator) is the formula for one standard deviation.

The facts of *Castaneda* can be plugged into the formula as follows:

Z = unknown
O = 339 (observed number of Mexican-American jurors)
N = 870 (total number of jurors selected)
P = .79 (the Mexican-American population, the basis of the probability assumption)

$$Z = \frac{339 - (870 \times .79)}{\sqrt{(870 \times .79)(1 - .79)}} = \frac{339 - 687}{\sqrt{687 \times .21}} = \frac{-348}{\sqrt{144}} = \frac{-348}{12}$$

$$Z = -29$$

With the outcome 29 standard deviations from the expected, the null hypothesis, that being a juror is unrelated to being a Mexican-American, is rejected. The Court in *Castaneda* concluded:

> Thus, in this case the standard deviation is approximately 29. As a general rule for such large samples, if the difference between the expected value and the observed number is greater than two or three standard deviations, then the hypothesis that the jury drawing was random would be suspect to a social scientist.

Id. The calculations for this formula are quite simple.

The result in *Castaneda* is shown graphically in Figure 4.4. The outcome X is −29 standard deviations from the expected result. The figure is a negative one because Mexican-American representation on juries fell far short of the expected outcome. (Only if the representation of Mexican Americans exceeded the expected would a positive standard deviation figure be involved.) The chance that this outcome could occur with the null hypothesis being true, that is, that being Mexican-American is unconnected with the chance of being selected for jury service, is infinitesimal.

The two- or three-standard deviation rule was accepted by the Supreme Court in *Hazelwood*. Surprisingly, the technique was not used by the Court in *Teamsters*, the case that set forth the probability assumptions underpinning the use of binomial distri-

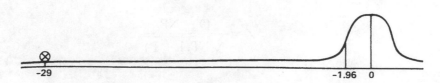

Figure 4.4

bution. The almost total exclusion of minority group members from line-driver jobs, only 13 of 1,828, made statistical techniques unnecessary to show discrimination. But it is possible to work the analysis in terms of the facts given in the case for defendant's employment in several cities where it operated. For employment at defendant's Atlanta terminal, the number of standard deviations, the Z score, is calculated as follows:

$$Z = \frac{O - NP}{\sqrt{NP(1 - P)}} = \frac{0 - (57 \times .22)}{\sqrt{(57 \times .22)(1 - .22)}} = \frac{-12.54}{\sqrt{9.78}} = \frac{-12.54}{3.13}$$

$$Z = -4.01$$

where

Z = unknown
O = zero (no minority line drivers)
N = 57 (number of Atlanta line drivers)
P = .22 (using metropolitan minority population figures)

In Atlanta, the null hypothesis is rejected: the outcome of 4 standard deviations far exceeds the two or three standard deviations guideline. But note also that the probability was determined by metropolitan area. Had city population been used, the showing would have been even more dramatic. If the minority population of the city of Atlanta, which was 51.31 percent, is used to establish the probability, the observed outcome is 7.76 standard deviations from the expected.

In these examples, the Z score (the number of standard deviations) is negative because the observed outcome of minority representation falls short of the expected outcome. Where the possibility that the statistical showing would be favorable to women or minority men (thereby producing a positive Z score) can be ruled out as defying logic, then the necessary conclusion that there is underrepresentation may be the basis for use of a "one-tailed" test of statistical significance. The one-tailed test means that the entire 5 percent chance of randomness all lies in the negative "tail," that is, the left side, of the bell-shaped curve of normal distribution. If the one-tailed test is appropriate, the Z score that justifies rejecting the null hypothesis is reduced to 1.65. Palmer v. Schultz (Kissinger), 815 F.2d 84 (D.C. Cir. 1987), rejected a one-tailed test: while women were clearly underrepresented in some Foreign Service jobs, they were overrepresented in others, so it could not be concluded that a positive Z score defied logic.

The Supreme Court decision in *Hazelwood* added three distinctions in the use of statistics. First, it distinguished between the use of general population statistics and the use of more limited labor pools reflecting the special qualifications needed for the job. In *Teamsters*, the general population was appropriate for comparison with the employer's workforce because "the job skill there involved — the ability to drive a truck — is one that many persons possess or can fairly readily acquire." *Hazelwood*. In contrast, the jobs in *Hazelwood* were teaching positions. "When special qualifications are required to fill particular jobs, comparisons to the general population (rather than to the smaller group of individuals who possess the necessary qualifications) may have little probative value." Thus, the Court used the pool of qualified teachers as the basis for comparison with defendant's workforce.

The second distinction made in *Hazelwood* is that pre-Act employment policies are not subject to attack. While plaintiff may make out a prima facie case relying on present employment totals, defendant can rebut plaintiff's case with statistics showing there was no post-Act discrimination. Plaintiff's statistical analysis may still show discrimination, but the *Hazelwood* Court stressed that, as a matter of law, any discrimination attributable to conduct before Title VII became effective is not subject to attack. Since Title VII has been generally applicable since at least 1972, this distinction will rarely be of any consequence today.

The third distinction in *Hazelwood* concerns the geographic area of concentration, the city of St. Louis. Plaintiff sought to use the entire metropolitan area. The Court remanded for a decision on what area was appropriate because the difference could determine the outcome. Assuming that post-Act hiring is the focus and further assuming that a pool of qualified teachers including those in the city of St. Louis is used as the basis for comparison, the expected percentage of minority group hires in 1972-1973 would be 15.4 percent. The Z score formula would yield a result of 5.6 standard deviations.

If the city of St. Louis is carved out of the geographic area, the qualified labor pool drops to 5.7 percent minority representation. With the new probability or expectancy of 5.7 percent, the result is a Z score of 1.5 standard deviations, which is less than the 1.96 cutoff showing statistical significance at the .05, or 1-chance-in-20, level. The 1.5 standard deviation figure means that there is a 14 percent chance that an outcome with this large a difference between the observed and the expected outcomes occurred randomly. The result is graphically shown in Figure 4.5, where X marks the observed outcome.

Statistical convention would have it that this showing is not sufficient to reject the null hypothesis. It could be accepted that race and teacher hiring were unrelated in the hiring by the Hazelwood district in 1972-1973. However, the Court did not decide whether that statistical convention must be followed in Title VII litigation. The *Hazelwood* Court, after working through the above examples, noted: "These observations are not intended to suggest that precise calculations of statistical significance are necessary in employing statistical proof. . . ." In the social sciences, judgment is used in deciding the level of statistical significance. It should also be a matter of judgment in Title VII litigation as to whether some showing less than the .05 level of

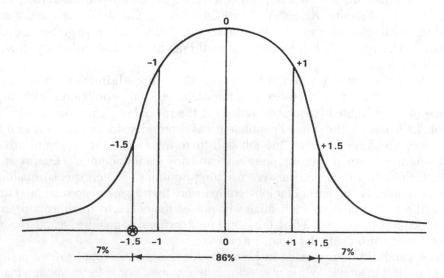

**Figure 4.5**

statistical significance (or the 1.96 Z score) is sufficient to support an inference of discrimination and thereby a rejection of the null hypothesis. As Professor Cohen has argued, the preponderance of the evidence test of civil liability reflects a 0.51 test of probability, rather than the 0.05 test used by social scientists. Neil B. Cohen, Confidence in Probability: Burdens of Persuasion in a World of Imperfect Knowledge, 60 N.Y.U. L. Rev. 385 (1985). Because Type I and Type II errors are of equal weight in terms of social policy in employment discrimination, the test of statistical significance, which sets the level of Type I error, can be set much lower than 0.05 in order to more nearly balance Type I and Type II errors.

Binomial distribution focuses on the relationship between two factors, the race or gender composition of the available labor pool versus that of the employer's workforce. While powerful where applicable, this technique is limited because it cannot take account of added variables sometimes involved in employment issues. For example, in *Hazelwood*, the Court used binomial distribution as a way of comparing the employer's workforce with the pool of qualified teachers. While useful once the pool of those who were qualified is defined, binomial distribution cannot define what factors were considered in determining the qualifications relied on in hiring teachers.

*Multiple Regression.*   Multiple regression is a technique used to study the influence of any number of factors, or variables. Its use in discrimination litigation was first approved by the Supreme Court in Bazemore v. Friday, although it had been previously employed by lower courts. See generally Julie Lee & Caitlin Liu, Measuring Discrimination in the Workplace: Strategies for Lawyers and Policymakers, 6 U. Chi. L. Sch. Roundtable 195 (1999), for description of the strengths and weaknesses of various multivariate analysis techniques, including multiple regression; Thomas J. Campbell, Regression Analysis in Title VII Cases: Minimum Standards, Comparable Worth, and Other Issues Where Law and Statistics Meet, 36 Stan. L. Rev. 1299 (1984); Barbara A. Norris, A Structural Approach to Evaluation of Multiple Regression Analysis as Used to Prove Employment Discrimination: The Plaintiff's Answer to Defense Attacks of "Missing Factors" and "Pre-Act Discrimination," 49 Law & Contemp. Probs. 65 (1986); Douglas Laycock, Statistical Proof and Theories of Discrimination, 49 Law & Contemp. Probs. 97 (1986). Note, Beyond the Prima Facie Case in Employment Discrimination Law: Statistical Proof and Rebuttal, 89 Harv. L. Rev. 387 (1975). Like the other techniques, multiple regression cannot be used to show what qualifications are actually needed to do a job, but it can be useful in finding what factors an employer relied on in a particular employment setting and the weight given to each factor.

The core notion of multiple regression is an extension of the notion of matching pairs. Suppose two employees are so similarly situated in education, experience in the industry, seniority, job title, and work performed that they are a matched pair. It would be suspicious if these two employees do not receive the same pay. If they are of different races or genders and the pay difference is not otherwise explained, there would be a prima facie case of employment discrimination. Multiple regression expands that notion so it is possible to compare the influence of many variables among a large group of employees. Once it is decided what variables are thought to bear on the employment situation, multiple regression makes it possible to hold these factors constant and then determine whether sex or race is also a statistically significant factor in setting salary.

Multiple regression is beyond simple graphical or mathematical statement, but the following may help to develop the concept. Assume someone suggests that the relevant factor in determining salary for an employer is education: the more education, the higher the pay. Graphically, each person's pay and years of education would look

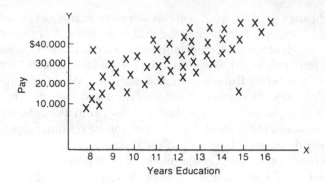

**Figure 4.6**

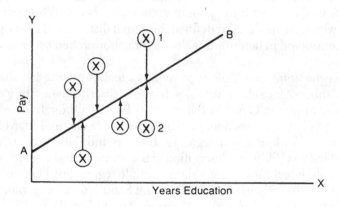

**Figure 4.7**

like the scattergram in Figure 4.6, with each X representing a particular person plotted on the graph by years of education and salary.

Notice that there appears to be some relationship between salary and years of education, but no straight-line relationship exists. To say it another way, there is no automatic rule that causes salary to go up a set amount of dollars for each increase of a year in education for every employee. But statistically it is possible to draw a "regression line" that is the "best fit" straight line to describe all the individual cases. Figure 4.7 illustrates such a linear regression. The notion is to balance out all the employees above the line with those below the line. In Figure 4.7, employee 1 has higher pay for the same education as employee 2, but those differences balance out if each is "regressed" to line A-B, the regression line, sometimes called the line of best fit.

When another variable — say, seniority — is suggested as being relevant in determining salary, the graphic description requires three dimensions, as shown in Figure 4.8.

Notice that, instead of a regression line, there is a three-dimensional plane that is the "best fit" description of the contribution of education and seniority to the determination of salary. Graphic demonstration stops at three dimensions, so it is not useful when more than two variables are to be taken into account in describing salary. Multiple regression is a statistical technique that, through the use of a computer, can demonstrate how any number of independent variables affect a continuous variable like salary.

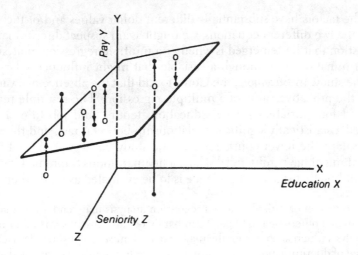

**Figure 4.8**

In short, multiple regression is "a method used to extract a systematic signal from the noise prescribed by the data." Franklin M. Fisher, Multiple Regression in Legal Proceedings, 80 Colum. L. Rev. 702, 706 (1980). Further, the result is quantifiable:

> The relationship between the dependent variable and the independent variable [race or sex] is then estimated by extracting the effects of the other major variables (the systematic part). When this has been done, one has the best available substitute for controlled experimentation. The results of multiple regression can be read as showing the effects of each variable on the dependent variable, holding the others constant. Moreover, those results allow one to make statements about the probability that the effect described has merely been observed as a result of chance fluctuation.

Multiple regression generates an equation that explains the relationship between the dependent variable (e.g., salary) and the independent variables (e.g., the factors used by the employer to determine salary). Note that the information used to generate the equation is drawn from the employer's own salary scheme. The resulting equation looks like this:

$$Y = a + b_1x_1 + b_2x_2 + b_3x_3 + b_4x_4 \ldots b_kx_k$$

In this equation, "Y" equals salary, "a" equals a constant dollar amount, "$b_1$" and "$b_2$" are dollar amounts, and "$x_1$" and "$x_2$" are factors relevant to the salary determination. For example, in an academic setting, "$x_1$" may equal number of years of seniority, while "$x_2$" equals number of years of education past undergraduate school, "$x_3$" equals number of articles written, and "$x_4$" equals number of committee chairs held. Each factor has a dollar value. Any individual faculty member's salary can be determined (approximately) by inserting that faculty member's characteristics into the equation. The factors and the dollar amounts associated with the factors are based on a study of the employer's salary system. If the factor "white" or "male" has a dollar value, we might suspect discrimination. An alternative approach is to generate two different equations — for example, one for women and another for men. Assuming an adequate p-value, if the factors have substantially different dollar values and/or the constant is different in the two different equations, we might again suspect discrimination.

One question that has emerged is whether a multiple regression analysis is probative of discrimination even though a variable that might influence salary is not included in the study. In *Bazemore*, the Court found that the absence of a variable does not destroy the probative value of a multiple regression. The multiple regression in the case used four variables — race, education, tenure, and job title. Though the study showed a statistically significant relationship between race and the dependent variable of salary, the lower courts rejected the study because it did not include all variables that might have influenced salary. The unanimous Supreme Court rejected that view, holding that statistical evidence is to be evaluated as is all other evidence.

> While the omission of variables from a regression analysis may render the analysis less probative than it otherwise might be, it can hardly be said, absent some other infirmity, that an analysis which accounts for the major factors "must be considered unacceptable as evidence of discrimination." . . . Normally, failure to include variables will affect the analysis' probativeness, not its admissibility.
>
> Importantly, it is clear that a regression analysis that includes less than "all measurable variables" may serve to prove a plaintiff's case. A plaintiff in a Title VII suit need not prove discrimination with scientific certainty; rather, his or her burden is to prove discrimination by a preponderance of the evidence. . . . Whether, in fact, such a regression analysis does carry the plaintiffs' ultimate burden will depend in a given case on the factual context of each case in light of all the evidence presented by both the plaintiff and the defendant.

The *Bazemore* Court did note that a multiple regression analysis could be so incomplete as to be inadmissible. See footnote 10. Presumably, the question would be whether the analysis was so incomplete that no reasonable trier of fact could credit it. Suppose, in *Bazemore*, that the plaintiff's statistical analysis controlled only for race and education, omitting "tenure" and "job title." Should it nevertheless have been admitted into evidence? See Joseph L. Gastwirth, Methods for Assessing the Sensitivity of Statistical Comparisons Used in Title VII Cases to Omitted Variables, 33 Jurimetrics J. 19 (1992) (using sensitivity analysis to assess whether the influence of a factor omitted from the analysis could be sufficient to explain the observed disparity).*

Mayer Freed and Daniel Polsby, in Comparable Worth in the Equal Pay Act, 51 U. Chi. L. Rev. 1078 (1984), criticized the court's use of multiple regression analysis in Melani v. Board of Higher Educ., 561 F. Supp. 769 (S.D.N.Y. 1983). In that case, the court accepted a multiple regression study that purported, after controlling for nearly 100 independent variables, to find a residual pay differential of $1,800 disfavoring females. Among other objections, Professors Freed and Polsby criticize the court for its reliance on a study that omitted the variable of academic department. If males were concentrated in higher-paid departments as compared to females, no inference of discrimination in pay would necessarily follow: "[I]t seems to us plainly wrong to suggest that a study that treats French teachers and teachers of computer science as fungible for purposes of making out a prima facie case of salary discrimination in a university . . . satisfies the requirement of threshold plausibility." Id. at 1109.

Does this observation properly take into account the litigation process? After *Bazemore*, the study is clearly admissible. Whether it is persuasive may depend on

---

*Professor Barnes has pointed out that the omission of a variable that does affect salary will make no difference unless the omitted variable is also correlated with race; it would thus tend to negate race as the explanation for the disparity shown. See David W. Barnes & John M. Conley, Statistical Evidence in Litigation, Section 8.16, and 1989 Supp. pp. 70-71.

whether the defendant can proffer evidence that the variable omitted — academic department — is likely to negate the conclusions because the employer shows that it is the department, and not gender, that explains differences in salary.

In short, if the regression analysis is minimally adequate in the sense of taking into account those variables which plausibly explain salary, the study should be admitted and establish a prima facie case. When the employer argues that the study has failed to take account of variables that would undermine the conclusion that salary was related to gender or race, it is up to the employer either to offer evidence of that fact or to produce its own studies using the variables it claims were involved that support upholding the null hypothesis, that salary is not related to sex or race.

From a statistician's perspective, the issue of the best regression analysis is characterized as one of "goodness of fit." Professor Thomas J. Campbell has suggested that the law use a statistical test of goodness of fit, the "R statistic." R expresses, as a percentage, the part of the total variance explained by the factors used in the study. He would set a minimum R score of .50. Thomas J. Campbell, Regression Analysis in Title VII Cases: Minimum Standards, Comparable Worth, and Other Issues Where Law and Statistics Meet, 36 Stan. L. Rev. 1299 (1984). Is that consistent with the preponderance of evidence standard emphasized in *Bazemore?*

A final point concerns what statisticians call practical (as opposed to statistical) significance. It is possible that a statistical study will show a statistically significant relationship between gender and salary, but one at such a low level that it may not be cognizable. For example suppose the regression showed that women were underpaid relative to men by $5 a year. No matter how robust the statistical proof, it is questionable whether a finding of discrimination ought to follow because the difference is so small. In the disparate impact chapter, we address a similar question in discussing quantum of impact. See pages 369-372.

## D.   DEFENSES TO DISPARATE TREATMENT CASES

There are three approaches to defending against a systemic disparate treatment case. The first is to challenge the factual basis on which plaintiff's case is predicated. Thus, the employer could deny that a formal policy exists or could challenge the facts on which plaintiff's case is based. Typically, where plaintiff demonstrates a systemic practice-based case using statistics, defendant must use statistical studies to counter plaintiff's statistical studies. *Bazemore* was such a case. The second line of defense is to challenge not the statistics plaintiff uses, but the inference of discriminatory intent the statistics raise. The third and final line of defense is to admit the discrimination but to assert a recognized defense.

### 1.   *Rebutting the Inference of Discriminatory Intent*

#### PERSONNEL ADMINISTRATOR v. FEENEY
#### 442 U.S. 256 (1979)

[The Court was faced with an equal protection challenge to a Massachusetts law granting military veterans absolute preference for state jobs. Because at that time

98 percent of the veterans were male, few women could realistically compete for jobs desired by veterans. The lower court found the consequences for women too inevitable to have been "unintended." The Supreme Court, per Justice Stewart, reversed the finding of unconstitutionality.]

The appellee's ultimate argument rests upon the presumption, common to the criminal and civil law, that a person intends the natural and foreseeable consequences of his voluntary actions. Her position was well stated in the concurring opinion in the District Court: "Conceding . . . that the goal here was to benefit the veteran, there is no reason to absolve the legislature from awareness that the means chosen to achieve this goal would freeze women out of all those state jobs actively sought by men. To be sure, the legislature did not wish to harm women. But the cutting-off of women's opportunities was an inevitable concomitant of the chosen scheme — as inevitable as the proposition that if tails is up, heads must be down. Where a law's consequences are that inevitable, can they meaningfully be described as unintended?"

This rhetorical question implies that a negative answer is obvious, but it is not. The decision to grant a preference to veterans was of course "intentional." So, necessarily, did an adverse impact upon nonveterans follow from that decision. And it cannot seriously be argued that the legislature of Massachusetts could have been unaware that most veterans are men. It would thus be disingenuous to say that the adverse consequences of this legislation for women were unintended, in the sense that they were not volitional or in the sense that they were not foreseeable.

"Discriminatory purpose," however, implies more than intent as volition or intent as awareness of consequences.[24] It implies that the decisionmaker, in this case a state legislature, selected or reaffirmed a particular course of action at least in part "because of," not merely "in spite of," its adverse effects upon an identifiable group.[25] Yet, nothing in the record demonstrates that this preference for veterans was originally devised or subsequently re-enacted because it would accomplish the collateral goal of keeping women in a stereotypic and predefined place in the Massachusetts Civil Service.

To the contrary, the statutory history shows that the benefit of the preference was consistently offered to "any person" who was a veteran. That benefit has been extended to women under a very broad statutory definition of the term veteran. The preference formula itself, which is the focal point of this challenge, was first adopted — so it appears from this record — out of a perceived need to help a small group of older Civil War veterans. It has since been reaffirmed and extended only to cover new veterans. When the totality of legislative actions establishing and extending the Massachusetts veterans' preference are considered, see Washington v. Davis, the law remains what it purports to be: a preference for veterans of either sex over nonveterans of either sex, not for men over women.

24. Proof of discriminatory intent must necessarily usually rely on objective factors, several of which were outlined in Arlington Heights v. Metropolitan Housing Development Corp., 429 U.S. 252, 266. The inquiry is practical. What a legislature or any official entity is "up to" may be plain from the results its actions achieve, or the results they avoid. Often it is made clear from what has been called, in a different context, "the give and take of the situation."

25. This is not to say that the inevitability or foreseeability of consequences of a neutral rule has no bearing upon the existence of discriminatory intent. Certainly, when the adverse consequences of a law upon an identifiable group are as inevitable as the gender-based consequences of [the veterans' preference] a strong inference that the adverse effects were desired can reasonably be drawn. But in this inquiry — made as it is under the Constitution — an inference is a working tool, not a synonym for proof. When, as here, the impact is essentially an unavoidable consequence of a legislative policy that has in itself always been deemed to be legitimate, and when, as here, the statutory history and all of the available evidence affirmatively demonstrate the opposite, the inference simply fails to ripen into proof.

## NOTES

1. *Feeney* could not have been brought under Title VII because § 712 explicitly excepts veterans' preference laws from attack under the statute.

2. Did the Court in *Feeney* reject the natural and probable consequences test of intent? Or did Massachusetts successfully rebut a prima facie case of intent inferred from the natural and probable consequences approach? Or was the Court simply convinced that, whatever the impact, gender discrimination was the last thing the legislature intended when it enacted the veterans' preference? Cf. footnote 24 in *Teamsters* (page 214).

3. Can you imagine anything that might rebut the inference of discriminatory intent (without necessarily challenging the underlying statistics) in *Teamsters*, *Hazelwood*, or *Bazemore*? In *Hazelwood*, for example, suppose the defendant claimed that residents of the school district had preference as teachers and it was Hazelwood's mostly white population that explained the scarcity of black teachers.

4. As with Title VII, a statistical showing of discrimination is not the end of the matter under the ADEA. The defendant can try to rebut the showing by offering nondiscriminatory reasons that explain the statistical picture and rebut the showing of intent to discriminate on age grounds. For example, suppose an employer could establish that a pattern of terminations occurred because older workers happened to be concentrated in a department that was eliminated as technologically obsolete.

## EEOC v. SEARS, ROEBUCK & CO.
### 839 F.2d 302 (7th Cir. 1988)

HARLINGTON WOOD, JR., Circuit Judge.

[The EEOC challenged Sears' hiring, promotion, and compensation practices as systemic disparate treatment on the basis of gender, with the principal issue being the concentration of men in higher-paying sales jobs compensated by commissions and the concentration of women in lower-paying sales jobs paid by the hour. Sears won in the trial court. The Seventh Circuit first held that the burden of persuasion on the issue of intent to discriminate remains at all times on the plaintiff. Second, the court reviewed the trial court's findings on that issue, using a clearly erroneous standard of review.]

The EEOC presented, almost exclusively, statistical evidence in the form of regression analyses based on information from employment applications of rejected sales applicants and Sears' computerized payroll records from 1973 through 1980. The EEOC based other regression analyses on information from Applicant Interview Guides Sears had administered at various times from 1978 through 1980 at two Sears stores in its Southwestern Territory. The EEOC attempted to bolster this statistical evidence through nonstatistical evidence regarding the subjective nature of Sears' selection process and allegedly discriminatory aspects of Sears' testing practices.

Sears did not respond with like regression analyses based on employment application and payroll records. Instead, most of Sears' evidence was directed at undermining two assumptions Sears claimed were faulty and fatal to the validity of the EEOC's statistical analysis — the assumptions of equal interests and qualifications of applicants for commission sales positions. This evidence consisted of testimony by Sears store managers, personnel managers, and other store officials, a study based on interviews of women in nontraditional jobs at Sears, national surveys and polls regarding the changing status of women in American society, morale surveys of Sears employees and 1976 and 1982 job interest surveys of Sears employees, national labor force data, and an analysis of the Applicant Interview Guides that attempts to measure differences in interest among men and women. Sears also presented evidence regarding its hiring figures, general evidence regarding the characteristics of commission salespersons including a case study of all commission sales hires in all stores, based on information in personnel files of applicants who were hired and sales performance data, evidence regarding the employment milieu at Sears, especially relating to commission selling and the structure of Sears, and evidence regarding its affirmative action efforts. . . .

The EEOC argues that Sears' "generalized interest evidence" is inadequate as a matter of law to refute the EEOC's statistical presentation. . . . The EEOC implies that Sears had the burden of responding with a more probative statistical analysis. The Supreme Court in *Teamsters* specifically stated, however, that "we do not . . . suggest that there are any particular limits on the type of evidence an employer may use." An employer may attempt to show that plaintiffs' proof is "either inaccurate or insignificant," or the [employer] may attempt to provide a "nondiscriminatory explanation for the apparently discriminatory result." Then-Justice, now Chief Justice Rehnquist, concurring in Dothard v. Rawlinson (reproduced at page 358), stated that defendants in a discrimination case "may endeavor [in rebuttal] to impeach the reliability of the statistical evidence, they may offer rebutting evidence, or they may disparage in arguments or in briefs the probative weight which the Plaintiffs' evidence should be accorded." See also Catlett v. Missouri Highway & Transportation Commission, 828 F.2d 1260, 1266 (8th Cir. 1987) (defendant may introduce evidence that a lesser interest in certain jobs on part of female applicants explains statistical disparity). . . . The cases cited by the EEOC to support its argument that Sears had the burden of rebutting its statistical analysis with more "refined, accurate and valid" statistical evidence did not state that the defendant must produce such evidence to succeed in rebutting the plaintiffs' case. Instead, those cases indicated that a defendant could or "was entitled to" use such a means of rebuttal. These cases involve disparate impact claims — without deciding whether these principles are applicable in a disparate treatment case, we can say that EEOC misconstrues the principles. These cases suggest, and the cases we have cited above confirm, that statistical evidence is only one method of rebutting a statistical case. We therefore reject the EEOC's contention that Sears' interest evidence, consisting of testimony of Sears' store witnesses, external labor force data, national survey data, and data from surveys of Sears' employees, is insufficient as a matter of law to undermine the EEOC's statistical evidence. . . .

The district judge found a plethora of problems in the statistical analyses that the EEOC had offered to support the claim that Sears discriminated against women in hiring into commission sales positions from 1973 to 1980. Before addressing the EEOC's specific challenges to the district court's criticisms of its statistical evidence, it is helpful to discuss three key findings made by the district court, which we believe are not clearly erroneous. Those findings are that during the period at issue in this case (1973-1980): (1) commission selling was significantly different from noncommission selling at Sears; (2) women were not as interested in commission selling as were men; and (3) women were not as qualified for commission selling as were men.

The finding that colors the district court's entire treatment of the EEOC's hiring as well as its promotion claims is that selling on commission at Sears is a very different job from "regular," or noncommission selling at Sears. We cannot say that finding is clearly erroneous. The court's description of commission and noncommission selling at Sears indicates that the two forms of selling differed in the type of merchandise sold, the risk involved, which was reflected in the manner of compensation, and the technical knowledge, expertise, and motivation involved. The district court describes the differences at length, thus we need only mention major differences. As the district court found, commission selling at Sears usually involved selling "big ticket" items, which are high-cost merchandise such as major appliances, furnaces, roofing, and sewing machines. Merchandise sold on a noncommission basis understandably was generally low-cost and included apparel, paint, and cosmetics. Commission selling involved some risk, especially before 1977. During that period commission salespersons generally received a commission ranging from 6% to 9% percent [sic] plus a "draw" each week. The draw usually did not exceed 70% of average or estimated earnings, but was subject to reduction if the employee's commission did not equal the amount of the draw. There was always a risk that the employee could lose some of the draw if the commissions did not equal the amount of the draw. After 1977, commission salespersons no longer faced deficits. In what the court noted was an effort "to reduce the financial risk of selling on commission in an effort to attract more women to commission sales," Sears paid commission salespersons a nominal salary plus a 3% commission. Noncommission salespersons were paid on a straight hourly rate, and full-time salespersons received 1% commission on all sales until January 1979 when the practice was discontinued. The district court found that commission selling often required salespersons to be available after the normal working hours of 8:00 a.m. to 5:00 p.m., sometimes required that they sell in people's homes, might require a license depending on the products sold, and required qualities usually not as necessary in regular selling, including a high degree of technical knowledge, expertise, and motivation.

The court's next two major findings, that there were different interests and qualifications among men and women for commission selling, were grounded in part on the court's recognition of differences between noncommission and commission selling at Sears. The court based these findings on the large amount of evidence presented by Sears on these issues. The court extensively discusses this evidence. Again, we cannot say that these findings are clearly erroneous.

Regarding the question of differing interests in general among men and women in commission selling, [the district] court found that "[t]he most credible and convincing evidence offered at trial regarding women's interest in commission sales at Sears was the detailed, uncontradicted testimony of numerous men and women who were Sears store managers, personnel managers and other officials, regarding their efforts to recruit women into commission sales." These witnesses testified to their only limited success in affirmative action efforts to persuade women to sell on commission, and testified that women were generally more interested in product lines like clothing, jewelry, and cosmetics that were usually sold on a noncommission basis, than they were in product lines involving commission selling like automotives, roofing, and furnaces. The contrary applied to men. Women were also less interested in outside sales which often required night calls on customers than were men, with the exception of selling custom draperies. Various reasons for women's lack of interest in commission selling included a fear or dislike of what they perceived as cut-throat competition, and increased pressure and risk associated with commission sales. Noncommission selling, on the other hand, was associated with more social contact and friendship, less pressure and less risk. This evidence was confirmed by a study of national surveys and polls from the mid-1930's through 1983 regarding the changing status of women in American society, from which a Sears expert made conclusions regarding women's interest in commission selling; morale surveys of Sears employees, which the court found "demonstrate[] that noncommission saleswomen were generally happier with their present jobs at Sears, and were much less likely than their male counterparts to be interested in other positions, such as commission sales"; a job interest survey taken at Sears in 1976; a survey taken in 1982 of commission and noncommission salespeople at Sears regarding their attitudes, interests, and the personal beliefs and lifestyles of the employees, which the court concluded showed that noncommission salesmen were "far more interested" in commission sales than were noncommission saleswomen, and national labor force data.

The court recognized the EEOC's expert witness testimony regarding women's general interests in employment, which essentially was that there were no significant differences between women and men regarding interests and career aspirations. We cannot determine the district court clearly erred in finding the evidence not credible, persuasive or probative. These expert witnesses used small samples of women who had taken traditional jobs when opportunities arose. Larger samples would have been more persuasive. In addition as the court found, "[n]one of these witnesses had any specific knowledge of Sears." The court found Sears' evidence clearly more persuasive on the issue of different interest in commission selling between men and women. The court also found significant Sears' evidence that women became increasingly willing to accept commission sales positions between 1970 and 1980 due to, among other things, changes in commission sales positions from mostly full-time to largely part-time (more women preferred part-time), change in compensation to salary plus commission (which eliminated a lot of risk), increased availability of day care, and a group of successful saleswomen who served as role models. . . .

In short, we hold that the district court did not clearly err in finding that women were not as interested in commission sales positions as were men.

We similarly find that the district court did not clearly err in concluding that women applicants had different qualifications than did men applicants. The court noted that the EEOC's Commission Sales Report indicated that "on average, female applicants in the 'sales' pool were younger, less educated, less likely to have commission sales experience, and less likely than male applicants to have prior work experience with the products sold on commission at Sears." The EEOC does not challenge this finding.

All three of the court's findings discussed above — that commission selling is significantly different from noncommission selling, that women were not equally interested with men in commission selling at Sears, and that women applicants were not equally qualified with men for commission selling at Sears — form the bases for the court's criticisms of the EEOC's statistics regarding hiring at Sears. . . .

CUDAHY, Circuit Judge, concurring in part and dissenting in part. . . .

Perhaps the most questionable aspect of the majority opinion is its acceptance of women's alleged low interest and qualifications for commission selling as a complete explanation for the huge statistical disparities favoring men. The adoption by the district court and by the majority of Sears' analysis of these arguments strikes me as extremely uncritical. Sears has indeed presented varied evidence that these gender-based differences exist, both in our society as a whole and in its particular labor pool. But it remains a virtually insuperable task to overcome the weight of the statistical evidence marshalled by the EEOC or the skepticism that courts ought to show toward defenses to Title VII actions that rely on unquantifiable traits ascribed to protected groups.

[T]he majority's more benign view tends to minimize the significance of Sears' contentions that women lack the interest and qualifications to sell on commission. Women, as described by Sears, the district court and the majority, exhibit the very same stereotypical qualities for which they have been assigned low-status positions throughout history. . . .

These conclusions, it seems to me, are of a piece with the proposition that women are by nature happier cooking, doing the laundry and chauffeuring the children to softball games than arguing appeals or selling stocks. The stereotype of women as less greedy and daring than men is one that the sex discrimination laws were intended to address. It is disturbing that this sort of thinking is accepted so uncritically by the district court and by the majority. Perhaps they have forgotten that women have been hugely successful in such fields as residential real estate, and door-to-door and other direct outside merchandising. There are abundant indications that women lack neither the desire to compete strenuously for financial gain nor the capacity to take risks.

Sears, the district court and the majority hang much of their refutation of the EEOC's hiring and promotion claims on the putative difference between men's and women's interest in undertaking commission sales. Huge statistical disparities in participation in various commission selling jobs are ascribed to differences in interest. Yet there is scarcely any recognition of the employer's role in shaping the interests of applicants. Even the majority is willing to concede that lack of opportunity may drive lack of interest, but dismisses the matter as a "chicken-egg" problem. . . .

## NOTES

1. The record revealed that women constituted 61 percent of the applicants for full-time sales jobs at Sears, but only 27 percent of the newly hired commission salespeople. Seventy-five percent of the non-commission sales force were women. Median hourly wages were about twice as high for commission as non-commission salespeople. See Vicki Schultz, Telling Stories About Women and Work: Judicial Interpretation of Sex Segregation in the Workplace in Title VII Cases Raising the Lack of Interest Argument, 103 Harv. L. Rev. 1749, 1752 nn.5-6 (1990). Do you think that the EEOC made out a prima facie case under *Teamsters*, *Hazelwood*, and *Bazemore* with these national statistics covering a number of years?

2. Given your understanding of *Bazemore*, should Sears have been required to rebut the EEOC's case with its own statistical studies? Does Sears' failure to introduce its own studies mean that Sears conceded the prima facie showing of intent to discriminate?

3. This case received much attention, from beginning to end. It was a massive attack on one of the nation's best-known retailers. This trial was the longest in the history of the Seventh Circuit, generating more than 20,000 pages of testimony. "Each side called numerous expert witnesses, some of whom contributed book-length reports to the trial record. . . ." Thomas Haskell & Sanford Levinson, Academic Freedom and Expert Witnessing: Historians and the *Sears* Case, 66 Tex. L. Rev. 1629, 1636-37 (1988). By choosing to rely almost entirely on statistics and by not presenting anecdotal evidence, the EEOC used a high-risk strategy that ultimately failed. Further, several other aspects contributed to the case's notoriety. First, Sears relied on a defense that split a seam within feminist thinking. Second, Sears relied on a feminist historian to aid its case. Finally, it appeared to many that Sears had created, and prevailed with, a potent new defense for employers in Title VII cases.

4. Sears based its defense on one school of feminist thinking that stresses the differences between men and women. The divergent life experiences of men and women lead them to develop different perspectives and attitudes. Carol Gilligan, In a Different Voice (1982), is the most prominent spokesperson for this view. See also Judy Auerbach, Linda Blum, Vicki Smith & Christine Williams, On Gilligan's In a Different Voice, 11 Feminist Stud. 149 (1985). This "difference" school contrasts with the "liberal" or "equality" view that women and men are essentially the same except for reproductive capacity. For an attempted reconciliation of these two themes, see Lucinda Finley, Choice and Freedom: Elusive Issues in the Search for Gender Justice, 96 Yale L.J. 914 (1987). See also Joan Williams, "It's Snowing Down South": How to Help Mothers and Avoid Recycling the Sameness/Difference Debate, 102 Colum. L. Rev. 812 (2002).

5. If women are different from men, those differences might influence the jobs they are interested in seeking, applying for, and accepting. The Sears commission sales workforce did not reflect the pool of applicants for all sales jobs, but did that result from the differences women bring to the job market, or intentional discrimination by Sears? Sears relied on Dr. Rosalind Rosenberg to make the point. In an offer of proof to the court, she wrote:

> Women's role in American society and in the American family unit has fostered the development of "feminine" values that have been internalized by women themselves and reinforced by society, through its customs, its culture, and its laws. . . . Throughout American history women have been trained from earliest childhood to develop the humane and nurturing values expected of the American mother. Thus trained, women have assumed primary responsibility for maintaining family relationships. . . . Women's participation in the labor force is affected by the values they have internalized. For example:
>
> a) Women tend to be more relationship centered and men tend to be more work centered. Although both men and women find satisfaction and a sense of self-worth in their jobs, men are more likely than women to derive their self-image from their work. Most employed women continue to derive their self-image from their role as wife and mother. Women tend to be more interested than men in the cooperative, social aspects of the work situation.
>
> b) Women are trained from earliest childhood to develop different expectations from men about what aspirations are socially acceptable. Women who challenged those expectations by choosing jobs typically pursued by men often experience doubts about their ability to do well. . . .
>
> c) Women are seen by themselves and society as less competitive than men and more concerned with protecting personal relationships.
>
> d) Men's more extensive experience in competitive sports prepares them for the competitiveness, aggressiveness, teamwork, and leadership required for many jobs.

Would this testimony rebut the inference of intent to discriminate in a systemic disparate treatment case? Would this evidence alone be sufficient to explain away the statistical evidence presented by the EEOC?

6. Does Sears' argument amount to little more than blaming the victim? But if women are the victims, who is the victimizer? If society has socialized women in certain ways, why is that Sears' fault? Does Title VII impose an affirmative duty on employers to re-socialize women or to alter job requirements to meet women's needs?

7. The EEOC countered with its own historian, Dr. Alice Kessler-Harris. In her written testimony to the court, she responded to Dr. Rosenberg:

[N]ew historical information calls into question the idea that women can "choose" not to work in certain areas, and insists that choice can be understood only within the framework of available opportunity. It flatly contradicts the notion that biology, culture, or socialization enables us to make statements about "all" women or about women generally. In particular, it provides the basis for refuting testimony that attributes to most women, and especially to those women who did work for wages, perceptions and attitudes that influenced the lives of relatively few. . . .

A more accurate interpretation of the history of women's work in the U.S. would take the following form. The structure of the labor force is the product of a complex interaction between labor force needs and a socialization process that reinforces desirable roles. Women's "interests" as well as their expectations are thus a consequence of life experiences that are reinforced or discouraged by the larger society. In an industrial society, a major part of the cycle of reinforcement is played by employers whose hiring policies significantly influence women's self-perception, their assessment of reasonable aspirations, and their announced goals. What appear to be women's choices, and what are characterized as women's "interests" are, in fact, heavily influenced by the opportunities for work made available to them. In the past, opportunities offered to women have been conditioned by society's perceptions of women and assumptions about them. Thus, women have been hired into limited numbers of jobs, and discriminated against in the work force generally. The resulting profile of "women's work" has been then perceived to be what the women "chose."

See also Schultz, supra note 1 at 1851. Coupled with the statistical showing, does this testimony prove that Sears did intend to discriminate? Given the testimony Sears introduced about its efforts to recruit women for commission jobs, what should the EEOC have done to find that Sears nevertheless intended to discriminate?

8. Taking Dr. Rosenberg's approach, what aspects of work culture would prove that Sears intended to keep women out of commission-paying sales jobs? What about job descriptions or application forms stressing that commission sales is competitive and requires aggressive tactics? Would evidence that competitive sales contests were used to motivate the workers be enough for a finding that Sears intended to discriminate on the basis of gender? Is it intentional discrimination to fail to alter the work culture for commission sales jobs to make it more compatible with the interests and values of women? Looking at it another way, is Sears merely perpetuating and then relying on already existing stereotypes about women? If so, is that intentional discrimination?

9. Did Sears win by attacking the basic underlying assumption of antidiscrimination laws: that different treatment of protected-class individuals is based on untrue stereotypes about those groups, rather than on real differences between those groups and the dominant culture? But did Congress decide in passing antidiscrimination laws that, even if protected groups have been socialized or deprived in ways that impair their ability to compete, employers cannot rely on those differences to further oppress these groups by depriving them of employment? Do antidiscrimination laws impose on employers an obligation to contribute to the re-socialization of protected-group individuals by providing them with employment opportunities?

10. The EEOC factored into its regression analyses the fact that women as a group had less interest in commission sales jobs than did men as a group. The studies still found a statistically significant relationship between gender and commission sales jobs. The parties were not disputing that women are less interested, but only how much less interested they were. The EEOC acknowledged that women were less interested, but presented statistical evidence of discrimination that quantified and took into

consideration that lower level of interest. If Sears agreed that women are less interested, but failed to quantify the impact of that lack of interest, how does this undermine the EEOC's case? How could the court possibly find in favor of Sears on this evidence?

11. Chapter 5 will consider how a requirement with a disparate racial or gender impact can be attacked. Title VII makes it illegal to use selection devices with an unjustified disparate impact. Thus, real differences between the races or genders should still be irrelevant to employment unless the trait at issue is needed for the job in question. While not claiming this is a legal mandate, Professor Lucinda Finley argues that, in a *Sears* situation, men and women should be liberated from the constrictions of gender roles.

> First, rather than blaming women and their nature for their underrepresentation in the high paying jobs, why not reexamine the jobs and their values? It may not be necessary for a salesperson to be an aggressive hustler willing to pester the customer to sell the commissioned items successfully. It may not be necessary to pit salespeople against each other; they could cooperate as a team working for the good of the division rather than the glory of the individual. There may be a way to accommodate the family responsibilities of women with the need for a salesperson to be available whenever a customer calls. Second, is the qualification personality profile really geared to the needs of the job, or does it merely describe those who have been doing the job and the way they have been doing it? Just because a particular set of traits seems to produce sales, another approach is not necessarily doomed to failure. It may be useful to reexamine the designation of some items as commission items and others, usually associated with women, as non-commission, and thus less "important" and remunerative to sell. The designations, which Sears might seek to attribute to sales volume and profit margin, may be more directly linked to the notion that some of the jobs will be done by men and some by women. Finally, should it be of any concern . . . that when a woman sees the male bias in the job itself, she may sense that she is not wanted or would suffer isolation and hazing on the job, and instead may cope with the odds against her by convincing herself that she really does not want what she probably would not get?

Finley, supra note 4, at 939. While it may not be intentional discrimination for an employer to require "masculine" traits for a job, such a requirement could be subject to disparate impact attack if substantially more women than men are excluded. As the next chapter makes clear, the employer's rebuttal to a prima facie case of disparate impact discrimination is to prove that its requirement is job related and necessary for business. Should the EEOC's attack against the "masculine" work culture of the commission sales jobs at Sears have been based on disparate impact analysis, rather than systemic disparate treatment analysis?

12. Mary Anne C. Case, Disaggregating Gender from Sex and Sexual Orientation: The Effeminate Man in the Law and Feminist Jurisprudence, 105 Yale L.J. 1, 37-38 (1995), argues that choosing "masculine" characteristics for jobs can itself be challenged. She describes four generations of sex-stereotyping cases:

> Briefly stated, the first generation focused on the assumption that an entire sex conformed to gender stereotypes; the second on the assumption that individual members of the sex did; the third on individuals penalized because their gender behavior did not conform to stereotypical expectations. Fourth-generation stereotyping claims, of the sort I endorse in this article, might take on the stereotyping of the job and its requirements rather than of the person holding or applying for it, challenging the assumption that qualities gendered masculine (or, more rarely, feminine) are essential to success rather than demanded merely by stereotypical expectations.

Professor Case argues that this use of gendered expectations can be challenged under disparate impact theory. But why isn't disparate treatment available?

13. Professor Vicki Schultz, in Telling Stories, supra note 1, and with Stephen Petterson, in Race, Gender, and Choice: An Empirical Study of the Lack of Interest Defense in Title VII Cases Challenging Job Segregation, 59 U. Chi. L. Rev. 1073 (1992), shows that the lack of interest defense was not born with the *Sears* decision. The conclusion of Schultz's study is that judges are more receptive to employer claims than in early race discrimination cases:

> During the 1965-89 period as [a] whole, the courts have required sex discrimination plaintiffs to meet more difficult standards of proof than race discrimination plaintiffs to refute the lack of interest argument. Since the late 1970s, the courts have also changed their approach to the lack of interest argument in race discrimination cases to one less favorable to plaintiffs. They have moved toward a conservative understanding of racial segregation that converges with the way they have always understood sex segregation in employment. . . . That this conversion occurred among judges of all political affiliations . . . suggests a significant transformation in judicial consciousness. After [the first] decade of efforts to enforce Title VII, federal judges apparently began to share the general public's belief that employment discrimination against minorities had been largely eradicated.

Id. at 1180-81.

14. The Seventh Circuit has applied similar analysis to a race discrimination case. In EEOC v. Consolidated Serv. Sys., 989 F.2d 233 (7th Cir. 1993), Judge Posner rejected a systemic disparate treatment challenge to the hiring practices of a small Korean-owned cleaning company. The EEOC established that 73 percent of applicants and 81 percent of hires were Korean as compared to less than 1 percent of the overall workforce in Cook County and 3 percent of the janitorial workforce. "It doesn't take a statistician to tell you that the difference between the percentage of Koreans in Consolidated's workforce and the percentage of Koreans in the relevant labor market, however exactly that market is defined, is not due to chance. But is it due to discrimination?" Id. at 234. The circuit court upheld the district judge's finding that this discrepancy resulted not from employer discrimination, but from the employer's reliance on word of mouth to obtain employees:

> If an employer can obtain all the competent workers he wants, at wages no higher than the minimum that he expects to have to pay, without beating the bushes for workers — without in fact spending a cent on recruitment — he can reduce his costs of doing business by adopting just the stance of Mr. Hwang. And this is no mean consideration to a firm whose annual revenues in a highly competitive business are those of a mom and pop grocery store. Of course if the employer is a member of an ethnic community, especially an immigrant one, this stance is likely to result in the perpetuation of an ethnically imbalanced work force. Members of these communities tend to work and to socialize with each other rather than with people in the larger community. The social and business network of an immigrant community racially and culturally distinct from the majority of Americans is bound to be largely confined to that community, making it inevitable that when the network is used for job recruitment the recruits will be drawn disproportionately from the community.

Id. at 235. Because of this, no inference of intentional discrimination could be drawn, "even if the employer would prefer to employ people drawn predominantly or even entirely from his own ethnic or, here, national-origin community. Discrimination is not preference or aversion; it is acting on the preference or aversion." Id. at 236.

Judge Posner went beyond arguing that word of mouth was a cheap method of recruiting to claim that it may be highly effective in obtaining a good workforce for two reasons:

> The first is that an applicant referred by an existing employee is likely to get a franker, more accurate, more relevant picture of working conditions than if he learns about the job from an employment agency, a newspaper ad, or a hiring supervisor. The employee can give him the real low-down about the job. The result is a higher probability of a good match, and a lower probability that the new hire will be disappointed or disgruntled, perform badly, and quit. Second, an employee who refers someone for employment may get in trouble with his employer if the person he refers is a dud; so word of mouth recruitment in effect enlists existing employees to help screen new applicants conscientiously.

Id. Did Judge Posner read Richard Epstein's book Forbidden Grounds? Why didn't he cite it? Are you persuaded?

15. If word-of-mouth hiring is merely strongly correlated with hiring members of one racial or ethnic group, *Biggins* tells us that this is nevertheless not racial discrimination. But even *Biggins* acknowledges that, if a factor is used because of its tendency to select members of one group, that constitutes intentional discrimination. How does Judge Posner know that Consolidated Service Systems used word-of-mouth hiring because it was efficient, rather than because it yielded the preferred results in terms of racial makeup? What evidence could the EEOC have presented to demonstrate that the employer used word-of-mouth hiring for the purpose of discriminating? Can we infer that an individual intends the natural and probable consequences of his or her actions? What limits does *Feeney* put on the ability to draw such an inference in Posner's example?

16. Other courts have relied on word-of-mouth hiring as circumstantial evidence of intent to discriminate. The Third Circuit said in EEOC v. Metal Serv. Co., 892 F.2d 341, 350-51 (3d Cir. 1990):

> Several courts have held that word-of-mouth hiring practices that carry forward racial imbalances are discriminatory. See Barnett v. W. T. Grant Co., 518 F.2d 543, 549 (4th Cir. 1975); Parham v. Southwestern Bell Tel. Co., 433 F.2d 421, 426-27 (8th Cir. 1970). This Court has held that word-of-mouth hiring which results in a relatively small number of minority applicants is circumstantial evidence which helps to establish a reasonable inference of an employer's discriminatory treatment of blacks as a class. . . . As the *Parham* court explained, the effects of such a word-of-mouth hiring process are patent:
>
> > [T]he Company's recruitment policy, . . . which depended primarily upon existing employees to refer new prospects for employment, operated to discriminate against blacks. . . . With an almost completely white work force, it is hardly surprising that such a system of recruitment produced few, if any, black applicants. As might be expected, existing white employees tended to recommend their own relatives, friends and neighbors, who would likely be of the same race.

Which approach is more persuasive?

17. What about age discrimination? In Mistretta v. Sandia Corp., 15 EPD (CCH) ¶7902 (D.N.M. 1977), *aff'd sub nom.* EEOC v. Sandia Corp., 639 F.2d 600 (10th Cir. 1980), the plaintiff showed an age-linked correlation between older workers and management layoff decisions. The defendant responded by having an expert testify that

performance, not age, explained the layoffs. He showed that the age-based correlation disappeared when performance ratings were factored in. Wouldn't this mean that, at Sandia at least, older workers were poorer performers? Isn't this possible? The court rejected this analysis as being dependent on the purity of the performance factor:

> [The theme of Sandia's defense is that performance ratings were the main ingredient in layoff decisions. T]he [rating] system . . . "is extremely subjective and has never been validated." . . . "[T]he evaluations were based on best judgment and opinion of the evaluators, but were not based on any definite identifiable criteria based on quality or quantity of work or specific performances that were supported by some kind of record."

Id. at 614. Suppose the defendant presented medical evidence tending to show that certain job-related abilities declined with increasing age. Would this justify a disproportionate age pattern as to the layoffs? But in *Sandia*, the defendant's experts "contest[ed] the notion that performance declines with age." Id. The defendant may have been caught in a bind: it tried to avoid impact liability and thereby forfeited the opportunity to claim that the age impact was no broader than the actual performance decline related to age. Remember that, after *Biggins*, even if performance correlates closely with age, relying on performance is not intentional age discrimination.

18. In their book Use of Statistics in Equal Employment Opportunity Litigation (1985), Walter B. Connolly, Jr., David W. Peterson, and Michael J. Connolly consider two additional ways age may differ from race or sex, ways that may have to be taken into account in statistical studies.

> [a] *The "Peter Principle."* In an organization consisting of many job levels . . . there may be a tendency for individuals to rise in the organization to a level at which they are barely able to perform. Limited in promotional opportunities by lackluster job performance, such people may witness the promotion from their job level of people more qualified but less senior than themselves. Thus, at any time, a given job level may consist of two types of people: those who have risen as far as is practical, and those who are apparently on their way to greater heights. Because those employees who are stuck in the level continue to accrue seniority, while those just passing through are continually replaced by people with generally less seniority, it is not unreasonable to expect that the more senior employees within a job level tend to be those whose careers have peaked. To the extent that age and seniority are correlated, it is also not unreasonable to expect that within a job level, the older employees will tend to be the less able performers.
>
> In an organization with such a structure, it seems clear that the people promoted from a given level during the course of a year may generally be younger than the people in that level who are not promoted. If the organization is required by legitimate business considerations to reduce the number of employees in a given level by discharging those who perform least satisfactorily, it is likely that the employees discharged from a given level will tend to be older than those who are not.[1]
>
> [b] *The Age-Wage Curve.* At a given instant, the relationship between average pay and employee age in an organization may be . . . a curve that rises with increasing age, but progressively less steeply. In such an organization the average amount by which the pay of, for example, thirty-five-year-olds exceeds that of thirty-year-olds is greater than the amount by which the average pay of sixty-year-olds exceeds that of fifty-five-year-olds. A pattern of this type could occur if an employer tended to give more substantial pay increases to younger employees than to older, according to some process unfair to older employees. However, this pattern could also arise as a result of practices that are quite

---

1. These possible implications of the "Peter Principle" were brought to our attention by Dr. William Chew. See also Peter Hull, The Peter Principle, Morrow, New York, 1969. . . .

benign, and hence, the existence of that pattern in an employer's labor force need not be probative of age-discriminatory practice.

One mechanism by which such a curve could arise is the following. Suppose an organization consists of some fixed number of job levels, each successively better paying, all persons at the same level being paid at the same rate. Suppose further that experience working at a job in any one level prepares an employee for a job in the next higher-paying level, so that typical career paths involve passage through successive levels. Suppose now that nearly all hiring is done for vacancies at the lowest-paying level and that nearly all other vacancies are filled by promotion from within. Finally, as an extreme case, suppose there are as many employees in one level as there are in any other level.

Consider now the experience of a typical employee hired at the bottom level. The departure of any employee in any level above her will create, by chain reaction, a vacancy at the next level above hers, for which she is in competition with others in her level. She is likely to have, therefore, many more opportunities for advancement than is someone at a higher level, who is competing with the same number of people as she, but whose advancement is contingent on the departure of one of the relatively small[2] number of people in levels above her. Hence, promotions are likely to come more frequently to persons at lower levels in this organization than to those at higher levels.

The longer an employee stays with this organization, the greater is the likelihood he or she will advance to the higher paying levels. However, in some average sense, this progress must slow as one nears the top level, because of the relatively small number of vacancies created by departures. Because no one can advance beyond the top level, the pay accorded persons in that level is an absolute upper limit on pay, that cannot be exceeded by employees of any seniority.

In this organization, it seems clear that on average, employees with little seniority will experience generally more rapid pay increases than those who, by virtue of their seniority, have risen to such heights in the organization that opportunities for further advancement are limited. If instead of age, we had plotted seniority along the horizontal axis in Figure 4.9, we should have seen a curve of the sort already shown. And because employees with long seniority tend to be older than those with less seniority, it would not be unusual to find that Figure 4.9 also depicts the relation between average pay and employee age as of some particular instant. And yet, there is no reasonable sense in which this employer's practices may be characterized as age discriminatory.

Id. at § 10.05. Do you agree with these objections? If so, how would you take them into account in analyzing an employer's workforce for age discrimination?

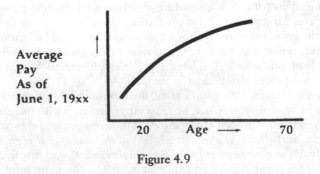

Figure 4.9

2. There are obviously more people in levels above the entry level than there are people above some higher level. Every departure above entry level creates an opening, by chain reaction, at the entry level; but only departures at the topmost levels create openings at the upper levels.

*PROBLEM 4.1*

Reread Problem 3.1, page 198. Can Jane Armstrong recover in a systemic disparate treatment case?

*PROBLEM 4.2*

Gotham Miniature Lamp Works makes light bulbs at its factory located on the north side of Gotham in a predominately Latino and Asian neighborhood. Most entry-level jobs require only basic manual dexterity and minimal ability to speak and understand English. Most incumbent workers are Latino or Asian. Almost all entry-level workers are hired by referral from incumbent employees. About 36 percent of the entry-level labor pool in Gotham is black, while 5 percent of entry-level workers in the company's workforce are black. The percentage of black applicants who were hired is 10 percent, while that for non-black applicants is 5 percent. Would the EEOC win if it challenged the company's word-of-mouth hiring?

## 2.   *Bona Fide Occupational Qualifications*

Section 703(e) of Title VII provides:

> Notwithstanding any other provision of this title . . . it shall not be an unlawful employment practice for an employer to hire and employ employees . . . on the basis of religion, sex, or national origin in those certain instances where religion, sex, or national origin is a bona fide occupational qualification reasonably necessary to the normal operation of that particular business or enterprise.

Although the bona fide occupational qualification (bfoq) defense does not reach race or color discrimination, it constitutes a potentially large loophole in Title VII's general prohibition of employment discrimination on the other three grounds. The Age Discrimination in Employment Act also provides a bfoq defense that uses language identical to Title VII.

The Court's first meaningful treatment of the bfoq was in Dothard v. Rawlinson, 433 U.S. 321 (1977). Although the Court's language was restrictive, indicating that the bfoq is "an extremely narrow exception to the general prohibition of discrimination on the basis of sex," id. at 334, it nevertheless upheld a rule requiring prison guards in "contact" positions to be the same gender as the inmates they guarded. The majority there stressed that Alabama's penitentiaries had been held unconstitutional because of their dangerous and inhumane conditions. Since there was no attempt to segregate inmates according to dangerousness, the 20 percent of male prisoners who were sex offenders were scattered throughout the dormitories. "In this environment of violence and disorganization, it would be an over-simplification to characterize [the rule against women] as an exercise in Romantic paternalism." Id. at 335. While Title VII normally allows individual women to decide whether jobs are too dangerous for them, in the Alabama prisons it was likely that women could not perform the essence of the correctional counselor's job — to maintain security:

> A woman's relative ability to maintain order in a male, maximum-security, unclassified penitentiary of the type Alabama now runs could be directly reduced by her

womanhood. There is a basis in fact for expecting that sex offenders who have criminally assaulted women in the past would be moved to do so again if access to women were established within the prison. There would also be a real risk that other inmates, deprived of a normal heterosexual environment, would assault women guards because they were women.

Id. at 336. Thus, an "employee's very womanhood" would undermine her ability to do the job. The dissent of Justice Marshall protested this analysis as justifying discrimination through the barbaric state of the prisons. Those conditions violate the Constitution and, therefore, cannot constitute "the normal operation of that particular business or enterprise" required by the bfoq defense. The notion that "the employee's very womanhood" makes assaults more likely

> regrettably perpetuates one of the most insidious of the old myths about women — that women, wittingly or not, are seductive sexual objects. The effect of the decision, made I am sure with the best of intentions, is to punish women because their very presence might provoke sexual assaults. It is women who are made to pay the price in lost job opportunities for the threat of depraved conduct by prison inmates. Once again, "[t]he pedestal upon which women have been placed has . . . , upon closer inspection, been revealed as a cage." It is particularly ironic that the cage is erected here in response to feared misbehavior by imprisoned criminals.

Id. at 345.

The Supreme Court's next encounter with the bfoq defense was not in a Title VII case challenging gender discrimination but in a suit under the Age Discrimination in Employment Act. In Western Air Lines v. Criswell, 472 U.S. 400 (1985), the Court made clear that it was adopting a uniform analysis applicable to both statutes. As originally enacted, the ADEA barred discrimination on account of age against those between the ages of 40 and 65. The upper limit was first extended to 70 and then removed entirely. The statute, however, has always permitted discrimination where age is "a bona fide occupational qualification." In Criswell, the Court was construing the ADEA during the period when the protected age bracket was 40 to 70. Criswell involved the question not reached in Thurston, whether age 60 was a bfoq for flight engineers. Flight engineers were the third "pilot" who monitored side-facing instrument panels in commercial aircraft of that era such as the Boeing 727 and the McDonnell Douglas DC-10. A regulation of the FAA banned people over age 60 from the other two pilot jobs — captain and first officer — but did not set any standard for flight engineers.

Defendant's evidence focused on the possibility that flight engineers would suffer a heart attack, the risks of which generally increased with age. Plaintiff's evidence focused on the fact that physiological deterioration was individualized and could be discovered through physical examinations that the FAA required for all flight engineers. Other airlines allowed flight engineers over age 60 to continue to fly without any apparent reduced safety records.

The jury was instructed that the "BFOQ defense is available only if it is reasonably necessary to the normal operation or essence of defendant's business." Having been informed that "the essence of Western's business is the safe transportation of their passengers," the jury was also instructed:

> One method by which defendant Western may establish a BFOQ in this case is to prove:
> (1) That in 1978, when these plaintiffs were retired, it was highly impractical for Western to deal with each second officer over age 60 on an individualized basis to determine his particular ability to perform his job safely; and

(2)  That some second officers over age 60 possess traits of a physiological, psychological or other nature which preclude safe and efficient job performance that cannot be
ascertained by means other than knowing their age.
    In evaluating the practicability to defendant Western of dealing with second officers
over age 60 on an individualized basis, with respect to the medical testimony, you
should consider the state of the medical art as it existed in July 1978.
The jury rendered a verdict for the plaintiffs, and awarded damages. . . .

Id. at 408. This jury instruction upon which a verdict for the plaintiff was reached was
based on authority developed in the lower courts, which the Supreme Court
adopted, in part because Congress had implicitly endorsed it in considering the 1978
amendments to the ADEA.

Every Court of Appeals that has confronted a BFOQ defense based on safety considerations has analyzed the problem consistently with the *Tamiami* standard. An EEOC regulation embraces the same criteria. Considering the narrow language of the BFOQ exception, the parallel treatment of such questions under Title VII, and the uniform
applications of the standard by the federal courts, the EEOC and Congress, we conclude that this two-part inquiry properly identifies the relevant considerations for resolving a BFOQ defense to an age-based qualification purportedly justified by considerations of safety.

Id. at 416. Another prong of the text, relatively rarely used, would also approve of a
bfoq if "all or substantially all" persons in the disfavored group "would be unable to
perform safely and efficiently the duties of the job involved." Id. at 414.

## NOTES

1. In Johnson v. Mayor and City Council of Baltimore, 472 U.S. 353 (1985), the
Supreme Court considered a claim that an age-55 mandatory retirement policy for
city firefighters was justified as a bfoq because a federal statute established mandatory
retirement at age 55 for certain federally employed firefighters. The Court recognized that, while the mere existence of a federal statute aimed at federal employees
could not justify the city's parallel policy, nevertheless the federal statute might bear
on the validity of that policy. The Court then examined the history of the federal law
and concluded that it did not represent a congressional determination that age under
55 is an occupational qualification for federal firefighters. The Court concluded,
therefore, that "it would be error for a court, faced with an age limit for firefighters,
to give any weight, much less conclusive weight, to the federal retirement provision."
Id. at 370.

2. The question is whether the test adopted by the *Criswell* Court is stringent
enough. In the gender context, an early Title VII decision, Rosenfeld v. Southern
Pacific Co., 444 F.2d 1219, 1225 (9th Cir. 1971), held that a bfoq can be established
only by proof that the job required "sexual characteristics, rather than characteristics
that might, to one degree or another, correlate with a particular sex." The court referred to sexual characteristics necessary for the successful performance of a job, such
as wet nurse, or when there is "a need for authenticity or genuineness, as in the case of
an actor or actress." Id. at 1224. Cf. The Crying Game (Miramax 1992). In short, the
major difference between *Criswell* and *Rosenfeld* seems to be that the latter case
would permit all women to be excluded only if all women were unqualified, whereas

the Fifth Circuit would, at least in circumstances where business essence is involved, permit bfoqs where some women were qualified as long as "substantially all" were not.

3. Colleges and universities cannot now retire tenured faculty at a given age unless they can establish a bfoq. Do you think that a college with a mandatory retirement policy could prevail in an ADEA suit? At what age? See Note, Questioning Age-Old Wisdom: The Legality of Mandatory Retirement of Tenured Faculty Under the ADEA, 105 Harv. L. Rev. 889 (1992) (arguing for a bfoq based in part on the need to create openings for younger faculty with new ideas). See generally National Research Council, Ending Mandatory Retirement for Tenured Faculty: The Consequence for Higher Education (1991).

## INTERNATIONAL UNION, UAW v. JOHNSON CONTROLS, INC.
### 499 U.S. 187 (1991)

Justice BLACKMUN delivered the opinion of the Court. . . .

### I

Respondent Johnson Controls, Inc., manufactures batteries. In the manufacturing process, the element lead is a primary ingredient. Occupational exposure to lead entails health risks, including the risk of harm to any fetus carried by a female employee.

Before the Civil Rights Act of 1964 became law, Johnson Controls did not employ any woman in a battery-manufacturing job. In June 1977, however, it announced its first official policy concerning its employment of women in lead-exposure work [which noted: "it would appear to be illegal discrimination to treat all who are capable of pregnancy as though they will become pregnant"].

Consistent with that view, Johnson Controls "stopped short of excluding women capable of bearing children from lead exposure," but emphasized that a woman who expected to have a child should not choose a job in which she would have such exposure. The company also required a woman who wished to be considered for employment to sign a statement that she had been advised of the risk of having a child while she was exposed to lead. . . .

Five years later, in 1982, Johnson Controls shifted from a policy of warning to a policy of exclusion. Between 1979 and 1983, eight employees became pregnant while maintaining blood lead levels in excess of 30 micrograms per deciliter. This appeared to be the critical level noted by the Occupational Safety and Health Administration (OSHA) for a worker who was planning to have a family. See 29 C.F.R. § 1910.1025 (1989). The company responded by announcing a broad exclusion of women from jobs that exposed them to lead:

> [I]t is [Johnson Controls'] policy that women who are pregnant or who are capable of bearing children will not be placed into jobs involving lead exposure or which could expose them to lead through the exercise of job bidding, bumping, transfer or promotion rights.

The policy defined "women . . . capable of bearing children" as "all women except those whose inability to bear children is medically documented." It further stated that an unacceptable work station was one where, "over the past year," an employee had recorded a blood lead level of more than 30 micrograms per deciliter or the work site had yielded an air sample containing a lead level in excess of 30 micrograms per cubic meter.

## II

[Plaintiffs filed a Title VII class action challenging the fetal-protection policy.] Among the individual plaintiffs were petitioners Mary Craig, who had chosen to be sterilized in order to avoid losing her job; Elsie Nason, a 50-year-old divorcee, who had suffered a loss in compensation when she was transferred out of a job where she was exposed to lead; and Donald Penney, who had been denied a request for a leave of absence for the purpose of lowering his lead level because he intended to become a father. . . .

[The district court granted summary judgment for defendant. The Seventh Circuit, en banc, affirmed by a 7-to-4 vote.] The majority held that the proper standard for evaluating the fetal-protection policy was the defense of business necessity; that Johnson Controls was entitled to summary judgment under that defense; and that even if the proper standard was a BFOQ, Johnson Controls still was entitled to summary judgment. . . .

[Judges Cudahy and Posner dissented. Both believed that the employer could prevail only by establishing a BFOQ. Judge Posner observed that a BFOQ must be "reasonably necessary to the normal operation" of a business which encompasses ethical, legal, and business concerns about the effects of an employer's activities on third parties.]

Judge Easterbrook, also in dissent and joined by Judge Flaum, agreed with Judges Cudahy and Posner that the only defense available to Johnson Controls was the BFOQ. He concluded, however, that the BFOQ defense would not prevail because respondent's stated concern for the health of the unborn was irrelevant to the operation of its business under the BFOQ. He also viewed the employer's concern as irrelevant to a woman's ability or inability to work under the Pregnancy Discrimination Act's amendment to Title VII. Judge Easterbrook also stressed what he considered the excessive breadth of Johnson Controls' policy. It applied to all women (except those with medical proof of incapacity to bear children) although most women in an industrial labor force do not become pregnant, most of those who do become pregnant will have blood lead levels under 30 micrograms per deciliter, and most of those who become pregnant with levels exceeding that figure will bear normal children anyway. "Concerns about a tiny minority of women cannot set the standard by which all are judged.". . .

## III

The bias in Johnson Controls' policy is obvious. Fertile men, but not fertile women, are given a choice as to whether they wish to risk their reproductive health for a particular job. Section 703(a) prohibits sex-based classifications in terms and conditions of employment, in hiring and discharging decisions, and in other employment decisions that adversely affect an employee's status. Respondent's fetal-protection policy explicitly discriminates against women on the basis of their sex. The policy excludes women with childbearing capacity from lead-exposed jobs and so creates a facial classification based on gender. Respondent assumes as much in its brief before this Court.

Nevertheless, the Court of Appeals assumed, as did the two appellate courts who already had confronted the issue, that sex-specific fetal-protection policies do not involve facial discrimination. These courts analyzed the policies as though they were facially neutral, and had only a discriminatory effect upon the employment opportunities of women. Consequently, the courts looked to see if each employer in question had established that its policy was justified as a business necessity. The business necessity standard is more lenient for the employer than the statutory BFOQ defense. The Court of Appeals . . . assumed that because the asserted reason for the sex-based exclusion (protecting women's unconceived offspring) was ostensibly benign, the policy was not sex-based discrimination. That assumption, however, was incorrect.

First, Johnson Controls' policy classifies on the basis of gender and childbearing capacity, rather than fertility alone. Respondent does not seek to protect the unconceived children of all its employees. Despite evidence in the record about the debilitating effect of lead exposure on the male reproductive system, Johnson Controls is concerned only with the harms that may befall the unborn offspring of its female employees. . . . This Court faced a conceptually similar situation in Phillips v. Martin Marietta Corp., 400 U.S. 542 (1971), and found sex discrimination because the policy established "one hiring policy for women and another for men — each having preschool-age children." Johnson Controls' policy is facially discriminatory because it requires only a female employee to produce proof that she is not capable of reproducing.

Our conclusion is bolstered by the Pregnancy Discrimination Act of 1978 (PDA) in which Congress explicitly provided that, for purposes of Title VII, discrimination "on the basis of sex" includes discrimination "because of or on the basis of pregnancy, childbirth, or related medical conditions." "The Pregnancy Discrimination Act has now made clear that, for all Title VII purposes, discrimination based on a woman's pregnancy is, on its face, discrimination because of her sex." Newport News Shipbuilding & Dry Dock Co. v. EEOC [reproduced at page 471]. In its use of the words "capable of bearing children" in the 1982 policy statement as the criterion for exclusion, Johnson Controls explicitly classifies on the basis of potential for pregnancy. Under the PDA, such a classification must be regarded, for Title VII purposes, in the same light as explicit sex discrimination. Respondent has chosen to treat all its female employees as potentially pregnant; that choice evinces discrimination on the basis of sex.

We concluded above that Johnson Controls' policy is not neutral because it does not apply to the reproductive capacity of the company's male employees in the same way as it applies to that of the females. Moreover, the absence of a malevolent motive does not convert a facially discriminatory policy into a neutral policy with a discriminatory effect. Whether an employment practice involves disparate treatment through explicit facial discrimination does not depend on why the employer discriminates but rather on the explicit terms of the discrimination. In *Martin Marietta*, the motives underlying the employers' express exclusion of women did not alter the intentionally discriminatory character of the policy. Nor did the arguably benign motives lead to consideration of a business necessity defense. The question in that case was whether the discrimination in question could be justified under §703(e) as a BFOQ. The beneficence of an employer's purpose does not undermine the conclusion that an explicit gender-based policy is sex discrimination under §703(a) and thus may be defended only as a BFOQ. . . .

In sum, Johnson Controls' policy "does not pass the simple test of whether the evidence shows 'treatment of a person in a manner which but for that person's sex would be different.'" Los Angeles Dept. of Water & Power v. Manhart. We hold that Johnson Controls' fetal-protection policy is sex discrimination forbidden under Title VII unless respondent can establish that sex is a "bona fide occupational qualification."

IV . . .

The BFOQ defense is written narrowly, and this Court has read it narrowly. See, e.g., Dothard v. Rawlinson; Trans World Airlines, Inc. v. Thurston. We have read the BFOQ language of § 4(f) of the Age Discrimination in Employment Act of 1967 (ADEA), which tracks the BFOQ provision in Title VII, just as narrowly. See Western Air Lines, Inc. v. Criswell. Our emphasis on the restrictive scope of the BFOQ defense is grounded on both the language and the legislative history of § 703.

The wording of the BFOQ defense contains several terms of restriction that indicate that the exception reaches only special situations. The statute thus limits the situations in which discrimination is permissible to "certain instances" where sex discrimination is "reasonably necessary" to the "normal operation" of the "particular" business. Each one of these terms — certain, normal, particular — prevents the use of general subjective standards and favors an objective, verifiable requirement. But the most telling term is "occupational"; this indicates that these objective, verifiable requirements must concern job-related skills and aptitudes.

The concurrence defines "occupational" as meaning related to a job. According to the concurrence, any discriminatory requirement imposed by an employer is "job-related" simply because the employer has chosen to make the requirement a condition of employment. In effect, the concurrence argues that sterility may be an occupational qualification for women because Johnson Controls has chosen to require it. This reading of "occupational" renders the word mere surplusage. "Qualification" by itself would encompass an employer's idiosyncratic requirements. By modifying "qualification" with "occupational," Congress narrowed the term to qualifications that affect an employee's ability to do the job.

Johnson Controls argues that its fetal-protection policy falls within the so-called safety exception to the BFOQ. Our cases have stressed that discrimination on the basis of sex because of safety concerns is allowed only in narrow circumstances. In Dothard v. Rawlinson, this Court indicated that danger to a woman herself does not justify discrimination. We there allowed the employer to hire only male guards in contact areas of maximum-security male penitentiaries only because more was at stake than the "individual woman's decision to weigh and accept the risks of employment." We found sex to be a BFOQ inasmuch as the employment of a female guard would create real risks of safety to others if violence broke out because the guard was a woman. Sex discrimination was tolerated because sex was related to the guard's ability to do the job — maintaining prison security. We also required in Dothard a high correlation between sex and ability to perform job functions and refused to allow employers to use sex as a proxy for strength although it might be a fairly accurate one.

Similarly, some courts have approved airlines' layoffs of pregnant flight attendants at different points during the first five months of pregnancy on the ground that the employer's policy was necessary to ensure the safety of passengers. See[, e.g.,] Harriss v. Pan American World Airways, Inc., 649 F.2d 670 (CA9 1980). In these cases, the courts pointedly indicated that fetal, as opposed to passenger, safety was best left to the mother.

We considered safety to third parties in Western Airlines, Inc. v. Criswell in the context of the ADEA. We focused upon "the nature of the flight engineer's tasks," and the "actual capabilities of persons over age 60" in relation to those tasks. Our safety concerns were not independent of the individual's ability to perform the assigned tasks, but rather involved the possibility that, because of age-connected debility, a flight engineer might not properly assist the pilot, and might thereby cause a safety emergency. Furthermore, although we considered the safety of third parties in

*Dothard* and *Criswell*, those third parties were indispensable to the particular business at issue. In *Dothard*, the third parties were the inmates; in *Criswell*, the third parties were the passengers on the plane. We stressed that in order to qualify as a BFOQ, a job qualification must relate to the "essence," or to the "central mission of the employer's business."

The concurrence ignores the "essence of the business" test and so concludes that "the safety to fetuses in carrying out the duties of battery manufacturing is as much a legitimate concern as is safety to third parties in guarding prisons (*Dothard*) or flying airplanes (*Criswell*)." By limiting its discussion to cost and safety concerns and rejecting the "essence of the business" test that our case law has established, the concurrence seeks to expand what is now the narrow BFOQ defense. Third-party safety considerations properly entered into the BFOQ analysis in *Dothard* and *Criswell* because they went to the core of the employee's job performance. Moreover, that performance involved the central purpose of the enterprise. . . . The concurrence attempts to transform this case into one of customer safety. The unconceived fetuses of Johnson Controls' female employees, however, are neither customers nor third parties whose safety is essential to the business of battery manufacturing. No one can disregard the possibility of injury to future children; the BFOQ, however, is not so broad that it transforms this deep social concern into an essential aspect of batterymaking.

Our case law, therefore, makes clear that the safety exception is limited to instances in which sex or pregnancy actually interferes with the employee's ability to perform the job. This approach is consistent with the language of the BFOQ provision itself, for it suggests that permissible distinctions based on sex must relate to ability to perform the duties of the job. Johnson Controls suggests, however, that we expand the exception to allow fetal-protection policies that mandate particular standards for pregnant or fertile women. We decline to do so. Such an expansion contradicts not only the language of the BFOQ and the narrowness of its exception but the plain language and history of the Pregnancy Discrimination Act.

The PDA's amendment to Title VII contains a BFOQ standard of its own: unless pregnant employees differ from others "in their ability or inability to work," they must be "treated the same" as other employees "for all employment-related purposes." This language clearly sets forth Congress' remedy for discrimination on the basis of pregnancy and potential pregnancy. Women who are either pregnant or potentially pregnant must be treated like others "similar in their ability . . . to work." In other words, women as capable of doing their jobs as their male counterparts may not be forced to choose between having a child and having a job.

The concurrence asserts that the PDA did not alter the BFOQ defense. The concurrence arrives at this conclusion by ignoring the second clause of the Act which states that "women affected by pregnancy, childbirth, or related medical conditions shall be treated the same for all employment-related purposes . . . as other persons not so affected but similar in their ability or inability to work. . . ."

The legislative history confirms what the language of the Pregnancy Discrimination Act compels. Both the House and Senate Reports accompanying the legislation indicate that this statutory standard was chosen to protect female workers from being treated differently from other employees simply because of their capacity to bear children. See Amending Title VII, Civil Rights Act of 1964, S. Rep. No. 95-331, pp. 4-6 (1977). . . .

This history counsels against expanding the BFOQ to allow fetal-protection policies. The Senate Report quoted above states that employers may not require a pregnant woman to stop working at any time during her pregnancy unless she is unable to do her work. Employment late in pregnancy often imposes risks on the unborn child, see Chavkin, Walking a Tightrope: Pregnancy, Parenting, and Work, in Double Exposure 196, 196-202 (W. Chavkin ed. 1984), but Congress indicated that the employer may take into account only the woman's ability to get her job done. See Becker, From Muller v. Oregon to Fetal Vulnerability Policies, 53 U. Chi. L. Rev. 1219, 1255-1256 (1986). With the PDA, Congress made clear that the decision to become pregnant or to work while being either pregnant or capable of becoming pregnant was reserved for each individual woman to make for herself.

We conclude that the language of both the BFOQ provision and the PDA which amended it, as well as the legislative history and the case law, prohibit an employer from discriminating against a woman because of her capacity to become pregnant unless her reproductive potential prevents her from performing the duties of her job. We reiterate our holdings in *Criswell* and *Dothard* that an employer must direct its concerns about a woman's ability to perform her job safely and efficiently to those aspects of the woman's job-related activities that fall within the "essence" of the particular business.[4]

V

We have no difficulty concluding that Johnson Controls cannot establish a BFOQ. Fertile women, as far as appears in the record, participate in the manufacture of batteries as efficiently as anyone else. Johnson Controls' professed moral and ethical concerns about the welfare of the next generation do not suffice to establish a BFOQ of female sterility. Decisions about the welfare of future children must be left to the parents who conceive, bear, support, and raise them rather than to the employers who hire those parents. Congress has mandated this choice through Title VII, as amended by the Pregnancy Discrimination Act. Johnson Controls has attempted to exclude women because of their reproductive capacity. Title VII and the PDA simply do not allow a woman's dismissal because of her failure to submit to sterilization.

Nor can concerns about the welfare of the next generation be considered a part of the "essence" of Johnson Controls' business. Judge Easterbrook in this case pertinently observed: "It is word play to say that 'the job' at Johnson [Controls] is to make batteries without risk to fetuses in the same way 'the job' at Western Air Lines is to fly planes without crashing."

Johnson Controls argues that it must exclude all fertile women because it is impossible to tell which women will become pregnant while working with lead. This argument is somewhat academic in light of our conclusion that the company may not exclude fertile women at all; it perhaps is worth noting, however, that Johnson Controls has shown no "factual basis for believing that all or substantially all women would be unable to perform safely and efficiently the duties of the job involved." Even on this sparse record, it is apparent that Johnson Controls is concerned about only a small

---

4. The concurrence predicts that our reaffirmation of the narrowness of the BFOQ defense will preclude considerations of privacy as a basis for sex-based discrimination. We have never addressed privacy-based sex discrimination and shall not do so here because the sex-based discrimination at issue today does not involve the privacy interests of Johnson Controls' customers. Nothing in our discussion of the "essence of the business test," however, suggests that sex could not constitute a BFOQ when privacy interests are implicated. See, e.g., Backus v. Baptist Medical Center, 510 F. Supp. 1191 (E.D. Ark. 1981), *vacated as moot*, 671 F.2d 1100 (CA8 1982) (essence of obstetrics nurse's business is to provide sensitive care for patient's intimate and private concerns).

minority of women. Of the eight pregnancies reported among the female employees, it has not been shown that any of the babies have birth defects or other abnormalities. The record does not reveal the birth rate for Johnson Controls' female workers but national statistics show that approximately nine percent of all fertile women become pregnant each year. The birthrate drops to two percent for blue collar workers over age 30. Johnson Controls' fear of prenatal injury, no matter how sincere, does not begin to show that substantially all of its fertile women employees are incapable of doing their jobs.

## VI

A word about tort liability and the increased cost of fertile women in the workplace is perhaps necessary. [At the Seventh Circuit, Judge Posner] expressed concern about an employer's tort liability and concluded that liability for a potential injury to a fetus is a social cost that Title VII does not require a company to ignore. It is correct to say that Title VII does not prevent the employer from having a conscience. The statute, however, does prevent sex-specific fetal-protection policies. These two aspects of Title VII do not conflict.

More than 40 States currently recognize a right to recover for a prenatal injury based either on negligence or on wrongful death. According to Johnson Controls, however, the company complies with the lead standard developed by OSHA and warns its female employees about the damaging effects of lead. It is worth noting that OSHA gave the problem of lead lengthy consideration and concluded that "there is no basis whatsoever for the claim that women of childbearing age should be excluded from the workplace in order to protect the fetus or the course of pregnancy." 43 Fed. Reg. 52952, 52966 (1978). Instead, OSHA established a series of mandatory protections which, taken together, "should effectively minimize any risk to the fetus and newborn child." See 29 C.F.R. § 1910.125(k)(ii) (1989). Without negligence, it would be difficult for a court to find liability on the part of the employer. If, under general tort principles, Title VII bans sex-specific fetal-protection policies, the employer fully informs the woman of the risk, and the employer has not acted negligently, the basis for holding an employer liable seems remote at best.

Although the issue is not before us, the concurrence observes that "it is far from clear that compliance with Title VII will preempt state tort liability." The cases relied upon by the concurrence to support its prediction, however, are inapposite. For example, in California Federal S. & L. Assn. v. Guerra, 479 U.S. 272, we considered a California statute that expanded upon the requirements of the PDA and concluded that the statute was not pre-empted by Title VII because it was not inconsistent with the purposes of the federal statute and did not require an act that was unlawful under Title VII. Here, in contrast, the tort liability that the concurrence fears will punish employers for complying with Title VII's clear command. When it is impossible for an employer to comply with both state and federal requirements, this Court has ruled that federal law pre-empts that of the States. . . .

If state tort law furthers discrimination in the workplace and prevents employers from hiring women who are capable of manufacturing the product as efficiently as men, then it will impede the accomplishment of Congress' goals in enacting Title VII. Because Johnson Controls has not argued that it faces any costs from tort liability, not to mention crippling ones, the pre-emption question is not before us. We therefore say no more than that the concurrence's speculation appears unfounded as well as premature.

The tort-liability argument reduces to two equally unpersuasive propositions. First, Johnson Controls attempts to solve the problem of reproductive health hazards by resorting to an exclusionary policy. Title VII plainly forbids illegal sex discrimination as a method of diverting attention from an employer's obligation to police the workplace. Second, the spectre of an award of damages reflects a fear that hiring fertile women will cost more. The extra cost of employing members of one sex, however, does not provide an affirmative Title VII defense for a discriminatory refusal to hire members of that gender. See *Manhart*. Indeed, in passing the PDA, Congress considered at length the considerable cost of providing equal treatment of pregnancy and related conditions, but made the "decision to forbid special treatment of pregnancy despite the social costs associated therewith."

We, of course, are not presented with, nor do we decide, a case in which costs would be so prohibitive as to threaten the survival of the employer's business. We merely reiterate our prior holdings that the incremental cost of hiring women cannot justify discriminating against them. . . .

Justice WHITE, with whom The Chief Justice and Justice KENNEDY join, concurring in part and concurring in the judgment.

The Court properly holds that Johnson Controls' fetal protection policy overtly discriminates against women, and thus is prohibited by Title VII unless it falls within the bona fide occupational qualification (BFOQ) exception. . . . The Court erroneously holds, however, that the BFOQ defense is so narrow that it could never justify a sex-specific fetal protection policy. I nevertheless concur in the judgment of reversal because on the record before us summary judgment in favor of Johnson Controls was improper. . . .

[A] fetal protection policy would be justified under the terms of the statute if, for example, an employer could show that exclusion of women from certain jobs was reasonably necessary to avoid substantial tort liability. Common sense tells us that it is part of the normal operation of business concerns to avoid causing injury to third parties, as well as to employees, if for no other reason than to avoid tort liability and its substantial costs. This possibility of tort liability is not hypothetical; every State currently allows children born alive to recover in tort for prenatal injuries caused by third parties, see W. Keeton, D. Dobbs, R. Keeton, & D. Owen, Prosser and Keeton on the Law of Torts § 55 p. 368 (5th ed. 1984), and an increasing number of courts have recognized a right to recover even for prenatal injuries caused by torts committed prior to conception, see 3 F. Harper, F. James, & O. Gray, Law of Torts § 18.3, pp. 677-678, n.15 (2d ed. 1986).

The Court dismisses the possibility of tort liability by no more than . . . speculation [which] will be small comfort to employers. First, it is far from clear that compliance with Title VII will pre-empt state tort liability, and the Court offers no support for that proposition. Second, although warnings may preclude claims by injured employees, they will not preclude claims by injured children because the general rule is that parents cannot waive causes of action on behalf of their children, and the parents' negligence will not be imputed to the children. Finally, although state tort liability for prenatal injuries generally requires negligence, it will be difficult for employers to determine in advance what will constitute negligence. Compliance with OSHA standards, for example, has been held not to be a defense to state tort or criminal liability. See National Solid Wastes Management Assn. v. Killian, 918 F.2d 671, 680, n.9 (CA7 1990) (collecting cases); see also 29 U.S.C. § 653(b)(4). Moreover, it is possible that employers will be held strictly liable, if, for example, their manufacturing process is considered "abnormally dangerous." See Restatement (Second) of Torts § 869, comment b (1979).

Prior decisions construing the BFOQ defense confirm that the defense is broad enough to include considerations of cost and safety of the sort that could form the basis for an employer's adoption of a fetal protection policy. . . .

*Dothard* and *Criswell* make clear that avoidance of substantial safety risks to third parties is inherently part of both an employee's ability to perform a job and an employer's "normal operation" of its business. Indeed, in both cases, the Court approved the statement in Weeks v. Southern Bell Telephone & Telegraph Co., 408 F.2d 228 (CA5 1969), that an employer could establish a BFOQ defense by showing that "all or substantially all women would be unable to perform *safely and efficiently* the duties of the job involved." (emphasis added). The Court's statement in this case that "the safety exception is limited to instances in which sex or pregnancy actually interferes with the employee's ability to perform the job" therefore adds no support to its conclusion that a fetal protection policy could never be justified as a BFOQ. On the facts of this case, for example, protecting fetal safety while carrying out the duties of battery manufacturing is as much a legitimate concern as is safety to third parties in guarding prisons (*Dothard*) or flying airplanes (*Criswell*).[5]

*Dothard* and *Criswell* also confirm that costs are relevant in determining whether a discriminatory policy is reasonably necessary for the normal operation of a business. In *Dothard*, the safety problem that justified exclusion of women from the prison guard positions was largely a result of inadequate staff and facilities. If the cost of employing women could not be considered, the employer there should have been required to hire more staff and restructure the prison environment rather than exclude women. Similarly, in *Criswell* the airline could have been required to hire more pilots and install expensive monitoring devices rather than discriminate against older employees. The BFOQ statute, however, reflects "Congress' unwillingness to require employers to change the very nature of their operations." Price Waterhouse v. Hopkins (plurality opinion).

The Pregnancy Discrimination Act (PDA), contrary to the Court's assertion, did not restrict the scope of the BFOQ defense. The PDA was only an amendment to the "Definitions" section of Title VII, and did not purport to eliminate or alter the BFOQ defense. Rather, it merely clarified Title VII to make it clear that pregnancy and related conditions are included within Title VII's antidiscrimination provisions. As we have already recognized, "the purpose of the PDA was simply to make the treatment of pregnancy consistent with general Title VII principles." . . .

In enacting the BFOQ standard, "Congress did not ignore the public interest in safety." The Court's narrow interpretation of the BFOQ defense in this case, however, means that an employer cannot exclude even pregnant women from an environment highly toxic to their fetuses. It is foolish to think that Congress intended such a result, and neither the language of the BFOQ exception nor our cases require it.[8]

5. I do not, as the Court asserts, reject the "essence of the business" test. Rather, I merely reaffirm the obvious — that safety to third parties is part of the "essence" of most if not all businesses. Of course, the BFOQ inquiry "'adjusts to the safety factor.'" As a result, more stringent occupational qualifications may be justified for jobs involving higher safety risks, such as flying airplanes. But a recognition that the importance of safety varies among businesses does not mean that safety is completely irrelevant to the essence of a job such as battery manufacturing.

8. The Court's interpretation of the BFOQ standard also would seem to preclude considerations of privacy as a basis for sex-based discrimination, since those considerations do not relate directly to an employee's physical ability to perform the duties of the job. The lower federal courts, however, have consistently recognized that privacy interests may justify sex-based requirements for certain jobs. See, e.g.,

II

Despite my disagreement with the Court concerning the scope of the BFOQ defense, I concur in reversing the Court of Appeals because that court erred in affirming the District Court's grant of summary judgment in favor of Johnson Controls. First, the Court of Appeals erred in failing to consider the level of risk-avoidance that was part of Johnson Controls' "normal operation." Although the court did conclude that there was a "substantial risk" to fetuses from lead exposure in fertile women, it merely meant that there was a high risk that some fetal injury would occur absent a fetal protection policy. That analysis, of course, fails to address the extent of fetal injury that is likely to occur. If the fetal protection policy insists on a risk-avoidance level substantially higher than other risk levels tolerated by Johnson Controls such as risks to employees and consumers, the policy should not constitute a BFOQ.

Second, even without more information about the normal level of risk at Johnson Controls, the fetal protection policy at issue here reaches too far. This is evident both in its presumption that, absent medical documentation to the contrary, all women are fertile regardless of their age, and in its exclusion of presumptively fertile women from positions that might result in a promotion to a position involving high lead exposure. . . .

Finally, the Court of Appeals failed to consider properly petitioners' evidence of harm to offspring caused by lead exposure in males. . . . The burden of proving that a discriminatory qualification is a BFOQ . . . rests with the employer. Thus, the court should have analyzed whether the evidence was sufficient for petitioners to survive summary judgment in light of respondent's burden of proof to establish a BFOQ. Moreover, the court should not have discounted the evidence as "speculative," merely because it was based on animal studies. We have approved the use of animal studies to assess risks, see Industrial Union Dept. v. American Petroleum Institute, 448 U.S. 607 (1980), and OSHA uses animal studies in establishing its lead control regulations, see United Steelworkers of America, AFL-CIO-CLC v. Marshall, 647 F.2d 1189, 1257, n.97 (1980). It seems clear that if the Court of Appeals had properly analyzed that evidence, it would have concluded that summary judgment against petitioners was not appropriate because there was a dispute over a material issue of fact. . . .

Justice SCALIA, concurring in the judgment.

I generally agree with the Court's analysis, but have some reservations, several of which bear mention.

First, I think it irrelevant that there was "evidence in the record about the debilitating effect of lead exposure on the male reproductive system." Even without such evidence, treating women differently "on the basis of pregnancy" constitutes discrimination "on the basis of sex," because Congress has unequivocally said so. Pregnancy Discrimination Act of 1978.

Second, the Court points out that "Johnson Controls has shown no factual basis for believing that all or substantially all women would be unable to perform safely . . . the duties of the job involved." In my view, this is not only "somewhat academic in light of our conclusion that the company may not exclude fertile women at all"; it is entirely irrelevant. By reason of the Pregnancy Discrimination Act, it would not matter

Fesel v. Masonic Home of Delaware, Inc., 447 F. Supp. 1346 (Del. 1978), aff'd, 591 F.2d 1334 (CA3 1979) (nurse's aide in retirement home).

if all pregnant women placed their children at risk in taking these jobs, just as it does not matter if no men do so.

Third, [as to possible liability under state tort law,] all that need be said in the present case is that Johnson has not demonstrated a substantial risk of tort liability — which is alone enough to defeat a tort-based assertion of the BFOQ exception.

Last, the Court goes far afield, it seems to me, in suggesting that increased cost alone — short of "costs . . . so prohibitive as to threaten survival of the employer's business" — cannot support a BFOQ defense. I agree with Justice White's concurrence that nothing in our prior cases suggests this, and in my view it is wrong. I think, for example, that a shipping company may refuse to hire pregnant women as crew members on long voyages because the on-board facilities for foreseeable emergencies, though quite feasible, would be inordinately expensive. In the present case, however, Johnson has not asserted a cost-based BFOQ. . . .

## NOTES

1. *Johnson Controls* rejected an attempt to sidestep the rigors of the bfoq as developed in *Dothard* and *Criswell* by employing the more lenient business necessity test. This defense is available in disparate impact cases, see Chapter 5, and several courts had applied it to fetal-protection policies by treating them as impact cases. *Johnson Controls* is significant for reasserting that business necessity applies *only* to disparate impact cases. The Civil Rights Act of 1991 codified the Court's decision in this respect by adding subsection (k)(2) to § 703 of Title VII: "A demonstration that an employment practice is required by business necessity may not be used as a defense against a claim of intentional discrimination under this title." *Johnson Controls* also is important for its holding that disparate treatment analysis (and, therefore, the bfoq defense) applies whenever an employer facially discriminates or acts on the basis of gender, regardless of whether it is motivated by animus. Compare *Biggins*.

2. *Johnson Controls* holds that the fetal-protection policy is discriminatory treatment entirely apart from the Pregnancy Discrimination Act. The implications of *Johnson Controls* for cases alleging pregnancy discrimination under § 701(k) are discussed in Chapter 7.

3. All the justices agreed that the defendant should not prevail. But what was the essence of the disagreement between the majority and the concurrences? The concurring justices would not have granted summary judgment to the employer. Does that mean a trial is necessary, or might they grant summary judgment to the plaintiffs? While some fetal-protection policies may be permissible according to Justice White, can the defendant's policy be justified on the facts before the Court? What would Justice Scalia say? Professor Susan S. Grover, in The Employer's Fetal Injury Quandary After *Johnson Controls*, 81 Ky. L.J. 639, 650 (1993), summarized the major points of disagreement among the justices.

> First, the justices disagreed on whether employers forced by federal law to expose fertile women to unavoidable fetal hazards could invoke the doctrine of federal preemption in order to escape state tort liability to the fetus. Second, the justices differed on whether the prospect of fetal tort liability could support a Title VII BFOQ even though the altruistic interest in fetal health could not.

Are those the only differences among the opinion for the Court and the concurring opinions? If state tort liability to fetuses is not preempted, can the costs of that liability ever rise to a level to make fetal protection the essence of a business and, therefore, the basis for a bfoq? Professor Grover predicts that state tort liability will not be preempted by Title VII and that tort liability that would ruin the business would establish a bfoq.

4. Is *Johnson Controls* consistent with *Dothard?* In both cases, third parties (fetuses or other prison guards and prisoners) could be affected by a woman's decision to perform a certain job. Is the difference that the third parties affected in *Dothard* are the essence of the business? Who defines that?

5. What is the danger of recognizing cost as the basis of a bona fide occupational qualification? Does the Court's opinion leave this possibility open?

6. What is the "essence" of a business? The test originated in Diaz v. Pan American Airways, Inc., 442 F.2d 385 (5th Cir. 1971), holding that the asserted superiority of stewardesses in being sexually attractive to male passengers and comforting to female passengers is peripheral to the airline's essential concern with safe transportation. Similarly, Smallwood v. United Airlines, Inc., 661 F.2d 303 (4th Cir. 1981), rejected a claim that a practice is essential if it enables the employer to make more money. The employer tried to justify its rule against hiring pilots who were more than 35 years old on the ground that training was expensive and that hiring young pilots allowed a longer period of peak productivity. Doesn't *Johnson Controls* confirm this view?

7. The Hooters chain of restaurants hires only women, who are scantily clad, to serve food to customers. The company defended its practice by arguing that, "A lot of places serve good burgers. The Hooters' Girls, with their charm and All-American sex appeal, are what our customers come for." N.Y. Times, Nov. 16, 1995, at A20, col. 5. The EEOC dropped its investigation against Hooters after the company's massive public relations campaign. A private action was then settled, under terms which allowed Hooters to continue to hire only women as waitstaff. The men who were discriminated against by this company policy did, however, receive monetary compensation. Hooters to Pay $3.75 Million in Sex Suit, USA Today, Oct. 1, 1997, at 1A. Is selling sex appeal a bfoq?

8. In Frank v. United Airlines, 216 F.3d 845 (9th Cir. 2000), female flight attendants challenged the airlines' maximum weight requirements requiring women to meet a standard for medium body frames while the standard for men corresponded to standards for large body frames. Women flight attendants were required to weigh 14 to 25 pounds less than male colleagues of the same height and age. The court found this to be a formal policy of sex discrimination and struck it down because the airline failed to justify it as a bfoq.

> United made no showing that having disproportionately thinner female than male flight attendants bears a relation to flight attendants' ability to greet passengers, push carts, move luggage, and, perhaps most importantly, provide physical assistance in emergencies. . . . Far from being "reasonably necessary" to the "normal operation" of United's business, the evidence suggests that, if anything, United's discriminatory weight requirements may have inhibited the job performance of female flight attendants.

Id. at 855. Why would United adopt such a policy? Is it to satisfy customer preference for conventional views of attractiveness? Gender-specific grooming requirements have been found not to violate Title VII, see pages 541-549. How do grooming requirements differ from the weight standards here?

9. In Healey v. Southwood Psychiatric Hospital, 78 F.3d 128 (3d Cir. 1996), plaintiff challenged a gender-specific rule for assigning child care specialists at a hospital for emotionally disturbed children and adolescents, some of whom had been sexually

abused. The court upheld summary judgment for the employer based on the bfoq defense:

> The "essence" of Southwood's business is to treat emotionally disturbed and sexually abused adolescents and children. Southwood has presented expert testimony that staffing both males and females on all shifts is necessary to provide therapeutic care. "Role modeling," including parental role modeling, is an important element of the staff's job, and a male is better able to serve as a male role model than a female and vice versa. A balanced staff is also necessary because children who have been sexually abused will disclose their problems more easily to a member of a certain sex, depending on their sex and the sex of the abuser. If members of both sexes are not on a shift, Southwood's inability to provide basic therapeutic care would hinder the "normal operation" of its "particular business." Therefore, it is reasonably necessary to the normal operation of Southwood to have at least one member of each sex available to the patients at all times.

Id. at 132-33. Plaintiff had introduced an affidavit that showed that another hospital did not use gender in staffing because it did not play a role in the staff's ability to provide necessary care to the patients. This did not raise a genuine issue of material fact because the "essence" of each institution was different. "Merck treats mentally retarded patients ranging from three to twenty-four years old whose developmental age is lower than their chronological age. Southwood's mission, in contrast, is to treat emotionally disturbed and sexually abused children and adolescents. Southwood's therapeutic mission depends on subtle interactions such as 'role modeling' rather than the more concrete behavior modification techniques practiced at Merck." Id. at 134.

10. Problems that the fetal-protection policy caused women in *Johnson Controls* may exist for African Americans. Suppose an employer barred black employees exhibiting sickle cell trait from certain assignments, claiming that sickle cell makes such blacks more vulnerable than whites to workplace hazards. The threshold question is whether this would constitute race discrimination. If so, the next issue is whether any defense is possible: the bfoq by its terms does not apply to race or color. Even were it judicially extended to race, would *Johnson Controls* allow the defense on these facts? Should the courts permit some racial differentiations? Can the FBI assign only white agents to infiltrate the Ku Klux Klan or only blacks to infiltrate the Black Panthers? Before you say yes, could a police department routinely assign black officers to black neighborhoods? See Patrolmen's Benevolent Assn. v. City of New York, 74 F. Supp. 2d 321 (S.D.N.Y. 1999) (suggesting that a police department's "operational needs" can be a compelling state interest under the Equal Protection Clause which might justify race-based decision making).

11. Title VII contains no BFOQ for race. The Seventh Circuit, however, adopted what amounts to a narrow, judicially crafted racial bfoq in Wittner v. Peters, 87 F.3d 916 (7th Cir. 1996), for a black lieutenant at a prison run like a boot camp. *Wittner* was an equal protection, not a Title VII, case. In Ferrill v. The Parker Group, Inc., 168 F.3d 468 (11th Cir. 1999), a § 1981 case, the Eleventh Circuit rejected a bfoq for racially segregating telemarketers aimed at getting out the vote for an election, with blacks calling blacks and whites calling whites. Given that Congress did not extend the bfoq defense to include race, does that mean courts should interpret § 1981 as not including a bfoq for race?

12. Is authenticity a compelling justification for a race bfoq in the entertainment industry? See Michael J. Frank, Justifiable Discrimination in the News and

Entertainment Industries: Does Title VII Need a Race or Color BFOQ?, 35 U.S.F. L. Rev. 473 (2001).

13. It has been argued that the existence of the bfoq defense to gender discrimination suggests that such discrimination is not generally to be equated with race discrimination. Granting such a conclusion, should courts be more permissive in accepting justifications for gender discrimination based on such factors as privacy and efficiency? See Mayer Freed & Daniel Polsby, Privacy, Efficiency, and the Equality of Men and Women: A Revisionist View of Sex Discrimination in Employment, 1981 Am. B. Found. Res. J. 583.

14. May a girls club discriminate against an unmarried pregnant employee? Before *Johnson Controls*, Chambers v. Omaha Girls Club, 834 F.2d 697 (8th Cir. 1987), *re-h'g denied*, 840 F.2d 583 (8th Cir. 1988), upheld a bfoq based on the need for a positive role model because the organization's major constituency was teen-age girls and one of that group's major concerns was unwed pregnancy. Three judges dissented, disapproving of the deference paid to an employer's subjective belief that an employee's unwed pregnancy rendered her unqualified for the position of arts and crafts teacher. Is the majority's result defendable after *Johnson Controls*?

15. Can personal privacy concerns of patients, clients, or inmates justify a bfoq defense? Justice White's concurrence feared the majority's opinion would do away with privacy bfoqs. The majority denied this. But how would a privacy-based policy be defended? See generally Deborah A. Calloway, Equal Employment and Third Party Privacy Interests: An Analytical Framework for Reconciling Competing Rights, 54 Fordham L. Rev. 327 (1985); Caroline S. Bratt, Privacy and the Sex BFOQ: An Immodest Proposal, 48 Alb. L. Rev. 923 (1984); Jillian B. Berman, Comment, Defining the "Essence of the Business": An Analysis of Title VII's Privacy BFOQ after *Johnson Controls*, 67 U. Chi. L. Rev. 749 (2000). The classic privacy example is the restroom attendant, although the problem may also arise in the context of prisons, hospitals, and nursing homes. The courts have been somewhat receptive to claims that members of one sex should be restricted from viewing unclothed members of the opposite sex or touching such persons, although the decisions have occasionally stressed that such concerns can be accommodated without infringing equal employment rights. See Fesel v. Masonic Home Inc., 447 F. Supp. 1346 (D. Del. 1978), *aff'd*, 591 F.2d 1334 (3d Cir. 1979), upholding limitations on male employment in a nursing home because of privacy concerns of female residents. That case, however, required the employer to also show that "it could not assign job responsibilities selectively in such a way that there would be minimal clash between the privacy interests of the customers and the nondiscrimination principle of Title VII." Id. at 1351. But see EEOC v. Sedita, 755 F. Supp. 808 (N.D. Ill. 1991) (insufficient proof to establish a women-only hiring rule as a bfoq, even though clients of the employer health club submitted a petition stating that it was an invasion of their privacy to have men working as instructors and the club owner also testified that members would quit the club).

In Robino v. Iranon, 145 F.3d 1109, 1109 (9th Cir. 1998), at issue was a rule, like the one in *Dothard*, that restricted some prison guard jobs to members of the same sex as the inmate:

> [W]e conclude that gender constitutes a BFOQ for the six [of 41] posts at issue here. . . .
> The plaintiffs further contend a BFOQ defense cannot be based on the privacy rights of
> the inmates and they correctly note that inmates' privacy rights are limited. . . . However, a person's interest in not being viewed unclothed by members of the opposite sex
> survives incarceration. . . . Whether or not the inmates could successfully assert their

own right to privacy is immaterial to this case. We are concerned here with a considered prison policy that takes into account security, rehabilitation, and morale. . . . The record amply supports the claimed BFOQ. WCCC adopted its current policy of assigning only female ACOs to posts that raise inmate privacy or safety concerns based on the serious allegations and the ensuing problems with morale among both the inmates and the ACOs. To comply with an EEOC settlement, it conducted an extensive survey of post duties before determining which posts should be designated female-only. Each designated female-only post is residential and requires the ACO on duty to observe the inmates in the showers and toilet areas for the prison's own security or provides unsupervised access to the inmates. The state's legitimate penological interests outweigh whatever interests the male ACOs may have in standing the watches of their choice.

See also Reed v. County of Casey, 184 F.3d 597 (6th Cir. 1999) (transfer of female guard to midnight shift was a bfoq when justified by need to supervise female prisoners and there were no satisfactory alternatives).

16. Whatever the correct view of privacy, it supports relatively narrow inroads into Title VII's proscriptions. It does, however, tend to merge into a problem that may have more general significance: when, if ever, is "customer preference" a basis for establishing a bfoq? The lower courts are divided on the question. EEOC v. Univ. of Texas Health Science Ctr., 710 F.2d 1091, 1095 (5th Cir. 1983), upheld as a bfoq an age-45 limitation on initial hiring of campus police in part because of testimony that "younger officers are better able to handle frequent confrontational episodes on campus because of their ability to relate to youthful offenders." By contrast, the Ninth Circuit rejected a bfoq claim in Fernandez v. Wynn Oil Co., 653 F.2d 1273 (9th Cir. 1981), where the defendant argued that the plaintiff could not be made vice-president of international operations because Latin American clients would react negatively to a woman in such a position. Although finding the defense not factually supported, the Ninth Circuit also held the defense inadequate as a matter of law because customer preference cannot justify gender discrimination. What does *Johnson Controls* suggest about this question? See also EEOC v. HI 40 Corp., Inc., 953 F. Supp. 301 (W.D. Mo. 1996) (being female was not a bfoq for counselors at weight loss centers, despite the centers' mostly female customers' preference for female counselors).

17. Religion as a bfoq has been rarely litigated, largely because those institutions most likely to use a religious test for employment are religious institutions that have a general exemption from Title VII's prohibition of discrimination on account of religion. See page 602. Note, however, that the use of a religious requirement by a secular company was upheld as a bfoq in Kern v. Dynalection Corp., 577 F. Supp. 1196 (N.D. Tex. 1983) (Saudi Arabian law forbidding non-Moslems from flying over certain holy areas justified Moslem faith as a bfoq for the position of helicopter pilot). Can *Kern* be extended? To the extent that Arab countries prohibit the employment of Jews, could an employer claim that not being a Jew is a bfoq? Or is that "racial" discrimination, not subject to bfoq analysis, if the prohibition includes both religious and non-religious Jews? For a discussion of when religion is viewed the same as race, see page 119.

## 3.  Voluntary Affirmative Action

In United Steelworkers of America v. Weber, 443 U.S. 193 (1979), a 5-2 majority upheld the employer's adoption and use of a voluntary affirmative action plan negotiated with the union representing its workers to create a training program for incumbent unskilled workers to fill skilled job categories. Until this plan was adopted, craft positions were filled by people with craft experience, typically learned in craft unions that historically excluded blacks from membership. Those unions did not represent the employer's workers. In order to resolve this problem, the plan reserved for black employees 50 percent of the openings in these newly created in-plant training programs until the percentage of black skilled craftworkers approximated the percentage of blacks in the local labor force.

After holding that Title VII's prohibition against racial discrimination does not condemn all private, voluntary, race-conscious affirmative action plans, the Court upheld the particular plan in the instant case.

> We need not today define in detail the line of demarcation between permissible and impermissible affirmative action plans. It suffices to hold that the challenged Kaiser-USWA affirmative action plan falls on the permissible side of the line. The purposes of the plan mirror those of the statute. Both were designed to break down old patterns of racial segregation and hierarchy. Both were structured to "open unemployment opportunities for Negroes in occupations which have been traditionally closed to them."
>
> At the same time, the plan does not unnecessarily trammel the interests of the white employees. The plan does not require the discharge of white workers and their replacement with new black hires. . . . Nor does the plan create an absolute bar to the advancement of white employees; half of those trained in the program will be white. Moreover, the plan is a temporary measure; it is not intended to maintain racial balance, but simply to eliminate a manifest racial imbalance.

Id. at 208.

Justice Rehnquist, joined by then-Chief Justice Burger, dissented.

> The operative sections of Title VII prohibit racial discrimination in employment *simpliciter*. Taken in its normal meaning, and as understood by all Members of Congress who spoke to the issue during the legislative debates, this language prohibits a covered employer from considering race when making an employment decision, whether the race be black or white. . . . We have never wavered in our understanding that Title VII "prohibits all racial discrimination in employment, without exception for any group of particular employees." . . .
>
> Thus, by a tour de force reminiscent not of jurists such as Hale, Holmes, and Hughes, but of escape artists such as Houdini, the Court eludes clear statutory language, "uncontradicted" legislative history, and uniform precedent in concluding that employers are, after all, permitted to consider race in making employment decisions.

Id. at 220-22.

## JOHNSON v. TRANSPORTATION AGENCY OF SANTA CLARA COUNTY
### 480 U.S. 616 (1987)

Justice BRENNAN delivered the opinion of the Court.

Respondent, Transportation Agency of Santa Clara County, California, unilaterally promulgated an Affirmative Action Plan applicable, inter alia, to promotions of employees. In selecting applicants for the promotional position of road dispatcher, the Agency, pursuant to the Plan, passed over petitioner Paul Johnson, a male employee, and promoted a female employee applicant, Diane Joyce. The question for decision is whether in making the promotion the Agency impermissibly took into account the sex of the applicants in violation of Title VII of the Civil Rights Act of 1964. . . .[2]

I

A

In December 1978, the Santa Clara County Transit District Board of Supervisors adopted an Affirmative Action Plan (Plan) for the County Transportation Agency. The Plan implemented a County Affirmative Action Plan, which had been adopted, declared the County, because "mere prohibition of discriminatory practices is not enough to remedy the effects of past practices and to permit attainment of an equitable representation of minorities, women and handicapped persons." Relevant to this case, the Agency Plan provides that, in making promotions to positions within a traditionally segregated job classification in which women have been significantly underrepresented, the Agency is authorized to consider as one factor the sex of a qualified applicant.

In reviewing the composition of its work force, the Agency noted in its Plan that women were represented in numbers far less than their proportion of the County labor force in both the Agency as a whole and in five of seven job categories. Specifically, while women constituted 36.4% of the area labor market, they composed only 22.4% of Agency employees. Furthermore, women working at the Agency were concentrated largely in EEOC job categories traditionally held by women: women made up 76% of Office and Clerical Workers, but only 7.1% of Agency Officials and Administrators, 8.6% of Professionals, 9.7% of Technicians, and 22% of Service and Maintenance Workers. As for the job classification relevant to this case, none of the 238 Skilled Craft Worker positions was held by a woman. The Plan noted that this underrepresentation of women in part reflected the fact that women had not traditionally been employed in these positions, and that they had not been strongly motivated to seek training or employment in them "because of the limited opportunities that have existed in the past for them to work in such classifications." . . .

The Agency stated that its Plan was intended to achieve "a statistically measurable yearly improvement in hiring, training and promotion of minorities and women throughout the Agency in all major job classifications where they are under-represented." As a benchmark by which to evaluate progress, the Agency stated that its long-term goal was to attain a work force whose composition reflected the proportion of minorities and women in the area labor force. Thus, for the Skilled Craft category in which the road dispatcher position at issue here was classified, the Agency's aspiration was that eventually about 36% of the jobs would be occupied by women.

The Plan acknowledged that a number of factors might make it unrealistic to rely on the Agency's long-term goals in evaluating the Agency's progress in expanding job opportunities for minorities and women. Among the factors identified were low turnover rates in some classifications, the fact that some jobs involved heavy labor, the small number of positions within some job categories, the limited number of entry positions leading to the Technical and Skilled Craft classifications, and the limited

2. No constitutional issue was either raised or addressed in the litigation below. We therefore decide in this case only the issue of the prohibitory scope of Title VII. Of course, where the issue is properly raised, public employers must justify the adoption and implementation of a voluntary affirmative action plan under the Equal Protection Clause. See Wygant v. Jackson Board of Education, 476 U.S. 267 (1986).

number of minorities and women qualified for positions requiring specialized training and experience. As a result, the Plan counseled that short-range goals be established and annually adjusted to serve as the most realistic guide for actual employment decisions. . . .

The Agency's Plan thus set aside no specific number of positions for minorities or women, but authorized the consideration of ethnicity or sex as a factor when evaluating qualified candidates for jobs in which members of such groups were poorly represented. One such job was the road dispatcher position that is the subject of the dispute in this case.

B

[In 1979, the Agency announced a vacancy for dispatcher in the Roads Division. Dispatchers assign road crews, equipment, and materials and maintain records. The position required a minimum of four years' experience with Santa Clara County. Twelve county employees applied, including Joyce and Johnson.] Joyce had worked for the County since 1970, serving as an account clerk until 1975. She had applied for a road dispatcher position in 1974, but was deemed ineligible because she had not served as a road maintenance worker. In 1975, Joyce transferred from a senior account clerk position to a road maintenance worker position, becoming the first woman to fill such a job. During her four years in that position, she occasionally worked out of class as a road dispatcher.

Petitioner Johnson began with the County in 1967 as a road yard clerk, after private employment that included working as a supervisor and dispatcher. He had also unsuccessfully applied for the road dispatcher opening in 1974. In 1977, his clerical position was downgraded, and he sought and received a transfer to the position of road maintenance worker. He also occasionally worked out of class as a dispatcher while performing that job.

Nine of the applicants, including Joyce and Johnson, were deemed qualified for the job, and were interviewed by a two-person board. Seven of the applicants scored above 70 on this interview, which meant that they were certified as eligible for selection by the appointing authority. The scores awarded ranged from 70 to 80. Johnson was tied for second with a score of 75, while Joyce ranked next with a score of 73. A second interview was conducted by three Agency supervisors, who ultimately recommended that Johnson be promoted. Prior to the second interview, Joyce had contacted the County's Affirmative Action Office because she feared that her application might not receive disinterested review.[5] The Office in turn contacted the Agency's Affirmative Action Coordinator, whom the Agency's Plan makes responsible for, inter alia, keeping the Director informed of opportunities for the Agency to accomplish its objectives

---

5. Joyce testified that she had had disagreements with two of the three members of the second interview panel. One had been her first supervisor when she began work as a road maintenance worker. In performing arduous work in this job, she had not been issued coveralls, although her male co-workers had received them. After ruining her pants, she complained to her supervisor, to no avail. After three other similar incidents, ruining clothes on each occasion, she filed a grievance, and was issued four pairs of coveralls the next day. Joyce had dealt with a second member of the panel for a year and a half in her capacity as chair of the Roads Operations Safety Committee, where she and he "had several differences of opinion on how safety should be implemented." In addition, Joyce testified that she had informed the person responsible for arranging her second interview that she had a disaster preparedness class on a certain day the following week. By this time about 10 days had passed since she had notified this person of her availability, and no date had yet been set for the interview. Within a day or two after this conversation, however, she received a notice setting her interview at a time directly in the middle of her disaster preparedness class. This same panel member had earlier described Joyce as a "rebel-rousing, skirt-wearing person."

under the Plan. At the time, the Agency employed no women in any Skilled Craft position, and had never employed a woman as a road dispatcher. The Coordinator recommended to the Director of the Agency, James Graebner, that Joyce be promoted.

Graebner, authorized to choose any of the seven persons deemed eligible, thus had the benefit of suggestions by the second interview panel and by the Agency Coordinator in arriving at his decision. After deliberation, Graebner concluded that the promotion should be given to Joyce. As he testified: "I tried to look at the whole picture, the combination of her qualifications and Mr. Johnson's qualifications, their test scores, their expertise, their background, affirmative action matters, things like that. . . . I believe it was a combination of all those."

The certification for naming Joyce as the person promoted to the dispatcher position stated that both she and Johnson were rated as well qualified for the job. The evaluation of Joyce read: "Well qualified by virtue of 18 years of past clerical experience including 3½ years at West Yard plus almost 5 years as a [road maintenance worker]." The evaluation of Johnson was as follows: "Well qualified applicant; two years of [road maintenance worker] experience plus 11 years of Road Yard Clerk. Has had previous outside Dispatch experience but was 13 years ago." Graebner testified that he did not regard as significant the fact that Johnson scored 75 and Joyce 73. . . .

. . . The District Court found that Johnson was more qualified for the dispatcher position than Joyce, and that the sex of Joyce was the *"determining factor* in her selection." The court acknowledged that, since the Agency justified its decision on the basis of its Affirmative Action Plan, the criteria announced in *Steelworkers v. Weber* should be applied in evaluating the validity of the Plan. It then found the Agency's Plan invalid on the ground that the evidence did not satisfy *Weber's* criterion that the Plan be temporary. . . .

## II

As a preliminary matter, we note that petitioner bears the burden of establishing the invalidity of the Agency's Plan. Only last Term, in Wygant v. Jackson Board of Education, 476 U.S. 267 (1986), we held that "[the] ultimate burden remains with the employees to demonstrate the unconstitutionality of an affirmative-action program," and we see no basis for a different rule regarding a plan's alleged violation of Title VII. This case also fits readily within the analytical framework set forth in McDonnell Douglas Corp. v. Green. Once a plaintiff establishes a prima facie case that race or sex has been taken into account in an employer's employment decision, the burden shifts to the employer to articulate a nondiscriminatory rationale for its decision. The existence of an affirmative action plan provides such a rationale. If such a plan is articulated as the basis for the employer's decision, the burden shifts to the plaintiff to prove that the employer's justification is pretextual and the plan is invalid. As a practical matter, of course, an employer will generally seek to avoid a charge of pretext by presenting evidence in support of its plan. That does not mean, however, as petitioner suggests, that reliance on an affirmative action plan is to be treated as an affirmative defense requiring the employer to carry the burden of proving the validity of the plan. The burden of proving its invalidity remains on the plaintiff.

The assessment of the legality of the Agency Plan must be guided by our decision in *Weber*.[6] In that case, the Court addressed the question whether the employer

6. Justice Scalia's dissent maintains that the obligations of a public employer under Title VII must be identical to its obligations under the Constitution, and that a public employer's adoption of an affirmative action plan therefore should be governed by *Wygant*. This rests on the following logic: Title VI embodies

violated Title VII by adopting a voluntary affirmative action plan designed to "eliminate manifest racial imbalances in traditionally segregated job categories." The respondent employee in that case challenged the employer's denial of his application
for a position in a newly established craft training program, contending that the employer's selection process impermissibly took into account the race of the applicants.
The selection process was guided by an affirmative action plan, which provided that
50% of the new trainees were to be black until the percentage of black skilled craftworkers in the employer's plant approximated the percentage of blacks in the local labor force. Adoption of the plan had been prompted by the fact that only 5 of 273, or
1.83%, of skilled craftworkers at the plant were black, even though the work force in
the area was approximately 39% black. Because of the historical exclusion of blacks
from craft positions, the employer regarded its former policy of hiring trained outsiders as inadequate to redress the imbalance in its work force.

We upheld the employer's decision to select less senior black applicants over the
white respondent, for we found that taking race into account was consistent with
Title VII's objective of "[breaking] down old patterns of racial segregation and hierarchy." As we stated:

> It would be ironic indeed if a law triggered by a Nation's concern over centuries of
> racial injustice and intended to improve the lot of those who had "been excluded from
> the American dream for so long" constituted the first legislative prohibition of all volun-
> tary, private, race-conscious efforts to abolish traditional patterns of racial segregation
> and hierarchy.[7]

We noted that the plan did not "unnecessarily trammel the interests of the white
employees," since it did not require "the discharge of white workers and their replacement with new black hires." Nor did the plan create "an absolute bar to the advancement of white employees," since half of those trained in the new program were
to be white. Finally, we observed that the plan was a temporary measure, not designed

---

the same constraints as the Constitution; Title VI and Title VII have the same prohibitory scope; therefore, Title VII and the Constitution are coterminous for purposes of this case. The flaw is with the second
step of analysis, for it advances a proposition that we explicitly considered and rejected in *Weber*. As we
noted in that case, Title VI was an exercise of federal power "over a matter in which the Federal Government was already directly involved," since Congress "was legislating to assure federal funds would not be
used in an improper manner." "Title VII, by contrast, was enacted pursuant to the commerce power to
regulate purely private decisionmaking and was not intended to incorporate and particularize the commands of the Fifth and Fourteenth Amendments. Title VII and Title VI, therefore, cannot be read in pari
materia." . . .

7. Justice Scalia's dissent maintains that *Weber*'s conclusion that Title VII does not prohibit voluntary
affirmative action programs "rewrote the statute it purported to construe." *Weber*'s decisive rejection of
the argument that the "plain language" of the statute prohibits affirmative action rested on (1) legislative
history indicating Congress' clear intention that employers play a major role in eliminating the vestiges of
discrimination, and (2) the language and legislative history of § 703(j) of the statute, which reflect a
strong desire to preserve managerial prerogatives so that they might be utilized for this purpose. As Justice
Blackmun said in his concurrence in *Weber*, "[I]f the Court has misperceived the political will, it has the
assurance that because the question is statutory Congress may set a different course if it so chooses." Congress has not amended the statute to reject our construction, nor have any such amendments even been
proposed, and we therefore may assume that our interpretation was correct.

Justice Scalia's dissent faults the fact that we take note of the absence of congressional efforts to amend
the statute to nullify *Weber*. It suggests that congressional inaction cannot be regarded as acquiescence
under all circumstances, but then draws from that unexceptional point the conclusion that any reliance
on congressional failure to act is necessarily a "canard." The fact that inaction may not always provide
crystalline revelation, however, should not obscure the fact that it may be probative to varying degrees.
*Weber*, for instance, was a widely publicized decision that addressed a prominent issue of public debate.
Legislative inattention thus is not a plausible explanation for congressional inaction. . . .

to maintain racial balance, but to "eliminate a manifest racial imbalance." As Justice Blackmun's concurrence made clear, *Weber* held that an employer seeking to justify the adoption of a plan need not point to its own prior discriminatory practices, nor even to evidence of an "arguable violation" on its part. Rather, it need point only to a "conspicuous . . . imbalance in traditionally segregated job categories." Our decision was grounded in the recognition that voluntary employer action can play a crucial role in furthering Title VII's purpose of eliminating the effects of discrimination in the workplace, and that Title VII should not be read to thwart such efforts.[8]

. . . The first issue is therefore whether consideration of the sex of applicants for Skilled Craft jobs was justified by the existence of a "manifest imbalance" that reflected underrepresentation of women in "traditionally segregated job categories." In determining whether an imbalance exists that would justify taking sex or race into account, a comparison of the percentage of minorities or women in the employer's work force with the percentage in the area labor market or general population is appropriate in analyzing jobs that require no special expertise, [citing *Teamsters* and *Weber*]. Where a job requires special training, however, the comparison should be with those in the labor force who possess the relevant qualifications. See *Hazelwood* (must compare percentage of blacks in employer's work ranks with percentage of qualified black teachers in area labor force in determining underrepresentation in teaching positions). The requirement that the "manifest imbalance" relate to a "traditionally segregated job category" provides assurance both that sex or race will be taken into account in a manner consistent with Title VII's purpose of eliminating the effects of employment discrimination, and that the interests of those employees not benefiting from the plan will not be unduly infringed.

A manifest imbalance need not be such that it would support a prima facie case against the employer, as suggested in Justice O'Connor's concurrence, since we do not regard as identical the constraints of Title VII and the Federal Constitution on voluntarily adopted affirmative action plans. Application of the "prima facie" standard in Title VII cases would be inconsistent with *Weber*'s focus on statistical imbalance,[10] and could inappropriately create a significant disincentive for employers to adopt an affirmative action plan. See *Weber* (Title VII intended as a "catalyst" for

----

8. Justice Scalia's suggestion that an affirmative action program may be adopted only to redress an employer's past discrimination was rejected in Steelworkers v. Weber because the prospect of liability created by such an admission would create a significant disincentive for voluntary action. As Justice Blackmun's concurrence in that case pointed out, such a standard would "[place] voluntary compliance with Title VII in profound jeopardy. The only way for the employer and the union to keep their footing on the 'tightrope' it creates would be to eschew all forms of voluntary affirmative action." . . .

10. The difference between the "manifest imbalance" and "prima facie" standards is illuminated by *Weber*. Had the Court in that case been concerned with past discrimination by the employer, it would have focused on discrimination in hiring skilled, not unskilled, workers, since only the scarcity of the former in Kaiser's work force would have made it vulnerable to a Title VII suit. In order to make out a prima facie case on such a claim, a plaintiff would be required to compare the percentage of black skilled workers in the Kaiser work force with the percentage of black skilled craft workers in the area labor market.

*Weber* obviously did not make such a comparison. Instead, it focused on the disparity between the percentage of black skilled craft workers in Kaiser's ranks and the percentage of blacks in the area labor force. Such an approach reflected a recognition that the proportion of black craft workers in the local labor force was likely as miniscule as the proportion in Kaiser's work force. The Court realized that the lack of imbalance between these figures would mean that employers in precisely those industries in which discrimination has been most effective would be precluded from adopting training programs to increase the percentage of qualified minorities. Thus, in cases such as *Weber*, where the employment decision at issue involves the selection of unskilled persons for a training program, the "manifest imbalance" standard permits comparison with the general labor force. By contrast, the "prima facie" standard would require comparison with the percentage of minorities or women qualified for the job for which the trainees are being trained, a standard that would have invalidated the plan in *Weber* itself.

employer efforts to eliminate vestiges of discrimination). A corporation concerned with maximizing return on investment, for instance, is hardly likely to adopt a plan if in order to do so it must compile evidence that could be used to subject it to a colorable Title VII suit.[11]

It is clear that the decision to hire Joyce was made pursuant to an Agency Plan that directed that sex or race be taken into account for the purpose of remedying underrepresentation. . . .

As an initial matter, the Agency adopted as a benchmark for measuring progress in eliminating underrepresentation the long-term goal of a work force that mirrored in its major job classifications the percentage of women in the area labor market.[13] Even as it did so, however, the Agency acknowledged that such a figure could not by itself necessarily justify taking into account the sex of applicants for positions in all job categories. For positions requiring specialized training and experience, the Plan observed that the number of minorities and women "who possess the qualifications required for entry into such job classifications is limited." The Plan therefore directed that annual short-term goals be formulated that would provide a more realistic indication of the degree to which sex should be taken into account in filling particular positions. The Plan stressed that such goals "should not be construed as 'quotas' that must be met," but as reasonable aspirations in correcting the imbalance in the Agency's work force. . . . From the outset, therefore, the Plan sought annually to develop even more refined measures of the underrepresentation in each job category that required attention.

[When Joyce was selected for the road dispatcher position, the Agency was still in the process of refining its short-term goals for Skilled Craft Workers in accordance with the Plan.]

We reject petitioner's argument that, since only the long-term goal was in place for Skilled Craft positions at the time of Joyce's promotion, it was inappropriate for the Director to take into account affirmative action considerations in filling the road dispatcher position. The Agency's Plan emphasized that the long-term goals were not to be taken as guides for actual hiring decisions, but that supervisors were to consider a host of practical factors in seeking to meet affirmative action objectives, including the fact that in some job categories women were not qualified in numbers comparable to their representation in the labor force.

By contrast, had the Plan simply calculated imbalances in all categories according to the proportion of women in the area labor pool, and then directed that hiring be governed solely by those figures, its validity fairly could be called into question. This is because analysis of a more specialized labor pool normally is necessary in determining underrepresentation in some positions. If a plan failed to take distinctions in qualifications into account in providing guidance for actual employment decisions, it would dictate mere blind hiring by the numbers. . . .

The Agency's Plan emphatically did *not* authorize such blind hiring. It expressly directed that numerous factors be taken into account in making hiring decisions,

---

11. In some cases, of course, the manifest imbalance may be sufficiently egregious to establish a prima facie case. However, as long as there is a manifest imbalance, an employer may adopt a plan even where the disparity is not so striking, without being required to introduce the nonstatistical evidence of past discrimination that would be demanded by the "prima facie" standard. See, e.g., *Teamsters* (statistics in pattern and practice case supplemented by testimony regarding employment practices). Of course, when there is sufficient evidence to meet the more stringent "prima facie" standard, be it statistical, nonstatistical, or a combination of the two, the employer is free to adopt an affirmative action plan.

13. Because of the employment decision at issue in this case, our discussion henceforth refers primarily to the Plan's provisions to remedy the underrepresentation of women. Our analysis could apply as well, however, to the provisions of the Plan pertaining to minorities.

including specifically the qualifications of female applicants for particular jobs. Thus, despite the fact that no precise short-term goal was yet in place for the Skilled Craft category in mid-1980, the Agency's management nevertheless had been clearly instructed that they were not to hire solely by reference to statistics. The fact that only the long-term goal had been established for this category posed no danger that personnel decisions would be made by reflexive adherence to a numerical standard.

Furthermore, in considering the candidates for the road dispatcher position in 1980, the Agency hardly needed to rely on a refined short-term goal to realize that it had a significant problem of underrepresentation that required attention. Given the obvious imbalance in the Skilled Craft category, and given the Agency's commitment to eliminating such imbalances, it was plainly not unreasonable for the Agency to determine that it was appropriate to consider as one factor the sex of Ms. Joyce in making its decision.[14] The promotion of Joyce thus satisfies the first requirement enunciated in *Weber*, since it was undertaken to further an affirmative action plan designed to eliminate Agency work force imbalances in traditionally segregated job categories.

We next consider whether the Agency Plan unnecessarily trammeled the rights of male employees or created an absolute bar to their advancement. In contrast to the plan in *Weber*, which provided that 50% of the positions in the craft training program were exclusively for blacks . . . , the Plan sets aside no positions for women. The Plan expressly states that "[the] 'goals' established for each Division should not be construed as 'quotas' that must be met." Rather, the Plan merely authorizes that consideration be given to affirmative action concerns when evaluating qualified applicants. As the Agency Director testified, the sex of Joyce was but one of numerous factors he took into account in arriving at his decision. The Plan thus resembles the "Harvard Plan" approvingly noted by Justice Powell in Regents of University of California v. Bakke, 438 U.S. 265, 316-319 (1978), which considers race along with other criteria in determining admission to the college. As Justice Powell observed: "In such an admissions program, race or ethnic background may be deemed a 'plus' in a particular applicant's file, yet it does not insulate the individual from comparison with all other candidates for the available seats." Similarly, the Agency Plan requires women to compete with all other qualified applicants. No persons are automatically excluded from consideration; all are able to have their qualifications weighed against those of other applicants.

In addition, petitioner had no absolute entitlement to the road dispatcher position. Seven of the applicants were classified as qualified and eligible, and the Agency Director was authorized to promote any of the seven. Thus, denial of the promotion unsettled no legitimate, firmly rooted expectation on the part of petitioner. Furthermore, while petitioner in this case was denied a promotion, he retained his employment with the Agency, at the same salary and with the same seniority, and remained eligible for other promotions.

[Finally, the Plan was intended to *attain* a balanced work force, not to maintain one. The absence of an explicit end date is not surprising because the Agency's approach was not expected to be successful immediately.] Express assurance that a program is only temporary may be necessary if the program actually sets aside positions according to specific numbers. This is necessary both to minimize the effect of the

14. In addition, the Agency was mindful of the importance of finally hiring a woman in a job category that had formerly been all male. The Director testified that, while the promotion of Joyce "made a small dent, for sure, in the numbers," nonetheless "philosophically it made a larger impact in that it probably has encouraged other females and minorities to look at the possibility of so-called 'non-traditional' jobs as areas where they and the agency both have samples of a success story."

program on other employees, and to ensure that the plan's goals "[are] not being used simply to achieve and maintain . . . balance, but rather as a benchmark against which" the employer may measure its progress in eliminating the underrepresentation of minorities and women. In this case, however, substantial evidence shows that the Agency has sought to take a moderate, gradual approach to eliminating the imbalance in its work force, one which establishes realistic guidance for employment decisions, and which visits minimal intrusion on the legitimate expectations of other employees. Given this fact, as well as the Agency's express commitment to "attain" a balanced work force, there is ample assurance that the Agency does not seek to use its Plan to maintain a permanent racial and sexual balance.

## III

. . . The Agency in the case before us has undertaken such a voluntary effort, and has done so in full recognition of both the difficulties and the potential for intrusion on males and nonminorities. The Agency has identified a conspicuous imbalance in job categories traditionally segregated by race and sex. It has made clear from the outset, however, that employment decisions may not be justified solely by reference to this imbalance, but must rest on a multitude of practical, realistic factors. It has therefore committed itself to annual adjustment of goals so as to provide a reasonable guide for actual hiring and promotion decisions. The Agency earmarks no positions for anyone; sex is but one of several factors that may be taken into account in evaluating qualified applicants for a position.[17] As both the Plan's language and its manner of operation attest, the Agency has no intention of establishing a work force whose permanent composition is dictated by rigid numerical standards.

We therefore hold that the Agency appropriately took into account as one factor the sex of Diane Joyce in determining that she should be promoted to the road dispatcher position. Accordingly, the judgment of the Court of Appeals is Affirmed.

[Justice STEVENS concurred, essentially on the grounds of stare decisis. In light of "the authoritative construction" of *Bakke* and *Weber*, he was compelled to accept this view even if he thought it "at odds with [his] understanding of the actual intent of the authors of the legislation."]

Justice O'CONNOR, concurring in the judgment. . . .

In my view, the proper initial inquiry in evaluating the legality of an affirmative action plan by a public employer under Title VII is no different from that required by

---

17. Justice Scalia's dissent predicts that today's decision will loose a flood of "less qualified" minorities and women upon the work force, as employers seek to forestall possible Title VII liability. . . .
A . . . more fundamental problem with Justice Scalia's speculation is that he ignores the fact that

[i]t is a standard tenet of personnel administration that there is rarely a single, "best qualified" person for a job. An effective personnel system will bring before the selecting official several fully-qualified candidates who each may possess different attributes which recommend them for selection. Especially where the job is an unexceptional, middle-level craft position, without the need for unique work experience or educational attainment and for which several well-qualified candidates are available, final determinations as to which candidate is "best qualified" are at best subjective.

Brief for the American Society for Personnel Administration as *Amicus Curiae* 9.
This case provides an example of precisely this point. Any differences in qualifications between Johnson and Joyce were minimal, to say the least. The selection of Joyce thus belies Justice Scalia's contention that the beneficiaries of affirmative action programs will be those employees who are merely not "utterly unqualified."

the Equal Protection Clause. In either case, consistent with the congressional intent to provide some measure of protection to the interests of the employer's nonminority employees, the employer must have had a firm basis for believing that remedial action was required. An employer would have such a firm basis if it can point to a statistical disparity sufficient to support a prima facie claim under Title VII by the employee beneficiaries of the affirmative action plan of a pattern or practice claim of discrimination.

In *Weber*, this Court balanced two conflicting concerns in construing §703(d): Congress' intent to root out invidious discrimination against any person on the basis of race or gender, and its goal of eliminating the lasting effects of discrimination against minorities. Given these conflicting concerns, the Court concluded that it would be inconsistent with the background and purpose of Title VII to prohibit affirmative action in all cases. As I read *Weber*, however, the Court also determined that Congress had balanced these two competing concerns by permitting affirmative action only as a remedial device to eliminate actual or apparent discrimination or the lingering effects of this discrimination. . . .

[I]n *Weber* the Court was careful to consider the effects of the affirmative action plan for black employees on the employment opportunities of white employees. Instead of a wholly standardless approach to affirmative action, the Court determined in *Weber* that Congress intended to permit affirmative action only if the employer could point to a "manifest . . . [imbalance] in traditionally segregated job categories." This requirement both "provides assurance . . . that sex or race will be taken into account in a manner consistent with Title VII's purpose of eliminating the effects of employment discrimination," and is consistent with this Court's and Congress' consistent emphasis on the value of voluntary efforts to further the antidiscrimination purposes of Title VII.

The *Weber* view of Congress' resolution of the conflicting concerns of minority and nonminority workers in Title VII appears substantially similar to this Court's resolution of these same concerns in *Wygant* which involved the claim that an affirmative action plan by a public employer violated the Equal Protection Clause. In *Wygant*, the Court was in agreement that remedying past or present racial discrimination by a state actor is a sufficiently weighty interest to warrant the remedial use of a carefully constructed affirmative action plan. The Court also concluded, however, that "[societal] discrimination, without more, is too amorphous a basis for imposing a racially classified remedy." Instead, we determined that affirmative action was valid if it was crafted to remedy past or present discrimination by the employer. Although the employer need not point to any contemporaneous findings of actual discrimination, I concluded in *Wygant* that the employer must point to evidence sufficient to establish a firm basis for believing that remedial action is required, and that a statistical imbalance sufficient for a Title VII prima facie case against the employer would satisfy this firm basis requirement. . . .

The *Wygant* analysis is entirely consistent with *Weber*. In *Weber*, the affirmative action plan involved a training program for unskilled production workers. There was little doubt that the absence of black craftworkers was the result of the exclusion of blacks from craft unions. *Weber* ("Judicial findings of exclusion from crafts on racial grounds are so numerous as to make such exclusion a proper subject for judicial notice"). The employer in *Weber* had previously hired as craftworkers only persons with prior craft experience, and craft unions provided the sole avenue for obtaining this experience. Because the discrimination occurred at entry into the craft union, the "manifest racial imbalance" was powerful evidence of prior race discrimination.

Under our case law, the relevant comparison for a Title VII prima facie case in those circumstances — discrimination in admission to entry-level positions such as membership in craft unions — is to the total percentage of blacks in the labor force. See *Teamsters*, cf. *Sheet Metal Workers* (observing that lower courts had relied on comparison to general labor force in finding Title VII violation by union). Here, however, the evidence of past discrimination is more complex. The number of women with the qualifications for entry into the relevant job classification was quite small. A statistical imbalance between the percentage of women in the work force generally and the percentage of women in the particular specialized job classification, therefore, does not suggest past discrimination for purposes of proving a Title VII prima facie case.

Unfortunately, the Court today gives little guidance for what statistical imbalance is sufficient to support an affirmative action plan. Although the Court denies that the statistical imbalance need be sufficient to make out a prima facie case of discrimination against women, the Court fails to suggest an alternative standard. Because both *Wygant* and *Weber* attempt to reconcile the same competing concerns, I see little justification for the adoption of different standards for affirmative action under Title VII and the Equal Protection Clause.

While employers must have a firm basis for concluding that remedial action is necessary, neither *Wygant* nor *Weber* places a burden on employers to prove that they actually discriminated against women or minorities. Employers are "trapped between the competing hazards of liability to minorities if affirmative action is not taken to remedy apparent employment discrimination and liability to nonminorities if affirmative action is taken." *Wygant* (O'Connor, J., concurring in part and concurring in judgment). Moreover, this Court has long emphasized the importance of voluntary efforts to eliminate discrimination. Thus, I concluded in *Wygant* that a contemporaneous finding of discrimination should not be required because it would discourage voluntary efforts to remedy apparent discrimination. A requirement that an employer actually prove that it had discriminated in the past would also unduly discourage voluntary efforts to remedy apparent discrimination. As I emphasized in *Wygant*, a challenge to an affirmative action plan "does not automatically impose upon the public employer the burden of convincing the court of its liability for prior unlawful discrimination; nor does it mean that the court must make an actual finding of prior discrimination based on the employer's proof before the employer's affirmative action plan will be upheld." Evidence sufficient for a prima facie Title VII pattern or practice claim against the employer itself suggests that the absence of women or minorities in a work force cannot be explained by general societal discrimination alone and that remedial action is appropriate. . . .

The long-term goal of the plan was "to attain a work force whose composition in all job levels and major job classifications approximates the distribution of women . . . in the Santa Clara County work force." If this long-term goal had been applied to the hiring decisions made by the Agency, in my view, the affirmative action plan would violate Title VII. "[I]t is completely unrealistic to assume that individuals of each [sex] will gravitate with mathematical exactitude to each employer . . . absent unlawful discrimination." *Sheet Metal Workers* (O'Connor, J., concurring in part and dissenting in part). Thus, a goal that makes such an assumption, and simplistically focuses on the proportion of women and minorities in the work force without more, is not remedial. Only a goal that takes into account the number of women and minorities qualified for the relevant position could satisfy the requirement that an affirmative action plan be remedial. This long-range goal, however, was never used as a guide for actual hiring decisions. Instead, the goal was merely a statement of aspiration wholly without operational significance. The affirmative action plan itself recognized the host of reasons why this goal was extremely unrealistic and as I read the record, the long-term goal was not applied in the promotion decision challenged in this case. Instead, the plan provided for the development of short-term goals, which alone were to guide the respondents, and the plan cautioned that even these goals "should not be construed as 'quotas' that must be met." . . .

At the time of the promotion at issue in this case, the short-term goals had not been fully developed. Nevertheless, the Agency had already recognized that the long-range goal was unrealistic, and had determined that the progress of the Agency should be judged by a comparison to the qualified women in the area work force. As I view the record, the promotion decision in this case was entirely consistent with the philosophy underlying the development of the short-term goals. . . .

The ultimate decision to promote Joyce rather than petitioner was made by James Graebner, the Director of the Agency. As Justice Scalia views the record in this case, the Agency Director made the decision to promote Joyce rather than petitioner solely on the basis of sex and with indifference to the relative merits of the two applicants. In my view, however, the record simply fails to substantiate the picture painted by Justice Scalia. The Agency Director testified that he "tried to look at the whole picture, the combination of [Joyce's] qualifications and Mr. Johnson's qualifications, their test scores, their experience, their background, affirmative action matters, things like that." Contrary to Justice Scalia's suggestion, the Agency Director knew far more than merely the sex of the candidates and that they appeared on a list of candidates eligible for the job. The Director had spoken to individuals familiar with the qualifications of both applicants for the promotion, and was aware that their scores were rather close. Moreover, he testified that over a period of weeks he had spent several hours making the promotion decision, suggesting that Joyce was not selected solely on the basis of her sex. Additionally, the Director stated that had Joyce's experience been less than that of petitioner by a larger margin, petitioner might have received the promotion. As the Director summarized his decision to promote Joyce, the underrepresentation of women in skilled craft positions was only one element of a number of considerations that led to the promotion of Ms. Joyce. While I agree with Justice Scalia's dissent that an affirmative action program that automatically and blindly promotes those marginally qualified candidates falling within a preferred race or gender category, or that can be equated with a permanent plan of "proportionate representation by race and sex," would violate Title VII, I cannot agree that this is such a case. Rather, as the Court demonstrates, Joyce's sex was simply used as a "plus" factor.

Justice SCALIA, with whom The Chief Justice joins, and with whom Justice WHITE joins in Parts I and II, dissenting.

. . . The Court today completes the process of converting [Title VII] from a guarantee that race or sex will not be the basis for employment determinations, to a guarantee that it often will. Ever so subtly, without even alluding to the last obstacles preserved by earlier opinions that we now push out of our path, we effectively replace the goal of a discrimination-free society with the quite incompatible goal of proportionate representation by race and by sex in the workplace.

I . . .

Several salient features of the plan should be noted. Most importantly, the plan's purpose was assuredly not to remedy prior sex discrimination by the Agency. It could not have been, because there was no prior sex discrimination to remedy. The majority, in cataloging the Agency's alleged misdeeds, neglects to mention the District Court's finding that the Agency "has not discriminated in the past, and does not discriminate in the present against women in regard to employment opportunities in general and promotions in particular." This finding was not disturbed by the Ninth Circuit.

Not only was the plan not directed at the results of past sex discrimination by the Agency, but its objective was not to achieve the state of affairs that this Court has dubiously assumed would result from an absence of discrimination — an overall work force "more or less representative of the racial and ethnic composition of the population in the community." *Teamsters.* Rather, the oft-stated goal was to mirror the racial and sexual composition of the entire county labor force, not merely in the Agency work force as a whole, but in each and every individual job category at the Agency. In a discrimination-free world, it would obviously be a statistical oddity for every job category to match the racial and sexual composition of even that portion of the county work force qualified for that job; it would be utterly miraculous for each of them to match, as the plan expected, the composition of the entire work force. Quite obviously, the plan did not seek to replicate what a lack of discrimination would produce, but rather imposed racial and sexual tailoring that would, in defiance of normal expectations and laws of probability, give each protected racial and sexual group a governmentally determined "proper" proportion of each job category. . . .

The fact of discrimination against Johnson is much clearer, and its degree more shocking, than the majority and Justice O'Connor's concurrence would suggest — largely because neither of them recites a single one of the District Court findings that govern this appeal, relying instead upon portions of the transcript which those findings implicitly rejected, and even upon a document (favorably comparing Joyce to Johnson) that was prepared after Joyce was selected. Worth mentioning, for example, is the trier of fact's determination that, if the Affirmative Action Coordinator had not intervened, "the decision as to whom to promote . . . would have been made by [the Road Operations Division Director]," who had recommended that Johnson be appointed to the position. Likewise, the even more extraordinary findings that James Graebner, the Agency Director who made the appointment, "did not inspect the applications and related examination records of either [Paul Johnson] or Diane Joyce before making his decision," and indeed "did little or nothing to inquire into the results of the interview process and conclusions which [were] described as of critical importance to the selection process." In light of these determinations, it is impossible to believe (or to think that the District Court believed) Graebner's self-serving statements relied upon by the majority and Justice O'Connor's concurrence, such as the assertion that he "tried to look at the whole picture, the combination of [Joyce's] qualifications and Mr. Johnson's qualifications, their test scores, their expertise, their background, affirmative action matters, things like that," (O'Connor, J., concurring in judgment). It was evidently enough for Graebner to know that both candidates (in the words of Johnson's counsel, to which Graebner assented) "met the M. Q.'s, the minimum. Both were minimally qualified." When asked whether he had "any basis," for determining whether one of the candidates was more qualified than the other, Graebner candidly answered, "No. . . . As I've said, they both appeared, and my conversations with people tended to corroborate, that they were both capable of performing the work."

After a 2-day trial, the District Court concluded that Diane Joyce's gender was "the determining factor," in her selection for the position. Specifically, it found that "[based] upon the examination results and the departmental interview, [Mr. Johnson] was more qualified for the position of Road Dispatcher than Diane Joyce," that "[but] for [Mr. Johnson's] sex, male, he would have been promoted to the position of Road Dispatcher," and that "[but] for Diane Joyce's sex, female, she would not have been appointed to the position. . . ." The Ninth Circuit did not reject these factual findings as clearly erroneous, nor could it have done so on the record before us. We are bound by those findings under Federal Rule of Civil Procedure 52(a).

## II

The most significant proposition of law established by today's decision is that racial or sexual discrimination is permitted under Title VII when it is intended to overcome the effect, not of the employer's own discrimination, but of societal attitudes that have limited the entry of certain races, or of a particular sex, into certain jobs. Even if the societal attitudes in question consisted exclusively of conscious discrimination by other employers, this holding would contradict a decision of this Court rendered only last Term. Wygant v. Jackson Board of Education held that the objective of remedying societal discrimination cannot prevent remedial affirmative action from violating the Equal Protection Clause. While Mr. Johnson does not advance a constitutional claim here, it is most unlikely that Title VII was intended to place a lesser restraint on discrimination by public actors than is established by the Constitution.[4] . . .

[T]oday's decision goes well beyond merely allowing racial or sexual discrimination in order to eliminate the effects of prior societal discrimination. The majority opinion often uses the phrase "traditionally segregated job category" to describe the evil against which the plan is legitimately (according to the majority) directed. As originally used in *Weber* that phrase described skilled jobs from which employers and unions had systematically and intentionally excluded black workers — traditionally segregated jobs, that is, in the sense of conscious, exclusionary discrimination. But that is assuredly not the sense in which the phrase is used here. It is absurd to think that the nationwide failure of road maintenance crews, for example, to achieve the Agency's ambition of 36.4% female representation is attributable primarily, if even substantially, to systematic exclusion of women eager to shoulder pick and shovel. It is a "traditionally segregated job category" not in the *Weber* sense, but in the sense

---

4. Justice O'Connor's concurrence at least makes an attempt to bring this Term into accord with last. Under her reading of Title VII, an employer may discriminate affirmatively, so to speak, if he has a "firm basis" for believing that he might be guilty of (nonaffirmative) discrimination under the Act, and if his action is designed to remedy that suspected prior discrimination. This is something of a halfway house between leaving employers scot-free to discriminate against disfavored groups, as the majority opinion does, and prohibiting discrimination, as do the words of Title VII. In the present case, although the District Court found that in fact no sex discrimination existed, Justice O'Connor would find a "firm basis" for the agency's belief that sex discrimination existed in the "inexorable zero": the complete absence, prior to Diane Joyce, of any women in the Agency's skilled positions. There are two problems with this: First, even positing a "firm basis" for the Agency's belief in prior discrimination, as I have discussed above, the plan was patently not designed to remedy that prior discrimination, but rather to establish a sexually representative work force. Second, even an absolute zero is not "inexorable." While it may inexorably provide "firm basis" for belief in the mind of an outside observer, it cannot conclusively establish such a belief on the employer's part, since he may be aware of the particular reasons that account for the zero. That is quite likely to be the case here, given the nature of the jobs we are talking about, and the list of "Factors Hindering Goal Attainment" recited by the Agency plan. The question is in any event one of fact, which, if it were indeed relevant to the outcome, would require a remand to the District Court rather than an affirmance.

that, because of longstanding social attitudes, it has not been regarded by women themselves as desirable work. . . . There are, of course, those who believe that the social attitudes which cause women themselves to avoid certain jobs and to favor others are as nefarious as conscious, exclusionary discrimination. Whether or not that is so (and there is assuredly no consensus on the point equivalent to our national consensus against intentional discrimination), the two phenomena are certainly distinct. And it is the alteration of social attitudes, rather than the elimination of discrimination, which today's decision approves as justification for state-enforced discrimination. This is an enormous expansion, undertaken without the slightest justification or analysis.

## III

I have omitted from the foregoing discussion the most obvious respect in which today's decision overleaps, without analysis, a barrier that was thought still to be overcome. . . . [U]ntil today the applicability of *Weber* to public employers remained an open question. . . . [T]his Court has repeatedly emphasized that *Weber* involved only a private employer. . . . [S]tate agencies, unlike private actors, are subject to the Fourteenth Amendment. . . . [I]t would be strange to construe Title VII to permit discrimination by public actors that the Constitution forbids.

In truth, however, the language of 42 U.S.C. § 2000e-2 draws no distinction between private and public employers, and the only good reason for creating such a distinction would be to limit the damage of *Weber*. It would be better, in my view, to acknowledge that case as fully applicable precedent, and to use the Fourteenth Amendment ramifications which *Weber* did not address and which are implicated for the first time here — as the occasion for reconsidering and overruling it. It is well to keep in mind just how thoroughly *Weber* rewrote the statute it purported to construe. The language of that statute, as quoted at the outset of this dissent, is unambiguous: it is an unlawful employment practice "to fail or refuse to hire or to discharge any individual, or otherwise to discriminate against any individual with respect to his compensation, terms, conditions, or privileges of employment, because of such individual's race, color, religion, sex, or national origin." *Weber* disregarded the text of the statute, invoking instead its "'spirit,'" and "practical and equitable [considerations] only partially perceived, if perceived at all, by the 88th Congress." It concluded, on the basis of these intangible guides, that Title VII's prohibition of intentional discrimination on the basis of race and sex does not prohibit intentional discrimination on the basis of race and sex, so long as it is "designed to break down old patterns of racial [or sexual] segregation and hierarchy," "does not unnecessarily trammel the interests of the white [or male] employees," "does not require the discharge of white [or male] workers and their replacement with new black [or female] hirees," "does [not] create an absolute bar to the advancement of white [or male] employees," and "is a temporary measure . . . not intended to maintain racial [or sexual] balance, but simply to eliminate a manifest racial [or sexual] imbalance." In effect, *Weber* held that the legality of intentional discrimination by private employers against certain disfavored groups or individuals is to be judged not by Title VII but by a judicially crafted code of conduct, the contours of which are determined by no discernible standard, aside from (as the dissent convincingly demonstrated) the divination of congressional "purposes" belied by the face of the statute and by its legislative history. We have been recasting that self-promulgated code of conduct ever since — and what it has led us to today adds to the reasons for abandoning it.

*NOTES*

1. Even Justices Stevens and O'Connor, who concur, appear to agree with Justice Scalia and the dissenters that the interpretation of the majority flies in the face of the literal terms of the statute. Does the majority agree? In *Weber,* the Court stressed that just because a situation appears to be within the literal language of a statute does not mean that the statute should necessarily be interpreted to include it. Legislative history may reveal the "true" intent of Congress. But Professor George Schatzki analyzed the legislative history after the decision in *Weber.*

> [W]hether or not the members of Congress thought of voluntary affirmative action, they did not discuss the issue. That being so, it is difficult for me to understand how either the majority or the dissent found much solace in the history. Justice Rehnquist stated, on the one hand, that Congress never thought about the matter; on the other hand, the justice was convinced the history rejected affirmative action. . . . I fail to see how the legislative history can lead someone to both of Rehnquist's conclusions — that Congress did not deal with affirmative action and that the Congress clearly rejected it.
>
> For the majority, Justice Brennan also overstates enormously the meaning of the legislative history. The truth is, Congress did not discuss or debate the issue.

George Schatzki, *United Steelworkers of America v. Weber:* An Exercise in Understandable Indecision, 56 Wash. L. Rev. 51, 66-67 (1980). If that is true, can a court nevertheless discern an intent about affirmative action from the overall thrust of the statute?

2. Obviously, Johnson believed that Joyce received a preference because she was a woman. Is that so clear? Read footnote 10 concerning the second interview panel. Might not the hiring of Joyce have reflected merely an effort to remove disadvantages imposed on Joyce because she was a woman? If so, that would not be "affirmative action," but only nondiscrimination. Justice O'Connor concludes that Joyce's sex was a "plus factor" in her hiring. Is she saying that sex discrimination did not occur? If a man's sex is a plus factor, does that violate Title VII? Is that Justice Scalia's point? Does it depend on whether it is a determinative factor, that is, whether it makes a difference in the final decision? The actual decision to name Joyce was made by Graebner. Does his quoted testimony show direct evidence of discrimination in favor of Joyce because she was a woman?

3. Did the employer concede that it was giving a woman a preference in promoting Joyce, rather than Johnson? What did the plaintiff have to show to make out a prima facie case of individual disparate treatment discrimination? If the employer did take the action pursuant to an affirmative action plan, why not admit it? Should an employer be able to argue in the alternative that the candidate who was promoted was the most qualified and, even if not, was the beneficiary of an affirmative action plan?

4. Courts have applied affirmative action concepts developed under Title VII to § 1981 claims alleging reverse discrimination. Thus, according to Schurr v. Resorts International Hotel, Inc., 196 F.3d 486 (3d Cir. 1999), if an affirmative action plan is valid under Title VII, then actions based upon it will not violate § 1981; however, a plan that is invalid under Title VII will not excuse racially motivated decisions challenged under § 1981.

5. Prior to *Johnson,* many had viewed the litigation structure of "reverse discrimination" cases as follows: the plaintiff must prove that a minority group member or female was preferred over him. The employer could then defend such a preference by showing, as an affirmative defense, that the preference was pursuant to a valid affirma-

tive action plan. Of course, the plaintiff and the defendant would frequently concede the racial or gender nature of the preference (as in *Weber* itself, where the plan was expressly intended to benefit blacks) and move immediately on to the validity of the plan. After *Johnson*, it is clear that this structure is inaccurate. The Court states that the plaintiff has the burden of showing that an affirmative action plan is invalid.

6. But not all "reverse discrimination" results from affirmative action plans. There may now be two alternative structures for such cases: the plaintiff may prove (1) he was the victim of an ad hoc racial or gender preference that was intentional discrimination or (2) he was the victim of a systematic racial or gender preference that the employer made pursuant to an affirmative action plan, which the plaintiff proves is invalid.

7. If this analysis is correct, why would a plaintiff ever try to show that the preference he was challenging was pursuant to an affirmative action plan? If it is simply challenged as ad hoc, won't the defendant have at least the burden of pleading and entering into evidence the fact that the challenged decision was the result of an affirmative action plan? Isn't this now a "legitimate, nondiscriminatory reason"? But how can an affirmative action plan ever be described as "nondiscriminatory"? See *Biggins*.

8. Will this approach prevent employers from arguing in the alternative (a) we did not favor a woman because of her sex and (b) we favored her because of her sex pursuant to an affirmative action plan?

9. Does *Price Waterhouse* or the 1991 Civil Rights Act alter the proof scheme *Johnson* established? Recall that the plurality in *Price Waterhouse* reserved the application of its holding to the affirmative action context. But Justice O'Connor and the three dissenters believed the *Price Waterhouse* approach should be fully applicable to reverse discrimination cases. In *Johnson*, the actual decision to name Joyce was made by Graebner. Under *Price Waterhouse* analysis, does his quoted testimony show "direct evidence" of discrimination in favor of Joyce because she is a woman? If so, presumably one way that the county could limit remedies is to persuade the trier of fact that Joyce would have been hired in any event. But another way is to show that favoring Joyce was pursuant to a valid affirmative action plan. As to the latter, does the burden of persuasion still rest on the plaintiff in accordance with *Johnson*?

10. What are the limits to voluntary affirmative action after *Johnson*? Is Justice Scalia correct that racial or gender balancing can now be pursued for its own sake? In United States v. Board of Educ. of the Township of Piscataway, 91 F.3d 1547 (3d Cir. 1996) (en banc), the school board decided to lay off one teacher from its high school's business education department. According to its collective bargaining agreement with the union, the board was required to lay off by seniority. Two teachers, Sharon Taxman, who is white, and Debra Williams, who is black, were tied in terms of seniority. They were also found to be equally qualified. Pursuant to an affirmative action plan and because Williams was the only African American in the business department, the school board retained Williams to maintain diversity among its teachers. Taxman was laid off. The Third Circuit, with 8 of 12 judges joining in the majority, found this violated Title VII both because the board's purpose of maintaining diversity in the workforce was not one of the remediation purposes for affirmative action approved in *Weber* and *Johnson* and because the plan unnecessarily trammeled the interests of nonminority employees:

> The Board admits that it did not act to remedy the effects of past employment discrimination. The parties have stipulated that neither the Board's adoption of its affirmative action policy nor its subsequent decision to apply it in choosing between Taxman and Williams was intended to remedy the results of any prior discrimination or

identified underrepresentation of Blacks within the Piscataway School District's teacher workforce as a whole. . . . Even though the Board's race-conscious action was taken to avoid what could have been an all-White faculty within the Business Department, the Board concedes that Blacks are not underrepresented in its teaching workforce as a whole or even in the Piscataway High School.

91 F.3d at 1563. Further, the affirmative action plan of the employer lacked the necessary definition and structure to ensure that it did not wrongly trammel the interests of nonminority employees. "[T]he Board's policy, devoid of goals and standards, is governed entirely by the Board's whim, leaving the Board free, if it so chooses, to grant racial preferences that do not promote even the policy's claimed purpose." Id. at 1564.

The Supreme Court granted certiorari in *Taxman* but the parties settled the dispute prior to its being argued. Accordingly, the Court dismissed the case, 522 U.S. 1010 (1997), thus avoiding any definitive decision. See Michael J. Zimmer, *Taxman*: Affirmative Action Dodges Five Bullets, 1 U. Pa. J. Lab. & Emp. L. 229 (1998).

11. In Ferrill v. The Parker Group, Inc. 168 F.3d 468, 474 (11th Cir. 1999), the court rejected an affirmative action defense where the employer operated a segregated set of telemarketers' jobs that were race-matched to the persons they called. "Although discrimination to remedy the effects of past discrimination is permitted under Title VII, and the defense is available to the § 1981 defendant, the [affirmative action] defense is not applicable to the case at bar. Ferrill's assignment to call African-Americans was not affirmative action . . . intended to correct racial imbalance. Rather, it was based on a racial stereotype that blacks would respond to blacks and on the assumption that Ferrill's race was directly related to her ability to do the job."

12. In Patrolmen's Benevolent Assn. v. City of New York, 310 F.3d 43 (2d. Cir. 2002), 22 African American and Hispanic officers sued the city after being transferred to the police precinct where Abner Louima had been brutalized. The city's defense of an "operational need" failed for the lack of objective evidence. In contrast, in Reynolds v. City of Chicago, 296 F.3d 524 (7th Cir. 2002), a challenge by white officers to the use of an affirmative action plan to promote a Hispanic sergeant to the rank of lieutenant ahead of white sergeants with higher test scores failed. The court found a compelling two-fold need for consideration of race: the need for Hispanic supervisors to "sensitize" non-Hispanic police officers and the need for "ambassadors" to the Hispanic community.

13. The opinions in *Johnson* differ over the implications of Congress's failure to amend Title VII to overturn *Weber*. The Civil Rights Act of 1991, 102 Pub. L. No. 166, 105 Stat. 1071, 1079 (1991), added a new section to Title VII, which provides:

> Section 116. Lawful Court Ordered Remedies, Affirmative Action, and Conciliation Agreement Not Affected.
> Nothing in the amendments made by this title shall be construed to affect court-ordered remedies, affirmative action, or conciliation agreements, that are in accordance with the law.

Michael J. Zimmer, *Taxman*: Affirmative Action Dodges Five Bullets, 1 U. Pa. J. Lab. & Emp. L. 229, 235 (1998), concludes that § 116 gives "no support to justify any change in the law of voluntary affirmative action. Further, by speaking about affirmative action in § 116, Congress has gone beyond the mere 'silent or passive assent' connoted by the word 'acquiescence.' Whether or not § 116 amounts to a full reenactment of *Weber/Johnson*, it is a statement recognizing the law in those cases. Thus, under any view, § 116 bolsters *Weber/Johnson* and the stare decisis effect that the courts should give to that law." See also Alfred W. Blumrosen & Ruth G. Blumrosen, The Flawed Foundations of *Piscataway High* — A Misleading Stipulation, an Absence of Representation, and Uncertainty About Informed Affirmative Action, 1 Rutgers L. Rev. 319 (1999); Ann C. McGinley & Michael J. Yelnosky, *Board of Education v. Taxman*, 4 Roger Williams U. L. Rev. 205 (1998); Ann C. McGinley, Affirmative Action Awash in Confusion: Backward-Looking Future-Oriented Justifications for Race Conscious Measures, 4 Roger Williams U. L. Rev. 209 (1998); Michael J. Yelnosky, Whither *Weber*, 4 Roger Williams U. L. Rev. 257 (1998).

14. Why are women underrepresented in fields such as mining, state police, and construction? Recall EEOC v. Sears, Roebuck & Co. (reproduced at page 253). If self-selection or the failure to consider certain kinds of jobs by women plays a part in maintaining segregated job categories, does that make the category less segregated or affirmative action less justified? Why would it be wrong for an employer to take affirmative action to bring women into positions that they would not have thought to seek for themselves? Could Sears have initiated an affirmative action plan to bring more women into commission sales jobs?

15. In Maitland v. Univ. of Minn., 155 F.3d 1013 (8th Cir. 1998), a male plaintiff challenged raises given to female employees pursuant to the settlement of their sex discrimination suit. The underlying case had involved disputed statistical models as to whether women were the victims of sex discrimination, or whether the disparities in their salaries were due to other factors. *Maitland* held that this dispute meant that there was a genuine issue as to whether the settlement was justified, that is, whether there was "a manifest or conspicuous imbalance in salaries based on gender," which the settlement was designed to address. Id. at 1018. In short, because it was not clear that there was ever a violation of Title VII as to the women who benefitted by the settlement, the male plaintiff's suit could go forward.

16. Recall the Court's concern in *Johnson* that the rights of non-minorities not be "unnecessarily trammeled." Could an affirmative action plan implemented by a consent decree or by a judgment in a litigated case trammel non-minority rights? See Chapter 10.

17. The ADEA poses interesting variations on the affirmative action theme. Since the statute restricts its protections to those age 40 and older, it permits discrimination in favor of older workers vis-à-vis persons under age 40. But the creation of a protected group of those age 40 and older means that discrimination on age grounds between covered individuals is also barred. Thus, an employer cannot, because of age, favor an applicant age 40 to one age 69, or vice versa. O'Connor v. Consolidated Coin Caters, Inc., 517 U.S. 308 (1996). While this view is taken by the EEOC's Interpretive Rules, 29 C.F.R. §§ 1625.1 et seq. (1993), those rules recognize an exception suggesting that greater benefits to older workers within the protected group may be permissible, id. § 1625.2(b). Might an employment preference in favor of older workers within the protected group be justified by an "affirmative action" rationale? Or, unlike affirmative action plans under Title VII, would such a preference discriminate against members of the very group that Congress thought was deserving of protection?

18. Professor Linda Hamilton Krieger, Civil Rights Perestroika: Intergroup Relations After Affirmative Action, 86 Cal. L. Rev. 1251, 1331-32 (1998), examined the implications of social cognition and identity theory for the debate over affirmative action. While recognizing some downsides to affirmative action, she concludes that it is justified because a colorblind model of nondiscrimination, an "objective" concept of merit, and individual disparate treatment adjudication are not equal to the task of controlling discrimination:

For better or worse, the application of insights from social cognition and social iden-tity theory complicates rather than simplifies the affirmative action debate. However, there is reason to fear that preferential forms of affirmative action, at least in some con-texts, may indeed exacerbate intergroup tensions and perpetuate rather than reduce subtle forms of intergroup bias. In other words, preferences appear to do harm as well as good.

On the other hand, insights derived from these fields suggest that we are not yet ready to abandon preferential forms of affirmative action for the simple reason that we have nothing adequate with which to replace them. Neither our political discourse nor our civil rights jurisprudence reflect an adequate understanding of what intergroup discrim-ination is, how or what causes it to occur, or what is required to reduce or eliminate it. We underestimate the stability, subtlety, and perniciousness of intergroup bias. Perhaps most importantly, we lack a coherent theory as to why improving intergroup relations should be a high priority in American political, economic, and cultural life.

These failures, and the confidence of anti-affirmative action activists, derive at least in part from two widely held but ultimately erroneous assumptions. The first assumption is that discrimination is conscious, intentional, and reasonably easy to identify. According to this view, by monitoring their thought processes, well-meaning, law-abiding people can and will refrain from discriminating. When discrimination does occur, it can be readily identified and negatively sanctioned. Nothing more than vigorous enforcement of existing laws prohibiting discrimination is needed to pave the way to an equal oppor-tunity society.

The second assumption holds that absent state-sanctioned or overt discrimination by private actors (which most would agree are waning), intergroup relations in the United States will improve or at least remain relatively tranquil, of their own accord. Intergroup harmony, rather than intergroup strife, is seen as a kind of default setting, necessitating little political intervention beyond the enactment and vigorous enforcement of laws prohibiting overt discrimination.

But tendencies toward intergroup discrimination are much more subtle, stable, and pernicious than these assumptions or their reflection in anti-affirmative action rhetoric admit. Social cognition teaches that much intergroup discrimination is both uninten-tional and unconscious. It occurs spontaneously as an unwanted artifact of normal cog-nitive functions associated with the processing of information about other people and can be corrected, if at all, only through further deliberate mental effort. Social identity theory and related research in experimental social psychology indicates that the tenden-cies to assist or excuse those with whom we feel closely identified and to subordinate the socially distant are far less tractable than we might wish.

See also Virginia Postel, The Lessons of the Grocery Shelf May Have Something to Say About Affirmative Action, N.Y. Times, Jan. 30, 2003, at C2 (consumers use "evoked sets" to make purchasing decisions, sets which often unconsciously exclude African Americans).

19. Professor Robert Post, Prejudicial Appearances: The Logic of American Anti-discrimination Law, 88 Cal. L. Rev. 1 (2000), challenges the idea that equal treat-ment entails color blindness. Using the blindness metaphor prevents us from asking the proper question antidiscrimination law should ask. From his "sociological" per-spective, the question is not how law should be used to transcend race and gender but is how law should be used to transform race and gender. He relies on Justice Bren-nan's approach in Weber as an example of the proper approach. See also Reva B. Siegel, Discrimination in the Eyes of the Law: How "Color Blindness" Discourse Disrupts and Rationalizes Social Stratification, 88 Cal. L. Rev. 77 (2000) (the aim of antidiscrimination law is to end social stratification).

20. The Court in *Johnson* avoided any constitutional decision. But, of course, the defendant was a public agency subject to constitutional constraints. The Court did not consider the constitutional question because the plaintiff did not raise it. In Justice O'Connor's view, the Court should have been guided by constitutional standards even though it was ruling under the statute. How would the Court have ruled if the plaintiff had invoked the Fourteenth Amendment? *Johnson* referred repeatedly to *Wygant,* limiting the extent to which affirmative action by government actors is permitted under the equal protection clause, but the Supreme Court has since restricted affirmative action even more.

## 4. Affirmative Action and the Constitution

### ADARAND CONSTRUCTORS v. PENA
### 515 U.S. 200 (1995)

Justice O'CONNOR, J., announced the judgment of the Court and delivered an opinion, which was for the Court except insofar as it might be inconsistent with the views expressed in Justice Scalia's concurrence.

Petitioner Adarand Constructors, Inc., claims that the Federal Government's practice of giving general contractors on government projects a financial incentive to hire subcontractors controlled by "socially and economically disadvantaged individuals," and in particular, the Government's use of race-based presumptions in identifying such individuals, violates the equal protection component of the Fifth Amendment's Due Process Clause. The Court of Appeals rejected Adarand's claim. We conclude, however, that courts should analyze cases of this kind under a different standard of review than the one the Court of Appeals applied. We therefore vacate the Court of Appeals' judgment and remand the case for further proceedings. . . .

[Adarand submitted the low bid on a subcontract to install guardrails on a federally funded highway construction project in Colorado. The prime contractor accepted instead the bid of Gonzales Construction Company because it received a bonus for subcontracting with small businesses, like Gonzales, that were controlled by "socially and economically disadvantaged individuals." In determining that status, federal contract law provided that "the contractor shall presume that socially and economically disadvantaged individuals include Black Americans, Hispanic Americans, Native Americans, Asian Pacific Americans, and other minorities, or any other individual found to be disadvantaged by the [Small Business Administration pursuant to section 8(a) of the Small Business Act."]

### III

The Government urges that "the Subcontracting Compensation Clause program is . . . a program based on disadvantage, not on race," and thus that it is subject only to "the most relaxed judicial scrutiny." To the extent that the statutes and regulations involved in this case are race neutral, we agree. The Government concedes, however, that "the race-based rebuttable presumption used in some certification determinations under the Subcontracting Compensation Clause" is subject to some heightened level of scrutiny. The parties disagree as to what that level should be. . . .

Adarand's claim arises under the Fifth Amendment to the Constitution, which provides that "No person shall . . . be deprived of life, liberty, or property, without due process of law." Although this Court has always understood that Clause to provide some measure of protection against *arbitrary* treatment by the Federal Government, it is not as explicit a guarantee of equal treatment as the Fourteenth Amendment, which provides that "No State shall . . . deny to any person within its jurisdiction the *equal* protection of the laws" (emphasis added). Our cases have accorded varying degrees of significance to the difference in the language of those two Clauses. We think it necessary to revisit the issue here.

A

Through the 1940s, this Court had routinely taken the view in non-race-related cases that, "unlike the Fourteenth Amendment, the Fifth contains no equal protection clause and it provides no guaranty against discriminatory legislation by Congress." Detroit Bank v. United States, 317 U.S. 329, 337 (1943). When the Court first faced a Fifth Amendment equal protection challenge to a federal racial classification, it adopted a similar approach, with most unfortunate results. In Hirabayashi v. United States, 320 U.S. 81 (1943), the Court considered a curfew applicable only to persons of Japanese ancestry. The Court observed — correctly — that "distinctions between citizens solely because of their ancestry are by their very nature odious to a free people whose institutions are founded upon the doctrine of equality," and that "racial discriminations are in most circumstances irrelevant and therefore prohibited." But it also cited *Detroit Bank* for the proposition that the Fifth Amendment "restrains only such discriminatory legislation by Congress as amounts to a denial of due process," and upheld the curfew because "circumstances within the knowledge of those charged with the responsibility for maintaining the national defense afforded a rational basis for the decision which they made."

Eighteen months later, the Court again approved wartime measures directed at persons of Japanese ancestry. Korematsu v. United States, 323 U.S. 214 (1944). . . .

In Bolling v. Sharpe, 347 U.S. 497 (1954), the Court for the first time explicitly questioned the existence of any difference between the obligations of the Federal Government and the States to avoid racial classifications. *Bolling* did note that "the 'equal protection of the laws' is a more explicit safeguard of prohibited unfairness than 'due process of law.'" But *Bolling* then concluded that, "in view of [the] decision that the Constitution prohibits the states from maintaining racially segregated public schools, it would be unthinkable that the same Constitution would impose a lesser duty on the Federal Government."

*Bolling's* facts concerned school desegregation, but its reasoning was not so limited. . . .

[Other cases] continued to treat the equal protection obligations imposed by the Fifth and the Fourteenth Amendments as indistinguishable. Loving v. Virginia, 308 U.S. 1 (1967), which struck down a race-based state law, cited *Korematsu* for the proposition that "the Equal Protection Clause demands that racial classifications . . . be subjected to the 'most rigid scrutiny.'" The various opinions in Frontiero v. Richardson, 411 U.S. 677 (1973), which concerned sex discrimination by the Federal Government, took their equal protection standard of review from Reed v. Reed, 404 U.S. 71 (1971), a case that invalidated sex discrimination by a State, without mentioning any possibility of a difference between the standards applicable to state and federal action. Thus, in 1975, the Court stated explicitly that "this Court's approach to Fifth Amendment equal protection claims has always been precisely the same as to equal protection claims under the Fourteenth Amendment." Weinberger v. Wiesenfeld, 420 U.S. 636, 638 (1975). We do not understand a few contrary suggestions appearing in cases in which we found special deference to the political branches of the Federal Government to be appropriate, e.g., Hampton v. Mow Sun Wong, 426 U.S. 88 (1976) (federal power over immigration), to detract from this general rule.

### B

Most of the cases discussed above involved classifications burdening groups that have suffered discrimination in our society. In 1978, the Court confronted the question whether race-based governmental action designed to benefit such groups should also be subject to "the most rigid scrutiny." Regents of Univ. of California v. Bakke, 438 U.S. 265 (1978) involved an equal protection challenge to a state-run medical school's practice of reserving a number of spaces in its entering class for minority students. The petitioners argued that "strict scrutiny" should apply only to "classifications that disadvantage 'discrete and insular minorities.'" Bakke did not produce an opinion for the Court, but Justice Powell's opinion announcing the Court's judgment rejected the argument. In a passage joined by Justice White, Justice Powell wrote that "the guarantee of equal protection cannot mean one thing when applied to one individual and something else when applied to a person of another color." He concluded that "racial and ethnic distinctions of any sort are inherently suspect and thus call for the most exacting judicial examination." On the other hand, four Justices in Bakke would have applied a less stringent standard of review to racial classifications "designed to further remedial purposes." And four Justices thought the case should be decided on statutory grounds.

Two years after Bakke, the Court faced another challenge to remedial race-based action, this time involving action undertaken by the Federal Government. In Fullilove v. Klutznick[, 448 U.S. 448 (1980),] the Court upheld Congress' inclusion of a 10% set-aside for minority-owned businesses in the Public Works Employment Act of 1977. As in Bakke, there was no opinion for the Court. Chief Justice Burger, in an opinion joined by Justices White and Powell, observed that "any preference based on racial or ethnic criteria must necessarily receive a most searching examination to make sure that it does not conflict with constitutional guarantees." That opinion, however, "did not adopt, either expressly or implicitly, the formulas of analysis articulated in such cases as [Bakke]." It employed instead a two-part test which asked, first, "whether the objectives of the legislation are within the power of Congress," and second, "whether the limited use of racial and ethnic criteria, in the context presented, is a constitutionally permissible means for achieving the congressional objectives." It then upheld the program under that test, adding at the end of the opinion that the program also "would survive judicial review under either 'test' articulated in the several Bakke opinions." Justice Powell wrote separately to express his view that the plurality opinion had essentially applied "strict scrutiny" as described in his Bakke opinion — i.e., it had determined that the set-aside was "a necessary means of advancing a compelling governmental interest" — and had done so correctly.

In Wygant v. Jackson Board of Education, 476 U.S. 262 (1986), the Court considered a Fourteenth Amendment challenge to another form of remedial racial classification. The issue in Wygant was whether a school board could adopt race-based preferences in determining which teachers to lay off. Justice Powell's plurality opinion observed that "the level of scrutiny does not change merely because the challenged classification operates against a group that historically has not been subject to governmental discrimination," and stated the two-part inquiry as "whether the layoff provision is supported by a compelling state purpose and whether the means chosen to accomplish that purpose are narrowly tailored." In other words, "racial classifications of any sort must be subjected to 'strict scrutiny.'" The plurality then concluded that the school board's interest in "providing minority role models for its minority students, as an attempt to alleviate the effects of societal discrimination," was not a compelling interest that could justify the use of a racial classification. It added that "societal discrimination, without more, is too amorphous a basis for imposing a racially classified remedy," and insisted instead that "a public employer . . . must ensure that, before it embarks on an affirmative-action program, it has convincing evidence that remedial action is warranted. That is, it must have sufficient evidence to justify the conclusion that there has been prior discrimination." Justice White concurred only in the judgment, although he agreed that the school board's asserted interests could not, "singly or together, justify this racially discriminatory layoff policy."

The Court's failure to produce a majority opinion in *Bakke*, *Fullilove*, and *Wygant* left unresolved the proper analysis for remedial race-based governmental action. . . .

The Court resolved the issue, at least in part, in 1989. Richmond v. J. A. Croson Co., 488 U.S. 469 (1989), concerned a city's determination that 30% of its contracting work should go to minority-owned businesses. A majority of the Court in *Croson* held that "the standard of review under the Equal Protection Clause is not dependent on the race of those burdened or benefited by a particular classification," and that the single standard of review for racial classifications should be "strict scrutiny." As to the classification before the Court, the plurality agreed that "a state or local subdivision . . . has the authority to eradicate the effects of private discrimination within its own legislative jurisdiction," but the Court thought that the city had not acted with "a 'strong basis in evidence for its conclusion that remedial action was necessary.'" The Court also thought it "obvious that [the] program is not narrowly tailored to remedy the effects of prior discrimination." With *Croson*, the Court finally agreed that the Fourteenth Amendment requires strict scrutiny of all race-based action by state and local governments. But *Croson* of course had no occasion to declare what standard of review the Fifth Amendment requires for such action taken by the Federal Government. *Croson* observed simply that the Court's "treatment of an exercise of congressional power in *Fullilove* cannot be dispositive here," because *Croson*'s facts did not implicate Congress' broad power under § 5 of the Fourteenth Amendment. . . .

Despite lingering uncertainty in the details, however, the Court's cases through *Croson* had established three general propositions with respect to governmental racial classifications. First, skepticism: "'any preference based on racial or ethnic criteria must necessarily receive a most searching examination,'" *Wygant*; *Fullilove*. Second, consistency: "the standard of review under the Equal Protection Clause is not dependent on the race of those burdened or benefited by a particular classification," *Croson*; see also *Bakke* (opinion of Powell, J.), i.e., all racial classifications reviewable under the Equal Protection Clause must be strictly scrutinized. And third, congruence: "equal protection analysis in the Fifth Amendment area is the same as that under the Fourteenth Amendment," Buckley v. Valeo. Taken together, these propositions lead to the conclusion that any person, of whatever race, has the right to demand that any governmental actor subject to the Constitution justify any racial classification subjecting that person to unequal treatment under the strictest judicial scrutiny. . . .

A year later, however, the Court took a surprising turn. [Metro Broadcasting v.

FCC, 497 U.S. 547 (1990),] involved a Fifth Amendment challenge to two race-based policies of the Federal Communications Commission. In *Metro Broadcasting*, the Court repudiated the long-held notion that "it would be unthinkable that the same Constitution would impose a lesser duty on the Federal Government" than it does on a State to afford equal protection of the laws. It did so by holding that "benign" federal racial classifications need only satisfy intermediate scrutiny, even though *Croson* had recently concluded that such classifications enacted by a State must satisfy strict scrutiny. "Benign" federal racial classifications, the Court said, " — even if those measures are not 'remedial' in the sense of being designed to compensate victims of past governmental or societal discrimination — are constitutionally permissible to the extent that they serve *important* governmental objectives within the power of Congress and are *substantially related* to achievement of those objectives." *Metro Broadcasting* (emphasis added). . . .

By adopting intermediate scrutiny as the standard of review for congressionally mandated "benign" racial classifications, *Metro Broadcasting* departed from prior cases in two significant respects. First, it turned its back on *Croson*'s explanation of why strict scrutiny of all governmental racial classifications is essential: "Absent searching judicial inquiry into the justification for such race-based measures, there is simply no way of determining what classifications are 'benign' or 'remedial' and what classifications are in fact motivated by illegitimate notions of racial inferiority or simple racial politics. Indeed, the purpose of strict scrutiny is to 'smoke out' illegitimate uses of race by assuring that the legislative body is pursuing a goal important enough to warrant use of a highly suspect tool. The test also ensures that the means chosen 'fit' this compelling goal so closely that there is little or no possibility that the motive for the classification was illegitimate racial prejudice or stereotype." We adhere to that view today, despite the surface appeal of holding "benign" racial classifications to a lower standard, because "it may not always be clear that a so-called preference is in fact benign." *Bakke.*

Second, *Metro Broadcasting* squarely rejected one of the three propositions established by the Court's earlier equal protection cases, namely, congruence between the standards applicable to federal and state racial classifications, and in so doing also undermined the other two — skepticism of all racial classifications, and consistency of treatment irrespective of the race of the burdened or benefitted group. Under *Metro Broadcasting*, certain racial classifications ("benign" ones enacted by the Federal Government) should be treated less skeptically than others; and the race of the benefited group is critical to the determination of which standard of review to apply. *Metro Broadcasting* was thus a significant departure from much of what had come before it.

The three propositions undermined by *Metro Broadcasting* all derive from the basic principle that the Fifth and Fourteenth Amendments to the Constitution protect persons, not groups. It follows from that principle that all governmental action based on race — a group classification long recognized as "in most circumstances irrelevant and therefore prohibited," *Hirabayashi* — should be subjected to detailed judicial inquiry to ensure that the personal right to equal protection of the laws has not been infringed. Accordingly, we hold today that all racial classifications, imposed by whatever federal, state, or local governmental actor, must be analyzed by a reviewing court under strict scrutiny. In other words, such classifications are constitutional only if they are narrowly tailored measures that further compelling governmental interests. To the extent that *Metro Broadcasting* is inconsistent with that holding, it is overruled. . . .

Justice Stevens chides us for our "supposed inability to differentiate between 'invidious' and 'benign' discrimination," because it is in his view sufficient that "people understand the difference between good intentions and bad." But, as we have just explained, the point of strict scrutiny is to "differentiate between" permissible and impermissible governmental use of race. And Justice Stevens himself has already explained in his dissent in *Fullilove* why "good intentions" alone are not enough to sustain a supposedly "benign" racial classification: "Even though it is not the actual predicate for this legislation, a statute of this kind inevitably is perceived by many as resting on an assumption that those who are granted this special preference are less qualified in some respect that is identified purely by their race. Because that perception — especially when fostered by the Congress of the United States — can only exacerbate rather than reduce racial prejudice, it will delay the time when race will become a truly irrelevant, or at least insignificant, factor. Unless Congress clearly articulates the need and basis for a racial classification, and also tailors the classification to its justification, the Court should not uphold this kind of statute." *Fullilove* (dissenting opinion); *Croson* ("Although [the legislation at issue] stigmatizes the disadvantaged class with the unproven charge of past racial discrimination, it actually imposes a greater stigma on its supposed beneficiaries."). These passages make a persuasive case for requiring strict scrutiny of congressional racial classifications.

Perhaps it is not the standard of strict scrutiny itself, but our use of the concepts of "consistency" and "congruence" in conjunction with it, that leads Justice Stevens to dissent. According to Justice Stevens, our view of consistency "equates remedial preferences with invidious discrimination," and ignores the difference between "an engine of oppression" and an effort "to foster equality in society," or, more colorfully, "between a 'No Trespassing' sign and a welcome mat." It does nothing of the kind. The principle of consistency simply means that whenever the government treats any person unequally because of his or her race, that person has suffered an injury that falls squarely within the language and spirit of the Constitution's guarantee of equal protection. It says nothing about the ultimate validity of any particular law; that determination is the job of the court applying strict scrutiny. The principle of consistency explains the circumstances in which the injury requiring strict scrutiny occurs. The application of strict scrutiny, in turn, determines whether a compelling governmental interest justifies the infliction of that injury. . . .

Justice Stevens also claims that we have ignored any difference between federal and state legislatures. But requiring that Congress, like the States, enact racial classifications only when doing so is necessary to further a "compelling interest" does not contravene any principle of appropriate respect for a co-equal Branch of the Government. It is true that various Members of this Court have taken different views of the authority § 5 of the Fourteenth Amendment confers upon Congress to deal with the problem of racial discrimination, and the extent to which courts should defer to Congress' exercise of that authority. We need not, and do not, address these differences today. For now, it is enough to observe that Justice Stevens' suggestion that any Member of this Court has repudiated in this case his or her previously expressed views on the subject, is incorrect. . . .

Finally, we wish to dispel the notion that strict scrutiny is "strict in theory, but fatal in fact." *Fullilove*. The unhappy persistence of both the practice and the lingering effects of racial discrimination against minority groups in this country is an unfortunate reality, and government is not disqualified from acting in response to it. As recently as 1987, for example, every Justice of this Court agreed that the Alabama Department of Public Safety's "pervasive, systematic, and obstinate discriminatory conduct" justified a narrowly tailored race-based remedy. See United States v. Paradise [reproduced at page 986]. When race-based action is necessary to further a compelling interest, such action is within constitutional constraints if it satisfies the "narrow tailoring" test this Court has set out in previous cases.

Justice SCALIA, concurring in part and concurring in the judgment.

In my view, government can never have a "compelling interest" in discriminating on the basis of race in order to "make up" for past racial discrimination in the opposite direction. See Richmond v. J. A. Croson Co. Individuals who have been wronged by unlawful racial discrimination should be made whole; but under our Constitution there can be no such thing as either a creditor or a debtor race. That concept is alien to the Constitution's focus upon the individual and its rejection of dispositions based on race or based on blood. To pursue the concept of racial entitlement — even for the most admirable and benign of purposes — is to reinforce and preserve for future mischief the way of thinking that produced race slavery, race privilege and race hatred. In the eyes of government, we are just one race here. It is American.

It is unlikely, if not impossible, that the challenged program would survive under this understanding of strict scrutiny, but I am content to leave that to be decided on remand.

Justice THOMAS, concurring in part and concurring in the judgment.

I agree with the majority's conclusion that strict scrutiny applies to all government classifications based on race. I write separately, however, to express my disagreement with the premise underlying Justice Stevens' and Justice Ginsburg's dissents: that there is a racial paternalism exception to the principle of equal protection. I believe that there is a "moral [and] constitutional equivalence," between laws designed to subjugate a race and those that distribute benefits on the basis of race in order to foster some current notion of equality. Government cannot make us equal; it can only recognize, respect, and protect us as equal before the law.

That these programs may have been motivated, in part, by good intentions cannot provide refuge from the principle that under our Constitution, the government may not make distinctions on the basis of race. As far as the Constitution is concerned, it is irrelevant whether a government's racial classifications are drawn by those who wish to oppress a race or by those who have a sincere desire to help those thought to be disadvantaged. There can be no doubt that the paternalism that appears to lie at the heart of this program is at war with the principle of inherent equality that underlies and infuses our Constitution.

These programs not only raise grave constitutional questions, they also undermine the moral basis of the equal protection principle. Purchased at the price of immeasurable human suffering, the equal protection principle reflects our Nation's understanding that such classifications ultimately have a destructive impact on the individual and our society. Unquestionably, "invidious [racial] discrimination is an engine of oppression." It is also true that "remedial" racial preferences may reflect "a desire to foster equality in society." But there can be no doubt that racial paternalism and its unintended consequences can be as poisonous and pernicious as any other form of discrimination. So-called "benign" discrimination teaches many that because of chronic and apparently immutable handicaps, minorities cannot compete with them without their patronizing indulgence. Inevitably, such programs engender attitudes of superiority or, alternatively, provoke resentment among those who believe that they have been wronged by the government's use of race. These programs stamp minorities with a badge of inferiority and may cause them to develop dependencies or to adopt an attitude that they are "entitled" to preferences. Indeed, Justice Stevens once recognized the real harms stemming from seemingly "benign" discrimination. See Fullilove v. Klutznick.

In my mind, government-sponsored racial discrimination based on benign prejudice is just as noxious as discrimination inspired by malicious prejudice. In each instance, it is racial discrimination, plain and simple.

Justice STEVENS, with whom Justice GINSBURG joins, dissenting. . . .

## I

The Court's concept of skepticism is, at least in principle, a good statement of law and of common sense. Undoubtedly, a court should be wary of a governmental decision that relies upon a racial classification. "Because racial characteristics so seldom provide a relevant basis for disparate treatment, and because classifications based on race are potentially so harmful to the entire body politic," a reviewing court must satisfy itself that the reasons for any such classification are "clearly identified and unquestionably legitimate." Fullilove v. Klutznick. But, as the opinions in *Fullilove* demonstrate, substantial agreement on the standard to be applied in deciding difficult cases does not necessarily lead to agreement on how those cases actually should or will be resolved. In my judgment, because uniform standards are often anything but uniform, we should evaluate the Court's comments on "consistency," "congruence," and stare decisis with the same type of skepticism that the Court advocates for the underlying issue.

## II

The Court's concept of "consistency" assumes that there is no significant difference between a decision by the majority to impose a special burden on the members of a minority race and a decision by the majority to provide a benefit to certain members of that minority notwithstanding its incidental burden on some members of the majority. In my opinion, that assumption is untenable. There is no moral or constitutional equivalence between a policy that is designed to perpetuate a caste system and one that seeks to eradicate racial subordination. Invidious discrimination is an engine of oppression, subjugating a disfavored group to enhance or maintain the power of the majority. Remedial race-based preferences reflect the opposite impulse: a desire to foster equality in society. No sensible conception of the Government's constitutional obligation to "govern impartially" should ignore this distinction. We should reject a concept of "consistency" that would view the special preferences that the National Government has provided to Native Americans since 1834 as comparable to the official discrimination against African Americans that was prevalent for much of our history.

The consistency that the Court espouses would disregard the difference between a "No Trespassing" sign and a welcome mat. It would treat a Dixiecrat Senator's decision to vote against Thurgood Marshall's confirmation in order to keep African Americans off the Supreme Court as on a par with President Johnson's evaluation of his nominee's race as a positive factor. It would equate a law that made black citizens ineligible for military service with a program aimed at recruiting black soldiers. An attempt by the majority to exclude members of a minority race from a regulated market is fundamentally different from a subsidy that enables a relatively small group of newcomers to enter that market. An interest in "consistency" does not justify treating differences as though they were similarities.

The Court's explanation for treating dissimilar race-based decisions as though they were equally objectionable is a supposed inability to differentiate between "invidious" and "benign" discrimination. But the term "affirmative action" is common and well understood. Its presence in everyday parlance shows that people understand the difference between good intentions and bad. As with any legal concept, some cases may be difficult to classify, but our equal protection jurisprudence has identified a critical difference between state action that imposes burdens on a disfavored few and state action that benefits the few "in spite of" its adverse effects on the many. *Feeney.* . . .

Moreover, the Court may find that its new "consistency" approach to race-based classifications is difficult to square with its insistence upon rigidly separate categories for discrimination against different classes of individuals. For example, as the law currently stands, the Court will apply "intermediate scrutiny" to cases of invidious gender discrimination and "strict scrutiny" to cases of invidious race discrimination, while applying the same standard for benign classifications as for invidious ones. If this remains the law, then today's lecture about "consistency" will produce the anomalous result that the Government can more easily enact affirmative-action programs to remedy discrimination against women than it can enact affirmative-action programs to remedy discrimination against African Americans — even though the primary purpose of the Equal Protection Clause was to end discrimination against the former slaves. When a court becomes preoccupied with abstract standards, it risks sacrificing common sense at the altar of formal consistency. . . .

## III

The Court's concept of "congruence" assumes that there is no significant difference between a decision by the Congress of the United States to adopt an affirmative-action program and such a decision by a State or a municipality. In my opinion that assumption is untenable. It ignores important practical and legal differences between federal and state or local decisionmakers.

In her plurality opinion in *Croson,* Justice O'Connor emphasized the importance of this distinction when she responded to the City's argument that *Fullilove* was controlling. She wrote:

> What appellant ignores is that Congress, unlike any State or political subdivision, has a specific constitutional mandate to enforce the dictates of the Fourteenth Amendment. The power to "enforce" may at times also include the power to define situations which Congress determines threaten principles of equality and to adopt prophylactic rules to deal with those situations. The Civil War Amendments themselves worked a dramatic change in the balance between congressional and state power over matters of race.

An additional reason for giving greater deference to the National Legislature than to a local law-making body is that federal affirmative-action programs represent the will of our entire Nation's elected representatives, whereas a state or local program may have an impact on nonresident entities who played no part in the decision to enact it. Thus, in the state or local context, individuals who were unable to vote for the local representatives who enacted a race-conscious program may nonetheless feel the effects of that program. This difference recalls the goals of the Commerce Clause, which permits Congress to legislate on certain matters of national importance while denying power to the States in this area for fear of undue impact upon out-of-state residents.

Presumably, the majority is now satisfied that its theory of "congruence" between the substantive rights provided by the Fifth and Fourteenth Amendments disposes of the objection based upon divided constitutional powers. But it is one thing to say (as no one seems to dispute) that the Fifth Amendment encompasses a general guarantee of equal protection as broad as that contained within the Fourteenth Amendment. It is another thing entirely to say that Congress' institutional competence and constitutional authority entitle it to no greater deference when it enacts a program designed to foster equality than the deference due a State legislature. The latter is an extraordinary proposition; and, as the foregoing discussion demonstrates, our precedents have rejected it explicitly and repeatedly.

Our opinion in *Metro Broadcasting* relied on several constitutional provisions to justify the greater deference we owe to Congress when it acts with respect to private individuals. In the programs challenged in this case, Congress has acted both with respect to private individuals and, as in *Fullilove*, with respect to the States themselves. When Congress does this, it draws its power directly from § 5 of the Fourteenth Amendment. That section reads: "The Congress shall have power to enforce, by appropriate legislation, the provisions of this article." One of the "provisions of this article" that Congress is thus empowered to enforce reads: "No State shall make or enforce any law which shall abridge the privileges or immunities of citizens of the United States; nor shall any State deprive any person of life, liberty, or property, without due process of law; nor deny to any person within its jurisdiction the equal protection of the laws." U.S. Const., Amdt. 14, § 1. The Fourteenth Amendment directly empowers Congress at the same time it expressly limits the States. This is no accident. It represents our Nation's consensus, achieved after hard experience throughout our sorry history of race relations, that the Federal Government must be the primary defender of racial minorities against the States, some of which may be inclined to oppress such minorities. A rule of "congruence" that ignores a purposeful "incongruity" so fundamental to our system of government is unacceptable. . . .

Justice GINSBURG, with whom Justice BREYER joins, dissenting.

. . . I write separately to underscore not the differences the several opinions in this case display, but the considerable field of agreement — the common understandings and concerns — revealed in opinions that together speak for a majority of the Court.

I

The statutes and regulations at issue, as the Court indicates, were adopted by the political branches in response to an "unfortunate reality": "the unhappy persistence of both the practice and the lingering effects of racial discrimination against minority groups in this country." The United States suffers from those lingering effects because, for most of our Nation's history, the idea that "we are just one race," (Scalia, J., concurring in part and concurring in judgment), was not embraced. For generations, our lawmakers and judges were unprepared to say that there is in this land no superior race, no race inferior to any other. In Plessy v. Ferguson, 163 U.S. 532 (1896), not only did this Court endorse the oppressive practice of race segregation, but even Justice Harlan, the advocate of a "color-blind" Constitution, stated: "The white race deems itself to be the dominant race in this country. And so it is, in prestige, in achievements, in education, in wealth and in power. So, I doubt not, it will continue to be for all time, if it remains true to its great heritage and holds fast to the principles of constitutional liberty." Not until Loving v. Virginia, which held unconstitutional Virginia's ban on interracial marriages, could one say with security that the Constitution and this Court would abide no measure "designed to maintain White Supremacy."

The divisions in this difficult case should not obscure the Court's recognition of the persistence of racial inequality and a majority's acknowledgment of Congress' authority to act affirmatively, not only to end discrimination, but also to counteract discrimination's lingering effects.

Those effects, reflective of a system of racial caste only recently ended, are evident in our workplaces, markets, and neighborhoods. Job applicants with identical resumes, qualifications, and interview styles still experience different receptions, depending on their race. White and African-American consumers still encounter different deals. People of color looking for housing still face discriminatory treatment by landlords, real estate agents, and mortgage lenders. Minority entrepreneurs sometimes fail to gain contracts though they are the low bidders, and they are sometimes refused work even after winning contracts. Bias both conscious and unconscious, reflecting traditional and unexamined habits of thought, keeps up barriers that must come down if equal opportunity and nondiscrimination are ever genuinely to become this country's law and practice.

Given this history and its practical consequences, Congress surely can conclude that a carefully designed affirmative action program may help to realize, finally, the "equal protection of the laws" the Fourteenth Amendment has promised since 1868.

II

The lead opinion uses one term, "strict scrutiny," to describe the standard of judicial review for all governmental classifications by race. But that opinion's elaboration strongly suggests that the strict standard announced is indeed "fatal" for classifications burdening groups that have suffered discrimination in our society. That seems to me, and, I believe, to the Court, the enduring lesson one should draw from Korematsu v. United States; for in that case, scrutiny the Court described as "most rigid," nonetheless yielded a pass for an odious, gravely injurious racial classification. A *Korematsu*-type classification, as I read the opinions in this case, will never again survive scrutiny: such a classification, history and precedent instruct, properly ranks as prohibited.

For a classification made to hasten the day when "we are just one race," however, the lead opinion has dispelled the notion that "strict scrutiny" is "'fatal in fact.'" Properly, a majority of the Court calls for review that is searching, in order to ferret out classifications in reality malign, but masquerading as benign. The Court's once lax review of sex-based classifications demonstrates the need for such suspicion. See, e.g., Hoyt v. Florida, 368 U.S. 57, 60 (1961) (upholding women's "privilege" of automatic exemption from jury service); Goesaert v. Cleary, 335 U.S. 464 (1948) (upholding Michigan law barring women from employment as bartenders). Today's decision thus usefully reiterates that the purpose of strict scrutiny "is precisely to distinguish legitimate from illegitimate uses of race in governmental decisionmaking," "to 'differentiate between' permissible and impermissible governmental use of race," to distinguish "'between a "No Trespassing" sign and a welcome mat.'"

Close review also is in order for this further reason. As Justice Souter points out, and as this very case shows, some members of the historically favored race can be hurt by catch-up mechanisms designed to cope with the lingering effects of entrenched racial subjugation. Court review can ensure that preferences are not so large as to trammel unduly upon the opportunities of others or interfere too harshly with legitimate expectations of persons in once-preferred groups. . . .

While I would not disturb the programs challenged in this case, and would leave their improvement to the political branches, I see today's decision as one that allows our precedent to evolve, still to be informed by and responsive to changing conditions.

## NOTES

1. In *Croson* and *Adarand*, a majority of five finally agreed that all racial classifications, whether established by state or national governmental actors and whether designed to redress discrimination or to engage in invidious discrimination, are to be judged by strict scrutiny: "[S]uch classifications are constitutional only if they are narrowly tailored measures that further compelling governmental interests."

2. Professor Jed Rubenfeld, The Anti Anti-discrimination Agenda, 111 Yale L.J. 1141 (2002), criticizes *Adarand* for transforming the equal protection question from one of "class" to one of "classifications." More generally, he compares the jurisprudence of the Court as to affirmative action with its decisions in other areas, such as restrictions on Congressional power under the commerce clause and § 5 of the Fourteenth Amendment, claiming that the best way to understand these cases, which are theoretically inconsistent in approach, is as advancing an anti-antidiscrimination agenda set by five justices of the Court:

> There are two basic defenses of *Adarand*; each is perfectly intelligible in its own terms, but each becomes much less intelligible when juxtaposed with other important equal protection doctrines. First, strict scrutiny for race-based affirmative action can be defended on the ground that affirmative action intentionally disadvantages whites. But this defense of *Adarand* in effect treats whites as a suspect class, a result contradicting everything the Court has ever said about the criteria required to make a group "suspect" for equal protection purposes.
>
> Second, strict scrutiny for race-based affirmative action can be defended on the ground that affirmative action unintentionally harms blacks (and other racial minorities) by promoting invidious racial stereotypes. But the effects-based defense of *Adarand* is very hard to reconcile with the Washington v. Davis [reproduced at page 404, holding that a test neutral on its face that disadvantages African Americans does not violate equal protection] doctrine. Under *Davis*, the Justices will say clearly and emphatically that harms to minorities, including the promotion of invidious racial stereotypes, are insufficient to trigger strict scrutiny unless these consequences were intended. Under *Adarand*, the Justices will say clearly and emphatically that the promotion of invidious racial stereotypes demands the application of strict scrutiny, even though this consequence was unintended. . . . But if the racial classifications in an affirmative action program demand strict scrutiny because of their unintended promotion of invidious racial stereotypes, then *Davis'* categorical denial of strict scrutiny to benignly intended race-neutral measures no longer makes sense. . . .
>
> Striving to take *Adarand* seriously on its own terms, we may see it as an effort to ensure the most rigorous judicial scrutiny of governmental action that runs a high risk of (inadvertently) promoting invidious racial stereotypes. The five Justices who decided *Adarand* explicitly defend their ruling in these terms. But given these Justices' simultaneous adherence to *Davis*, which refuses strict scrutiny for governmental action that demonstrably (but inadvertently) promotes invidious racial stereotypes, their statements should not be credited.

Id. at 1175-76.

3. What governmental interests are compelling for equal protection purposes? In Wygant v. Jackson Board of Educ., 476 U.S. 267 (1986), the Court was unanimous that the use of race-conscious decision-making to provide a remedy for the victims of proven discrimination was a compelling interest. A majority, however, rejected as compelling an interest in remedying societal discrimination. Does that mean that, on remand in *Adarand*, the statute will be struck down unless the federal government shows that it discriminated against African Americans and/or Chicanos?

4. The remedial justification has often been argued to reach only affirmative action intended to redress prior discrimination by the state agency in question. But private discrimination in the past was endemic. Can a state actor use affirmative action to redress the consequences of such discrimination? See Ian Ayres & Frederick E. Vars, When Does Private Discrimination Justify Public Affirmative Action?, 98 Colum. L. Rev. 1577 (1998) (a majority of the Justices in *Croson* explicitly recognized private discrimination as a justification for a racial set-aside).

5. In Hopwood v. Texas, 78 F.3d 932 (5th Cir. 1996), the court rejected diversity as a compelling governmental interest justifying the use of affirmative action by a law school. "[A]ny consideration of race or ethnicity by the law school for the purpose of achieving a diverse student body is not a compelling interest under the Fourteenth Amendment." Id. at 944. In contrast to *Hopwood*, the Sixth Circuit in Grutter v. Bollinger, 288 F.3d 732 (6th Cir. 2002), found diversity as a compelling governmental interest and upheld the University of Michigan Law School's admission policy as indistinguishable from the "Harvard" plan Justice Powell said was constitutional in *Bakke*. The Supreme Court granted certiorari in *Grotter* and a companion case involving undergraduate admissions at the University of Michigan. 123 S. Ct. 617 (2002). In Johnson v. Board of Regents of the University of Georgia, 263 F.3d 1234, 1248 (11th Cir. 2001), the court refrained from deciding whether student body diversity is a compelling state interest but asserted that "no five Justices in *Bakke* expressly held that student body diversity is a compelling state interest."

6. In Boston Police Super. Officers Fedn. v. City of Boston, 147 F.3d 13 (1st Cir. 1998), the court rejected a challenge to the Boston police department's bypassing of white candidates on a promotion test list in order to promote an African American whose score on the test was a point lower than the white's. The compelling governmental interest was to remedy past discrimination by the police department. Looking back at a long history of discrimination, the court held that affirmative action was still necessary. While a consent decree had been entered in 1972 to remedy initial appointment discrimination, the effects of past discrimination were still present in the rank of lieutenant. The narrowly tailored test was satisfied because there was only one point difference in test scores and, within a short period, the white plaintiffs were all promoted. Similarly, McNamara v. City of Chicago, 138 F.3d 1219 (7th Cir. 1998), upheld an affirmative action plan intended to boost the number of minorities in the rank of firefighter captain against an equal protection challenge. The court held that a combination of statistical and anecdotal evidence supported the district court's finding that, until the mid-1980s, the fire department "endeavored with considerable success to make the department uncongenial to blacks and Hispanics." Id. at 1224. The city's plan was valid when the increase in minorities "is a plausible lower-bound estimate of the shortfall in minority representation among fire captains that is due to the fire department's intentional discrimination in the past." Id.

7. The federal government has long-established requirements for affirmative action plans for federal employees and federal contractors. See Executive Order 11,246, 30 Fed. Reg. 12,319 (1965); Revised Guide No. 4, 41 C.F.R. §§ 60-2.1 to 2.32

(1996). The validity of Executive Order 11,246 has been upheld as within the executive power of the president or authorized — expressly or impliedly — by Congress. Contractors Assn. v. Secretary of Labor, 442 F.2d 159 (3d Cir. 1971). See generally Michael Brody, Congress, the President, and Federal Equal Employment Policymaking: A Problem of Separation of Powers, 60 B.U. L. Rev. 239 (1980). But see Chrysler Corp. v. Brown, 441 U.S. 281 (1979) (OFCCP regulations authorizing the disclosure of affirmative action information did not satisfy the "authorized by law" language of the Trade Secret Act, 18 U.S.C.S. § 1905 (2003)). Even if Executive Order 11,246 and its regulations are valid in terms of being within the power of the executive branch, are they consistent with equal protection principles? After *Adarand*, what is the status of these regulations?

In theory, of course, affirmative action need not mandate reverse discrimination in the sense of preferring less-qualified minorities and women over white males; rather, it simply seeks to ensure the kind of balanced workforce that is reasonably to be expected when employees are recruited, hired, and promoted on the basis of legitimate job requirements. See Legal Aid Socy. v. Brennan, 608 F.2d 1319, 1343 (9th Cir. 1979) ("Nothing in the decree . . . requires preferential treatment or discrimination on the basis of race or sex. We therefore need not consider when if ever racial and sexual preferences and discrimination undertaken to comply with Executive Order 11,246 can be lawful under either Title VII or the Constitution."). But in practice, an employer might well favor a protected class member over a white male in order to satisfy the goals imposed by the plan. *Legal Aid Society*, in fact, recognized this possibility: "Employers may find it expedient to adopt, indeed compliance officials may require, affirmative action programs that involve preference and discrimination. Both administrative and judicial remedies will be available to test the lawfulness of such provisions on the basis of a specific record." Id. at 1334. That was, of course, the allegation in *Johnson*. While the affirmative action plan there satisfied Title VII, would it be upheld under the equal protection clause?

8. Not only must an interest be compelling, but the government action pursuing it must also be narrowly tailored to achieve that interest. In Podberesky v. Kirwan, 38 F.3d 147 (4th Cir. 1994), the court accepted as a compelling state interest the use of race to remedy the present effects of the past discrimination of a state actor that had earlier racially segregated, but it nevertheless found that the University of Maryland's plan was not narrowly tailored to serve that interest. In contrast, in Hunter v. Regents of the University of California, 190 F.3d 1061 (9th Cir. 1999), the challenged admissions process satisfied the strict scrutiny standard because the state had a compelling interest in providing effective education and the research school's use of race and ethnicity was narrowly tailored to achieve the necessary laboratory environment to produce effective research results.

9. *Weber* and *Johnson* hold that, in passing Title VII, Congress did not intend to ban voluntary affirmative action. While employees of public employers will now surely use *Croson* and *Adarand* to attack affirmative action, what effect do these two holdings have on the voluntary use of affirmative action by private employers? *Croson* and *Adarand* do not require Congress to ban affirmative action by statute, but do these cases suggest that the present Supreme Court will find that *Weber* and *Johnson* are wrong in their interpretation of what Congress intended in enacting Title VII?

10. In Hill v. Ross, 183 F.3d 586 (7th Cir. 1999), the court reversed a grant of summary judgment in favor of a college in a reverse sex discrimination suit. Plaintiff proffered sufficient evidence to find that a dean blocked a department recommendation

to hire a male professor, and left the position vacant, because he desired to hire more women. A reasonable jury could find that "Dean Ross used Hill's sex not as one factor among many, but as the sole basis for his decision." Id. at 588. This would be impermissible under both *Johnson* and *Wygant,* much less under the stricter standard of *Adarand.* Further, the university did not contend that its affirmative action plan was "essential to eradicate the consequences of prior discrimination." Id. at 589. In any event, however, the plan did not *require* Dean Ross's action. While that plan encouraged "outreach" to minorities and women, it did not require any specific number of hires, and therefore did not justify the dean's action. Finally, the court found that the equal protection clause required an "exceedingly persuasive" justification for any gender discrimination, and the university — having denied past discrimination against women — did not offer any justification at all. If a justification had been offered, *Johnson* would require the plaintiff to overcome it, but no such burden needs to be carried by the plaintiff if the defendant simply denies discrimination.

11. In Texas v. Lesage, 528 U.S. 18 (1999), the Supreme Court addressed the rights of individual plaintiffs attacking an affirmative action plan. At issue was the University of Texas's claim that, even if the plaintiff proved it had used an impermissible racial preference, the case should still be dismissed since plaintiff would not have been admitted in any event. The Court's per curiam opinion agreed to the extent that

> The government can avoid liability by proving that it would have made the same decision without the impermissible motive.
>
> Simply put, where a plaintiff challenges a discrete governmental decision as being based on an impermissible criterion and it is undisputed that the government would have made the same decision regardless, there is no cognizable injury warranting relief under §1983.

Id. at 20. The Court did recognize an exception: "a plaintiff who challenges an ongoing race-conscious program and seeks forward-looking relief need not affirmatively establish that he would receive the benefit in question if race were not considered. The relevant injury in such cases is 'the inability to compete on an equal footing'" (quoting Northeastern Fla. Chapter, Associated Gen. Contractors of America v. Jacksonville, 508 U.S. 656, 666 (1993)). Id. With respect to damages, this analysis follows the *Price Waterhouse* approach, which was superceded by the 1991 Amendments for Title VII cases but continues to apply to § 1983 claims. As for injunctive relief, apparently no harm other than a dignitary offense need be established for a § 1983 suit.

12. How would you argue *Adarand* on remand if you represented the government? Does the articulated standard of review actually make any difference if strict scrutiny can be satisfied?

13. What if a construction firm owned and run by females applies for and is awarded the contract pursuant to the federal preference program at issue in *Adarand*? In United States v. Virginia, 518 U.S. 515 (1996), the Court struck down, on equal protection grounds, the exclusion of women from the Virginia Military Institute. In doing so, the Court applied the following standard of review:

> Without equating gender classifications, for all purposes, to classifications based on race or national origin, the Court has carefully inspected official action that closes a door or denies opportunity to women (or to men). To summarize the Court's current directions for cases of official classification based on gender: Focusing on the differential treatment or denial of opportunity for which relief is sought, the reviewing court must determine whether the proffered justification is "exceedingly persuasive." The burden of

justification is demanding and it rests entirely on the State. The State must show "at least that the [challenged] classification serves 'important governmental objectives and that the discriminatory means employed' are 'substantially related to the achievement of those objectives.'" The justification must be genuine, not hypothesized or invented post hoc in response to litigation. And it must not rely on overbroad generalizations about the different talents, capacities, or preferences of males and females.

Does this standard apply at all to affirmative action benefitting women? If not, what standard applies? Rational relationship? Or strict scrutiny? If the VMI standard does apply to affirmative action benefitting women, does that mean it is easier to sustain affirmative action for women than for African Americans?

All members of the VMI Court were in agreement that intermediate scrutiny applies to cases involving gender classifications, but Chief Justice Rehnquist concurred, citing extensive precedent that the proferred justification need not be "exceedingly persuasive," but merely serve "important governmental objectives." Justice Scalia's dissent argued that Virginia's decision to find one all-male was substantially related to its important educational interests.

14. In *Adarand*, Justice Stevens criticized the majority's view of "consistency," which would allow the government to "more easily enact affirmative-action programs to remedy discrimination against women than it can enact affirmative-action programs to remedy discrimination against African Americans. . . ." This is true, writes the Justice, "even though the primary purpose of the Equal Protection Clause was to end discrimination against the former slaves." Does this mean that affirmative action programs based on race should be subject to the less-exacting intermediate scrutiny, or should the standard of review for gender-based affirmative action programs be raised? If Justice Stevens is correct, can the fact that it is easier to implement an affirmative action program benefitting women than it would be for African Americans be reconciled with the original intent of the equal protection clause? If the lower level of scrutiny for gender-based classifications is grounded in the idea that women do not require as much protection against invidious discrimination as African Americans do, should the standards be reversed for affirmative-action cases?

15. For the Fifth Circuit, this debate may be moot. In Dallas Fire Fighters Assn. v. City of Dallas, 150 F.3d 438 (1998), the court applied strict scrutiny to race-based affirmative action decisions and intermediate scrutiny to gender-based affirmative action decisions. Neither passed constitutional muster, since, according to the court, the city showed little evidence of prior race- or gender-based discrimination.

16. The Supreme Court affirmative action cases have so far dealt with preferences for minority group members in employment decisions. What about non-preferential affirmative action involving outreach and recruitment? Do those plans involve the use of racial classifications that trigger strict scrutiny? See Michelle Adams, The Last Wave of Affirmative Action, 1998 Wis. L. Rev. 1395, 1463 (1998) ("race-conscious, non-preferential affirmative action programs ensure enhanced and vigorous competition for benefits such as employment . . . and seek to even what has historically been an extraordinarily skewed playing field. As such, these programs promote the American ideal of a truly colorblind society and are necessary to ensure equal opportunity for all its citizens."). In Clough v. City of New Haven, 2002 U.S. App. LEXIS 3511, p. *7 (2d Cir. 2002), the court held that where the intent underlying a consent decree was "to remedy past discrimination against minorities [that] does not amount to a forbidden racial classification or an intent to discriminate against non-minority candidates unless it involves measures like quotas, set-asides, or preferential grading that prevent non-minorities from competing for positions."

17. Justice Stevens referred to "special preferences" the federal government has historically accorded Native Americans. The extent to which constitutional principles may be used to attack "affirmative action" involving Native Americans is explored in Carole Goldberg, American Indians and "Preferential Treatment," 49 UCLA L. Rev. 943 (2002).

18. Peter H. Schuck, Affirmative Action: Past, Present, and Future, 20 Yale L. & Pol'y Rev. 1, 3 (2002):

> My chief concern here is not with the constitutionality of ethno-racial affirmative action, but with its wisdom as public policy. In my view — much too briefly stated — the Constitution should be interpreted to permit Congress to adopt a law preferring blacks so long as it does not violate the heightened constitutional protection that other racial minorities enjoy. At the time of the Fourteenth Amendment, after all, Congress did just that. Congress enacts laws every day that favor one group over another, laws that if rational are constitutional. That being so, Congress has the power to favor blacks at the expense of the white majority if it believes that this would be sound policy. Whether it can favor blacks over other disadvantaged ethno-racial minorities, as affirmative action sometimes does, is less clear.

Professor Shuck, nevertheless, argues that such a law should not be adopted. "But my larger point is that even if an ethno-racial preference could meet the Court's standard, it should not be adopted and that most proposals for reform would be impractical, ineffective, or make matters even worse." Id. at 4.

19. Abraham L. Wickelgren, The Efficiency of Affirmative Action with Purely Historical Discrimination, at http://papers.ssrn.com/sol3/results.cfm (2002), argues that affirmative action is economically efficient since firms that act rationally will "favor more able workers over more qualified ones."

> Because ability and class both affect educational attainment, . . . higher ability minorities will earn less even after discrimination ends. . . . This implies that minorities remain more able than non-minorities of similar educational attainment, so non-discriminatory firms will voluntarily practice affirmative action when there has been past discrimination. This suggests that the recent laws and court decisions restricting governmental affirmative action impede the government's ability to act efficiently.

## PROBLEM 4.3

If Johnson attacked the constitutionality of Santa Clara's decision to promote Joyce, what standard of review would apply? Would Santa Clara's affirmative action plan and the specific decision to promote Joyce survive constitutional attack? What arguments would you make for Johnson? What arguments would you make for Santa Clara?

# Chapter 5

# Systemic Disparate
# Impact Discrimination

While disparate treatment discrimination is the purposeful exclusion of minorities or women from jobs, disparate impact discrimination exists when employment policies, regardless of intent, adversely affect one group more than another and cannot be adequately justified. This chapter presents the structure of disparate impact analysis, the policies subject to disparate impact analysis, and defenses to a disparate impact case.

As we will see, the disparate impact theory clearly applies under Title VII of the Civil Rights Act of 1964, 42 U.S.C.S. §§ 2000e to 2000e-17 (2003), and the Americans with Disabilities Act ("ADA"), 42 U.S.C.S. §§ 12111 et seq. (2003). It may also operate under the Age Discrimination in Employment Act ("ADEA"), 29 U.S.C.S. §§ 631-634 (2003), but neither Congress nor the Supreme Court has spoken definitively on this point. The Supreme Court has held that disparate impact is *not* available under 42 U.S.C.S. § 1981 (2003), General Bldg. Contractors Assn. v. Pennsylvania, 458 U.S. 375 (2002), or under 42 U.S.C.S. § 1983 (2003) in suits enforcing the equal protection clause of the United States Constitution, e.g., Personnel Administrator of Massachusetts v. Feeney, 442 U.S. 256, 272 (1979).

Even under Title VII, where disparate impact originated as a theory of liability, recent developments have altered the landscape. The theory originated in 1971 in Griggs v. Duke Power Co., 401 U.S. 424, and was elaborated on in a number of Supreme Court decisions until 1989, when Wards Cove Packing Co. v. Atonio, 490 U.S. 642, radically reconceptualized the law. Congress, in turn, revived disparate impact analysis as the centerpiece (and most controversial) part of the Civil Rights Act of 1991.*

This chapter proceeds as follows. Section A introduces the concept and policy justifications of disparate impact analysis. Section B then addresses the contemporary structure of disparate impact law emerging from the amendments to Title VII added by the Civil Rights Act of 1991. Section C deals with the exceptions to disparate impact analysis for professionally developed tests and bona fide seniority and merit systems.

# A.   THE CONCEPT OF DISPARATE IMPACT DISCRIMINATION

## GRIGGS v. DUKE POWER CO.
### 401 U.S. 424 (1971)

Chief Justice BURGER delivered the opinion of the Court.

We granted the writ in this case to resolve the question whether an employer is prohibited by the Civil Rights Act of 1964, Title VII, from requiring a high school education or passing of a standardized general intelligence test as a condition of employment in or transfer to jobs when (a) neither standard is shown to be significantly related to successful job performance, (b) both requirements operate to disqualify Negroes at a substantially higher rate than white applicants, and (c) the jobs in question formerly had been filled only by white employees as part of a longstanding practice of giving preference to whites.

Congress provided, in Title VII of the Civil Rights Act of 1964, for class actions for enforcement of provisions of the Act and this proceeding was brought by a group of incumbent Negro employees against Duke Power Company. All the petitioners are employed at the Company's Dan River Steam Station, a power generating facility located at Draper, North Carolina. At the time this action was instituted, the Company had 95 employees at the Dan River Station, 14 of whom were Negroes; 13 of these are petitioners here.

The District Court found that prior to July 2, 1965, the effective date of the Civil Rights Act of 1964, the company openly discriminated on the basis of race in the hiring and assigning of employees at its Dan River plant. The plant was organized into five operating departments: (1) Labor, (2) Coal Handling, (3) Operations, (4) Maintenance, and (5) Laboratory and Test. Negroes were employed only in the Labor Department where the highest paying jobs paid less than the lowest paying jobs in the other four "operating" departments in which only whites were employed.[2] Promotions

---

* The controversy over the Civil Rights Act of 1991 centered primarily on the effort to make it easier for employees to prevail in disparate impact cases. The intensity of that controversy, however, may seem strange since only a small percentage of the total federal employment discrimination caseload involves disparate impact claims. See John J. Donohue III & Peter Siegelman, The Changing Nature of Employment Discrimination Litigation, 43 Stan. L. Rev. 983, 989 (1991) (only 101 of the 7,613 employment civil rights cases brought in 1989 alleged disparate impact discrimination). Others have argued, however, that the number of litigated cases is not a good measure of the significance of the disparate impact theory since employees may alter their policies in response to the risk such cases impose.

2. A Negro was first assigned to a job in an operating department in August 1966, five months after charges had been filed with the Equal Employment Opportunity Commission. The employee, a high

were normally made within each department on the basis of job seniority. Transferees into a department usually began in the lowest position.

In 1955 the Company instituted a policy of requiring a high school education for initial assignment to any department except Labor, and for transfer from the Coal Handling to any "inside" department (Operations, Maintenance, or Laboratory). When the Company abandoned its policy of restricting Negroes to the Labor Department in 1965, completion of high school also was made a prerequisite to transfer from Labor to any other department. From the time the high school requirement was instituted to the time of trial, however, white employees hired before the time of the high school education requirement continued to perform satisfactorily and achieve promotions in the "operating" departments. Findings on this score are not challenged.

The Company added a further requirement for new employees on July 2, 1965, the date on which Title VII became effective. To qualify for placement in any but the Labor Department it became necessary to register satisfactory scores on two professionally prepared aptitude tests, as well as to have a high school education. Completion of high school alone continued to render employees eligible for transfer to the four desirable departments from which Negroes had been excluded if the incumbent had been employed prior to the time of the new requirement. In September 1965 the Company began to permit incumbent employees who lacked a high school education to qualify for transfer from Labor or Coal Handling to an "inside" job by passing two tests — the Wonderlic Personnel Test, which purports to measure general intelligence, and the Bennett Mechanical Comprehension Test. Neither was directed or intended to measure the ability to learn to perform a particular job or category of jobs. The requisite scores used for both initial hiring and transfer approximated the national median for high school graduates.[3]

The District Court had found that while the Company previously followed a policy of overt racial discrimination in a period prior to the Act, such conduct had ceased. The District Court also concluded that Title VII was intended to be prospective only and, consequently, the impact of prior inequities was beyond the reach of corrective action authorized by the Act.

. . . The Court of Appeals noted . . . that the District Court was correct in its conclusion that there was no showing of a racial purpose or invidious intent in the adoption of the high school diploma requirement or general intelligence test and that these standards had been applied fairly to whites and Negroes alike. It held that, in the absence of a discriminatory purpose, use of such requirements was permitted by the Act. In so doing, the Court of Appeals rejected the claim that because these two requirements operated to render ineligible a markedly disproportionate number of Negroes, they were unlawful under Title VII unless shown to be job related. . . .

The objective of Congress in the enactment of Title VII is plain from the language of the statute. It was to achieve equality of employment opportunities and remove barriers that have operated in the past to favor an identifiable group of white employees over other employees. Under the Act, practices, procedures, or tests neutral on their face, and even neutral in terms of intent, cannot be maintained if they operate to "freeze" the status quo of prior discriminatory employment practices.

school graduate who had begun in the Labor Department in 1953, was promoted to a job in the Coal Handling Department.

3. The test standards are thus more stringent than the high school requirement, since they would screen out approximately half of all high school graduates.

The Court of Appeals' [judges] agreed that, on the record in the present case, "whites register far better on the Company's alternative requirements" than Negroes.[6] This consequence would appear to be directly traceable to race. Basic intelligence must have the means of articulation to manifest itself fairly in a testing process. Because they are Negroes, petitioners have long received inferior education in segregated schools and this Court expressly recognized these differences in Gaston County v. United States, 395 U.S. 285 (1969). There, because of the inferior education received by Negroes in North Carolina, this Court barred the institution of a literacy test for voter registration on the ground that the test would abridge the right to vote indirectly on account of race. Congress did not intend by Title VII, however, to guarantee a job to every person regardless of qualifications. In short, the Act does not command that any person be hired simply because he was formerly the subject of discrimination, or because he is a member of a minority group. Discriminatory preference for any group, minority or majority, is precisely and only what Congress has proscribed. What is required by Congress is the removal of artificial, arbitrary, and unnecessary barriers to employment when the barriers operate invidiously to discriminate on the basis of a racial or other impermissible classification.

Congress has now provided that tests or criteria for employment or promotion may not provide equality of opportunity merely in the sense of the fabled offer of milk to the stork and the fox. On the contrary, Congress has now required that the posture and condition of the job-seeker be taken into account. It has — to resort again to the fable — provided that the vessel in which the milk is proffered be one all seekers can use. The Act proscribes not only overt discrimination but also practices that are fair in form, but discriminatory in operation. The touchstone is business necessity. If an employment practice which operates to exclude Negroes cannot be shown to be related to job performance, the practice is prohibited.

On the record before us, neither the high school completion requirement nor the general intelligence test is shown to bear a demonstrable relationship to successful performance of the jobs for which it was used. Both were adopted, as the Court of Appeals noted, without meaningful study of their relationship to job-performance ability. Rather, a vice president of the Company testified, the requirements were instituted on the Company's judgment that they generally would improve the overall quality of the work force.

The evidence, however, shows that employees who have not completed high school or taken the tests have continued to perform satisfactorily and make progress in departments for which the high school and test criteria are now used. The promotion record of present employees who would not be able to meet the new criteria thus suggests the possibility that the requirements may not be needed even for the limited purpose of preserving the avowed policy of advancement within the Company. In the context of this case, it is unnecessary to reach the question whether testing requirements that take into account capability for the next succeeding position or related future promotion might be utilized upon a showing that such long-range requirements

6. In North Carolina, 1960 census statistics show that, while 34% of white males had completed high school, only 12% of Negro males had done so. U.S. Bureau of the Census, U.S. Census of Population: 1960, Vol. 1, Characteristics of the Population, pt. 35, Table 47.

Similarly, with respect to standardized tests, the EEOC in one case found that use of a battery of tests, including the Wonderlic and Bennett tests used by the Company in the instant case, resulted in 58% of whites passing the tests as compared with only 6% of the blacks. Decision of EEOC, CCH Empl. Prac. Guide, ¶17,304.53 (Dec. 2, 1966). See also Decision of EEOC 70-552, CCH Empl. Prac. Guide, ¶6139 (Feb. 19, 1970).

fulfill a genuine business need. In the present case the Company has made no such showing.

The Court of Appeals held that the Company had adopted the diploma and test requirements without any "intention to discriminate against Negro employees." We do not suggest that either the District Court or the Court of Appeals erred in examining the employer's intent; but good intent or absence of discriminatory intent does not redeem employment procedures or testing mechanisms that operate as "built-in headwinds" for minority groups and are unrelated to measuring job capability.

The Company's lack of discriminatory intent is suggested by special efforts to help the undereducated employees through Company financing of two-thirds the cost of tuition for high school training. But Congress directed the thrust of the Act to the *consequences* of employment practices, not simply the motivation. More than that, Congress has placed on the employer the burden of showing that any given requirement must have a manifest relationship to the employment in question.

The facts of this case demonstrate the inadequacy of broad and general testing devices as well as the infirmity of using diplomas or degrees as fixed measures of capability. History is filled with examples of men and women who rendered highly effective performance without the conventional badges of accomplishment in terms of certificates, diplomas, or degrees. Diplomas and tests are useful servants, but Congress has mandated the common sense proposition that they are not to become masters of reality.

The Company contends that its general intelligence tests are specifically permitted by § 703(h) of the Act.[8] That section authorizes the use of "any professionally developed ability test" that is not "designed, intended or *used* to discriminate because of race. . . ." (Emphasis added.)

The Equal Employment Opportunity Commission, having enforcement responsibility, has issued guidelines interpreting Section 703(h) to permit only the use of job-related tests.[9] The administrative interpretation of the Act by the enforcing agency is entitled to great deference. Since the Act and its legislative history support the Commission's construction, this affords good reason to treat the guidelines as expressing the will of Congress.

Section 703(h) was not contained in the House version of the Civil Rights Act but was added in the Senate during extended debate. For a period, debate revolved around claims that the bill as proposed would prohibit all testing and force employers to hire unqualified persons simply because they were part of a group formerly subject to job discrimination. Proponents of Title VII sought throughout the debate to assure the critics that the Act would have no effect on job-related tests. Senators Case of New Jersey and Clark of Pennsylvania, co-managers of the bill on the Senate floor, issued a

---

8. Section 703(h) applies only to tests. It has no applicability to the high school diploma requirement.
9. EEOC Guidelines on Employment Testing Procedures, issued August 24, 1966, provide:

> The Commission accordingly interprets "professionally developed ability test" to mean a test which fairly measures the knowledge or skills required by the particular job or class of jobs which the applicant seeks, or which fairly affords the employer a chance to measure the applicant's ability to perform a particular job or class of jobs. The fact that a test was prepared by an individual or organization claiming expertise in test preparation does not, without more, justify its use within the meaning of Title VII.

> The EEOC position has been elaborated in the new Guidelines on Employee Selection Procedures, 29 C.F.R. § 1607, 35 Fed. Reg. 12333 (Aug. 1, 1970). These guidelines demand that employers using tests have available "data demonstrating that the test is predictive of or significantly correlated with important elements of work behavior which comprise or are relevant to the job or jobs for which candidates are being evaluated." Id., at § 1607.4(c).

memorandum explaining that the proposed Title VII "expressly protects the employer's right to insist that any prospective applicant, Negro or white, *must meet the applicable job qualifications*. Indeed, the very purpose of Title VII is to promote hiring on the basis of job qualifications, rather than on the basis of race or color." 110 Cong. Rec. 7247.[11] (Emphasis added.) Despite these assurances, Senator Tower of Texas introduced an amendment authorizing "professionally developed ability tests." Proponents of Title VII opposed the amendment because, as written, it would permit an employer to give any test, "whether it was a good test or not, so long as it was professionally designed. Discrimination could actually exist under the guise of compliance with the statute." 110 Cong. Rec. 13504 (remarks of Sen. Case).

The amendment was defeated and two days later Senator Tower offered a substitute amendment which was adopted verbatim and is now the testing provision of § 703(h). Speaking for the supporters of Title VII, Senator Humphrey, who had vigorously opposed the first amendment, endorsed the substitute amendment, stating: "Senators on both sides of the aisle who were deeply interested in Title VII have examined the text of this amendment and have found it to be in accord with the intent and purpose of that title." 110 Cong. Rec. 13724. The amendment was then adopted. From the sum of the legislative history relevant in this case, the conclusion is inescapable that the EEOC's construction of § 703(h) to require that employment tests be job related comports with congressional intent.

Nothing in the Act precludes the use of testing or measuring procedures; obviously they are useful. What Congress has forbidden is giving these devices and mechanisms controlling force unless they are demonstrably a reasonable measure of job performance. Congress has not commanded that the less qualified be preferred over the better qualified simply because of minority origins. Far from disparaging job qualifications as such, Congress has made such qualifications the controlling factor, so that race, religion, nationality, and sex become irrelevant. What Congress has commanded is that any tests used must measure the person for the job and not the person in the abstract. . . .

## WARDS COVE PACKING CO. v. ATONIO
### 490 U.S. 642 (1989)

Justice WHITE delivered the opinion of the Court.

---

11. The Court of Appeals majority, in finding no requirement in Title VII that employment tests be job related, relied in part on a quotation from an earlier Clark-Case interpretive memorandum addressed to the question of the constitutionality of Title VII. The Senators said in that memorandum:

> There is no requirement in Title VII that employers abandon bona fide qualifications tests where, because of differences in background and education, members of some groups are able to perform better on these tests than members of other groups. An employer may set his qualifications as high as he likes, he may test to determine which applicants have these qualifications, and he may hire, assign, and promote on the basis of test performance. [110 Cong. Rec. 7213.]

However, nothing there stated conflicts with the later memorandum dealing specifically with the debate over employer testing, 110 Cong. Rec. 7247 (quoted from in the text above), in which Senators Clark and Case explained that tests which measure "applicable job qualifications" are permissible under Title VII. In the earlier memorandum Clark and Case assured the Senate that employers were not to be prohibited from using tests that determine *qualifications*. Certainly a reasonable interpretation of what the Senators meant, in light of the subsequent memorandum directed specifically at employer testing, was that nothing in the Act prevents employers from requiring that applicants be fit for the job.

I

The claims before us are disparate-impact claims, involving the employment practices of petitioners, two companies that operate salmon canneries in remote and widely separated areas of Alaska. The canneries operate only during the salmon runs in the summer months. They are inoperative and vacant for the rest of the year. In May or June of each year, a few weeks before the salmon runs begin, workers arrive and prepare the equipment and facilities for the canning operation. Most of these workers possess a variety of skills. When salmon runs are about to begin, the workers who will operate the cannery lines arrive, remain as long as there are fish to can, and then depart. The canneries are then closed down, winterized, and left vacant until the next spring. During the off-season, the companies employ only a small number of individuals at their headquarters in Seattle and Astoria, Oregon, plus some employees at the winter shipyard in Seattle.

The length and size of salmon runs vary from year to year, and hence the number of employees needed at each cannery also varies. Estimates are made as early in the winter as possible; the necessary employees are hired, and when the time comes, they are transported to the canneries. Salmon must be processed soon after they are caught, and the work during the canning season is therefore intense. For this reason, and because the canneries are located in remote regions, all workers are housed at the canneries and have their meals in company-owned mess halls.

Jobs at the canneries are of two general types: "cannery jobs" on the cannery line, which are unskilled positions; and "noncannery jobs," which fall into a variety of classifications. Most noncannery jobs are classified as skilled positions.[3] Cannery jobs are filled predominantly by nonwhites: Filipinos and Alaska Natives. The Filipinos are hired through, and dispatched by, Local 37 of the International Longshoremen's and Warehousemen's Union pursuant to a hiring hall agreement with the local. The Alaska Natives primarily reside in villages near the remote cannery locations. Noncannery jobs are filled with predominantly white workers, who are hired during the winter months from the companies' offices in Washington and Oregon. Virtually all of the noncannery jobs pay more than cannery positions. The predominantly white noncannery workers and the predominantly nonwhite cannery employees live in separate dormitories and eat in separate mess halls.

In 1974, respondents, a class of nonwhite cannery workers who were (or had been) employed at the canneries, brought this Title VII action against petitioners. Respondents alleged that a variety of petitioners' hiring/promotion practices — e.g., nepotism, a rehire preference, a lack of objective hiring criteria, separate hiring channels, a practice of not promoting from within — were responsible for the racial stratification of the work force and had denied them and other nonwhites employment as noncannery workers on the basis of race. Respondents also complained of petitioners' racially segregated housing and dining facilities. . . .

[The Court of Appeals held that disparate impact analysis applied to subjective hiring practices. It found that respondents established a prima facie case of disparate impact in hiring for both skilled and unskilled noncannery positions and remanded], instructing the District Court that it was the employer's burden to prove that any

3. The noncannery jobs were described as follows by the Court of Appeals: "Machinists and engineers are hired to maintain the smooth and continuous operation of the canning equipment. Quality control personnel conduct the FDA-required inspections and record keeping. Tenders are staffed with a crew necessary to operate the vessel. A variety of support personnel are employed to operate the entire cannery community, including, for example, cooks, carpenters, store-keepers, bookkeepers, beach gangs for dock yard labor and construction, etc."

disparate impact caused by its hiring and employment practices was justified by business necessity. . . .

## II

In holding that respondents had made out a prima facie case of disparate impact, the Court of Appeals relied solely on respondents' statistics showing a high percentage of nonwhite workers in the cannery jobs and a low percentage of such workers in the noncannery positions. Although statistical proof can alone make out a prima facie case, the Court of Appeals' ruling here misapprehends our precedents and the purposes of Title VII, and we therefore reverse.

"There can be no doubt," as there was when a similar mistaken analysis had been undertaken by the courts below in *Hazelwood*, "that the . . . comparison . . . fundamentally misconceived the role of statistics in employment discrimination cases." The "proper comparison [is] between the racial composition of [the at-issue jobs] and the racial composition of the qualified . . . population in the relevant labor market." [It is such a comparison — between the racial composition of the qualified persons in the labor market and the persons holding at-issue jobs — that generally forms the proper basis for the initial inquiry in a disparate impact case.] Alternatively, in cases where such labor market statistics will be difficult if not impossible to ascertain, we have recognized that certain other statistics — such as measures indicating the racial composition of "otherwise-qualified applicants" for at-issue jobs — are equally probative for this purpose. See, e.g., New York City Transit Authority v. Beazer, 440 U.S. 568 (1979).[6]

It is clear to us that the Court of Appeals' acceptance of the comparison between the racial composition of the cannery work force and that of the noncannery work force, as probative of a prima facie case of disparate impact in the selection of the latter group of workers, was flawed for several reasons. Most obviously, with respect to the skilled noncannery jobs at issue here, the cannery work force in no way reflected "the pool of *qualified* job applicants" or the "*qualified* population in the labor force." Measuring alleged discrimination in the selection of accountants, managers, boat captains, electricians, doctors, and engineers — and the long list of other "skilled" noncannery positions found to exist by the District Court, by comparing the number of nonwhites occupying these jobs to the number of nonwhites filling cannery worker positions is nonsensical. If the absence of minorities holding such skilled positions is due to a dearth of qualified nonwhite applicants (for reasons that are not petitioners' fault), petitioners' selection methods or employment practices cannot be said to have had a "disparate impact" on nonwhites.

One example illustrates why this must be so. Respondents' own statistics concerning the noncannery work force at one of the canneries at issue here indicate that approximately 17% of the new hires for medical jobs, and 15% of the new hires for officer worker positions, were nonwhite. If it were the case that less than 15 to 17% of the applicants for these jobs were nonwhite and that nonwhites made up a lower percentage of the relevant qualified labor market, it is hard to see how respondents, without more, would have made out a prima facie case of disparate impact. Yet, under the Court of Appeals' theory, simply because nonwhites comprise 52% of the cannery

6. In fact, where "figures for the general population might . . . accurately reflect the pool of qualified job applicants," we have even permitted plaintiffs to rest their prima facie cases on such statistics as well. See, e.g., Dothard v. Rawlinson.

workers at the cannery in question respondents would be successful in establishing a prima facie case of racial discrimination under Title VII.

Such a result cannot be squared with our cases or with the goals behind the statute. The Court of Appeals' theory, at the very least, would mean that any employer who had a segment of his work force that was — for some reason — racially imbalanced, could be haled into court and forced to engage in the expensive and time-consuming task of defending the "business necessity" of the methods used to select the other members of his work force. The only practicable option for many employers would be to adopt racial quotas, insuring that no portion of their work forces deviated in racial composition from the other portions thereof; this is a result that Congress expressly rejected in drafting Title VII. See 42 U.S.C. § 2000e-2(j). . . . The Court of Appeals' theory would "leave the employer little choice . . . but to engage in a subjective quota system of employment selection. This, of course, is far from the intent of Title VII." Albemarle Paper Co. v. Moody, 422 U.S. 405, 449 (1975) (Blackmun, J., concurring in judgment).

The Court of Appeals also erred with respect to the unskilled noncannery positions. Racial imbalance in one segment of an employer's work force does not, without more, establish a prima facie case of disparate impact with respect to the selection of workers for the employer's other positions, even where workers for the different positions may have somewhat fungible skills (as is arguably the case for cannery and unskilled noncannery workers). As long as there are no barriers or practices deterring qualified nonwhites from applying for noncannery positions, if the percentage of selected applicants who are nonwhite is not significantly less than the percentage of qualified applicants who are nonwhite, the employer's selection mechanism probably does not operate with a disparate impact on minorities.[8] Where this is the case, the percentage of nonwhite workers found in other positions in the employer's labor force is irrelevant to the question of a prima facie statistical case of disparate impact. As noted above, a contrary ruling on this point would almost inexorably lead to the use of numerical quotas in the workplace, a result that Congress and this Court have rejected repeatedly in the past.

Moreover, isolating the cannery workers as the potential "labor force" for unskilled noncannery positions is at once both too broad and too narrow in its focus. It is too broad because the vast majority of these cannery workers did not seek jobs in unskilled noncannery positions; there is no showing that many of them would have done so even if none of the arguably "deterring" practices existed. Thus, the pool of cannery workers cannot be used as a surrogate for the class of qualified job applicants because it contains many persons who have not (and would not) be noncannery job applicants. Conversely, if respondents propose to use the cannery workers for comparison purposes because they represent the "qualified labor population" generally, the group is too narrow because there are obviously many qualified persons in the labor market for noncannery jobs who are not cannery workers.

The peculiar facts of this case further illustrate why a comparison between the percentage of nonwhite cannery workers and nonwhite noncannery workers is an

---

8. We qualify this conclusion — observing that it is only "probable" that there has been no disparate impact on minorities in such circumstances — because bottom-line racial balance is not a defense under Title VII. See Connecticut v. Teal. Thus, even if petitioners could show that the percentage of selected applicants who are nonwhite is not significantly less than the percentage of qualified applicants who are nonwhite, respondents would still have a case under Title VII, if they could prove that some particular hiring practice has a disparate impact on minorities, notwithstanding the bottom-line racial balance in petitioners' work force.

improper basis for making out a claim of disparate impact. Here, the District Court found that nonwhites were "overrepresent[ed]" among cannery workers because petitioners had contracted with a predominantly nonwhite union (local 37) to fill these positions. As a result, if petitioners (for some permissible reason) ceased using local 37 as its hiring channel for cannery positions, it appears (according to the District Court's findings) that the racial stratification between the cannery and noncannery workers might diminish to statistical insignificance. Under the Court of Appeals' approach, therefore, it is possible that *with no change whatsoever* in their hiring practices for noncannery workers — the jobs at issue in this lawsuit — petitioners could make respondents' prima facie case of disparate impact "disappear." But *if* there would be no prima facie case of disparate impact in the selection of noncannery workers absent petitioners' use of local 37 to hire cannery workers, surely petitioners' reliance on the union to fill the cannery jobs not at issue here (and its resulting "overrepresentation" of nonwhites in those positions) does not — standing alone — make out a prima facie case of disparate impact. Yet it is precisely such an ironic result that the Court of Appeals reached below.

Consequently, we reverse the Court of Appeals' ruling that a comparison between the percentage of cannery workers who are nonwhite and the percentage of noncannery workers who are nonwhite makes out a prima facie case of disparate impact.

## III

Since the statistical disparity relied on by the Court of Appeals did not suffice to make out a prima facie case, any inquiry by us into whether the specific challenged employment practices of petitioners caused that disparity is pretermitted, as is any inquiry into whether the disparate impact that any employment practice may have had was justified by business considerations.[9] Because we remand for further proceedings, however, on whether a prima facie case of disparate impact has been made in defensible fashion in this case, we address two other challenges petitioners have made to the decision of the Court of Appeals.

### A

First is the question of causation in a disparate-impact case. The law in this respect was correctly stated by Justice O'Connor's opinion last Term in Watson v. Fort Worth Bank & Trust [reproduced at page 342]:

> [W]e note that the plaintiff's burden in establishing a prima facie case goes beyond the need to show that there are statistical disparities in the employer's work force. The plaintiff must begin by identifying the specific employment practice that is challenged. . . . Especially in cases where an employer combines subjective criteria with the use of more rigid standardized rules or tests, the plaintiff is in our view responsible for isolating and identifying the specific employment practices that are allegedly responsible for any observed statistical disparities.

9. As we understand the opinions below, the specific employment practices were challenged only insofar as they were claimed to have been responsible for the overall disparity between the number of minority cannery and noncannery workers. The Court of Appeals did not purport to hold that any specified employment practice produced its own disparate impact that was actionable under Title VII. This is not to say that a specific practice, such as nepotism, if it were proved to exist, could not itself be subject to challenge if it had a disparate impact on minorities. Nor is it to say that segregated dormitories and eating facilities in the workplace may not be challenged under 42 U.S.C. § 2000e-2(a)(2) without showing a disparate impact on hiring or promotion.

. . . Our disparate-impact cases have always focused on the impact of *particular* hiring practices on employment opportunities for minorities. Just as an employer cannot escape liability under Title VII by demonstrating that, "at the bottom line," his work force is racially balanced (where particular hiring practices may operate to deprive minorities of employment opportunities), see Connecticut v. Teal, 457 U.S. [440, 450 (1980) reproduced at page 347], a Title VII plaintiff does not make out a case of disparate impact simply by showing that, "at the bottom line," there is racial imbalance in the work force. As a general matter, a plaintiff must demonstrate that it is the application of a specific or particular employment practice that has created the disparate impact under attack. Such a showing is an integral part of the plaintiff's prima facie case in a disparate-impact suit under Title VII.

Here, respondents have alleged that several "objective" employment practices (e.g., nepotism, separate hiring channels, rehire preferences), as well as the use of "subjective decision making" to select noncannery workers, have had a disparate impact on nonwhites. Respondents base this claim on statistics that allegedly show a disproportionately low percentage of nonwhites in the at-issue positions. However, even if on remand respondents can show that nonwhites are underrepresented in the at-issue jobs in a manner that is acceptable under the standards set forth above, this alone will not suffice to make out a prima facie case of disparate impact. Respondents will also have to demonstrate that the disparity they complain of is the result of one or more of the employment practices that they are attacking here, specifically showing that each challenged practice has a significantly disparate impact on employment opportunities for whites and nonwhites. To hold otherwise would result in employers being potentially liable for "the myriad of innocent causes that may lead to statistical imbalances in the composition of their work forces." *Watson.*

Some will complain that this specific causation requirement is unduly burdensome on Title VII plaintiffs. But liberal civil discovery rules give plaintiffs broad access to employers' records in an effort to document their claims. Also, employers falling within the scope of the Uniform Guidelines on Employee Selection Procedures, 29 CFR § 1607.1 et seq. (1988), are required to "maintain . . . records or other information which will disclose the impact which its tests and other selection procedures have upon employment opportunities of persons by identifiable race, sex, or ethnic group[s]." See § 1607.4(A). This includes records concerning "the individual components of the selection process" where there is a significant disparity in the selection rates of whites and nonwhites. See § 1607.4(C). Plaintiffs as a general matter will have the benefit of these tools to meet their burden of showing a causal link between challenged employment practices and racial imbalances in the work force. . . .

B

If, on remand, respondents meet the proof burdens outlined above, and establish a prima facie case of disparate impact with respect to any of petitioners' employment practices, the case will shift to any business justification petitioners offer for their use of these practices. This phase of the disparate-impact case contains two components: first, a consideration of the justifications an employer offers for his use of these practices; and second, the availability of alternative practices to achieve the same business ends, with less racial impact. See, e.g., Albemarle Paper Co. v. Moody. We consider these two components in turn.

*(1)*

Though we have phrased the query differently in different cases, it is generally well established that at the justification stage of such a disparate-impact case, the dispositive issue is whether a challenged practice serves, in a significant way, the legitimate employment goals of the employer. See, e.g., Watson v. Fort Worth Bank & Trust; New York City Transit Authority v. Beazer; Griggs v. Duke Power Co. The touchstone of this inquiry is a reasoned review of the employer's justification for his use of the challenged practice. A mere insubstantial justification in this regard will not suffice, because such a low standard of review would permit discrimination to be practiced through the use of spurious, seemingly neutral employment practices. At the same time, though, there is no requirement that the challenged practice be "essential" or "indispensable" to the employer's business for it to pass muster: this degree of scrutiny would be almost impossible for most employers to meet, and would result in a host of evils we have identified above.

In this phase, the employer carries the burden of producing evidence of a business justification for his employment practice. The burden of persuasion, however, remains with the disparate-impact plaintiff. . . . "[T]he ultimate burden of proving that discrimination against a protected group has been caused by a specific employment practice remains with the plaintiff *at all times.*" *Watson* (emphasis added). This rule conforms with the usual method for allocating persuasion and production burdens in the federal courts, see Fed. Rule Evid. 301, and more specifically, it conforms to the rule in disparate-treatment cases that the plaintiff bears the burden of disproving an employer's assertion that the adverse employment action or practice was based solely on a legitimate neutral consideration. See Texas Dept. of Community Affairs v. Burdine. We acknowledge that some of our earlier decisions can be read as suggesting otherwise. But to the extent that those cases speak of an employers' "burden of proof" with respect to a legitimate business justification defense, see, e.g., Dothard v. Rawlinson, 433 U.S. 321 (1977) [reproduced at page 358], they should have been understood to mean an employer's production — but not persuasion — burden. The persuasion burden here must remain with the plaintiff, for it is he who must prove that it was "because of such individual's race, color," etc., that he was denied a desired employment opportunity. See 42 U.S.C. § 2000e-2(a).

*(2)*

Finally, if on remand the case reaches this point, and respondents cannot persuade the trier of fact on the question of petitioners' business necessity defense, respondents may still be able to prevail. To do so, respondents will have to persuade the factfinder that "other tests or selection devices, without a similarly undesirable racial effect, would also serve the employer's legitimate [hiring] interest[s]"; by so demonstrating, respondents would prove that "[petitioners were] using [their] tests merely as a 'pretext' for discrimination." *Albemarle Paper Co.*; see also *Watson*. If respondents, having established a prima facie case, come forward with alternatives to petitioners' hiring practices that reduce the racially disparate impact of practices currently being used, and petitioners refuse to adopt these alternatives, such a refusal would belie a claim by petitioners that their incumbent practices are being employed for nondiscriminatory reasons.

Of course, any alternative practices which respondents offer up in this respect must be equally effective as petitioners' chosen hiring procedures in achieving petitioners' legitimate employment goals. Moreover, "[f]actors such as the cost or other burdens of proposed alternative selection devices are relevant in determining whether they would be equally as effective as the challenged practice in serving the employer's legitimate business goals." *Watson.* "Courts are generally less competent than employers to structure business practices," Furnco Construction Corp. v. Waters, 438 U.S. 567 (1978); consequently, the judiciary should proceed with care before mandating that an employer must adopt a plaintiff's alternative selection or hiring practice in response to a Title VII suit. . . .

Justice STEVENS, with whom Justice BRENNAN, Justice MARSHALL, and Justice BLACKMUN join, dissenting.

Fully 18 years ago, this Court unanimously held that Title VII of the Civil Rights Act of 1964 prohibits employment practices that have discriminatory effects as well as those that are intended to discriminate. Griggs v. Duke Power Co. Federal courts and agencies consistently have enforced that interpretation, thus promoting our national goal of eliminating barriers that define economic opportunity not by aptitude and ability but by race, color, national origin, and other traits that are easily identified but utterly irrelevant to one's qualification for a particular job. Regrettably, the Court retreats from these efforts in its review of an interlocutory judgment respecting the "peculiar facts" of this lawsuit. Turning a blind eye to the meaning and purpose of Title VII, the majority's opinion perfunctorily rejects a longstanding rule of law and underestimates the probative value of evidence of a racially stratified work force.[4] I cannot join this latest sojourn into judicial activism. . . .

Decisions of this Court and other federal courts repeatedly have recognized that while the employer's burden in a disparate-treatment case is simply one of coming forward with evidence of legitimate business purpose, its burden in a disparate-impact case is proof of an affirmative defense of business necessity. Although the majority's opinion blurs that distinction, thoughtful reflection on common-law pleading principles clarifies the fundamental differences between the two types of "burdens of proof." In the ordinary civil trial, the plaintiff bears the burden of persuading the trier of fact that the defendant has harmed her. See, e.g., 2 Restatement (Second) of Torts §§ 328 A, 433 B (1965) (hereinafter Restatement). The defendant may undercut plaintiff's efforts both by confronting plaintiff's evidence during her case in chief and by submitting countervailing evidence during its own case. But if the plaintiff proves the existence of the harmful act, the defendant can escape liability only by persuading

---

4. Respondents constitute a class of present and former employees of petitioners, two Alaskan salmon canning companies. The class members, described by the parties as "nonwhite," include persons of Samoan, Chinese, Filipino, Japanese, and Alaska Native descent, all but one of whom are United States citizens. Fifteen years ago they commenced this suit, alleging that petitioners engage in hiring, job assignment, housing, and messing practices that segregate nonwhites from whites in violation of Title VII. Evidence included this response in 1971 by a foreman to a college student's inquiry about cannery employment:

> We are not in a position to take many young fellows to our Bristol Bay canneries as they do not have the background for our type of employees. Our cannery labor is either Eskimo or Filipino and we do not have the facilities to mix others with these groups.

Some characteristics of the Alaska salmon industry described in this litigation — in particular, the segregation of housing and dining facilities and the stratification of jobs along racial and ethnic lines — bear an unsettling resemblance to aspects of a plantation economy. See generally Plantation, Town, and County, Essays on the Local History of American Slave Society 163-334 (E. Miller & E. Genovese eds. 1974). Indeed the maintenance of inferior, segregated facilities for housing and feeding nonwhite employees, strikes me as a form of discrimination that, although it does not necessarily fit neatly into a disparate-impact or disparate-treatment mold, nonetheless violates Title VII. Respondents, however, do not press this theory before us.

the factfinder that the act was justified or excusable. See, e.g., Restatement §§ 454-461, 463-467. The plaintiff in turn may try to refute this affirmative defense. Although the burdens of producing evidence regarding the existence of harm or excuse thus shift between the plaintiff and the defendant, the burden of proving either proposition remains throughout on the party asserting it.

In a disparate-treatment case there is no "discrimination" within the meaning of Title VII unless the employer intentionally treated the employee unfairly because of race. Therefore, the employee retains the burden of proving the existence of intent at all times. If there is direct evidence of intent, the employee may have little difficulty persuading the factfinder that discrimination has occurred. But in the likelier event that intent has to be established by inference, the employee may resort to the *McDonnell/Burdine* inquiry. In either instance, the employer *may* undermine the employee's evidence but has no independent burden of persuasion.

In contrast, intent plays no role in the disparate-impact inquiry. The question, rather, is whether an employment practice has a significant, adverse effect on an identifiable class of workers — regardless of the cause or motive for the practice. The employer may attempt to contradict the factual basis for this effect; that is, to prevent the employee from establishing a prima facie case. But when an employer is faced with sufficient proof of disparate impact, its only recourse is to justify the practice by explaining why it is necessary to the operation of business. Such a justification is a classic example of an affirmative defense.

Failing to explore the interplay between these distinct orders of proof, the Court announces that our frequent statements that the employer shoulders the burden of proof respecting business necessity "should have been understood to mean an employer's production — but not persuasion — burden." Our opinions always have emphasized that in a disparate-impact case the employer's burden is weighty. "The touchstone," the Court said in *Griggs*, "is business necessity." Later, we held that prison administrators had failed to "rebu[t] the prima facie case of discrimination by showing that the height and weight requirements are . . . essential to effective job performance," Dothard v. Rawlinson. I am thus astonished to read that the "touchstone of this inquiry is a reasoned review of the employer's justification for his use of the challenged practice. . . . [T]here is no requirement that the challenged practice be . . . 'essential.'" This casual — almost summary — rejection of the statutory construction that developed in the wake of *Griggs* is most disturbing. I have always believed that the *Griggs* opinion correctly reflected the intent of the Congress that enacted Title VII. Even if I were not so persuaded, I could not join a rejection of a consistent interpretation of a federal statute. Congress frequently revisits this statutory scheme and can readily correct our mistakes if we misread its meaning.

Also troubling is the Court's apparent redefinition of the employees' burden of proof in a disparate-impact case. No prima facie case will be made, it declares, unless the employees "isolat[e] and identif[y] the specific employment practices that are allegedly responsible for any observed statistical disparities." This additional proof requirement is unwarranted. It is elementary that a plaintiff cannot recover upon proof of injury alone; rather, the plaintiff must connect the injury to an act of the defendant in order to establish prima facie that the defendant is liable. E.g., Restatement § 430. Although the causal link must have substance, the act need not constitute the sole or primary cause of the harm. §§ 431-433; cf. Price Waterhouse v. Hopkins. Thus in a disparate-impact case, proof of numerous questionable employment practices ought to fortify an employee's assertion that the practices caused racial disparities. Ordinary principles of fairness require that Title VII actions be tried like "any lawsuit." The changes the majority makes today, tipping the scales in favor of employers, are not faithful to those principles.

## II

Petitioners seek reversal of the Court of Appeals and dismissal of this suit on the ground that respondents' statistical evidence failed to prove a prima facie case of discrimination. . . . I believe that respondents' evidence deserves greater credit than the majority allows.

Statistical evidence of discrimination should compare the racial composition of employees in disputed jobs to that "'of the qualified . . . population in the relevant labor market.'" That statement leaves open the definition of the qualified population and the relevant labor market. Our previous opinions demonstrate that in reviewing statistical evidence, a court should not strive for numerical exactitude at the expense of the needs of the particular case.

The District Court's findings of fact depict a unique industry. Canneries often are located in remote, sparsely populated areas of Alaska. Most jobs are seasonal, with the season's length and the canneries' personnel needs varying not just year to year but day to day. To fill their employment requirements, petitioners must recruit and transport many cannery workers and noncannery workers from States in the Pacific Northwest. Most cannery workers come from a union local based outside Alaska or from Native villages near the canneries. Employees in the noncannery positions — the positions that are "at issue" — learn of openings by word of mouth; the jobs seldom are posted or advertised, and there is no promotion to noncannery jobs from within the cannery workers' ranks.

In general, the District Court found the at-issue jobs to require "skills," ranging from English literacy, typing, and "ability to use seam micrometers, gauges, and mechanic's hand tools" to "good health" and a driver's license. All cannery workers' jobs, like a handful of at-issue positions, are unskilled, and the court found that the intensity of the work during canning season precludes on-the-job training for skilled noncannery positions. It made no findings regarding the extent to which the cannery workers already are qualified for at-issue jobs: individual plaintiffs testified persuasively that they were fully qualified for such jobs,[22] but the court neither credited nor discredited this testimony. Although there are no findings concerning wage differentials, the parties seem to agree that wages for cannery workers are lower than those for noncannery workers, skilled or unskilled. The District Court found that "nearly all" cannery workers are nonwhite, while the percentage of nonwhites employed in the entire Alaska salmon canning industry "has stabilized at about 47% to 50%." The precise stratification of the work force is not described in the findings, but the parties seem to agree that the noncannery jobs are predominantly held by whites.

Petitioners contend that the relevant labor market in this case is the general population of the "'external' labor market for the jobs at issue." While they would rely on the District Court's findings in this regard, those findings are ambiguous. At one point the District Court specifies "Alaska, the Pacific Northwest, and California" as "the geographical region from which [petitioners] draw their employees," but its next finding refers to "this relevant geographical area for cannery worker, laborer, and other nonskilled jobs." There is no express finding of the relevant labor market for noncannery jobs.

---

22. Some cannery workers later became architects, an Air Force officer, and a graduate student in public administration. Some had college training at the time they were employed in the canneries.

Even assuming that the District Court properly defined the relevant geographical area, its apparent assumption that the population in that area constituted the "available labor supply," is not adequately founded. An undisputed requirement for employment either as a cannery or noncannery worker is availability for seasonal employment in the far reaches of Alaska. Many noncannery workers, furthermore, must be available for preseason work. Yet the record does not identify the portion of the general population in Alaska, California, and the Pacific Northwest that would accept this type of employment. This deficiency respecting a crucial job qualification diminishes the usefulness of petitioners' statistical evidence. In contrast, respondents' evidence, comparing racial compositions within the work force, identifies a pool of workers willing to work during the relevant times and familiar with the workings of the industry. Surely this is more probative than the untailored general population statistics on which petitioners focus.

Evidence that virtually all the employees in the major categories of at-issue jobs were white, whereas about two-thirds of the cannery workers were nonwhite, may not by itself suffice to establish a prima facie case of discrimination.[26] But such evidence of racial stratification puts the specific employment practices challenged by respondents into perspective. Petitioners recruit employees for at-issue jobs from outside the work force rather than from lower paying, overwhelmingly nonwhite, cannery worker positions. Information about availability of at-issue positions is conducted by word of mouth;[27] therefore, the maintenance of housing and mess halls that separate the largely white noncannery work force from the cannery workers, coupled with the tendency toward nepotistic hiring,[28] are obvious barriers to employment opportunities for nonwhites. Putting to one side the issue of business justifications, it would be quite wrong to conclude that these practices have no discriminatory consequence. . . .[29]

## III

The majority's opinion begins with recognition of the settled rule that "a facially neutral employment practice may be deemed violative of Title VII without evidence of the employer's subjective intent to discriminate that is required in a

26. The majority suggests that at-issue work demands the skills possessed by "accountants, managers, boat captains, electricians, doctors, and engineers." It is at least theoretically possible that a disproportionate number of white applicants possessed the specialized skills required by some at-issue jobs. In fact, of course, many at-issue jobs involved skills not at all comparable to these selective examples. Even the District Court recognized that in a year-round employment setting, "some of the positions which this court finds to be skilled, e.g., truck driving on the beach, [would] fit into the category of jobs which require skills that are readily acquirable by persons in the general public."

27. As the Court of Appeals explained in its remand opinion: "Specifically, the companies sought cannery workers in Native villages and through dispatches from ILWU Local 37, thus securing a work force for the lowest paying jobs which was predominantly Alaska Native and Filipino. For other departments the companies relied on informal word-of-mouth recruitment by predominantly white superintendents and foremen, who recruited primarily white employees. That such practices can cause a discriminatory impact is obvious."

28. The District Court found but downplayed the fact that relatives of employees are given preferential consideration. But "of 349 nepotistic hires in four upper-level departments during 1970-75, 332 were of whites, 17 of nonwhites," the Court of Appeals noted. "If nepotism exists, it is by definition a practice of giving preference to relatives, and where those doing the hiring are predominantly white, the practice necessarily has an adverse impact on nonwhites."

29. The Court suggests that the discrepancy in economic opportunities for white and nonwhite workers does not amount to disparate impact within the meaning of Title VII unless respondents show that it is "petitioners' fault." This statement distorts the disparate-impact theory, in which the critical inquiry is whether an employer's practices operate to discriminate. Whether the employer intended such discrimination is irrelevant.

'disparate-treatment' case." It then departs from the body of law engendered by this disparate-impact theory, reformulating the order of proof and the weight of the parties' burdens. Why the Court undertakes these unwise changes in elementary and eminently fair rules is a mystery to me.

I respectfully dissent.

## NOTES

1. Why should a showing of adverse impact alone, without intent to discriminate, be sufficient to establish illegal discrimination? Is it because defendants may be acting with intent to discriminate, but proof of such intent is not available to plaintiff? Duke Power imposed the challenged rules just as Title VII became effective. Was the Supreme Court merely trying to get around the lower court's finding of no intent to discriminate? But *Wards Cove* involved a longstanding method of running the Alaska fish canning business, which had long been quite segregated, just like Duke Power's operation before 1965. Why the different outcomes? See generally Julia Lamber, Discretionary Decisionmaking: The Application of Title VII's Disparate Impact Theory, 1985 U. Ill. L. Rev. 869; Steven Willborn, The Disparate Impact Model of Discrimination: Theory and Limits, 34 Am. U. L. Rev. 799 (1985); Paulette Caldwell, Reaffirming the Disproportionate Effects Standard of Liability in Title VII Litigation, 46 U. Pitt. L. Rev. 555 (1985). See also Rosemary G. Hunter & Elaine W. Shoben, Disparate Impact Discrimination: American Oddity or Internationally Accepted Concept?, 19 Berkeley J. Emp. & Lab. L. 108 (1998).

2. *Griggs* dealt with an educational prerequisite as well as test results, which probably correlate highly with increased level and quality of education. These requirements were imposed in a state that segregated African Americans in underfunded and inferior school systems. Is it this de jure discrimination in education that caused blacks in North Carolina to be disproportionately affected by Duke Power's rule? In *Wards Cove*, the cause of the impact was the racial segregation in membership of the union and the residential segregation of the areas surrounding the canneries on one hand and the very different labor market in the lower 48 states used for noncannery recruitment on the other. Is that the reason for the different approaches? Ramona L. Paetzold & Steven L. Willborn, in Deconstructing Disparate Impact: A View of the Model Through New Lenses, 74 N.C. L. Rev. 325, 353-354 (1995), argue that the cause of impact is irrelevant to the disparate impact theory:

> The employment practice was one cause of the disparate impact in *Griggs*; if the employer had not required a high school diploma, the criterion obviously could not have caused a disparate impact on blacks. But the disparate impact was also "caused" by the social conditions that resulted in a lower proportion of blacks than whites with high school diplomas. The high school diploma requirement would not have caused a disparate impact if social conditions had produced the same proportion of high school graduates within the black and white subpopulations. Every disparate impact case depends on an interaction of at least two "causes" in this sense. In *Griggs*, each of the two relevant "causes" (the employment criterion and the social conditions) was necessary to cause the disparate impact on blacks. If either had been absent, no disparate impact would have been present. . . .
>
> Ordinary disparate impact cases, then, view causation with blinders. The law treats the employer's criterion as the cause of a disparity, even though it may be only one of a wide array of factors necessary to produce the disparity. Ordinary disparate impact cases

view causation with blinders, not because the cases arise in a single-cause context, but because they ignore causes external to the employer that contribute to the impact. The blinders necessarily mean that employers may be held legally responsible for impacts that are "caused" in substantial part by factors external to the employers.

See also Kathryn Abrams, Title VII and the Complex Female Subject, 92 Mich. L. Rev. 2479, 2524 (1994).

3. In upholding the disparate impact theory against an attack based on the Eleventh Amendment in an action against a state, In re Employment Discrimination Litigation Against the State of Alabama, 198 F.3d 1305, 1322 (11th Cir. 1999), found disparate impact theory to be within the power of Congress under § 5 of the Fourteenth Amendment because it is a method of rooting out intentional discrimination.

> Our analysis of the mechanics of a disparate impact claim has led us unavoidably to the conclusion that although the form of the disparate impact inquiry differs from that used in a case challenging state action direction under the Fourteenth Amendment, the core injury targeted by both methods of analysis remains the same: intentional discrimination.

That circuit's view was repeated in EEOC v. Joe's Stone Crab, Inc., 220 F.3d 1263, 1274 (11th Cir. 2000) (reproduced at page 438): "In essence, disparate impact theory is a doctrinal surrogate for eliminating unprovable acts of intentional discrimination hidden behind facially neutral policies or practices." Do you agree that *Griggs* and *Wards Cove* can be so viewed? Is this consistant with the view of Professors Paetzold and Willborn?

4. Professor Paulette Caldwell believes that one purpose of Title VII is to increase productive efficiency by allowing individuals to achieve their full economic potential. Reaffirming the Disproportionate Effects Standard of Liability in Title VII Litigation, 46 U. Pitt. L. Rev. 555 (1985). Caldwell's point is that, in the long run, efficiency will be improved if the pool of potential workers is widened by adding persons whose full potential would never be developed if denied entry-level positions. Is this what Chief Justice Burger meant when he wrote in *Griggs* that "[h]istory is filled with examples of men and women who rendered highly effective performance without the conventional badges of accomplishment in terms of certificates, diplomas, and degrees?" If so, does it have anything to do with intent to discriminate?

5. Whatever the underlying justifications of impact liability, is disparate impact at odds with the basic premise of antidiscrimination legislation: because members of protected groups are indistinguishable from similarly situated members of the majority, they ought not be treated differently in the workplace? Skin color does not make a worker less effective, nor does advancing age necessarily make her less efficient. While group differences may exist, disparate treatment ignores those differences and focuses instead on members of the protected group who are similarly situated to nonprotected individuals.

In contrast, impact analysis not only acknowledges, but also focuses on, differences between groups. Individuals will be entitled to a remedy precisely because they are members of a group that is different. The impact approach, however, does not abandon the equality principle that similarly situated individuals should be treated equally. The business necessity defense is designed to permit the employer to rely on differences between employees when those differences are relevant to the job. Employers are prohibited from considering only differences that are not related to job performance. Thus, for purposes of qualifying for work, the underlying premise remains true: protected group members should be treated equally when their work qualifications are the same.

6. Disparate impact liability effectively creates a duty for employers to identify and eliminate employment practices that unnecessarily operate as "built-in headwinds" for protected groups that have not yet achieved economic parity with white males. Viewed in this light, disparate impact can be considered a form of liability for negligence — an employer who does not intend to discriminate may nonetheless be liable for failing to exercise its duty of care toward protected group members. See David Benjamin Oppenheimer, Negligent Discrimination, 141 U. Pa. L. Rev. 899 (1993). Obviously, this approach is a far cry from intent to discriminate.

7. *Wards Cove* generated a national controversy about the disparate impact theory that was ultimately resolved by the enactment of the Civil Rights Act of 1991. While that statute also addresses other Supreme Court decisions that Congress viewed as cutting back on civil rights protection, the focus of debate was on "quotas," *Wards Cove*, and the appropriate structure of the disparate impact theory. During the debates, proponents argued that a strong impact theory was needed to open up job opportunities to minorities and women. Opponents vociferously claimed that disparate impact would result in quotas by encouraging employers to hire minorities and women, without regard to qualifications, merely to avoid potential liability. What do you think of the argument? Did *Griggs* encourage quota hiring? Did *Wards Cove* restructure *Griggs* to minimize that result?

8. Ian Ayres & Peter Siegelman, The Q-Word as Red Herring: Why Disparate Impact Liability Does Not Induce Hiring Quotas, 74 Tex. L. Rev. 1487 (1996), challenge the quota claim. They note that prior authors, including John J. Donohue III & Peter Siegelman, The Changing Nature of Employment Discrimination Litigation, 43 Stan. L. Rev. 983, 1015-1021, 1023-1032 (1991), and Richard Posner, The Efficiency and the Efficacy of Title VII, 136 U. Pa. L. Rev. 513, 519 (1987), recognized tension between protecting applicants against discrimination in hiring and protecting workers from discriminatory firing after they have been hired. Antidiscrimination law forbids both kinds of conduct, but they argue the two prohibitions are inherently at odds. "By making it harder to fire certain workers, employment discrimination law tends to make these workers less attractive prospects at the hiring stage. An employer would prefer to hire someone who can be easily fired (should that prove necessary) than an otherwise identical applicant whose firing would be subject to legal scrutiny. Thus, protection against discriminatory firing acts as a kind of tax on hiring those to whom it is extended." 74 Tex. L. Rev. at 1488-1489. Ayres & Siegelman then argue that, "far from producing hiring quotas that induce employers to discriminate in favor of minorities, disparate impact liability may actually induce hiring discrimination against minorities (and other protected groups)." Id. at 1489. By making it harder to fire protected workers, the authors argue that disparate impact liability discourages probationary employment generally and might even lead employers to discriminate deliberately against protected workers at the hiring stage. Id. at 1491. Does this suggest that both proponents and opponents of the 1991 Amendments were wrong in their assessments? Paul Oyer & Scott Schaefer, Sorting, Quotas, and the Civil Rights Act of 1991: Who Hires When It's Hard to Fire?, 45 J.L. & Econ. 41 (2002) (data suggest firms more susceptible to litigation substitute away from protected workers but no evidence that firms with fewer protected workers substitute toward this group). You might reconsider whether this argument makes sense at the end of this chapter. You should also consider whether disparate impact liability is different from systemic disparate treatment liability in this regard.

9. The Court's use of statistics in *Griggs* is unsophisticated — even naive — compared with later refinements. The impact statistics on high school diplomas and tests were not linked in any direct way to the defendant's practices. Nevertheless, *Griggs* is a landmark case because of its validation of a statistical approach to discrimination litigation. Further, the decision establishes another critical point: when data that relates directly to the practices of the defendant itself is not available, a plaintiff may make out a prima facie case with more general statistics, leaving the defendant to show the inapplicability of those statistics to its practices. See Espinoza v. Farah Mfg. Co., 414 U.S. 86 (1973). Is this approach to establishing a prima facie case of impact excessively generous to the plaintiff?

10. What about the statistics in *Wards Cove*? On the surface, the comparison between the racial breakdown of those working in cannery jobs and those in noncannery jobs was more dramatic than those in *Griggs*. Plaintiffs in *Wards Cove* sought to prove the discriminatory impact of a number of neutral hiring practices, including "nepotism, a rehire preference, a lack of objective hiring criteria, separate hiring channels, [and] a practice of not promoting from within." Assuming that these practices were used in hiring unskilled noncannery workers, how should plaintiffs have proceeded to establish disparate impact? If the unskilled noncannery workforce is predominately white, nepotism and rehire preferences are likely to yield predominately white hiring. But to what group should the workforce numbers be compared to determine whether the results are disparate? Or is the problem that these specific practices were not linked to the disparate racial bottom line? What does footnote 9 mean? Did plaintiffs fail to prove that there was nepotism or fail to prove the racial impact of the nepotism?

11. *Wards Cove* states that the "proper comparison [is] between the racial composition of [the at-issue jobs] and the racial composition of the qualified . . . population in the relevant labor market." The concept of the relevant labor market is borrowed from Hazelwood School District v. United States (reproduced at page 218), a systemic disparate treatment case. Is the relevant labor market concept as used in disparate treatment cases appropriate for disparate impact analysis? Remember that in Teamsters v. United States (reproduced at page 210), the relevant labor market was the general population, while, in *Hazelwood*, it was persons in the relevant geographic area who were certified to teach. In Alexander v. Fulton County, Ga., 207 F.3d 1303 (11th Cir. 2000), the court held that the general population was inappropriate for law enforcement positions. In *Teamsters*, there was no reason to believe that the population interested in and otherwise qualified for truck-driving jobs varied much from the general population. That was obviously not true in *Hazelwood*. In both cases, however, the issue was whether the statistics supported an inference of discriminatory intent. The Court was seeking to identify the pool from which the employer drew its employees so it could compare that group with the group selected in order to determine whether the difference between the two was significant enough to suggest intentional discrimination.

The question in a disparate impact case is not whether the statistics provide an inference of discriminatory intent but whether the employer's neutral employment practice has a disparate impact on a statutorily protected group. What group are we interested in — the applicant pool, or the labor pool from which the employer recruited, or the labor pool in the geographic area surrounding the workplace, or the general population (where?). The applicant pool is perhaps the most relevant comparison group because it is directly affected by the employer's practices. The applicant pool, however, might be distorted by the employer's choice of recruitment sources, or posted qualifications, or reputation for discrimination. The employer's choice of labor pool may not be appropriate because that pool may be distorted (compared to what?). The geographic area "around" the workplace may not be appropriate because the job in question may require a broader search, and, in any event, defining what constitutes an appropriate commuting distance is difficult. Is the most relevant choice the labor pool from which a reasonable nondiscriminatory employer would draw its employees? But a reasonable employer who had no intention to discriminate might select a labor pool that is very homogenous just because it is convenient. Should that pool be compared with the most diverse pool of qualified applicants available in order to determine whether there is impact? Does impact analysis impose on employers a duty to seek out the most diverse labor pool?

12. Isn't the employment practice the *Wards Cove* plaintiffs should have challenged the practice of recruiting all noncannery workers in the lower 48 states and failing to recruit for at least the unskilled noncannery jobs when it recruited through the union and among Native Americans in Alaska? It was the practice that produced the virtually all white noncannery job work force. Would the employer have any good reason for not recruiting for these jobs through the union and the immediately surrounding area?

13. The *Wards Cove* majority remodeled disparate impact law (1) by requiring a highly focused showing that particular employment practices caused a disparate impact (2) by reducing the employer's rebuttal obligations from a showing of job-relatedness and business necessity to "a reasoned review of the employer's justification"; and (3) by redefining the rebuttal stage to a burden of production, not persuasion. As a result, disparate impact law looked more like disparate treatment law, though still without an intent to discriminate element.

## B. THE STRUCTURE OF DISPARATE IMPACT LAW AFTER THE 1991 CIVIL RIGHTS ACT

Congress responded to *Wards Cove*, as well as to a number of other Supreme Court decisions cutting back civil rights laws, by enacting the Civil Rights Act of 1991. Those amendments added § 703(k) to Title VII to provide a statutory basis for disparate impact law. In order to understand the significance of the new statutory provision, it is important to focus both on the new provision and to understand its historical background. This treatment will proceed by first addressing plaintiff's prima facie case; second, it will examine the defendant's rebuttal of job relatedness and business necessity; and third, it will examine the plaintiff's surrebuttal of showing an alternative employment practice that the employer refuses to adopt. The chapter will conclude by analyzing the affirmative defenses articulated in § 703(h) and by considering whether they, too, are subject to plaintiff's surrebutal.

Section 703(k)(1) sets forth the new statutory action for disparate impact discrimination:

> (A) An unlawful employment practice based on disparate impact is established under this title only if —
> (i) a complaining party demonstrates that a respondent uses a particular employment practice that causes a disparate impact on the basis of race, color, religion, sex, or national origin and the respondent fails to demonstrate that the challenged practice is job related for the position in question and consistent with business necessity; or
> (ii) the complaining party makes the demonstration described in subparagraph (C)

with respect to an alternative employment practice and the respondent refuses to adopt such alternative employment practice.

(B)(i) With respect to demonstrating that a particular employment practice causes a disparate impact as described in subparagraph (A)(i), the complaining party shall demonstrate that each particular challenged employment practice causes a disparate impact, except that if the complaining party can demonstrate to the court that the elements of a respondent's decisionmaking process are not capable of separation for analysis, the decisionmaking process may be analyzed as one employment practice.

(ii) If the respondent demonstrates that a specific employment practice does not cause the disparate impact, the respondent shall not be required to demonstrate that such practice is required by business necessity.

New § 701(m) defines "demonstrates" as carrying the burden of production and persuasion.

## 1.  *Plaintiff's Proof of a Prima Facie Case*

### a.  A Particular Employment Practice

Section 703(k)(1)(A)(i) states the general rule for a disparate impact case: plaintiff carries the burden of persuasion that the employer "uses a particular employment practice that causes disparate impact on the basis of race, color, religion, sex, or national origin." This embraces two questions that arose before the 1991 Amendments: (1) is every employment-related action of an employer a qualifying "employment practice"; and (2) how does a plaintiff establish that a disparate impact resulted from a "particular" practice as opposed to a congeries of causes?

### WATSON v. FORT WORTH BANK & TRUST
#### 487 U.S. 977 (1988)

Justice O'CONNOR announced the judgment of the Court [and delivered its opinion with respect to the portions reproduced below]:

I

Petitioner Clara Watson, who is black, was hired by respondent Fort Worth Bank and Trust (the Bank) as a proof operator in August 1973. In January 1976, Watson was promoted to a position as teller in the Bank's drive-in facility. In February 1980, she sought to become supervisor of the tellers in the main lobby; a white male, however, was selected for this job. Watson then sought a position as supervisor of the drive-in bank, but this position was given to a white female. In February 1981, after Watson had served for about a year as a commercial teller in the Bank's main lobby, and informally as assistant to the supervisor of tellers, the man holding that position was promoted. Watson applied for the vacancy, but the white female who was the supervisor of the drive-in bank was selected instead. Watson then applied for the vacancy created at the drive-in; a white male was selected for that job. The Bank, which has about 80 employees, had not developed precise and formal criteria for evaluating candidates for the positions for which Watson unsuccessfully applied. It relied instead on the subjective judgment of supervisors who were acquainted with the candidates and with the nature of the jobs to be filled. All the supervisors involved in denying Watson the four promotions at issue were white. . . .

[The district court rejected both Watson's disparate treatment and disparate impact claims, and the Court of Appeals affirmed the finding of no proof of disparate treatment and also held that "a Title VII challenge to an allegedly discretionary promotion system is properly analyzed under the disparate treatment model rather than the disparate impact model."]

## II

### A

. . . In Griggs v. Duke Power Co., this Court held that a plaintiff need not necessarily prove intentional discrimination in order to establish that an employer has violated [Title VII]. In certain cases, facially neutral employment practices that have significant adverse effects on protected *groups* have been held to violate the Act without proof that the employer adopted those practices with a discriminatory intent. The factual issues and the character of the evidence are inevitably somewhat different when the plaintiff is exempted from the need to prove intentional discrimination. The evidence in these "disparate impact" cases usually focuses on statistical disparities, rather than specific incidents, and on competing explanations for those disparities.

The distinguishing features of the factual issues that typically dominate in disparate impact cases do not imply that the ultimate legal issue is different than in cases where disparate treatment analysis is used. Nor do we think it is appropriate to hold a defendant liable for unintentional discrimination on the basis of less evidence than is required to prove intentional discrimination. Rather, the necessary premise of the disparate impact approach is that some employment practices, adopted without a deliberately discriminatory motive, may in operation be functionally equivalent to intentional discrimination. . . .

This Court has repeatedly reaffirmed the principle that some facially neutral employment practices may violate Title VII even in the absence of a demonstrated discriminatory intent. We have not limited this principle to cases in which the challenged practice served to perpetuate the effects of pre-Act intentional discrimination. Each of our subsequent decisions, however, like *Griggs* itself, involved standardized employment tests or criteria. See, e.g., Albemarle Paper Co. v. Moody, 422 U.S. 405 (1975) (written aptitude tests); Washington v. Davis (written test of verbal skills); Dothard v. Rawlinson (height and weight requirements); New York City Transit Authority v. Beazer (rule against employing drug addicts); Connecticut v. Teal (written examination). In contrast, we have consistently used conventional disparate treatment theory, in which proof of intent to discriminate is required, to review hiring and promotion decisions that were based on the exercise of personal judgment or the application of inherently subjective criteria. See, e.g., McDonnell Douglas Corp. v. Green (discretionary decision not to rehire individual who engaged in criminal acts against employer while laid off).

Our decisions have not addressed the question whether disparate impact analysis may be applied to cases in which subjective criteria are used to make employment decisions. . . . [T]he Courts of Appeals are in conflict on the issue. In order to resolve this conflict, we must determine whether the reasons that support the use of disparate impact analysis apply to subjective employment practices, and whether such analysis can be applied in this new context under workable evidentiary standards.

B

The parties present us with stark and uninviting alternatives. Petitioner contends that subjective selection methods are at least as likely to have discriminatory effects as are the kind of objective tests at issue in *Griggs* and our other disparate impact cases. Furthermore, she argues, if disparate impact analysis is confined to objective tests, employers will be able to substitute subjective criteria having substantially identical effects, and *Griggs* will become a dead letter. Respondent and the United States (appearing as amicus curiae) argue that conventional disparate treatment analysis is adequate to accomplish Congress' purpose in enacting Title VII. They also argue that subjective selection practices would be so impossibly difficult to defend under disparate impact analysis that employers would be forced to adopt numerical quotas in order to avoid liability.

We are persuaded that our decisions in *Griggs* and succeeding cases could largely be nullified if disparate impact analysis were applied only to standardized selection practices. . . .

We are also persuaded that disparate impact analysis is in principle no less applicable to subjective employment criteria than to objective or standardized tests. In either case, a facially neutral practice, adopted without discriminatory intent, may have effects that are indistinguishable from intentionally discriminatory practices. It is true, to be sure, that an employer's policy of leaving promotion decisions to the unchecked discretion of lower level supervisors should itself raise no inference of discriminatory conduct. Especially in relatively small businesses like respondent's, it may be customary and quite reasonable simply to delegate employment decisions to those employees who are most familiar with the jobs to be filled and with the candidates for those jobs. It does not follow, however, that the particular supervisors to whom this discretion is delegated always act without discriminatory intent. Furthermore, even if one assumed that any such discrimination can be adequately policed through disparate treatment analysis, the problem of subconscious stereotypes and prejudices would remain. In this case, for example, petitioner was apparently told at one point that the teller position was a big responsibility with "a lot of money . . . for blacks to have to count." Such remarks may not prove discriminatory intent, but they do suggest a lingering form of the problem that Title VII was enacted to combat. If an employer's undisciplined system of subjective decisionmaking has precisely the same effects as a system pervaded by impermissible intentional discrimination, it is difficult to see why Title VII's proscription against discriminatory actions should not apply. In both circumstances, the employer's practices may be said to "adversely affect [an individual's] status as an employee, because of such individual's race, color, religion, sex, or national origin." 42 U.S.C. § 2000e-2(a)(2). We conclude, accordingly, that subjective or discretionary employment practices may be analyzed under the disparate impact approach in appropriate cases.

[Since the lower court had not evaluated the statistical evidence to determine if a prima facie disparate impact case was made out, the case was remanded with the caution that "[i]t may be that the relevant data base is too small to permit any meaningful statistical analysis. . . ."]

*NOTES*

1. *Watson* lists the previous disparate impact cases decided by the Court that show the potential range of application of disparate impact analysis. There were, however, doubts about the kinds of practices to which the disparate impact theory applied. *Watson* resolved one of these questions, rejecting the decisions of some lower courts that disparate impact was limited to objective practices. Section 703(k) apparently codifies this thrust of *Watson* insofar as it applies to "a particular employment practice" without qualification. Thus, a plaintiff who can identify a particular employment practice with the requisite impact will establish a prima facie case without regard to whether the practice is "objective" or "subjective."

2. The *Watson* plurality, and later the *Wards Cove* majority, counterbalanced the expansion of disparate impact to subjective practices by cutting back on the sweep of the impact theory. But the 1991 codification of disparate impact renders this aspect of the decisions no longer relevant.

3. Lower courts have rejected disparate impact claims because plaintiffs failed to identify a particular or specific employment policy that was causally connected to the racial imbalance shown. See Anderson v. Douglas & Lomason Co., Inc., 26 F.3d 1277 (5th Cir. 1994); Munoz v. Orr, 200 F.3d 291 (5th Cir. 2000). While § 703(k) speaks of "a particular employment practice" without qualification, some lower court decisions viewed some employer conduct as beyond disparate impact. E.g., Finnegan v. Trans World Air Lines, Inc., 967 F.2d 1161 (7th Cir. 1992) (an employer's change in fringe benefits is not subject to disparate impact attack). The same court created a "passivity" exception to the employment practices that are subject to disparate impact attack. In EEOC v. Chicago Miniature Lamp Works, 947 F.2d 292 (7th Cir. 1991), the employer relied on "word-of-mouth" recruitment by incumbent workers to fill job openings. Citing *Wards Cove*, the court reversed the finding of disparate impact liability.

> The EEOC does not allege that Miniature affirmatively engaged in word-of-mouth recruitment of the kind where it told or encouraged its employees to refer applicants for entry-level jobs. Instead, it is uncontested that Miniature passively waited for applicants who typically learned of opportunities from current Miniature employees. The court erred in considering passive reliance on employee word-of-mouth recruiting as a particular employment practice for the purposes of disparate impact. The practices here are undertaken solely by employees. Therefore, disparate impact liability against Miniature must be reversed.

Are either *Finnegan* or *Chicago Miniature Lamps* still good law under § 703(k)? Perhaps the Seventh Circuit has reconsidered. In DeClue v. Central Ill. Light Co., 223 F.3d 434 (7th Cir. 2000), the employer's failure to provide restroom facilities for its employees was found to have a disparate impact on women. Would that have fallen within the "passivity" exception?

4. Another attempt to create an exception to disparate impact was Council 31 v. Ward, 978 F.2d 373, 375 (7th Cir. 1992), which considered whether "an 'employment practice' [must] be more than a single decision by an employer to be actionable under a disparate impact theory." The Illinois Department of Employment Security layoffs in divisional offices located in Chicago affected a disproportionate number of black employees. The trial court dismissed the case: the plaintiffs had failed to identify a "specific employment practice" because an "employment practice" must be a "repeated, customary method of operation." The Seventh Circuit reversed, noting that

previous cases had applied impact analysis to single employment decisions and that "the distinction drawn by the district court is analytically unmanageable — almost any repeated course of conduct can be traced back to a single decision." Id. at 377. After trial, however, judgment for defendants was affirmed because the trial judge accepted defendant's expert witness report that there was no impact because, "[t]he parties agreed that if you look at all employees (full-time employees and intermittent employees), the RIF affected blacks and nonblacks proportionately." 169 F.3d 1068, 1073.

5. In Bramble v. American Postal Workers Union, 135 F.3d 21 (1st Cir. 1998), the union changed its compensation so that union officers who were retired from the postal service received much less pay than union officers still actively employed by the postal service for their union work. The court found that disparate impact analysis did not apply: "Where an employer targets a single employee and implements a policy which has, to date, affected only that one employee, there is simply no basis for a disparate impact claim." Is this too "particular" an employment practice to be within § 703(k)? Or is it not regular enough to be a "practice"? But if that is true, is *Council 31* correctly decided?

6. In EEOC v. Joe's Stone Crab, Inc., reproduced at page 438, the court held that where there was evidence that the owners and management personnel responsible for hiring wait staff referred to the position "as a male server type job by tradition," which could be the basis for finding the existence of a facially discriminatory policy, there was no basis for using the disparate impact theory: "No specific *facially neutral* employment practice of Joe's can be *causally connected* to the statistical disparity between the percentage of women in the qualified labor pool and the percentage of women hired as food servers by Joe's." See also DiBiase v. SmithKline Beecham Corp., 48 F.3d 719 (3d Cir. 1995) (facially discriminatory policy could not be attacked under disparate impact).

7. Some employment practices may cause a disparate impact but nevertheless may not be cognizable because they are not within Title VII's concerns. In Garcia v. Spun Steak Co., 998 F.2d 1480 (9th Cir. 1993), the plaintiff challenged an employer policy requiring its bilingual workers to speak only English while working on the job. There was no dispute that any adverse effects would be felt by those of Hispanic origin. Rather,

> the dispute centers on whether the policy causes any adverse effects at all, and if it does, whether the effects are significant. The Spanish-speaking employees argue that the policy adversely affects them in the following ways: (1) it denies them the ability to express their cultural heritage on the job; (2) it denies them a privilege of employment that is enjoyed by monolingual speakers of English; and (3) it creates an atmosphere of inferiority, isolation, and intimidation.

Id. at 1486-87. With respect to expressing cultural heritage, the court wrote, "Title VII is concerned only with disparities in the treatment of workers; it does not confer substantive privileges. . . . Just as a private employer is not required to allow other types of self-expression, there is nothing in Title VII which requires an employer to allow employees to express their cultural identity." Id. at 1487. As for denying the workers a privilege given to monolingual employees (i.e., the right to speak their primary language on the job), "[w]hen the privilege is defined at its narrowest (as merely the ability to speak on the job), we cannot conclude that those employees fluent in both English and Spanish are adversely impacted by the policy. Because they are able to speak English, bilingual employees can engage in conversation on the job." Id. It was only non-English speakers who were denied the privilege to talk while working; such persons might have a disparate impact claim, but only if the rule actually bothered them. Finally, as to the hostile environment claim, the court held that an English-only rule did not necessarily create an abusive environment, although in some circumstances it might. Do you agree with this analysis? Why was the environment claim treated as a disparate impact question? Hostile environment discrimination is covered in Chapter 7.

8. Prior to the 1991 Amendments, courts sometimes differentiated between § 703(a)(2), to which disparate impact analysis applied, because it used the language *"tend to"* deprive individuals of employment opportunities, and § 703(a)(1), which speaks directly of practices that discriminate. In Lynch v. Freeman, 817 F.2d 380 (6th Cir. 1987), the Tennessee Valley Authority provided workers filthy toilets, frequently lacking toilet paper. The district court found that the impact on women was real, but not substantial. The Sixth Circuit reversed:

> Any employment practice that adversely affects the health of female employees while leaving male employees unaffected has a significantly discriminatory impact. The district court erred as a matter of law in concluding that Ms. Lynch failed to make out a prima facie case. The court found that "all females were placed at a higher risk of urinary tract infections by using unsanitary portable toilets or by avoiding the use of such toilets and holding their urine." The court also found that men were not exposed to the same risks from using the toilets because of "anatomical differences between the sexes." It was error, after the plaintiff had made out a prima facie case, to require anything else of her.

Id. at 388. Judge Boggs dissented, arguing that working conditions are beyond disparate impact attack under § 703(a)(2). In the wake of the 1991 Civil Rights Act, shouldn't his analysis be rejected?

## CONNECTICUT v. TEAL
### 457 U.S. 440 (1982)

Justice BRENNAN delivered the opinion of the Court.

We consider here whether an employer sued for violation of Title VII of the Civil Rights Act of 1964 may assert a "bottom line" theory of defense. Under that theory, as asserted in this case, an employer's acts of racial discrimination in promotions — effected by an examination having disparate impact — would not render the employer liable for the racial discrimination suffered by employees barred from promotion if the "bottom line" result of the promotional process was an appropriate racial balance. We hold that the "bottom line" does not preclude respondent-employees from establishing a prima facie case, nor does it provide petitioner-employer with a defense to such a case.

Four of the respondents, Winnie Teal, Rose Walker, Edith Latney, and Grace Clark, are black employees of the Department of Income Maintenance of the State of Connecticut. Each was promoted provisionally to the position of Welfare Eligibility Supervisor and served in that capacity for almost two years. To attain permanent status as supervisors, however, respondents had to participate in a selection process that required, as the first step, a passing score on a written examination. This written test was administered on December 2, 1978, to 329 candidates. Of these candidates, 48 identified themselves as black and 259 identified themselves as white. The results of the examination were announced in March 1979. With the passing score set at 65,[3]

---

3. The mean score on the examination was 70.4 percent. However, because the black candidates had a mean score 6.7 percentage points lower than the white candidates, the passing score was set at 65, apparently in an attempt to lessen the disparate impact of the examination.

54.17 percent of the identified black candidates passed. This was approximately 68 percent of the passing rate for the identified white candidates.[4] The four respondents were among the blacks who failed the examination, and they were thus excluded from further consideration for permanent supervisory positions. . . .

More than a year after this action was instituted, and approximately one month before trial, petitioners made promotions from the eligibility list generated by the written examination. In choosing persons from that list, petitioners considered past work performance, recommendations of the candidates' supervisors and, to a lesser extent, seniority. Petitioners then applied what the Court of Appeals characterized as an affirmative action program in order to ensure a significant number of minority supervisors. Forty-six persons were promoted to permanent supervisory positions, 11 of whom were black and 35 of whom were white. The overall result of the selection process was that, of the 48 identified black candidates who participated in the selection process, 22.9 percent were promoted and of the 259 identified white candidates, 13.5 percent were promoted. It is this "bottom-line" result, more favorable to blacks than to whites, that petitioners urge should be adjudged to be a complete defense to respondents' suit. . . .

## II

### A . . .

Petitioners' examination, which barred promotion and had a discriminatory impact on black employees, clearly falls within the literal language of § 703(a)(2), as interpreted by *Griggs*. The statute speaks, not in terms of jobs and promotions, but in terms of *limitations* and *classifications* that would deprive any individual of employment *opportunities*.[9] A disparate impact claim reflects the language of § 703(a)(2) and Congress' basic objectives in enacting that statute: "to achieve equality of employment *opportunities* and remove barriers that have operated in the past to favor an identifiable group of white employees over other employees." (Emphasis added.) When an employer uses a nonjob-related barrier in order to deny a minority or woman applicant employment or promotion, and that barrier has a significant adverse effect on minorities or women, then the applicant has been deprived of an employment *opportunity* "because of . . . race, color, religion, sex, or national origin." In other words, § 703(a)(2) prohibits discriminatory "artificial, arbitrary, and unnecessary barriers to employment" that "limit . . . or classify . . . applicants for employment . . . in any way which would deprive or tend to deprive any individual of employment *opportunities*." (Emphasis added.) . . .

In short, the District Court's dismissal of respondents' claim cannot be supported on the basis that respondents failed to establish a prima facie case of employment discrimination under the terms of § 703(a)(2). The suggestion that disparate impact

---

4. . . . Petitioners do not contest the District Court's implicit finding that the examination itself resulted in disparate impact under the "eighty percent rule" of the Uniform Guidelines on Employee Selection Procedures adopted by the Equal Employment Opportunity Commission. Those guidelines provide that a selection rate that "is less than [80 percent] of the rate for the group with the highest rate will generally be regarded . . . as evidence of adverse impact." 29 C.F.R. § 1607.4D (1981).

9. In contrast, the language of § 703(a)(1), 42 U.S.C. § 2000e-2(a)(1), if it were the only protection given to employees and applicants under Title VII, might support petitioners' exclusive focus on the overall result. That subsection makes it an unlawful employment practice "to fail or refuse to hire or to discharge any individual, or otherwise to discriminate against any individual with respect to his compensation, terms, conditions or privileges of employment because of such individual's race, color, religion, sex, or national origin."

should be measured only at the bottom line ignores the fact that Title VII guarantees these individual respondents the *opportunity* to compete equally with white workers on the basis of job-related criteria. Title VII strives to achieve equality of opportunity by rooting out "artificial, arbitrary and unnecessary" employer-created barriers to professional development that have a discriminatory impact upon individuals. Therefore, respondents' rights under § 703(a)(2) have been violated, unless petitioners can demonstrate that the examination given was not an artificial, arbitrary, or unnecessary barrier, because it measured skills related to effective performance in the role of Welfare Eligibility Supervisor. . . .

## III

Having determined that respondents' claim comes within the terms of Title VII, we must address the suggestion of petitioners and some *amici curiae* that we recognize an exception, either in the nature of an additional burden on plaintiffs seeking to establish a prima facie case or in the nature of an affirmative defense, for cases in which an employer has compensated for a discriminatory pass-fail barrier by hiring or promoting a sufficient number of black employees to reach a nondiscriminatory "bottom line." We reject this suggestion, which is in essence nothing more than a request that we redefine the protections guaranteed by Title VII.

Section 703(a)(2) prohibits practices that would deprive or tend to deprive "*any individual* of employment opportunities." The principal focus of the statute is the protection of the individual employee, rather than the protection of the minority group as a whole. Indeed, the entire statute and its legislative history are replete with references to protection for the individual employee. See, e.g., §§ 703(a)(1), (b), (c), 704(a), as amended; 110 Cong. Rec. 7213 (1964) (interpretive memorandum of Sens. Clark and Case) ("discrimination is prohibited as to any individual"); 110 Cong. Rec. 8921 (remarks of Sen. Williams) ("Every man must be judged according to his ability. In that respect, all men are to have an equal opportunity to be considered for a particular job.").

In suggesting that the "bottom line" may be a defense to a claim of discrimination against an individual employee, petitioners and *amici* appear to confuse unlawful discrimination with discriminatory intent. The Court has stated that a nondiscriminatory "bottom line" and an employer's good faith efforts to achieve a nondiscriminatory work force, might in some cases assist an employer in rebutting the inference that particular action had been intentionally discriminatory: "Proof that [a] work force was racially balanced or that it contained a disproportionately high percentage of minority employees is not wholly irrelevant on the issue of intent when that issue is yet to be decided." Furnco Construction Corp. v. Waters. See also Teamsters v. United States, n.20. But resolution of the factual question of intent is not what is at issue in this case. Rather, petitioners seek simply to justify discrimination against respondents, on the basis of their favorable treatment of other members of respondents' racial group. Under Title VII, "A racially balanced work force cannot immunize an employer from liability for specific acts of discrimination." Furnco Construction Corp. v. Waters. . . .

It is clear that Congress never intended to give an employer license to discriminate against some employees on the basis of race or sex merely because he favorably treats other members of the employees' group. We recognized in Los Angeles Dept. of Water & Power v. Manhart [reproduced at page 200], that fairness to the class of women employees as a whole could not justify unfairness to the individual female employee because the "statute's focus on the individual is unambiguous." Similarly, in Phillips v. Martin Marietta Corp., 400 U.S. 542 (1971) (per curiam), we recognized that a rule barring employment of all married *women* with preschool children, if not a bona fide occupational qualification under §703(e), violated Title VII, even though female applicants without preschool children were hired in sufficient numbers that they constituted 75 to 80 percent of the persons employed in the position plaintiff sought.

Petitioners point out that *Furnco, Manhart,* and *Phillips* involved facially discriminatory policies, while the claim in the instant case is one of discrimination from a facially neutral policy. The fact remains, however, that irrespective of the form taken by the discriminatory practice, an employer's treatment of other members of the plaintiffs' group can be "of little comfort to the victims of . . . discrimination." Teamsters v. United States. Title VII does not permit the victim of a facially discriminatory policy to be told that he has not been wronged because other persons of his or her race or sex were hired. That answer is no more satisfactory when it is given to victims of a policy that is facially neutral but practically discriminatory. Every *individual* employee is protected against both discriminatory treatment and against "practices that are fair in form, but discriminatory in operation." Griggs v. Duke Power Co. Requirements and tests that have a discriminatory impact are merely some of the more subtle, but also the more pervasive, of the "practices and devices which have fostered racially stratified job environments to the disadvantage of minority citizens." McDonnell Douglas Corp. v. Green. . . .

Justice POWELL, with whom the Chief Justice, Justice REHNQUIST, and Justice O'CONNOR join, dissenting.

. . . Although [the language of §703(a)(2)] suggests that discrimination occurs only on an individual basis, . . . our disparate impact cases consistently have considered whether the result of an employer's *total selection process* had an adverse impact upon the protected group. If this case were decided by reference to the total process — as our cases suggest that it should be — the result would be clear. Here 22.9 percent of the blacks who entered the selection process were ultimately promoted, compared with only 13.5 percent of the whites. To say that this selection process had an unfavorable "disparate impact" on blacks is to ignore reality.

The Court, disregarding the distinction drawn by our cases, repeatedly asserts that Title VII was designed to protect individual, not group, rights. It emphasizes that some individual blacks were eliminated by the disparate impact of the preliminary test. But this argument confuses the *aim* of Title VII with the legal theories through which its aims were intended to be vindicated. It is true that the aim of Title VII is to protect individuals, not groups. But in advancing this commendable objective, Title VII jurisprudence has recognized two distinct methods of proof. In one set of cases — those involving direct proof of discriminatory intent — the plaintiff seeks to establish direct, intentional discrimination against him. In that type case, the individual is at the forefront throughout the entire presentation of evidence. In disparate impact cases, by contrast, the plaintiff seeks to carry his burden of proof by way of *inference* — by showing that an employer's selection process results in the rejection of a disproportionate number of members of a protected group to which he belongs. From such a showing a fair inference then may be drawn that the rejected applicant, as a member of that disproportionately excluded group, was himself a victim of that process's "built-in headwinds." *Griggs.* But this method of proof — which actually *defines* disparate impact theory under Title VII — invites the plaintiff to prove discrimination by reference to the group rather than to the allegedly affected individual.[3] There can be no violation of Title VII on the basis of disparate impact in the absence of disparate impact on a *group*.

In this case the plaintiff seeks to benefit from a conflation of "discriminatory treatment" and "disparate impact" theories. But he cannot have it both ways. Having undertaken to prove discrimination by reference to one set of group figures (used at a preliminary point in the selection process), the plaintiff then claims that *non*discrimination cannot be proved by viewing the impact of the entire process on the group as a whole. The fallacy of this reasoning — accepted by the Court — is transparent. It is to confuse the individualistic *aim* of Title VII with the methods of proof by which Title VII rights may be vindicated. The respondent, as an individual, is entitled to the full personal protection of Title VII. But, having undertaken to prove a violation of his rights by reference to group figures, respondent cannot deny petitioner the opportunity to rebut his evidence by introducing figures of the same kind. Having pleaded a disparate impact case, the plaintiff cannot deny the defendant the opportunity to show that there was no disparate impact. . . .

Where, under a facially neutral employment process, there has been no adverse effect on the group — and certainly there has been none here — Title VII has not been infringed. . . .

## III

Today's decision takes a long and unhappy step in the direction of confusion. Title VII does not require that employers adopt merit hiring or the procedures most likely to permit the greatest number of minority members to be considered for or to qualify for jobs and promotions. See Texas Dept. of Community Affairs v. Burdine; *Furnco*. Employers need not develop tests that accurately reflect the skills of every individual candidate; there are few if any tests that do so. Yet the Court seems unaware of this practical reality, and perhaps oblivious to the likely consequences of its decision. By its holding today, the Court may force employers either to eliminate tests or rely on expensive, job-related, testing procedures, the validity of which may or may not be sustained if challenged. For state and local governmental employers with limited funds, the practical effect of today's decision may well be the adoption of simple quota hiring.[8] This arbitrary method of employment is itself unfair to individual applicants, whether or not they are members of minority groups. And it is not likely to produce a competent workforce. Moreover, the Court's decision actually may result in employers employing *fewer* minority members [by discouraging voluntary affirmative action plans].

3. . . . . Regardless of whether the plaintiff's prima facie case must itself focus on the defendant's overall selection process or whether it is sufficient that the plaintiff establish that at least one pass-fail barrier has resulted in disparate impact, the employer's presentation of evidence showing that its overall selecting procedure does not operate in a discriminatory fashion certainly dispels any inference of discrimination. In such instances, at the close of evidence, the plaintiff has failed to show disparate impact by a preponderance of the evidence.

8. Another possibility is that employers may integrate consideration of test results into one overall hiring decision based on that "factor" *and* additional factors. Such a process would not, even under the Court's reasoning, result in a finding of discrimination on the basis of disparate impact unless the actual hiring decisions had a disparate impact on the minority group. But if employers integrate test results into a single-step decision, they will be free to select *only* the number of minority candidates proportional to their representation in the workforce. If petitioner had used this approach, it would have been able to hire substantially fewer blacks without liability on the basis of disparate impact. The Court hardly could have intended to encourage this.

*NOTES*

1. *Teal* asks: when an employer uses more than one practice to select its workers, may the plaintiff focus on each practice, or is she limited to the "bottom line" effect of all the practices considered together? *Teal* permits an attack on any practice with an identifiable impact, and, just as importantly, renders a nondiscriminatory bottom line no defense to an impact on a particular practice. Is *Teal* still good law after the 1991 Civil Rights Act?

2. Answering that question might require an interpretation of "particular employment practice." The "plain meaning" of this term suggests an intent to separate out multicomponent selection processes into their individual parts. This is confirmed by § 703(k)(1)(B), which requires the plaintiff to show that "each particular challenged employment practice causes an impact, except that if the complaining party can demonstrate to the court that the elements of [an employer's] decisionmaking process cannot be separated for analysis, the decisionmaking process may be analyzed as one employment practice."

3. Resort to the legislative history of the Civil Rights Act confirms this, but the Act itself has a provision limiting judicial use of legislative history. Section 105(b) of the Act says, "No statements other than [a specified] interpretive memorandum shall be considered legislative history of, or relied upon in any way as legislative history in construing or applying, any provision of this Act that relates to *Wards Cove* — business necessity/cumulation/alternative employment practice." Presumably, the "particular employment practice" question is within this limitation, perhaps due to the "cumulation" language. Resort to the referenced Interpretative Memorandum of October 25, 1991, on this point does seem helpful:

> When a decision-making process includes particular, functionally-integrated practices which are components of the same criterion, standard, method of administration, or test, such as the height and weight requirements designed to measure strength in Dothard v. Rawlinson, the particular functionally-integrated practices may be analyzed as one employment practice.

Clearly, an entire multiple-choice exam is one employment practice under this definition. But why are the height and weight requirements in *Dothard*, which are in some ways quite different, nevertheless viewed as one practice?

4. Does *Teal* provide the answer? The employer there used a sequential, multistep procedure: passing the test was a condition for being considered at the next level. In the last footnote of his dissent, Justice Powell suggested that the decision could be avoided by integrating the test into a single, but multifactored, decision. Under his view, the bottom line would then become the only focus. Is that what the new statute envisions? If so, the interpretive memorandum's citation to *Dothard* would be wrong because the height requirement and the weight requirement were separate: an applicant could satisfy one and fail the other. Perhaps the point, however, is that the requirements can be passed and failed. They are not, like Justice Powell's hypothetical, just factors to be weighed. A person who is too short will not be employed, regardless of his or her strengths in other regards.

5. How would the new statute apply to *Teal* if that case were decided today? Plaintiffs were able to pinpoint the written test as having a racial impact because the employer kept records of the scores of all the test takers. Thus, they could establish the disparate impact of a "particular employment practice." While the test in *Teal* was objective, there may be subjective evaluation systems that nevertheless rely on scoring systems that could be used to determine whether a disparate impact existed.

6. In *Teal* itself, the non-test elements that made up the promotion process varied from objective criteria, like seniority, to subjective elements, such as the recommendations of the candidate's supervisors. Since these elements were not scored, the only way to determine their impact was to look at the "bottom line." But the "bottom line" was that those elements did *not* have a disparate impact on African Americans; instead, they were (at least collectively) "more favorable to blacks than to whites." Thus, today the plaintiffs in *Teal* would still not be able to attack any part of the selection process except for the written test.

7. Suppose in *Teal*, the test did not cause a disparate impact on African Americans but the rest of the process did result in a disparate impact at the "bottom line." Since the rest of the process is multicomponent, § 703(k)(1)(A)(i) suggests that plaintiffs would not be able to establish a prima facie case. Of course, § 703(k)(1)(B)(i) does recognize a bottom line exception to (A)(i)'s general rule that the plaintiff must identify a "particular employment practice."

8. In Stout v. Potter, 276 F.3d 1118 (9th Cir. 2002), plaintiffs challenged the selection process for promoting postal inspectors to the position of Inspector in Charge. While there was no impact if the comparison was between the representation of women in the pool of postal inspectors and the final results of the promotion process, the court rejected defendant's claim that such a result barred plaintiffs' action. Instead, the focus of plaintiffs' claim was impact at the level of a review panel that initially screened all applicants who came from the pool of inspectors, sending only the most qualified forward to a separate selection committee. Focusing on the outcome of the review panel, plaintiffs' still failed to establish a prima facie case of disparate impact because of sex. "Female applicants comprised 13.3 percent (2 of 15) of all those interviewed [by the selection committee] and 15.8 percent (6 of 38) of the original applicant pool. The percentage of interviewees who are female is nearly proportional to the percentage of applicants who are female. The 2.5 percent difference is not a substantial or significant statistical disparity." Id. at 1123. Applying the EEOC's "four-fifths" rule produced the same result. "[T]he selection rate for female applicants to be interviewed was 33 percent (2 of 6) and the rate for male applicants was 41 percent (13 of 32). This means that the selection of women was 81 percent of the rate of interview for men, again demonstrating that no disparate impact was shown." Id. at 1124. Was the real problem that the sample size was too small to be able to draw any conclusions about impact?

9. Assuming that plaintiff can establish a prima facie case by showing that a subjective evaluation system did cause a disparate impact, how can the employer justify such a system? In a portion of her opinion in *Watson* joined by only a plurality of the Court, Justice O'Connor expressed concern that "validating" subjective employment criteria could prove to be nearly impossible:

> Some qualities — for example, common sense, good judgment, originality, ambition, loyalty, and tact — cannot be measured accurately through standardized testing techniques. Moreover, success at many jobs in which such qualities are crucial cannot itself be measured directly. Opinions often differ when managers and supervisors are evaluated, and the same can be said for many jobs that involve close cooperation with one's co-workers or complex and subtle tasks like the provision of professional services or personal counseling. Because of these difficulties, we are told, employers will find it impossible to eliminate subjective selection criteria and impossibly expensive to defend such practices in litigation.

487 U.S. at 991-92. How will Justice O'Connor's concerns be addressed in the wake of the 1991 amendments? We will explore employer justifications for practices with a disparate impact later in this chapter.

10. Susan Sturm, Second Generation Employment Discrimination: A Structural Approach, 101 Colum. L. Rev. 458, 485-90 (2001), writes:

> Employers engage in subjective decisionmaking whenever they make employment decisions that require the exercise of judgment and discretion. These practices could involve individuals, such as promotion and job assignment decisions resulting from interviews, references, and collective or individual assessments of the relative merits of candidates, or groups, such as decisions about defining the pool from which to select employees for a particular position. For a variety of reasons, decisions requiring the exercise of individual or collective judgment that are highly unstructured tend to reflect, express, or produce biased outcomes. This bias has been linked to patterns of underrepresentation or exclusion of members of nondominant groups. . . .
>
> The Court . . . failed in *Watson* to carry through on the structuralist insight that prompted disparate impact's application to subjective employment practices in the first place. The conduct that was being challenged was not the individual expression of bias per se, or the exclusionary impact of the particular qualification being sought through the subjective process. It was instead the failure of the employer's decisionmaking system to minimize the expression of bias. Given the structural nature of the problem, it made sense to define employers' business necessity defense as an inquiry about their system's adequacy. This possibility was not considered by the Court in *Watson*. . . .
>
> If subjective employment practices produce a disparate impact on women or people of color, this disparity operates as a signal of the possibility that the system is contributing to the production or expression of bias. [Some lower courts have started to assess] the subjective decisionmaking process to determine whether it provided adequate steps to minimize or eliminate the expression of bias. The emphasis is on whether the degree of unaccountable or unstructured exercise of discretion is warranted. To make this determination, courts will look at the available alternatives. Are there systems of decisionmaking that will permit the exercise of discretion, but will institute standards and processes that minimize the expression of bias?

Does Professor's Sturm's view re-invigorate disparate impact as a means of rooting out unintended discrimination, even if such impact is the result of unconscious prejudices?

11. Professor Tristin Green, although agreeing with Professor Sturm that the employer's harmful action in these circumstances is its failure to minimize discriminatory bias in individual decision-making, questions whether disparate impact theory is capable of supporting the inquiry needed for change:

> If one were to point to an employer's use of an identifiable subjective criteria, such as "friendliness" or "leadership ability," which, even when applied neutrally to all individuals, has a disparate impact on members of certain groups, the employer should be required under proper application of disparate impact theory to justify that criteria as job related and consistent with business necessity. . . . In practice, however, the larger problem with subjectivity in decision-making for the anti-discrimination project is its tendency to enable, facilitate, or permit the operation of discriminatory bias in decision makers. In other words, the discrimination is typically not in the requirement of friendliness or leadership ability itself; the employer's search for applicants with that characteristic may indeed be job related and justified by business necessity. Rather, the discrimination arises in the application of that criteria by members of the white majority according to dominant definitions of that term. . . .
>
> Disparate impact doctrine, with its conceptual focus on neutral barriers with adverse consequence, tends to present litigants and courts with a dichotomous decision. Either the job requirement or employment practice that has an adverse impact can be justified in terms of business necessity, and thus its use does not amount to unlawful discrimina-

tion and can be retained, or the job requirement cannot be so justified, and thus its use amounts to unlawful discrimination and must be eliminated. It is neither realistic nor sensible, however, to combat the operation of discriminatory bias in the modern workplace along such dichotomous lines. Rather than requiring the elimination of the practice itself, we need to begin exploring the ways in which employers can be held accountable for managing diversity within modern structures and practices to minimize the operation of discriminatory bias. The complex, contextual nature of the problem requires a correspondingly innovative, problem-based, collaborative solution that does not fit easily within the existing disparate impact remedial paradigm.

Discrimination in Workplace Dynamics: Toward a Structural Account of Disparate Treatment Theory, 38 Harv. C.R.-C.L. L. Rev. 91, 142-43 (2002).

12. Is an employer's use of a particular labor market to recruit workers a particular employment practice within the general rule of § 703(k)(1)(A)(i)? Recall that *Wards Cove* restricted that application of disparate impact law. In NAACP, Newark Branch v. Town of Harrison, 940 F.2d 792 (3d Cir. 1991), the town's residents-only rule had a disparate impact because Harrison was almost exclusively white, while nearby areas, such as Newark, were predominately black. In short, Harrison had defined a geographic labor market, but the plaintiff challenged that very definition as creating an adverse impact. Why is Newark the relevant comparison in *Harrison?*

13. In United States v. City of Warren, Michigan, 138 F.3d 1083, 1093 (6th Cir. 1998), the city imposed a residents-only rule for its hiring and refused to advertise outside of predominantly white Macomb County, a suburb of Detroit. The Sixth Circuit reversed a decision for the defendant that had concluded that the plaintiff had not introduced statistical evidence showing that these practices had an impact:

> Because of the concurrence of the residency requirement and the challenged recruiting practices, the statistical proof which *Wards Cove* generally requires was unattainable in this case. . . . *Wards Cove* does not[, however,] preclude the United States' claim for failing to isolate and quantify the effects of Warren's discriminatory employment practices simply because two practices, both of which the district court has held to be unlawful [as applied to police and firefighter jobs], converged to discourage black applicants. Indeed, such a result would be anomalous and contrary to *Wards Cove's* explicit recognition that when, as here, certain employment practices obscure labor-market statistics, alternative statistical analysis suffices to establish a prima facie disparate impact case.

14. Can disparate impact be used to attack policy decisions of employers such as the decision to require all employees to sign agreements to arbitrate all disputes arising out of employment? See Miriam A. Cherry, Not-So-Arbitrary Arbitration: Using Title VII Disparate Impact Analysis to Invalidate Employment Contracts That Discriminate, 21 Harv. Women's L.J. 267 (1998). While a policy limited to arbitrating claims of, say, race discrimination could have a disparate impact on African Americans, how would a plaintiff prove impact if the policy applied to all employment disputes?

15. The 1991 Civil Rights Act created a specific exception to the application of disparate impact discrimination for some employment practices dealing with illegal drug use. Section 703(k)(3) provides that "a rule barring the employment of an individual who currently and knowingly uses or possesses a controlled substance . . . other than the use or possession of a drug taken under the supervision of a licensed health care professional, . . . shall be considered an unlawful employment practice under this title only if such rule is adopted or applied with an intent to discriminate because of race, color, sex, or national origin." This appears to resolve the tension within disparate im-

pact doctrine resulting from New York City Transit Auth. v. Beazer, 440 U.S. 568 (1979), which involved a disparate impact challenge to an employer rule prohibiting employment of people on methadone maintenance. In upholding the employer's rule, the Court imposed a very high threshold showing of impact sufficient to make out a prima facie case and then, in dicta, suggested a low burden on the employer to justify the rule under the business necessity defense. The Court did this without suggesting it was applying special rules because a drug rule was involved. But §703(k) now specifically excludes the application of disparate impact analysis to employer rules dealing with the illegal use of drugs. Ironically, §703(k)(3) would not exempt the rule in *Beazer* since that rule involved the legal use of drugs. Presumably, if *Beazer* arose again today, it would be subject to normal disparate treatment analysis under §703(k)(1).

16. Like *Griggs, Teal* involved a written test. The codification of disparate impact in the Civil Rights Act of 1991 should generally result in scrutiny of such tests for their adverse impact on minorities. However, the 1991 Act added a provision that bears on the use of tests, and may affect disparate impact application. Section 703(l), added in 1991, provides:

> It shall be an unlawful employment practice for a respondent, in connection with the selection or referral of applicants or candidates for employment or promotion, to adjust the scores of, use different cutoff scores for, or otherwise alter the results of, employment related tests on the basis of race, color, religion, sex, or national origin.

Does this mean that an employer cannot avoid disparate impact liability by modifying its tests? In Hayden v. County of Nassau, 180 F.3d 42 (2d Cir. 1999), a police department, in conformity with a consent decree in an earlier employment discrimination case, developed an entrance examination. After the exam was administered, the test scores were analyzed to determine whether it was valid and whether it had an adverse impact on minority applicants. That analysis resulted in the department using only nine of the 25 sections of the test: those sections were valid and using only them minimized the adverse impact on minority applicants. White and Latino applicants challenged this use, claiming it violated §703(l). The court rejected that challenge because the exam was scored the same for all test takers:

> The statute, on its face, clearly prohibits methods which utilize different scoring techniques or adjust candidates' scores on the basis of race. . . . The legislative history of the statute also confirms that it intended to prohibit "race norming" and other methods of using different cutoffs for different races or altering scores based on race. See generally 137 Cong. Rec. S15476 (1991). In the case before us, the 1994 exam was scored in the same manner for all applicants; no differential cutoffs were employed.

Id. at 53.

### b.   The New "Bottom Line" Exception of the 1991 Civil Rights Act

While §703(k)(1)(A)(i) generally requires plaintiff to identify particular employment practices that cause the impact, the statute does provide an exception in which the entire decision-making process of the employer is treated as one employment practice, with bottom-line statistics allowed to show impact. Thus, new §703(k)(1)(B) now provides:

> With respect to demonstrating that a particular employment practice causes a disparate impact as described in subparagraph (A)(i), the complaining party shall demonstrate

that each particular challenged employment practice causes a disparate impact, except that if the complaining party can demonstrate to the court that the elements of a respondent's decisionmaking process are not capable of separation for analysis, the decisionmaking process may be analyzed as one employment practice.

If the plaintiff cannot identify particular employment practices, but can show a discriminatory bottom line, how can she demonstrate that the process is not capable of separation? Should the standard be one of reasonably diligent efforts? What if the plaintiff's difficulty in identifying a particular employment policy is caused by the employer's failure to maintain records or its destruction of relevant records? Should the employer be permitted to escape liability by failing to maintain records? Does the question whether practices are capable of separation relate to whether separation is theoretically possible or practically possible?

Recall Justice Powell's *Teal* hypothetical, where the employer considers many factors, whether those factors are objective, subjective, or mixed, but does not "score" any of them. Presumably § 703(k)(1)(B)(i) would apply, enabling plaintiff to establish a prima facie case based on the bottom-line statistics of the people hired or promoted by the entire process compared to the people considered in the process. But in *Teal* itself, there was no discrimination at the bottom line. Justice Powell's approach would shield the employer under the amended statute.

In Chavez v. Coors Brewing Co., 1999 U.S. App. LEXIS 5300 (10th Cir. 1999), the company downsized its maintenance department, with incumbent employees who were selected for new "senior specialist" positions excluded from the reduction-in-force.

> Working closely with a professor at Colorado State University, Martine and his staff designed a selection process to fill the new senior specialist positions (submission of questionnaires to employees regarding essential skills, establishment of screening criteria, development of an appropriate exam) to ensure the process was standardized, reliable, job-related, and procedurally fair. All applicants were required to have a Colorado journeyman's license. The selection committee examined each applicant's attendance record, safety rate, prior evaluations, welding quality, training records, score on a written test designed to identify the desired skills, interview, computer skills, and certification in additional crafts. Martine and his staff then ranked the applicants by their scores, and the top candidates received offers for the new positions.

Id. at *3. Plaintiff claimed the senior specialist job category had an adverse impact on Hispanics because only one of five Hispanic applicants (20 percent) was selected, while nineteen of forty-three (44 percent) of non-Hispanic candidates were selected. The Tenth Circuit held that plaintiff failed to identify any particular aspect of the selection process that had a disparate impact on Hispanics. "A general assault on the racial composition of the workforce will not suffice to create an actionable disparate impact claims." Id. at *10. Assuming the "bottom line" exception of § 703(k)(1)(B) applied, plaintiff nevertheless failed to establish a prima facie case because the statistical evidence was based on too small a sample. "The small number of *overall* applicants for the senior specialist positions renders a statistical analysis relatively unhelpful." Id. at *13.

Assuming a plaintiff can make out a prima facie case based on the bottom line exception to the general requirement that plaintiff identify a particular employment practice causing the impact, the burden of persuasion shifts to the defendant to prove either (1) that the specific practices that make up the decision-making process do not cause the impact; or (2) that the remaining practices are justified as job related and consistent with business necessity; or (3) that those practices fall within the § 703(h) defenses. The first defense arises from § 703(k)(1)(B)(ii), which provides: "If the respondent demonstrates that a specific employment practice does not cause the disparate impact, the respondent shall not be required to demonstrate that such practice is required by business necessity."

## PROBLEM 5.1

Fogey.com is an e-commerce business that is growing rapidly. Alice Aortop is in charge of hiring, and she says that she interviews every applicant and subjectively evaluates each one looking for "creativity, decisiveness, ambition, loyalty and ability to create buzz!" Assuming that comparatively few of the African-American and Latino applicants are hired, can the "bottom-line" number of minority group members be used to make out a prima facie case of disparate impact discrimination since the subjective evaluation system is a particular employment practice? Or since factors such as creativity, decisiveness, etc., are relied upon, must the plaintiff first convince the judge that these elements are not capable of separation for analysis because he is using bottom-line statistics to prove disparate impact?

### c.    The Employer Uses the Practice

Section 703(k)(1)(A)(i) requires that plaintiff prove that the employer "*uses* a particular employment practice that causes a disparate impact." This requires a causal link between the practice used by the employer and the resulting impact.

## DOTHARD v. RAWLINSON
### 433 U.S. 321 (1977)

Justice STEWART delivered the opinion of the Court. . . .

I

At the time she applied for a position as correctional counselor trainee, Rawlinson was a 22-year-old college graduate whose major course of study had been correctional psychology. She was refused employment because she failed to meet the minimum 120-pound weight requirement established by an Alabama statute. The statute also establishes a height minimum of 5 feet 2 inches. . . .

Like most correctional facilities in the United States, Alabama's prisons are segregated on the basis of sex. Currently the Alabama Board of Corrections operates four major all-male penitentiaries. . . . The Board also operates the Julia Tutwiler Prison for Women, the Frank Lee Youth Center, the Number Four Honor Camp, the State Cattle Ranch, and nine Work Release Centers, one of which is for women. The Julia Tutwiler Prison for Women and the four male penitentiaries are maximum-security institutions. Their inmate living quarters are for the most part large dormitories, with communal showers and toilets that are open to the dormitories and hallways. The Draper and Fountain penitentiaries carry on extensive farming operations, making necessary a large number of strip searches for contraband when prisoners re-enter the prison buildings.

A correctional counselor's primary duty within these institutions is to maintain security and control of the inmates by continually supervising and observing their activities. To be eligible for consideration as a correctional counselor, an applicant must possess a valid Alabama driver's license, have a high school education or its equivalent, be free from physical defects, be between the ages of 20½ years and 45 years at the time of appointment, and fall between the minimum height and weight requirements of 5 feet 2 inches, and 120 pounds, and the maximum of 6 feet 10 inches, and 300 pounds. Appointment is by merit, with a grade assigned each applicant based on experience and education. No written examination is given. . . .

II . . .

A

The gist of the claim that the statutory height and weight requirements discriminate against women does not involve an assertion of purposeful discriminatory motive. It is asserted, rather, that these facially neutral qualification standards work in fact disproportionately to exclude women from eligibility for employment by the Alabama Board of Corrections. We dealt in Griggs v. Duke Power Co. and Albemarle Paper Co. v. Moody [reproduced at page 401] with similar allegations that facially neutral employment standards disproportionately excluded Negroes from employment, and those cases guide our approach here.

Those cases make clear that to establish a prima facie case of discrimination, a plaintiff need only show that the facially neutral standards in question select applicants for hire in a significantly discriminatory pattern. Once it is thus shown that the employment standards are discriminatory in effect, the employer must meet "the burden of showing that any given requirement [has] . . . a manifest relationship to the employment in question." Griggs v. Duke Power Co. If the employer proves that the challenged requirements are job related, the plaintiff may then show that other selection devices without a similar discriminatory effect would also "serve the employer's legitimate interest in 'efficient and trustworthy workmanship.'" Albemarle Paper Co. v. Moody, quoting McDonnell Douglas Corp. v. Green.

Although women 14 years of age or older compose 52.75% of the Alabama population and 36.89% of its total labor force, they hold only 12.9% of its correctional counselor positions. In considering the effect of the minimum height and weight standards on this disparity in rate of hiring between the sexes, the District Court found that the 5'2" requirement would operate to exclude 33.29% of the women in the United States between the ages of 18-79, while excluding only 1.28% of men between the same ages. The 120-pound weight restriction would exclude 22.29% of the women and 2.35% of the men in this age group. When the height and weight restrictions are combined, Alabama's statutory standards would exclude 41.13% of the female population while excluding less than 1% of the male population.[12] Accordingly, the District Court found that Rawlinson had made out a prima facie case of unlawful sex discrimination.

The appellants argue that a showing of disproportionate impact on women based on generalized national statistics should not suffice to establish a prima facie case. They point in particular to Rawlinson's failure to adduce comparative statistics con-

12. Affirmatively stated, approximately 99.76% of the men and 58.87% of the women meet both these physical qualifications. From the separate statistics on height and weight of males it would appear that

cerning actual applicants for correctional counselor positions in Alabama. There is no requirement, however, that a statistical showing of disproportionate impact must always be based on analysis of the characteristics of actual applicants. See Griggs v. Duke Power Co. The application process itself might not adequately reflect the actual potential applicant pool, since otherwise qualified people might be discouraged from applying because of a self-recognized inability to meet the very standards challenged as being discriminatory. See Teamsters v. United States. A potential applicant could easily determine her height and weight and conclude that to make an application would be futile. Moreover, reliance on general population demographic data was not misplaced where there was no reason to suppose that physical height and weight characteristics of Alabama men and women differ markedly from those of the national population.

For these reasons, we cannot say that the District Court was wrong in holding that the statutory height and weight standards had a discriminatory impact on women applicants. The plaintiffs in a case such as this are not required to exhaust every possible source of evidence, if the evidence actually presented on its face conspicuously demonstrates a job requirement's grossly discriminatory impact. If the employer discerns fallacies or deficiencies in the data offered by the plaintiff, he is free to adduce countervailing evidence of his own. In this case no such effort was made.

B

We turn, therefore, to the appellants' argument that they have rebutted the prima facie case of discrimination by showing that the height and weight requirements are job related. These requirements, they say, have a relationship to strength, a sufficient but unspecified amount of which is essential to effective job performance as a correctional counselor. In the District Court, however, the appellants produced no evidence correlating the height and weight requirements with the requisite amount of strength thought essential to good job performance. Indeed, they failed to offer evidence of any kind in specific justification of the statutory standards.[14]

If the job-related quality that the appellants identify is bona fide, their purpose could be achieved by adopting and validating a test for applicants that measures strength directly. Such a test, fairly administered, would fully satisfy the standards of Title VII because it would be one that "measure[s] the person for the job and not the person in the abstract." Griggs v. Duke Power Co. But nothing in the present record even approaches such a measurement. . . .

[Justice REHNQUIST, joined by the Chief Justice and Justice BLACKMUN, filed a concurring opinion.]

---

after adding the two together and allowing for some overlap the result would be to exclude between 2.35% and 3.63% of males from meeting Alabama's statutory height and weight minima. None of the parties has challenged the accuracy of the District Court's computations on this score, however, and the discrepancy is in any event insignificant in light of the gross disparity between the female and male exclusions. Even under revised computations the disparity would greatly exceed the 34% to 12% disparity that served to invalidate the high school diploma requirement in the Griggs case.

14. [T]he appellants contend that the establishment of the minimum height and weight standards by statute requires that they be given greater deference than is typically given private employer-established job qualifications. The relevant legislative history of the 1972 amendments extending Title VII to the States as employers does not, however, support such a result. Instead, Congress expressly indicated the intent that the same Title VII principles be applied to governmental and private employers alike. See H.R. Rep. No. 92-238, p. 17 (1971); S. Rep. No. 92-415, p. 10 (1971). . . .

Justice WHITE, dissenting.

. . . I have . . . trouble agreeing that a prima facie case of sex discrimination was made out by statistics showing that the Alabama height and weight requirements would exclude a larger percentage of women in the United States than of men. As in *Hazelwood*, the issue is whether there was discrimination in dealing with actual or potential applicants; but in *Hazelwood* there was at least a colorable argument that the racial composition of the area-wide teacher work force was a reasonable proxy for the composition of the relevant applicant pool and hence that a large divergence between the percentage of blacks on the teaching staff and the percentage in the teacher work force raised a fair inference of racial discrimination in dealing with the applicant pool. In *Dothard*, however, I am unwilling to believe that the percentage of women applying or interested in applying for jobs as prison guards in Alabama approximates the percentage of women either in the national or state population. A plaintiff could, of course, show that the composition of the applicant pool was distorted by the exclusion of nonapplicants who did not apply because of the allegedly discriminatory job requirement. But no such showing was made or even attempted here; and although I do not know what the actual fact is, I am not now convinced that a large percentage of the actual women applicants, or of those who are seriously interested in applying, for prison guard positions would fail to satisfy the height and weight requirements. Without a more satisfactory record on this issue, I cannot conclude that appellee Rawlinson has either made out a prima facie case for the invalidity of the restrictions or otherwise proved that she was improperly denied employment as a prison guard. There being no showing of discrimination, I do not reach the question of justification. . . .

## NOTES

1. Is the impact on women of height and weight minima the result of societal discrimination? Why is using a non-job-related barrier to the employment of women unfair even if the source of the barrier is not discrimination?

2. Could *Dothard* be analyzed as a disparate treatment case? Is the disparity caused by the neutral criteria sufficient to raise an inference of intent? Compare *Teamsters*. Even if the disparity is significant, remember *Feeney*, where the Court, in the equal protection context, declined to equate knowledge of a significant impact with intent. But in *Dothard*, does the employer's use of a gender-explicit exclusion, treated in another portion of the opinion (see page 265), coupled with the impact of the neutral criteria, suggest that the employer selected the criteria with a discriminatory purpose?

3. Does plaintiff's proof of national height and weight statistics satisfy § 703(k)(1)(A)(i)'s requirement that plaintiff prove that the employer "uses" a practice that causes impact? Justice White's dissent would require the plaintiff to prove that the employer's use caused impact. Should the disparate impact theory be available to challenge, at least at a prima facie level, employment practices that, if used by employers generally, would cause a disparate impact?

4. Or is Justice White's point that perhaps only taller, heavier women are interested in prison guard positions in the first place, so that there is no actual (as opposed to theoretic) impact by the employer's policy. Do you think plaintiff's showing in *Dothard* should suffice under § 703(k)(1)(B)?

5. The Supreme Court has not been entirely consistent in approach. In New York City Transit Auth. v. Beazer, 440 U.S. 568 (1979), plaintiffs, seeking attorneys' fees after having won on constitutional grounds, invoked Title VII to challenge an em-

ployer rule disqualifying people taking methadone, a drug used in the treatment of heroin addiction. Plaintiffs showed that 81 percent of all Transit Authority (TA) employees suspected of drug use were black or Hispanic and, less certainly, that between 62 percent and 65 percent of all methadone-maintained people in New York City were black or Hispanic. The Supreme Court rejected that challenge in part because of the inadequate showing of impact.

> [R]espondents have only challenged the rule to the extent that it is construed to apply to methadone users, and [the statistics about overall drug use tell] us nothing about the racial composition of the employees suspected of using methadone. Nor does the record give us any information about the number of black, Hispanic, or white persons who were dismissed for using methadone. . . . We do not know . . . how many of these persons [in methadone maintenance programs] ever worked or sought to work for TA. This statistic therefore reveals little if anything about the racial composition of the class of TA job applicants and employees receiving methadone treatment.

Id. at 585. Was the majority unduly severe in its statistical analysis of the showing of impact? Could an inference be drawn that these statistics indicated a racial impact for the methadone rule? The lesson seems to be that plaintiffs must introduce data that focus more directly on the effect of defendant's use of the challenged rule. The Court suggests that the relevant group for deriving impact statistics is the Transit Authority's applicant pool. But wouldn't individuals on maintenance who are aware of the TA's methadone restriction not bother to apply? Is *Beazer* still good law, now that §703(k)(3) has exempted from disparate impact attack employer rules barring the illegal use of drugs?

6. The plaintiffs in *Beazer* presented impact evidence based on general population statistics. In contrast, the Court seemed to rely on the "relevant labor market" concept developed in the disparate treatment context. Assuming that this concept applies to a disparate impact case, what is the relevant labor market for prison guards? Is it the general population, interested individuals in the general population, or applicants?

7. Is it appropriate to borrow the relevant labor market concept and apply it in the impact context precisely as it is applied in the disparate treatment context? When statistics are used to create an inference of discriminatory intent, the relevant comparison population is the population from which the employer actually selected employees. Unless it can be proved that the employer chose its labor market discriminatorily (e.g., selecting employees from a certain college *because* the student population of that college is predominately white or requiring a college degree *because* that requirement screens out minority group members), the only relevant group is the group it actually considered. It is the comparison between that group and the resulting workforce that will reveal disparities from which intentional disparate treatment can be inferred. But what is the appropriate comparison group in a disparate impact case? What population must be impacted by the challenged employment practice?

8. In Caviale v. State of Wisconsin, Dept. of Health & Social Servs., 744 F.2d 1289 (7th Cir. 1984), the plaintiff challenged the employer's decision to consider only "career executives" for a job opening. Only 2 of the 200 members of this pool were women. The court rejected the *Beazer*-based argument that the employer-defined pool of career executives constituted the group of qualified persons for the job. Rather, it constructed a pool of those who met the minimum objective qualifications for the job, a much broader pool than the career executive group. The employer's decision to define the pool more narrowly, therefore, had a disparate impact on the ba-

sis of gender. Which of these labor pools would be relevant if the plaintiffs in *Caviale* sought to establish systemic disparate treatment? In an impact case, once the employer's choice of labor market is questioned, how should the court construct an alternative labor market in order to determine the existence of impact?

9. Thomas v. Washington County Sch. Bd., 915 F.2d 922 (4th Cir. 1990), found disparate impact because the school board relied on word-of-mouth hiring and nepotism in the context of a predominately white workforce. While plaintiff's statistics were inadequate because they focused on the general population, rather than the qualified labor pool, the board was liable because "when the work force is predominantly white, nepotism and similar practices which operate to exclude outsiders may discriminate against minorities as effectively as any intentionally discriminatory policy." Id. at 925. Is the court correct in finding it unnecessary to present a comparison population to establish impact? Reliance on nepotism and word-of-mouth hiring in a predominately white workforce would seem to arbitrarily exclude minority groups. But what if the plant is located in a geographic area that is predominately white for hundreds of miles around? Or what if blacks are not interested in the jobs for other reasons? Cf. Newark Branch, NAACP v. City of Bayonne, 134 F.3d 113 (3d Cir. 1998) (residency requirement did not in fact have a disparate impact on African Americans although statistics suggested it was likely to have such an impact).

10. How should the "qualified labor market" be defined? A student note, Scott Baker, Comment, Defining "Otherwise Qualified Applicants": Applying an Antitrust Relevant-Market Analysis to Disparate Impact Cases, 67 U. Chi. L. Rev. 725 (2000), argues that both the applicant flow method and the proxy labor market method (usually derived from current holders of the jobs at issue) are inappropriate and that courts should look to antitrust principles of market definition to construct the appropriate labor market for analysis.

11. Ramona L. Paetzold & Steven L. Willborn, in Deconstructing Disparate Impact: A View of the Model Through New Lenses, 74 N.C. L. Rev. 325, 356 (1995), argue that the plaintiff in a disparate impact case need not prove actual causation:

> [D]isparate impact cases . . . [do] not require that the plaintiff prove that the employer's criterion has actually produced a disparate impact in the workplace. In *Griggs*, for example, the same disparate impact on blacks may have occurred even if the employer had not utilized the high school diploma requirement. Employees applying for the jobs at issue in *Griggs* also had to attain a certain score on a general "intelligence" test that approximated the national median score for high school graduates. Blacks as a class may have suffered from the same (or even a greater) disparate impact as a result of the test requirement. The disparate impact model as applied in *Griggs*, then, did not require any proof that the criterion at issue actually produced a disparate impact; it merely required proof that the criterion at issue would have screened out protected class members disproportionately if applied independently of any other factors at play in the selection process.

Do you agree? Is *Beazer* consistent with this view? If that is an accurate statement of the law under *Griggs*, is it still valid under § 703(k)(A)(1)?

12. In Espinoza v. Farah Mfg. Co., 414 U.S. 86, 93 (1973), the Court allowed the employer to rebut plaintiff's showing that a rule requiring American citizenship had a disparate impact on those born outside the United States by presenting statistics that the rule did not have that effect at its plant:

> [P]ersons of Mexican ancestry make up more than 96% of the employees at the company's San Antonio division, and 97% of those doing the work for which Mrs. Espinoza

applied. While statistics such as these do not automatically shield an employer from a charge of unlawful discrimination, the plain fact of the matter is that Farah does not discriminate against persons of Mexican national origin with respect to employment in the job Mrs. Espinoza sought.

13. Section 703(k)(1)(B)(ii) now provides that if the employer "demonstrates that a specific employment practice does not cause the disparate impact, the [employer] shall not be required to demonstrate that such practice is required by business necessity." This subsection (ii) follows subsection (i), which creates the bottom-line exception to the general rule of § 703(k)(1)(A)(i) that plaintiffs must point to a particular employment practice that the employer uses that causes a disparate impact. Thus, it is clear that subsection (ii) creates an affirmative defense to a prima facie case based on bottom line statistics pursuant to subsection (i). The broader question is whether subsection (ii) also creates an affirmative defense to a prima facie case based on the general rule of § 703(k)(1)(A)(i) where the plaintiff does identify a particular employment practice that causes a disparate impact.

The argument against applying the subsection (ii) affirmative defense to a prima facie case based on § 703(k)(1)(A)(i) is that the burden of persuasion on the same point — whether the challenged practice causes a disparate impact — would then be on both parties. A response is that these two provisions, when read together, first require the plaintiff to carry the burden of persuasion that the employer used a practice that causes a disparate impact, which burden can be satisfied with national statistics as in *Dothard* and *Griggs*. Once the plaintiff satisfies that burden, the employer may prevail by proving the affirmative defense created by § 703(k)(1)(B)(ii), as the employer did in *Espinoza*, that its own use of the practice did not cause a disparate impact.

14. The courts are confused on this issue. In Johnson v. Uncle Ben's Inc., 965 F.2d 1363 (5th Cir. 1992), the court rejected national statistics as an appropriate comparison for determining the disparate impact of alleged (but not clearly proven) education requirements on the promotion of black employees at Uncle Ben's Inc. (UBI):

> The national population . . . is not the qualified labor pool against which UBI's workforce should be compared. The effect of educational requirements on the ability of Blacks in the national population to get promotions at UBI has little relevance. . . . The question is whether and how specific educational requirements affected *UBI employees* seeking promotions. It is not obvious that Black UBI employees in the pool of employees qualified for promotion to higher levels would not have the skills or education allegedly required for promotion.

Id. at 1369. Similarly, in Thomas v. Metroflight, Inc., 814 F.2d 1506 (10th Cir. 1987), the plaintiff challenged a "no-spouse rule," requiring the "voluntary" resignation of one of the spouses working in the same department or the discharge of the less-senior spouse. In seven of the previous instances of intrafirm marriage, the rule was not violated because the spouses worked in different departments, accommodations were made by reclassifying one spouse's work assignment, or the violation was simply allowed. In addition to the plaintiff, one other female employee was discharged because of the rule. The court, while citing authority that no-spouse rules in practice often result in discrimination against women, found that plaintiff failed to make out a showing of impact by the at-issue rule. See generally Timothy Chandler, Spouses Need Not Apply: The Legality of Anti-Nepotism and No-Spouse Rules, 39 San Diego L. Rev. 31 (2002) ("[E]mployees, primarily women, affected by the application of these rules have raised challenges under various legal theories. Their primary argument has been that while neutral on their face, anti-nepotism and no-spouse rules significantly burden women to a larger extent than men. Courts, however, have been ambivalent about the treatment afforded to challenges to the application of these rules. In general, courts continue to treat these rules as sex-neutral, and deny employees affected by them any form of relief. This article argues that the view that anti-nepotism and no-spouse rules are sex-neutral ignores the real life employment experiences of married women. These rules are antiquated policies, based on a traditional, conservative view of appropriate gender roles."); Barbara M. Albert, Note, The Combined Effect of No-Spouse Rules and At-Will Doctrines on Career Families Where Both Spouses Are in the Same Field, 36 Brandeis J. Fam. L. 251 (1998); Leonard Bierman & Cynthia D. Fisher, Antinepotism Rules Applied to Spouses: Business and Legal Viewpoints, 35 Lab. L.J. 634 (1984); Joan G. Wexler, Husbands and Wives: The Uneasy Case for Antinepotism Rules, 62 B.U. L. Rev. 75 (1982); Henry Beu-Zvi, (Mrs.) Alice Doesn't Work Here Anymore: No-Spouse Rules and the American Working Woman, 19 UCLA L. Rev. 199 (1981). Did the court correctly focus on the evidence at the defendant's workplace, or did the plaintiff fail to provide sufficient proof of the general impact of antispouse and antinepotism policies?

15. Fudge v. City of Providence Fire Dept., 766 F.2d 650, 658 (1st Cir. 1985), which involved a challenge to the employer's use of a written examination, reached just the opposite conclusion. While the plaintiff showed that the test had an adverse impact on the minorities who took it, the court here ruled against the plaintiffs because the impact might not exist more generally:

> The focus in Title VII cases is upon the discriminatory impact a test would have on all blacks and all whites in the relevant population. Where only sample data is available, the disparate impact observed in a single sample of individuals drawn from the relevant population and administered the exam may not justify the conclusion that the test has a discriminatory impact upon the population as a whole. For one sample given the test, the passage rate for blacks may be much lower than that of whites, while for a second sample, drawn from the same population and given the same test, the opposite result may occur. Thus, the issue is: what is the probability that the disparity in passage rates that appeared in the sample would occur by chance if in fact there would be no difference in the passage rates of blacks and whites in the relevant population.

16. *Fudge* and *Thomas* can't both be right, can they? In any event, these cases were decided on the law before the 1991 Civil Rights Act added new § 703(k). How would these cases be decided now?

17. In a post-1991 case, Pietras v. Board of Fire Commrs., 180 F.3d 468 (2d Cir. 1999), plaintiff challenged a physical agility test (PAT) used by a fire department. The most difficult part of the test was the "charged hose drag," which involved dragging a 280-pound, water-filled hose over a distance of 150 feet in four minutes. The experience of the employer when it imposed the test was that "95% (63 out of 66)" of the males passed "while the female pass rate was only 57% (4 out of 7)." Acknowledging that the experience of the employer provided a small sample, the court nevertheless upheld a finding of disparate impact based on expert testimony "of the practices of other fire departments." Liability then attached because "the record is bereft of any evidence that a four minutes time-limit to finish the PAT was job-related."

*PROBLEM 5.2*

The Naperville police department chief wants to replace the traditional police re-volver used as standard equipment with the much more powerful Smith & Wesson Model 59 service revolver. The Model 59 is very powerful and is quite large, with a wide hand grip. National data show that over 50 percent of all women and about 10 percent of all men would be unable to handle the gun because of the size of the hand grip. Assume the police chief asks you if there would be any legal problem with the department adopting the Model 59. What more facts would you like to know before you render an opinion? Could you recommend that the department take any steps before requiring that the Model 59 be used by all department officers that might help insulate the department from disparate impact liability?

### d.  The Amount of Impact

Section 703(k)(1)(A)(i) requires plaintiff to prove that the practice she challenges "causes a disparate impact" but it does not define "disparate" in terms of the amount of impact that suffices.

*Statistical Techniques to Establish Disparate Impact.*  Statistical techniques can be used to more accurately determine whether an employment policy creates a disparate impact. In this regard, there are two basic problems that often are confused. One is whether there is any impact. In statistical terms, this is phrased in terms of the probability that a particular sample is representative of the universe (the large group it represents). Second is whether the amount, or quantum, of impact is sufficient: must a policy have a greatly disparate impact (80 percent of whites satisfy it, while only 10 percent of blacks do), or is any impact enough (93 percent of males qualify as compared to 91 percent of females)?

The Supreme Court decisions in disparate impact cases have not involved the use of sophisticated statistical techniques. Instead, the cases essentially "eyeballed" the numbers to find impact. Two circuits, however, have required studies showing statistical significance in order to make out a prima facie case of disparate impact. In Fudge v. City of Providence Fire Dept., 766 F.2d 650, 658 (1st Cir. 1985), the court concluded:

> Widely accepted statistical techniques have been developed to determine the likelihood an observed disparity resulted from mere chance. Where a plaintiff relies exclusively on a narrow base of data, as here, it is crucial for the court to consider the possibility that chance could account for the observed disparity.
>
> We think that in cases involving a narrow data base, the better approach is for the courts to require a showing that the disparity is statistically significant, or unlikely to have occurred by chance, applying basic statistical tests as the method of proof.

See also Thomas v. Metroflight, Inc., 814 F.2d 1506 (10th Cir. 1987).

The Uniform Guidelines on Employee Selection Procedures, 29 C.F.R. § 1607.4D (1993), adopted by federal civil rights enforcement agencies, including the EEOC, create a standard of the impact necessary to trigger enforcement efforts:

A selection rate for any race, sex, or ethnic group which is less than four-fifths (4/5) (or eighty percent) of the rate for the group with the highest rate will generally be regarded by the Federal enforcement agencies as evidence of adverse impact, while a greater than four-fifths rate will generally not be regarded by Federal enforcement agencies as evidence of adverse impact.[*]

In EEOC v. Joint Apprenticeship Comm., 164 F.3d 89 (2d Cir. 1998), the EEOC challenged a high school diploma prerequisite for admission to an apprenticeship program. Of African-American applicants, 2.27% failed to have high school diplomas, while only 1.07% of white applicants lacked a diploma. The district court applied the EEOC's four-fifths rule to the rate, even though "96.3% of Black and 98.6% of White applicants possessed a high school diploma or GED." Id. at 97. The Second Circuit found that the district court erred in relying on the fail rather than the pass rate because those who failed were such a small sample. "Under these circumstances, we find that the application of the four-fifths rule to this particular fail ratio was inappropriate, because such a small sample would tend to prove inherently unreliable results." Id. at 119. In Bullington v. United Air Lines, Inc., 186 F.3d 1301 (10th Cir. 1999), impact was shown where the female pass rate for interviews was 27.9% and the male pass rate was 46.6%. The female pass rate was only 60% of the male pass rate. In Firefighters Inst. For Racial Equality v. City of St. Louis, 220 F.3d 898 (8th Cir. 2000), impact was shown when 18.8% of whites but only 8% of African-Americans passed. The African American pass rate was only 43% of the white pass rate.

1. *The Statistical Significance of Results from Samples.*   What is it that must be shown in a "statistically significant" way? Statisticians often deal with "sample" problems. In the plaintiffs' attack on a test, suppose the initial question is whether that test had an adverse impact on African Americans. There is no doubt about the adverse impact on the blacks in the group that actually took the test. They fared worse than whites who took the same test. But this group was only a sample of a larger universe — the universe of all black and white potential test-takers. If you are interested in the impact on this universe, the question is whether, had the test been given to the universe, the same results would have been obtained.

Suppose Employer A administers a particular test and uses the results to hire 100 employees. Suppose further that 100 blacks and 100 whites apply for jobs, but that 70 whites pass the test as compared with 30 blacks. Does the test have a disparate racial impact? If the answer is yes, can this situation be distinguished from that of

---

[*] The Uniform Guidelines utilize a passing rate to calculate whether the four-fifths rule applies. That seems prima facie appropriate, but other bases have been argued:

In determining the amount of adverse impact necessary to constitute "substantial" adverse impact, the various courts of appeals have utilized several different sets of data and have not always been consistent in their choices. The comparison chosen can itself control the determination of whether adverse impact is "substantial." The most commonly used comparison has been that of majority pass rate to minority pass rate. A number of courts have, however, compared minority fail rates with majority fail rates. Whether the court focuses on pass or fail rates can make a significant difference in the apparent magnitude of the disparity. For example, in Green v. Missouri Pacific Railroad[, 523 F.2d 1290 (8th Cir. 1975)], the minority to majority fail rate of 2.5:1, if stated in terms of majority to minority pass rate, is a mere 1.03:1. The Seventh and Ninth Circuits have adopted an entirely different comparison. Those courts would compare the percentage of minority applicants to the percentage of minority hirees. Again, depending on whether the court focuses upon pass rates, fail rates, or minority applicants versus hirees, the apparent disparity can be minimized or maximized.

Dean Booth & James L. Mackay, Legal Constraints on Employment Testing and Evolving Trends in the Law, 29 Emory L.J. 121, 153-154 (1980).

Employer *B*, which hired only 10 persons, 7 whites and 3 blacks from a pool of 10 whites and 10 blacks?

For a statistician, the answer is yes: the larger the sample size is, the more certain it is that the test discriminates against blacks generally. Thus, in the case of Employer *B*, had one more black passed the test (4) and one less white (6), the 70 percent versus 30 percent pass rate would have dropped to 60 percent versus 40 percent. Individual variations, rather than race, are more likely to explain discrepancies in such small samples. If one fewer white (69) and one more black (31) had passed Employer *A*'s test, the ratio would still be almost the same: for whites, 69 percent rather than 70 percent; for blacks, 31 percent rather than 30 percent.

Before we go on to further consider statistical proof of impact, remember that statistical techniques are useful only if they prove something relevant. Recall *Hazelwood*, where the trial court used statistical evidence comparing the percentage of minority teachers with the percentage of minority students was presented. The difficulty with this evidence is that it did not provide a legally relevant comparison. Systemic discriminatory intent is inferred by comparing the percentage of minority members in the relevant labor market with the percentage of minority teachers in the employer's workforce. The disparity between minority teachers and minority students is irrelevant.

With respect to disparate impact, reconsider our earlier discussion following *Wards Cove* concerning appropriate comparison groups for purposes of establishing a case of disparate impact. What groups are relevant? Is the question whether a test has a disparate impact on the actual applicants who took the test or whether the test has a disparate impact on otherwise qualified individuals in the general population? If disparate impact is established by proving impact on actual applicants, then it is irrelevant that the group of test-takers may not be representative of the otherwise qualified individuals in the population as a whole. Remember *Dothard* and the question whether the height and weight criteria might not have had a disparate impact if one looked only at the group of individuals interested in working as guards, rather than at the otherwise qualified general population. Whether the sample of individuals applying for the job in question is representative of the population as a whole matters only if disparate impact is established by showing an impact on the general population, rather than on the interested applicant pool or some other comparison group. As you consider the methods of proving disparate impact described below, keep in mind that, regardless of the statistical technique applied, considerable thought must be given to whether the comparison groups being used are appropriate and legally relevant.

Once the relevant comparison group has been selected, the commonsense insight regarding sample size can be utilized in a more rigorous fashion by using accepted statistical techniques. Recall the discussion of the two- or three standard deviation test in Chapter 4 (pages 241-247). It is for this reason that courts have sometimes found disparate impact analysis inapplicable: the sample is too small to yield any statistically significant results. In Fudge v. City of Providence Fire Dept., 766 F.2d 650 (1st Cir. 1985), the defendant changed the test often enough that the plaintiffs could not look to other test administrations to provide an adequate sample. See also Fallis v. Kerr-McGee Corp., 944 F.2d 743 (10th Cir. 1991) (ADEA) (nine employees too few). Similarly, in Mems v. City of St. Paul, 224 F.3d 735 (8th Cir. 2000), the court found that the sample size ranging from 3 to 7 was too small to be statistically significant. The court also held that grouping all minorities together for the purpose of determining the examination's impact on African Americans would be improper.

Two statistical techniques have been suggested by Professor Elaine Shoben to analyze whether race (or gender) is related to particular employer selection devices. Differential Pass-Fail Rates in Employment Testing: Statistical Proof Under Title VII, 91 Harv. L. Rev. 793 (1978). They are the techniques of testing the difference between independent proportions and chi square.

Shoben's work was in large part a response to the "four-fifths" rule found in the Uniform Guidelines on Employee Selection Procedures. Professor Shoben has, quite rightly, taken the Uniform Guidelines to task for the rule, demonstrating that sample size should be a factor in any analysis of the impact of a particular selection device. Consider the following example:

|  | Employer I | | Employer II | |
|---|---|---|---|---|
|  | Blacks | Whites | Blacks | Whites |
| Total Applicants | 50 | 250 | 600 | 1,000 |
| Number Selected | 35 | 200 | 420 | 800 |
| Passing Rate | 70% | 80% | 70% | 80% |
| Ratio of Black to White Rates | 7/8 | | 7/8 | |

Professor Shoben's central thesis is that, while both employers satisfy the four-fifths test, more sophisticated statistical techniques would demonstrate a racial correlation for Employer II because the probability of that result from the larger sample, if independent of race, is less than 0.05. The Seventh Circuit appears to have followed Professor Shoben's approach in Bew v. City of Chicago, 252 F.3d 891 (7th Cir. 2001). Even though 98.24% of the African American testtakers passed compared with 99.96% of the whites so the four-fifths rule was not violated, the challenged test had a disparate impact because there was evidence that there was a statistically significant correlation between race and test failure. The fact that the difference in magnitude between the pass rates was so small was not relevant because the difference was statistically significant.

2. *Real But Small Impact.* It may be, however, that Professor Shoben undervalues one consideration implicit in the four-fifths test: perhaps not every racially correlated selection device should be considered prima facie illegal under Title VII. Rather, court intervention may not be warranted unless the difference in selection rates is large enough to be considered practically (not just statistically) significant. In other words, is the harm done of sufficient magnitude to justify legal intervention? This possibility can be seen by moving away from sample-related problems to situations in which the racial, gender, or ethnic impact of an entire universe is known. Suppose two tests are given to every person in the relevant labor market (e.g., all persons in a particular town). Test A yields two curves of performance, one for men and one for women. There is obviously a gender impact, the female median being 20 points lower than the male median. If a passing score is set at the male median, 75, half the men would be qualified, but a much smaller percentage of the women would be. The curves in Figure 5.1 might reflect something like the situation in *Dothard.**

Suppose, however, that Test B yields disparate gender impact, but with a much smaller margin, such as that shown in Figure 5.2. Given the fact that the whole universe is represented, there is no doubt as to the gender correlation, but the impact adverse to women is slight. If a passing score is set at the male median — so that 50 percent of males are hired — 49 percent of females will also qualify.

* The curves have been drawn to reflect equal numbers of test-takers for purposes of clarity of presentation. This is likely to be true in a significant number of sex discrimination cases. In the typical race case, however, the universe of blacks is smaller than the universe of whites. Thus, the black curve will be smaller than the white curve.

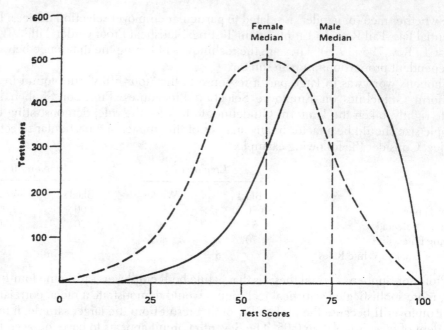

Figure 5.1

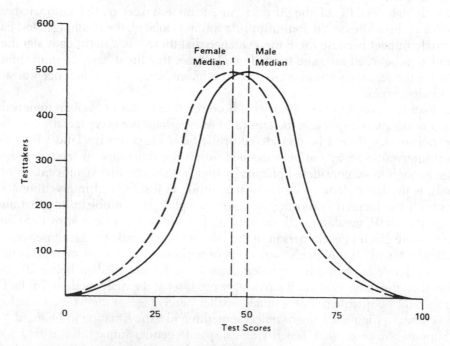

Figure 5.2

The Uniform Guidelines, therefore, may be attempting to offer a quantitative substantiality test to answer the question of whether there is statistically significant gender correlation. In other words, the guidelines may be suggesting that an observed disparity must be tested for *both* statistical significance and magnitude. So viewed, the four-fifths test has a focus different from that which Professor Shoben analyzes. Of course, this is not to suggest that the four-fifths rule is the right rule, even if corrected by statistical techniques to focus on whether any statistically demonstrable racial correlation exists. For example, David Baldus and James Cole suggest that absolute difference in pass rates (e.g., $50\% - 49\% = 1\%$) is a better measure of magnitude than the proportion of pass rates. David C. Baldus & James W. L. Cole, Statistical Proof of Discrimination 336 (1989).

At any rate, the guidelines' rough-and-ready four-fifths rule seems more appropriate when viewed as what it is: a policy allocating scarce enforcement resources. The government cannot challenge every discriminatory impact and accordingly will challenge only those that are "substantial," as defined by the four-fifths rule. In *Teal*, the Supreme Court stressed that purpose and, therefore, reduced the chances that a version of that rule will be adopted by the courts — not as an enforcement parameter, but as a standard of liability. See Connecticut v. Teal, 457 U.S. 440, 453 n.12 (1982). Professor Shoben's work seems to argue for statistically proven racial impact as the only necessity for a prima facie case. But, in addition to real impact, should something more than a small impact be necessary? The language of *Griggs* seems to suggest that the impact must be "substantial," but Albemarle Paper Co. v. Moody, 422 U.S. 405 (1975), speaks of "significance." Do both of these words refer only to the difficulty of proving the fact of impact unless the racial differences are large? Or might one or the other refer to the magnitude of the difference, perhaps implicit in the four-fifths rule? Does *Albemarle* use "significance" in a statistical sense or, as a layperson might, as synonymous with "substantial"? If the former, statistical techniques permit confident appraisals of the fact of impact with smaller differences as the sample size grows larger.

A few lower courts have discussed the problem. In Thomas v. Metroflight, Inc., 814 F.2d 1506, 1511 n.4 (10th Cir. 1987), the court distinguished statistical significance from substantiality of impact and found disparate impact was not established simply because statistical significance was found:

> *Hazelwood* does not say that "statistically significant" is "significantly discriminatory" as used in *Dothard*. Beyond a requirement of statistical significance, the Court may require in disparate impact cases that the disparity be "substantial" as well. One possible index of substantial disparity is suggested by Department of Justice guidelines: "Under the so-called 80% rule promulgated by the EEOC, the difference must not only be statistically significant, but the hire rate for the allegedly discriminated group must also be less than 80% of the rate for the favored group." Meier, Sacks and Zabell, What Happened in *Hazelwood*: Statistics, Employment Discrimination, and the 80% Rule, 1984 A.B.F. Research J. 139.

See also Frazier v. Garrison Ind. Sch. Dist., 980 F.2d 1514, 1524 (5th Cir. 1993).

Finally, to focus on the quantum of racial correlation in impact cases, rather than on the mere fact of correlation, would result in a major difference between impact and treatment cases: the purpose of statistics in treatment cases such as *Teamsters* and *Hazelwood* is to infer, from a racial correlation, a motive to discriminate. That motive, of course, is enough to make out a prima facie case. A statistically significant disproportion of blacks triggers the defendant's burden of coming forward with a non-racial justification. Impact theory, however, holds intent unnecessary. And not only is racial intent unnecessary, but also it is frequently not present. With Figure 5.2, for example, an employer could scarcely know the disparate impact from eyeballing the test results; therefore, the test was almost certainly not chosen because it filters out females somewhat more than males. But the impact is real. Is it enough to require employer justification? Is it enough to require court intervention? Or is some greater quantum of impact needed? These questions remain unanswered.

3. *The Impact Is to a Protected Group.* Title VII protects all persons against employment discrimination because of race, color, sex, religion, and national origin. McDonald v. Santa Fe Trail Transp. Co. [reproduced at page 111]. That protection extends to disparate treatment discrimination but it is not clear that disparate impact theory is available to whites or males. All of the disparate impact cases decided by the Supreme Court involved claims by women or minority men. *Griggs* emphasized that Title VII was "to achieve equality of employment opportunities and remove barriers that have operated in the past to favor an identifiable group of white employees over other employees." 401 U.S. at 429-30 (1971). The strong suggestion is that whites and males could not utilize the theory.

City of Los Angeles v. Manhart, 435 U.S. 702, 710 n.20 (1978), came closer to so stating. That case dealt with the argument that equalizing both pension benefits and contributions for men and women to eliminate the use of an illegal gender classification would produce a disparate impact on men, who as a group do not live as long as women. The Court suggested that men would not be able to use the disparate impact theory. "Even a completely neutral practice will inevitably have some disproportionate impact on one group or another. *Griggs* does not imply, and this Court has never held, that discrimination must always be inferred from such consequences."

If disparate impact analysis is ultimately justified by past societal discrimination against women and minority groups, it may not be appropriate to permit white males to use *Griggs* to attack rules that operate to disadvantage them. Cf. Craig v. Alabama State Univ., 804 F.2d 682 (11th Cir. 1986) (disparate impact claim by white faculty applicant to predominately black university). Suppose a cutback in military expenditures by the government causes defense employers to lay off workers, predominately white males. Could white male engineers and physicists use *Griggs* to attack a cab company rule against hiring applicants with advanced degrees because their educational background made them "overqualified" to drive cabs? If an advanced education does not interfere with the ability to drive a cab, is this rule fair? Even if unfair, should it be legal? A federal court dismissed an equal protection attack on a New London hiring policy that rejected police applicants who scored too *high* on a Wonderlic pre-employment test. Jordan v. City of New London, 1999 U.S. Dist. LEXIS 14289 (D. Conn. 1999). *Jordan* was affirmed on the ground that there was a rational basis for the practice. Jordan v. City of New London, 225 F.3d 645 (2d Cir. 2000). Suppose the white plaintiff brought a Title VII disparate impact case, and suppose that the rule disproportionately excluded whites. Is there a claim? In Foss v. Thompson, 242 F.3d 1131 (9th Cir. 2001), a male plaintiff lost his job when he was not allowed to bump into another position during a reduction in force because he lacked a nursing degree. He claimed that a job description stating that "it is desirable that the incumbent [for the job of Managed Care Coordinator/Nurse Specialist] possess a minimum of [a] Bachelor of Science in Nursing degree" had disparate impact on men since nurses were overwhelmingly female. The court dismissed his claim, holding that "the proper analysis turns on the percentage of men and women who are otherwise qualified but lack a nursing degree." Id. at 1134. The dissent argued that the practice at issue was the requirement of a nursing degree, which clearly had an adverse impact on men: "The employer has a requirement for the managed care coordinator position (in this office but not most of its offices) that effectively and practically limits the job to persons of one sex. With that requirement, nine out of ten people who can fill the job are limited to one sex. And 100% of the people who got the position in the Portland Area Office were of one sex. Without it, the sex distribution of those filing the job is pretty evenly balanced [by plaintiff's showing that in the Indian Health Service offices that do not require a nursing degree a slight majority of managed care coordinators are male]. That is enough to allow the trier of fact to infer that the requirement 'causes a disparate impact on the basis of . . . sex." Id. at 1137. There was no discussion of whether disparate impact was available to a male plaintiff. Do you think, nevertheless, that was on the mind of the majority?

The 1991 Civil Rights Act does not explicitly limit disparate impact to women and minorities. Indeed, its "plain language" seems to permit any racial group or either gender adversely affected by a particular employment practice to make a claim. Or could Congress' adoption of a term which was limited to minorities and women prior to 1991 suggest an intent to use that term as it had evolved in the courts?

If whites and males as well as women and minority men may all use disparate impact analysis to attack whatever employer policy adversely affected their group, should employers be advised to ensure that all of their practices can be justified by business necessity and job relatedness, since all policies are likely to have an adverse impact on some group in society? Does this make Title VII too intrusive into employer discretion? Even if the answer is yes, isn't that the plain language meaning of § 703(k)(1)(A)?

## 2. Defendant's Rebuttal

There are five rebuttal possibilities available to the employer to respond to a prima facie case of disparate impact discrimination.

### a. The Employer's Use Does Not Cause Impact

Even before the 1991 Act, the employer could try to undermine the plaintiff's showing of a prima facie case by introducing evidence that the data plaintiff relied on was flawed. That rebuttal possibility does not change the basic rule that the plaintiff has the burden of persuasion to prove a prima facie case. Section 703(k)(1)(A)(i) states the general rule that "a complaining party demonstrates that a respondent uses a particular employment practice that causes a disparate impact," with "demonstrate" being separately defined in § 701(m) as "meets the burdens of production and persuasion." Section 703(k)(1)(B)(ii), however, appears to create an affirmative defense that imposes on the employer the burden of persuasion to prove that "a specific employment practice does not cause the disparate impact."

Since the burden of persuasion cannot be on both the plaintiff and the defendant on the same issue, this apparent conflict must be resolved by differentiating the types of proof used by plaintiff to establish the prima facie case. If the plaintiff makes out a prima facie case based on data showing the experience of the employer's use of the challenged practice, the employer may rebut such a showing by challenging the accuracy of the evidence that plaintiff relied upon. The defendant, presumably, does not carry the burden of persuasion when it merely undermines the evidence the plaintiff uses to establish a prima facie case. However, if the plaintiff establishes disparate impact by national data or with the experience of other employers, § 701(k)(1)(B)(ii) then accords the employer an affirmative defense (as to which it has the burden of persuasion) that its *own* use of the practice does not have a disparate impact.

In Council 31, AFSCME v. Doherty, 169 F.3d 1068 (7th Cir. 1999), the plaintiff presented evidence that an employer's layoff criteria had a disparate impact on black employees. The court allowed the defendant to rebut the impact by showing that the plaintiff had not accounted for all persons who were subject to the challenged practice, and when all persons were accounted for, no disparate impact existed. The plaintiff's expert had assessed impact by looking only at full-time workers. When both full and part-time workers were considered, no impact existed. Because the court found no reason not to include the part-time workers, as all were targeted for layoff, plaintiff had no impact claim.

### b.   Business Necessity and Job Relatedness

## LANNING v. SOUTHEASTERN PENNSYLVANIA
## TRANSPORTATION AUTHORITY
### 181 F.3d 478 (3d Cir. 1999)

MANSMANN, Circuit Judge.

In this appeal, we must determine the appropriate legal standard to apply when evaluating an employer's business justification in an action challenging an employer's cutoff score on an employment screening exam as discriminatory under a disparate impact theory of liability. We hold today that under the Civil Rights Act of 1991, a discriminatory cutoff score on an entry level employment examination must be shown to measure the minimum qualifications necessary for successful performance of the job in question in order to survive a disparate impact challenge. Because we find that the District Court did not apply this standard in evaluating the employer's business justification for its discriminatory cutoff score in this case, we will reverse the District Court's judgment and remand for reconsideration under this standard. . . .

I . . .

A

SEPTA is a regional mass transit authority that operates principally in Philadelphia, Pennsylvania. In 1989, in response to a perceived need to upgrade the quality of its transit police force, SEPTA . . . began to consider methods by which it might upgrade the physical fitness level of its police officers.

In 1991, SEPTA hired Dr. Paul Davis to develop an appropriate physical fitness test for its police officers.[2] Dr. Davis initially met with SEPTA officials in order to ascertain SEPTA's objectives. Dr. Davis determined that SEPTA was interested in enhancing the level of fitness, physical vigor and general productivity of its police force. Once Dr. Davis had determined SEPTA's objectives, he went on a ride-along with SEPTA transit police and, over the course of two days and approximately twenty hours, rode the SEPTA trains in order to obtain a perspective on the expectations of SEPTA transit officers.

Dr. Davis next conducted a study with twenty experienced SEPTA officers, desig-

---

2. Dr. Davis is an expert exercise physiologist who has extensive experience in designing physical fitness employment tests for various law enforcement agencies.

nated "subject matter experts" (SMEs), in an effort to determine what physical abilities are required to perform the job of SEPTA transit officer. From the responses Dr. Davis received in this study, he determined that running, jogging, and walking were important SEPTA transit officer tasks and that SEPTA officers were expected to jog almost on a daily basis.

Dr. Davis then asked the SMEs to determine what level of physical exertion was necessary to perform these tasks. The SMEs estimated that it was reasonable to expect them to run one mile in full gear in 11.78 minutes. Dr. Davis rejected this estimate as too low based upon his determination that any individual could meet this requirement. Ultimately, Dr. Davis recommended a 1.5 mile run within 12 minutes. Dr. Davis explained that completion of this run would require that an officer possess an aerobic capacity of 42.5 mL/kg/min, the aerobic capacity that Dr. Davis determined would be necessary to perform the job of SEPTA transit officer.[3] Dr. Davis recommended that SEPTA use the 1.5 mile run as an applicant screening test. Dr. Davis understood that SEPTA officers would not be required to run 1.5 miles within 12 minutes in the course of their duties, but he nevertheless recommended this test as an accurate measure of the aerobic capacity necessary to perform the job of SEPTA transit police officer. Based upon Dr. Davis' recommendation, SEPTA adopted a physical fitness screening test for its applicants which included a 1.5 mile run within 12 minutes. Beginning in 1991, the 1.5 mile run was administered as the first component of the physical fitness test; if an applicant failed to run 1.5 miles in 12 minutes, the applicant would be disqualified from employment as a SEPTA transit officer.

It is undisputed that for the years 1991, 1993, and 1996, an average of only 12% of women applicants passed SEPTA's 1.5 mile run in comparison to the almost 60% of male applicants who passed. For the years 1993 and 1996, the time period in question in this litigation, the pass rate for women was 6.7% compared to a 55.6% pass rate for men. In addition, research studies confirm that a cutoff of 12 minutes on a 1.5 mile run will have a disparately adverse impact on women. SEPTA concedes that its 1.5 mile run has a disparate impact on women.

In conjunction with the implementation of its physical fitness screening test, SEPTA also began testing incumbent officers for aerobic capacity in 1991. SEPTA policy requires any officer who fails any portion of the incumbent fitness test to retest on the failed element within three months. For each portion of the physical fitness test that an incumbent officer fails, an interim goal is set for that officer.

SEPTA initially disciplined those incumbent officers who failed the fitness test. Due to protests by the incumbent officers' union, however, SEPTA discontinued its discipline policy and instead implemented an incentive program that rewarded incumbent officers for passing their interim fitness goals.

According to SEPTA's internal documents, significant percentages of incumbent officers of all ranks have failed SEPTA's physical fitness test. By 1996, however, 86% of incumbent officers reached SEPTA's physical fitness standards. SEPTA has never taken any steps to determine whether incumbent officers who have failed the physical fitness test have adversely affected SEPTA's ability to carry out its mission.

SEPTA has promoted incumbent officers who have failed some or all of the components of the physical fitness test. SEPTA has also given special recognition, com-

3. Dr. Davis initially decided that an aerobic capacity of 50 mL/kg/min was necessary to perform the job of SEPTA transit police officer. After determining that institution of such a high standard would have a draconian effect on women applicants, however, Dr. Davis decided that the goals of SEPTA could be satisfied by using a 42.5 mL/kg/min standard.

mendations, and satisfactory performance evaluations to incumbent officers who have failed the physical fitness test. SEPTA has never disciplined, terminated, removed, reassigned, suspended or demoted any transit officer for failing to perform the physical requirements of the job.

In addition, due to a clerical error, SEPTA hired a female officer in 1991 who failed the 1.5 mile run. This officer has subsequently been "decorated" by SEPTA and has been nominated repeatedly for awards such as Officer of the Year and Officer of the Quarter. SEPTA has commended her for her outstanding performance as a police officer and has chosen her to serve as one of SEPTA's two defensive tactics instructors.

SEPTA employs an extremely low number of women in its transit police force. The District Court found that, as of July 1997, SEPTA employed only 16 women in its 234 member police force. Only two of these women hold ranks higher than that of patrol officer.

[Five women who failed SEPTA's 1.5 mile run brought a Title VII class action against SEPTA. The Department of Justice also filed suit on behalf of the United States.]

After litigation commenced, SEPTA hired expert statisticians to submit reports examining the statistical relationship between the aerobic capacity of SEPTA's officers and their number of arrests, "arrest rates"[7] and number of commendations. In these reports, the statisticians concluded that there was a statistically significant correlation between high aerobic capacity and arrests, arrest rates and commendations. In addition, one expert prepared a report that estimated that 51.9% of the persons arrested for serious crimes between 1991 and 1996 had an aerobic capacity of 48 mL/kg/min and 27% of those arrested had an aerobic capacity of less than 42 mL/kg/min.[8] Based upon these reports, the District Court held that SEPTA established that its aerobic capacity requirement is job related and consistent with business necessity.

The District Court also found support for this conclusion in an expert report submitted on behalf of SEPTA by Dr. Robert Moffatt. Dr. Moffatt simulated a training course and concluded that officers with aerobic capacities of 45 mL/kg/min or better had a 7-8% decrement in their ability to perform physical activities after a run of approximately three minutes; officers with an aerobic capacity of less than 45 mL/kg/min exhibited a 30% decrement in physical ability after the same run. The District Court found that Dr. Moffatt's study demonstrates "the manifest relationship of aerobic capacity to the critical and important duties of a SEPTA transit police officer. . . ."

II . . .

Because SEPTA concedes that its 1.5 mile run has a disparate impact on women, the first prong of the disparate impact analysis is not at issue in this appeal. Rather, this appeal focuses our attention on the proper standard for evaluating whether SEPTA's 1.5 mile run is "job related for the position in question and consistent with business necessity" under the Civil Rights Act of 1991. Because the Act instructs that this standard incorporates only selected segments of prior Supreme Court jurisprudence on the business necessity doctrine, we examine the history of this doctrine in order to resolve this threshold issue.

7. "Arrest rates" were tabulated by expressing the number of arrests made by an officer as a percentage of the number of incident reports involving that officer.
8. The category of "serious crimes" includes homicide, rape, robbery, aggravated assault, burglary, theft, and auto theft. This category of arrests accounts for approximately ten percent of all reported incidents and seven percent of all reported arrests.

A

The disparate impact theory of discrimination under Title VII was judicially created in the seminal case of Griggs v. Duke Power Co. In embracing disparate impact, the Court recognized that Title VII was meant not only to proscribe overt discrimination, but also to prohibit "practices that are fair in form, but discriminatory in operation." *Griggs*. The Court made clear that what is required by Title VII is "the removal of artificial, arbitrary, and unnecessary barriers to employment when the barriers operate invidiously to discriminate on the basis of racial or other impermissible classification." Accordingly, the Court announced that in evaluating practices fair in form but discriminatory in operation, "[t]he touchstone is business necessity."

The Court, however, was unclear in articulating what an employer must show to demonstrate business necessity. The Court couched the employer's burden in terms of showing that its practice is "related to job performance"; "bear[s] a demonstrable relationship to successful performance of the jobs for which it was used"; has "a manifest relationship to the employment in question"; and is "demonstrably a reasonable measure of job performance." In applying this standard, however, the Court rejected the employer's justification in *Griggs* that its standardized intelligence tests and diploma requirements generally would improve the overall quality of the work force in its power plant. The Court held that, although these requirements may be useful, they could not be used to exclude disproportionately a protected group when the employer failed to show that they do not test an applicant's ability to perform the job in question.

The Court next spoke to the issue of business necessity in Albemarle Paper Co. v. Moody. In *Albemarle*, an employer sought to justify the use of verbal exam and high school diploma requirements in determining whether to promote employees to more skilled positions in its paper mill. In preparation for trial, the employer hired an industrial psychologist to complete validation studies showing that the tests were job related because they had a statistically significant correlation with supervisorial ratings in several groups of the jobs in question. The Court, nevertheless, rejected the employer's contention that its requirements were job related.

The Court held that "discriminatory tests are impermissible unless shown, by professionally acceptable methods, to be 'predicative of or significantly correlated with important elements of work behavior which comprise or are relevant to the job or jobs for which candidates are being evaluated.'" In so holding, the Court noted that the Equal Employment Opportunity Commission (EEOC) Guidelines for professional standards of test validation are entitled to great deference in determining whether an employer has demonstrated that its requirements are job related. The Court rejected the employer's validation studies as inadequate in several respects under the EEOC Guidelines. . . .

The next Title VII case to raise the business necessity issue for the Court's consideration was Dothard v. Rawlinson. In *Dothard*, female applicants challenged a prison's minimum height and weight requirements for its prison guard positions as violative of Title VII. On the issue of business necessity, the Court made clear that "a discriminatory employment practice must be shown to be necessary to safe and efficient job performance to survive a Title VII challenge." The Court rejected the prison's assertion that height and weight requirements have a relationship to the unspecified amount of strength essential to effective job performance, holding that if strength is a bona fide job related quality, the prison could test for it directly by adopting and validating a fairly administered strength test.

The Court's next definitive statement on the business necessity doctrine is found in Wards Cove Packing Co., Inc. v. Atonio, where a majority of the Court deviated from its previous business necessity jurisprudence in adopting a more liberal test for business necessity.[11] According to the Court:

> [T]he dispositive issue is whether a challenged practice serves, in a significant way, the legitimate employment goals of the employer. The touchstone of this inquiry is a reasoned review of the employer's justification for his use of the challenged practice. A mere insubstantial justification in this regard will not suffice, because such a low standard of review would permit discrimination to be practiced through the use of spurious, seemingly neutral employment practices. At the same time, though, there is no requirement that the challenged practice be "essential" or "indispensable" to the employer's business for it to pass muster. . . .

In addition, the Court made clear that at the business necessity stage of Title VII litigation, the employer bears only the burden of production; the burden of persuasion remains on the disparate impact plaintiff at all times. Id. As we have previously recognized, the Wards Cove standard may reasonably be viewed as a departure from the more stringent business necessity standard under Griggs and its progeny.

### B

In response to Wards Cove, Congress enacted the Civil Rights Act of 1991. One of the primary purposes of the Act was "to codify the concepts of 'business necessity' and 'job related' enunciated by the Supreme Court in Griggs v. Duke Power Co., and in the other Supreme Court decisions prior to Wards Cove." Civil Rights Act of 1991, Pub. L. No. 102-166, § 3, 105 Stat. 1071, 1071 (1992). As part of this codification of Griggs, the Act made clear that both the burden of production and the burden of persuasion in establishing business necessity rest with the employer. See 42 U.S.C. § 2000e-2(k).

In addition, the Act codified the business necessity doctrine by using the following language:

An unlawful employment practice based on disparate impact is established under this subchapter only If —

(i) a complaining party demonstrates that a respondent uses a particular employment practice that causes a disparate impact on the basis of race, color, religion, sex, or national origin and the respondent fails to demonstrate that the challenged practice is *job related for the position in question and consistent with business necessity;* or

(ii) the complaining party makes the demonstration described in subparagraph (C) with respect to an alternative employment practice and the respondent refuses to adopt such alternative employment practice.

---

11. Two cases prior to Wards Cove forecast some of the changes to come. In New York City Transit Auth. v. Beazer, the Court disposed of a Title VII case by holding that the plaintiffs failed to establish a prima facie case of disparate impact. The Court, however, commented on the business necessity doctrine in dicta. In a footnote, the Court stated that even if a prima facie case had been established, the employer would have shown business necessity by establishing that its practice significantly serves its legitimate business goals of safety and efficiency. Similarly, a plurality opinion in Watson v. Fort Worth Bank & Trust, suggested that employers could meet their burden of establishing business necessity simply by advancing a legitimate business reason for the practice in question. While the language in these cases clearly foreshadowed the Court's holding in Wards Cove, this language had never been embraced by a majority of the Court as the binding standard for business necessity prior to Wards Cove.

42 U.S.C. § 2000e-2(k)(1)(A) (emphasis added). The Act further instructs that in interpreting its business necessity language, "[n]o statements other than the interpretive memorandum . . . shall be considered legislative history of, or relied upon in any way as legislative history. . . ." [§ 105(b).] The interpretive memorandum referenced in this portion of the Act states in relevant part:

> The terms "business necessity" and "job related" are intended to reflect the concepts enunciated by the Supreme Court in *Griggs*, and in the other Supreme Court decisions prior to *Wards Cove*.

137 Cong. Rec. 28,680 (1991). After the passage of the Act, proponents of both a strict test for business necessity and a more liberal requirement claimed victory in the standard adopted by the Act.[12]

## III

The Supreme Court has yet to interpret the "job related for the position in question and consistent with business necessity" standard adopted by the Act. In addition, our sister courts of appeals that have applied the Act's standard to a Title VII challenge have done so with little analysis. See, e.g., Fitzpatrick v. City of Atlanta, 2 F.3d 1112, 1117-18 (11th Cir.1993) (noting that Civil Rights Act of 1991 statutorily reversed *Wards Cove* but ruling in favor of employer because practice was demonstrably necessary to meet an "important business goal"); Bradley v. Pizzaco of Nebraska, Inc., 7 F.3d 795, 797-98 (8th Cir. 1993) (noting that *Griggs* standard was reinstated by the Act and holding that employer failed to meet *Griggs* standard).

Because the Act proscribes resort to legislative history with the exception of one short interpretive memorandum endorsing selective caselaw, our starting point in interpreting the Act's business necessity language must be that interpretive memorandum. The memorandum makes clear that Congress intended to endorse the business necessity standard enunciated in *Griggs* and not the *Wards Cove* interpretation of that standard. By Congress' distinguishing between *Griggs* and *Wards Cove*, we must conclude that Congress viewed *Wards Cove* as a significant departure from *Griggs*. Accordingly, because the Act clearly chooses *Griggs* over *Wards Cove*, the Court's interpretation of the business necessity standard in *Wards Cove* does not survive the Act.[13]

We turn now to articulate the standard for business necessity — one most consistent with *Griggs* and its pre-*Ward Cove* progeny. The laudable mission begun by the Court in *Griggs* was the eradication of discrimination through the application of practices fair in form but discriminatory in practice by eliminating unnecessary barriers to employment opportunities. In the context of a hiring exam with a cutoff score

---

12. See Andrew C. Spiropoulos, Defining the Business Necessity Defense to the Disparate Impact Cause of Action: Finding the Golden Mean, 74 N.C. L. Rev. 1479, 1516-20 (1996) (outlining the respective positions of both sides to the debate); compare also Michael Carvin, Disparate Impact Claims Under the New Title VII, 68 Notre Dame L. Rev. 1153 (1993) (arguing that *Wards Cove* is still good law after Civil Rights Act of 1991); with Susan S. Grover, The Business Necessity Defense in Disparate Impact Discrimination Cases, 30 Ga. L. Rev. 387 (1996) (arguing for a strict business necessity standard under the Act); Note, The Civil Rights Act of 1991: The Business Necessity Standard, 106 Harv. L. Rev. 896 (1993) (asserting that *Wards Cove* does not survive the Act).

13. We are cognizant that a contrary argument has been advanced in which it is asserted that *Wards Cove* remains the controlling standard. See Carvin, supra note 12, at 1157-64. Pursuant to the argument, the business necessity standard announced in *Wards Cove* simply clarified *Griggs* and therefore is not inconsistent with the Act's command to apply the standard enunciated in *Griggs*. In addition, it is asserted

shown to have a discriminatory effect, the standard that best effectuates this mission is implicit in the Court's application of the business necessity doctrine to the employer in *Griggs*, i.e., that a discriminatory cutoff score is impermissible unless shown to measure the minimum qualifications necessary for successful performance of the job in question. Only this standard can effectuate the mission begun by the Court in *Griggs*; only by requiring employers to demonstrate that their discriminatory cutoff score measures the minimum qualifications necessary for successful performance of the job in question can we be certain to eliminate the use of excessive cutoff scores that have a disparate impact on minorities as a method of imposing unnecessary barriers to employment opportunities.

The evolution of the Court's articulation of the business necessity doctrine in both *Albemarle* and *Dothard* reinforces the conclusion that this standard is both implicit in *Griggs* and central to its mission. In *Albemarle*, the Court explained that discriminatory tests must be validated to show that they are "predictive of . . . important elements of work behavior which comprise . . . the job . . . for which candidates are being evaluated" and that the scores of the higher level employees do not necessarily validate a cutoff score for the minimum qualifications to perform the job at an entry level. This is simply another way of saying that discriminatory cutoff scores must be validated to show they measure the minimum qualifications necessary for successful performance of the job. Similarly, in *Dothard*, the Court made clear that "a discriminatory employment practice," such as a discriminatory cutoff score on an entry level exam, "must be shown to be necessary to safe and efficient job performance to survive a Title VII challenge."

Taken together, *Griggs*, *Albemarle* and *Dothard* teach that in order to show the business necessity of a discriminatory cutoff score an employer must demonstrate that its cutoff measures the minimum qualifications necessary for successful performance of the job in question. Furthermore, because the Act instructs us to interpret its business necessity language in conformance with *Griggs* and its pre-*Wards Cove* progeny, we must conclude that the Act's business necessity language incorporates this standard.

Our conclusion that the Act incorporates this standard is further supported by the business necessity language adopted by the Act. Congress chose the terms "job related for the position in question" and "consistent with business necessity." Judicial application of a standard focusing solely on whether the qualities measured by an entry level exam bear some relationship to the job in question would impermissibly write out the business necessity prong of the Act's chosen standard. With respect to a discriminatory cutoff score, the business necessity prong must be read to demand an inquiry into whether the score reflects the minimum qualifications necessary to perform successfully the job in question. See also EEOC Guidelines, 29 C.F.R. § 1607.5(H) (noting that cutoff scores should "be set so as to be reasonable and consistent with normal expectations of acceptable proficiency within the work force.").

In addition, Congress' decision to emphasize the importance of the policies underlying the disparate impact theory of discrimination through its codification supports application of this standard to discriminatory cutoff scores. The disparate impact the-

---

that due to the legislative history of the Act, it would be improper to apply a strict business necessity standard. This argument, however, ignores two important aspects of the Act which constrain our interpretation of the standard adopted. First, the interpretive memorandum's distinction between *Griggs* and *Wards Cove* casts significant doubt on the assertion that Congress read *Wards Cove* as simply a clarification of *Griggs*. Second, the Act precludes us from considering the legislative history upon which this argument relies for support. Accordingly, we find this argument to be devoid of merit.

ory of discrimination combats not intentional, obvious discriminatory policies, but a type of covert discrimination in which facially neutral practices are employed to exclude, unnecessarily and disparately, protected groups from employment opportunities. Inherent in the adoption of this theory of discrimination is the recognition that an employer's job requirements may incorporate societal standards based not upon necessity but rather upon historical, discriminatory biases.[14] A business necessity standard that wholly defers to an employer's judgment as to what is desirable in an employee therefore is completely inadequate in combating covert discrimination based upon societal prejudices. Only a business necessity doctrine that examines discriminatory cutoff scores in light of the minimum qualifications that are necessary to perform the job in question successfully can address adequately this subtle form of discrimination.[15]

Accordingly, we hold that the business necessity standard adopted by the Act must be interpreted in accordance with the standards articulated by the Supreme Court in *Griggs* and its pre–*Wards Cove* progeny which demand that a discriminatory cutoff score be shown to measure the minimum qualifications necessary for the successful performance of the job in question in order to survive a disparate impact challenge.[16]

## IV

Although the District Court purported to apply the Act's "job related to the position in question and consistent with business necessity" standard to SEPTA's cutoff score on its 1.5 mile run, it is clear from the District Court's memorandum opinion that it did not apply the standard we have found to be implicit in *Griggs* and incorpo-

14. For an interesting discussion on male-oriented biases in the labor market see Maxine N. Eichner, Getting Women Work That Isn't Women's Work: Challenging Gender Biases in the Workplace Under Title VII, 97 Yale L.J. 1397 (1988).

15. We need not be concerned that implementation of this standard will result in forcing employers to adopt quotas, a result that would be inconsistent with the mandates of Title VII. If an employer can demonstrate that its discriminatory cutoff score reflects the minimum qualifications necessary for successful job performance, it will be able to continue to use it. If not, the employer must abandon that cutoff score, but is free to develop either a non-discriminatory practice which furthers its goals, or an equally discriminatory practice that can meet this standard. Nothing in the *Griggs* business necessity standard requires employers to hire employees in numbers to reflect the ethnic, racial or gender make-up of the community.

The following example based upon the facts of this case illustrates this point. Assuming that SEPTA's 1.5 mile run has a disparate impact on women and that SEPTA can not show that the 12 minute cutoff measures the minimum aerobic capacity necessary to be a successful transit officer, it does not follow that SEPTA would then be required to hire women in equal proportion to men. Several options would be available to SEPTA. For example, SEPTA could: 1) abandon the test as a hiring requirement but maintain an incentive program to encourage an increase in the officers' aerobic capacities; 2) validate a cutoff score for aerobic capacity that measures the minimum capacity necessary to successfully perform the job and maintain incentive programs to achieve even higher aerobic levels; or 3) institute a non-discriminatory test for excessive levels of aerobic capacity such as a test that would exclude 80% of men as well as 80% of women through separate aerobic capacity cutoffs for the different sexes. Each of these options would help SEPTA achieve its stated goal of increasing aerobic capacity without running afoul of Title VII and none of these options require hiring by quota.

16. Relying upon Spurlock v. United Airlines, Inc., 475 F.2d 216 (10th Cir. 1972), and like cases from our sister courts of appeals, the dissent asserts that this standard should not apply to SEPTA because the job of SEPTA transit officer implicates issues of public safety. Under the Act, however, our interpretation of the business necessity language is limited to "the concepts enunciated by the Supreme Court in *Griggs,* and in the other *Supreme Court* decisions prior to *Wards Cove.*" See 137 Cong. Rec. 28,680 (1991) (emphasis added). Because the Supreme Court never adopted the holding of *Spurlock* prior to *Wards Cove,* it is clear that, under the Act, we are not to consider *Spurlock* as authoritative. Furthermore, if Congress had intended to endorse the holding of *Spurlock,* it could have done so affirmatively. Accordingly, because the Act limits our interpretation to Supreme Court jurisprudence and does not otherwise endorse *Spurlock,* we are not at liberty to adopt the holding of *Spurlock* at this juncture. Moreover, to the extent that *Spurlock* and other cases from our sister courts of appeals can be read to suggest that minimum

rated by the Act. The District Court rejected the formulation of the *Griggs* standard found in *Dothard*, characterizing it as dicta, and relied instead upon language found in *Beazer*. As our prior discussion makes clear, the *Beazer* language is dicta and the *Dothard* standard is binding under the Act. Moreover, the *Beazer* dicta upon which the District Court relied mirrors the standard adopted by *Wards Cove*. As we previously stated, the *Wards Cove* standard does not survive the Act.

The District Court's application of its understanding of business necessity to SEPTA's business justification further illustrates that the District Court did not apply the correct legal standard. As an initial matter, the District Court seemed to conclude that Dr. Davis' expertise alone is sufficient to justify the 42.5 mL/kg/min aerobic capacity cutoff measured by the 1.5 mile run.[18] This conclusion disregards the teachings of *Griggs*, *Albemarle* and *Dothard* in which the Court made clear that judgment alone is insufficient to validate an employer's discriminatory practices.[19] More fundamentally, however, nowhere in its extensive opinion did the District Court consider whether Dr. Davis' 42.5 mL/kg/min cutoff reflects the minimum aerobic capacity necessary to perform successfully the job of SEPTA transit police officer.

---

qualifications do not apply to certain types of employment, these cases are inconsistent with the teachings of *Griggs* and are accordingly uninformative under the Act.

Furthermore, to the limited extent that the Supreme Court's pre-*Wards Cove* jurisprudence instructs that public safety is a legitimate consideration, application of the business necessity standard to SEPTA is consistent with that jurisprudence because the standard itself takes public safety into consideration. If, for example, SEPTA can show on remand that the inability of a SEPTA transit officer to meet a certain aerobic level would significantly jeopardize public safety, this showing would be relevant to determine if that level is necessary for the successful performance of the job. Clearly a SEPTA officer who poses a significant risk to public safety could not be considered to be performing his job successfully. We are accordingly confident that application of the business necessity standard to SEPTA is fully consistent with the Supreme Court's pre-*Wards Cove* jurisprudence as required by the Act.

18. While relying predominantly upon Dr. Davis' expertise, the District Court does point to a study which Dr. Davis completed for Anne Arundel County, Maryland in which he concluded that a 42.5 mL/kg/min aerobic capacity predicted success as an Anne Arundel County police officer. Absent a finding that the work of an Anne Arundel County police officer is comparable to SEPTA transit officer work, a finding the District Court did not make, reliance on this validation study is misplaced. See 29 C.F.R. § 1607.7(B)(2); see also 29 C.F.R. § 1607.7(B)(3) (explaining that validation studies created for other employers must also include a study of "test fairness"). Furthermore, it is unclear from Dr. Davis' report whether the Anne Arundel study's 42.5 mL/kg/min cutoff actually measures for qualities significant to SEPTA transit police performance. Compare Davis Report (noting that 42.5 mL/kg/min level for Anne Arundel study is significant for carrying an unspecified amount of weight and generally effecting arrests) with Davis Report (stating "[t]ransit police officers are more likely to have incidents come to them, as opposed to responding to the scene of an event. By mission, the presence of the officer is that of a deterrent, maintaining maximum visibility. Occasionally, officers will come upon criminal activities such as assaults or robberies, but for the most part, the officer will attempt to control a situation such as disorderly conduct or force compliance (paying fares) without having to make an arrest."); see also Davis Report (quoting experienced officer as stating "[t]he most important factors in my opinion of being a good officer is to be able to think clearly at all times an [sic] verbalize and or articulate when dealing with all people. . . . Running quickly is physically demanding, although in the transit system, most dealings are close, physical altercations."). In addition, it is unclear from the record whether the Anne Arundel study itself was properly validated.

19. The danger of allowing an employer to carry its burden by relying simply upon an expert's unvalidated judgment as to an appropriate cutoff score in a testing device is illustrated by this case. In determining an appropriate cutoff for aerobic capacity, Dr. Davis rejected the SMEs' estimate of the minimal qualifications necessary to perform the job even though these SMEs were experienced transit officers. Dr. Davis then determined that "a SEPTA transit officer needs an aerobic capacity of 50 mL/kg/min to successfully perform a number of tasks." Dr. Davis, however, revised this requirement, finding that "the goals of SEPTA could be satisfied by using a 42.5 mL/kg/min standard" after determining that the higher limit would have a "draconian" effect on women. There is no indication in the District Court's opinion as to how Dr. Davis determined that the lower standard would be sufficient. Where, as here, the cutoff score chosen has a discriminatory disparate impact, *Griggs* prohibits the establishment of exactly this type of arbitrary barrier to employment opportunities.

Instead, the District Court upheld this cutoff because it was "readily justifiable."[20] The validation studies of SEPTA's experts upon which the District Court relied to support this conclusion demonstrate the extent to which this standard is insufficient under the Act. The general import of these studies is that the higher an officer's aerobic capacity, the better the officer is able to perform the job. Setting aside the validity of these studies, this conclusion alone does not validate Dr. Davis' 42.5 mL/kg/min cutoff under the Act's business necessity standard.[21] At best, these studies show that aerobic capacity is related to the job of SEPTA transit officer. A study showing that "more is better," however, has no bearing on the appropriate cutoff to reflect the minimal qualifications necessary to perform successfully the job in question. Dr. Siskin's testimony is particularly instructive on this point. Dr. Siskin testified that in view of the linear relationship between aerobic capacity and the arrest parameters, any cutoff score can be justified since higher aerobic capacity levels will get you more field performance (i.e., "more is better"). Under the District Court's understanding of business necessity, which requires only that a cutoff score be "readily justifiable," SEPTA, as well as any other employer whose jobs entail any level of physical capability, could employ an unnecessarily high cutoff score on its physical abilities entrance exam in an effort to exclude virtually all women by justifying this facially neutral yet discriminatory practice on the theory that more is better.[22] This result contravenes *Griggs* and demonstrates why, under *Griggs*, a discriminatory cutoff score must be shown to

20. The District Court seems to have derived this standard from the Principles for the Validation and Use of Personnel Selection Procedures ("SIOP Principle"), principles published by the Society for Industrial and Organizational Psychology as a professional guideline for conducting validation research and personnel selection. To the extent that the SIOP Principles are inconsistent with the mission of *Griggs* and the business necessity standard adopted by the Act, they are not instructive.

21. The Court has cautioned that studies done in anticipation of litigation to validate discriminatory employment tests that have already been given must be examined with great care due to the danger of lack of objectivity. *Albemarle*. . . . A critical evaluation of the statistical studies relied upon by the District Court in this case, reveals several aspects of these studies that we find to be, at a minimum, disconcerting.

The following concerns are only a representative sample of possible deficiencies in these studies: 1) While the ability to make an arrest may be an important aspect of the job, the absolute number of arrests or "arrest rates" do not necessarily correlate with successful job performance. See App. at 3132 (noting that SEPTA officer should generally attempt to control a situation without having to make an arrest); 2) The study on arrests and arrest rates examined a disproportionately large number of officers with an aerobic capacity over 42 mL/kg/min compared to the number of officers with an aerobic capacity under that level which likely skewed the results. See also, 29 C.F.R. § 1607.14(B)(6) (noting that "[r]eliance upon a selection procedure which is significantly related to a criterion measure, but which is based upon a study involving a large number of subjects and has a low correlation coefficient will be subject to close review if it has a large adverse impact."); 3) The comparison of aerobic capacity with commendations is not helpful absent finding as to the subjective considerations involved in awarding commendations. See *Albemarle*; 4) The studies' emphasis on arrests for "serious crimes" is suspect; these arrests account for only 7% of all arrests and therefore represent only a small aspect of the job. See generally 29 C.F.R. § 1607.14(B)(6) (noting that reliance on single selection instrument which is related to only one of many job duties will be subject to close review); 5) SEPTA's table on the field performance of its officers belies the contention that there is a strict linear relationship of arrests to aerobic capacity; officers at less than 37 mL/kg/min had an average arrests of 13.6 compared to officers with at least a 48 mL/kg/min level who had average arrests of 13.9; 6) The study on the average aerobic capacity of perpetrators has little meaning unless SEPTA can show that arrests of these perpetrators are typically aerobic contests; because SEPTA police are armed, such a showing is unlikely.

Because we are remanding for the District Court to reconsider this evidence in light of the *Griggs* standard, we need not rule on whether any of the District Court's prior findings as to these studies were clearly erroneous. We comment here on the validity of these studies only to draw the District Court's attention to these concerns and to encourage the District Court to take a critical look at these studies, if necessary, on remand.

22. Such a result has the potential to have a significant detrimental impact on the amount and type of employment opportunities available to women. Obviously, under a "more is better" theory, employers

measure the minimum qualifications necessary to perform successfully the job in question.[23]

## V

For the foregoing reasons, it is clear to us that the District Court did not employ the business necessity standard implicit in *Griggs* and incorporated by the Act which requires that a discriminatory cutoff score be shown to measure the minimum qualifications necessary for successful performance of the job in question in order to survive a disparate impact challenge. We will therefore vacate the judgment of the District Court and remand this appeal for the District Court to determine whether SEPTA has carried its burden of establishing that its 1.5 mile run measures the minimum aerobic capacity necessary to perform successfully the job of SEPTA transit police officer.[24] . . .

WEISS, Circuit Judge, dissenting:

The "minimum qualifications" criterion of business justification does not apply to all types of employment. When public safety is at stake, a lighter burden is placed on employers to justify their hiring requirements. Because I believe that the latter standard applies in this case, I would affirm.

## I . . .

Unlike many metropolitan police departments, SEPTA officers are deployed alone and on foot, engaging in physical activities more frequently than other law enforcement agencies. . . .

SEPTA officers must occasionally ask for assistance from their comrades. . . . These calls are divided into two categories, "officer assists" and "officer backups." An "assist" requires officers to respond immediately. Often the only method available to get to

---

such as police departments, fire departments and correctional facilities could develop physical tests with unnecessarily high cutoffs that would effectively exclude women from their ranks. Perhaps less obvious, however, is the impact that this result could have on industries where strength is even minimally related to the job in question. For example, all companies engaged in delivery, construction or any other type of physical labor would be permitted to develop unnecessary strength requirements on the theory that "more is better" or "the stronger the worker, the faster the job gets done." This result is clearly unacceptable given the policies underlying both Title VII and the disparate impact theory of discrimination.

23. This is not to say that studies that actually prove that "more is better" are always irrelevant to validation of an employer's discriminatory practice. For example, a content validated exam, such as a typing exam for the position of typist, which demonstrates that the applicants who score higher on the exam will exhibit better job performance may justify a rank-ordering hiring practice that is discriminatory. In such a case, a validation study proving that "more is better" may suffice to validate the rank-order hiring. This is true, however, in only the rarest of cases where the exam tests for qualities that fairly represent the totality of a job's responsibilities. It is unlikely that such a study could validate rank hiring with a discriminatory impact based upon physical attributes in complex jobs such as that of police officer in which qualities such as intelligence, judgment, and experience surely play a critical role. This is especially true in SEPTA's case, where the record indicates that SEPTA patrol officers encounter "running assists," the most strenuous task upon which SEPTA's aerobic capacity testing predominately was justified, at an average rate of only twice per year.

24. The District Court rejected as irrelevant the plaintiffs' evidence that incumbent officers had failed the physical fitness test yet successfully performed the job and that other police forces function well without an aerobic capacity admission test. Under the standard implicit in *Griggs* and incorporated into the Act, this evidence tends to show that SEPTA's cutoff score for aerobic capacity does not correlate with the minimum qualifications necessary to perform successfully the job of SEPTA transit officer. Accordingly, this evidence is relevant and should be considered by the District Court on remand.

the scene quickly is a run of five to eight city blocks. An officer responding to an "assist" must preserve enough energy to deal effectively with a situation once arriving on the scene. SEPTA averages about 380 running assists per year. "Backups" are not as critical as "assists," so officers generally use a "paced jog." SEPTA averages about 1,920 "backups" annually.

For help in attaining its fitness goals, SEPTA turned to Dr. Paul Davis, an acknowledged expert in the field who had recommended corrective measures for numerous law enforcement and government agencies. At the time Dr. Davis began his research for SEPTA, an officer's equipment load was 12 pounds; it is now nearly 26 pounds. Dr. Davis found that officers need "sound, intact, disease-free cardiovascular system[s]" to effectively perform their jobs. These requirements implicate aerobic capacity, i.e., the ability of the body to utilize oxygen during sustained physical activities such as running, swimming, and cycling. Aerobic capacity is commonly measured in units of milliliters of oxygen per kilogram of body weight per minute — "mL/kg/min," or "mL."

SEPTA officers typically run or jog on a daily basis from three to eight city blocks for periods of three to ten minutes. They also engage in stair climbing, which requires a capacity of 54 mL. In light of this and other evidence, Dr. Davis concluded that SEPTA transit officers need an aerobic capacity of 50 mL. After determining that such a level would have a "draconian" effect on female applicants, however, Dr. Davis lowered his recommendation to 42.5 mL. That capacity could be demonstrated by running 1.5 miles in 12 minutes, a test that was adopted for applicants.

Dr. Davis had done a similar study for a fire department in St. Paul, Minnesota, which — in setting a standard of 45 mL — required applicants to run 1.5 miles in 11 minutes and 40 seconds. Eighty percent of male applicants and 76% of female applicants passed this test.

In addition to Dr. Davis' testimony, SEPTA also presented evidence from other experts to demonstrate a statistically significant correlation between aerobic capacity and the number of arrests made by individual SEPTA officers. Furthermore, of 207 commendations, 96% went to officers with an average capacity of 46 mL. Of these awards, 198 involved arrests, and 116 involved a foot pursuit, use of force or other physical exertion. Another study indicated that 51.9% of offense perpetrators had a capacity of 48 mL or higher, with only 27% having lower than a 42 mL rating.

The record demonstrates that a smaller percentage of female applicants passed the running test than males, but that nearly all women who trained for it were able to pass. The named plaintiffs and some of the class members who failed demonstrated, for the most part, a "cavalier" attitude towards the running test. Videotapes showed some of these applicants walking at the halfway point, either because they were indifferent or unable to run for even that short a period of time. Thus, although there was a significant disparity between the pass-fail rates of male and female applicants, the extent of the difference appears to have been exaggerated to some extent by the approach taken by some of the applicants.

A physiologist, Dr. Lynda Ransdell, testified that 40% of all women starting at an aerobic capacity of 35 to 37 mL can train to pass the running test in eight weeks, and that 10% of all women between 20 and 29 years of age can do so without any training. She concluded that the average sedentary woman can achieve SEPTA's performance standard with only moderate training. SEPTA sent applicants a letter outlining recommended training techniques that Dr. Ransdell testified were adequate.

Plaintiffs introduced the testimony of Dr. William McArdle, who suggested the use of a "relative fitness" test in which all applicants would be required to meet the 50th percentile of aerobic capacity for their gender — approximately 42 mL for males, and 36 mL for females. However, Dr. Robert Moffatt, a defense expert who conducted tests of the aerobic capacity necessary to perform a SEPTA officer's duties, disagreed. He stated that female officers with a capacity of 36 mL would not be able to capably perform their duties after running to an "assist" or a "backup." Dr. Bernard Siskin, another defense expert, found that the arrest rate for females with a 36 mL capacity was significantly lower than that of males with a 42 mL capacity.

The District Court rejected Dr. McArdle's proposal because it would not serve SEPTA's business goal of providing a police force capable of performing the physical requirements of the job nearly as well as the existing test. Instead, the court found that "Dr. Davis' study, standing alone, met the professional standards for construct validation and satisfies defendant's burden of demonstrating job relatedness and business necessity." Moreover, his study had sufficient empirical support for an aerobic capacity requirement of 42.5 mL.

## II

The dispute in this case centers on the applicable standard of business justification under the Civil Rights Act of 1991. . . .[1]

The 1990 bill, which had been vetoed by the President [because of fears it would lead to "quota hiring"] had used the phrase "required by business necessity," rather than "consistent with business necessity," as used in the 1991 Act. The substitution of the word "consistent" was considered to indicate a standard less stringent than would "required." In that light, a fair reading of the 1991 Act is "the challenged practice is job related for the position in question and in harmony with business necessity."

It may fairly be said that the language ultimately adopted in the 1991 Act reflects an "agreement to disagree" and a return of the dispute to the courts for resolution. In short, unable to muster a veto-proof majority for either view, Congress "punted." This conclusion is underscored by Congress' highly unusual admonition that the courts consider only a designated "interpretive memorandum" as legislative history, rather than the more elaborate committee reports and other materials that customarily reveal the extent of the controversy between various views. . . .

Congress' reference to the *Griggs* line of Supreme Court decisions, however, does little to clear the air because the language in those opinions has caused confusion. The problem can ultimately be traced back to *Griggs* itself. In that case, which involved power-plant jobs, the Court held that a high school completion requirement and general intelligence tests that disproportionately disqualified black applicants were not significantly job related. The Court said: "The touchstone is business necessity." However, the very next sentence reads, "[i]f an employment practice . . . cannot be shown to be related to job performance, the practice is prohibited." Thus, the Court speaks of both "necessity" and "job-relatedness" in the same breath.

In the following paragraph, we read that neither employment requirement is "shown to bear a demonstrable relationship to successful performance of the jobs for

---

1. In addition to the law review commentaries cited by the majority, see also Rosemary Alito, Disparate Impact Discrimination Under the 1991 Civil Rights Act, 45 Rutgers L. Rev. 1011, 1033 (1993) ("Only . . . cases requiring proof of job-relatedness and a reasonable need for the challenged practice accord[ ] with both the statutory language of the 1991 Act and the applicable Supreme Court precedent."); Kingsley R. Browne, The Civil Rights Act of 1991: A "Quota Bill," A Codification of *Griggs*, A Partial Return to *Wards Cove*, or All of the Above?, 43 Case W. Res. L. Rev. 287, 349 (1993) ("business necessity" has the same meaning as the *Wards Cove* phrase "serves, in a significant way").

which it was used. Both were adopted . . . without meaningful study of their relationship to job-performance ability." The Court also refers to "testing mechanisms [that are] unrelated to measuring job capability," "job-related tests," and states that "any given requirement must have a manifest relationship to the employment in question." Not once does the opinion repeat or expound upon "business necessity." Unquestionably, "job-relatedness" is *Griggs'* dominant thread. . . .

[After *Albemarle*, the] Court next considered appropriate criteria in Washington v. Davis [reproduced at page 404], which involved written tests that allegedly had a discriminatory impact on black applicants for police officer positions. Although the suit was not brought under Title VII, the Court discussed *Griggs* and *Albemarle*. The district judge had concluded "that a positive relationship between the test and training course performance was sufficient to validate the [test], wholly aside from its possible relationship to actual performance as a police officer." Significantly, the Supreme Court remarked that such a conclusion was not foreclosed by either *Griggs* or *Albemarle* and "it seems to us the much more sensible construction of the job-relatedness requirement." Dismissing challenges to the test, the Court remarked that "some minimum verbal and communicative skill would be very useful, if not essential, to satisfactory progress in the training regimen."

In another case, Dothard v. Rawlinson [reproduced at page 358], the Court held that height and weight requirements for prison guards could not stand. The ruling was based on the employer's failure to produce any evidence to correlate those standards with "the requisite amount of strength thought essential to good job performance." In a footnote, *Dothard* repeated *Griggs'* statement that "[t]he touchstone is business necessity," and further stated that "a discriminatory employment practice must be shown to be necessary to safe and efficient job performance to survive a Title VII challenge." Earlier in the body of the opinion, the Court explained that the employer must show that a requirement has "'a manifest relationship to the employment in question.'"

In yet another context, the Court upheld an employer's prohibition of employment to users of methadone, despite claims of disparate impact on blacks and Hispanics. See New York City Transit Authority v. Beazer, 523 U.S. 83 (1979). To the Court, the employer's narcotics rule, even in its application to methadone users, was "job related."

*Beazer* quoted the District Court's observation that "those goals [i.e., safety and efficiency] are significantly served by — even if they do not require — [the employer's] rule as it applies to all methadone users including those who are seeking employment in non-safety-sensitive positions." The Supreme Court concluded that "[t]he record thus demonstrates that [the employer's] rule bears a 'manifest relationship to the employment in question.'"

The *Beazer* Court observed that most of the affected job positions were "attended by unusual hazards and must be performed by 'persons of maximum alertness and competence.'" Other positions were "critical" or "safety sensitive," and many involved "danger to [the employees] or to the public."

## III

As the preceding sketch of pre-*Wards Cove* opinions demonstrates, the Supreme Court's articulations of the appropriate standards are far from clear. Phrases such as "business necessity," "demonstrable relationship to successful performance of the job," "manifest relationship to the employment in question," "genuine business needs," and "essential to good job performance," have been used interchangeably. These varying formulations bring to mind Justice Holmes' observation, "A word is not a crystal, transparent and unchanged, it is the skin of a living thought and may vary greatly in color and content according to the circumstances and the time in which it is used." Towne v. Eisner, 245 U.S. 418, 425.

My study of the standard for business justification as set forth by the Civil Rights Act of 1991 convinces me that it remains essentially the same as it was in the pre-*Wards Cove* era. However, other than its holding on burden of proof, it does not seem that *Wards Cove* was a revolutionary pronouncement. Until the Supreme Court reexamines the subject, however, courts will continue to struggle with the often inconsistent phraseology employed in *Griggs* and its progeny. The definition and application of the appropriate standard for business justification will depend on the context in which it is raised. There are significant factual differences in the cases that explain, to some extent, the differing formulations. *Albemarle* and *Griggs* applied greater scrutiny when the disparate impact affected entry to lower-level jobs, where it is fair to assume that no special qualifications would be generally expected.

In contrast, *Beazer* and *Washington* raised an additional important consideration — public safety. *Beazer* concerned jobs involving serious dangers to employees as well as to transit passengers. In *Washington*, a written test demonstrating an applicant's ability to complete police officer training was job-related, even apart from its relationship to actual performance as a police officer. The impact of public safety concerns on employee qualifications is inescapable, and serves to differentiate those positions from lower-level, nonsafety-sensitive ones.

The Courts of Appeals have explicitly recognized the relevance of safety considerations in a series of decisions beginning with Spurlock v. United Airlines, Inc., 475 F.2d 216 (10th Cir. 1972). In that case, an airline required that applicants for flight officer positions have a college degree and a minimum of 500 flight hours. The Court, citing *Griggs*, held that where "the job clearly requires a high degree of skill and the economic and human risks involved in hiring an unqualified applicant are great, the employer bears a correspondingly lighter burden to show his employment criteria are job related." Because, in the case of pilots, "[t]he risks involved in hiring an unqualified applicant are staggering . . . [t]he courts . . . should proceed with great caution before requiring an employer to lower his pre-employment standards for such a job."

Another leading case, Davis v. City of Dallas, 777 F.2d 205 (5th Cir. 1985), applied the *Spurlock* doctrine to criteria for hiring police officers. The City required a specific amount of college education, no history of recent marijuana usage, and a negative history of traffic violations. Despite findings of disparate impact, the Court upheld the requirements. Having reviewed the many cases following *Spurlock*, the Court had "no difficulty . . . equating the position of police officer in a major metropolitan area such as Dallas with other jobs that courts have found to involve the important public interest in safety." The degree of public risk and responsibility alone "would warrant examination of the job relatedness of the . . . education requirement under the lighter standard imposed under *Spurlock* and its progeny." . . .

Observing the nature of the positions at issue in *Griggs* and *Albemarle*, *Davis* noted that in neither case did the Supreme Court suggest that those jobs "were noteworthy for their dangerousness or importance to the public welfare." In contrast, the employment under consideration in *Davis* directly implicated public safety concerns. It is interesting that Justice Blackmun, in Watson v. Fort Worth Bank & Trust, objecting to what he considered to be a tendency to weaken the employer's burden, cited *Davis* favorably, stating that "[t]he proper means of establishing business necessity will vary with the type and size of the business in question."[5]

In a post-*Wards Cove* case involving firefighters, the Court of Appeals for the Eleventh Circuit noted that such "safety claims would afford the City an affirmative defense, for protecting employees from workplace hazards is a goal that, as a matter of law, has been found to qualify as an important business goal for Title VII purposes." *Fitzpatrick v. City of Atlanta*, 2 F.3d 1112, 1119 (11th Cir. 1993) (citing *Beazer; Dothard*). Thus, "[m]easures demonstrably necessary to meeting the goal of ensuring worker safety are therefore deemed to be 'required by business necessity' under Title VII."

## IV

The issues that separate the parties are straightforward. Plaintiffs do not seriously contest the fact that aerobic capacity is a valid predictor of efficient job performance as a transit police officer. They do not challenge the finding that running for 1.5 miles is an effective way to measure aerobic capacity. Nor apparently do they suggest that 42.5 mL is an inappropriate cut-off for male applicants: they implicitly accept this standard by advancing Dr. McArdle's alternative test, which would use that score for males and a lower one for females.

Even the government plaintiff concedes that an employer may improve its workforce. *Griggs*, in turn, stressed that tests "must measure the person for the job and not the person in the abstract." SEPTA's running test attempts to do just that, i.e., improve the caliber of its police force by selecting new hires to fit appropriately heightened performance standards.

A fair appraisal of the plaintiffs' objection is that the running test's cut-off requires female applicants to run faster than a majority of women can run without training. However, nearly all of the women who did train were able to pass the test. Also, not all males were able to pass, although their failure percentages were substantially lower.

Plaintiffs complain that SEPTA cannot point to any instances where a perpetrator of a crime got away, or an offense was committed because of an officer's lack of aerobic capacity. But as noted by *Fitzpatrick*, "[t]he mere absence of unfortunate incidents is not sufficient" to preclude a particular safety requirement because otherwise, such "measures could be instituted only once accidents had occurred rather than in order to avert accidents."

Here, where applicants have it within their power to prepare for the running test, they may properly be expected to do so. In view of the important public safety concerns at issue, it is not unreasonable to expect all applicants — female or male — to take the necessary steps in order to qualify for the positions.

The question then, is whether SEPTA's standard is permissible under the terms of the Civil Rights Act of 1991 and the relevant precedents. The District Court rejected the plaintiffs' contention that "business necessity" under the statute is governed by a footnote in *Dothard* that states: "[A] discriminatory employment practice must be shown to be necessary to safe and efficient job performance. . . ." Rather, looking to *Griggs* and *Beazer*, the District Court stated that SEPTA need only show that its tests "significantly serve, but are neither required by nor necessary to, the employer's

---

5. In the analogous context of the defense of bona fide occupational qualification, the Supreme Court has stated: "'The greater the safety factor, measured by the likelihood of harm and the probable severity of that harm in case of an accident, the more stringent may be the job qualifications. . . .'" *Western Air Lines, Inc. v. Criswell.*

legitimate business interests" — in other words, that it "bears a manifest relationship" to the employment in question.

In disagreeing with the criteria used by the District Court, the majority holds that "a discriminatory cutoff score is impermissible unless shown to measure the minimum qualifications necessary for successful performance of the job in question." The difficulties presented by this standard are illustrated by the testimony of Dr. McArdle, the plaintiffs' expert. In essence, he proposed that female applicants be expected to meet 50% of their aerobic capacity, translating to 36 mL, but that males continue at the 50% level of 42.5 mL. That standard would, of course, have less adverse impact on women, but according to the findings of the District Court, would also have a detrimental impact on the effectiveness of the SEPTA transit police.

With this in mind, I cannot agree that the majority's standard is the correct one for this case. Reducing standards towards the lowest common denominator is particularly inappropriate for a police force. Undoubtedly, candidates who fail the running test — female or male — may have other qualities of particular value to SEPTA, but they must possess the requisite aerobic capacity as well. No matter how laudable it is to reduce job discrimination, to achieve this goal by lowering important public safety standards presents an unacceptable risk.

Aerobic capacity is an objective, measurable factor which gauges the ability of a human being to perform physical activity. The aerobic demands on the human system are affected by absolutes such as the distance traveled, the speed, the number of steps to be climbed, and similar factors. Governmental agency pronouncements will not shorten distances, reduce the number of steps, or decrease the aerobic capacity of perpetrators to match the reduced standards of officers, male or female. Some males and more females cannot meet the necessary requirements. Based on the facts established at trial, those individuals simply cannot perform the job efficiently. To the extent that they cannot, their hire adversely affects public safety.

The current Uniform Guidelines on Employee Selection Procedures, 29 C.F.R. § 1607 ("EEOC Guidelines"), are not as strict as the standard suggested by the majority. In discussing cut-off scores, the Guidelines explicitly state that "they should normally be set so as to be reasonable and consistent with normal expectations of acceptable proficiency within the work force." 29 C.F.R. § 1607.5(H) (1998). Further, the EEOC Guidelines standard — "predictive of or significantly correlated with important elements" — has been cited by the Supreme Court with approval on several occasions. See *Albemarle* (quoting former 29 C.F.R. § 1607.4(c)); *Griggs* (quoting same); see also 29 C.F.R. § 1607.5(B) (1998).

Further, *Albemarle*'s reference to "minimal qualifications" was directed only to the inappropriateness of using a test geared towards higher-level jobs as a screen for entry-level positions. This holding, which is minimally relevant to the matter at hand, is doubly inapplicable when the job affects public safety. See *Davis*.[9]

I see no need to remand this case to the District Court. Whatever standard is used, the findings of fact require an affirmance. Although the District Court rejected the plaintiffs' argument that the *Dothard* footnote, rather than *Beazer*, supplied the proper standard, the factual findings make it clear that under either formulation, the District Court reached the correct result.

The *Dothard* footnote states that the challenged practice must be "necessary to safe and efficient job performance." The District Court, also in a footnote, wrote

9. The plaintiffs also suggest that SEPTA's validation studies were insufficient. However, strict compliance with the EEOC Guidelines is not necessary in all cases. See *Beazer; Washington.* In cases involving public safety, courts have held that empirical validation is not required.

"physical fitness is only one trait or ability required of SEPTA officers, [but] it is a trait or ability that is necessary for and critical to the successful performance of the job, and thus SEPTA should be able to test for such a trait." This finding more than complies with *Dothard's* footnote by concluding that not only is physical fitness "necessary" to safe and efficient job performance as SEPTA officers, but that it is "critical" to successful performance of these jobs. Moreover, the finding clearly meets even the criterion that cut-off scores "measure the minimum qualifications necessary for *successful performance* of the job." (Emphasis added.)

Nor can there be any doubt that the factual findings here satisfy *Griggs'* requirement of "business necessity." Unquestionably, SEPTA's test is job-related and there can be no doubt that physical fitness, and particularly aerobic capacity, is necessary for adequate performance of the job of a SEPTA transit officer. The findings are convincing that 42.5 mL is a reasonable cut-off point for determining the physical ability necessary for successful performance of the job. Consequently, even under the plaintiffs' reading of the 1991 Act, which relies so much on *Dothard*, the judgment in favor of the defendant should be affirmed.

To my mind, the correct standard for this case is that of *Spurlock-Davis*, one that places greater emphasis on the safety of the public and fellow officers. I have no doubt that this line of cases survives the Civil Rights Act of 1991, because those opinions — as noted in Congress' "interpretive memorandum" — "reflect the concepts enunciated" in Supreme Court decisions prior to *Wards Cove*. See *Watson*; *Beazer*; *Washington*; *Smith*; *Fitzpatrick*. Safety concerns are clearly "concepts" considered by the Supreme Court and applied in various factual circumstances by the Courts of Appeals, both in pre and post-*Wards Cove* cases. Nothing in the legislative history casts any doubt on the continued viability of these opinions.

Although it did not cite *Spurlock-Davis*, the District Court stated in its conclusions of law that "employers such as SEPTA should be encouraged to improve the efficiency of its workforce, especially where public safety is implicated by the particular job as it is with SEPTA." More emphatically, it stated that "[t]he Court simply will not condone dilution of readily obtainable physical abilities standards that serve to protect the public safety in order to allow unfit candidates, whether they are male or female, to become SEPTA transit police officers."

### NOTES

1. While earlier Title VII cases used "business necessity" and "job related" in discussing the employer's defense, the 1991 Act requires both. How does the majority apply this standard? Is the dissent disagreeing with the approach of the majority or arguing for a less rigorous application of the standard because public safety is involved?

2. Is the aerobic test "job related"? Yes — in the sense that everyone who passes it will be fit, at least aerobically, for the job. It may not be "job related" if that term means that those who fail the test are not fit to be police officers. Would the aerobic test pass muster if the defense standard was either job related *or* consistent with business necessity, but not job related *and* consistent with business necessity?

3. Is the majority looking to business necessity to justify its conclusion that the aerobic test must measure only the minimum qualifications necessary for the job? What is wrong with the "more is better" approach? Is it that more may be *better* for business but not *necessary*?

4. The dissent, by comparing the 1990 and 1991 versions, presents plausible legislative history that Congress meant to water down the standard when it changed "required by business necessity" to "consistent with business necessity." But isn't that use of legislative history prohibited by the terms of the 1991 Act? Can a court look to a dictionary definition of "consistent" without violating the 1991 Act, as long as it does not point to anything in the legislative history of the Act as to the meaning of the term?

5. The dissent would apply a lower standard where safety to the public was involved. In *Watson*, Justice O'Connor even suggested deference to the employer's judgment when subjective practices were at issue. In Finnegan v. Trans World Airlines, Inc., 967 F.2d 1161 (7th Cir. 1992), Judge Posner, emphasizing that "*this* case makes no sense in disparate impact terms," found that changes in fringe benefits were not subject to disparate impact attack to avoid requiring the employer to prove business necessity. Is there any basis in the statute for different levels of scrutiny depending on what practice is at issue?

6. The dissent also stresses that all applicants, male and female, "have it within their power to prepare for the running test," and can be expected to perform well if they do so. Is this relevant to the proper test? In most prior disparate impact cases, the at-issue practice was not one that employees or applicants could easily satisfy. Is Judge Weiss ruling out disparate impact analysis when disfavored individuals can comply with the challenged requirement but choose not to?

7. On the other hand, SEPTA did not require aerobic fitness of current employees, although it did encourage such fitness. How could a specified level of fitness be "necessary" if most employees need not attain or maintain it?

8. Dr. McArdle, the plaintiffs' expert, proposed that "female applicants be expected to meet 50% of their aerobic capacity, translating to 36 mL, but that males continue at the 50% level of 42.5 mL." Does that mean that the test is harder for women than for men? Would it be disparate treatment of men if SEPTA adopted McArdle's suggestion?

9. On remand, the 42.5 mL test was upheld as justified by business necessity. See 308 F.3d 286 (3d Cir. 2002) (2–1). The court described what the "minimum qualifications necessary" standard meant in terms of the evidence in the case:

> SEPTA argued that the run test measures the "minimum qualifications necessary" because the relevant studies indicate that individuals who fail the test will be much less likely to successfully execute critical policing tasks. For example, the District Court credited a study that evaluated the correlation between a successful run time and performance on 12 job standards. The study found that individuals who passed the run test had a success rate on the job standards ranging from 70% to 90%. The success rate of the individuals who failed the run test ranged from 5% to 20%.[ ] The District Court found that such a low rate of success was unacceptable for employees who are regularly called upon to protect the public. In so doing, the District Court implicitly defined "minimum qualifications necessary" as meaning "likely to be able to do the job."

Id. at 290. The basis for upholding the new physical fitness test was the judgment that SEPTA management had decided to upgrade the physical fitness of its transit police officers. "It is undisputed that SEPTA management wanted to improve the crime fighting ability of SEPTA's force and the fitness of its officers." Id. at 288. The reason was to improve public safety, which was an appropriate basis for taking the actions it did: "the business necessity standard takes public safety into consideration." Id. at 289. The opinion also stressed that it was reasonable to expect women to take the necessary steps to train to meet the aerobic standard.

10. How does the business necessity defense compare to the bfoq defense to intentional disparate treatment discrimination? Does the absence of an intent element in disparate impact cases justify a business necessity defense that is more deferential to the employer's judgment? Or does that make no difference?

11. Professor Susan S. Grover, The Business Necessity Defense in Disparate Impact Discrimination Cases, 30 Ga. L. Rev. 387 (1996), argues that the correct test is a uniform, high standard, while Michael Garvin, Disparate Impact Claims Under the New Title VII, 68 Notre Dame L. Rev. 1153 (1993), claims that § 703(k) did not really change *Wards Cove*. Andrew C. Spiropoulos, Defining the Business Necessity Defense to the Disparate Impact Cause of Action: Finding the Golden Mean, 74 N.C. L. Rev. 1479, 1485 (1996), argues that the Supreme Court opinions articulated two very different versions of the business necessity defense: a strict one that would be very difficult for employers to meet, and a lenient one that would give employers more discretion. He contends that fulfilling the objectives of Title VII to remove artificial barriers to employment while preserving legitimate employer prerogatives requires establishing different standards for different types of jobs. A more flexible standard of business necessity under the 1991 Amendment should be applied to qualifications for positions that, because of their difficulty, great responsibility, or special risks to the public, require skills or intangible qualities that cannot be measured empirically. In the vast majority of jobs where such qualifications are not necessary, the stricter standards of necessity should apply. Linda Lye, Comment, Title VII, Tangled Tale: The Erosion and Confusion of Disparate Impact and the Business Necessity Defense, 19 Berkeley J. Emp. & Lab. L. 315 (1998), proposes to synthesize one test out of the two requirements that the practice be "job related and consistent with business necessity":

> [A]n employer must demonstrate that a challenged practice is a reasonable predictor of effective performance of job duties, which are duties defined in light of the employer's important business goals. Under this standard, an employer could not define the duties of the job to encompass tasks utterly irrelevant to the overall mission of the business and then exclude job candidates based on their inability to perform those peripheral duties. By requiring the job duties — the performance of which the challenged practice must measure — to be defined in light of important business goals, this interpretation gives meaning to the statute's requirement of consistency with business necessity.

Id. at 355-56. How would this approach resolve *Lanning*? The comment proposes a three-step inquiry into whether a challenged employment practice is justified: "The inquiry would thus involve three questions: (1) does the challenged practice reasonably predict an applicant's ability to perform a job duty? (2) has the employer identified an important business goal? And (3) does the job duty effectively further that goal?" See also David E. Hollar, Comment, Physical Ability Tests and Title VII, 67 U. Chi. L. Rev. 777 (2000).

## PROBLEM 5.3

Rath Packing had a rule prohibiting the employment of spouses of current employees. The plaintiff has succeeded in establishing that the no-spouse rule has a disparate impact on the employment of women. Rath asserts that the rule is necessary to promote optimum production and employee performance because spousal relationships in the workplace create situations that are problematic for the employer and employees — problems of efficiency, productivity, and ease of management. Rath says that its no-spouse rule is directed at problems that occurred in the past when married couples worked at Rath. The problems include dual absenteeism, vacation scheduling, supervision, and pressure to hire spouses. During a three-year period for which information on absenteeism is available, employees with spouses working at Rath exhibited a lower absentee rate than did those without spouses working there. Rath was able to point to one incident of habitual dual absenteeism, which was perceived by Rath management as having a significant disruptive effect on plant operations. Vacation scheduling for spouses impacted on the efficiency of Rath's production until Rath instituted a policy allowing employees to trade vacation time. Since the new policy went into effect, actual scheduling problems have been reduced significantly, but spouses remain dissatisfied with the procedure, and disgruntled fellow workers often apply for vacation times sought by less senior spousal employees in order to prevent couples from securing a joint vacation. Rath cites one instance where spousal supervision resulted in complaints of favoritism to and harassment of the supervised spouse. Is the no-spouse rule justified by business necessity? See EEOC v. Rath Packing Co., 787 F.2d 318 (8th Cir. 1986).

### 3. Alternative Employment Practices

Early disparate impact cases, particularly Albemarle Paper Co. v. Moody, 422 U.S. 405, 425 (1975), described the litigation structure of a disparate impact case as including a plaintiff's surrebuttal, even if the employer proves the challenged practice is justified as job-related and consistent with business necessity or, arguably, that it is sheltered by § 703(h):

> If an employer does then meet the burden of proving that its tests are "job related," it remains open to the complaining party to show that other tests or selection devices, without a similarly undesirable racial effect, would also serve the employer's legitimate interest in "efficient and trustworthy workmanship." Such a showing would be evidence that the employer was using its tests merely as a "pretext" for discrimination.

It was not clear whether "pretext" was used as a state-of-mind concept, as in *McDonnell Douglas*, or merely as a kind of shorthand for a "less restrictive alternative" analysis. Under the latter view, if an equally effective alternate practice with a lesser impact is available, how could a challenged practice be a business "necessity"? In subsequent cases, the Court seemed to shift back and forth between the two views.

The Civil Rights Act of 1991 seems to solve this problem. While a plaintiff presumably can always prevail by establishing intent to discriminate, "pretext" is not a formal part of disparate impact analysis. Rather, the new statute adds § 703(k)(1)(A) to Title VII. We have already discussed the first prong of that analysis when plaintiff shows a particular employment practice with a disparate impact, and the employer fails to establish job relation and business necessity. § 703(k)(1)(A)(i). But a disparate impact violation also exists when, despite the employer's successful proof of job relation and business necessity, the plaintiff "makes the demonstration described in subparagraph C with respect to an alternative employment practice and the [employer] refuses to adopt such alternative employment practice." § 703(k)(1)(A)(ii). Subparagraph (C), in turn, defines alternative employment practice by stating that "the demonstration referred to in subparagraph (A)(ii) shall be accordance with the law as it existed on

June 4, 1989, with respect to the concept of 'alternative employment practice.'" The Court's decision in *Wards Cove* was issued on June 5, 1989, suggesting that Congress meant "alternative employment practice" to embrace the law prior to *Wards Cove*, as it had explicitly provided with respect to business necessity and job relatedness.

This is curious, however, because it was *Wards Cove* that first spoke of "alternative business practices" with a less discriminatory impact. Further, that case viewed the failure to adopt such alternatives as raising doubts about the employer's intent. Prior to June 4, 1989, that is, prior to *Wards Cove*, the closest phrase to "alternative employment practices" was Justice O'Connor's plurality opinion in Watson v. Fort Worth Bank & Trust, 487 U.S. 977 (1988), which had permitted the plaintiff to demonstrate less discriminatory "alternative selection devices" in response to the defendant's business necessity showing. Justice O'Connor went on to note that "[f]actors such as the cost or other burdens of proposed alternative selection devices are relevant in determining whether they would be equally as effective as the challenged practice in serving the employer's legitimate business goals." Id. at 998.

Before *Watson*, the Court had not spoken of "alternative employer practices." For example, *Dothard* noted the plaintiff's opportunity to show less discriminatory "selection devices." Thus, "'[i]f the employer proves that the challenged requirements are job related, the plaintiff may then show that other selection devices without a similar discriminatory effect would also serve the employer's legitimate interest in "efficient and trustworthy workmanship."'" 433 U.S. 321, 329 (1977). Earlier, *Albemarle* had used similar language but described the showing as establishing "pretext" for an employer's job-related tests. *Beazer* also viewed the plaintiff's rebuttal opportunity as establishing that the employer's neutral rule was merely a pretext for intentional discrimination.

In light of this history, what does the statute mean? The phrasing of the statute more or less tracks the language in *Wards Cove*,* but without referring to pretext or disparate treatment. And a common element in the Court's prior impact cases was that the plaintiff could establish liability by showing less discriminatory alternatives. Thus, the prior law and the new statute are consistent to the extent that § 703(k)(1)(A)(ii) is read to allow proof of liability without regard to intent. What has disappeared is the possibility that such alternatives were merely a way of finding intentional discrimination. This strengthens the plaintiff's position by allowing her to prevail without the need to show intent; of course, a plaintiff who can show intentional discrimination will prevail under the disparate treatment theory.

However, proving "alternative employment practices" liability may not be easy. Does the statute impose on the plaintiff the burden to establish such alternatives? What evidence must the employee present? Must the alternative practice be nondiscriminatory or merely less discriminatory in effect? What if the alternative devices are effective, but not *equally* effective? What if they are more costly? *Watson* indicates that "cost and other burdens" are relevant in determining whether an alternative selection device is *equally* effective. And *Watson* does precede *Wards Cove*, so it satisfies that requirement for application. But this language in *Watson* appears only in the plurality opinion, which may not constitute an opinion of "the Court." In addition, by adopting the law in effect before *Wards Cove*, arguably Congress intended to reject

---

* Section 703(k)(1)(A) speaks of "alternative employment practice," substituting "employment" for "business" in the *Wards Cove* phrasing, but § 703(k)(1)(B) bars the use of any but prescribed legislative history in construing the Act insofar as it "relates to *Wards Cove*-business necessity/cumulation/alternative *business* practice." (Emphasis added.)

*Wards Cove*'s requirement that alternative selection practices be equally effective and no more costly in order to support liability.

Under the statute, a successful alternative selection practice claim also requires that the employer "refuse" to adopt the alternative practice. Does the plaintiff have the burden of proving that the employer refused? "Refuse" seems to mean more than mere failure to use the alternative practice. Would proof that the employer knew of the existence of the practice and failed to adopt it suffice? What if an employee proposed an alternative practice by placing it in the employer's suggestion box? What if the alternative practice is offered during discovery or at trial and the employer fails or "refuses" to adopt it? Is liability established?

Prior to *Wards Cove*, plaintiffs had an opportunity to prove less discriminatory alternatives or pretext after the employer met its burden with respect to business necessity. *Wards Cove*, in contrast, identified a separate claim based on a prima facie showing of impact, taken together with a demonstration that the employer had refused to adopt less discriminatory alternatives. Reconsider the language of § 703(k)(1)(A). Which approach has the statute adopted?

But doesn't the availability of less discriminatory alternatives necessarily indicate that the employer's standard, even if job related, is *not* a business necessity? Unlike the definition of business necessity, the Act does not specifically limit the definition of alternative employment practices to prior Supreme Court decisions. It merely requires that proof "shall be in accordance with the law as it existed on June 4, 1989." As of June 4, 1989, the EEOC's Uniform Guidelines on Employee Selection Procedures required employers, as part of their burden of justifying discriminatory selection procedures, to account for alternative procedures that they should have known about. See 29 C.F.R. §§ 1607.3, 1607.15A(9) (1993). Are such regulations "law"? After the 1991 Civil Rights Act, could a plaintiff present evidence of less discriminatory alternatives in order to rebut the employer's case of business necessity? The advantage, of course, would be that the plaintiff might have enough evidence to prevent the defendant from carrying its burden of persuasion, even if the plaintiff's proof would not carry her burden on alternative business practice. Does the presence of an alternative form of liability grounded in alternative employment practices preclude the plaintiff from using the same evidence to rebut business necessity?

Does this beg a more fundamental question: What is the purpose of disparate impact liability? Is it a back-door method of smoking out discriminatory intent, analogous to a res ipsa loquitur inference in tort law, an effort to compensate groups who have been disadvantaged historically, or is it simply designed to force employers to use the least discriminatory methods available to select employees?

## FITZPATRICK v. CITY OF ATLANTA
### 2 F.3d 1112 (11th Cir. 1993)

ANDERSON, Circuit Judge:

This suit was brought against the City of Atlanta ("the City") by several African-American firefighters employed by the Atlanta Department of Public Safety, Bureau of Fire Services ("the Fire Department") who suffer from a medical condition on account of which they cannot shave their faces. Plaintiffs challenge a fire department regulation that requires all firefighters to be clean-shaven. They allege . . . that this "no-beard" rule has a discriminatory disparate impact on African-Americans in violation of Title VII of the 1964 Civil Rights Act. . . . The City defends the policy, contending that the respirator masks used by firefighters cannot safely be worn by bearded men. The district court granted summary judgment for the City and the firefighters have appealed. For the reasons set forth below, we affirm the judgment of the district court.

## I.  FACTS AND PROCEDURAL HISTORY

In order to breathe in smoke-filled environments, firefighters must wear respirators, otherwise known as positive pressure self-contained breathing apparatuses ("SCBA's"). For the SCBA mask to operate properly and safely, its edges must be able to seal securely to the wearer's face. The parties do not dispute that a wearer's long facial hair can interfere with the forming of a proper seal. In an attempt to address the hazard posed by such hair, the City Fire Department until 1982 enforced a policy requiring all male firefighters to be completely clean-shaven.

The twelve plaintiff-appellant firefighters in this case are all African-American men who suffer from pseudofolliculitis barbae ("PFB"), a bacterial disorder which causes men's faces to become infected if they shave them. It is generally recognized that PFB disproportionately afflicts African-American men. . . .

[Originally] firefighters with PFB were permitted to participate in a program known as the "shaving clinic." Shaving clinic participants were allowed to wear very short "shadow" beards, which were not to exceed length limits specified by a dermatologist employed by the City. . . . It was believed that so long as the shadow beards were kept very short, the SCBA masks would still be able to seal sufficiently well to enable the firefighters to use them safely.

In 1988 . . . [o]n the recommendation of . . . the City's then-Assistant Commissioner of Public Safety, the Fire Department decided that shadow beards would no longer be permitted, on the grounds that even shadow beards may interfere with the safe use of SCBA's.

. . . Under the new policy, firefighters who cannot be clean-shaven must be removed from firefighting duty. Such persons may be transferred to non-firefighting positions within the Department, if suitable openings are available. They may also apply for other available positions with the City but are accorded no special priority and must compete on an equal basis with other eligible candidates. Under the new policy such persons are granted the right to be temporarily reassigned from firefighting duties for a one-time period of ninety days. Male firefighters who cannot shave and for whom non-firefighting positions are not available within the Department are terminated, once they have exhausted their ninety days of temporary reassignment. . . .

[The court found that the employer rule prohibiting all beards was justified by business necessity, and then turned to whether there was a less discriminatory alternative.]

[I]n order for the City to be entitled to summary judgment on the disparate impact claim, there must also be no genuine issue of fact with respect to whether a less discriminatory comparably effective alternative to the no-beard rule is available. The existence of a less discriminatory alternative is an issue on which the firefighters, the non-movants, would bear the burden of proof at trial. Thus, our analysis of whether there exists a genuine issue as to this material fact begins with an examination of whether the City has carried the movant's initial burden applicable for issues on which the movant would not bear the burden of proof at trial.

In such circumstances, the movant may carry the initial burden by adducing evidence affirmatively negating the material fact at issue, or else by showing an absence of evidence on the part of the non-movant to prove the fact at trial. As discussed above, the City has cited the OSHA, ANSI, and NIOSH safety standards which advise that safety requires that SCBA-wearers be clean-shaven. We believe that this evidence affirmatively demonstrates, not only that being clean-shaven is a business necessity for firefighters, but also that any proposed less discriminatory alternatives to the no-beard rule that would not require firefighters to be clean-shaven would not be adequately safe. Thus the evidence is sufficient to satisfy the City's initial burden as the summary judgment movant on the less discriminatory alternative issue.

Responsibility then devolves upon the firefighters to adduce evidence creating a genuine issue as to the availability of a comparably safe, less discriminatory alternative. The firefighters have proposed two possible alternatives to the City's rule requiring firefighters to be clean-shaven. The first is simply reinstitution of the shadow beard shaving clinic. However, in order for the shadow beard program to constitute a legitimate less discriminatory alternative, shadow beards must adequately serve the Fire Department's acknowledged business need, namely, safety. As we have explained above in addressing the City's business necessity defense, the firefighters have failed to create a genuine issue that shadow beards are safe. Thus, for the same reason, they have also failed to create a genuine issue that the shaving clinic would be a comparably effective alternative to the shadow beard ban.

The second possible alternative suggested by the firefighters is shaving only the portion of the face where the SCBA seal would come into contact with the skin. However, in the two sentences of their summary judgment papers in which they propose this alternative, the firefighters cite no evidence to show that partial shaving would be a viable and safe alternative. Moreover, as a matter of common knowledge, it is apparent that partial shaving would pose the same PFB problems as full-face shaving, and thus it is doubtful that the firefighters could have adduced evidence that partial shaving constitutes a viable less discriminatory alternative. Thus, the firefighters have failed to carry their summary judgment rebuttal burden of creating a genuine issue as to the viability of either of the two less discriminatory alternatives they propose. . . .

## NOTES

1. According to *Fitzpatrick*, who bears the burden of persuasion on the issue of alternative business practice or less discriminatory alternative? Why? Does the court require the plaintiffs to show pretext in the sense of discriminatory intent?

2. The employees' proffered alternative practice of permitting shadow beards clearly is less discriminatory. Why do they lose on this issue? Must alternative less discriminatory practices be equally or more effective to prevail? Why? What if the business practice did not involve worker safety?

3. Notice that the employees were permitted to offer evidence of an alternative business practice to rebut the employer's showing of business necessity. Is this consistent with the language of the 1991 Civil Rights Act?

4. In Lanning v. Southeastern Pa. Transp. Auth. (reproduced at page 373), the Third Circuit majority reversed the district court finding's that a physical fitness test of aerobic ability was justified by business necessity. It, therefore, did not need to address the alternative practice question. The dissenting judge, who would affirm the judgment for the employer, did address the issue of alternative employment practice.

The [plaintiffs] propose a number of alternative practices that they suggest would have a lesser disparate impact while still serving SEPTA's goals. First, they suggest that SEPTA select medically fit applicants who pass fitness requirements at the end of their training at the Philadelphia Police Academy. Second, as noted earlier, they argue in favor of a relative fitness test (i.e., one with a lower cut-off point for females). Third, they prompt SEPTA to propose an alternative.

For plaintiffs to establish a satisfactory alternative, they must "make[ ] the demonstration described in [42 U.S.C. § 2000e-2(k)(1)(C)] with respect to an alternative employment practice and [establish that] the [employer] refuses to adopt such alternative employment practice." 42 U.S.C. § 2000e-2(k)(1)(A)(ii). To meet this burden, the plaintiffs' proposed alternatives must have less disparate impact and "also serve the employer's legitimate interest in 'efficient and trustworthy workmanship.'" *Albemarle.* As stated in *Watson,* the alternative test must "be equally as effective as the challenged practice in serving the employer's legitimate business goals."

The District Court found that none of the plaintiffs' proposals served SEPTA's legitimate interest in having a more physically fit work force. If SEPTA may require an aerobic capacity of 42.5 mL after training at the police academy, as plaintiffs propose, it is unclear how that practice would be any less discriminatory than requiring it before hire. In short, that plan would simply require that training be on "company time" rather than on that of the applicants.

As to the relative fitness test proposed by the plaintiffs' expert, the factual findings demonstrate that officers with a capacity of 36 mL do not serve SEPTA's needs as well as the required standard of 42.5 mL. Finally, the proposal that SEPTA come forward with an alternative is not an alternative at all. Thus, plaintiffs have failed to meet their burden to establish an alternative employment practice.

Given that there was evidence that, with training, women could pass the aerobic test, doesn't plaintiffs' first alternative work as an alternative under the test Judge Weiss advocates? As to using a relative fitness test, Judge Weiss added footnote 11, suggesting that § 703(l) might bar such action:

> The Civil Rights Act of 1991 presents another potential barrier to the relative fitness test. Subsection 2000e-2(l) prohibits "in connection with the selection or referral of applicants or candidates for employment . . . use [of] different cutoff scores for . . . employment related tests on the basis of sex[.]" By its plain language, 42 U.S.C. § 2000e-2(l) arguably prohibits a relative fitness test. The District Court concluded that this provision did not apply. I have some doubt on that ruling, but need not reach that issue because I would affirm on other bases.

Oddly, the majority which upheld the district court's finding of business necessity on remand did not address the alternative practice question, 308 F.3d 286 (3d Cir. 2002), although the dissent by Judge McKee reiterated several possibilities. Id. at 294-95.

5. For an argument, based on Justice Scalia's plain meaning approach to statutory interpretation, that § 703(k)(1)(A)(ii) creates a new right of action, independent of the basic § 703(k)(1)(A)(i) group disparate impact action, see Michael J. Zimmer, Individual Disparate Impact Law: On the Plain Meaning of the 1991 Civil Rights Act, 30 Loy. U. Chi. L.J 473 (1998). Essentially, Professor Zimmer argues that § 703 (k)(1)(A) expressly recognizes two ways of establishing a disparate treatment claim. Paragraph (i) more or less codifies the traditional notion that a practice is subject to disparate impact attack if it has an unjustified impact on race, gender or other protected groups. But, because it is phrased in the disjunctive, paragraph (ii) is expressly drafted as an alternative method of establishing a violation, and does not include any requirement of proof of disparity of impact on anyone. A violation occurs if:

(ii) the complaining party makes the demonstration described in subparagraph (c) with respect to an alternative employment practice and the respondent refuses to adopt such alternative employment practice.

This reading would have the odd result of Congress labeling something "disparate impact" without any requirement of proving any disparity of impact on any group. But requiring a showing of disparate impact under (ii) would contravene the plain meaning of the text.

If this view is taken, § 703(k)(1)(A)(ii) would create an entirely new "individual disparate impact" action. An individual protected by Title VII would be able to establish a disparate impact claim under § 703(k)(1)(A)(ii) simply by proving (1) that the employer took adverse action based on an "employment practice," (2) that an alternative practice exists that serves the employer's interests yet would not adversely affect the plaintiff, and (3) that the employer refused to adopt the better alternative. Contrary to pre-existing Title VII law, this new cause of action neither includes an intent to discriminate or pretext element nor requires any showing of group impact. How would this new cause of action for "individual disparate impact" work for an employee who was discharged, allegedly for excessive tardiness? Aren't there many alternatives available in most workplaces that would allow for flexibility in starting times?

6. An advantage of joining an individual disparate impact action with one for individual disparate treatment is the interaction of the two: to the extent the employer characterizes its action as not being based on an employment practice, the adverse action will then appear to be ad hoc, perhaps subjective, and therefore more likely to be found the product of intent to discriminate. To the extent the employer claims the non-discriminatory basis for its adverse action against plaintiff is merely the application of a neutral employment policy or practice, it may be conceding the first part of the § 703(k)(1)(A)(ii) action. That still requires plaintiff to prove that an alternative exists that satisfies the employer's legitimate interests and that the employer refused to adopt it. See Chapter 6.

If faced with deciding which of the two theories to employ, plaintiffs would prefer the individual disparate treatment action since it provides for the possibility of compensatory and punitive damages as well as a right to trial by jury, rights that are not available in the individual disparate impact action.

7. As we will see in the next section, Title VII has several defenses to its broad sweep. We have already met the bona fide occupational qualification defense to intentional gender, religion, or national origin discrimination in Chapter 4. In addition, § 703(h) creates exceptions for professionally developed employment tests (as we saw in *Griggs*), for bona fide seniority systems, and for bona fide merit systems. But 703(k)(1)(A)(ii) is not, by its express terms, limited to a surrebuttal to the defendant's proof of business necessity. Its plain meaning suggests that plaintiff can demonstrate an alterative employment practice to practices that are sheltered by § 703(h), including professionally developed tests, bona fide seniority systems, and bona fide merit systems. We will revisit this use of § 703(k)(1)(A)(ii) after surveying these three defenses.

## C.  SECTION 703(h) EXCEPTIONS

In addition to the job relatedness/business necessity defense to disparate impact discrimination, Title VII offers three other statutory defenses in disparate impact cases.

Section 703(h) creates exceptions for professionally developed employment tests, for bona fide seniority systems, and for bona fide merit systems.

## 1.  Professionally Developed Tests

Section 703(h) provides that, notwithstanding any other provision of Title VII, it shall not

> be an unlawful employment practice for an employer to give and to act upon the results of any professionally developed ability test provided that such test, its administration or action upon the results is not designed, intended or used to discriminate because of race, color, religion, sex or national origin.

As indicated in *Griggs*, the EEOC took the position early in the life of Title VII that, where there was a disparate impact, § 703(h) incorporated the strict validation standards that industrial psychologists established for themselves for any test or selection device. With the acceptance of that position in *Griggs*, § 703(h) operates less as an exception than as a fundamental part of the broad interpretation given Title VII.

## ALBEMARLE PAPER CO. v. MOODY
### 422 U.S. 405 (1975)

Justice STEWART delivered the opinion of the Court.

. . . Like the employer in *Griggs*, Albemarle uses two general ability tests, the Beta Examination, to test nonverbal intelligence, and the Wonderlic Test (Forms A and B), the purported measure of general verbal facility which was also involved in the *Griggs* case. Applicants for hire into various skilled lines of progression at the plant are required to score 100 on the Beta Exam and 18 on one of the Wonderlic Test's two alternative forms.

The question of job relatedness must be viewed in the context of the plant's operation and the history of the testing program. The plant, which now employs about 650 persons, converts raw wood into paper products. It is organized into a number of functional departments, each with one or more distinct lines of progression, the theory being that workers can move up the line as they acquire the necessary skills. The number and structure of the lines have varied greatly over time. For many years, certain lines were themselves more skilled and paid higher wages than others, and until 1964 these skilled lines were expressly reserved for white workers. In 1968, many of the unskilled "Negro" lines were "end-tailed" onto skilled "white" lines, but it apparently remains true that at least the top jobs in certain lines require greater skills than the top jobs in other lines. In this sense, at least, it is still possible to speak of relatively skilled and relatively unskilled lines.

In the 1950's while the plant was being modernized with new and more sophisticated equipment, the Company introduced a high school diploma requirement for entry into the skilled lines. Though the Company soon concluded that this requirement did not improve the quality of the labor force, the requirement was continued until the District Court enjoined its use. In the late 1950's the Company began using the Beta Examination and the Bennett Mechanical Comprehension Test (also involved in the *Griggs* case) to screen applicants for entry into the skilled lines. The Bennett Test was dropped several years later, but use of the Beta Test continued.

The Company added the Wonderlic Tests in 1963, for the skilled lines, on the theory that a certain verbal intelligence was called for by the increasing sophistication of the plant's operations. The Company made no attempt to validate the test for job relatedness, and simply adopted the national "norm" score of 18 as a cut-off point for new job applicants. After 1964, when it discontinued overt segregation in the lines of progression, the Company allowed Negro workers to transfer to the skilled lines if they could pass the Beta and Wonderlic Tests, but few succeeded in doing so. Incumbents in the skilled lines, some of whom had been hired before adoption of the tests, were not required to pass them to retain their jobs or their promotion rights. The record shows that a number of white incumbents in high-ranking job groups could not pass the tests.

Four months before this case went to trial, Albemarle engaged an expert in industrial psychology to "validate" the job relatedness of its testing program. He spent a half day at the plant and devised a "concurrent validation" study, which was conducted by plant officials, without his supervision. The expert then subjected the results to statistical analysis. The study dealt with 10 job groupings, selected from near the top of nine of the lines of progression. Jobs were grouped together solely by their proximity in the line of progression; no attempt was made to analyze jobs in terms of the particular skills they might require. All, or nearly all, employees in the selected groups participated in the study — 105 employees in all, but only four Negroes. Within each job grouping, the study compared the test scores of each employee with an independent "ranking" of the employee, relative to each of his coworkers, made by two of the employee's supervisors. . . .

For each job grouping, the expert computed the "Phi coefficient" of statistical correlation between the test scores and an average of the two supervisorial rankings. Consonant with professional conventions, the expert regarded as "statistically significant" any correlation that could have occurred by chance only five times, or fewer, in 100 trials. On the basis of these results, the District Court found that "[t]he personnel tests administered at the plant have undergone validation studies and have been proven to be job related." Like the Court of Appeals, we are constrained to disagree.

The EEOC has issued "Guidelines" for employers seeking to determine, through professional validation studies, whether their employment tests are job related. 29 C.F.R. pt. 1607. These Guidelines draw upon and make reference to professional standards of test validation established by the American Psychological Association.[29] The EEOC Guidelines are not administrative "regulations" promulgated pursuant to formal procedures established by the Congress. But, as this Court has heretofore noted, they do constitute "[t]he administrative interpretation of the Act by the enforcing agency," and consequently they are "entitled to great deference."

The message of these Guidelines is the same as that of the *Griggs* case — that discriminatory tests are impermissible unless shown, by professionally acceptable methods, to be "predictive of or significantly correlated with important elements of work behavior which comprise or are relevant to the job or jobs for which candidates are being evaluated." 29 C.F.R. § 1607.4(c).

Measured against the Guidelines, Albemarle's validation study is materially defective in several respects:

(1) Even if it had been otherwise adequate, the study would not have "validated" the Beta and Wonderlic test battery for all of the skilled lines of progression for which the

29. American Psychological Association, Standards for Educational and Psychological Tests and Manuals (1966) (hereafter APA Standards). A volume of the same title, containing modifications, was issued in 1974. . . .

two tests are, apparently, now required. The study showed significant correlations for the Beta Exam in only three of the eight lines. Though the Wonderlic Test's Form A and Form B are in theory identical and interchangeable measures of verbal facility, significant correlations for one form but not for the other were obtained in four job groupings. In two job groupings neither form showed a significant correlation. Within some of the lines of progression, one form was found acceptable for some job groupings but not for others. Even if the study were otherwise reliable, this odd patchwork of results would not entitle Albemarle to impose its testing program under the Guidelines. A test may be used in jobs other than those for which it has been professionally validated only if there are "no significant differences" between the studied and unstudied jobs. 29 C.F.R. § 1607.4(c)(2). The study in this case involved no analysis of the attributes of, or the particular skills needed in, the studied job groups. There is accordingly no basis for concluding that "no significant differences" exist among the lines of progression, or among distinct job groupings within the studied lines of progression. Indeed, the study's checkered results appear to compel the opposite conclusion.

(2) The study compared test scores with subjective supervisorial rankings. While they allow the use of supervisorial rankings in test validation, the Guidelines quite plainly contemplate that the rankings will be elicited with far more care than was demonstrated here. Albemarle's supervisors were asked to rank employees by a "standard" that was extremely vague and fatally open to divergent interpretations. As previously noted, each "job grouping" contained a number of different jobs, and the supervisors were asked, in each grouping, to "determine which [employees] they felt irrespective of the job that they were actually doing, but in their respective jobs, did a better job than the person they were rating against. . . ." There is no way of knowing precisely what criteria of job performance the supervisors were considering, whether each of the supervisors was considering the same criteria or whether, indeed, any of the supervisors actually applied a focused and stable body of criteria of any kind.[32] There is, in short, simply no way to determine whether the criteria *actually* considered were sufficiently related to the Company's legitimate interest in job-specific ability to justify a testing system with a racially discriminatory impact.

(3) The Company's study focused, in most cases, on job groups near the top of the various lines of progression. In Griggs v. Duke Power Co., the Court left open "the question whether testing requirements that take into account capability for the next succeeding position or related future promotion might be utilized upon a showing that such long-range requirements fulfill a genuine business need." The Guidelines take a sensible approach to this issue, and we now endorse it:

> If job progression structures and seniority provisions are so established that new employees will probably, within a reasonable period of time and in a great majority of cases, progress to a higher level, it may be considered that candidates are being evaluated for jobs at that higher level. However, where job progression is not so nearly automatic, or the time span is such that higher level jobs or employees' potential may be expected to change in significant ways, it shall be considered that candidates are being evaluated for a job at or near the entry level. 29 C.F.R. § 1607.4(c)(1).

The fact that the best of those employees working near the top of a line of progression score well on a test does not necessarily mean that that test, or some particular cutoff

---

32. It cannot escape notice that Albemarle's study was conducted by plant officials, without neutral, on-the-scene oversight, at a time when this litigation was about to come to trial. Studies so closely controlled by an interested party in litigation must be examined with great care.

score on the test, is a permissible measure of the minimal qualifications of new workers entering lower level jobs. In drawing any such conclusion, detailed consideration must be given to the normal speed of promotion, to the efficacy of on-the-job training in the scheme of promotion, and to the possible use of testing as a promotion device, rather than as a screen for entry into low-level jobs. The District Court made no findings on these issues. The issues take on special importance in a case, such as this one, where incumbent employees are permitted to work at even high-level jobs without passing the company's test battery. See 29 C.F.R. § 1607.11.

(4) Albemarle's validation study dealt only with job-experienced, white workers; but the tests themselves are given to new job applicants, who are younger, largely inexperienced, and in many instances nonwhite. The APA Standards state that it is "essential" that "[t]he validity of a test should be determined on subjects who are at the age or in the same educational or vocational situation as the persons for whom the test is recommended in practice." PC 5.41. The EEOC Guidelines likewise provide that "[d]ata must be generated and results separately reported for minority and non-minority groups wherever technically feasible." 29 C.F.R. § 1607.5(b)(5). In the present case, such "differential validation" as to racial groups was very likely not "feasible," because years of discrimination at the plant have insured that nearly all of the upper level employees are white. But there has been no clear showing that differential validation was not feasible for lower level jobs. More importantly, the Guidelines provide:

> If it is not technically feasible to include minority employees in validation studies conducted on the present work force, the conduct of a validation study without minority candidates does not relieve any person of his subsequent obligation for validation when inclusion of minority candidates becomes technically feasible. 29 C.F.R. § 1607.5(b)(1). . . .

For all these reasons, we agree with the Court of Appeals that the District Court erred in concluding that Albemarle had proved the job relatedness of its testing program and that the respondents were consequently not entitled to equitable relief. . . .

## WASHINGTON v. DAVIS
### 426 U.S. 229 (1976)

Justice WHITE, for the Court.

[Plaintiff in *Davis* relied on Title VII authority to attack the use of a pre-employment test in a case against the District of Columbia brought under 42 U.S.C. § 1981 and the equal protection component of the Fifth Amendment. After rejecting the use of *Griggs's* disparate impact analysis in constitutional equal protection law, the Court treated the statutory issue.]

. . . The District Court also assumed that Title VII standards were to control the case, identified the determinative issue as whether Test 21 was sufficiently job related and proceeded to uphold use of the test because it was "directly related to a determination of whether the applicant possesses sufficient skills requisite to the demands of the curriculum a recruit must master at the police academy." The Court of Appeals reversed because the relationship between Test 21 and training school success, if demonstrated at all, did not satisfy what it deemed to be the crucial requirement of a direct relationship between performance on Test 21 and performance on the police-man's job.

We agree with petitioners and the federal parties that this was error. The advisability of the police recruit training course informing the recruit about his upcoming job, acquainting him with its demands, and attempting to impart a modicum of required skills seems conceded. It is also apparent to us, as it was to the District Judge, that some minimum verbal and communicative skill would be very useful, if not essential, to satisfactory progress in the training regimen. Based on the evidence before him, the District Judge concluded that Test 21 was directly related to the requirements of the police training program and that a positive relationship between the test and training-course performance was sufficient to validate the former, wholly aside from its possible relationship to actual performance as a police officer. This conclusion of the District Judge that training-program validation may itself be sufficient is supported by regulations of the Civil Service Commission, by the opinion evidence placed before the District Judge, and by the current views of the Civil Service Commissioners who were parties to the case. Nor is the conclusion foreclosed by either *Griggs* or Albemarle Paper Co. v. Moody; and it seems to us the much more sensible construction of the job-relatedness requirement. . . .

## NOTES

1. How do the test validation requirements fit into the general structure of disparate impact analysis? If a test is validated, does that mean the business necessity/job relatedness defense has been satisfied, or is test validation a separate defense in a disparate impact case? In Contreras v. City of Los Angeles, 656 F.2d 1267 (9th Cir. 1981), a testing case, the court opted for a relaxed interpretation of the business necessity defense, but nevertheless concluded that "discriminatory tests are impermissible unless shown, by professionally accepted methods, to be predictive of or significantly correlated with important elements of work behavior which comprise or are relevant to the job or jobs for which candidates are being evaluated." Id. at 1276.

2. Is the point of *Contreras* that test validation is just different from the ordinary applications of business necessity? Cf. *Griggs* and *Beazer*. Why should that be true? Tests have historically played a significant role in excluding African Americans and other minorities from a wide range of jobs.

3. No matter how courts interpret the 1991 Civil Rights Act defense of job relatedness and business necessity, they are unlikely to conclude that every neutral employment criterion subject to disparate impact analysis must be "validated" in the sense that § 703(h) requires validation. If "tests" are subject to more stringent proof of job relatedness by virtue of § 703(h), then it becomes necessary to distinguish between employment tests and other neutral criteria used by employers to make employment-related decisions. What is a test? Consider the use of paper-and-pencil "honesty" or "integrity" tests used as pre-employment screening devices. Do such "tests" require validation? Is it wise to discourage, through § 703(h), the use of neutral or objective testing, given that an employer may opt instead for far more subjective criteria? See *Albemarle*, Blackmun, J. concurring.

4. *Albemarle*'s close comparison of the employer's validation study to the EEOC Uniform Guidelines provoked criticism. Dean Booth & James L. Mackay, in Legal

Constraints on Employment Testing and Evolving Trends in the Law, 29 Emory L.J. 121, 125 (1980), describe the reaction to strict adherence to the guidelines:

> If read literally, the 1970 Guidelines set forth requirements for validation so stringent as to effectively preclude almost all use of employment testing. In this regard, Dr. William Enneis, the senior industrial psychologist employed by the EEOC since 1966 and the principal draftsman of the 1970 Guidelines, testified in 1974 that he was aware of only three or four criterion-related validation studies which met all of the requirements of the 1970 Guidelines. Professional criticism of the 1970 Guidelines has been severe. The Psychological Corporation, a respected and long established developer of psychological tests, has taken the position that the 1970 Guidelines are "unreasonable, unrealistic, and unworkable." The Division of Industrial-Organizational Psychology of the American Psychological Association . . . has criticized the rigid application of the 1970 Guidelines as leading to "professionally unrealistic and effectively unattainable requirements."

The 1970 guidelines did reflect the extant standards of industrial psychologists. Why were the test experts opposed to their own standards?

5. As a matter of testing theory, the fundamental flaw of the validation study in *Albemarle* was the failure of the test expert to do a job analysis of any of the jobs for which the tests were used. Would the Court have treated the study more favorably if it had not been an eve-of-litigation effort?

6. Did the Court in Washington v. Davis change its mind about the deference owed the EEOC guidelines? *Washington* was not a Title VII case because, at the time the action was commenced, public employees were not protected by Title VII.

7. *Albemarle* refers to EEOC guidelines requiring differential validation by race, thus suggesting that different scores could predict different levels of performance for blacks and whites. This technique may have been invalidated by the Civil Rights Act of 1991, which changed the law of employment testing by prohibiting "race norming." Section 703(l) now provides:

> It shall be an unlawful employment practice for a respondent, in connection with the selection or referral of applicants or candidates for employment or promotion, to adjust the scores of, use different cutoff scores for, or otherwise alter the results of, employment related tests on the basis of race, color, religion, sex, or national origin.

While this provision does not specifically bar differential validation in testing, what would be the use of such validation if lower-scoring individuals could not be hired on the basis that they were likely to perform as well as higher-scoring whites? Or does the phrasing of the statute permit an employer to hire lower-scoring individuals so long as their scores are not adjusted and different cutoff scores are not used? In Billish v. City of Chicago, 989 F.2d 890 (7th Cir. 1993), the court upheld a challenge by white firefighters where the city had raised minority candidates' scores sufficiently to avoid having a racial impact under the EEOC guidelines. The court found this would have violated the new § 703(l). Would it be race norming for an employer, pursuant to an affirmative action plan, to promote a minority group member with a lower test score than a white? *Billish* upheld precisely that claim by the white firefighters, but on different grounds. Today, would the question simply be whether § 703(l) was violated?

8. There are three ways by which a study may be validated: criterion-related validation, construct-related validation, and content validation. In criterion-related validation, the general criterion selected is performance on the job. For example, if a job analysis reveals that good job performance requires good vision, good hearing, or

motor dexterity, the employer can devise tests for those skills, and validate them by comparing test performance to job performance. In a criterion-related validation, the employer tests individuals, but then hires them without regard to their performance on the tests to see if good test performance really predicts good job performance.

A variation of this technique is "concurrent validation," such as that attempted in *Albemarle*. As compared to criterion validation, the basic difference is that the current employees are tested, and the tests are validated by comparing the test results to job performance ratings. In theory, concurrent validation is less reliable since the employees tested may not be a random sample of the individuals who will be given the tests in the future.

Another form of validation is construct validation. This requires a testing expert to analyze the job and construct a test that she thinks will measure traits necessary for success on the job. Construct validation is appropriate for traits more abstract than those subject to criterion-related validation. Thus, traits such as intelligence, mechanical comprehension, and verbal fluency are subject to construct validation.

Perhaps most intuitively appealing is content validation, which, at its simplest, is simply using a sample of the work done on the job as the test. If the sample is really representative of the job, success on the test necessarily implies success on the job.

That any job requires skills appropriate for only one type of validation technique is debatable. Take a job that includes typing as a major function. Obviously, a typing test can be validated by content validation if the test reflects the kind of typing the job requires. Criterion-related validation can be used if a motor function, such as finger dexterity, is viewed as the skill shared by people who could likely become good typists. Even construct validation can be used if the predominate mental trait of good typists is the ability to withstand boredom. If you were an employer, what kind of test would you use to improve your chance of winning a case challenging the test?

9. The Uniform Guidelines on Employee Selection Procedures, effective September 25, 1978, still look to the standards the industrial psychologists set for themselves. The test professionals, however, have relaxed their professional standards in line with the positions they took as amici in Washington v. Davis. See Division 14, American Psychological Association (Industrial-Organizational Psychology), Principles for the Validation and Use of Personnel Selection Procedures (1979). The Uniform Guidelines now provide that any one of the validation strategies is acceptable where appropriate. However, while the presumption of the EEOC guidelines has been eliminated, the same presumption still exists in the professional standards of industrial psychology. So, while the test expert should decide what type of validation strategy to use based on the skills, functions, and traits revealed in the job analysis, criterion validation is preferred because it is based on a comparison of two sets of data — test scores and job performance scores — that results in a number, the correlation coefficient, which is a mathematical expression of the relationship between test scores and job performance. In contrast, content validation starts with one empirical basis — job analysis data — and requires the test expert to argue that the test is, in fact, a sample of critical job behaviors shown in the analysis.

10. Guardians Assn. v. Civil Service Comm., 630 F.2d 79, 92 (2d Cir. 1980), described the legal significance of choosing a test validation theory. After first noting that construct validation could be used only if empirically validated, the court wrote:

> This content-construct distinction has a significance beyond just selecting the proper technique for validating the exam; it frequently determines who wins the lawsuit. Content validation is generally feasible while construct validation is frequently impossible.

Even the Guidelines acknowledge that construct validation requires "an extensive and arduous effort." The principal difficulty with construct validation is that it requires a technique that includes a criterion-related study. Developing such data is difficult, and tests for which it is required have frequently been declared invalid. As a result, a conclusion that construct validation is required would often decide a case against a test-maker, once a disparate racial impact has been demonstrated.

## GILLESPIE v. WISCONSIN
### 771 F.2d 1035 (7th Cir. 1985)

COFFEY, Circuit Judge:

. . . Ronald A. Gillespie is the named plaintiff of a class of approximately forty unsuccessful minority applicants for the position of Personnel Specialist I or Personnel Manager I with the State of Wisconsin. The examination challenged by Gillespie was the first step in the hiring process for these positions. Candidates whose scores on the written examination were above an acceptable level were invited to an interview. Responses to the interviewers were evaluated by the respective interviewers and each candidate was given a score. The candidates' written exam scores and the interview scores were totaled with veteran and/or minority applicants having points added to their total scores. Based on these total scores, the candidates were ranked on a list of certified candidates eligible for appointment to vacant state positions.

The Wisconsin Department of Employment Relations ("DER") developed the new written examination in question as former tests utilized by the Department were previously held to have had an inordinate adverse impact on minority applicants. As an initial step in the test development process, the DER convened a committee of "job specialists" who not only had personnel experience in positions similar to the Personnel Specialist/Personnel Manager I positions but also supervised employees in these positions. The job specialists were asked to analyze the positions in order that they might determine what tasks were required of a Personnel Specialist/Personnel Manager I to perform and to identify the knowledges, skills or abilities necessary to perform these tasks. The job specialists delineated the skills, abilities and knowledges required as: an ability to write standard English; interpersonal skills; decision-making; the ability to work under pressure; and the ability to establish priorities. After the committee reviewed and discussed the skills, abilities, and knowledge required, they rated each as to their respective importance.

Deborah Koyen, a DER employee specializing in recruiting and in developing employment examinations, utilized the list of knowledges, skills, and abilities to construct the written examination. In determining what form of test to implement, Koyen interviewed other government personnel departments concerning the type of test they utilize to screen applicants for entry level professional positions such as the Personnel Specialist/Personnel Manager I positions. After reviewing, weighing and considering their responses, the adverse impact of the previous test (the multiple-choice test), and the skills to be measured by the written test, Koyen decided to construct an essay type rather than a multiple-choice question and answer examination. The test written by Koyen was designed to test the applicants' abilities to use standard English and to analyze and organize information, leaving interpersonal skills to be tested at the interview level. The essay examination contained three questions. In the first question, the applicants were given a narrative description of a groundkeeper's duties and were given instructions on how to write a job description utilizing the narrative description. The instructions also contained an example of a complete job description. These extensive instructions on how to write a job description were also included in an instruction packet to be sent to applicants before the examination to aid the applicant in preparing for the exam. The second question directed the applicants to write a memorandum to another department member requesting certain information required for a departmental meeting. The third question presented statistical information about the minority enrollment in two schools and posed a hypothetical recruiting trip in which the recruiter, whose goal was to contact potential minority applicants, had time only to visit one school. The applicants were asked two questions: First, they were asked to choose which school to visit and to justify that choice. Secondly, they were asked what additional information about the schools they would like to have had before making their selection. Koyen presented the test to the job specialists and the committee agreed that the examination tested the necessary basic skills required for the position.

Furthermore, Koyen administered this test to lower level personnel specialists at the Division of Personnel to determine if the questions and the instructions were clear. Koyen also devised a grading system, established rating criteria, and trained graders to evaluate the examination. Koyen gave the graders sample examination answers to grade and examined the results of this trial grading to see if the graders understood the rating criteria and whether the respective graders applied the rating criteria in the same manner.

The test was given on February 9, 1980 to 451 applicants. Koyen divided the sixteen employees who were to grade the examinations into eight teams of two graders. The papers were distributed among the teams and each paper assigned to a team was evaluated by both graders. In addition, ten to twelve papers were given to all the grading teams. The teams were not told that all the graders were evaluating these particular papers. Koyen ran statistical tests of the reliability of the scores both between and within the grading teams and found that the graders were reliable in their application of the rating criteria. Koyen and other DER employees next examined the scores to determine a proper cut-off point; only applicants whose scores were above the cut-off point would be invited to the interviews. In arriving at the cut-off score, the DER attempted to maximize the number of minority applicants to be invited to the interview while at the same time restricting the total number of invitees in order that the interviewers might not be overwhelmed. One hundred eighty-four candidates, including eleven minority applicants, were invited to the interviews and, after the completion of the interviewing and rating process, nine applicants, three of which were minorities, were offered positions.

[The District Court determined] that the written examination had an adverse impact on minority applicants. Advancing to the second stage of the analysis of a disparate impact claim — whether the test was job-related . . . the district court found that the examination was job-related and was designed to directly measure specific skills important to job performance. Finally, the court determined that the plaintiff failed to show that other tests without a similarly undesirable disparate impact would serve the defendants' legitimate interest in obtaining qualified applicants.

A test is job-related if it measures traits that are significantly related to the applicant's ability to perform the job. *Griggs.* The Uniform Guidelines on Employee Selections Procedures provide that an employer may conduct professional validation studies to determine whether its employment tests are job-related. The Uniform Guidelines draw upon current psychological literature on psychometrics as well as standards of test validation established by the American Psychological Association.

§ 1607.5C. The Uniform Guidelines recognize three methods of validating employment tests: criterion-related, content, and construct validity. § 1607.5B. The choice of validation strategy depends upon the type of inference the user wishes to draw from the test scores. . . .

## A.  Appropriateness of the Choice of a Content Validation Strategy . . .

### 2.  Whether the Choice of a Content Validation Strategy Was Appropriate for the Characteristics to Be Measured

Gillespie points to the district court's finding that one purpose of the test was to measure an applicant's ability to prepare written position descriptions and argues that the testing of this ability was inappropriate because writing a job description is a skill readily learned within the first few months of employment. The Uniform Guidelines caution that, "[i]n general, users should avoid making employment decisions on the basis of measures of knowledges, skills or abilities which are normally learned in a brief orientation period, and which have an adverse impact." § 1607.5F. Use of tests which measure knowledge of factual information that will be acquired in a training program, "risks favoring applicants with prior exposure to that information, a course likely to discriminate against a disadvantaged minority." Guardians Assn. of New York City v. Civil Service Commn. of City of New York, 630 F.2d 79, 94 (2d Cir. 1980). A test must measure ability rather than factual information normally acquired during the training period. Id. The defendant in this action developed an extensive set of instructions for writing job descriptions and not only included these instructions with the test but also forwarded the instructions to the applicants before the test to aid the applicants in preparing for the exam. Specifically, the testimony at trial established that the defendants' express purpose in providing the instructions before the test was to remove the advantage some applicants may have gained from writing job descriptions in previous jobs, and to allow the applicants an opportunity to discuss the instructions with other persons, plus giving the applicants the opportunity to practice applying the instructions. The district court found that the test was developed to measure the applicants' abilities. A district court's findings of fact will not be overturned unless it is clearly erroneous. Fed. R. Civ. P. 52(a). On the basis of this record, we hold that the district court properly found that the test measured abilities — i.e., the abilities "to communicate in standard written English [and to] prepare basic written position descriptions" — rather than factual information normally acquired during the training period.

The one argument of the plaintiff's that merits discussion is that "skills in decision-making and priority setting . . . are mere rephrasings of such traits as common sense and judgment, items specifically precluded from a content-validated examination." The Uniform Guidelines prohibit testing for constructs with a content-validated test. . . . The specific issue raised by Gillespie is whether a plaintiff sufficiently demonstrates that a content validated test attempted to measure a construct merely by alleging that the test's goals are "rephrasings" of a construct.

Gillespie's free use of the lay definitions of "skills, decision-making and priority setting" fails to acknowledge that psychometricians and the Uniform Guidelines utilize operational definitions of terms. The Guidelines specifically provide:

> Where the job analysis also identified the knowledges, skills, and abilities used in work behavior(s), an operational definition for each knowledge in terms of a body of learned information and for each skill and ability in terms of observable behaviors and outcomes, and the relationship between each knowledge, skill, ability and each work behavior, as well as the method used to determine this relationship, should be provided (essential).

§ 1607.15C(3). By resorting to lay definitions of terms in his "rephrasing," the plaintiff asks the court to ignore the Guidelines explicit requirement that knowledges, skills and abilities be operationally defined. Furthermore, the plaintiff's reliance on lay definitions distracts attention from a critical question under Title VII in determining whether a content validation strategy could be used — whether the trait is too abstract to be measured with a content validated test. Accordingly, we hold that "rephrasing" the goal of the test as a construct is insufficient to prove that a content validated test attempted to measure a construct rather than existing job skills, knowledge or behavior.

The test for determining whether a characteristic is too abstract to be measured by a content validated test is given by the Uniform Guidelines:

> . . . . The closer the content and the context of the selection procedures are to work samples or work behaviors, the stronger is the basis for showing content validity. As the content of the selection procedure less resembles a work behavior, or the setting and manner of the administration of the selection procedure less resemble the work situation, or the result less resembles the work product, the less likely the selection procedure is to be content valid, and the greater the need for other evidence of validity.

§ 1607.14C(4). Thus, the court must evaluate the test for: (1) the degree to which the nature of the examination procedure approximates the job conditions; (2) whether the test measures abstract or concrete qualities; and (3) the combination of these factors, i.e., whether the test attempts to measure an abstract trait with a test that fails to closely approximate the working situation.

After analyzing Gillespie's misstatements of the standards to be applied, we reach the ultimate issue of whether the content validation strategy adopted by the DER was appropriate under the circumstances. Both Deborah Koyen and Daniel Wallock, a testing expert employed by the DER, testified that the purpose of the written examination was to screen out those persons who did not possess the fundamental skills necessary to perform as a Personnel Specialist/Personnel Manager I. A test that screens candidates for fundamental skills may be validated by the content validation procedure. Furthermore, a review of the characteristics to be measured by the test and of the form of the test reveals that a content validation method was appropriate. The abilities to communicate in standard written English, to prepare a written job description, and to place the analysis of a recruiting problem in acceptable form are concrete, observable and quantifiable characteristics. Moreover, planning a recruiting trip and writing a job description and a memorandum closely simulate the actual work performed by a Personnel Specialist/Personnel Manager I. Because the test measured concrete characteristics in a form that simulated actual work behavior, we hold that the content validation procedure could be employed to validate the test.

### B.    SUFFICIENCY OF THE CONTENT VALIDATION STUDY
####     CONDUCTED BY THE DER

Gillespie argues that the job analysis performed by the DER as part of its content validation of the written test was inadequate, thus rendering the content validation study insufficient, because the job specialists were not trained in psychometrics and were unfamiliar with the job of Personnel Specialist/Personnel Manager I. . . . An examination of the record reveals that the job specialists had either worked as Personnel Specialists or Managers or had supervised employees in these positions. Since the record amply demonstrates that the employees were knowledgeable about the positions, they were qualified to be job specialists. Because the position analysis was conducted by qualified job specialists who identified the necessary knowledges, skills and abilities required for the work and also ranked and weighted the elements as to the importance for the position, we hold that the plaintiff's contention that the position analysis was inadequate fails to find support in the record.

We turn now to Gillespie's second attack on the sufficiency of the content validation study, his contention that the skills measured by the test did not reflect the work done in the personnel positions. Gillespie alleges that the test was not representative of the tasks performed by Personnel Specialist/Personnel Manager I because the examination did not test all or nearly all skills required. Title VII does not require an employer to test all or nearly all skills required for the occupation. To be representative for Title VII purposes, an employment test must neither: (1) focus exclusively on a minor aspect of the position; nor (2) fail to test a significant skill required by the position. Testimony at trial established that the ability to communicate in standard written English, to analyze and organize information, and to use these skills to write, edit or review job descriptions; to write memoranda; or to plan recruiting trips were vitally important in performing as a Personnel Specialist/Personnel Manager I; thus, the record reveals that the test did not focus exclusively on a minor aspect of the work. Moreover, the plaintiff does not suggest that the examination failed to test a significant skill required by the position. Accordingly, we hold that the examination was representative because it tested skills necessary for adequate performance as a Personnel Specialist/Personnel Manager I.

## C. RELIABILITY AND USE OF THE TEST SCORES . . .

Gillespie also argues that the cut-off score was not logically chosen and that the DER improperly used the scores on the written examination to rank-order the applicants. An employer using a test to screen job applicants must fulfill two requirements to justify the choice of a cut-off score: The test scores must be reliable, *Guardians*, and the employer must have some justifiable reasoning for adopting the cut-off score. Id. APA Standards at 66-67. Grader reliability is determined by having a sample of test papers independently scored by two examiners and correlating the two scores thus obtained by each examinee. An employer may establish a justifiable reason for a cut-off score by, for example, "using a professional estimate of the requisite ability levels, or, at the very least by analyzing the test results to locate a logical 'breakpoint' in the distribution of scores." *Guardians*. Koyen testified that two examiners graded each applicant's paper. Additionally, all of the examiners scored one batch of papers. Koyen statistically analyzed the test results to determine how well each grader's score correlated with the other grader on the team. Further, Koyen's examination of the scores of the tests that were graded by all of the examiners determined how well the teams correlated with one another. Thus, the record reveals that Koyen determined the reliability of the scores with recognized psychometric techniques. Furthermore, Koyen and Wallock testified that the cut-off point was selected in order that the DER could interview as many minority candidates as possible while at the same time assuring that the candidates possessed the minimum skills necessary to perform as a Personnel Specialist/Personnel Manager I. In addition to selecting as many qualified minority applicants as possible, the cut-off score was set so that the interviewers would not be overwhelmed by the sheer number of candidates. Therefore, the record demonstrates that the DER's cut-off score was based upon an estimate of the ability levels needed, maximized the number of minority candidates and preserved the integrity of the interview process. The plaintiff has failed to demonstrate that the cut-off score chosen by the DER was illogical and unjustified.

Finally, we turn to Gillespie's contention that the DER improperly used the written examination scores to rank-order the applicants. "Use of a selection procedure on a ranking basis may be supported by content validity if there is evidence from job analysis or other empirical data that what is measured by the selection procedure is associated with differences in levels of job performance." EEOC Questions and Answers, Q. 62. Gillespie contends in his appellate brief, that the testimony of his expert, Dr. Raynor, established that the written examination score caused a disparate impact on the final, rank-ordered score. However, on cross-examination Gillespie's own expert witness stated that his testimony had not addressed the questions of whether "there was any statistically adverse impact as to the composite exam or as to the oral exam." We hold that the plaintiff failed to demonstrate that the use of the written exam scores in determining a final score caused a disparate impact on minority applicants.

## NOTES

1. Where the job entails reading and writing, content validation is available for tests that provide a sample of the reading and writing required in the job itself. Content validation has even been stretched to apply to multiple-choice tests for police officer jobs, jobs that did not include answering multiple-choice questions. In Guardians Assn. v. Civil Service Comm., 630 F.2d 79, 92 (2d Cir. 1980), the court noted: "Content validation is generally feasible while construct [or criterion] validation is frequently impossible." Therefore, if the defendants could not show that content validation was appropriate, plaintiff would prevail. But in deciding which strategy would be used, the court thought the appropriate analogy was a spectrum:

> [I]t would seem that abilities, at least those that require any thinking, and constructs are simply different segments along a continuum reflecting a person's capacity to perform various categories of tasks. This continuum starts with precise capacities and extends to increasingly abstract ones — from the capacity for filling out forms to the capacity for exercising judgment.
>
> Recognition that abilities and constructs are not entirely distinct leads to a conclusion that a validation technique for purposes of determining Title VII compliance can best be selected by a functional approach that focuses on the nature of the job. The crucial question under Title VII is job relatedness — whether or not the abilities being tested for are those that can be determined by direct, verifiable observation to be required or desirable for the job.

Id. at 93. The answer to that question should be based on the job analysis. But that avoids the question of how well the test works. The theory underlying content validation is that a sample of the job will be a good test of the abilities necessary to do the job. Once the content of the test is divorced from the content of the job, however, there is no basis for drawing that conclusion. In Association of Mexican-American Educators v. State of California, 183 F.3d 1055 (9th Cir. 1999), the court held that the California teaching credential exam did not violate Title VII because the state was not acting as an employer in using it. Nevertheless, in dicta, the court said the test was content valid because the skills the test addressed were necessary for teachers, even though there was no showing that the test was in any way a sample of the job of teaching. Similarly, in Williams v. Ford Motor Co., 187 F.3d 533 (6th Cir. 1999), the court upheld a paper-and-pencil test used for unskilled labor positions in an automobile plant because the job analysis was well done; again, there was no showing that the test was in any way a sample of the jobs for which it was used. See also Firefighters Inst. for Racial Equality v. City of St. Louis, 220 F.3d 898 (8th Cir. 2000) (multiple-choice exam for fire chiefs content valid); Bryant v. City of Chicago, 200 F.3d 1092 (7th Cir. 2000) (multiple-choice exam for police lieutenants content valid).

2. By way of comparison, criterion-related validation, which uses a statistical comparison between the scores test-takers earn on the test and their scores performing the job, provides both a statistical and an inferential basis for concluding that the test does predict job performance. The *Guardians* court concluded that the exam tested for three abilities that were involved in police work: the ability to remember details, the ability to fill out forms, and the ability to apply general principles to specific facts. Assuming that those abilities are necessary to do police work, there was still no proof that a person who scored well on the test would excel at remembering details, filling out forms, or applying general principles to specific facts when confronted with the need to do so as a police officer.

3. The *Guardians* court was concerned that limiting content validation to job samples would render the technique inappropriate for validating tests for admission to a training program: "If the attributes the test attempts to measure are too general, they are likely to be regarded as constructs, in which event validation is usually too difficult to be successful; if the attributes are fairly specific, they are likely to be appropriate for content validation, but this too will prove unsuccessful because the specific attributes will usually be learned in a training program or on the job." 630 F.2d at 92. Compare Commonwealth of Pennsylvania v. Flaherty, 983 F.2d 1267 (3d Cir. 1993), where the court thought a training program was essential to police officer skill development and thus allowed test scores to be correlated with performance in the police academy. Is this criterion-related validation or content validation?

4. The *Gillespie* court did not address the reliability of rank ordering the test results. The court in *Guardians* commented on the error of measurement, which is the variation that occurs in scoring when a person retakes the same or a similar test:

> [E]rror of measurement . . . is a statistical phenomenon indicating the degree to which scores on successive tests will be subject to inevitable random variation, no matter how carefully the test-makers have eliminated or at least lessened the effects of extraneous factors within their control. The error of measurement can be calculated by use of the standard deviation concept. For any test, regardless of how carefully it was prepared, statistical analysis, based on the normal distribution curve, shows that there is a 68% probability that successive scores would fall within a range of one standard deviation from an actual score and a 95% probability . . . that successive scores would fall within a range of two standard deviations from the actual score.

630 F.2d at 102. Simply put, if there is no clear difference between the meanings of scores of 94 and 95 on a test because the error of measurement would find the two scores equivalent, then rank ordering the test scores, so that people with scores of 95 get jobs before people scoring 94, is not justified in terms of any real difference in ability. In Bryant v. City of Chicago, 200 F.3d 1092, 1099-1100 (7th Cir. 2000), the court upheld the use of rank ordering on a content validated test: "[W]hen an exami-

nation measures ability with sufficient differentiating power to justify rank-ordering, it is permissible for the City to set a cutoff score at the point where the rank-ordering provides the number of promotions to fill the City's available openings."

5. In *Guardians*, the court upheld the police test as content valid, but held that the validation was too weak to support using the particular cutoff score or rank ordering. In Berkman v. City of New York, 812 F.2d 52 (2d Cir. 1987), the Second Circuit upheld rank ordering the results of a physical ability test for firefighters based on speed of completion. "Completion in less than four minutes was scored 100, completion in each of the six 30-second intervals between four and seven minutes was scored downward from 95 to 70 in five-point steps, and completion in more than seven minutes was considered failing. This produced seven passing grades or 'bands.'" Id. at 55. Does the use of bands solve the error of measurement problem? No women and 6,780 men received scores in the two highest bands. The test, combined with the results of a written exam, would be used to offer firefighter positions to 6,500 firefighters over four years. Does that mean that functionally, if not formally, everybody in the lowest bands "failed" the test? In Pietras v. Board of Fire Commissioners of the Farmingville Fire District, 180 F.3d 468 (2d Cir. 1999), a test was found to be invalid because the defendant used as a test score the average time in which job incumbents, who were mostly male, had completed the challenged agility test. Because there was no showing that this time reflected the demands of the job and since many successful incumbents were below average on the test, the requirement was not job-related.

6. In Williams v. Ford Motor Co., 187 F.3d 533 (6th Cir. 1999), the court affirmed as criterion related a pencil-and-paper test for unskilled labor jobs in automobile plants. Using a "concurrent" strategy, the employer picked a sample of 105 employees who had passed the test and been hired. It then compared their test scores with supervisor evaluations. The coefficient correlation between the test scores and the supervisor rates was .30, showing a low but positive relationship between the two. The court did not consider significant the claim that concurrent validation could not show how well or poorly applicants who were not hired because of low test scores would perform as workers.

7. In Allen v. Entergy Corp., 181 F.3d 902 (8th Cir. 1999), the court affirmed as a criterion-related validation an aptitude test for operations and maintenance workers in a fossil fuel power plant. Each employee was required to take an aptitude test in a basic area other than the worker's own craft to determine his suitability for continued employment in new "multi-craft" positions that were to be created. Those who did not pass the test after two attempts were laid off. The court found that the tests were job-related and plaintiffs failed to show that seniority in the previous single-craft positions would be an equally accurate predictor of success in the new multi-craft positions.

## 2. Bona Fide Seniority Systems

Section 703(h) also provides an exception to Title VII liability for seniority systems:

[I]t shall not be an unlawful employment practice for an employer to apply different standards of compensation, or different terms, conditions, or privileges of employment pursuant to a bona fide seniority or merit system . . . provided that such differences are not the result of an intention to discriminate because of race, color, religion, sex, or national origin.

# LESTER C. THUROW, THE ZERO SUM SOCIETY
## 188-189 (1980)

Imagine a race with two groups of runners of equal ability. Individuals differ in their running ability, but the average speed of the two groups is identical. Imagine that a handicapper gives each individual in one of the groups a heavy weight to carry. Some of those with weights would still run faster than some of those without weights, but on average, the handicapped group would fall farther and farther behind the group without the handicap.

Now suppose that someone waves a magic wand and all of the weights vanish. Equal opportunity has been created. If the two groups are equal in their running ability, the gap between those who never carried weights and those who used to carry weights will cease to expand, but those who suffered the earlier discrimination will never catch up. If the economic baton can be handed on from generation to generation, the current effects of past discrimination can linger forever.

If a fair race is one where everyone has an equal chance to win, the race is not fair even though it is now run with fair rules. To have a fair race, it is necessary to (1) stop the race and start over, (2) force those who did not have to carry weights to carry them until the race has equalized, or (3) provide extra aid to those who were handicapped in the past until they catch up.

While these are the only three choices, none of them is a consensus choice in a democracy. Stopping the race and starting over would involve a wholesale redistribution of physical and human wealth. This only happens in real revolution, if ever. This leaves us with the choice of handicapping those who benefitted from the previous handicaps or giving special privileges to those who were previously handicapped. Discrimination against someone unfortunately always means discrimination in favor of someone else. The person gaining from discrimination may not be the discriminator, but she or he will have to pay part of the price of eliminating discrimination. This is true regardless of which technique is chosen to eliminate the current effects of past discrimination.

An individualistic ethic is acceptable if society has never violated this individualistic ethic in the past, but it is unacceptable if society has not, in fact, lived up to its individualistic ethic in the past. To shift from a system of group discrimination to a system of individual performance is to perpetuate the effects of past discrimination into the present and the future. The need to practice discrimination (positive or negative) to eliminate the effects of past discrimination is one of the unfortunate costs of past discrimination. To end discrimination is not to create "equal opportunity."

---

In Quarles v. Philip Morris, 279 F. Supp. 505 (E.D. Va. 1968), a system of formal race segregation among different departments ended, but the departmental seniority system continued. Blacks, wishing to transfer to formerly white departments, would lose their seniority once they transferred. Declaring that "Congress did not intend to freeze an entire generation of Negro employees into discriminatory patterns that existed before the act," the court created the "present effects of past discrimination" concept of liability. "[T]he present differences in departmental seniority of Negroes and whites that result from the company's intentional, racially discriminatory hiring policy before January 1, 1965 [the effective date of Title VII] are not validated by the proviso of § 703(h)."

Despite uniform adoption of the present effects concept of discrimination among the lower courts, the Supreme Court disavowed the approach in International Brotherhood of Teamsters v. United States, 431 U.S. 324 (1977), and United Airlines, Inc. v. Evans, 431 U.S. 553 (1977). In *Teamsters* the collective bargaining agreement created separate seniority lines for city driver jobs and line driver jobs. Blacks had been confined to the city driver jobs and excluded from the better line driver positions. To move to the better jobs, minority drivers would have to surrender their city driver seniority. The Supreme Court held that the mere perpetuation of earlier discrimination does not make a seniority provision in a collective bargaining agreement illegal. "[A]n otherwise neutral, legitimate seniority system does not become unlawful under Title VII simply because it may perpetuate pre-Act discrimination." Because of § 703(h), Title VII has no effect on the legality of a seniority system even where, owing to discrimination that occurred before Title VII became effective, women and minority males were handicapped in their present ability to compete for jobs. "[T]hat conclusion is inescapable even in a case, such as this one, where the pre-Act discriminatees are incumbent employees who accumulated seniority in other bargaining units."

That the Supreme Court repudiated the present effects of past discrimination concept was made clear in United Airlines, Inc. v. Evans, 431 U.S. 553 (1977). The plaintiff had been discharged under a no-marriage policy, which policy was struck down as discriminating against women in an action not brought by the plaintiff in this suit. When the employer rescinded the policy, the plaintiff reapplied and was rehired but was denied her previously accumulated seniority. Because the plaintiff had not timely challenged her original discharge and because the discriminatory policy underlying her original discharge was no longer in force when she was rehired, she had nothing to timely attack as discriminatory except the operation of the seniority system, which carried into the present the past effects of the company's discrimination against her. The essence of her claim was that she had less seniority than she would have had absent that earlier discriminatory discharge. Despite this present effect of past discrimination, the Court found she had no cause of action. The plaintiff "is correct in pointing out that the seniority system gives present effect to a past act of discrimination. But United was entitled to treat that past act [her discharge] as lawful after [she] failed to file a charge of discrimination within [the statutory time limit]."

*Teamsters* and *Evans* demonstrate the demise of the present effects test of discrimination as a separate theory of liability. The Court turned *Quarles* on its head: by including § 703(h), Congress did intend to freeze an entire generation of employees in the discriminatory patterns that existed before Title VII was enacted.

Just as important, the *Teamsters* Court also treats § 703(h) as creating a defense to disparate impact claims for actions taken pursuant to a bona fide seniority system. "Were it not for § 703(h), the seniority system in this case would seem to fall under the *Griggs* rationale." Thus, whenever the plaintiff establishes a prima facie case of disparate impact discrimination, one possible defense is that the barrier to employment opportunity that plaintiff has shown is really the product of a bona fide seniority system.

Since § 703(h) is an exception from liability for disparate impact discrimination, the seniority system issue should be an affirmative defense with the burden of proof and persuasion on the defendant. If the employer succeeds in carrying the burden of establishing its affirmative defense, then the plaintiff has a surrebuttal step of proving that the system had its genesis in intentional discrimination.

The first element of the defense may be for the employer to show that the seniority system is part of a collective bargaining agreement negotiated by union and management. An employer attempting to defend against a disparate impact case may not be successful if all that can be shown is that the employer unilaterally uses seniority to determine job benefits and burdens. It is true that, by its terms, § 703(h) does not specify that the defense applies only to seniority systems that are part of collective bargaining agreements between unions and management. But all of the Supreme Court cases involving the § 703(h) defense have involved labor contracts. And, in one case involving seniority but not a collective bargaining agreement, the Supreme Court did not even address § 703(h). In Nashville Gas Co. v. Satty, 434 U.S. 136 (1977), the employer required pregnant employees to take a formal leave of absence that carried with it the loss of accumulated seniority. Although the Court concluded that the employer's "policy of denying accumulated seniority to female employees returning from pregnancy leave violated section 703(a)(2) of Title VII," the opinion nowhere dealt with § 703(h). The most obvious reason is that the seniority rules in the case were unilaterally promulgated by the employer and did not involve a union-negotiated collective bargaining agreement. Since seniority is one of the classic issues of unionism and since Congress knew that when it enacted § 703(h), the affirmative defense provided by that section should apply only to seniority systems that have been collectively bargained by labor and management.

An ADA case recently cast doubt on whether a seniority system must be the product of a collective bargaining agreement to be protected by § 703(h). In U.S. Airways, Inc. v. Barnett, 122 S. Ct. 1516 (2002), defendant had unilaterally promulgated a seniority system. Plaintiff requested as an accommodation that the seniority system not be applied to protect him from losing a position to an employee with greater seniority. The Court held that, "in the run of cases," a requested accommodation that would conflict with the rules of a seniority system is not reasonable. Whether or not the seniority system is the product of collective bargaining, such systems generally create expectations by employees of fair treatment and encourage employee loyalty. Those values would be undermined were an employer required to demonstrate, on a case-by-case basis, special circumstances that would permit it to adhere to the system in the face of a requested accommodation. Such case-by-case analysis "might well undermine the employees' expectations of consistent, uniform treatment — expectations upon which the seniority system's benefits depend." Id. at 122 S. Ct. 1524. Nonetheless, a plaintiff may present evidence showing that, under the particular circumstances of his case, an exception to the seniority system would in fact be reasonable. While Barnett is not a Title VII case, it may well be that even unilaterally promulgated seniority systems will be held to be sheltered from disparate impact liability by § 703(h).

The second element of the defense is for the employer to prove that its challenged policy is a traditional component of a system of seniority. First, there must in fact be a system; the ad hoc or occasional use of seniority by an employer will not fall within the exception since that is not the systematic use of seniority. Second, while seniority connotes length of service, the Supreme Court has rejected the bright-line test of what is sheltered by § 703(h) in favor of a broader test set by commonly accepted notions of what constitutes a seniority system.

In California Brewers Assn. v. Bryant, 444 U.S. 598 (1980), plaintiffs challenged a clause in a collective bargaining agreement in the state's brewing industry that required a temporary employee to work at least 45 weeks in a single calendar year in order to become a permanent employee. Permanent employees were entitled to greater benefits than temporary employees, and no black had ever attained permanent-employee status because of the operation of the 45-week rule. While the court of appeals had found that the 45-week rule was not a seniority system nor part of a seniority system because it was independent of total time worked or overall length of service, the Supreme Court reversed. "'[S]eniority' is a term that connotes length of employment. A 'seniority system' is a scheme that, alone or in tandem with non-'seniority' criteria, allots to employees ever improving employment rights and benefits as their relative lengths of pertinent employment increase." Since § 703(h) by its terms protects seniority systems and since Title VII was passed against a backdrop of labor policy favoring unregulated bargaining between labor and management, even those parts of a seniority system that do not turn on length of service are sheltered from disparate impact liability:

> In order for any seniority system to operate at all, it has to contain ancillary rules that accomplish certain necessary functions, but which may not themselves be directly related to length of employment. For instance, every seniority system must include rules that delineate how and when the seniority time clock begins ticking, as well as rules that specify how and when a particular person's seniority may be forfeited. Every seniority system must also have rules that define which passages of time will "count" toward the accrual of seniority and which will not. Every seniority system must, moreover, contain rules that particularize the types of employment conditions that will be governed or influenced by seniority, and those that will not. Rules that serve these necessary purposes do not fall outside § 703(h) simply because they do not, in and of themselves, operate on the basis of some factor involving the passage of time.

Id. at 607-08.

This might suggest that a seniority system is whatever a union and management say it is. But the Court stopped short of allowing all employment practices to be sheltered from disparate impact attack just because they were set forth in a clause or article of a collective bargaining agreement entitled "seniority." Section 703(h) does not sweep within its protection "employment rules that depart fundamentally from commonly accepted notions concerning the acceptable contours of a seniority system, simply because those rules are dubbed 'seniority' provisions or have some nexus to an arrangement that concededly operates on the basis of seniority." Id. at 608. For example, an educational prerequisite used as a threshold requirement for entering a seniority track is not sheltered by § 703(h) just because it was included in an article in a labor contract dealing with seniority. Further examples that would not be protected by § 703(h) are aptitude or physical tests, or a standard that gives effect to subjectivity.

The final step in the analysis of the seniority system defense is plaintiff's surrebuttal that the operation of the seniority system is the product of intentional disparate treatment discrimination. In Pullman-Standard v. Swint, 456 U.S. 273 (1982), the Court treated a challenge to the bona fides of a department seniority system having a disparate impact on black workers, who would be required to forfeit their departmental seniority if they transferred to a different department, including departments that had been restricted to whites before passage of Title VII. The Supreme Court held the court of appeals had violated Rule 52 of the Federal Rules of Civil Procedure, which requires that findings of fact not be set aside unless clearly erroneous. The Supreme Court treated the issue as a question of fact as to whether there existed disparate treatment discrimination:

> [H]ere the District Court was not faulted for misunderstanding or applying an erroneous definition of intentional discrimination. It was reversed for arriving at what the Court of Appeals thought was an erroneous finding as to whether the differential impact of the sen-

iority system reflected an intent to discriminate on account of race. That question, as we see it, is a pure question of fact, subject to Rule 52's clearly erroneous standard.

Id. at 287. Prior to *Swint,* there was considerable confusion as to whether the surre-buttal in a seniority system case utilized normal principles of disparate treatment dis-crimination or whether some special test applied only to seniority cases. One source of the confusion was that in *Teamsters* the seniority system, with separate seniority for line and city drivers, seemed to be integral to the successful exclusion of blacks and Hispanics from the line driver jobs, which was found to be intentional disparate treat-ment in the same decision. The second source was language in *Teamsters* preserving the outcome, if not the reasoning, of the earlier cases brought under the present-effects-of-past-discrimination theory:

> Insofar as the result in *Quarles* and in the cases that followed it depended upon findings that the seniority systems were themselves "racially discriminatory" or had their "genesis in racial discrimination," . . . the decisions can be viewed as resting upon the proposi-tion that a seniority system that perpetuates the effects of pre-Act discrimination cannot be bona fide if an intent to discriminate entered into its very adoption.

Treating the language "genesis in racial discrimination" as establishing a special test for reviewing seniority systems, James v. Stockham Valves & Fittings Co., 559 F.2d 310 (5th Cir. 1977), adopted a four-factor test to evaluate whether a seniority system was bona fide. After *Swint,* it now seems clear that there is no special test for seniority systems. The four factors from *James,* while not the exclusive way to analyze a chal-lenge to the bona fides of a seniority system, may be of assistance because they do help to focus on the question of intent. The factors are:

(1) whether the seniority system operates to discourage all employees equally from transferring between seniority units;
(2) whether the seniority units are in the same or separate bargaining units (if the latter, whether that structure is rational and in conformance with industry practice);
(3) whether the seniority system has its genesis in racial discrimination; and
(4) whether the system was negotiated and has been maintained free from any il-legal purpose.

## 3. Bona Fide Merit and Piecework Systems

Section 703(h) sets forth an exception to disparate impact liability for bona fide merit and piecework systems:

> [I]t shall not be an unlawful employment practice for an employer to apply different standards of compensation, or different terms, conditions, or privileges of employment pursuant to a bona fide . . . merit system, or a system which measures earnings by quan-tity or quality of production . . . provided that such differences are not the result of an in-tention to discriminate.

Systems that measure compensation by quantity of production are piecework sys-tems: the more a worker produces, the more he or she is paid. Since quantity of pro-duction obviously is a factor in determining a quality of a worker, piecework systems (sometimes called incentive systems) are one type of merit system. A system that mea-sures compensation by quality of production may also be part of a piecework system in the sense that rejects do not count for pay. A quality-of-production system might be broader, however, in that it involves the evaluation of the quality-of-worker performance. In that sense the quality-of-production notion is really just another name for a merit system. The general concept of this exception is that better job performance is rewarded.

The only substantial gloss on the merit system defense comes from a police test case. In Guardians Assn. v. Civil Service Commn., 633 F.2d 232 (2d Cir. 1980), *aff'd on other grounds*, 463 U.S. 582 (1983), the defendants, having failed to show that a challenged test to select police recruits was job related, argued that the rank ordering of applicants by test scores constituted the application of a bona fide merit system, which was exempt from attack by disparate impact discrimination. While the plaintiffs argued that, by its terms, the merit system defense did not encompass hiring practices, the court did not decide this question; instead it held that "a hiring system that ranks applicants according to their performance on discriminatory examinations cannot claim the status of a 'bona fide merit system' within the meaning of the statute." Id. at 252. Further, the court distinguished the merit system defense from the seniority defense established in *Teamsters*:

> There was no contention in *Teamsters* that the seniority system under scrutiny did not measure precisely what it purported to measure, that is, the length of time a given employee had been on the job. . . . [T]he merit system in the instant case does not measure what it purports to measure. . . . Once it has been determined that an examination has a disproportionate impact on minority groups that it is not job-related, one cannot logically characterize a system of hiring solely on the basis of the results of the test as a "merit" system — for whatever the test does measure it does not have merit: it does not measure fitness for the job in question, which is surely the only logical meaning of the term "merit" in the hiring context.

The application of the *Griggs* job-related test in *Guardians* was straightforward because defendants were merely trying to protect an employment test that had not been validated pursuant to the treatment of tests under § 703(h). The question is whether in other situations the seniority system precedents are appropriate in a merit system case. Suppose, for example, that an employer sets up a system of evaluation of employees to assess their job performance, with the results of that merit determination used to make promotions or to grant wage increases. If the results were to have a disparate impact on women or minority males, would the employer have a stronger argument than the employer did in *Guardians* that the systematic use of merit should be sheltered from disparate impact attack by the operation of § 703(h), just as a seniority system is sheltered by that section's treatment of bona fide seniority systems? The *Guardians* court would say no: "Section 703(h) makes sense only if the term 'bona fide merit system' is understood to refer to merit in areas related to the necessities of the business, not 'merit' in the abstract." While piecework systems are by their nature job related and seniority pursuant to a seniority system is clearly defined, merit determinations beyond quantity of production are open to abstract, vague, and therefore potentially discriminatory influences. Thus, the merit system defense is justified only if the employer demonstrates that the system is job related.

## 4.   *Yet Another Surrebuttal?*

As we have seen, not only does § 703(h) create exceptions for professionally developed employment tests, bona fide seniority systems, and bona fide merit systems, but

§ 703(k)(1)(A)(ii) also permits an employee to show that alternative employment practices exist that are less discriminatory. Section 703(k)(1)(A)(ii), is not, by its express terms, limited to a surrebuttal of the defendant's proof of business necessity. Its plain meaning suggests that plaintiff can demonstrate an alterative employment practice to practices that are sheltered by § 703(h), including professionally developed tests, bona fide seniority systems, and bona fide merit systems. This suggests that, in theory at least, *Teamsters* has been opened to attack since seniority systems are typically demanded of employers by unions; historically, employers have resisted seniority as destructive of management prerogatives. Non-unionized employers rarely utilize seniority systems except for benefits such as vacations and other fringe benefits. In practice, how likely is it that a plaintiff will be able to show a viable alternative employment practice if the defendant establishes a bona fide seniority system as opposed to validating a professionally developed test? In Bryant v. City of Chicago, 200 F.3d 1092 (7th Cir. 2000), plaintiff proved that a test had a disparate impact and the defendant then proved that the test had been properly validated. The court held that at that point the "burden shifts back to the plaintiff to prove that there was another available method of evaluation which was equally valid and less discriminatory that the defendant refused to use." Id. at 1094. See also AMAE v. California, 231 F.3d 572 (9th Cir. 2000) (en banc); Fitzpatrick v. City of Atlanta, 2 F.3d 1112 (11th Cir. 1993); Bullington v. United Air Lines, Inc., 186 F.3d 1301 (10th Cir. 1999); Allen v. Entergy Corp., 181 F.3d 902 (8th Cir. 1999); Price v. City of Chicago, 251 F.3d 656 (7th Cir. 2001).

### NOTE ON IMPACT ANALYSIS UNDER THE ADEA

There is no clear answer to whether the disparate impact theory applies under the Age Discrimination in Employment Act. That Act was passed in 1967 and, therefore, preceded the *Griggs* decision. Nevertheless, the ADEA's parallels to Title VII led many to believe that the same theories should apply under both statutes. The Supreme Court has never resolved the question. The issue was first raised in Geller v. Markham, 635 F.2d 1027 (2d Cir. 1980). There the Second Circuit applied disparate impact analysis to invalidate a school district policy restricting teacher hires to persons in lower pay grades. Because the grades increased with experience, the policy had a disparate impact on older teachers. Plaintiff's expert testified that 92.6 percent of Connecticut teachers between 40 and 65 years old (the protected age group under the ADEA at that time) had more than five years' experience as compared to only 62 percent of teachers under 40. The Second Circuit found that plaintiff had established disparity of impact and that defendant's cost-saving justification did not constitute a business necessity. The Supreme Court denied certiorari, but did so over the dissent of then-Justice Rehnquist. He doubted both the invocation of disparate impact under the ADEA and its application in the case at bar:

> This Court has never held that proof of discriminatory impact can establish a violation of the ADEA, and it certainly has never sanctioned a finding of a violation where the statistical evidence revealed that a policy, neutral on its face, has such a significant impact on all candidates, not simply the protected age group.

451 U.S. at 948. Further, Justice Rehnquist questioned the lower court's rejection of defendant's cost-justification defense. More recently, in Hazen Paper Co. v. Biggins

(reproduced at page 87), Justice Kennedy, citing *Geller*, again questioned the extension of disparate impact analysis to the ADEA. Justice Kennedy was joined by Justices Rehnquist and Thomas. The opinion for the Court by Justice O'Connor emphasized that the ADEA is not violated where the employment decision is "wholly motivated by the factors other than age, . . . even if the motivating factor is correlated with age." 507 U.S. at 611. But the Court explicitly noted, "[W]e have never decided whether a disparate impact theory of liability is available under the ADEA, . . . and we need not do so here. Respondent claims only that he received disparate treatment." Most recently, the court granted certiorari to resolve the issue, but after oral argument, dismissed the writ as improvidently granted. Adams v. Florida Power Co., 535 U.S. 228 (2002).

Circuit decisions immediately after *Geller* were generally receptive to the theory. E.g., Leftwich v. Harris-Stowe State College, 702 F.2d 686 (8th Cir. 1983); Allison v. Western Union Tel. Co., 680 F.2d 1318 (11th Cir. 1982).* Cf. Massarsky v. General Motors Corp., 706 F.2d 111 (3d Cir. 1983). Further, the EEOC believes that disparate impact applies under the ADEA, 29 C.F.R. § 1625.7(d) (1993).

Since *Biggins*, however, five appellate courts have squarely held that disparate impact is inapplicable to ADEA cases, Mullin v. Raytheon Co., 164 F.3d 696 (1st Cir. 1999); Ellis v. United Airlines, Inc., 73 F.3d 999 (10th Cir. 1996); Lyon v. Ohio Educ. Assn. & Profl. Staff Union, 53 F.3d 135 (6th Cir. 1995); EEOC v. Francis W. Parker School, 41 F.3d 1073 (7th Cir. 1994) (2-1); Adams v. Florida Power Co., 255 F.3d 1322 (11th Cir. 2001), *cert. dismissed as improvidently granted*, 535 U.S. 228 (2002). See generally Mack A. Player, *Wards Cove Packing* or Not *Wards Cove Packing?* That is Not the Question: Some Thoughts on Impact Analysis Under the Age Discrimination in Employment Act, 31 U. Rich. L. Rev. 819 (1997) (arguing in favor of impact analysis but urging a less demanding business necessity defense by focusing on "reasonable factors other than age"); Steven Kaminshine, The Cost of Older Workers, Disparate Impact, and the Age Discrimination in Employment Act, 42 Fla. St. L. Rev. 229, 275-78 (1990); Mack Player, Title VII Impact Analysis Applied to the Age Discrimination in Employment Act: Is a Transplant Appropriate?, 14 U. Tol. L. Rev. 1261 (1983); Judith Johnson, Semantic Cover for Age Discrimination: Twilight of the ADEA, 42 Wayne L. Rev. (1995); Earl M. Maltz, The Legacy of *Griggs v. Duke Power Co.*: A Case Study in the Impact of a Modernist Statutory Precedent, 1994 Utah L. Rev. 1353. See also Keith R. Fentonmiller, The Continuing Validity of Disparate Impact Analysis for Federal-Sector Age Discrimination Claims, 47 Am. U. L. Rev. 1071, 1072-73 (1998) ("the unique statutory language of section 15, combined with its legislative history and parallel to corresponding provisions of Title VII mandate the continuing application of disparate impact analysis in ADEA cases against the federal government" regardless of whether disparate impact is more generally applied under that statute).

Relevant to the debate about the applicability of disparate impact under the ADEA is § 4(f)(1), which allows differentiations on the basis of "reasonable factors other than age." See page 658. It has been argued that this section suggests that criteria not motivated by age considerations are permissible or at least subject to a less strict standard of justification than "business necessity." Pamela S. Krop, Note, Age Discrimi-

---

* The Eighth Circuit, while reaffirming the application of disparate impact analysis to ADEA claims, required the plaintiff to show an impact on the entire over-40 group. It therefore affirmed summary judgment against the EEOC, which had claimed only that the employer's reduction in force had a disparate impact on employees aged 55 and older. EEOC v. McDonnell Douglas Corp., 191 F.3d 948 (8th Cir. 1999). Accord, Lowe v. Commack Union Sch. Dist., 886 F.2d 1364 (2d Cir. 1990).

nation and the Disparate Impact Doctrine, 34 Stan. L. Rev. 837, 844-45 (1982). But the phrasing of this exception in the ADEA contrasts sharply with its Equal Pay Act counterpart, which permits wage discriminations when they are based on "any other factor other than sex." 29 U.S.C.S. § 206(d)(1) (2003). The ADEA does not permit *any* other-than-age factor, but only *reasonable* other-than-age factors. Arguably, by this language the ADEA explicitly adopts a version of the disparate impact concept of business necessity by applying a test of reasonableness to factors that are not age based in the intent sense. The contrary argument focuses on the structure of the defense: "It shall not be unlawful . . . to take any action otherwise prohibited . . . where the differentiation is based on reasonable factors other than age." 29 U.S.C.S. § 623(f)(1) (2003). If disparate impact discrimination is not "otherwise prohibited" by the text of the Act, the "reasonable factors" defense is not a proper basis for creating liability. But could one respond that disparate impact age discrimination is illegal and that the reasonable factors defense is simply a statutory expression of the business necessity defense?

The First Circuit, in Mullin v. Raytheon Co., 164 F.3d 696 (1st Cir. 1999), proffered another reason why the ADEA does not support a disparate impact cause of action — the legislative asymmetry caused by the 1991 Amendments, where Congress explicitly created a cause of action for disparate impact in Title VII, but not in the ADEA. This argument may seem strained, since the 1991 Congress' failure to amend the ADEA could not, under normal principles of statutory interpretation, shed any light on the intent of the 1967 Congress that enacted the statute. But *Raytheon* does raise an interesting question. Assuming disparate impact applies under the ADEA, how does *Wards Cove* affect the analysis? Presumably, the *Wards Cove* Court believed that its analysis was a proper interpretation of Title VII as originally written. Wouldn't the same analysis then necessarily apply under the ADEA if it includes a disparate impact theory? The Civil Rights Act of 1991 amends Title VII as to disparate impact, but not the ADEA. Is *Wards Cove*, then, still good law under the ADEA? If so, does that case restrict the theory so much that the underlying question whether disparate impact applies under the ADEA becomes unimportant? See Faulkner v. Super Value Stores, Inc., 3 F.3d 1419, 1429 n.8 (10th Cir. 1993) (applicability of Civil Rights Act of 1991 to ADEA remains an open question). In Houghton v. SIPCO, Inc., 38 F.3d 953 (8th Cir. 1994), the court ordered a new trial because the jury was improperly instructed that, once the plaintiff proved a prima facie case, defendants must show by a preponderance of the evidence that their actions were justified by business necessity. Id. at 959. The proper charge should not place the burden of proof on the defendant and must use the *Wards Cove* standard of business justification. Id. See Howard Eglit, The Age Discrimination in Employment Act, Title VII, and the Civil Rights Act of 1991: Three Acts and a Dog That Didn't Bark, 39 Wayne L. Rev. 1096 (1993).

# Chapter 6

## The Interrelation of the Disparate Treatment and Disparate Impact Theories of Discrimination

The individual disparate treatment, systemic disparate treatment, and disparate impact approaches to discrimination have each developed separately. The courts have yet to synthesize these approaches into a coherent field theory of employment discrimination law. This chapter will attempt to lay the groundwork for that synthesis.

### PROBLEM 6.1

You are an attorney who has been visited by a potential client, Ann Able, who claims she was denied a promotion because she is an African American.

The employer, Shuffled Papers Inc., hires many people for entry-level clerical jobs. In a metropolitan area with an 18 percent minority population, the entry level is made up of 16 percent blacks and Hispanics — 160 of the 1,000 clericals. Persons promoted to supervisor come from the pool of clericals; other than promoting from within, no announced policy describes the promotion process. Openings are not posted, and people apparently are simply picked for promotion by the managers, who are predominately white and male. Only 2 of the 50 supervisors are minority group members.

Able asked her supervisor, Bernie Baker, if she could be promoted. He told her that he thought she was well qualified and that he would suggest her name to his manager. After several other people were promoted, Able asked Baker why she had not been chosen. He told her that she was "in the running," but had to wait until her turn came.

In your initial discussions with the lawyer for Shuffled Papers, you were told that, to be considered for promotion to supervisor, a clerical employee must have two years of college and three years of experience. All of the supervisors satisfy those prerequisites, but some clericals, including Able, also satisfy them. Twenty percent of the white clerical workers meet these minimum requirements, while only 10 percent of the black clerical workers have both three years of experience and two years of college.

Evaluate Able's case in light of all three general theories of discrimination.

---

As you read through the following material, reconsider what theories of liability are available to you on behalf of Able and what defenses Shuffled Papers can assert in response to each theory of liability.

## A.   KEEPING DISPARATE TREATMENT AND DISPARATE IMPACT ANALYSIS DISTINCT

Disparate impact analysis is neither necessary nor relevant in a pure disparate treatment case. The point is obvious with respect to individual disparate treatment: a plaintiff typically will present her case by focusing on facts relevant to her situation; there will be no need to develop broader theories. Similarly, the employer will not seek to justify, in business necessity terms, an individual employment decision. Under individual disparate treatment analysis, the employer's usual strategy will be to show a "legitimate, nondiscriminatory reason" for its actions. Because this is easier to establish than "business necessity," few employers will try to shoulder the heavier burden.

It is true that a plaintiff bringing an individual case of disparate treatment might try to establish that the employer's "legitimate, nondiscriminatory reason" has a disparate impact. Such a case, however, will then become a garden-variety disparate impact case. More typically, the plaintiff asserting an individual disparate treatment theory will put into evidence discriminatory patterns of employer conduct not to show disparate impact, but to raise an inference of systemic disparate treatment. This will enable the trier of fact to place the claims of intentional individual discrimination in the proper context and will help with the plaintiff's proof of pretext, as McDonnell Douglas Corp. v. Green (reproduced at page 97) suggested.

The inapplicability of disparate impact analysis to systemic disparate treatment claims is less obvious, but no less clear upon consideration. With respect to formal systems of disparate treatment, the Supreme Court has several times spoken directly. First, in Los Angeles Dept. of Water & Power v. Manhart (reproduced at page 200), the employer used a gender-explicit criterion to differentiate pension contributions, but tried to argue that the use of gender was merely a proxy for real differences in longevity between men and women. The Court first held that an employment practice requiring "2,000 individuals to contribute more money into a fund than 10,000 other employees simply because each of them is a woman, rather than a man, . . . does not pass the simple test of whether the evidence shows 'treatment of a person in a manner which but for that person's sex would be different.'" Thus, it constitutes discrimination and a violation of Title VII unless within an exemption. 435 U.S. 702, 711 (1978). The Court rejected, among several asserted justifications, a cost-based defense because Title VII has no provision permitting discrimination when cost savings are involved. The defendant, by arguing that the higher costs of providing benefits for women as a group explained the requirement of higher contributions from every woman, was claiming that the absence of a disparate impact on women was a defense to a claim of disparate treatment of them. That is, the employer claimed that, since the difference between the longevity of men and women was real, the formal gender classification did not have any discriminatory effect on women because the class of women received as much as the class of men. *Manhart* thus stands for the proposition that the absence of disparate impact does not prevent a finding of disparate treatment liability where facial discrimination is concerned. Similarly, in Trans World Airlines, Inc. v. Thurston (reproduced at page 206), the Court stressed that the absence of a disparate impact does not affect a suit challenging a formal discriminatory policy under the Age Discrimination in Employment Act.

The Court's third encounter with the relationship between the two systemic theories where facial discrimination was involved proved the most definitive. In International Union, UAW v. Johnson Controls, Inc. (reproduced at page 268), the Supreme Court was confronted with several circuit court decisions upholding fetal-protection policies on the grounds they were a "business necessity." The Court rejected this approach: such policies facially discriminate on the basis of gender and pregnancy, and business necessity is not a defense to intentional discrimination. Rather, it can be employed only to defend a disparate impact attack. This result was codified by the Civil Rights Act of 1991, which added § 703(k)(2), 42 U.S.C.S. § 2000e-2(k)(2) (2003), to Title VII: "A demonstration that an employment practice is required by business necessity may not be used as a defense against a claim of intentional discrimination under this title."

This amendment also resolved a question not formally raised by *Manhart*, *Thurston*, or *Johnson Controls*: the application of disparate impact analysis where the plaintiff, unable to show formal systemic disparate treatment, seeks to establish disparate treatment by showing a pattern or practice of conduct that gives rise to an inference of intentional discrimination. The seminal case, of course, is Teamsters v. United States (reproduced at page 210). The language of § 703(k)(2) makes clear that the employer in such a case may not prevail by proving business necessity. Rather, as we have seen, it may prevail by disproving the pattern or by offering an alternative explanation for the inference of discriminatory intent the plaintiff seeks to draw. It should be noted, however, that — while business necessity is not a formal defense in this setting — the employer's nondiscriminatory reasons for acting in a certain way may rebut an inference of discriminatory intent that would otherwise be drawn from statistics or other circumstances.

## B.   THE RELATIONSHIP BETWEEN DISPARATE IMPACT AND TREATMENT WHERE THERE IS A STATISTICAL SHOWING OF EFFECTS

Where a formal employment policy is not involved, the common thread to both systemic theories, disparate treatment and disparate impact, is finding discrimination from the effects of an employer's decisions. In disparate treatment, of course, the effects create an inference of discriminatory intent; in disparate impact, the effects by themselves establish a violation unless the defendant can show business necessity. What is the relationship between the two distinct modes of analysis when both rest on a similar factual showing?

The Supreme Court has not spoken clearly on the relationship between disparate treatment and disparate impact theories where the prima facie case of disparate treatment is based on statistical evidence. Footnote 15 of *Teamsters* (reproduced at page 210), which gives a thumbnail comparison of the two systemic theories, concludes: "Either theory may, of course, be applied to a particular set of facts." Under this approach, a plaintiff could use the systemic disparate treatment theory in tandem with the disparate impact theory to maximize the chances of a successful attack. As applied to *Teamsters*, the plaintiff could have claimed not merely that the defendant intentionally discriminated against blacks and Hispanics, but also that, even if the inference of intent to discriminate could be rebutted, the employer used policies that had a disparate impact.

The second, perhaps countervailing, authority came from Furnco Construction Co. v. Waters, 438 U.S. 567, 575 n.6 (1978), involving an attack on a hiring system in which the employer, instead of maintaining a permanent workforce, appointed a superintendent for each new job and delegated to him the task of finding a workforce. The superintendents hired only bricklayers they knew to be qualified and, therefore, did not accept applications at the job site. Such a system would seem vulnerable to attack under the disparate impact theory because white superintendents would tend not to know black workers, but that theory was not before the Supreme Court. See Julia Lamber, Discretionary Decisionmaking: The Application of Title VII's Disparate Impact Theory, 1985 U. Ill. L. Rev. 869, 877 n.28; Alfred W. Blumrosen, The Legacy of *Griggs*: Social Progress and Subjective Judgments, 63 Chi.-Kent L. Rev. 1 (1987); Jane Rigler, Title VII and the Applicability of Disparate Impact Analysis to Subjective Selection Criteria, 88 W. Va. L. Rev. 25 (1985); Julia Lamber, Alternatives to Challenged Employee Selection Criteria: The Significance of Nonstatistical Evidence in Disparate Impact Cases Under Title VII, 1985 Wis. L. Rev. 1. Nevertheless, then-Justice Rehnquist in footnote 6 distinguished disparate treatment and impact claims in language that seemed to suggest disparate impact doctrine could be used only when a test or other "particularized" requirement was involved. Under this approach, there would presumably be separate domains for each theory.

The possibility of such a bifurcated approach generated considerable scholarly debate and a split among the courts of appeals. Ultimately, as we have seen, the Supreme Court refused to limit disparate impact analysis to "objective" employment practices. In Watson v. Fort Worth Bank & Trust (reproduced at page 342), a majority of the Court agreed that subjective as well as objective selection procedures are subject to impact analysis. The significance of this was, however, simultaneously undercut by the plurality's dilution of the entire theory. In Wards Cove Packing Co. v. Atonio (reproduced at page 326), a majority emerged that substantially modified disparate impact law along the lines suggested by the *Watson* plurality. At that point, then, presumably all employment practices were subject to either systemic disparate treatment or disparate impact attack, but the utility of the impact theory was questionable.

With the passage of the Civil Rights Act of 1991, this picture changed radically. Section 703(k)(1)(A), 42 U.S.C.S. § 2000e-2(k)(1)(A) (2003), now provides for establishing an "unlawful employment practice" by the disparate impact theory. This presumably reaches all employment practices and, therefore, confirms the *Watson* decision that the theory reaches both objective and subjective practices. It remains true, however, that disparate treatment attacks may be preferred by plaintiffs because prevailing on this issue effectively wins the case (except where a bona fide occupational qualification or affirmative action is involved), while proof of disparate impact leaves the defendant able to prevail by showing business necessity.

As we have seen, however, the 1991 Act redefined the disparate impact theory to the extent that it applies to multicomponent employment practices. Without repeating the analysis in Chapter 5, the statute adopted earlier restrictions on the disparate impact theory by requiring the plaintiff to "demonstrate that each particular challenged employment practice causes a disparate impact, except that if the complaining party can demonstrate to the court that the elements of a respondent's decisionmaking process are not capable of separation for analysis, the decisionmaking process may be analyzed as one employment practice." § 703(k)(1)(B).

This would seem to create a distinction between the two systemic models: a plaintiff can now use the impact theory to challenge any practice, whether "objective" or "subjective," but only so long as she can identify the practice and show that it (as distinguished from other components of the process) has a disparate impact. A plaintiff may, however, utilize bottom-line or "snapshot" statistics to make out a disparate treatment case. Such bottom-line statistics can be used under the disparate impact model only if she can also show that "the elements of a respondent's decisionmaking process are not capable of separation for analysis."

In broad outline, this describes the relationship between the two systemic theories, but a more refined analysis suggests intriguing interactions that may not be immediately apparent. For example, Segar v. Smith, 738 F.2d 1249 (D.C. Cir. 1984), which preceded many of the developments we have surveyed, nevertheless raises some possibilities regarding the way the two theories work in tandem. Chief Judge J. Skelly Wright wrote the opinion for the court in this suit against the Drug Enforcement Agency in which the plaintiffs used both systemic theories. He stressed that both theories can rest on the same proof:

> Though allocations of proof differ [for each theory], an important point of convergence exists in class actions like the present case. Both pattern or practice disparate treatment claims and disparate impact claims are attacks on the systemic results of employment practices. The pattern or practice claim amounts to an allegation that an observed disparity is the systemic result of an employer's intentionally discriminatory practices. The disparate impact claim amounts to an allegation that an observed disparity is the systemic result of a specific employment practice that cannot be justified as necessary to the employer's business. *Consequently the proof of each claim will involve a showing of disparity between the minority and majority groups in an employer's work force.*

Id. at 1267 (emphasis added). If the plaintiff makes out a prima facie case of systemic disparate treatment by "providing evidence — often in statistical form — of a disparity in the position of members of the plaintiff class and *comparably qualified* whites," id. (emphasis in original), the defendant must respond, either by refuting the claim that a disparity exists or by "offer[ing] an explanatory defense; such a defense amounts to a claim that an observed disparity has not resulted from illegal discrimination." Id.

The refutation path we have already explored, but the "explanatory defense" has further implications:

> To rebut a disparate treatment challenge the employer can argue that the observed disparity between the plaintiff class and the majority group does not support an inference

of intentional discrimination because there is a legitimate, nondiscriminatory explanation for the disparity. For example, the defendant might come forward with some additional job qualification — not sufficiently perceptible to plaintiffs to have permitted them to account for it in their initial proof — that the plaintiff class lacks, thus explaining the disparity. . . .

[T]he employer's effort to rebut the pattern or practice claim by articulating a legitimate nondiscriminatory explanation may have the effect of putting before the court all elements of a traditional disparate impact case. By its explanation of an observed disparity the employer will typically pinpoint an employment practice (or practices) having a disparate impact on a protected class. And to rebut plaintiffs' case the employer will typically be required to introduce evidence showing that the employment practice in fact caused the observed disparity. In this situation, between the plaintiffs' prima facie showing of disparity and the defendant's rebuttal explanation of the disparity, the essential elements of a disparate impact case will have been placed before the trier of fact. Such a case is ripe for resolution using disparate impact analysis. Though the plaintiffs in a disparate treatment case bear the burden of persuasion as to the existence of a disparity, the defendant bears the burden of proving the business necessity of the practices causing the disparity. Thus when an employer defends a disparate treatment challenge by claiming that a specific employment practice causes the observed disparity, and this defense sufficiently rebuts the plaintiffs' initial case of disparate treatment, the defendant should at this point face a burden of proving the business necessity of the practice.

The only difference between this situation and the traditional disparate impact case is that in the latter the plaintiff articulates the employment practice causing the adverse impact and forces the employer to defend it, while in the former the employer articulates the employment practice and must then go on to defend it.

Id. at 1268-70.

To understand this, consider a simple hypothetical. Plaintiff launches a disparate treatment attack, showing that the employer's workforce, which consists of non-skilled workers, is 99 percent white in a geographic labor market that is 23 percent minority. Her statistician finds the correlation between race and employment statistically significant. Defendant responds by arguing that it does not intentionally discriminate in hiring; rather, it employs only workers who reside in the town in which it is located, and the town happens to be 99 percent white. See NAACP, Newark Branch v. Town of Harrison, 940 F.2d 792 (3d Cir. 1991). In statistical terms, defendant is showing a co-variable — residence — that is related to race and is arguing that it is residence, not race, that explains its actions.*

Putting aside burdens of proof, the persuasiveness of defendant's rebuttal of the inference of discrimination raised by plaintiff's statistics turns entirely on whether the employer utilizes an intent-neutral practice that happens to have a disparate impact on blacks. Proof of that, as Segar v. Smith suggests, may mean that defendant can avoid disparate treatment liability, but only by showing disparate impact liability — although it can avoid both if it also shows that the policy producing the impact is justified by business necessity. See also Powers v. Alabama Dept. of Educ., 854 F.2d 1285 (11th Cir. 1988).

---

* Of course, the employer might have chosen to employ only town residents precisely because this policy would exclude blacks. This issue will be resolved by exploring the reasons for the adoption of the policy. Note that, in cases like this, the employer has defined the labor market by its policy. Unless the motivations for that definition can be attacked, the employer's practices can be analyzed under disparate treatment only in terms of whether it discriminated within the market it defined. A disparate impact challenge, however, can be broader: the very definition of the labor market may create the adverse impact. See notes 6-10 on pages 362-363.

As the *Segar* court recognized, this "damned if you do and damned if you don't" approach raised opposition, but the cases resisting such analysis have been basically superseded by subsequent developments, most notably *Watson* and the Civil Rights Act of 1991. While the continued authority of *Segar* itself may be questioned, the case is a relatively straightforward meshing of the two theories. Indeed, it is difficult to avoid the conclusion that, no matter who proves the various elements of a disparate impact claim, once it is shown, the employer can defend only by establishing business necessity. Further, *Segar* stressed that its analysis is not as radical as it might first appear:

> An employer will face the justificatory burden only after a plaintiff class has shown a disparity in the positions of members of the class and the majority group who appear to be comparably qualified; if plaintiffs fail to make their prima facie case, the employer never faces this justificatory burden. But if the plaintiffs have made their prima facie case, the employer, to avoid liability under the disparate treatment theory, will have to advance some nondiscriminatory explanation for the disparity. An employer's claim that it cannot isolate the cause of the disparity will be unlikely to deflect the force of the inference of discrimination from plaintiffs' proof. The defendant will in all likelihood point to a specific job qualification or performance/evaluation rating as the explanation for the observed disparity. Thus application of disparate impact in this situation will not . . . place on the employer any additional burden of articulation; to rebut the disparate treatment claim the employer will have had to articulate which employment practices cause an observed disparity. Nor will the employer be forced to justify all of its employment practices. The employer will be required to show the job relatedness of only the practice or practices identified as the cause of the disparity.

738 F.2d at 1271.

Can this result be avoided? The defendants might claim that Title VII specifies that "[a]n unlawful employment practice based on disparate impact is established under this title only if (i) *a complaining party* demonstrates that a respondent uses a particular employment practice that causes a disparate impact. . . ." § 703(k)(1)(A)(ii) (emphasis added). Under a literal interpretation, the defendants' proof would not satisfy this standard. This, however, not only carries literalism beyond reason, but also fails to account for the litigation process. Frequently, a plaintiff's proof consists precisely of the defendant's stipulations and admissions. Further, it seems senseless to require the plaintiff through elaborate discovery to prove what the employer claims is the truth anyway.

How does the Civil Rights Act of 1991 bear on this question? By restricting a disparate impact attack to "a particular employment practice that causes a disparate impact," the statute narrows the possibility that the plaintiff will use a statistical showing of the defendant's overall employment picture to support a disparate impact challenge. Such a claim is allowed only when the plaintiff can also show that the individual components of the whole process are not capable of separation.

But the new statute does not bar the plaintiff from using such proof to make out a systemic disparate treatment case. The statute does contain a no-cause defense — "If the respondent demonstrates that a specific employment practice does not cause the disparate impact, the respondent shall not be required to demonstrate that such practice is required by business necessity," § 703(k)(1)(B)(ii) — which is by its terms inapposite to a systemic disparate treatment challenge. Presumably, then, the defendant is left under the new statute basically where it was when Segar v. Smith was decided: to avoid a finding of disparate treatment, it can prove a practice giving rise to disparate impact. This is, in fact, the converse of § 703(k)(1)(B)(ii).

If this is correct, why would an employer come forth with a "neutral" reason for a statistical disparity? Remember that the only defense to disparate treatment is the bfoq, which is difficult to establish. And in race cases, the statute theoretically provides no defense at all except for affirmative action. Thus, it may be important for the defendant to shift the analysis from disparate treatment to disparate impact, where it has at least the defense of business necessity.

Another possible limitation on the use of the two theories in tandem relates to what quantum of impact is sufficient to make out a plaintiff's case under each theory. The previous discussion has assumed a showing of discriminatory effects sufficient to establish a prima facie case of disparate treatment. If the plaintiff cannot muster such evidence, the treatment case will fail, and he can then prevail only by showing sufficient evidence of disparate impact — either of a particular practice or of the bottom line if the employer's process cannot be separated into its component parts.

Certainly, some have argued that a greater level of impact is necessary to show disparate treatment than would suffice for a disparate impact claim. Indeed, why would a plaintiff ever rely on disparate impact if a prima facie case of disparate treatment could be established based on the same evidence of impact? Consider this question as applied to, say, height and weight prerequisites. If they are set so high that virtually no women can satisfy them, does that make out both systemic disparate treatment and impact cases? Suppose plaintiff shows that the passing rate for blacks on a pre-employment test is 70 percent of that for whites. That would seem sufficient to make out a prima facie case of disparate impact. Does it also make out a prima facie case of disparate treatment?

Answering these questions requires revisiting the bases of each theory. These cases are basically statistical, and from the point of view of statistical analysis, the question is always the same, whether the law is assessing the proof from an impact or a treatment perspective. The question, for a statistician, is whether gender or race is correlated with employment decisions. Statisticians do not draw cause and effect inferences; they simply determine how probable it is that a given result could follow if race (or sex or age) were unrelated to the decision-making process. In making that assessment, statisticians can help the court determine whether there is a cognizable disparity (e.g., whether the results from a sample are likely to reflect the universe from which they were drawn) and/or the quantum of disparity (e.g., whether black employees are excluded at a rate twice that of white employees).

But it is not a statistical question whether the correlation results from the intentional use of race or sex as opposed to the use of factors (such as education and height) that themselves correlate with race or sex. In the weight and height example, the employer could have used those factors without any intent to discriminate against women, even though it was aware that women would suffer disproportionately. This is, of course, the point of Personnel Administrator v. Feeney (reproduced at page 251). The application of intentional discrimination theory depends, then, not on the statistical correlation, but on a judgment (informed by other evidence) as to whether discriminatory intent was likely to explain such a correlation. In some cases, of course, common sense indicates that no intent to discriminate can be inferred from a given disparity. For example, where the disparity is real, but the quantum of difference is very small, it is highly unlikely that an employer motivated by discriminatory intent would choose a device that had a very limited effect in achieving its exclusionary goals.

The Supreme Court has not addressed this question, and the lower courts seem confused by it. While there is authority requiring a showing of statistical significance to establish a disparate impact case, e.g., Fudge v. City of Providence Fire Dept., 766

F.2d 650 (1st Cir. 1985), it is not clear whether the plaintiffs must show such significance in a systemic disparate treatment case based primarily on statistics. See also Thomas v. Metroflight, Inc., 814 F.2d 1506, 1511 n.4 (10th Cir. 1987). It is true, however, that a systemic treatment case could adduce individual instances of discrimination and that the statistical showing might not need to be as rigorous in light of such nonstatistical proof.

On the other hand, could it be argued that, absent some anecdotal proof of discrimination, even proof of statistical significance is not a sufficient basis to infer intent to discriminate? Statistical significance establishes at most that race is correlated with the employment decision; it cannot establish that the decision-maker was motivated by racial reasons. If race is highly correlated with some other factor on which the employer relies in its decisions, the defendant may not have been guilty of intentional discrimination. Is the defendant's opportunity to show such a nondiscriminatory reason sufficient to ensure a fair result?

In impact cases, statistics serve a different purpose. Rather than providing an indirect basis to infer intent, they prove more or less directly that an employment practice correlates with race. Is this difference relevant to either the quantum or the significance of the disparity that must be proved by the plaintiff?

Some decisions seem to focus on the quantum of impact. We saw in Chapter 5 that the fact of impact is not necessarily enough if the disparity between the favored and the disfavored groups is not large. The *Metroflight* court wrote that "[b]eyond a requirement of statistical significance, the Court may require in disparate impact cases that the disparity be 'substantial' as well." Id. Can the same be said for disparate treatment cases? Won't a small disparity also undercut any inference of discrimination that might be drawn from the evidence? Indeed, isn't the intuitive view that a large impact is necessary to draw an inference of intent?

Some have suggested that there is a two-tier test for disparate treatment and disparate impact. A higher showing is needed to prove disparate treatment and to shift to the employer the burden of coming forth with a justification, even if the employer does so by claiming that the disparity is merely the result of policies with a disparate impact. But a lower showing will trigger a finding of disparate impact if it is statistically significant, although if it is too low, there may be no prima facie violation of Title VII. Are any of these points clarified by the following case?

## FISHER v. TRANSCO SERVICES-MILWAUKEE, INC.
### 979 F.2d 1239 (7th Cir. 1992)

DILLIN, District Judge.

. . . At all relevant times prior to March of 1984, The Great Atlantic & Pacific Tea Company, Inc. (A&P), through its subsidiary Kohl's Food Stores, Inc., owned and operated a retail grocery warehouse where plaintiffs-appellants Fisher and Kirchhoff had worked since 1970 as order selectors (selectors). As selectors, appellants were responsible for processing requests for goods, which included retrieving and loading the goods, and completing some required paperwork.

In March of 1984, A&P contracted with Transco Service Corporation, through its subsidiary, defendant-appellee Transco Services-Milwaukee, Inc. (Transco), to operate the warehouse. Approximately five months after the transfer of management, Transco instituted A&P's "Measured Day Work Program" in order to measure and evaluate the performance of its full-time selectors, including appellants.

At the heart of A&P's Program was a computer which analyzed each incoming order and assigned the number of "leveled minutes" needed for a selector to complete it. In calculating this time, the computer considered the goods requested, particularly their sizes, weights, and locations in the warehouse, and made adjustments for such variables as the distance between the starting area and the loading platform, and the degree of difficulty in loading a particular good.

Every leveled minute of work assigned to a selector earned the selector a proportional number of "rest allowance minutes" for personal needs. The leveled minutes and rest allowance minutes were summed to determine the "standard minutes" needed to complete an order. A selector's performance was calculated by taking the ratio of standard minutes to the actual time expended.

During an eight hour day, which is 480 minutes, a selector was expected under the Program to perform 407 minutes of leveled work and receive 73 minutes of rest allowance. At all times relevant, Transco expected a standard-to-actual ratio of one to one, i.e., 100 percent. Any selector who failed to maintain this ratio on a weekly basis might be subject to discipline.

Specifically, until all selectors achieved a 100 percent performance ratio, those selectors whose performance ratios fell into the lower 20 percent of those working that week were subject to progressive discipline. After the first week of low production, counseling and an oral warning were to be given. If a second week of low production occurred, additional counseling and a written warning were to be given. If a third, another written warning, as well as a one-day suspension; for a fourth, a written warning and a three day suspension. Finally, if the employee's performance level fell in the bottom 20 percent for a fifth time, the employee became subject to discharge. The weeks of poor performance did not need to be consecutive, but if discipline was administered, a one week grace period was to be granted before discipline would again be given.

[According to Transco, the plaintiffs failed to rank in the upper 80 percent of selectors for five weeks each. Both were terminated. They were age 42 and 45 at termination. Plaintiffs claimed they had been erroneously disciplined three times and should not have been terminated]. There is evidence to support these contentions.

Transco ended its Program on August 3, 1985, after 48 weeks. During this time 1,182 weekly measurements were taken, of which only 20 were at or above the 100 percent level. As a result of the Program, 11 out of the 52 selectors who worked for at least five weeks were fired, of whom 10 were age 40 or older.

To succeed in this action, Fisher and Kirchhoff must prove that they would not have been discharged "but for" their age. There exist two possible theories under which Fisher and Kirchhoff may assert their claims. First, they may argue that they have suffered disparate treatment because of their age. Second, they may assert that their employer's practice, while not necessarily intended, resulted in a significant disparate impact upon its older workers.

We will first consider the theory of disparate treatment. Under it, appellants may prove their claim in two ways. First they may meet their burden head on by presenting evidence, direct or circumstantial, that age was the determining factor in their discharge. Second, and the more common, they may utilize the indirect, burden-shifting method of proof used in Title VII cases. See McDonnell Douglas Corp. v. Green. Appellants have opted for the latter.

Under the indirect method of proving disparate treatment, appellants must set forth a prima facie case to create a presumption of discrimination. In discharge cases such as the present, plaintiffs must show that (1) they were in the protected class (persons over the age of 40), (2) they were doing their jobs well enough to meet their employer's legitimate expectations, (3) they were discharged or demoted, and (4) the employer sought a replacement for them.

If the plaintiff is successful, the burden of production shifts to his employer to articulate a legitimate, nondiscriminatory reason for the discharge. If such an articulation is forthcoming, the presumption dissolves, and the burden of production shifts back to the plaintiff to show that the employer's proffered reason is a pretext for discrimination.

It is clear that appellants were members of the class protected by the ADEA, and that they were discharged. In addition, we agree with appellants that until this appeal Transco had not challenged the contention that appellants were replaced and cannot do so now. Thus, remaining at issue is whether the appellants were performing their jobs well enough to meet Transco's legitimate expectations.

Transco's expectations as to the appellants' performances are wholly dependent upon the Program alleged by appellants to be a pretext for discrimination. We find that in this situation, the issue of legitimate performance is best merged with the issue of pretext. This approach is logical, for if the conditions placed upon the appellants by the Program are found to be illegitimate, it follows that Transco's expectations were likely pretextual, and vice-versa. Further, to hold otherwise would unnecessarily insulate Transco from the burden of articulating a nondiscriminatory reason for the discharge of the appellants. This would clearly not further the purpose of the ADEA.

For the above reasons, we believe that the appellants have effectively created a rebuttable presumption of discrimination. Thus, the burden of production is shifted to Transco to articulate a legitimate reason for appellants' discharge. This burden is not difficult to satisfy. Transco "need not persuade the court that it was actually motivated by the proffered reasons." Texas Department of Community Affairs v. Burdine. It is sufficient if its proffered reason raises a genuine issue of material fact as to whether it discriminated against the plaintiff. Id.

Transco relies upon appellants' poor performance under the Program as the basis for discharging the appellants. Since the Program was created after extensive studies, we find that Transco has met its burden of production. Therefore, the burden of production now shifts back to Fisher and Kirchhoff to show that the Program was really a pretext for discrimination. In support of a finding of pretext, appellants contend that Transco's Program was unreasonable in its demands and was not implemented in a neutral manner.

Despite the fact that Transco's standard under the Program, i.e., a 100 percent performance level, was seemingly unreasonable in that this level was achieved very rarely by any selector, and in most weeks was not achieved at all, we agree with the District Court that this does not, standing alone, show intentional discrimination. However, we believe that this standard, when coupled with the alleged manner of the Program's implementation, raises a genuine issue of material fact as to the Program being a pretext for age discrimination.

Appellants argue that erroneous disciplines occurred under the Program twenty-two times, of which 18 were applied against older workers and four against younger ones, and that the rate at which Transco disciplined workers decreased substantially after it had terminated several of its older workers. Because of this, appellants contend that eight younger workers who should have been fired were not, and that six older workers, including appellants, were fired when they should not have been.

[Some errors were indeed committed.] For example, for the week ending 10/13/84, 35 selectors were measured and none achieved a 100 percent level. Thus, seven of these constituted the lower 20 percent. However, appellant Fisher, who had received a performance level of 70.0% was disciplined despite his being one percent above the 20 percent cut-off, while a younger selector, who had a level of 69.7%, was not.

Transco argues that this error and others "are nothing more than rounding problems in . . . [appellants' expert's] data base." However, this is merely an assertion and is not documented. In sum, we believe that whether the alleged errors present in Transco's implementation of the Program, coupled with the very high standards under the Program, render the Program a pretext for age discrimination presents a genuine issue of material fact.

Next to consider is the least developed aspect of this case, the appellants' claim of disparate impact. To establish unlawful disparate impact under the ADEA, as under Title VII, an employee must first show that an employer utilizes a particular employment practice that results in a disparate impact upon a protected class of workers. If the employee makes such a showing, the employer must then set forth how the challenged practice serves, in a significant way, its legitimate employment goals, i.e., the business necessity of the practice. However, no proof of discriminatory intent is necessary.

Eleven terminations took place as a result of the Program, and 52 selectors were involved, of which 27 were age 40 or above. Of the 11 terminated, 10 were of a protected age. It is true that we, like other courts, are reluctant to render conclusions in a disparate impact claim based upon small statistical samples. However, this is not a hard and fast rule and generally some substantial evidence of the unreliability of the statistics is asserted before it is applied. In this case, where 10 of 27 older employees were terminated, as against 1 of 25 younger ones, it does not require expertise in differential equations to observe that an adverse ratio of approximately 10 to 1 is disproportionate. Thus, while the statistical analysis will have to be fully developed and presented at trial, we believe that the granting of summary judgment in favor of Transco on this issue by the District Court was premature.

The District Court found in the alternative that even if the appellants could show a disparate impact, the appellants had not rebutted Transco's claim that the Program was justified by business necessity. We disagree.

The standard required under the Program was so high that out of 1,182 attempts to meet it, the workers were successful only 20 times. Moreover, the Program was abandoned after 48 weeks, after several older employees had been eliminated, and was replete with errors in its administration. Under these circumstances, we believe that the District Court's grant of summary judgment was inappropriate. Simply put, whether the Program implemented at Transco was consistent with business necessity likewise presents a genuine issue of material fact.

### NOTES

1. We saw in Chapter 5 that it is not clear that the disparate impact theory applies under the ADEA, but this case could arise as easily if the Measured Day Work Program resulted in adverse impact on women or minorities. In any event, *Transco* offers an opportunity to assess the interaction of disparate treatment and disparate impact theories.

2. Disparate treatment is relatively easy to analyze: Fisher, for example, seems to have been treated worse than the plan would, in theory, permit. In these

circumstances, the discharge of an older worker might itself establish a prima facie case because one might expect an employer with an elaborate plan for rating job performance to ensure that the plan was implemented correctly. A failure to do so to the disadvantage of an older worker might be sufficient to create a prima facie case.

3. The plaintiffs had more than this: not only were there two older workers who sued, but they also offered evidence that instances of erroneous discipline occurred more frequently against older workers and that "the rate at which Transco disciplined workers decreased substantially after it had terminated several of its older workers." In short, the plaintiffs presented evidence from which it could be found "that eight younger workers who should have been fired were not, and that six older workers, including appellants, were fired when they should not have been."

4. Whether all this proof was necessary merely to make out a prima facie case of disparate treatment discrimination is debatable, but the disproportionate effects on older workers clearly became relevant (indeed, critical) when the employer proffered a nondiscriminatory explanation. Obviously, a mere mistake by the employer in implementing its system, however unfortunate, would not justify relief under the ADEA. For the plaintiffs to prevail, then, they would have to establish that the supposed "mistakes" were really pretexts for Transco's efforts to discharge older workers. A pattern of "mistaken" dismissals that disproportionately fell on older workers would tend to rebut the mistake claim.

5. In this regard, the pattern of treating older workers less favorably than younger workers is offered not to prove mere disparate impact, but rather to provide a basis for the trier of fact's inferring that an age-discriminatory motive underlay the supposedly neutral Measured Day Work Program. Assuming the only evidence at trial is that which was proffered in the summary judgment motion, who is likely to prevail before a jury? Is your answer affected by the fact that, no matter what the instructions, a jury is unlikely to be sympathetic to an employer who not only mistakenly fired two workers, but also failed to offer them their jobs back when it realized its mistake?

6. Is there sufficient showing of impact to raise an inference of intentional age discrimination, even if the evidence of the mistakes is factored out of the operation of the system? If the jury concludes that the employer's mistakes in administering were just that and that the mistakes did not support the inference that the Measured Day Work Program was adopted with an intent to discriminate on the basis of age, must the jury render a verdict in favor of the employer on the systemic disparate treatment theory? What significance should be given to the fact that the system was abandoned?

7. Is the level of showing of impact sufficient to make out a prima facie case of disparate impact discrimination? Is there sufficient showing of impact to make out a prima facie case of disparate impact if the evidence of the mistakes in administration is factored out of the challenge to the system as an employment practice of the employer? Should a lesser showing of impact than is necessary to raise an inference of systemic disparate treatment be sufficient to make out a disparate impact case?

8. Presumably, neither side will be able to put on different statistical evidence, although each may offer different expert analyses of the data. Does this decision *require* the factfinder to find disparity of impact? Does the opinion mean at a minimum that the factfinder is *permitted* to find such impact, even if expert testimony cannot establish any statistical significance to the age impact?

9. For disparate treatment, the age pattern of the supposed "mistakes" seems probative on the intent issue, even if there is not enough data for a statistical analysis. But is a statistical analysis necessary for the impact theory? After all, the conceptual underpinning of the theory is that the practice in question (the Measured Day Work

Program) has an impact on older workers generally, not merely the particular persons who happened to be employed in this case. Could a jury be allowed to make that finding absent testimony that there is a statistically significant relationship between age and the system?

10. If there were such a relationship, wouldn't it suggest that older workers are less efficient? If so, wouldn't it be permissible to discharge less efficient workers? The problem is not with efficiency per se — selecting workers to fire on the basis of efficiency would undoubtedly be justified as a business necessity and obviously has a strong job relation — but rather with the Measured Day Work Program as a test for efficiency. The employer's mistakes in implementing the system and its abandonment suggest that, as a measure for efficiency, the system is flawed.

11. What about the defenses to disparate impact discrimination? The Measured Day Work Program seems to be job related because it is a means of analyzing the elements of the job and judging how well people were performing them. Do the mistakes in administration undermine the claim that the system is job related? Is necessary for business? How necessary is a system that, at best, is administered so sloppily?

12. Is the Measured Day Work Program a professionally developed test? Looking back at the methods for validating these tests, isn't this system an example of a content valid test? It is, after all, more than just a sample of the job; it is a measurement of the people actually doing the job. What significance should the mistakes in administration have in determining whether the test is valid?

13. Is the Measured Day Work Program an example of a bona fide merit system? Section 703(h) provides that "it shall not be an unlawful employment practice for an employer to apply . . . different terms, conditions, or privileges of employment pursuant to a bona fide . . . merit system, or a system which measures earnings by quantity or quality of production . . . provided that such differences are not the result of an intention to discriminate because of race, color, religion, sex, or national origin. . . ." Given the mistakes in administration, the system may not have been a good measurement of merit or quantity of production, but does that mean the defense is not available to the employer?

## EEOC v. JOE'S STONE CRAB, INC.
### 220 F.3d 1263 (11th Cir. 2000)

MARCUS, Circuit Judge:

This is the paradigmatic "hard" case, and we have labored for many months to reach the right result. On appeal, Defendant, Joe's Stone Crab, Inc. ("Joe's"), challenges the district court's entry of judgment in favor of [the EEOC], on its gender-based disparate impact claims under Title VII. Joe's is a landmark Miami Beach seafood restaurant which from 1986 to 1990 hired 108 male food servers and zero female food servers. After the EEOC filed its discrimination charge in June 1991, Joe's hired 88 food servers from 1991 to 1995, nineteen, or roughly 21.7%, of whom were female. The district court concluded that while Joe's was not liable for intentional discrimination, it was liable for disparate impact discrimination based on these statistical disparities. After thorough review, we vacate the district court judgment, and remand for reconsideration of the EEOC's intentional discrimination claim consistent with this opinion.

In our view, the facts of this case render a disparate impact finding inappropriate. A disparate impact claim requires the identification of a specific, facially-neutral, employment practice causally responsible for an identified statistical disparity. On this record, the district court has identified no *facially-neutral* practice responsible for the gender disparity in Joe's food server population and we can find none. However, some of the district court's subsidiary findings suggest that there may have been *facially-discriminatory* practices of Joe's that were responsible for the identified hiring disparity, although the district court expressly rejected the EEOC's intentional discrimination claim in summary fashion. . . .

I . . .

Joe's Stone Crab, Inc. is a fourth-generation, family-owned seafood restaurant and Miami Beach landmark. During the stone crab season, which lasts from October to May, the restaurant is extremely busy — serving up to 1450 patrons each weeknight and up to 1800 patrons each weekend night. Today, the restaurant employs between 230 and 260 employees; of those, approximately 70 are food servers. Throughout its history, Joe's has experienced extremely low food server turnover — a result of Joe's family ethos, generous salary and benefits package, and its seven-month employment season. From 1950 onward, however, the food servers have been almost exclusively male. . . .

To hire new food servers, Joe's conducts a "roll call" every year on the second Tuesday in October. Although Joe's rarely advertises, significantly, the district court found that the roll call is "widely known throughout the local food server community," and typically attracts over 100 applicants for only a limited number of slots. At a typical roll call, each applicant completes a written application and an individual interview. Selected applicants then enter a three-day training program where they shadow experienced servers. Upon successful completion of the program, they then become permanent hires. Until the EEOC's charge, roll call interviews and hiring selections were handled exclusively by the daytime maitre d' with occasional interview assistance from other staff members. Hiring decisions were made by the daytime maitre d' on the basis of four subjective factors (appearance, articulation, attitude, and experience) and without upper management supervision or the benefit of instructive written or verbal policies. After the EEOC's discrimination charge in 1991, Joe's changed its roll call format somewhat. All applicant interviews were conducted by three members of Joe's management. In addition, each applicant was required to take and pass a "tray test," which involved the lifting and carrying of a loaded serving tray, or else be automatically disqualified from a food server position. The district court found the tray test to be a "legitimate indicator of an individual's ability to perform an essential component of a food server's job at Joe's," and that "women have the physical strength to carry serving trays," In addition to its description of Joe's hiring process, the district court also made several subsidiary findings relating to the historical operation of the roll call system. The district court observed that while "women have predominated as owner/managers," "most of Joe's female employees have worked in positions traditionally viewed as 'women's jobs,' e.g., as cashiers or laundry workers. Food servers generally have been male." Although Joe's hired female food servers during World War II, most of these positions "reverted to men at the conclusion of the war." Further, the district court found that, "from 1950 on, the food serving staff has been almost exclusively male. Indeed, one striking exception proves the rule. Dotty Malone worked as a food server at Joe's for seventeen years, and for most of this time she was the lone female on a serving staff that ranged between twenty-four and thirty-two."

In explaining this historical dearth of female food servers, the district court found that Joe's maintained an "Old World" European tradition, in which the highest level of food service is performed by men, in order to create an ambience of "fine dining" for its customers. The district court elaborated:

> The evidence presented at trial does not establish that Joe's management had an express policy of excluding women from food server positions. To the contrary, the evidence portrays owner/managers who have been courageous in opposing overt discrimination. For example, Joe's was picketed for two years when the owners insisted on hiring African-American employees who had been excluded from union membership because of race. What the evidence in this case does prove is that Joe's management acquiesced in and gave silent approbation to the notion that male food servers were preferable to female food servers.

As evidence for this finding, the district court cited three pieces of witness testimony. First, the district court pointed to the testimony of Grace Weiss, Joe's owner, who stated, "I cannot explain the predominance of male servers, but perhaps it has to do with the very heavy trays to be carried, *the ambience of the restaurant*, and the extremely low turnover in servers." (Emphasis added by the district court.) Second, the district court highlighted the testimony of Roy Garrett, a longtime maitre d' of Joe's with hiring authority, who explained that Joe's had a "tradition" that food server positions were "a male server type of job". . . .

Finally, the district court referred to the testimony of Joe's own restaurant industry expert, Karen McNeil, for a historical explanation of the "male-only" server tradition.

> It has been an attitude and standard, it comes from Europe. In all of Europe you will find in all of the grade three restaurants in Europe, there is an impression that service at that high level is the environment of men, and that it ought to be that way. And I think that that attitude a few decades ago came and was felt a little bit here in this country. . . . Those [European] opinions and those sensibilities, I think were in fact carried here by restauranteurs who hoped to create something serious. If you wanted to create a serious restaurant that would become known in the community, that would become one of the community's great restaurants, you did what they did in Europe, you modeled yourself after them. I don't think anybody thought about it. They said, well, men did it there. It tended to be men here, too, who had those skill sets, and so men were [sic] automatically became the labor pool.

The district court added that "Joe's [had] sought to emulate Old World traditions by creating an ambience in which tuxedo-clad men served its distinctive menu."

With this historical background in place, the district court then focused on Joe's female hiring statistics for the relevant pre- and post-charge periods. For the pre-charge period of 1986-1990, the number of female food server applicants at Joe's annual hiring roll calls was minuscule. While there is little available evidence as to the actual numbers of female applicants at these roll calls (because Joe's historically did not retain any employment data from its roll calls), the district court determined, and both parties agreed, that during this period, no more than two or three women per year (or, at most, 3% of the overall applicant class) actually attended the roll calls. In that same period, 108 new male food servers were hired while *zero* women were hired. During the post-charge period (from 1991 to 1995), many more women (in all, 22% of the actual applicant pool) applied for food server positions. Of Joe's 88 new food server hires during this period, 19 were women. These post-charge figures translate into a female hiring percentage of 21.7% — a percentage almost exactly proportional to the percentage of females in the actual applicant pool. . . .

However, in making its findings, the district court found this actual applicant flow data "unreliable because it is skewed." Relying on hearsay trial testimony from local female food servers, the district court found that Joe's public reputation for not hiring women encouraged women to self-select out of the hiring process — thereby skewing the actual applicant flow. . . . Although the district court noted that female food server applications to Joe's dramatically increased as a result of publicity about the EEOC charge, it still found Joe's post-charge applicant pool data (depicting a female applicant pool of 22%) unreliable after comparing it with hiring rates, between 30% and 40% female, for other area seafood restaurants.

Having found the actual applicant pool data wholly unreliable, the district court discarded it and then set about selecting alternative non-applicant labor market data. The EEOC's expert witness, a labor economist, suggested a qualified female labor pool of 44.1% based on 1990 census data for female food servers living and/or working in the Miami Beach area (a labor pool which included cocktail and buffet servers). Not surprisingly, the district court rejected this figure in part because there was no demonstration that this female labor pool necessarily was qualified to work at Joe's. Instead, the district court "refined" the relevant labor pool to include all female servers who lived or worked on Miami Beach and earned between $25,000 and $50,000 — thereby "using past earning capacity as a proxy for experience, and by extension, experience as a proxy for qualification." Solely based on this alternative methodology, the district court was able to find "that at all relevant times, 31.9% of the available labor pool has been female.". . .

## II . . .

[W]e have struggled on appeal to find the proper resolution of this case. As we explain in detail, we believe that the district court's factual findings simply do not support a legal conclusion that Joe's is liable for *disparate impact* discrimination. Based on the district court's findings, no specific *facially-neutral* employment practice of Joe's can be *causally connected* to the statistical disparity between the percentage of women in the qualified labor pool and the percentage of women hired as food servers by Joe's.

### A. DISPARATE IMPACT . . .

The disparate impact framework under Title VII by now is well-settled. "Since *Griggs*, Congress has codified the appropriate burdens of proof in a disparate impact case in 42 U.S.C. § 2000e-2(k) (1994), and a settled jurisprudence has arisen to implement the methodology." *In re Employment* [Litigation Against the State of Alabama], 198 F.3d 1305, 1311 (11th Cir. 1999). As correctly identified by the district court, a plaintiff in a sex discrimination suit must establish three elements: *first,* that there is a significant statistical disparity between the proportion of women in the available labor pool and the proportion of women hired; *second,* that there is a specific, facially-neutral, employment practice which is the alleged cause of the disparity; and *finally,* and most critically in this case, that a causal nexus exists between the specific employment practice identified and the statistical disparity shown. . . .

As for the first prong of the analysis, it is critical to observe that no statistically-significant disparity exists between the percentage of women who actually *applied* to

Joe's and the percentage of women who were *hired* as servers by Joe's. The record indicates that for the pre-charge period (October 1986 to June 1991) very few female food servers applied to Joe's, "perhaps 3% of [all] applicants," out of an actual applicant pool of between 80 and 120 people a year. In this five-year time period, 108 male food servers were hired and no women were hired. Despite the fact that no women were hired during this period, Joe's pre-charge hiring rate demonstrated no significant statistical disparity because so few women actually applied for food server positions.[11] For the post-charge period (July 1991 to December 1995), the district court found that, on average, 22.02% of Joe's food server applicants were women and that Joe's hired roughly 21.7% women for these positions. . . .

This insight is important for disparate impact analysis because the mere fact that Joe's hired no women in the pre-charge period is not, alone, sufficient to impose upon Joe's Title VII liability. To hold otherwise would be to impose liability upon Joe's based on "bottom line" reasoning which the Supreme Court has expressly forbade. In *Watson*, the Supreme Court made clear that Title VII liability could not be based solely on "bottom line" statistical imbalances in an employer's workforce. . . .

This disdain for "bottom line" reasoning reflects the belief that holding employers liable for statistical imbalances *per se* is inconsistent with Title VII's plain language and statutory purpose. Section 703(j) of Title VII, 42 U.S.C. 2000e-2(j), in fact, explicitly rejects the notion that employers must adopt numerical hiring quotas or "grant preferential treatment . . . on account of an imbalance which may exist with respect to the total number or percentage of persons . . . in comparison with the total number or percentage . . . in any community." . . . As a result, a plaintiff must do more than simply identify a workforce imbalance to establish a prima facie disparate impact case; it must causally connect a facially-neutral employment practice to the identified disparity.

In this case, the district court could create a statistically-significant disparity only by first throwing out the actual applicant data as a point of comparison and instead comparing the percentage of women hired for server positions at Joe's with the percentage of women in the "qualified" labor pool. The district court recognized that the number of women who actually applied for server positions at Joe's was disproportionately low when compared with the number of women in the Miami Beach area who were seemingly qualified for such positions. There was, in fact, a significant statistical disparity between the percentage of female applicants to Joe's during the pre- and post-charge periods and the percentage of female applicants to comparable area restaurants. Joe's female applicant percentage of 3% and 22.02% for the pre-and post-charge periods respectively varied sharply from the female applicant percentage of area restaurants which ranged from 29.5% to 42.1%. As a result of these findings, the district court found the actual *applicant* flow data to be "unreliable because it is skewed." It concluded that the data was skewed because of the pronounced self-selection of women out of Joe's hiring process. The district court then expressly rejected the actual *applicant* flow data in favor of an *alternative* labor pool consisting of those

11. While it is true that during this period Joe's hired 108 men and zero women, this zero hiring percentage is deceptive. So few women applied to Joe's during this time period (perhaps one to three a year or, at most, fifteen in total as compared to 80 to 120 men or, at most, 600 men in total) that Joe's zero hiring rate is not significantly deviant from what Joe's female hiring rate ought to be according to laws of random probability (around 1.5% at best). "The mere absence of minority employees in [particular] positions does not suffice to prove a prima facie case of discrimination. . . ." Carter v. Bull, 33 F.3d 450, 456 (4th Cir. 1994) (citing Moore v. Hughes Helicopters, Inc., 708 F.2d 475, 484 (9th Cir. 1983).

local food servers who were theoretically "available" and "qualified" to work at Joe's.[13] After hearing testimony from the expert witnesses of both parties, the district court arrived at an "eligible" labor pool, based on 1990 census data refined for qualification/ experience on the basis of past earning capacity, which was 31.9% female. The district court then used this alternative labor data and compared it to Joe's actual hire statistics. By comparing Joe's pre-charge female hiring percentage (0%) with the percentage of women in the qualified labor market (31.9%), the district court created a legally-cognizable statistical disparity.[14]

Assuming this substitution of data was appropriate, in order to establish disparate impact discrimination, the EEOC still was required to show a causal link between some *facially-neutral* employment practice of Joe's and the statistical disparity. In other words, the EEOC was required to prove that at least one facially neutral employment practice proximately caused the disparity. This finding is essential to avoid the potential conflation of disparate treatment and disparate impact claims. As we have noted, the central difference between disparate treatment and disparate impact claims is that disparate treatment requires a showing of discriminatory intent and disparate impact does not. *See In re Employment.* In fact, the judicial doctrine of disparate impact was created in *Griggs* specifically to redress *facially-neutral* policies or practices which visited disproportionate effects on groups protected by Title VII. . . .

The central problem in this case, however, is that the district court has identified no *facially-neutral* employment practice responsible for the gender disparity in Joe's

13. On appeal, Joe's challenges the district court's use of this alternative labor data as clear error. *See Kilgo* [v. Bowman Transp. Inc.], 789 F.2d 859, 869-870 & n.10 [(11th Cir. 1986)] (suggesting that the decision to reject actual applicant market data for alternative labor market data is necessarily fact-intensive and reviewed for clear error). Joe's contends that the district court improperly relied on hearsay reputation evidence in finding the actual applicant flow data unreliable. Joe's also argues that the district court erred in using "refined" census data to define the relevant labor market for Miami Beach food servers qualified to work at Joe's. The district court narrowed the labor pool to those Miami Beach food servers who made between $25,000 and $50,000 — a salary range comparable to what Joe's food servers earn. Joe's claims that the district court's methodology of using *income* as a proxy for job *qualifications* in no way assures that the labor pool actually consists only of those food servers who have the special food-serving skills requisite to work at Joe's. In the disparate impact context, we have explained that the "definition of a qualified applicant pool will shift with the nature of the job or job benefit, and the nature of the challenged employment practice at issue." *In re Employment.* We also have observed that "'when special qualifications are required to fill particular jobs,'" the use of certain statistics such as general population figures "becomes troublesome." Id. at 1313 (quoting Hazelwood School Dist. v. United States); *see also* Alexander v. Fulton County, Ga., 207 F.3d 1303, 1327-28 (11th Cir. 2000) (noting that class-based disparate treatment statistics showing that a given minority is underrepresented in the work force by comparison with the general population is generally useful only for claims involving jobs with low skill levels where the applicant pool can be considered roughly coextensive with the general population); Peightal v. Metropolitan Dade County, 26 F.3d 1545, 1554 (11th Cir. 1994) (stating that "for positions requiring minimal training or for certain entry level positions, statistical comparison to the racial composition of the relevant population suffices, whereas positions requiring special skills necessitate a determination of the number of minorities qualified to undertake the particular task"). We have had no prior occasion to determine specifically whether salary is an adequate proxy for food server job qualifications at a fine dining establishment. Because we conclude *infra* that the district court erred in finding that the EEOC established disparate impact discrimination, *even* if we accept the alternative labor pool data, we need not address whether the alternative labor pool selected by the district court was comprised of "qualified" potential applicants.

14. When this same 31.9% figure was applied to Joe's post-charge hiring statistics, a slight disparity, bordering on the significant, was found. The statistical variation was between 1.96 to 2.07 under "standard deviation" analysis. However, no particular numerical deviation is required to establish a prima facie case; instead courts employ a case-by-case approach dependent on the particularized case facts. *See Watson.* In addition, our caselaw has recognized that post-charge hiring behavior is less probative than pre-charge conduct because a business may be improving its hiring practices to avoid liability or large damages in their pending discrimination case. *See* James v. Stockham Valves & Fittings Co., 559 F.2d 310, 325 n.18 (5th Cir. 1977); Rowe v. General Motors Corp., 457 F.2d 348, 359 (5th Cir. 1972).

food server population, and we can find none. The EEOC and the district court have identified, at most, two neutral employment practices on which to ground a disparate impact analysis: first, Joe's word of mouth recruiting, and second, Joe's "undirected and undisciplined delegation of hiring authority to subordinate staff," resulting in its subjective "roll call" hiring process. Disparate impact analysis fails in this case because neither neutral practice can be causally connected to the gender disparity.

First, there is no evidence that Joe's word-of-mouth recruiting method caused any disparity between the percentage of women in the qualified labor pool and the percentage of women actually hired by Joe's as servers. Notably, this is not a case where Joe's formal recruiting practices or its informal word-of-mouth recruiting network kept women from learning about available jobs at Joe's. Compare United States v. Georgia Power Co., 474 F.2d 906, 925 (5th Cir. 1973) (finding that word-of-mouth recruiting system can operate as a "'built-in headwind'" isolating blacks from "web of information" relating to job openings). Rather, the district court specifically found quite the opposite, namely that local female food servers *knew* about the availability of positions at Joe's and the logistical details of Joe's hiring roll calls. . . .

Nor is there any evidence that Joe's facially-neutral, albeit undisciplined and subjective, hiring practices caused the disparity the district court found between the percentage of women in the qualified labor pool and the percentage of women actually hired as servers by Joe's. There is no evidence that Joe's subjective hiring criteria either caused women not to apply to Joe's or caused those who applied not to be hired. . . .

The district court, recognizing that it could not causally connect Joe's neutral, albeit subjective, recruiting and hiring practices with the disparity between the percentage of women in the qualified labor pool and the percentage of women actually hired as servers by Joe's, identified Joe's *reputation* as a discriminator against women as the causal agent for the disparity. . . .

We conclude that the district court's use of reputation was, on the face of this record, both problematic and inadequate for several independent reasons. First, reputation itself is neither a specific act or a practice. It is far more amorphous. Reputation is "'a prevalent or common belief, a general name, the opinion of a number of persons.'" Reputation is the community "picture" of an individual or corporate entity formed over a number of years. Reputation has never been used, as far as we can tell, as a facially-neutral employment act or practice for disparate impact purposes. . . . Indeed, no case has ever used reputation as a bridge connecting a neutral hiring practice to a statistical disparity in order to establish disparate impact liability where the neutral employment practices alone did not cause the disparity.

In addition, even if reputation could somehow be used in theory as a causal bridge, in this case there is no logical or factual connection between any facially-neutral component of Joe's employment practices and Joe's reputation as a discriminator. Nothing in this record indicates that Joe's recruitment by "word-of-mouth" rather than through other recruiting mechanisms such as print or television advertising contributed in any way to Joe's reputation for discrimination. Nor is there any evidence that the use of appearance, articulation, attitude, and experience as hiring criteria contributed to Joe's reputation for discrimination. Indeed, there is no suggestion from either party that these hiring criteria are themselves somehow illegitimate or discriminatory. . . . [W]here Joe's neutral hiring and recruiting practices did not cause its reputation, we think it is wholly inappropriate to use reputation as the causal bridge connecting neutral practices to a statistical disparity for the purposes of establishing Joe's disparate impact liability. See Lewis v. Tobacco Workers' Int'l Union, 577 F.2d 1135, 1143 (4th Cir. 1978) (holding that an employer cannot be found liable under Title

VII simply because potential minority applicants subjectively believe the company will not hire them because of their race where this belief is not attributable to the employer's conduct). . . .

While a company may be held liable for a discriminatory reputation if there is evidence it caused or perpetuated that reputation through some *intentional* affirmative act, *see Morrow; Rath Packing,* we know of no federal circuit that has found an employer liable under Title VII on the basis of a reputation for discrimination it did not cause. *See Lewis.* Nor are we prepared to impose on an employer an affirmative duty under Title VII to ameliorate a public reputation not attributable to its own employment conduct. In fact, we are unaware of any case that requires a Title VII employer to affirmatively dispel a negative public image *not* of its own making or else be subject to a finding of Title VII discrimination.

That said, the record extant and some of the district court's findings of fact can be read to support the alternate conclusion that Joe's management *intentionally* excluded women from food serving positions in order to provide its customers with an "Old World," fine-dining ambience. Thus, for example, the district court found that "Joe's management acquiesced in and gave silent approbation to the notion that male food servers were preferable to female food servers." At another point in its findings, the district court observed that "Joe's sought to emulate Old World traditions by creating an ambience in which tuxedo-clad men served its distinctive menu." Moreover, the district court apparently also credited the testimony of one of Joe's former hiring maitre d', Roy Garrett, who explained that Joe's was "a male server type of job" by tradition. As a result, the district court said that "women have systematically been excluded from the most lucrative entry level position, that of server." Finally, the district court found that this historical practice of hiring only men was responsible for Joe's "male-only" reputation. The district court held that "Joe's reputation in the community, which reflected the restaurant's historical hiring practice, led potential female applicants not to apply for server positions. Joe's reputation, therefore, was largely responsible for the gender skew in the pool of applicants at the annual roll call."

But, these factual findings do not mesh easily with a disparate impact theory because they suggest that Joe's hiring system was not in practice *facially-neutral,* but rather was *facially-discriminatory* on the basis of gender. They suggest the conclusion that in fact Joe's had a desired preference for male servers and that this preference influenced the hiring decisions of Joe's decisionmakers, resulting in the deliberate and systematic exclusion of women as food servers. If this were true, Joe's could be found liable for intentional discrimination in violation of Title VII . . .

At bottom then, this case really centers around the theory that women refrained from making the "futile gesture," *Teamsters,* of applying to Joe's when they knew that Joe's only hired men as food servers. If Joe's reputation came from anything causally attributable to the restaurant, it emanated from Joe's own purportedly discriminatory hiring practices, *not* from the specific facially neutral practices identified by the district court. [The facts of this case may be read to suggest] that Joe's hiring decisionmakers systematically excluded female applicants from consideration, that over time this male-only preference became common knowledge, and that eventually most potential, qualified, female applicants self-selected out of Joe's hiring process precisely because of its reputation for intentional sex discrimination. Indeed, the subsidiary factual findings in this case could be read in simple syllogistic form: first, "Old World" fine-dining meant hiring only tuxedo-clad *male* servers; second, Joe's sought to emulate "Old World" fine-dining; and finally, Joe's therefore only hired male servers. If this is what the district court meant to find, it is indicative of something quite different from the theory of disparate impact. But we cannot affirm a disparate impact judgment where the case centers entirely around allegations and evidence of *intentional* discrimination. The record does not support it, and to do so would unwisely conflate the distinct theories of disparate impact and disparate treatment.

## B.  REMAND

We are left then with two unattractive choices on appeal: first, we can affirm the liability judgment on an alternate theory of Title VII liability such as *disparate treatment* or *pattern or practice discrimination,* as the EEOC suggests, or we can remand so that the district court may reconsider its factual findings and conclusions of law. Although the district court's findings may be read to suggest a pattern or practice on the part of Joe's to intentionally discriminate on the basis of sex in its hiring of food servers, we are not prepared to draw this conclusion in the face of the district court's having expressly rejected this theory; rather we think a remand to the district court is the wiser choice.

We reach this conclusion for three principal reasons. First, we are deeply troubled by and unable to easily square the fundamental inconsistency between the district court's express rejection of the EEOC's intentional discrimination claim and several of its subsidiary factual findings that Joe's hired male servers only in order to create an "Old World" fine dining ambience. . . .

Second, after carefully reading the trial transcript, we believe the district court's conclusion that the EEOC has not met its burden of proving intentional discrimination may have been based on an erroneous view of Title VII case law. . . . In light of the district court's seemingly unambiguous findings that "Joe's has been a 'male server type' establishment for the better part of the century" and that "women have systematically been excluded from the most lucrative entry level position, that of server," we emphasize that a finding of disparate treatment requires no more than a finding that women were intentionally treated differently by Joe's because of or on account of their gender. To prove the discriminatory intent necessary for a disparate treatment or pattern or practice claim, a plaintiff need not prove that a defendant harbored some special "animus" or "malice" towards the protected group to which she belongs. In the race discrimination context, we recently have explained that "ill will, enmity, or hostility are not prerequisites of intentional discrimination." Ferrill v. Parker Group, Inc., 168 F.3d 468, 473 n.7 (11th Cir. 1999). In *Ferrill,* for example, we held a defendant, who acted without racial animus but consciously and intentionally made job assignments based on racial stereotypes, liable for intentional discrimination. . . .

Simply put, Title VII prohibits "the entire spectrum of disparate treatment of men and women resulting from sex stereotypes," Los Angeles Dept. of Water & Power v. Manhart, even where the stereotypes are benign or not grounded in group animus. Therefore, if Joe's deliberately and systematically excluded women from food server positions based on a sexual stereotype which simply associated "fine-dining ambience" with all-male food service, it then could be found liable under Title VII for intentional discrimination regardless of whether it also was motivated by ill-will or malice toward women.

Moreover, in light of the district court's findings that "Joe's management acquiesced in and gave silent approbation to the notion that male food servers were preferable to female food servers," and that "what prevailed at Joe's, albeit not mandated by written policy or verbal direction, was the ethos that female food servers were not to be hired," we also emphasize that under our controlling case law, either under a disparate treatment or a pattern or practice theory, Plaintiff need not show that hiring decisions were made pursuant to an *express* policy or directive from Joe's owners. It is enough to show in a disparate treatment case that a particular employment decision was made because of sex and in a pattern or practice case that employment decisions were generally made deliberately because of sex, regardless of whether in either context a *formal* or *express* policy of discrimination existed from the employer. *See Teamsters*; Harris v. Shelby County Bd. of Educ., 99 F.3d 1078, 1083 (11th Cir. 1996). . . .

Finally, before we remand, we take a moment to explicate in more detail settled law concerning the requirements of Title VII liability based on a finding of intentional discrimination. There are two theories of intentional discrimination under Title VII: disparate treatment and pattern or practice discrimination. Disparate treatment claims require proof of discriminatory intent either through direct or circumstantial evidence. *See Harris* (observing that a "'plaintiff must, by either direct or circumstantial evidence, demonstrate by a preponderance of the evidence that the employer had a discriminatory intent'" to prove a disparate treatment claim). "Direct evidence is evidence that establishes the existence of discriminatory intent behind the employment decision without any inference or presumption." Standard v. A.B.E.L. Servs., Inc., 161 F.3d 1318, 1330 (11th Cir. 1998). Absent direct evidence, a plaintiff may prove intentional discrimination through the familiar *McDonnell Douglas* paradigm for circumstantial evidence claims. . . .

In contrast, a pattern and practice claim either may be brought by the EEOC if there is "reasonable cause to believe that any person or group of persons is engaged in a pattern or practice" of discrimination, 42 U.S.C. § 2000e-6(a) (1994); *see also In re Employment,* or by a class of private plaintiffs under 42 U.S.C. § 2000e, et. seq., *see* Cox v. American Cast Iron Pipe Co., 784 F.2d 1546, 1549 (11th Cir. 1986). In such suits, the plaintiffs must establish "'that [sex] discrimination was the company's standard operating procedure.'" *Cox; see also* Franks v. Bowman Transportation Co., 424 U.S. 747, 772 (1976). To meet this burden of proof, a plaintiff must "prove more than the mere occurrence of isolated or accidental or sporadic discriminatory acts. It has to establish by a preponderance of the evidence that [ ] discrimination [is] the company's standard operating procedure — the regular rather than unusual practice." *Teamsters* (footnote and internal quotation marks omitted). While "pattern or practice cases are a variant of the disparate treatment theory and thus 'proof of discriminatory motive is critical,'" statistical evidence often is used to establish the existence of a pattern or practice. Lujan v. Franklin County Bd. of Educ., 766 F.2d 917, 929 (6th Cir. 1985). A plaintiff may establish a pattern or practice claim "through a combination of strong statistical evidence of disparate impact coupled with anecdotal evidence of the employer's intent to treat the protected class unequally." Mozee v. American Commercial Marine Service Co., 940 F.2d 1036, 1051 (7th Cir. 1991) We also point out that "direct evidence of an intent to discriminate" may be used to establish a pattern or practice claim. *Lujan.* Finally, we observe that in determining pattern or practice liability, the government is not required to prove that any particular employee was a victim of the pattern or practice; it need only establish a prima facie case that such a policy existed.[22]

22. Once this pattern or practice is established, the burden of proof then shifts to the employer to demonstrate that the government's showing of a pattern or practice of discrimination is either inaccurate or insignificant. If the employer fails to rebut the government's prima facie case, the resulting finding of a discriminatory pattern or practice may give rise to an inference that all persons subject to the policy were its victims and are entitled to appropriate remedies. As we have explained previously, "once a pattern and practice of discrimination is established, a rebuttable presumption that [the] plaintiff was discriminated

HULL, Circuit Judge, specially concurring in part and dissenting in part:

I also agree with the majority that disparate *impact* liability requires a showing that facially-neutral employment practices caused the lack of female food servers at Joe's. I disagree, however, with the majority's conclusion that the district court "identified no *facially-neutral* practice responsible for the gender disparity in Joe's food server population and we can find none." I disagree because the district court (1) did single out certain employment practices that are facially neutral and (2) did not err in finding that these practices *caused* the gender disparity in Joe's food servers. In my view, the district court's finding of disparate *impact* liability should be affirmed in full.

Alternatively, even if, as the majority concludes, the district court's subsidiary factual findings suggest that *facially-discriminatory* practices at Joe's actually caused the gender disparity and thus its findings support only disparate *treatment* liability, we should affirm on that alternate ground. A remand for more work by this trial court is unnecessary. . . .

Because the evidence overwhelmingly showed a legally significant gender disparity in Joe's food servers, the majority opinion necessarily focuses on the second and third prongs of a prima facie disparate impact case — whether the EEOC and the district court identified *facially-neutral* employment practices as *causing* this gender disparity. The majority concludes they did not. I conclude they did.

The main facially-neutral employment practice identified by the district court was management's lack of *any* hiring guidelines and policies and the resultant "undirected and undisciplined delegation of hiring authority to subordinate staff." Within the ambit of "undirected and undisciplined delegation of hiring authority to subordinate staff," the district court included these facially-neutral practices: (1) management's lack of any written or even oral guidelines for its staff to follow in hiring; (2) the staff's use of mainly a subjective interview process and "subjective intuition" for hiring its servers; (3) management's sitting in on the roll call process but providing no input; and (4) lack of any managerial oversight and lack of any standardization, as exemplified by management's failure to raise a question when the subordinate staff filled 108 consecutive vacancies with only male servers. The majority states that "the subjective hiring criteria did not harm women once they entered the application process." I disagree because the record evidence supports the district court's findings that it did. Many qualified women attended Joe's roll calls and were interviewed, but were not hired. . . .

Another major employment practice at Joe's, which the district court identified as causing the gender disparity, was Joe's use of only a "word-of-mouth" roll call system for recruiting new servers. The district court pointed out that year after year only a few women came to the roll call due to Joe's well-known historical practice of hiring, and using, only tuxedo-clad men as servers. The district court emphasized that Joe's did not advertise in the newspaper or elsewhere that it was an equal opportunity employer or that Joe's hired both men and women as servers. Instead, Joe's continued recruiting through only the "word-of-mouth" roll call on the first Tuesday in October — just as it had done for decades.

The majority stresses that the particular date of the roll call was widely known in the Miami Beach community, and that no woman testified that she failed to apply because she was unaware of the roll call. However, the district court found that Joe's

___

against because of her sex and is entitled to recovery obtains. The employer may overcome this presumption only with clear and convincing evidence that job decisions made when the discriminatory policy was in force were not made in pursuit of that policy." *Cox*, 784 F.2d at 1559 (citing *Teamsters.*)

historical practice of hiring only men as servers was also well known in that community and caused women servers to self-select out and not come to Joe's roll call. Joe's *own conduct* caused the dearth of women applicants. The district court, in effect, found women refrained from making the futile gesture of attending the roll call when they knew Joe's hired only men as servers.

Although the undisciplined delegation of hiring, subjective interview process, and the use of a roll call are facially-neutral employment practices, the district court also referenced "Joe's history of being an all-male server establishment." Excluding women as servers — even if to create a fine dining ambience of tuxedo-clad men — is a facially-discriminatory practice, as the majority notes. However, Joe's past discriminatory hiring is part of the factual background against which the district court analyzed whether the above facially-neutral practices caused the gender disparity to continue. The district court's order raised the precise question of whether "Joe's undirected and undisciplined delegation of hiring authority caused the disparity between the number of women hired as servers and the number of women available, or are forces outside the hiring process — such as a deteriorating neighborhood, low turnover, or the heavy lifting required of servers — to blame?"

In short, the district court considered the above facially-neutral employment practices, not in a vacuum, but in the context of Joe's historical discriminatory practice of excluding women as food servers. The district court properly considered Joe's historical discriminatory practices, and the "males-only" reputation Joe's created for itself, as relevant background evidence in examining whether Joe's facially-neutral employment practices *caused and continued* the gender disparity in Joe's food servers. In doing so, the district court did not err because it is well settled that past discrimination is admissible to demonstrate that facially-neutral employment practices continue to perpetuate the effects of past discrimination.

Against this historical backdrop, then, the district court found that management's continued unguided and undisciplined delegation of hiring authority, without any written or verbal policies or guidelines, allowed Joe's subordinate staff (a) to recruit servers by using only its "word-of-mouth" roll call system even though that system had proved to recruit mostly male applicants, and (b) to continue to hire only males as food servers based on their "gut feelings" regardless of the qualified women who did apply. In this manner, the facially-neutral practices caused the gender disparity. . . .

Additionally, the district court correctly found that Joe's facially-neutral recruiting and hiring practices did not address the entrenched "male-only" hiring and "male-only" reputation Joe's created for itself and thereby further caused the gender disparity to continue. The district court found that, at a minimum, Joe's needed to advertise that it now hired both men and women as servers. Instead, Joe's continued reliance on the facially-neutral, "word-of-mouth" roll call caused the gender disparity in its applicant pool and, in turn, its hires, to continue. Furthermore, as to the women who did apply, the district court found that "without additional guidance and structuring by management, there is no assurance that female applicants who [do] attend roll call will be treated even-handedly." . . .

Thus, I conclude that the district court's findings — that Joe's specific *facially-neutral* recruiting and hiring practices *caused* the gender disparity in its serving staff — are not clearly erroneous. . . .

Alternatively, even if, as the majority concludes, the district court's subsidiary factual findings that Joe's systematically excluded women as food servers show that disparate *treatment* analysis is more appropriate in this case than disparate *impact* analysis, I would affirm the district court's liability finding on that basis. . . .

## NOTES

1. On remand, the district court found that Joe's had "engaged in intentional disparate treatment sex discrimination." 136 F. Supp. 2d 1311, 1313 (S.D. Fla. 2001). Are you surprised? Weren't the facts as originally found pretty clear that Joe's did intend to discriminate?

2. Isn't *Joe's* a case where "intent" exists in terms of perceptions and stereotypes of which the owners may not even have been aware? Is this a classic example of Professor Krieger's theory of cognitive misperceptions influenced by unconscious use of "stereotypes, scripts and schemas to interpret, encode and retrieve information relevant to social judgments"? See pages 84-85. Is that the point of the court's discussion in the "Remand" section of the opinion, that the district court may have been looking for animus, not merely for "intentional" discrimination? But when citing an earlier decision for this proposition, Ferrill v. Parker Group, Inc., 168 F.3d 468, 473 n.7 (11th Cir. 1999), the court described that case as involving "consciously and intentionally [making] job assignments based on racial stereotypes."

3. Christine Jolls, Is There a Glass Ceiling? 25 Harv. Women's L.J. 1, 5-7 (2002), discusses in connection with *Joe's Stone Crab* an empirical study of discrimination in wait staff selection. The study, David Neumark, Sex Discrimination in Restaurant Hiring: An Audit Study, 111 Q.J. Econ. 915 (1996), is a "restaurant audit study," using testers. It involved the odds of applicants' receiving interviews at 65 Philadelphia restaurants, and basically consisted of fictional male and female names on resumes submitted. Professor Jolls writes:

> . . . Neumark's methodology is tightly tethered to the question of unlawful sex discrimination because at the point at which the employer's decision to interview is made, the *only* information in its possession is the resume, and thus there is simply no plausible explanation other than unlawful discrimination for different interview frequencies in response to male versus female resumes; this is so because each resume used in the study was sometimes associated with a male name and sometimes with a female name, so that on average the set of male resumes and the set of female resumes were identical. . . .
>
> Neumark's results are striking. Resumes with male names led to interviews in sixty-one percent of cases at high-price restaurants (where pay is higher than at middle- and low-price restaurants), whereas female resumes led to interviews in only twenty-six percent of cases at such restaurants. Clearly, high-price restaurants exhibited a strong preference for waiters over waitresses with on-average-identical resumes. . . .
>
> After establishing that male resumes are far more likely than (on-average-identical) female resumes to lead to interviews, Neumark goes on to examine the likelihood that male and female candidates ultimately receive job offers. He finds, not surprisingly, that male candidates are far more likely than female candidates ultimately to receive job offers at high-price restaurants; males received offers in forty-eight percent of cases, whereas females received offers in only nine percent of cases. These results are in principle more open to question than the interview results, for different success rates could reflect the behavior or demeanor of candidates during interviews; indeed, sometimes it is even suggested that individuals interested in participating in discrimination studies may also be individuals who (consciously or otherwise) end up behaving in ways that lend support to the discrimination theory in which they believe. However, the similarity between the interview disparities (which cannot be attributed to candidates' behavior) and the offer disparities supports the idea that discrimination may be driving the offer disparities . . . .

This evidence would support disparate treatment liability, but what is its application to *Joe's*? Contrary to the tester study, women were selected in proportion to their representation in the application pool — at least after the EEOC started investigating. Do Neumark's findings suggest that Joe's "Old World" image was fueled by conscious or subconscious views that male waiters were better?

4. As for disparate impact, Joe's hired women (1) proportional to their representation in the application pool but (2) less than their representation in the labor market that the district court constructed. The only possible explanation for the discrepancy is that women did not want to work at Joe's. Is this simply the *Sears* lack of interest defense? Or did the EEOC attempt to prove that it is not the women's lack of interest in the abstract but that Joe's discouraged their interest?

5. The Eleventh Circuit wrote: "The central problem in this case, however, is that the district court has identified no *facially-neutral* employment practice responsible for the gender disparity in Joe's food server population, and we can find none." Why wasn't Joe's adoption of an "Old World" atmosphere rather than a funkier Miami Beach approach a practice that caused (or at least contributed to) the problem? Why isn't that a practice that can be challenged? Is it because it is not an *employment* practice but a general business practice?

6. Instead, the EEOC and district court both focused on Joe's "word of mouth recruiting" and its "undirected and undisciplined delegation of hiring authority to subordinate staff," resulting in its subjective "roll call" hiring process. Is that because these were the only "employment" practices involved? Isn't the appeals court clearly right that, in light of the other findings, these practices did not cause women to fail to apply in numbers proportionate to their representation in the area labor market?

7. The Eleventh Circuit asserted that, to establish disparate impact, a plaintiff must prove that "there is a significant statistical disparity between the proportion of women in the available labor pool and the proportion of women hired." What is wrong with that formulation? Does it disregard the holding in *Teal*? The dissent disagrees on disparate impact analysis because a number of qualified women who attended the roll call were not hired. But how does that fact prove that there was a disparate impact when women were hired in proportion to their representation in the applicant pool? A number of qualified males who attended the roll call were probably also not hired.

8. The dissent suggests that, had Joe's abandoned the roll call approach, women would have applied in greater numbers. Apparently, the dissenting judge believed that the continued use of the roll call signaled to the world a "business as usual" approach, which, combined with the "Old World" ambience, discouraged women from applying. Is this implausible?

9. Does the Eleventh Circuit rule out "reputation" as a practice subject to disparate impact attack, or is Joe's Stone Crab's reputation irrelevant to this analysis because there is no nexus shown between the selection methods challenged and that reputation? The court's citation of Lewis v. Tobacco Workers' Intl. Union, 577 F.2d 1135, 1143 (4th Cir. 1978) suggests that an employer cannot be liable for any consequences of its reputation if it does not engage in acts that justify this reputation.

10. What was the point of the Eleventh Circuit's mini-review of disparate treatment law at the end of its Remand discussion? Was it trying to offer the district court an avenue to find disparate treatment liability? If so, which avenue — direct evidence, circumstantial evidence, pattern or practice liability? Do you find the discussion helpful in resolving this case?

11. Does this case suggest that the line between the disparate treatment and disparate impact theories is not as sharp as you might have thought?

## NOTE ON THE RELATIONSHIP BETWEEN INDIVIDUAL AND SYSTEMIC DISPARATE TREATMENT CASES

Most cases of individual disparate treatment are litigated entirely apart from any systemic claims and, therefore, are unaffected by either of the systemic theories. There are, however, instances in which the individual cases are brought in the shadow of broader-based attacks on the defendant's employment policies, either because the individual claims are being litigated in a class action that makes systemic attacks or because the individual claims are considered in the context of a government enforcement action. See Chapter 9 regarding class actions.

The basic question is whether the resolution of the systemic claims can help or hinder the individual cases being litigated. As a start, it is clear that, when one of the systemic theories is proven, the prosecution of individual cases of discrimination is facilitated. This can be seen from Franks v. Bowman Transp. Co., 424 U.S. 747 (1976), in which the Supreme Court established the relationship between systemic disparate treatment and individual disparate treatment where liability is established on the systemic claim. Essentially, the Court held that demonstrating a systemic pattern of intentional discrimination creates a presumption that the individual members of the racial group in question had themselves been discriminated against on account of race. See Chapter 10. Thus, the employer can avoid granting relief to individual members of the class only if it can carry the burden of persuasion that each individual was not a victim of discrimination.

In Cooper v. Federal Reserve Bank of Richmond, 467 U.S. 867 (1984), the Court considered the converse question: the effect on individual claims of a class action that failed to prove systemic disparate treatment discrimination. The failure of the systemic claims does not cut off the right of individuals making up the class to advance claims of individual disparate treatment.

> The crucial difference between an individual's claim of discrimination and a class action alleging a general pattern or practice of discrimination is manifest. The inquiry regarding an individual's claim is the reason for a particular employment decision, while "at the liability stage of a pattern-or-practice trial the focus often will not be on individual hiring decisions, but on a pattern of discriminatory decision-making."

Id. at 876. The members of the class are barred by res judicata from bringing another class action against the employer alleging systemic disparate treatment discrimination for the time period. But because the claims of individual disparate treatment made by individual class members have never been litigated, individual claims (other than those of the named plaintiff) are not precluded merely because the systemic claim has been litigated.

In sum, even when it is established that there is no practice or policy of discrimination, individual plaintiffs can still claim that the challenged action was the product of individual disparate treatment. For example, even if the "inexorable zero" representation of women in an employer's workforce was the product of several hiring prerequisites that were each justified by business necessity, plaintiff could show that she met those prerequisites, but nevertheless was not hired. That would make out a prima facie case of individual disparate treatment.

## C.   RECONCILING THE TENSION BETWEEN DISPARATE TREATMENT AND DISPARATE IMPACT

Professor Douglas A. Laycock, in Statistical Proof and Theories of Discrimination, 49 Law & Contemp. Probs. 97, 98-99 (1986), argues that there is a fundamental inconsistency between the statistical showings for the two systemic theories:

> The [Teamsters] Court explicitly assumes that but for discrimination, the employer's work force would in the long run mirror the racial composition of the labor force from which it was hired. That conclusion requires the further implicit assumption that the black and white populations are substantially the same in all relevant ways, so that any differences in result are attributable to discrimination.
>
> Some variation of that assumption is critical to all statistical evidence of disparate treatment. It is a powerful and implausible assumption: the two populations are assumed to be substantially the same in their distribution of skills, aptitudes, and job preferences. Two hundred and fifty years of slavery, nearly a century of Jim Crow, and a generation of less virulent discrimination are assumed to have had no effect: the black and white populations are assumed to be substantially the same. All the differential socialization of little girls that feminists justifiably complain about is assumed to have had no effect; the male and female populations are assumed to be substantially the same.
>
> This assumption, which is so critical to statistical disparate treatment cases, is fundamentally inconsistent with the policy premise of disparate impact theory. The explicit premise of disparate impact theory is that women and minorities have suffered from discrimination. Measures of skill and merit are suspect because discrimination has left many minorities with fewer and less developed skills. Griggs, the seminal disparate impact case, relies explicitly on the history of segregated and inferior education for blacks in North Carolina schools. So disparate impact theory insists that employers require only those skills essential to the job. To require skills unnecessarily is to exclude minorities unnecessarily.
>
> It should now be clear what is wrong with the one-two punch of turning all disparate treatment defenses into disparate impact claims: the two theories are inconsistent. The disparate treatment half of the strategy assumes that the black and white populations, or the male and female populations, are identical. The disparate impact half simultaneously assumes that they are greatly different. This pair of inconsistent assumptions lets the plaintiff "prove" discrimination, but the proof is invalid.

Are you persuaded by Professor Laycock's argument?

Certainly, his predicates are correct: disparate treatment involves treating people differently despite the fact they are alike. Disparate impact assumes people from different groups are different. If applicant A is, in fact, different from applicant B in some way other than his race, the employer can rely on that difference to treat the two differently with impunity — so far as disparate treatment is concerned. And that is true regardless of whether the employer's reasons are based on job relation or business necessity — or are even rational. We saw that an employer could prefer a white Aries to a black Capricorn so long as the decision was truly based on zodiacal considerations.

But disparate impact liability focuses on the reasons an employer gives. While reliance on employees' astrological signs would not have a disparate impact, use of other factors might. If a private employer used service in the armed forces as a basis for hiring, it certainly would tend to exclude women. This requirement might or might not be justified as a business necessity.

The point is relatively simple: employers may not intentionally use prohibited factors; employers may use any other criteria unless they have a disparate impact, in which case they may be used only if justified.

Suppose plaintiff shows snapshot statistics revealing that an employer has promoted men almost exclusively from a pool that includes many women workers.* In response to the disparate treatment claim, the employer explains that it has a policy of promoting the tallest person among those eligible applicants. As a result, while tall women occasionally were promoted over short men, most of the promotions went to men. If the finder of fact believes the company's story that it was height and not gender that caused the almost total exclusion of women from promotions, that would exonerate the company of disparate treatment liability. But given the disparity of impact, the employer has still acted illegally if height is not job related.

Isn't the simple answer to Professor Laycock's criticism that Title VII presumes that the relevant groups (blacks and whites or males and females) are the same unless the employer demonstrates that they are different in ways that are relevant to the employer's business? Statistically, women are shorter than men, and statistically, blacks are less well educated than whites. Nevertheless, the employer must treat the two groups as the same unless it can show that height or educational requirements are necessary to the job in question.

At this point, the law of employment discrimination might be summed up as follows: disparate treatment is not allowed because subjective bias is not a permissible basis for denying employment opportunities to individuals in our society; but even a pure motivation will not save practices that are not justified by business necessity and that have the effect of carrying the consequences of societal discrimination into the job market. So stated, disparate treatment and disparate impact principles seem to work in conjunction to achieve the basic goals of Title VII. But are the principles always consistent? May they come into conflict?

As indicated previously, in Los Angeles Dept. of Water & Power v. Manhart, 435 U.S. 702 (1978) (reproduced at page 200), the Supreme Court held that the lack of disparate impact on one gender (or racial group) does not justify disparate treatment of that group. But what of the other side of that coin? Doesn't the absence of disparate impact on, say, women who are being treated disparately mean that, if women were treated equally with men, there would be a disparate impact on men?

If the employer collected equal pension contributions from men and women and paid out equal monthly retirement benefits, women as the longer-lived class would collect more total benefits than would the class of men.† That would seem to show

---

* Not many years ago that would have been a good description of school systems in the United States, particularly elementary schools. Even today, men are disproportionately represented as principals in elementary schools compared to their numbers in the teacher workforce.

† Footnote 19 of *Manhart* suggests that the employer already had the problem of equal contributions producing disparate impact with its death benefit plan: requiring equal contributions from men and women for equal life insurance benefits creates an adverse impact on women who receive less for their contributions; as a group, women live longer than men and so should be charged a lower premium. The Court indicated that, under defendant's argument, "this neutral finding of death benefits is unfair to women as a class." 435 U.S. at 710.

an adverse impact on males. Footnote 20 of *Manhart* tries to resolve the tension of disparate impact resulting from equal treatment:

> A variation on the Department's fairness theme is the suggestion that a gender-neutral pension plan would itself violate Title VII because of its disproportionately heavy impact on male employees. Cf. Griggs v. Duke Power Co. This suggestion has no force in the sex discrimination context because each retiree's total pension benefits are ultimately determined by his actual life span; any differential in benefits paid to men and women in the aggregate is thus "based on [a] factor other than sex," and consequently immune from challenge under the Equal Pay Act, 29 U.S.C. § 206(d). Even under Title VII itself — assuming disparate-impact analysis applies to fringe benefits, cf. Nashville Gas Co. v. Satty, 434 U.S. 136, 144-45 — the male employees would not prevail. Even a completely neutral practice will inevitably have some disproportionate impact on one group or another. *Griggs* does not imply, and this Court has never held, that discrimination must always be inferred from such consequences.

Id. at 710 n.20. The meaning of this passage is far from clear. Indeed, the Court seems to make three points. First, it states that the determination of total benefits is based on each individual's actual life span and is thus immune under the "factor other than sex" exception in the Equal Pay Act. This might suggest that the disparate impact theory does not exist under that statute. Beyond this possibility, the Court does not explain why a disparity of impact against men resulting from benefits paid over the lives of all employees is not a violation.

Second, the reference to Nashville Gas Co. v. Satty, although tentative in its phrasing, invokes the possibility that impact analysis applies not to cases brought under § 703(a)(1) (which bars discrimination), but only to cases brought under § 703(a)(2) (which bars classifications that "tend to deprive" individuals of employment opportunities). However, the Supreme Court never squarely held that a different mode of analysis applies to the two subsections of § 703(a), and, whatever the status of this theory when *Manhart* was decided, it does not survive the Civil Rights Act of 1991.

Third, footnote 20 in *Manhart* may imply that there is no tension between the two theories because disparate impact is not available to men (and, by implication, whites). Imagine a new employer who is considering what employee selection procedure to adopt. Using a written test will result in 90 percent white employees and 10 percent black employees. In contrast, a structured interview will result in 70 percent whites and 30 percent blacks. Isn't it clear that whether the employer picks the test or the structured interview, there will be a disparate impact on some group? If disparate impact protected only racial minorities, no dilemma would exist. What would be the basis for such a rule?

As we have seen in Chapter 5, in Craig v. Alabama State University, 804 F.2d 682 (11th Cir. 1986), the court applied disparate impact analysis on behalf of a white, but in the process characterized the plaintiff, a white, as a minority group member. The employer was a predominately black state university. Does this case mean that whites can challenge barriers to their employment opportunities using disparate impact analysis against any employer? Or might the court be adapting Title VII to the special problem of de jure segregation in the South? Might any such rule be somewhat more subtle: what if a male challenged practices at an institution whose employees were predominately women? Perhaps disparate impact is available to any group that is a minority at the employer in question. Does that explain *Craig?*

Is the unavailability of the disparate impact theory to whites and males generally implicit in the *Griggs* doctrine? Suppose Duke Power is ordered to alter its testing requirements because of their unjustified impact on blacks. Wouldn't the new tests have a disparate impact on whites, at least when compared with the results from the old tests? Even if it is implicit in *Griggs*, does this distinction survive the passage of the Civil Rights Act of 1991?

Note that, even if whites and males cannot use disparate impact analysis, the employer must still concern itself with disparities among protected groups. Favoring veterans is likely to disproportionately help blacks as opposed to whites, but is likely to adversely affect females as compared to males. While whites may not be able to challenge the policy, women can.

## NOTE ON NATURE VERSUS NURTURE

One of the most explosive topics in public policy debates today is the extent to which racial or gender differences are innate as opposed to acquired. There are undoubtedly biological differences between the races and the sexes, but the focus of the debate has been not on factors such as skin color or XY chromosomes, but on whether such traits as intelligence and aggressiveness are race- or gender-linked in a biological sense.

In most instances, this debate is simply irrelevant for employment discrimination purposes. If, for example, women are less aggressive than men, it does not matter whether the difference results from nature or nurture. Thus, under the individual disparate treatment theory, an employer may not stereotype a particular woman as less aggressive than a male competitor, but must assess the two rivals' aggressiveness individually. The systemic disparate treatment theory would also bar a policy treating all women as less aggressive than all men, even if women as a group were less aggressive.

It is true, however, that differences between groups will become relevant to employment discrimination litigation in two circumstances. First, plaintiffs must show that groups are different in a disparate impact case. For example, a plaintiff might challenge an employer's aggressiveness requirement under the disparate impact theory by showing that it had a disparate adverse impact on women, forcing the employer to defend it as a business necessity. Second, as we saw in EEOC v. Sears, Roebuck & Co. (reproduced at page 253), an employer might want to show that groups are different in order to rebut the inference of discriminatory intent raised by a systemic disparate treatment case. Both sides in *Sears* agreed that women fared less well in promotions to big-ticket sales jobs, but differed radically in their explanation why. The EEOC inferred discriminatory intent from the statistical showing, but Sears convinced the court that the explanation was not "demand side" discrimination, but "supply side" reticence: female employees did not want the higher-paid, but higher-pressure, jobs to the same degree that men did.

Nevertheless, the cause of the difference (as opposed to the existence of the difference) seems unimportant. It did not matter in Dothard v. Rawlinson (reproduced at page 358) why women were shorter and lighter than men; what was critical was the disparity of impact on women produced by the employer's height and weight requirements. Such requirements might also have a disparate impact on racial or national origin grounds. Again, it would not matter whether a race is genetically smaller if it were excluded by such a policy. In *Sears*, the defendant's expert, Professor Rosalind Rosenberg of Barnard College, credited socialization, not biology, for the differences she identified. While she viewed women as preferring cooperative to competitive jobs, Thomas Haskell & Sanford Levinson, in Academic Freedom and

Expert Witnessing: Historians and the *Sears* Case, 66 Tex. L. Rev. 1629, 1652 (1988), stress that neither Rosenberg nor any other Sears expert asserted that this characteristic results from innate differences. Rosenberg did not treat gender roles as caused by "women's choices alone, and she was careful to present differences of interest as a matter of statistical distributions, not inherent features of gender. She freely allowed that the current allocation of roles is 'reinforced externally through social pressures and governmental action' as well as 'internally through the internalization of norms.'" Id.

Although Professor Rosenberg did not claim that biology determined these differences, and indeed attributed them in large part to societal discrimination, her testimony generated a firestorm of criticism. Professors Haskell and Levinson recount some of the criticisms of her, including charges that she was "immoral," was "unprofessional," had "betrayed" feminism, and had launched "an attack on working women and sexual equality, an attack on the whole concept of affirmative action." Id. at 1630-32. The Coordinating Committee of Women in the History Profession passed a resolution declaring that "'as feminist scholars we have a responsibility not to allow our scholarship to be used against the interests of women struggling for equity in our society.'" Id. at 1692. Others have differed with Haskell and Levinson on both the academic freedom issue and their analysis of *Sears* and Professor Rosenberg's testimony. See, e.g., Joan W. Scott, Deconstructing Equality-Versus-Difference: On the Uses of Poststructuralist Theory for Feminism, 14 Feminist Stud. 33 (1988); Alice Kessler-Harris, Academic Freedom and Expert Witnessing: A Response to Haskell and Levinson, 67 Tex. L. Rev. 429 (1988).

Regardless of the merits of this dispute, the reality remains that Sears employed feminist scholarship as to differences between men and women in order to avoid Title VII liability. This, in turn, sharpened the debate between feminists stressing equality and feminists stressing differences and made more pointed the efforts to achieve a coherent synthesis. See generally Kathryn Abrams, Gender Discrimination and the Transformation of Workplace Norms, 42 Vand. L. Rev. 1183 (1989). This debate, however, has often ignored the simple fact that, as Title VII is structured, differences between men and women are important for disparate impact analysis. As a consequence, recognition of differences remains a two-edged sword. Professor Rosenberg's testimony could easily have been used on behalf of plaintiffs in another setting — a disparate impact challenge.

In any event and whatever the theoretic constructs, feminist writings have not tried to attribute differences between men and women to biology — other than those that necessarily flow from the male and female roles in reproduction. However, there are some who stress biological or genetic bases of broad-based differences between men and women. For example, Richard A. Epstein, in Gender Is for Nouns, 41 DePaul L. Rev. 981, 990 (1992), writes:

> The nurturing instincts usually attributable to women are a set of attitudinal adaptations that reduce the cost of doing activities that help promote the survival of both her and her offspring. . . . If nurturing brings greater pleasure or requires lower costs for women than for men, then we should expect to see women devote a greater percentage of their resources to it than men.

Epstein suggests that we might, for example, expect men to be better in architecture (an occupation heavily dependent on spatial abilities) and women to dominate in occupations "such as counselling and guidance, that demand more of the nurturing and intuitive skill associated with the female roles in child rearing. . . ." Id. at 991. See also Kingsley R. Browne, Women at War: An Evolutionary Perspective, 49 Buffalo

L. Rev. 51 (2001) (evidence points to inherent psychological differences between the sexes, which plays an important role in considering whether women should be integrated into the military).

Such writings have triggered understandably strong reactions. E.g., Kathryn Abrams, Social Construction, Roving Biologism, and Reasonable Women: A Response to Professor Epstein, 41 DePaul L. Rev. 1021 (1992). Even feminists who have stressed female differences have rarely attributed those differences to biology, probably because those who have emphasized biological differences in the past have typically done so in order to confine women to secondary roles in society. Even if that is not Professor Epstein's purpose, it may well be the effect of arguments such as his: nurturing roles have, at least as a matter of economics, been traditionally low-valued in the employment market. Feminists who argue that society ought to celebrate, rather than belittle, ways in which women differ from men wonder why writers like Epstein do not argue the superiority of female traits: in increasingly interdependent work settings, the asserted superiority of women in building relationships and smoothing over confrontations should be valued more highly than "male" traits, such as aggression, which are becoming more and more anachronistic. See generally Martha Minow, The Supreme Court, 1986 Term — Foreword: Justice Engendered, 101 Harv. L. Rev. 10, 62 (1987).

The political origins and uses of research into biological differences have been particularly marked in the ways in which scientists and quasi-scientists have approached racial differences. Identifying such differences has not proceeded by some effort to string out human traits along some continuum and then neutrally decide which race has more of one trait or less of another. Rather, originating around the turn of the twentieth century, efforts to differentiate the races were characterized by attempts to demonstrate the racial inferiority of non-white groups. See generally Stephen Jay Gould, The Mismeasure of Man (1981). Such efforts were further cast into disrepute when charges of fraud were leveled at Sir Cyril Burt, who published a study of twins separated early in life purporting to show that 80 percent of IQ is inherited. In the 1970s, doubts about the validity of the study led the British Psychological Society to find that he had been guilty of fraud. While Burt continues to have his defenders and detractors, see Peter Lennon, Mind Games — IQ, The Guardian, July 18, 1992, at 4, other research has continued the underlying controversy. Arthur Jensen, in How Much Can We Boost IQ and Scholastic Achievement?, 39 Harv. Educ. Rev. 1, 82 (1969), concluded that the average difference between IQ scores of blacks as a group and whites as a group can be explained only by genetic differences between the two racial groups. Similarly, William Shockley, in Dysgenics, Geneticity and Raceology: A Challenge to the Intellectual Responsibility of Educators, 72 Phi Delta Kappan 297 (1972), attributed differences in black-white IQ to biological causes. Such studies have been questioned because of their source of funding. Lennon, supra. See generally Richard Delgado et al., Can Science Be Inopportune? Constitutional Validity of Governmental Restrictions on Race-IQ Research, 31 UCLA L. Rev. 128 (1983). Other studies have found that the so-called persistent IQ gap between blacks and whites is not persistent at all. Daniel Goleman, An Emerging Theory on Blacks' I.Q. Scores, N.Y. Times, Apr. 10, 1988, at 12-22. That article concludes on an ironic note:

> There is one aspect of IQ research which American researchers have singularly failed to take to its logical conclusion. In the United States, orientals (Japanese and Chinese) always score higher than whites. But while heredity scientists feel continually obliged, with a Walrus and Carpenter air of regret, to make the point that blacks are inferior to whites there is a notable reluctance to highlight the fact that whites should, by the same tests, be judged inferior to orientals.

The debate over genetic racial differences in intelligence broke out anew with the publication in 1994 of The Bell Curve: Intelligence and Class Structure in American Life by Richard Herrnstein and Charles Murray. This book's central thesis is that social ills can largely be traced to low intelligence and that intelligence is largely inherited. Because blacks consistently score lower than whites on standard intelligence tests and other criteria, the book also argues that blacks as a race are significantly less intelligent than whites as a race. Needless to say, The Bell Curve prompted an enormous amount of criticism of its methods and conclusions. E.g., Stephen J. Gould, The Mismeasure of Man (rev. ed. 1996) at 367; F. Allan Hanson, Testing, "The Bell Curve," and the Social Construction of Intelligence, 10 Tikkun 22 (1995).

This brings us back to the scientific bases of sex-linked differences beyond those obviously related to reproduction. See generally Cynthia Fuchs Epstein, Deceptive Distinctions: Sex, Gender, and the Social Order (1988); Carol Tarvis, The Mismeasure of Woman (1992). Scientific research, often conducted by women, has sought to identify such differences. Doreen Kimura, in Sex Differences in the Brain, Scientific American, Sept. 1992, at 118, 119, writes:

> Women and men differ not only in physical attributes and reproductive function but also in the way in which they solve intellectual problems. It has been fashionable to insist that these differences are minimal, the consequence of variations in experience during development. The bulk of the evidence suggests, however, that the effects of sex hormones on brain organization occur so early in life that from the start the environment is acting on differently wired brains in girls and boys. Such differences make it almost impossible to evaluate the effects of experience independent of physiological predisposition.

She goes on to conclude that sex differences "in intellectual function seem to lie in patterns of ability rather than in overall level of intelligence (IQ)." Id. Thus,

> [m]en, on average, perform better than women on certain spatial tasks. In particular, men have an advantage in tests that require the subject to imagine rotating an object or manipulating it in some other way. They outperform women in mathematical reasoning tests and in navigating their way through a route. Further, men are more accurate in tests of target-directed motorskills — that is, in guiding or intercepting projectiles.
>
> Women tend to be better than men at rapidly identifying matching items, a skill called perceptual speed. They have greater verbal fluency, including the ability to find words that begin with a specific letter or fulfill some other constraint. Women also outperform men in arithmetic calculation and in recalling landmarks from a route. Moreover, women are faster at certain precision manual tasks, such as placing pegs in designated holes on a board.

Id. Based on Kimura's research, some differences are slight, but others are large. Less significant than the observation of such differences, however, is the conclusion that "[d]iffering patterns of ability between men and women most probably reflect different hormonal influences on their developing brains." Id. at 120. Much of the data relied on to reach this conclusion is from animal studies, but some is drawn from studies of humans, including studies of girls exposed to excess androgens in the prenatal or neonatal stage, which can occur because of a genetic defect called congenital adrenal hyperplasia. Professor Kimura speculates that sex-role specialization during evolution explains the differences she observes. She concludes: "The finding of consistent and, in some cases, quite substantial sex differences suggests that men and women may have different occupational interests and capabilities, independent of societal influences." Id. at 125. See also Doreen Kimura, Sex and Cognition (1999).

Had her research been conducted earlier, should Sears have called Professor Kimura to buttress Professor Rosenberg's testimony?

More recently, Kingsley R. Browne published a lengthy article, Sex and Temperament in Modern Society: A Darwinian View of the Glass Ceiling and the Gender Gap, 27 Ariz. L. Rev. 971 (1995), which questions whether most differences in female achievement (the "glass ceiling" limiting women's access to the highest levels of employer hierarchies and the gender gap in wages) result from discrimination. Instead, he argues, a substantial part of these phenomena is

> the product of basic biological sex differences in personality and temperament. These differences have resulted from differential reproductive strategies that have been adopted by the two sexes during human history and are every bit as much a product of natural selection as our bipedal locomotion and opposable thumbs. Although these temperamental traits evolved in our hunting-and-gathering ancestral environment, they remain with us today whether or not they remain adaptive.

Id. at 984. Professor Browne is not explicit about how acceptance of such a view should affect the law of employment discrimination, but it is apparent that such an approach would lead to a very different analysis from that of those who argue that most sex differences are socially constructed. Following the publication of the article, Professor Browne published a more detailed analysis of his views on sexual harassment, the gender gap, and the "glass ceiling." Kingsley R. Browne, Biology at Work: Rethinking Sexual Equality (2002) ("removing barriers to inequality will not achieve equality" because biological differences exist between men and women that affect their behavior in the workplace).

While many feminists and others resist biological explanations for race or sex differences, some advocates of gay rights seem to welcome them. Professor Kimura also noted intriguing studies suggesting that "sexual behavior may reflect further anatomic differences," including a smaller brain region (an interstitial nucleus of the anterior hypothalamus) in homosexual than in heterosexual men. Kimura, supra at 125. A 1993 study published in 261 Science 321 noted a disproportionately high number of gay men found among the relatives on the mothers' side of gay males being studied. Dean H. Hamer, Stella Hu, Victoria L. Magnuson, Nan Hu & Angela Pattatucci, A Linkage Between DNA Markers on the X Chromosome and Male Sexual Orientation, 261 Science 321-27. The researchers then analyzed the X chromosome received from the mother in 40 pairs of homosexual brothers, finding that 33 brother pairs shared a similar pattern of genetic material in a particular area on the X chromosomes. This was unusual because these chromosomes normally vary greatly in brothers. The researchers, therefore, suspect a genetic origin for homosexuality. But see Alan P. Medinger, Study of Twins Has Important Implications, http://www.messiah.edu/hpages/facstaff/chase/h/articles/regenera/twins.htm (last visited Dec. 6, 2002). If further research confirms this tendency, some legal scholars think that laws regulating homosexual behavior will be undermined as unconstitutional. Presumably, that is because it is unfair to punish individuals for an immutable characteristic, much as race or sex. But see Janet E. Halley, Sexual Orientation and the Politics of Biology: A Critique of the Argument from Immutability, 46 Stan. L. Rev. 503 (1994). Are you persuaded? There are, of course, other possible uses for such information — attempts to biologically engineer sexual orientation or abort homosexual fetuses. See William A. Henry III, Born Gay?, Time, July 26, 1993, at 36. Cf. A. Dean Byrd & Stony Olsen, Homosexuality: Innate and Immutable?, 14 Regent U. L. Rev. 383 (2000/2001) (arguing that, even though homosexuality is biologically influenced, it is subject to successful treatment if the patient truly wants to change).

# Chapter 7

# Special Problems in Applying Title VII, Section 1981, and the ADEA

## A. INTRODUCTION

The broad theories developed in Part II generally control any Title VII suit. Distinctive problems, however, have arisen in applying these concepts to different types of discrimination. For example, the Supreme Court has had to determine whether alienage discrimination violates the statutory ban on national origin discrimination and the extent of Title VII's duty of employer "accommodation" with reference to the religious beliefs and practices of employees. In addition, some consideration is needed of an important provision in Title VII designed to prohibit retaliation for opposing discrimination.

This chapter considers the following topics. Section B treats the threshold question of coverage of Title VII, § 1981, and the Age Discrimination in Employment Act (ADEA). The next five sections deal with distinctive problems under Title VII. Thus, section C addresses several issues concerning gender discrimination, including pregnancy, sexual harassment, grooming and dress codes, and sexual orientation. Section D focuses on the problem of discrimination on the basis of religion, including the duty to accommodate. Section E examines national origin discrimination and alienage restrictions. Section F considers questions of union liability. In section G, we turn to a topic common to Title VII and the ADEA: retaliation for resisting discrimination. Finally, section H considers distinctive problems that arise under the ADEA.

461

## B.   COVERAGE OF TITLE VII,
##      SECTION 1981, AND THE ADEA

We have seen that the basic prohibitions of both Title VII and the ADEA are directed at "employers," "employment agencies," and "labor organizations." Civil Rights Act of 1964, §703(a)-(c), 42 U.S.C.S. §2000e-2(a)-(c) (2003); ADEA, 29 U.S.C.S. §623(a)-(c) (2003). It is these entities that are prohibited from engaging in discrimination. Each of these terms is defined separately. For example, subject to exceptions, the term "employer" is defined by Title VII as "a person engaged in an industry affecting commerce who has fifteen or more employees for each working day in each of twenty or more calendar weeks in the current or preceding calendar year, and any agent of such person." §701(b), 42 U.S.C.S. §2000e(b) (2003). The ADEA is phrased identically, except that "employers" includes only those who have 20 or more employees. 29 U.S.C.S. §630(b) (2003).

These definitions are, however, to a large extent circular. An "employer" must have "employees," but the statutes define "employee" as "an individual employed by an employer." §701(f), 42 U.S.C.S. §2000e(f) (2003); 29 U.S.C.S. §630(f) (2003). The critical concept for these statutes, then, is what constitutes "employment." That term, however, is not defined by either Title VII or the ADEA, leaving courts to struggle with where "employment" begins and other legal relationships end.

### HISHON v. KING & SPALDING
#### 467 U.S. 69 (1984)

[Chief Justice BURGER wrote for the unanimous Court:
In 1972, Elizabeth Hishon became an associate of the defendant law firm, a firm of more than 50 partners and about 50 associates. She claimed that the prospect of partnership was an important factor in her initial decision to accept employment and that defendant had used that prospect as a recruiting device to induce her to join the firm. She claimed that the firm had represented that advancement to partnership after five or six years was a matter of course for associates who received satisfactory evaluations and that associates were promoted to partnership "on a fair and equal basis." Hishon sued after being considered and rejected for partnership, alleging sex discrimination.]

Petitioner alleges that respondent is an "employer" to whom Title VII is addressed. She then asserts that consideration for partnership was one of the "terms, conditions, or privileges of employment" as an associate with respondent. If this is correct, respondent could not base an adverse partnership decision on "race, color, religion, sex, or national origin."

Once a contractual relationship of employment is established, the provisions of Title VII attach and govern certain aspects of that relationship. In the context of Title VII, the contract of employment may be written or oral, formal or informal; an informal contract of employment may arise by the simple act of handing a job applicant a shovel and providing a workplace. The contractual relationship of employment triggers the provision of Title VII governing "terms, conditions, or privileges of employment." Title VII in turn forbids discrimination on the basis of "race, color, religion, sex, or national origin."

Because the underlying employment relationship is contractual, it follows that the "terms, conditions, or privileges of employment" clearly include benefits that are part of an employment contract. Here, petitioner in essence alleges that respondent made a contract to consider her for partnership.[6] Indeed, this promise was allegedly a key contractual provision which induced her to accept employment. If the evidence at trial establishes that the parties contracted to have petitioner considered for partnership, that promise clearly was a term, condition, or privilege of her employment. Title VII would then bind respondents to consider petitioner for partnership as the statute provides, i.e., without regard to petitioner's sex. The contract she alleges would lead to the same result.

Petitioner's claim that a contract was made, however, is not the only allegation that would qualify respondent's consideration of petitioner for partnership as a term, condition, or privilege of employment. An employer may provide its employees with many benefits that it is under no obligation to furnish by an express or implied contract. Such a benefit, though not a contractual right of employment, may qualify as a "privileg[e]" of employment under Title VII. A benefit that is part and parcel of the employment relationship may not be doled out in a discriminatory fashion, even if the employer would be free under the employment contract simply not to provide the benefit at all. Those benefits that comprise the "incidents of employment," or that form "an aspect of the relationship between the employer and employees" may not be afforded in a manner contrary to Title VII.

Several allegations in petitioner's complaint would support the conclusion that the opportunity to become a partner was part and parcel of an associate's status as an employee at respondent's firm, independent of any allegation that such an opportunity was included in associates' employment contracts. Petitioner alleges that respondent's associates could regularly expect to be considered for partnership at the end of their "apprenticeships," and it appears that lawyers outside the firm were not routinely so considered. Thus, the benefit of partnership consideration was allegedly linked directly with an associate's status as an employee, and this linkage was far more than coincidental: Petitioner alleges that respondent explicitly used the prospect of ultimate partnership to induce young lawyers to join the firm. Indeed, the importance of the partnership decision to a lawyer's status as an associate is underscored by the allegation that associates' employment is terminated if they are not elected to become partners. These allegations, if proved at trial, would suffice to show that partnership consideration was a term, condition, or privilege of an associate's employment at respondent's firm, and accordingly that partnership consideration must be without regard to sex. . . .

Justice POWELL, concurring. . . .

I write to make clear my understanding that the Court's opinion should not be read as extending Title VII to the management of a law firm by its partners. The reasoning of the Court's opinion does not require that the relationship among partners be characterized as an "employment" relationship to which Title VII would apply. The relationship among law partners differs markedly from that between employer and

6. Petitioner not only alleges that respondent promised to consider her for partnership, but also that it promised to consider her on a "fair and equal basis." This latter promise is not necessary to petitioner's Title VII claim. Even if the employment contract did not afford a basis for an implied condition that the ultimate decision would be fairly made on the merits, Title VII itself would impose such a requirement. If the promised consideration for partnership is a term, condition, or privilege of employment, then the partnership decision must be without regard to "race, color, religion, sex, or national origin."

employee — including that between the partnership and its associates.[2] The judgmental and sensitive decisions that must be made among the partners embrace a wide range of subjects.[3] The essence of the law partnership is the common conduct of a shared enterprise. The relationship among law partners contemplates that decisions important to the partnership normally will be made by common agreement . . . or consent among the partners. . . .

## NOTES

1. As *Hishon* stresses, the Title VII prohibition of discrimination by "employers" is limited to discrimination in the employment relationship. Consequently, discrimination, even by persons who qualify as statutory "employers," does not infringe on Title VII unless it occurs in an employment context. See note 12.

2. *Hishon* reasoned that plaintiff, as an associate with the firm, was plainly an employee. If, as she claimed, a term of her employment was to be considered for partnership, Title VII required the firm to consider her without regard to sex. Once the firm made her a partner, however, could she then be subjected to sex discrimination? Similarly, the ADEA clearly covers King & Spalding in its relationships with its associates. But a firm rule requiring all partners to retire at age 65 presumably would not be discrimination in employment, but only discrimination in the partnership arrangements and outside the ADEA. Or suppose King & Spalding acquired partners only by "lateral entry," that is, by inviting into the partnership persons not previously affiliated with the firm. Because such persons are not employees and are being offered "partnership," not "employment," Title VII and the ADEA probably would not apply.

3. As stated in the concurrence, "[a]n employer may not evade the strictures of Title VII simply by labeling its employees as 'partners.'" But what test will be used to determine who is a "partner"? In some large organizations, partners may be employees within the meaning of Title VII and the ADEA. Simpson v. Ernst & Young, 100 F.3d 436 (6th Cir. 1996) (holding "partner" to be an employee). See generally Leigh Pokora, Comment, Partners as Employees Under Title VII: The Saga Continues, 22 Ohio N.U. L. Rev. 249 (1995). Some other business organizations pose a similar problem. "Stockholder-employees" in professional corporations have been held to be employees for purposes of the antidiscrimination statutes. Wells v. Clackamas Gastroenterology Assocs., P.C., 271 F.3d 903 (9th Cir. 2001), *cert. granted*, 123 S. Ct. 31 (2002). Contra EEOC v. Dowd & Dowd, Ltd., 736 F.2d 1177 (7th Cir. 1984). See also Trainer v. Apollo Metal Specialties, Inc., 2002 U.S. App. LEXIS 25,654 (10th Cir. 2002) (controlling shareholder was also an employee). Are members of limited liability companies employees? See generally Daniel S. Klienberger, "Magnificent Circularity" and the Churkendoose: LLC Members and Federal Employment Law, 22 Okla. City U. L. Rev. 477 (1997).

2. Of course, an employer may not evade the strictures of Title VII simply by labeling its employees as "partners." Law partnerships usually have many of the characteristics that I describe generally here.

3. These decisions concern such matters as participation in profits and other types of compensation; work assignments; approval of commitments in bar association, civic or political activities; questions of billing; acceptance of new clients; questions of conflicts of interest; retirement programs; and expansion policies. Such decisions may affect each partner of the firm. Divisions of partnership profits, unlike shareholders' rights to dividends, involve judgments as to each partner's contribution to the reputation and success of the firm. This is true whether the partner's participation in profits is measured in terms of points or percentages, combinations of salaries and points, salaries and bonuses, and possibly in other ways.

Even if certain organizational relationships are beyond Title VII and the ADEA, other legal protections may apply. Mark S. Kende, in Shattering the Glass Ceiling: A Legal Theory for Attacking Discrimination Against Women Partners, 46 Hastings L.J. 17 (1994), argued the implied covenant of good faith and fair dealing in the association's charter can be interpreted to prohibit participants from discriminating against each other on the basis of gender. In addition, § 1981 prohibits race and alienage discrimination in the formation, terms, and administration of contracts.

4.  A related question is whether a person who renders personal services for another is an "employee" or an "independent contractor." Title VII and the ADEA do not protect "independent contractors." E.g., EEOC v. North Knox Sch. Corp., 154 F.3d 744 (7th Cir. 1998). The distinction between "employees" and "independent contractors" arose under the common law in deciding whether a principal was liable for the torts of his agent: such liability attached if the agent was an employee, but not if he was an independent contractor. The distinction turned primarily on the degree of control the principal exerted over the work of the agent. If the control was substantial, the principal was liable for his agent's work-related torts. If the degree of control was less, the agent was labeled an "independent contractor" and the principal generally was not liable. See Hunt v. State of Missouri, 297 F.3d 735 (8th Cir. 2002) (employees of temporary agency were correctly found to be employees of the defendant employer when it controlled their job performance). The Restatement (Second) of Agency § 220(1) (1958) lists ten factors by which the degree of control can be measured.

5.  Should the common law approach be applied under Title VII and the ADEA? Perhaps terms used by Congress, such as "employee," should be taken in their traditional common law sense. But a second test, the "economic realities" approach, was developed under the Fair Labor Standards Act long before Title VII was enacted. See, e.g., Bartels v. Birmingham, 332 U.S. 126, 130 (1947). Basically, this approach looks to the degree of economic dependency of the putative employee on the principal to decide if an "employment" relationship exists: the greater the dependency, the more likely the person is an "employee." See, e.g., Armbruster v. Quinn, 711 F.2d 1332, 1340 (6th Cir. 1983). A third approach is called the "hybrid" test. Under this approach, the characterization decision turns primarily on the degree of the principal's control, but the degree of economic dependency on the principal is also considered. See, e.g., Oestman v. National Farmers Union Ins. Co., 958 F.2d 303 (10th Cir. 1992).

In Nationwide Mutual Insurance Co. v. Darden, 503 U.S 318 (1992), the Supreme Court held that common law agency principles govern the definition of "employee" under ERISA. The Court indicated that, where a statute is not helpful in defining "employee," the courts should look to the common law definition. The Court stated that "[a]gency law principles comport, moreover, with our recent precedents and with the common understanding reflected in these precedents, of the difference between an employee and an independent contractor." Id. at 327. In short, Darden declared that, where the statute is unclear, a court should not infer a broader meaning than the common law definition of employee.

Darden suggests that neither the economic realities nor the hybrid test is applicable to Title VII and the ADEA. However, each of the three tests has purportedly been applied in recent decisions. E.g., EEOC v. North Knox Sch. Corp., 154 F.3d 744 (7th Cir. 1998) (economic realities test); Cilecek v. Inova Health Sys. Servs., 115 F.3d 256 (4th Cir. 1997) (common law test); Lambertsen v. Utah Dept. of Corrections, 79 F.3d 1024 (10th Cir. 1996) (hybrid test). When one looks beneath the courts' labels, however, Darden has pushed the courts toward the common law approach. In fact, some courts now deny that the economic realities and hybrid tests substantially differ from the common law test. E.g., Simpson v. Ernst & Young, 100 F.3d 436 (6th Cir. 1996); Wilde v. County of Kandiyohi, 15 F.3d 103 (8th Cir. 1993). See generally Lewis L. Maltby & David C. Yamada, Beyond "Economic Realities": The Case for Amending Federal Employment Discrimination Laws to Include Independent Contractors, 38 B.C. L. Rev. 239 (1997).

6. These problems do not typically arise under § 1981. That statute reaches substantially all contractual relations, not merely employment. See Runyon v. McCrary, 427 U.S. 160 (1976). Thus, § 1981 reaches relationships that do not constitute "employment" under Title VII, such as partnership or independent contractor status. E.g., Danco, Inc. v. Wal-Mart Stores, Inc., 178 F.3d 8 (1st Cir. 1999) (corporate independent contractor, but not its owner or employees, protected by § 1981). Further, § 1981 reaches all employers, except the federal government, thus covering employers exempt from Title VII. Of course, § 1981 bars only racial and alienage discrimination: Hishon could not have succeeded on her sex discrimination claim under that statute.

Nevertheless, some limitations on the reach of § 1981 may exist. Concurring in Runyon v. McCrary, 427 U.S. 160, 187-188 (1976) (private school violates § 1981 by excluding black children), Justice Powell attempted to identify "personal contracts" beyond the reach of § 1981: "[where] the choice made by the offeror is selective, it reflects 'a purpose of exclusiveness' other than the desire to bar members of the Negro race. Such a purpose, certainly in most cases, would invoke associational rights long respected." That decision also recognized that various constitutional bases, such as freedom of association, free exercise of religion, and the right of privacy are potential limits on § 1981 liability. For example, there may be a free exercise of religion defense to refusing to hire an applicant of a particular race when church dogma requires racial segregation. Brown v. Dade Christian Schs., Inc., 556 F.2d 310 (5th Cir. 1977). The right of association, however, was no defense for the private school's refusal to accept black children in *Runyon*. Freedom of association claims also were rejected in Roberts v. United States Jaycees, 468 U.S. 609 (1984), and in a portion of *Hishon* not reproduced.

7. Recent decisions have divided over whether § 1981 is applicable to at-will employment. The only appellate decisions to have analyzed the question in detail have concluded that it is, at least when at-will employment is contractual under state law. Perry v. Woodward, 199 F.3d 1126 (10th Cir. 1999); Spriggs v. Diamond Auto Glass, 165 F.3d 1015 (4th Cir. 1999); Fadeyi v. Planned Parenthood Assn., 160 F.3d 1048 (5th Cir. 1998). Indeed, *Fadeyi* seems to go further, implying that § 1981 is applicable to employment at will regardless of state law. In contrast, several recent district court decisions have held that § 1981 is not applicable to at-will employment, apparently assuming that state law did not regard at-will employment as contractual. E.g., Moorer v. Grumman Aerospace Corp., 964 F. Supp. 665 (E.D.N.Y. 1997), *aff'd on grounds stated below*, 162 F.3d 1148 (2d Cir. 1998). See also Gonzales v. Ingersoll Milling Mach. Co., 133 F.3d 1025 (7th Cir. 1998).

8. "Employment agencies" and "labor organizations" have posed few problems, Charles A. Sullivan, Michael J. Zimmer & Rebecca Hanner White, Employment Discrimination Law and Practice § 1.06 (3d ed. 2002), although unions that are sued in their employer capacity (rather than in their representative capacity) may have to qualify as "employers" in order to be covered. Ferroni v. Teamsters, Chauffeurs & Warehousemen Local No. 222, 297 F.3d 1146 (10th Cir. 2002). However, a number of questions have arisen with the definition of "employer."

The main issue has been whether the defendant employed the requisite number of employees for the required time period. Although hourly, part-time, and on-leave employees count, Walters v. Metropolitan Educ. Enters., 519 U.S. 202 (1997), others clearly do not, including partners, Burke v. Friedman, 556 F.2d 867 (7th Cir. 1977), corporate directors, McGraw v. Warren County Oil Co., 707 F.2d 990 (8th Cir. 1983), and independent contractors, Ost v. West Suburban Travelers Limousine, Inc., 88 F.3d 435 (7th Cir. 1996). Sometimes two or more entities may be aggregated in order to find a statutory employer. E.g., Kang v. U. Lim Am., Inc., 296 F.3d 810 (9th Cir. 2002); Papa v. Katy Indus., Inc., 166 F.3d 937 (7th Cir. 1999); Lambertsen v. Utah Dept. of Corr., 79 F.3d 1024 (10th Cir. 1996). Where a foreign corporation has an office in the United States, the courts are divided on whether the corporation's foreign employees are counted. See Morelli v. Cedel, 141 F.3d 39 (2d Cir. 1996), and the cases cited there. A similar problem is whether one counts only the employees of an instrumentality of a state (or political subdivision) or all the employees of the state (or political subdivision). See, e.g., Bristol v. Bd. of County Comm'rs, 312 F.3d 1213 (10th Cir. 2002); Palmer v. Ark. Council on Econ. Educ., 154 F.3d 892 (8th Cir. 1998). Finally, a few district court decisions have recently shown concern for whether particular employers satisfy the "commerce" requirement in the statute. E.g., Vasquez v. Visions, Inc., 2002 U.S. Dist. LEXIS 1091 (N.D. Ill. Jan. 23, 2002) (nonprofit corporation with de minimis connection to interstate commerce not covered by Title VII).

9. Both Title VII and the ADEA generally reach state and local governmental employers. The Eleventh Amendment clearly permits private Title VII enforcement against state employers, but private ADEA suits may not be brought against state employers. Private suits under the ADA may not be brought against the state where Title I is concerned, although there is conflicting authority under Title II. See pages 920-924. In any event, both statutes exempt from their definition of "employee" elected officers and "any person chosen by such officer to be on such officer's personal staff, or an appointee on the policy-making level or an immediate adviser with respect to the exercise of the constitutional or legal powers of the office." 42 U.S.C.S. § 2000e(f) (2003); 29 U.S.C.S. § 630(f) (2003). E.g., EEOC v. Bd. of Trustees of Wayne County Community College, 723 F.2d 509 (6th Cir. 1983) (community college president is a policy-maker within the meaning of the statute). Such persons, however, may have protection under a related statute. See pages 923-924.

10. Section 1981 also reaches the contractual relationships of state and local governmental employers. Any doubt was resolved by the 1991 Civil Rights Act's addition of paragraph (c), providing that "[t]he rights protected by this section are protected against impairment by nongovernmental discrimination and impairment under color of State law." However, the recovery of compensatory and punitive damages from a governmental entity may be subject to several limitations. See note 6, pages 949-950. There may also be Eleventh Amendment questions about private suits. See pages 920-924.

11. Almost all federal civilian employment is also covered by Title VII and the ADEA through separate provisions in each law. § 717, 42 U.S.C.S. § 2000e-16 (2003); 29 U.S.C.S. § 633(a) (2003). The remaining federal civilian employees are protected by either the Civil Rights Act of 1991 or the Congressional Accountability Act of 1995, Pub. L. No. 104-1, 109 Stat. 3. Section 1981, however, does not reach federal employment. Brown v. General Serv. Admin., 425 U.S. 820, 825 (1976) (Title VII exclusive discrimination remedy for federal employment within its scope); Lee v. Hughes, 145 F.3d 1272 (11th Cir. 1998).

12. Some courts expand Title VII's reach in a way that is not obvious. In Sibley Meml. Hosp. v. Wilson, 488 F.2d 1338 (D.C. Cir. 1973), a male private-duty nurse challenged the defendant hospital's refusal to assign him to care for female patients.

The hospital responded that neither the plaintiff nor the hospital contemplated an employment relationship between them; rather, the employment relationship was between the nurse and his patients. The hospital contended, therefore, that it was not an "employer." The court held that Title VII prohibits an "employer" from discriminating against any "individual" (not merely against "employees") with regard to employment; therefore, the hospital's discriminatory referral practices were actionable because they "interfer[ed] with an individual's employment opportunities with another employer." Id. at 1341. Accord Zaklama v. Mt. Sinai Med. Ctr., 842 F.2d 291 (11th Cir. 1988). But see Bender v. Suburban Hosp., 159 F.3d 186 (4th Cir. 1998), and Diggs v. Harris Hosp.-Methodist, Inc., 847 F.2d 270 (5th Cir. 1988) (assuming arguendo that interference with third-person employment constituted a violation, interference with a physician's opportunities to care for private patients did not constitute interference with an employment relationship). But even *Sibley* jurisdictions balk when the "other employer" is a corporation wholly owned by the plaintiff. Hayden v. La-Z-Boy Chair Co., 9 F.3d 617 (7th Cir. 1993). See generally Andrew O. Schiff, Note, The Liability of Third Parties Under Title VII, 18 U. Mich. J.L. Reform 167 (1984); Michael B. Metzger & John F. Suhre, The Jurisdictional Reach of Title VII, 34 Sw. L.J. 817 (1980). Should the courts extend *Sibley* to state licensing decisions? See Association of Mexican-Am. Educators v. California, 231 F.3d 572 (9th Cir. 2000) (en banc); Darks v. City of Cincinnati, 745 F.2d 1040 (6th Cir. 1984).

13. There are miscellaneous exemptions in the antidiscrimination statutes. Title VII, for example, exempts a "bona fide private membership club." § 701(b)(2), 42 U.S.C.S. § 2000e(b)(2) (2003). At the time this exception was recognized, there was reason to believe that it was constitutionally required. But in a portion of the *Hishon* opinion not reproduced above, the Court held that King & Spalding had no constitutional right of association that prevented the application of Title VII to partnership decisions. See also New York State Club Assn. v. City of New York, 487 U.S. 1 (1988) (upholding constitutionality of amendment to New York City Human Rights Law substantially narrowing its "private club" exemption); Roberts v. United States Jaycees, 468 U.S. 609 (1984). Another Title VII exception is for Indian tribes. § 701(b), 42 U.S.C.S. § 2000e(b) (2003). While this exception is not expressly included in the ADEA, it has been read into the statute. E.g., EEOC v. Fond du Lac Heavy Equip. Co., 986 F.2d 246 (8th Cir. 1993). See also EEOC v. Kavok Tribe Hous. Auth., 260 F.3d 1071 (9th Cir. 2001). See generally Vicki J. Limas, Application of Federal Labor and Employment Statutes to Native American Tribes: Respecting Sovereignty and Achieving Consistency, 26 Ariz. St. L.J. 681 (1994).

14. Other exceptions to Title VII, § 1981, and the ADEA may be found in other federal laws. In Sumitomo Shoji, America, Inc. v. Avagliano, 457 U.S. 176 (1982), the Supreme Court considered a claim that, by virtue of the Friendship, Commerce, and Navigation Treaty between the United States and Japan, the defendant was immune from Title VII for discrimination against non-Japanese in filling certain positions. The Court rejected the defense on the ground that the defendant, a New York-incorporated subsidiary of a Japanese corporation, did not qualify as a "company of Japan," but indicated that a true "company of Japan" can invoke this defense. See also Papaila v. Uniden Am. Corp., 51 F.3d 54 (5th Cir. 1995) (U.S. subsidiary can invoke treaty where discrimination dictated by parent).

The most important authority on these questions since *Sumitomo Shoji* dealt with a similar treaty between the United States and Korea. MacNamara v. Korean Air Lines, 863 F.2d 1135 (3d Cir. 1988), held that the "target of [the treaty] was legislation that forced foreign employers to hire host country personnel." Id. at 1144. It therefore concluded that the treaty simply allowed the use of citizenship as a criterion for employment. So read, the court found no direct conflict with Title VII, which does not prohibit the use of citizenship. The court went on to hold, however, that the treaty does preclude Title VII liability for any disparate impact resulting from use of a citizenship requirement. The effect of *MacNamara* is to prohibit a beneficiary of the treaty from intentionally discriminating, even in its executive positions, on the basis of age, sex, religion, or race. The court did not consider whether the treaty would provide a defense under the Immigration Reform and Control Act of 1986 (IRCA), which prohibits discrimination against United States citizens and authorized aliens. See page 633. See generally Daniel H. Tabak, Note, Friendship Treaties and Discriminatory Practices, 28 Colum. J.L. & Soc. Probs. 475 (1995).

More controversially, the Fourth Circuit has held that the IRCA has the effect of excluding "unauthorized aliens" from the protection of Title VII and the ADEA, at least with regard to hiring decisions. Chaudhry v. Mobil Oil Corp., 186 F.3d 502 (4th Cir. 1999); Egbuna v. Time-Life Libraries, Inc., 153 F.3d 184 (4th Cir. 1998) (en banc and per curiam). This ruling is discussed on page 634.

15. As originally enacted, Title VII did not extend to the employment of Americans outside the United States. EEOC v. Arabian Am. Oil Co., 499 U.S. 244 (1991). The Civil Rights Act of 1991 prospectively overruled this decision by adding a sentence to the definition of "employee": "With respect to employment in a foreign country, such term includes an individual who is a citizen of the United States." § 701(f), 42 U.S.C.S. § 2000e(f) (2003). The breadth of this provision was, however, limited by the simultaneous addition of § 702(b), 42 U.S.C.S. § 2000e-1(b) (2003), which allowed discrimination "with respect to an employee . . . in a foreign country if compliance [with Title VII] would cause such employer . . . to violate the law of the foreign country in which such workplace is located." Thus, if foreign law excluded women from certain occupations, the exemption would immunize discrimination against American women applicants for those positions. See Mahoney v. RFE/RL, Inc., 47 F.3d 447 (D.C. Cir. 1995) (exemption applied when application of the ADEA would require violating a collective bargaining agreement in a country where such departures are illegal without approval by government-established "works councils").

Although U.S. citizens abroad are now "employees," the new statute expressly excludes foreign companies acting abroad from coverage. Section 702(c)(2), 42 U.S.C.S. § 2000e-1(c)(2) (2003), provides that Title VII "shall not apply with respect to the foreign operations of an employer that is a foreign person not controlled by an American employer." In short, American corporations operating abroad are covered, but "foreign persons" are not. The remaining question is the extent to which foreign affiliates of American corporations may be treated as American employers. This is addressed in § 702(c)(1), 42 U.S.C.S. § 2000e-1(c)(1) (2003), which extends Title VII to foreign corporations that are "controlled" by American corporations.

These provisions closely parallel those Congress had earlier added to the ADEA. 29 U.S.C.S. § 623(h) (2003). See generally Louise P. Zanar, Note, Recent Amendments to the Age Discrimination in Employment Act, 19 Geo. Wash. J. Intl. L. & Econ. 165 (1985).

## C.  SEX DISCRIMINATION

Sex discrimination claims have raised a series of difficult problems flowing from what the term "sex" means under Title VII. This section considers four areas in which definitional problems have manifested themselves: pregnancy; sexual harassment; gender-based grooming and dress codes; and discrimination on the basis of sexual orientation or preference. The section on sexual harassment also addresses harassment based on membership in other protected classes. These cases are discussed here because most of the law in this area originated with sexual harassment cases. Finally, the fifth part of the section on sex discrimination will briefly consider the problem of achieving wage equality for women under Title VII and the Equal Pay Act (EPA), 29 U.S.C.S. § 206(d) (2003).

## 1.  Pregnancy

The central theme of employment discrimination law is the notion that similarly situated individuals should receive equal treatment by employers. In previous chapters, we have seen courts struggle to remain true to this theme even though the groups protected by antidiscrimination laws are not, in fact, always similarly situated. First, the statutes have been interpreted to permit (but not require) employers to engage in affirmative action because courts recognize that some of the groups protected by the antidiscrimination laws are not similarly situated as a result of past discrimination. Second, differences among groups sometimes cause neutral work rules to have a disparate impact on the employment opportunities of different groups. Even though these neutral rules treat similarly situated employees equally, employers cannot use them unless they are job related and consistent with business necessity. Impact analysis, however, remains true to the equality principle by allowing job-related differences to support different treatment. Third, we will see in section D that Title VII requires employers to accommodate religious differences, a candid recognition that some religious practices distinguish religious employees from secular society.

These exceptions to the equality principle reflect an alternative theme for employment discrimination law: *equalizing employment opportunity* even for groups who are different in some respects. Title VII's prohibition against discrimination on the basis of pregnancy highlights the tension between equal treatment and equal opportunity inherent in the antidiscrimination laws. Pregnancy, childbirth, and related medical conditions affect a woman's ability to work. Most women who carry a child to term will require six to eight weeks of leave to deliver the child and physically recover from childbirth. Women who work in jobs that require physical activity also may be impaired during the latter months of their pregnancy. Given these differences, what constitutes discrimination on the basis of pregnancy? What is *equal* treatment? Is equal treatment sufficient to provide pregnant women with equal employment opportunities?

This section will first explore Title VII's response to discrimination on the basis of pregnancy and will then consider whether Title VII adequately addresses the problems faced by fertile women in the workplace. In this latter regard, we will examine the most recent statute addressing this and similar problems, the Family and Medical Leave Act of 1993 (FMLA).

The Supreme Court's first encounter with the question of pregnancy discrimination was not auspicious. In General Electric Co. v. Gilbert, 429 U.S. 125 (1976), the Court concluded that discrimination on the basis of pregnancy was not discrimination on the basis of sex within the meaning of Title VII. *Gilbert* involved an employer-sponsored disability insurance plan that excluded pregnancy from coverage. The Court followed Fourteenth Amendment equal protection precedent established in Geduldig v. Aiello, 417 U.S. 484 (1974), holding that pregnancy classifications are not gender classifications. In reaching its result, the *Gilbert* Court quoted from a footnote in *Geduldig*:

> The lack of identity between the excluded disability [pregnancy] and gender as such . . . becomes clear upon the most cursory analysis. The program divides potential recipients into two groups — pregnant women and nonpregnant persons. While the first group is exclusively female, the second includes members of both sexes.

429 U.S. at 135. Congress soon overruled *Gilbert* by passing the Pregnancy Discrimination Act of 1978 (PDA), Pub. L. No. 95-555, 92 Stat. 2076 (Oct. 31, 1978), which amended Title VII to include a new § 701(k):

> The terms "because of sex" or "on the basis of sex" include, but are not limited to, because of or on the basis of pregnancy, childbirth, or related medical conditions; and women affected by pregnancy, childbirth, or related medical conditions shall be treated the same for all employment-related purposes, including receipt of benefits under fringe benefit programs, as other persons not so affected but similar in their ability or inability to work, and nothing in section 703(h) of this title shall be interpreted to permit otherwise. . . .

The Supreme Court's first decision considering pregnancy discrimination after the PDA was ironic in two respects. First, the Court struck down a pregnancy limitation because it discriminated against *male* employees; and second, the Court analyzed the PDA less in terms of its language dealing with pregnancy discrimination than as casting light on Title VII's basic prohibition against sex discrimination.

## NEWPORT NEWS SHIPBUILDING & DRY DOCK CO. v. EEOC
### 462 U.S. 669 (1983)

[This case involved an employer-sponsored medical plan that provided the same hospitalization coverage for male and female employees but that differentiated between female employees and spouses of male employees by imposing a cap on the pregnancy-related hospital benefits for spouses of male workers. The Court held that the employer's plan discriminated against its male employees: "[T]he Pregnancy Discrimination Act, not only overturned the specific holding in General Electric v. Gilbert, but also rejected the test of discrimination employed by the Court in that case." The majority concluded that, in passing the PDA, Congress adopted the dissenters' view in *Gilbert* that the defendant's exclusion of pregnancy-related disabilities was illegal. In that case, Justice Brennan had thought it facially discriminatory to have "a policy that, but for pregnancy, offers protection for all risks, even those that are 'unique to' men or heavily male dominated." Justice Stevens had stressed that the plan discriminated because it distinguished "between persons who face a risk of pregnancy — [i.e., women] and those who do not." While this reasoning failed to convince the majority in *Gilbert*, it did persuade Congress in passing the PDA.]

[I]f a private employer were to provide complete health insurance coverage for the dependents of its female employees, and no coverage at all for the dependents of its male employees, it would violate Title VII. Such a practice would not pass the simple test of Title VII discrimination that we enunciated in Los Angeles Department of Water & Power v. Manhart, for it would treat a male employee with dependents "in a manner which but for that person's sex would be different." The same result would be reached even if the magnitude of the discrimination were smaller. For example, a plan that provided complete hospitalization coverage for the spouses of female employees but did not cover spouses of male employees when they had broken bones would violate Title VII by discriminating against male employees.

Petitioner's practice is just as unlawful. Its plan provides limited pregnancy-related benefits for employees' wives, and affords more extensive coverage for employees' spouses for all other medical conditions requiring hospitalization. Thus, the husbands of female employees receive a specified level of hospitalization coverage for all conditions; the wives of male employees receive such coverage except for pregnancy-related conditions. Although *Gilbert* concluded that an otherwise inclusive plan that singled out pregnancy-related benefits for exclusion was nondiscriminatory on its face, because only women can become pregnant, Congress has unequivocally rejected that reasoning. The 1978 Act makes clear that it is discriminatory to treat pregnancy-related conditions less favorably than other medical conditions. Thus, petitioner's plan unlawfully gives married male employees a benefit package for their dependents that is less inclusive than the dependency coverage provided to married female employees.

[The Court stressed that the issue was not pregnancy coverage per se: there is no requirement that an employer provide any medical insurance at all.]

## NOTES

1. What does it mean to discriminate on the basis of pregnancy? Does the statute flatly bar discrimination because of pregnancy? Surprisingly, failing to hire a woman because she is pregnant does not necessarily violate Title VII. In Marafino v. St. Louis County Circuit Court, 707 F.2d 1005 (8th Cir. 1983), failure to hire a pregnant woman as a judicial law clerk who would require a leave of absence soon after starting work was held to be lawful because the employer would not have hired *anyone* who required a leave of absence shortly after beginning work. Accord Marshall v. American Hosp. Assn., 157 F.3d 520 (7th Cir. 1998) (no violation to discharge employee who required pregnancy leave during the busiest time of the year prior to an important annual conference). Even so, won't pregnant women be more easily identified than others as persons who will require leave?

2. One analysis of the PDA offers two different meanings of the statute based on the two clauses in the law:

> One reading . . . suggests that the second clause [women affected by pregnancy . . . shall be treated the same as other persons not so affected but similar in their ability or inability to work] gives substance to the first [the terms "because of sex" or "on the basis of sex" include, but are not limited to, because of or on the basis of pregnancy . . .], which is viewed as primarily definitional. Thus the prohibition of differential treatment means that pregnant women shall not be singled out because of their disability, but rather shall be treated the same as any other employees, based on their ability to work. . . . An alternative reading places greater emphasis on the fact that Congress specifically amended Title VII to remedy problems of pregnancy discrimination. [It focuses on the first clause of the amendments.]

. . . Following this [alternative] reading, Title VII . . . prohibits, for example, an employer from discharging an employee because she is pregnant, regardless of the treatment of a similarly disabled but non-pregnant employee — because the employee would not be fired but for her pregnancy.

Andrew Weissmann, Note, Sexual Equality Under the Pregnancy Discrimination Act, 83 Colum. L. Rev. 690, 694-96 (1983). See also Wendy W. Williams, Equality's Riddle: Pregnancy and the Equal Treatment/Special Treatment Debate, 13 N.Y.U. Rev. L. & Soc. Change 325 (1985).

3. To appreciate the difference between the two approaches, suppose an employer has a no leave policy for everyone. Does Title VII require that employer to provide leave to pregnant women? Stout v. Baxter Healthcare Corp., 282 F.3d 856, 861 (5th Cir. 2002) (although a "no leave" policy would affect all or substantially all pregnant women, no treatment or impact claim was stated; "To hold otherwise would be to transform the PDA into a guarantee of medical leave for pregnant employees, something we have specifically held that the PDA does not do.").

4. Sometimes, a policy will facially discriminate on the basis of pregnancy and will be struck down on that basis. See EEOC v. W & O Inc., 213 F.3d 600 (11th Cir. 2000) (restaurant's policy prohibiting pregnant waitresses from serving tables after the fifth month of pregnancy was discriminatory on its face). However, pregnancy discrimination, like other sex discrimination, can be justified if "not being pregnant" is a bfoq. If the discrimination is not facial, the employer may simply deny that pregnancy had anything to do with the adverse employment decision. Litigating cases in which the employer denies acting on the basis of pregnancy is nearly indistinguishable from litigating other individual disparate treatment claims. The issue is whether pregnancy was the basis of the employer's decision. To prevail, however, there must be evidence the defendant knew plaintiff was pregnant. See Prebilich-Holland v. Gaylord Entm't Co., 297 F.3d 438 (6th Cir. 2002).

5. In Tamimi v. Howard Johnson Co., 807 F.2d 1550 (11th Cir. 1987), plaintiff was discharged, allegedly for failing to abide by a newly promulgated policy that desk clerks wear makeup. The court upheld a finding of pregnancy discrimination:

[T]here is no doubt that if plaintiff had not become pregnant, she would not have been dismissed from her job. To require that plaintiff wear makeup because she appears less attractive when pregnant, even though the employer had no such requirement of plaintiff or any other employee prior to plaintiff's pregnancy, is a form of sexual discrimination.

Id. at 1554. No bfoq defense was established because defendant did not demonstrate that female employees had to wear makeup to maintain the defendant's "public image."

6. Are these individual disparate treatment claims based on the first clause, the second clause, or both clauses of the PDA? In these cases, the second clause of the PDA seems to do no more than explicitly require what is implicit in all Title VII disparate treatment cases: equal treatment of similarly situated individuals.

7. But is there a middle ground? Can the employer admit that the employee's pregnancy was relevant to the challenged employment decision but nevertheless win without establishing a bfoq? Marafino, 707 F.2d at 1006 n.2, indicates that the answer is yes, and a number of other decisions take the same position. In EEOC v. Detroit-Macomb Hosp. Ctr., 1992 U.S. App. LEXIS 647 (6th Cir. 1992), a nurse's aide who was medically restricted from entering isolation rooms to protect her unborn child was placed on involuntary leave until after the birth. Although the medical restriction

was necessitated by Jancowicz's pregnancy and was the basis of the decision to place her on leave, the court found no violation of the PDA because "non-pregnant workers with temporary disabilities and medical restrictions have been placed on disability leave similar to Jancowicz's." Id. at *3-4.

8. These cases seem inconsistent with the first clause of the PDA, but perhaps they are consistent with the second clause. The second clause can be viewed as defining "legitimate, nondiscriminatory reason" to include reasons that relate to pregnancy, but that apply to other disabilities as well. Alternatively, is it a defense — decisions based on pregnancy are permitted if similarly disabled individuals are treated in the same way?

9. Suppose an employer fires an unmarried pregnant woman. May it escape liability under the first clause of § 701(k) by claiming that it discriminated not because of pregnancy, but because of "immorality"? The courts seem to believe that it is permissible to discharge pregnant women as part of a policy against sexual immorality so long as the employer does (or would) also discharge men who engaged in premarital sex. E.g., Cline v. Catholic Diocese, 206 F.3d 651, 658 (6th Cir. 1999) ("The central question in this case, therefore, is whether St. Paul's nonrenewal of Cline's contract constituted discrimination based on her pregnancy as opposed to a gender-neutral enforcement of the school's premarital sex policy. While the former violates Title VII, the latter does not.").

10. The Fifth and Sixth Circuits disagree on the appropriate comparison to be made in pregnancy discrimination cases. The Sixth Circuit held that the appropriate comparison is with employees who are similarly situated *solely* with respect to their ability or inability to work. In Ensley-Gaines v. Runyon, 100 F.3d 1220 (6th Cir. 1996), the employer denied light duty to a pregnant employee on the ground that her work limitation, unlike the work limitations of accommodated employees, was not due to a job-related injury. The Sixth Circuit found discrimination because pregnant employees must be treated the same as other workers with similar work limitations *regardless of the source of the limitation.* Id. at 1226. The Fifth Circuit disagreed, finding no discrimination under similar circumstances. Urbano v. Continental Airlines, 138 F.3d 204, 208 (5th Cir. 1998). The court compared the pregnant employee with other employees who were *similar both in terms of their work restriction and in terms of the source of the restriction.* Applying this analysis, the pregnant employee was not discriminated against because she was treated the same as other employees who had similar work restrictions and whose injuries or illnesses were not employment related. Accord, Spivey v. Beverly Enterprises, 196 F.3d 1309 (11th Cir. 1999).

11. Is it pregnancy discrimination to treat a pregnant worker less favorably than other pregnant workers? See Deneen v. Northwest Airlines, 132 F.3d 431 (8th Cir. 1998) (yes).

12. Is it pregnancy discrimination to require clerical employees to submit to pregnancy tests in a pre-employment physical? See Norman-Bloodsaw v. Lawrence Berkeley Lab., 135 F.3d 1260 (9th Cir. 1998) (yes).

13. Is it pregnancy discrimination for an employer to refuse to accommodate an employee's need to pump breast milk? See Martinez v. NBC, Inc., 49 F. Supp. 2d 305 (S.D.N.Y. 1999) (no); Diana Kasdan, Note, Reclaiming Title VII and the PDA: Prohibiting Workplace Discrimination Against Breastfeeding Women, 76 N.Y.U. L. Rev. 309 (2001) (yes). Could it be argued that the PDA, by rejecting the analysis in *Gilbert,* established that discrimination based on *any* characteristic that is exclusive to women constitutes sex discrimination? Is breastfeeding "a related medical condition"? Is it sex discrimination for an employer's prescription drug plan to exclude

coverage for contraceptives? See Erickson v. Bartell Drug Co., 141 F. Supp. 2d 1266 (W.D. Wash. 2001) (yes). In Mauldin v. Wal-Mart Stores, Inc., 2002 WL 2022334 (N.D. Ga. 2002), a federal judge recently granted class action status to female employees challenging Wal-Mart's exclusion of contraceptive coverage. What if a plan excludes coverage for Viagra? Is that sex discrimination? For a suggestion that exclusion of contraceptives from prescription coverage also may violate the ADA, see Melissa Cole, Beyond Sex Discrimination: Why Employers Discriminate Against Women with Disabilities When Their Employee Health Plans Exclude Contraceptives from Prescription Coverage, 43 Ariz. L. Rev. 501 (2001).

What if a plan excludes coverage for certain infertility treatments? Is that sex discrimination if the exclusions are treatments that are only performed on women? Saks v. Franklin Covey Co., 2003 U.S. App. LEXIS 549 (2d Cir. 2003) (no).

## TROUPE v. MAY DEPARTMENT STORES CO.
### 20 F.3d 734 (7th Cir. 1994)

[Kimberly Hern Troupe, a department store saleswoman, was placed on probation for repeated tardiness ascribed to severe morning sickness. During her probation, Troupe was late to work 11 more days. On the day before she planned to begin her maternity leave, Troupe was fired. She testified at trial that her supervisor told her that the company discharged her because she was not expected to return to work after she had her baby.

In an opinion written by Judge POSNER, the Seventh Circuit found that Troupe was not a victim of pregnancy discrimination. Although the timing of Troupe's discharge suggested discrimination, her repeated tardiness and her supervisor's statement that she was being terminated because no one expected her to return to work after her maternity leave suggested alternative explanations. Judge Posner framed the main issue on appeal as whether discharge of a pregnant employee to avoid paying the costs of maternity leave is discrimination under the PDA. "Standing alone," he asserted, "it is not."]

If the discharge of an unsatisfactory worker were a purely remedial measure rather than also, or instead, a deterrent one, the inference that Troupe wasn't really fired because of her tardiness would therefore be a powerful one. But that is a big "if." We must remember that after two warnings Troupe had been placed on probation for sixty days and that she had violated the implicit terms of probation by being as tardy during the probationary period as she had been before. If the company did not fire her, its warnings and threats would seem empty. Employees would be encouraged to flout work rules knowing that the only sanction would be a toothless warning or a meaningless period of probation. . . .

[Title VII does not bar a financially motivated dismissal, but requires a finding that the employer] failed to exhibit comparable rapacity toward similarly situated employees. . . . We must imagine a hypothetical Mr. Troupe, who is as tardy as Ms. Troupe was, also because of health problems, and who is about to take a protracted sick leave growing out of those problems at an expense to Lord & Taylor equal to that of Ms. Troupe's maternity leave. If Lord & Taylor would have fired our hypothetical Mr. Troupe, this implies that it fired Ms. Troupe not because she was pregnant but because she cost the company more than she was worth to it. . . .

Employers can treat pregnant women as badly as they treat similarly affected but nonpregnant employees. . . . The Pregnancy Discrimination Act requires the employer to ignore an employee's pregnancy, but . . . not her absence from work, unless the employer overlooks the comparable absences of nonpregnant employees . . . in which event it would not be ignoring pregnancy after all. . . .

Troupe would be halfway home if she could find one nonpregnant employee had not been fired when about to begin a leave similar in length to hers.

[The court observed that its emphasis on comparative evidence could pose problems for a plaintiff in a situation lacking a comparison group but reserved that issue for a case in which it is raised.]

## NOTES

1. Insofar as *Troupe* accepts as nondiscriminatory the employer's concern that Troupe might not come back after leave, scholars have argued that "Kimberly Troupe appears to have fallen victim to sex stereotyping" because Lord & Taylor would probably not have concluded that a similarly situated employee, about to take disability leave, would not return to work after the leave. See Ann C. McGinley & Jeffrey W. Stempel, Condescending Contradiction: Richard Posner's Pragmatism and Pregnancy Discrimination, 46 Fla. L. Rev. 193, 221 (1994). By permitting the defendant to assume that Troupe would not return to work after her baby was born, Judge Posner allowed use of exactly the type of stereotype about women, especially pregnant women, that the PDA was intended to overcome. Id.

2. In Maldanado v. U.S. Bank, 186 F.3d 759 (7th Cir. 1999), the bank fired an employee upon learning she was pregnant, reasoning that her due date would render her unable to work during the summer, a particularly busy time of the year for persons in the plaintiff's position. The Seventh Circuit reversed summary judgment in the bank's favor, holding that an "employer cannot take anticipatory action unless it has a good faith basis, supported by sufficiently strong evidence, that the normal inconveniences of an employee's pregnancy will require special treatment." Id. at 767. Is the Seventh Circuit's opinion in *Maldanado* reconcilable with its decision in *Troupe*?

3. The *Troupe* court, like most courts, interprets the PDA to prohibit only conduct that treats pregnant women differently than "similarly situated" nonpregnant people. In *Troupe*, however, the court narrows the statute's protection by adopting restrictive rules about proving different treatment based on pregnancy. Does the court take into account the significance of the employer's disability and maternity leave policy? By adopting a leave policy, hasn't the employer acknowledged that disabled employees will receive leave if they meet the stated requirements? If so, depriving Troupe of her leave is inconsistent with the written policy, leaving no explanation for her termination other than her pregnancy.

4. In Byrd v. Lakeshore Hospital, 30 F.3d 1380 (11th Cir. 1994), the court took a different approach. The plaintiff missed ten days of work within two months due to pregnancy-related medical complications. In compliance with Lakeshore's sick leave policy, Byrd applied accrued sick leave to her absences, giving her supervisors sufficient notice on each occasion. Nevertheless, Lakeshore fired her for unsatisfactory performance. The court of appeals specifically rejected the defendant's claim that Byrd must show that other employees used the guaranteed sick leave benefits or were retained despite using them. Id. at 1383. According to the court,

> the only logical inference to be drawn in this case is that the Lakeshore policy customarily was followed. A contrary result would amount to a presumption . . . that Lakeshore

Hospital commonly discharges employees for taking their allotted sick leave time. If such is the case, then the burden was on Lakeshore to prove this unusual scenario. The effect of our decision today is simple: it is a violation of the PDA for an employer to deny a pregnant employee the benefits commonly afforded temporarily disabled workers in similar positions, or to discharge a pregnant employee for using those benefits.

Id. at 1383-84.

In the Supreme Court's second encounter with the PDA, an employer challenged a California statute that mandated benefits for pregnant employees on the ground that it was preempted by Title VII.

### CALIFORNIA FEDERAL SAVINGS & LOAN ASSOCIATION v. GUERRA
#### 479 U.S. 272 (1987)

Justice MARSHALL delivered the opinion of the Court.

The question presented is whether Title VII of the Civil Rights Act of 1964, as amended by the Pregnancy Discrimination Act of 1978, pre-empts a state statute that requires employers to provide leave and reinstatement to employees disabled by pregnancy.

### I

California's Fair Employment and Housing Act (FEHA) . . . prohibits discrimination in employment and housing. In September 1978, California amended the FEHA to proscribe certain forms of employment discrimination on the basis of pregnancy. . . . It requires these employers to provide female employees an unpaid pregnancy disability leave of up to four months. Respondent Fair Employment and Housing Commission, the state agency authorized to interpret the FEHA, has construed § 12945(b)(2) to require California employers to reinstate an employee returning from such pregnancy leave to the job she previously held, unless it is no longer available due to business necessity. In the latter case, the employer must make a reasonable, good faith effort to place the employee in a substantially similar job. The statute does not compel employers to provide *paid* leave to pregnant employees. Accordingly, the only benefit pregnant workers actually derive from § 12945(b)(2) is a qualified right to reinstatement.

### II . . .

Lillian Garland was employed by Cal Fed as a receptionist for several years. In January 1982, she took a pregnancy disability leave. When she was able to return to work in April of that year, Garland notified Cal Fed, but was informed that her job had been filled and that there were no receptionist or similar positions available.

### III

#### A

In determining whether a state statute is pre-empted by federal law and therefore invalid under the Supremacy Clause of the Constitution, our sole task is to ascertain the intent of Congress. See Shaw v. Delta Air Lines, Inc., 463 U.S. 85, 95 (1983). Federal law may supersede state law in several different ways. First, when acting within constitutional limits, Congress is empowered to pre-empt state law by so stating in express terms. Second, congressional intent to pre-empt state law in a particular area may be inferred where the scheme of federal regulation is sufficiently comprehensive to make reasonable the inference that Congress "left no room" for supplementary state regulation. Rice v. Santa Fe Elevator Corp., 331 U.S. 218, 230 (1947). Neither of these bases for pre-emption exists in this case. Congress has explicitly disclaimed any intent categorically to pre-empt state law or to "occupy the field" of employment discrimination law.

As a third alternative, in those areas where Congress has not completely displaced state regulation, federal law may nonetheless pre-empt state law to the extent it actually conflicts with federal law. Such a conflict occurs either because "compliance with both federal and state regulations is a physical impossibility," Florida Lime & Avocado Growers, Inc. v. Paul, 373 U.S. 132 (1963), or because the state law stands "as an obstacle to the accomplishment and execution of the full purposes and objectives of Congress." Hines v. Davidowitz, 312 U.S. 52, 67 (1941). Nevertheless, pre-emption is not to be lightly presumed.

This third basis for pre-emption is at issue in this case. In two sections of the 1964 Civil Rights Act, §§ 708 and 1104, Congress has indicated that state laws will be pre-empted only if they actually conflict with federal law. Section 708 of Title VII provides:

> Nothing in this title shall be deemed to exempt or relieve any person from any liability, duty, penalty, or punishment provided by any present or future law of any State or political subdivision of a State, other than any such law which purports to require or permit the doing of any act which would be an unlawful employment practice under this title. § 2000e-7.

Section 1104 of Title XI, applicable to all titles of the Civil Rights Act, establishes the following standard for pre-emption:

> Nothing contained in any title of this Act shall be construed as indicating an intent on the part of Congress to occupy the field in which any such title operates to the exclusion of State laws on the same subject matter, nor shall any provision of this Act be construed as invalidating any provision of State law unless such provision is inconsistent with any of the purposes of this Act, or any provision thereof. § 2000h-4.

Accordingly, there is no need to infer congressional intent to pre-empt state laws from the substantive provisions of Title VII; these two sections provide a "reliable indicium of congressional intent with respect to state authority" to regulate employment practice.

Sections 708 and 1104 severely limit Title VII's pre-emptive effect. Instead of pre-empting state fair employment laws, § 708 "'simply left them where they were before the enactment of title VII.'" Shaw. Similarly, § 1104 was intended primarily to "assert the intention of Congress to preserve existing civil rights laws." 110 Cong. Rec. 2788 (1964) (remarks of Rep. Meader). The narrow scope of preemption available under §§ 708 and 1104 reflects the importance Congress attached to state antidiscrimination laws in achieving Title VII's goal of equal employment opportunity. The legislative history of the PDA also supports a narrow interpretation of these provisions, as does our opinion in Shaw.

In order to decide whether the California statute requires or permits employers to violate Title VII, as amended by the PDA, or is inconsistent with the purposes of the statute, we must determine whether the PDA prohibits the States from requiring employers to provide reinstatement to pregnant workers, regardless of their policy for disabled workers generally.

### B

Petitioners argue that the language of the federal statute itself unambiguously rejects California's "special treatment" approach to pregnancy discrimination, thus rendering any resort to the legislative history unnecessary. They contend that the second clause of the PDA forbids an employer to treat pregnant employees any differently than other disabled employees. Because "[t]he purpose of Congress is the ultimate touchstone" of the pre-emption inquiry, however, we must examine the PDA's language against the background of its legislative history and historical context. As to the language of the PDA, "[i]t is a 'familiar rule, that a thing may be within the letter of the statute and yet not within the statute, because not within its spirit, nor within the intention of its makers.'" Steelworkers v. Weber.

It is well established that the PDA was passed in reaction to this Court's decision in General Electric Co. v. Gilbert. "When Congress amended Title VII in 1978, it unambiguously expressed its disapproval of both the holding and the reasoning of the Court in the *Gilbert* decision." *Newport News.* By adding pregnancy to the definition of sex discrimination prohibited by Title VII, the first clause of the PDA reflects Congress' disapproval of the reasoning in *Gilbert.* Rather than imposing a limitation on the remedial purpose of the PDA, we believe that the second clause was intended to overrule the holding in *Gilbert* and to illustrate how discrimination against pregnancy is to be remedied. . . . Accordingly, subject to certain limitations,[17] we agree with the Court of Appeals' conclusion that Congress intended the PDA to be "a floor beneath which pregnancy disability benefits may not drop — not a ceiling above which they may not rise."

The context in which Congress considered the issue of pregnancy discrimination supports this view of the PDA. Congress had before it extensive evidence of discrimination *against* pregnancy, particularly in disability and health insurance programs like those challenged in *Gilbert.* The reports, debates, and hearings make abundantly clear that Congress intended the PDA to provide relief for working women and to end discrimination against pregnant workers. In contrast to the thorough account of discrimination against pregnant workers, the legislative history is devoid of any discussion of preferential treatment of pregnancy, beyond acknowledgments of the existence of state statutes providing for such preferential treatment. Opposition to the PDA came from those concerned with the cost of including pregnancy in health and disability benefit plans and the application of the bill to abortion, not from those who favored special accommodation of pregnancy.

In support of their argument that the PDA prohibits employment practices that favor pregnant women, petitioners and several amici cite statements in the legislative history to the effect that the PDA does not *require* employers to extend any benefits to pregnant women that they do not already provide to other disabled employees. . . . We do not interpret these references to support petitioners' construction of the statute.

---

17. For example, a State could not mandate special treatment of pregnant workers based on stereotypes or generalizations about their needs and abilities.

On the contrary, if Congress had intended to *prohibit* preferential treatment, it would have been the height of understatement to say only that the legislation would not *require* such conduct. It is hardly conceivable that Congress would have extensively discussed only its intent not to require preferential treatment if in fact it had intended to prohibit such treatment.

We also find it significant that Congress was aware of state laws similar to California's but apparently did not consider them inconsistent with the PDA. . . .

Title VII, as amended by the PDA, and California's pregnancy disability leave statute share a common goal. The purpose of Title VII is "to achieve equality of employment opportunities and remove barriers that have operated in the past to favor an identifiable group of . . . employees over other employees." *Griggs*. Rather than limiting existing Title VII principles and objectives, the PDA extends them to cover pregnancy. As Senator Williams, a sponsor of the Act, stated: "The entire thrust . . . behind this legislation is to guarantee women the basic right to participate fully and equally in the workforce, without denying them the fundamental right to full participation in family life." 123 Cong. Rec. 29658 (1977).

Section 12945(b)(2) also promotes equal employment opportunity. By requiring employers to reinstate women after a reasonable pregnancy disability leave, § 12945(b)(2) ensures that they will not lose their jobs on account of pregnancy disability. . . .

We emphasize the limited nature of the benefits § 12945(b)(2) provides. The statute is narrowly drawn to cover only the period of *actual physical disability* on account of pregnancy, childbirth, or related medical conditions. Accordingly, unlike the protective labor legislation prevalent earlier in this century, § 12945(b)(2) does not reflect archaic or stereotypical notions about pregnancy and the abilities of pregnant workers. A statute based on such stereotypical assumptions would, of course, be inconsistent with Title VII's goal of equal employment opportunity.

c

Moreover, even if we agreed with petitioners' construction of the PDA, we would nonetheless reject their argument that the California statute requires employers to violate Title VII. Section 12945(b)(2) does not prevent employers from complying with both the federal law (as petitioners construe it) and the state law. This is not a case where "compliance with both federal and state regulations is a physical impossibility," or where there is an "inevitable collision between the two schemes of regulation." Section 12945(b)(2) does not compel California employers to treat pregnant workers better than other disabled employees; it merely establishes benefits that employers must, at a minimum, provide to pregnant workers. Employers are free to give comparable benefits to other disabled employees, thereby treating "women affected by pregnancy" no better than "other persons not so affected but similar in their ability or inability to work." Indeed, at oral argument, petitioners conceded that compliance with both statutes "is theoretically possible."

Petitioners argue that "extension" of the state statute to cover other employees would be inappropriate in the absence of a clear indication that this is what the California Legislature intended. They cite cases in which this Court has declined to rewrite underinclusive state statutes found to violate the Equal Protection Clause. This argument is beside the point. Extension is a remedial option to be exercised by a court once a statute is found to be invalid.

IV

Thus, petitioners' facial challenge to § 12945(b)(2) fails. The statute is not pre-empted by Title VII, as amended by the PDA, because it is not inconsistent with the purposes of the federal statute, nor does it require the doing of an act which is unlawful under Title VII.

## NOTES

1. How does the Court in *Guerra* define pregnancy discrimination?

2. What did *Guerra* say about employers' obligations under the PDA to accommodate pregnancy? The Court indicated that the second clause of the PDA provides "a floor beneath which pregnancy disability benefits may not drop — not a ceiling above which they may not rise." What is the nature of that floor? Are employers *required*, under the PDA, to accommodate pregnant women with maternity leave, light duty, or modified work assignments when they do not provide such accommodations for other similarly disabling conditions?

3. The EEOC's Questions and Answers on the Pregnancy Discrimination Act indicate that employers must process a pregnant employee's requests for benefits based on her pregnancy in the same way as any other employee's request. 29 C.F.R. pt. 1604 app. questions 5, 6. As we have seen previously, courts have required employers to accommodate pregnant employees' needs only when failing to accommodate treats pregnant women differently from other employees who are similarly able or unable to work. See, e.g., EEOC v. Ackerman, Hood & McQueen, Inc., 956 F.2d 944, 948 (10th Cir. 1992) (pregnant worker entitled to be excused from overtime work because employer had previously granted work schedule requests for personal and medical reasons).

4. Commentators have noted that the PDA, as currently interpreted, is inadequate to deal with the needs of pregnant women for accommodation in the workplace. These commentators suggest a variety of responses ranging from reinterpreting the PDA to enacting new legislation. See Deborah A. Calloway, Accommodating Pregnancy in the Workplace, 25 Stetson L. Rev. 1 (1995); Samuel Issacharoff & Elyse Rosenblum, Women and the Workplace: Accommodating the Demands of Pregnancy, 94 Colum. L. Rev. 2154 (1994); Ann C. McGinley & Jeffrey W. Stempel, Condescending Contradiction: Richard Posner's Pragmatism and Pregnancy Discrimination, 46 Fla. L. Rev. 193 (1994).

5. The Court in *Guerra* concluded that preferential treatment of pregnancy, as compared with other disabilities, is *permitted* under the PDA. How did the Court reach this conclusion? Is it consistent with the language of the amendment? Is this the result Congress would have wanted had it addressed the issue when it was considering the Pregnancy Discrimination Act?

6. In his concurrence, Justice Stevens characterized the preferential treatment permitted by the majority as analogous to voluntary affirmative action permitted in United Steelworkers of America v. Weber, 443 U.S. 193 (1979). But *Weber* and subsequent affirmative action cases impose limits on affirmative action plans in order to protect the rights of other employees. What limits does *Guerra* place on an employer's right to voluntarily provide preferential treatment to pregnant women as compared with similarly disabled individuals?

7. The *Guerra* Court noted that California's statute "is narrowly drawn to cover only the period of actual physical disability" related to pregnancy. Does preferential treatment for pregnant women that is not so limited violate the PDA or Title VII's general prohibition against sex discrimination? Does the Court provide any other limitations for voluntary preferential treatment?

8. In Harness v. Hartz Mountain Corp., 877 F.2d 1307 (6th Cir. 1989), Harness suffered a heart attack, and Hartz immediately placed him on unpaid leave pursuant to a policy allowing a maximum of 90 days of leave. When Harness was not medically fit to return to work after 90 days, he was "considered to have resigned [his] position because of illness." Id. at 1308. Harness sued, contending that Hartz's leave policy accorded more favorable treatment to pregnant employees by allowing them up to a year's leave, thereby discriminating against male employees. Although deciding the case under Kentucky law, the Sixth Circuit wrote:

> [T]he pregnancy leave policy of Hartz gives preferential treatment to pregnant employees. Such employees are permitted to take up to one year of unpaid leave for "maternity related reasons." Other employees, such as Harness, are allowed only 90 days of unpaid sick leave. Since the *Guerra* Court held, however, that such preferential treatment is permissible under the PDA, it follows that the preferential treatment accorded pregnant employees under the Hartz policy is permissible under KRS §§ 344.030(6) and 344.040(1).

Id. at 1310. Is this consistent with *Guerra?* *

9. What if Hartz had provided disability leave for pregnant women, but no leave at all for Harness? Would such a system violate Title VII? What if an employer provided "light duty" for pregnant employees, but not for other employees similarly disabled? Does it matter that both men and women suffer from nonpregnancy-related disabilities? Are these situations examples of permissible "preferential treatment" or prohibited discrimination? Could such preferential treatment be justified on the ground that neutral leave provisions, light-duty provisions, and medical restriction provisions may have a disparate impact on pregnant workers?

10. Some civil rights groups aligned themselves with the employer in *Guerra*. What was their fear in upholding the California law? One possibility is ideological: "protective" laws have traditionally "protected" women right out of job opportunities, and it is better to resist such statutes, no matter how well intended. Another possibility is practical: the expenses incident to compliance provide an incentive to employers not to hire women. How does the majority deal with the problem of "protective" legislation that operates to restrict the employment opportunities of women? What is the impact of the FMLA on this issue? See page 485.

11. Recall the Supreme Court's decision in International Union UAW v. Johnson Controls, Inc., 499 U.S. 187 (1991). *Johnson Controls* described the PDA as containing "a BFOQ of its own" in the second clause, providing that pregnant women must be treated the same as other persons "similar in their ability or inability to work." The concurrence, in contrast, quoted *Guerra*: "[T]he purpose of the PDA was simply to make the treatment of pregnancy consistent with general Title VII principles." Does the second clause of the PDA define pregnancy discrimination or does it provide a statutory defense to pregnancy discrimination? Who bears the burden of proof on the

*Harness* was decided before the effective dates of the ADA and the FMLA. An employee like Harness probably would now be protected under one or both of those statutes and therefore, would not need to allege sex discrimination. See Chapter 8.

question whether the employer has treated pregnant women the same as other similarly situated individuals?

12.  Is there any difference between the second clause of the PDA and the bfoq defense? Would *Johnson Controls* have come out differently without the PDA?

13.  Is disparate impact a viable theory under the PDA? The *Guerra* Court noted the issue but did not address it. In his dissent, however, Justice White wrote that "[w]hatever remedies Title VII would otherwise provide for victims of disparate impact, Congress expressly ordered pregnancy to be treated in the same manner as other disabilities." 479 U.S. at 297 n.1. Was Justice White saying that the second clause of the PDA bars the application of the disparate impact theory? If so, does the codification of the disparate impact theory in the Civil Rights Act of 1991 alter that conclusion?

14.  Certainly it would seem that if a practice disproportionately disadvantaged women, even if it were because of pregnancy, disparate impact theory would be available. But would a disparate impact claim be stated if the practice disproportionately disadvantaged pregnant women, as opposed to women as a whole? See Garcia v. Woman's Hosp. of Tex., 97 F.3d 810 (5th Cir. 1996) (permitting a disparate impact claim if proof of impact on pregnant women was shown).

15.  What if an employer provides no leave to its employees and the impact of this failure to provide leave falls more harshly on women because of their need for pregnancy related leaves? Would an impact claim be viable? See Stout v. Baxter Healthcare Corp., 282 F.3d 856, 861 (5th Cir. 2002) (although a "no leave" policy would affect all or substantially all pregnant women, no treatment or impact claim stated).

## NOTE ON ACCOMMODATING PREGNANCY UNDER THE PDA AND THE AMERICANS WITH DISABILITIES ACT

The Americans with Disabilities Act (ADA) requires employers to provide reasonable accommodations to qualified employees with disabilities unless such accommodation would impose an undue hardship on the employer. 42 U.S.C.S. § 12112(b)(5)(A) (2003). In order to be qualified, an individual must be able to perform the essential functions of the job in question with or without reasonable accommodation. See Chapter 8. The EEOC's interpretive guidance concludes that, because pregnancy is not an impairment, it is not a disability. Pregnant women, therefore, are not entitled to the ADA's protection. 29 C.F.R. pt. 1630 app. § 1630.2(h), (j). Although normal pregnancies are not covered under the ADA, complications or conditions arising out of pregnancy may be covered.

One commentator has argued that the EEOC's interpretation of the ADA's coverage conflicts with legislative intent. In Note, Substantive Equality and Antidiscrimination: Accommodating Pregnancy Under the Americans with Disabilities Act, 82 Geo. L.J. 193 (1993), Colette G. Matzzie contends that the ADA's broad language, the absence of an explicit statutory exclusion for pregnancy, and Congress's broad remedial purpose in enacting the ADA all support including pregnancy within its coverage. Id. at 217-18.

Even if the ADA does not directly protect pregnant women, however, the ADA may indirectly accord pregnant women rights to accommodation under the PDA. Pregnancy is at least a temporarily disabling condition. Pregnant employees viewing their situation as comparable to those of individuals with disabilities may demand the same accommodations to which disabled employees are entitled under the ADA. Deborah

Calloway, Accommodating Pregnancy in the Workplace, 25 Stetson L. Rev. 1, 29-30 (1995). Individuals covered by the ADA may, like pregnant women, require flexible work rules or medical leave or relief from tasks such as climbing stairs and lifting heavy weights. If an employer, in compliance with the ADA's reasonable accommodation requirement, grants leave, provides flexible work rules, or assigns a disabled employee to light duty, the PDA would seem to require that employer to provide the same accommodations to pregnant employees who have similar needs.

The Sixth Circuit's interpretation of the PDA, which requires pregnant women to be treated the same as employees similar in their ability or inability to work, regardless of the source of the limiting condition, would seemingly allow pregnancy discrimination claims based on a comparison with the treatment of individuals protected by the ADA. The argument would be that the PDA requires employers to treat individuals with similar work limitations the same way — the temporary or chronic nature of the limitation would be irrelevant. Ensley-Gaines v. Runyon, 100 F.3d 1220 (6th Cir. 1996). In contrast, the Fifth and Eleventh Circuits would find no violation as long as some other similarly limited employee was treated in the same way — for example, an employee with an injury not qualifying as a disability under the ADA. Spivey v. Beverly Enterprises, 196 F.3d 1309 (11th Cir. 1999); Urbano v. Continental Airlines, 138 F.3d 204 (5th Cir. 1996).

### NOTE ON RELATED MEDICAL CONDITIONS

Suppose medical testimony establishes that a pregnant woman is unable to work for only six weeks. If she asks for more time, isn't she seeking leave not for *childbearing*, but for *childrearing*? Does Title VII require employers to grant such leave? Can childrearing be considered "pregnancy, childbirth, or related medical conditions"? See Fisher v. Vassar Coll., 70 F.3d 1420 (2d Cir. 1995) (choice to remain home for an extended period following birth of a child is not the inevitable consequence of pregnancy or a medical condition related to pregnancy as required by the PDA).

Under *Guerra*, does Title VII allow an employer to provide maternity leave for childrearing without providing "paternity" leave for fathers who wish to care for their children? See Martin H. Malin, Fathers and Parental Leave, 72 Tex. L. Rev. 1047 (1994); Steven Keyes, Note, Affirmative Action for Working Mothers: Does *Guerra's* Preferential Treatment Rationale Extend to Childrearing Leave Benefits?, 60 Fordham L. Rev. 309 (1991). In Shafer v. Board of Public Education, 903 F.2d 243 (3d Cir. 1990), the court found that denying a one-year unpaid leave of absence to Shafer, a male teacher, to care for his son violated Title VII. The controlling collective bargaining agreement provided up to one year of leave for "female teachers and other female personnel" for "personal reasons relating to childbearing or childrearing." Is *Shafer* correct under *Guerra*? What if an employer grants childrearing leave but only to mothers who breast-feed their infants? Would a male employee who sought childrearing leave have a reverse discrimination claim?

In Turic v. Holland Hospitality Inc., 849 F. Supp. 544 (W.D. Mich. 1994), *aff'd in part, rev'd in part*, 85 F.3d 1211 (6th Cir. 1996), the court held that the phrase "related medical conditions" encompasses a woman's right to have an abortion. Id. at 549. The court based its conclusions on the EEOC Guidelines and the PDA's legislative history. The plaintiff was discharged because she contemplated having an abortion, thereby offending the hotel's "very Christian staff." The court saw no difference between intending to have an abortion and actually having one for purposes of PDA protection. See id. at 550. Is infertility a "related medical condition" covered by the PDA? What about the ADA? See Bragdon v. Abbot (reproduced at page 680) (impairment that substantially limits the ability to reproduce is a disability).

### NOTE ON THE FAMILY AND MEDICAL LEAVE ACT

Some of the problems faced by pregnant women and parents of small children are addressed by the Family and Medical Leave Act of 1993 (FMLA), 29 U.S.C.S. § 2601 (2003), which ensures up to 12 weeks of unpaid leave for a variety of purposes, including the birth or adoption of a child. See Family & Medical Leave Act, 58 Fed. Reg. 31,794 (1993) (DOL's Interim Final Rule). The Department of Labor (DOL) recognizes that "[c]ircumstances may require that leave for the birth of a child, or for placement for adoption or foster care, be taken prior to the actual birth or placement." Id. at 31,798 (summary and discussion of § 825.112). The DOL has indicated, however, that "[a]n employee's entitlement to FMLA leave for birth or placement of a child expires 12 months after the birth or placement." Id. at 31,801 (summary and discussion of § 825.201).

The FMLA reduces, but by no means eliminates, the importance of the PDA for pregnant workers. The FMLA applies only to employers with 50 or more employees. Further:

> To be "eligible," an employee must have worked for the employer: (1) For at least 12 months and (2) for at least 1,250 hours during the year preceding the start of the leave, and (3) be employed at a worksite where the employer employs at least 50 employees within a 75-mile radius. . . .

Id. at 31,798 (summary and discussion of §§ 825.110 and 825.111). Thus, part-time employees, first-year employees, and employees who work for small employers are not entitled to leave under the FMLA. The exclusion of small employers is important because pregnancy discrimination claims "are often against small firms whose policies may be more 'paternalistic' than those of major corporations." 137 LRRM (BNA) 331.

In addition, the FMLA does not resolve disputes regarding pregnancy accommodations other than unpaid leave. See generally Michael Selmi, Family Leave and the Gender Wage Gap, 78 N.C. L. Rev. 707, 711-12 (2000), who contends that gender inequality remains pervasive in today's workplace because men have not changed their behavior and women thus continue to bear primary responsibility for child care and childrearing. Accordingly, he asserts, "things have continued for the most part as they were: women have less of an attachment to the labor force than men (though the differences are narrowing), miss more work than men, take more time off when they have children, and generally work fewer hours. All of these factors contribute to a cumulative workplace disadvantage that exacts a heavy price in terms of salary, promotions, and responsibility." See also Laura T. Kessler, The Attachment Gap: Employment Discrimination Law, Women's Cultural Caregiving, and the Limits of Economic and Liberal Legal Theory, 34 U. Mich. J.L. Reform 371 (2001) (analyzing the law's failure to address the work/family conflicts that disproportionately affect women).

In March 2002, the Supreme Court issued its first FMLA decision. In Ragsdale v. Wolverine Worldwide, Inc., 535 U.S. 81 (2002), the Court rejected a regulation promulgated by the Department of Labor that allowed time off to count against an employee's 12 weeks of FMLA leave only if the employer notified the employee that the leave was being designated as FMLA leave. Ragsdale was unable to show that she had been harmed by her employer's failure to provide notice; under those circumstances, the regulation was deemed invalid.

### PROBLEM 7.1

Charlene works in a company mail room. Her duties include helping to unload bags of mail from the mail trucks. She also sorts mail and works at the front counter serving customers. Charlene is in her sixth month of pregnancy and has been advised by her doctor not to lift the heavy mailbags at work. When she asked her employer to permit her to limit her work to sorting mail and working at the counter for the remaining period of her pregnancy, the employer refused and put her on leave without pay, promising to return her to her job after the baby was delivered and she became well enough to perform all of the duties of her job. Charlene's employer has no pregnancy leave policy and no long-term disability policy. The employer permits employees to take two weeks of sick leave each year. Employees who require more than two weeks of sick leave are discharged. Charlene filed suit under the PDA, alleging discrimination on the basis of her pregnancy. A male employee, who recently suffered injuries in a car accident also has filed suit, complaining that, rather than receiving leave without pay and a promise of reinstatement, he was discharged after using up his allotted two weeks of sick leave. What rights and remedies (if any) do these employees have?

## 2.  Sexual and Other Discriminatory Harassment

In this section, we consider employees' rights to a workplace in which they are free from sexual and other discriminatory harassment. Under Title VII, employees have a cause of action for harassment when it discriminates on the basis of membership in a protected group. Sexual harassment imposes different conditions of employment on women because of their gender. Harassment also is actionable, however, when aimed at racial, religious, or ethnic groups or at older or disabled workers. Sexual harassment is unique, however, because, unlike other discriminatory behavior, it often may be nearly indistinguishable from "normal" social relations between men and women.

Sexual harassment and other discriminatory harassment can violate Title VII even if the victim suffers no adverse employment decision or economic impact as a result. Moreover, sexual and other discriminatory harassment frequently is practiced in violation of, rather than in compliance with, company policy. Further, harassers often are satisfying their own personal interests, rather than seeking to further their employer's interests. This attribute of discriminatory harassment raises a new issue: what is the employer's liability for harassment by supervisors and co-workers in violation of company policy? Finally, because controlling discriminatory harassment in the workplace by disciplining harassing employees may relieve an employer of liability, discriminatory harassment raises questions about the rights of employees who perpetrate this form of discrimination.

# MERITOR SAVINGS BANK v. VINSON
## 477 U.S. 57 (1986)

Justice REHNQUIST delivered the opinion of the Court.

I

[In 1974, Michelle Vinson met Sidney Taylor, a vice-president of Meritor Savings Bank and manager of one of its branch offices. Taylor hired her and became her supervisor. Vinson started as a trainee, but ultimately was promoted to assistant branch manager, working at the same branch until her discharge in 1978. "[I]t is undisputed that her advancement there was based on merit alone." In late 1978, Vinson took sick leave and finally was discharged for excessive use of that leave. Vinson sued both Taylor and the bank, claiming that she had "constantly been subjected to sexual harassment" by Taylor during her four years of employment.]

At . . . trial, the parties presented conflicting testimony about Taylor's behavior during respondent's employment. Respondent testified that during her probationary period as a teller-trainee, Taylor treated her in a fatherly way and made no sexual advances. Shortly thereafter, however, he invited her out to dinner and, during the course of the meal, suggested that they go to a motel to have sexual relations. At first she refused, but out of what she described as fear of losing her job she eventually agreed. According to respondent, Taylor thereafter made repeated demands upon her for sexual favors, usually at the branch, both during and after business hours; she estimated that over the next several years she had intercourse with him some 40 or 50 times. In addition, respondent testified that Taylor fondled her in front of other employees, followed her into the women's restroom when she went there alone, exposed himself to her, and even forcibly raped her on several occasions. These activities ceased after 1977, respondent stated, when she started going with a steady boyfriend.

Respondent also testified that Taylor touched and fondled other women employees of the bank, and she attempted to call witnesses to support this charge. But while some supporting testimony apparently was admitted without objection, the District Court did not allow her "to present wholesale evidence of a pattern and practice relating to sexual advances to other female employees in her case in chief, but advised her that she might well be able to present such evidence in rebuttal to the defendants' cases." Respondent did not offer such evidence in rebuttal. Finally, respondent testified that because she was afraid of Taylor she never reported his harassment to any of his supervisors and never attempted to use the bank's complaint procedure.

Taylor denied respondent's allegations of sexual activity, testifying that he never fondled her, never made suggestive remarks to her, never engaged in sexual intercourse with her, and never asked her to do so. He contended instead that respondent made her accusations in response to a business-related dispute. The bank also denied respondent's allegations and asserted that any sexual harassment by Taylor was unknown to the bank and engaged in without its consent or approval.

The District Court denied relief, but did not resolve the conflicting testimony about the existence of a sexual relationship between respondent and Taylor. It found instead that:

[i]f [respondent] and Taylor did engage in an intimate or sexual relationship during the time of [respondent's] employment with [the bank], that relationship was a voluntary

one having nothing to do with her continued employment at [the bank] or her advancement or promotions at that institution.

The court ultimately found that respondent "was not the victim of sexual harassment and was not the victim of sexual discrimination" while employed at the bank. . . .


II . . .

Respondent argues, and the Court of Appeals held, that unwelcome sexual advances that create an offensive or hostile working environment violate Title VII. Without question, when a supervisor sexually harasses a subordinate because of the subordinate's sex, that supervisor "discriminate[s]" on the basis of sex. Petitioner apparently does not challenge this proposition. It contends instead that in prohibiting discrimination with respect to "compensation, terms, conditions, or privileges" of employment, Congress was concerned with what petitioner describes as "tangible loss" of "an economic character," not "purely psychological aspects of the workplace environment." In support of this claim petitioner observes that in both the legislative history of Title VII and this Court's Title VII decisions, the focus has been on tangible, economic barriers erected by discrimination.

We reject petitioner's view. First, the language of Title VII is not limited to "economic" or "tangible" discrimination. The phrase "terms, conditions, or privileges of employment" evinces a congressional intent "'to strike at the entire spectrum [of] disparate treatment of men and women'" in employment. Los Angeles Dept. of Water and Power v. Manhart. Petitioner has pointed to nothing in the Act to suggest that Congress contemplated the limitation urged here.

Second, in 1980 the EEOC issued Guidelines specifying that "sexual harassment," as there defined, is a form of sex discrimination prohibited by Title VII. As an "administrative interpretation of the Act by the enforcing agency," Griggs v. Duke Power Co., these guidelines, "'while not controlling upon the courts by reason of their authority, do constitute a body of experience and informed judgment to which courts and litigants may properly resort for guidance.'" General Electric v. Gilbert (quoting Skidmore v. Swift & Co., 323 U.S. 134, 140 (1944)). The EEOC Guidelines fully support the view that harassment leading to noneconomic injury can violate Title VII.

In defining "sexual harassment," the Guidelines first describe the kinds of workplace conduct that may be actionable under Title VII. These include "[u]nwelcome sexual advances, requests for sexual favors, and other verbal or physical conduct of a sexual nature." 29 C.F.R. § 1604.11(a) (1985). Relevant to the charges at issue in this case, the Guidelines provide that such sexual misconduct constitutes prohibited "sexual harassment," whether or not it is directly linked to the grant or denial of an economic quid pro quo, where "such conduct has the purpose or effect of unreasonably interfering with an individual's work performance or creating an intimidating, hostile, or offensive working environment." § 1604.11(a)(3).

In concluding that so-called "hostile environment" (i.e., non quid pro quo) harassment violates Title VII, the EEOC drew upon a substantial body of judicial decisions and EEOC precedent holding that Title VII affords employees the right to work in an environment free from discriminatory intimidation, ridicule, and insult. Rogers v. EEOC, 454 F.2d 234 (5th Cir. 1971), was apparently the first case to recognize a cause of action based upon a discriminatory work environment.

In *Rogers*, the Court of Appeals for the Fifth Circuit held that a Hispanic complainant could establish a Title VII violation by demonstrating that her employer created an offensive work environment for employees by giving discriminatory service to its Hispanic clientele. The court explained that an employee's protections under Title VII extend beyond the economic aspects of employment:

> [T]he phrase "terms, conditions or privileges of employment" in [Title VII] is an expansive concept which sweeps within its protective ambit the practice of creating a working environment heavily charged with ethnic or racial discrimination. . . . One can readily envision working environments so heavily polluted with discrimination as to destroy completely the emotional and psychological stability of minority group workers. . . .

Courts applied this principle to harassment based on race, religion, and national origin. Nothing in Title VII suggests that a hostile environment based on discriminatory sexual harassment should not be likewise prohibited. The Guidelines thus appropriately drew from, and were fully consistent with, the existing case law.

Since the Guidelines were issued, courts have uniformly held, and we agree, that a plaintiff may establish a violation of Title VII by proving that discrimination based on sex has created a hostile or abusive work environment. As the Court of Appeals for the Eleventh Circuit wrote in Henson v. Dundee, 682 F.2d 897, 902 (1982):

> Sexual harassment which creates a hostile or offensive environment for members of one sex is every bit the arbitrary barrier to sexual equality at the workplace that racial harassment is to racial equality. Surely, a requirement that a man or woman run a gauntlet of sexual abuse in return for the privilege of being allowed to work and make a living can be as demeaning and disconcerting as the harshest of racial epithets.

Of course, as the courts in both *Rogers* and *Henson* recognized, not all workplace conduct that may be described as "harassment" affects a "term, condition, or privilege" of employment within the meaning of Title VII. For sexual harassment to be actionable, it must be sufficiently severe or pervasive "to alter the conditions of [the victim's] employment and create an abusive working environment." Respondent's allegations in this case — which include not only pervasive harassment but also criminal conduct of the most serious nature — are plainly sufficient to state a claim for "hostile environment" sexual harassment.

The question remains, however, whether the District Court's ultimate finding that respondent "was not the victim of sexual harassment" effectively disposed of respondent's claim. The Court of Appeals recognized, we think correctly, that this ultimate finding was likely based on one or both of two erroneous views of the law. First, the District Court apparently believed that a claim for sexual harassment will not lie absent an economic effect on the complainant's employment. . . . Since it appears that the District Court made its findings without ever considering the "hostile environment" theory of sexual harassment, the Court of Appeals' decision to remand was correct.

Second, the District Court's conclusion that no actionable harassment occurred might have rested on its earlier "finding" that "[i]f [respondent] and Taylor did engage in an intimate or sexual relationship . . . , that relationship was a voluntary one." But the fact that sex-related conduct was "voluntary," in the sense that the complainant was not forced to participate against her will, is not a defense to a sexual harassment suit brought under Title VII. The gravamen of any sexual harassment claim is that the alleged sexual advances were "unwelcome." 29 C.F.R. § 1604.11(a) (1985). While the question whether particular conduct was indeed unwelcome presents difficult problems of proof and turns largely on credibility determinations committed to the trier of fact, the District Court in this case erroneously focused on the "voluntariness" of respondent's participation in the claimed sexual episodes. The correct inquiry is whether respondent by her conduct indicated that the alleged sexual advances were unwelcome, not whether her actual participation in sexual intercourse was voluntary.

Petitioner contends that even if this case must be remanded to the District Court, the Court of Appeals erred in one of the terms of its remand. Specifically, the Court of Appeals stated that testimony about respondent's "dress and personal fantasies," which the District Court apparently admitted into evidence, "had no place in this litigation." The apparent ground for this conclusion was that respondent's voluntariness vel non in submitting to Taylor's advances was immaterial to her sexual harassment claim. While "voluntariness" in the sense of consent is not a defense to such a claim, it does not follow that a complainant's sexually provocative speech or dress is irrelevant as a matter of law in determining whether he or she found particular sexual advances unwelcome. To the contrary, such evidence is obviously relevant. The EEOC Guidelines emphasize that the trier of fact must determine the existence of sexual harassment in light of "the record as a whole" and "the totality of circumstances, such as the nature of the sexual advances and the context in which the alleged incidents occurred." 29 C.F.R. § 1604.11(b) (1985). Respondent's claim that any marginal relevance of the evidence in question was outweighed by the potential for unfair prejudice is the sort of argument properly addressed to the District Court. In this case the District Court concluded that the evidence should be admitted, and the Court of Appeals' contrary conclusion was based upon the erroneous, categorical view that testimony about provocative dress and publicly expressed sexual fantasies "had no place in this litigation." While the District Court must carefully weigh the applicable considerations in deciding whether to admit evidence of this kind, there is no per se rule against its admissibility.

## NOTES

1. Because the alleged conduct by Taylor was so egregious, it may not be clear from *Meritor* that one central theoretical problem with the sexual harassment cause of action is deciding what constitutes harassment. At one pole, a violation will be established if accepting sexual advances is an explicit or apparent quid pro quo for obtaining, retaining, or advancing in a job. The Court in *Meritor* clearly prohibits less egregious conduct than this, holding that a contaminated work environment also is prohibited. At the other extreme, however, defining harassment becomes problematic. Is every "pass" a Title VII violation? Every "pass" by a supervisor? Does harassment by co-workers (or even subordinates) violate Title VII? Is mere exposure to raw language harassment? What about compliments or criticisms regarding an employee's appearance? Although the line between harassment and acceptable social behavior is unclear, many cases concern behavior that any reasonable person, male or female, would recognize as harassment.

2. The Court admitted evidence of Vinson's dress and sexual fantasies. In rape cases, defendants commonly seek to make the moral character of the victim an issue. Might such a defense be raised in a sexual harassment case? What is the appropriate judicial response? Consider the relevance of dress or past conduct to the question

whether sexual advances were unwelcome. Rule 412 of the Federal Rules of Evidence regulates the admissibility of evidence of past sexual conduct. In trials relating to sexual misconduct, Rule 412 makes inadmissible

> evidence offered to prove that any alleged victim engaged in other sexual behavior . . . [or] . . . to prove any alleged victim's sexual predisposition . . . [unless] its probative value substantially outweighs the danger of harm to any victim and of unfair prejudice to any party. Evidence of an alleged victim's reputation is admissible only if it has been placed in controversy by the alleged victim.

What effect is this rule of evidence likely to have on sexual harassment litigation? See Rodriguez-Hernandez v. Miranda-Valez, 132 F.3d 848 (1st Cir. 1998) (sexual history of plaintiff properly excluded under Rule 412). See generally Andrea A. Curcio, Rule 412 Laid Bare: A Procedural Rule That Cannot Adequately Protect Sexual Harassment Plaintiffs from Embarrassing Exposure, 67 U. Cin. L. Rev. 125 (1998) (contending that Rule 412 has not fully achieved its purpose of protecting plaintiffs from exploration of their consensual sexual activities); Ethan A. Heinz, Comment, The Conflicting Mandates of FRE 412 and FRCP 26: Should Courts Allow Discovery of a Sexual Harassment Plaintiff's Sexual History?, 1999 U. Chi. Legal F. 519 (exploring the effect of Rule 412 on what information is discoverable); Jacqueline H. Sloan, Comment, Extending Rape Shield Protection to Sexual Harassment Actions: New Federal Rule of Evidence 412 Undermines *Meritor Savings Bank v. Vinson*, 25 Sw. U. L. Rev. 363 (1996) (Rule 412 shifts the focus of sexual harassment litigation away from the conduct of the plaintiff and back toward the conduct of the defendant).

3. The 1991 Civil Rights Act expanded the remedies available in Title VII cases to include compensatory and punitive damages and damages for emotional distress. Prior to these amendments, Title VII provided only equitable remedies, which were largely ineffective in hostile environment cases because plaintiffs could secure only attorneys' fees and injunctive relief against further violations. By providing emotional distress and punitive damages, the 1991 Act reinvigorated Title VII's prohibition of harassment. The amount of damages available is limited, however, depending on the size of the plaintiff's employer. See Chapter 10. Further, courts may hold, as they have in tort suits, that a plaintiff seeking damages for mental and emotional distress places her mental state in controversy, justifying an order to undergo psychiatric examination. See, e.g., Patterson v. P.H.P. Healthcare, 90 F.3d 927 (5th Cir. 1996) (unlawfully discharged black employee's testimony about his emotional response to being referred to as "porch monkey" or "nigger" does not support more than nominal damages absent corroborating expert medical or psychological evidence of sleeplessness, anxiety, or depression). See Chapter 10.

4. Why wouldn't the district court allow plaintiff to introduce evidence of Taylor's harassment of other employees as part of her prima facie case? Doesn't that evidence make Taylor's denial that he harassed Vinson less credible? Why didn't plaintiff produce such evidence in rebuttal when she apparently was permitted to?

5. Although the vast majority of sexual harassment complaints are brought by female employees, male employees also are subjected to sexual harassment by females. For example, in Huebschen v. Department of Health & Social Servs., 716 F.2d 1167 (7th Cir. 1983), a male complained that his female supervisor retaliated against him after their romantic relationship turned sour. Theoretically, should complaints by male employees be subject to the same analysis as claims by female employees? What about harassment by members of the same sex?

### a.   Harrassment "Because of" Sex

## ONCALE v. SUNDOWNER OFFSHORE SERVICES, INC.
### 523 U.S. 75 (1998)

Justice SCALIA delivered the opinion of the Court.

This case presents the question whether workplace harassment can violate Title VII's prohibition against "discrimination . . . because of . . . sex," when the harasser and the harassed employee are of the same sex.

### I

The District Court having granted summary judgment for respondent, we must assume the facts to be as alleged by petitioner Joseph Oncale. The precise details are irrelevant to the legal point we must decide, and in the interest of both brevity and dignity we shall describe them only generally. In late October 1991, Oncale was working for respondent Sundowner Offshore Services on a Chevron U.S.A., Inc., oil platform in the Gulf of Mexico. He was employed as a roustabout on an eight-man crew which included respondents John Lyons, Danny Pippen, and Brandon Johnson. Lyons, the crane operator, and Pippen, the driller, had supervisory authority. On several occasions, Oncale was forcibly subjected to sex-related, humiliating actions against him by Lyons, Pippen and Johnson in the presence of the rest of the crew. Pippen and Lyons also physically assaulted Oncale in a sexual manner, and Lyons threatened him with rape.

Oncale's complaints to supervisory personnel produced no remedial action; in fact, the company's Safety Compliance Clerk, Valent Hohen, told Oncale that Lyons and Pippen "picked [on] him all the time too," and called him a name suggesting homosexuality. Oncale eventually quit — asking that his pink slip reflect that he "voluntarily left due to sexual harassment and verbal abuse." When asked at his deposition why he left Sundowner, Oncale stated "I felt that if I didn't leave my job, that I would be raped or forced to have sex."

[The district court held that "Mr. Oncale, a male, has no cause of action under Title VII for harassment by male co-workers." The Fifth Circuit affirmed.]

### II

Title VII of the Civil Rights Act of 1964 provides, in relevant part, that "it shall be an unlawful employment practice for an employer . . . to discriminate against any individual with respect to his compensation, terms, conditions, or privileges of employment, because of such individual's race, color, religion, sex, or national origin." . . .

Title VII's prohibition of discrimination "because of . . . sex" protects men as well as women, *Newport News*, and in the related context of racial discrimination in the workplace we have rejected any conclusive presumption that an employer will not discriminate against members of his own race. "Because of the many facets of human motivation, it would be unwise to presume as a matter of law that human beings of one definable group will not discriminate against other members of that group." Castaneda v. Partida, 430 U.S. 482 (1977). In Johnson v. Transportation Agency, Santa Clara County [reproduced at page 283], a male employee claimed that his employer discriminated against him because of his sex when it preferred a female employee for promotion. Although we ultimately rejected the claim on other grounds, we did not consider it significant that the supervisor who made that decision was also a man. If our precedents leave any doubt on the question, we hold today that nothing in Title VII necessarily bars a claim of discrimination "because of . . . sex" merely because the plaintiff and the defendant (or the person charged with acting on behalf of the defendant) are of the same sex.

Courts have had little trouble with that principle in cases like *Johnson*, where an employee claims to have been passed over for a job or promotion. But when the issue arises in the context of a "hostile environment" sexual harassment claim, the state and federal courts have taken a bewildering variety of stances. Some, like the Fifth Circuit in this case, have held that same-sex sexual harassment claims are never cognizable under Title VII. Other decisions say that such claims are actionable only if the plaintiff can prove that the harasser is homosexual (and thus presumably motivated by sexual desire). Compare McWilliams v. Fairfax County Board of Supervisors, 72 F.3d 1191 (4th Cir. 1996), with Wrightson v. Pizza Hut of America, 99 F.3d 138 (4th Cir. 1996). Still others suggest that workplace harassment that is sexual in content is always actionable, regardless of the harasser's sex, sexual orientation, or motivations. See Doe v. Belleville, 119 F.3d 563 (7th Cir. 1997).

We see no justification in the statutory language or our precedents for a categorical rule excluding same-sex harassment claims from the coverage of Title VII. As some courts have observed, male-on-male sexual harassment in the workplace was assuredly not the principal evil Congress was concerned with when it enacted Title VII. But statutory prohibitions often go beyond the principal evil to cover reasonably comparable evils, and it is ultimately the provisions of our laws rather than the principal concerns of our legislators by which we are governed. Title VII prohibits "discrimination . . . because of . . . sex" in the "terms" or "conditions" of employment. Our holding that this includes sexual harassment must extend to sexual harassment of any kind that meets the statutory requirements.

Respondents and their amici contend that recognizing liability for same-sex harassment will transform Title VII into a general civility code for the American workplace. But that risk is no greater for same-sex than for opposite-sex harassment, and is adequately met by careful attention to the requirements of the statute. Title VII does not prohibit all verbal or physical harassment in the workplace; it is directed only at "discrimination . . . because of . . . sex." We have never held that workplace harassment, even harassment between men and women, is automatically discrimination because of sex merely because the words used have sexual content or connotations. "The critical issue, Title VII's text indicates, is whether members of one sex are exposed to disadvantageous terms or conditions of employment to which members of the other sex are not exposed." [Harris v. Forklift Systems, Inc., reproduced at page 507.]

Courts and juries have found the inference of discrimination easy to draw in most male-female sexual harassment situations, because the challenged conduct typically involves explicit or implicit proposals of sexual activity; it is reasonable to assume those proposals would not have been made to someone of the same sex. The same chain of inference would be available to a plaintiff alleging same-sex harassment, if there were credible evidence that the harasser was homosexual. But harassing conduct need not be motivated by sexual desire to support an inference of discrimination on the basis of sex. A trier of fact might reasonably find such discrimination, for example, if a female victim is harassed in such sex-specific and derogatory terms by another woman as to make it clear that the harasser is motivated by general hostility to the presence of women in the workplace. A same-sex harassment plaintiff may also, of course, offer direct comparative evidence about how the alleged harasser treated members of both sexes in a mixed-sex workplace. Whatever evidentiary route the plaintiff chooses to follow, he or she must always prove that the conduct at issue was not merely tinged with offensive sexual connotations, but actually constituted "discrimination . . . because of . . . sex."

And there is another requirement that prevents Title VII from expanding into a general civility code: As we emphasized in *Meritor* and *Harris*, the statute does not reach genuine but innocuous differences in the ways men and women routinely interact with members of the same sex and of the opposite sex. The prohibition of harassment on the basis of sex requires neither asexuality nor androgyny in the workplace; it forbids only behavior so objectively offensive as to alter the "conditions" of the victim's employment. "Conduct that is not severe or pervasive enough to create an objectively hostile or abusive work environment — an environment that a reasonable person would find hostile or abusive — is beyond Title VII's purview." *Harris*. We have always regarded that requirement as crucial, and as sufficient to ensure that courts and juries do not mistake ordinary socializing in the workplace — such as male-on-male horseplay or intersexual flirtation — for discriminatory "conditions of employment."

We have emphasized, moreover, that the objective severity of harassment should be judged from the perspective of a reasonable person in the plaintiff's position, considering "all the circumstances." *Harris*. In same-sex (as in all) harassment cases, that inquiry requires careful consideration of the social context in which particular behavior occurs and is experienced by its target. A professional football player's working environment is not severely or pervasively abusive, for example, if the coach smacks him on the buttocks as he heads onto the field — even if the same behavior would reasonably be experienced as abusive by the coach's secretary (male or female) back at the office. The real social impact of workplace behavior often depends on a constellation of surrounding circumstances, expectations, and relationships which are not fully captured by a simple recitation of the words used or the physical acts performed. Common sense, and an appropriate sensitivity to social context, will enable courts and juries to distinguish between simple teasing or roughhousing among members of the same sex, and conduct which a reasonable person in the plaintiff's position would find severely hostile or abusive. . . .

## NOTES

1. The Fifth Circuit had concluded that male-on-male harassment was not actionable under Title VII. *Oncale* makes clear that, regardless of the gender of the harasser and victim, the central issue for purposes of establishing liability under Title VII is whether the terms and conditions of the victim's employment were altered because of or on the basis of sex.

2. Although *Oncale* establishes that same-sex harassment is actionable under Title VII, the question remains, when is harassment because of or on the basis of sex? The Court confirms prior opinions in which an inference of sex-based discrimination was based on sexual advances made by a heterosexual toward a victim of the opposite sex. Consistent with this logic, the Court indicates that sexual advances by a homosexual toward an individual of the same sex also may give rise to the inference that such action is "because of sex." See La Day v. Catalyst Tech. Inc., 302 F.3d 474 (5th Cir. 2002) (discussing what proof will establish the alleged harasser was homosexual). For

criticism of this focus on the sexual orientation of the harasser, see Katherine M. Franke, What's Wrong with Sexual Harassment?, 49 Stan. L. Rev. 691, 732 (1997).

3. Steven Wilborn, Taking Discrimination Seriously: *Oncale* and the Fate of Exceptionalism in Sexual Harassment Law, 7 Wm. & Mary Bill Rts. J. 677 (1999), argues that pre-*Oncale* law was misguided because the "standard model" of sexual harassment either ignored discrimination entirely or treated it as a purely formal element. Thus, the "sexual nature" of verbal or physical conduct sufficed, at least where the two individuals were of different sexes. He views *Oncale* as refocusing attention on whether the conduct at issue is discriminatory, not merely in the same-sex scenario but even when members of the opposite sex are involved. One consequence of this would be the elimination of the heterosexual presumption — discrimination would have to be proven in harassment as in other cases. While sexually tinged words or actions would be a relevant factor, they would not necessarily suffice even between members of the opposite sex. See Ocheltree v. Scollon Productions, 308 F.3d 351 (4th Cir. 2002) (sexual speech, though "repulsive," not directed at plaintiff because of sex); EEOC v. Harbert-Yeargin, Inc., 266 F.3d 498 (6th Cir. 2001) (jury verdict in favor of same-sex harassment victim reversed; unwanted touchings or poking of genital area were insufficient evidence that harasser acted because of plaintiff's gender); Rizzo v. Sheahan, 266 F.3d 705 (7th Cir. 2001) ("sexually explicit comments made to a mother by her supervisor in reference to her 15-year-old daughter" deplorable and offensive but not motivated by the employee's sex). See also Rebecca Hanner White, There's Nothing Special About Sex: The Supreme Court Mainstreams Sexual Harassment, 7 Wm. & Mary Bill Rts. J. 725, 734 (1999) ("The fact that harassment is sexual in nature may (and often will) be powerful evidence that the victim is suffering harassment because of her sex. The defendant may, however, avoid liability if the fact finder is convinced that the victim was not a target of harassment because of her sex, whether or not the harassment was sexual in nature.").

Professor David S. Schwartz, When Is Sex Because of Sex? The Causation Problem in Sexual Harrassment Law, 150 U. Pa. L. Rev. 1697 (2002), takes a different view. He advocates a "sex per se" rule that would find sexual conduct sufficient to satisfy the "because of sex" requirement. As he notes, "Insofar as the employer's business judgment is not implicated in harassment cases — in contrast to cases involving arguably rational personnel decisions — the need for a causation analysis to fulfill the gatekeeping function is considerably less." Id. at 1718. The Ninth Circuit appears to agree. In Rene v. MGM Grand Hotel Inc., 305 F.3d 1061 (9th Cir. 2002) (en banc), a sexual harassment claim by a gay man was permitted to go forward because the conduct complained of was sexual in nature: "The physical attacks to which Rene was subjected, which targeted body parts clearly linked to his sexuality were 'because of' . . . sex," Judge Fletcher's opinion stated, adding that "Rene's tormentors did not grab his elbow or poke their fingers in his eye. They grabbed his crotch and poked their fingers in his anus."

4. On remand, what evidence would you present to establish that Oncale's coworkers were harassing him because of his sex? What evidence would you present on behalf of the employer to prove an alternative motivation such as jealousy or dislike? Professor Catherine J. Lanctot, The Plain Meaning of *Oncale*, 7 Wm. & Mary Bill Rts. J. 913, 926 (1999), reports "an emerging split in the lower courts over whether the Court's intent in *Oncale* was to encourage more frequent use of summary judgment to resolve harassment claims, or whether, instead, the Court's emphasis on 'common sense' and 'context' signaled a desire to leave such questions to juries rather than to federal judges."

5. Franke, supra note 2, at 696-97, categorizes the same-sex cases that arose before *Oncale* as involving three distinct situations:

> The first set of cases involve [sic] a gay male supervisor who seeks sexual favors from or creates a sexually hostile environment for his male subordinates or coworkers. . . .
>
> The second set of cases involve [sic] nongay same-sex harassment. Here, the defendant is either heterosexual, or at least not alleged to be gay, and is charged with exhibiting sexual behavior in the workplace in such a way that another male employee regards as both unwelcome and offensive. In these cases, the harasser neither wants to have sex with the plaintiff, nor does he desire to have sex with members of the class of people to which the plaintiff belongs. Rather than sexually objectifying the plaintiff, the harasser engages in sexual behavior that is designed to or has the effect of making the plaintiff annoyed, uncomfortable, offended, humiliated, intimidated, or otherwise victimized by the defendant's conduct.
>
> The third set of same-sex sexual harassment cases are [sic] similar to those just described but differ from them in one significant way: the harassing conduct of a sexual nature was undertaken because of the plaintiff's gender identity. That is, the plaintiff was not sufficiently masculine according to the individual defendant's standards of proper masculine presentation, the gender rules of the particular workplace, or according to masculine gender normativity as defined by the culture more generally.

The first set of cases presumably easily falls within *Oncale*, but after *Oncale*, what is the appropriate response to the second situation? Professor Franke recognizes that the second set is hardest for the courts to recognize as "sex" discrimination. Would Justice Scalia? See generally Charles R. Calleros, Same-Sex Harassment, Textualism, Free Speech and *Oncale*: Laying the Groundwork for a Coherent and Constitutional Theory of Sexual Harassment Liability, 7 Geo. Mason L. Rev. 1, 13 (1998) (reading *Oncale* to suggest that the nature of the harassment might be gender discrimination even in a workplace with only one sex represented). How would you establish that such conduct is "based on sex"?

6. As to the third set of cases, Professor Franke asserts that "by and large, courts have been unwilling to recognize this kind of sexual harassment — between men as a way of policing hetero-masculine gender norms — as a form of discrimination because of sex and therefore actionable as sex discrimination." Franke, at 698. She argues, "What makes it sex discrimination, as opposed to the actions of 'a philanderer, a terrible person, and a cheapskate,' or a racist for that matter, is not the fact that the conduct is sexual, but that the sexual conduct is being used to enforce or perpetuate gender norms and stereotypes." Id. at 745. Cf. Nichols v. Azteca Rest. Enterprises, Inc., 256 F.3d 864 (9th Cir. 2001) (discrimination against male for acting too feminine is actionable under Title VII); Camille Hébert, Sexual Harassment as Discrimination "Because of . . . Sex": Have We Come Full Circle?, 27 Ohio N.U. L. Rev. 439 (2001) (plaintiff harassed for failure to conform to gender stereotypes would meet the "because of . . . sex" requirement.). See also Hilary S. Axam & Deborah Zalesne, Simulated Sodomy and Other Forms of Heterosexual "Horseplay": Same-Sex Sexual Harassment, Workplace Gender Hierarchies, and the Myth of the Gender Monolith Before and After *Oncale*, 11 Yale J.L. & Feminism 155, 160 (1999) (by failing "to acknowledge the sex-discriminatory purpose and effect of gender stereotypes and sexual humiliation directed at men by other men" the lower courts "have adopted unduly restrictive conceptions" of sex; *Oncale* does not sufficiently reject this approach). In this regard, consider the relevance of the Court's recognition in *Price Waterhouse* (reproduced at page 152) that gender stereotyping is direct evidence of sex discrimination under Title VII.

7. If Oncale's employer can establish that his co-workers harassed him because he is a homosexual, can he nonetheless establish an actionable claim under Title VII? How? In subsection C.4 of this chapter, we will see that discrimination on the basis of sexual preference is not generally actionable under Title VII. Given the lack of federal protection against sexual orientation discrimination, there has been considerable debate in the literature about whether recognizing same-sex harassment as actionable will alleviate or contribute to the subordination of gays and lesbians in the workplace. See generally Richard F. Storrow, Same-Sex Sexual Harassment Claims After *Oncale*: Defining the Boundaries of Actionable Conduct, 47 Am. U. L. Rev. 677 (1998).

8. Shepherd v. Slater Steel Corp., 168 F.3d 998 (7th Cir. 1999), read *Oncale* to establish two prongs by which same-sex harassment may be gender discrimination:

(1) credible evidence that the harasser is gay or lesbian — in which case it is reasonable to assume that the harasser would not harass members of the other sex (or at least not with "explicit or implicit proposals of sexual activity"); and (2) proof that the plaintiff was harassed in "such sex-specific and derogatory terms" as to reveal an antipathy to persons of plaintiff's gender.

Id. at 1009. In the case before it, the court found sufficient evidence that defendant's harassment was "borne of sexual attraction" to give rise to the inference that plaintiff was harassed because he was male. The court distinguished other cases in which "sexual references were essentially incidental to what was otherwise run-of-the-mill horseplay and vulgarity." Id. at 1010. The court found more difficult the evidence that a woman had been harassed as well. While recognizing that a fact-finder could find defendant's harassment to be "bisexual and therefore beyond the reach of Title VII," id. at 1011, it recognized that a contrary inference was also supportable. See also Higgins v. New Balance Athletic Shoe, Inc., 194 F.3d 252 (1st Cir. 1999), which rejected a claim based on harassment because of sexual orientation, but in the process suggested that, had plaintiff established a record below, it might have found sex discrimination in either (1) the fact that sexual orientation harassment was directed only at men, not women; or (2) because plaintiff's harassment was predicated on his failure to conform to male stereotypes.

9. As *Shepherd* suggests, a test case is the "equal opportunity harasser," the person who directs offensive conduct and remarks against both men and women. At least under the "equality" approach, such a person is not guilty of sex discrimination under Title VII. Charles R. Calleros, The Meaning of "Sex": Homosexual and Bisexual Harassment under Title VII, 20 Vt. L. Rev. 55, 70-78 (1995). See Ramona L. Paetzold, Same-Sex Harassment: Can It Be Sex-Related for Purposes of Title VII?, 1 Emp. Rts. & Employ. Pol'y J. 25 (1997). But under the "sexual conduct is discriminatory" approach, the result might be different. What about the antisubordination principle? While this theory might prohibit all sexual harassment because of its tendency to subordinate women in the workplace, might such subordination be implicit in any attempt to confine either sex to traditional gender roles? Does *Oncale* foreclose liability in this situation?

10. If *Oncale* requires a reconsideration of what "because of sex" means, perhaps the following extract from Vicki Schultz, Reconceptualizing Sexual Harassment 107 Yale L.J. 1683, 1686-87, 1689 (1998), will help with that task:

Although th[e] sexual desire-dominance paradigm represented progress when it was first articulated as the foundation for quid pro quo sexual harassment, using the paradigm to conceptualize hostile work environment harassment has served to exclude from legal understanding many of the most common and debilitating forms of harassment faced by women (and many men) at work each day. The prevailing paradigm privileges conduct thought to be motivated by sexual designs — such as sexual advances — as the core sex- or gender-based harassment. Yet much of the gender-based hostility and abuse that women (and some men) endure at work is neither driven by the desire for sexual relations nor even sexual in content. . . .

This Article challenges the sexual desire-dominance paradigm . . . [T]he paradigm is underinclusive: It omits — and even obscures — many of the most prevalent forms of harassment that make workplaces hostile and alienating to workers based on their gender. Much of what is harmful to women in the workplace is difficult to construe as sexual in design. Similarly, many men are harmed at work by gender-based harassment that fits only uneasily within the parameters of a sexualized paradigm. The prevailing paradigm, however, may also be overinclusive. By emphasizing the protection of women's sexual selves and sensibilities over and above their empowerment as workers, the paradigm permits — or even encourages — companies to construe the law to prohibit some forms of sexual expression that do not promote gender hierarchy at work. The focus of harassment law should not be on sexuality as such. The focus should be on conduct that consigns people to gendered work roles that do not further their own aspirations or advantage.

One of Schultz's solutions is for courts to make an "assumption, which could take the form of a rebuttable presumption" of illegal harassment when the harassment is directed at women who work in traditionally segregated job categories. Professor Steven Willborn agrees with Professor Schultz that harassment ought to be brought back to discrimination law, but takes issue with her "presumption" that harassment in sex-segregated workplaces is discriminatory. He finds no support for that approach in the cases, views it as "much broader than the evidence on which it is based," and believes Professor Schultz is unclear about what conduct should trigger it. While no presumption is appropriate, sex segregation may be relevant in determining whether certain conduct is discriminatory. Steven L. Willborn, Taking Discrimination Seriously: *Oncale* and the Fate of Exceptionalism in Sexual Harassment Law, 7 Wm. & Mary Bill Rts. J. 677, 717-18 (1999). See also Rebecca Hanner White, There's Nothing Special About Sex: The Supreme Court Mainstreams Sexual Harassment, 7 Wm. & Mary Bill Rts. J. 725, 735-36 (1999) (Schultz's "approach makes sense intuitively, and is consistent with *Oncale*, provided that courts keep in mind that only an inference of sex-discrimination is created, not a conclusive method of proof. After all, a woman in a male-dominated workplace may be harassed because she is a woman, or she may be harassed because she is a jerk."). Professor Schultz elaborated further on her views in Talking About Harassment, 9 J.L. & Poly. 417 (2002). See also Henry L. Chambers, Jr., A Unifying Theory of Sex Discrimination, 34 Ga. L. Rev. 1591, 1594 (2000) ("[H]ostile work environment and disparate treatment theory should combine to produce a new cause of action that makes actionable any non-harassing, gender-related conduct that creates a hostile work environment.").

## NOTE ON "REVERSE HARASSMENT" AND "PERSONAL RELATIONSHIPS"

Many sexual harassment cases have involved what might be called extortion — an employee is forced to choose between employment and sexual relations. But what about sex as bribery — an employee using his or her sexual attractiveness to obtain an advantage relative to other employees? Is this actionable under Title VII? Does it matter if the disfavored employees and the favored employee are of the opposite sex?

"Reverse harassment" was litigated in DeCintio v. Westchester County Medical Center, 807 F.2d 304 (2d Cir. 1986). Male respiratory therapists complained that their department head discriminated against them by adopting promotion standards designed to disqualify them and to favor a female applicant with whom he was romantically involved. The court found no Title VII violation:

> Ryan's conduct, although unfair, simply did not violate Title VII. Appellees were not prejudiced because of their status as males; rather, they were discriminated against because Ryan preferred his paramour. Appellees faced exactly the same predicament as that faced by any woman applicant for the promotion: No one but Guagenti could be considered for the appointment because of Guagenti's special relationship to Ryan. That relationship forms the basis of appellees' sex discrimination claims. Appellees' proffered interpretation of Title VII prohibitions against sex discrimination would involve the EEOC and federal courts in the policing of intimate relationships. Such a course, founded on a distortion of the meaning of the word "sex" in the context of Title VII, is both impracticable and unwarranted.

Id. at 308. The court emphasized that Title VII protects individuals from discrimination on the basis of status, "not on his or her sexual affiliations." Id. at 306-07. Isn't this precisely the reasoning that led to early Title VII decisions in which courts declined to find liability for quid pro quo sexual harassment?

The court in DeCintio distinguished sexual harassment claims because the issue there is "the coercive nature of the employer's acts, rather than the fact of the relationship itself." Id. at 307. But doesn't Oncale confirm that the basis of sexual harassment liability is the notion that, "but for" an individual's sex, he or she would not be subjected to harassment? Didn't the plaintiffs in DeCintio lose a job opportunity that, "but for" their gender, they would have had? For a recent decision following DeCintio, see Schobert v. Illinois Dept. of Transp., 304 F.3d 725 (7th Cir. 2002). See generally Mary C. Manemann, Comment, The Meaning of "Sex" in Title VII: Is Favoring an Employee Lover a Violation of the Act?, 83 Nw. U. L. Rev. 612 (1989).

DeCintio found no discrimination in part because both women and men were barred from the job because they did not have a "special relationship" with Ryan. But in harassment cases, the plaintiff need not prove that all women or men are harassed. As the court in Oncale stated, "Courts and juries have found the inference of discrimination easy to draw in most male-female sexual harassment situations, because the challenged conduct typically involves explicit or implicit proposals of sexual activity; it is reasonable to assume those proposals would not have been made to someone of the same sex." 523 U.S. at 80. Why doesn't the same assumption work here? Other women do not have a relationship with Ryan, but assuming he prefers heterosexual relationships, only men are precluded from seeking to establish such a relationship.

Did the plaintiffs in DeCintio lose because the court was unwilling to recognize a Title VII discrimination claim for an employee because he was *not* a victim of sexual harassment? Is that result justified because another woman could not sue? Could a female plaintiff have complained about Ryan's actions? Compare King v. Palmer, 778 F.2d 878 (D.C. Cir. 1985) (employer liable when a male supervisor passed over a qualified woman in favor of a female with whom he was having a sexual relationship), with Womack v. Runyon, 147 F.3d 1298 (11th Cir. 1998) (preferential treatment based on consensual relationship between supervisor and employee does not constitute sexual harassment under Title VII); Taken v. Oklahoma Corp. Comm., 125 F.3d

1366 (10th Cir. 1997) (promotion of girlfriend over two other female candidates does not violate Title VII).

Should the employer be liable for quid pro quo harassment in sexual favoritism cases because the implicit message is that promotion is available only to those who have a sexual relationship with the supervisor? In Dirksen v. City of Springfield, 842 F. Supp. 1117 (C.D. Ill. 1994), the court found quid pro quo harassment where a supervisor told the plaintiff that promotion was conditioned on sexual relations with him and then, while she was on leave, replaced her with a woman with whom he was having a sexual relationship.

Suppose Guagenti, after being hired by Ryan, refused to continue their romantic relationship and Ryan discharged her. Would she have a claim of quid pro quo harassment? In Green v. Administrators of Tulane Educational Fund, 284 F.3d 642 (5th Cir. 2002), the court rejected Tulane's argument that harassment triggered by the ending of a consensual relationship was merely "personal animosity" and not actionable. The court found the harassing behavior was causally related to plaintiff's gender; plaintiff was harassed because she refused to continue to have a "casual" sexual relationship after the breakup. What if there had been no demand for casual sex after the breakup? Would harassing her simply because she was once a consensual sexual partner be actionable? Cf. Pipkins v. City of Temple Terrace, 267 F.3d 1197 (11th Cir. 2001) (disappointment in failed relationship not because of sex); Succar v. Dade County Sch. Bd., 229 F.3d 1343 (11th Cir. 2000) (co-worker harassment not based on gender but result of anger over plaintiff's termination of relationship). On the other hand, if, in a race discrimination case, the court concludes that an employer treated an individual differently because of personal dislike unconnected with race, the employer will prevail. See St. Mary's Honor Ctr. v. Hicks (reproduced at page 130). Should that same reasoning control in a sexual harassment case? Is Ryan's attraction to Guagenti unrelated to her sex?

Consider Phillips v. Martin Marietta, 400 U.S. 542 (1971), in which an employer refused to hire women with preschool age children because of concerns about absenteeism. The Court found sex discrimination because sex plus some other factor — young children — caused the discrimination. Harassing a *particular* woman could be characterized the same way — sex plus attractiveness.

Professor Ellen Paul, however, has questioned the entire theory of sexual harassment as a form of sex discrimination under Title VII:

> Does sexual harassment conform to th[e] disparate treatment paradigm? . . . In the former, a supervisor demands sexual favors in return for job benefits because of sexual desire, and he selects his target because he finds her sexually attractive. In the latter, the supervisor refuses to hire, to promote, or to reward a female employee as he would a comparable male, because he has an animus of some sort against women.
>
> What is missing from the former and is present in the latter is an essential attribute of discrimination: that is, that any member of the scorned group will trigger the response of the person who practices discrimination. . . . Discrimination, concededly, is difficult to define, but one of its essential attributes is that it fastens upon all members of the group to be scorned (or devalued by a negative stereotype). Thus, something essentially different from discrimination in this classic sense seems to be occurring in quid pro quo sexual harassment. . . . [T]he discriminator scorns or devalues all members of a group, while the sexual harasser only targets someone whom he finds attractive. While it is undoubtedly true that many practitioners of sexual harassment are recidivists, their targets are not just any female simply because she is female. . . . [T]ypically, many women work together and only one or some may suffer flagrantly intolerable treatment.

Ellen F. Paul, Sexual Harassment as Sex Discrimination: A Defective Paradigm, 8
Yale L. & Poly. Rev. 333, 349-50 (1990). Do you agree with this analysis? Is Professor
Paul wrong that one of the essential attributes of discrimination is "that it fastens
upon all members of the group to be scorned (or devalued by a negative stereotype)"?
What about an employer who discriminates against African Americans or females
only if they are assertive? Why doesn't sex plus attractiveness equal gender discrimination within *Martin Marietta?* Presumably, a heterosexual male supervisor is unlikely to harass attractive male employees. Even if Paul's arguments do not succeed in
undermining the entire theory of sexual harassment as sex discrimination, has she accurately identified a weakness in cases in which a male employee in a workplace full
of women imposes sexual advances on one particular woman because he finds her attractive? Does the analysis in *Oncale* provide any help in resolving these issues?

### NOTE ON OTHER DISCRIMINATORY HARASSMENT

Sexual harassment claims have predominated among the hostile environment
cases under Title VII, but as the Court noted in *Meritor,* the first case to recognize
hostile environment as a basis for liability under Title VII concerned an employer
who "created an offensive work environment for employees by giving discriminatory
service to its Hispanic clientele." Even before the 1991 statutory amendments provided enhanced damages for discrimination, there was a revival of litigation over
work environments contaminated by racial, national origin, or age discrimination.
See, e.g., EEOC v. Beverage Canners, Inc., 897 F.2d 1067 (11th Cir. 1990) (frequent
racist comments and racial epithets create a hostile environment in violation of Title
VII); Blake v. J. C. Penney Co., 894 F.2d 274 (8th Cir. 1990) (age-based harassment
actionable under ADEA).

An illustrative case is Daniels v. Essex Group, Inc., 937 F.2d 1264 (7th Cir. 1991),
where Daniels complained that, over the course of a decade, he was subjected to
racist jokes and name-calling; a black dummy dripping fake blood was hung near his
workstation; racist and threatening graffiti were scrawled on bathroom walls; a co-
worker called him "nigger," threatened to beat him up, and threatened his four-year-
old son; and a bullet was shot into his house near his bedroom window. The Seventh
Circuit determined that Daniels had demonstrated both that the racial harassment altered the terms and conditions of his employment and that the harassment "would
have adversely affected the work performance and well-being of a reasonable person."
Id. at 1274. The Seventh Circuit has also ruled that a white district sales manager's
use of the word "nigger" on just two occasions constituted racial harassment even
though black employees in the same workplace sometimes used the word. See
Rodgers v. Western-Southern Life Ins. Co., 12 F.3d 668 (7th Cir. 1993); Swinton v.
Potomac Corp., 270 F.3d 794 (9th Cir. 2001), *cert. denied,* 122 S. Ct. 1609 (2002)
(affirming one million dollar punitive damage award under §1981 in case of racial
harassment involving repeated use of the word "nigger" and racial "jokes").

Sexual harassment claims have themselves come full circle. Women are complaining not only of unwelcome sexual advances but also of environments that are hostile to
women in other ways. The courts have found that harassing conduct of a non-sexual
nature can constitute sexual harassment, sometimes called gender harassment. For example, in Berkman v. City of New York, 580 F. Supp. 226 (E.D.N.Y. 1983), *aff'd,* 755
F.2d 913 (2d Cir. 1985), the court found harassment against female probationary
firefighters hired pursuant to a consent decree in a previous discrimination case. They

were subjected to crude comments, graffiti, cartoons, and practical jokes apparently designed to insult and annoy, rather than to solicit sexual favors. See also Gorski v. New Hampshire Dept. of Corr., 290 F.3d 466 (1st Cir. 2002) (remarks and conduct directed toward plaintiff's pregnancy or because of her pregnancy stated a claim based on a hostile work environment); Haugerud v. Amery Sch. Dist., 259 F.3d 678 (7th Cir. 2001) (conduct was not sexual, but sole female custodian presented sufficient evidence that it was directed toward her because of her sex); Williams v. General Motors Corp., 187 F.3d 553 (6th Cir. 1999) ("conduct underlying sexual harassment claim need not be overtly sexual in nature"); Smith v. Sheahan, 189 F.3d 529 (7th Cir. 1999) (physical assault created hostile work environment for female jail guard).

While any harassment claim under Title VII must allege harassment based on membership in a statutorily protected group, complaints of discriminatory harassment involve many of the same issues discussed in this subsection concerning sexual harassment. While recognizing the benefits of analogizing race and sexual harassment, one commentator, however, has cautioned of the dangers:

> [S]ome courts have used explicit and implicit analogies between race and sex to make it more difficult to establish the existence of racial harassment, by importing the standards for sexual harassment into the standards of proof for racial harassment claims. Accordingly, some courts have begun to use language suggesting that "welcomeness" may be an issue in racial harassment claims, so that it becomes relevant to ask whether the target of harassment somehow invited that behavior. The movement of courts toward a more "gender-neutral" . . . perspective for judging sexually harassing conduct may also cause courts to reject the relevance of the experience of racial minorities with racially threatening and offensive conduct. The use of the standard developed in the context of sexual harassment requiring that conduct be "severe or pervasive" in order to be actionable has led the courts to conclude that even quite damaging and serious racially motivated behavior, including references to lynching or racially motivated assault, is insufficient to state a cause of action for racial harassment. The use of standards of employer liability developed in connection with sexual harassment claims in the context of racial harassment claims may well leave many employees victimized by racially hostile workplaces and no remedy for this discriminatory and damaging behavior. Analogies between race and sex may also lead courts to conclude that even racially explicit conduct is not racially motivated, similar to the conclusions drawn by some courts that sexually explicit conduct is not motivated by gender.

L. Camille Hébert, Analogizing Race and Sex in Workplace Harassment Claims, 58 Ohio St. L.J. 819, 878-79 (1997). In National Railroad Passenger Corp. v. Morgan, 536 U.S. 101 (2002), however, the Court asserted that "[h]ostile work environment claims based on racial harassment are reviewed under the same standard as those based on sexual harassment." Id. at n.10, p. 2074. Issues unique to other discriminatory harassment will be noted throughout this section.

### b.  "Unwelcome" Conduct

### BURNS v. McGREGOR ELECTRONIC INDUSTRIES
#### 989 F.2d 959 (8th Cir. 1993)

LAY, Senior Circuit Judge.

[The court referred to its earlier opinion, published at 955 F.2d 559, 560-63

(1992), for the "grisly and shocking facts supporting a finding of unwelcome sexual harassment." In that earlier opinion, the court described the following facts:

> Burns testified that during her . . . employment with McGregor, manager-trainee Marla Ludvik often made sexual comments as Burns left the restroom, such as "have you been playing with yourself in there?" Ludvik also made almost daily comments to other workers that she did not think Burns took douches, that she saw Burns riding in [owner] Oslac's car, and that Burns was going out with Oslac. Ludvik tried to convince Burns to date male employees. . . .
>
> . . . Burns testified that Oslac showed her advertisements for pornographic films in Penthouse magazine, talked about sex, asked her to watch pornographic movies with him, and made lewd gestures, such as ones imitating masturbation. . . . Oslac asked Burns for dates at least once a week. . . . Burns testified that . . . Oslac visited the plant from 11:00 a.m. Monday until 9:00 a.m. Tuesday of each week and that he spent most of this time with her. He continued to ask for dates and wanted to engage in oral sex so she would "be able to perform [her] work better." When Burns refused a date, Oslac told her, "I'm tired of your fooling around and always turning me down. You must not need your job very bad." Believing that Oslac intended to fire her, she accepted an invitation to dinner at his apartment on the condition that her mother would join them. Burns testified that her mother refused to go, so her father, Daniel Burns, went with her. . . . Oslac appeared shocked when Burns' father appeared at the dinner with Burns. After the meal, Daniel Burns told Oslac he knew what was going on and for Oslac "to leave the girls alone at work."
>
> Burns further testified that . . . Ludvik, who was then a supervisor, circulated a petition to have Burns fired because nude photographs of her, taken by her father, appeared in two motorcycle magazines — Easyrider and In the Wind. One full frontal view of Burns revealed a pelvic tatoo; two photographs highlighted jewelry attached to her pierced nipples. Burns testified that she had willingly allowed her father to do the piercing and photography. She did not take copies of the magazines into the plant. Former employee Deborah Johnson testified that she saw Ludvik showing employees the magazine and the petition. Burns testified that after Oslac learned about the nude photos from Ludvik, he told her, "They're ganging up on you and trying to get rid of you. If you don't go out with me, I might just let them do it." Oslac then asked Burns to pose nude for him in the plant in return for overtime pay. . . .
>
> Burns testified that the overall work environment was "hostile and offensive.". . . [D]uring the last six weeks of her . . . employment at McGregor she overheard [a coworker] tell a fellow worker that "he should throw [Burns] over the [conveyor] belts" and commit an act of sodomitic intercourse upon her. [The co-worker] denied making the statement attributed to him by Burns about "throwing her over the belts." He admitted on direct examination, however, that he had called Burns names — "anything nasty."

[Evidence from other co-workers corroborated Burns' testimony.]

In its first opinion, issued in July 1990, the district court found that there is "no doubt" that Paul Oslac, the owner of McGregor Electronic, made unwelcome sexual advances toward Burns . . . when she was . . . employed at the McGregor, Iowa company. However, the district court found that plaintiff exaggerated the severity and pervasiveness of the sexual harassment and its effect on her. The trial court observed that Burns had previously appeared in provocative poses in a lewd magazine called Easyriders. Some employees brought the magazine to work and circulated it. Oslac and other male workers repeatedly made harassing comments to Burns about the photographs. Based on Burns's past behavior and the district judge's observation of her at trial, the trial court found that although the sexual advances at work were considered by Burns to be unwelcome, she would not have been offended by these advances and by the sexual innuendo from other employees and supervisors. . . .

In the decision . . . before us, the trial court explained that it believes there are two elements necessary for establishing sexual harassment: (1) whether the conduct was unwelcome because it was not solicited or invited, and (2) whether the conduct was offensive to the plaintiff.

We believe the trial court erred in requiring proof that the conduct at issue was unwelcome and offensive. . . . "The gravamen of any sexual harassment claim is that the alleged sexual advances were 'unwelcome.'" Meritor Savs. Bank v. Vinson. . . . "[T]he threshold for determining that conduct is unwelcome" is whether it was uninvited and offensive. . . . [F]or the court to find that the conduct was unwelcome but not offensive was internally inconsistent as a matter of law. Whether the behavior is unwelcomed is to be determined by weighing whether the conduct was uninvited and offensive. . . .

The district court found that notwithstanding the fact that the employer's conduct was unwelcome and created a hostile work environment, the plaintiff was not an "affected" individual in that she did not regard the conduct of her employer as undesirable or offensive. This finding was premised on the fact that plaintiff had appeared in non-work related nude poses in lewd magazines. . . . The district court reasoned that a person who would appear nude in a national magazine could not be offended by the behavior which took place at the McGregor plant. . . .

The plaintiff's choice to pose for a nude magazine outside work hours is not material to the issue of whether plaintiff found her employer's work-related conduct offensive. This is not a case where Burns posed in provocative and suggestive ways at work. Her private life, regardless how reprehensible the trier of fact might find it to be, did not provide lawful acquiescence to unwanted sexual advances at her work place by her employer. To hold otherwise would be contrary to Title VII's goal of ridding the work place of any kind of unwelcome sexual harassment. . . .

The trial court made explicit findings that the conduct was not invited or solicited despite her posing naked for a magazine distributed nationally. The court believed, however, that because of her outside conduct, including her "interest in having her nude pictures appear in a magazine containing much lewd and crude sexually explicit material," the uninvited sexual advances of her employer were not "in and of itself offensive to her." The court explained that Burns "would not have been offended if someone she was attracted to did or said the same thing."

We hold that such a view is unsupported in law. If the court intended this as a standard or rationale for a standard, it is clearly in error. This rationale would allow a complete stranger to pursue sexual behavior at work that a female worker would accept from her husband or boyfriend. This standard would allow a male employee to kiss or fondle a female worker at the workplace. None of the plaintiff's conduct, which the court found relevant to bar her action, was work related. Burns did not tell sexual stories or engage in sexual gestures at work. She did not initiate sexual talk or solicit sexual encounters with co-employees. Under the trial court's rationale, if a woman taught part-time sexual education at a high school or college, a court would be compelled to find that sexual language, even though uninvited when directed at her in the work place, would not offend her as it might someone else who was not as accustomed to public usage of the terms. . . .

We need not remand for reconsideration since we find that it is undisputed that the trial court has determined that the respondent's conduct was unwelcomed by the plaintiff and was such that a hypothetical reasonable woman would consider the conduct sufficiently severe or pervasive to alter the conditions of employment and create an abusive work environment. The evidence that plaintiff had engaged in posing for nude pictures in Easyriders magazine, although relevant to the totality of the events that ensued, cannot constitute a defense to her claim of a hostile sexual harassment environment at the work place when, as here, the trial court has determined that it did not constitute an invitation to engage in sexual discourse. . . .

### NOTES

1. Does a woman lose her right to complain of sexual harassment by engaging in "welcoming" behavior? What is "welcoming behavior"? Does it include body language and style of dress? Does a female employee have a right to dress provocatively without being subjected to sexual solicitation and touching? The court noted that Burns did not pose in provocative and suggestive ways at work. *Meritor* stated that Vinson's style of dress was "obviously relevant" to the question whether she welcomed Taylor's sexual advances. Does this mean that an employee who dresses in a sexually attractive manner loses her right to be free of sexual harassment?

2. Neither *Burns* nor *Meritor* directly considered whether "welcoming" is a question of objective appearance or subjective interest. The definition of "unwelcome" used by both courts, requiring the conduct to be both uninvited and offensive, suggests that "welcomeness" is subjective. In Henson v. City of Dundee, 682 F.2d 897 (11th Cir. 1982), the Eleventh Circuit expressly adopted a subjective standard, stating that the conduct "must be unwelcome in the sense that the employee . . . regarded the conduct as undesirable or offensive." Id. at 903.

3. Does a woman who has a private consensual sexual relationship with a married co-worker "welcome" sexual advances at work? See Stacks v. Southwestern Bell Yellow Pages, Inc., 27 F.3d 1316 (8th Cir. 1994) (no).

4. If a woman uses foul language or tells off-color jokes at work, has she "welcomed" conduct that might otherwise constitute sexual harassment? Compare Wyerick v. Bayou Steel Corp., 887 F.2d 1271 (5th Cir. 1989) (three sexual comments made in response to numerous sexual remarks and gestures did not constitute sufficient welcoming behavior for summary judgment), with Reed v. Shepard, 939 F.2d 484 (7th Cir. 1991) (participation in conduct on which complaint is based is a defense).

In determining whether a victim's behavior precludes recovery because she welcomed sexually charged comments or behavior, courts seem to weigh the victim's conduct against that of the alleged perpetrators. Compare Carr v. Allison Gas Turbine Div., 32 F.3d 1007 (7th Cir. 1994) (plaintiff's bawdy behavior and use of foul language did not constitute welcoming behavior justifying four years of extensive harassment that included derogatory sexual comments, foul names, sex-related pranks, and sexual graffiti and pictures), with Balletti v. Sun-Sentinel Co., 909 F. Supp. 1539, 1548 (S.D. Fla. 1995) (plaintiff's vulgar language and conduct including pulling down a co-worker's pants and exposing his buttocks was worse than anything she complained about).

5. Why is a woman who engages in welcoming behavior fair game for sexual harassment? Has she consented to be harassed? Or does the conduct simply cease to be harassment? Why is harassment prohibited only if it is unwelcome? See Susan Estrich, Sex at Work, 43 Stan. L. Rev. 813 (1991) (arguing for the elimination of the welcomeness inquiry); Mary F. Radford, By Invitation Only: The Proof of

Welcomeness in Sexual Harassment Cases, 72 N.C. L. Rev. 499 (1994) (arguing that defendants should bear the burden of proving welcomeness).

6.  If a woman has not actively welcomed sexual conduct or speech in the work-place, what must she do to establish that such behavior is unwelcome? Is it enough for her to testify she found the conduct unwelcome, or must she affirmatively indi-cate to the harasser, in words or in conduct, that she found the conduct unwelcome?

7.  If harassing conduct is sufficiently severe that a reasonable person would find it offensive (such as a supervisor grabbing a female employee's breasts or a male em-ployee's genitals in front of a group of other employees), is the conduct unwelcome even in the absence of any communication to that effect from the victim?

8.  In Harris v. Forklift Systems, Inc. (reproduced at page 507), the plaintiff did not expressly inform her boss that his conduct was offensive until just before she quit her job. After she informed him, there only was one additional incident of harassment. If Harris failed to communicate through "body language" that Hardy's offensive re-marks were unwelcome, was his conduct so outrageous that it was unnecessary for Harris to communicate that it was unwelcome? On remand, the district court limited Harris' case to the single harassing incident that occurred after she complained be-cause the company president was unaware that she was offended until she informed him that his remarks and conduct were unwelcome. Harris v. Forklift Sys. Inc., 66 Fair Emp. Prac. Cas. (BNA) 1886 (M.D. Tenn. 1994).

9.  What is the relationship between "severe or pervasive" and "unwelcome"? Can conduct be severe or pervasive, but nonetheless welcome? Is the issue of "welcome-ness" a separate question from whether the employee "subjectively perceive[d] the environment as abusive"? See Harris (reproduced at page 507).

10.  Can an employee waive her right to be free of harassment at work by her sex-ual behavior outside of the workplace? If a woman welcomes sexual attention in one context, does she necessarily welcome it in another context? Is Burns foreclosed from refusing sexual advances at work? Are her co-workers and supervisors free to respond to her off-duty behavior with sexual advances and raw language until she clearly indi-cates her displeasure with such behavior? When a woman appears in Playboy or dances at a nude bar or works as a prostitute, what do these activities say about her willingness to be solicited for sex or to engage in sexual activity in other contexts?

11.  One question with respect to welcoming behavior has not yet been litigated in the circuit courts but is likely to arise. It relates to establishments such as Hooters res-taurants that hire women as waitresses, dress them in outfits designed to be provoca-tive, and advertise not just the food but also the sexually attractive personnel. If a Hooters waitress complains of sexual harassment by customers, can the employer say that she welcomed harassment by taking the job or that putting up with some level of harassment is a bfoq? The same question arises with respect to dancers in clubs.

12.  Does the issue of "welcomeness" have any relevance in racial harassment cases? What does it mean to "welcome" racial harassment? See L. Camille Hébert, Analogizing Race and Sex in Workplace Harassment Claims, 58 Ohio St. L.J. 819, 878-79 (1997).

13.  What is the relationship between "unwelcomeness," an element on which the plaintiff bears the burden of proof, and the employer's affirmative defense outlined in Ellerth, reproduced at page 516? Does the affirmative defense make the "welcome-ness" inquiry unnecessary? For discussion of this point, see Henry L. Chambers, Jr., (Un)Welcome Conduct and the Sexually Hostile Work Environment, 53 Ala. L. Rev. 733 (2002).

### c.  Severe or Pervasive Harassment

## HARRIS v. FORKLIFT SYSTEMS, INC.
### 510 U.S. 17 (1993)

O'CONNOR, J., delivered the opinion for a unanimous Court. . . .

### I.

Teresa Harris worked as a manager at Forklift Systems, Inc., an equipment rental company, from April 1985 until October 1987. Charles Hardy was Forklift's president.

The Magistrate found that, throughout Harris' time at Forklift, Hardy often insulted her because of her gender and often made her the target of unwanted sexual innuendos. Hardy told Harris on several occasions, in the presence of other employees, "You're a woman, what do you know" and "We need a man as the rental manager"; at least once, he told her she was "a dumb ass woman." Again in front of others, he suggested that the two of them "go to the Holiday Inn to negotiate [Harris'] raise." Hardy occasionally asked Harris and other female employees to get coins from his front pants pocket. He threw objects on the ground in front of Harris and other women, and asked them to pick the objects up. He made sexual innuendos about Harris' and other women's clothing.

In mid-August 1987, Harris complained to Hardy about his conduct. Hardy said he was surprised that Harris was offended, claimed he was only joking, and apologized. He also promised he would stop, and based on this assurance Harris stayed on the job. But in early September, Hardy began anew: While Harris was arranging a deal with one of Forklift's customers, he asked her, again in front of other employees, "What did you do, promise the guy . . . some [sex] Saturday night?" On October 1, Harris collected her paycheck and quit.

Harris then sued Forklift, claiming that Hardy's conduct had created an abusive work environment for her because of her gender. The [district court] found this to be "a close case," but held that Hardy's conduct did not create an abusive environment. The court found that some of Hardy's comments "offended [Harris], and would offend the reasonable woman," but that they were not "so severe as to be expected to seriously affect [Harris'] psychological well-being." A reasonable woman manager under like circumstances would have been offended by Hardy, but his conduct would not have risen to the level of interfering with that person's work performance.

> Neither do I believe that [Harris] was subjectively so offended that she suffered injury. . . . Although Hardy may at times have genuinely offended [Harris], I do not believe that he created a working environment so poisoned as to be intimidating or abusive to [Harris].

. . . We granted certiorari to resolve a conflict among the Circuits on whether conduct, to be actionable as "abusive work environment" harassment (no quid pro quo harassment issue is present here), must "seriously affect [an employee's] psychological well-being" or lead the plaintiff to "suffer injury." . . .

II

Title VII of the Civil Rights Act of 1964 makes it "an unlawful employment practice for an employer . . . to discriminate against any individual with respect to his compensation, terms, conditions, or privileges of employment, because of such individual's race, color, religion, sex, or national origin." As we made clear in *Meritor,* this language "is not limited to 'economic' or 'tangible' discrimination. The phrase 'terms, conditions, or privileges of employment' evinces a congressional intent 'to strike at the entire spectrum of disparate treatment of men and women' in employment," which includes requiring people to work in a discriminatorily hostile or abusive environment. When the workplace is permeated with "discriminatory intimidation, ridicule, and insult," that is "sufficiently severe or pervasive to alter the conditions of the victim's employment and create an abusive working environment," Title VII is violated.

This standard, which we reaffirm today, takes a middle path between making actionable any conduct that is merely offensive and requiring the conduct to cause a tangible psychological injury. As we pointed out in *Meritor,* "mere utterance of an . . . epithet which engenders offensive feelings in an employee," does not sufficiently affect the conditions of employment to implicate Title VII. Conduct that is not severe or pervasive enough to create an objectively hostile or abusive work environment — an environment that a reasonable person would find hostile or abusive — is beyond Title VII's purview. Likewise, if the victim does not subjectively perceive the environment to be abusive, the conduct has not actually altered the conditions of the victim's employment, and there is no Title VII violation.

But Title VII comes into play before the harassing conduct leads to a nervous breakdown. A discriminatorily abusive work environment, even one that does not seriously affect employees' psychological well-being, can and often will detract from employees' job performance, discourage employees from remaining on the job, or keep them from advancing in their careers. Moreover, even without regard to these tangible effects, the very fact that the discriminatory conduct was so severe or pervasive that it created a work environment abusive to employees because of their race, gender, religion, or national origin offends Title VII's broad rule of workplace equality. The appalling conduct alleged in *Meritor,* and the reference in that case to environments "'so heavily polluted with discrimination as to destroy completely the emotional and psychological stability of minority group workers,'" quoting Rogers v. EEOC, merely present some especially egregious examples of harassment. They do not mark the boundary of what is actionable.

We therefore believe the District Court erred in relying on whether the conduct "seriously affected plaintiff's psychological well-being" or led her to "suffer injury." Such an inquiry may needlessly focus the factfinder's attention on concrete psychological harm, an element Title VII does not require. Certainly Title VII bars conduct that would seriously affect a reasonable person's psychological well-being, but the statute is not limited to such conduct. So long as the environment would reasonably be perceived, and is perceived, as hostile or abusive, there is no need for it also to be psychologically injurious.

This is not, and by its nature cannot be, a mathematically precise test. We need not answer today all the potential questions it raises, nor specifically address the EEOC's new regulations on this subject, see 58 Fed. Reg. 51266 (1993) (proposed 29 C.F.R. §§ 1609.1, 1609.2); see also 29 C.F.R. § 1604.11 (1993). But we can say that whether an environment is "hostile" or "abusive" can be determined only by looking at all the circumstances. These may include the frequency of the discriminatory conduct; its severity; whether it is physically threatening or humiliating, or a mere offensive utterance; and whether it unreasonably interferes with an employee's work performance. The effect on the employee's psychological well-being is, of course, relevant to determining whether the plaintiff actually found the environment abusive. But while psychological harm, like any other relevant factor, may be taken into account, no single factor is required.

## III

Forklift, while conceding that a requirement that the conduct seriously affect psychological well-being is unfounded, argues that the District Court nonetheless correctly applied the *Meritor* standard. We disagree. Though the District Court did conclude that the work environment was not "intimidating or abusive to [Harris]," it did so only after finding that the conduct was not "so severe as to be expected to seriously affect plaintiff's psychological well-being," and that Harris was not "subjectively so offended that she suffered injury." The District Court's application of these incorrect standards may well have influenced its ultimate conclusion, especially given that the court found this to be a "close case." . . .

Justice SCALIA, concurring.

Meritor Savings Bank v. Vinson held that Title VII prohibits sexual harassment that takes the form of a hostile work environment. The Court stated that sexual harassment is actionable if it is "sufficiently severe or pervasive 'to alter the conditions of [the victim's] employment and create an abusive work environment.'" Today's opinion elaborates that the challenged conduct must be severe or pervasive enough "to create an objectively hostile or abusive work environment — an environment that a reasonable person would find hostile or abusive."

"Abusive" (or "hostile," which in this context I take to mean the same thing) does not seem to me a very clear standard — and I do not think clarity is at all increased by adding the adverb "objectively" or by appealing to a "reasonable person's" notion of what the vague word means. Today's opinion does list a number of factors that contribute to abusiveness, but since it neither says how much of each is necessary (an impossible task) nor identifies any single factor as determinative, it thereby adds little certitude. As a practical matter, today's holding lets virtually unguided juries decide whether sex-related conduct engaged in (or permitted by) an employer is egregious enough to warrant an award of damages. One might say that what constitutes "negligence" (a traditional jury question) is not much more clear and certain than what constitutes "abusiveness." Perhaps so. But the class of plaintiffs seeking to recover for negligence is limited to those who have suffered harm, whereas under this statute "abusiveness" is to be the test of whether legal harm has been suffered, opening more expansive vistas of litigation.

Be that as it may, I know of no alternative to the course the Court today has taken. One of the factors mentioned in the Court's nonexhaustive list — whether the conduct unreasonably interferes with an employee's work performance — would, if it were made an absolute test, provide greater guidance to juries and employers. But I see no basis for such a limitation in the language of the statute. Accepting *Meritor's* interpretation of the term "conditions of employment" as the law, the test is not whether work has been impaired, but whether working conditions have been discriminatorily altered. I know of no test more faithful to the inherently vague statutory language than the one the Court today adopts. For these reasons, I join the opinion of the Court.

*NOTES*

1. *Harris* reaffirms the *Meritor* standard, which requires that, "[f]or sexual harassment to be actionable, it must be sufficiently severe or pervasive 'to alter the conditions of [the victim's] employment and create an abusive working environment.'" What does this standard reveal about drawing the line between acceptable social behavior and actionable sexual harassment? Does *Harris* make the standard any clearer than it was after *Meritor*? What should the district court find on remand? Was Hardy's conduct "severe" or "pervasive" or both? If the harassment in this case was not severe, when did it become pervasive enough to be actionable?

2. A number of courts have applied the *Harris* standard. In DeAngelis v. El Paso Municipal Police Officers Assn., 51 F.3d 591 (5th Cir. 1995), the Fifth Circuit rejected a harassment claim based on four derogatory references to a female police sergeant printed in a police union newsletter column at irregular intervals over a period of two and one-half years. Similarly, the Seventh Circuit in Saxton v. AT&T, 10 F.3d 526 (7th Cir. 1993), found insufficient evidence of sexual harassment where an employee alleged that her supervisor fondled and forcibly kissed her during an after-work meeting at a nightclub and, weeks later, made forcible advances in a park on the way back to work after lunch. The employee admonished the supervisor, and after the incident in the park, there were no further incidents. The behavior, while inappropriate, was not actionable because, even if the plaintiff felt harassed, the court found that a reasonable person would not have considered the relatively isolated incidents sufficiently severe to constitute harassment.

The Seventh Circuit also found insufficient evidence of harassment in Baskerville v. Culligan Intl. Co., 50 F.3d 428 (7th Cir. 1995). In *Baskerville*, a secretary cited nine incidents involving her supervisor over a six-month period, including calling her a pretty girl, grunting in approval of a leather skirt, saying his office was hot after she came in, and saying he was lonely in his hotel room. The court noted that the supervisor never touched or assaulted the plaintiff, never asked her to have sex, and never threatened her or exposed himself or showed her dirty pictures. "He never said anything to her that could not be repeated on prime-time television." Id. at 431. See also Duncan v. Gen. Motors Corp., 300 F.3d 928 (8th Cir. 2002) (reversing jury verdict in plaintiff's favor because pattern of advances and "boorish behavior" not sufficiently severe or pervasive). Are these results consistent with the standard articulated in *Harris*? For a study of sexual harassment cases in the federal courts, concluding that a successful claim is most likely to involve sexualized conduct directed toward an individual, see Ann Juliano & Stewart Schwab, The Sweep of Sexual Harassment Cases, 86 Cornell L. Rev. 548 (2001).

3. The Second Circuit has held that judges should be cautious in granting summary judgment in sexual harassment cases because juries are better qualified to evaluate appropriate behavior in the workplace:

> Today, while gender relations in the workplace are rapidly evolving, and views of what is appropriate behavior are diverse and shifting, a jury made up of a cross-section of our heterogenous communities provides the appropriate institution for deciding whether borderline situations should be characterized as sexual harassment.

Gallagher v. Delaney, 139 F.3d 338, 342 (2d Cir. 1998). See Theresa M. Beiner, Let the Jury Decide: The Gap Between What Judges and Reasonable People Believe Is Sexually Harrassing, 75 S. Cal. L. Rev. 791 (2002) (cautioning against summary judgment as a matter of law because "reasonable people believe that conduct is sexually harassing in situations that courts fail to acknowledge"). Is this a good solution to the problem of defining actionable sexual harassment? Are decisions by juries capable of setting new standards of behavior? Consider the following remarks in another Second Circuit case:

> American popular culture can, on occasion, be highly sexist and offensive. What *is*, is not always what is right, and reasonable people can take justifiable offense at comments that the vulgar among us, even if they are a majority, would consider acceptable.

Torres v. Pisano, 116 F.3d 625, 633 n.7 (2d Cir. 1997). If those who believe vulgar comments are acceptable constitute a majority of the population, how can juries be expected to improve sexist behavior in the workplace?

4. One way to approach this problem is to admit expert testimony as to what constitutes sexual harassment. See Donna Shestowsky, Note, Where Is the Common Knowledge? Empirical Support for Requiring Expert Testimony in Sexual Harassment Trials, 51 Stan. L. Rev. 357 (1999), who argues that federal courts often exclude expert testimony in sexual harassment cases "because they assume that what constitutes sexual harassment is 'common knowledge' and therefore expert opinion on the matter would not be helpful to the trier of fact." She asserts, however, that "empirical evidence finding that men and women have vastly different perceptions of sexual harassment indicates that a common knowledge base for determining reasonable behavior does not exist."

5. After *Harris*, courts continue to disagree about what a plaintiff must show to establish a hostile work environment. The Sixth Circuit requires plaintiffs to demonstrate that the harassment "had the effect of unreasonably interfering with the plaintiff's work performance and creating an intimidating, hostile, or offensive working environment. . . ." Harrison v. Metro Govt. of Nashville, 80 F.3d 1107, 1118 (6th Cir. 1996) (quoting Rabidue v. Osceola Refining Co., 805 F.2d 611, 619 (6th Cir. 1986)). The Tenth Circuit, in contrast, has held that a woman who continues to enjoy her work and intends to stay on the job can, nonetheless, establish that she has been a victim of hostile environment harassment. Davis v. United States Postal Serv., 142 F.3d 1334 (10th Cir. 1998). Under this standard a sexual harassment claimant is "not required to prove that her tangible productivity or work performance declines or that her ability to do her job was impaired." Smith v. Norwest Fin. Acceptance, 129 F.3d 1408, 1413 (10th Cir. 1997). Which approach is more consistent with *Harris*?

6. The primary issue resolved in *Harris* is that the victim of harassment need not establish that she or he suffered serious psychological injury in order to recover under Title VII. But can an employee win a harassment suit merely by establishing that a reasonable person would have been offended? What does the Court mean when it states that, "if the victim does not subjectively perceive the environment to be abusive, the conduct has not actually altered the conditions of the victim's employment, and there is no Title VII violation"?

7. Do the Court's examples clarify the meaning of actionable sexual harassment? What is a "mere offensive utterance"? What if the president of a company refers to a female vice-president as a "cunt" or a "whore" at a meeting with an important client? Should this conduct be actionable? See Howley v. Town of Stratford, 217 F.3d 141 (2d Cir. 2000). Is the president's tone of voice relevant? Does it matter if he is joking or insulting her in anger or merely making an offhand remark? What about rumors? In Spain v. Gallegos, 26 F.3d 439 (3d Cir. 1994), false rumors that a female

employee was having an affair with her male supervisor constituted actionable sexual harassment.

8.  Courts have sometimes resisted finding actionable harassment based only on offensive comments. In Clark County School District v. Breeden (reproduced at page 638), the Supreme Court held that no reasonable person could believe that telling a single joke with a sexual innuendo constituted actionable harassment. See, e.g., Skouby v. Prudential Ins. Co., 130 F.3d 794 (7th Cir. 1997) (male employees' banter about attending striptease club and presentation to plaintiff of eight to ten drawings with sexual themes not severe or pervasive); Sprague v. Thorn Americas, Inc., 129 F.3d 1355 (10th Cir. 1997) (sporadic comments over 16-month period did not create a hostile environment; comments included joking request to undo her top button, reference to PMS, staring down her dress and joking about it, and referring to a jewelry item as "kinky"); Black v. Zaring Homes, Inc., 104 F.3d 822 (6th Cir. 1997) (numerous comments at real estate meetings referring to property adjacent to Hooters Restaurant as "Titsville" or "Twin Peaks," joking about client named "Busam" and whether plaintiff was seen dancing on the tables at a nearby biker bar insufficient to create a hostile environment). Courts have been more open to finding a hostile environment based on verbal harassment when the comments are alleged to be "commonplace," "ongoing," and "continuing" over a long period of time. See Abeita v. TransAmerica Mailings, Inc., 159 F.3d 246 (6th Cir. 1998). However in McCowan v. All Star Maintenance, 273 F.3d 917 (10th Cir. 2001), the court found a jury question present on a hostile work environment claim, even though the plaintiffs worked for only three weeks. Throughout their employment, they were subjected to vulgar and offensive speech, including such terms as "burrito-eating motherfuckers" and "stupid fucking Mexicans." The court overturned the lower court's grant of summary judgment, leaving it to the jury to determine whether the conduct was sufficiently severe or pervasive.

9.  As employers become educated about the impropriety and illegality of harassing conduct and speech, it is likely that they will be careful not to use obviously harassing language. Will subtlety avoid a violation? Is it harassment when an employee is subjected to derogatory statements directed at "all of you" or "one of them" when it is clear that the reference is to protected group members? See Aman v. Cort Furniture Rental Corp., 85 F.3d 1074, 1078 (3d Cir. 1996).

10.  Should it be possible to pursue a pattern and practice or class action case of hostile environment sexual harassment? What problems do you see? How should a court deal with the subjective aspect of a harassment claim in a class action context? See EEOC v. Mitsubishi Motor Mfg., 990 F. Supp. 1059 (C.D. Ill. 1998) (allowing a pattern and practice sexual harassment action); Jenson v. Eveleth Taconite Co., 824 F. Supp. 847 (D. Minn. 1993) (finding class-wide liability for sexual harassment).

11.  Contaminated workplace sexual harassment is often "pervasive" precisely because a number of incidents — no one of which may suffice — occur over a period of time and collectively alter the plaintiff's terms and conditions of employment. Title VII, however, has a very short period in which to file a charge with EEOC — 180 or 300 days from a violation. This raises a question of whether events occurring before that period can be the basis of a sexual harassment claim. In National R.R. Passenger Corp. v. Morgan, 536 U.S. 101 (2002) (reproduced at page 842), the Supreme Court held that "the entire scope of a hostile work environment claim, including behavior alleged outside the statutory time period, is permissible for the purposes of assessing liability, so long as any act contributing to that hostile environment takes place within the statutory time period." 536 U.S. at 117.

12. In discussing the requirement that conduct be severe or pervasive to be actionable, the *Oncale* Court states, "in same-sex (as in all) harassment cases, that inquiry requires careful consideration of the social context in which particular behavior occurs and is experienced by its target." Does this mean that it is not possible to establish sexual harassment when females are hired to work in a previously all male blue-collar workplace where sexually explicit language and pictures have long been commonplace? In Williams v. General Motors, 187 F.3d 553 (6th Cir. 1999), the court held that the standard for establishing sexual harassment does not vary with the work environment. The same standard applies, therefore, whether the complaint is asserted in a coarse blue-collar environment or in a more refined professional environment. Is this holding consistent with *Oncale*? Consider the following:

> It is true that the severity of alleged harassment must be assessed in light of the social mores of American workers and workplace culture, see *Oncale*, but nothing in *Oncale* even hints at the idea that prevailing culture can excuse discriminatory actions. Employers who tolerate workplaces marred by exclusionary practices and bigoted attitudes cannot use their discriminatory pasts to shield them from the present-day mandate of Title VII.

Smith v. Sheahan, 189 F.3d 529 (7th Cir. 1999). See generally, Michael J. Frank, The Social Context Variable in Hostile Environment Litigation, 77 Notre Dame L. Rev. 437 (2002); Amanda Helm Wright, Note, From the Factory to the Firm: Clarifying Standards for Blue-Collar and White-Collar Sexual Harassment Claims Under Title VII of the Civil Rights Act of 1964, 2001 U. Ill. L. Rev. 1085.

## NOTE ON LIABILITY FOR SINGLE INCIDENTS OF HARASSMENT

Is it possible for a single incident of harassment to be actionable? The *Meritor* Court's formulation requires that harassment be severe *or* pervasive. Doesn't this formulation suggest that a single serious incident could suffice?

In the highly publicized case of Jones v. Clinton, 990 F. Supp. 657 (E.D. Ark. 1998), the district court granted summary judgment, concluding that the single incident of harassment alleged by the plaintiff, although "boorish and offensive" was not sufficiently severe to constitute sexual harassment. Although the case was pursued under the equal protection clause, the court applied standards developed under Title VII. Jones alleged that then-Governor Clinton invited her to his hotel room, exposed himself to her, and requested her to perform oral sex. Jones asserted that she in no way invited this behavior.

Some courts have been willing to find serious single incidents of harassment sufficient to establish liability under Title VII, especially if the complaint involves physical contact. See, e.g., Ferris v. Delta Air Lines, Inc., 277 F.3d 128 (2d Cir. 2001), *cert. denied*, 123 S. Ct. 110 (2002) (single incident of rape satisfies severity prong); Smith v. Sheahan, 189 F.3d 529 (7th Cir. 1999) (male employee physically assaulted female county jail guard and seriously injured her wrist); Lockard v. Pizza Hut, Inc., 162 F.3d 1062 (10th Cir. 1998) (customer grabbed plaintiff's hair and breast); Tomka v. Seiler Corp., 66 F.3d 1295 (2d Cir. 1995) (plaintiff allegedly was raped by three managers following a business dinner).

Courts have been reluctant, however, to find actionable harassment for single incidents of *verbal* harassment, even in cases involving seriously offensive comments.

See, e.g., Gross v. Burggraf Constr. Co., 53 F.3d 1531, 1542 (10th Cir. 1995) (perpetrator stated "sometimes don't you just want to smash a woman in the face"); EEOC v. Champion Intl. Corp., No. 93C20279, 1995 U.S. Dist. LEXIS 11808 (N.D. Ill. 1995) (employee exposed himself to plaintiff and said, "suck my dick, you black bitch"). This reluctance is consistent with courts' unwillingness to find actionable harassment based solely on offensive verbal remarks. Are these cases correctly decided?

In contrast, in Howley v. Town of Stratford, 217 F.3d 141 (2d Cir. 2000), the court found that references to plaintiff as a "fucking whining cunt" who received her job because she performed oral sex were enough to send the case to a jury. Similarly, the Seventh Circuit in Daniels v. Essex Group, Inc., 937 F.2d 1264, 1274 n.4 (7th Cir. 1991), suggested facts that could constitute racial harassment in a single incident even in the absence of physical contact:

> The Ku Klux Klan's effect on blacks calls to mind the example of a case in which only one isolated instance of harassment would be enough to establish the existence of a hostile work environment. If a black worker's colleagues came to work wearing the white hoods and robes of the Klan and proceeded to hold a cross-burning on the premises, all with the knowledge of the employer, this single incident would doubtless give rise to the employer's liability for racial harassment under Title VII.

State courts sometimes have proven more willing than federal courts to find actionable harassment based on a single serious incident of verbal harassment. See, e.g., Nadeau v. Rainbow Rugs, 675 A.2d 973 (Me. 1996) (company president created hostile environment by offering to pay for sex with female employee); Taylor v. Metzger, 706 A.2d 685 (N.J. 1997) (county sheriff referring to black female officer as a "jungle bunny" establishes racial harassment in violation of New Jersey law).

## NOTE ON THE REASONABLE PERSON STANDARD

*Harris* judges harassment by an objective standard. Thus, the fact that the victim feels harassed is not sufficient: a reasonable person in her position must feel harassed. Is it fair to permit employers and their agents to persist in behavior that an employee has identified as offensive just because a less-sensitive "reasonable" person would not object? Should harassment be judged from the perspective of a reasonable woman or victim? *Harris* does not address this issue directly.

Prior to *Harris*, the Ninth Circuit adopted a standard evaluating the severity and pervasiveness of sexual harassment from the perspective of the victim. Ellison v. Brady, 924 F.2d 872 (9th Cir. 1991). In support of this standard, the court stated:

> If we only examined whether a reasonable person would engage in allegedly harassing conduct, we would run the risk of reinforcing the prevailing level of discrimination. . . . We therefore prefer to analyze harassment from the victim's perspective. A complete understanding of the victim's view requires, among other things, an analysis of the different perspectives of men and women. Conduct that many men consider unobjectionable may offend many women.

Id. at 878. The Ninth Circuit's analysis in *Ellison* found support in Professor Kathryn Abrams' article, Gender Discrimination and the Transformation of Workplace Norms, 42 Vand. L. Rev. 1183, 1203 (1989), in which she noted that the characteristically male view depicts sexual harassment as comparatively harmless amusement and stated that:

> While many women hold positive attitudes about uncoerced sex, their greater physical and social vulnerability to sexual coercion can make women wary of sexual encounters. Moreover, American women have been raised in a society where rape and sex-related violence have reached unprecedented levels, and a vast pornography industry creates continuous images of sexual coercion, objectification and violence. Finally, women as a group tend to hold more restrictive views of both the situation and type of relationship in which sexual conduct is appropriate. Because of the inequality and coercion with which it is so frequently associated in the minds of women, the appearance of sexuality in an unexpected context or a setting of ostensible equality can be an anguishing experience.

Id. at 1205. See also Nancy Ehrenreich, Pluralist Myths and Powerless Men: The Ideology of Reasonableness in Sexual Harassment Law, 99 Yale L.J. 1177, 1207-08 (1990) (men tend to view some forms of sexual harassment as "harmless social interactions to which only overly-sensitive women would object"). The debate over the appropriate standard for assessing reasonableness in the context of discriminatory harassment cases has attracted considerable attention in the academic community. See Gillian K. Hadfield, Rational Women: A Test for Sex-Based Harassment, 83 Cal. L. Rev. 1151 (1995) (Title VII should be violated if a "rational woman" would choose a job where the conduct in question does not exist over a job where it did exist, assuming both jobs offered "substantially equivalent benefits"); Jane L. Dolkart, Hostile Environment Harassment: Equality, Objectivity, and the Shaping of Legal Standards, 43 Emory L.J. 151 (1994) (proposing a contextualized reasonable victim standard "placing the reasonable person in the situation of the victim, with the experiences and perceptions of the victim"); Robert Adler & Ellen Peirce, The Legal, Ethical, and Social Implications of the "Reasonable Woman" Standard in Sexual Harassment Cases, 61 Fordham L. Rev. 773 (1993).

After *Harris*, the Ninth Circuit modified its standard for evaluating sexual harassment in an attempt to reconcile *Ellison* with the standard applied in *Harris*: "[w]hether the workplace is objectively hostile must be determined from the perspective of a reasonable person with the same fundamental characteristics." Fuller v. City of Oakland, 47 F.3d 1522, 1527 (9th Cir. 1995). How does this change the standard adopted in *Ellison*? Is this new standard consistent with *Harris*?

In Radtke v. Everett, 501 N.W.2d 155 (Mich. 1993), the Michigan Supreme Court explained its rejection of a "reasonable woman" standard for sexual harassment claims:

> The "chief advantage of [the reasonable person] standard" is that it enables triers of fact "to look to a community standard rather than an individual one, and at the same time to express their judgment of what that standard is in terms of the conduct of a human being." 2 Restatement Torts, 2d, § 283, comment c, p. 13.
> Furthermore, the reasonable person standard examines the totality of the circumstances to ensure a fair result. Hence, [it] is sufficiently flexible to incorporate gender as one factor, without destroying the vital stability provided by uniform standards of conduct.
> The gender-conscious standard . . . places undue emphasis on gender . . . while it inappropriately deemphasizes society's need for uniform standards of conduct. Hence, a gender-conscious standard eliminates community standards and replaces them with standards formulated by a subset of the community. An acceptance of a gender-conscious standard and the logic undergirding it would inexorably lead to the

fragmentation of legal standards to the detriment of society. After all, the diversity that is Michigan — a multitude of ethnic groups, national origins, religions, races, cultures, as well as divergences in wealth and education — would demand as many standards. Yet one standard of conduct has always regulated this diverse population, and to hold otherwise would weave great discord and unnecessary confusion into the law.

. . . [A]lthough well intended, a gender-conscious standard could reintrench the very sexist attitudes it is attempting to counter. . . . Courts utilizing the reasonable woman standard pour into the standard stereotypic assumptions of women which infer women are sensitive, fragile, and in need of a more protective standard. Such paternalism degrades women and is repugnant to the very ideals of equality that the act is intended to protect.

Id. at 166-67. Who has the better argument — the Ninth Circuit or the Michigan Supreme Court? Even if Title VII ultimately is interpreted to apply a reasonable person standard, a reasonable victim standard may be available to plaintiffs under applicable state antidiscrimination statutes. See, e.g., Lehmann v. Toys 'R Us, Inc., 626 A.2d 445 (N.J. 1993) (adopting a reasonable woman standard for assessing sexual harassment claims under the New Jersey Law Against Discrimination).

### d.   Vicarious Liability

## BURLINGTON INDUSTRIES, INC. v. ELLERTH
### 524 U.S. 742 (1998)

Justice KENNEDY delivered the opinion of the Court.

We decide whether, under Title VII of the Civil Rights Act of 1964, an employee who refuses the unwelcome and threatening sexual advances of a supervisor, yet suffers no adverse, tangible job consequences, can recover against the employer without showing the employer is negligent or otherwise at fault for the supervisor's actions.

### I

Summary judgment was granted for the employer, so we must take the facts alleged by the employee to be true. The employer is Burlington Industries, the petitioner. The employee is Kimberly Ellerth, the respondent. From March 1993 until May 1994, Ellerth worked as a salesperson in one of Burlington's divisions in Chicago, Illinois. During her employment, she alleges, she was subjected to constant sexual harassment by her supervisor, one Ted Slowik.

In the hierarchy of Burlington's management structure, Slowik was a mid-level manager. . . . He had authority to make hiring and promotion decisions subject to the approval of his supervisor, who signed the paperwork. According to Slowik's supervisor, his position was "not considered an upper-level management position," and he was "not amongst the decision-making or policy-making hierarchy." Slowik was not Ellerth's immediate supervisor. Ellerth worked in a two-person office in Chicago, and she answered to her office colleague, who in turn answered to Slowik in New York.

Against a background of repeated boorish and offensive remarks and gestures which Slowik allegedly made, Ellerth places particular emphasis on three alleged incidents where Slowik's comments could be construed as threats to deny her tangible job benefits. In the summer of 1993, while on a business trip, Slowik invited Ellerth to the hotel lounge, an invitation Ellerth felt compelled to accept because Slowik was her boss. When Ellerth gave no encouragement to remarks Slowik made about her breasts, he told her to "loosen up" and warned, "[y]ou know, Kim, I could make your life very hard or very easy at Burlington."

In March 1994, when Ellerth was being considered for a promotion, Slowik expressed reservations during the promotion interview because she was not "loose enough." The comment was followed by his reaching over and rubbing her knee. Ellerth did receive the promotion; but when Slowik called to announce it, he told Ellerth, "you're gonna be out there with men who work in factories, and they certainly like women with pretty butts/legs."

In May 1994, Ellerth called Slowik, asking permission to insert a customer's logo into a fabric sample. Slowik responded, "I don't have time for you right now, Kim — unless you want to tell me what you're wearing." Ellerth told Slowik she had to go and ended the call. A day or two later, Ellerth called Slowik to ask permission again. This time he denied her request, but added something along the lines of, "are you wearing shorter skirts yet, Kim, because it would make your job a whole heck of a lot easier."

A short time later, Ellerth's immediate supervisor cautioned her about returning telephone calls to customers in a prompt fashion. In response, Ellerth quit. She faxed a letter giving reasons unrelated to the alleged sexual harassment we have described. About three weeks later, however, she sent a letter explaining she quit because of Slowik's behavior.

During her tenure at Burlington, Ellerth did not inform anyone in authority about Slowik's conduct, despite knowing Burlington had a policy against sexual harassment. In fact, she chose not to inform her immediate supervisor (not Slowik) because "'it would be his duty as my supervisor to report any incidents of sexual harassment.'" On one occasion, she told Slowik a comment he made was inappropriate.

. . . The District Court granted summary judgment to Burlington. The Court found Slowik's behavior, as described by Ellerth, severe and pervasive enough to create a hostile work environment, but found Burlington neither knew nor should have known about the conduct. . . .

The Court of Appeals en banc reversed in a decision which produced eight separate opinions and no consensus for a controlling rationale. . . . The disagreement revealed in the careful opinions of the judges of the Court of Appeals reflects the fact that Congress has left it to the courts to determine controlling agency law principles in a new and difficult area of federal law. We granted certiorari to assist in defining the relevant standards of employer liability.

## II

At the outset, we assume an important proposition yet to be established before a trier of fact. It is a premise assumed as well, in explicit or implicit terms, in the various opinions by the judges of the Court of Appeals. The premise is: a trier of fact could find in Slowik's remarks numerous threats to retaliate against Ellerth if she denied some sexual liberties. The threats, however, were not carried out or fulfilled. Cases based on threats which are carried out are referred to often as *quid pro quo* cases, as distinct from bothersome attentions or sexual remarks that are sufficiently severe or pervasive to create a hostile work environment. The terms *quid pro quo* and hostile work environment are helpful, perhaps, in making a rough demarcation between cases in which threats are carried out and those where they are not or are absent altogether, but beyond this are of limited utility.

Section 703(a) of Title VII forbids "an employer" —

(1) to fail or refuse to hire or to discharge any individual, or otherwise to discriminate against any individual with respect to his compensation, terms, conditions or privileges of employment, because of such individual's . . . sex.

"*Quid pro quo*" and "hostile work environment" do not appear in the statutory text. The terms appeared first in the academic literature, found their way into decisions of the Courts of Appeals, and were mentioned in this Court's decision in *Meritor*.

In *Meritor*, the terms served a specific and limited purpose. There we considered whether the conduct in question constituted discrimination in the terms or conditions of employment in violation of Title VII. We assumed, and with adequate reason, that if an employer demanded sexual favors from an employee in return for a job benefit, discrimination with respect to terms or conditions of employment was explicit. Less obvious was whether an employer's sexually demeaning behavior altered terms or conditions of employment in violation of Title VII. We distinguished between *quid pro quo* claims and hostile environment claims, and said both were cognizable under Title VII, though the latter requires harassment that is severe or pervasive. The principal significance of the distinction is to instruct that Title VII is violated by either explicit or constructive alterations in the terms or conditions of employment and to explain the latter must be severe or pervasive. The distinction was not discussed for its bearing upon an employer's liability for an employee's discrimination. On this question *Meritor* held, with no further specifics, that agency principles controlled.

Nevertheless, as use of the terms grew in the wake of *Meritor*, they acquired their own significance. The standard of employer responsibility turned on which type of harassment occurred. If the plaintiff established a quid pro quo claim, the Courts of Appeals held, the employer was subject to vicarious liability. The rule encouraged Title VII plaintiffs to state their claims as quid pro quo claims, which in turn put expansive pressure on the definition. The equivalence of the quid pro quo label and vicarious liability is illustrated by this case. The question presented on certiorari is whether Ellerth can state a claim of quid pro quo harassment, but the issue of real concern to the parties is whether Burlington has vicarious liability for Slowik's alleged misconduct, rather than liability limited to its own negligence. . . .

We do not suggest the terms *quid pro quo* and hostile work environment are irrelevant to Title VII litigation. To the extent they illustrate the distinction between cases involving a threat which is carried out and offensive conduct in general, the terms are relevant when there is a threshold question whether a plaintiff can prove discrimination in violation of Title VII. When a plaintiff proves that a tangible employment action resulted from a refusal to submit to a supervisor's sexual demands, he or she establishes that the employment decision itself constitutes a change in the terms and conditions of employment that is actionable under Title VII. For any sexual harassment preceding the employment decision to be actionable, however, the conduct must be severe or pervasive. Because Ellerth's claim involves only unfulfilled threats, it should be categorized as a hostile work environment claim which requires a showing of severe or pervasive conduct. For purposes of this case, we accept the District Court's finding that the alleged conduct was severe or pervasive. The case before us involves numerous alleged threats, and we express no opinion as to whether a single unfulfilled threat is sufficient to constitute discrimination in the terms or conditions of employment.

When we assume discrimination can be proved, however, the factors we discuss below, and not the categories *quid pro quo* and hostile work environment, will be controlling on the issue of vicarious liability. That is the question we must resolve.

## III

We must decide, then, whether an employer has vicarious liability when a supervisor creates a hostile work environment by making explicit threats to alter a subordinate's terms or conditions of employment, based on sex, but does not fulfill the threat. We turn to principles of agency law, for the term "employer" is defined under Title VII to include "agents." . . .

As *Meritor* acknowledged, the Restatement (Second) of Agency (1957) (hereinafter Restatement), is a useful beginning point for a discussion of general agency principles. . . .

### A

Section 219(1) of the Restatement sets out a central principle of agency law:

> A master is subject to liability for the torts of his servants committed while acting in the scope of their employment.

An employer may be liable for both negligent and intentional torts committed by an employee within the scope of his or her employment. Sexual harassment under Title VII presupposes intentional conduct. While early decisions absolved employers of liability for the intentional torts of their employees, the law now imposes liability where the employee's "purpose, however misguided, is wholly or in part to further the master's business." W. Keeton, D. Dobbs, R. Keeton & D. Owen, Prosser and Keeton on Law of Torts § 70, p. 505 (5th ed. 1984) (hereinafter Prosser and Keeton on Torts). In applying scope of employment principles to intentional torts, however, it is accepted that "it is less likely that a willful tort will properly be held to be in the course of employment and that the liability of the master for such torts will naturally be more limited." F. Mechem, Outlines of the Law of Agency § 394, p. 266 (P. Mechem 4th ed., 1952). The Restatement defines conduct, including an intentional tort, to be within the scope of employment when "actuated, at least in part, by a purpose to serve the [employer]," even if it is forbidden by the employer. Restatement §§ 228(1)(c), 230.

As Courts of Appeals have recognized, a supervisor acting out of gender-based animus or a desire to fulfill sexual urges may not be actuated by a purpose to serve the employer. The harassing supervisor often acts for personal motives, motives unrelated and even antithetical to the objectives of the employer. There are instances, of course, where a supervisor engages in unlawful discrimination with the purpose, mistaken or otherwise, to serve the employer.

The general rule is that sexual harassment by a supervisor is not conduct within the scope of employment.

### B

Scope of employment does not define the only basis for employer liability under agency principles. In limited circumstances, agency principles impose liability on employers even where employees commit torts outside the scope of employment. The principles are set forth in the much-cited § 219(2) of the Restatement:

> (2) A master is not subject to liability for the torts of his servants acting outside the scope of their employment, unless:
>
> (a)  the master intended the conduct or the consequences, or
>
> (b)  the master was negligent or reckless, or
>
> (c)  the conduct violated a non-delegable duty of the master, or
>
> (d)  the servant purported to act or to speak on behalf of the principal and there was reliance upon apparent authority, or he was aided in accomplishing the tort by the existence of the agency relation.

Subsection (a) addresses direct liability, where the employer acts with tortious intent, and indirect liability, where the agent's high rank in the company makes him or her the employer's alter ego. None of the parties contend Slowik's rank imputes liability under this principle. There is no contention, furthermore, that a non-delegable duty is involved. See § 219(2)(c). So, for our purposes here, subsections (a) and (c) can be put aside.

Subsections (b) and (d) are possible grounds for imposing employer liability on account of a supervisor's acts and must be considered. Under subsection (b), an employer is liable when the tort is attributable to the employer's own negligence. Thus, although a supervisor's sexual harassment is outside the scope of employment because the conduct was for personal motives, an employer can be liable, nonetheless, where its own negligence is a cause of the harassment. An employer is negligent with respect to sexual harassment if it knew or should have known about the conduct and failed to stop it. Negligence sets a minimum standard for employer liability under Title VII; but Ellerth seeks to invoke the more stringent standard of vicarious liability.

Subsection 219(2)(d) concerns vicarious liability for intentional torts committed by an employee when the employee uses apparent authority (the apparent authority standard), or when the employee "was aided in accomplishing the tort by the existence of the agency relation" (the aided in the agency relation standard). As other federal decisions have done in discussing vicarious liability for supervisor harassment, we begin with § 219(2)(d).

### C

As a general rule, apparent authority is relevant where the agent purports to exercise a power which he or she does not have, as distinct from where the agent threatens to misuse actual power. In the usual case, a supervisor's harassment involves misuse of actual power, not the false impression of its existence. Apparent authority analysis therefore is inappropriate in this context. If, in the unusual case, it is alleged there is a false impression that the actor was a supervisor, when he in fact was not, the victim's mistaken conclusion must be a reasonable one. When a party seeks to impose vicarious liability based on an agent's misuse of delegated authority, the Restatement's aided in the agency relation rule, rather than the apparent authority rule, appears to be the appropriate form of analysis.

### D

We turn to the aided in the agency relation standard. In a sense, most workplace tortfeasors are aided in accomplishing their tortious objective by the existence of the agency relation: Proximity and regular contact may afford a captive pool of potential victims. Were this to satisfy the aided in the agency relation standard, an employer would be subject to vicarious liability not only for all supervisor harassment, but also for all co-worker harassment, a result enforced by neither the EEOC nor any court of appeals to have considered the issue. The aided in the agency relation standard, therefore, requires the existence of something more than the employment relation itself.

At the outset, we can identify a class of cases where, beyond question, more than the mere existence of the employment relation aids in commission of the harassment: when a supervisor takes a tangible employment action against the subordinate. Every Federal Court of Appeals to have considered the question has found vicarious liability when a discriminatory act results in a tangible employment action. In *Meritor*, we acknowledged this consensus ("The courts have consistently held employers liable for the discriminatory discharges of employees by supervisory personnel, whether or not the employer knew, or should have known, or approved of the supervisor's actions"). Although few courts have elaborated how agency principles support this rule, we think it reflects a correct application of the aided in the agency relation standard.

In the context of this case, a tangible employment action would have taken the form of a denial of a raise or a promotion. The concept of a tangible employment action appears in numerous cases in the Courts of Appeals discussing claims involving race, age, and national origin discrimination, as well as sex discrimination. Without endorsing the specific results of those decisions, we think it prudent to import the concept of a tangible employment action for resolution of the vicarious liability issue we consider here. A tangible employment action constitutes a significant change in employment status, such as hiring, firing, failing to promote, reassignment with significantly different responsibilities, or a decision causing a significant change in benefits. Compare Crady v. Liberty Nat. Bank & Trust Co. of Ind., 993 F.2d 132, 136 (7th Cir. 1993) ("A materially adverse change might be indicated by a termination of employment, a demotion evidenced by a decrease in wage or salary, a less distinguished title, a material loss of benefits, significantly diminished material responsibilities, or other indices that might be unique to a particular situation"), with Flaherty v. Gas Research Institute, 31 F.3d 451, 456 (7th Cir. 1994) (a "bruised ego" is not enough); Kocsis v. Multi-Care Management, Inc., 97 F.3d 876, 887 (6th Cir. 1996) (demotion without change in pay, benefits, duties, or prestige insufficient); and Harlston v. McDonnell Douglas Corp., 37 F.3d 379, 382 (8th Cir. 1994) (reassignment to more inconvenient job insufficient).

When a supervisor makes a tangible employment decision, there is assurance the injury could not have been inflicted absent the agency relation. A tangible employment action in most cases inflicts direct economic harm. As a general proposition, only a supervisor, or other person acting with the authority of the company, can cause this sort of injury. A co-worker can break a co-worker's arm as easily as a supervisor, and anyone who has regular contact with an employee can inflict psychological injuries by his or her offensive conduct. But one co-worker (absent some elaborate scheme) cannot dock another's pay, nor can one co-worker demote another. Tangible employment actions fall within the special province of the supervisor. The supervisor has been empowered by the company as a distinct class of agent to make economic decisions affecting other employees under his or her control.

Tangible employment actions are the means by which the supervisor brings the official power of the enterprise to bear on subordinates. A tangible employment decision requires an official act of the enterprise, a company act. The decision in most cases is documented in official company records, and may be subject to review by higher level supervisors. The supervisor often must obtain the imprimatur of the enterprise and use its internal processes.

For these reasons, a tangible employment action taken by the supervisor becomes for Title VII purposes the act of the employer. Whatever the exact contours of the aided in the agency relation standard, its requirements will always be met when a supervisor takes a tangible employment action against a subordinate. In that instance, it would be implausible to interpret agency principles to allow an employer to escape liability, as *Meritor* itself appeared to acknowledge.

Whether the agency relation aids in commission of supervisor harassment which does not culminate in a tangible employment action is less obvious. Application of the standard is made difficult by its malleable terminology, which can be read to either expand or limit liability in the context of supervisor harassment. On the one hand, a supervisor's power and authority invests his or her harassing conduct with a particular threatening character, and in this sense, a supervisor always is aided by the agency relation. See *Meritor.* (Marshall, J., concurring in judgment) ("It is precisely because the supervisor is understood to be clothed with the employer's authority that he is able to impose unwelcome sexual conduct on subordinates"). On the other hand, there are acts of harassment a supervisor might commit which might be the same acts a co-employee would commit, and there may be some circumstances where the supervisor's status makes little difference.

It is this tension which, we think, has caused so much confusion among the Courts of Appeals which have sought to apply the aided in the agency relation standard to Title VII cases. The aided in the agency relation standard, however, is a developing feature of agency law, and we hesitate to render a definitive explanation of our understanding of the standard in an area where other important considerations must affect our judgment. In particular, we are bound by our holding in *Meritor* that agency principles constrain the imposition of vicarious liability in cases of supervisory harassment. See *Meritor* ("Congress' decision to define 'employer' to include any 'agent' of an employer, 42 U.S.C. § 2000e(b), surely evinces an intent to place some limits on the acts of employees for which employers under Title VII are to be held responsible"). Congress has not altered *Meritor's* rule even though it has made significant amendments to Title VII in the interim. Although *Meritor* suggested the limitation on employer liability stemmed from agency principles, the Court acknowledged other considerations might be relevant as well. For example, Title VII is designed to encourage the creation of antiharassment policies and effective grievance mechanisms. Were employer liability to depend in part on an employer's effort to create such procedures, it would effect Congress' intention to promote conciliation rather than litigation in the Title VII context and the EEOC's policy of encouraging the development of grievance procedures. See 29 CFR § 1604.11(f) (1997); EEOC Policy Guidance on Sexual Harassment, 8 BNA FEP Manual 405:6699 (Mar. 19, 1990). To the extent limiting employer liability could encourage employees to report harassing conduct before it becomes severe or pervasive, it would also serve Title VII's deterrent purpose. As we have observed, Title VII borrows from tort law the avoidable consequences doctrine, and the considerations which animate that doctrine would also support the limitation of employer liability in certain circumstances.

In order to accommodate the agency principles of vicarious liability for harm caused by misuse of supervisory authority, as well as Title VII's equally basic policies of encouraging forethought by employers and saving action by objecting employees, we adopt the following holding in this case and in Faragher v. Boca Raton, also decided today. An employer is subject to vicarious liability to a victimized employee for an actionable hostile environment created by a supervisor with immediate (or successively higher) authority over the employee. When no tangible employment action is taken, a defending employer may raise an affirmative defense to liability or damages, subject to proof by a preponderance of the evidence. The defense comprises two necessary elements: (a) that the employer exercised reasonable care to prevent and correct promptly any sexually harassing behavior, and (b) that the plaintiff employee unreasonably failed to take advantage of any preventive or corrective opportunities provided by the employer or to avoid harm otherwise. While proof that an employer had promulgated an anti-harassment policy with complaint procedure is not necessary in every instance as a matter of law, the need for a stated policy suitable to the employment circumstances may appropriately be addressed in any case when litigating the first element of the defense. And while proof that an employee failed to fulfill the corresponding obligation of reasonable care to avoid harm is not limited to showing any unreasonable failure to use any complaint procedure provided by the employer, a demonstration of such failure will normally suffice to satisfy the employer's burden under the second element of the defense. No affirmative defense is available, however, when the supervisor's harassment culminates in a tangible employment action, such as discharge, demotion, or undesirable reassignment.

## IV

Relying on existing case law which held out the promise of vicarious liability for all *quid pro quo* claims, Ellerth focused all her attention in the Court of Appeals on proving her claim fit within that category. Given our explanation that the labels *quid pro quo* and hostile work environment are not controlling for purposes of establishing employer liability, Ellerth should have an adequate opportunity to prove she has a claim for which Burlington is liable.

Although Ellerth has not alleged she suffered a tangible employment action at the hands of Slowik, which would deprive Burlington of the availability of the affirmative defense, this is not dispositive. In light of our decision, Burlington is still subject to vicarious liability for Slowik's activity, but Burlington should have an opportunity to assert and prove the affirmative defense to liability. . . .

## NOTES

1.  In a part of *Meritor* not reproduced previously, the Court addressed, but did not fully resolve one of the major issues in sexual harassment cases — under what circumstances is the *employer* liable for harassment in the workplace? The *Meritor* Court did not impose liability automatically:

> . . . Congress' decision to define "employer" to include any "agent" of an employer, 42 U.S.C. § 2000e(b), surely evinces an intent to place some limits on the acts of employees for which employers under Title VII are to be held responsible. For this reason, we hold that the Court of Appeals erred in concluding that employers are always automatically liable for sexual harassment by their supervisors. For the same reason, absence of notice to an employer does not necessarily insulate that employer from liability.
>    . . . [W]e reject petitioner's view that the mere existence of a grievance procedure and a policy against discrimination, coupled with respondent's failure to invoke that procedure, must insulate petitioner from liability. While those facts are plainly relevant, the situation before us demonstrates why they are not necessarily dispositive. Petitioner's

general nondiscrimination policy did not address sexual harassment in particular, and thus did not alert employees to their employer's interest in correcting that form of discrimination. Moreover, the bank's grievance procedure apparently required an employee to complain first to her supervisor, in this case Taylor. Since Taylor was the alleged perpetrator, it is not altogether surprising that respondent failed to invoke the procedure and report her grievance to him. Petitioner's contention that respondent's failure should insulate it from liability might be substantially stronger if its procedures were better calculated to encourage victims of harassment to come forward.

477 U.S. at 72-73. Resolving this issue is particularly important because, although Title VII defines "employer" to include "any agent" of an employer, courts have not always been willing to hold individual employees personally liable for their discriminatory conduct. See Chapter 10. If employers are not liable for their supervisor's conduct, it is possible that neither the individual harasser nor the employer will be liable in some circumstances.

2. In Faragher v. City of Boca Raton, 524 U.S. 775 (1998), a companion case to *Ellerth*, the Court also considered the liability of an employer for the harassing actions of its supervisor. *Faragher* adopted the same holding as in *Ellerth*. See id. at 802-08. Did the Court in *Ellerth* and *Faragher* create a rule of liability that is fair to plaintiffs? Is this rule fair to defendants?

3. When *Meritor* was decided, the only remedy for hostile environment harassment was injunctive relief. The Court, in *Ellerth* and in footnote 4 of *Faragher*, emphasized the importance of following *Meritor*'s holding relieving employers of automatic liability for supervisor harassment on the ground that Congress enacted the 1991 Amendments, with their imposition of compensatory and emotional distress damages, with *Meritor*'s limitation on liability in mind.

4. Prior to *Ellerth*, courts held that, if the harasser is himself in a high enough position in the employer's hierarchy, the actions and knowledge of the harasser are imputed to the employer, what *Ellerth* referred to as "alter ego" liability. Kotcher v. Rosa & Sullivan Appliance Ctr., Inc., 957 F.2d 59 (2d Cir. 1992). In *Faragher*, the Court addressed imputed liability:

> [It was not] exceptional that standards for binding the employer were not in issue in *Harris*. In that case of discrimination by hostile environment, the individual charged with creating the abusive atmosphere was the president of the corporate employer, who was indisputably within that class of an employer organization's officials who may be treated as the organization's proxy.

524 U.S. at 790. *Ellerth* also notes the possibility of "direct liability, where the employer acts with tortious intent, and indirect liability, where the agent's high rank in the company makes him or her the employer's alter ego." 524 U.S. at 758. Is the defense created in *Ellerth* and *Faragher* available in cases in which the harasser's actions are imputed to the employer under the "alter ego" or "proxy" approach?

5. Is any individual with supervisory status necessarily a supervisor for purposes of imposing vicarious liability under *Ellerth* and *Faragher*? The analysis of *Ellerth* and *Faragher* suggests the answer is no. See Swinton v. Potomac Corp., 270 F.3d 794 (9th Cir. 2001), *cert. denied*, 122 S. Ct. 1609 (2002) (actions of supervisor who had no supervisory authority over the plaintiff could not subject employer to vicarious liability).

6. After *Ellerth*, can sexual harassment by a supervisor be "within the scope of employment" of the supervisor? Suppose a supervisor, in order to boost sales, requires female employees to wear revealing attire that generates severe and pervasive

responses by customers? See EEOC v. Sage Realty Co., 507 F. Supp. 599 (S.D.N.Y. 1981). If employer liability can be based on harassment being "within the scope of employment" of a supervisor, is the defense created in *Ellerth* available or is it available only when "agency" is based on the "aided in the agency relation" approach and no "tangible employment actions" are involved?

7. A key issue in the wake of *Ellerth* and *Faragher* is what constitutes a tangible employment action. "Determining whether the complaining employee has suffered a tangible employment action is the indispensable first step in every supervisor sexual harassment/vicarious liability case under Title VII." Casiano v. AT&T Corp., 213 F.3d 278, 284 (5th Cir. 2000) (see also "Supervisor Sexual Harassment Roadmap" at app., 213 F.3d at 288). Deciding whether a tangible employment action has occurred is often outcome determinative since the employer may not assert the affirmative defense if a supervisor's discrimination results in a tangible employment action. But courts have yet to agree on what constitutes a tangible employment action. Is a lateral transfer a tangible employment action if an employee's pay is not affected? Is being assigned different tasks? Being denied perks such as travel to conferences?

One commentator, Rebecca Hanner White, De Minimis Discrimination, 47 Emory L.J. 1121, 1158 (1998), asserts that the best way to determine whether an action is tangible within the meaning of *Ellerth* and *Faragher* is to look to the agency theory relied on in those cases and thus to examine whether the action is one the supervisor's authority *as supervisor* enabled him to take. If so, it should be deemed a tangible employment action:

> Only a supervisor can transfer, reassign, or negatively evaluate a worker, but supervisors and co-workers alike may use racial epithets, may hurt an employee's feelings, or smack an employee on the rear. When the supervisor "brings the official power of the enterprise to bear on subordinates" — a "decision in most cases . . . documented in official company records and . . . subject to review by higher level supervisors" — such action, if discriminatorily motivated, will be attributed to the employer. . . . Accordingly, it is not the economic or materially adverse nature of the discrimination that makes [the employer vicariously liable] but the fact that it involves an action only supervisors can inflict on their subordinates.

In Jin v. Metropolitan Life Insurance Co., 310 F.3d 84 (2d Cir. 2002), the court employed a similar analysis to find that a supervisor's insistence that an employee engage in sex acts or be fired was a tangible employment action when the employee submitted to the demands. Even if the employee suffered no economic harm, it was the supervisor's position of power to terminate or retain plaintiff and to require her to report to his private office where the abuse occurred that enabled him to take the actions.

Professor White's approach to "tangible employment actions" is broader than that followed by numerous lower courts. Is it too broad? Professor Michael Harper suggests a somewhat different analysis. He asserts that a tangible employment action should be viewed as any supervisory action that is recorded or reported, as it would be "readily available for review." Michael C. Harper, Employer Liability for Harassment Under Title VII: A Functional Rationale for *Faragher* and *Ellerth*, 36 San Diego L. Rev. 41 (1999). For an article analyzing the lower courts' approaches to "tangible employment actions" and criticizing these approaches, see Susan Grover, After *Ellerth*: The Tangible Employment Action in Sexual Harassment Analysis, 35 U. Mich. J.L. Reform 809 (2002).

8. Is constructive discharge a tangible employment action? The lower courts disagree on this point. See Jackson v. Arkansas Dept. of Educ., 272 F.3d 1020 (8th Cir.

2001), *cert. denied*, 122 S. Ct. 2366 (2002) (yes); Durham Life Ins. Co. v. Evans, 166 F.3d 139 (3d Cir. 1999) (yes); Caridad v. Metro-N. Commuter R.R., 191 F.3d 283 (2d Cir. 1999) (no). See Sara Kagay, Note, Applying the *Ellerth* Defense to Constructive Discharge: An Affirmative Answer, 85 Iowa L. Rev. 1035 (2000).

9.  If a plaintiff alleges that discriminatory harassment culminated in a tangible employment action, but also asserts a hostile work environment claim, does the existence of the tangible employment action preclude assertion of the affirmative defense for the hostile work environment claim? See Ogden v. Wax Works, Inc., 214 F.3d 999 (8th Cir. 2000) (raising, but not resolving, this question).

10.  In National Railroad Passenger Corp. v. Morgan (reproduced at page 842), the Court distinguished between claims involving a "discrete discriminatory or retaliatory act" and those alleging a hostile work environment in determining whether actions occurring outside the 180/300 day time period are actionable. See Chapter 9. The Court held that each discrete discriminatory act starts the clock running and must be the subject of a timely filed charge to be actionable. However, because hostile work environment claims often evolve over time, all acts contributing to the environment may be considered, so long as one act contributing to the hostile environment occurred within the time period. Are the terms "discrete act" and "tangible employment action" synonymous?

11.  When no tangible employment action has occurred, *Ellerth* permits the employer to assert an affirmative defense. What facts must a defendant prove to establish this defense?

## MATVIA v. BALD HEAD ISLAND MANAGEMENT, INC.
### 259 F.3d 261 (4th Cir. 2001)

TRAXLER, Circuit Judge:

Christina Matvia appeals from the grant of summary judgment in favor of Bald Head Island Management ("BHIM") on her claims of sexual harassment. . . . We affirm.

I

On June 16, 1997, BHIM hired Matvia as a housekeeper. One month later, BHIM transferred Matvia to the position of Maintenance Worker I in the Contractor Service Village ("CSV"). Her supervisor at the CSV was Richard Terbush. Beginning in September 1997, Matvia became the recipient of unwanted attentions from Terbush:

- Terbush approached Matvia, said he needed a hug, and proceeded to hug her;
- Terbush told Matvia, who had just dyed her hair brown, that he would have to fantasize about a brunette rather than a blond;
- Terbush informed Matvia that he no longer had sexual relations with his wife;
- Terbush placed a pornographic picture on Matvia's desk;
- Terbush told Matvia she looked good enough to eat;
- Terbush frequently placed his arm around Matvia when they were riding in a golf cart and massaged her shoulder;
- Terbush repeatedly told Matvia that he loved her and had a crush on her;
- Terbush, on December 10, 1997, told Matvia that he had a dream that she sued him for sexual harassment and warned her that if she did bring suit she would be in big trouble; and

- Terbush, five days after recounting his dream, pulled Matvia close to him in the golf cart, tried to kiss her, and struggled with Matvia until she was able to escape.

Matvia became physically ill after the attempted kiss and went home early. The next day Terbush told BHIM officials what had happened in the cart and was suspended pending an investigation. Matvia participated in the investigation and also pressed criminal charges against Terbush. On December 31, BHIM fired Terbush for sexually harassing Matvia.

While the harassment was ongoing, BHIM had in place a policy against sexual harassment. The policy is printed in the employee handbook which Matvia signed for at her orientation. The policy defines sexual harassment as "unwelcome or unwanted conduct of a sexual nature, whether verbal or physical." Examples of sexual harassment are given, and employees are encouraged to report improper behavior to their supervisor, the personnel department, or the chief operating officer.

According to Matvia, after Terbush's termination co-workers and managers at BHIM altered their behavior towards her. Co-workers would move away if she sat near them on BHIM's buses or ferries; the bus drivers, who were often at the CSV, would stop talking among themselves when Matvia entered the room; the bus drivers traduced [sic. Ed.: While the word is used in obsolete constuction to mean "calumniously blame," its most common meaning is "to convey from one place to another." OED (2d ed. 1989)] Matvia while on their routes; and members of management stopped saying "hello" to Matvia while waiting for the ferry. . . .

## II . . .

To prevail on a Title VII hostile work environment claim, Matvia must establish four elements: (1) unwelcome conduct, (2) based on Matvia's gender, (3) sufficiently pervasive or severe to alter the conditions of employment and to create a hostile work environment, and (4) some basis for imputing liability to BHIM. The district court assumed the first three elements had been established, but granted summary judgment on the fourth element in light of the affirmative defense outlined in Faragher v. City of Boca Raton, and Burlington Industries, Inc. v. Ellerth.

The affirmative defense of *Faragher* and *Ellerth* allows an employer to avoid strict liability for a supervisor's sexual harassment of an employee if no tangible employment action was taken against the employee. Examples of tangible employment action include "discharge, demotion, or undesirable reassignment." If entitled to raise the affirmative defense, the employer must establish: "(a) that the employer exercised reasonable care to prevent and correct promptly any sexually harassing behavior, and (b) that the plaintiff employee unreasonably failed to take advantage of any preventative or corrective opportunities provided by the employer or to avoid harm otherwise."

### A. TANGIBLE EMPLOYMENT ACTION

Matvia contends that the affirmative defense is not available because there was tangible employment action. However, Matvia was not discharged, demoted, or reassigned — in fact, during her tenure at BHIM she received a raise, promotion, and good evaluations. She claims that these positive events happened because she silently suffered Terbush's advances and therefore there was tangible employment action. See Brown v. Perry, 184 F.3d 388, 395 (4th Cir. 1999) (implying that receipt of a promotion can be a tangible employment action under *Faragher* and *Ellerth*).

However, in the present case there is no evidence that Matvia received benefits in exchange for acquiescing in Terbush's advances. Regarding Matvia's promotion from Maintenance Worker I to Maintenance Worker II and the accompanying increase in pay, Matvia testified that she and a co-worker received this status change because "we took on a lot more responsibilities" when the CSV began fuel sales. Terbush, according to Matvia's testimony, "thought that me and the other worker should receive more because we were doing more work." Indeed, in requesting that his subordinates be reclassified to the category of Maintenance Worker II, Terbush observed that "these employees are woefully underpaid" in light of their additional responsibilities. Clearly, the promotion and raise were not unique to Matvia — the other worker Terbush supervised received the same benefit. Moreover, Matvia never alleged that Terbush offered her the promotion and pay increase in exchange for sexual favors. Matvia's own testimony indicates that these benefits were conferred because she and her colleague acquired additional responsibilities. Hence, the raise and promotion do not amount to tangible employment action.

Similarly, the evaluations indicating that Matvia was performing at a "satisfactory" level and that her employment should be continued do not amount to tangible employment actions. There are no allegations that Terbush promised Matvia a satisfactory evaluation in exchange for sexual favors, or that Matvia was performing at an unsatisfactory level but received a satisfactory rating in exchange for her tolerance of Terbush's unwelcome conduct. The evaluations were routine matters and cannot operate to prevent BHIM from raising the affirmative defense.

In sum, there was no tangible employment action in this case. While Matvia is entitled to all reasonable inferences from the evidence, her theory of "silent sufferance" would transform any ordinary employment action into tangible employment action. For example, under her theory, so long as sexual harassment is present, an upgrade in equipment used by the employee, a grant of sick leave, or any other mundane, non-adverse action would constitute tangible employment action and thus deprive the employer of the affirmative defense. *Faragher* and *Ellerth* simply do not lend themselves to a result that would make a grant of summary judgment in favor of the employer an impossibility. Of course, this does not mean that the affirmative defense is available when supervisors guilty of sexual harassment do bestow benefits in exchange for an employee's silence. However, in the present case there is no evidence that Matvia received her pay increase, promotion, or satisfactory evaluations in exchange for refraining from reporting the unwelcome conduct. Accordingly, BHIM is entitled to raise the affirmative defense outlined in *Faragher* and *Ellerth*.

### B.   PREVENTION AND CORRECTION OF IMPROPER BEHAVIOR

Matvia argues that BHIM did not take reasonable care to prevent and correct sexually harassing behavior because BHIM's antiharassment policy was not an effective preventative program. Our cases have held that dissemination of "an effective antiharassment policy provides compelling proof" that an employer has exercised reasonable care to prevent and correct sexual harassment. Evidence showing that the employer implemented the policy in bad faith or was deficient in enforcing the policy will rebut this proof.

Matvia does not allege that the policy was implemented in bad faith, but rather argues that it was deficient because BHIM employees did not understand it. Tellingly, Matvia points to no language in the policy rendering it ambiguous or difficult to follow. Nor does she suggest how the policy against sexual harassment could have been made any clearer. Her only evidence of the alleged deficiency is deposition testimony in which BHIM employees had trouble recalling the details of their orientation briefings. . . . .

The failure to recollect the details of an orientation session does not mean that the employee does not understand the sexual harassment policy. . . . The record also contains numerous affidavits from BHIM employees indicating an awareness of the policy against sexual harassment and the company officials to whom harassment could be reported. In the face of a policy that clearly defines sexual harassment and to whom harassment should be reported, Matvia cannot survive summary judgment by claiming that employees failed to recall their orientation briefings. Hence, Matvia's contention that BHIM lacked an effective preventative program must fail.

As for correction of sexually harassing behavior, BHIM suspended Terbush without pay four days after he attempted to kiss Matvia. Twelve days later, after completing an investigation, BHIM terminated Terbush. As this sequence of events indicates, shortly after it learned of Terbush's improper conduct, BHIM took prompt corrective action as required by Faragher and Ellerth.

Questioning the adequacy of BHIM's corrective action, Matvia focuses her arguments not on BHIM's suspension and termination of Terbush, but on the ostracism she suffered at the hands of the bus drivers and others. The first prong of the affirmative defense, however, focuses on the employer's exercise of "reasonable care to prevent and correct promptly any sexually harassing behavior." *Faragher; Ellerth.* Matvia alleges no sexually harassing behavior occurring after the date of the attempted kiss. Though co-workers were often uncivil towards Matvia, they did not sexually harass her. Accordingly, BHIM's response to the ostracism and vilification of Matvia, which was bereft of a sexual component, is irrelevant to the first prong of the affirmative defense.

### C. FAILURE TO TAKE ADVANTAGE OF PREVENTATIVE OR CORRECTIVE OPPORTUNITIES

Matvia argues that her reluctance to report Terbush's conduct was not unreasonable. According to circuit precedent, "evidence that the plaintiff failed to utilize the company's complaint procedure will normally suffice to satisfy [the company's] burden under the second element of the defense." Barrett v. Applied Radiant Energy Corp., 240 F.3d 262, 267 (4th Cir. 2001). If Title VII's prohibitions against sexual harassment are to be effective, employees must report improper behavior to company officials. See *Faragher,* (observing "that a victim [of sexual harassment] has a duty to use such means as are reasonable under the circumstances to avoid or minimize the damages that result from violations of the statute"); Parkins v. Civil Constructors, Inc., 163 F.3d 1027, 1038 (7th Cir. 1998) (observing that "the law against sexual harassment is not self-enforcing and an employer cannot be expected to correct harassment unless the employee makes a concerted effort to inform the employer that a problem exists"). Otherwise, the harasser's conduct would continue, perhaps leading other employees to infer that such behavior is acceptable in the workplace.

Matvia contends that she needed time to collect evidence against Terbush so company officials would believe her. But *Faragher* and *Ellerth* command that a victim of sexual harassment report the misconduct, not investigate, gather evidence, and then approach company officials. Sexual harassment cases often involve the word of the harasser versus the word of the harassed employee, but this is no different from any other case where the outcome depends on the credibility of the parties' testimony.

Though we understand why Matvia would want tangible evidence to buttress her version of events, this cannot excuse her failure to report Terbush's unwelcome conduct.

Matvia also argues that it was proper to refrain from reporting Terbush so she could determine whether he was a "predator" or merely an "interested man" who could be politely rebuffed. According to Matvia, she discovered that Terbush was a predator just days before the attempted kiss in the golf cart and consequently she should not be penalized for failing to take preventative or corrective action. We disagree. As an initial matter, our case law makes no distinction between "predators" and "interested men." So long as the conduct is unwelcome, based on the employee's gender, and sufficiently pervasive or severe to alter the conditions of employment, the label given to the harasser is immaterial. Moreover, even if we were to use Matvia's proffered nomenclature, the gravity and numerosity of the incidents make clear that Terbush was not merely an interested man who could be politely rebuffed. Matvia informed Terbush that her husband would not appreciate his conduct and she often turned her back to him and left the room when Terbush's actions or comments made her feel uncomfortable. Nonetheless, Terbush persisted in harassing her. In light of this long-term and persistent harassment, Matvia cannot be excused from failing to report Terbush to BHIM officials.

Next, Matvia points to the actions of the bus drivers and argues that she reasonably feared retaliation from co-employees. Without question, the reporting of sexual harassment can place "the harassed employee in an awkward and uncomfortable situation." Barrett. Not only is it embarrassing to discuss such matters with company officials, but after the harassed employee overcomes this hurdle she may have to deal with a negative reaction from coworkers. While such events might cause an employee stress, the unpleasantness cannot override the duty to report sexual harassment. The reporting requirement is so essential to the law of sexual harassment that we "have refused to recognize a nebulous fear of retaliation as a basis for remaining silent." Barrett. The bringing of a retaliation claim rather than failing to report sexual harassment, is the proper method for dealing with retaliatory acts. Consequently, Matvia's fear that her co-workers would react negatively is insufficient to deprive BHIM of the affirmative defense.

Finally, Matvia argues that the attempted kiss alone should be considered in assessing the hostility of her work environment, and because she contacted BHIM soon after the incident, BHIM cannot as a matter of law establish that Matvia unreasonably failed to invoke the company's anti-harassment policy. From the filing of her complaint, Matvia has characterized the inappropriate behavior as beginning "after Terbush became Plaintiff's supervisor." In an effort to avoid the affirmative defense set forth in Faragher and Ellerth, Matvia now asks this court to ignore the numerous incidents of sexual harassment enumerated in her complaint and discussed in her deposition testimony, and to instead focus only on the final indignity she suffered. This we cannot do. The evidence reveals a pattern of behavior beginning in September 1997 and ending December 15. The only way we can assess whether Matvia "failed to take advantage of any preventative or corrective opportunities provided by the employer," is to examine Matvia's actions from the time the unwelcome conduct began. Matvia's pick-and-choose method would make a mockery of this inquiry and would violate the basic tenets of fairness.

In short, though Terbush's advances began in September 1997 and ended on December 15, BHIM did not learn of the harassment until December 16. BHIM had an effective anti-harassment policy in place that Matvia failed to utilize. Hence, BHIM has established the second prong of the affirmative defense. . . .

*NOTES*

1. Matvia contended that because she silently suffered Terbush's advances, she was rewarded with a raise, a promotion, and good evaluations and that a tangible employment action thus was present. The Fourth Circuit appears to agree that job benefits bestowed in exchange for an employee's silence about ongoing harassment would preclude the affirmative defense but finds Matvia did not prove the actions occurred because of her forbearance. Is her theory correct? Is a raise or promotion received because an employee does not report a supervisor's sexual advance a tangible employment action within the meaning of *Ellerth* and *Faragher*? Compare Jin v. Metropolitan Life Ins., 310 F.3d 84 (2d Cir. 2002).

2. In *Matvia*, the employer had promulgated and disseminated an antiharassment policy that defined sexual harassment and identified multiple reporting channels. The court finds this to be "compelling proof" that the employer has exercised reasonable care to prevent and correct harassment, leaving it to the employee to rebut with evidence the policy was implemented in bad faith or not effectively enforced. Is this approach consistent with placing on the defendant the burden of proving the affirmative defense? Should a policy that looks good on paper be sufficient prima facie proof that the employer has met this prong of the defense?

3. That harassment has occurred, despite the employer's efforts, does not mean the employer did not exercise reasonable care to prevent harassment. As noted by the Seventh Circuit, "the law does not require success — it only requires that an employer act reasonably to prevent harassment." In Shaw v. Autozone, Inc., 180 F.3d 806 (7th Cir. 1999), the employer was found to have acted reasonably because it distributed to every employee a policy clearly stating that the employer would not tolerate sexual harassment, provided multiple mechanisms for reporting and resolving complaints, and regularly conducted training sessions. What if the employer conducts training sessions, but does not ensure that they are attended and understood by all employees, particularly supervisory employees?

4. Although the Supreme Court stated that an employer need not necessarily have promulgated an antiharassment policy to satisfy its duty of reasonable care, it is the unusual case in which an employer will prevail absent such a policy. Although courts have been reluctant to lay down a rigid list of requirements that an antiharassment policy must meet to be considered effective, it is helpful to the employer if the policy not only prohibits sexual harassment but also gives some explanation or description of what is meant by sexual harassment. See Molnar v. Booth, 229 F.3d 593 (7th Cir. 2000). Particularly important is the presence of alternative avenues for reporting harassment; often it is the immediate supervisor who is engaging in the harassment, and thus, a requirement that an employee report harassment to her supervisor will likely render the policy ineffective. See Madray v. Publix Supermarkets, Inc., 208 F.3d 1290 (11th Cir. 2000). Moreover, clear identification of to whom within the organization complaints are to be made is important. See Gentry v. Export Packing Co., 238 F.3d 842 (7th Cir. 2001). The policy's assurance against retaliation has been important to some courts. See, e.g., Barrett v. ARECO, 240 F.3d 262 (4th Cir. 2000). For a description of features an antiharassment policy should contain, see Paul Buchanan & Courtney W. Wisall, The Evolving Understanding of Workplace Harassment and Employer Liability: Implications of Recent Supreme Court Decisions Under Title VII, 34 Wake Forest L. Rev. 55 (1999).

5. Professor Susan Sturm, in Second Generation Employment Discrimination: A Structural Approach, 101 Colum. L. Rev. 458 (2001), approves the law's encour-

agement of employer initiatives aimed at achieving workplace equality. She examines structures put into place at several large employers that treat discrimination and harassment as but a subset of workplace problems that need to be resolved, a problem-solving approach that may be more effective than litigation at rooting out the subconscious bias that characterizes much of today's discrimination. However, one commentator has questioned the Court's willingness to allow training programs to ground an affirmative defense, suggesting that the effectiveness of these programs in deterring harassing behavior has yet to be shown. See Susan Bisom-Rapp, An Ounce of Prevention Is a Poor Substitute for a Pound of Cure: Confronting the Developing Jurisprudence of Education and Prevention in Employment Discrimination Law, 22 Berkeley J. Emp. & Lab. L. 1 (2001); Susan Bisom-Rapp, Fixing Watches with Sledgehammers: The Questionable Embrace of Employee Sexual Harassment Training by the Legal Profession, 24 U. Ark. Little Rock L. Rev. 147 (2001).

6. In addition to taking reasonable care to prevent harassment, the employer also must establish that it took reasonable steps to correct the harassment. Matvia's employer suspended Terbush and then terminated him following the investigation. But the court finds the company's response to the "ostracism and vilification of Matvia" irrelevant to this prong of the affirmative defense because the conduct lacked a sexual component. Is this correct? Can an employer that tolerates misconduct directed toward an employee because she has complained of sexual harassment be acting reasonably to correct the harassment? Cf. Wyatt v. Hunt Plywood Co., 297 F.3d 405 (5th Cir. 2002).

7. Is termination of the harasser always a necessary or proper course of action? Employers who discipline harassers in order to avoid liability under Title VII must be careful to avoid liability to the harassing employee. Employees who have individual employment contracts, civil service rights, or academic tenure, or who work under the protection of a policy manual or a collective bargaining agreement may be protected against discharge without just cause.

Employers who have disciplined harassers have been sued for violating the rights of the harassing employees. See, e.g., Duffy v. Leading Edge Prods. Inc., 44 F.3d 308 (5th Cir. 1995) (unsuccessful defamation suit); Chalmers v. Quaker Oats Co., 61 F.3d 1340 (7th Cir. 1995) (unsuccessful ERISA suit); Scherer v. Rockwell Intl. Corp., 975 F.2d 356 (7th Cir. 1992) (unsuccessful breach of contract claim). In Pierce v. Commonwealth Life Ins. Co., 40 F.3d 796 (6th Cir. 1994), a supervisor demoted for violating the employer's sexual harassment policy asserted that, because the victim, who was a willing participant, was not disciplined, he was a victim of reverse discrimination. Id. at 799. The court ruled, however, that his status as a supervisor was a legitimate, nondiscriminatory reason justifying different treatment. Id. at 803-804. See also Amy Payne, Note, Protecting the Accused in Sexual Harassment Investigations: Is the Fair Credit Reporting Act an Answer?, 87 Va. L. Rev. 381 (2001) (arguing against application of the FRCA to sexual harassment investigations, despite an FTC ruling interpreting the Act to reach such investigations when conducted by individuals outside the company, usually attorneys).

8. What if the employee who complains about harassment asks the employer to keep her complaint confidential? In Torres v. Pisano, 116 F.3d 625 (2d Cir. 1997), the Second Circuit ruled that an employee's confidentiality request insulated the employer from liability for its failure to act. Id. at 627. The court emphasized that some complaints, such as those alleging harassment of other employees, may require the employer to breach the trust of an employee who has requested confidentiality, but found that this was not such a case. Id. at 639. Is the Second Circuit's approach consistent with *Ellerth* and *Faragher*? Could there be a difference between liability to the

employee who asks that no action be taken and liability to later victims of harassment if the complaining person's request is honored?

9. The affirmative defense also requires that the defendant prove that the employee unreasonably failed to take advantage of preventive or corrective opportunities. Matvia contended that the final incident was sufficiently severe and that because she did not unreasonably fail to avoid harm for that incident, she should have a claim. The court disagrees, reasoning that her actions throughout the period of harassment must be assessed. Is this correct? Must a victim complain at the earliest opportunity to preserve her claim? Was Matvia acting reasonably when she waited to determine whether Terbush was an interested man or a predator?

10. In Watts v. Kroger Co., 147 F.3d 460 (5th Cir. 1998), the Fifth Circuit affirmed summary judgment in favor of the employer on the ground that the employer took prompt remedial action after Watts complained to her store manager that her supervisor was harassing her. After *Ellerth* and *Faragher*, the Fifth Circuit withdrew its opinion and subsequently reversed its judgment on the ground that the employer could not, as a matter of law, establish that Watts "unreasonably failed to take advantage of any preventive or corrective opportunities provided by the employer." Although Watts alleged that her supervisor had harassed her for nearly a year, she did not complain until the harassment intensified. The court believed that a jury might find it "not unreasonable" to hold off complaining under these circumstances. *Watts*, 170 F.3d 505, 510 (5th Cir. 1999). However, in Wyatt v. Hunt Plywood Co., 297 F.3d 405 (5th Cir. 2002), the court held that plaintiff's failure to report harassment by her boss and his supervisor was unreasonable, precluding her from recovering for a four-month period of harassment that culminated in her supervisor's pulling her pants down in view of other employees. When plaintiff then complained, both her supervisor and his boss were fired, and no further acts of sexual harassment occurred.

11. Is a woman's reasonableness in not reporting harassment to be analyzed objectively or subjectively? Might a reasonable woman standard be appropriate here? There are some studies about why women are frequently reluctant to report sexual harassment. See Phoebe A. Morgan, Risking Relationships: Understanding the Litigation Choices of Sexually Harassed Women, 33 L. & Socy. Rev. 67 (1999). Commentators discussing the appropriateness of permitting an employer to satisfy the second prong of the affirmative defense by relying on a woman's failure to report harassing behavior include Theresa M. Beiner, Sex, Science and Social Knowledge: The Implications of Social Science Research on Imputing Liability to Employers for Sexual Harassment, 7 Wm. & Mary J. Women & Law 273 (2001); Joanna L. Grossman, The First Bite Is Free: Employer Liability for Sexual Harassment, 61 U. Pitt. L. Rev. 671 (2000); Theresa M. Beiner, Using Evidence of Women's Stories in Sexual Harassment Cases, 24 U. Ark. Little Rock L. Rev. 117 (2001); Linda Hamilton Krieger, Employer Liability for Sexual Harassment — Normative, Descriptive, and Doctrinal Interactions: A Reply to Professors Beiner and Bisom-Rapp, 24 U. Ark. L. Rev. 169 (2001).

12. As was true in *Matvia*, courts generally have not been sympathetic to plaintiffs' claims that they delayed reporting because they feared retaliation. See Leopold v. Baccarat, Inc., 239 F.3d 243 (2d Cir. 2001); Harrison v. Eddy Potash, Inc., 248 F.3d 1014 (10th Cir.), *cert. denied*, 534 U.S. 1019 (2001). See generally B. Glenn George, Employer Liability for Sexual Harassment: The Buck Stops Where?, 34 Wake Forest L. Rev. 1 (1999). In *Matvia*, however, retaliatory acts in fact occurred, and yet summary judgment for the employer was granted because the employee had no evidence, but only a suspicion that she would be retaliated against, at the time she delayed reporting. Why isn't the fact that retaliatory behavior occurred sufficient at least to create a fact question on the reasonableness of the plaintiff's fear of retaliation?

13. Is the lower courts' requirement that plaintiffs speak up at the earliest opportunity in some tension with the Supreme Court's decision in Clark County v. Breeden, reproduced at page 638, holding that complaint of sexual conduct that obviously was not severe or pervasive enough to state a claim for a hostile work environment was not protected from retaliation. For discussion of the interaction between the antiretaliation provisions of Title VII and the use of internal complaint procedures, see Edward Marshall, Excluding Participation in Internal Complaint Mechanisms From Absolute Retaliation Protection: Why Everyone, Including the Employer, Loses, 5 Emp. Rts. & Employ. Pol'y J. 549 (2001). In finding the affirmative defense met, the *Matvia* court stated that plaintiff's recourse for retaliatory acts was to bring a retaliation claim. Matvia, however, did bring a retaliation claim, but that action was dismissed for want of an adverse action. See infra pages 656-657.

14. What happens if a supervisor commits a severe act of harassment, such as a rape or attempted rape, and the employee immediately reports the harassment to her employer? If the employer has a strong antiharassment policy in place and engages in prompt and effective corrective action, can the employer still be vicariously liable for the hostile work environment? Since it is the employer's burden to establish *both* prongs of the affirmative defense, the answer should be yes. The employer would be unable to establish the second prong of the defense because the employee has acted reasonably. See Frederick v. Sprint/United Mgt. Co., 246 F.3d 1305 (11th Cir. 2001); Harrison v. Eddy Potash Inc., 248 F.3d 1014 (10th Cir. 2001), *cert. denied*, 534 U.S. 1019 (2001); Casiano v. AT&T Corp., 213 F.3d 278 (5th Cir. 2000); Johnson v. West, 218 F.3d 725 (7th Cir. 2000). However, some courts nonetheless are answering the question in the negative. John H. Marks, Smoke, Mirrors, and the Disappearance of "Vicarious" Liability: The Emergence of a Dubious Summary-Judgment Safe Harbor for Employers Whose Supervisory Personnel Commit Hostile Environment Workplace Harassment, 38 Hous. L. Rev. 1401 (2002) (reviewing and critiquing this group of cases). See also David Sherwyn, Michael Heise & Zev J. Eigen, Don't Train Your Employees and Cancel Your 1-800 Harassment Hotline: An Empirical Examination of the Flaws in the Affirmative Defense to Sexual Harassment Charges, 69 Fordham L. Rev. 1265 (2001).

15. In light of *Ellerth* and the availability of damages under the 1991 Act, how would you advise employers? Is there any way for an employer to avoid liability short of taking aggressive and serious steps to ensure that no supervisory harassment occurs? How should an employer respond if it has reason to believe that a supervisor has been harassing employees, but the victims are unwilling to make a formal complaint? Are restrictions of socio-sexual activity among employees an appropriate response? What about "dating waivers," i.e., documents executed by employees "desiring to undertake and pursue a mutually consensual social and/or amorous relationship"? Niloofar Nejat-Bina, Employers as Vigilant Chaperones Armed with Dating Waivers: The Intersection of Unwelcomeness and Employer Liability in Hostile Work Environment Sexual Harassment Law, Berkeley J. Empl. & Labor L. 325, 343 (1999) (quoting form prepared by law firm for employer use).

## NOTE ON EMPLOYER LIABILITY FOR HARASSMENT BY CO-WORKERS AND CUSTOMERS

Before *Ellerth*, courts generally agreed that the employer is liable for the harassing conduct of coworkers only if the employer knew or should have known of the harassment and failed to take adequate corrective action. Did *Ellerth* change this rule? Who bears the burden of establishing that the employer knew or should have known about co-worker harassment? The lower courts continue to hold employers liable for harassment by co-workers only if the employer knew or should have known of the harassment and failed to take corrective measures. As one circuit has observed, the difference between employer liability for supervisory harassment as opposed to co-worker harassment essentially comes down to which party bears the burden of proof. The factors examined in determining whether the affirmative defense has been satisfied are very similar to those looked at in employer liability for co-worker harassment. However, when it is a supervisor's harassment that is at issue, it is the employer that bears the burden of proving the affirmative defense. In co-worker harassment cases, it is the plaintiff's burden to prove the employer's negligence. Swinton v. Potomac Corp., 270 F.3d 794 (9th Cir. 2001), *cert. denied*, 535 U.S. 1018 (2002).

Even in cases of co-worker harassment, the issue of who the "employer" is and when the employer "knows" about the harassment can arises. Does *Ellerth* indicate how to resolve the issue of who the "employer" is for purposes of receiving complaints about harassment by co-workers? Is it sufficient that the worker inform his or her supervisor of harassment by a co-worker if the employer's harassment policy assigns the task of taking complaints to the human resources department? After *Ellerth*, who bears the burden of establishing that an appropriate agent of the employer knew or should have known of co-worker harassment? Williamson v. City of Houston, 148 F.3d 462 (5th Cir. 1998) (employer's policy directing employees to report harassment to supervisors establishes that supervisor's knowledge of harassment is imputed to the employer). In deciding whether an individual's knowledge may be imputed to the employer under the "knew or should have known standard," the Ninth Circuit held that one who has authority over either the harasser or the harassee's terms or conditions of employment *or* who has an official or de facto duty to serve as a conduit of information will have his knowledge imputed to the employer. Swinton v. Potomac Corp., 270 F.3d 794 (9th Cir. 2001), *cert. denied*, 122 S. Ct. 1609 (2002). In *Swinton*, because the employment manual directed employees to report harassing conduct to their supervisors, a supervisor's knowledge that a subordinate was being harassed was imputed to the employer. The court further held the manual's directive to report harassing conduct to supervisors made those supervisors managerial employees within the meaning of the *Kolstad* standard for punitive damages. See Chapter 10. Is this the correct test for imputing knowledge? For assessing punitive damages?

Must the employer have knowledge that the plaintiff herself had been the victim of harassment, or will knowledge of harassment of other co-workers by the perpetrator be sufficient to establish liability? Ferris v. Delta Air Lines, Inc., 277 F.3d 128 (2d Cir.), *cert. denied*, 123 S. Ct. 110 (2001) (employer knowledge that worker had raped other co-workers sufficient basis for imputing liability). What if it is common knowledge throughout a department that an employee is being sexually harassed by a co-worker? What if the whole department is aware that a supervisor is harassing an employee, but the human resources officer who handles harassment complaints is unaware? In *Faragher*, the Court commented on situations where knowledge of harassing behavior is widespread:

> There have . . . been myriad cases [that] have held employers liable on account of actual knowledge by the employer, or high-echelon officials of an employer organization, of sufficiently harassing action by subordinates, which the employer or its informed officers

have done nothing to stop. In such instances, the combined knowledge and inaction may be seen as demonstrable negligence, or as the employer's adoption of the offending conduct and its results, quite as if they had been authorized affirmatively as the employer's policy.

*Faragher* at 788. Is the *Ellerth* defense available when employer liability is based on negligent failure to take action to stop known harassing conduct? If the defense is available, could such an employer meet its requirements?

Is notice to the employer *always* a prerequisite to liability for co-worker harassment? What if the employer's policies provide no avenue for complaint? See Distasio v. Perkin-Elmer Corp., 157 F.3d 55, 63-64 (2d Cir. 1998) (plaintiff's allegation that her supervisor threatened her with the loss of her job if she reported a co-worker's harassing behavior, if proven, would render the employer liable for unreported incidents of harassment).

Is an employer liable for sexual harassment by customers? Suppose a sales representative must regularly deal with a customer's purchasing agent who harasses her. Does her employer have a duty to protect her? How far does this duty reach? Must it cease doing business with the harasser's firm if other methods fail? Quinn v. Green Tree Credit Corp.,159 F.3d 759, 766 (2d Cir. 1998), held that an employer's duty with respect to controlling harassment by customers is the same as its duty with respect to co-worker harassment — the employer is responsible for sexual harassment if it knows or should have known of it unless it can demonstrate immediate and appropriate corrective action. We will further consider the problem of employees whose jobs subject them to harassment by customers in the following section concerning grooming and dress codes.

Once an employer has notice that a co-worker, customer, or client is harassing an employee, what constitutes an adequate response? The Tenth Circuit has ruled that responses that are "reasonably calculated to end the harassment" are adequate to insulate the employer from liability even if new incidents of harassment occur. See Adler v. Wal-Mart Stores, Inc., 144 F.3d 664, 676 (10th Cir. 1998). Other courts also have been sympathetic to employers' attempts to control harassment by co-workers, customers, clients, and anonymous harassers. See, e.g., Folkerson v. Circus Circus Enterprises, 107 F.3d 754 (9th Cir. 1997) (casino not liable for customer's harassment of professional mime because casino warned offensive patrons and assigned a large male employee to follow her and notify security of problems); Hirras v. National R.R. Passenger Corp., 95 F.3d 396 (5th Cir. 1996) (by taking complaints seriously, conducting prompt and thorough investigation, and referring complaints to law enforcement, railroad responded adequately to complaints about anonymous harassing calls, notes, and graffiti even though harasser was never identified); Sanchez v. Alvarado, 101 F.3d 223, 228-29 (1st Cir. 1996) (consistent investigation and graduated disciplinary response to harassment complaints adequate even though co-worker's harassment not immediately stopped). In Swenson v. Potter, 271 F.3d 1184 (9th Cir. 2001), the court addressed the employer's obligation to take steps reasonably calculated to end the harassment in a case involving co-worker harassment. The inquiry has two steps. First, what were the temporary steps taken while the matter was under investigation? The court said an employer must, at a minimum, attempt to eliminate contact between the accuser and accused that is not business related. Second, what are the permanent remedial steps that have been taken? A harasser need not necessarily be punished if there is insufficient evidence to support discipline.

## NOTE ON THE FIRST AMENDMENT IMPLICATIONS
## OF SEXUAL HARASSMENT LIABILITY

The First Amendment implications of regulating sexual harassment in the workplace are broad-reaching and complex. This note provides no more than a brief introduction to the issue. One source of further information is Professor Eugene Volokh's website on free speech and workplace harassment, which is located at http://www.law.ucla.edu/faculty/volokh/harass. See also Kingsley R. Browne, Zero Tolerance for the First Amendment: Title VII's Regulation of Employee Speech, 27 Ohio N.U. L. Rev. 563 (2001); Eugene Volokh, Freedom of Speech, Cyperspace, and Harassment Law, 2001 Stan. Tech. L. Rev. 3; Charles R. Calleros, Title VII and the First Amendment: Content-Neutral Regulation, Disparate Impact, and the "Reasonable Person," 58 Ohio St. L.J. 1217 (1997); Cynthia L. Estlund, Freedom of Expression in the Workplace and the Problem of Discriminatory Harassment, 75 Tex. L. Rev. 687 (1997); Nicholas Wolfson, Hate Speech, Sex Speech, Free Speech (1997); Kingsley R. Browne, Title VII as Censorship: Hostile-Environment Harassment and the First Amendment, 52 Ohio St. L.J. 481 (1991).

Hostile environment sexual harassment liability frequently is based on sexually offensive, obscene, or denigrating speech. For example, in Robinson v. Jacksonville Shipyards, 760 F. Supp. 1486 (M.D. Fla. 1991), the court cited 29 separate instances of pornographic pictures posted throughout the workplace. The offensive pinups included numerous pictures of naked women with their pubic area or buttocks exposed, a naked woman with "USDA Choice" stamped on her chest, pictures suggestive of sexually submissive behavior, and naked women engaged in sexual activity. Id. at 1495-96. Robinson also complained about comments including "Hey pussycat, come here and give me a whiff"; "The more you lick it, the harder it gets"; "You rate about an 8 or 9 on a scale of 10"; "women are only fit company for something that howls"; and "there's nothing worse than having to work around women." Id. at 1498. Robinson also complained about graffiti on the walls of her working areas, including "lick me you whore dog bitch," "eat me," "pussy," and "cunt." Id. at 1499. Other female workers at the shipyard were subjected to equally explicit sexual remarks. The court considered and rejected Jacksonville Shipyards' assertion that imposing liability based on the pictures and speech would violate the First Amendment. See id. at 1535-36.

The speech at issue in *Robinson* is, unfortunately, typical of sexual harassment cases. Some harassment cases, however, have involved speech that is not as sexually oriented as that in *Robinson* and more clearly political in nature. See Eugene Volokh, What Speech Does "Hostile Work Environment" Harassment Law Restrict, 85 Geo. L.J. 627 (1997) (presenting evidence that employers seeking to avoid liability for sexual harassment restrict a broad range of political, religious, and social commentary). For example, in Lipsett v. University of Puerto Rico, 864 F.2d 881, 903-04 (1st Cir. 1988), a female resident stated a Title VII claim by alleging that she was subjected to comments that women should not be surgeons. Lipsett also complained about unwelcome sexual advances, pinups degrading women, and sexually charged nicknames. Consider also the speech in *Harris*. Could that be characterized as political?

Before considering the First Amendment implications of prohibiting harassing speech, it is necessary to clarify the issue. Evidence of sexist or racist speech in the workplace is relevant in employment discrimination litigation for a variety of reasons. First, sex or race stereotyping or expressions of bias and prejudice may provide evidence that an employer made decisions on the basis of sex or race, rather than for nondiscriminatory reasons. See Price Waterhouse v. Hopkins (reproduced at page 152). The government, through Title VII, imposes liability in such cases not because of what was said but because of the discriminatory *actions* taken. The speech merely provides evidence of motive and does not, therefore, create significant First Amendment problems of restricting speech. Similarly, sexual propositions may be evidence of quid pro quo sexual harassment. The employer may inform a female employee, for example, that she will not receive an employment benefit unless she cooperates by providing him with sexual favors. If she rejects the advance and suffers an adverse action, the proposition evidences the Title VII violation. Second, as in *Robinson* and *Lipsett,* sexist or racist speech may provide the basis for claiming that the employer is maintaining a hostile environment in violation of Title VII. The speech is *not merely evidence* of discriminatory conduct. It is prohibited because it is offensive enough to contaminate the work setting for women or minorities. The *speech itself* is restricted and forms the basis of liability. Hostile environment cases that rely primarily on speech, rather than on actual or proposed conduct, most clearly implicate First Amendment rights.

The First Amendment implications of sexual harassment liability are minimal when *private* employers voluntarily choose to regulate the speech absent any government coercion. In such cases, the actions of the private employer do not implicate the Constitution because no government action is involved. Of course, government employers who control the speech of their own employees are subject to some First Amendment restrictions. Moreover, when courts impose Title VII liability on private employers on the basis of their speech or their agents' speech, First Amendment concerns are implicated. Just as common law defamation is subject to First Amendment restrictions, New York Times v. Sullivan, 376 U.S. 254 (1964), so, too, is Title VII harassment law.

The Supreme Court has recognized categories of speech that the government may prohibit or restrict in some circumstances without violating the First Amendment. Several of these categories, including fighting words, offensive speech, and obscenity, are potentially applicable or analogous to speech that creates a discriminatory, hostile environment. While some speech at issue in sexual harassment cases readily fits within these categories, other speech does not.

Not only is classifying sexually harassing speech as an unprotected category of speech difficult, but prohibiting discriminatory harassing speech raises further First Amendment problems. Viewpoint restrictions have nearly always been considered violations of the First Amendment, and the Court specifically held that prohibiting discriminatory fighting words *because* they express a particular point of view violates the First Amendment. See R.A.V. v. City of St. Paul, Minnesota, 505 U.S. 377 (1992) (R.A.V. challenged a statute on which a cross-burning prosecution was based; the statute prohibited symbols known to arouse "anger, alarm, or resentment in others on the basis of race, color, creed, religion, or gender"). Nevertheless, *R.A.V.* suggested that Title VII's prohibition of sexual harassment is distinguishable from the St. Paul statute:

> [S]ince words can in some circumstances violate laws directed not against speech but against conduct (a law against treason, for example, is violated by telling the enemy the nation's defense secrets), a particular content-based subcategory of a proscribable class of speech can be swept up incidentally within the reach of a statute directed at conduct rather than speech. Thus, for example, sexually derogatory "fighting words," among

other words, may produce a violation of Title VII's general prohibition against sexual discrimination in employment practices, 42 U.S.C. § 2000e-2; 29 C.F.R. § 1604.11 (1991). See also 18 U.S.C. § 242; 42 U.S.C. §§ 1981, 1982. Where the government does not target conduct on the basis of its expressive content, acts are not shielded from regulation merely because they express a discriminatory idea or philosophy.

505 U.S. at 389. Does the Court's distinction apply to all hostile environment cases or only those based on "fighting words"? What does the Court mean by "'fighting words' among other words" in the context of sexual harassment? What about obscene and indecent speech? What about the pinups in *Robinson*? Could a court find that artwork depicting naked women creates a discriminatory environment without violating the First Amendment? What about statements like "there's nothing worse than having to work around women"? Does the Court's attempt to distinguish sexual harassment cases extend to other discriminatory hostile environment cases involving communicative "conduct"? Note that the R.A.V. Court's attempt to distinguish hostile environment liability clearly was dicta.

Since *R.A.V.*, the Court has decided Harris v. Forklift Systems Inc. (reproduced at page 507). The sexually harassing behavior in that case was primarily evidenced by offensive remarks. Although the constitutionality of imposing liability on the employer for those remarks was raised in briefs submitted in that case, the Court did not address the issue in its opinion. Are these remarks fighting words? Does the Court's dicta in *R.A.V.* explain why Hardy's statements are not protected by the First Amendment?

In the public sector, the Supreme Court has, outside of the harassment context, developed First Amendment doctrine to accommodate both government employees' free speech rights and government employers' interest in controlling the behavior of their own employees in the workplace. In this context, the Court has ruled that public employees may not be disciplined or discharged for engaging in speech on a matter of public concern unless the government can assert some interest in restricting that speech, such as disruption of the workplace, that outweighs the employees' interest in speaking. See Charles A. Sullivan, Deborah A. Calloway & Michael J. Zimmer, Cases and Materials on Employment Law 647-59 (1993).

Both prongs of the analysis are illustrated by Tindle v. Caudell, 56 F.3d 966 (8th Cir. 1995), in which the Eighth Circuit found that an employee who was suspended for appearing in blackface at an office Halloween party was not protected by the First Amendment. The costume was not intended to express any message on a matter of public concern, and his interest in wearing the costume did not outweigh the department's interest in maintaining discipline and harmonious working relationships. Id. at 971. See also Jeffries v. Harleston, 52 F.3d 9, 13 (2d Cir. 1995) (demotion of professor at a public college for anti-Semitic remarks does not violate the First Amendment because trustees who voted to demote the professor reasonably believed that the speech would disrupt college operations). Similarly, the Sixth Circuit held that a university coach's discharge for using the word "nigger" in addressing players did not violate the First Amendment because his speech did not involve a matter of public concern and the university had a countervailing interest in defining valid means of motivating players. In the course of its opinion, however, the court stated, that the university's policy prohibiting behavior "that subjects an individual to an intimidating, hostile or offensive educational, employment or living environment" is overbroad, vague, and a content- and viewpoint-discrimination violation of the First Amendment. Dambrot v. Central Mich. Univ., 55 F.3d 1177, 1182 (6th Cir. 1995).

Along this line, Saxe v. State College Area School District, 240 F.3d 200 (3d Cir. 2001), invalidated a school district's antiharassment policy on the basis that it was overbroad in prohibiting speech beyond what antidiscrimination statutes prohibit; the court also refused to recognize any "harassment exception" to the First Amendment. "[T]here is no question that the free speech clause protects a wide variety of speech that listeners may consider deeply offensive, including statements that impugn another's race or national origin or that denigrate religious beliefs." Id. at 204. Employees also prevailed on the basis of the First Amendment in Johnson v. Los Angeles County Fire Dept., 865 F. Supp. 1430, 1434 (C.D. Cal. 1994), where a county fire department prohibited employees from reading Playboy magazine in private at the workplace. The court concluded that reading the magazine amounted to expression relating to matters of public concern because it contained articles relating to politics, sports, arts, and entertainment. Id. at 1436. The ban was content-oriented because it was based on the department's disagreement with the manner in which the magazine portrays women. The department's interest in eliminating sexual harassment was not weighty enough to support a content-based restriction. Id. at 1439.

In cases in which private employers have asserted First Amendment defenses to disciplinary responses to sexual and racial harassment, courts have used a variety of approaches to find that Title VII liability complies with the First Amendment. See, e.g., Baty v. Willamette Indus., 172 F.3d 1232 (10th Cir. 1999) (First Amendment defense rejected because employer did not seek to express itself through its employees' speech, the speech constituted discriminatory conduct, workers are a captive audience, Title VII is narrowly drawn and serves a compelling state interest, and speech may be curtailed to remedy harm inflicted on other employees); Aguilar v. Avis Rent-A-Car System, 980 P.2d 846 (Cal. 1999) (remedial injunction against racist speech in the workplace did not violate prohibition against prior restraints because injunction targeted words not because of their expressive content, but because of their secondary effect of altering the terms and conditions of employment of minority employees by creating a discriminatory and hostile work environment); Jenson v. Eveleth Taconite Co., 824 F. Supp. 847 (D. Minn. 1993) (First Amendment defense asserted against hostile environment case arising from sexual graffiti, photographs, and language; court disagreed, treating employees in the workplace as a captive audience and relying on R.A.V.'s notion of speech as conduct).

## NOTE ON ALTERNATIVE REMEDIES FOR HARASSMENT

Title VII is not the only source of remedies for sexual and other harassment in the employment setting. Harassment also can be attacked under state employment discrimination statutes, and state employees may assert a violation of their constitutional right to equal protection. Resort to state tort claims, such as intentional infliction of emotional distress and assault, may also be desirable in order to improve on Title VII remedies. See generally Krista J. Schoenheider, Comment, A Theory of Tort Liability for Sexual Harassment in the Workplace, 134 U. Pa. L. Rev. 1461 (1986). See also Truman v. United States, 26 F.3d 592, 595 (5th Cir. 1994) (sexual harassment claim for intentional infliction of emotional distress not barred by Federal Tort Claims Act's exceptions to waiver of sovereign immunity); McGanty v. Staudenraus, 901 P.2d 841, 860 (Or. 1995) (employee who alleges that she was sexually harassed and abused by supervisor and that employer knew or should have known these acts would cause severe emotional distress states a claim for intentional infliction of emotional distress even though she did not allege that supervisor or employer had specific purpose of inflicting distress).

Although the Civil Rights Act of 1991 amended Title VII to provide for punitive and compensatory damages, § 102 limits the amount of damages that can be awarded. See Chapter 10. Because the limits range from $50,000 to $300,000, depending on the size of the employer, plaintiffs may continue to pursue tort remedies. In addition, as we saw in *Meritor,* Title VII hostile environment cases typically have required harassed employees to show a pattern of harassment in order to prevail. In contrast, a claim of assault or intentional infliction of emotional distress can be stated based on a single incident of discriminatory harassment. In some jurisdictions, however, workers' compensation statutes may provide the exclusive remedy for intentional infliction of mental distress on the job. See Jane B. Korn, The Fungible Woman and Other Myths of Sexual Harassment, 67 Tul. L. Rev. 1363 (1993). Note, also, that state law claims that cannot be resolved without interpreting a collective bargaining agreement may be preempted by federal law. Compare McCormick v. AT&T Technologies, Inc., 934 F.2d 531, 536-38 (4th Cir. 1991) (claim preempted), and Baker v. Farmers Elec. Co-op, Inc., 34 F.3d 274, 280-81 (5th Cir. 1994) (claim preempted), with Jackson v. Kimel, 992 F.2d 1318, 1326-28 (4th Cir. 1993) (claim not preempted).

## 3. *Grooming and Dress Codes*

Perhaps the most blatant remaining form of gender discrimination in employment is employer dress and grooming codes, which frequently have disparate standards for males and females. How can such standards survive Title VII's prohibition of gender discrimination? In Willingham v. Macon Telegraph Publishing Co., 507 F.2d 1084, 1091-92 (5th Cir. 1975) (en banc), the Fifth Circuit denied a man's challenge to an employer's rule prohibiting male (but not female) employees from having hair longer than shoulder length:

> Equal employment *opportunity* may be secured only when employers are barred from discriminating against employees on the basis of immutable characteristics, such as race and national origin. Similarly, an employer cannot have one hiring policy for men and another for women *if* the distinction is based on some fundamental right. But a hiring policy that distinguishes on some other ground, such as grooming codes or length of hair, is related more closely to the employer's choice of how to run his business than to equality of employment opportunity. In [Phillips v. Martin Marietta, 400 U.S. 532 (1971),] the Supreme Court condemned a hiring distinction based on having pre-school age children, an existing condition not subject to change. In Sprogis v. United Air Lines[, 444 F.2d 1194 (7th Cir. 1971)], the Seventh Circuit reached a similar result with respect to marital status. We have no difficulty with the result reached in those cases; but nevertheless perceive that a line must be drawn between distinctions grounded on such fundamental rights as the right to have children or to marry and those interfering with the manner in which an employer exercises his judgment as to the way to operate a business. Hair length is not immutable and in the situation of employer vis à vis employee enjoys no constitutional protection. If the employee objects to the grooming code he has the right to reject it by looking elsewhere for employment, or alternatively he may choose to subordinate his preference by accepting the code along with the job. . . .
>
> We adopt the view, therefore, that distinctions in employment practices between men and women on the basis of something other than immutable or protected characteristics

do not inhibit employment *opportunity* in violation of Sec. 703(a). Congress sought only to give all persons equal access to the job market, not to limit an employer's right to exercise his informed judgment as to how best to run his shop.

We are in accord also with the alternative ground. . . . "From all that appears, equal job opportunities are available to both sexes. It does not appear that defendant fails to impose grooming standards for female employees; thus in this respect each sex is treated equally."

*Willingham* has received general acceptance from the courts of appeals. The mere fact of gender-specific differences in dress and grooming codes does not violate Title VII. See, e.g., Harper v. Blockbuster Entertainment Corp., 139 F.3d 1385 (11th Cir. 1998) (different hair length standards for men and women do not violate Title VII); Tavora v. New York Mercantile Exch., 101 F.3d 907 (2d Cir. 1997) (same).

No one seems to doubt that permitting female, but not male, employees to have shoulder-length hair is sex discrimination in an analytic sense. What, then, is the justification for permitting it? Does *Willingham* establish a de minimis test: if the sex distinctions in question are too trivial, they do not warrant federal court intervention? That would explain the court's distinction between cases involving hair length and cases involving "fundamental rights," a concept that seems to have been borrowed from equal protection doctrine. Remember, also, that some courts have required different treatment to have material adverse effects in order to constitute discrimination. Or is *Willingham* an example of a "volition" exception to Title VII: employer requirements that can easily be met by an employee are not within the statutory proscription?

Declining protection because the different treatment is trivial is consistent with the court's treatment of sexual harassment that is not sufficiently serious or pervasive to create a hostile environment. But sexual harassment becomes actionable as a quid pro quo case when job benefits are contingent on acceptance of the discriminatory remarks or conduct. What if an employee is threatened with the loss of his job on the ground that his hair is too long? How can this be viewed as trivial?

In the last sentence of the *Willingham* extract, the court suggests that imposing grooming standards on both men and women is simply not disparate treatment. But isn't Willingham's complaint that those grooming standards are different and that the difference is sex based? Do you agree?

Many commentators look on grooming cases as *sui generis*. But don't these cases reflect stereotypes so ingrained that they are not even recognized as such? See Karl E. Klare, Power/Dressing: Regulation of Employee Appearance, 26 New Eng. L. Rev. 1395 (1992). Why is it that an employer can legally prohibit males from wearing dresses or eye shadow? Is it because there is something wrong with males assuming "female" roles? Is a man wrong to assume such roles in turn because females are inferior and a man demeans himself by aping them? Is it merely coincidence that society looks more favorably on women who appropriate "male" attire (e.g., the pants suit) than the other way around? Perhaps the courts are simply applying what they perceive as legislative intent: whatever Congress *said*, it did not *mean* to bar this kind of employer rule. Isn't it clear that Congress did not intend Title VII to require a unisex dress code?

While the mere existence of disparate grooming codes is not illegal, employers who require female employees to dress in provocative clothes may be guilty of sexual harassment. Is it ever permissible for an employer to require its female employees to wear provocative clothing? What about a club that features strippers or nude dancers? Does Title VII mean to prohibit employing women in such positions?

Several decisions have found Title VII violated when the employer's dress code did not treat women equally. In Carroll v. Talman Federal Savings & Loan Assn., 604 F.2d 1028 (7th Cir. 1979), the court considered a dress code allowing males to wear "customary business attire," but requiring women to wear uniforms. Although disclaiming any intent to pass on the reasonableness of general employer dress regulations, the court distinguished the case before it where the disparate treatment was demeaning to women: "While there is nothing offensive about uniforms per se, when some employees are uniformed and others not there is a natural tendency to assume that the uniformed women have a lesser professional status than their male colleagues attired in normal business clothes." Id. at 1033. In a footnote, the court was even more explicit:

> [W]e do not view the recognition of different dress norms for males and females to be offensive or illegal stereotyping. What is offensive is the compulsion to wear employer-identified uniforms and the assumption on which the employer openly admits that rule is based: that women cannot be expected to exercise good judgment in choosing business apparel, whereas men can.

Id. at 1033 n.17. Does *Carroll* establish "separate but equal" as the standard governing Title VII appearance cases? If so, is it consistent with *Willingham?* See also Gerdom v. Continental Airlines, Inc., 692 F.2d 602 (9th Cir. 1982) (en banc). Different standards of dress for different positions (e.g., "dress" clothes versus casual) do not violate Title VII. See Lowe v. Angelo's Italian Foods, Inc., 87 F.3d 1170 (10th Cir. 1996).

In Frank v. United Air Lines, 216 F.3d 845 (9th Cir. 2000), the court struck down an airline's weight standards for flight attendants as facially discriminatory. United based men's weight limits on large body frames, while women's weight limits were based on medium body frames. Because the standards imposed unequal burdens on men and women, they were unlawful. The court declined to decide whether different weight limits for men and women in and of themselves would be unlawful. While acknowledging that separate but equal dress and grooming codes for men and women have been upheld, it questioned whether weight limits should receive similar treatment.

## CRAFT v. METROMEDIA, INC.
### 766 F.2d 1205 (8th Cir. 1985)

GIBSON, Circuit Judge.

[When Christine Craft was demoted from co-anchor to reporter by KMBC-TV, she sued the station's owner and operator, Metromedia, Inc. Her suit focused on whether KMBC had stricter standards for on-air appearance for females than for males. KMBC, having slipped in its local news ratings, had determined to adopt the co-anchor format used by its two major competitors in Kansas City. Furthermore, because of the perceived "coldness" of its anchor, Scott Feldman, the new position was to be filled by a female to "soften" its news presentation.]

Craft accepted the coanchor position at KMBC and at the station's request stopped in Dallas for a meeting with Lynn Wilford of Media Associates before reporting to Kansas City. She made her debut as coanchor on January 5, 1981, and the testimony is essentially uncontradicted that [news director] Shannon and [general manager]

Replogle immediately began having concerns about her clothing and makeup. Wilford came to Kansas City on January 14 to work with Craft on dress as well as on various aspects of her presentation technique. It was during this visit that Wilford for the only time applied Craft's makeup, and the results on the 6 p.m. news were so unsatisfactory that Craft was allowed to remove the makeup before the 10 p.m. broadcast.

In the following months Shannon continued to make occasional suggestions or criticisms as to certain articles of Craft's clothing, and Craft was provided with materials, including the book *Women's Dress for Success*, on wardrobe and makeup. Then, beginning in April, KMBC arranged for Macy's Department Store to provide clothing for Craft in exchange for advertising time. Craft was assisted by a consultant from Macy's in selecting outfits. She would then return to the KMBC studio, try on the clothing, and appear before camera so tapes could be made to send to Wilford for review.

[Media Associates researched viewer perceptions of KMBC's newscasts by conducting four "focus group" discussions in which groups of ten viewed sample video tapes of local news programs and then reacted. The response to Craft's appearance was "overwhelmingly negative." Replogle and Shannon met with Craft to discuss this result. Replogle told her that management was ready to work with her to overcome the problems. Craft ultimately agreed to cooperate, and her wardrobe was more closely supervised, including instituting a "clothing calendar," showing what clothes were to be worn. A follow-up telephone survey of 400 randomly selected persons in the viewing area pursued issues raised by the focus groups. The participants were asked to rank Craft against her female co-anchor competitors in response to 14 statements, 4 of which dealt with "good looks" or the dress of and image of a "professional anchor woman." Craft trailed in almost every category. As a result, Craft was replaced by KMBC.]

Craft's attacks on the district court's disposition of her Title VII sex discrimination claim are essentially factual, rather than legal as she contends. Her central position is that KMBC's appearance standards were based on stereotyped characterizations of the sexes and were applied to women more constantly and vigorously than they were applied to men. . . .

[Craft argues] that the district court clearly erred in failing to find that KMBC enforced appearance standards more strictly as to female than as to male on-air personnel. In support of her position she points to the evidence most favorable to her, which shows that only females were subject to daily scrutiny of their appearance or were ever required to change clothes at the station before going on the air and that no male was ever directed to take time from his journalistic duties to select clothing, with the help of a consultant, from Macy's and to test that clothing on camera for the approval of another consultant. The district court, however, concluded that such facts, in light of other evidence, showed only that KMBC was concerned with the appearance of all its on-air personnel and that it took measures appropriate to individual situations, characteristics, and shortcomings.

The court found that KMBC had only gradually increased its attentions to Craft's appearance, with the institution of the clothing calendar representing the culmination of efforts made necessary when lesser suggestions, such as those complied with by other personnel, proved ineffective.

The evidence shows that one female, Brenda Williams, had never been the subject of criticism for her appearance while numerous males on occasion had been given specific directions as to their individual shortcomings. Mike Placke, for example, had been told to lose weight, to get better fitting clothes, to refrain from wearing sweaters under jackets, and to tie his necktie in a certain manner. Similarly, Michael Mahoney had been told to lose weight and to pay more attention to his wardrobe and hairstyle, while Bob Werley had been told to try wearing contact lenses and to get a hair piece and had been given a makeup chart on a form similar to that used with Craft. An interpretation of this record as showing that KMBC enforced its appearance standards equally as to males and females in response to individual problems is neither "illogical" nor "implausible" and has "support in inferences that may be drawn from the facts." We cannot conclude that the district court erred in this respect.

Our determination is not altered by the testimony, cited by Craft, of the consultant Wilford or of other female KMBC employees to the effect that the station put more emphasis on the appearance of females. This testimony represents only the opinions and impressions of the witnesses as to KMBC's policy, and the district court by implication rejected such opinions, making its own finding to the contrary on the record. . . . Finally, the district court attributed the use in the survey of questions on appearance and good looks only as to female anchors as prompted not by sexual bias but by the concerns raised as to Craft by the focus groups. The viewers were asked to rank the male anchors on more points concerning personality and "coldness," Feldman's perceived weaknesses. The inclusion of a makeup criterion and a requirement that Craft not deviate from her clothing calendar in the "standards of performance" by which her work was to be evaluated, in contrast to the absence of any appearance objectives in Feldman's "standards of performance," similarly just reflected management's efforts to pursue with personnel their individual weaknesses.[10]

[Craft further argues] that even if KMBC was evenhanded in applying its appearance standards, the district court erred in failing to recognize that the standards themselves were discriminatory. She contends that she was forced to conform to a stereotypical image of how a woman anchor should appear. The evidence included a communication from the consultant, Wilford, to Shannon suggesting that Craft purchase more blouses with "feminine touches," such as bows and ruffles, because many of her clothes were "too masculine." The general wardrobe hints for females developed by Media Associates warned that women with "soft" hairstyles and looks should wear blazers to establish their authority and credibility while women with short "masculine" hairstyles shouldn't wear "masculine" clothing in dark colors and with strong lines because they would appear too "aggressive." The district court found that Craft had been hired to "soften" KMBC's news presentation.

. . . Craft's argument is that these differing standards as to females reflect customer preferences, which a number of cases have held cannot justify discriminatory practices. E.g., Diaz v. Pan American World Airways, 442 F.2d 385, 389 (5th Cir. 1971).

The district court, however, found that KMBC's appearance standards were based instead on permissible factors. While there may have been some emphasis on the feminine stereotype of "softness" and bows and ruffles and on the fashionableness of female anchors, the evidence suggests such concerns were incidental to a true focus on consistency of appearance, proper coordination of colors and textures, the effects of studio lighting on clothing and makeup, and the greater degree of conservatism thought necessary in the Kansas City market. The "dos" and "don'ts" for female

---

10. Feldman's temper and personality, for example, were his special problems. He frequently argued with the female producers, and management had spoken to him about his "throwing curve balls" during newscasts to fluster other on-air personnel. In addition he had been sharply reprimanded for referring to Craft in the newsroom as "that girl."

anchors addressed the need to avoid, for example, tight sweaters or overly "sexy" clothing and extreme "high fashion" or "sporty" outfits while the male "dos" and "don'ts" similarly cautioned against "frivolous" colors and "extreme" textures and styles as damaging to the "authority" of newscasters. These criteria do not implicate the primary thrust of Title VII, which is to prompt employers to "discard outmoded sex stereotypes posing distinct employment disadvantages for one sex." Knott v. Missouri Pacific Railroad, 527 F.2d 1249, 1251 (8th Cir. 1975).

Courts have recognized that the appearance of a company's employees may contribute greatly to the company's image and success with the public and thus that a reasonable dress or grooming code is a proper management prerogative. E.g., Fagan v. National Cash Register Co., 481 F.2d 1115, 1124-25 (D.C. Cir. 1973). Evidence showed a particular concern with appearance in television; the district court stated that reasonable appearance requirements were "obviously critical" to KMBC's economic well-being; and even Craft admitted she recognized that television was a visual medium and that on-air personnel would need to wear appropriate clothes and makeup. . . .

We further reject the argument of Craft that the perception, discussed above, that she would add warmth and "comfortability" to the newscast defined a stereotypical "female" role, secondary to that of the male anchor, into which she was forced in terms of story assignments and division of duties. First, we observe that the research survey asked participants to rank both male and female anchors in response to the statement "comfortable to watch." In addition, the district court rejected Craft's factual contention that Feldman was assigned the lead story more frequently and was given more live stories while she was assigned the human interest, personal, and humorous stories. The court, for example, while acknowledging the testimony of news producer Sandra Woodward that she initially was instructed to give Feldman about two-thirds of the lead stories, also accepted testimony of Shannon that that policy had been designed to ease the transition to coanchors for Craft and the viewers and was discontinued after a few weeks, after which time the lead stories were equitably divided. . . .

## NOTES

1. Didn't KMBC admit to violating Title VII by favoring a female co-anchor to offset Feldman's "coldness"? Is female warmth a bfoq for the position of co-anchor? Even assuming that this is sex discrimination, Craft would not sue on that basis because she benefitted from it. But is it completely irrelevant to her suit? Or does it suggest that KMBC would try to feminize Craft once she was hired?

2. Wasn't a large part of Craft's problem that she was being compared to female coanchors at other stations in the various viewer surveys? Isn't that discriminatory and, therefore, necessarily illegal unless being a woman is a bfoq for the position in the first place? Under this view, isn't the district court's failure to find discrimination in the face of such direct evidence "clearly erroneous"?

3. Suppose Craft could demonstrate that viewers were collectively guilty of gender discrimination; that is, they had different standards for female anchors than for males. Would that help or hurt her case? Could a station refuse to hire a black anchor because significant numbers of its viewers would change channels? Does the bfoq defense make sex discrimination different?

4. Granting that the station had an interest in the appearance of all on-air personnel, did it discriminate in the way it accomplished its ends? After all, the *Carroll*

court held the defendant liable on such grounds. If the question was whether women were treated the same as men, why didn't the station arrange with Macy's to provide a wardrobe for Feldman? Isn't that evidence of disparate treatment of Craft?

5. What is the court's theory in this case? Does it agree with the district court and *Willingham* that sex-based grooming and dress standards simply are not disparate treatment? Under that theory, there is no need to consider further whether such treatment is justified under Title VII.

6. What is the harm in this approach? Isn't it obvious that, in a visual "entertainment" medium such as television news, the employer has a legitimate interest in the appearance of its on-air employees? Consider the application of grooming and dress standards in the context of producing a movie. Certainly, a director must impose sex-based requirements on the actors and actresses. But consider the grooming and dress standards for a female attorney. A supervising attorney might decide that it will help win a case if a female litigator who is representing an alleged rapist dresses in feminine attire. Is it permissible under Title VII for the firm to require the attorney to dress femininely? What if a female associate is required to dress in feminine clothes and wear makeup as a condition of becoming partner in a law firm?

7. Does Price Waterhouse v. Hopkins (reproduced at page 152) require reconsideration of the *Craft* case? The *Price Waterhouse* Court recounted the facts:

> There were clear signs . . . that some of the partners reacted negatively to Hopkins' personality because she was a woman. One partner described her as "macho"; another suggested that she "overcompensated for being a woman"; a third advised her to take "a course at charm school." Several partners criticized her use of profanity; in response, one partner suggested that those partners objected to her swearing only "because it's a lady using foul language." Another supporter explained that Hopkins "had matured from a tough-talking somewhat masculine hard-nosed mgr to an authoritative, formidable, but much more appealing lady ptr candidate." But it was the man who . . . bore responsibility for explaining to Hopkins the reasons for the Policy Board's decision to place her candidacy on hold who delivered the coup de grace: in order to improve her chances for partnership, Thomas Beyer advised, Hopkins should "walk more femininely, talk more femininely, dress more femininely, wear make-up, have her hair styled, and wear jewelry."

490 U.S. at 235. Craft lost her job because her clothes were not sufficiently soft and feminine. Hopkins was denied partnership in part because her personality and appearance were not sufficiently feminine. Can these two cases be distinguished?

8. The thrust of *Price Waterhouse*, as codified by the Civil Rights Act of 1991, is that an employer violates Title VII if gender is a motivating factor in an employment decision. The Court concluded that the lower court correctly found that a number of the partners' comments "showed sex stereotyping at work." 490 U.S. at 251. The Court further held that stereotyping can be evidence of sex discrimination. Don't the focus groups, the comparison with other female co-anchors, and the question in the survey show that stereotyping was at work? Given the importance of these efforts and the fact that Craft ultimately lost her job because of the results, the sex stereotypes could scarcely be viewed as merely stray remarks.

9. *Willingham* and *Craft* suggest that sex-based grooming and dress codes do not violate Title VII either because they are de minimis infringements or because they do not discriminate at all. Under either of these approaches, clothing rules based on societal standards may be applied in any context without justification. Treating dress codes as neutral rules with a disparate impact would impose on employers the obligation to establish the job relatedness and business necessity of dress codes, but

characterizing sex-based rules as neutral in order to permit the application of a business necessity defense was clearly rejected by the Supreme Court in both *Manhart* and *Johnson Controls*. This result was codified by the Civil Rights Act of 1991. Are the dress and grooming cases still good law?

10.  Mary Anne C. Case, Disaggregating Gender from Sex and Sexual Orientation: The Effeminate Man in the Law and Feminist Jurisprudence, 105 Yale L.J. 1, 68-69 (1995), writes:

> Put quite tendentiously, my contention in pressing quite strongly the claim that sex-specific clothing regulations constitute disparate treatment of a sort prohibited by Title VII is that the world will not be safe for women in frilly pink dresses — they will not, for example, generally be as respected as either men or women in gray flannel suits — unless and until it is made safe for men in dresses as well. Rather than eliminate feminine styles, in clothing and elsewhere, I would prefer to enable them to be more generally valued. While I do not approve and do not mean to encourage the societal tendency to devalue most things limited to women and to value them only insofar as men feel free to engage in them, I do note it, as have many scholars and commentators. In light of this tendency, it seems that one of the most effective ways to improve the value of something coded feminine — whether something as serious as being the primary caregiver for one's child or as seemingly trivial and frivolous as wearing a dress, makeup, or jewelry — is to make it accessible to and acceptable in men.

11.  Can *Craft* be justified as an informal application of the bfoq defense? Is that the real difference between *Craft*, on the one hand, and *Price Waterhouse* and *Carroll*, on the other? Television is a "visual medium," while accounting and banking are not. Would the bfoq defense have provided a more honest analysis of a setting that was fraught with sex-based distinctions even before Craft was hired?

12.  If the problem of grooming and dress code discrimination were handled under the rubric of bfoq, would that solve the theoretical problems posed by grooming and dress code cases? Television is not the only context in which an employer might assert that "feminine" appearance and attractiveness are bona fide occupational qualifications. Airlines, for example, have attempted to justify policies restricting positions to females based on a need to project a certain image and cater to customer preferences. Although the courts have rejected this argument in the context of single-sex hiring policies, see, e.g., Wilson v. Southwest Airlines Co., 517 F. Supp. 292, 302 (N.D. Tex. 1981), could an employer more credibly assert that ultrafeminine attire is a bfoq for women employed as dancers or waitresses in a nightclub?

13.  Litigants with complaints regarding grooming and dress codes should also explore the possibility of a claim under state or local antidiscrimination provisions. The District of Columbia Human Rights Act, for example, prohibits discrimination based on personal appearance. D.C. Code Ann. § 2-140211. In one case, a transsexual employee stated a claim for personal appearance discrimination under that provision. The employee allegedly was discharged "because she is a transsexual and retains some masculine traits." Underwood v. Archer Mgmt. Servs., Inc., 857 F. Supp. 96, 97 (D.D.C. 1994).

14.  Professor Katharine T. Bartlett suggests that community norms concerning dress and appearance cannot be fully removed from the process of furthering workplace equality:

> For the most part, courts have rationalized dress and appearance requirements by reference, directly or indirectly, to community norms. Based on these norms, courts may

excuse dress and appearance requirements they deem trivial in their impact on employees, or neutral in affecting men and women alike, or essential to the employer's lawful business objectives. These rationalizations have been criticized by scholars, who argue that reliance on community norms constitutes an acceptance or legitimation of the very gender stereotypes that Title VII was established to eliminate. The proposed solution is that community norms be put off limits as a basis for justifying discriminatory standards and that mandatory dress and appearance codes be found unlawful under Title VII.

. . . Critics assume that it is possible, and desirable, to evaluate dress and appearance rules without regard to the norms and expectations of the community — that is, according to stable or universal versions of equality that are uninfected by community norms. I question this assumption, arguing that equality, no less than other legal concepts, cannot transcend the norms of the community that has produced it. I argue, further, that eliminating dress and appearance discrimination against women in the workplace is not as simple a matter as the critics suggest. . . . [I]n evaluating dress and appearance codes, my focus is . . . on whether . . . they further gender-based disadvantage in the workplace. Because what constitutes disadvantage, as well as what it takes to reduce that disadvantage and even what reducing disadvantage means, can only be determined in context, in relation to a particular set of circumstances, I conclude that the evaluation of equality claims under Title VII requires more, not less, attention to community norms. . . .

. . . The law shapes, and is shaped by, community norms, in an ongoing series of negotiations over form and function, over ideals and reality, and over difference, disadvantage, and the difference between the two. In this process of negotiation, only those versions of equality that incorporate past understandings, as well as new insights, will be stable enough to form the basis of even better future versions. Viewing community norms as a central part of this process rather than as an evil that can or should be ignored reflects this premise.

Only Girls Wear Barrettes: Dress and Appearance Standards, Community Norms, and Workplace Equality, 92 Mich. L. Rev. 2541, 2543-46 (1994).

15. Professor Mark Linder has detailed how dress codes requiring women to wear heels endanger women's health as well as their right to equality in the workplace. See Smart Women, Stupid Shoes, and Cynical Employers: The Unlawfulness and Adverse Health Consequences of Sexually Discriminatory Workplace Footwear Requirements for Female Employees, 22 J. Corp. L. 295 (1997).

## PROBLEM 7.2

You work as an employment lawyer. Cindy, a waitress at a local nightclub, seeks your advice. While working, she is required to dress in hot pants and a tight t-shirt that leaves her midriff bare. There are no waiters at the club, although two of the three bartenders are male. The bartenders dress in long pants, long-sleeved shirts, and vests. Cindy complains that she frequently is subjected to obscene remarks and sexual advances by male customers as she walks through the club taking orders and delivering drinks. She has complained to the manager. The manager responded by ejecting a customer when she complained that he touched her. Her complaints about the customers' remarks, however, have gone unheeded. The manager's response: "That goes with the turf." Cindy also is unhappy that she is required to wear an outfit designed to appeal to the sexual fantasies of her male customers. She wants to know if she has been a victim of sexual harassment and whether she has a right to insist on wearing less-revealing clothes. Cindy's friend Alice, who works as a dancer in the club, also is distressed by the remarks made by the men in the crowd and by the skimpy clothes she is required to wear. Do these women have any rights under Title VII? See Sexual Ornament or Invitation to Harassment at Hooters Bar? L.A. Times, Aug. 8, 1993, at A18.

## 4.  Discrimination on the Basis of Sexual Preference

### DESANTIS v. PACIFIC TELEPHONE
### & TELEGRAPH CO.
#### 608 F.2d 327 (9th Cir. 1979)

CHOY, J.: Male and female homosexuals brought three separate federal district court actions claiming that their employers or former employers discriminated against them in employment decisions because of their homosexuality. They alleged that such discrimination violated Title VII of the Civil Rights Act of 1964. The district courts dismissed the complaints as failing to state claims. . . .

[Strailey was fired by the Happy Times Nursery School after working two years as a teacher, allegedly because he wore a small gold ear-loop to school. DeSantis, Boyle, and Simard claimed that Pacific Telephone & Telegraph Co. (PT & T) discriminated against them because of their homosexuality. DeSantis alleged that he was not hired because a PT & T supervisor believed he was a homosexual. Boyle claimed to have been continually harassed by co-workers and forced to quit to preserve his health. Simard alleged similar harassment, but claimed that it was inflicted by his supervisors as well as his co-workers. Lundin and Buckley alleged that PT & T discriminated against them because of their known lesbian relationship and eventually fired them.]

Appellants argue first that the district courts erred in holding that Title VII does not prohibit discrimination on the basis of sexual preference. They claim that in prohibiting certain employment discrimination on the basis of "sex," Congress meant to include discrimination on the basis of sexual orientation. They add that in a trial they could establish that discrimination against homosexuals disproportionately affects men and that this disproportionate impact and correlation between discrimination on the basis of sexual preference and discrimination on the basis of "sex" requires that sexual preference be considered a subcategory of the "sex" category of Title VII. See 42 U.S.C. § 2000e-2.

### A.  CONGRESSIONAL INTENT IN PROHIBITING "SEX" DISCRIMINATION

In Holloway v. Arthur Anderson & Co., 566 F.2d 659 (9th Cir. 1977), plaintiff argued that her employer had discriminated against her because she was undergoing a sex transformation and that this discrimination violated Title VII's prohibition on sex discrimination. This court rejected that claim, writing:

> The cases interpreting Title VII sex discrimination provisions agree that they were intended to place women on an equal footing with men.
> Giving the statute its plain meaning, this court concludes that Congress had only the traditional notions of "sex" in mind. Later legislative activity makes this narrow definition even more evident. Several bills have been introduced to amend the Civil Rights Act to prohibit discrimination against "sexual preference." None have been enacted into law.

Congress has not shown any intent other than to restrict the term "sex" to its traditional meaning. Therefore, this court will not expand Title VII's application in the absence of Congressional mandate. The manifest purpose of Title VII's prohibition against sex discrimination in employment is to ensure that men and women are treated equally, absent a bona fide relationship between the qualifications for the job and the person's sex.

Following *Holloway*, we conclude that Title VII's prohibition of "sex" discrimination applies only to discrimination on the basis of gender and should not be judicially extended to include sexual preference such as homosexuality. See Smith v. Liberty Mutual Insurance Co., 569 F.2d 325, 326-27 (5th Cir. 1978).

## B.  DISPROPORTIONATE IMPACT

Appellants argue that recent decisions dealing with disproportionate impact require that discrimination against homosexuals fall within the purview of Title VII. They contend that these recent decisions, like Griggs v. Duke Power Co., establish that any employment criterion that affects one sex more than the other violates Title VII. . . . They claim that in a trial they could prove that discrimination against homosexuals disproportionately affects men both because of the greater incidence of homosexuality in the male population and because of the greater likelihood of an employer's discovering male homosexuals compared to female homosexuals.

Assuming that appellants can otherwise satisfy the requirement of *Griggs*, we do not believe that *Griggs* can be applied to extend Title VII protection to homosexuals. In finding that the disproportionate impact of educational tests on blacks violated Title VII, the Supreme Court in *Griggs* sought to effectuate a major congressional purpose in enacting Title VII: protection of blacks from employment discrimination. . . .

The *Holloway* court noted that in passing Title VII Congress did not intend to protect sexual orientation and has repeatedly refused to extend such protection. Appellants now ask us to employ the disproportionate impact decisions as an artifice to "bootstrap" Title VII protection for homosexuals under the guise of protecting men generally.

This we are not free to do. Adoption of this bootstrap device would frustrate congressional objectives as explicated in *Holloway*, not effectuate congressional goals as in *Griggs*. It would achieve by judicial "construction" what Congress did not do and has consistently refused to do on many occasions. It would violate the rule that our duty in construing a statute is to "ascertain . . . and give effect to the legislative will." We conclude that the *Griggs* disproportionate impact theory may not be applied to extend Title VII protection to homosexuals.

## C.  DIFFERENCES IN EMPLOYMENT CRITERIA

Appellants next contend that recent decisions have held that an employer generally may not use different employment criteria for men and women. They claim that if a male employee prefers males as sexual partners, he will be treated differently from a female who prefers male partners. They conclude that the employer thus uses different employment criteria for men and women and violates the Supreme Court's warning in Phillips v. Martin Marietta Corp.: "The Court of Appeals therefore erred in reading this section as permitting one hiring policy for women and another for men. . . ."

We must again reject appellants' efforts to "bootstrap" Title VII protection for homosexuals. While we do not express approval of an employment policy that differentiates according to sexual preference, we note that whether dealing with men or women the employer is using the same criterion: it will not hire or promote a person who prefers sexual partners of the same sex. Thus this policy does not involve different decisional criteria for the sexes.

## D.   INTERFERENCE WITH ASSOCIATION

Appellants argue that the EEOC has held that discrimination against an employee because of the race of the employee's friends may constitute discrimination based on race in violation of Title VII. See EEOC Dec. No. 71-1902, [1972] Empl. Prac. Guide (CCH) ¶6281; EEOC Dec. No. 71-969, [1972] Empl. Prac. Guide (CCH) ¶6193. They contend that analogously discrimination because of the sex of the employee's sexual partner should constitute discrimination based on sex.

Appellants, however, have not alleged that appellees have policies of discriminating against employees because of the gender of their friends. That is, they do not claim that the appellees will terminate anyone with a male (or female) friend. They claim instead that the appellees discriminate against employees who have a certain type of relationship — i.e., homosexual relationship — with certain friends. As noted earlier, that relationship is not protected by Title VII. Thus, assuming that it would violate Title VII for an employer to discriminate against employees because of the gender of their friends, appellants' claims do not fall within this purported rule.

## E.   EFFEMINACY

Appellant Strailey contends that he was terminated by the Happy Times Nursery School because that school felt that it was inappropriate for a male teacher to wear an earring to school. He claims that the school's reliance on a stereotype — that a male should have a virile rather than an effeminate appearance — violates Title VII.

In *Holloway* this court noted that Congress intended Title VII's ban on sex discrimination in employment to prevent discrimination because of gender, not because of sexual orientation or preference. Recently the Fifth Circuit similarly read the legislative history of Title VII and concluded that Title VII thus does not protect against discrimination because of effeminacy. Smith v. Liberty Mutual Insurance Co. We agree and hold that discrimination because of effeminacy, like discrimination because of homosexuality or transsexualism (*Holloway*), does not fall within the purview of Title VII. . . .

SNEED, J. (concurring and dissenting).
. . . I respectfully dissent from subpart B which holds that male homosexuals have not stated a Title VII claim under the disproportionate impact theories of Griggs v. Duke Power Co. My position is not foreclosed by our holding, with which I agree, that Title VII does not afford protection to homosexuals, male or female. The male appellants' complaint, as I understand it, is based on the contention that the use of homosexuality as a disqualification for employment, which for *Griggs'* purposes must be treated as a facially neutral criterion, impacts disproportionately on males because of the greater visibility of male homosexuals and a higher incidence of homosexuality among males than females.

To establish such a claim will be difficult because the male appellants must prove that as a result of the appellee's practices there exists discrimination against males qua males. That is, to establish a prima facie case under *Griggs* it will not be sufficient to show that appellees have employed a disproportionately large number of female *homosexuals* and a disproportionately small number of male *homosexuals*. Rather it will be necessary to establish that the use of homosexuality as a bar to employment disproportionately impacts on *males*, a class that enjoys Title VII protection. Such a showing perhaps could be made were male homosexuals a very large proportion of the total applicable male population.

My point of difference with the majority is merely that the male appellants in their *Griggs* claim are not using that case "as an artifice to 'bootstrap' Title VII protection for homosexuals under the guise of protecting men generally." Their claim, if established properly, would in fact protect males generally. I would permit them to try to make their case and not dismiss it on the pleadings. . . .

## NOTES

1. One way to find that Title VII bars discrimination against persons engaging in certain kinds of sexual conduct is to read "sex" in § 703 to mean "sexual conduct," not merely "gender." Was that the thrust of the plaintiffs' argument?

2. Why wasn't a simple disparate treatment theory applicable? Plaintiff DeSantis argued that he was discriminated against for engaging in conduct (sexual relations with males) that would not be held against him were he a female. Why is this not persuasive?

3. The Ninth Circuit recently disavowed the *DeSantis*'s court's refusal to recognize a claim based on a male's failure to conform to masculine stereotypes. In Nichols v. Azteca Restaurant Enterprises, Inc., 256 F.3d 864 (9th Cir. 2001), the court held plaintiff had stated a claim under Title VII when he alleged he was discriminated against for acting "too feminine." It said *Price Waterhouse* prohibits discrimination based on sex stereotyping and thus, to the extent *DeSantis* conflicts with *Price Waterhouse*, it is no longer good law.

4. Consider Mary Anne C. Case, Disaggregating Gender from Sex and Sexual Orientation: The Effeminate Man in the Law and Feminist Jurisprudence, 105 Yale L.J. 1, 2-3 (1995), who writes:

> The word "gender" has come to be used synonymously with the word "sex" in the law of discrimination. In women's studies and related disciplines, however, the two terms have long had distinct meanings, with gender being to sex what masculine and feminine are to male and female. Were that distinct meaning of gender to be recaptured in the law, great gains both in analytic clarity and in human liberty and equality might well result. For, as things now stand, the concept of gender has been imperfectly disaggregated in the law from sex on the one hand and sexual orientation on the other. Sex and orientation exert the following differential pull on gender in current life and law: When individuals diverge from the gender expectations for their sex — when a woman displays masculine characteristics or a man feminine ones — discrimination against her is now treated as sex discrimination while his behavior is generally viewed as a marker for homosexual orientation and may not receive protection from discrimination. This is most apparent from a comparison of *Price Waterhouse v. Hopkins* . . . with cases upholding an employer's right to fire or not to hire males specifically because they were deemed "effeminate."
> 
> This differential treatment has important implications for feminist theory. It marks the continuing devaluation, in life and in law, of qualities deemed feminine. The man

who exhibits feminine qualities is doubly despised, for manifesting the disfavored qualities and for descending from his masculine gender privilege to do so. The masculine
woman is today more readily accepted. Wanting to be masculine is understandable; it
can be a step up for a woman, and the qualities associated with masculinity are also associated with success.

We are in danger of substituting for prohibited sex discrimination a still acceptable
gender discrimination, that is to say, discrimination against the stereotypically feminine,
especially when manifested by men, but also when manifested by women. Ann
Hopkins, I fear, may have been protected only because of the doubleness of her bind: It
was nearly impossible for her to be both as masculine as the job required and as feminine as gender stereotypes require. But the Supreme Court seems to have had no
trouble with the masculine half of Hopkins's double bind; there is little indication, for
example, that the Court would have found it to be sex discrimination if a prospective accounting partner had instead been told to remove her makeup and jewelry and to go to
assertiveness training class instead of charm school.

Do you agree? Professor Case recognizes the irony that "gender" has come to be
interchangeable with "sex" in legal literature largely as the result of now-Justice Ruth
Bader Ginsburg's work in challenging sex discrimination. Further, the most prominent other recent effort to return to "sex" as opposed to "gender" is by Richard A. Epstein, in Gender Is for Nouns, 41 De Paul L. Rev. 981 (1992), scarcely an
admirer of antidiscrimination laws.

5. As for disparate impact, how did the court distinguish *Griggs*? Is *DeSantis*
merely a "legislative intent" decision; that is, whatever "normal" impact analysis
means, Congress did not intend it to be used to prohibit discrimination against gays?
If so, did the court correctly divine the "intent" of Congress? Did Congress envision
the many ways in which disparate impact theory would be used? Is there any way
other than such inferred legislative intent to justify the decision? Assuming that argument fails, will anti-gay policies have a disparate impact on men?

6. In Faraca v. Clements, 506 F.2d 956 (5th Cir. 1975), the court found race discrimination in a refusal to hire a white married to a black when blacks married to
blacks had been hired. Accord Parr v. Woodmen of World Life Ins. Co., 791 F.2d
888, 891-92 (11th Cir. 1986). If the race of a spouse can establish racial discrimination, why can't the gender of a sex partner establish gender discrimination? See also
Loving v. Virginia, 388 U.S. 1 (1967) (striking down state law banning interracial
marriages, although Virginia argued that it did not discriminate against either race).

7. The absence of a federal statute prohibiting discrimination on the basis of sexual orientation has led to a number of other legal theories attacking such conduct. In
public employment, sexual orientation discrimination has been challenged on the
basis of the right of privacy, due process, free speech, and equal protection. Most constitutional attacks have had very limited success.

8. Development of expansive protection based on the right of privacy was cut short
by Bowers v. Hardwick, 478 U.S. 186 (1986), in which the Supreme Court rejected a
privacy attack on a Georgia criminal statute used to prosecute consensual homosexual conduct. In *Bowers*, the Court rejected the argument that the right to privacy
cases, which deal with such issues as raising and educating children, family relationships, procreation, marriage, contraception, and divorce, should be extended to include the right to consensual homosexual sodomy. The Court agreed that the due
process clause protects the substantive right to privacy because certain fundamental
rights are "implicit in the concept of ordered liberty[;] . . . neither liberty nor justice
would exist if [they] were sacrificed"; put differently, some rights are "deeply rooted in

this Nation's history and tradition." Id. at 191. But sodomy was considered an offense at common law and prohibited by all 13 states when the Bill of Rights was ratified; it was prohibited by all 50 states until 1961 and was still outlawed by 24 states at the time of *Bowers*. Accordingly, the right to engage in consensual homosexual sodomy is not "deeply rooted in this Nation's history and tradition," nor is it "implicit in the concept of ordered liberty." Further, the Court refused to create a new due process right not supported by "express constitutional authority" because "the Court is most vulnerable and comes nearest to illegitimacy when it deals with judge-made constitutional law having little or no cognizable root in the language or design of the Constitution." Id. at 194. However, the continued viability of *Bowers* recently was called into question when the Supreme Court granted certiorari in a case upholding a state statute that penalized certain acts only if performed between members of the same sex. Lawrence v. State, 41 S.W.3d 349 (Tex. App. 2001), *cert. granted*, 2002 U.S. LEXIS 8680 (2002).

9. Equal protection analysis, although initially ineffective, recently has provided some significant victories. See generally Cass R. Sunstein, Sexual Orientation and the Constitution: A Note on the Relationship Between Due Process and Equal Protection, 55 U. Chi. L. Rev. 1161 (1988). Most courts have declined to apply strict or intermediate scrutiny, upholding sexual orientation classifications using the minimum rationality test. E.g., Steffan v. Perry, 41 F.3d 677 (D.C. Cir. 1994); High Tech Gays v. Defense Indus. Sec. Clearance Office, 895 F.2d 563 (9th Cir. 1990); Ben-Shalom v. Marsh, 881 F.2d 454 (7th Cir. 1989); Woodward v. United States, 871 F.2d 1068 (Fed. Cir. 1989); Baker v. Wade, 769 F.2d 289 (5th Cir. 1985).

10. However, the Supreme Court, although applying rationality review, nonetheless found that a law discriminating on the basis of sexual preference can violate equal protection. In Romer v. Evans, 517 U.S. 620 (1996), the Supreme Court considered an equal protection challenge to Amendment 2 to the Colorado state constitution, which was adopted after a statewide referendum. The amendment was drafted in response to local ordinances banning discrimination on the basis of sexual orientation. It provided that neither Colorado nor any of its local governmental units "shall enact, adopt or enforce any statute, regulation, ordinance or policy whereby homosexual, lesbian or bisexual orientation, conduct, practices or relationships shall constitute or otherwise be the basis of or entitle any person or class of persons to have or claim any minority status, quota preferences, protected status or claim of discrimination." Stating that it was applying rational basis scrutiny, a majority invalidated the amendment:

> Amendment 2 fails, indeed defies, even this conventional inquiry. First, the amendment has the peculiar property of imposing a broad and undifferentiated disability on a single named group, an exceptional and, as we shall explain, invalid form of legislation. Second, its sheer breadth is so discontinuous with the reasons offered for it that the amendment seems inexplicable by anything but animus toward the class that it affects; it lacks a rational relationship to legitimate state interests.

517 U.S. at 632. Justice Scalia issued a dissent (joined by the Chief Justice and Justice Thomas), which scathingly criticized the majority:

> The Court has mistaken a Kulturkampf for a fit of spite. The constitutional amendment before us here is not the manifestation of a "'bare . . . desire to harm'" homosexuals, but is rather a modest attempt by seemingly tolerant Coloradans to preserve traditional sexual mores against the efforts of a politically powerful minority to revise those mores through use of the laws.

That objective, and the means chosen to achieve it, are . . . unimpeachable under any
constitutional doctrine hitherto pronounced (hence the opinion's heavy reliance upon
principles of righteousness rather than judicial holdings). . . .

Id. at 1629. The impact of *Romer* on more general questions of homosexual limitations, for example, in the military, remains to be seen. Justice Scalia viewed the
decision as an overruling of Bowers v. Hardwick, but the majority certainly did not
expressly do so. Subsequent lower court cases have continued to uphold some discrimination against gays as consistent with equal protection principles. E.g., Holmes v.
California Army Natl. Guard, 124 F.3d 1126 (9th Cir. 1997); Shahar v. Bowers, 114
F.3d 1097 (11th Cir. 1997). However, in Lovell v. Comsewogue Sch. Dist., 214 F.
Supp. 2d 519 (E.D.N.Y. 2002), the court found that a lesbian teacher's claim of discrimination and harassment based on her sexual orientation was actionable under
the Equal Protection Clause.

11. Some challenges based on state constitutions have also been successful. On
the same day and in the same city where *DeSantis* was handed down, the Supreme
Court of California decided Gay Law Students Assn. v. Pacific Telephone & Telegraph Co., 595 P.2d 592 (Cal. 1979), holding that homosexuals could sue a public
utility for employment discrimination under the equal protection clause of the
California constitution.

12. In response to the lack of protection for homosexuals under federal law, a
number of states and municipalities have enacted their own civil rights legislation expressly covering sexual orientation. Such statutes typically protect against discrimination on the basis of affectional or sexual orientation, normally defined as including
heterosexuality, bisexuality, and homosexuality. For a comprehensive listing, see
www.lambdalegal.org. See generally Developments in the Law — Employment
Discrimination, 109 Harv. L. Rev. 1568 (1996); Roberta Achtenberg, Sexual Orientation and the Law §§ 5.01-5.07 (1992); Peter M. Cicchino, Bruce R. Deming &
Katherine M. Nicholson, Note, Sex, Lies, and Civil Rights: A Critical History of the
Massachusetts Gay Civil Rights Bill, 26 Harv. C.R.-C.L. L. Rev. 549, 556-57 (1991).

13. Resistance to legislative efforts to afford protection to homosexuals has been
fierce. Legislation in most states has been defeated, and in some states where antidiscrimination statutes have been enacted, opponents have sought to repeal them by referendum. Romer v. Evans, 517 U.S. 620 (1996), invalidated on equal protection
grounds a referendum-adopted amendment to the Colorado state constitution that
restricted the ability of the state or its subdivisions to enact laws protecting gays.
While the sweep of *Romer* may be limited, cf. Equality Foundation of Greater
Cincinnati v. City of Cincinnati, 128 F.3d 289 (6th Cir. 1997) (upholding charter
amendment restricting city's power to enact ordinances according gays "minority or
protected status"), *Romer* clearly reinforces the gains gay rights advocates have
achieved in state legislatures and in many localities.

14. The Americans with Disabilities Act states explicitly that "homosexuality and
bisexuality are not impairments and as such are not disabilities." It separately states
that "transvestism, transsexualism, pedophilia, voyeurism, gender identity disorders
not resulting from physical impairments, or other sexual behavior disorders" are not
disabilities. 42 U.S.C.S. § 12211 (2003); see also 42 U.S.C.S. § 12208 (2003). AIDS-
related discrimination, however, is within the statute, which may protect homosexuals from discrimination, especially if male homosexuals are the victims of discrimination because they are perceived to be suffering from AIDS or perceived to be at risk of
that disease.

On the state level, a similar approach to the disability question usually is taken.

Sommers v. Iowa Civil Rights Commn., 337 N.W.2d 470, 476 (Iowa 1983). For example, while the *Sommers* court acknowledged that there are differences between transsexualism and homosexuality or transvestism and that "adverse societal attitude" may make "obtaining and retaining employment" difficult for transsexuals, it refused to classify transsexualism as a disability: it lacked "the inherent propensity to limit major life activities." See generally Patricia Cain, Stories from the Gender Garden: Transsexuals and Anti-Discrimination Laws, 75 Denver U. L. Rev. 1321 (1998).

15.  Although Title VII does not bar discrimination against homosexuals per se, it is now clear that the statute's prohibitions on sexual harassment protect individuals who are sexually harassed by employees of the same gender, so long as the harassment is because of sex. See Oncale v. Sundowners Offshore Servs., Inc. (reproduced at page 492).

16.  Federal legislation to bar discrimination based on sexual orientation continues to be introduced and debated by Congress. In Do Gay Rights Laws Matter?: An Empirical Assessment, 75 S. Cal. L. Rev. 65 (2001), William B. Rubenstein addressed the question of the prevalence of sexual orientation claims:

> My findings belie the heretofore unexamined assumption that gay rights claims are rarely filed. Using a low-end estimate of the number of gay people in the workforce, I find that in six of ten surveyed states, the incidence of sexual orientation filings falls somewhere between the incidence of sex and race discrimination filings. In two other states, the prevalence of sexual orientation filings exceeds that of both race and gender. In only two states does the incidence of sexual orientation filings fall below both race and gender filings. Even assuming a high portion of gay people in the workforce, the frequency with which gay workers file claims of sexual orientation discrimination is far closer to the rates at which women file gender discrimination claims and people of color file race discrimination claims than the raw numbers suggest.

Professor Rubenstein's study, however, was dependent on the admittedly difficult task of estimating how many gays were in the workforce in order to calculate the rate of filings by such individuals as compared to the filings by minorities and women alleging race and sex discrimination.

## BOY SCOUTS OF AMERICA v. DALE
### 530 U.S. 640 (2000)

Chief Justice REHNQUIST delivered the opinion of the Court.

Petitioners are the Boy Scouts of America and the Monmouth Council, a division of the Boy Scouts of America. . . . The Boy Scouts is a private, not-for-profit organization engaged in instilling its system of values in young people. The Boy Scouts asserts that homosexual conduct is inconsistent with the values it seeks to instill. Respondent is James Dale, a former Eagle Scout whose adult membership in the Boy Scouts was revoked when the Boy Scouts learned that he is an avowed homosexual and gay rights activist. The New Jersey Supreme Court held that New Jersey's public accommodations law requires that the Boy Scouts admit Dale. This case presents the question whether applying New Jersey's public accommodations law in this way violates the Boy Scouts' First Amendment right of expressive association. We hold that it does.

James Dale entered scouting in 1978 at the age of eight by joining Monmouth Council's Cub Scout Pack 142. Dale became a Boy Scout in 1981 and remained a Scout until he turned 18. By all accounts, Dale was an exemplary Scout. In 1988, he achieved the rank of Eagle Scout, one of Scouting's highest honors.

Dale applied for adult membership in the Boy Scouts in 1989. The Boy Scouts approved his application for the position of assistant scoutmaster of Troop 73. Around the same time, Dale left home to attend Rutgers University. After arriving at Rutgers, Dale first acknowledged to himself and others that he is gay. He quickly became involved with, and eventually became the copresident of, the Rutgers University Lesbian/Gay Alliance. In 1990, Dale attended a seminar addressing the psychological and health needs of lesbian and gay teenagers. A newspaper covering the event interviewed Dale about his advocacy of homosexual teenagers' need for gay role models. In early July 1990, the newspaper published the interview and Dale's photograph over a caption identifying him as the copresident of the Lesbian/Gay Alliance.

Later that month, Dale received a letter from Monmouth Council Executive James Kay revoking his adult membership. Dale wrote to Kay requesting the reason for Monmouth Council's decision. Kay responded by letter that the Boy Scouts "specifically forbid membership to homosexuals."

[In 1992, Dale filed a state court complaint alleging that the Boy Scouts had violated New Jersey's public accommodations statute, which prohibits discrimination on the basis of sexual orientation in places of public accommodation. The New Jersey Supreme Court held that the Boy Scouts was subject to the public accommodations law. It rejected the Boy Scouts' claims that such a ruling violated its federal constitutional rights of association. Board of Directors of Rotary Intl. v. Rotary Club of Duarte, 481 U.S. 537, 544 (1987).] With respect to the right to intimate association, the court concluded that the Boy Scouts' "'large size, nonselectivity, inclusive rather than exclusive purpose, and practice of inviting or allowing nonmembers to attend meetings, establish that the organization is not 'sufficiently personal or private to warrant constitutional protection' under the freedom of intimate association.'" (quoting *Duarte*). With respect to the right of expressive association, the court "agreed that Boy Scouts expresses a belief in moral values and uses its activities to encourage the moral development of its members." But the court concluded that it was "not persuaded . . . that a shared goal of Boy Scout members is to associate in order to preserve the view that homosexuality is immoral." . . . The court also determined that New Jersey has a compelling interest in eliminating "the destructive consequences of discrimination from our society," and that its public accommodations law abridges no more speech than is necessary to accomplish its purpose. . . .

## II

In Roberts v. United States Jaycees, 468 U.S. 609, 622 (1984), we observed that "implicit in the right to engage in activities protected by the First Amendment" is "a corresponding right to associate with others in pursuit of a wide variety of political, social, economic, educational, religious, and cultural ends." This right is crucial in preventing the majority from imposing its views on groups that would rather express other, perhaps unpopular, ideas. Government actions that may unconstitutionally burden this freedom may take many forms, one of which is "intrusion into the internal structure or affairs of an association" like a "regulation that forces the group to accept members it does not desire." Forcing a group to accept certain members may impair the ability of the group to express those views, and only those views, that it intends to express. Thus, "[f]reedom of association . . . plainly presupposes a freedom not to associate."

The forced inclusion of an unwanted person in a group infringes the group's freedom of expressive association if the presence of that person affects in a significant way the group's ability to advocate public or private viewpoints. New York State Club

Assn., Inc. v. City of New York, 487 U.S. 1 (1988). But the freedom of expressive association, like many freedoms, is not absolute. We have held that the freedom could be overridden "by regulations adopted to serve compelling state interests, unrelated to the suppression of ideas, that cannot be achieved through means significantly less restrictive of associational freedoms." *Roberts.* To determine whether a group is protected by the First Amendment's expressive associational right, we must determine whether the group engages in "expressive association." The First Amendment's protection of expressive association is not reserved for advocacy groups. But to come within its ambit, a group must engage in some form of expression, whether it be public or private.

Because this is a First Amendment case where the ultimate conclusions of law are virtually inseparable from findings of fact, we are obligated to independently review the factual record to ensure that the state court's judgment does not unlawfully intrude on free expression. The record reveals the following. The Boy Scouts is a private, nonprofit organization. According to its mission statement:

> It is the mission of the Boy Scouts of America to serve others by helping to instill values in young people and, in other ways, to prepare them to make ethical choices over their lifetime in achieving their full potential.
>
> The values we strive to instill are based on those found in the Scout Oath and Law:
>
> **Scout Oath:**
> On my honor I will do my best
> To do my duty to God and my country
> and to obey the Scout Law;
> To help other people at all times;
> To keep myself physically strong,
> mentally awake, and morally straight.
>
> **Scout Law:**
> A *Scout is:*
>
> Trustworthy Obedient
> Loyal Cheerful
> Helpful Thrifty
> Friendly Brave
> Courteous Clean
> Kind Reverent.

Thus, the general mission of the Boy Scouts is clear: "To instill values in young people." The Boy Scouts seeks to instill these values by having its adult leaders spend time with the youth members, instructing and engaging them in activities like camping, archery, and fishing. During the time spent with the youth members, the scoutmasters and assistant scoutmasters inculcate them with the Boy Scouts' values — both expressly and by example. It seems indisputable that an association that seeks to transmit such a system of values engages in expressive activity. . . .

Given that the Boy Scouts engages in expressive activity, we must determine whether the forced inclusion of Dale as an assistant scoutmaster would significantly affect the Boy Scouts' ability to advocate public or private viewpoints. This inquiry necessarily requires us first to explore, to a limited extent, the nature of the Boy Scouts' view of homosexuality.

The values the Boy Scouts seeks to instill are "based on" those listed in the Scout Oath and Law. The Boy Scouts explains that the Scout Oath and Law provide "a positive moral code for living; they are a list of 'do's' rather than 'don'ts.' The Boy Scouts asserts that homosexual conduct is inconsistent with the values embodied in the Scout Oath and Law, particularly with the values represented by the terms "morally straight" and "clean."

Obviously, the Scout Oath and Law do not expressly mention sexuality or sexual orientation. And the terms "morally straight" and "clean" are by no means self-defining. Different people would attribute to those terms very different meanings. For example, some people may believe that engaging in homosexual conduct is not at odds with being "morally straight" and "clean." And others may believe that engaging in homosexual conduct is contrary to being "morally straight" and "clean." The Boy Scouts says it falls within the latter category . . .

The Boy Scouts asserts that it "teaches that homosexual conduct is not morally straight," and that it does "not want to promote homosexual conduct as a legitimate form of behavior." We accept the Boy Scouts' assertion. We need not inquire further to determine the nature of the Boy Scouts' expression with respect to homosexuality. But because the record before us contains written evidence of the Boy Scouts' viewpoint, we look to it as instructive, if only on the question of the sincerity of the professed beliefs.

A 1978 position statement to the Boy Scouts' Executive Committee, signed by Downing B. Jenks, the President of the Boy Scouts, and Harvey L. Price, the Chief Scout Executive, expresses the Boy Scouts' "official position" with regard to "homosexuality and Scouting":

**Q.** May an individual who openly declares himself to be a homosexual be a volunteer Scout leader?

**A.** No. The Boy Scouts of America is a private, membership organization and leadership therein is a privilege and not a right. We do not believe that homosexuality and leadership in Scouting are appropriate. We will continue to select only those who in our judgment meet our standards and qualifications for leadership.

Thus, at least as of 1978 — the year James Dale entered Scouting — the official position of the Boy Scouts was that avowed homosexuals were not to be Scout leaders. [Two subsequent position statements — both promulgated but, like the 1978 statement, not published after Dale became an assistant scoutmaster was revoked, with one after this litigation was commenced — reemphasized the Boy Scout's position that "homosexuals do not provide a desirable role model for Scouts."]

The Boy Scouts publicly expressed its views with respect to homosexual conduct by its assertions in prior litigation. For example, throughout a California case with similar facts filed in the early 1980's, the Boy Scouts consistently asserted the same position with respect to homosexuality that it asserts today. We cannot doubt that the Boy Scouts sincerely holds this view.

We must then determine whether Dale's presence as an assistant scoutmaster would significantly burden the Boy Scouts' desire to not "promote homosexual conduct as a legitimate form of behavior." As we give deference to an association's assertions regarding the nature of its expression, we must also give deference to an association's view of what would impair its expression. That is not to say that an expressive association can erect a shield against antidiscrimination laws simply by asserting that mere acceptance of a member from a particular group would impair its message. But here Dale, by his own admission, is one of a group of gay Scouts who have "become leaders in their community and are open and honest about their sexual orientation." Dale was the copresident of a gay and lesbian organization at college and remains a gay rights activist. Dale's presence in the Boy Scouts would, at the very least, force the organization to send a message, both to the youth members and the world, that the Boy Scouts accepts homosexual conduct as a legitimate form of behavior.

*Hurley* [v. Irish-American Gay, Lesbian & Bisexual Group, 515 U.S. 557 (1995)] is illustrative on this point. There we considered whether the application of Massachusetts' public accommodations law to require the organizers of a private St. Patrick's Day parade to include among the marchers an Irish-American gay, lesbian, and bisexual group, GLIB, violated the parade organizers' First Amendment rights. We noted that the parade organizers did not wish to exclude the GLIB members because of their sexual orientations, but because they wanted to march behind a GLIB banner. . . .

Here, we have found that the Boy Scouts believes that homosexual conduct is inconsistent with the values it seeks to instill in its youth members; it will not "promote homosexual conduct as a legitimate form of behavior." As the presence of GLIB in Boston's St. Patrick's Day parade would have interfered with the parade organizers' choice not to propound a particular point of view, the presence of Dale as an assistant scoutmaster would just as surely interfere with the Boy Scout's choice not to propound a point of view contrary to its beliefs.

The New Jersey Supreme Court determined that the Boy Scouts' ability to disseminate its message was not significantly affected by the forced inclusion of Dale as an assistant scoutmaster because of the following findings:

> Boy Scout members do not associate for the purpose of disseminating the belief that homosexuality is immoral; Boy Scouts discourages its leaders from disseminating any views on sexual issues; and Boy Scouts includes sponsors and members who subscribe to different views in respect of homosexuality.

We disagree with the New Jersey Supreme Court's conclusion drawn from these findings.

First, associations do not have to associate for the "purpose" of disseminating a certain message in order to be entitled to the protections of the First Amendment. An association must merely engage in expressive activity that could be impaired in order to be entitled to protection. For example, the purpose of the St. Patrick's Day parade in *Hurley* was not to espouse any views about sexual orientation, but we held that the parade organizers had a right to exclude certain participants nonetheless.

Second, even if the Boy Scouts discourages Scout leaders from disseminating views on sexual issues — a fact that the Boy Scouts disputes with contrary evidence — the First Amendment protects the Boy Scouts' method of expression. If the Boy Scouts wishes Scout leaders to avoid questions of sexuality and teach only by example, this fact does not negate the sincerity of its belief discussed above.

Third, the First Amendment simply does not require that every member of a group agree on every issue in order for the group's policy to be "expressive association." The Boy Scouts takes an official position with respect to homosexual conduct, and that is sufficient for First Amendment purposes. . . .

Having determined that the Boy Scouts is an expressive association and that the forced inclusion of Dale would significantly affect its expression, we inquire whether the application of New Jersey's public accommodations law to require that the Boy Scouts accept Dale as an assistant scoutmaster runs afoul of the Scouts' freedom of expressive association. We conclude that it does.

State public accommodations laws were originally enacted to prevent discrimination in traditional places of public accommodation — like inns and trains. See, e.g.,

*Hurley*; Romer v. Evans, 517 U.S. 620 (1996) (describing the evolution of public accommodations laws). Over time, the public accommodations laws have expanded to cover more places. New Jersey's statutory definition of "'[a] place of public accommodation'" is extremely broad. The term is said to "include, but not be limited to," a list of over 50 types of places. N.J. Stat. Ann. § 10:5-5(1) (West Supp. 2000). Many on the list are what one would expect to be places where the public is invited. For example, the statute includes as places of public accommodation taverns, restaurants, retail shops, and public libraries. But the statute also includes places that often may not carry with them open invitations to the public, like summer camps and roof gardens. In this case, the New Jersey Supreme Court went a step further and applied its public accommodations law to a private entity without even attempting to tie the term "place" to a physical location. As the definition of "public accommodation" has expanded from clearly commercial entities, such as restaurants, bars, and hotels, to membership organizations such as the Boy Scouts, the potential for conflict between state public accommodations laws and the First Amendment rights of organizations has increased.

We recognized in cases such as Roberts and Duarte that States have a compelling interest in eliminating discrimination against women in public accommodations. But in each of these cases we went on to conclude that the enforcement of these statutes would not materially interfere with the ideas that the organization sought to express. In Roberts, we said "indeed, the Jaycees has failed to demonstrate . . . any serious burden on the male members' freedom of expressive association." In Duarte, we said ["the evidence fails to demonstrate that admitting women to Rotary Clubs will affect in any significant way the existing members' ability to carry out their various purposes."]

We thereupon concluded in each of these cases that the organizations' First Amendment rights were not violated by the application of the States' public accommodations laws.

In *Hurley*, we said that public accommodations laws "are well within the State's usual power to enact when a legislature has reason to believe that a given group is the target of discrimination, and they do not, as a general matter, violate the First or Fourteenth Amendments." But we went on to note that in that case "the Massachusetts [public accommodations] law has been applied in a peculiar way" because "any contingent of protected individuals with a message would have the right to participate in petitioners' speech, so that the communication produced by the private organizers would be shaped by all those protected by the law who wish to join in with some expressive demonstration of their own." And in the associational freedom cases such as *Roberts, Duarte*, and *New York State Club Assn.*, after finding a compelling state interest, the Court went on to examine whether or not the application of the state law would impose any "serious burden" on the organization's rights of expressive association. So in these cases, the associational interest in freedom of expression has been set on one side of the scale, and the State's interest on the other. . . .

In *Hurley*, we applied traditional First Amendment analysis to hold that the application of the Massachusetts public accommodations law to a parade violated the First Amendment rights of the parade organizers. Although we did not explicitly deem the parade in *Hurley* an expressive association, the analysis we applied there is similar to the analysis we apply here. We have already concluded that a state requirement that the Boy Scouts retain Dale as an assistant scoutmaster would significantly burden the organization's right to oppose or disfavor homosexual conduct. The state interests embodied in New Jersey's public accommodations law do not justify such a severe intrusion on the Boy Scouts' rights to freedom of expressive association. That being the case, we hold that the First Amendment prohibits the State from imposing such a requirement through the application of its public accommodations law.

Justice Stevens' dissent makes much of its observation that the public perception of homosexuality in this country has changed. Indeed, it appears that homosexuality has gained greater societal acceptance. But this is scarcely an argument for denying First Amendment protection to those who refuse to accept these views. The First Amendment protects expression, be it of the popular variety or not. . . .

. . . We are not, as we must not be, guided by our views of whether the Boy Scouts' teachings with respect to homosexual conduct are right or wrong; public or judicial disapproval of a tenet of an organization's expression does not justify the State's effort to compel the organization to accept members where such acceptance would derogate from the organization's expressive message. "While the law is free to promote all sorts of conduct in place of harmful behavior, it is not free to interfere with speech for no better reason than promoting an approved message or discouraging a disfavored one, however enlightened either purpose may strike the government." *Hurley*. . . .

Justice STEVENS, with whom Justice SOUTER, Justice GINSBURG, and Justice BREYER join, dissenting. . . .

The majority holds that New Jersey's law violates BSA's right to associate and its right to free speech. But that law does not "impose any serious burdens" on BSA's "collective effort on behalf of [its] shared goals," Roberts v. United States Jaycees, nor does it force BSA to communicate any message that it does not wish to endorse. New Jersey's law, therefore, abridges no constitutional right of the Boy Scouts.

I . . .

In this case, Boy Scouts of America [BSA] contends that it teaches the young boys who are Scouts that homosexuality is immoral. Consequently, it argues, it would violate its right to associate to force it to admit homosexuals as members, as doing so would be at odds with its own shared goals and values. This contention, quite plainly, requires us to look at what, exactly, are the values that BSA actually teaches.

[The dissent then parses the BSA's mission statement, stressing that BSA describes itself as having a "representative membership," which it defines as "boy membership [that] reflects proportionately the characteristics of the boy population of its service area." It notes that the Boy Scout Handbook and Scoutmaster's Handbooks do not define "morally straight" or "clean" by any reference to homosexual conduct. "It is plain as the light of day that neither one of these principles — "morally straight" and "clean" — says the slightest thing about homosexuality. Indeed, neither term in the Boy Scouts' Law and Oath expresses any position whatsoever on sexual matters."]

II

The Court seeks to fill the void by pointing to a statement of "policies and procedures relating to homosexuality and Scouting" signed by BSA's President and Chief Scout Executive in 1978 and addressed to the members of the Executive Committee of the national organization. The letter says that the BSA does "not believe that homosexuality and leadership in Scouting are appropriate." But when the entire 1978 letter is read, BSA's position is far more equivocal . . . :

Four aspects of the 1978 policy statement are relevant to the proper disposition of this case. First, at most this letter simply adopts an exclusionary membership policy.

But simply adopting such a policy has never been considered sufficient, by itself, to prevail on a right to associate claim.

Second, the 1978 policy was never publicly expressed — unlike, for example, the Scout's duty to be "obedient." It was an internal memorandum, never circulated beyond the few members of BSA's Executive Committee. It remained, in effect, a secret Boy Scouts policy. Far from claiming any intent to express an idea that would be burdened by the presence of homosexuals, BSA's public posture — to the world and to the Scouts themselves — remained what it had always been: one of tolerance, welcoming all classes of boys and young men. In this respect, BSA's claim is even weaker than those we have rejected in the past.

Third, it is apparent that the draftsmen of the policy statement foresaw the possibility that laws against discrimination might one day be amended to protect homosexuals from employment discrimination. Their statement clearly provided that, in the event such a law conflicted with their policy, a Scout's duty to be "obedient" and "obey the laws," even if "he thinks [the laws] are unfair" would prevail in such a contingency. . . . The statement does not address the question whether the publicly proclaimed duty to obey the law should prevail over the private discriminatory policy if, and when, a conflict between two should arise — as it now has in New Jersey. At the very least, then, the statement reflects no unequivocal view on homosexuality. . . .

Fourth, the 1978 statement simply says that homosexuality is not "appropriate." It makes no effort to connect that statement to a shared goal or expressive activity of the Boy Scouts. Whatever values BSA seeks to instill in Scouts, the idea that homosexuality is not "appropriate" appears entirely unconnected to, and is mentioned nowhere in, the myriad of publicly declared values and creeds of the BSA. That idea does not appear to be among any of the principles actually taught to Scouts. Rather, the 1978 policy appears to be no more than a private statement of a few BSA executives that the organization wishes to exclude gays — and that wish has nothing to do with any expression BSA actually engages in. . . .

### III

BSA's claim finds no support in our cases. We have recognized "a right to associate for the purpose of engaging in those activities protected by the First Amendment — speech, assembly, petition for the redress of grievances, and the exercise of religion." *Roberts*. And we have acknowledged that "when the State interferes with individuals' selection of those with whom they wish to join in a common endeavor, freedom of association . . . may be implicated." But "the right to associate for expressive purposes is not . . . absolute"; rather, "the nature and degree of constitutional protection afforded freedom of association may vary depending on the extent to which . . . the constitutionally protected liberty is at stake in a given case." Indeed, the right to associate does not mean "that in every setting in which individuals exercise some discrimination in choosing associates, their selective process of inclusion and exclusion is protected by the Constitution." New York State Club Assn., Inc. v. City of New York, 487 U.S. 1, 13 (1988). For example, we have routinely and easily rejected assertions of this right by expressive organizations with discriminatory membership policies, such as private schools,[10] law firms,[11] and labor organizations.[12] In fact, until today, we have never

---

10. Runyon v. McCrary, 427 U.S. 160, 175-176 (1979).
11. Hishon v. King & Spaulding, 467 U.S. 69, 78 (1984).
12. Railway Mail Ass'n v. Corsi, 324 U.S. 88, 93-94 (1945).

once found a claimed right to associate in the selection of members to prevail in the face of a State's antidiscrimination law. To the contrary, we have squarely held that a State's antidiscrimination law does not violate a group's right to associate simply because the law conflicts with that group's exclusionary membership policy.

In Roberts v. United States Jaycees, we addressed just such a conflict. The Jaycees was a nonprofit membership organization "'designed to inculcate in the individual membership . . . a spirit of genuine Americanism and civic interest, and . . . to provide . . . an avenue for intelligent participation by young men in the affairs of their community.'" The organization was divided into local chapters, described as "'young men's organizations,'" in which regular membership was restricted to males between the ages of 18 and 35. But Minnesota's Human Rights Act, which applied to the Jaycees, made it unlawful to "'deny any person the full and equal enjoyment of . . . a place of public accommodation because of . . . sex.'" The Jaycees, however, claimed that applying the law to it violated its right to associate — in particular its right to maintain its selective membership policy.

We rejected that claim. Cautioning that the right to associate is not "absolute," we held that "infringements on that right may be justified by regulations adopted to serve compelling state interests, unrelated to the suppression of ideas, that cannot be achieved through means significantly less restrictive of associational freedoms." We found the State's purpose of eliminating discrimination is a compelling state interest that is unrelated to the suppression of ideas. We also held that Minnesota's law is the least restrictive means of achieving that interest. The Jaycees had "failed to demonstrate that the Act imposes any serious burdens on the male members' freedom of expressive association." Though the Jaycees had "taken public positions on a number of diverse issues, [and] . . . regularly engage in a variety of . . . activities worthy of constitutional protection under the First Amendment," there was "no basis in the record for concluding that admission of women as full voting members will impede the organization's ability to engage in these protected activities or to disseminate its preferred views." "The Act," we held, "requires no change in the Jaycees' creed of promoting the interest of young men, and it imposes no restrictions on the organization's ability to exclude individuals with ideologies or philosophies different from those of its existing members."

We took a similar approach in Board of Directors of Rotary Int'l v. Rotary Club of Duarte. . . .[13]

Several principles are made perfectly clear by Jaycees and Rotary Club. First, to prevail on a claim of expressive association in the face of a State's antidiscrimination law, it is not enough simply to engage in some kind of expressive activity. Both the Jaycees and the Rotary Club engaged in expressive activity protected by the First Amendment, yet that fact was not dispositive. Second, it is not enough to adopt an openly avowed exclusionary membership policy. Both the Jaycees and the Rotary Club did that as well. Third, it is not sufficient merely to articulate some connection

13. BSA urged on brief that under the New Jersey Supreme Court's reading of the State's antidiscrimination law, "Boy Scout Troops would be forced to admit girls as members" and "Girl Scout Troops would be forced to admit boys." The New Jersey Supreme Court had no occasion to address that question, and no such issue is tendered for our decision. I note, however, the State of New Jersey's observation that BSA ignores the exemption contained in New Jersey's law for "any place of public accommodation which is in its nature reasonably restricted exclusively to one sex," including, but not limited to, "any summer camp, day camp, or resort camp, bathhouse, dressing room, swimming pool, gymnasium, comfort station, dispensary, clinic or hospital, or school or educational institution which is restricted exclusively to individuals of one sex."

between the group's expressive activities and its exclusionary policy. The Rotary Club, for example, justified its male-only membership policy by pointing to the "'aspect of fellowship . . . that is enjoyed by the [exclusively] male membership'" and by claiming that only with an exclusively male membership could it "operate effectively" in foreign countries. *Rotary Club.*

Rather, in *Jaycees,* we asked whether Minnesota's Human Rights Law requiring the admission of women "imposed any *serious burdens*" on the group's "collective effort on behalf of [its] *shared goals.*" (emphases added). Notwithstanding the group's obviously publicly stated exclusionary policy, we did not view the inclusion of women as a "serious burden" on the Jaycees' ability to engage in the protected speech of its choice. Similarly, in *Rotary Club,* we asked whether California's law would "affect in any *significant way* the existing members' ability" to engage in their protected speech, or whether the law would require the clubs "to abandon their *basic goals.*" (emphases added); see also Hurley v. Irish-American Gay, Lesbian and Bisexual Group of Boston, Inc., 515 U.S. 557, 581 (1995); New York State Club Assn. (to prevail on a right to associate claim, the group must "be able to show that it is organized for specific expressive purposes and that it will not be able to advocate its desired viewpoints nearly as effectively if it cannot confine its membership to those who share the same sex, for example, or the same religion"); NAACP v. Alabama ex rel. Patterson, 357 U.S. 449, 462-63 (1958) (asking whether law "entailed the likelihood of a substantial restraint upon the exercise by petitioner's members of their right to freedom of association" and whether law is "likely to affect adversely the ability of petitioner and its members to pursue their collective effort to foster beliefs"). The relevant question is whether the mere inclusion of the person at issue would "impose any serious burden," "affect in any significant way," or be "a substantial restraint upon" the organization's "shared goals," "basic goals," or "collective effort to foster beliefs." Accordingly, it is necessary to examine what, exactly, are BSA's shared goals and the degree to which its expressive activities would be burdened, affected, or restrained by including homosexuals.

The evidence before this Court makes it exceptionally clear that BSA has, at most, simply adopted an exclusionary membership policy and has no shared goal of disapproving of homosexuality. BSA's mission statement and federal charter say nothing on the matter; its official membership policy is silent; its Scout Oath and Law — and accompanying definitions — are devoid of any view on the topic. . . .

## IV

The majority pretermits this entire analysis. It finds that BSA in fact "'teaches that homosexual conduct is not morally straight.'" This conclusion, remarkably, rests entirely on statements in BSA's briefs. Moreover, the majority insists that we must "give deference to an association's assertions regarding the nature of its expression" and "we must also give deference to an association's view of what would impair its expression." So long as the record "contains written evidence" to support a group's bare assertion, "we need not inquire further." Once the organization "asserts" that it engages in particular expression, "we cannot doubt" the truth of that assertion.

This is an astounding view of the law. I am unaware of any previous instance in which our analysis of the scope of a constitutional right was determined by looking at what a litigant asserts in his or her brief and inquiring no further. . . .

Surely there are instances in which an organization that truly aims to foster a belief at odds with the purposes of a State's antidiscrimination laws will have a First Amendment right to association that precludes forced compliance with those laws. But that right is not a freedom to discriminate at will, nor is it a right to maintain an exclusionary membership policy simply out of fear of what the public reaction would be if the group's membership were opened up. It is an implicit right designed to protect the enumerated rights of the First Amendment, not a license to act on any discriminatory impulse. To prevail in asserting a right of expressive association as a defense to a charge of violating an antidiscrimination law, the organization must at least show it has adopted and advocated an unequivocal position inconsistent with a position advocated or epitomized by the person whom the organization seeks to exclude. If this Court were to defer to whatever position an organization is prepared to assert in its briefs, there would be no way to mark the proper boundary between genuine exercises of the right to associate, on the one hand, and sham claims that are simply attempts to insulate nonexpressive private discrimination, on the other hand. . . .

## V

Even if BSA's right to associate argument fails, it nonetheless might have a First Amendment right to refrain from including debate and dialogue about homosexuality as part of its mission to instill values in Scouts. It can, for example, advise Scouts who are entering adulthood and have questions about sex to talk "with your parents, religious leaders, teachers, or Scoutmaster," and, in turn, it can direct Scoutmasters who are asked such questions "not undertake to instruct Scouts, in any formalized manner, in the subject of sex and family life" because "it is not construed to be Scouting's proper area." Dale's right to advocate certain beliefs in a public forum or in a private debate does not include a right to advocate these ideas when he is working as a Scoutmaster. And BSA cannot be compelled to include a message about homosexuality among the values it actually chooses to teach its Scouts, if it would prefer to remain silent on that subject. . . .

In its briefs, BSA implies, even if it does not directly argue, that Dale would use his Scoutmaster position as a "bully pulpit" to convey immoral messages to his troop, and therefore his inclusion in the group would compel BSA to include a message it does not want to impart. Even though the majority does not endorse that argument, I think it is important to explain why it lacks merit, before considering the argument the majority does accept.

BSA has not contended, nor does the record support, that Dale had ever advocated a view on homosexuality to his troop before his membership was revoked. Accordingly, BSA's revocation could only have been based on an assumption that he would do so in the future. But the only information BSA had at the time it revoked Dale's membership was a newspaper article describing a seminar at Rutgers University on the topic of homosexual teenagers that Dale attended. . . .

Nothing in that article, however, even remotely suggests that Dale would advocate any views on homosexuality to his troop. . . .

To be sure, the article did say that Dale was co-president of the Lesbian/Gay Alliance at Rutgers University, and that group presumably engages in advocacy regarding homosexual issues. But surely many members of BSA engage in expressive activities outside of their troop, and surely BSA does not want all of that expression to be carried on inside the troop. . . .

The majority, though, does not rest its conclusion on the claim that Dale will use his position as a bully pulpit. Rather, it contends that Dale's mere presence among the Boy Scouts will itself force the group to convey a message about homosexuality — even if Dale has no intention of doing so. The majority holds that "the presence of an avowed homosexual and gay rights activist in an assistant scoutmaster's uniform sends a distinct . . . message," and, accordingly, BSA is entitled to exclude that message. In particular, "Dale's presence in the Boy Scouts would, at the very least, forces the organization to send a message, both to the youth members and the world, that the Boy Scouts accepts homosexual conduct as a legitimate form of behavior."

The majority's argument relies exclusively on Hurley v. Irish-American Gay, Lesbian and Bisexual Group of Boston, Inc. . . . [In *Hurley*, we] first pointed out that the St. Patrick's Day parade — like most every parade — is an inherently expressive undertaking. Next, we reaffirmed that the government may not compel anyone to proclaim a belief with which he or she disagrees. We then found that GLIB's marching in the parade would be an expressive act suggesting the view "that people of their sexual orientations have as much claim to unqualified social acceptance as heterosexuals." Finally, we held that GLIB's participation in the parade "would likely be perceived" as the parade organizers' own speech — or at least as a view which they approved — because of a parade organizer's customary control over who marches in the parade. Though *Hurley* has a superficial similarity to the present case, a close inspection reveals a wide gulf between that case and the one before us today.

First, it was critical to our analysis that GLIB was actually conveying a message by participating in the parade — otherwise, the parade organizers could hardly claim that they were being forced to include any unwanted message at all. Our conclusion that GLIB was conveying a message was inextricably tied to the fact that GLIB wanted to march in a parade, as well as the manner in which it intended to march. We noted the "inherent expressiveness of marching [in a parade] to make a point," and in particular that GLIB was formed for the purpose of making a particular point about gay pride. More specifically, GLIB "distributed a fact sheet describing the members' intentions" and, in a previous parade, had "marched behind a shamrock-strewn banner with the simple inscription 'Irish American Gay, Lesbian and Bisexual Group of Boston.'" "[A] contingent marching behind the organization's banner," we said, would clearly convey a message. Indeed, we expressly distinguished between the members of GLIB, who marched as a unit to express their views about their own sexual orientation, on the one hand, and homosexuals who might participate as individuals in the parade without intending to express anything about their sexuality by doing so.

Second, we found it relevant that GLIB's message "would likely be perceived" as the parade organizers' own speech. That was so because "parades and demonstrations . . . are not understood to be so neutrally presented or selectively viewed" as, say, a broadcast by a cable operator, who is usually considered to be "merely 'a conduit' for the speech" produced by others. Rather, parade organizers are usually understood to make the "customary determination about a unit admitted to the parade."

Dale's inclusion in the Boy Scouts is nothing like the case in *Hurley*. His participation sends no cognizable message to the Scouts or to the world. Unlike GLIB, Dale did not carry a banner or a sign; he did not distribute any fact sheet; and he expressed no intent to send any message. If there is any kind of message being sent, then, it is by the mere act of joining the Boy Scouts. Such an act does not constitute an instance of symbolic speech under the First Amendment. . . .

The only apparent explanation for the majority's holding, then, is that homosexuals are simply so different from the rest of society that their presence alone — unlike any other individual's — should be singled out for special First Amendment treatment. Under the majority's reasoning, an openly gay male is irreversibly affixed with the label "homosexual." That label, even though unseen, communicates a message that permits his exclusion wherever he goes. His openness is the sole and sufficient justification for his ostracism. Though unintended, reliance on such a justification is tantamount to a constitutionally prescribed symbol of inferiority. As counsel for the Boy Scouts remarked, Dale "put a banner around his neck when he . . . got himself into the newspaper. . . . He created a reputation. . . . He can't take that banner off. He put it on himself and, indeed, he has continued to put it on himself." . . .

Furthermore, it is not likely that BSA would be understood to send any message, either to Scouts or to the world, simply by admitting someone as a member. . . .

## VI

Unfavorable opinions about homosexuals "have ancient roots." Bowers v. Hardwick, 478 U.S. 186, 192 (1986). Like equally atavistic opinions about certain racial groups, those roots have been nourished by sectarian doctrine. (Burger, C. J., concurring); Loving v. Virginia, 388 U.S. 1, 3 (1967). See also Mathews v. Lucas, 427 U.S. 495, 520 (1976) (Stevens, J., dissenting) ("Habit, rather than analysis, makes it seem acceptable and natural to distinguish between male and female, alien and citizen, legitimate and illegitimate; for too much of our history there was the same inertia in distinguishing between black and white"). Over the years, however, interaction with real people, rather than mere adherence to traditional ways of thinking about members of unfamiliar classes, have modified those opinions. A few examples: The American Psychiatric Association's and the American Psychological Association's removal of "homosexuality" from their lists of mental disorders; a move toward greater understanding within some religious communities; Justice Blackmun's classic opinion in Bowers; Georgia's invalidation of the statute upheld in Bowers; and New Jersey's enactment of the provision at issue in this case. . . .

That such prejudices are still prevalent and that they have caused serious and tangible harm to countless members of the class New Jersey seeks to protect are established matters of fact that neither the Boy Scouts nor the Court disputes. That harm can only be aggravated by the creation of a constitutional shield for a policy that is itself the product of a habitual way of thinking about strangers. As Justice Brandeis so wisely advised, "we must be ever on our guard, lest we erect our prejudices into legal principles."

If we would guide by the light of reason, we must let our minds be bold. I respectfully dissent.

Justice SOUTER, with whom Justice GINSBURG and Justice BREYER join, dissenting.

I join Justice Stevens's dissent but add this further word on the significance of Part VI of his opinion. There, Justice Stevens describes the changing attitudes toward gay people and notes a parallel with the decline of stereotypical thinking about race and gender. The legitimacy of New Jersey's interest in forbidding discrimination on all these bases by those furnishing public accommodations is, as Justice Stevens indicates, acknowledged by many to be beyond question. The fact that we are cognizant of this laudable decline in stereotypical thinking on homosexuality should not, however, be taken to control the resolution of this case.

. . . The right of expressive association does not, of course, turn on the popularity of the views advanced by a group that claims protection. Whether the group appears to this Court to be in the vanguard or rearguard of social thinking is irrelevant to the group's rights. I conclude that BSA has not made out an expressive association claim, therefore, not because of what BSA may espouse, but because of its failure to make sexual orientation the subject of any unequivocal advocacy, using the channels it customarily employs to state its message. . . .

If, on the other hand, an expressive association claim has met the conditions Justice Stevens describes as necessary, there may well be circumstances in which the antidiscrimination law must yield, as he says. It is certainly possible for an individual to become so identified with a position as to epitomize it publicly. When that position is at odds with a group's advocated position, applying an antidiscrimination statute to require the group's acceptance of the individual in a position of group leadership could so modify or muddle or frustrate the group's advocacy as to violate the expressive associational right. While it is not our business here to rule on any such hypothetical, it is at least clear that our estimate of the progressive character of the group's position will be irrelevant to the First Amendment analysis if such a case comes to us for decision.

*NOTES*

1. Although *Dale* involved a state law relating to sexual orientation discrimination in public accommodations, it is a constitutional decision that seems applicable to federal employment discrimination statutes like Title VII. Its meaning, therefore, could be critical for the efficacy of antidiscrimination laws, depending on how broadly it is construed. For the development of this expressive association right, see Daniel A. Farber, Speaking in the First Person Plural: Expressive Associations and the First Amendment, 85 Minn. L. Rev. 1483 (2001).

2. The obvious first question is to whom the right of "expressive association" applies? Is a for-profit corporation by definition an entity that has no right of expressive association? Corporations clearly have First Amendment rights, First Natl. Bank of Boston v. Bellotti, 435 U.S. 765 (1978), but perhaps the right of expressive association is narrower than the right of free speech. The Court indicates that the right "is not reserved for advocacy groups. But to come within its ambit, a group must engage in some form of expression, whether it be public or private." Doesn't every corporation engage in "some form of expression"? Professor Richard A. Epstein, The Constitutional Perils of Moderation: The Case of the Boy Scouts, 74 S. Cal. L. Rev. 119 (2000), takes the polar position that all private associations that are not monopolists should have the same expressive association rights as the Boy Scouts even though that "calls for the constitutional invalidation of much of the Civil Rights Act, including Title VII insofar as it relates to employment." Id. at 139.

3. Professor Evelyn Brody's article, Entrance, Voice, and Exit: The Constitutional Bounds of the Right of Association, 35 U.C. Davis L. Rev. 821, 823 (2002), delves deeper in the organizational structure of nonprofits and poses a series of questions:

> [T]he typical American nonprofit organization is a corporation that lacks both shareholders and members, so are there any "associates" whose rights are entitled to protection, or is the corporation's freedom of speech all that constitutionally matters? [R]egardless of whether an organization comprises members, not all private entities operate "democratically"; does the law care? Finally, even if voice is democratic, how do we protect dissenters if exit is not voluntary?

4. Professor Dale Carpenter, Expressive Association and Anti-Discrimination Law After *Dale*: A Tripartite Approach, 85 Minn. L. Rev. 1515 (2001), traces the

importance of expressive association rights for the development and protection of the gay community. He criticizes the dissent for focusing on the message of the association as being content-based discrimination. Primarily based on Justice O'Connor's concurrence in *Roberts*, Professor Carpenter develops a tripartite distinction among expressive associations — expressive associations, quasi-expressive associations, and commercial associations. Quasi-expressive associations are those that are expressive in very important respects but which also enter the marketplace of commerce to a substantial degree. Because Dale was a scout leader, the Boy Scouts would be justified in excluding him as a homosexual whether it was an expressive or a quasi-expressive association. If, however, the person excluded was an employee or a scout, then the distinction between expressive and quasi-expressive would be determinative. The argument that the Boy Scouts was a quasi-expressive association is that it has entered the marketplace with extensive marketing of Boy Scout equipment and uniforms, even to the extent of owning and operating retail stores. See also Adrianne K. Zahner, Note: A Comprehensive Approach to Conflicts Between Antidiscrimination Laws and Freedom of Expressive Association After *Boy Scouts of America v. Dale*, 77 Chi.-Kent L. Rev. 373 (2001). In Chicago Area Council of Boy Scouts of America v. City of Chicago Commn. on Human Relations, 748 N.E.2d 759 (Ill. App. Ct. 2001), the court remanded to the Commission the question whether the claimant was seeking a non-expressive position with the Boy Scouts. In Boy Scouts of America v. Till, 136 F. Supp. 2d 1295 (S.D. Fla. 2001), the court held that a school board had created a limited public forum by allowing different groups to use school facilities after school hours. Because of that, it could not bar the Boy Scouts from using the facilities based on either the school board policy or a contract provision in its lease prohibiting discrimination by those using the facilities because of sexual orientation.

5. Some private business owners want to organize their businesses along religious lines because they view their religious beliefs and practices as key to their otherwise secular businesses, see infra page 605. Does *Dale* now give them a constitutional right to hire only members of the owners' religion? See Steven G. Gey, The No Religion Zone: Constitutional Limitations on Religious Association in the Public Sphere, 85 Minn. L. Rev. 1885 (2001).

6. The Court in *Dale* writes that the "forced inclusion of an unwanted person" infringes on a group's expressive association "if the presence of that person affects in a significant way the group's ability to advocate public or private viewpoints." Were you satisfied that the Boy Scouts' ability to advocate its views would be significantly affected by the admission of Dale? Or is the point that having to admit Dale would require having to admit other homosexuals (or homosexual activists), and that would significantly affect the Scouts' expressive goals? Lacking any evidence that, as a scoutmaster, Dale said anything to anybody about sexuality, much less sexual orientation, does this decision simply boil down to upholding discrimination based on his status as a homosexual? To put it another way, does *Dale* preclude a state from proscribing individual disparate treatment discrimination on the basis of sexual orientation? Does it really matter whether the employer actually had taken an expressive position opposed to homosexuality?

7. The New Jersey Supreme Court had held that there was a compelling state interest in eliminating discrimination; presumably, this would justify an infringement on First Amendment rights, so long as the infringement were narrowly tailored to further the intrusion. The *Dale* Court speaks of compelling state interests as overriding First Amendment concerns, but never directly addresses the New Jersey court's holding that the public accommodation statute was justified by a compelling state interest. Why?

8. Is a possible answer to the previous question the Court's emphasis on the sweep of the state's public accommodation law as not being limited to "places"? But surely that is a characteristic of modern antidiscrimination statutes. Certainly, Title VII and the ADA sweep very broadly.

9. Or was the problem that the state law protects against sexual orientation discrimination? Would the Court have so easily struck down the same law to the extent that it prevented an association from discriminating against African Americans? Are *Roberts* and *Duarte* still good law regarding membership rules against women? If those cases are still good law, is the majority in *Dale* differentiating the extent of protection afforded freedom of association based on whether the issue is sex or sexual orientation discrimination? Before *Dale*, the distinction between *Roberts* and *Duarte* on one hand and *Hurley* on the other was that the gay activist marchers in *Hurley* were advocating gay and lesbian rights by their very act of marching in the parade. Can the organizers of the St. Patrick's Day parade now exclude from the march anyone they consider to be a homosexual, even if the person is simply marching in the parade, advocating whatever all the other marchers are advocating?

10. Rules of general application can often be applied to the press without violating the First Amendment. For example, a newspaper could be subjected to the same tax as other business organizations. Any adverse effects on its reporting would be merely incidental. Similarly, free exercise is not implicated by rules of general application, even if the effects on religious organizations can be extreme. Employment Div. v. Smith, 494 U.S. 890 (1990). Under such an analysis, *Dale* would be wrongly decided. Why isn't that principle applied to the right of expressive association? Is that right stronger than the rights of free press and free exercise, which are expressly found in the First Amendment? See Laurence H. Tribe, Disentangling Symmetries: Speech, Association, Parenthood, 28 Pepp. L. Rev. 641 (2001).

11. Professor Jed Rubenfeld, The Anti-Antidiscrimination Agenda, 111 Yale L.J. 1141 (2002), takes a global view of recent Supreme Court decisions reflecting the new federalism and Eleventh Amendment restrictions on congressional authority. *Dale*, which prohibits the states from proscribing discrimination on the basis of sexual orientation, is problematic in this context. Rubenfeld posits that the only intellectually honest way to read these cases as a whole is to see them as carrying out an anti-antidiscrimination agenda by five members of the Court. *Dale* reveals "all three critical elements [demonstrating the anti-antidiscrimination agenda]: (1) the sudden embrace of unwritten constitutional law, in stark contrast to the insistent textualism of the 'federalism' cases; (2) the declaration of a judicial duty to balance interests and to decide how needful the challenged law is, which is in stark contrast to the 'federalism' cases' categorical logic, that purports to eschew such considerations; and, above all, (3) the fortuitous conclusion that states cannot pass precisely the kind of measure that, according to the 'federalism' cases lies at the heart of the state legislative prerogative." Id. at 1156.

12. Pi Lambda Phi Fraternity, Inc. v. University of Pittsburgh, 229 F.3d 435 (3d Cir. 2000), held that a local chapter of a fraternity, suspended by the University because several fraternity members were arrested after drugs were found in the fraternity house, did not possess rights of protected intimate association. In Central Texas Nudists v. County of Travis, No. 03-00-00024-CV, 2000 Tex. App. LEXIS 8136 (Tex. App. 2000), *cert. denied*, 534. U.S. 952 (2001), the court held that a naturist association and its members did not have a right to expressive association, based on nudism, in order to challenge a rule that access to a clothing-optional public park be limited to those over age 18. Are these cases rightly decided?

13. Professor Andrew Koppelman, Signs of the Times: Dale v. Boy Scouts of America and the Changing Meaning of Nondiscrimination, 23 Cardozo L. Rev. 1819, 1819-20 (2002), writes:

> All antidiscrimination laws are unconstitutional in all their applications. Citizens are allowed to disobey laws whenever obedience would be perceived as endorsing some message. Both of these propositions are absurd. However, [Dale] stands for at least one of them, and perhaps both. The already voluminous commentary on Dale is too polite, because almost all of it fails to notice the sheer lunacy of what the Court said. The Court's disastrous opinion offers a useful cautionary lesson in First Amendment jurisprudence: determinations of what is protected speech cannot defer either to individual speakers or to the culture as a whole, because such deference produces bizarre results.

14. Taking a different tack, Madhavi Sunder, in Cultural Dissent, 54 Stan. L. Rev. 495 (2001), writes:

> Gay Scoutmasters contest what it means to be a "Boy Scout." Female Pueblo Indians denounce tribal rules as sexist. Muslim women reinterpret the Koran and emphasize women's right to religion and equality. In the twenty-first century, exposure to modernity and globalization has created a society that now more than ever is characterized by cultural dissent: challenges by individuals within a culture to modernize, or broaden, the traditional terms of cultural membership. Cultural dissent symbolizes a movement away from imposed cultural identities to a new age of autonomy, choice, and reason within culture. But current law, stuck in a nineteenth-century view of culture as imposed, distinct, and homogeneous, elides cultural dissent. Under current law, cultural dissenters have either a right to culture (with no right to contest cultural meaning) or a right to equality (with no right to cultural membership), but not to both.

Id. Professor Sunder criticizes Dale for, in the name of preserving cultural distinctiveness, applying freedom of association law to authorize "the exclusion of those whose speech challenges cultural norms." Id. He argues that "[l]aw's conception of culture matters. As cultures become more internally diverse and members appeal to courts to determine a culture's meaning, increasingly, it will be law, not culture, that regulates cultural borders." He argues instead for a "cultural dissent" approach to cultural conflict which would "prevent law from becoming complicit in the backlash project of suppressing internal cultural reform." Id. at 496.

## 5. Equal Pay for Equal Work

The problem of achieving wage equity for women in the workplace has presented unique challenges for employment discrimination law. The Equal Pay Act (EPA), 29 U.S.C.S. § 206(d) (2003), which is specifically directed at discrimination against women with respect to wages, takes an equal treatment approach, but with a different twist: in determining whether individuals are similarly situated, an EPA case begins by focusing on the equality of the work performed, rather than on the similarity of the workers. Because the structure of an EPA case is different from that of a Title VII case, which also reaches wage discrimination, Congress sought to harmonize the two statutes by directing, in § 703(h) of Title VII, that wage differentials "authorized by the Equal Pay Act" do not violate Title VII. The confusing case law resulting from this provision highlights the differences and similarities between the two approaches to discrimination. The problem of reconciling the two statutes has been further exacerbated by the persistence of gender segregation in the workforce, which has presented the law with a problem that neither statute is designed to reach.

As we discussed in Chapter 2, any legislation intended to guarantee workers' rights may theoretically impair economic efficiency. The conflict between fairness and efficiency is no more graphically represented than in the context of wage regulation. When the government undertakes to regulate wages, the potential for possibly upsetting the "natural" balance of a market-driven economy is obvious. On the other hand, what could be more unfair than arbitrarily paying equally qualified or equally productive workers different amounts? In this section, we briefly explore the legal approaches to achieving wage equity for female workers.

### a.  The Basic Statutory Prohibition of the Equal Pay Act

The Equal Pay Act predates Title VII and continues to play a role in attacks on gender-based wage discrimination for at least two reasons. First, the absence of Title VII's administrative requirements and the availability of "liquidated damages" sometimes makes the EPA the preferred statutory remedy. Second, Title VII contains a provision that attempts to harmonize the substantive law under the two statutes. Consequently, the law generated under the EPA affects the development of Title VII principles.

While Title VII broadly proscribes sex discrimination, the EPA is much narrower and more technical in its prohibitions. The basic prohibition, 29 U.S.C.S. § 206(d)(1) (2003), states:

> No employer having employees subject to any provisions of this section shall discriminate, within any establishment in which such employees are employed, between employees on the basis of sex by paying wages to employees in such establishment at a rate less than the rate at which he pays wages to employees of the opposite sex in such establishment for equal work on jobs the performance of which requires equal skill, effort, and responsibility, and which are performed under similar working conditions, except where such payment is made pursuant to (i) a seniority system; (ii) a merit system; (iii) a system which measures earnings by quantity or quality of production; or (iv) a differential based on any other factor other than sex.

The EPA is deceptive in its brevity. Almost all of its operative words have become terms of art, requiring considerable explication.

It is possible to identify in the basic prohibition of the Equal Pay Act four requirements for making out a prima facie case. A plaintiff must prove that two workers of opposite sex (1) in the same "establishment" are (2) receiving unequal pay (3) "on the basis of sex" (4) for work that is "equal." Once a prima facie case is made out, however, several defenses are available.

*The "Establishment" Requirement.*  The word "establishment" might suggest that different pay in different work sites cannot violate the Act. However, the few Equal Pay Act decisions that have addressed the establishment concept hold that the mere existence of physically separate operations is not necessarily fatal to EPA application. Brennan v. Goose Creek Consol. Ind. Sch. Dist., 519 F.2d 53 (5th Cir. 1975). Relevant considerations include:

> the degree of central authority for employment relations, the movement between locations by the employees, and whether duties and working conditions are similar. Where

there is central control of hiring, salary, and records, as well as employee movement between physical locations, there is a greater chance that a multi-location employer will be considered to operate a single "establishment."

D'Alema v. Appalachian Communities, 55 FEP (BNA) 1426, 1428 (N.D. Ga. 1991); see 29 C.F.R. § 1620.9(b).

*Unequal Pay.* While comparing base pay would seem straightforward, problems arise. For example, can inflation be taken into account in deciding whether pay is unequal? Consider a female employed at $15,000 a year beginning on March 5, 2003, who succeeded a male employee in the same job who was paid $15,000 on March 5, 2002. Can she claim that her pay is less in "real dollars"?

Fringe benefits can create complicated questions of unequal pay. The EEOC defines "wages" to include all payments made "as a remuneration for employment," including vacation and holiday pay and premium pay overtime work. 29 C.F.R. § 1620.10.

Another issue arises because the EPA bars discrimination not in pay, but in "rate" of pay. Thus, in Bence v. Detroit Health Corp., 712 F.2d 1024 (6th Cir. 1983), a chain of health spas operated men's spas and women's spas in the same establishment on alternate days of the week. The chain violated the EPA by paying 5 percent sales commissions to women selling memberships on women's days and 7.5 percent sales commissions to men selling memberships to men on men's days. Id. at 1026. The defendant argued that, because there were more potential female customers than male customers, "a male manager and a female manager, sitting at the same desk in the same spa and expending the same amount of effort, under totally equal conditions" will earn the same total amount of money despite the different commission rate. Id. at 1026-27. The court rejected this argument because: "Evaluation of employer's compensation on a 'per sale' basis makes it apparent that it paid female managerial personnel at a lower rate than their male counterparts. This is precisely what the Equal Pay Act forbids." Id. at 1028.

*Equal Work.* The Equal Pay Act requires equal pay only for "equal work on jobs the performance of which requires equal skill, effort and responsibility, and which are performed under similar working conditions." The plaintiff must demonstrate the "equalness" of two jobs as part of the prima facie case. But jobs need not be identical in order to be "equal." The test is "substantial equality." Corning Glass Works v. Brennan, 417 U.S. 188 n.24 (1974). Nevertheless, jobs cannot be too different and still be equal. The Act itself defines the elements of job comparison — skill, effort, responsibility, and working conditions.

In approaching the question of equal work, the courts have had to ascertain the underlying facts of each case and then formulate legal rules to assess the significance of those facts. The process is complicated by what may be called the "individual" versus the "class" approach to equal work questions. In the individual approach, the courts compare the plaintiff's work with the work of one or more comparable male workers. In the class approach, the courts compare a predominately female job classification to a predominately male one. The individual approach has been used for professional jobs, such as that of college teachers, see, e.g., Hein v. Oregon College of Educ., 718 F.2d 910 (9th Cir. 1983), while the class approach has been utilized for blue-collar positions. See, e.g., Schultz v. Wheaton Glass Co., 421 F.2d 259 (3d Cir. 1970).

In either case, however, factual analysis is the first step — that is, identifying the elements of the jobs to be compared and determining what, if any, common core exists. This task poses few peculiar problems. The second step — deciding how much jobs can differ and still be equal — is far more complex. At one end of the spectrum is the rare case of two jobs that are factually identical. In such cases the jobs are necessarily equal. This situation, however, is primarily limited to cases in which a male and a female occupy the same job successively. At the other end of the spectrum, the jobs being compared will have no common elements. Although one could argue that factually distinct jobs are equal in some ultimate sense — say, with regard to value, skill, or effort — no court has adopted this view. Rather, the courts have held that "comparable work" is not within the EPA because comparing jobs on some abstract measure of value is not consistent with the legislative intent underlying the EPA.

Between these two poles, the hard cases remain — at what point does different work become equal enough? Obviously, there must be a substantial, perhaps predominate, core of tasks common to the jobs; past this requirement, the significance of the ways in which the jobs differ must be considered. Needless to say, the greater the common core is and the less significant the tasks peculiar to each job are, the more likely a court is to find equal work.

Courts have not hesitated to apply a de minimis test to minor job differences. For example, catheterizations performed infrequently by male orderlies, but not by female nurses' aides, do not constitute unequal work. See Brennan v. South Davis Community Hosp., 538 F.2d 859 (10th Cir. 1976). But the de minimis approach cannot be read too broadly because of the remaining variable — the quality of the disparate tasks. Thus two jobs, each composed of 95 percent common tasks, may constitute unequal work if the 5 percent differing tasks require greatly differing skills, effort, or responsibilities.

*On the Basis of Sex.*   Even wage differentials between employees of the opposite sex doing equal work do not violate the EPA unless the differentials are "on the basis of sex." The plaintiff presumably also has the burden of proving this element. It has been argued that this burden can be carried merely by demonstrating that a single person of the opposite sex receives unequal wages for equal work in the same establishment. See Corning Glass Works v. Brennan, 417 U.S. 188 (1974); EEOC v. White & Son Enters., 881 F.2d 1006 (11th Cir. 1989); Hennick v. Schwans Sales Enters., 168 F. Supp. 2d 938 (N.D. Iowa 2001).

But what if individual negotiation is the basis for salary determination, so that some females earn more than some male counterparts and some males earn as little as the lowest-paid females? Recognizing a prima facie case based on evidence that two opposite-sex employees perform equal work for unequal pay creates an anomaly, illustrated by the following table:

| Wage Level | Employee |
| --- | --- |
| $10,000 | Male 1  Female 1 |
| $ 9,000 | Male 2  Female 2 |

If all four employees perform equal work in the same establishment, Male 2 can make out a prima facie case by comparing his salary with that of Female 1, and Female 2 can make out a prima facie case by comparing her salary with that of Male 1.

Thus, we have two cases of apparent sex-based wage discrimination stemming from one compensation scheme — one anti-male and the other anti-female.

One solution is to accept the anomaly, relying on the fact that the employer can rebut by various methods we will consider shortly. Second, one could impose additional requirements, such as proof of either (a) subjective employer intent to discriminate or (b) a pattern of pay inequality disfavoring one sex. Even if such additional evidence of a sex basis is not *required* for a prima facie case, it clearly is permitted.

**Breaking an Equal Pay Act Prima Facie Case.**   A defendant may avoid liability through four statutory defenses. Equal pay is not required for equal work if the unequal wage payment "is made pursuant to (i) a seniority system; (ii) a merit system; (iii) a system which measures earnings by quantity or quality of production; or (iv) a differential based on any other factor other than sex." 29 U.S.C.S. § 206(d)(1) (2003). The defendant bears the burden of establishing any exception. Corning Glass Works v. Brennan, 417 U.S. 188, 190-91 (1974).

The EPA approach is different from proof of individual disparate treatment under Title VII. There, once the plaintiff establishes a prima facie case, the defendant has a burden of production, to identify a "legitimate, nondiscriminatory reason" for its action. Although such reasons can be equated with the four exceptions to the EPA, the EPA defendant bears the burden of persuasion, not production, to establish the exceptions.

The bulk of litigation relating to the defendant's rebuttal defense has focused on the catch-all "any other factor other than sex" defense. See, e.g., Stanley v. Univ. of S. Cal., 178 F.3d 1069 (9th Cir. 1999). In Los Angeles Dept. of Water & Power v. Manhart, 435 U.S. 702, 710 n.20 (1978), the Court made clear that a factor cannot be "other than sex" for EPA purposes if it would violate Title VII's disparate treatment test. Similarly, appellate courts have consistently rejected employer defenses that reveal a compensation scheme rooted in discriminatory intent.

"Factors" explaining sex-based differential in pay that may themselves be discriminatory include "market rate" in a market that values men more than women. See Brock (Donovan) v. Georgia Southwestern Coll., 765 F.2d 1026 (11th Cir. 1985). Factors that, under appropriate circumstances, can satisfy the employer's burden to show "any other factor other than sex" include shift differentials, job classification or rating systems, temporary reassignment, temporary or part-time employment, education, and experience. See EEOC Interpretive Rules, 29 C.F.R. § 1620.26(b).

State claims of Eleventh Amendment immunity under the Equal Pay Act have been rejected. The statute has been found to validly abrogate state immunity from suit. See Cherry v. Univ. of Wis. Sys. Bd. of Regents, 265 F.3d 541 (7th Cir. 2001); Hundertmark v. Florida Dept. of Transp., 205 F.3d 1272 (11th Cir. 2000).

### b.  Using Title VII to Attack Gender-Based Wage Discrimination

The Equal Pay Act's threshold requirement of "equal work" drastically narrows the situations to which it applies. It seems certain that gender-based wage discrimination is prevalent where the job differences preclude applying the EPA. Such situations range from cases of similar work (work that almost qualifies as substantially equal) to instances of pure "comparable work" (work that is totally different in terms of job tasks, but nevertheless comparable in terms of "skill," "effort," or "worth").

Because the EPA does not apply to unequal work cases, the only source of redress for wage discrimination in such a setting is Title VII. Invoking Title VII, however, raises two problems. First, does Title VII prohibit wage discrimination on the basis of sex? The statute's prohibition of sex discrimination in "compensation" clearly answers this question in the affirmative. Nonetheless, the second question is whether the Bennett Amendment excludes from Title VII all sex-based wage discrimination that is not prohibited by the EPA. The Bennett Amendment, found in § 703(h), 42 U.S.C.S. § 2000e-2(h) (2003), provides:

> It shall not be an unlawful employment practice under [Title VII] for any employer to differentiate upon the basis of sex in determining the amount of wages or compensation paid or to be paid to employees of such employer if such differentiation is authorized by the provisions of [the Equal Pay Act].

While it is clear that this provision legalizes, for Title VII purposes, wage discrimination permitted by the four exceptions to the EPA, a real controversy arose over whether the Bennett Amendment goes further — perhaps exempting from Title VII any sex-based wage discrimination not reached by the EPA. That view would, of course, render wage discrimination involving unequal work immune from attack under either statute.

The Supreme Court considered the scope of the Bennett Amendment in County of Washington v. Gunther, 452 U.S. 161 (1981), where the defendant paid lower wages to female guards in the female section of the county jail than to male guards in the male section. The trial court dismissed the EPA claims, finding the work not substantially equal. The court also found the claim excluded from Title VII coverage because it failed the equal work standard of the EPA. The Supreme Court reversed:

> The language of the Bennett Amendment suggests an intention to incorporate only the affirmative defenses of the Equal Pay Act into Title VII. The Amendment bars sex-based wage discrimination claims under Title VII where the pay differential is "authorized" by the Equal Pay Act. Although the word "authorized" sometimes means simply "to permit," it ordinarily denotes affirmative enabling action. Black's Law Dictionary, 122 (5th ed. 1979) defines "authorize" as "[t]o empower: to give a right or authority to act." The question, then is what wage practices have been affirmatively authorized by the Equal Pay Act.
>
> The Equal Pay Act is divided into two parts: a definition of the violation, followed by four affirmative defenses. The first part can hardly be said to "authorize" anything at all: it is purely prohibitory. The second part, however, in essence "authorizes" employers to differentiate in pay on the basis of seniority, merit, quantity or quality of production, or any other factor other than sex, even though such differentiation might otherwise violate the Act. It is to these provisions, therefore, that the Bennett Amendment must refer.

Id. at 168-69.

In the wake of *Gunther*, there are two major questions concerning wage discrimination claims under Title VII. First, when an employee uses Title VII to challenge discrimination between jobs that are "equal" within the meaning of the EPA, must the Title VII analysis track the EPA approach? For example, under the EPA, the employer bears the burden of establishing that wage discrepancies are not sex based and the EPA, unlike Title VII, may not proscribe neutral rules that have a disparate impact on the basis of sex. Second, what analysis should be used in Title VII cases not involving equal work?

The Ninth Circuit in Kouba v. Allstate Ins. Co., 691 F.2d 873 (9th Cir. 1982), applied EPA burdens to a Title VII wage discrimination suit, imposing the burden of persuasion on the employer to establish that using prior salaries to set minimum compensation is a "factor other than sex" within the meaning of the EPA. The circuits are split on whether to follow EPA burdens or a traditional Title VII approach in claims of sex-based salary discrimination. Compare Maxwell v. City of Tucson, 803 F.2d 444 (9th Cir. 1986) (defendant bears the burden of proving any other factor other than sex); Marcoux v. State of Me., 797 F.2d 1100 (1st Cir. 1986) (same); McKee v. Bi-State Dev. Agency, 801 F.2d 1014 (8th Cir. 1986) (same), with Fallon v. Illinois, 882 F.2d 1206 (7th Cir. 1989) (Title VII burdens applied); Peters v. City of Shreveport, 818 F.2d 1148 (5th Cir. 1987) (same).

A number of other issues arise in Title VII claims of sex-based wage discrimination. First, if employers have the burden of justifying wage disparities by establishing a "factor other than sex," what constitutes a "factor other than sex"? Second, should this term be defined under Title VII the same way it is defined under the EPA? Third, can a policy be a "factor other than sex" if it has a disparate impact on the basis of sex? Fourth, can a policy be a "factor other than sex" if it is not based on a business reason? Fifth, in cases that do not involve equal work, do the EPA burdens and defenses apply at all in Title VII litigation? Sixth, does the Bennett Amendment permit a claim that an employer's neutral rule has a disparate impact on the basis of sex? The courts have struggled with these questions without achieving a consensus.

### c. Narrowing the Gap Between Men's and Women's Earnings: Comparable Worth

The theory of "comparable worth," as the Supreme Court described it in *Gunther*, allows a plaintiff to "claim increased compensation on the basis of a comparison of the intrinsic worth or difficulty of their job with that of other jobs in the same organization or community." 452 U.S. at 166.

The theory of comparable worth is predicated on several propositions. First, women are concentrated in relatively few occupations. Second, women are underpaid relative to men. Third, the concentration of women in a few occupations (typically the lower-paid ones) accounts for a portion of the wage gap between women and men, who are spread over more diverse and typically higher-paid occupations. Fourth, a portion of the pay differential between women's and men's jobs is caused by discrimination, rather than by legitimate wage-setting factors, such as skill, education, training, experience, responsibility, working conditions, or the production value of the job.

The concentration of women in relatively few lower-paid occupations and the persistence of an "earnings gap" between women and men is well established. There is considerable controversy, however, about the reasons for the concentration and the "earnings gap." Opponents of comparable worth assert that the wage gap results from female preferences for certain working conditions and question whether there is any practical way to implement comparable worth in a market economy. Opponents also question whether job evaluation systems accurately value disparate jobs.

Comparable worth advocates have sought to implement comparable worth in a variety of ways. First, they have litigated, seeking equal pay for *substantially* equivalent work under the EPA, and equal pay for comparable work under Title VII. Second, they have lobbied for legislative relief. Third, they have sought to negotiate equal pay for comparable work.

Occupational segregation renders the EPA an ineffective tool for improving the economic status of women because there are relatively few cases of higher-paid males doing "equal work." Although "substantially equal" work may satisfy the equal work requirement, see Schultz v. Wheaton Glass Co., 421 F.2d 259 (3d Cir. 1970), the legislative history of the EPA indicates that Congress did not intend to require equal pay for comparable worth. Given this history, courts probably will not expand the "substantially equal" concept sufficiently to embrace a full-blown comparable worth approach. Awareness of the limitations inherent in the EPA has prompted comparable worth advocates to turn to Title VII with broader comparable worth claims.

What is the appropriate Title VII analysis in cases of alleged wage discrimination in which the work is not equal? Suppose Title VII bars wage discrimination between comparable jobs. What standards should be used to determine the comparability of jobs? Although the disparate treatment theory might resolve cases of "similar" (even if not equal) work by finding an intent to discriminate, the more common problem may be undervaluing whole classes of jobs that are predominately held by women. Or, put simply, does Title VII require a secretary to be paid the same as a custodian? The Supreme Court answered the basic question of Title VII's reach in Gunther, but has offered little help in resolving the more general question of comparable worth.

The clear thrust of Gunther is that a plaintiff may prevail in such cases as long as she can prove that her compensation results from discrimination. The most obvious way to do so is to establish disparate treatment either by formal discriminatory policies of the employer or by "direct" evidence of discriminatory intent — that is, admissions by agents of the defendant. Examples of compensation policies that are formally discriminatory are found in Los Angeles Dept. of Water & Power v. Manhart (reproduced at page 200) and Arizona Governing Comm. v. Norris, 463 U.S. 1073 (1983).

A second method of proving discrimination is by employer admissions. Clearly, after Gunther, "if an employer hired a woman for a unique position in the company and then admitted that her salary would have been higher had she been male," 452 U.S. at 178-79, a Title VII violation would be found. International Union of Electrical Workers v. Westinghouse Electric Corp., 631 F.2d 1094 (3d Cir. 1980), was predicated on employer admissions. The plaintiff claimed that present wage practices could be traced back to the 1930s when there was explicit gender discrimination in paying males more than females for jobs rated the same. Id. at 1097.

Even if discriminatory intent cannot be established either by facially discriminatory policies or by employer admissions, Title VII generally provides three other methods of proving discrimination — systemic disparate treatment proven by statistical evidence, individual disparate treatment proven by inference, and disparate impact.

The Ninth Circuit has addressed claims of comparable worth wage discrimination in two cases. See Spaulding v. Univ. of Wash., 740 F.2d 686 (9th Cir. 1983); American Fed. of State, County, and Municipal Employees (AFSCME) v. State of Wash., 770 F.2d 1401 (9th Cir. 1985). These cases provide examples of the difficulties faced in using Title VII to remedy wage discrepancies between jobs that are not equal.

Spaulding was a lawsuit by faculty in the predominantly female nursing department alleging discrimination in setting their salaries as compared with faculty in other departments. Applying the disparate treatment theory, the court found that the nursing faculty jobs were not substantially equal to faculty jobs in other departments. This finding provided a legitimate nondiscriminatory reason for the difference in pay. The nursing faculty was unable to introduce any other evidence to support an inference of discrimination. The court declined to infer discrimination arising from paying different wages to workers in positions that are comparable or similar, but not equal.

Turning to disparate impact, the nursing faculty asserted that the wage disparity was caused by "the facially neutral policy or practice of the University of setting wages according to market prices." The court ruled that reliance on market prices is not the sort of "policy" to which disparate impact analysis applies:

> Every employer constrained by market forces must consider market values in setting his labor costs. Naturally, market prices are inherently job-related, although the market may embody social judgments as to the worth of some jobs. Employers relying on the market are, to that extent, "price-takers." They deal with the market as a given and do not meaningfully have a "policy" about it in the relevant Title VII sense. . . . [A]llowing plaintiffs to establish reliance on the market as a facially neutral policy for Title VII purposes would subject employers to liability for pay disparities with respect to which they have not, in any meaningful sense, made an independent judgment.

Id. at 708. The Supreme Court's decision in *Watson* (reproduced at page 342) that disparate impact theory is not limited to discrete, objective employment practices and the 1991 Amendment's codification of the disparate impact theory undermine the Ninth Circuit's unwillingness to recognize reliance on market prices as the kind of policy that can be analyzed under the disparate impact theory. Nevertheless, may the *Spaulding* result be defended on the ground that, even if reliance on the market establishes a prima facie case of disparate impact, such reliance is job related and a business necessity?

A further reason why reliance on the market may not provide a basis for disparate impact liability is that the "market" may be viewed as "any other factor other than sex" under the EPA. The EPA may not recognize factors with a disparate impact as discriminatory and therefore *not* "other than sex." If this is the case and if EPA defenses are incorporated into all Title VII sex-based wage discrimination claims, then disparate impact is unavailable in these cases by virtue of the Bennett Amendment.

The Ninth Circuit's consideration of *AFSCME* provides further insight into the difficulties of addressing wage disparities between job classifications under Title VII. In *AFSCME*, the State of Washington commissioned a study "to determine whether a wage disparity existed between employees in jobs help predominantly by women and jobs held predominantly by men." 770 F.2d at 1403. The state identified disparities, but did not implement a comparable worth compensation program for several years. Id. It was the failure to promptly remedy the sex-based wage disparities identified by the study that formed the basis of the plaintiff's complaint of sex discrimination. See id. at 1403-04.

The court once again rejected the argument that the disparities violated Title VII under the disparate impact theory because the disparities stemmed from market forces. Id. at 1406. AFSCME argued that the state acted with discriminatory intent because, once the study revealed that market forces undervalue women, the state intentionally discriminated by continuing to rely on market forces to set wages. The court rejected this argument because the state did not create the market disparity and there was no evidence that it relied on the market *because of* the disparity. See id. at 1406-07. "While the Washington legislature may have the discretion to enact a comparable worth plan if it chooses to do so, Title VII does not obligate it to eliminate an economic inequality that it did not create." Id. at 1407.

*AFSCME* seems consistent with the Supreme Court holding that knowledge of the consequences of adopting an employment practice with an adverse effect on one gender — in this case, using the market to set wage levels — does not prove that the employer intended to discriminate. To be liable, the employer must act *because of* the gender effect, not merely despite it. *Feeney* (reproduced at page 251). *AFSCME* and *Spaulding* illustrate some of the difficulties encountered by plaintiffs who seek to promote comparable worth through litigation under Title VII. See generally Martha Chamallas, Review, The Market Excuse, 68 U. Chi. L. Rev. 579 (2001) (reviewing Robert L. Nelson & William P. Bridges, Legalizing Gender Inequality: Courts, Markets, and Unequal Pay for Women in America (1999)).

Many employees have sought to address the issue of comparable worth politically. Several states have collected data on comparable worth and some have subsequently made comparable worth adjustments for state and municipal employees. One reason for the success of efforts to incorporate comparable worth into the public employee wage setting is that government employers frequently set public-sector wages on the basis of job evaluation studies.

In the private sector, comparable worth has been pursued with some success through union representation and the contract negotiation process. See, e.g., Linda M. Blum, Between Feminism and Labor: The Significance of the Comparable Worth Movement (1991); Toni Gilpin, Gary Isaac, Dan Letwin & Jack McKivigan, On Strike for Respect: The Yale Strike of 1984-85 (1988).

## D.   DISCRIMINATION ON ACCOUNT OF RELIGION

Title VII prohibits discrimination because of religion. The statute's definition of religion, however, introduces a kind of discrimination we have not encountered before — the failure to reasonably accommodate religious practices and observances. In addition, the statute generates complications by permitting religious discrimination by certain religious employers and also by permitting such discrimination when religion is a bona fide occupational qualification. Overarching all of these statutory provisions is the First Amendment. In some cases, employees resort to the free exercise clause to supplement Title VII's statutory protections, and in some cases churches and other religious institutions invoke the free exercise clause to limit the intrusion of Title VII and other antidiscrimination statutes into their operations. Finally, the establishment clause plays a part in this complicated mix, limiting the extent to which the state can favor religion by its enactments in this area.

### 1.   Nondiscrimination and the Special Duty to Accommodate Employees' Religious Practices

Religious discrimination cases often proceed on the same general theories of discrimination as race and gender cases. Thus, there are cases in which the plaintiff claims that the defendant admitted its religious motivation, e.g., EEOC v. Wiltel, Inc., 81 F.3d 1508 (10th Cir. 1996); Blalock v. Metal Trades, Inc., 775 F.2d 703 (6th Cir. 1985), and others in which the courts must infer an impermissible purpose from more circumstantial evidence, e.g., Turpen v. Missouri-Kansas-Texas R.R. Co., 736 F.2d 1022 (5th Cir. 1984). See also Mandell v. County of Suffolk, 2003 U.S. App.

LEXIS 650, *16 (2d Cir. 2003) (comments by police chief could permit reasonable jury to infer that he viewed Christianity "as a necessary part of a good police officer's make-up."). See Laura S. Underkufer, "Discrimination" on the Basis of Religion: An Examination of Attempted Value Neutrality in Employment, 30 Wm. & Mary L. Rev. 581 (1989).

## VAN KOTEN v. FAMILY HEALTH MANAGEMENT, INC.
### 1998 U.S. App. LEXIS 1837 (7th Cir. Feb. 6, 1998)

Dr. Robert J. Van Koten filed a complaint alleging that the defendants willfully and intentionally discriminated against him by discharging him because of his religious beliefs in violation of Title VII of the Civil Rights Act of 1964. The district court granted the defendants' motion for summary judgment, finding that Van Koten failed to demonstrate a genuine issue of material fact over whether the defendants had knowledge of his religious beliefs. On appeal Van Koten argues that the defendants did have knowledge of his religious beliefs. We affirm the district court's decision, although on the different ground that Van Koten failed to show that there was a genuine issue of material fact that the nondiscriminatory reason given for his discharge was a pretext for religious discrimination.

Van Koten is a licensed chiropractor in Illinois. He asserts that he has held a sincere and bona-fide belief in the Wiccian religion since 1973. He describes the Wiccian religion (also known as Wicca, the Craft, or the Old Religion) as "a monistic and pantheistic, positive, shamanistic, nature based religion that is predicated on a simple set of ethics and morality which promulgates avoidance of harm to other people, promoting brotherly love and harmony with, and respect for, all life forms." Van Koten's religious beliefs include that Halloween is a holy day, respect for all life and consequently a vegetarian diet, astrology, psychic abilities, and reincarnation.

Van Koten was hired by Family Health Management (FHM) as a chiropractor on September 21, 1994. Although his contract was with FHM, he was "leased out" to Chiromed Physicians (Chiromed). On November 1, 1994, Chris Meinecke, the clinic manager, approached Van Koten and accused him of not following proper procedure by failing to fill out a diagnosis form on a patient. Van Koten responded by stating "fuck the procedure." Van Koten argues that he always followed the defendants' procedures and that he believed that forms had to be filled out only when a patient paid for services through insurance, rather than out-of-pocket.

On November 2, 1994, Duane F. Meyers, the sole shareholder and chief executive officer of FHM and Chiromed, discharged Van Koten allegedly due to his "profane refusal to follow procedures which were required in his employment." Van Koten states that on November 2, Meyers told him during a lunch discussion that, "I think it's time we go our separate ways," and made a comment about "trying to fit a square peg into a round hole." Van Koten also asserts that he asked why he was being terminated and Meyers responded, "I don't want this to be a character assassination."

The defendants moved for summary judgment on the basis that Meyers was not aware of Van Koten's religion and therefore could not have been motivated to discharge him on the basis of his religious beliefs. Meyers stated in an affidavit that he was not advised of any of Van Koten's religious beliefs until after Van Koten was terminated. Meyers asserts that the first time he learned of Van Koten's religious beliefs was when he received a notice of right to sue from the Illinois Department of Human Rights dated November 18, 1994.

Van Koten argues that the defendants, and Meyers in particular, knew about his religious beliefs. The only direct evidence that Van Koten had presented a religious belief to Meyers occurred on or about October 15, 1994, when Van Koten had a discussion with Meyers over lunch. During this conversation, Van Koten informed Meyers "that he had purchased a vegetarian meal because he was a vegetarian due to his religious beliefs."

In addition to directly informing Meyers of his religious belief in a vegetarian diet, Van Koten states that there is a possibility that Meyers might also have learned of his religious beliefs from co-workers. However, Van Koten admitted at his deposition that he never used the word Wicca at work. Van Koten installed a program on his office computer that allowed him to prepare astrology charts during non-business hours. Van Koten believes that he uses psychic abilities to orally interpret these charts. He prepared astrology charts and gave oral interpretations to those co-workers who requested them for themselves or their families. As part of his interpretation of the charts, he referred to the sun as the father and the moon as the mother. Van Koten argues that in making these references, he communicated that he believed that the sun and moon were gods. Van Koten asserts that any of the employees that he prepared astrology charts for could have informed Meyers of his belief in astrology. Additionally, Van Koten states that Meyers could have learned of his religious belief in astrology on or about October 20, 1994, when Meyers observed a crowd of people gathered around Van Koten's office and was informed by an employee that Van Koten was preparing astrology charts. However, Van Koten stated at his deposition that he never informed anyone at work that astrology was part of his religion.

Van Koten also argues that Meyers could have learned of his religious belief that Halloween was a holy day. On October 31, 1994, Van Koten stated in front of several co-workers, including Meinecke, Cheryl Wilkinson, Bonnie Lauff, and Randy Provick, that he considered Halloween to be the "holiest day of the year in his religion." Van Koten further argues that the proximity between making this statement and his discharge two days later supports that his termination was motivated by his religious beliefs.

Lastly, Van Koten asserts that an inference can be drawn that Provick informed Meyers of Van Koten's religious beliefs. In addition to hearing his statement about Halloween, Van Koten states that "on previous occasions Provick made unsolicited comments to [him] about being 'brutally agnostic' and asked [him] probing questions regarding [his] belief system." Van Koten argues that Provick had ample opportunity to tell Meyers about Van Koten's statement that Halloween was his holiest day, because on November 1, 1994, Meyers spent two to three hours with Provick in Provick's office with the door closed.

Under Title VII it is unlawful for an employer "to fail or refuse to hire or to discharge any individual, or otherwise to discriminate against any individual with respect to his compensation, terms, conditions, or privileges of employment, because of such individual's . . . religion." 42 U.S.C. § 2000e-2(a)(1). "The term 'religion' includes all aspects of religious observance and practice, as well as belief, unless an employer demonstrates that he is unable to reasonably accommodate to an employee's or prospective employee's religious observance or practice without undue hardship on the conduct of the employer's business." 42 U.S.C. § 2000e(j). "An unlawful employment practice is established when the complaining party demonstrates that . . . religion . . . was a motivating factor for any employment practice, even though other factors also motivated the practice." 42 U.S.C. § 2000e-2(m).

As there was no direct evidence of discrimination in this case, the district court properly applied the indirect, burden-shifting approach established in McDonnell

Douglas Corp. v. Green. In *McDonnell Douglas*, the Supreme Court noted that the elements of the prima facie case may vary depending on the facts presented in Title VII cases. The district court stated that a claimant normally meets the burden of establishing a prima facie case if he demonstrates that he: (1) is a member of a protected class; (2) was qualified for the job in question; (3) was discharged; and (4) that the position remained open after his discharge to similarly qualified candidates. The district court also stated that this case requires the claimant, as part of his prima facie test, to establish an additional element: (5) that the employer had knowledge of the employee's religious beliefs. The district court determined that Van Koten met each of the factors of the prima facie test except for the newly added knowledge requirement.

Although the district court based its determination on the use of the above prima facie test, we need not consider if this is the appropriate test because "we of course may affirm the judgment of the district court on any ground supported by the record." The record contains sufficient information for this court to assume that a prima facie case had been made, and affirm the district court's judgment because Van Koten failed to raise a genuine issue of material fact that the legitimate nondiscriminatory reason given for his discharge was a pretext for religious discrimination. . . .

Although the defendants' brief does not include a detailed discussion of the reason for discharging Van Koten, it does explain that he was fired because of his "profane refusal to follow procedures." The record also contains sufficient documentation to establish a legitimate reason for discharge. "Where the defendant has done everything that would be required of him if the plaintiff had properly made out a prima facie case, whether the plaintiff really did so is no longer relevant." United States Postal Service Bd. of Governors v. Aikens, 460 U.S. 711 (1983).

The defendants [sic] reference to a profane refusal to follow procedure relates to Van Koten's response of "fuck the procedure" to Meinecke on November 1, 1994. Van Koten admits that he made this comment. . . . Duane Meyers also stated in his answers to interrogatories that Van Koten was fired for making this profane comment. The record contains additional documentation from November 1 and 2, that shows that Van Koten frequently left morning meetings early, belittled staff, acted callous and shallow, and was rude to patients. Based on the information available in the record, the defendants gave a legitimate, nondiscriminatory reason for discharging Van Koten.

Van Koten asserts that the reason for his discharge was a pretext for religious discrimination. He first argues that the fact that his discharge occurred only two days after his statement that Halloween is a holy day, supports a finding of pretext. Although the proximity between adverse employment actions and allegedly discriminatory incidents can imply a genuine issue of material fact over the cause of discharge, such is not the case here. Regardless of whether the prima facie test for this case would include a knowledge requirement, defendants' knowledge of Van Koten's religious beliefs would also be relevant to the issue of pretext. Smith v. Cook County, 74 F.3d 829, 834 (7th Cir. 1996) (the same evidence can be relevant to both the prima facie case and to the question of pretext). The record does not support a finding that there is a genuine issue of material fact that Meyers was unaware that Halloween was a holy day for Van Koten. Van Koten attempts to argue that Meyers could have learned of this belief from an employee who heard Van Koten state that Halloween was a holy day. However, subjective beliefs and speculation of a plaintiff are insufficient to create a genuine issue of material fact. Further, this court has held that an employee's desired inference that a co-worker informed decision makers of his disability prior to his discharge was not reasonable and was "unsupported speculation." In fact, the only religious belief that Van Koten has demonstrated Meyers knew of was that he was a vegetarian for religious reasons. . . .

## NOTES

1. *Van Koten* is a straightforward disparate treatment case, with the only variation on the situations we have seen being the claim that plaintiff's religion was the reason for his discharge. Unlike race, sex, and age, however, an individual's religious beliefs are not necessarily apparent. Thus, *Van Koten* raises the threshold question whether the employer knew about the plaintiff's religion. While the Seventh Circuit does not explicitly adopt this requirement, it seems clearly correct. Accord Lubetsky v. Applied Card Sys., 296 F.3d 1301 (11th Cir. 2002) (plaintiff had to adduce evidence that decision-maker knew of his religion to establish prima facie case). Do you agree with the district court that there was insufficient basis to go to the jury on that issue? Isn't it pretty unusual in America today to celebrate Halloween as one's "holiest day"? Isn't it likely that such a statement would be the topic of office gossip? Of course, even if employer knowledge is part of the prima facie case, the religion of certain employees may be more easily ascertainable. E.g., Rosen v. Thornburgh, 928 F.2d 528, 534 (2d Cir. 1991) ("We believe that a trier of fact might reasonably conclude that Rosen's religion was apparent from his surname as well as from the vocal anti-semitism engendered by his presence. . . .").

2. The district court in *Van Koten* altered the *McDonnell Douglas* analysis by requiring proof that the employer knew of plaintiff's religion. In Shapolia v. Los Alamos National Laboratory, 992 F.2d 1033 (10th Cir. 1993), where plaintiff claimed he was terminated because he was not a Mormon like his supervisors, the court also indicated that the *McDonnell Douglas* prima facie case elements could not be applied as in "straightforward sex and race discrimination discharge cases":

> First, use of the "protected class" factor in this case would be misleading because it suggests some identifiable characteristic of the plaintiff in order to give rise to Title VII protection. However, in this case, it is the religious beliefs of the employer, and the fact that Shapolia does not share them, that constitute the basis of the claim. Where discrimination is not targeted against a particular religion, but against those who do not share a particular religious belief, the use of the protected class factor is inappropriate. Second, because the discrimination is targeted against non-Mormons, and non-Mormons constitute a majority of society, the case resembles those cases of reverse discrimination [where plaintiff must "establish background circumstances that support an inference that the defendant is one of those unusual employers who discriminates against the majority"].

Id. at 1038. *Shapolia* then described the appropriate prima facie case: "[P]laintiff must show (1) that he was subjected to some adverse employment action; (2) that, at the time the employment action was taken, the employee's job performance was satisfactory; and (3) some additional evidence to support the inference that the employment actions were taken because of a discriminatory motive based upon the employee's failure to hold or follow his or her employer's religious beliefs." Id. See also Habib v. Nationsbank, 279 F.3d 563 (8th Cir. 2001) (court ruled that the third prong of a prima facie case was not established when a Muslim woman accommodated with five breaks a day to pray failed to show that she was discharged because of religious discrimination when she refused to submit a doctor's note for an absence). Is *Van Koten's* requirement of employer knowledge of the employee's religion just an application of the third prong of *Shapolia?*

3. *Shapolia* might suggest that the plaintiff must at least prove that he and the defendant are of different religions. But perhaps that it not enough. Americans practice dozens or hundreds of different religions. See the Religious Movements Homepage at the University of Virginia, www.religiousmovements.org. Assuming the defendant knew of Van Koten's religion, was there any "additional evidence" to justify an inference of religious discrimination against him? Is it enough that Wicca is a "nontraditional" religion, easily ridiculed? See also Paul Horwitz, Scientology in Court: A Comparative Analysis and Some Thoughts on Selected Issues in Law And Religion, 47 DePaul L. Rev. 85 (1997); Tuan N. Samahon, Note, The Religion Clauses and Political Asylum: Religious Persecution Claims and the Religious Membership — Conversion Imposter Problem, 88 Geo. L.J. 2211 (2000).

4. Or is the *Van Koten* court less concerned with whether the defendant knew of plaintiff's religion than whether it fired him because of that religion, given his profanity and his disdain for office procedures? But isn't it likely that Wiccans are viewed with hostility by others? Might it be more likely that Van Koten would be fired for being a witch than for being, say, a Methodist?

5. Is Wicca a religion? What is a "religion"? Wicca has been recognized as a religion for First Amendment purposes. Maberry v. McKune, 24 F. Supp. 2d 1222 (D. Kan. 1998), and the military has approved the practice of Wicca at its bases. See US Army Defends Military Witches, Irish Times, June 9, 1999, at 11. See also Brown v. Woodland Joint Unified Sch. Dist., 27 F.3d 1373 (9th Cir. 1994) (assuming without deciding that Wicca is a religion for purposes of a challenge to school district's use of readings alleged to promote witchcraft).

6. Perhaps because of the diversity of religions in the United States, most successful religion cases seem to turn on some statements by the employer implicating religious bias, even if circumstantial evidence also played a role. E.g., Campos v. City of Blue Springs, Mo., 289 F.3d 546 (8th Cir. 2002) (evidence supported determination that a city youth outreach counselor who observed tenets of Native American spirituality was discriminated against and constructively discharged because she was not Christian); EEOC v. Univ. of Chi. Hosps., 276 F.3d 326 (7th Cir. 2002) (a reasonable inference could be made that a hospital recruiter's constructive discharge was based on religious discrimination by her employer); Abramson v. William Paterson Coll. of N.J., 260 F.3d 265 (3d Cir. 2001) (reversing summary judgment for employer because factfinder could find plaintiff's treatment was due to his religious faith and practice); Shanoff v. Illinois Dept. of Human Servs., 258 F.3d 696 (7th Cir. 2001) (a reasonable jury could conclude that harassment due to race and religion created a hostile work environment).

7. Van Koten's employer did know he was a vegetarian. Could he have been lawfully fired for being a vegetarian? The answer might be more complicated than it seems. Many vegetarians have religious bases for their lifestyle, but many others are vegetarians for health reasons. Still others have what might be called philosophical or moral reasons for not consuming animals. What constitutes a "religious" belief? Applying state law, a California court held that an individual who was not hired by an employer because he refused, on the basis of his vegan beliefs, to be innoculated with a mumps vaccine (grown in chicken embryos) was not a victim of religious discrimination because the vegan belief system is a secular philosophy lacking any apparent spiritual or otherworldly component. Friedman v. Southern Cal. Permanente Medi-

cal Group, 125 Cal. Rptr. 2d 663 (2d Dist. 2002). Similarly, Van Koten's employer knew that he practiced astrology. Is astrology a religion?

8. When can a practice or belief be linked to religion? Compare Hall v. Baptist Memorial Hosp., 215 F.3d 618 (6th Cir. 2000), where the court refused to find that it was the religious aspect of a discharged employee's leadership in a church promoting gay issues that led to her being fired, with Altman v. Minnesota Dept. of Corr., 251 F.3d 1199 (8th Cir. 2001) (discipline of religious employees who read Bible during gay sensitivity training might have been discriminatory). In Peterson v. Wilmur Communs., Inc., 205 F. Supp. 2d 1014, 1015 (E.D. Wis. 2002), the court granted summary judgment on liability to an individual who had been demoted from a supervisory position (in which he supervised several persons of color). It found that his white supremacist beliefs were religious. He was a member of the "World Church of the Creator," which preached "Creativity, the central tenet of which is white supremacy. Creativity teaches that all people of color are 'savage' and intent on 'mongrelizing the White Race,' that African-Americans are subhuman and should be 'shipped back to Africa'; that Jews control the nation and have instigated all wars in this century and should be driven from power, and that the Holocaust never occurred, but if it had occurred, Nazi Germany 'would have done the world a tremendous favor.'" The Church described itself as a religion, although it did not include belief in a God or an afterlife. Compare the suit filed by an individual who was fired for refusing to remove an eyebrow ring. Salt Lake Tribune, Oct. 19, 2002. She claimed that the ring was part of her religion, the Church of Body Modification, whose website is http://www.churchofbodmod.com/.

9. As originally enacted, Title VII barred discrimination against religion but did not define the term. In its 1972 Amendments to Title VII, Congress added a provision which operates less to define what constitutes a religion than to expand the scope of protection. Section 701(j) now provides:

> The term "religion" includes all aspects of religious observance and practice, as well as belief, unless an employer demonstrates that he is unable to reasonably accommodate to an employee's or prospective employee's religious observance or practice without undue hardship on the conduct of the employer's business.

Accordingly, the prohibition of discrimination on account of religion would seem to bar not only discriminating against a person because of his beliefs (e.g., Wiccan) but also discrimination against him because of his "religious observances and practices." If the employer had fired Van Koten because he was a vegetarian, and if vegetarianism was a practice or observance of his Wiccan religion, wouldn't there be a violation of Title VII?

10. In military service cases concerning conscientious objector status, the Supreme Court first formulated a definition of a religious-based belief as a "sincere and meaningful belief which occupies in the life of its possessor a place parallel to that filled by the God of those admittedly qualifying for the exemption." United States v. Seeger, 380 U.S. 163, 176 (1965). Later, the definition was expanded to include moral and ethical beliefs that assumed the function of a religion in the registrant's life. Only if the belief "rests solely upon considerations of policy, pragmatism, or expediency" does it fail to qualify. Welsh v. United States, 398 U.S. 333, 342-43 (1970). See generally Rebecca Redwood French, From *Yoder* to Yoda: Models of Traditional, Modern, and Postmodern Religion in United States Constitutional Law, 41 Ariz. L. Rev. 49 (1999); Dmitri N. Feofanov, Defining Religion: An Immodest

Proposal, 23 Hofstra L. Rev. 309 (1994); Kent Greenawalt, Religion as a Concept in Constitutional Law, 72 Cal. L. Rev. 753 (1984); Jesse Choper, Defining "Religion" in the First Amendment, 1982 U. Ill. L. Rev. 579. Is this the definition of religion under Title VII? See generally Kent Greenawalt, Title VII and Religious Liberty, 33 Loy. U. Chi. L.J. 1, 32-35 (2001); Barbara L. Kramer, Reconciling Religious Rights and Responsibilities, 30 Loy. U. Chi. L.J. 439 (1999). Could an atheist qualify as one who had a "religious" belief? If so, how could normal practices of an employer ever conflict with those beliefs? See Young v. Southwestern Sav. & Loan Assn., 509 F.2d 140 (5th Cir. 1975) (atheist need not participate in prayer activities held at a secular employer). But see Kolodziej v. Smith, 588 N.E.2d 634 (Mass. 1992) (an employer may require management-level employees to attend a seminar on interpersonal relationships that, while nondenominational, used Bible references).

11. In Pime v. Loyola University, 803 F.2d 351 (7th Cir. 1986), plaintiff, a Jew, complained that he was denied a teaching position when the philosophy department voted to reserve the next three tenure-track vacancies for Jesuits. While the majority rejected the attack on other grounds, Judge Posner's concurrence argued that the defendant was not guilty of "religious" discrimination:

> Pime was turned down for a tenure-track position in Loyola's philosophy department not because he is a Jew, not because he is not a Catholic, but because he is not a member of the Jesuit order. I therefore do not think he has been deprived of an employment opportunity because of his religion. It is true that you cannot be a Jesuit if you are not a Catholic; but only a tiny fraction of Catholics are Jesuits. If Pime were a Catholic but not a Jesuit he would be just as ineligible for the position as he is being a Jew, yet it would be odd indeed to accuse Loyola of discriminating against Catholics because it wanted to reserve some positions in its philosophy department for Jesuits, thus excluding most Catholics from consideration.

803 F.2d at 354. Judge Posner's argument is reminiscent of the pre-1978 treatment of pregnancy. The Supreme Court, however, rejected a similar argument in Phillips v. Martin Marietta Co., 400 U.S. 542 (1970), where the employer, which discriminated against women with preschool children, claimed that it did not engage in gender discrimination because it was gender "plus" the age of the children that disqualified an applicant. The Court held that sex plus another factor still equaled sex discrimination. Is Judge Posner consistent with *Phillips* in concluding that religion (Catholic) plus another factor (being a Jesuit) is not religious discrimination? Cf. Maguire v. Marquette University, 814 F.2d 1213 (7th Cir. 1987), where the plaintiff, a Catholic woman, sought an appointment in the theology department of a Catholic university, but was barred by a similar Jesuit preference. The court found that the failure to hire the plaintiff was not because she was female, but because her views about abortion were not in compliance with the position of the Catholic church. "Given the plaintiff's controversial beliefs regarding abortion, Marquette would have reached the same decision even if she were a man." Id. at 1218. Assuming the decision was not sex discrimination, was it religious discrimination? If so, that would be permissible only if the employer were within a religious entity exemption, see page 602, or religious beliefs were a bfoq, see page 604.

12. Even if a belief is "religious," it must still be sincerely held to fall within the statute's protection. How can an employer show his worker is not sincere? Would a person's prior conduct inconsistent with the professed belief show that sincerity was lacking? See EEOC v. Union Independiente De La Autoridad De Acueductos y Alcantarillados de P.R., 279 F.3d 49, 56-57 (1st Cir. 2002) (summary judgment

denied where the sincerity of a claimed Seventh Day Adventist was put in issue by the defendant through "specific undisputed evidence of conduct on Cruz's part that is contrary to the tenets of his professed religious belief [including that] Cruz lied on an employment application; that he is divorced; that he took an oath before a notary upon becoming a public employee; and that he works five days a week (instead of the six days required by his faith)."

13. Suppose the defendant had discriminated against plaintiff on the basis of his religion. Is that ever permissible?

a. Normal "mixed motives" analysis applies: while it is a violation of the statute for religion to be a motivating factor in an employment decision, an employer may limit the plaintiff's remedies by demonstrating that it would have taken the same action for nondiscriminatory reasons. In Cowan v. Strafford R-VI Sch. Dist., 140 F.3d 1153 (8th Cir. 1998), plaintiff sent home with her second graders a "magic rock" and a note saying that the rock "will always let you know that you can do anything that you set your mind to. To make your rock work, close your eyes, rub it and say to yourself three times, 'I am a special and terrific person, with talents of my own.'" Her principal then told the teachers during a staff meeting that "she was concerned about the perception of the school in the community with regard to teaching New Ageism, and she instructed teachers to avoid magical notions in their teaching. In conjunction with this discussion, she announced a seminar coordinated by a local pastor [and grandfather of one of Cowan's second graders], Reverend Stark, that was devoted to the issue of New Ageism and the infiltration of New Age thinking in the public schools." Id. at 1156. At the end of that school year, Cowan's contract was not renewed. Applying Price Waterhouse, a jury found for Cowan, which was affirmed on appeal:

> A plaintiff in a discrimination case under Title VII can proceed under the Price Water-house mixed motives analysis if an employee first establishes that religion was a motivating factor in the employment decision. Then the burden of persuasion shifts to the defendant, who must show that it would have made the same decision even in the absence of the illegal criteria. A plaintiff is entitled to have her case analyzed under the mixed motives standard if she presents "evidence of conduct or statements by persons involved in the decision making process that may be viewed as directly reflecting the alleged discriminatory attitude."

Id. at 1158. See also Brown v. Polk County, Iowa, 61 F.3d 650 (8th Cir. 1995) (en banc) (finding no reasonable factfinder could determine that plaintiff would have been fired but for his religious activities).

b. We will see that Title VII contains exemptions permitting discrimination on account of religion. The first may seem obvious: certain religious organizations are permitted to discriminate on account of religion (but not on the basis of race, sex, or other prohibited ground). See page 602.

c. Another exemption is the bona fide occupational qualification — which may be used even by secular employers in appropriate cases. Suppose Van Koten's employer were a veterinarian and did not believe it appropriate to employ a witch because of the popular association of witches with devil worship and animal sacrifice. Does it matter that Wiccans are vegetarians and renounce animal sacrifice? What about members of a religion that does sacrifice animals? Cf. Church of Lukumi Babalu Aye v. Hialeah, 508 U.S. 520 (1993) (ordinance prohibiting ritual animal sacrifice targets religion and violates the First Amendment because it is not narrowly tailored to serve the asserted government interests).

d. Religious restrictions may also be upheld when necessary to avoid establishment clause problems. This defense, which has arisen in response to constitutional challenges to public employer restrictions on employees' religious expression, would analytically be a bfoq in a Title VII suit. See page 604. See Knight v. Conn. Dept. of Pub. Health, 275 F.3d 156 (2d Cir. 2001) (agency could bar employee's proselytizing of clients); Marchi v. Bd. of Cooperative Educ. Servs., 173 F.3d 469 (2d Cir. 1999) (establishment clause concerns justified restricting employee's free exercise clause rights by prohibiting teacher's use of religious references in dealing with students and their parents); Helland v. South Bend Community Sch. Corp., 93 F.3d 327 (7th Cir. 1996) (upholding discharge of a public school teacher for reading the Bible aloud to a fifth-grade class because of a compelling government interest against teaching religion in public schools). See also Bishop v. Aronov, 926 F.2d 1066 (11th Cir. Ala. 1991) (upholding restrictions on college instructor's introduction of religion into physiology classes against both free speech and free exercise attacks). But see Tucker v. Cal. Dept. of Educ., 97 F.3d 1204 (9th Cir. 1996) (invalidating on free speech grounds a state employer's policy barring religious artifacts outside of the owners' "closed offices or defined cubicles" and also barring religious advocacy during work hours or in the workplace); Brown v. Polk County, Iowa, 61 F.3d 650 (8th Cir. 1995) (en banc) (employee successfully challenged his discharge for religious activities when public employer could not establish disruption or other harm). Can these cases be squared by the notion that religious activity, even advocacy, is protected by the Constitution (and perhaps Title VII) so long as impressionable individuals, such as children, are not subjected to it?

14. Note that the original statute would have barred discrimination against religion in the sense of prohibiting employers from treating believers differently than other persons. But the original statute would not have prevented an employer from treating every employee the same, even if the effect were felt primarily by those of a particular religious persuasion. The 1972 Amendments to Title VII, in making clear that an employer could not discriminate on the basis of practices or observances (in addition to beliefs), created a special theory of liability for religious discrimination. An employer must not only avoid discrimination but also "reasonably accommodate" an employee's religious observance unless to do so would be "an undue hardship on the conduct of the employer's business."

15. Accommodating religious practices reflected a congressional concern with the problems of those whose religions forbid work on their Sabbath or other holy day. For example, both Seventh Day Adventists and Orthodox Jews have strict limitations on the kinds of work they can perform on their Sabbaths, and Jews are also limited with respect to such high holy days as Yom Kippur. In fact, the vast majority of "accommodation" cases involve refusals by employers to adjust work schedules to the religious observances of particular employees. But the language of the statute is not limited to excusing employees from work when their religion forbids labor or demands religious practices. It reaches a broad spectrum of other activities, which may range from wearing distinctive clothes, to not shaving, to displaying religious icons.

16. The broad formulation of the reasonable accommodation provision suggests that religious observances are privileged as opposed to secular practice. But the law on reasonable accommodation of religion has evolved in a much less stringent fashion than the statute's language might suggest, and much less stringently than has the similar reasonable accommodation requirement under the Americans with Disabilities Act. See Chapter 8. Despite the statute's broad language, the Supreme Court has read § 701(j) provision quite narrowly. See generally Debbie N. Kaminer, Title VII's

Failure to Provide Meaningful and Consistent Protection of Religious Employees: Proposals for an Amendment, 21 Berkeley J. Empl. & Lab. L. 575 (2000) (arguing that "Congress intended § 701(j) to guarantee a higher level of accommodation than that required by the courts today" and that an amendment is necessary to clarify employer accommodation obligations).

The first question is what accommodation is "reasonable." This inquiry focuses on the relationship between the employee's religious needs and the employer's offered accommodation. In Ansonia Bd. of Educ. v. Philbrook, 479 U.S. 60 (1986), the Court held that the fit did not have to be very tight. In that case, a teacher needed six days off to attend required religious services and asked the employer to accommodate him by allowing him to use three of his paid personal days for this purpose. The employer refused because the collective bargaining agreement specified three paid days for religious observances. The Supreme Court found that the agreement offered a reasonable accommodation of religion through the time provided for religious observance, even though it did not completely satisfy plaintiff's religious-based needs. Once an employer has made a reasonable accommodation, the employer has fully satisfied its duty under § 701(j). The Court declared:

> We find no basis in either the statute or its legislative history for requiring an employer to choose any particular reasonable accommodation. By its very terms the statute directs that any reasonable accommodation by the employer is sufficient to meet its accommodation obligation. . . . Thus, where the employer has already reasonably accommodated the employee's religious needs, the statutory inquiry is at an end. The employer need not further show that each of the employee's alternative accommodations would result in undue hardship. As [Trans World Airlines v.] *Hardison* illustrates, the extent of undue hardship on the employer's business is at issue only where the employer claims that it is unable to offer any reasonable accommodation without such hardship. Once the Court of Appeals assumed that the school board had offered to Philbrook a reasonable alternative, it erred by requiring the board to nonetheless demonstrate the hardship of Philbrook's alternatives.
>
>     . . . Under the approach articulated by the Court of Appeals, however, the employee is given every incentive to hold out for the most beneficial accommodation, despite the fact that an employer offers a reasonable resolution of the conflict. This approach, we think, conflicts with both the language of the statute and the views that led to its enactment. We accordingly hold that an employer has met its obligation under § 701(j) when it demonstrates that it has offered a reasonable accommodation to the employee.

Id. at 68-69. See also Dachman v. Shalala, 2001 U.S. App. LEXIS 9888 (4th Cir. May 18, 2001) (no discrimination against Jewish employee who was permitted to leave work early enough to be home for her Sabbath but not early enough to do certain preparations for it). How can an accommodation be "reasonable" if it does not accommodate the religious observance at issue?

It is only if the employer fails to offer any reasonable accommodation that the second issue, whether a requested accommodation poses an undue hardship for the employer, becomes relevant. In Trans World Airlines, Inc. v. Hardison, 432 U.S. 63 (1977), referred to in *Philbrook*, the Court defined undue hardship quite narrowly in a case in which a Saturday Sabbatarian asked that a shift schedule requiring Saturday work be modified for him. He proposed a number of alternatives, but the Court found each to involve an undue hardship under a de minimis cost test: "To require TWA to bear more than a de minimis cost in order to give Hardison Saturdays off is an undue hardship." Id. at 84. Hardship would flow either from TWA paying other employees premium rates to do Hardison's work or from TWA allocating days off on a religious basis: if Hardison were given Saturdays off for religious reasons, other employees would lose their opportunity to have Saturdays off. The Court concluded:

> ... Title VII does not contemplate such unequal treatment. The repeated, unequivocal emphasis of both the language and the legislative history of Title VII is on eliminating discrimination in employment, and such discrimination is proscribed when it is directed against majorities as well as minorities. Indeed, the foundation of Hardison's claim is that TWA and IAM engaged in religious discrimination in violation of § 703(a)(1) when they failed to arrange for him to have Saturdays off. It would be anomalous to conclude that by "reasonable accommodation" Congress meant that an employer must deny the shift and job preference of some employees, as well as deprive them of their contractual rights, in order to accommodate or prefer the religious needs of others, and we conclude that Title VII does not require an employer to go that far.
>
> ... Like abandonment of the seniority system, to require TWA to bear additional costs when no such costs are incurred to give other employees the days off that they want would involve unequal treatment of employees on the basis of their religion. By suggesting that TWA should incur certain costs in order to give Hardison Saturdays off the Court of Appeals would in effect require TWA to finance an additional Saturday off and then to choose the employee who will enjoy it on the basis of his religious beliefs. While incurring extra costs to secure a replacement for Hardison might remove the necessity of compelling another employee to work involuntarily in Hardison's place, it would not change the fact that the privilege of having Saturdays off would be allocated according to religious beliefs.
>
> As we have seen, the paramount concern of Congress in enacting Title VII was the elimination of discrimination in employment. In the absence of clear statutory language or legislative history to the contrary, we will not readily construe the statute to require an employer to discriminate against some employees in order to enable others to observe their Sabbath.

Id. at 80-85. Subsequent lower court cases have confirmed that "[t]he cost of hiring an additional worker or the loss of production that results from not replacing a worker who is unavailable due to a religious conflict can amount to undue hardship." Lee v. ABF Freight System, Inc., 22 F.3d 1019, 1023 (10th Cir. 1994). Further, de minimis cost "entails not only monetary concerns, but also the employer's burden in conducting its business." Brown v. Polk County, Iowa, 61 F.3d 650, 655 (8th Cir. 1995). However, the mere fact that a seniority system is involved does not preclude reasonable accommodation, because some practices may be accommodated without violating the system. Balint v. Carson City, Nev., 180 F.3d 1047 (9th Cir. 1999). Cf. Thomas v. Natl. Assn. of Letter Carriers, 225 F.3d 1149 (10th Cir. 2000) (undue hardship to accommodate Sabbath observer by violating collective bargaining agreement); Virts v. Consolidated Freightways Corp. of Del., 285 F.3d 508 (6th Cir. 2002) (undue hardship for trucking company to accommodate a Christian truck driver who refused to make overnight runs with female drivers because it would require violating a collective bargaining agreement under which drivers are dispatched in the order of seniority). Other cases have refused to find as "reasonable" accommodating an employee's unwillingness to work with other individuals: Weber v. Roadway Exp., Inc., 199 F.3d 270 (5th Cir. 2000) (accommodating driver's religious objections to being partnered with female driver would unduly burden other workers); Broff v. North Miss. Health Serv., Inc., 244 F.3d 495 (5th Cir. 2001) (undue hardship to accommodate counselor's religious beliefs by not assigning her patients who wished help with homosexual or extramarital relations). Finally, an accommodation is not reasonable where it would require the employer to violate federal laws. Thus, an employee's religious-based refusal to provide an employer with his Social Security number was a valid basis for refusing to hire him because federal immigration and tax laws required that the employer obtain this information. Sutton v. Providence St. Joseph Medical Ctr., 192 F.3d 826 (9th Cir. 1999).

Despite the overall guidance provided by the Supreme Court in *Philbrook* and *Hardison*, the lower courts have had to wrestle with a number of issues at the intersection of nondiscrimination and reasonable accommodation.

## WILSON v. U.S. WEST COMMUNICATIONS
### 58 F.3d 1337 (8th Cir. 1995)

GIBSON, Senior Circuit Judge. . . .

[Christine L.] Wilson worked for U.S. West for nearly 20 years before U.S. West transferred her to another location as an information specialist, assisting U.S. West engineers in making and keeping records of the location of telephone cables. This facility had no dress code. In late July 1990, Wilson, a Roman Catholic, made a religious vow that she would wear an anti-abortion button "until there was an end to abortion or until [she] could no longer fight the fight." The button was two inches in diameter and showed a color photograph of an eighteen to twenty-week old fetus. The button also contained the phrases "Stop Abortion," and "They're Forgetting Someone." Wilson chose this particular button because she wanted to be an instrument of God like the Virgin Mary. She believed that the Virgin Mary would have chosen this particular button. She wore the button at all times, unless she was sleeping or bathing. She believed that if she took off the button she would compromise her vow and lose her soul.

Wilson began wearing the button to work in August 1990. Another information specialist asked Wilson not to wear the button to a class she was teaching. Wilson explained her religious vow and refused to stop wearing the button.

The button caused disruptions at work. Employees gathered to talk about the button. U.S. West identified Wilson's wearing of the button as a "time robbing" problem. Wilson acknowledged that the button caused a great deal of disruption. A union representative told Wilson's supervisor, Mary Jo Jensen, that some employees threatened to walk off their jobs because of the button. Wilson's co-workers testified that they found the button offensive and disturbing for "very personal reasons," such as infertility problems, miscarriage, and death of a premature infant, unrelated to any stance on abortion or religion.

In early August 1990, Wilson met with her supervisors, Jensen and Gail Klein, five times. Jensen and Klein are also Roman Catholics against abortion. Jensen and Klein told Wilson of co-workers' complaints about the button and anti-abortion T-shirt Wilson wore which also depicted a fetus. Jensen and Klein told Wilson that her co-workers were uncomfortable and upset and that some were refusing to do their work. Klein noted a 40 percent decline in the productivity of the information specialists since Wilson began wearing the button.

Wilson told her supervisors that she should not be singled out for wearing the button because the company had no dress code. She explained that she "just wanted to do [her] job," and suggested that co-workers offended by the button should be asked not to look at it. Klein and Jensen offered Wilson three options: (1) wear the button only in her work cubicle, leaving the button in the cubicle when she moved around the office; (2) cover the button while at work; or (3) wear a different button with the same message but without the photograph. Wilson responded that she could neither cover nor remove the button because it would break her promise to God to wear the button and be a "living witness." She suggested that management tell the other information specialists to "sit at their desk[s] and do the job U.S. West was paying them to do."

[For a time, Wilson took personal and vacation days off, but she] returned to work on September 18, 1990, and disruptions resumed. Information specialists refused to go to group meetings with Wilson present. The employees complained that the button made them uneasy. Two employees led grievances based on Wilson's button. Employees accused Jensen of harassment for not resolving the button issue to their satisfaction. Eventually, U.S. West told Wilson not to report to work wearing anything depicting a fetus, including the button or the T-shirt. U.S. West told Wilson again that she could cover or replace the button or wear it only in her cubicle. U.S. West sent Wilson home when she returned to work wearing the button and fired her for missing work unexcused for three consecutive days. Wilson sued U.S. West, claiming that her firing constituted religious discrimination.

An employee establishes a prima facie case of religious discrimination by showing that: (1) the employee has a bona fide religious belief that conflicts with an employment requirement; (2) the employee informed the employer of this belief; (3) the employee was disciplined for failing to comply with the conflicting employment requirement. Bhatia v. Chevron U.S.A., Inc., 734 F.2d 1382, 1383 (9th Cir. 1984). The parties stipulated that Wilson's "religious beliefs were sincerely held," and the district court ruled that Wilson made a prima facie case of religious discrimination. The court then considered whether U.S. West could defeat Wilson's claim by demonstrating that it offered Wilson a reasonable accommodation. An employer is required to "reasonably accommodate" the religious beliefs or practices of their employees unless doing so would cause the employer undue hardship. 42 U.S.C. § 2000e(j); Ansonia Board of Education v. Philbrook.

The court considered the three offered accommodations and concluded that requiring Wilson to leave the button in her cubicle or to replace the button were not accommodations of Wilson's sincerely held religious beliefs because: (1) removing the button at work violated Wilson's vow to wear the button at all times; and (2) replacing the button prohibited Wilson from wearing the particular button encompassed by her vow. However, the court concluded that requiring Wilson to cover the button while at work was a reasonable accommodation. The court based this determination on its factual finding that Wilson's vow did not require her to be a living witness. The court reasoned that covering the button while at work complied with Wilson's vow but also reduced office turmoil. The court also concluded that, even if Wilson's vow required her to be a living witness, U.S. West could not reasonably accommodate Wilson's religious beliefs without undue hardship. The court entered judgment for U.S. West, and Wilson appeals. . . .

I . . .

The district court's finding that Wilson's vow did not require her to be a living witness is supported by the record. First, the stipulation that Wilson's religious beliefs were sincerely held does not cover the details of her religious vow. Second, there is evidence that Wilson's vow did not always include the requirement that she be a living witness. Indeed, the evidence suggests that Wilson first mentioned the living witness requirement only after her supervisor suggested that she cover the button. Wilson's answer to an interrogatory asking her to explain her vow did not mention any living witness requirement, but explained that her vow was "to acknowledge the sanctity of the unborn by wearing the pro-life button until the days [sic] that abortions were no longer performed." Although Wilson testified at trial that wearing the button would allow her to be a "living witness to the truth," on cross-examination, she admitted that, in an interview given in August 1990 to a reporter for The Catholic Voice, she said nothing about being a living witness. Klein testified that he never heard Wilson use the word witness in explaining her vow, but rather, that he understood Wilson's vow was to "wear the button until abortions were ended." Accordingly, the district court's finding is supported by the evidence and is not clearly erroneous.

## II

We next consider Wilson's argument that the district court erred as a matter of law in concluding that U.S. West offered to reasonably accommodate Wilson's religious views. Wilson argues that her religious beliefs did not require her or any other employee to miss or rearrange work schedules, as typically causes a reasonable accommodation dispute. She argues that it was her co-workers' response to her beliefs that caused the workplace disruption, not her wearing the button. Wilson contends that U.S. West should have focused its attention on her co-workers, not her. Wilson's brief states: "Quite frankly, . . . Klein and Jensen should have simply instructed the troublesome co-workers to ignore the button and get back to work."

The district court, however, succinctly answered Wilson's argument: Klein was unable to persuade the co-workers to ignore the button. Although Wilson's religious beliefs did not create scheduling conflicts or violate dress code or safety rules, Wilson's position would require U.S. West to allow Wilson to impose her beliefs as she chooses. Wilson concedes the button caused substantial disruption at work. To simply instruct Wilson's co-workers that they must accept Wilson's insistence on wearing a particular depiction of a fetus as part of her religious beliefs is antithetical to the concept of reasonable accommodation.

Moreover, U.S. West did not oppose Wilson's religious beliefs, but rather, was concerned with the photograph. The record demonstrates that U.S. West did not object to various other religious articles that Wilson had in her work cubicle or to another employee's anti-abortion button. It was the color photograph of the fetus that offended Wilson's co-workers, many of whom were reminded of circumstances unrelated to abortion. Indeed, many employees who opposed Wilson's button shared Wilson's religion and view on abortion.

Wilson also argues that requiring her to cover the button is not a reasonable accommodation. . . . [S]he argues that the accommodation offered required her to abandon her religious beliefs, and therefore, that the accommodation was no accommodation at all. Having affirmed the finding that Wilson's religious vow did not require her to be a living witness, we summarily reject this argument. U.S. West's proposal allowed Wilson to comply with her vow to wear the button and respected the desire of co-workers not to look at the button. Hence, the district court did not err in holding that U.S. West reasonably accommodated Wilson's religious beliefs.

## III

Finally, Wilson argues that the district court erred in concluding that her suggested proposals would be an undue hardship for U.S. West.

In *Ansonia Board of Education*, the Supreme Court held that an employer is not required to select the employee's proposal of reasonable accommodation and that any reasonable accommodation by the employer is sufficient to comply with the statute. "The employer violates the statute unless it 'demonstrates that [it] is unable to reasonably accommodate . . . an employee's . . . religious observance or practice without undue hardship on the conduct of the employer's business.'" When the employer reasonably accommodates the employee's religious beliefs, the statutory inquiry ends. The employer need not show that the employee's proposed accommodations would cause an undue hardship. Undue hardship is at issue "only where the employer claims that it is unable to offer any reasonable accommodation without such hardship."

Because we hold that U.S. West offered Wilson a reasonable accommodation, our inquiry ends, and we need not consider Wilson's argument that her suggested accommodations would not cause undue hardship.

## NOTES

1. Did the *Wilson* court inquire too closely into the nature of plaintiff's religious beliefs in its findings about whether she was a "living witness"? Did the court mean that the Catholic Church did not require such conduct? Is that the same as saying that plaintiff's conduct was not "religious"? There was no question that Wilson's beliefs were sincere. But were they religious? Compare Altman v. Minn. Dept. of Corr., 251 F.3d 1199 (8th Cir. 2001) (reprimand for reading Bible during sensitivity training on gay and lesbian issues raised triable issue of religious discrimination).

2. Must an employer accommodate every practice related to even a bona fide religious belief? Is that the point of *Wilson* — that her religion did not *require* her to wear the button, even if it may have permitted or encouraged her to do so? A number of courts have rejected claims because the employee did not allege or prove that her religious beliefs *required* certain conduct, even if they admittedly motivated it. Chalmers v. Tulon Co., 101 F.3d 1012 (4th Cir. 1996) (religious beliefs did not require plaintiff to send letters to co-workers criticizing their lives); Vetter v. Farmland Indus., 120 F.3d 749 (8th Cir. 1997) (plaintiff's desire to live in a different town was more personal preference than religious belief even though the employer's residency requirement made it more inconvenient for the employee to attend religious services); Tiano v. Dillard Dept. Store, 139 F.3d 679 (9th Cir. 1998) (an employer who would not give an employee time off from work during the busy season for a religious pilgrimage did not violate Title VII when it fired her for not coming to work since the worker did not prove that her beliefs required her to go on the pilgrimage during peak season). Where does the statute say that a religious practice or observance must be required to be accommodated? In fact, the whole notion of "required" religious observances seems to reflect a very Western, even Christian, view of religion.

3. A very different view was taken in Dorr v. First Kentucky Natl. Corp., No. 84-5067, 1986 WL 398289, at *1 (6th Cir. July 17, 1986). Plaintiff alleged he lost his job at the bank because of his involvement with Integrity, an organization affiliated with the Episcopal church that advocates equal rights for homosexual men and women. While not questioning that Dorr's involvement stemmed from sincere religious convictions, "the court found that Dorr's Integrity activities were not an outgrowth of his religious beliefs." Id. at 11. The Sixth Circuit disagreed:

> The court characterized Dorr's testimony at trial as asserting that his leadership and activity were required by his beliefs, and then discredited this testimony based on Dorr's deposition in which he indicated that his religion did not "require" him to serve

as president of Integrity and take a public stance on gay rights. The court saw an inconsistency in these two positions and from this determined that Dorr's beliefs as stated at trial — that his participation was required — were not sincerely held. The court properly refrained from inquiring into whether Dorr's religion in fact required his Integrity activities; rather, the court judged whether Dorr sincerely believed it did.

The difficulty in the court's treatment of this issue is its focus on what Dorr believed was "required" of him. The concept of religion embraced by the statute is not, we think, one of an external set of forces and rules that compel an individual to act one way or another. To speak of what Dorr believes is required of him — a concept raised in questioning by opposing counsel, not by Dorr — is to be concerned with too narrow a portion of religious belief. The question is not one of compulsion, but of motivation. Therefore, to find that Dorr does not sincerely believe that he is required to serve as Integrity's President does not complete the inquiry; that participation may still be motivated by his religious beliefs. Put another way, his sincerely held religious beliefs may motivate his activity even though they do not require it.

Id. at 13. *Dorr* was subsequently *vacated*, 1986 U.S. App. LEXIS 33065 (6th Cir. 1986). While it no longer has any precedential value, isn't its analysis correct? See also Anderson v. U.S.F. Logistics (IMC), Inc., 274 F.3d 470 (7th Cir. 2001) (district court would "probably" have erred if it viewed plaintiff's desire to use "have a blessed day" with customers as subject to a lesser requirement of accommodation because it was not required by her religion). In Pielich v. Massasoit Greyhound, Inc., 668 N.E.2d 1298 (Mass. 1996), the Supreme Judicial Court invalidated a state antidiscrimation statute which did not protect two employees' sincere religious beliefs that their Roman Catholicism prohibited them from working on Christmas. The lower court had determined that Roman Catholic religion imposed no such prohibition, and that, therefore, the employees' beliefs, while sincere, were unprotected. In the wake of *Pielich*, the state legislation revised the statute to protect sincerely held religious beliefs "without regard to whether such beliefs are approved, espoused, prescribed or required by an established church or other religious institution or organization." Mass. Gen. L. ch. 151 B, § 4(1A) (1996). Would such a broad approach to Title VII put too large a burden on employers, requiring them to accommodate any act based on a worker's religious motivation?

4. Why is *Wilson* an accommodation case? Would plaintiff have been better off eschewing any accommodation claim and, instead, arguing that she was simply discharged because of her religion? Reread the statute. While "undue hardship" is a defense to a reasonable accommodation claim, it is not a defense to a charge of disparate treatment religious discrimination. It is true that bfoq might be a defense in theory, but did U.S. West establish the elements of a bfoq?

5. Or is the employer entitled to raise the accommodation issue — that it could not reasonably accommodate plaintiff's religious beliefs without undue hardship — as a defense to an individual disparate treatment case? In Brown v. Polk County, Iowa, 61 F.3d 650 (8th Cir. 1995) (en banc) the plaintiff made a straightforward claim that he was terminated because of his religion. The employer then raised accommodation as a defense: it argued that, because plaintiff never explicitly asked for accommodation of his religious activities, he could not claim the protections of Title VII. The court seemed to accept this approach. While it held against the defendant on the facts, it did suggest that the employer could prevail if it could show that any accommodation of the plaintiff's religious expression was an undue hardship. 61 F.3d at 655. How could that be? Is "undue hardship" another name for bfoq in this setting?

6. Can an employer respond to a claim of religious discrimination, first, by denying that religion was involved in the decision plaintiff is challenging and, second, by claiming that, even if religion was a motivating factor in its decision, the employer could not reasonably accommodate the religious practices without undue hardship? Who bears the burden of persuasion in such a scenario?

7. Was Wilson "harassed" because of her religious beliefs? Or was she "harassing" others because of her religious beliefs? We examined sexual and other kinds of harassment in the preceding section, but religious harassment raises some distinctive issues. Indeed, the EEOC has attempted to formulate guidelines for religious harassment with little success. See, e.g., Michael D. Moberly, Bad News for Those Proclaiming the Goods News?: The Employer's Ambiguous Duty to Accommodate Religious Proselytizing, 42 Santa Clara L. Rev. 1 (2001); Kent Greenawalt, Title VII and Religious Liberty, 33 Loy. U. Chi. L.J. 1 (2001); Eugene Volokh, Freedom of Speech, Religious Harassment Law, and Religious Accommodation Law. 33 Loy. U. Chi. L.J. 57 (2001); Betty L. Dunkum, Where to Draw the Line: Handling Religious Harassment Issues in the Wake of the Failed EEOC Guidelines, 71 Notre Dame L. Rev. 953 (1996); Terry Morehead Dworkin & Ellen R. Peirce, Is Religious Harassment "More Equal?," 26 Seton Hall L. Rev. 44 (1995); David L. Gregory, Religious Harassment in the Workplace: An Analysis of the EEOC's Proposed Guidlines, 56 Mont. L. Rev. 119 (1995). President Clinton issued Guidelines on Religious Exercise and Religious Expression in the Federal Workplace, August 14, 1997, which have also come under intense attack. Stephen S. Kao, The President's Guidelines on Religious Exercise and Religious Expression in the Federal Workplace: A Restatement or Reinterpretation of Law?, 8 B.U. Pub. Int. L.J. 251 (1999).

The problem, of course, is that one person's harassment is another person's free exercise of religion. In this regard, Title VII poses a problem within itself: both the person expressing herself religiously and the person who is offended by that expression may seek the protection of the statute. Further, the Constitution can come into play. To the extent that the statute curbs religious expression, it implicates free exercise notions. Cf. Note on the First Amendment Implications of Sexual Harassment Liability, page 537. See also Thomas C. Berg, Religious Speech in the Workplace: Harassment or Protected Speech?, 22 Harv. L.J. & Pub. Pol'y 954, 959 (1999). Some issues in this regard might be clear: an employer who barred wearing a crucifix while permitting other jewelry is discriminating on the basis of religion. And even a bar on all jewelry (or all symbolic jewelry) might trigger a duty to accommodate. On the other hand, more directed expressions of religion — such as in *Wilson* itself or the employee who wrote her co-workers letters criticizing their morals, Chalmers v. Tulon Co., 101 F.3d 1012 (4th Cir. 1996) — are problematic.

8. Title VII bars religious discrimination, and will typically be the only federal statute implicated when religious discrimination by a private employer is concerned. However, where the employer is a governmental agency, the First Amendment also comes into play. It is generally thought "that in the governmental employment context, the first amendment [free exercise clause] protects at least as much religious activity as Title VII does." Brown v. Polk County, Iowa, 61 F.3d 650, 654 (8th Cir. 1995) (en banc). See also United States v. Bd. of Educ., 911 F.2d 882, 890 (3d Cir. 1990) ("at the very least, undue hardship is a lower standard than compelling state interest"). The *Brown* court went on to state that "if a governmental employer has violated Title VII, it has also violated the guarantees of the first amendment." 61 F.3d at 654. This formulation makes it possible that the First Amendment protects discrimination that Title VII would permit, although it is not clear that the courts will so hold in

practice. In Fraternal Order of Police Newark Lodge No. 12 v. City of Newark, 170 F.3d 359 (3d Cir. 1999), the court held that a city's refusal to accommodate officers whose religion required them to wear beards violated the free exercise clause, at least where the city permitted officers with medical conditions that limited shaving to wear beards. But see Daniels v. City of Arlington, 246 F.3d 500 (5th Cir. 2001) (city could bar display of cross as part of "no pin" policy for uniformed officers); United States v. Bd. of Educ. for Sch. Dist. of Phila., 911 F.2d 882 (3d Cir. 1990) (no accommodation required for female Muslim public school teacher who wished to wear a head scarf and a long, loose dress in the face of a statute prohibiting school teachers from wearing clothes indicating membership in a religion). Cf. Goldman v. Weinberger, 475 U.S. 503 (1986) (Air Force could constitutionally enforce a uniform dress requirement prohibiting the wearing of headgear indoors even though it restricted an Orthodox Jewish officer from wearing a yarmulke, a religious headpiece required by his religious beliefs; the Court emphasized the special situation of the military).

9. The Religious Freedom Restoration Act, 42 U.S.C.S. § 2000 bb-4 (2003), may also apply to federal employment decisions. See generally, Gregory P. Magarian, How to Apply the Religious Freedom Restoration Act to Federal Law without Violating the Constitution, 99 Mich. L. Rev. 1903 (2001). But see La Voz Radio de la Communidad v. FCC, 223 F.3d 313 (6th Cir. 2000) (expressing doubt that RFRA may constitutionally apply to the federal government).

10. Brown v. Polk County, Iowa, 61 F.3d 650, 654 (8th Cir. 1995) (en banc), did reject the argument that a defendant could not violate the duty to accommodate unless the employee explicitly requested an accommodation for his religious activities. See also Heller v. EBB Auto Co., 8 F.3d 1433, 1439 (9th Cir. 1993) (employer need have "only enough information about an employee's religious needs to permit the employer to understand the existence of a conflict between the employee's religious practices and the employer's job requirements"). But see Chalmers v. Tulon Co., 101 F.3d 1012, 1020 (4th Cir. 1996) ("Knowledge that an employee has strong religious beliefs does not place an employer on notice that she might engage in any religious activity, no matter how unusual.").

11. In *Wilson*, the response of co-workers to the religious practices of the plaintiff was at issue in determining whether the employer attempted to reasonably accommodate plaintiff and whether the accommodations plaintiff desired were an undue hardship. If co-worker backlash against having a female or an African-American supervisor or customer hostility to women or minority employees is not a justification for an employer's race or gender discrimination, why is co-worker backlash relevant in a religious discrimination case? Would co-worker hostility to an employee wearing a crucifix or a Star of David justify asking the wearer to remove or cover it? See generally Theresa M. Beiner & John M.A. DiPappa, Hostile Environments and the Religious Employee, 19 U. Ark. Little Rock L.J. 577 (1997).

12. When a professional basketball player refused for religious reasons to abide by an NBA rule requiring players to "line up in a designated position" for the playing of the national anthem, he was suspended by his team. Did the Denver Nuggets violate their duty to accommodate? Or would fan reaction justify the suspension, either as an undue hardship or a bfoq? See K. B. Koenig, Note: Mahmoud Abdul-Rauf's Suspension for Refusing to Stand for the National Anthem: A "Free Throw" for the NBA and Denver Nuggets, or a "Slam Dunk" Violation of Abdul-Rauf's Title VII Rights?, 76 Wash. U. L.Q. 327 (1998).

13. Perhaps some religious practices cannot be reasonably accommodated. In Chalmers v. Tulon Co., 101 F.3d 1012, 1020 (4th Cir. 1996), the plaintiff was fired

for sending letters to co-workers criticizing their personal lives. "Chalmers' religious accommodation claim would nonetheless fail . . . because Chalmers' conduct is not the type that an employer can possibly accommodate, even with notice." The court recognized that some religious practices, like Sabbath observances and wearing religious garb, could be accommodated with "indirect and minimal burdens, if any, on other employees." Accord Knight v. Conn. Dept. of Pub. Health, 275 F.3d 156, 168 (2d Cir. 2001) ("even assuming appellants did make out their prima facie cases, the accommodation they now seek is not reasonable. Permitting appellants to evangelize while providing services to clients would jeopardize the state's ability to provide services in a religion-neutral matter"). Cf. Anderson v. U.S.F. Logistics (IMC), Inc., 274 F.3d 470 (7th Cir. 2001) (it was a reasonable accommodation to permit worker to use "have a blessed day" with customers other than the one who objected since her religious belief did not entail using it all the time). However, "where an employee contends that she has a religious need to impose personally and directly on fellow employees, invading their privacy and criticizing their personal lives, the employer is placed between a rock and a hard place. If Tulon had the power to authorize Chalmers to write such letters, and if Tulon had granted Chalmers' request to write the letters, the company would subject itself to possible suits from [co-workers] claiming that Chalmers' conduct violated their religious freedoms or constituted religious harassment." Id. at 1021.

14. In Ryan v. United States Dept. of Justice, 950 F.2d 458 (7th Cir. 1991), the court found that the FBI need not agree to the only accommodation acceptable to the agent — that the agency discontinue investigating antiwar groups. "Ryan proposed no course other than discontinuing investigations of the sort to which he is opposed which would be capitulation rather than accommodation." Id. at 461. Similarly, in Rodriguez v. City of Chicago, 156 F.3d 771 (7th Cir. 1998), plaintiff police officer alleged that the city discriminated against him by refusing to exempt him from an assignment to guard an abortion clinic. The court held that the city had satisfied "its duty to accommodate Officer Rodriguez by providing him the opportunity, through the [collective bargaining agreement], to transfer to a district that did not have an abortion clinic with no reduction in his level of pay or benefits." This was a "paradigm" of reasonable accommodation, Chief Judge Posner concurred, saying that "police officers and firefighters have no right under Title VII . . . [to] recuse themselves from having to protect persons of whose activities they disapprove for religious (or any other) reasons." Requiring any accommodation would lead "to the loss of public confidence in governmental protective services if the public knows that its protectors are at liberty to pick and choose whom to protect." Accord Shelton v. Univ. Med. & Dentistry of N.J., 223 F.3d 220 (3d Cir. 2000) (moving labor/delivery nurse to another department was reasonable accommodation of her beliefs concerning abortion). But neither Rodriguez nor Sheldon held that a right to transfer was required: they simply held that that was a sufficient accommodation. And does Judge Posner's position effectively negate any duty of accommodation? Are all these cases just applications of Philbrook — once an employer offers an accommodation, the duty is discharged, even if the religious practice is not fully accommodated?

15. Although Hardison obviously limited the extent to which employers must accommodate employees unable to work on particular days because of religious beliefs, the determination is made on a case-by-case basis, and the courts sometimes find that accommodation could be arranged without undue hardship. E.g., EEOC v. Ilona of Hungary, 108 F.3d 1569 (7th Cir. 1997) (violation to refuse unpaid leave to two Jewish employees for Yom Kippur). See Karen Engle, The Persistence of Neutrality: The

Failure of the Religious Accommodation Provision to Redeem Title VII, 76 Tex. L. Rev. 317, 321 (1997) ("Courts considering claims for religious accommodation, contrary to common belief, have been unable to break out of the neutrality paradigm that is predominant in the other categories. Rather than taking an accommodationist approach, courts in the religion cases either follow . . . an integrationist approach — primarily found in the race and national origin cases — or a separationist approach — most commonly found in the sex cases. This inability of religious accommodation to overcome integrationist and separationist ideology is one of many examples of the dominance of the nondiscrimination-neutrality norm in American law.").

16.  The structure of accommodation law for religious beliefs and practices is quite strict and does not seem consistent with the plain meaning of § 701(j) or its legislative history. Senator Randolph, the sponsor of § 701(j), argued that the Amendment would protect employees who were members of religious sects that "believe there should be steadfast observance of the Sabbath and require that the observance of the day of worship, the day of the Sabbath, be other than on Sunday. On this day of worship work is prohibited where the day should fall on Friday, or Saturday, or Sunday." 118 Cong. Rec. 705 (1972). Why has the Supreme Court decided to underenforce § 701(j)? Might it be a concern that full enforcement would violate the establishment clause of the First Amendment? See Note on the Establishment Clause, page 605.

## NOTE ON RELIGIOUS INSTITUTIONS' EXEMPTION FROM THE PROHIBITION OF RELIGIOUS DISCRIMINATION

Religious entities are exempted from Title VII's prohibition of discrimination on the basis of religion. See Corporation of the Presiding Bishop v. Amos, 483 U.S. 327 (1987). Even religious employers, however, are barred from discriminating on the other grounds prohibited by Title VII. E.g., Bollard v. California Province of Socy. of Jesus, 196 F.3d 940 (9th Cir. 1999) (a valid Title VII sexual harassment claim was stated against a religious order). This structure raises several questions, two of which frequently arise in tandem: is an employer "religious," and, if so, is the discrimination it practices "religious" in nature?

Title VII has several exemptions from its prohibition of religious discrimination for religious institutions. Section 702(a), 42 U.S.C.S. § 2000e-1(a) (2003), provides that "This title shall not apply . . . to a religious corporation, association, educational institution, or society with respect to the employment of individuals of a particular religion to perform work connected with carrying on" the activities of such an entity. See Killinger v. Samford Univ., 113 F.3d 196 (11th Cir. 1997). Section 2000e-1(e) provides that the equal employment provisions of the Act do not apply to employment by an "educational institution" of individuals "of a particular religion" if the educational institution is "owned, supported, controlled or managed by a particular religion" or a religious corporation, "if the curriculum of such school . . . is directed toward the propagation of a particular religion." The latter exemption has been construed narrowly. For example, it does not exempt an institution "merely 'affiliated' with a religious organization." EEOC v. Townley Eng'g & Mfg. Co., 859 F.2d 610, 617 (9th Cir. 1988), nor exempt a school which is merely nominally religious. EEOC v. Kamehameha Schs./Bishop Estate, 990 F.2d 458 (9th Cir. 1993). The test is whether the institution is "primarily secular" or "primarily religious," taking into account its "ownership and affiliation, purpose, faculty, student body, student activities, and curriculum." Id. at 461. See also Pime v. Loyola Univ., 803 F.2d 351 (7th Cir. 1986) (while having a long Jesuit history, Loyola University was a nonprofit corporation with bylaws that required only that the president and one-third plus one of the board of trustees be Jesuits. All students were required to take three theology classes, but those courses need not cover Catholic theology).

Two contrary views of whether religious institutions should be able to take religious beliefs and practices into account in hiring have emerged recently. Jane Rutherford, Equality as the Primary Constitutional Value: The Case for Applying Employment Discrimination Laws to Religion, 81 Cornell L. Rev. 1049, 1126-28 (1996), launches an attack on the entire concept of immunizing religions from anti-discrimination laws:

> The problems of discrimination persist because they are deeply imbedded in our common culture. Law, alone, has been unable to eradicate bias. The only hope is broad scale change in social and cultural values. One part of that culture is a religious heritage that is pervasively discriminatory. Section 702 . . . allows religious groups to discriminate on religious grounds, and courts sometimes permit religious institutions to discriminate on the basis of race, sex, age, or disability. Such Congressional or judicial exceptions to civil rights laws violate the Free Exercise Clause because they limit the rights of minorities, women, the aged, and the disabled to practice their religious beliefs on the same terms as the dominant groups. Church leaders have a greater chance of having their religious views incorporated into religious doctrine because of this access to power. When minorities, women, the aged and the disabled are excluded from religious hierarchies, their views are significantly less likely to be acknowledged. Those excluded from leadership positions are denied the right to participate in their own religion. . . . The First Amendment should not be permitted to be used as a shield to protect such subordinating conduct. Nevertheless, applying anti-discrimination laws to religions poses free exercise problems for religious groups. Some fear that empowering the government to enforce civil rights laws against religions would completely dismantle religion. That view puts too little faith in religion, however. It assumes that discrimination is the central tenet and that nothing would be left if religion were forced to treat minorities, women, the aged, and the disabled as equals.
>
> Nevertheless, religions do risk intrusions on free exercise rights. Courts faced with these decisions are caught in a dilemma. Any decision intrudes on a free exercise right, either of the religious groups or those excluded. The only solution to the dilemma is to look outside the religion clauses for a principled way to decide. That principle may be found in the primacy of equality.

A contrary view is taken by Robert John Araujo, "The Harvest Is Plentiful, But the Laborers Are Few": Hiring Practices and Religiously Affiliated Universities, 30 U. Rich. L. Rev. 713, 724 (1996). According to Araujo, religiously affiliated schools should be able to extend apostolic preference not only to co-religionists but to all other employment candidates who are allied with and supportive of the institution's religiously inspired mission. Such preferential hiring practices could help promote and sustain the diversity that is important to American culture and education. See also Jack M. Battaglia, Religion, Sexual Orientation, and Self-Realization: First Amendment Principles and Anti-Discrimination Laws, 76 U. Det. Mercy L. Rev. 189 (1999); G. Sidney Buchanan, The Power of Government to Regulate Class Discrimination by Religious Entities: A Study in Core Values, 43 Emory L.J. 1189 (1994); Shelley K. Wessels, The Collision of Religious Exercise and Governmental Nondiscrimination Policies, 41 Stan. L. Rev. 1201 (1989); David A. Fielder, Serving God or Caesar: Constitutional Limits on the Regulation of Religious Employers, 51 Mo. L. Rev. 779 (1986); Bruce N. Bagni, Discrimination in the Name of the Lord: A Critical

Evaluation of Discrimination by Religious Organizations, 79 Colum. L. Rev. 1514 (1979).

### NOTE ON BFOQ DEFENSE TO RELIGIOUS DISCRIMINATION

Because of the exemptions for religious institutions, church-related organizations rarely need to rely on the bfoq defense. In some cases, however, institutions that were not within the exemption, but were nevertheless religiously oriented, have used the defense. For example, Pime v. Loyola University, 803 F.2d 351 (7th Cir. 1986), found a bfoq established for reserving tenured lines for Jesuits in Loyola's philosophy department, although it did not find Loyola to be a religious employer. Judge Fairchild wrote for the majority in *Pime*:

> It appears to be significant to the educational tradition and character of the institution that students be assured a degree of contact with teachers who have received the training and accepted the obligations which are essential to membership in the Society of Jesus. It requires more to be a Jesuit than just adherence to the Catholic faith, and it seems wholly reasonable to believe that the educational experience at Loyola would be differ-ent if Jesuit presence were not maintained. As priests, Jesuits perform rites and sacra-ments, and counsel members of the university community, including students, faculty, and staff. One witness expressed the objective as keeping a presence "so that students would occasionally encounter a Jesuit."
>
> It is true that it has not been shown that Jesuit training is a superior academic qualification, applying objective criteria, to teach the particular courses. It is also true that in looking at claims of BFOQ, courts have considered only the content of the par-ticular job at issue. Yet it seems to us that here the evidence supports the more general proposition that having a Jesuit presence in the Philosophy faculty is "reasonably neces-sary to the normal operation" of the enterprise, and that fixing the number at seven out of 31 is a reasonable determination. . . .

803 F.2d at 353-54. Judge Posner feared that the majority was reading the bfoq test too broadly under then-existing authority.

*Pime* was decided before International Union, UAW v. Johnson Controls (repro-duced at page 268), which narrowed the bfoq exemption. Is *Pime* still good law? EEOC v. Kamehameha Schs./Bishop Estate, 990 F.2d 458 (9th Cir. 1993), rejected a bfoq for hiring Protestants to teach in the Kamehameha schools. The district court had so found, because a "Protestant presence is significant to the educational and normal operation" of the schools, much as a Jesuit presence was desirable at Loyola. The Ninth Circuit reversed:

> Even if *Pime* were an accurate statement of the law in light of *Johnson Controls*, how-ever, it could not bear the weight the Schools would have it carry. *Pime* approved a Jesuit "presence" of four positions in the Philosophy Department of Loyola University, a school with "a long Jesuit tradition" and a largely Catholic student body. The court fo-cused on the tradition and character of the school and the desire of administrators "'that students would *occasionally* encounter a Jesuit.'" (emphasis added). The court stated it was "wholly reasonable to believe that the educational experience at Loyola would be different if a Jesuit presence were not maintained." In this case, the Schools will have a Protestant "presence" equal to or greater than the Jesuit "presence" at Loyola even if the proportion of Protestants on the faculty falls well below one hundred percent, and there is no indication the educational experience at the Schools will be any different if

some of the teachers are not Protestants. Moreover, the Schools seek to retain a wholly Protestant faculty at a school whose student body has a majority of non-Protestant students and whose tradition and character is rooted more in Hawaiian history and culture than in specific principles of Protestantism.

Id. Further, the origins of the Protestant-only requirement in the will that established the schools did not alter the result. "The will suggests only that Mrs. Bishop was stating a personal preference based on her own experience in missionary schools. This kind of personal preference is not a BFOQ when expressed by a living employer, and there is no reason to reach a different conclusion because the preference is expressed posthumously." Id. at 466.

All of these employers had some religious connection. Is it possible for a purely secular employer to establish a bfoq? See Kern v. Dynalection Corp., 577 F. Supp. 1196 (N.D. Tex. 1983) (Saudi Arabian law forbidding non-Muslims from flying over certain holy areas justified Muslim faith as a bfoq for the position of helicopter pilot). See also Piatti v. Jewish Cmty. Ctrs., 1993 Mass. Super. LEXIS 328 (Mass. Super. Ct. 1993) (finding being a practicing Jew to be a bfoq under state law for position at Jewish Community Center). Professor Steven D. Jamar argues that Title VII is underprotective of religion by failing to take account of what he calls religious secular employers, that is, employers who view religious beliefs and practices as key to their otherwise secular businesses. Professor Jamar argues that it is wrong for Title VII to assume that secular employers must eschew religion. Accommodating Religion at Work: A Principled Approach to Title VII and Religious Freedom, 40 N.Y.L. L. Rev. 719, 788-89 (1996). Is it wrong for the law to require a secular employer to eschew religious-based notions of how to run a business, or must employees be expected to accommodate to their employer's decision to run the business based on religious values, beliefs, and practices?

## NOTE ON THE ESTABLISHMENT CLAUSE

Possible constitutional limitations on Title VII's treatment of religion have not been well received. One attack that did reach the Supreme Court was a challenge to the exemption of religious institutions from the statute's prohibition on religious discrimination. Corporation of the Presiding Bishop v. Amos, 483 U.S. 327 (1987), involved the Deseret Gymnasium in Salt Lake City, Utah, a nonprofit facility, open to the public, but operated by two religious corporations, both associated with The Church of Jesus Christ of Latter-day Saints, sometimes called the Mormon Church. A building engineer sued when he was discharged in 1981 because he failed to qualify for "a temple recommend, that is, a certificate that he is a member of the Church and eligible to attend its temples." Id. at 330. When the defendants moved to dismiss on the basis that § 702 shielded them from liability, plaintiff contended that § 702 would violate the establishment clause if it were construed to allow religious employers to discriminate in hiring for non-religious jobs. The Supreme Court upheld the § 702 exemption:

"This Court has long recognized that the government may (and sometimes must) accommodate religious practices and that it may do so without violating the Establishment Clause." Hobbie v. Unemployment Appeals Commn. of Fla., 480 U.S. 136 (1987). It is well established, too, that "[t]he limits of permissible state accommodation to religion are by no means co-extensive with the noninterference mandated by the Free

> Exercise Clause." Walz v. Tax Commn., 397 U.S. 664 (1970). There is ample room under the Establishment Clause for "benevolent neutrality which will permit religious exercise to exist without sponsorship and without interference." At some point, accommodation may devolve into "an unlawful fostering of religion," *Hobbie*, but this is not such a case, in our view.

Id. at 334. The Court found no occasion to re-examine the much-criticized three-pronged test for establishment clause validity of Lemon v. Kurtzman, 403 U.S. 602 (1971), since "the exemption involved here is in no way questionable under *Lemon*." 483 U.S. at 327.

*Amos* first held that § 702 had a "secular legislative purpose." To be secular, such a purpose did not have to be wholly unrelated to religion. A permissible purpose was "to alleviate significant governmental interference with the ability of religious organizations to define and carry out their religious missions." Id. at 335. Although an exemption for religious activities only might have been adequate "in the sense that the Free Exercise Clause required no more," Congress could validly choose to reduce the "significant burden on a religious organization to require it, on pain of substantial liability, to predict which of its activities a secular court will consider religious. The line is hardly a bright one, and an organization might understandably be concerned that a judge would not understand its religious tenets and sense of mission. Fear of potential liability might affect the way an organization carried out what it understood to be its religious mission." Id. at 336.

The second prong of *Lemon* — that the law have "a principal or primary effect . . . that neither advances nor inhibits religion" — was also satisfied. While religions are somewhat assisted, "[a] law is not unconstitutional simply because it allows churches to advance religion, which is their very purpose. For a law to have forbidden 'effects' under *Lemon*, it must be fair to say that the government itself has advanced religion through its own activities and influence." Id. at 337. Nor was it determinative that the statute accords the benefit only to religious organizations. "Where, as here, government acts with the proper purpose of lifting a regulation that burdens the exercise of religion, we see no reason to require that the exemption come packaged with benefits to secular entities." Id. at 338.

Finally, the Court found the third part of *Lemon* easily satisfied — the exemption did not impermissibly entangle church and state. Indeed, "the statute effectuates a more complete separation of the two and avoids the kind of intrusive inquiry into religious belief" that might be required of a less complete exemption. Justice O'Connor and Justices Brennan and Marshall separately concurred, each stressing that the opinion reached only nonprofit entities, and that a different result might follow if the religious organization was for-profit. Justice O'Connor, in addition, criticized the *Lemon* test.

A second constitutional challenge on establishment clause grounds has been to the whole notion of reasonable accommodation. It is clear that a duty to accommodate employees' religious beliefs may go too far. In Estate of Thornton v. Caldor, Inc., 472 U.S. 703 (1985), the Court struck down a Connecticut statute which prohibited employers from requiring an employee to work on his Sabbath. That statute was not limited to "reasonable" accommodation, but required accommodation by the employer, regardless of the burden imposed. In a later case, the statute struck down in *Thornton* was described as effectively having given "the force of law to an employee's designation of his sabbath day and required accommodation by the employer regardless of the burden that constituted for the employer or other employees." *Amos*, 483 U.S. at

337-38, n.15. Title VII, which provides only for "reasonable" accommodation and provides employer protection for undue hardship, is presumably distinguishable. In Protos v. Volkswagen of America, Inc., 797 F.2d 129 (3d Cir. 1986), Volkswagen was held to have violated § 701(j) by failing to accommodate plaintiff's religious-based need to be free of Saturday overtime. Because the employer always scheduled a crew of relief operators to substitute for absent employees, it would not have cost the employer more to accommodate plaintiff. Volkswagen claimed that, so read, the reasonable accommodation requirement violated the establishment clause. The court rejected this argument, relying on Lemon v. Kurtzman. It distinguished *Thornton*:

> Unlike the Connecticut statute, Title VII does not require absolute deference to the religious practices of the employee, allows for consideration of the hardship to other employees and to the company, and permits an evaluation of whether the employer has attempted to accommodate the employee. Volkswagen contends that as applied in this case, Title VII provided a primary benefit to religion because Protos sought an absolute guarantee of exemption from all Saturday labor. However, in determining whether she was entitled to such a guarantee, the court considered the impact accommodating her would have on "secular interests of the workplace," *Thornton*, and found that given the nature of Protos's assembly line position and Volkswagen's method of providing substitutes for absent employees, her absence would not significantly affect those interests. Any effect the statute had of advancing religion, therefore, would appear to be incidental to its primary effect of promoting freedom of conscience and prohibiting discrimination in the workplace.

Id. at 136. Because the accommodation requirement had a secular purpose — "to relieve individuals of the burden of choosing between their jobs and their religious convictions," id. — and would not lead to excessive government entanglement with religion, it was constitutional.

It may be with the establishment clause in mind that the Supreme Court has so narrowly construed the duty of reasonable accommodation in both *Hardison* and *Philbrook*. Certainly, the Court's reading is far narrower than the literal language would suggest, and far narrower than the similarly phrased duty of reasonable accommodation under the Americans with Disabilities Act. See Chapter 8. And the Supreme Court has a history of reading statutes to avoid having to face constitutional questions under the religion clauses of the First Amendment. E.g., NLRB v. Catholic Bishop, 440 U.S. 490 (1979) (interpreting National Labor Relations Act not to reach religiously affiliated schools in order to avoid free exercise problems). However, it might be argued that the constitutional landscape has changed. Would the Court that decided *Amos* strike down a literal interpretation of Title VII's duty of reasonable accommodation?

## COMBS v. CENTRAL TEXAS ANNUAL CONFERENCE
## OF THE UNITED METHODIST CHURCH
### 173 F.3d 343 (5th Cir. 1999)

W. EUGENE DAVIS, Circuit Judge:

Reverend Pamela Combs appeals the dismissal of her Title VII sex and pregnancy discrimination suit against the First United Methodist Church of Horst ("First United") and the Central Texas Annual Conference of the United Methodist Church

("Central Texas Conference"). The sole question presented in this appeal is whether the district court correctly determined that the Free Exercise Clause of the First Amendment precluded it from considering Reverend Combs's employment discrimination case. For the reasons that follow, we conclude that the district court was correct and affirm.

## I

. . . The facts of this case, when viewed in [the light most favorable to plaintiff], are summarized as follows.

Reverend Combs is a graduate of the New Orleans Theological Seminary. In 1988, she was ordained as a Baptist minister. In 1993, she was hired as First United's Singles Minister. In late 1994, she was appointed First United's Associate Minister. In this new position, she served communion, assisted in baptisms, performed marriages, and led funerals.

In February 1995, as part of the long process of having her ordination recognized within the Methodist Church, she was interviewed by the United Methodist Board of Ordained Ministry, which unanimously recommended to the Bishop of the Central Texas Conference that she be ordained. In June 1995, she was appointed by the Bishop, Joe A. Wilson, to serve for the next year as a minister at First United.

In October 1995, Reverend Combs, who was — and still is — married, announced that she was pregnant. She requested and was granted maternity leave for the expected childbirth. In March 1996, she had her annual interview with the United Methodist Board of Ordained Ministry. The board again recommended unanimously that Reverend Combs continue with the process of having her ordination recognized within the Methodist Church.

Around this time, Reverend Combs questioned why her pay was substantially lower than that of the male ministers she had replaced. She also requested a housing allowance because she and her family had moved out of the parsonage to free up space for other church use. In response, the Staff Parish Relations Committee made several adjustments to her compensation package.

In April 1996, Reverend Combs took some accrued vacation time and began her eight-week maternity leave, as provided for clergy by the rules of the United Methodist Church Book of Discipline. On April 17, 1996, she gave birth. Unfortunately, however, Reverend Combs suffered serious post-partum complications, which required hospitalization, surgery, heavy medication, and extensive rest.

During this period of incapacitation, Reverend Combs's position within First United was questioned by her pastor and immediate supervisor, Dr. John Fielder. He challenged her competence, performance, and honesty. In addition, one of First United's oversight committees stated that she was a lay employee rather than a member of the clergy. The church then denied her the maternity benefits she had been granted and demanded she repay those benefits that had already been paid to her.

Nevertheless, in June 1996, the Bishop of the Central Texas Conference reappointed Reverend Combs as an Associate Minister for First United. However, when Reverend Combs returned to work on June 17, 1996, she was told by Dr. Fielder that she had been terminated and that she was required to leave the premises immediately. The next day, Reverend Combs went to the Staff Parish Relations Committee. The committee stated that Dr. Fielder said she had resigned and that the committee had accepted her resignation. Reverend Combs protested that she had not resigned, but to no avail. Reverend Combs then brought the matter to the attention of the Central Texas Conference. However, she found no support from that organization either.

. . . Reverend Combs sued both the Central Texas Conference and First United, alleging discrimination on the basis of her sex and her pregnancy in violation of Title VII. She alleged that the deprivation of her benefits and her termination were the conclusion of a practice of discrimination that included disparate salary and treatment while she was employed.

[The district court dismissed Reverend Comb's suit, holding that "the First Amendment prohibits civil review of the Defendants' decision to terminate Reverend Combs."] Reverend Combs now appeals this dismissal.[1]

## II

The question before us is whether the Free Exercise Clause of the First Amendment deprives a federal court of jurisdiction to hear a Title VII employment discrimination suit brought against a church by a member of its clergy, even when the church's challenged actions are not based on religious doctrine.

All parties agree that prior to 1990, the district court decision would have been correct. In McClure v. Salvation Army, 460 F.2d 553, 560 (5th Cir. 1972), this Court established a church-minister[3] exception to the coverage of Title VII. In this appeal, however, Reverend Combs questions whether McClure and its church-minister exception still stand in light of the Supreme Court's decision in Employment Division, Department of Human Resources of Oregon v. Smith, 494 U.S. 872 (1990). To resolve this question, we start by reviewing McClure and move from that case forward.

## A

[Mrs. Billie McClure, a Salvation Army officer alleged discrimination on the basis of her sex. The Court held she stated a claim under Title VII but that] the Salvation Army was a church and . . . Mrs. McClure was an ordained minister within that church. These findings required the Court to address two further questions: Was the Salvation Army exempt from Title VII under Section 702's religious exemption? If not, did the First Amendment exempt the Salvation Army's treatment of Mrs. McClure from federal review under Title VII?

In answering the first question, the Court concluded that although Section 702 exempts religious organizations from Title VII's coverage for religious discrimination, it does not provide a blanket exemption for all discrimination. Title VII still prohibits a religious organization from discriminating on the basis of race, color, sex, or national origin. Because Mrs. McClure was alleging discrimination on the basis of her sex, this Court held that her claim did not fall within the Section 702 exemption.

After determining that Mrs. McClure's claim fell within the statutory coverage of Title VII, the Court addressed whether the Free Exercise Clause of the First Amendment permitted such a claim by a minister against her church. The Court began by

1. All parties agree that, at least for the purposes of this appeal, the following facts are true: Reverend Combs was a member of the clergy performing traditional clerical functions; both Defendants are churches and at least one of them employed Reverend Combs; and Reverend Combs's claims are based purely on sex and pregnancy and do not directly involve matters of religious dogma or ecclesiastical law. In addition, for the purposes of this appeal, we assume that Reverend Combs's allegations are sufficient to support a finding of discrimination.

3. Courts have called this exception both the church-minister exception and the ministerial exception. We use both terms interchangeably.

noting that the First Amendment has built a "wall of separation" between church and state. After describing this wall, the Court stated:

> Only in rare instances where a "compelling state interest in the regulation of a subject within the State's constitutional power to regulate" is shown can a court uphold state action which imposes even an "incidental burden" on the free exercise of religion. In this highly sensitive constitutional area "'only the gravest abuses, endangering paramount interests, give occasion for permissible limitation.'" Sherbert v. Verner, 374 U.S. 398 (1963).

This Court then emphasized the importance of the relationship between an organized church and its ministers, describing it as the church's "lifeblood." The Court reviewed a series of cases in which the Supreme Court had placed matters of church government and administration beyond the regulation of civil authorities (citing and describing Watson v. Jones, 80 U.S. (13 Wall.) 679 (1871) (affirming state court decision not to become involved in factional dispute within church); Gonzalez v. Roman Catholic Archbishop of Manila, 280 U.S. 1 (1929) (declining, absent fraud, collusion, or arbitrariness, to involve secular courts in matters purely ecclesiastical); Kedroff v. St. Nicholas Cathedral, 344 U.S. 94 (1952) (holding that legislation transferring control of Russian Orthodox churches from Patriarch of Moscow to convention of North American churches is unconstitutional interference with the free exercise of religion); Kreshik v. St. Nicholas Cathedral, 363 U.S. 190 (1960) (overturning, as unconstitutional involvement in matters of church administration, state court ruling that Patriarch of Moscow did not control Russian Orthodox churches within North America); Presbyterian Church v. Mary Elizabeth Blue Hull Memorial Presbyterian Church, 393 U.S. 440 (1969) (warning against civil court involvement in church property litigation)).

After reviewing this Supreme Court precedent, the *McClure* Court determined that applying Title VII to the employment relationship between the Salvation Army and Mrs. McClure "would involve an investigation and review . . . [that] would . . . cause the State to intrude upon matters of church administration and government which have so many times before been proclaimed to be matters of a singular ecclesiastical concern." Thus, the Court held that applying Title VII to the relationship under consideration "would result in an encroachment by the State into an area of religious freedom which it is forbidden to enter by the principles of the free exercise clause of the First Amendment." The Court therefore affirmed the district court's dismissal of Mrs. McClure's claim.

Most of our sister circuits adopted the church-minister exception articulated in *McClure*. See, e.g., Natal v. Christian and Missionary Alliance, 878 F.2d 1575 (1st Cir. 1989); Rayburn v. General Conf. of Seventh-day Adventists, 772 F.2d 1164 (4th Cir. 1985); Hutchison v. Thomas, 789 F.2d 392, 393 (6th Cir. 1986); Young v. Northern Illinois Conf. of United Methodist Church, 21 F.3d 184 (7th Cir. 1994); Scharon v. St. Luke's Episcopal Presbyterian Hosp., 929 F.2d 360, 363 (8th Cir. 1991); Minker v. Baltimore Annual Conf. of United Methodist Church, 894 F.2d 1354, 1358 (D.C. Cir. 1990). Although the Supreme Court itself has never adopted the *McClure* exception, it is the law of this circuit and much of the rest of the country.

**B**

Reverend Combs contends in this appeal that the *McClure* church-minister exception cannot stand in light of the Supreme Court's decision in Employment Division, Department of Human Resources of Oregon v. Smith, 494 U.S. 872 (1990).

In *Smith*, Alfred Smith and Galen Black were fired by their employer because of their sacramental use of peyote — a controlled substance under Oregon law — within the Native American Church. Oregon denied unemployment benefits to Smith and Black because they were terminated for "misconduct" — a violation of Oregon criminal law. Smith and Black argued that the Free Exercise Clause of the First Amendment prohibited Oregon from denying them benefits solely because they ingested peyote for sacramental purposes. In order to resolve this issue, the Supreme Court considered whether Oregon was constitutionally permitted to include the religious use of peyote within its general criminal prohibition of that drug.

The Supreme Court determined that Oregon's prohibition on all peyote use did not violate the First Amendment: "the right of free exercise does not relieve an individual of the obligation to comply with a valid and neutral law of general applicability on the ground that the law proscribes (or prescribes) conduct that his religion prescribes (or proscribes)." In arriving at this conclusion, the Supreme Court specifically rejected the "compelling state interest" test set forth in Sherbert v. Verner. The Court then held that because Oregon was constitutionally permitted to prohibit Smith's and Black's ingestion of peyote, Oregon was also constitutionally permitted to deny them unemployment benefits when their dismissal resulted from their use of the drug.

Congress attempted to reverse *Smith* legislatively by passing the Religious Freedom Restoration Act of 1993 ("RFRA"), codified at 42 U.S.C. § 2000bb et seq. (1994), which granted religious organizations broad immunity from neutrally applicable laws. One of the stated goals of RFRA was to restore the compelling interest test from *Sherbert* that the Supreme Court had rejected in *Smith*.

The Supreme Court, however, held RFRA to be unconstitutional. In its 1997 decision in City of Boerne v. Flores, 521 U.S. 507 (1997), the Supreme Court adopted its earlier analysis in *Smith*. In a passage now quoted by Reverend Combs, the Court stated, "When the exercise of religion has been burdened in an incidental way by a law of general application, it does not follow that the persons affected have been burdened more than other citizens, let alone burdened because of their religious beliefs."

Reverend Combs's argument that *McClure* cannot stand in light of the Supreme Court's decisions in *Smith* and *Boerne* is relatively straightforward: First, in *Smith* and *Boerne*, the Supreme Court held that the First Amendment does not bar the application of facially neutral laws even when these laws burden the exercise of religion. Second, *McClure* was based on the now-rejected "compelling interest" test. For these reasons, Reverend Combs argues that *McClure* no longer controls and therefore she should be permitted to pursue her Title VII discrimination claim against First United and the Central Texas Conference.

*1*

A well-reasoned opinion from the D.C. Circuit recently considered the precise question presented to us. In E.E.O.C. v. Catholic University, 83 F.3d 455 (D.C. Cir. 1996), that court was asked whether, in light of *Smith*, a professor who was also a Catholic nun could sue Catholic University for sex discrimination in the denial of her application for tenure. In resolving this issue, the D.C. Circuit addressed the post-*Smith* validity of the ministerial exception.

The D.C. Circuit began its analysis by making the important distinction between two different strands of free exercise law. The court stated, "government action may burden the free exercise of religion, in violation of the First Amendment, in two quite different ways: by interfering with a believer's ability to observe the commands or practices of his faith, . . . and by encroaching on the ability of a church to manage its internal affairs." The court emphasized that the Supreme Court has shown a particular reluctance to interfere with a church's selection of its own clergy (citing Gonzalez v. Roman Catholic Archbishop of Manila; Serbian Eastern Orthodox Diocese v. Milivojevich).

The [*Catholic University*] court concluded that *Smith* did not address the Free Exercise Clause's protection to a church against government encroachment into the church's internal management. Rather, *Smith* only addressed the strand of Free Exercise Clause protection afforded an individual to practice his faith. Thus, the *Catholic University* court determined that the language in *Smith* that the plaintiff relied on — "the right of free exercise does not relieve an individual of the obligation to comply with a valid and neutral law of general applicability . . ." — did not mean that a church, as opposed to an individual, is never entitled to relief from a neutral law of general application.

The D.C. Circuit provided two main reasons for its conclusion. First, the court stated that:

> The burden on free exercise that is addressed by the ministerial exception is of a fundamentally different character from that at issue in *Smith* and in the cases cited by the [Supreme] Court in support of its holding. The ministerial exception is not invoked to protect the freedom of an individual to observe a particular command or practice of his church. Rather it is designed to protect the freedom of the church to select those who will carry out its religious mission. Moreover, the ministerial exception does not present the dangers warned of in *Smith*. Protecting the authority of a church to select its own ministers free of government interference does not empower a member of that church, by virtue of his beliefs, to become a law unto himself. Nor does the exception require judges to determine the centrality of religious beliefs before applying a "compelling interest" test in the free exercise field.

Second, the D.C. Circuit acknowledged that the Supreme Court had rejected the "compelling interest" test cited by some courts (including *McClure*) when invoking the ministerial exception. The court observed, however, that many courts applying the exception rely on a long line of Supreme Court cases standing for the fundamental proposition that churches should be able to "decide for themselves, free from state interference, matters of church government as well as those of faith and doctrine." (quoting *Kedroff*). The D.C. Circuit concluded, "we cannot believe that the Supreme Court in *Smith* intended to qualify this century-old affirmation of a church's sovereignty over its own affairs."

2

We agree with both the reasoning and the conclusion of the D.C. Circuit. Especially important is that court's distinction between the two strands of free exercise cases — restrictions on an individual's actions that are based on religious beliefs and encroachments on the ability of a church to manage its internal affairs. Reverend Combs acknowledges this distinction, but argues that it does not determine the outcome of this case. Instead, Reverend Combs contends that *Smith* and *Boerne* indicate that the constitutional protection for religious freedom is impermissibly broadened when it grants churches immunity from employment actions by clergy when such actions are not based on questions of religious dogma or ecclesiastical law. We disagree.

*Smith*'s language is clearly directed at the first strand of free exercise law, where an individual contends that, because of his religious beliefs, he should not be required to conform with generally applicable laws. The concerns raised in *Smith* are quite different from the concerns raised by Reverend Combs's case, which pertains to interference in internal church government. We concur wholeheartedly with the D.C. Circuit's conclusion that *Smith*, which concerned individual free exercise, did not purport to overturn a century of precedent protecting the church against governmental interference in selecting its ministers.

We also disagree with Reverend Combs's argument that *McClure* is no longer good law because it relied on the "compelling state interest" test rejected by the Supreme Court in *Smith*. Our review of *McClure* reveals that although this Court presented the "compelling state interest" test in its general discussion of First Amendment law, the test is never applied or even mentioned later in the opinion. Thus, it is unclear how much this Court was actually relying on this test. Moreover, even if the *McClure* panel was relying on the *Sherbert* test, we hold that the church-minister exception survives *Sherbert*'s demise. As the D.C. Circuit observed in *Catholic University*, the primary doctrinal underpinning of the church-minister exception is not the *Sherbert* test, but the principle that churches must be free "to decide for themselves, free from state interference, matters of church government as well as those of faith and doctrine." *Kedroff.* This fundamental right of churches to be free from government interference in their internal management and administration has not been affected by the Supreme Court's decision in *Smith* and the demise of *Sherbert*.

### 3

The final point to address is Reverend Combs's argument that *Catholic University* is distinguishable from this case because a resolution of Sister McDonough's claim in *Catholic University* would have required an evaluation of church doctrine, while there would be no such need in this case.

Sister McDonough was denied tenure at Catholic University at least in part because the reviewing committees decided that her teaching and scholarship failed to meet the standards required of a tenured member of Catholic University's Canon Law Faculty. Indeed at trial, the parties introduced an "extensive body of conflicting testimony" concerning the quality of Sister McDonough's publications. We agree that the district court would have been placed in an untenable position had it been required to evaluate the merits of Sister McDonough's canon law scholarship. Having a civil court determine the merits of canon law scholarship would be in violent opposition to the constitutional principle of the separation of church and state. See Presbyterian Church v. Mary Elizabeth Blue Hull Memorial Presbyterian Church, 393 U.S. 440, 445 (1969) (civil courts are not permitted to determine ecclesiastical questions). Reverend Combs argues that because the resolution of her claim, in contrast to that of Sister McDonough, requires no evaluation or interpretation of religious doctrine, her claim should be allowed to proceed.

Not long after our decision in *McClure*, this Court rejected a similar argument in Simpson v. Wells Lamont Corp., 494 F.2d 490 (5th Cir. 1974).[7] As this Court observed in *Simpson*, the First Amendment concerns are two-fold. The first concern is that secular authorities would be involved in evaluating or interpreting religious

---

7. In *Simpson*, the plaintiff argued that the *McClure* exception should not apply to his racial discrimination claim because it was unrelated to church dogma. This Court disagreed, however, and determined that the First Amendment protection relative to the relationship between a church and a minister extended beyond purely dogmatic issues.

doctrine. The second quite independent concern is that in investigating employment discrimination claims by ministers against their church, secular authorities would necessarily intrude into church governance in a manner that would be inherently coercive, even if the alleged discrimination were purely nondoctrinal. This second concern is the one present here. This second concern alone is enough to bar the involvement of the civil courts.

In short, we cannot conceive how the federal judiciary could determine whether an employment decision concerning a minister was based on legitimate or illegitimate grounds without inserting ourselves into a realm where the Constitution forbids us to tread, the internal management of a church. . . .

## NOTES

1. Since *Combs*, several more circuits have applied the ministerial exception to preclude suits against churches: EEOC v. Roman Catholic Diocese of Raleigh, N.C., 213 F.3d 795 (4th Cir. 2000) (ministerial exception held to bar application of Title VII to church's dismissal of music teacher because "selection, presentation, and teaching music were an integral part of Catholic worship and belief"); Gellington v. Christian Methodist Episcopal Church, Inc., 203 F.3d 1299 (11th Cir. 2000) (establishment clause prohibited judicial review of minister's termination because application of Title VII would create excessive entanglement between church and state); Starkman v. Evans, 198 F.3d 173 (5th Cir. 1999) (choir director qualifies as "minister" for purposes of the ministerial exception because she "participated in religious rituals and had numerous religious duties"); Bryce v. Episcopal Church in the Diocese of Colo., 289 F.3d 648 (10th Cir. 2002) (ministerial exception bars sexual harassment claim by a lesbian youth minister who was fired because her relationship with her partner violated Episcopal doctrine that teaches that people should be married and faithful or single and celibate).

2. Title VII, as written, would reach Reverend Combs' claim. The court, however, treats Title VII as limited by the free exercise clause, and in doing so has to distinguish Employment Div., Dept. of Human Resources v. Smith, 494 U.S. 872 (1990). As *Combs* indicated, in *Smith* the Supreme Court announced a new approach to free exercise-mandated exceptions to statutes of general application. Plaintiffs there challenged the state's denial of unemployment compensation benefits after they had been fired from their private-sector jobs because of their sacramental use of the drug peyote. Writing for the Court, Justice Scalia found no support in the Court's precedents for the proposition that an individual's religious practices might relieve her from the duty to comply with a criminal law of general application. Id. at 878-79. Further, he rejected using the compelling governmental interest test in these cases. Id. at 886-87. For the free exercise clause to be implicated, the law in question presumably would have to be aimed at religious practices. Cf. Church of Lukumi Babalu Aye v. Hialeah, 508 U.S. 520 (1993) (ordinance prohibiting ritual animal sacrifice targets religion and violates the First Amendment because it is not narrowly tailored to serve the asserted government interests).

3. Title VII is clearly a law of general application which does not target religion for its antidiscrimination command. Why is *Smith* inapplicable? What test does the *Combs* court use?

4. *Smith* did not overrule all prior cases that seemed to subject laws of general application to strict scrutiny. Rather, *Smith* distinguished them as involving "hybrid"

constitutional claims, that is, cases involving "not the Free Exercise Clause alone, but the Free Exercise Clause in conjunction with other constitutional protections." 490 U.S. at 872, 873. These included Wisconsin v. Yoder, 406 U.S. 205 (1972) (free exercise coupled with right of parents to educate students). In addition to reading *Smith* as inapplicable to intrusions on church governance of internal affairs, *Catholic University* also distinguished *Smith* because Title VII's application to church ministers would also implicate two constitutional protections — the free exercise clause and the establishment clause problem of excessive entanglement. Did the Supreme Court in describing this hybrid exception to *Smith* have in mind that the rule would not apply to free exercise claims that were joined with establishment clause problems? The other hybrid cases Justice Scalia cited in *Smith* involved free speech issues as well as free exercise issues.

5. In Fraternal Order of Police Newark Lodge No. 12 v. City of Newark, 170 F.3d 359 (3d Cir. 1999), the court held that a city's refusal to accommodate officers whose religion required them to wear beards violated the free exercise clause, at least where the city permitted officers with medical conditions that limited shaving to wear beards. Although the no-beard rule seemed a rule of general application within the meaning of *Smith*, the court found *Smith* inapplicable since the city already made an exception for medical conditions. Does this distinction make sense to you? Applying heightened scrutiny, the court found no sufficient justification for the policy as applied to religious observers.

6. Does the *Combs* court too quickly dismiss RFRA as a basis for overriding Title VII? The Religious Freedom Restoration Act (RFRA), 42 U.S.C.S. § 2000bb (2003), whose stated purpose was to overturn *Smith*, provides:

(a) In general. — Government shall not substantially burden a person's exercise of religion even if the burden results from a rule of general applicability, except as provided in subsection (b).

(b) Exception. — Government may substantially burden a person's exercise of religion only if it demonstrates that application of the burden to the person —

(1) is in furtherance of a compelling governmental interest; and

(2) is the least restrictive means of furthering that compelling governmental interest.

The statute defines "government" to include the federal, state, and local governments. § 5. The Act "applies to all Federal and State law, and the implementation of that law, whether statutory or otherwise, and whether adopted before or after the enactment of this Act." § 6(a).

In City of Boerne v. Flores, 521 U.S. 507 (1997), the Supreme Court found RFRA unconstitutional as applied to the states.\* However, it has yet to be determined whether RFRA is constitutional as applied to the federal government. *Boerne* dealt extensively with the limitations on congressional power under § 5 of the Fourteenth Amendment, concluding that RFRA was not within that grant of authority to Congress. There is some language that suggests that Congress may also have gone too far insofar as it intruded into the judiciary's role, id. at 535-36, but it is not clear that *Boerne* intended to strike down RFRA as applied to federal action. See Christians v. Crystal Evangelical Church, 141 F.3d 854 (8th Cir. 1998) (necessary and proper clause and bankruptcy clause suggested RFRA; application to bankruptcy question). See generally, Gregory P. Magarian, How to Apply the Religious Freedom Restoration Act to

---

\*The invalidation of RFRA has led to renewed interest in state versions of the statute. See Symposium, Restoring Religious Freedom in the States, 32 U.C. Davis L. Rev. 513 et seq. (1999).

Federal Law without Violating the Constitution, 99 Mich. L. Rev. 1903 (2001). If it is constitutional as applied to Title VII, wouldn't RFRA in effect statutorily amend Title VII to incorporate the ministerial exception? Might it broaden the exception beyond the scope accorded it by *Catholic University* or *Combs?* Or might Title VII be applied as written — there is a compelling governmental interest in eliminating discrimination? Does Boy Scouts of Am. v. Dale, reproduced at page 557, bear on the question?

7. In Ryan v. United States Dept. of Justice, 950 F.2d 458, 461 (7th Cir. 1991), an FBI agent challenged his discharge for refusing to investigate antiwar groups because of his religious beliefs. Ryan claimed a free exercise-required exception to the FBI's insubordination rule. The court rejected the claim:

> After Employment Division v. Smith, any argument that failure to accommodate Ryan's religiously motivated acts violates the free exercise clause of the first amendment is untenable. *Smith* holds that rules neutral with respect to religion satisfy that clause. The FBI did not hold Ryan's faith against him; it judged his deeds, not his beliefs, and treated him no more severely than it would have treated an agent who refused a direct order for secular reasons. Title VII requires of the FBI more than the Constitution in its own right.

Would *Ryan* come out differently under RFRA, if it still applies to the federal government? Does that statute reach government *employment?*

8. Even if there is a ministerial exception, the antidiscrimination statutes may apply to some church actions. Bollard v. Cal. Socy. of Jesus, 196 F.3d 940 (9th Cir. 1999) (Title VII sexual harassment suit stated a claim where the challenged conduct neither involved a church selecting its ministers nor was religious in nature).

9. In Government Regulation of Religion Through Labor and Employment Discrimination Laws, 22 Stet. L. Rev. 27, 28 (1992), Professor David Gregory describes the law today as insufficiently protective of religious individuals and excessively protective of traditional religious institutions.

# E. NATIONAL ORIGIN AND ALIENAGE DISCRIMINATION

This section addresses two related kinds of employment discrimination, national origin discrimination and alienage discrimination. These are addressed in three separate statutes. The section first treats the Title VII proscription of national origin discrimination. It then turns to the § 1981 proscription of alienage (or citizenship) discrimination. Finally, it examines the Immigration Reform and Control Act of 1986 (IRCA), Pub. L. No. 99-603, 100 Stat. 3359 (1986), which proscribes both national origin and alienage discrimination.

## 1. National Origin Discrimination

In the nineteenth century, the Irish were informed by a sign in a store window that they "need not apply" for a position. Italian immigrants in the twentieth century suffered similar discrimination. More recently, persons with a Spanish language ancestry have been discriminated against, sometimes in subgroups such as Puerto Ricans, Cubans, or Chicanos, sometimes as part of a more loosely defined "Hispanic" or "Latino" group. Individuals of Portuguese origin or descent, whether from Portugal or South America, may also suffer from the discrimination aimed at "Latino" groups, although their primary language is Portuguese, rather than Spanish. Nor are these the only groups to be victimized by discrimination. World events can trigger hostility toward persons associated with particular nations or regions. The Iranian hostage incident, for example, resulted in discrimination against Iranians in the United States, and recurrent Mid-East crises have led to discrimination against Arabs, which has heightened in the wake of September 11. See generally, Leti Volpp, The Citizen and the Terrorist, 49 U.C.L.A. L. Rev. 1575 (2002); Kevin R. Johnson, The End of "Civil Rights" as We Know It?: Immigration and Civil Rights in the New Miillenium, 49 U.C.L.A. L. Rev. 1481 (2002).

The only Supreme Court decision on Title VII's prohibition of national origin discrimination is Espinoza v. Farah Manufacturing Co., 414 U.S. 86 (1973). The employer refused to hire a citizen of Mexico, who was a lawfully admitted resident alien, because she was not a citizen of the United States. She then brought a Title VII action, claiming national origin discrimination. In defining "national origin," the Court looked to the legislative history:

> The only direct definition given the phrase "national origin" is in the following remark made on the floor of the House of Representatives by Congressman Roosevelt, Chairman of the House Subcommittee which reported the bill: "It means the country from which you or your forebears came. . . . You may come from Poland, Czechoslovakia, England, France, or any other country."

Id. at 89 (quoting 110 Cong. Rec. 2549 (1964)). Since "national origin" refers to the country from which a person or her ancestors came, it does not refer to a person's citizenship status. From a disparate treatment perspective, the evidence did not show any intent to discriminate against Espinoza because of her Mexican ancestry. The Court then applied disparate impact analysis. However, Espinoza's claim also failed under this analysis because the statistical evidence did not show that the defendant's citizenship requirement had a disproportionate impact on persons of Mexican ancestry. In fact, the statistics revealed that the employer had an exceedingly high percentage of employees with Mexican ancestry. The Court concluded by stating that Title VII does protect aliens from sex, race, religion, color, and national origin discrimination by employers, thus reiterating its holding that Title VII simply does not prohibit alienage discrimination.

*Espinoza* did appear to settle three points. First, Title VII's prohibition of national origin discrimination prohibits discrimination based on ancestry, not discrimination based on alienage. Second, both disparate treatment and the disparate impact analyses are applicable in determining national origin discrimination. (Any lingering doubt about the applicability of the disparate impact analysis was removed by the addition of § 703(k)(l)(A)(i), 42 U.S.C.S. § 2000e-2(k)(1)(A)(i) (2003), in the Civil Rights Act of 1991.) Third, Title VII does protect aliens from employment discrimination on the basis of race, color, sex, religion, and national origin.

The *Espinoza* opinion, however, was unclear on two other points. First, does Title VII's protection of aliens extend to aliens who cannot legally work in the United States? This problem will be considered later in connection with the IRCA. Second, did the Court hold that the term "national origin" does not include a United States national origin?

An inference that Title VII does not protect those with a United States national origin might be drawn from the Court's reason for rejecting Espinoza's disparate impact claim. Farah's citizens-only policy clearly had an adverse disparate impact on applicants with solely a Mexican ancestry (like Espinoza) when compared with applicants with a United States ancestry (including Farah's Mexican-American employees). Yet the Court held that Espinoza was required to prove a disparate impact on persons of Mexican ancestry as compared with persons of some other foreign ancestry. It must follow that an employer that hired only citizens of European countries would not violate Title VII because of the policy's disparate impact on applicants with a United States national origin. If so, the explanation would seem to be that the term "national origin" does not include a United States national origin. Contra, e.g., Chaiffetz v. Robertson Research Holding, Ltd., 798 F.2d 731 (5th Cir. 1986) (Title VII protects those with a United States national origin).

National origin discrimination can pose difficult proof and conceptual problems.

## EEOC v. SEARS ROEBUCK & CO.
### 243 F.3d 846 (4th Cir. 2001)

DIANA GRIBBON MOTZ, Circuit Judge: . . .

### I

Santana, born in Mexico in 1960, has olive skin and speaks with an Hispanic accent. He moved to this country in 1971 and has since become a naturalized citizen of the United States. In 1979, after graduating from high school, Santana enlisted in the United States Marine Corps and has continually served as a Marine since that time.

During much of his adult life, Santana has also worked for Sears. In 1985, while he was stationed at a Marine base in Tustin, California, Sears hired Santana as a part-time loss prevention agent to provide undercover store security in its Costa Mesa, California store. Except for a one-year military leave of absence when he was stationed abroad, for the next ten years, Santana continued to work as a part-time loss prevention agent at the Costa Mesa store. In late 1995, the Marines transferred Santana to the Marine Corps Air Station in Cherry Point, North Carolina.

In preparation for this transfer in October 1995, Santana visited North Carolina. During his visit, Santana went to the Sears store in Morehead City, North Carolina to inquire about job opportunities for the same position he had held for ten years in California — specifically part-time loss prevention agent. Santana spoke with William Mansfield, the loss prevention manager in the Morehead City store. Mansfield assured Santana that the Morehead City store could use someone with his experience and that there would be a job waiting for him when he arrived. Mansfield then gave Santana a business card with the telephone number of the store's operations manager, Teri Katsekes, and said he would talk to Katsekes about Santana and his background and experience.

[From California, Santana had the Costa Mesa Sears send a transfer form to the personnel department at the Morehead City store. He then called Katsekes, by telephone, and told Katsekes that he would be available for work in around the last week in December. Katsekes responded that the store would be glad to have him in the North Carolina store and to get in touch when he arrived. He did so, but despite repeated visits to the store, and submitting three applications, one of which indicated that he would also accept "any other position" with Sears, Sears did not contact Santana until October 1996.]

In October, Patty Haynes, a human resources specialist at the Morehead City store, telephoned Santana and invited him to come in for an interview. During this interview, Haynes commented on Santana's accent and asked where he was "[o]riginally from." Santana answered that he had been born in Mexico City. At the conclusion of the interview, Haynes offered Santana a position as a stock clerk. When Santana referred to his loss prevention experience, Haynes realized that he was "the guy from California" and remembered his previous applications.

Haynes then took Santana to meet with Katsekes, who interviewed him in the office of the store manager, Patricia Kiely; according to Santana, Katsekes told him that Kiely was on vacation at the time. Santana remembered this because Katsekes apologized for the messiness of the desk during the interview, explaining that it was not her office, where she normally conducted interviews, but that she was "standing in" for store manager Kiely, using Kiely's desk, while Kiely was on vacation. Santana maintains that, during the interview, Katsekes became increasingly disinterested and abrupt due to his accent, although she did not comment on the accent, as Haynes had. Nevertheless, at the conclusion of the interview, Katsekes offered Santana a part-time loss prevention position, sent him for a routine drug screening, and stated that he would begin work right after a satisfactory drug screening result was received. Two days later, on October 25, 1996, Santana underwent a drug screening test; the negative result was sent to Sears.

On November 1, 1996, Santana returned to the store to give Haynes a copy of his social security card and asked when he could begin work. Haynes told him that "the trainer was sick." When Santana demurred that he had been trained and worked for the company for ten years, she replied that company policy required retraining. A week later, on November 8, 1996, Santana telephoned Haynes, again inquiring when he could start work. Haynes told him that a background investigation was being conducted and that he would be called by November 12. During this time, Santana spoke twice with David Mrazick, the loss prevention manager who had replaced Mansfield; Mrazick indicated that there was an immediate need for someone in the loss prevention department, that he was impressed by Santana's experience, and that he would speak to "management" on Santana's behalf.

Despite this, no one at Sears contacted Santana about starting work. When Santana did not hear from Sears, he telephoned the store repeatedly; he also contacted Sears loss prevention officials in California, including that region's manager, to see if they could determine the reason for the delay. After these telephone calls failed to yield an answer, on November 22, Santana went to the store to speak with Haynes or Katsekes; Haynes saw him and told him Katsekes would telephone him by November 26. On November 27, after Santana had not heard from Katsekes, he called her. At that time she told him that he was not going to be hired after all because Sears had hired someone else in his place and the store did not have the payroll to hire yet another person. Subsequently, Santana learned that Virginia Born, a Caucasian woman, had been hired as a part-time loss prevention agent two weeks earlier, on November 12, 1996.

Upon hearing that he was not going to be hired, Santana immediately telephoned Sears corporate headquarters to complain about the way he had been treated. After Santana related his story, an employee in the corporate office asked if he was willing to take any available position at the Morehead City Sears; Santana stated that he was. Shortly thereafter, the corporate employee called him and said that the Morehead City store was going to find him a position before December 6 and someone would call him by November 29. When Santana did not hear from anyone, he called on December 2, 1996 and talked to Haynes, who said she did not know anything about finding him a position. The Morehead City Sears never employed Santana.

In early 1997, Santana filed an EEOC claim against Sears alleging discrimination on the basis of national origin. Sears assigned David Cross, the Fair Employment Manager for the South Central region, to respond to the charge. Cross contacted Katsekes and Haynes in the course of preparing this response and asked why Santana had not been hired. Based on their explanations, Cross submitted a position statement for Sears to the EEOC. The position statement acknowledged Santana "had a number of years" experience in loss prevention at a Sears store in California, and that his job history was "a positive one." The Sears position statement asserted that the Morehead City store did not hire Santana before October 1996 because "he had not shown up or contacted the unit" and, although store employees repeatedly tried to contact him, they were "unable to do so." When Santana "finally showed up," he was told "that the position had been filled," and he responded that he "had been on deployment with the military." Thereafter, Santana "constantly inquired about any open positions in the unit." Recognizing that Santana "would be an asset" to the store, Sears interviewed him and requested "additional hours and payroll for its" loss prevention division, but the request was denied. Sears maintained that they did not hire Santana because there were no hours available in loss prevention.

During discovery, Sears offered another story. Katsekes testified that it was difficult to find experienced loss prevention employees and that she was interested in hiring the "loss prevention agent from a California Sears store" that Mansfield told her about, but Mansfield was unable to locate this person in late 1995 or early 1996 at his work number, and was told by someone that he was on deployment. (Mansfield ended his employment with Sears in 1996 and did not testify or submit an affidavit.) Katsekes could not identify who told Sears this, and acknowledged that no effort was made to contact the California loss prevention agent at his home. She did not testify that this agent had been deployed by the Marines or had told the store he had been deployed. Moreover, Katsekes did not dispute that Santana had filed employment applications in January, March, and July 1996 but she maintained that she was "never aware of [the earlier] applications" and that the first time she saw his July application was in October 1996 when she interviewed him.

Katsekes admitted that the reasons she gave to Cross, and that he in turn gave to the EEOC in 1997, for refusing to hire Santana in October 1996 were inaccurate. She explained that she did have an available loss prevention position when she interviewed Santana because she had determined to "take those hours from somewhere else in the store" and "put on extra Loss Prevention help." Katsekes testified that she had been impressed with Santana's loss prevention experience and offered him a job, contingent on his passing a drug test and background check, "[h]owever . . . after the interview" she "was instructed not to go any further with the application." Katsekes acknowledged that a few weeks after she interviewed Santana, a Caucasian woman, Virginia Born, was hired as a part-time loss prevention associate. Sears records produced to Santana indicate that on November 12, 1996, Sears hired Born, who had no loss prevention experience, no previous employment history with Sears, and less education than Santana. Katsekes admitted that "[w]ith respect to education and prior experience," she would "have to say Mr. Santana" was more qualified than Born.

In her 1999 deposition, Katsekes testified that the reason Sears did not employ the better qualified Santana was not what she previously told Cross, but rather that, a few hours after her interview with Santana, Mrazick came into her office and told her that store manager Patricia Kiely "decided that we're not going to go any further with this application." Katsekes maintained that she did not ask either Mrazick or Kiely the reason for this decision because she was angry at Kiely for overruling her without an explanation. Katsekes further testified that she did not inform Santana or Cross or the EEOC that Kiely had overruled her decision to hire Santana because she thought it reflected badly on the store.

Kiely testified in her deposition (taken in 1999, several months after Katsekes's) that in October 1996, when Mrazick told her that Katsekes "was getting ready to hire a guy from California with asset protection experience," she told him she "did not want that to happen," without explaining her reasons. Kiely maintained that in the beginning of 1996, she had a telephone conversation with Ann Manherz, a Sears regional manager, who mentioned in passing an unnamed "asset protection agent from California that had some sexual harassment issues," and Kiely mistakenly thought Santana "could be that person." (Sears does not contend and has not contended that Santana was in fact the individual to whom Manherz had referred.) Kiely acknowledged that she did not investigate or attempt to confirm that Santana was the suspected individual. Rather, she "assumed" that he was the individual Manherz had spoken about and therefore decided not to hire him. Kiely further asserted that, at the time she decided not to hire Santana, she had not met or seen Santana, and that she did not know his national origin or even his name.

["Ann Manherz had no recollection of speaking with Kiely, Katsekes, or Haynes but could . . . have had a conversation with Ms. Kiely about a loss prevention agent being accused of sexual harassment," since she was aware, in early 1996, that a loss prevention agent from a California store, who had been accused of sexual harassment, was looking for work in the Southeast. But she did not know Santana and did not talk about him specifically with Kiely.]

After discovery was completed, the district court granted Sears's motion for summary judgment. . . .

II

. . . Plainly, Santana satisfies all four elements of a prima facie case: (i) as a Hispanic Mexican-American, he is a member of a protected class, (ii) he applied and was well qualified for a position as a part-time loss prevention associate at Sears, (iii) despite his qualifications, Sears rejected him, and (iv) the position remained open, Sears continued to seek to fill it, and did shortly fill it by hiring a less qualified Caucasian woman.

Indeed, the prima facie case here is a strong one. The evidence as to Santana's year-long job seeking odyssey — including his numerous visits to the store, contacts with store personnel, and the filing of three different job applications — is uncontroverted. Unlike some cases, here the EEOC presented overwhelming evidence that Santana diligently applied for the job denied him.

Furthermore the uncontroverted evidence clearly demonstrates that Santana, again unlike some discrimination claimants, was well qualified for the position he so eagerly sought. In fact, his previous ten years of experience as a part-time loss prevention agent with Sears would seem to make him as qualified as any person could be for this position.

It is also beyond question that Santana satisfied the third and fourth elements of the prima facie case, namely that, despite his qualifications, Sears rejected his application for employment and then quickly filled the position by hiring a Caucasian woman. While employers often insist in hiring cases such as this one that the person chosen for the job over the plaintiff was better qualified, here even Sears concedes, as it must, that Santana's education and experience were superior to the Caucasian woman hired in his stead, who had never before worked for Sears, had less education, and had no loss prevention experience. In sum, Santana presented uncontroverted evidence of a strong prima facie case — despite his repeated applications, his superb qualifications, and his expressed willingness to accept any available position, Sears refused to hire him at the Morehead City store and instead hired a Caucasian woman who, Sears itself concedes, was less qualified than Santana.

Once a plaintiff establishes a prima facie case, the burden then shifts to the employer to "produc[e] evidence that the plaintiff was rejected, or someone else was preferred, for a legitimate, nondiscriminatory reason." In this case, Sears has, over time, proffered several reasons for its failure to hire Santana, including the selection of someone else, a lack of available hours in the loss prevention department, and the belief that Santana had been investigated for sexual harassment in the past. Sears now insists that only this last explanation — the belief that Santana was the person described by Manherz who had been investigated for sexual harassment — is the true reason for its failure to hire Santana. If this is the reason Sears did not hire Santana — although this belief ultimately proved to be unfounded — it nonetheless constitutes a legitimate non-discriminatory explanation.

Once an employer offers a legitimate, non-discriminatory explanation for the challenged employment decision, "the plaintiff must than have an opportunity to prove . . . that the legitimate reasons offered by the defendant were not its true reasons, but were a pretext for discrimination." The Supreme Court recently clarified the plaintiff's burden at the pretext stage in *Reeves v. Sanderson Plumbing Prods., Inc.* [reproduced at page 136]. The Court reiterated that evidence of pretext, combined with the plaintiff's prima face case, does not *compel* judgment for the plaintiff, because "[i]t is not enough . . . to disbelieve the employer; the factfinder must [also] believe the plaintiff's explanation of intentional discrimination." However, the *Reeves* Court made plain that, under the appropriate circumstances, "a plaintiff's prima facie case, combined with sufficient evidence to find that the employer's asserted justification is false, may permit the trier of fact to conclude that the employer unlawfully discriminated."

Here, looking at the totality of the circumstances, there is ample evidence from which a factfinder could conclude that, in the words of the *Reeves* Court, Sears's "asserted justification is false." Indeed, the fact that Sears has offered different justifications at different times for its failure to hire Santana is, in and of itself, probative of pretext.

Moreover, a factfinder could infer from the late appearance of Sears's current justification that it is a post-hoc rationale, not a legitimate explanation for Sears's decision not to hire Santana. Katsekes interviewed and offered Santana a job in October 1996; the first time Katsekes claimed that Kiely overruled her decision to hire Santana was in her deposition in May 1999, over two and a half years later. Katsekes stated that she chose not to tell Santana at the time that her decision to hire him had been overruled by Kiely because she thought it reflected badly on the store. This explanation certainly seems possible. But, Katsekes had another opportunity to disclose Kiely's involvement in the decision not to hire Santana, namely in 1997, when Cross contacted her in the course of preparing his response to Santana's EEOC Charge of Discrimination, and she did not do so. Instead, Katsekes told Cross that no hours were available in loss prevention — an explanation that she conceded years later at her deposition was not accurate and is further belied by the fact that Virginia Born was hired as a loss prevention associate less than three weeks after Katsekes interviewed Santana.

Katsekes's failure to tell Cross or the EEOC of Kiely's involvement seems curious. If Kiely had instructed Katsekes not to hire Santana, why would Katsekes not tell this to Cross? She could hardly be embarrassed to disclose this fact to Cross, a fellow Sears employee, and, as an operations manager, she must have known the importance of responding truthfully and completely to an EEOC discrimination charge. Furthermore, would she not have realized that Cross would want to talk to Kiely, if Kiely had indeed made the ultimate decision not to hire Santana? It seems probable that Katsekes would have mentioned Kiely's involvement during the EEOC investigation, if not before. Given that she did not do so, a trier of fact would certainly be entitled to infer that this explanation is nothing more than a post hoc rationale, invented for the purposes of litigation.

Apart from the late appearance of Sears's current explanation, there is additional evidence from which a factfinder could infer that it is unworthy of belief. Kiely claims that she ordered Katsekes not to hire Santana because, based on a casual conversation with Manherz eight months earlier, she believed that Santana had been investigated for sexual harassment. While Sears now acknowledges that this belief was incorrect, it contends that a mistaken belief, honestly held, is not a pretext for discrimination. In this case, however, the evidence does *not* support Sears's contention that Kiely honestly believed that Santana was the individual investigated for sexual harassment. Kiely admits that, at the time she rejected Santana, she did not know the name of the individual to whom Manherz referred and did not make any attempt to verify that Santana was, in fact, that individual. A juror could easily find it implausible that Kiely would reject a qualified applicant, such as Santana, without first substantiating that he was, in fact, the individual accused of sexual harassment. This is particularly true given that both Kiely and Katsekes testified that the Morehead City store had difficulty finding people experienced in loss prevention, as Santana was. The credibility of Kiely's explanation is further undermined by the fact that, until after this litigation was underway, she admittedly failed to reveal to anyone, including Mrazick or Katsekes, the now-asserted reason for her claimed directive not to hire Santana.

In sum, the EEOC made out a strong prima facie case of national origin discrimination and offered ample evidence to discredit Sears's proffered non-discriminatory reason for its failure to hire Santana. Under *Reeves*, this showing is sufficient to permit a trier of fact to "infer the ultimate fact of discrimination from the falsity of the employer's explanation." Indeed, *Reeves* teaches that when "the employer's justification has been eliminated, discrimination may well be the most likely alternative explanation, especially since the employer is in the best position to put forth the actual reason for its decision.". . .

Thus, the only remaining question is whether Sears has presented evidence such that "no rational factfinder" could conclude that Sears's refusal to hire Santana was motivated by national origin discrimination. Sears maintains that it has. Specifically, Sears contends that it has presented evidence proving that: (1) the person who decided not to hire Santana was Kiely, and (2) Kiely did not know Santana's national origin. That argument must fail, however, because, although Sears has certainly presented evidence that could lead a factfinder to these conclusions, Sears has not presented evidence that requires this. Rather, ample evidence in the record would permit a reasonable trier of fact to reject either or both of these conclusions.

Sears maintains that Kiely, not Katsekes, decided to revoke the job offer to Santana. While that is certainly Sears's contention, there is a good deal of record evidence that discredits it. For example, Katsekes failed to tell anyone that Kiely was the decision-maker either at the time of Santana's job application or during the EEOC adminis-trative process. The trier of fact could reasonably infer from Katsekes's failure to dis-close Kiely's involvement until litigation had begun that the explanation is simply untrue, and that the relevant decision-maker in this case was Katsekes, not Kiely. Furthermore, Santana testified, in the kind of detail that imbues his testimony with credibility, that when Katsekes interviewed him, she did so in Kiely's untidy office, ex-plaining that Kiely was on vacation. If a factfinder credits this testimony, and Sears apparently offered no attendance records or other evidence to counter it, then Sears's contention that, within hours of Santana's interview, Kiely ordered Katsekes not to hire Santana appears unlikely.

Moreover, on the present record, it is undisputed that in the weeks following Santana's interview, Mrazick told Santana he would talk to "management" on Santana's behalf, Haynes told Santana his start date would begin after training and the background check were completed, and Katsekes continued to evade Santana's inquiries as to a start date. Indeed, Katsekes did not notify Santana for more than a month that she was withdrawing the job offer and during that time she hired a Cau-casian woman for the job that had been offered to Santana. A factfinder could infer from this evidence that Katsekes, not Kiely, decided not to follow through on the job offer to Santana; that remembering Santana's accent and national origin, Katsekes be-came increasingly less enthusiastic about Santana as a candidate and for this reason, she delayed finalizing his start date; and that when Katsekes found a less "foreign" candidate, she determined to hire that person and revoke her offer to Santana. Of course, a finder of fact might not so conclude, but there is certainly evidence, now uncontroverted, that permits this inference.

Even if a factfinder should conclude that Kiely was the relevant decisionmaker, a factfinder might not accept Sears's second contention — that Kiely did not know Santana's national origin. As the EEOC notes, Kiely's assertion to this effect "is not supported by any other testimony in the record." In fact, Katsekes stated in her affidavit not that Mrazick told her to stop activity on the application of the unnamed California loss prevention agent, but that "Ms. Kiely had directed [Mrazick] to tell me that the store would not hire *Mr. Santana*," (emphasis added), suggesting that Kiely did know Santana by his "Hispanic sounding" name.

Moreover, Santana testified that he was in the Morehead City store very frequently over a year-long period, during which time he repeatedly talked with store personnel about job openings and submitted three job applications; even Sears conceded that Santana "constantly inquired" about open positions. Given this uncontroverted evi-dence, a jury might conclude that Kiely, the manager of this small store, would over time have heard Santana's name or seen him and ascertained that this Hispanic man was the loss prevention agent from California. Furthermore, there is no dispute that numerous other members of the store's management — Katsekes, Haynes, Mansfield and Mrazick — who undoubtedly regularly discussed personnel matters with Kiely, did know of Santana's national origin. A jury might well infer that, in these discus-sions, they mentioned Santana's national origin to Kiely.

Because there is evidence from which a factfinder could conclude that Katsekes made the decision to revoke the job offer, or that Kiely did know Santana's national origin, a factfinder would be entitled to reject Sears's contentions that Kiely was the sole decision-maker and that she did not know of Santana's national origin. In other words, Sears has failed to demonstrate that "no rational factfinder could conclude that" Sears's refusal to hire Santana was motivated by illegal discrimination. *Reeves.*

Nor does the lack of direct evidence of anti-Hispanic animus or the fact that Sears has hired other Hispanics compel this conclusion. Since no direct evidence of animus is necessary to prove employment discrimination, its absence hardly compels a factfinder to conclude that the employer did not discriminate. Moreover, simply because Sears hired other Hispanic individuals in other departments does not mean that its failure to hire Santana was free from discriminatory intent. This is not to say that a trier of fact might not ultimately rely on this evidence in returning a verdict for Sears. But this evidence does not compel the grant of summary judgment to Sears because it does not foreclose the possibility that a factfinder could conclude that national origin discrimination was the true reason for Sears's failure to hire Santana. . . .

In sum, under the rule announced in *Reeves,* there is sufficient evidence in this case for a trier of fact to conclude that Santana was the victim of illegal discrimination. The EEOC, on behalf of Santana, has proven a strong prima facie case of national origin discrimination and has raised significant questions as to the validity of Sears's proffered non-discriminatory reason for its failure to hire Santana. Perhaps at trial, the EEOC will be unable to convince the factfinder that discrimination was the true reason for Sears's failure to hire Santana. But on this record, we cannot hold that "no rational factfinder could conclude" that intentional discrimination was the true motivation for Sears's decision. *Reeves.* Accordingly, the district court erred in granting summary judgment to Sears. . . .

NIEMEYER, Circuit Judge, dissenting:

It appears to me, regretfully, that the majority may have permitted the plaintiff's personal suspicions, coupled with Sears' clumsiness in giving its reasons for not hiring plaintiff, to become the *prima facie* case for national origin discrimination. [T]he majority is incorrect in holding that a rational factfinder could conclude that Sears' decision not to hire Santana was based on *national origin* discrimination. *See* Reeves v. Sanderson Plumbing Prods., Inc.

[The dissent accepted that it was Patricia Kiely who had vetoed Santana, and that "Kiely had never met him. It argued that "the Morehead Sears store did *not* discriminate by reason of national origin and was prepared to hire Hispanics" because Haynes and Katsekes had offered Santana a job and during the period in question, "Sears had hired other Hispanics in the store for various positions."]

*NOTES*

1. The dissent posits that Kiely, the decision-maker, never knew Santana's national origin and, therefore, could not have acted because of it. The legal principle seems clear, at least for a disparate treatment challenge, but why is not there a basis for believing that either Katsekes made the decision or that she at least told Kiely more about Santana — including his name and accent? And, if the decision-maker did not know Santana's national origin, why was it important for the dissent that Sears did not otherwise discriminate against Hispanics? Is the dissent suggesting that, had Kiely known Santana's name, summary judgment still would be appropriate because no jury could infer that Sears acted for discriminatory reasons?

2. The dissent finds evidence of national origin discrimination "completely lacking" because there is no more indication of such discrimination "than there is that [plaintiff] was a victim of age discrimination or gender discrimination." Is the dissent's point that national origin ought not to be inferred, even when the adverse employment action is exceedingly strange on traditional criteria?

3. There may be a germ of truth here — suppose Santana's name was instead Standish and his forebears had come to the United States on the Mayflower. Could a reasonable jury infer national origin discrimination against those of English origin? The notion of national origin discrimination may implicate background circumstances, such as hostility to certain groups. Indeed, while the term "Hispanic" includes a wide range of races and racial mixes, many people view most Hispanics as non-white. The court notes Mr. Santana's "olive skin." Does this explain the majority's readiness to infer a discriminatory motive here, when it might not in the case of the hypothetical Mr. Standish?

4. To test this proposition, ask whether Mr. Santana would have created a jury issue for the dissent had he been African American. Then ask yourself whether the majority would have found a jury issue on sex discrimination on the same facts, including that both decision-makers were women.

5. One basis of inferring that Kiely knew Mr. Santana's national origin was his name. The "name game" can pose interesting questions. In a discrimination case, a defendant described the plaintiff as not having an "American name." The defendant's own name was Germanic in origin, and the other "American" names he compared to the plaintiff's were of Irish, Italian, and Polish origin. It was patently clear that the defendant was distinguishing in his own mind between older and newer immigrants to the United States. Such evidence might create a *Price Waterhouse* case, or at least reinforce the inference of bias derived from the conduct of the defendant. But in other cases, names will be ambiguous, and especially given the tendency of women to take their husband's names, names are often deceptive indicators of national origin.

6. The dissent's reliance on Sears's willingness to hire other Hispanics is worth examining. It is certainly irrelevant if the Sears decision-maker was unaware of Santana's national origin. But is the dissent suggesting that, even were Kiely to have admitted knowing Santana's name, proof of nondiscrimination toward other Hispanics would have precluded a jury question? Surely the majority is correct that proof of no systemic prejudice is not sufficient to reject an individual claim, at least in a large organization where hiring might not always be done by the same person. But maybe the dissent's point is more nuanced: while such discrimination is possible, plaintiff must put on more proof of it to get to a jury.

7. There are a number of problems in this regard. First, there are Hispanics and Hispanics. It is not clear that the other Hispanics Sears hired were of Mexican origin. It is possible that an employer might reject a Mexican while hiring, say, a person of Cuban dissent. How does this possibility fit into the litigation structure. Would the EEOC have been better advised to claim discrimination against Mexicans rather than discrimination against Hispanics? Second, isn't it possible that managers who disliked certain groups might nevertheless be willing to employ them in specific positions? Finally, maybe it was not Santana's national origin per se but his accent that posed the problem. Surely, there are people who will accept "Americanized" workers but reject those who are not. Again, how are these possibilities accounted for in the litigation structure?

8. As viewed by the majority, *Sears* is a straightforward *McDonnell Douglas* case. Plaintiff proves a strong prima facie case (strong, apparently in that the decision is especially odd on normal merit principles), defendant puts into evidence a legitimate

nondiscriminatory reason, and plaintiff offers a number of bases to question that reason — including the different stories told over time and the implausibility of Kiely's acting as she now claims to have acted. *Reeves* then dictates that the case go to the jury. Is the dissent simply resisting *Reeves* and requiring "pretext plus" evidence?

9. One possible reason for discrimination against Mr. Santana was his accent. This is, in fact, a recurrent basis for national origin discrimination claims. E.g., Carino v. University of Okla., 750 F.2d 815, 816 (10th Cir. 1984); Berke v. Ohio Dept. of Public Welfare, 628 F.2d 980, 981 (6th Cir. 1980). Suppose, however, the defendant admitted that it had not hired plaintiff because of his accent, but also claimed that the accent was so "thick" as to impair his ability to communicate? In Fragante v. City & County of Honolulu, 888 F.2d 591 (9th Cir. 1989), plaintiff — who had emigrated from the Phillipines — was denied a position involving contact with the public. He had obtained the highest score on the Civil Service Examination "which tested, among other things, word usage, grammar and spelling." Id. at 594. The district court found that Fragante's oral skills were "hampered by his accent or manner of speaking," and concluded that Fragante lacked the bfoq of being able to communicate effectively with the public. Id. at 594. The Ninth Circuit's opinion, however, is confused. The court first held that foreign accent discrimination constitutes national origin discrimination. It then intermixed the bfoq defense and the *McDonnell Douglas/ Burdine* analysis, concluding that the plaintiff had failed to prove that the employer's job-related reason was a pretext. But if the plaintiff failed to prove his foreign accent was a factor in the employer's decision, there was no need to consider the bfoq defense, and if he proved his foreign accent was a factor, one would think that the only issues were whether the defendant had established a bfoq or mixed-motives defense. In the court's view, however, the defendant's claim that "the deleterious effect his Filipino accent had upon his ability to communicate orally, not merely because he had such an accent" was a legitimate, nondiscriminatory reason for his non-selection.

10. Was the *Fragante* court correct in holding that foreign accent discrimination is a form of national origin discrimination? *Sears* seems to also accept this view. But accent discrimination does not single out persons with particular national origins. Further, some people with a foreign national origin do not have a foreign accent, and some people with a United States national origin have an accent. Should a foreign accent and a foreign national origin be regarded as "analytically distinct" pursuant to Hazen Paper Co. v. Biggins (reproduced at page 87)? Of course, the *Biggins* approach would find a Title VII violation when foreign accent discrimination was used as a proxy for national origin discrimination. Can foreign accent discrimination be shown to have a disparate impact on persons with a particular national origin without the concept of a United States national origin?

11. Two cases have viewed employer consideration of a foreign accent as not necessarily national origin discrimination. Both involved college teaching positions that required the ability to communicate in English. Each court stated that, in such circumstances, consideration of a foreign accent is equivocal evidence of an intent to discriminate on the basis of national origin. In the end, both plaintiffs failed to prove discrimination. Jiminez v. Mary Washington Coll., 57 F.3d 369 (4th Cir. 1995); Bina v. Providence Coll., 39 F.3d 21 (1st Cir. 1994). See also del la Cruz v. New York City Human Res. Admin., 82 F.3d 16 (2d Cir. 1996) (lawful to replace bilingual Puerto Rican who had difficulty writing English with better writer when job requires good writing skills). But see Hasham v. Cal. State Bd. of Equalization, 200 F.3d 1035 (7th Cir. 2000) (comment that foreign accent cannot be understood supports inference of national origin discrimination).

12. Professor Mari J. Matsuda, in Voices of America: Accent, Antidiscrimination Law, and a Jurisprudence for the Last Reconstruction, 100 Yale L.J. 1329, 1384-1385 (1991), attacked the defendant's evaluation of speaking ability:

> The evaluation of Fragante was shoddy. . . . The interviewers who found Fragante's accent "difficult" did not identify any incidences of misunderstanding during the interview. The lack of standard interview questions, the irrationality of the rating sheet, and the absence in the interview process of training or instruction in either speech assessment or the obligation of nondiscrimination reveal a weak system of evaluation. . . . Significantly, the evaluation process did not include a functional component. That is, Fragante's speech was never tested in a real or simulated job setting. . . .
>
> The evaluation process invited discretion and subjective judgment. As the sociolinguistic evidence would have predicted, a candidate with an accent identified as foreign and inferior is unlikely to survive such a subjective process. . . . There is significant evidence on the record that every listener in the courtroom could understand Mr. Fragante during direct and cross-examinations, which required speech more complex than that described by the employer as necessary for the job.

But was the critical issue Fragante's ability to do the job or the agency's intent to discriminate? Did the plaintiff or the defendant effectively have the burden of persuasion on the job-relatedness issue? From a bfoq standpoint, the defendant would have to prove more than merely that it was reasonable in its judgment. Is that why the *Fragante* court intermixed the discrimination question?

13. Can employer rules requiring that only English be spoken in the workplace survive Title VII? In Garcia v. Gloor, 618 F.2d 264, 270 (5th Cir. 1980), a rule requiring bilingual sales personnel to speak only English on the job was upheld:

> [Title VII] does not support an interpretation that equates the language an employee prefers to use with his national origin. To a person who speaks only one tongue or to a person who has difficulty using another language than the one spoken in his home, language might well be an immutable characteristic like skin color, sex or place of birth. However, the language a person who is multi-lingual elects to speak at a particular time is by definition a matter of choice. . . . In some circumstances, the ability to speak or the speaking of a language other than English might be equated with national origin, but this case concerns only a requirement that persons capable of speaking English do so while on duty.

In fact, the employees were required to speak English to English-speaking customers and Spanish to Spanish-speaking customers, but to speak only English with co-workers. Was Garcia discharged because he was Hispanic or because he spoke a language other than English? Although the *Gloor* court seemed to believe that the choice of which language to speak was volitional for bilingual workers, socio-linguistic scholarship suggests that such individuals often "code switch," that is, speak a combination of languages without always being conscious of which language(s) they are using. See generally Mark Colon, Note, Line Drawing, Code Switching, and Spanish as Second-Hand Smoke: English-Only Workplace Rules and Bilingual Employees, 20 Yale L. & Poly. Rev. 227, 251 (2002) ("Contrary to the majority rule, the research into code switching indicates that adhering to an English-only requirement is not simply a matter of preference for many "fully" bilingual speakers, and that code switching cannot typically be turned off and on in response to a rule. This is particularly true for bilingual speakers who grew up in communities where code switching is an accepted and common form of communication.").

14. In another case, bilingual meatpacking employees challenged an employer's requirement that they speak only English at work, claiming that the rule both had a disparate impact and created a hostile work environment. The court rejected the disparate impact claim on the ground that Title VII requires a significant impact, not just inconvenience. Regarding the hostile environment claim, the court held that an English-only rule does not by itself create a hostile environment, although it might if imposed in the context of an environment of discrimination or if enforced in a draconian and harassing manner. Garcia v. Spun Steak Co., 998 F.2d 1480 (9th Cir. 1993). See David Ruiz Cameron, How the Garcia Cousins Lost Their Accents: Understanding the Language of Title VII Decisions Approving English-Only Rules as the Product of Racial Dualism, Latino Invisibility, and Legal Indeterminacy, 10 La Raza L.J. 261 (1998). The EEOC recently clarified its position on English-only rules, permitting such a rule only when adopted for a non-discriminatory reason and when it is justified by business necessity. http://www.eeoc.gov/origin/index.html.

15. Government imposition of English-only rules also raises First Amendment issues. See Yniguez v. Mofford, 42 F.3d 1217 (9th Cir. 1995) (striking down Arizona constitutional amendment making English the state's official language), *vacated as moot*, 520 U.S. 43 (1997). See generally Drucilla Cornell & William W. Bratton, Deadweight Costs and Intrinsic Wrongs of Nativism: Economics, Freedom, and Legal Suppression of Spanish, 84 Cornell L. Rev. 595 (1999) (rejecting the argument of "linguistic self-defense" as a justification for English-only rules).

16. Employer rules requiring the ability to speak English have generally withstood attack under Title VII. In Garcia v. Rush-Presbyterian-St. Luke's Med. Ctr., 660 F.2d 1217, 1222 (7th Cir. 1981), the court said:

> Rush requires employees in nearly all job classifications to speak and read English in some fashion. Plaintiffs contend that this requirement results in unlawful discrimination against Latinos. They did not produce evidence, nor is there any in the record to show that Latinos were excluded from Rush's workforce at a greater rate than persons of other national origins, by virtue of such requirement standing alone, or in connection with other employee selection procedures. The requirement that an employee speak and read English in some fashion did not have an adverse impact on Latinos; nor were Latinos treated differently than all other persons with regard to the requirement. The ability to speak and read some English is a necessary, job-related requirement for every job in this highly sophisticated medical care institution.

The *Rush* court seemed to be saying that there was no showing of disparate impact and the rule was a business necessity. How would you have shown that Latinos suffer a disparity of impact? But disparate impact aside, why isn't the rule disparate treatment discrimination? Perhaps to cover that possibility, the court went on to write:

> Thus some facility in English is at Rush a Bona Fide Occupational Qualification (BFOQ). The question of language in a large modern hospital in an urban area is, if we may interject some judicial notice, difficult, and anyone who has been so lucky or unlucky as to be a patient in such an institution probably has had some personal experience with it. Such an institution is apt to be somewhat of a Tower of Babel. We would suppose that English is most likely to be the common language of a majority of patients and staff alike, and, therefore, a deficiency in English is the language deficiency most likely to be troublesome with an employee of a hospital located well in the interior of a supposedly English-speaking nation.

*Id.* at 1222. Aside from the bfoq defense, does a disparate treatment theory run afoul of the *Biggins* analysis of discriminatory intent?

17. Juan F. Perea, in Ethnicity and Prejudice: Reevaluating "National Origin" Discrimination Under Title VII, 35 Wm. & Mary L. Rev. 805, 807-08 (1994), stresses the limits of the Title VII prohibition:

> Courts have been largely unsympathetic to claims of discrimination as experienced by persons whose ethnicity differs from that of the majority. . . . Employees may be fired or disciplined for speaking languages other than English in the workplace, even if employees are doing their jobs at the time or if their conversations do not interfere with job performance. Persons who speak with "foreign" accents may be denied employment, despite excellent qualifications and verbal skills, because of the discomfort and displeasure they cause interviewers. African American women may be denied the ability to express their ethnic identity by wearing their hair in cornrows.

He goes on to argue, however,

> that the "national origin" term does not, and cannot, correctly encompass the protection of ethnic traits or ethnicity. Indeed, the concept of "national origin" discrimination is not helpful in describing accurately or recognizing the kind of discrimination that should be prohibited under Title VII. The continuing and exclusive reliance on "national origin" as the statutory source of protection in Title VII against discrimination because of ethnic traits is increasingly incompatible with more ethnic diversity in the workplace and the predictably increasing demand for equal treatment.

*Id.* at 809-10. Should Title VII be amended to prohibit discrimination on the basis of "ethnic traits or ethnicity"?

18. As the dissent in *Sears* implies, national origin discrimination under Title VII does not receive the same level of judicial scrutiny as claims of race discrimination. Why not? Should Latinos, instead of claiming national origin discrimination, claim race discrimination when they challenge English-language rules? Gary A. Greenfield & Don B. Kates, Jr., in Mexican Americans, Racial Discrimination, and the Civil Rights Act of 1866, 63 Cal. L. Rev. 662, 730-31 (1975), have traced the treatment of Mexican Americans as a racial group and concluded that, beyond the temporary obstacles faced by all immigrants, they have faced "the additional barriers of racism." Can Puerto Ricans also claim that they have been treated as a racial minority?

19. Under Title VII, Native Americans have been treated as a racial minority, Morton v. Mancari, 417 U.S. 535 (1974), and have also been protected from discrimination on the basis of national origin, Brito v. Zia Co., 478 F.2d 1200 (10th Cir. 1973). Moreover, § 703(i), 42 U.S.C.S. § 2000e-2(i) (2003), allows preferential treatment of Indians by businesses near reservations. In Livingston v. Ewing, 601 F.2d 1110 (10th Cir. 1979), a museum's rule prohibiting the sale of handcrafted jewelry made by persons other than American Indians did not violate Title VII because of § 703(i). In *Mancari*, the Court found that a Bureau of Indian Affairs rule providing employment preferences for "qualified Indians" had not been repealed when Title VII was extended to protect federal employees; the Court also upheld the preference against an equal protection challenge. A recent decision, however, held that Title VII does not permit an on-reservation employer to prefer Navajos over Hopis. Dawavendewa v. Salt River Project Agric. Improv. & Power Dist., 154 F.3d 1117 (9th Cir. 1998).

20. Does § 1981 prohibit a broader form of national origin discrimination? In Donaire v. NME Hosp., Inc., 27 F.3d 507 (11th Cir. 1994), the plaintiff alleged

employment discrimination due to his Philippine birth and ancestry. The district court dismissed the claim, holding that § 1981 does not protect persons from "foreign ethnic" or "foreign ancestry" discrimination. Relying on the Supreme Court's decision in *Saint Francis College*, discussed at pages 117-119, the appellate court held that § 1981 does prohibit discrimination based on foreign ancestry or ethnicity. Is § 1981 applicable in a "foreign accent" case? What did the Supreme Court mean by "ancestry or ethnic characteristics"? Does § 1981 protect black employees who wear cornrows and Latino employees who speak Spanish? See also Amini v. Oberlin College, 259 F.3d 493 (6th Cir. 2001) (§ 1981 protects those with a "Middle Eastern" race).

21. National origin discrimination in employment is also prohibited by the IRCA, but, as will be seen, the IRCA excludes from coverage any national origin discrimination prohibited by Title VII.

## 2.  *Alienage Discrimination*

In Espinoza v. Farah Manufacturing Co., 414 U.S. 86 (1973), the Supreme Court held that alienage or citizenship discrimination is not included within Title VII's prohibition of national origin discrimination. Consequently, Farah Manufacturing did not violate Title VII by hiring only United States citizens. The Court, however, did not consider whether alienage discrimination was prohibited by § 1981, which accords "all persons within the jurisdiction of the United States" the same right to make and enforce contracts "as is enjoyed by white citizens."

The limited appellate authority indicates that § 1981 prohibits alienage discrimination in both state and private employment. The Second Circuit has squarely held that § 1981 prohibits private employers from discriminating against aliens on the basis of their lack of citizenship. Anderson v. Conboy, 156 F.3d 167 (2d Cir. 1998). The same result must flow from Duane v. GEICO, 37 F.3d 1036 (4th Cir. 1994), which held that § 1981 prohibits alienage discrimination in the making of private insurance contracts. These two decisions rested on both the plain meaning of the statute and a careful examination of the statute's legislative history. A pre-1991 Fifth Circuit decision, Bhandari v. First Natl. Bank of Commerce, 829 F.2d 1343 (5th Cir. 1987) (en banc), *vacated and remanded*, 492 U.S. 901, *reaffirmed on remand*, 887 F.2d 609 (1989), thought that § 1981 prohibited alienage discrimination in state employment, but held the statute did not reach private employment. However, since *Bhandari* was decided, Congress enacted § 1981(c), which expressly provides that § 1981 reaches both state and private discrimination. Presumably, the Fifth Circuit would now agree that § 1981 also prohibits alienage discrimination in private employment. Accord Chacko v. Texas A&M Univ., 960 F. Supp. 1180 (S.D. Tex. 1997), *aff'd*, 149 F.3d 1175 (5th Cir. 1998). See generally, Angela M. Ford, Note, Private Alienage Discrimination and the Reconstruction Amendments: The Constitutionality of 42 U.S.C. § 1981, 49 U. Kan. L. Rev. 457 (2001).

This interpretation of § 1981 will give rise to several subsidiary issues. The most obvious is whether § 1981 also prohibits alienage discrimination against aliens who cannot legally work in the United States. Although § 1981 protects "all persons within the jurisdiction of the United States," the IRCA, as will be discussed in the next subsection, prohibits employment of "unauthorized aliens." The *Conboy* court attempted to reconcile § 1981 and the IRCA by commenting that an unauthorized alien who was denied employment *because of his unauthorized status* has not experienced alienage discrimination. But the truly difficult problem is presented where employment is denied partly or entirely on the basis of the unauthorized alien's lack of United States citizenship.

Where employment has been denied on the basis of an unauthorized alien's lack of citizenship, two approaches are possible. First, the courts could apply the usual disparate treatment principles, including the mixed-motives and after-acquired evidence doctrines. If the employer considered both the alien's unauthorized status and his lack of citizenship, a mixed-motives defense may preclude liability or limit damages, depending on whether courts apply *Price Waterhouse* or the approach in the 1991 Civil Rights Act. See page 174. If the employer acted on the alien's lack of citizenship but later discovered the alien's unauthorized status, the after-acquired evidence defense may limit the available relief. See page 999. Second, rather than applying the usual disparate treatment principles, the courts might hold that the IRCA has placed unauthorized aliens outside the scope of § 1981's protection. These alternative approaches were debated in the several opinions in Egbuna v. Time-Life Libraries, Inc., 95 F.3d 353 (4th Cir.), *vacated,* 1996 U.S. App. LEXIS 33089 (1996), *opinion issued,* 153 F.3d 184 (1998), where the en banc court held that an unauthorized alien could not maintain a Title VII action alleging a discriminatory refusal to hire. Which approach would best further the purposes of both § 1981 and the IRCA? Does *Espinoza*'s statement that aliens are protected by Title VII (see pages 617-618) suggest the first approach is correct?

A recent Supreme Court decision under the National Labor Relations Act, however, suggests a third approach as the proper solution to the problem. In Hoffman Plastic Compounds, Inc. v. NLRB, 535 U.S. 137 (2002), the Court (5-4) set aside a NLRB backpay award to an unauthorized alien who had fraudulently obtained employment, but who then had been unlawfully discharged due to his union activity. Chief Justice Rehnquist explained:

> We therefore conclude that allowing the Board to award backpay to illegal aliens would unduly trench upon explicit statutory prohibitions critical to federal immigration policy, as expressed in IRCA. It would encourage the successful evasion of apprehension by immigration authorities, condone prior violations of the immigration laws, and encourage future violations. However broad the Board's discretion to fashion remedies when dealing only with the NLRA, it is not so unbounded as to authorize this sort of an award.
>
> Lack of authority to award backpay does not mean that the employer gets off scot-free. The Board here has already imposed other significant sanctions against Hoffman — sanctions Hoffman does not challenge. These include orders that Hoffman cease and desist its violations of the NLRA, and that it conspicuously post a notice to employees setting forth their rights under the NLRA and detailing its prior unfair practices. Hoffman will be subject to contempt proceedings should it fail to comply with these orders. We have deemed such "traditional remedies" sufficient to effectuate national labor policy regardless of whether the "spur and catalyst" of backpay accompanies them.

Id. at 1284-85. Should an unauthorized alien be allowed to obtain a prohibitory injunction and attorneys' fees (but no other relief) in a § 1981 action establishing alienage discrimination?

Another issue is whether § 1981 prohibits discrimination against United States citizens on the basis of their citizenship. One court, which thought that § 1981 prohibited alienage discrimination, nevertheless held that § 1981 does not protect United States citizens from citizenship discrimination. Chaiffetz v. Robertson Research

Holding, Ltd., 798 F.2d 731, 735 (5th Cir. 1986). Although the court recognized that § 1981 protects whites as well as racial minorities from race discrimination (see *Santa Fe Trail Transportation*, page 111), the court rejected the analogy between race and alienage discrimination, reasoning that "discrimination against Americans can never be discrimination based on *alienage*." Are you persuaded?

Even if § 1981 does protect United States citizens from citizenship discrimination, a foreign company may have a treaty right to discriminate in favor of its fellow citizens when filling certain positions in the United States. See Sumitomo Shoji Am., Inc. v. Avagliano, 457 U.S. 176 (1982). The treaty right may also extend to an American subsidiary of a foreign company when the subsidiary acted pursuant to its parent's dictates. Papaila v. Uniden Am. Corp., 51 F.3d 54 (5th Cir. 1995).

A final issue is whether some type of bfoq or business necessity defense is available in a § 1981 alienage discrimination action. Section 1981 does not mention any affirmative defense and there does not appear to be any case law to support such a defense. However, the IRCA permits citizenship discrimination when such discrimination is required by "law, regulation, or executive order" or a government contract. 8 U.S.C.S. § 1324b(a)(2)(C) (2003). Should these defenses be read into § 1981? Are not these defenses both too broad and too narrow? Can you imagine circumstances in which a United States citizenship would be job-related? Do the events of September 11 change your answer?

Aliens have sometimes successfully attacked state-imposed citizens-only rules for employment and professional licensing by bringing § 1983 actions raising equal protection claims. See generally Michael Scaperlanda, Partial Membership: Aliens and the Constitutional Community, 81 Iowa L. Rev. 707 (1996); Linda S. Bosniak, Membership, Equality, and the Difference That Alienage Makes, 69 N.Y.U. L. Rev. 1047 (1994). Congress, however, by virtue of its power over immigration and naturalization, has broader authority to limit the employment opportunities of aliens than states have. See Nyquist v. Mauclet, 432 U.S. 1 (1977); Matthews v. Diaz, 426 U.S. 67 (1976).

The IRCA, which is covered in the next subsection, also prohibits discrimination on the basis of citizenship. That statute protects United States citizens and authorized aliens, but denies such protection to unauthorized aliens. However, the IRCA provides those who are protected with a less generous remedy than does § 1981.

## 3.   *The Immigration Reform and Control Act of 1986*

A novel approach to the employment of aliens is found in the Immigration Reform and Control Act of 1986, Pub. L. No. 99-603, 100 Stat. 3359 (1986). That statute requires employers to discriminate against unauthorized aliens, but also prohibits employers from discriminating against aliens who are authorized to work in the United States. In addition, the statute prohibits national origin discrimination and discrimination against United States citizens.

Section 101 of the IRCA, 8 U.S.C.S. § 1324a (2003), prohibits the hiring, recruiting, and referral for fee of "unauthorized aliens." An alien is any person who is not a citizen of the United States. An "unauthorized alien" is an alien who is not lawfully admitted for permanent residence or authorized to be employed by the IRCA or the Attorney General. An employer, on learning that it has hired an unauthorized alien, must terminate the employee or face substantial penalties. In making employment decisions, the employer is required to document the individual's work authorization and identity. The employer is also required to attest that it made such an examination.

In Collins Foods Intl., Inc. v. INS, 948 F.2d 549 (9th Cir. 1991), the court reversed a finding that the employer had constructive knowledge of a person's status as an unauthorized alien. Constructive knowledge could not be inferred from (1) the employer offering the job on the telephone before checking the applicant's documentation, and (2) the employer, while checking the documentation when the applicant arrived to work, failing to compare his Social Security card with the sample in the INS Service Manual. The court said that "Congress did not intend the statute to cause employers to become experts in identifying and examining a prospective employee's employment authorization documents." Id. at 554. Further, expanding liability by using the constructive knowledge doctrine would cause employers to discriminate against people because of their national origin or citizenship. "To guard against unknowing violations, the employer may, again, avoid hiring anyone with an appearance of alienage. To preserve Congress' intent in passing the employer sanctions provisions of IRCA, then, the doctrine of constructive knowledge must be sparingly applied." Id. at 555. Cf. Mester Mfg. Co. v. INS, 879 F.2d 561 (9th Cir. 1989) (violation to continue employment without further inquiry after INS questioned documentation and the employee was an unauthorized alien).

Section 101 may provide the employer with a defense in an employment discrimination action by an unauthorized alien. Consider Egbuna v. Time-Life Libraries, Inc., 153 F.3d 184 (4th Cir. 1998) (en banc), where an unauthorized alien filed a Title VII action alleging that he had been denied employment in retaliation for his testimony in connection with an EEOC charge. The court affirmed summary judgment for the defendant, holding that § 101 rendered the plaintiff ineligible for employment. Because the court did not indicate that the employer had acted on the basis of the applicant's unauthorized status, the opinion must mean that the applicant was simply beyond the protection of Title VII. Strangely, the court did not think it necessary to distinguish *Espinoza*, where prior to the IRCA, the Supreme Court broadly stated that aliens are protected by Title VII. See pages 617-618. There is language in the opinion, however, which suggests a different result might have ensued if the unauthorized alien had been hired and then subjected to discrimination. In any event, the Fourth Circuit's ruling approach is questionable. As indicated in the preceding subsection, cases like *Egbuna* can and perhaps should be decided through application of the usual disparate treatment principles.

Section 201 of the IRCA, 8 U.S.C.S. § 1255a (2003), granted amnesty to certain aliens who resided continuously in the United States in an unlawful status since before January 1, 1982. To have received amnesty, an alien had to apply by May 6, 1988, and show such continuous residence and no serious criminal violations. An alien whose application was granted is protected from deportation and is entitled to receive a work authorization.

While § 101 requires an employer to discriminate against unauthorized aliens, § 102, 8 U.S.C.S. § 1324b (2003), makes it an "unfair immigration-related employment practice" for an employer to discriminate against either an individual because of his national origin or a "protected individual" because of his citizenship status. A "protected individual" means a citizen of the United States or an alien who "is lawfully admitted for permanent residence, is granted the status of an alien lawfully admitted for temporary residence under [the amnesty provisions described above], is admitted as a refugee . . . , or is granted asylum. . . ." 8 U.S.C.S. § 1324b(a)(3) (2003). These provisions, however, leave many lawfully present aliens unprotected against discrimination on account of their alienage. See Michael A. Scaperlanda, The Paradox of a Title: Discrimination Within the Anti-Discrimination Provisions of the Immigration Reform and Control Act of 1986, 1988 Wis. L. Rev. 1043.

Moreover § 102 also contains some provisions that restrict its scope. One provision excludes from coverage any national origin discrimination that is prohibited by Title VII, and another permits discrimination based on citizenship when such discrimination is required by "law, regulation, or executive order" or a federal or state contract. Finally, § 102 is inapplicable to employers with three or fewer employees. 8 U.S.C.S. § 1324b(a)(2)(A-C) (2003).

Section 102 was added to prevent employers from seeking to avoid the IRCA's requirements by simply not hiring any "foreign-appearing" individuals. Section 102, coupled with Title VII's prohibition of national origin discrimination, was intended to safeguard the rights of American citizens and authorized aliens. There is considerable doubt about the success of this effort. The General Accounting Office issued a report estimating that 19 percent of more than 4 million employers began discriminatory practices as a result of the IRCA, Daily Labor Report, no. 62, Mar. 30, 1990, at A-9, prompting calls for its repeal. See generally Michael Crocenzi, Comment, IRCA-Related Discrimination: Is It Time to Repeal the Employer Sanctions?, 96 Dick. L. Rev. 673 (1992).

Does the IRCA really protect native-born Americans from discrimination because of their citizenship? The plain language of the statute supports the claim. The legislative history, however, shows that Congress acted primarily to protect recently naturalized American citizens and immigrants intending to become citizens — those who might otherwise be subject to discrimination on the basis of the appearance that they are not United States citizens. Nevertheless, should a court apply the plain language of the statute as the Supreme Court did in regard to the race discrimination claims of whites in McDonald v. Santa Fe Trail Transportation Co. (reproduced at page 111)? See also Oncale v. Sundowner Offshore Servs., Inc. (reproduced at page 492) and Eileen M. Mullen, Rotating Japanese Managers in American Subsidiaries of Japanese Firms: A Challenge for American Employment Discrimination Law, 45 Stan. L. Rev. 725, 765-66 (1993).

Special procedures apply to IRCA discrimination claims. See 8 U.S.C.S. § 1324b(b)-(j) (2003). Complaints are to be lodged with the special counsel for immigration-related unfair employment practices, an office in the Department of Justice. There is a 180-day limit for filing complaints. If the special counsel has not acted within 120 days, the complaining party may proceed privately by filing a complaint directly with an administrative law judge. Findings of discrimination can result in civil penalties of up to $1,000 for each individual discriminated against and $2,000 for a repeat offender, plus backpay, reinstatement, and attorneys' fees.

A deficiency in these procedures has appeared. In Hensel v. Office of the Chief Hearing Officer, 38 F.3d 505 (10th Cir. 1994), the petitioner had been denied a position in a medical facility that was jointly operated by a federal and a state agency. She claimed discrimination because of her United States citizenship. After an administrative law judge dismissed her complaint, she petitioned for judicial review, naming the federal and state agencies. The Tenth Circuit upheld both the federal agency's defense of sovereign immunity and the state agency's defense of Eleventh Amendment immunity, concluding that the IRCA contained no provisions that would overcome these defenses. Could the petitioner have avoided the Eleventh Amendment defense by naming a state official as a respondent?

The scope of the protection accorded by the IRCA remains to be developed. President Ronald Reagan, on signing the bill, stated that individuals filing discrimination complaints must prove the employer acted with discriminatory intent. But some members of Congress contested that reading of the law. See Immigration Law Sets Off Dispute over Job Rights for Legal Aliens, N.Y. Times, Nov. 23, 1986, at A1. From the viewpoint of statutory interpretation, § 101 requires that an employer knowingly hire an illegal alien in order to be guilty under the law. Section 102 says nothing about a state-of-mind element for an employer that discriminates against a person protected by the act. The structure of the statute, therefore, arguably supports the claim that there is no state-of-mind element in § 102.

## F.   UNION LIABILITY

In 1935, Congress passed the Wagner Act, which, as amended and now called the National Labor Relations Act (NLRA), 29 U.S.C.S. §§ 151 et seq. (2003), established the legal structure for the relationship between unions and employers. The act made no provisions for the problems of race or gender discrimination and, as originally passed, did not include any direct control of the activities of unions.

Despite the absence of statutory language, one of the first theories of federal law available to attack employment discrimination was the duty of fair representation. In Steele v. Louisville & Nashville R.R., 323 U.S. 192 (1944), the Court created a federal cause of action on behalf of black railroad employees who claimed that the union that was legally charged with representing them was bargaining with the employer to have them replaced. While the statute did not give these black workers the right to become members of the union that represented them, the Court found that a union granted exclusive bargaining representative status over some workers under the NLRA had the duty to represent them fairly. "While the majority of the craft chooses the bargaining representative, when chosen it represents, as the Act by its terms makes plain, the craft or class, and not the majority. The fair interpretation of the statutory language is that the organization chosen to represent a craft is to represent all its members, the majority as well as the minority, and it is to act for and not against those whom it represents." Id. at 202.

In 1964, in Title VII's § 703, Congress directly barred discrimination by unions. Section 703(c)(1) prohibits a union from discriminating in union membership, "or otherwise to discriminate"; subsection (2) prohibits a union from limiting, segregating, or classifying members or applicants "in any way which would deprive or tend to deprive any individual of employment opportunities"; and subsection (3) prohibits a union from causing an employer to discriminate against an individual.

In Goodman v. Lukens Steel Co., 482 U.S. 656 (1987), the Supreme Court construed § 703(c). The lower court had found that the union had failed to challenge the employer's discriminatory discharge of black probationary employees, had failed to assert race discrimination as a ground for grievances, and had tolerated the employer's racial harassment. The union argued that it could only be liable for an employer's action if, under § 703(c)(3), the union had caused the employer to discriminate. The Court rejected that narrow reading of Title VII and referred to § 703(c)(1), which made it an unlawful practice for a union to "exclude or to expel from its membership, or *otherwise to discriminate against*" any individual (emphasis added).

In contrast to the broad approach of the majority, which would prohibit discrimination by unions in their representation of workers, Justice Powell, joined by Justices

Scalia and O'Connor, would have construed § 703(c) more narrowly. "§ 703(c)(1) prohibits direct discrimination by a union against its members; it does not impose upon a union an obligation to remedy discrimination by the employer. Moreover, § 703(c)(3) specifically addresses the union's interaction with the employer by outlawing efforts by the union to 'cause or attempt to cause an employer to discriminate against an individual in violation of this section.'" Id. at 688. See also Thorn v. Amalgamated Transit Union, 305 F.3d 826 (8th Cir. 2002) (no affirmative duty for union to investigate and take steps to remedy employer discrimination).

Neither the majority nor the dissent referred to § 703(c)(2), which prohibits a union from classifying any individual "in any way which would deprive or tend to deprive any individual of employment opportunities." Under § 703(c)(2), it would appear that a union would be liable for classifying individuals by race in failing to assert grievances because of the race of the grievants, since that failure would tend to deprive those individuals of the employment opportunity of participating in the grievance process.

## G.   RETALIATION

In addition to prohibiting discrimination on the grounds of race, sex, religion, national origin, and age, Title VII, § 1981, and the ADEA create a remedy for certain retaliatory conduct. Retaliation is also prohibited by the Americans with Disabilities Act as treated in Chapter 8. Section 704(a) of Title VII, 42 U.S.C.S. § 2000e-3(a) (2003), provides:

> It shall be an unlawful employment practice for an employer to discriminate against any of his employees or applicants for employment . . . because he has opposed any practice made an unlawful employment practice by this title, or because he has made a charge, testified, assisted, or participated in any manner in an investigation, proceeding, or hearing under this title.

The ADEA prohibits retaliation in substantially identical language. 29 U.S.C.S. § 623(d) (2003).

Even though § 1981 does not expressly prohibit retaliation, recent appellate decisions have interpreted the statute as doing so. E.g., Hawkins v. 1115 Legal Serv. Care, 163 F.3d 684 (2d Cir. 1998); Kim v. Nash Finch Co., 123 F.3d 1046 (8th Cir. 1997). However, this interpretation cannot be considered settled. The Supreme Court's decision in Patterson v. McLean Credit Union, 491 U.S. 164 (1989), which limited § 1981 to discrimination relating to contract formation and enforcement, cast grave doubt on earlier decisions that had also interpreted § 1981 as prohibiting retaliation. Although *Patterson* was overturned by the addition of § 1981(b) in the Civil Rights Act of 1991, the statutory language does not expressly address retaliation. Nevertheless, the legislative history of § 1981(b) expressly states that Congress intended the provision to also prohibit retaliation. See Andrews v. Lakeshore Rehab. Hosp., 140 F.3d 1405 (11th Cir. 1998). See also Suzanne E. Riley, Comment, Employees' Retaliation Claims Under 42 U.S.C. § 1981: Ramifications of the Civil Rights Act of 1991, 79 Marq. L. Rev. 579 (1996).

This section will focus on retaliation decisions under Title VII and the ADEA. The relevant provision in each statute consists of two separate clauses that present distinct legal questions. The first bars retaliation for "oppos[ing] . . . any practice made an unlawful employment practice." This "opposition clause" encompasses more types of conduct than the second clause, the "free access" or "participation" clause, which proscribes retaliation "because [an employee or applicant] has made a charge, testified, assisted, or participated . . . in an investigation, proceeding, or hearing" under the relevant statute.

## CLARK COUNTY SCHOOL DISTRICT v. BREEDEN
### 532 U.S. 268 (2001)

PER CURIAM.

Under Title VII of the Civil Rights Act of 1964, 42 U.S.C. § 2000e-3(a), it is unlawful "for an employer to discriminate against any of his employees . . . because [the employee] has opposed any practice made an unlawful employment practice by [Title VII], or because [the employee] has made a charge, testified, assisted, or participated in any manner in an investigation, proceeding, or hearing under [Title VII]." In 1997, respondent filed a § 2000e-3(a) retaliation claim against petitioner Clark County School District. The claim as eventually amended alleged that petitioner had taken two separate adverse employment actions against her in response to two different protected activities in which she had engaged. . . .

On October 21, 1994, respondent's male supervisor met with respondent and another male employee to review the psychological evaluation reports of four job applicants. The report for one of the applicants disclosed that the applicant had once commented to a co-worker, "I hear making love to you is like making love to the Grand Canyon." At the meeting respondent's supervisor read the comment aloud, looked at respondent and stated, "I don't know what that means." The other employee then said, "Well, I'll tell you later," and both men chuckled. Respondent later complained about the comment to the offending employee, to Assistant Superintendent George Ann Rice, the employee's supervisor, and to another assistant superintendent of petitioner. Her first claim of retaliation asserts that she was punished for these complaints.

The Court of Appeals for the Ninth Circuit has applied § 2000e-3(a) to protect employee "opposition" not just to practices that are actually "made . . . unlawful" by Title VII, but also to practices that the employee could reasonably believe were unlawful. We have no occasion to rule on the propriety of this interpretation, because even assuming it is correct, no one could reasonably believe that the incident recounted above violated Title VII.

Title VII forbids actions taken on the basis of sex that "discriminate against any individual with respect to his compensation, terms, conditions, or privileges of employment." 42 U.S.C. § 2000e-2(a)(1). Just three Terms ago, we reiterated, what was plain from our previous decisions, that sexual harassment is actionable under Title VII only if it is "so 'severe or pervasive' as to 'alter the conditions of [the victim's] employment and create an abusive working environment.'" Faragher v. Boca Raton, 524 U.S. 775, 786 (1998) (quoting Meritor Savings Bank, FSB v. Vinson [reproduced at page 487] (some internal quotation marks omitted)). See also Burlington Industries, Inc. v. Ellerth [reproduced at page 516] (Only harassing conduct that is "severe or pervasive" can produce a "constructive alteration in the terms or conditions of employment."); Oncale v. Sundowner Offshore Services, Inc. [reproduced at page 492] (Title VII "forbids only behavior so objectively offensive as to alter the 'conditions' of the victim's employment"). Workplace conduct is not measured in isolation; instead, "whether an environment is sufficiently hostile or abusive" must be judged "by 'look-ing at all the circumstances,' including the 'frequency of the discriminatory conduct; its severity; whether it is physically threatening or humiliating, or a mere offensive ut-terance; and whether it unreasonably interferes with an employee's work perform-ance.'" Faragher v. Boca Raton, 524 U.S. at 787-788 (quoting Harris v. Forklift Sys-tems, Inc. [reproduced at page 507]). Hence, "[a] recurring point in [our] opinions is that simple teasing, offhand comments, and isolated incidents (unless extremely seri-ous) will not amount to discriminatory changes in the 'terms and conditions of em-ployment.'" Faragher v. Boca Raton.

No reasonable person could have believed that the single incident recounted above violated Title VII's standard. The ordinary terms and conditions of respon-dent's job required her to review the sexually explicit statement in the course of screening job applicants. Her co-workers who participated in the hiring process were subject to the same requirement, and indeed, in the District Court respondent "con-ceded that it did not bother or upset her" to read the statement in the file. Her super-visor's comment, made at a meeting to review the application, that he did not know what the statement meant; her co-worker's responding comment; and the chuckling of both are at worst an "isolated incident" that cannot remotely be considered "ex-tremely serious," as our cases require, Faragher v. Boca Raton. The holding of the Court of Appeals to the contrary must be reversed.

Besides claiming that she was punished for complaining to petitioner's personnel about the alleged sexual harassment, respondent also claimed that she was punished for filing charges against petitioner with the Nevada Equal Rights Commission and the Equal Employment Opportunity Commission (EEOC) and for filing the present suit. Respondent filed her lawsuit on April 1, 1997; on April 10, 1997, respondent's supervisor, Assistant Superintendent Rice, "mentioned to Allin Chandler, Executive Director of plaintiff's union, that she was contemplating transferring plaintiff to the position of Director of Professional Development Education,"; and this transfer was "carried through" in May. In order to show, as her defense against summary judg-ment required, the existence of a causal connection between her protected activities and the transfer, respondent "relied wholly on the temporal proximity of the filing of her complaint on April 1, 1997 and Rice's statement to plaintiff's union representa-tive on April 10, 1997 that she was considering transferring plaintiff to the [new] po-sition." The District Court, however, found that respondent did not serve petitioner with the summons and complaint until April 11, 1997, one day after Rice had made the statement, and Rice filed an affidavit stating that she did not become aware of the lawsuit until after April 11, a claim that respondent did not challenge. Hence, the court concluded, respondent "had not shown that any causal connection exists be-tween her protected activities and the adverse employment decision."

The Court of Appeals reversed, relying on two facts: The EEOC had issued a right-to-sue letter to respondent three months before Rice announced she was contemplat-ing the transfer, and the actual transfer occurred one month after Rice learned of respondent's suit. The latter fact is immaterial in light of the fact that petitioner con-cededly was contemplating the transfer before it learned of the suit. Employers need not suspend previously planned transfers upon discovering that a Title VII suit has been filed, and their proceeding along lines previously contemplated, though not yet definitively determined, is no evidence whatever of causality.

As for the right-to-sue letter: Respondent did not rely on that letter in the District Court and did not mention it in her opening brief on appeal. Her demonstration of causality all along had rested upon the connection between the transfer and the filing of her lawsuit — to which connection the letter was irrelevant. When, however, petitioner's answering brief in the Court of Appeals demonstrated conclusively the lack of causation between the filing of respondent's lawsuit and Rice's decision, respondent mentioned the letter for the first time in her reply brief. The Ninth Circuit's opinion . . . suggests that the letter provided petitioner with its first notice of respondent's charge before the EEOC, and hence allowed the inference that the transfer proposal made three months later was petitioner's reaction to the charge. This will not do.

First, there is no indication that Rice even knew about the right-to-sue letter when she proposed transferring respondent. And second, if one presumes she knew about it, one must also presume that she (or her predecessor) knew *almost two years earlier* about the protected action (filing of the EEOC complaint) that the letter supposedly disclosed. . . . The cases that accept mere temporal proximity between an employer's knowledge of protected activity and an adverse employment action as sufficient evidence of causality to establish a prima facie case uniformly hold that the temporal proximity must be "very close," Neal v. Ferguson Constr. Co., 237 F.3d 1248, 1253 (CA10 2001). See e.g., Richmond v. Oneok, Inc., 120 F.3d 205, 209 (CA10 1997) (3-month period insufficient); Hughes v. Derwinski, 967 F.2d 1168, 1174-1175 (CA7 1992) (4-month period insufficient). Action taken (as here) 20 months later suggests, by itself, no causality at all.

In short, neither the grounds that respondent presented to the District Court, nor the ground she added on appeal, nor even the ground the Court of Appeals developed on its own, sufficed to establish a dispute substantial enough to withstand the motion for summary judgment. The District Court's granting of that motion was correct. The judgment of the Court of Appeals is reversed.

## NOTES

1. Shirley Breeden presented two distinct claims of retaliation. One was for opposition conduct (her internal complaints), while the other was for participation conduct (her filing of charges to the state agency and the EEOC). Many courts and commentators have perceived a sharp distinction between the protections of the "opposition" clause and the "participation" clause. While a plaintiff invoking the opposition clause must demonstrate a reasonable, good faith belief that the conduct complained of is unlawful, the protections of the participation clause have been almost absolute. One of the first "participation" cases, Pettway v. American Cast Iron Pipe Co., 411 F.2d 998 (5th Cir. 1969), set the tone for these decisions by finding actionable retaliation when a worker was fired for filing an allegedly false and malicious charge with the EEOC — namely, that the employer had bought off an EEOC investigator. The court wrote:

> There can be no doubt about the purpose of § 704(a). In unmistakable language it is to protect the employee who utilizes the tools provided by Congress to protect his rights. The Act will be frustrated if the employer may unilaterally determine the truth or falsity of charges and take independent action.

Id. at 1004-05. See also Glover v. S.C. Law Enf., 170 F.3d 411 (4th Cir. 1999) (unreasonable deposition testimony protected by participation clause); Clover v. Total Sys. Serv., Inc., 176 F.3d 1346 (11th Cir. 1999) (reasonable belief not needed for participation clause protections to be triggered). But see Fine v. Ryan Intl. Airlines, 305 F.3d 746, 752 (7th Cir. 2002) (improper to retaliate against employee for filing lawsuit that was based on reasonable, good faith belief; improper to retaliate unless claim is "completely groundless."); Johnson v. ITT Aerospace, 272 F.3d 498 (7th Cir. 2001) (filing frivolous charges against employer not protected); Barnes v. Small, 840 F.2d 972 (D.C. Cir. 1988) (although plaintiff's letters to the agency head were sufficiently related to race discrimination proceedings to be protected, discharge was permissible because the letters were both false and malicious).

2. After the *Breeden* Court disposed of the plaintiff's "opposition clause" claim by deciding that no reasonable person could believe that she had been sexually harassed, it went on to consider the causation issue on her "participation" clause claim. Doesn't *Breeden* thus establish that the participation clause prohibits retaliation even where the underlying discrimination claim lacks a reasonable basis? Why should that be so? What if the plaintiff's charge and suit had been filed in bad faith? Cf. Christiansburg Garmet Co. v. EEOC (reproduced at page 1012) (Supreme Court holding that employer can be awarded attorneys' fees for Title VII action that was "frivolous, unreasonable, or groundless" or in bad faith).

3. At the same time, the *Breeden* Court questioned, although it did not decide, whether the opposition clause's protections attach if the challenged practice is not in fact unlawful. In other words, a reasonable, good faith belief that the employer has acted unlawfully may not suffice under the opposition clause. While the statutory language certainly supports limiting the statute's protections only to opposition to conduct that is in fact unlawful, would such an interpretation be consistent with the policy objectives of § 704? See Robinson v. Shell Oil , 519 U.S. 337 (1997) (since policy of § 704 furthered by including former employees within the protections of the statute, they are within the protected class). Prior to *Robinson*, courts generally agreed that a reasonable, good faith belief is sufficient; the challenged conduct need not actually be unlawful.

4. Because the protections afforded by these two clauses differ, perhaps dramatically, what is the line between participation, as opposed to opposition, conduct? Internal complaints of discrimination, it appears from *Breeden*, are opposition, not participation, conduct. Is this consistent with the affirmative defense set forth in *Ellerth*, reproduced at page 516? If the affirmative defense is aimed at encouraging plaintiffs to utilize internal complaint mechanisms, why not protect employees from retaliation when they do what the affirmative defense essentially requires them to do? This argument was made to the Eleventh Circuit by the EEOC and rejected. EEOC v. Total Sys. Servs., Inc., 221 F.3d 1171 (11th Cir. 2000).

5. Is *Breeden* inconsistent with *Ellerth* in yet a more fundamental way? If a purpose of the affirmative defense is to encourage victims to report offensive conduct before it becomes severe or pervasive, thereby allowing employers to promptly correct the conduct, see Casiano v. AT&T, 213 F.3d 278 (5th Cir. 2000), why should retaliation against employees who do what *Ellerth* encourages plaintiffs to do *not* be protected? For discussion of the interaction between § 704 and internal complaint procedures, see Edward Marshall, Excluding Participation in Internal Complaint Mechanisms From Absolute Retaliation Protection: Why Everyone, Including the Employer, Loses, 5 Emp. Rts. & Employ. Pol'y J. 549 (2001); Dorothy E. Larkin, Note, Participation Anxiety: Should Title VII's Participation Clause Protect Employees Participating in Internal Investigations, 33 Ga. L. Rev. 1181 (1999).

6. What happens if the employer requires, as a condition of employment, that an employee agree to arbitrate discrimination claims? Would participation in arbitration

proceedings fall under the opposition or the participation clause? See Edward Marshall, Title VII's Participation Clause and Circuit City Stores v. Adams: Making the Foxes Guardians of the Chickens, 24 Berkeley J. Emp. & Lab. L. — (2002). Is an employee's refusal to sign an arbitration agreement protected activity? See EEOC v. Luce, Forward, Hamilton & Scripps, 303 F.3d 994 (9th Cir. 2002) (no); Weeks v. Harden Mfg. Corp., 291 F.3d 1307 (11th Cir. 2002) (same).

7. Although the lower courts have held that a reasonable, good faith belief is both necessary and sufficient, it is clear that reasonableness is not to be determined by the ultimate success of the underlying claim. While the conduct of which Breeden complained is a far cry from the "severe or pervasive" conduct envisioned by the Court in *Meritor* and its progeny, how much of a difference is there between conduct that will support a claim of hostile work environment and that which will support a reasonable, good faith belief that the workplace is hostile?

8. On the participation claim, the *Breeden* Court thought it "immaterial" that the transfer was finalized a month after suit was filed, reasoning that the transfer was contemplated earlier. Should the trier of fact have been allowed to determine the decision-maker's motivation in finalizing the transfer? Would a contrary ruling in practice have required employers to "suspend previously planned transfers upon discovering that a Title VII suit has been filed"? Must a plaintiff now present evidence regarding the proximity between the decision-maker's knowledge of the protected activity and his initial contemplation of the adverse employment action?

9. Does *Breeden* mean that the plaintiff always loses on a summary judgment motion where the employer has denied retaliation and the plaintiff's only evidence of causation is that the adverse employment action occurred three months or more after the decision-maker learned of the protected activity? What if the decision-maker began contemplating such action within three months of learning of the protected activity? See Franzoni v. Hartmarx Corp., 300 F.3d 767 (7th Cir. 2002) (six-month time lapse between charge of discrimination and termination, standing alone, insufficient proof of causation).

10. Does the mixed-motives approach in the 1991 Civil Rights Act, §§ 703(m), 706(g)(2)(B), apply in a Title VII retaliation case? Most circuits have now stated that *Price Waterhouse*, not § 703(m), is controlling in Title VII retaliation actions involving mixed-motives. Pennington v. City of Huntsville, 261 F.3d 1262 (11th Cir. 2001); Speedy v. Rexnord Corp., 243 F.3d 397 (7th Cir. 2001); Matima v. Celli, 228 F.3d 68 (2d Cir. 2000); Norbeck v. Basin Elec. Power Co-op, 215 F.3d 848 (8th Cir. 2000) (dicta); Kubicko v. Ogden Logistics Servs., 181 F.3d 544 (4th Cir. 1999); Woodson v. Scott Paper Co., 109 F.3d 913 (3d Cir. 1997); Tanca v. Nordberg, 98 F.3d 680 (1st Cir. 1996).

## 1.  Protected Conduct

As we saw in *Breeden*, participation conduct has received greater protection than opposition conduct. While opposition conduct must be supported by a reasonable, good faith belief that the employer has acted unlawfully (if not a finding that the employer's action was in fact unlawful), no such determination appears to be required for participation conduct.

The clauses differ in another important way. The form of participation activities generally will not take the plaintiff outside the protection of the Act. Courts have found employers guilty of unlawful retaliation when they act on *any* ground related to filing a discrimination charge. See, e.g., EEOC v. Bd. of Governors of State

Colls. and Univs., 957 F.2d 424 (7th Cir. 1992) (invalidating a collective bargaining agreement provision terminating grievance proceedings when a lawsuit is filed; the policy constitutes retaliation, although not motivated by malice); East v. Romine, Inc., 518 F.2d 332 (5th Cir. 1975) (employer refused to hire applicant who had filed several previous charges on the ground that she was a "litigious" person); Barela v. United Nuclear Corp., 462 F.2d 149 (10th Cir. 1972) (employer refused to hire applicant who was suing a former employer for reinstatement because he was unlikely to be permanent). That the employer is invoking a neutral rule that would have been applied to employees engaging in other forms of litigation does not mean those rules may be applied to persons who have engaged in participation activities under employment discrimination statutes. In a sense, § 704's participation clause entitles plaintiffs to special treatment.

The extent to which this protection can be carried is illustrated by Womack v. Munson, 619 F.2d 1292 (8th Cir. 1980), in which the black plaintiff, after being hired by the county prosecutor, filed a Title VII suit against his former employer, the county sheriff. The prosecutor immediately questioned the plaintiff about the suit, investigated his responses, and shortly thereafter discharged him. In the course of the investigation, the plaintiff first admitted physically abusing black suspects while working for the sheriff, but subsequently denied it. Although the Eighth Circuit did not seem to doubt that either lying or physical abuse of prisoners would be grounds for dismissing a law enforcement officer, the opinion stressed that the physical abuse of black suspects was a focus of the plaintiff's suit against the sheriff. The court concluded that "the admission and denial of abuse by Womack are so inextricably related to the allegation in the complaint that they cannot be considered independently of one another." Id. at 1297. It was, therefore, clear that the prosecutor fired the plaintiff because of allegations in his complaint, that is, because he "made a charge . . . or participated in any manner in a . . . proceeding" under Title VII. See also Merritt v. Dillard Paper Co., 120 F.3d 1181 (11th Cir. 1997).

But what about the opposition clause? Can the form the employee's opposition takes remove her from the protections of the Act? As should be obvious from McDonnell Douglas Corp. v. Green, reproduced at page 97, the answer is yes. Recall that Greeen had engaged in a "stall in" to protest alleged discrimination by the company, and the company had asserted his participation in those activities as the explanation for why Green was not rehired. Although the *McDonnell Douglas* Court did not directly rule on § 704(a), as that claim was not before it, the Court, in language broad enough to embrace § 704(a), wrote: "Nothing in Title VII compels an employer to absolve and rehire one who has engaged in such deliberate, unlawful activity against it." Id. at 803.

How far does *McDonnell Douglas* go in allowing an employer to discriminate because of an employee's "opposition"? Is it merely a "law and order" decision in that it permits retaliation where the opposition violates criminal statutes, or can it be read more broadly? In justifying its ruling, the Court looked to the "disloyalty doctrine" under the National Labor Relations Act. The opinion quoted from NLRB v. Fansteel Metallurgical Corp., 306 U.S. 240 (1939) (sitdown strikers' discharge upheld), which set out the core concept: some acts of protest by employees, even if done for a protected purpose, are sufficiently disloyal to justify discharge. See also NLRB v. Electrical Workers Local 1229, 346 U.S. 464 (1953) (Court upheld the discharge of engineers who distributed handbills that disparaged the employer's product, but did not mention a labor dispute). Should the *Fansteel* approach be transplanted to Title VII and the ADEA?

The Supreme Court again addressed the issue in Emporium Capwell Co. v. Western Addition Community Org., 420 U.S. 50 (1975), holding that the NLRA does not protect concerted action by minority employees who seek to bargain directly with their employer about employment discrimination when the employees are represented by a union. Although *Emporium Capwell* is not dispositive of any Title VII question, the Court suggested that the employees' call for a consumer boycott of their employer, with handbills referring to the employer as a "20th Century colonial plantation," a "racist pig" and a "racist store," *might* fall outside the protections of the statute.

What does it take for opposition to what the employee reasonably and in good faith believes is unlawful discrimination to fall outside the protection of the statute? Given that some forms of opposition are unprotected, how should the burdens of production and proof apply? Is it plaintiff's burden to persuade that the form the opposition takes is protected by the statute? Need the employer only articulate the form the opposition conduct took as a legitimate, nondiscriminatory reason for its retaliatory action, thereby distinguishing the conduct from the expression? Or should the employer be required to prove that any retaliation for the form of opposition conduct was justified? Does the following case assist you in thinking about and answering these questions?

## JENNINGS v. TINLEY PARK COMMUNITY CONSOLIDATED SCHOOL DISTRICT NO. 146
### 864 F.2d 1368 (7th Cir. 1988)

CUMMINGS, Circuit Judge.

. . . Jennings was employed by the Tinley Park (Illinois) Community Consolidated School District No. 146 from November 1973 until June 1979, serving as secretary to the Superintendent of the School District, Robert Procunier. Jennings' employment ended on June 15, 1979, when she was discharged by Procunier due to events and conduct surrounding a protest of alleged unlawful discrimination based upon sex.

The alleged sex discrimination concerned a disparity in pay between the School District's secretaries and custodians. . . . All secretaries were female; all custodians were male. Custodians were paid one and one-half times their hourly rate for overtime work as approved by a supervisor. Secretaries were not paid for overtime work. Defendants argued that secretaries were not required to work overtime.

[In February 1979, the secretaries sent a letter to the school board, which was given to Procunier to present, objecting to the pay disparity. They also requested permission from Procunier to meet bimonthly and later provided Procunier with the minutes. Eventually, Procunier informed them of a salary schedule he proposed to present to the school board. The secretaries opposed the schedule because it continued the pay disparity. They formed an ad hoc committee to attend the school board meeting, giving their minutes to Procunier. He and Jennings again discussed the secretaries' concerns. At the board meeting, Procunier proposed his salary schedule, which was adopted despite the secretaries' opposition.]

In response to the School Board action . . . , the secretaries decided to prepare their own salary schedule, one that would contradict Procunier's. Jennings was the principal draftsman. The final draft, entitled "P.S. Salary Study" . . . was signed collectively by the Committee of Concerned Secretaries, and individually by, among others,

Jennings. This action, in contrast to the other meetings and activities, was done without Procunier's knowledge.

Rather than deliver the P.S. Salary Study to Procunier and instruct him to present it to the School Board at the next meeting (apparently scheduled for June 19th), as they had done previously, the secretaries decided to deliver individually the P.S. Salary Study to each Board member on June 1. Jennings was responsible for delivering a copy to Procunier, who heretofore was unaware of the P.S. Salary Study. Although delivery of the P.S. Salary Study to School Board members began at 2:00 p.m., and despite seeing and speaking to Procunier throughout the day — in fact Procunier asked Jennings to arrange a meeting with the secretaries so that Procunier could address their concerns — she did not deliver a copy to Procunier, nor inform him of its existence, until 3:50 p.m. that same day. Because of the timing of the delivery, Procunier was unable to respond to individual School Board members' inquiries which began that same day.

Following receipt of the P.S. Salary Study, the working relationship between Procunier and Jennings deteriorated. Procunier distanced himself from Jennings. Whereas prior to June 1, the delivery date of the P.S. Salary Study, Procunier had Jennings open the mail and the two would then review it together, after June 1 Procunier instructed her to leave the unopened mail in his office. He also instructed her not to answer phone calls on his personal line, as she had done in the past. A chair was removed from Procunier's office, apparently so that Jennings would have no place to sit.

On June 13, Procunier met with Jennings to discuss the timing and direct delivery of the P.S. Salary Study to Board members. Procunier expressed his displeasure at not being informed of its preparation and especially at not receiving a copy sooner. Jennings responded that some of the secretaries did not trust Procunier to present the P.S. Salary Study to the School Board, and thus the reason for the extraordinary delivery to Board members. Procunier replied that if such was the case, he expected Jennings to stand up and vouch for his trustworthiness, and if Jennings was unable to do this, then he could not in turn trust her.

On June 15, Procunier again met with Jennings and informed her that because she had not been loyal and supportive, he would recommend to the School Board that she be terminated. The reasons for her discharge were set forth in a letter . . . :

> . . . The very important element of mutual trust and support which is so essential in the relationship of a personal secretary to the administrator responsible for an operation similar to this school district has been seriously undermined. As a result of your reluctance to inform me [in advance] of actions which you and other secretaries took relative to communication with the Board of Education, you have created a situation which is antagonistic to the close, confidential working relationship which is necessary in this office.
>
> The deterioration of the level of trust and support leaves no alternative open to me.

The sole rationale for Jennings' termination was her conduct arising out of the preparation and delivery of the P.S. Salary Study as it related to Procunier, her supervisor. No other secretary was terminated or disciplined for participating in the P.S. Salary Study or for delivering it directly to Board members. . . .

. . . A claim of retaliatory discharge in contravention of Title VII prompts a three-step analysis. . . . First, the plaintiff has the burden of proving a prima facie case of discrimination based upon opposition to an unlawful employment practice. The plaintiff meets this burden by establishing that: (1) she was engaged in statutorily protected expression, viz., opposition to a seemingly unlawful employment practice; (2) she

suffered an adverse employment action; and, (3) there was a causal connection between the statutorily protected expression and the adverse employment action. The
plaintiff need not establish that the action she was protesting was actually an unlawful
employment practice; but rather only that she had a reasonable belief that the action
was unlawful.

Second, assuming the plaintiff is able to establish a prima facie case, the burden
shifts to the defendant to "articulate some legitimate nondiscriminatory reason" for
the adverse employment action. Disciplining an employee for protesting apparently
unlawful employment discrimination is, of course, not a legitimate, nondiscriminatory reason. However, courts have held that a decision to discipline an employee
whose conduct is unreasonable, even though borne out of legitimate protest, does not
violate Title VII.

Finally, if the defendant is able to carry its burden of articulating some legitimate,
nondiscriminatory reason for the adverse action, the burden then shifts to the plaintiff to show that the defendant's articulated reason was truly pretextual for the defendant's actual discriminatory motive.

[District Judge Norgle's significant findings of fact] are: mutual trust and confidence between Procunier and Jennings were essential to the proper functioning of
the workplace; Jennings told Procunier she did not trust him to deliver the salary
study to the School Board; Jennings' belief that Procunier would not deliver the salary study to the School Board was unreasonable; the salary study was not presented to
Procunier prior to being delivered to members of the School Board in order to enhance its effectiveness; Procunier discharged Jennings because of the form of her protest, i.e., not informing Procunier of the salary study or giving him a copy before it
was delivered to the School Board; Jennings' discharge was based upon a loss of trust
and confidence by Procunier, which was reasonable under the circumstances. . . .]

In *Jennings I* [796 F.2d 962 (7th Cir. 1986)], this Court expressed some doubt as to
whether mere "disloyalty" can ever be the sole legitimate nondiscriminatory reason
for discharging an employee protesting unlawful employment practices. [Citing
EEOC v. Crown Zellerbach Corp., 720 F.2d 1008 (9th Cir. 1983)], the panel majority observed that almost every form of opposition to an employment practice is in
some sense disloyal.

In *Crown Zellerbach*, a group of minority employees, seeking to remedy what they
perceived to be unlawful employment discrimination . . . wrote letters not only to the
employer's corporate parent requesting an open meeting to discuss the situation, but
also to local officials, protesting the failure of public officials to investigate. The group
picketed the office of the Mayor of Los Angeles. The group also lodged an administrative complaint with the Office of Federal Contract Compliance, charging that the
employer's practices did not conform to Executive Order 11246, and this was later
borne out by a General Services Administration investigation. All of this activity apparently was readily known by the employer. Finally, the group discovered through
the company newspaper that the employer was to receive an award from the Los
Angeles School District, a significant customer, for sponsorship of a program designed to provide career guidance to students at a predominantly Hispanic school.
The group, believing that the employer did not merit an award for undertaking affirmative action, then wrote a letter to the School Board, composed of elected
officials, to inform it of the "bigoted position of racism" and of various discrimination
charges that had been filed against the company.

As a consequence, the employer fired the group of employees for "disloyalty." The
Ninth Circuit applied a reasonableness test to determine whether the conduct could

provide a legitimate nondiscriminatory basis for the discharge. Holding for the employees, the court determined that disloyalty alone would not suffice as reason for discharge, remarking that otherwise virtually any opposition, no matter how reasonable, could be chilled in that opposition by definition connotes overtures of disloyalty. Rather, the court determined that the letter to the School Board was an appropriate response to a decision by a body of elected officials to bestow an affirmative action award upon the employer.

The Ninth Circuit carefully distinguished cases in which an employee's opposition to perceived unlawful employment practices was determined to be unreasonable. In particular, the court distinguished Hochstadt v. Worcester Foundation for Experimental Biology, 545 F.2d 222 (1st Cir. 1976), where the manner of opposition by an employee was held unreasonable. Although the First Circuit in *Hochstadt* expressly determined that the employee's conduct was "disloyal," it was also clear that the employee's conduct resulted in her poor work performance and also in fellow employees' diminished performance and reduced morale. The employee in *Hochstadt* would have been fired based on her employment performance alone without reference to the crux of her opposition.

The standard adopted in *Crown Zellerbach* remains applicable in this case. The issue before us is whether Jennings' conduct gave rise to a legitimate nondiscriminatory reason for her discharge, despite the fact that the substance of her protest was protected. Although the district court held that "objection to the form of the protest cannot be easily divorced from an objection to the protest itself," that is exactly the result compelled by *Crown Zellerbach*. The substance of the secretaries' protest, unlawful sex discrimination, is of course protected. But the outcome here depends on whether in pursuing her protest, Jennings exceeded the cloak of statutory protection by engaging in unreasonable conduct.

The district court found, and we do not question, that in order to enhance its effectiveness Procunier was not informed of the P.S. Salary Study, nor given an advance copy. Despite seeing and speaking to Procunier throughout the day, Jennings deliberately chose to keep him in the dark instead of following past practice of letting him present such a study to the Board. Accordingly Procunier, the proponent of the competing salary schedule, was not given an opportunity to respond promptly to the School Board members' inquiries. Judge Norgle determined that the decision to withhold notice from Procunier and then surprise him with the P.S. Salary Study after the School Board members had been receiving their own copies, was unreasonable. Judge Norgle's findings compel the conclusion that Jennings' decision was a conscious effort to hamper a supervisor's ability to respond to his superiors for the purpose of accomplishing her own ends.

. . . As a consequence of the crucial findings below, it follows as a matter of law that the cloak of statutory protection does not extend to deliberate attempts to undermine a superior's ability to perform his job. As in *Hochstadt*, when an employee engaged in opposition to a perceived unlawful employment practice participates in conduct which does not further the protest, but rather merely hinders another person's ability to perform his job, that employee relinquishes statutory protection. Here Jennings relinquished Title VII statutory protection. The substance of her protest was protected; she could not have been disciplined for her opposition to a reasonably perceived unlawful employment practice. Her decision to sandbag Procunier, however, was not entitled to protection. Perhaps if she had shown that Procunier was initially unresponsive, hostile or adversarial, such action might have been reasonable. But such was not the case. The facts indicate that Procunier was responsive, albeit his responses were not what the secretaries wanted to hear. The work environment was not disturbed because Procunier lessened Jennings' responsibilities; rather the environment was disturbed due to her decision to hinder her supervisor's ability to do his job. The record before Judge Norgle supports his conclusion that an adversarial relationship developed because of Jennings' unreasonable conduct.

An employee need not always inform a supervisor of her plans to, and substance of, protest. There are doubtless times where such a requirement would chill the rights of employees to engage in reasonable protest. Rather, we hold only that an employee may not use legitimate opposition to perceived unlawful employment discrimination as a gratuitous opportunity to embarrass a supervisor or thwart his ability to perform his job. Jennings' actions to hinder Procunier's ability to perform his job were purely gratuitous. If Procunier had been likely to disrupt or prevent legitimate opposition, contrary to what the district court found, the outcome of this litigation might be different.

Today's decision is not an affirmation of the "loyalty" defense that was questioned in *Jennings I*. It is doubtful whether loyalty alone can be a legitimate, nondiscriminatory reason for disciplining an employee engaged in opposition to an unlawful employment practice. The issue here is not simply loyalty; it is whether a supervisor can discipline an employee who deliberately interferes with the supervisor's efficacy in relationship to his superiors, particularly when the employee is in a position to repeat the interference. This decision recognizes that it is not unreasonable for a supervisor who has been thwarted once vis-à-vis his superiors to expect a repetition and to take action to avoid another attempt. An employer may in such circumstances discipline the employee, not because of her opposition, not because of a sense of disloyalty, but rather because of the employee's deliberate decision to disrupt the work environment, including her superior's standing with his own superiors. . . .

## NOTES

1. *Jennings II* follows the approach adopted by the circuit courts in relying on the *McDonnell Douglas* method of drawing inferences to determine an employer's motivation when there is no direct evidence. This includes three stages: the plaintiff establishes a prima facie case, the employer articulates a nondiscriminatory reason for its actions, and the plaintiff rebuts by proving pretext.

2. As for the prima facie case, the court's statement of the three elements is generally recognized: (1) plaintiff engaged in protected expression, (2) she suffered an adverse employment action, and (3) there was a causal link between the former and the latter. Some courts also add a fourth requirement: employer knowledge of the employee's expression. See, e.g., Gordon v. New York City Bd. of Educ., 232 F.3d 111 (2d Cir. 2002). Others consider employer knowledge as embraced within the causation element. But see Stone v. City of Indianapolis Pub. Utils. Div., 281 F.3d 640 (7th Cir.), *cert. denied*, 123 S. Ct. 79 (2002) (describing two paths to avoid summary judgment: direct evidence of causation or a modified *McDonnell Douglas* prima facie case that would require the plaintiff "to show that after filing the charge only he, and not any similarly situated employee who did not file a charge, was subjected to an adverse employment action even though he was performing his job in a satisfactory manner"). Id. at 644.

3. *McDonnell Douglas*, reproduced at page 97, establishes that some conduct is too unreasonable to be protected. At the same time, as *Crown Zellerbach* indicates, the mere fact that the employer perceives the conduct to be disloyal does not deprive

it of protection. Are some forms of opposition so beyond the pale as to prevent plaintiff from establishing a prima facie case? Or, so long as the opposition is directed toward unlawful discrimination, is the first element of the prima facie case met, leaving it to the employer to articulate the form as a legitimate, nondiscriminatory reason for its action? How does *Jennings II* answer that question?

Reread Slack v. Havens, reproduced at page 79. The employees there refused to work because of their belief that discrimination had motivated their job assignment. If they had been wrong in their allegations of discrimination, would the refusal to work have been a protected or unprotected form of opposition? See Hazel v. Postmaster Gen., 7 F.3d 1 (1st Cir. 1993) (refusal to work not protected).

4. The *Jennings II* court had little problem with the plaintiff's prima facie case. The defendant's nondiscriminatory reason, however, caused difficulties. Not every reason will satisfy the employer's burden of production: some reasons may amount to admitting retaliation. Did Procunier lose "trust" in the plaintiff because of her protected expression or her unprotected conduct? The employer did not seem to contend that there was anything inappropriate in the preparation of the study; rather, he criticized the plaintiff's failure to inform him before circulating it. Certainly, Jennings's conduct falls far short of the illegal conduct in *McDonnell Douglas*. But was it unreasonable? Can failures of tact or politeness deprive an employee of § 704(a)'s protections?

5. Can *Jennings II*, with its "reasonableness approach," be read as a case of employer retaliation but with justification? (Compare the bfoq defense (see page 265), which basically justifies discrimination.) If so, was the question not really whether Jennings's conduct was protected, but whether Procunier, in fact, had lost confidence in her? Should someone be forced to have an assistant he does not trust? In the prior appeal, one judge suggested that trust and confidence are "bona fide occupational qualifications," at least for certain employees. But the language of the bfoq provision does not reach retaliation. Wouldn't the antiretaliation provision be rendered nugatory if an executive did not have to work with an assistant he distrusts?

What if an employer believes an employee lied during an investigation of sexual harassment? Will the employer's reasonable, good faith belief that the employee was not telling the truth constitute a legitimate, nondiscriminatory reason for firing her? Or is protection lost only if the employee in fact lied? See EEOC v. Total Sys. Servs., Inc., 221 F.3d 1171 (11th Cir. 2000) (reasonable, good faith belief that employee lied entitles employer to terminate employee).

6. Are the courts really establishing a balancing test? See O'Day v. McDonnell Douglas Helicopter Co., 79 F.3d 756 (9th Cir. 1996) (acknowledging use of balancing test). If so, what goes on the scales? See Cruz v. Coach Stores, Inc., 202 F.3d 560 (2d Cir. 2000) (slapping co-worker in response to sexual harassment); Douglas v. DynMcDermott Petro. Oper. Co., 144 F.3d 364 (5th Cir. 1998) (unethical disclosure by attorney); O'Day v. McDonnell Douglas Helicopter Co., supra (employee searched his supervisor's desk and showed the discovered documents to other employees). What if the employee is a high-level affirmative action official? Johnson v. Univ. of Cincinnati, 215 F.3d 561 (6th Cir. 2000) (Title VII protects VP for Human Resources advocating on behalf of women and minorities). Is the validity of the allegation or the employer's reaction a factor? What about the extent of any resulting disruption? See Robbins v. Jefferson Cty. Sch. Dist., 186 F.3d 1253 (10th Cir. 1999), *abrogated on other grounds*, Boyler v. Cordant Techs., Inc., 2003 U.S. App. LEXIS 628 (10th Cir. 2003). Could even substantial disruption be outweighed by employer provocation? Should the court consider whether the plaintiff was more disruptive than necessary or whether the plaintiff had ulterior motivations?

7. Suppose an employee did not engage in protected activity, but the employer mistakenly believes that he did and fires him for that reason. Would the employee have a retaliation claim? Fogleman v. Mercy Hosp., Inc., 283 F.3d 561 (3d Cir. 2002) (yes). The *Fogelman* court also found, however, that retaliation against an individual because his father engaged in protected activity was not within the reach of the ADEA's antiretaliation provision, although it was actionable under the ADA. See page 805.

8. The *Jennings II* court may have thought that there could be no retaliation without animus or hostility. But is that true? Or does the opposition clause, like the participation clause, sometimes privilege conduct that an employer would not have to tolerate were the conduct not in opposition to unlawful discriminatory practices? Cf. § 8(a)(1) of the National Labor Relations Act, 29 U.S.C.S. § 158 (a)(1) (2003).

## 2.   *Adverse Action*

The second element of the prima facie face case recently has become a critical issue. Courts are dismissing retaliation cases on the basis that the retaliation complained of was not sufficiently adverse. What is an adverse employment action? Is an adverse action an element of the prima facie case or is it needed for a claim, even when direct evidence of retaliation is present? Can retaliation by co-workers result in a § 704 violation?

### RAY v. HENDERSON
### 217 F.3d 1234 (9th Cir. 2000)

B. FLETCHER, Circuit Judge:

In this case we are called upon to determine whether William J. Ray suffered adverse employment actions after complaining of harassment at his workplace. We hold that in our circuit an adverse employment action is adverse treatment that is reasonably likely to deter employees from engaging in protected activity. Under this standard, we conclude that Ray suffered cognizable adverse employment actions when his employer, in retaliation for Ray's complaints concerning management's treatment of women employees, eliminated employee meetings, eliminated its flexible starting time policy, instituted a "lockdown" of the workplace, and cut Ray's salary. We also hold that Ray has a cognizable claim for retaliation based on his supervisors' creation of a hostile work environment. . . .

III . . .

To make out a prima facie case of retaliation, an employee must show that (1) he engaged in a protected activity; (2) his employer subjected him to an adverse employment action; and (3) a causal link exists between the protected activity and the adverse action. See Steiner v. Showboat Operating Co., 25 F.3d 1459, 1464 (9th Cir. 1994). If a plaintiff has asserted a prima facie retaliation claim, the burden shifts to the defendant to articulate a legitimate nondiscriminatory reason for its decision. If the defendant articulates such a reason, the plaintiff bears the ultimate burden of demonstrating that the reason was merely a pretext for a discriminatory motive.

The parties do not contest that Ray engaged in protected activities when he complained of the treatment of women at the Willits Post Office both informally and formally with the EEOC.[3] The heart of this dispute is whether Ray suffered cognizable adverse employment actions. Ray asserts that he suffered from changes in workplace policy and pay, as well as from a hostile work environment. We first examine the definition of an adverse employment action. We then discuss whether the changes in workplace policy and pay constitute adverse employment actions, and whether Ray has established a causal link between his protected activities and those adverse employment actions. Finally, we examine whether Ray's allegation that he was subjected to a hostile work environment in retaliation for engaging in protected activity is cognizable under the anti-retaliation provisions of Title VII.

## IV

The circuits are currently split as to what constitutes an adverse employment action. Although we have yet to articulate a rule defining the contours of an adverse employment action, our prior cases situate us with those circuits that define adverse employment action broadly. Other circuits that define adverse employment action broadly are the First, Seventh, Tenth, Eleventh and D.C. Circuits. An intermediate position is held by the Second and Third Circuits. The most restrictive view of adverse employment actions is held by the Fifth and Eighth Circuits. Below, we set forth the Ninth Circuit's position within this split, and explain the case law in the other circuits. Then, we examine what guidelines we should follow in analyzing whether an action constitutes an adverse employment action.

We have found that a wide array of disadvantageous changes in the workplace constitute adverse employment actions. While "mere ostracism" by co-workers does not constitute an adverse employment action, see Strother v. Southern California Permanente Medical Group, 79 F.3d 859, 869 (9th Cir. 1996), a lateral transfer does. In Yartzoff v. Thomas, 809 F.2d 1371, 1376 (9th Cir. 1987), we held that "transfers of job duties and undeserved performance ratings, if proven, would constitute 'adverse employment decisions.'" The Yartzoff decision was in line with our earlier decision in St. John v. Employment Development Dept., 642 F.2d 273, 274 (9th Cir. 1981), where we held that a transfer to another job of the same pay and status may constitute an adverse employment action.

Similarly, in Hashimoto v. Dalton, 118 F.3d 671, 676 (9th Cir. 1997), we found that the dissemination of an unfavorable job reference was an adverse employment action "because it was a 'personnel action' motivated by retaliatory animus." We so found even though the defendant proved that the poor job reference did not affect the prospective employer's decision not to hire the plaintiff: "That this unlawful personnel action turned out to be inconsequential goes to the issue of damages, not liability."

In Strother, we examined the case of an employee who, after complaining of discrimination, was excluded from meetings, seminars and positions that would have made her eligible for salary increases, was denied secretarial support, and was given a more burdensome work schedule. We determined that she had suffered from adverse employment actions.

---

3. As the statutory language quoted above indicates, filing a complaint with the EEOC is a protected activity. See 42 U.S.C. § 2000e-3(a). Making an informal complaint to a supervisor is also a protected activity. See Equal Employment Opportunity Commission v. Hacienda Hotel, 881 F.2d 1504, 1514 (9th Cir. 1989). . . .

These cases place the Ninth Circuit in accord with the First, Seventh, Tenth, Eleventh and D.C. Circuits. These Circuits all take an expansive view of the type of actions that can be considered adverse employment actions. See Wyatt v. City of Boston, 35 F.3d 13 (1st Cir. 1994) (adverse employment actions include "demotions, disadvantageous transfers or assignments, refusals to promote, unwarranted negative job evaluations and toleration of harassment by other employees"); Knox v. Indiana, 93 F.3d 1327 (7th Cir. 1996) (employer can be liable for retaliation if it permits "actions like moving the person from a spacious, brightly lit office to a dingy closet, depriving the person of previously available support services . . . or cutting off challenging assignments"); Corneveaux v. CUNA Mutual Ins. Group, 76 F.3d 1498 (10th Cir. 1996) (employee demonstrated adverse employment action under the ADEA by showing that her employer "required her to go through several hoops in order to obtain her severance benefits"); Berry v. Stevinson Chevrolet, 74 F.3d 980 (10th Cir. 1996) (malicious prosecution by former employer can be adverse employment action); Wideman v. Wal-Mart Stores, Inc., 141 F.3d 1453 (11th Cir. 1998) (adverse employment actions include an employer requiring plaintiff to work without lunch break, giving her a one-day suspension, soliciting other employees for negative statements about her, changing her schedule without notification, making negative comments about her, and needlessly delaying authorization for medical treatment); Passer v. American Chemical Soc., 935 F.2d 322 (D.C. Cir. 1991) (employer's cancellation of a public event honoring an employee can constitute adverse employment action under the ADEA, which has an anti-retaliation provision parallel to that in Title VII).

The Second and Third circuits hold an intermediate position within the circuit split. They have held that an adverse action is something that materially affects the terms and conditions of employment. See Robinson v. City of Pittsburgh, 120 F.3d 1286 (3d Cir. 1997) ("retaliatory conduct must be serious and tangible enough to alter an employee's compensation, terms, conditions, or privileges of employment . . . to constitute [an] 'adverse employment action'"); Torres v. Pisano, 116 F.3d 625 (2nd Cir. 1997) (to show an adverse employment action employee must demonstrate "a materially adverse change in the terms and conditions of employment") (quoting McKenney v. New York City Off-Track Betting Corp., 903 F. Supp. 619 (S.D.N.Y. 1995)).

The Fifth and Eighth Circuits, adopting the most restrictive test, hold that only "ultimate employment actions" such as hiring, firing, promoting and demoting constitute actionable adverse employment actions. See Mattern v. Eastman Kodak Co., 104 F.3d 702 (5th Cir. 1997) (only "ultimate employment decisions" can be adverse employment decisions); Ledergerber v. Stangler, 122 F.3d 1142 (8th Cir. 1997) (transfer involving only minor changes in working conditions and no reduction in pay or benefits is not an adverse employment action).

The government urges us to turn from our precedent, and to adopt the Fifth and Eighth Circuit rule that only "ultimate employment actions" such as hiring, firing, promoting and demoting constitute actionable adverse employment actions.[5] But we

---

5. The government relies on Burlington Industries, Inc. v. Ellerth [reproduced at page 516] for the proposition that only ultimate employment actions such as "hiring, firing, failing to promote, reassignment with significantly different responsibilities [and] a decision causing a significant change in benefits" constitute adverse employment actions. But the discussion in Burlington Industries cited by the government concerns the types of employment actions which, if taken by a supervisor, would subject the employer to vicarious liability for harassment. Although the Supreme Court cited to circuit-level Title VII cases that defined "adverse employment actions," the Court specifically declined to adopt the holdings of those cases: "Without endorsing the specific results of those decisions, we think it prudent to import the concept of a tangible employment action for resolution of the vicarious liability issue we consider here." Id. at 761. Therefore, we reject the contention that Burlington Industries set forth a standard for adverse employment actions in the anti-retaliation context.

cannot square such a rule with our prior decisions. Actions that we consider adverse employment actions, such as the lateral transfers in *Yartzoff* and *St. John*, the unfavorable reference that had no affect on a prospective employer's hiring decisions in *Hashimoto*, and the imposition of a more burdensome work schedule in *Strother* are not ultimate employment actions. Nor, for that matter, does the test adopted by the Second and Third Circuits comport with our precedent. While some actions that we consider to be adverse (such as disadvantageous transfers or changes in work schedule) do "materially affect the terms and conditions of employment," others (such as an unfavorable reference not affecting an employee's job prospects) do not.

The EEOC has interpreted "adverse employment action" to mean "any adverse treatment that is based on a retaliatory motive and is reasonably likely to deter the charging party or others from engaging in protected activity." EEOC Compliance Manual Section 8, "Retaliation," Par. 8008 (1998). Although EEOC Guidelines are not binding on the courts, they "constitute a body of experience and informed judgment to which courts and litigants may properly resort for guidance." Meritor Savings Bank v. Vinson [reproduced at page 487]; see also Gutierrez v. Municipal Court, 838 F.2d 1031 (9th Cir. 1988). We find the EEOC test to be consistent with our prior holdings, and with the holdings in the First, Seventh, Tenth, Eleventh and D.C. Circuits.

The EEOC test covers lateral transfers, unfavorable job references, and changes in work schedules. These actions are all reasonably likely to deter employees from engaging in protected activity. Nonetheless, it does not cover every offensive utterance by co-workers, because offensive statements by co-workers do not reasonably deter employees from engaging in protected activity.

As we stated in *Hashimoto*, the severity of an action's ultimate impact (such as loss of pay or status) "goes to the issue of damages, not liability." Instead of focusing on the ultimate effects of each employment action, the EEOC test focuses on the deterrent effects. In so doing, it effectuates the letter and the purpose of Title VII. According to 42 U.S.C. § 2000e-3(a), it is unlawful "for an employer to discriminate" against an employee in retaliation for engaging in protected activity. This provision does not limit what type of discrimination is covered, nor does it prescribe a minimum level of severity for actionable discrimination. See *Knox* ("There is nothing in the law of retaliation that restricts the type of retaliatory act that might be visited upon an employee who seeks to invoke her rights by filing a complaint."). . . .

Because the EEOC standard is consistent with our prior case law and effectuates the language and purpose of Title VII, we adopt it, and hold that an action is cognizable as an adverse employment action if it is reasonably likely to deter employees from engaging in protected activity.[6]

We now turn to the question of whether the actions alleged by Ray constitute adverse employment actions under this standard, whether Ray has provided sufficient evidence of a causal link between his protected activities and the adverse employment actions, and whether he can overcome the USPS' proffered nondiscriminatory reasons for the actions.

V

Ray claims that, in retaliation for his complaints, his supervisors eliminated the Employee Involvement program, eliminated the flexible start-time policy, instituted

---

6. The first part of the EEOC's definition of adverse employment action, which requires that the action be "based on a retaliatory motive," collapses into the "causal link" prong of the prima facie test for retaliation.

lockdown procedures, and reduced his workload — and his pay — disproportionately to the reductions faced by other employees.

We conclude that all four qualify as adverse employment actions. The actions decreased Ray's pay, decreased the amount of time that he had to complete the same amount of work, and decreased his ability to influence workplace policy, and thus were reasonably likely to deter Ray or other employees from complaining about discrimination in the workplace. . . .

## VI

We now examine whether Ray's allegation that he was subjected to a hostile work environment is cognizable under the anti-retaliation provisions of Title VII. We have not previously decided whether a hostile work environment may be the basis for a retaliation claim under Title VII. However, the Second, Seventh and Tenth Circuits have held that an employer may be liable for a retaliation-based hostile work environment. See Richardson v. New York State Dep't of Correctional Serv., 180 F.3d 426 (2nd Cir. 1999) ("co-worker harassment, if sufficiently severe, may constitute adverse employment action so as to satisfy the second prong of the retaliation *prima facie* case"); Drake v. Minnesota Mining & Mfg. Co., 134 F.3d 878 (7th Cir. 1998) ("retaliation can take the form of a hostile work environment"); Gunnell v. Utah Valley State College, 152 F.3d 1253 (10th Cir. 1998) ("co-worker hostility or retaliatory harassment, if sufficiently severe, may constitute 'adverse employment action' for purposes of a retaliation claim").

We agree with our sister circuits. Harassment is obviously actionable when based on race and gender. Harassment as retaliation for engaging in protected activity should be no different — it is the paradigm of "adverse treatment that is based on retaliatory motive and is reasonably likely to deter the charging party or others from engaging in protected activity." EEOC Compliance Manual Par. 8008.

Harassment is actionable only if it is "sufficiently severe or pervasive to alter the conditions of the victim's employment and create an abusive working environment." Harris v. Forklift Systems, Inc. [reproduced at page 507]. It must be both objectively and subjectively offensive. See Faragher v. City of Boca Raton, 524 U.S. 775, 787 (1998). To determine whether an environment is sufficiently hostile, we look to the totality of the circumstances, including the "frequency of the discriminatory conduct; its severity; whether it is physically threatening or humiliating, or a mere offensive utterance; and whether it unreasonably interferes with an employee's work performance." Id.

Not every insult or harassing comment will constitute a hostile work environment. . . .

Repeated derogatory or humiliating statements, however, can constitute a hostile work environment. In *Hacienda Hotel*, for example, we found that the plaintiffs had demonstrated sufficiently "severe or pervasive" harassment by demonstrating that one supervisor "repeatedly engaged in vulgarities, made sexual remarks, and requested sexual favors" while another supervisor "frequently witnessed, laughed at, or herself made these types of comments." And in Draper v. Coeur Rochester, Inc., 147 F.3d 1104, 1109 (9th Cir. 1998), we found that the appellant's allegations that her supervisor had regularly made sexual remarks about her throughout her employment, and that he laughed at her complaints to him, raised a genuine factual issue regarding a hostile work environment.

Here, after Ray made his complaint about the treatment of women at the Willits Post Office, he was targeted for verbal abuse related to those complaints for a period lasting over one and half years. His supervisors regularly yelled at him during staff meetings; they called him a "liar," a "troublemaker," and a "rabble rouser," and told him to "shut up." Additionally, Ray was subjected to a number of pranks, and was falsely accused of misconduct.

Not only did his supervisors make it harder for Ray to complete his own tasks, they made Ray an object lesson about the perils of complaining about sexual harassment in the workplace. Carey and Briggs made it clear to the other staff members that disadvantageous changes in management style were due to Ray's complaints. Carey linked the change to a fixed starting time to Ray's letter to Carey's supervisor. He canceled the Employee Involvement meetings in response to Ray's complaints. Carey and Briggs also fostered animus in other employees whose working conditions were affected. Other employees began to distance themselves from Ray, and some stopped talking to him. In November of 1995, the difficulties at work rose to such a level that Ray took stress leave from his job.

We conclude that Ray has presented evidence that is, for purposes of summary judgment, sufficient to raise a genuine issue of fact as to whether he was subjected to a hostile work environment. We therefore hold that the district court erred in granting summary judgment on the hostile work environment-based retaliation claim.

## NOTES

1. As the Ninth Circuit explains, the Fifth and the Eighth Circuits have taken a very narrow approach concerning when retaliation is actionable, requiring that an "ultimate" employment action occur. While other circuits have rejected such an extreme approach, there is no uniformity within those circuits as to how adverse an action need be before a claim will be stated. The Sixth Circuit, for example, has held that neither a temporary suspension nor a reassignment to a more physically demanding job was adverse enough to support a retaliation claim, and it thus reversed a jury verdict in favor of the plaintiff. See White v. Burlington Northern & Santa Fe Ry. Co., 310 F.3d 443 (6th Cir. 2002). See generally Joel A. Kravetz, Deterrence vs. Material Harm: Finding the Appropriate Standard to Define An 'Adverse Action' in Retaliation Claims Brought Under the Applicable Equal Employment Opportunity Statutes, 4 U. Pa. J. Lab. & Emp. L. 315 (2002); Matthew J. Wiles, Comment, Defining Adverse Employment Action in Title VII Claims for Employer Retaliation, 27 U. Day. L. Rev. 217 (2001); Melissa A. Essary & Terence D. Friedman, Retaliation Claims Under Title VII, the ADEA, and the ADA: Untouchable Employees, Uncertain Employers, Unresolved Courts, 63 Mo. L. Rev. 115 (1998); Rebecca Hanner White, De Minimis Discrimination, 47 Emory L.J. 1121 (1998).

2. Is treating an employee *more favorably* because the employer believes he will claim discrimination an adverse employment action? In Cullom v. Brown, 209 F.3d 1035 (7th Cir. 2000), the court rejected such a contention. "While Title VII prevents employers from punishing their employees for complaining about discrimination, it does not prevent an employer from unjustifiably rewarding an employee to avoid a discrimination claim." Id. at 1041. Do you agree?

3. Is a "tangible employment action" as referenced in *Ellerth*, reproduced at page 516, the same thing as an adverse employment action? The Ninth Circuit resists equating the two. Why? Are there good reasons to hold employers automatically liable for supervisory retaliation when they would not be automatically liable if the supervisory action were because of sex? For discussion of the intersection of these lines of cases, see Susan Grover, After *Ellerth*: the Tangible Employment Action in Sexual Harassment Analyses, 35 U. Mich. J. L. Ref. 809 (2002).

4. In Clark County v. Breeden, reproduced at page 638, the plaintiff complained that she had been transferred in response to her participation conduct. Although the Supreme Court dismissed her claim for want of causation, it did not question whether she had suffered an adverse action. Does that mean the Court regards lateral transfers as actionable retaliation?

Some cases hold that retaliation can result from acts beyond the employment relationship. E.g., Robinson v. Shell Oil Co., 519 U.S. 337 (1997) (former employee given inaccurate references); Aviles v. Cornell Forge Co., 183 F.3d 598 (7th Cir. 1999) (false police report about employee). Taken together, do *Robinson* and *Breeden* support a broad approach to what constitutes an adverse action?

5. Occasionally a question has arisen as to whether an employer can violate the antidiscrimination statutes by bringing suit in retaliation for protected conduct, as, for example, bringing defamation charges against an employee who has alleged discrimination. The Supreme Court recently addressed a similar issue under the National Labor Relations Act. In BE & K Construction Co. v. NLRB, 536 U.S. 516 (2002), the Supreme Court, in light of First Amendment concerns, held that the NLRA did not prohibit reasonably based but unsuccessful suits filed with a retaliatory purpose. In that case, however, the retaliatory purpose was inferred from the fact that the conduct, which the lawsuit admittedly was aimed at stopping, was found protected. The Board's rule thus would have penalized employers who resorted to litigation to stop what the employer reasonably believes to be illegal acts. The Court did not decide whether such lawsuits would be unlawful if they "would not have been filed but for a motive to impose the costs of the litigation process, regardless of the outcome." Id. at 2401. While Title VII was not before it, the strong suggestion of *BE&K Construction Co.* is that employer resort to the legal system, even if aimed at conduct determined to be protected, will not be actionable unless the suit is baseless. Would a baseless suit, motivated by a retaliatory purpose, be actionable, even though no adverse employment action had occurred?

6. Is an adverse action merely an element of the prima facie case, or will action that is not sufficiently adverse not be actionable at all, even if retaliatory motive is admitted or proved? Suppose an employer promulgated a policy that the offices of every employee who files a charge of discrimination be painted red. In that case, a retaliatory policy would exist; motive need not be inferred. Would the policy be actionable retaliation? For an argument that it would, see White, supra note 1. Would the Ninth Circuit agree? Would the Fifth?

7. The Ninth Circuit in *Henderson* recognized a claim for supervisory "retaliatory harassment," patterned on the standards for a claim of a sexually hostile work environment. This theory essentially views "severe or pervasive" retaliatory conduct that "alters the working environment" as an adverse employment action. When the retaliatory harassment occurs at the hands of supervisory employees, will the employer be vicariously liable unless it establishes the affirmative defense set forth in *Ellerth*? Will the affirmative defense be available in cases of retaliatory harassment, or does the existence of severe or pervasive retaliatory harassment itself defeat the affirmative defense? What if it is co-workers, not supervisors, who engage in retaliatory harassment? Will a claim exist? See Richardson v. New York State Dept. of Corr. Serv., 180 F.3d 426 (2d Cir. 1999) (employer liability extends to the retaliatory actions of co-workers that the employer knew or should have known about and failed to correct).

8. In Matvia v. Bald Head Island, reproduced at page 526, the plaintiff alleged co-worker retaliation, but the court rejected her claim, finding no adverse employment action. "Matvia does not allege that BHIM instructed her co-workers to ostracize her; rather she simply alleges that BHIM failed to correct the co-workers' behavior." Is

the Fourth Circuit contending the co-worker conduct was not sufficiently severe or pervasive, or is it declining to hold employers liable for retaliatory actions of co-workers? Note that in Munday v. Waste Management, Inc., 126 F.3d 239 (4th Cir. 1997), the Fourth Circuit stated that "In no case in this circuit have we found an adverse employment action to encompass a situation where the employer has instructed employees to ignore and spy on an employee who engaged in protected activity." Id. at 243. Wouldn't such conduct tend to discourage employees from opposing discrimination or filing charges? If so, shouldn't it be actionable? Since the conduct occurred at the direction of supervisors should it be viewed as "tangible" or "adverse" and thus attributable to the employer, whether or not it was severe or pervasive? For discussion of co-worker retaliatory harassment, see Kari Jahnke, Protecting Employees from Employees: Applying Title VII's Anti-Retaliation Provisions to CoWorker Harassment, 19 Law & Ineq. J. 101 (2001); Christopher M. Courts, Note, An Adverse Employment Action — Not Just an Unfriendly Place to Work: Co-Worker Retaliatory Harassment Under Title VII, 87 Iowa L. Rev. 235 (2001).

9. Additional sources discussing retaliation questions include Douglas E. Ray, Title VII Retaliation Cases: Creating a New Protected Class, 58 U. Pitt. L. Rev. 405 (1997); Edward C. Walterscheid, A Question of Retaliation: Opposition Conduct as Protected Expression Under Title VII of the Civil Rights Act of 1964, 29 B.C. L. Rev. 391 (1988).

# H.  AGE DISCRIMINATION

The legal treatment of age discrimination has a considerably different history than the law's approach to other kinds of discrimination. For example, while most of the bases of Title VII's prohibitions are paralleled by heightened scrutiny under the equal protection clause, age discrimination has been subject to only rational basis review.* Even the Age Discrimination in Employment Act initially took a somewhat ambivalent approach to its mission. As originally passed in 1967, it barred discrimination only between the ages of 40 and 65, thus leaving untouched the traditional retirement age of 65. While the upper age limit was first extended to 70 and ultimately lifted entirely by Congress, the ADEA still contains several explicit exemptions from its reach that indicate the ambivalence with which age discrimination has been viewed.

---

*In Massachusetts Bd. of Retirement v. Murgia, 427 U.S. 307, 315 (1976), the Supreme Court rejected an equal protection attack against a Massachusetts statute mandating retirement for state troopers at age 50. Holding that older citizens are not a "suspect class," the Court applied minimal scrutiny. Under that rational relationship analysis, the Court upheld the statute because it rationally furthered the state's interest in the physical fitness of state troopers: "Since physical ability generally declines with age, mandatory retirement at 50 serves to remove from police service those whose fitness for uniformed work presumptively has diminished with age." Id. The fact that other means to determine fitness were available did not destroy the rationality of the age-50 rule. See also Vance v. Bradley, 440 U.S. 93 (1979).

The passage of the Age Discrimination in Employment Act in 1967 pretermitted much development on the constitutional front, but courts have continued to routinely sustain age classifications against constitutional attack. E.g., Maresca v. Cuomo, 475 N.E.2d 95 (N.Y. 1984). The most recent Supreme Court encounter with the question was Gregory v. Ashcroft, 501 U.S. 452 (1991) which involved a Missouri constitutional provision requiring judges to "retire at the age of seventy years." In light of federalism concerns, the Court held that Congress had not spoken clearly enough to exclude judges from the ADEA exemption for "appointees on the policy-making level." As for the plaintiffs' equal protection claim, the Court applied the rational basis test to uphold mandatory retirement.

Basic coverage questions under the ADEA were considered in section B. The age bfoq and the seniority system exceptions were discussed in Chapters 3 and 5. Several other exceptions of continuing significance will be considered in this section.

## 1.  *"Good Cause" and "Reasonable Factors Other Than Age"*

The ADEA provides that "[i]t shall not be unlawful . . . to discharge or otherwise discipline an individual for good cause." § 4(f)(3), 29 U.S.C.S. § 623(f)(3) (2003). It seems clear that the ADEA does not require that the employer demonstrate the kind of "good cause" that might be appropriate before tenured or civil service employees are fired. Similarly, it is not unlawful "to take any action otherwise prohibited . . . where the differentiation is based on reasonable factors other than age." § 4(f)(1), 29 U.S.C.S. § 623(f)(1) (2003). This would seem to be merely a broader statement of the principle embodied in the "good cause" section: adverse action against older workers — but on bases other than age — is valid. See Abdu-Brisson v. Delta Airlines, Inc., 239 F.3d 456 (airline successfully challenged an age discrimination claim by adducing nondiscriminatory grounds, industry practices and cost savings, as reasons for its actions with respect to seniority, benefits, and pay of newly acquired former Pan Am pilots).

The phrasing of the statute and the EEOC's Interpretive Rules makes clear that age must play no part in "reasonable factors." 29 C.F.R. § 1625.7(c) (2002). The employer cannot, then, admit age discrimination while claiming some justification, such as economic necessity. In short, any factor that reflects an intent to discriminate because of age cannot establish a defense. E.g., EEOC v. Commonwealth of Mass., 987 F.2d 64 (1st Cir. 1993) (state statute requiring public employees over 70 to take an annual medical examination not a reasonable factor other than age). This is hardly surprising because the provision seems to parallel the pretext analysis in disparate treatment cases. For example, the higher labor costs associated with the employment of older employees do not constitute "reasonable factors other than age" (although at some level such costs might constitute a bfoq). See generally Mark Brodin, Costs, Profits, and Equal Employment Opportunity, 62 Notre Dame L. Rev. 318 (1987). With respect to any light the reasonable factors other than age provision may shed on the use of the disparate impact theory in ADEA cases, see pages 423-424.

## 2.  *Bona Fide Executive Exception*

Although mandatory retirement is generally prohibited by the ADEA, "bona fide executives" can be mandatorily retired at age 65 under certain circumstances:

> [A]ny employee who has attained 65 years of age, and who, for the 2-year period immediately before retirement, is employed in a bona fide executive or high policymaking position, if such employee is entitled to an immediate nonforfeitable annual retirement benefit from a pension, profit-sharing, savings or deferred compensation plan, or any combination of such plans, of the employer of such employee, which equals, in the aggregate, at least $44,000.

§ 12(c)(1), 29 U.S.C.S. § 631(c)(1) (2003). See also 29 C.F.R. § 1625.12 (1996). The exception obviously is highly qualified. First, a "bona fide executive" remains fully protected by the ADEA until age 65. Even thereafter, such an executive may not be discriminated against on age grounds except for mandatory retirement. Second, the statute's requirements for the exception are conjunctive: to be subject to the provision, the employee must both (1) be in a "bona fide executive" or "high policymaking position" and (2) receive the defined benefits of $44,000 a year. See 29 C.F.R. § 1625.12 (1996); Passer v. American Chem. Socy., 935 F.2d 322 (D.C. Cir. 1991) (head of division with 25 employees and $4 million budget qualified); Whittlesey v. Union Carbide Corp., 742 F.2d 724 (2d Cir. 1984) (corporation's chief in-house labor counsel not within the exception). See Patrick McGeehan, Dealing with Aging Executives Who Just Won't Quit, N.Y. Times, Feb. 2, 2003, at 3-1.

### 3. Exception for Police and Firefighters

Much of the early case law interpreting the ADEA bfoq defense focused on mandatory retirement for police officers and firefighters. Congress has essentially resolved the controversy by exempting mandatory retirement at age 55 from the reach of the statute. As amended in 1996 by 104 Pub. L. No. 208, § 119, the ADEA now permits states or political subdivisions "to fail or refuse to hire or to discharge any individual because of such individual's age" with respect to "the employment of an individual as a firefighter or as a law enforcement officer," provided that the action is taken "pursuant to a bona fide hiring or retirement plan that is not a subterfuge to evade the purposes of this Act." 29 U.S.C.S. § 623(j) (2003). See Kopec v. City of Elmhurst, 193 F.3d 894 (7th Cir. 1999). Both "firefighter" and "law enforcement officer" are defined broadly. See EEOC v. State of Ill., 986 F.2d 187 (7th Cir. 1993) (special agents of Division of Criminal Investigation counted as state police and, therefore, were law enforcement officers); EEOC v. Commonwealth of Mass., 864 F.2d 933 (1st Cir. 1988) (department of motor vehicles examiners were "law enforcement officers," in part because they were armed).

### 4. Bona Fide Employee Benefit Plans

The ADEA's bona fide employee benefit plan provision is a significant exception to the statute's general prohibition of age discrimination. Understanding this provision has been complicated by its technical language and its tortuous history. The Supreme Court has twice interpreted the exception broadly to permit age discrimination, and each time Congress has amended the ADEA to narrow the exemption. These, and other amendments, including the sweeping Older Workers Benefit Protection Act (OWBPA), Pub. L. No. 101-521, 104 Stat. 978 (1990), provided essential clarification of the exemption.

As it presently exists, the ADEA prohibits discrimination in "compensation, terms, conditions, or privileges of employment," § 623(a)(1), which "encompasses all employee benefits, including such benefits provided pursuant to a bona fide employee benefit plan." § 630(l). Thus, the general rule is no age discrimination, although there have been disputes as to what constitutes age discrimination in the context of benefit plans. Compare Solon v. Gary Community Sch. Corp., 180 F.3d 844 (7th Cir. 1999) (early retirement plan that gave those retiring at 58 four years of incentive payments and those retiring at 62 no incentives constitutes age discrimination unless saved by statutory defenses), with Lyon v. Ohio Educ. Assn., 53 F.3d 135 (6th Cir. 1995) (plan imputing years of service for purposes of computing early retirement benefits did not discriminate on the basis of age even though the younger the worker electing to retire the more years were imputed and the greater the pension). See also

DiBiase v. Smith-Kline Beecham Co., 48 F.3d 719 (3d Cir. 1995) (no discrimination when employer offered equal benefits to all those waiving rights, even though older workers had more rights to waive). Several courts have refused to find age discrimination where older workers are offered more benefits than younger workers, even when both are within the protected class. E.g., Stokes v. Westinghouse Savannah River Co., 206 F.3d 420 (4th Cir. 2000); May v. Shuttle, Inc., 129 F.3d 165 (D.C. Cir. 1997).

Assuming that an employer discriminates on the basis of age, however, § 4(f)(2), 29 U.S.C.S. § 623(f)(2)(B) (2003), creates an exception:

> It shall not be unlawful for an employer, employment agency, or labor organization . . . (2) to take any action otherwise prohibited [by the ADEA] (B) to observe the terms of a bona fide employee benefit plan
>     (i) where, for each benefit or benefit package, the actual amount of payment made or cost incurred on behalf of an older worker is no less than that made or incurred on behalf of a younger worker, as permissible under section 1625.10, title 29, Code of Federal Regulations. . . . Notwithstanding [this exception] no such employee benefit plan shall require or permit the involuntary retirement of any individual . . . because of the age of such individual.

29 U.S.C.S. § 623(f)(2) (2003).

Congress intended the exemption from its prohibition of age discrimination to be limited to discrimination in "fringe benefits," rather than base compensation or other privileges of employment. The language barring using the benefit plan exception to require mandatory retirement was added to legislatively overrule United Air Lines, Inc. v. McMann, 434 U.S. 192 (1977), which had construed the original benefit plan exception to allow mandatory retirement. E.g., EEOC v. Commonwealth of Mass., 987 F.2d 64, 74 (1st Cir. 1993) (statute requiring employees over 70 to take an annual medical examination not within the exception because it "acts as a conditional involuntary retirement program"). Similarly, the language requiring "equal costs or equal benefits" was added by the Older Workers Benefit Protection Act (OWBPA) to reverse Public Employees Retirement Sys. of Ohio v. Betts, 492 U.S. 158, 160 (1989), which had invalidated the EEOC regulations that the statute now incorporates by reference.

In short, the exemption as currently drafted permits age-based discrimination only in the payment of fringe benefits, and then only within parameters defined by EEOC regulations. To reinforce the narrowness of the exception, the plan must still be "bona fide," and Congress has specifically provided that employers relying on this exemption "shall have the burden of proving that such actions are lawful in any enforcement proceeding brought under this Act." § 623(f).

To understand the current statutory provision, it is important to appreciate that certain fringe benefit costs rise with age. Life insurance and health insurance are typical examples. As amended, the ADEA now explicitly adopts the "equal benefits or equal costs" principle, which the EEOC first announced in its regulations. In short, an employer may provide equal benefits for all workers. There is, then, no age discrimination, and no violation. If, however, an employer chooses to provide lower benefits for older workers, it must cost-justify that decision. Thus, lower benefits for older workers are permitted "where, for each benefit or benefit package, the actual amount of payment made or cost incurred on behalf of an older worker is no less than that made or incurred on behalf of a younger worker." For example, suppose the cost of $100,000 of employer-provided life insurance is $1,000 for workers aged 40. If the same $1,000 will buy only $70,000 of insurance for workers aged 60, the employer may provide them that lesser benefit. Note that the employer could not exclude workers over 60 entirely from such a benefit — that exclusion would not be cost-justified, and would therefore be outside the exception. The EEOC's regulations, which the statute incorporates, also specify how cost justification works: employers are permitted to define the average cost of workers in age brackets of no more than five years to compare with the average cost of workers in the next younger bracket. For example, if the average cost of 55- to 59-year-olds is in parity with the average cost for workers aged 50 to 54, the benefit is cost-justified as between these groups. The statutory reference to "benefit or benefit package" reflects Congress' decision to allow employers to cost-justify either each benefit or a package of benefits. So an employer might lump health and life insurance together, and cost-justify age distinctions for the entire package.

While these provisions radically reduce employer discretion to discriminate on account of age, Congress did provide some relief for employers by approving "safe harbor" age discrimination. Thus, the statute allows "coordination of benefits" in order to reduce plan costs. For example, a defined benefit plan under ERISA may be keyed to Social Security benefits, § 4(*l*)(1)(B), 29 U.S.C.S. § 623(*l*)(1)(B) (2003), which permits plans to take into account an employee's age insofar as it relates to Social Security benefits. A similar coordination of benefits problem arises with respect to Medicare. Benefit plans frequently reduce or terminate medical benefits upon eligibility for Medicare, which is, of course, largely age-dependent. The EEOC has approved of Medicare-carve out plans (those which reduce plan benefits for Medicare-eligible participants), but indicated opposition to other kinds of Medicare "coordination" plans. Retirees, although no longer employees, have standing to bring ADEA suits for discrimination in benefit plans. Erie County Retirees Assn. v. County of Erie, 220 F.3d 193 (3d Cir. 2000), and one district court has held that a reduction of benefits for Medicare-eligible retirees violated the ADEA, Erie County Retirees Assn. v. County of Erie, Pa., 140 F. Supp. 2d 466 (W.D. Pa. 2001). Cf. Gutchen v. Bd. of Governors of the Univ. of R.I., 148 F. Supp. 2d 151 (D.R.I. 2001) (plaintiffs failed to state a case for discrimination since, unlike *Erie County*, plaintiffs did not allege that their medical coverage was inferior to that enjoyed by younger retirees; they never claimed that their stipend, when combined with Medicare benefits, purchased less medical coverage than those retirees who were not eligible for Medicare). See generally, Christopher E. Condeluci, Comment: Winning the Battle, But Losing the War: Purported Age Discrimination May Discourage Employers From Providing Retiree Medical Benefits, 35 J. Marshall L. Rev. 709 (2002). Despite the authority finding ADEA violations in such situations, the EEOC has rescinded its policy of enforcing the law against such benefit plans. http://www.eeoc.gov/docs/benefits-rescind.html.

Another safe harbor resolved the question whether severance pay could be reduced by retirement benefits, which was heavily litigated before the new amendments. Employers may reduce any severance pay "made available as a result of a contingent event unrelated to age" by the value of retiree health benefits and the value of "additional" pension benefits following from such a contingency. § 4(*l*)(2)(A), 29 U.S.C.S. § 623(*l*)(2)(A) (2003). See Stokes v. Westinghouse Savannah River Co., 206 F.3d 420 (4th Cir. 2000). Similarly, a bona fide benefit plan may reduce long-term disability benefits by the amount of pension benefits that the employee "voluntarily elects to receive" or for which she is eligible upon having "attained the later of age 62 or normal retirement age." § 4(*l*)(3), 29 U.S.C.S. § 623(*l*)(3) (2003). Cf. Kalvinskas v. Cal. Inst. of Tech., 96 F.3d 1305 (9th Cir. 1996) (employer violated the ADEA when it offset disability benefits by benefits that an employee could receive only by retiring; the offset essentially forced the employee to retire, and was not within § 623(*l*)(3)'s "safe harbor" because the employee was not eligible for benefits until he retired). While these provisions may depart from the basic cost-justification principle, their adoption by Congress resolves most questions about their legitimacy. See generally Catherine R. Urban, Section (4)(f)(2) of the Age Discrimination in Employment Act: No Justification for Cost Justification?, 24 Ind. L. Rev. 161 (1990); David A. Niles, Comment, The Older Workers Benefit Protection Act: Painting Age Discrimination Law with a Watery Brush, 40 Buff. L. Rev. 869 (1992).

Finally, there is the question of defined contribution pension plans and the significance of using a "normal retirement age" (NRA) in such plans. The ADEA, as amended by the OWBPA, now explicitly provides that an ERISA pension benefit plan may specify "a minimum age as a condition for normal or early retirement benefits." § 4(*l*)(1)(A), 29 U.S.C.S. § 623(*l*)(1)(A) (2003). The ADEA also makes it unlawful "to establish or maintain an employee pension benefit plan which requires or permits" any age-based reduction in employee benefit accrual or any age-based reduction in allocations to the employer's account, depending on whether the employer utilizes a defined benefit plan or a defined contribution plan. However, benefits can still be limited by years of service or of plan participation. In brief, the amended statute allows defined benefit plans to specify a level of benefits by setting an NRA while at the same time ensuring that employees who work past NRA continue to accrue more benefits. However, benefit accrual by all workers, including those who continue past NRA, may be limited by other factors. See Atkins v. Northwest Airlines, Inc., 967 F.2d 1197 (8th Cir. 1992).

There is a continuing dispute about "cash balance" retirement plans. Neither the EEOC nor the IRS has issued final regulations, although the most recent proposed IRS regulations would broadly validate such plans. 67 Fed. Reg. 76,123 (Dec. 11, 2002). See Mary Williams Walsh, It May Be Time to Plumb Your Pension's Depth, N.Y. Times, Dec. 15, 2002, Business Section, p.8. The only court decision on point upheld most aspects of the plan before it, Eaton v. Onan Corp., 117 F. Supp. 2d 812 (S.D. 2000). This has not stilled the continuing controversy. One commentator captures the problem:

> The common characterization of the cash balance plan is that it is a defined benefit pension designed to look like a defined contribution arrangement. The conventional defined benefit plan promises a retiree an annuity based on the retiree's earnings history and her completed years of service. The most common defined benefit formula is the "final average" format under which the retiree's annuity is a percentage of her highest paid years multiplied by a factor reflecting the retiree's length of service. For example, a final average defined benefit formula might be fifty percent of the participant's average compensation for her three highest paid years multiplied by a years of service fraction, the numerator of which is the retiree's actual years of service and the denominator of which is thirty, representing the number of years in a career spent entirely with the employer sponsoring the plan. . . .
>
> In short, for pension purposes, the last years of an employee's career are particularly significant if covered by a traditional final average formula defined benefit pension plan; a central factor arousing concern about the conversion to cash balance arrangements is the resulting deprivation to employees of the pension impact of these late-career years. . . .
>
> Unlike defined benefit plans, which specify the amount the employee will receive from her retirement plan, defined contribution arrangements specify the employer's funding commitment without guaranteeing or limiting the total to which those funds will grow by the time of retirement. In simplest terms, a defined benefit pension, as its name implies, grants the employee an output specified in terms of retirement income

while a defined contribution arrangement, as its equally apt moniker indicates, grants the employee an input specified in terms of employer contributions.

Let us now suppose that, in lieu of a defined benefit plan, an employer embraces a typical defined contribution formula: ten percent of current compensation. Under this defined contribution format, the employer contributes, for an employee earning $20,000 annually, $2000, which is placed in an individual account for the employee. The employee is not guaranteed the ultimate amount to which this $2000 contribution will grow by retirement via investment earnings nor is there any limit to which this contribution may burgeon via such earnings. Rather, each year (or more frequently), the employee's account, holding cumulative employer contributions, is credited with investment returns and charged with investment losses. . .

Under a defined benefit plan, the employer, having specified a retirement income the employee will receive, incurs the risk of bad investment experience (since the employer must make up any shortfall to provide the employee with the promised benefit) and recoups the rewards of good investment experience (since a more amply-funded plan requires less additional employer contributions to finance promised benefits). In contrast, in the defined contribution context, the employee absorbs the risk of poor investment performance (since such performance decreases the employee's account balance and, hence, her retirement income) and garners superior investment return (since such return augments the balance of the employee's account). . . .

Cash balance plans mimic defined contribution arrangements since the employee's pension entitlement under a cash balance formula is specified in terms of a theoretical account balance. However, cash balance plans are defined benefit schemes since the plan (and, ultimately, the employer) guarantee the employee this theoretical balance — no more, no less.

Edward A. Zelinsky, The Cash Balance Controversy, 19 Va. Tax Rev. 683, 683-94 (2000). The initiation of cash balance plans is relatively uncontroversial, but the conversion of plans, especially from final average pay to cash balance, is very controversial. That is because, as compared to final average pay plans, cash balance plans reduce older workers' expected benefits. "[I]nstead of averaging pay in the later, more lucrative years of employment as most traditional defined benefit pensions do, cashbalance plans require employees to accrue a flat percentage of pay annually over their careers." Coleman J. F. Cannon, Cashing in on Older Workers: Age Discrimination Claims in Cash-Balance Pension Plans, 19 Law & Ineq. J. 31, 38 (2001).

There is a wide divergence of opinion on the legality of such conversions. Cannon contends that plaintiff will have a hard time establishing either age discrimination or violation of the equal cost/equal benefit rule. Id. at 61-62. See also Jonathan Barry Forman & Amy Nixon, Cash Balance Pension Plan Conversions, 25 Okla. City U. L. Rev. 379 (2000). Professor Zelinsky, by contrast, argues that cash balance plans, while perhaps justifiable on policy grounds, nevertheless violate the plain language of the ADEA:

> While designed to mimic defined contribution plans, cash balance arrangements are defined benefit plans pursuant to which plans, and ultimately sponsoring employers, guarantee specified benefits. Thus, the relevant test for age discrimination in the cash balance context is the plan's outputs [and, under this analysis, such a plan is deemed discriminatory as to age if "under the plan, an employee's benefit accrual is ceased, or the rate of an employee's benefit accrual is reduced, because of the attainment of any age."]
>
> The Code and ERISA further specify that an employee's accrued benefit in a defined benefit plan is "an annual benefit commencing at normal retirement age." Since cash balance plans delineate each employee's pension entitlement, not as a traditional

annuity, but as a notional account balance, to determine a cash balance participant's accrued benefit as such benefit is defined statutorily, it is necessary to convert the participant's ersatz account balance under the plan into a deferred annuity projected to start a normal retirement.

Such conversion reveals that, as a cash balance participant gets older, the same dollar contribution to the plan for her purchases less in annuity terms since there is less time for that contribution to accrue investment earnings before retirement and the commencement of previously deferred annuity payments. In defined contribution terms, cash balance plans are not age discriminatory since hypothetical contributions (i.e., inputs) for employees typically do not decrease with age. However, cash balance plans are defined benefit arrangements which, as a statutory matter, measure for age discrimination in terms of outputs, i.e., the annuity purchased as of normal retirement. In such annuity terms, the same dollar contribution each year purchases successively smaller amounts at retirement as the participant ages and thus has one less year for the contribution to accumulate investment earnings prior to payout at normal retirement.

Placing these arithmetic realities against the language of the statutes, each year, as an employee gets older, the same dollar contribution results in a reduced rate of benefit accrual since the employee's incremental accrued benefit — measured, per the statutes, as a deferred annuity to commence at retirement — declines as the employee successively attains later ages and thus gets closer to retirement. By the same token, the same cash balance contribution for two employees of different ages produces for the older employee a smaller accrued benefit measured as the projected annuity to be purchased with that contribution at normal retirement.

Cash balance pensions can avoid this problem by annually increasing theoretical contributions as the participant ages, thereby keeping stable the annuity value of those contributions. In practice, however, I am skeptical that many cash balance pensions utilize this or any similar formula. Nevertheless, this possibility highlights the fact-and plan-specific nature of the age discrimination inquiry in the cash balance context.

Edward A. Zelinsky, The Cash Balance Controversy Revisited: Age Discrimination and Fidelity to the Statutory Text, 20 Va. Tax Rev. 557, 562 (2001).

## 5.   *Early Retirement Incentive Plans*

The Older Workers Benefit Protection Act (OWBPA) also attempted to resolve the question of when early retirement incentive plans are permissible. Incentive programs have become an increasingly common employer strategy in corporate downsizing. Typically, such plans involve both carrots and sticks. The employer creates a "window of opportunity" during which employees can obtain greater retirement benefits if they elect early retirement. When the window shuts, the enhanced benefits disappear. Further, while the early retirement incentive plan rarely will directly threaten termination of those who do not accept, these incentive plans typically are offered by companies in the process of downsizing. There often is, therefore, an implicit threat that layoffs will follow if enough workers do not accept the early retirement incentive. See generally Michael C. Harper, Age-Based Exit Incentives, Coercion, and the Prospective Waiver of ADEA Rights: The Failure of the Older Workers Benefit Protection Act, 79 Va. L. Rev. 1271 (1993); Judith McMorrow, Retirement and Worker Choice: Incentives to Retire and the Age Discrimination in Employment Act, 29 B.C. L. Rev. 347 (1988).

In the past, employees challenged such plans, claiming that they had accepted early retirement only because of the implicit threat of discharge. E.g., Henn v. Natl. Geographic Socy., 819 F.2d 824 (7th Cir. 1987). Ironically, other plaintiffs sometimes sued because they were not offered an opportunity to participate. E.g., Cipriano v. Bd. of Educ., 785 F.2d 51 (2d Cir. 1986). The OWBPA amended the ADEA to address both these problems while striking a balance between employer and employee interests. Its success in doing so has been the subject of dispute.

First, the ADEA permits a benefit plan "that is a voluntary early retirement incentive plan" consistent with the purposes of the Act. § 4(f)(2)(B)(ii), 29 U.S.C.S. § 623(f)(2)(B)(ii) (2003). To some extent, this simply asks courts to evaluate the plan in light of the general purposes of the ADEA without much specific guidance. This should tend to invalidate retirement incentive plans that exclude older workers, as in *Cipriano*, although it does not forbid them outright. Harper, supra at 1312-18. Cf. Katz v. Regents of Univ. of Cal., 229 F.3d 831 (9th Cir. 2000) (exclusion of members of one retirement plan from incentive retirement offer not shown to be disparate impact age discrimination although excluded plan had more older members than included plan).

Second, however, the statute provides that a pension plan will not violate the statute "solely because . . . [it] provides for the attainment of a minimum age as a condition of eligibility for normal or early retirement benefits." § 4(*l*)(1)(a), 29 U.S.C.S. § 623(*l*)(1)(a) (2003). This latter provision would help resolve cases where younger workers sue. See generally Peter N. Swan, Early Retirement Incentives with Upper Age Limits Under the Older Workers Benefits Protection Act, 19 J.C. & U.L. 53 (1992).

The statute conditions legality on consistency with the purposes of the ADEA, an uncertain standard, and does not create a safe harbor for minimum retirement ages, but merely provides that designating an early retirement age is not a per se violation. Nevertheless, courts have tended to view such plans favorably. See Fagan v. N.Y. State Elec. & Gas Corp., 186 F.3d 127 (2d Cir. 1999) (existence of the early retirement plan is not evidence of age discrimination since the ADEA creates a safe harbor for such plans that are "consistent with the relevant purpose or purposes" of the ADEA; neither management expression of pleasure that older workers were being retired nor explicit link of plaintiff's status to the retirement plan destroyed the safe harbor).

Further, employees who do not accept the incentive plan may have no standing to challenge it, and those who do sign may find themselves unable to attack even a plan that is, in some sense, illegal because the OWBPA also authorizes "knowing and voluntary" waivers of ADEA rights. OWBPA does specify a rigorous laundry list of substantive and procedural requirements before a waiver of ADEA rights will be deemed "knowing and voluntary." While these requirements technically do not apply to other discrimination statutes, the courts may look to the OWBPA for guidance in considering waivers under those laws. The new provision governs any waiver of ADEA rights, including after an ADEA suit is filed. Nevertheless, the principal use of all these provisions is to validate early retirement incentive plans. An employee who agrees to a plan that is illegal will, therefore, waive his rights if his consent is "knowing and voluntary" within the requirements of the Act.*

OWBPA establishes minimum conditions for all waivers.† It amended the ADEA

---

* It has been suggested that the effect of a waiver might be limited if a former employee's cause of action did not arise until after the waiver is executed. Since the ADEA prohibits prospective waivers, a holding that a cause of action does not arise until an ex-employee has reason to know that his termination was based on age would make many waivers ineffective. Richard J. Lussier, Title II of the Older Workers Benefit Protection Act: A License for Age Discrimination?, 35 Harv. J. Leg. 189, 202 (1998).

† It has been held that the statute does not provide any substantive rights; it merely defines the requirements for having an effective waiver. Thus, Ellison v. Premier Salons Intl., Inc., 164 F.3d 1111 (8th Cir. 1999), held that an early retirement offer to employees may be revoked during the statutory 21-day period the law prescribed for their opportunity to consider the offer. OWBPA did not turn an otherwise revocable offer into an irrevocable one.

by providing that "an individual may not waive any right or claim under this Act unless the waiver is knowing and voluntary." § 7(f), 29 U.S.C.S. § 626(f) (2003).* Not only does the party asserting the validity of the waiver — typically the employer — have the burden of establishing that a waiver qualifies, § 7(f)(3), 29 U.S.C.S. § 626(f)(3), but the ADEA further provides that, to be knowing and voluntary, an agreement must *at least* (A) be "written in a manner calculated to be understood"; (B) make specific reference to ADEA claims; (C) not waive rights arising after its execution; (D) be supported by "consideration in addition to anything of value to which the individual already is entitled"; (E) advise the individual in writing to consult an attorney; (F) provide at least 21 days for the employee to consider her decision; and (G) provide a seven-day period during which the waiver may be revoked. § 7(f)(1), 29 U.S.C.S. § 626(f)(1) (2003). There are also additional requirements when the waiver is sought as part of a program offered to a group of workers, such as an early retirement incentive plan. § 7(f)(1)(H), 29 U.S.C.S. § 626(f)(1)(H) (2003). First, the notice period is expanded from 21 days to 45 days. Second, the employer must provide the group being offered the plan with detailed information concerning it, including job titles and ages of those selected for the program. See Raczak v. Ameritech Corp., 103 F.3d 1257 (6th Cir. 1997). Obviously, this kind of information can help recipients assess the legality of the plan from the perspective of a systemic violation.

The courts have tended to strictly enforce the requirements of OWBPA for a valid release, e.g., American Airlines, Inc. v. Cordoza-Rodriguez, 133 F.3d 111 (1st Cir. 1998) (release invalidated for failure to explicitly advise employees to consult an attorney), an approach which was taken by the Supreme Court in its first encounter with the statute.

## OUBRE v. ENTERGY OPERATIONS, INC.
### 522 U.S. 422 (1998)

Justice KENNEDY delivered the opinion of the Court.

An employee, as part of a termination agreement, signed a release of all claims against her employer. In consideration, she received severance pay in installments. The release, however, did not comply with specific federal statutory requirements for a release of claims under the Age Discrimination in Employment Act of 1967. After receiving the last payment, the employee brought suit under the ADEA. The employer claims the employee ratified and validated the nonconforming release by retaining the monies paid to secure it. The employer also insists the release bars the action unless, as a precondition to filing suit, the employee tenders back the monies received. We disagree and rule that, as the release did not comply with the statute, it cannot bar the ADEA claim. . . .

[Dolores Oubre received a poor performance rating. Her supervisor gave her the option of either improving her performance or accepting a severance package. She had 14 days to consider her options, during which she consulted with attorneys. Oubre decided to accept, and she signed a release], in which she "agree [d] to waive, settle, release, and discharge any and all claims, demands, damages, actions, or causes of action . . . that I may have against Entergy. . . ." In exchange, she received six installment payments over the next four months, totaling $6,258.

---

*Even a valid waiver does not affect the EEOC's enforcement powers nor interfere with an employee's right to file a charge with the Commission. § 7(f)(4), 29 U.S.C.S. § 626(f)(4) (2003).

The Older Workers Benefits Protection Act (OWBPA) imposes specific require-ments for releases covering ADEA claims. 29 U.S.C. §§ 626(f)(1)(B), (F), (G). In procuring the release, Entergy did not comply with the OWBPA in at least three re-spects: (1) Entergy did not give Oubre enough time to consider her options. (2) En-tergy did not give Oubre seven days after she signed the release to change her mind. And (3) the release made no specific reference to claims under the ADEA.

Oubre filed [suit] alleging constructive discharge on the basis of her age in viola-tion of the ADEA and state law. Oubre has not offered or tried to return the $6,258 to Entergy, nor is it clear she has the means to do so. [Entergy was awarded summary judgment on the basis that] Oubre had ratified the defective release by failing to re-turn or offer to return the monies she had received. . . .

## II

The employer rests its case upon general principles of state contract jurisprudence. As the employer recites the rule, contracts tainted by mistake, duress, or even fraud are voidable at the option of the innocent party. See 1 Restatement (Second) of Con-tracts § 7, and Comment b (1979). The employer maintains, however, that before the innocent party can elect avoidance, she must first tender back any benefits received under the contract. See, e.g., Dreiling v. Home State Life Ins. Co., 515 P.2d 757, 766-767 (Kan. 1973). If she fails to do so within a reasonable time after learning of her rights, the employer contends, she ratifies the contract and so makes it binding. Re-statement (Second) of Contracts, supra, § 7, Comments d, e. The employer also in-vokes the doctrine of equitable estoppel. As a rule, equitable estoppel bars a party from shirking the burdens of a voidable transaction for as long as she retains the benefits received under it. See, e.g., Buffum v. Peter Barceloux Co., 289 U.S. 227, 234 (1933) (citing state case law from Indiana and New York). Applying these prin-ciples, the employer claims the employee ratified the ineffective release (or faces estoppel) by retaining all the sums paid in consideration of it. The employer, then, re-lies not upon the execution of the release but upon a later, distinct ratification of its terms.

These general rules may not be as unified as the employer asserts. And in equity, a person suing to rescind a contract, as a rule, is not required to restore the consider-ation at the very outset of the litigation. See 3 Restatement (Second) of Contracts, supra, § 384, and Comment b; Restatement of Restitution § 65, Comment d (1936); D. Dobbs, Law of Remedies § 4.8, p. 294 (1973). Even if the employer's statement of the general rule requiring tender back before one files suit were correct, it would be unavailing. The rule cited is based simply on the course of negotiation of the parties and the alleged later ratification. The authorities cited do not consider the question raised by statutory standards for releases and a statutory declaration making non-conforming releases ineffective. It is the latter question we confront here.

In 1990, Congress amended the ADEA by passing the OWBPA. The OWBPA pro-vides: "An individual may not waive any right or claim under [the ADEA] unless the waiver is knowing and voluntary. . . . [A] waiver may not be considered knowing and voluntary unless at a minimum" it satisfies certain enumerated requirements, includ-ing the three listed above. 29 U.S.C. § 626(f)(1).

The statutory command is clear: An employee "may not waive" an ADEA claim unless the waiver or release satisfies the OWBPA's requirements. The policy of the Older Workers Benefit Protection Act is likewise clear from its title: It is designed to protect the rights and benefits of older workers. The OWBPA implements Congress' policy via a strict, unqualified statutory stricture on waivers, and we are bound to take Congress at its word. Congress imposed specific duties on employers who seek releases of certain claims created by statute. Congress delineated these duties with precision and without qualification: An employee "may not waive" an ADEA claim unless the employer complies with the statute. Courts cannot with ease presume ratification of that which Congress forbids.

The OWBPA sets up its own regime for assessing the effect of ADEA waivers, separate and apart from contract law. The statute creates a series of prerequisites for knowing and voluntary waivers and imposes affirmative duties of disclosure and waiting periods. The OWBPA governs the effect under federal law of waivers or releases on ADEA claims and incorporates no exceptions or qualifications. The text of the OWBPA forecloses the employer's defense, notwithstanding how general contract principles would apply to non-ADEA claims.

The rule proposed by the employer would frustrate the statute's practical operation as well as its formal command. In many instances a discharged employee likely will have spent the monies received and will lack the means to tender their return. These realities might tempt employers to risk noncompliance with the OWBPA's waiver provisions, knowing it will be difficult to repay the monies and relying on ratification. We ought not to open the door to an evasion of the statute by this device.

Oubre's cause of action arises under the ADEA, and the release can have no effect on her ADEA claim unless it complies with the OWBPA. In this case, both sides concede the release the employee signed did not comply with the requirements of the OWBPA. Since Oubre's release did not comply with the OWBPA's stringent safeguards, it is unenforceable against her insofar as it purports to waive or release her ADEA claim. As a statutory matter, the release cannot bar her ADEA suit, irrespective of the validity of the contract as to other claims.

In further proceedings in this or other cases, courts may need to inquire whether the employer has claims for restitution, recoupment, or setoff against the employee, and these questions may be complex where a release is effective as to some claims but not as to ADEA claims. We need not decide those issues here, however. It suffices to hold that the release cannot bar the ADEA claim because it does not conform to the statute. Nor did the employee's mere retention of monies amount to a ratification equivalent to a valid release of her ADEA claims, since the retention did not comply with the OWBPA any more than the original release did. The statute governs the effect of the release on ADEA claims, and the employer cannot invoke the employee's failure to tender back as a way of excusing its own failure to comply. . . .

Justice BREYER, with whom Justice O'CONNOR joins, concurring.

. . . I write these additional words because I believe it important to specify that the statute need not, and does not, thereby make the worker's procedurally invalid promise totally void, i.e., without any legal effect, say, like a contract the terms of which themselves are contrary to public policy. See 1 Restatement (Second) of Contracts, §7, Comment a; 2 id., §178. Rather, the statute makes the contract that the employer and worker tried to create voidable, like a contract made with an infant, or a contract created through fraud, mistake or duress, which contract the worker may elect either to avoid or to ratify. See 1 id., §7 and Comment b. . . .

That the contract is voidable rather than void may prove important. For example, an absolutely void contract, it is said, "is void as to everybody whose rights would be affected by it if valid." 17A Am. Jur. 2d, Contracts §7, p. 31 (1991). Were a former worker's procedurally invalid promise not to sue absolutely void, might it not become legally possible for an employer to decide to cancel its own reciprocal obligation, say, to pay the worker, or to provide ongoing health benefits — whether or not the worker in question ever intended to bring a lawsuit? It seems most unlikely that Congress, enacting a statute meant to protect workers, would have wanted to create — as a result of an employer's failure to follow the law — any such legal threat to all workers, whether or not they intend to bring suit. To find the contract voidable, rather than void, would offer legal protection against such threats.

At the same time, treating the contract as voidable could permit an employer to recover his own reciprocal payment (or to avoid his reciprocal promise) where doing so seems most fair, namely, where that recovery would not bar the worker from bringing suit. Once the worker (who has made the procedurally invalid promise not to sue) brings an age-discrimination suit, he has clearly rejected (avoided) his promise not to sue. As long as there is no "tender-back" precondition, his (invalid) promise will not have barred his suit in conflict with the statute. Once he has sued, however, nothing in the statute prevents his employer from asking for restitution of his reciprocal payment or relief from any ongoing reciprocal obligation. See Restatement of Restitution § 47, Comment b (1936) ("A person who transfers something to another believing that the other thereby comes under a duty to perform the terms of a contract . . . is ordinarily entitled to restitution for what he has given if the obligation intended does not arise and if the other does not perform"); Dobbs, supra, at 994 (restitution is often allowed where benefits are conferred under voidable contract). A number of older state cases indicate, for example, that the amount of consideration paid for an invalid release can be deducted from a successful plaintiff's damages award. . . .

Justice SCALIA, dissenting.

I agree with Justice Thomas that the [OWBPA] does not abrogate the common-law doctrines of "tender back" and ratification. Because no "tender back" was made here, I would affirm the judgment. . . .

Justice THOMAS, with whom Chief Justice REHNQUIST joins, dissenting.

The Older Workers Benefit Protection Act imposes certain minimum requirements that waivers of claims under the Age Discrimination in Employment Act of 1967 must meet in order to be considered "knowing and voluntary." The Court of Appeals held that petitioner had ratified a release of ADEA claims that did not comply with the OWBPA by retaining the benefits she had received in exchange for the release, even after she had become aware of the defect and had decided to sue respondent. The majority does not suggest that the Court of Appeals was incorrect in concluding that petitioner's conduct was sufficient to constitute ratification of the release. Instead, without so much as acknowledging the long-established principle that a statute "must 'speak directly' to the question addressed by the common law" in order to abrogate it, United States v. Texas, 507 U.S. 529, 534 (1993) (quoting Mobil Oil Corp. v. Higginbotham, 436 U.S. 618, 625 (1978)), the Court holds that the OWBPA abrogates both the common-law doctrine of ratification and the doctrine that a party must "tender back" consideration received under a release of legal claims before bringing suit. Because the OWBPA does not address either of these common-law doctrines at all, much less with the clarity necessary to abrogate them, I respectfully dissent. . . .

## NOTES

1. *Oubre* makes clear that releases within OWBPA are subject to very strict requirements. But OWBPA reaches only ADEA claims, not claims under other

antidiscrimination statutes. While employers are likely to formulate releases to satisfy OWBPA in order to gain maximum protection, what principles will govern releases of Title VII, ADA, or § 1981 claims? See Jan W. Henkel, Waiver of Claims Under the Age Discrimination in Employment Act After *Oubre v. Entergy Operations, Inc.*, 35 Wake Forest L. Rev. 395, 422-23 (2000) ("Courts are likely to extend the holding in *Oubre* to other discrimination statutes.").

2.  Prior to OWBPA, the courts took different approaches to the question of releases. Some courts have seen two distinct modes of analysis arising in waiver cases. One is the application of normal contract principles. O'Shea v. Commercial Credit Corp., 930 F.2d 358 (4th Cir. 1991); Lancaster v. Buerkle Buick Honda Co., 809 F.2d 539 (8th Cir. 1987). The second is a more rigorous "totality of the circumstances" approach, looking to both the language of the agreement and the circumstances surrounding its signing. Melanson v. Browning-Ferris Indus., 281 F.3d 272 (1st Cir. 2002); Torrez v. Public Serv. Corp., 908 F.2d 687 (10th Cir. 1990); Borman v. AT&T Communications, Inc., 875 F.2d 399 (2d Cir. 1989). Which approach should govern instances not covered by the OWBPA? See generally Alfred W. Blumrosen, Ruth G. Blumrosen, Marco Carmigani & Thomas Daly, Downsizing and Employee Rights, 50 Rutgers L. Rev. 943, 1019-1020 (1998) (Title VII waivers should be required to meet OWBPA requirements).

3.  OWBPA provides certain minimum conditions for the validity of waivers. But its overarching requirement is that any waiver be "knowing and voluntary." This suggests that even a waiver that satisfies the specific requirements of the statute may still not be valid. Presumably, undue influence, duress, or fraud would also invalidate a waiver. Bennett v. Coors Brewing Co., 189 F.3d 1221, 1228 (10th Cir. 1999) (OWBPA "factors are not exclusive and other circumstances, outside the express statutory requirements, may impact whether a waiver under the OWBPA is knowing and voluntary").

4.  The *Oubre* majority did not wholly deprive employers of remedies for breach of a release that is not within OWBPA. Rather, it made clear that the employer may be able to recover back the money paid by a claim for "restitution recoupment or setoff." What did the Court mean? Does Justice Breyer's concurrence help?

5.  Might an employer still be held liable by the employee as a matter of contract law, even though a waiver is not effective under OWBPA? Is that Justice Breyer's point? EEOC regulations provide that employers may not abrogate agreements, even if they are successfully challenged under OWBPA. 29 C.F.R. § 1623(d). But see Kiren Dosanjh, Old Rules Need Not Apply: The Prohibition of Ratification and "Tender Back" in Employees' Challenges to ADEA Waivers, 3 J. Legal Advoc. & Prac. 5 (2001) (employers who meet their statutory obligations in drafting ADEA waivers are protected through that statute and not common law principles which could be used to undermine legal protections extended to older employees).

6.  Michael C. Harper, in Age-Based Exit Incentives, Coercion, and the Prospective Waiver of ADEA Rights: The Failure of the Older Workers Benefit Protection Act, 79 Va. L. Rev. 1271, 1277-79 (1993), argues that this scheme, in effect, encourages age discrimination:

> To understand how conditional exit incentive offers can be used to induce retirement from employees who would prefer continued employment, consider how a typical offer of this type would be weighed by an offeree. Assume that an employer announces to its workforce that because of general recessionary conditions or deep cuts in the demand for its particular product, employment will have to be cut by thirty percent over the next

four months. The employer also announces at the same time that in order to avoid as many involuntary layoffs as possible, it will offer retirement incentives to all employees over the age of fifty-five. . . . The offer is conditional, however, because the benefits will only be granted to those who voluntarily retire within the next two months. Those offerees who are involuntarily laid off, or those offerees who decide to retire after the expiration of the two month period, will not obtain the benefits. Finally, assume that the employer does not specify how it will determine who will be laid off to achieve the necessary residual amount of reductions in staff after the closure of the voluntary retirement window.

A post-fifty-five-year-old offeree in this typical exit window scenario might well rationally accept early retirement even though she prefers continuing employment. The reason is that the offeree must include in her calculations the chance that she will be terminated without the extra benefits offered for voluntary retirement. Thus, an offeree who prefers employment to retirement with increased benefits might prefer the latter to the perceived chance of continued employment plus the perceived chance of termination without enhanced benefits. Clearly it is the conditional nature of the retirement incentive that makes the two preferences consistent, that, in other words, makes it rational for an offeree to accept the incentive even though she prefers continued employment. This is highly significant for an employer wanting to rid itself of more older workers than could be justified by individualized comparisons of the productivity of all its workers. . . .

The waiver provisions of the OWBPA only enhance this result. Indeed, Professor Harper argues that the statute functionally approves a prospective waiver of ADEA rights, id. at 1294, although the OWBPA expressly bars such waivers. Harper argues instead that "[t]he only practical way to prevent employers from using retirement incentives to effect the termination of particular workers selected on the basis of age who would prefer continued employment is to prohibit age-based incentives from being temporally or otherwise conditioned." Id. at 1329. Do you agree? Would there be other consequences? Will employers cease offering such incentives? See also Judith A. McMorrow, Retirement Incentives in the Twenty-First Century: The Move Toward Employer Control of the ADEA, 31 U. Rich. L. Rev. 795 (1997) (arguing that a combination of OWBPA and the increasing use of arbitration largely removes the operation of the retirement incentive system from public scrutiny); Eileen Silverstein, From Statute to Contract: The Law of the Employment Relationship Reconsidered, 18 Hofstra Lab. & Emp. L.J. 479, 525 (2001) ("A fundamental problem with enforcing waivers-for-private gain is the inability of employees and applicants to assess the choices offered, because there is no contemporaneous and concrete employment dispute at the time the employees or applicants agree to forego litigation over past and present claims or to submit future claims to arbitration.").

## PROBLEM 7.3

Employer adopted a "rule of 75" plan for early retirement, that is, for retirement before the "normal retirement age" of 62 under the basic company retirement plan. The "rule of 75" plan allows workers whose age plus years of service at the employer total 75 or more to retire and receive $600 a month until they are 62 (at which point benefits under the basic retirement plan begin).

Employee A, who is 60, will never be eligible for early retirement because she began working for the company only ten years ago. She is upset because employee B just took early retirement; he is 48 years old and began working for the company at age 18. Employee *C* is also contemplating early retirement. He is 60 years old; he has fewer years with the employer than *B*, having worked there for 15 years, but his age and years of service do equal 75. He is upset, however, because *B* will receive 14 years of early retirement benefits, while he (*C*) will receive only two years. Finally, employee *D* is upset. She joined the company 20 years ago and thus has five more years of service than *C*. But because she is only 45 now, she will not be able to take early retirement for another ten years.

Do any of the employees have a claim of violation of the ADEA? Be sure to consider whether there is age discrimination to begin with and, if so, whether a defense applies. If you need more information to answer this question, specify what data might be helpful.

This problem is based on the facts of *Dorsch v. L. B. Foster Co.*, 782 F.2d 1421 (7th Cir. 1986), but it is not so clear that a reading of that opinion will help you to correctly answer the question, especially because the ADEA has since been amended.

# PART III

---

# ALTERNATIVE APPROACHES
# TO DISCRIMINATION

# Chapter 8

# Disability Discrimination

## A. INTRODUCTION

The Americans with Disabilities Act of 1990 (ADA), Pub. L. No. 101-336, prohibits employment discrimination against persons with disabilities. Title I, 42 U.S.C.S. §§ 12111-12117 (2003), covers most employment agencies, labor organizations, and employers,* including state and local governments. However, the Eleventh Amendment bars private suits against nonconsenting states. See pages 920-924.

Title II, 42 U.S.C.S. §§ 12131-12134 (2003), which generally prohibits disability discrimination by state and local governments, may also prohibit such entities from discriminating in employment. Thus, private employers are subject only to Title I, but state and local public employers may be subject to both Title I and Title II. The circuits are split, however, on whether Title II encompasses employment discrimination claims by government employees. See section G.

---

* Section 102(a) of Title I, 42 U.S.C.S. §12112(a) (2003), prohibits disability discrimination by a "covered entity." Section 101(2), §12111(2), defines a "covered entity" as an "employer, employment agency, labor organization, or joint labor-management committee." This definition is not as broad as first appears. For example, §101(5)(A), id. §12111(5)(A), defines an "employer" as a "person" engaged in an "industry affecting commerce" and having 15 or more employees for 20 or more weeks. Federal executive agency employees are protected by the Rehabilitation Act of 1973, 29 U.S.C.S. §§701-795(I) (2003). Employees of the House of Representatives and the instrumentalities of Congress are protected by §509(b), (c) of the ADA, 42 U.S.C.S. §12209(b), (c) (2003). Other federal employees are protected by entirely different sources of law. This subject is discussed further in section H.

Before Congress enacted the ADA, the most comprehensive federal legislation prohibiting disability discrimination was the Rehabilitation Act of 1973, 29 U.S.C.S. §§ 701-795(I) (2003). This Act requires most federal contractors and federal executive agencies to take affirmative action to employ and promote qualified persons with disabilities. The Act also protects such persons from disability discrimination in any program or activity that either receives federal financial assistance or is conducted by a federal executive agency. Although the Eleventh Amendment bars private ADA suits against state governments under Title I, and perhaps under Title II, many state employees with disabilities may be protected by the Rehabilitation Act because the programs or activities for which they work receive federal financial assistance. See section H. There seem to be few Eleventh Amendment problems with claims against state entities under the Rehabilitation Act because, by accepting federal funds, states have been deemed to have waived their immunity from suit for the program or agency receiving those funds. See, e.g., Koslow v. Pennsylvania, 302 F.3d 161 (3d Cir. 2002); Kvorjak v. Maine, 259 F.3d 48 (1st Cir. 2001); Douglas v. California Dept. of Youth Auth., 271 F.3d 812 (9th Cir. 2001) (collecting cases).

Protecting individuals with disabilities from discrimination in employment poses difficult practical and legal problems. The primary practical difficulty is the scope and severity of discrimination on the basis of disability. The following excerpt from the legislative history of the ADA suggests the dimensions of the problem:

> Individuals with disabilities experience staggering levels of unemployment and poverty. . . . Two-thirds of all disabled Americans between the age of 16 and 64 are not working at all; yet, a large majority of those not working say that they want to work. . . .
> Despite the enactment of Federal legislation such as the Education for All Handicapped Children Act of 1975 and the Rehabilitation Act of 1973, a U.S. Census Bureau Report issued in July, 1989 reported the following findings:
> (A) The percentage of men with a work disability working full time fell 7 percent from 30 percent in 1981 to 23 percent in 1988.
> (B) The income of workers with disabilities dropped sharply compared to other workers. In 1980, men with disabilities earned 23 percent less than men with no work disability, and by 1988 this had dropped to 36 percent less than their counterparts. In 1980, women with disabilities earned 30 percent less than women with no disabilities, and by 1988 this had dropped to 38 percent less than their counterparts.
> . . . In 1984, fifty percent of all adults with disabilities had household incomes of $15,000 or less. Among non-disabled persons, only twenty-five percent had household incomes in this wage bracket.

H.R. Rep. No. 101-485, pt. 2, at 32 (1990), *reprinted in* 1990 U.S.C.C.A.N. 303, 314.
An earlier report of the United States Commission on Civil Rights provides further insight into the problem:

> [S]tudies indicate that only in a tiny percentage of cases is inability to perform a regular, full-time job the reason a handicapped person is not employed.
> Frequently, employer prejudices exclude handicapped persons from jobs. Biases operate subtly, sometimes unconsciously, to eliminate handicapped job applicants in the application, screening, testing, interviewing, and medical examination process:
> > Often, the employer makes erroneous assumptions regarding the effect of a person's disability on his or her ability to perform on the job. In most cases the disabled person is never given an opportunity to disprove those assumptions; in some cases, the disabled person never knows why he or she didn't get the job.

Deborah Kaplan, Employment Rights: History, Trends and Status, in Law Reform in Disability Rights, Vol. 2 (Berkeley: Disability Rights Education and Defense Fund, 1981), p. E-4. . . .

The majority of unemployed handicapped people, if given the chance, are quite capable of taking their places in the job market. Numerous studies indicate that handicapped workers, when assigned appropriate positions, perform as well as or better than their nonhandicapped fellow workers. . . .

. . . Studies have demonstrated that, for every educational level, the average wage rate of disabled people is below that of the nondisabled population. . . .

Such differences in wage levels cannot be explained by any differential in productivity. Studies dating back to a massive 1948 Department of Labor study of disabled and nondisabled workers have consistently concluded that handicapped and nonhandicapped workers are equally productive. A recent survey of such research studies concluded: "the existing literature appears to show both that the disabled who are working are as productive in their jobs as their co-workers and that employers perceive the handicapped as being comparably productive."

United States Commission on Civil Rights, Accommodating the Spectrum of Individual Abilities 13, 29-31 (1983).

Congress, in enacting the ADA, found that discrimination against individuals with disabilities is pervasive, takes a variety of forms, and costs the United States billions of dollars in unnecessary expenses, which result from the dependency and non-productivity of those with disabilities. See ADA § 2(a)(1)-(9).

While the scope and severity of disability discrimination are daunting, the difficult legal problems associated with ending disability discrimination result primarily from the fact that disabilities are sometimes relevant to an individual's ability to work. Some disabilities deprive people of the physical and/or mental prerequisites to perform essential job functions. Prohibiting "discrimination" against such individuals would unduly interfere with employers' ability to select a qualified workforce. Other disabled individuals may be qualified to work but only if the employer accommodates their disability in some way. These individuals, unlike most other statutorily protected groups, require some form of accommodation or different treatment in order to enjoy equal access to employment opportunities and benefits. Guaranteeing equal treatment for similarly situated individuals is an inadequate legal response to the problem of promoting employment for individuals who may require different treatment or accommodation.

The ADA seeks to deal with these problems in two separate ways. First, the statute broadens the defenses available to employers as compared with other antidiscrimination statutes. Employers are permitted to engage in disparate treatment on the basis of disability if the disabled employee is unable to perform the essential functions of the job. In addition, employers are free to use qualification standards that screen out disabled individuals if those qualifications are job related and consistent with business necessity.

Counterbalancing this, disabled individuals have rights beyond those guaranteed to most other groups protected by antidiscrimination legislation. The centerpiece of disability discrimination law is the employer's affirmative duty to provide reasonable accommodation to ensure that individuals with disabilities secure equal employment opportunities and benefits. The focus of the duty to accommodate is on equal employment opportunity, rather than on equal treatment.

As a result, employers are legally obligated to treat covered employees equally or differently depending on the circumstances — employers *must treat individuals with disabilities equally* if they are qualified and their disabilities do not require accommodation; employers are *permitted to treat such individuals differently* if their disabilities cannot be accommodated; and employers *are required to treat such individuals differently* if reasonable accommodations are necessary to ensure equal employment opportunity and benefits.

Further, accommodation providing equal opportunity for individuals with disabilities can be costly for employers. The ADA, therefore, includes an "undue hardship" defense, which makes cost, almost always irrelevant under other antidiscrimination statutes, an expressly enumerated statutory defense to discrimination based on the duty to accommodate.

The focus of this chapter will be Title I of the ADA. Because the language of the ADA and associated regulations borrows extensively from Rehabilitation Act law, this chapter will rely on both ADA and Rehabilitation Act precedents, along with the ADA regulations and Interpretive Guidance of the Equal Employment Opportunity Commission (EEOC), to develop the concepts of disability discrimination under the ADA. As we will see, however, the courts do not always defer to the EEOC's regulations and interpretation of the statute.

The language of the pre-ADA Rehabilitation Act and accompanying regulations differs in some respects from Title I of the ADA. First, § 504 of the Rehabilitation Act prohibits discrimination "solely" on the basis of disability, while Title I of the ADA tracks Title VII's language. Second, prior to the 1990 Rehabilitation Act Amendments, that Act differed from the ADA in a variety of ways, including not expressly denying coverage to current users of illegal drugs, not expressly permitting employers to discipline employees whose current alcohol use interferes with job performance, and not expressly mentioning transfer to a vacant position as a possible reasonable accommodation. See Section 504 Compliance Handbook, Vol. 1, ¶213 (Thompson Publishing Group, 1999). As amended in 1992, the EEOC regulations for Title I of the ADA govern § 504. Thus, although Congress expressed an intent to borrow Rehabilitation Act law and the Act now conforms to Title I with respect to the substantive rules of employment discrimination, Rehabilitation Act precedent should be viewed with some caution. Even cases decided relatively recently may have arisen prior to the 1990 and 1992 Amendments or may borrow inappropriately from earlier Rehabilitation Act precedent. As we proceed through the materials, significant substantive differences between the ADA and the Rehabilitation Act will be noted. See section H for further discussion of the Rehabilitation Act.

Section B of this chapter focuses on what constitutes a "disability" under the ADA, a threshold question that has generated considerable litigation. Section C explores the concepts of "essential function," "reasonable accommodation," and "undue hardship" in the context of considering what it means to be a "qualified" individual with a disability under Title I of the ADA. Section D examines discriminatory qualification standards, including the provision that employers may discriminate against employees who pose a "direct threat" to health or safety. Section E explores the process of proving and defending against disability discrimination claims, including disparate treatment and failing to provide reasonable accommodation. Section F addresses special problems under the ADA, including coverage for individuals addicted to drugs or alcohol, medical examinations and inquiries, retaliation, harassment, relationships with covered individuals, health and disability insurance plans, and rights under the National Labor Relations Act and the Family and Medical Leave Act. The chapter concludes with sections G and H, which survey Title II of the ADA and the Rehabilitation Act.

## B.  THE MEANING OF "DISABILITY"

In contrast to other statutes prohibiting discrimination in employment, establishing membership in the ADA's protected classification often requires extensive legal analysis. Generally speaking, to claim protection under the ADA, a plaintiff must be "a qualified individual with a disability"; that is, the plaintiff must be an individual with a disability who can perform essential job functions with or without reasonable accommodation.

Section 3(2) defines "disability" as

(A)  a physical or mental impairment that substantially limits one or more of the major life activities of . . . [an] individual;
(B)  a record of such an impairment; or
(C)  being regarded as having such an impairment.

However, §§ 508 and 511 expressly exclude certain practices or conditions from this definition. Many of these are sex related, such as homosexuality, bisexuality, transvestism, pedophilia, transexualism, and exhibitionism. Also excluded are compulsive gambling, kleptomania, pyromania, and disorders resulting from the current illegal use of psychoactive drugs.

The EEOC's ADA regulations broadly define the terms "physical or mental impairment" and "major life activities."* Moreover, the regulations provide that an individual is substantially limited if totally or significantly restricted in her ability to perform major life activities in comparison with "the average person in the general population." 29 C.F.R. § 1630.2(j)(1)(i)(ii) (2002). Factors to be considered in determining whether an individual is substantially limited include:

(i)  The nature and severity of the impairment;
(ii)  The duration or expected duration of the impairment; and
(iii)  The permanent or long term impact, or the expected permanent or long term impact of or resulting from the impairment.

29 C.F.R. § 1630.2(j)(2).

ADA coverage does not depend on establishing an actual, present disability. An individual who has a "record" of a physical or mental impairment that substantially limits a major life activity is within the definition of disability. Even if such a person does not currently have such an impairment or was previously misclassified as having such an impairment, he is within the definition if he has a record of such an impairment. 29 C.F.R. § 1630.2(k).

---

* Section 1630.2(h) of the regulations defines physical or mental impairment as:

(1)  Any physiological disorder or condition, cosmetic disfigurement, or anatomical loss affecting one or more of the following body systems: neurological, musculoskeletal, special sense organs, respiratory (including speech organs), cardiovascular, reproductive, digestive, genito-urinary, hemic and lymphatic, skin, and endocrine; or
(2)  Any mental or psychological disorder, such as mental retardation, organic brain syndrome, emotional or mental illness, and specific learning disabilities.

Section 1630.2(i) defines "major life activities" as "caring for oneself, performing manual tasks, walking, seeing, hearing, speaking, breathing, learning, and working."

An additional method of establishing a "disability" is to show that an employer regarded the individual as having a disability. The ADA regulations define "regarded as having such an impairment" to mean:

(1)  Has a physical or mental impairment that does not substantially limit major life activities but is treated by a covered entity as constituting such limitation;

(2)  Has a physical or mental impairment that substantially limits major life activities only as a result of the attitudes of others toward such impairment; or

(3)  Has none of the impairments [discussed above] but is treated by a covered entity as having a substantially limiting impairment.

29 C.F.R. § 1630.2(*l*).

The Supreme Court considered the meaning of this three-pronged definition of disability for the first time in School Board of Nassau County v. Arline, 480 U.S. 273 (1987). Although *Arline* was a Rehabilitation Act case, it continues to be significant because the definition of "handicapped individual"* under the Rehabilitation Act is identical to the definition of individual with a disability under the ADA. In *Arline*, the school board had fired plaintiff, an elementary school teacher, because it believed her active tuberculosis posed a threat to the health of others. Essentially, the school board contended that a person with a contagious disease was not within the protections of the Rehabilitation Act if the adverse employment action was based on the employee's contagiousness and not on the condition itself. In finding Arline to be a handicapped individual, the Supreme Court refused to allow the school board to disassociate the contagious effects of the teacher's impairment from the impairment itself. As the Court stated, "Arline's contagiousness and her physical impairment each resulted from the same underlying condition, tuberculosis. It would be unfair to allow an employer to seize upon the distinction between the effects of a disease on others and the effects of a disease on a patient and use that distinction to justify discriminatory intent."

In light of *Arline*'s holding that a contagious disease can be a "disability," a person who has developed acquired immune deficiency syndrome (AIDS) is undoubtedly an "individual with a disability" under both the Rehabilitation Act and the ADA. Active AIDS clearly qualifies as a physical impairment and also substantially limits major life activities. But *Arline* left open the question whether a person can be considered "handicapped" *solely* on the basis of contagiousness. Is a person who tests positively for the antibodies produced in reaction to HIV, the virus that causes AIDS, an "individual with a disability"? The Supreme Court addressed this issue in its first ADA case confronting the definition of disability. Although Bragdon v. Abbot was a Title III case involving public accommodation discrimination, note that the definition of disability in the ADA applies to Titles I and II as well.

## 1.  Actual Disability

### BRAGDON v. ABBOTT
#### 524 U.S. 624 (1998)

Justice KENNEDY delivered the opinion of the Court in which Justices STEVENS, SOUTER, GINSBURG, and BREYER, joined.

---

* This term was used in the Rehabilitation Act until the Rehabilitation Act Amendments of 1986, Pub. L. No. 88-506, 100 Stat. 1807, replaced it with the term "individual with handicaps." This was replaced with "individual with a disability" in the Rehabilitation Act Amendments of 1992, Pub. L. No. 102-569, 106 Stat. 4344. These amendments, however, did not change the definition.

We address in this case the application of the Americans with Disabilities Act of 1990 (ADA) to persons infected with the human immunodeficiency virus (HIV). We granted certiorari to review, first, whether HIV infection is a disability under the ADA when the infection has not yet progressed to the so-called symptomatic phase. . . .

## I

Respondent Sidney Abbott has been infected with HIV since 1986. When the incidents we recite occurred, her infection had not manifested its most serious symptoms. On September 16, 1994, she went to the office of petitioner Randon Bragdon in Bangor, Maine, for a dental appointment. She disclosed her HIV infection on the patient registration form. Petitioner completed a dental examination, discovered a cavity, and informed respondent of his policy against filling cavities of HIV-infected patients. He offered to perform the work at a hospital with no added fee for his services, though respondent would be responsible for the cost of using the hospital's facilities. Respondent declined.

Respondent sued petitioner under . . . § 302 of the ADA, alleging discrimination on the basis of her disability. . . . [Section 302 of Title III of the ADA prohibits discrimination on the basis of disability "by any person who . . . operates a place of public accommodation." The term "public accommodation" is defined to include the "professional office of a health care provider." § 12181(7)(F).]

## II

We first review the ruling that respondent's HIV infection constituted a disability under the ADA. The statute defines disability as:

(A)  a physical or mental impairment that substantially limits one or more of the major life activities of such individual;
(B)  a record of such an impairment; or
(C)  being regarded as having such impairment.

§ 12102(2). We hold respondent's HIV infection was a disability under subsection (A) of the definitional section of the statute. In light of this conclusion, we need not consider the applicability of subsections (B) or (C).

Our consideration of subsection (A) of the definition proceeds in three steps. First, we consider whether respondent's HIV infection was a physical impairment. Second, we identify the life activity upon which respondent relies (reproduction and child bearing) and determine whether it constitutes a major life activity under the ADA. Third, tying the two statutory phrases together, we ask whether the impairment substantially limited the major life activity. In construing the statute, we are informed by interpretations of parallel definitions in previous statutes and the views of various administrative agencies which have faced this interpretive question.

### A

The ADA's definition of disability is drawn almost verbatim from the definition of "handicapped individual" included in the Rehabilitation Act of 1973, and the definition of "handicap" contained in the Fair Housing Amendments Act of 1988. Congress' repetition of a well-established term carries the implication that Congress intended the term to be construed in accordance with pre-existing regulatory interpretations. In this case, Congress did more than suggest this construction; it adopted a specific statutory provision in the ADA directing as follows:

> Except as otherwise provided in this chapter, nothing in this chapter shall be construed to apply a lesser standard than the standards applied under title V of the Rehabilitation Act of 1973 or the regulations issued by Federal agencies pursuant to such title.

42 U.S.C. § 12201(a). The directive requires us to construe the ADA to grant at least as much protection as provided by the regulations implementing the Rehabilitation Act.

### 1

The first step in the inquiry under subsection (A) requires us to determine whether respondent's condition constituted a physical impairment. The Department of Health, Education and Welfare (HEW) issued the first regulations interpreting the Rehabilitation Act in 1977. The regulations are of particular significance because, at the time, HEW was the agency responsible for coordinating the implementation and enforcement of § 504. The HEW regulations, which appear without change in the current regulations issued by the Department of Health and Human Services, define "physical or mental impairment" to mean:

> (A) any physiological disorder or condition, cosmetic disfigurement, or anatomical loss affecting one or more of the following body systems: neurological; musculoskeletal; special sense organs; respiratory, including speech organs; cardiovascular; reproductive, digestive, genito-urinary; hemic and lymphatic; skin; and endocrine; or
> (B) any mental or psychological disorder, such as mental retardation, organic brain syndrome, emotional or mental illness, and specific learning disabilities.

45 CFR § 84.3(j)(2)(i) (1997). In issuing these regulations, HEW decided against including a list of disorders constituting physical or mental impairments, out of concern that any specific enumeration might not be comprehensive. 42 Fed. Reg. 22685 (1977), reprinted in 45 CFR pt. 84, App. A, p. 334 (1997). The commentary accompanying the regulations, however, contains a representative list of disorders and conditions constituting physical impairments, including "such diseases and conditions as orthopedic, visual, speech, and hearing impairments, cerebral palsy, epilepsy, muscular dystrophy, multiple sclerosis, cancer, heart disease, diabetes, mental retardation, emotional illness, and . . . drug addiction and alcoholism." Id.

In 1980, the President transferred responsibility for the implementation and enforcement of § 504 to the Attorney General. See, e.g., Exec. Order No. 12250, 3 CFR § 298 (1981). The regulations issued by the Justice Department, which remain in force to this day, adopted verbatim the HEW definition of physical impairment quoted above. 28 CFR § 41.31(a)(1) (1997). In addition, the representative list of diseases and conditions originally relegated to the commentary accompanying the HEW regulations were incorporated into the text of the regulations. Id.

HIV infection is not included in the list of specific disorders constituting physical impairments, in part because HIV was not identified as the cause of AIDS until 1983. HIV infection does fall well within the general definition set forth by the regulations, however.

The disease follows a predictable and, as of today, an unalterable course. Once a person is infected with HIV, the virus invades different cells in the blood and in body tissues. Certain white blood cells, known as helper T-lymphocytes or CD4+ cells, are particularly vulnerable to HIV. The virus attaches to the CD4 receptor site of the target cell and fuses its membrane to the cell's membrane. HIV is a retrovirus, which means it uses an enzyme to convert its own genetic material into a form indistinguishable from the genetic material of the target cell. The virus' genetic material migrates to the cell's nucleus and becomes integrated with the cell's chromosomes. Once integrated, the virus can use the cell's own genetic machinery to replicate itself. Additional copies of the virus are released into the body and infect other cells in turn.

The virus eventually kills the infected host cell. CD4+ cells play a critical role in coordinating the body's immune response system, and the decline in their number causes corresponding deterioration of the body's ability to fight infections from many sources. Tracking the infected individual's CD4+ cell count is one of the most accurate measures of the course of the disease.

The initial stage of HIV infection is known as acute or primary HIV infection. In a typical case, this stage lasts three months. The virus concentrates in the blood. The assault on the immune system is immediate. The victim suffers from a sudden and serious decline in the number of white blood cells. There is no latency period. Mononucleosis-like symptoms often emerge between six days and six weeks after infection, at times accompanied by fever, headache, enlargement of the lymph nodes (lymphadenopathy), muscle pain (myalgia), rash, lethargy, gastrointestinal disorders, and neurological disorders. Usually these symptoms abate within 14 to 21 days. HIV antibodies appear in the bloodstream within 3 weeks; circulating HIV can be detected within 10 weeks.

After the symptoms associated with the initial stage subside, the disease enters what is referred to sometimes as its asymptomatic phase. The term is a misnomer, in some respects, for clinical features persist throughout, including lymphadenopathy, dermatological disorders, oral lesions, and bacterial infections. Although it varies with each individual, in most instances this stage lasts from 7 to 11 years. The virus now tends to concentrate in the lymph nodes, though low levels of the virus continue to appear in the blood. It was once thought the virus became inactive during this period, but it is now known that the relative lack of symptoms is attributable to the virus' migration from the circulatory system into the lymph nodes. The migration reduces the viral presence in other parts of the body, with a corresponding diminution in physical manifestations of the disease. The virus, however, thrives in the lymph nodes, which, as a vital point of the body's immune response system, represents an ideal environment for the infection of other CD4+ cells.

A person is regarded as having AIDS when his or her CD4+ count drops below 200 cells/mm3 of blood or when CD4+ cells comprise less than 14% of his or her total lymphocytes.[Medical citations omitted.] During this stage, the clinical conditions most often associated with HIV, such as pneumocystis carninii pneumonia, Kaposi's sarcoma, and non-Hodgkin's lymphoma, tend to appear. In addition, the general systemic disorders present during all stages of the disease, such as fever, weight loss, fatigue, lesions, nausea, and diarrhea, tend to worsen. In most cases, once the patient's CD4+ count drops below 10 cells/mm3, death soon follows.

In light of the immediacy with which the virus begins to damage the infected person's white blood cells and the severity of the disease, we hold it is an impairment from the moment of infection. As noted earlier, infection with HIV causes immediate abnormalities in a person's blood, and the infected person's white cell count continues to drop throughout the course of the disease, even when the attack is concentrated in the lymph nodes. In light of these facts, HIV infection must be regarded as a physiological disorder with a constant and detrimental effect on the infected person's hemic and lymphatic systems from the moment of infection. HIV infection satisfies the statutory and regulatory definition of a physical impairment during every stage of the disease.

### 2

The statute is not operative, and the definition not satisfied, unless the impairment affects a major life activity. Respondent's claim throughout this case has been that the HIV infection placed a substantial limitation on her ability to reproduce and to bear children. Given the pervasive, and invariably fatal, course of the disease, its effect on major life activities of many sorts might have been relevant to our inquiry. Respondent and a number of amici make arguments about HIV's profound impact on almost every phase of the infected person's life. In light of these submissions, it may seem legalistic to circumscribe our discussion to the activity of reproduction. We have little doubt that had different parties brought the suit they would have maintained that an HIV infection imposes substantial limitations on other major life activities. . . .

We have little difficulty concluding that [reproduction is a major life activity]. As the Court of Appeals held, "the plain meaning of the word 'major' denotes comparative importance" and "suggests that the touchstone for determining an activity's inclusion under the statutory rubric is its significance." Reproduction falls well within the phrase "major life activity." Reproduction and the sexual dynamics surrounding it are central to the life process itself.

While petitioner concedes the importance of reproduction, he claims that Congress intended the ADA only to cover those aspects of a person's life which have a public, economic, or daily character. The argument founders on the statutory language. Nothing in the definition suggests that activities without a public, economic, or daily dimension may somehow be regarded as so unimportant or insignificant as to fall outside the meaning of the word "major." The breadth of the term confounds the attempt to limit its construction in this manner.

As we have noted, the ADA must be construed to be consistent with regulations issued to implement the Rehabilitation Act. Rather than enunciating a general principle for determining what is and is not a major life activity, the Rehabilitation Act regulations instead provide a representative list, defining the term to include "functions such as caring for one's self, performing manual tasks, walking, seeing, hearing, speaking, breathing, learning, and working." 45 CFR § 84.3(j)(2)(ii) (1997); 28 CFR § 41.31(b)(2) (1997). As the use of the term "such as" confirms, the list is illustrative, not exhaustive.

These regulations are contrary to petitioner's attempt to limit the meaning of the term "major" to public activities. The inclusion of activities such as caring for one's self and performing manual tasks belies the suggestion that a task must have a public or economic character in order to be a major life activity for purposes of the ADA. On the contrary, the Rehabilitation Act regulations support the inclusion of reproduction as a major life activity, since reproduction could not be regarded as any less important than working and learning. Petitioner advances no credible basis for confining major life activities to those with a public, economic, or daily aspect. . . . [R]eproduction is a major life activity for the purposes of the ADA.

### 3

The final element of the disability definition in subsection (A) is whether respondent's physical impairment was a substantial limit on the major life activity she asserts. The Rehabilitation Act regulations provide no additional guidance.

Our evaluation of the medical evidence leads us to conclude that respondent's infection substantially limited her ability to reproduce in two independent ways. First, a woman infected with HIV who tries to conceive a child imposes on the man a significant risk of becoming infected. The cumulative results of 13 studies collected in a 1994 textbook on AIDS indicates that 20% of male partners of women with HIV became HIV-positive themselves, with a majority of the studies finding a statistically significant risk of infection.

Second, an infected woman risks infecting her child during gestation and childbirth, i.e., perinatal transmission. Petitioner concedes that women infected with HIV face about a 25% risk of transmitting the virus to their children. Published reports available in 1994 confirm the accuracy of this statistic.

Petitioner points to evidence in the record suggesting that antiretroviral therapy can lower the risk of perinatal transmission to about 8%. . . . It cannot be said as a matter of law that an 8% risk of transmitting a dread and fatal disease to one's child does not represent a substantial limitation on reproduction.

The Act addresses substantial limitations on major life activities, not utter inabilities. Conception and childbirth are not impossible for an HIV victim but, without doubt, are dangerous to the public health. This meets the definition of a substantial limitation. The decision to reproduce carries economic and legal consequences as well. There are added costs for antiretroviral therapy, supplemental insurance, and long-term health care for the child who must be examined and, tragic to think, treated for the infection. The laws of some States, moreover, forbid persons infected with HIV from having sex with others, regardless of consent.

In the end, the disability definition does not turn on personal choice. When significant limitations result from the impairment, the definition is met even if the difficulties are not insurmountable. For the statistical and other reasons we have cited, of course, the limitations on reproduction may be insurmountable here. Testimony from the respondent that her HIV infection controlled her decision not to have a child is unchallenged. In the context of reviewing summary judgment, we must take it to be true. Fed. Rule Civ. Proc. 56(e). We agree with the District Court and the Court of Appeals that no triable issue of fact impedes a ruling on the question of statutory coverage. Respondent's HIV infection is a physical impairment which substantially limits a major life activity, as the ADA defines it. In view of our holding, we need not address the second question presented, i.e., whether HIV infection is a per se disability under the ADA.

B

Our holding is confirmed by a consistent course of agency interpretation before and after enactment of the ADA. Every agency to consider the issue under the Rehabilitation Act found statutory coverage for persons with asymptomatic HIV. Responsibility for administering the Rehabilitation Act was not delegated to a single agency, but we need not pause to inquire whether this causes us to withhold deference to agency interpretations under Chevron U.S.A. Inc. v. Natural Resources Defense Council, Inc., 467 U.S. 837, 844 (1984). It is enough to observe that the well-reasoned views of the agencies implementing a statute "constitute a body of experience and informed judgment to which courts and litigants may properly resort for guidance." Skidmore v. Swift & Co., 323 U.S. 134, 139-140 (1944).

One comprehensive and significant administrative precedent is a 1988 opinion issued by the Office of Legal Counsel of the Department of Justice (OLC) concluding that the Rehabilitation Act "protects symptomatic and asymptomatic HIV-infected individuals against discrimination in any covered program." Application of Section 504 of the Rehabilitation Act to HIV-Infected Individuals, 12 Op. Off. Legal Counsel 264, 264-265 (Sept. 27, 1988) (preliminary print) (footnote omitted). Relying on a letter from Surgeon General C. Everett Koop stating that, "from a purely scientific perspective, persons with HIV are clearly impaired" even during the asymptomatic phase, OLC determined asymptomatic HIV was a physical impairment under the Rehabilitation Act because it constituted a "physiological disorder or condition affecting the hemic and lymphatic systems." Id., at 271 (internal quotation marks omitted). OLC determined further that asymptomatic HIV imposed a substantial limit on the major life activity of reproduction. . . . In addition, OLC indicated that "the life activity of engaging in sexual relations is threatened and probably substantially limited by the contagiousness of the virus." Either consideration was sufficient to render asymptomatic HIV infection a handicap for purposes of the Rehabilitation Act. In the course of its Opinion, OLC considered, and rejected, the contention that the limitation could be discounted as a voluntary response to the infection. The limitation, it reasoned, was the infection's manifest physical effect. Without exception, the other agencies to address the problem before enactment of the ADA reached the same result.

Every court which addressed the issue before the ADA was enacted in July 1990, moreover, concluded that asymptomatic HIV infection satisfied the Rehabilitation Act's definition of a handicap. We are aware of no instance prior to the enactment of the ADA in which a court or agency ruled that HIV infection was not a handicap under the Rehabilitation Act.

Had Congress done nothing more than copy the Rehabilitation Act definition into the ADA, its action would indicate the new statute should be construed in light of this unwavering line of administrative and judicial interpretation. All indications are that Congress was well aware of the position taken by OLC when enacting the ADA and intended to give that position its active endorsement. [See, e.g.], H.R. Rep. No. 101-485, pt. 2, p. 52 (1990) (endorsing the analysis and conclusion of the OLC Opinion). . . .

We find the uniformity of the administrative and judicial precedent construing the definition significant. When administrative and judicial interpretations have settled the meaning of an existing statutory provision, repetition of the same language in a new statute indicates, as a general matter, the intent to incorporate its administrative and judicial interpretations as well. The uniform body of administrative and judicial precedent confirms the conclusion we reach today as the most faithful way to effect the congressional design.

c

Our conclusion is further reinforced by the administrative guidance issued by the Justice Department to implement the public accommodation provisions of Title III of the ADA. As the agency directed by Congress to issue implementing regulations, see 42 U.S.C. § 12186(b), to render technical assistance explaining the responsibilities of covered individuals and institutions, § 12206(c), and to enforce Title III in court, § 12188(b), the Department's views are entitled to deference. See *Chevron*.

The Justice Department's interpretation of the definition of disability is consistent with our analysis. The regulations acknowledge that Congress intended the ADA's definition of disability to be given the same construction as the definition of handicap in the Rehabilitation Act. 28 CFR § 36.103(a) (1997); id., pt. 36, App. B, pp. 608, 609. The regulatory definition developed by HEW to implement the Rehabilitation Act is incorporated verbatim in the ADA regulations. § 36.104. The Justice Department went further, however. It added "HIV infection (symptomatic and asymptomatic)" to the list of disorders constituting a physical impairment. § 36.104(1)(iii). . . .

We also draw guidance from the views of the agencies authorized to administer other sections of the ADA [EEOC, the Attorney General, and the Secretary of Transportation]. These agencies, too, concluded that HIV infection is a physical impairment under the ADA. Most categorical of all is EEOC's conclusion that "an individual who has HIV infection (including asymptomatic HIV infection) is an individual with a disability." EEOC Interpretive Manual § 902.4(c)(1), p. 902-21; accord, id., § 902.2(d), p. 902-14, n. 18. In the EEOC's view, "impairments . . . such as HIV infection, are inherently substantially limiting." 29 CFR pt. 1630, App., p. 350 (1997); EEOC Technical Assistance Manual II-4; EEOC Interpretive Manual § 902.4(c)(1), p. 902-21.

The regulatory authorities we cite are consistent with our holding that HIV infection, even in the so-called asymptomatic phase, is an impairment which substantially limits the major life activity of reproduction.

## NOTES

1. As *Bragdon* makes clear, determining whether a disability exists requires examination of three separate elements: whether there is (a) physical or mental impairment that (b) substantially limits (c) one or more major life activities. Analysis of each of these elements must occur, regardless of which of the three routes to disability status is at issue.

2. As in *Bragdon*, whether an impairment exists is often not difficult to determine. But sometimes it is. The EEOC has stated that the term "physical or mental impairment" does not include physical characteristics, such as weight, height, and eye color, that are in the "normal range" and are not the result of a physiological disorder. The Interpretive Guidance also excludes common personality traits, illiteracy, economic disadvantages, and temporary physical conditions. Advanced age also is excluded, although physical and mental impairments associated with aging are not. See 29 C.F.R. pt. 1630, app. § 1630.2(h), (j). Could you argue that the EEOC's interpretation is incorrect with respect to any of these conditions?

3. Is any physical characteristic outside the normal range an "impairment"? Consider unusual strength or high intelligence. Are these impairments (because they are out of the normal range), but not disabilities (because they do not substantially impair life activities)? Or are they not impairments at all because they are out of the normal range on the "positive," rather than the "negative," side?

4. Pregnancy shares many of the characteristics of a disability as defined by the ADA. Nonetheless, the EEOC ADA Guidance suggests that pregnancy is not a disability covered by the statute because pregnancy is not an *impairment*. See 29 C.F.R. pt. 1630, app. § 1630.2(h). One commentator has argued that pregnancy is covered by the ADA. See Collette G. Matzzie, Substantive Equality and Antidiscrimination: Accommodating Pregnancy Under the Americans with Disabilities Act, 82 Geo. L.J. 193 (1993). Another commentator has argued that, even if pregnancy as such is not a disability, pregnancy is disabling for many women. The article then goes on to assess whether the denial of coverage for contraceptives in an employer's insurance program

violates the ADA. See Melissa Cole, Beyond Sex Discrimination: Why Employers Discriminate Against Women with Disabilities When Their Employee Health Plans Exclude Contraceptives from Prescription Coverage, 42 Ariz. L. Rev. 501 (2001).

5. Can a physical condition that is caused at least in part by voluntary conduct constitute an impairment? The First Circuit considered this issue in Cook v. Rhode Island Dept. of Mental Health, 10 F.3d 17 (1st Cir. 1993). Bonnie Cook worked for seven years as an institutional attendant for mentally retarded persons at a residential facility. After leaving her job voluntarily in 1986, she reapplied for the identical position in 1988 at which time she stood 5'2" tall and weighed over 320 pounds. In medical terms, she was morbidly obese, meaning that she weighed either more than twice her optimal weight or more than 100 pounds over her optimal weight. See Merck Manual 950, 953 (15th ed. 1987). She was not hired because her morbid obesity "compromised her ability to evacuate patients in case of an emergency and put her at greater risk of developing serious ailments." Id. at 21. In response to her claim of discrimination under the Rehabilitation Act, the defendant argued that "'mutable' conditions are not the sort of impairments" covered by the Act because Cook could "simply lose weight and rid herself of any concomitant disability." Id. at 23. Although the court questioned whether "immutability is a prerequisite to the existence" of an "impairment," the court found evidence in the record to support a finding that the dysfunctional metabolism underlying morbid obesity is permanent. The defendant also argued that morbid obesity cannot be an impairment because it is "caused, or at least exacerbated, by voluntary conduct." The court responded:

> The Rehabilitation Act contains no language suggesting that its protection is linked to how an individual became impaired, or whether an individual contributed to his or her impairment. On the contrary, the Act indisputably applies to numerous conditions that may be caused or exacerbated by voluntary conduct, such as alcoholism, AIDS, diabetes, cancer resulting from cigarette smoking, heart disease resulting from excesses of various types, and the like. Consequently, voluntariness, like mutability, is relevant only in determining whether a condition has a substantially limiting effect.

Id. at 24. Nonetheless, the court found as a matter of fact that: "Given the plethoric evidence introduced concerning the physiological roots of morbid obesity, the jury certainly could have concluded that the metabolic dysfunction and failed appetite-suppressing neural signals were beyond plaintiff's control and rendered her effectively powerless to manage her weight." Id. Do you find the First Circuit's legal position persuasive? Can excessive weight be distinguished from the other "voluntary" conditions listed by the court? Should "voluntary" conditions be covered impairments? Note that the EEOC would not regard "common obesity" as an impairment.

6. A related question is whether temporary impairments are covered by the Rehabilitation Act or the ADA. In Toyota Motor Mfg. Co. v. Williams [reproduced at page 691], the Supreme Court stated that, to substantially limit performance of manual tasks, "the impairment's impact must also be permanent or long-term." Subsequent to Toyota, the Fourth Circuit concluded that a medical condition necessitating surgery and a recovery period requiring a nine-month leave of absence was temporary and thus not substantially limiting. See Pollard v. High's of Baltimore, Inc., 281 F.3d 462 (4th Cir. 2002). Even if not permanent, isn't this "long-term"?

7. A wide range of impairments are genetically based: "Many serious genetic diseases, such as adult polycystic kidney disease (APKD), hemochromatosis, and Huntington's disease (HD), do not manifest themselves until middle age or later. Is

an individual who carries an allele for a late-onset disorder covered under the ADA prior to the onset of any symptoms?" Mark A. Rothstein, Genetic Discrimination in Employment and the Americans with Disabilities Act, 29 Hous. L. Rev. 23, 43 (1992). In May 2002, the EEOC settled its first case challenging genetic testing. A $2.2 million settlement was reached with Burlington Northern Santa Fe Railway Co. on behalf of 36 workers who underwent genetic testing for carpal tunnel syndrome. The company also agreed to discontinue use of genetic testing. (70 U.S.L.W. No. 44, page 2730, May 21, 2002.) See also Frances H. Miller & Philip A. Huvos, Genetic Blueprints, Employer Cost-Cutting, and the Americans with Disabilities Act, 46 Admin. L. Rev. 369 (1994); Larry Gostin, Genetic Discrimination: The Use of Genetically Based Diagnostic and Prognostic Tests by Employers and Insurers, 17 Am. J.L. & Med. 109 (1991). Is an individual with a genetic propensity to disease impaired? If so, does this impairment substantially limit any major life activity?

8. In Vande Zande v. Wisconsin Dept. of Admin. [reproduced at page 235], Vande Zande, who is paralyzed from the waist down, sought reasonable accommodations under the ADA relating to pressure ulcers caused by her paralysis. Her employer argued that, because her ulcers were intermittent and episodic impairments, they did not fit the definition of a disability. The Seventh Circuit disagreed:

> [A]n intermittent impairment that is a characteristic manifestation of an admitted disability is, we believe, a part of the underlying disability. . . . Often the disabling aspect of a disability is, precisely, an intermittent manifestation of the disability, rather than the underlying impairment. The AIDS virus progressively destroys the infected person's immune system. The consequence is a series of opportunistic diseases which . . . often prevent the individual from working. If they are not part of the disability, then people with AIDS do not have a disability which seems to us a very odd interpretation of the law, and one expressly rejected by the regulations. We hold that Vande Zande's pressure ulcers are a part of her disability.

Id. at 544. Vande Zande's treatment of the symptom of a disability is consistent with the Supreme Court's treatment of contagiousness in Arline.

9. At issue in Bragdon was whether reproduction was a "major life activity." The Court's holding that reproduction is a major life activity has significance beyond the question whether HIV infection is a disability within the meaning of the ADA. Prior to Bragdon, the lower courts were split on this question. The regulations list reproduction among the body systems that, if disordered, meet the definition of "impairment." Reproduction, however, is not specified in § 1630.2(i), which lists examples of major life activities that, when substantially limited by an impairment, constitute disabilities. Bragdon adds reproduction to that list, opening the door for disability claims by individuals who suffer from impairments that cause them to be infertile or that require treatment to improve fertility.

10. Bragdon acknowledges that the § 1630.2(i) list of major life activities is not exclusive. After Bragdon, what other activities are major life activities under the ADA? In Toyota Motor Mfg. Co. v. Williams [reproduced at page 691], the Supreme Court held that performing manual activities is a major life activity. What about the ability to eat, drink, sleep, drive a car, think, or get along with people? Are these major life activities under the ADA? See Amir v. St. Louis Univ., 184 F.3d 1017 (8th Cir. 1999) (eating and drinking are major life activities; getting along with others might be); Pack v. Kmart Corp., 166 F.3d 1300 (10th Cir. 1999) (sleep is a major life activity; concentration is not); Taylor v. Phoenixville Schools, 184 F.3d 296 (3d Cir. 1999)

(thinking is a major life activity); Hayes v. United Parcel Serv., Inc., 2001 U.S. App. LEXIS 19096 (6th Cir. 2001) (sitting is a major life activity); Reeves v. Johnson Controls World Servs., Inc., 140 F.3d 144 (2d Cir. 1998) ("everyday mobility" is not a major life activity where agoraphobia restricted ability to cross bridges and overpasses, enter tunnels, and board trains). For a discussion of cases before and after *Bragdon* confronting the question of what constitutes a major life activity, see Curtis D. Edmonds, Snakes and Ladders: Expanding the Definition of "Major Life Activity" in the Americans with Disabilities Act, 33 Tex. Tech. L. Rev. 321 (2002).

11. In Furnish v. SVI Systems, Inc., 270 F.3d 445 (7th Cir. 2001), the court distinguished an impairment's effect on a body system from the impairment's impact on activities, rejecting a claim that liver function was a major life activity. "[Plaintiff] argues that Hepatitis B should be a disability because it is a chronic illness that affects the functioning of a major organ. However, under the ADA, even a serious illness such as Hepatitis B does not equate with a disability. Only when the impact of the illness substantially limits a major life activity — such as working — is an individual considered disabled within the meaning of the ADA." Id. at 450. Is this correct? Should the court have taken the next step and reasoned that, if an impairment in fact does substantially limit the functioning of a major organ then it necessarily will limit one or more major life activities? Or would doing so be inconsistent with *Bragdon*'s focus on the activity relied on by the plaintiff in framing her case?

12. Must a particular major life activity be identified in determining disability status? Justice Ginsburg's concurrence in *Bragdon* addressed ADA coverage for HIV-infected individuals:

> HIV infection, as the description set out in the Court's opinion documents, has been regarded as a disease limiting life itself. The disease inevitably pervades life's choices: education, employment, family and financial undertakings. It affects the need for and, as this case shows, the ability to obtain health care because of the reaction of others to the impairment. No rational legislator, it seems to me apparent, would require nondiscrimination once symptoms become visible but permit discrimination when the disease, though present, is not yet visible. I am therefore satisfied that the statutory and regulatory definitions are well met. HIV infection is "a physical . . . impairment that substantially limits . . . major life activities," or is so perceived, 42 U.S.C. §§ 12102(2)(A),(C), including the afflicted individual's family relations, employment potential, and ability to care for herself, see 45 CFR § 84.3(j)(2)(ii) (1997); 28 CFR § 41.31(b)(2) (1997).

524 U.S. at 624. Justice Ginsburg suggests that HIV infection is substantially limiting in part because it will later develop into a seriously debilitating illness. If this is so, what about multiple sclerosis, which in its early stages can be relatively asymptomatic, but which may ultimately be seriously disabling? Consider the impact of the EEOC Interpretive Guidance:

> Some impairments may be disabling for particular individuals but not for others, depending on the stage of the disease or disorder, the presence of other impairments that combine to make the impairment disabling or any number of other factors.

29 C.F.R. pt. 1630, app. § 1630.2(j).

13. An issue that has caused considerable controversy is whether working is a major life activity and what it means to be substantially limited in the ability to work.

Consideration of this question is deferred to the notes after Sutton v. United Air Lines, Inc., 527 U.S. 471 (1999), reproduced at page 699.

14. *Bragdon* resolves the issue of ADA coverage for *most* individuals who are infected with HIV. Does the decision provide any assistance to HIV-infected plaintiffs who are unable to bear children for reasons other than their HIV infection? What about an HIV-infected woman who had her fallopian tubes tied prior to her infection? Is such an individual "substantially limited" for other reasons? In Blanks v. Southwestern Bell Corp., 310 F.3d 398 (5th Cir. 2002), the court held that an HIV positive worker who did not intend to have more children failed to establish a disability under the ADA. Does the *Bragdon* opinion support an argument that HIV infection is substantially limiting because it restricts an individual's freedom to engage in sexual intercourse? Does the Court's analysis suggest that sexual intercourse might be characterized as a major life activity?

The Court further explored what it means for an impairment to substantially limit a major life activity in the following case.

## TOYOTA MOTOR MANUFACTURING, KENTUCKY, INC. v. WILLIAMS
### 534 U.S. 184 (2002)

Justice O'CONNOR delivered the opinion of the Court.

Under the Americans with Disabilities Act of 1990 (ADA or Act), a physical impairment that "substantially limits one or more . . . major life activities" is a "disability." 42 U.S.C. § 12102(2)(A). Respondent, claiming to be disabled because of her carpal tunnel syndrome and other related impairments, sued petitioner, her former employer, for failing to provide her with a reasonable accommodation as required by the ADA. See § 12112(b) (5)(A). The District Court granted summary judgment to petitioner, finding that respondent's impairments did not substantially limit any of her major life activities. The Court of Appeals for the Sixth Circuit reversed, finding that the impairments substantially limited respondent in the major life activity of performing manual tasks, and therefore granting partial summary judgment to respondent on the issue of whether she was disabled under the ADA. We conclude that the Court of Appeals did not apply the proper standard in making this determination because it analyzed only a limited class of manual tasks and failed to ask whether respondent's impairments prevented or restricted her from performing tasks that are of central importance to most people's daily lives.

## I

Respondent began working at petitioner's automobile manufacturing plant in Georgetown, Kentucky, in August 1990. She was soon placed on an engine fabrication assembly line, where her duties included work with pneumatic tools. Use of these tools eventually caused pain in respondent's hands, wrists, and arms. . . . Respondent consulted a personal physician who placed her on permanent work restrictions that precluded her from lifting more than 20 pounds or from "frequently lifting or carrying of objects weighing up to 10 pounds," engaging in "constant repetitive . . . flexion or extension of [her] wrists or elbows," performing "overhead work," or using "vibratory or pneumatic tools."

In light of these restrictions, for the next two years petitioner assigned respondent to various modified duty jobs. . . . [P]etitioner placed respondent on a team in Quality Control Inspection Operations (QCIO). QCIO is responsible for four tasks: (1) "assembly paint"; (2) "paint second inspection"; (3) "shell body audit"; and (4) "ED surface repair." Respondent was initially placed on a team that performed only the first two of these tasks, and for a couple of years, she rotated on a weekly basis between them. . . . The parties agree that respondent was physically capable of performing both of these jobs and that her performance was satisfactory.

During the fall of 1996, petitioner announced that it wanted QCIO employees to be able to rotate through all four of the QCIO processes. . . . A short while after the shell body audit job was added to respondent's rotations, she began to experience pain in her neck and shoulders. . . . Respondent requested that petitioner accommodate her medical conditions by allowing her to return to doing only her original two jobs in QCIO, which respondent claimed she could still perform without difficulty.

The parties disagree about what happened next. According to respondent, petitioner refused her request and forced her to continue working in the shell body audit job, which caused her even greater physical injury. According to petitioner, respondent simply began missing work on a regular basis. Regardless, it is clear that on December 6, 1996, the last day respondent worked at petitioner's plant, she was placed under a no-work-of-any-kind restriction by her treating physicians. On January 27, 1997, respondent received a letter from petitioner that terminated her employment, citing her poor attendance record. . . .

[The District Court granted summary judgment for defendant, finding that at the time respondent requested accommodation, she was not disabled within the meaning of the statute because her impairment did not substantially limit any major life activity. It further found that at the time of her termination she was not a qualified individual with a disability because her doctor had precluded her from performing any work whatsoever.]

The Court of Appeals for the Sixth Circuit reversed the District Court's ruling on whether respondent was disabled at the time she sought an accommodation. . . . The Court of Appeals held that in order for respondent to demonstrate that she was disabled due to a substantial limitation in the ability to perform manual tasks at the time of her accommodation request, she had to "show that her manual disability involved a 'class' of manual activities affecting the ability to perform tasks at work." Respondent satisfied this test, according to the Court of Appeals, because her ailments "prevented her from doing the tasks associated with certain types of manual assembly line jobs, manual product handling jobs and manual building trade jobs (painting, plumbing, roofing, etc.) that require the gripping of tools and repetitive work with hands and arms extended at or above shoulder levels for extended periods of time." In reaching this conclusion, the court disregarded evidence that respondent could "tend to her personal hygiene [and] carry out personal or household chores," finding that such evidence "does not affect a determination that her impairment substantially limited her ability to perform the range of manual tasks associated with an assembly line job." Because the Court of Appeals concluded that respondent had been substantially limited in performing manual tasks and, for that reason, was entitled to partial summary judgment on the issue of whether she was disabled under the Act, it found that it did not need to determine whether respondent had been substantially limited in the major life activities of lifting or working, or whether she had had a "record of" a disability or had been "regarded as" disabled.

We granted certiorari to consider the proper standard for assessing whether an individual is substantially limited in performing manual tasks. We now reverse the Court of Appeals' decision to grant partial summary judgment to respondent on the issue whether she was substantially limited in performing manual tasks at the time she sought an accommodation. . . .

## II

The ADA requires covered entities, including private employers, to provide "reasonable accommodations to the known physical or mental limitations of an otherwise qualified individual with a disability who is an applicant or employee, unless such covered entity can demonstrate that the accommodation would impose an undue hardship." 42 U.S.C. § 12112(b)(5)(A) (1994 ed.). The Act defines a "qualified individual with a disability" as "an individual with a disability who, with or without reasonable accommodation, can perform the essential functions of the employment position that such individual holds or desires." § 12111(8). In turn, a "disability" is:

(A) a physical or mental impairment that substantially limits one or more of the major life activities of such individual;
(B) a record of such an impairment; or
(C) being regarded as having such an impairment.

§ 12102(2). . . .

## III

The question presented by this case is whether the Sixth Circuit properly determined that respondent was disabled under subsection (A) of the ADA's disability definition at the time that she sought an accommodation from petitioner. 42 U.S.C. § 12102(2)(A). The parties do not dispute that respondent's medical conditions, which include carpal tunnel syndrome, myotendinitis, and thoracic outlet compression, amount to physical impairments. The relevant question, therefore, is whether the Sixth Circuit correctly analyzed whether these impairments substantially limited respondent in the major life activity of performing manual tasks. Answering this requires us to address an issue about which the EEOC regulations are silent: what a plaintiff must demonstrate to establish a substantial limitation in the specific major life activity of performing manual tasks.

Our consideration of this issue is guided first and foremost by the words of the disability definition itself. "Substantially" in the phrase "substantially limits" suggests "considerable" or "to a large degree." See Webster's Third New International Dictionary 2280 (1976) (defining "substantially" as "in a substantial manner" and "substantial" as "considerable in amount, value, or worth" and "being that specified to a large degree or in the main"); see also 17 Oxford English Dictionary 66-67 (2d ed. 1989) ("substantial": "relating to or proceeding from the essence of a thing; essential"; "of ample or considerable amount, quantity, or dimensions"). The word "substantial" thus clearly precludes impairments that interfere in only a minor way with the performance of manual tasks from qualifying as disabilities. Cf. Albertson's, Inc. v. Kirkingburg [reproduced at page 769]. (explaining that a "mere difference" does not amount to a "significant restriction" and therefore does not satisfy the EEOC's interpretation of "substantially limits").

"Major" in the phrase "major life activities" means important. See Webster's, supra, at 1363 (defining "major" as "greater in dignity, rank, importance, or interest"). "Major life activities" thus refers to those activities that are of central importance to daily life. In order for performing manual tasks to fit into this category — a category that includes such basic abilities as walking, seeing, and hearing — the manual tasks in question must be central to daily life. If each of the tasks included in the major life activity of performing manual tasks does not independently qualify as a major life activity, then together they must do so.

That these terms need to be interpreted strictly to create a demanding standard for qualifying as disabled is confirmed by the first section of the ADA, which lays out the legislative findings and purposes that motivate the Act. See 42 U.S.C. § 12101. When it enacted the ADA in 1990, Congress found that "some 43,000,000 Americans have one or more physical or mental disabilities." § 12101(a)(1). If Congress intended everyone with a physical impairment that precluded the performance of some isolated, unimportant, or particularly difficult manual task to qualify as disabled, the number of disabled Americans would surely have been much higher. Cf. Sutton v. United Air Lines, Inc. [reproduced at page 699] (finding that because more than 100 million people need corrective lenses to see properly, "had Congress intended to include all persons with corrected physical limitations among those covered by the Act, it undoubtedly would have cited a much higher number [than 43 million disabled persons] in the findings").

We therefore hold that to be substantially limited in performing manual tasks, an individual must have an impairment that prevents or severely restricts the individual from doing activities that are of central importance to most people's daily lives. The impairment's impact must also be permanent or long-term. See 29 CFR §§ 1630.2(j)(2)(ii)-(iii) (2001).

It is insufficient for individuals attempting to prove disability status under this test to merely submit evidence of a medical diagnosis of an impairment. Instead, the ADA requires those "claiming the Act's protection . . . to prove a disability by offering evidence that the extent of the limitation [caused by their impairment] in terms of their own experience . . . is substantial." Albertson's, Inc. v. Kirkingburg (holding that monocular vision is not invariably a disability, but must be analyzed on an individual basis, taking into account the individual's ability to compensate for the impairment). That the Act defines "disability" "with respect to an individual," 42 U.S.C. § 12102(2), makes clear that Congress intended the existence of a disability to be determined in such a case-by-case manner. See Sutton v. United Air Lines, Inc.; Albertson's, Inc. v. Kirkingburg; cf. Bragdon v. Abbott (relying on unchallenged testimony that the respondent's HIV infection controlled her decision not to have a child, and declining to consider whether HIV infection is a *per se* disability under the ADA); 29 CFR pt. 1630, App. § 1630.2(j) (2001) ("The determination of whether an individual has a disability is not necessarily based on the name or diagnosis of the impairment the person has, but rather on the effect of that impairment on the life of the individual."). ("The determination of whether an individual is substantially limited in a major life activity must be made on a case-by-case basis.")

An individualized assessment of the effect of an impairment is particularly necessary when the impairment is one whose symptoms vary widely from person to person. Carpal tunnel syndrome, one of respondent's impairments, is just such a condition. While cases of severe carpal tunnel syndrome are characterized by muscle atrophy and extreme sensory deficits, mild cases generally do not have either of these effects and create only intermittent symptoms of numbness and tingling. Carniero, Carpal

Tunnel Syndrome: The Cause Dictates the Treatment, 66 Cleveland Clinic J. Medicine 159, 161-162 (1999). Studies have further shown that, even without surgical treatment, one quarter of carpal tunnel cases resolve in one month, but that in 22 percent of cases, symptoms last for eight years or longer. See DeStefano, Nordstrom, & Uierkant, Long-term Symptom Outcomes of Carpal Tunnel Syndrome and its Treatment, 22A J. Hand Surgery 200, 204-205 (1997). When pregnancy is the cause of carpal tunnel syndrome, in contrast, the symptoms normally resolve within two weeks of delivery. See Ouellette, Nerve Compression Syndromes of the Upper Extremity in Women, 17 Journal of Musculoskeletal Medicine 536 (2000). Given these large potential differences in the severity and duration of the effects of carpal tunnel syndrome, an individual's carpal tunnel syndrome diagnosis, on its own, does not indicate whether the individual has a disability within the meaning of the ADA.

## IV

The Court of Appeals' analysis of respondent's claimed disability suggested that in order to prove a substantial limitation in the major life activity of performing manual tasks, a "plaintiff must show that her manual disability involves a 'class' of manual activities," and that those activities "affect the ability to perform tasks at work." Both of these ideas lack support.

The Court of Appeals relied on our opinion in Sutton v. United Air Lines, Inc., for the idea that a "class" of manual activities must be implicated for an impairment to substantially limit the major life activity of performing manual tasks. But Sutton said only that *"when the major life activity under consideration is that of working*, the statutory phrase 'substantially limits' requires . . . that plaintiffs allege that they are unable to work in a broad class of jobs." (emphasis added). Because of the conceptual difficulties inherent in the argument that working could be a major life activity, we have been hesitant to hold as much, and we need not decide this difficult question today. In *Sutton*, we noted that even assuming that working is a major life activity, a claimant would be required to show an inability to work in a "broad range of jobs," rather than a specific job. But *Sutton* did not suggest that a class-based analysis should be applied to any major life activity other than working. Nor do the EEOC regulations. In defining "substantially limits," the EEOC regulations only mention the "class" concept in the context of the major life activity of working. 29 CFR § 1630.2(j)(3) (2001) ("With respect to the major life activity of *working*[,] the term *substantially limits* means significantly restricted in the ability to perform either a class of jobs or a broad range of jobs in various classes as compared to the average person having comparable training, skills and abilities"). Nothing in the text of the Act, our previous opinions, or the regulations suggests that a class-based framework should apply outside the context of the major life activity of working.

While the Court of Appeals in this case addressed the different major life activity of performing manual tasks, its analysis circumvented *Sutton* by focusing on respondent's inability to perform manual tasks associated only with her job. This was error. When addressing the major life activity of performing manual tasks, the central inquiry must be whether the claimant is unable to perform the variety of tasks central to most people's daily lives, not whether the claimant is unable to perform the tasks associated with her specific job. Otherwise, *Sutton's* restriction on claims of disability based on a substantial limitation in working will be rendered meaningless because an inability to perform a specific job always can be recast as an inability to perform a "class" of tasks associated with that specific job.

There is also no support in the Act, our previous opinions, or the regulations for the Court of Appeals' idea that the question of whether an impairment constitutes a disability is to be answered only by analyzing the effect of the impairment in the workplace. Indeed, the fact that the Act's definition of "disability" applies not only to Title I of the Act, 42 U.S.C. §§ 12111-12117, which deals with employment, but also to the other portions of the Act, which deal with subjects such as public transportation, §§ 12141-12150, 42 U.S.C. §§ 12161-12165, and privately provided public accommodations, §§ 12181-12189, demonstrates that the definition is intended to cover individuals with disabling impairments regardless of whether the individuals have any connection to a workplace.

Even more critically, the manual tasks unique to any particular job are not necessarily important parts of most people's lives. As a result, occupation-specific tasks may have only limited relevance to the manual task inquiry. In this case, "repetitive work with hands and arms extended at or above shoulder levels for extended periods of time," the manual task on which the Court of Appeals relied, is not an important part of most people's daily lives. The court, therefore, should not have considered respondent's inability to do such manual work in her specialized assembly line job as sufficient proof that she was substantially limited in performing manual tasks.

At the same time, the Court of Appeals appears to have disregarded the very type of evidence that it should have focused upon. It treated as irrelevant "the fact that [respondent] can . . . tend to her personal hygiene [and] carry out personal or household chores." Yet household chores, bathing, and brushing one's teeth are among the types of manual tasks of central importance to people's daily lives, and should have been part of the assessment of whether respondent was substantially limited in performing manual tasks.

The District Court noted that at the time respondent sought an accommodation from petitioner, she admitted that she was able to do the manual tasks required by her original two jobs in QCIO. In addition, according to respondent's deposition testimony, even after her condition worsened, she could still brush her teeth, wash her face, bathe, tend her flower garden, fix breakfast, do laundry, and pick up around the house. The record also indicates that her medical conditions caused her to avoid sweeping, to quit dancing, to occasionally seek help dressing, and to reduce how often she plays with her children, gardens, and drives long distances. But these changes in her life did not amount to such severe restrictions in the activities that are of central importance to most people's daily lives that they establish a manual-task disability as a matter of law. On this record, it was therefore inappropriate for the Court of Appeals to grant partial summary judgment to respondent on the issue whether she was substantially limited in performing manual tasks, and its decision to do so must be reversed. . . .

Accordingly, we reverse the Court of Appeals' judgment granting partial summary judgment to respondent and remand the case for further proceedings consistent with this opinion. . . .

## NOTES

1. The decision in *Toyota* was unanimous, presumably because of the very narrow holding of the case. The Court did not determine whether Williams' impairment substantially limited her ability to perform manual tasks. Nor did it determine whether Williams' impairment substantially limited her ability to perform any other major life activity.

2. Alternatively, Williams had contended that lifting and working were major life activities and that her impairment substantially limited those activities as well. The appeals court did not rule on those contentions, and neither did the Supreme Court. Is lifting a major life activity? Is working? On the latter question, see the Court's decision in *Sutton*, reproduced at page 699.

3. At the district court level, Williams also had alleged that housework, gardening, and playing with her children were major life activities, but she did not appeal the district court's rejection of those contentions. In light of the Court's language in *Toyota*, do you agree with her decision to abandon those contentions?

4. Importantly, the Court agreed with the Sixth Circuit that performing manual tasks *is* a major life activity. But it held that the manual tasks, either singly or together, must be "central to daily life." If a particular manual task is central to daily life, is it a major life activity, standing alone? When would one need a combination of tasks central to daily life for their performance to be a major life activity? What are the manual tasks "central to daily life"? Is using one's arms and hands to communicate with others a manual task? See Thornton v. McClatchy Newspapers, Inc., 261 F.3d 789 (9th Cir. 2001), *amended*, 292 F.3d 1045 (9th Cir. 2002).

5. The Sixth Circuit had focused only on a "class" of manual tasks that were work related. The appeals court had not determined that Williams was substantially limited in her ability to work, and yet the only limitations it had considered were those that were work related. Was the Court concerned that the Sixth Circuit may have been trying to circumvent the rigors of establishing that an individual is substantially limited in her ability to work? See *Sutton*, reproduced at page 699.

On remand, would Williams be better served by emphasizing her contention that working is a major life activity and the impairment's impact on her ability to work? But see McKay v. Toyota Motor Mfg., U.S.A., Inc., 110 F.3d 369 (6th Cir. 1997) (plaintiff whose carpal tunnel syndrome precluded repetitive factory work not substantially limited in the major life activity of working).

6. The primary question before the *Toyota* Court was whether Williams's impairment *substantially limited* her major life activity of performing manual tasks. The Court answered that question by stating that only if the impairment "prevents or severely restricts the individual from doing activities that are of central importance to most people's daily lives" will it be substantially limiting. Moreover, the impairment's impact must also be permanent or long-term. Is the Court's approach to "substantially limits" in *Toyota* consistent with its approach to that term in *Bragdon v. Abbott*?

7. The EEOC has promulgated regulations that define "substantially limited" to mean "unable to perform a major life activity that the average person in the general population can perform" or "significantly restricted as to the condition, manner or duration under which an individual can perform a particular major life activity as compared to the condition, manner, or duration under which the average person in the general population can perform that same major life activity." 29 C.F.R. § 1630.2(j) (2001). The regulations state that the following factors should be considered: "the nature and severity of the impairment; the duration or expected duration of the impairment; and the permanent or long-term impact, or the expected permanent or long-term impact of or resulting from the impairment." §§ 1630.2(j)(2)(i)-(iii). Although the *Toyota* Court quoted these regulations (and assumed their reasonableness) in a portion of the opinion, not produced, it pointedly declined to decide whether the EEOC's regulations were entitled to any deference. The Court noted, however, that the regulations did not address the precise issue confronting the Court, that is, what constitutes a substantial limitation on the performance of manual tasks.

8. To prove that a limitation is substantial as compared with the average person, must the plaintiff come forward with some sort of comparative evidence of his limitations vis a vis the general population? In Hayes v. United Parcel Serv., Inc., 2001 U.S. App. LEXIS 19096 (6th Cir. 2001), the court answered no, when plaintiff could sit only 20 to 25 minutes. "Common sense and life experiences will permit finders of fact to determine whether someone who cannot sit for more than this period of time is significantly restricted as compared to the average person." However, when the major life activity is working, some courts have required plaintiffs to present specific evidence about the relevant labor market and the jobs her impairment precludes her from performing. See Thornton v. McClatchy Newspapers, Inc., 261 F.3d 789 (9th Cir. 2001), *amended,* 292 F.3d 1045 (9th Cir. 2002) (journalist who could keyboard or write only for very brief periods each day not substantially limited in major life activity of working).

9. Bristol v. Board of County Commissioners, 281 F.3d 1148, 1156 (10th Cir. 2002), *vacated in part on other grounds,* 312 F.3d 1213 (10th Cir. 2002), stated that determining whether something constitutes an impairment or a major life activity is a question for the court, but whether the impairment *substantially limits* the major life activity is a question of fact for the jury. Would the *Toyota* Court agree?

10. Although the *Toyota* holding is narrow, its language is very broad, insisting that the definition of disability be "interpreted strictly to create a demanding standard for qualifying as disabled." Why? Given that disability status is but a threshold step toward protected status under Title I, is the Court's interpretation of "disability" raising the bar too high?

11. Understand the catch-22 the Court's construction of "disability" potentially poses for persons such as Williams. One who can perform basic life functions despite her impairment may have a difficult time establishing she is disabled. However, once Williams's condition worsened to the point where she was placed on a "no work of any kind" restriction, her termination was held by both lower courts to be lawful. She was no longer a "qualified" individual, whether or not she had a disability.

12. In Muller v. Costello, 187 F.3d 298 (2d Cir. 1999), a corrections officer suffered from bronchitis and asthma that made it difficult for him to breathe in smoky environments. Exposure to smoke at work caused him to suffer sufficiently serious breathing problems that he was required to leave work for one to ten days at a time, visit his doctor, and on some occasions report to a hospital emergency room. Muller's medical evidence indicated that his lung function diminished 45 percent when exposed to irritants. The court, however, ruled that Muller was not substantially limited with respect to breathing. The court reasoned that: "Other than Muller's difficulties while at work at Midstate, what we are left with is testimony that Muller was physically active outside of work, that he could potentially have severe reactions to environmental irritants, and that, on one occasion, he did have such a reaction." Id. at 314. Does *Toyota* suggest *Muller* was correctly decided? See also Mack v. Great Dane, Inc., 308 F.3d 776 (7th Cir. 2002) (impairment's impact on ability to lift at work insufficient to establish disability because no evidence of impact on lifting outside the workplace).

13. In Albertson's v. Kirkingburg, reproduced at page 769, the Supreme Court held that the fact that an impairment requires an individual to perform a major life activity differently does not mean it is substantially limiting. As the Court stated,

[T]he Ninth Circuit . . . conclud[ed] that because Kirkingburg had presented "uncontroverted evidence" that his vision was effectively monocular, he had demonstrated that "the manner in which he sees differs significantly from the manner in which most people see." That difference in manner, the court held, was sufficient to establish disability. . . . But in several respects the Ninth Circuit was too quick to find a disability. First, although the EEOC definition of "substantially limits" cited by the Ninth Circuit requires a "significant restriction" in an individual's manner of performing a major life activity, the court appeared willing to settle for a mere difference. By transforming "significant restriction" into "difference," the court undercut the fundamental statutory requirement that only impairments causing "substantial limitations" in individuals' ability to perform major life activities constitute disabilities. While the Act "addresses substantial limitations on major life activities, not utter inabilities," Bragdon v. Abbott, it concerns itself only with limitations that are in fact substantial.

527 U.S. at 461. In EEOC v. United Parcel Serv., Inc., 306 F.3d 794 (9th Cir. 2002), the Ninth Circuit concluded that because plaintiffs with monocular vision could use their eyesight as most people do in daily life, they were not substantially limited in the major life activity of seeing.

14. One issue concerning "substantial limitation" arose in many disability cases. Individuals with impairments that can be controlled or corrected asserted that whether their impairments are substantially limiting should be assessed without considering the medication or devices that ameliorate the impact of their impairments. The Supreme Court resolved this issue in the following case.

## SUTTON v. UNITED AIR LINES, INC.
### 527 U.S. 471 (1999)

Justice O'CONNOR delivered the opinion of the Court. . . .

I

. . . Petitioners are twin sisters, both of whom have severe myopia. Each petitioner's uncorrected visual acuity is 20/200 or worse in her right eye and 20/400 or worse in her left eye, but "with the use of corrective lenses, each . . . has vision that is 20/20 or better." Consequently, without corrective lenses, each "effectively cannot see to conduct numerous activities such as driving a vehicle, watching television or shopping in public stores," but with corrective measures, such as glasses or contact lenses, both "function identically to individuals without a similar impairment."

In 1992, petitioners applied to respondent for employment as commercial airline pilots. They met respondent's basic age, education, experience, and FAA certification qualifications. After submitting their applications for employment, both petitioners were invited by respondent to an interview and to flight simulator tests. Both were told during their interviews, however, that a mistake had been made in inviting them to interview because petitioners did not meet respondent's minimum vision requirement, which was uncorrected visual acuity of 20/100 or better. Due to their failure to meet this requirement, petitioners' interviews were terminated, and neither was offered a pilot position.

In light of respondent's proffered reason for rejecting them, petitioners [filed suit] alleging that respondent had discriminated against them "on the basis of their disability, or because [respondent] regarded [petitioners] as having a disability" in violation of the ADA.

The District Court dismissed petitioners' complaint for failure to state a claim upon which relief could be granted. Because petitioners could fully correct their visual impairments, the court held that they were not actually substantially limited in any major life activity and thus had not stated a claim that they were disabled within the meaning of the ADA. . . . [T]he Court of Appeals for the Tenth Circuit affirmed the District Court's judgment.

The Tenth Circuit's decision is in tension with the decisions of other Courts of Appeals. . . .

## II

The ADA prohibits discrimination by covered entities, including private employers, against qualified individuals with a disability. . . . 42 U.S.C. § 12112(a); see also § 12111(2). . . . [A] "Disability" is defined as:

(A) a physical or mental impairment that substantially limits one or more of the major life activities of such individual;
(B) a record of such an impairment; or
(C) being regarded as having such impairment.

§ 12102(2). Accordingly, to fall within this definition one must have an actual disability (subsection (A)), have a record of a disability (subsection (B)), or be regarded as having one (subsection (C)).

The parties agree that the authority to issue regulations to implement the Act is split primarily among three Government agencies. According to the parties, the EEOC has authority to issue regulations to carry out the employment provisions in Title I of the ADA, §§ 12111-12117, pursuant to § 12116. . . . The Attorney General is granted authority to issue regulations with respect to Title II, subtitle A, §§ 12131-12134, which relates to public services. See § 12134. . . . Finally, the Secretary of Transportation has authority to issue regulations pertaining to the transportation provisions of Titles II and III. See § 12149(a); § 12164; § 12186(a)(1); § 12143(b). . . . Moreover, each of these agencies is authorized to offer technical assistance regarding the provisions they administer. See § 12206(c)(1).

No agency, however, has been given authority to issue regulations implementing the generally applicable provisions of the ADA, see §§ 12101-12102, which fall outside Titles I-V. Most notably, no agency has been delegated authority to interpret the term "disability." § 12102(2). Justice Breyer's contrary, imaginative interpretation of the Act's delegation provisions is belied by the terms and structure of the ADA. The EEOC has, nonetheless, issued regulations to provide additional guidance regarding the proper interpretation of this term. After restating the definition of disability given in the statute, see 29 CFR § 1630.2(g) (1998), the EEOC regulations define the three elements of disability: (1) "physical or mental impairment," (2) "substantially limits," and (3) "major life activities." See id. at §§ 1630.2(h)-(j). Under the regulations, a "physical impairment" includes

any physiological disorder, or condition, cosmetic disfigurement, or anatomical loss affecting one or more of the following body systems: neurological, musculoskeletal, special sense organs, respiratory (including speech organs), cardiovascular, reproductive, digestive, genito-urinary, hemic and lymphatic, skin, and endocrine.

§ 1630.2(h)(1). The term "substantially limits" means, among other things, "unable to perform a major life activity that the average person in the general population can perform;" or

> significantly restricted as to the condition, manner or duration under which an individual can perform a particular major life activity as compared to the condition, manner, or duration under which the average person in the general population can perform that same major life activity.

§ 1630.2(j). Finally, "major life activities means functions such as caring for oneself, performing manual tasks, walking, seeing, hearing, speaking, breathing, learning, and working." § 1630.2(i). Because both parties accept these regulations as valid, and determining their validity is not necessary to decide this case, we have no occasion to consider what deference they are due, if any.

The agencies have also issued interpretive guidelines to aid in the implementation of their regulations. For instance, at the time that it promulgated the above regulations, the EEOC issued an "Interpretive Guidance," which provides that "the determination of whether an individual is substantially limited in a major life activity must be made on a case by case basis, without regard to mitigating measures such as medicines, or assistive or prosthetic devices." 29 CFR pt. 1630, App. § 1630.2(j) (1998) (describing § 1630.2(j)). The Department of Justice has issued a similar guideline. See 28 CFR pt. 35, App. A, § 35.104 ("The question of whether a person has a disability should be assessed without regard to the availability of mitigating measures, such as reasonable modification or auxiliary aids and services"); pt. 36, App. B, § 36.104 (same). Although the parties dispute the persuasive force of these interpretive guidelines, we have no need in this case to decide what deference is due.

## III

With this statutory and regulatory framework in mind, we turn first to the question whether petitioners have stated a claim under subsection (A) of the disability definition, that is, whether they have alleged that they possess a physical impairment that substantially limits them in one or more major life activities. Because petitioners allege that with corrective measures their vision "is 20/20 or better," they are not actually disabled within the meaning of the Act if the "disability" determination is made with reference to these measures. Consequently, with respect to subsection (A) of the disability definition, our decision turns on whether disability is to be determined with or without reference to corrective measures.

Petitioners maintain that whether impairment is substantially limiting should be determined without regard to corrective measures. They argue that, because the ADA does not directly address the question at hand, the Court should defer to the agency interpretations of the statute, which are embodied in the agency guidelines issued by the EEOC and the Department of Justice. These guidelines specifically direct that the determination of whether an individual is substantially limited in a major life activity be made without regard to mitigating measures. See 29 CFR pt. 1630, App. § 1630.2(j); 28 CFR pt. 35, App. A, § 35.104 (1998); 28 CFR pt. 36, App. B, § 36.104.

Respondent, in turn, maintains that an impairment does not substantially limit a major life activity if it is corrected. It argues that the Court should not defer to the agency guidelines cited by petitioners because the guidelines conflict with the plain meaning of the ADA. The phrase "substantially limits one or more major life activities," it explains, requires that the substantial limitations actually and presently exist. Moreover, respondent argues, disregarding mitigating measures taken by an individual defies the statutory command to examine the effect of the impairment on the major life activities "of such individual." And even if the statute is ambiguous, respondent claims, the guidelines' directive to ignore mitigating measures is not reasonable, and thus this Court should not defer to it.

We conclude that respondent is correct that the approach adopted by the agency guidelines — that persons are to be evaluated in their hypothetical uncorrected state — is an impermissible interpretation of the ADA. Looking at the Act as a whole, it is apparent that if a person is taking measures to correct for, or mitigate, a physical or mental impairment, the effects of those measures — both positive and negative — must be taken into account when judging whether that person is "substantially limited" in a major life activity and thus "disabled" under the Act. The dissent relies on the legislative history of the ADA for the contrary proposition that individuals should be examined in their uncorrected state (opinion of Stevens, J.). Because we decide that, by its terms, the ADA cannot be read in this manner, we have no reason to consider the ADA's legislative history.

Three separate provisions of the ADA, read in concert, lead us to this conclusion. The Act defines a "disability" as "a physical or mental impairment that *substantially limits* one or more of the major life activities" of an individual. § 12102(2)(A) (emphasis added). Because the phrase "substantially limits" appears in the Act in the present indicative verb form, we think the language is properly read as requiring that a person be presently — not potentially or hypothetically — substantially limited in order to demonstrate a disability. A "disability" exists only where an impairment "substantially limits" a major life activity, not where it "might," "could," or "would" be substantially limiting if mitigating measures were not taken. A person whose physical or mental impairment is corrected by medication or other measures does not have an impairment that presently "substantially limits" a major life activity. To be sure, a person whose physical or mental impairment is corrected by mitigating measures still has an impairment, but if the impairment is corrected it does not "substantially limit" a major life activity.

The definition of disability also requires that disabilities be evaluated "with respect to an individual" and be determined based on whether an impairment substantially limits the "major life activities of such individual." § 12102(2). Thus, whether a person has a disability under the ADA is an individualized inquiry. See Bragdon v. Abbott (declining to consider whether HIV infection is a per se disability under the ADA); 29 CFR pt. 1630, App. § 1630.2(j) ("The determination of whether an individual has a disability is not necessarily based on the name or diagnosis of the impairment the person has, but rather on the effect of that impairment on the life of the individual").

The agency guidelines' directive that persons be judged in their uncorrected or unmitigated state runs directly counter to the individualized inquiry mandated by the ADA. The agency approach would often require courts and employers to speculate about a person's condition and would, in many cases, force them to make a disability determination based on general information about how an uncorrected impairment usually affects individuals, rather than on the individual's actual condition. For instance, under this view, courts would almost certainly find all diabetics to be disabled, because if they failed to monitor their blood sugar levels and administer insulin, they would almost certainly be substantially limited in one or more major life activities. A diabetic whose illness does not impair his or her daily activities would therefore be considered disabled simply because he or she has diabetes. Thus, the guidelines approach would create a system in which persons often must be treated as members of a group of people with similar impairments, rather than as individuals. This is contrary to both the letter and the spirit of the ADA.

The guidelines approach could also lead to the anomalous result that in determining whether an individual is disabled, courts and employers could not consider any negative side effects suffered by an individual resulting from the use of mitigating measures, even when those side effects are very severe. This result is also inconsistent with the individualized approach of the ADA.

Finally, and critically, findings enacted as part of the ADA require the conclusion that Congress did not intend to bring under the statute's protection all those whose uncorrected conditions amount to disabilities. Congress found that "some 43,000,000 Americans have one or more physical or mental disabilities, and this number is increasing as the population as a whole is growing older." § 12101(a)(1). This figure is inconsistent with the definition of disability pressed by petitioners.

[As to the "likely source" of the 43,000,000 number cited in the 1990 statute, the Court stated that "the exact source of the 43 million figure is not clear" but concluded that it was probably based on a report of the National Council on Disability titled "On the Threshold of Independence" (1988). That report] stated that 37.3 million individuals have "difficulty performing one or more basic physical activities," including "seeing, hearing, speaking, walking, using stairs, lifting or carrying, getting around outside, getting around inside, and getting into or out of bed." Id. at 19. The study from which it drew this data took an explicitly functional approach to evaluating disabilities. See U.S. Dep't of Commerce, Bureau of Census, Disability, Functional Limitation, and Health Insurance Coverage: 1984/85, p. 2 (1986). . . . The 5.7 million gap between the 43 million figure in the ADA's findings and the 37.3 million figure in the report can . . . probably be explained as an effort to include in the findings those who were excluded from the National Council figure. . . .

Regardless of its exact source, however, the 43 million figure reflects an understanding that those whose impairments are largely corrected by medication or other devices are not "disabled" within the meaning of the ADA. The estimate is consistent with the numbers produced by studies performed during this same time period that took a similar functional approach to determining disability. . . . By contrast, nonfunctional approaches to defining disability produce significantly larger numbers. [T]he 1986 National Council on Disability report estimated that there were over 160 million disabled under the "health conditions approach." Toward Independence, at 10.

Because it is included in the ADA's text, the finding that 43 million individuals are disabled gives content to the ADA's terms, specifically the term "disability." Had Congress intended to include all persons with corrected physical limitations among those covered by the Act, it undoubtedly would have cited a much higher number of disabled persons in the findings. That it did not is evidence that the ADA's coverage is restricted to only those whose impairments are not mitigated by corrective measures.

The dissents suggest that viewing individuals in their corrected state will exclude from the definition of "disabled" those who use prosthetic limbs or take medicine for epilepsy or high blood pressure. This suggestion is incorrect. The use of a corrective device does not, by itself, relieve one's disability. Rather, one has a disability under subsection A if, notwithstanding the use of a corrective device, that individual is substantially limited in a major life activity. For example, individuals who use prosthetic limbs or wheelchairs may be mobile and capable of functioning in society but still be disabled because of a substantial limitation on their ability to walk or run. The same may be true of individuals who take medicine to lessen the symptoms of an impairment so that they can function but nevertheless remain substantially limited. Alternatively, one whose high blood pressure is "cured" by medication may be regarded as disabled by a covered entity, and thus disabled under subsection C of the definition. The use or non-use of a corrective device does not determine whether an individual is disabled; that determination depends on whether the limitations an individual with an impairment actually faces are in fact substantially limiting.

Applying this reading of the Act to the case at hand, we conclude that the Court of Appeals correctly resolved the issue of disability in respondent's favor. As noted above, petitioners allege that with corrective measures, their visual acuity is 20/20 and that they "function identically to individuals without a similar impairment." In addition, petitioners concede that they "do not argue that the use of corrective lenses in itself demonstrates a substantially limiting impairment." Accordingly, because we decide that disability under the Act is to be determined with reference to corrective measures, we agree with the courts below that petitioners have not stated a claim that they are substantially limited in any major life activity.

[The Court's discussion of whether the plaintiffs were "regarded as having a disability" is reproduced at page 716.]

Justice STEVENS, with whom Justice BREYER joins, dissenting.

When it enacted the Americans with Disabilities Act in 1990, Congress certainly did not intend to require United Air Lines to hire unsafe or unqualified pilots. Nor, in all likelihood, did it view every person who wears glasses as a member of a "discrete and insular minority." Indeed, by reason of legislative myopia it may not have foreseen that its definition of "disability" might theoretically encompass, not just "some 43,000,000 Americans," 42 U.S.C. § 12101(a)(1), but perhaps two or three times that number. Nevertheless, if we apply customary tools of statutory construction, it is quite clear that the threshold question whether an individual is "disabled" within the meaning of the Act — and, therefore, is entitled to the basic assurances that the Act affords — focuses on her past or present physical condition without regard to mitigation that has resulted from rehabilitation, self-improvement, prosthetic devices, or medication. One might reasonably argue that the general rule should not apply to an impairment that merely requires a nearsighted person to wear glasses. But I believe that, in order to be faithful to the remedial purpose of the Act, we should give it a generous, rather than a miserly, construction.

There are really two parts to the question of statutory construction presented by this case. The first question is whether the determination of disability for people that Congress unquestionably intended to cover should focus on their unmitigated or their mitigated condition. If the correct answer to that question is the one provided by eight of the nine Federal Courts of Appeals to address the issue, and by all three of the Executive agencies that have issued regulations or interpretive bulletins construing the statute — namely, that the statute defines "disability" without regard to ameliorative measures — it would still be necessary to decide whether that general rule should be applied to what might be characterized as a "minor, trivial impairment." Arnold v. United Parcel Service, Inc., 136 F.3d 854, 866, n. 10 (CA1 1998) (holding that unmitigated state is determinative but suggesting that it "might reach a different result" in a case in which "a simple, inexpensive remedy," such as eyeglasses, is available "that can provide total and relatively permanent control of all symptoms"). I shall therefore first consider impairments that Congress surely had in mind before turning to the special facts of this case.

I

. . . The three parts of [the definition of disability] do not identify mutually exclusive, discrete categories. On the contrary, they furnish three overlapping formulas aimed at ensuring that individuals who now have, or ever had, a substantially limiting impairment are covered by the Act.

An example of a rather common condition illustrates this point: There are many individuals who have lost one or more limbs in industrial accidents, or perhaps in the service of their country in places like Iwo Jima. With the aid of prostheses, coupled with courageous determination and physical therapy, many of these hardy individuals can perform all of their major life activities just as efficiently as an average couch potato. If the Act were just concerned with their present ability to participate in society, many of these individuals' physical impairments would not be viewed as disabilities. Similarly, if the statute were solely concerned with whether these individuals viewed themselves as disabled — or with whether a majority of employers regarded them as unable to perform most jobs — many of these individuals would lack statutory protection from discrimination based on their prostheses.

The sweep of the statute's three-pronged definition, however, makes it pellucidly clear that Congress intended the Act to cover such persons. The fact that a prosthetic device, such as an artificial leg, has restored one's ability to perform major life activities surely cannot mean that subsection (A) of the definition is inapplicable. Nor should the fact that the individual considers himself (or actually is) "cured," or that a prospective employer considers him generally employable, mean that subsections (B) or (C) are inapplicable. But under the Court's emphasis on "the present indicative verb form" used in subsection (A), that subsection presumably would not apply. And under the Court's focus on the individual's "present — not potential or hypothetical" — condition and on whether a person is "precluded from a broad range of jobs," subsections (B) and (C) presumably would not apply.

In my view, when an employer refuses to hire the individual "because of" his prosthesis, and the prosthesis in no way affects his ability to do the job, that employer has unquestionably discriminated against the individual in violation of the Act. Subsection (B) of the definition, in fact, sheds a revelatory light on the question whether Congress was concerned only about the corrected or mitigated status of a person's impairment. If the Court is correct that "[a] 'disability' exists only where" a person's "present" or "actual" condition is substantially impaired, there would be no reason to include in the protected class those who were once disabled but who are now fully recovered. Subsection (B) of the Act's definition, however, plainly covers a person who previously had a serious hearing impairment that has since been completely cured. See School Bd. of Nassau Cty. v. Arline. Still, if I correctly understand the Court's opinion, it holds that one who continues to wear a hearing aid that she has worn all her life might not be covered — fully cured impairments are covered, but merely treatable ones are not. The text of the Act surely does not require such a bizarre result.

The three prongs of the statute, rather, are most plausibly read together not to inquire into whether a person is currently "functionally" limited in a major life activity, but only into the existence of an impairment — present or past — that substantially limits, or did so limit, the individual before amelioration. This reading avoids the counterintuitive conclusion that the ADA's safeguards vanish when individuals make themselves more employable by ascertaining ways to overcome their physical or mental limitations. To the extent that there may be doubt concerning the meaning of the statutory text, ambiguity is easily removed by looking at the legislative history. . . .

The ADA originated in the Senate. The Senate Report states that "whether a person has a disability should be assessed without regard to the availability of mitigating measures, such as reasonable accommodations or auxiliary aids." S. Rep. No. 101-116, p. 23 (1989). The Report further explained, in discussing the "regarded as" prong:

> [An] important goal of the third prong of the [disability] definition is to ensure that persons with medical conditions that are under control, and that therefore do not currently limit major life activities, are not discriminated against on the basis of their medical conditions. For example, individuals with controlled diabetes or epilepsy are often denied jobs for which they are qualified. Such denials are the result of negative attitudes and misinformation.

When the legislation was considered in the House of Representatives, its Committees reiterated the Senate's basic understanding of the Act's coverage, with one minor modification: They clarified that "correctable" or "controllable" disabilities were covered in the first definitional prong as well. The Report of the House Committee on the Judiciary states, in discussing the first prong, that, when determining whether an individual's impairment substantially limits a major life activity, "the impairment should be assessed without considering whether mitigating measures, such as auxiliary aids or reasonable accommodations, would result in a less-than-substantial limitation." H. R. Rep. No. 101-485, pt. III, p. 28 (1990). The Report continues that "a person with epilepsy, an impairment which substantially limits a major life activity, is covered under this test," as is a person with poor hearing, "even if the hearing loss is corrected by the use of a hearing aid."

The Report of the House Committee on Education and Labor likewise states that "whether a person has a disability should be assessed without regard to the availability of mitigating measures, such as reasonable accommodations or auxiliary aids." To make matters perfectly plain, the Report adds:

> For example, a person who is hard of hearing is substantially limited in the major life activity of hearing, *even though the loss may be corrected through the use of a hearing aid.* Likewise, persons with impairments, such as epilepsy or diabetes, which substantially limit a major life activity are covered under the first prong of the definition of disability, *even if the effects of the impairment are controlled by medication.*

(Emphasis added.)

All of the Reports, indeed, are replete with references to the understanding that the Act's protected class includes individuals with various medical conditions that ordinarily are perfectly "correctable" with medication or treatment.

In addition, each of the three Executive agencies charged with implementing the Act has consistently interpreted the Act as mandating that the presence of disability turns on an individual's uncorrected state. . . . At the very least, these interpretations "constitute a body of experience and informed judgment to which [we] may properly resort" for additional guidance. Skidmore v. Swift & Co., 323 U.S. 134, 139-140 (1944). See also *Bragdon.* . . .

In my judgment, the Committee Reports and the uniform agency regulations merely confirm the message conveyed by the text of the Act — at least insofar as it applies to impairments such as the loss of a limb, the inability to hear, or any condition such as diabetes that is substantially limiting without medication. The Act generally protects individuals who have "correctable" substantially limiting impairments from unjustified employment discrimination on the basis of those impairments. The question, then, is whether the fact that Congress was specifically concerned about protecting a class that included persons characterized as a "discrete and insular minority" and that it estimated that class to include "some 43,000,000 Americans" means that we should construe the term "disability" to exclude individuals with impairments that Congress probably did not have in mind.

## II

. . . If a narrow reading of the term "disability" were necessary in order to avoid the danger that the Act might otherwise force United to hire pilots who might endanger the lives of their passengers, it would make good sense to use the "43,000,000 Americans" finding to confine its coverage. There is, however, no such danger in this case. If a person is "disabled" within the meaning of the Act, she still cannot prevail on a claim of discrimination unless she can prove that the employer took action "because of" that impairment, 42 U.S.C. § 12112(a), and that she can, "with or without reasonable accommodation, . . . perform the essential functions" of the job of a commercial airline pilot. See § 12111(8). Even then, an employer may avoid liability if it shows that the criteria of having uncorrected visual acuity of at least 20/100 is "job-related and consistent with business necessity" or if such vision (even if correctable to 20/20) would pose a health or safety hazard. §§ 12113(a) and (b).

This case, in other words, is not about whether petitioners are genuinely qualified or whether they can perform the job of an airline pilot without posing an undue safety risk. The case just raises the threshold question whether petitioners are members of the ADA's protected class. It simply asks whether the ADA lets petitioners in the door. . . . Inside that door lies nothing more than basic protection from irrational and unjustified discrimination because of a characteristic that is beyond a person's control. Hence, this particular case, at its core, is about whether, assuming that petitioners can prove that they are "qualified," the airline has any duty to come forward with some legitimate explanation for refusing to hire them because of their uncorrected eyesight, or whether the ADA leaves the airline free to decline to hire petitioners on this basis even if it is acting purely on the basis of irrational fear and stereotype.

I think it quite wrong for the Court to confine the coverage of the Act simply because an interpretation of "disability" that adheres to Congress' method of defining the class it intended to benefit may also provide protection for "significantly larger numbers" of individuals than estimated in the Act's findings. . . .

Accordingly, although I express no opinion on the ultimate merits of petitioners' claim, I am persuaded that they have a disability covered by the ADA. I therefore respectfully dissent.

Justice BREYER, dissenting.

We must draw a statutory line that either (1) will include within the category of persons authorized to bring suit under the Americans with Disabilities Act of 1990 some whom Congress may not have wanted to protect (those who wear ordinary eyeglasses), or (2) will exclude from the threshold category those whom Congress certainly did want to protect (those who successfully use corrective devices or medicines, such as hearing aids or prostheses or medicine for epilepsy). Faced with this dilemma, the statute's language, structure, basic purposes, and history require us to choose the former statutory line, as Justice Stevens (whose opinion I join) well explains. I would add that, if the more generous choice of threshold led to too many lawsuits that ultimately proved without merit or otherwise drew too much time and attention away from those whom Congress clearly sought to protect, there is a remedy. The Equal Employment Opportunity Commission (EEOC), through regulation, might draw finer definitional lines, excluding some of those who wear eyeglasses (say, those with certain vision impairments who readily can find corrective lenses), thereby cabining the overly broad extension of the statute that the majority fears.

The majority questions whether the EEOC could do so, for the majority is uncertain whether the EEOC possesses typical agency regulation-writing authority with respect to the statute's definitions. The majority poses this question because the section of the statute, 42 U.S.C. § 12116, that says the EEOC "shall issue regulations" also says these regulations are "to carry out *this subchapter*" (namely, § 12111 to § 12117, the employment subchapter); and the section of the statute that contains the three-pronged definition of "disability" precedes "this subchapter," the employment subchapter, to which § 12116 specifically refers. (Emphasis added.)

Nonetheless, the employment subchapter, i.e., "*this* subchapter," includes other provisions that use the defined terms, for example a provision that forbids "discriminating against a qualified individual with a disability because of the disability." § 12112(a). The EEOC might elaborate through regulations the meaning of "disability" in this last-mentioned provision, if elaboration is needed in order to "carry out" the substantive provisions of "this subchapter." An EEOC regulation that elaborated the meaning of this use of the word "disability" would fall within the scope both of the basic definitional provision and also the substantive provisions of "this" later subchapter, for the word "disability" appears in both places.

There is no reason to believe that Congress would have wanted to deny the EEOC the power to issue such a regulation, at least if the regulation is consistent with the earlier statutory definition and with the relevant interpretations by other enforcement agencies. The physical location of the definitional section seems to reflect only drafting or stylistic, not substantive, objectives. And to pick and choose among which of "this subchapter['s]" words the EEOC has the power to explain would inhibit the development of law that coherently interprets this important statute.

## NOTES

1.  On the question whether Congress intended to cover individuals whose impairments would be substantially limiting without treatment, who has the better argument, the majority or the dissent? Is the statute unambiguous on this issue? Is the EEOC's interpretation of the statute unreasonable? In footnote 3 of his dissent, Justice Stevens reminds the Court that in General Elec. Co. v. Gilbert (see pages 470-471), "the majority rejected an EEOC guideline and the heavy weight of authority in the federal courts of appeals in order to hold that Title VII did not prohibit discrimination on the basis of pregnancy-related conditions" only to be "swiftly 'overruled'" by Congress in the Pregnancy Discrimination Act of 1978. Has the Court misread congressional intent in *Sutton*? Remember that the question in this case is not whether the petitioners were qualified to fly but rather whether they are members of the ADA's protected class.

2.  In his article, Subordination, Stigma, and "Disability," 86 Va. L. Rev. 397 (2000), Samuel R. Bagenstos argues that a subordination-based approach to disability status would have been a preferable way of resolving both *Bragdon* and *Sutton*, although he believes the results in those cases would have been the same. He contends that disability should be understood as a "condition in which people — because of present, past, or perceived 'impairments' — are viewed as somehow outside of the

'norm' for which society's institutions are designed and therefore are likely to have systematically less opportunity to participate in important areas of public and private life." Id. at 401. "Rather than treating the statute as providing all-purpose protection against irrational or arbitrary conduct that is taken on the basis of a physical or mental condition, my approach ties the ADA's reasonable accommodation and antidiscrimination protections directly to the circumstances that justify them — circumstances where members of a subordinated group challenge the practices that enact and enforce their subordinated status." Id. at 452.

3. Does the Court's requirement that "a person be presently — not potentially or hypothetically — substantially limited in order to demonstrate a disability" resolve the question whether individuals with genetic predisposition for a disease are covered by the ADA? What about an individual stricken by multiple sclerosis in the early stages of the disease? What about an HIV-infected child too young to be sexually active? What would you argue on behalf of such individuals? See Sorensen v. University of Utah Hosp., 194 F.3d 1084 (10th Cir. 1999) (nurse diagnosed with multiple sclerosis not disabled because not currently substantially limited).

4. Murphy v. United Parcel Serv., 527 U.S. 516 (1999), decided the same day as *Sutton*, considered the disability discrimination claim of a mechanic dismissed from his job because of high blood pressure. The plaintiff asserted that the disability determination should be made without reference to the medication he took to control his blood pressure, a claim the Court rejected in light of its resolution of this issue in *Sutton*. Murphy, however, did not seek review of the lower court's conclusion that, when medicated, Murphy's high blood pressure did not substantially limit him in any major life activity. The Court therefore, did not consider "whether petitioner is 'disabled' due to limitations that persist despite his medication or the negative side effects of his medication." After *Sutton*, plaintiffs like Murphy must develop factual records to support that their impairment is substantially limiting even when controlled by medication. See Gordon v. E. L. Hamm & Assocs. Inc., 100 F.3d 907 (11th Cir. 1996) (medical conditions that necessitate disabling treatments may be "substantially limiting" within the meaning of the ADA); Christian v. St. Anthony Med. Ctr., 117 F.3d 1051 (7th Cir. 1997) (same).

5. If the effects of mitigating measures must be taken into account in assessing disability status, what happens if it is the medication that causes the impairment to substantially limit a major life activity? Remember that the court in *Bragdon* stated that "[r]eproduction and the sexual dynamics surrounding it are central to the life process itself." Many medications, including antidepressants such as Prozac, substantially impair sexual function. Are individuals who take such medications "disabled" under the ADA? See McAlindin v. County of San Diego, 192 F.3d 1226 (9th Cir. 1999) (factual issue exists as to whether an employee who suffers from panic disorder is substantially limited in major life activity of engaging in sexual relations because he has testified that he is impotent as a result of medications he is taking). If so, would not far more than 43 million individuals be covered by the ADA?

6. Should an individual be covered by the ADA if his impairment is substantially limiting only because he fails to control an otherwise controllable illness such as diabetes or a psychiatric disorder? See Siefken v. Village of Arlington Heights, 65 F.3d 664 (7th Cir. 1995) (no; diabetes); Van Stan v. Fancy Colours & Co., 125 F.3d 563 (7th Cir. 1997) (no; bipolar disorder). See Sarah Shaw, Comment, Why Courts Cannot Deny ADA Protection to Plaintiffs Who Do Not Use Available Mitigating Measures for Their Impairments, 90 Cal. L. Rev. 1981 (2002). Does *Sutton* suggest that a diabetic who is careless about monitoring his or her sugar level is disabled, while a well-controlled diabetic is not?

7. In Albertsons, Inc. v. Kirkingburg, reproduced at page 769, decided the same day as *Sutton*, the plaintiff had monocular vision, but his brain had subconsciously adjusted to the impairment. Although the Ninth Circuit had ignored the impact of those adjustments, the Court held that a body's coping mechanisms that mitigate an impairment must be considered in assessing disability status. "We see no principled basis for distinguishing between measures undertaken with artificial aids, like medications and devices, and measures undertaken, whether consciously or not, with the body's own systems." Id. at 565.

8. The *Kirkingburg* Court also criticized the Ninth Circuit's determination that monocular vision was a per se disability, emphasizing, as it had in *Sutton*, the need for a case-by-case determination of whether a disability exists. *Kirkingburg* makes clear that even impairments that seem obviously disabling must be examined on a case-by-case basis to determine if they are, in fact, substantially limiting. The Court also indicated that this decision must be based on detailed medical evidence, specific to the individual, demonstrating the precise way in which an impairment substantially limits major life activities. For a critique of the Court's insistence on an individualized determination of disability status, see Wendy E. Parmet, Individual Rights and Class Discrimination: The Fallacy of an Individualized Determination of Disability, 9 Temp. Pol. & Civ. Rts. L. Rev. 283 (2000).

9. *Kirkingburg* states, on the other hand, that individuals with monocular vision do not have "an onerous burden" to show that they are disabled. Is the Court saying that some impairments obviously are substantially limiting and therefore require little evidence to support a finding of disability? But see EEOC v. United Parcel Serv., Inc., 306 F.3d 794 (9th Cir. 2002) (monocular vision did not substantially limit major life activity of seeing).

10. Can workplace accommodations be taken into account in determining whether an individual's disability substantially limits his ability to work? See Black v. Roadway Express, Inc., 297 F.3d 445 (6th Cir. 2002) (no).

### NOTE ON DEFERENCE TO THE EEOC

The EEOC is a federal administrative agency charged with the administration and enforcement of Title VII, the ADEA, and the ADA. Importantly, each of these statutes requires a complaining party to file charges with the EEOC prior to filing suit. The EEOC enforcement process is explored in Chapter 9. Additionally, we have seen in a number of cases that the EEOC may be a plaintiff in Title VII litigation, bringing suit on behalf of workers it contends are victims of discrimination.

To what extent, however, is the EEOC entitled to meaningful deference from the courts in its *interpretation* of the statutes it administers? This question was presented to, but not answered by, the Court in *Sutton*. As we have seen in earlier chapters, the Court's willingness to defer to EEOC interpretations of Title VII's substantive provisions has been limited. Although Congress gave the EEOC the power to issue procedural regulations under Title VII, it withheld from the agency the power to issue substantive regulations under that statute. See United States v. Mead Corp., 533 U.S. 218 (2001); General Elec. Co. v. Gilbert, 429 U.S. 125, 140-42 (1976) (Because "Congress . . . did not confer upon the EEOC authority to promulgate rules or regulations," the level of deference afforded depends on "the thoroughness evident in its consideration, the validity of its reasoning, its consistency with earlier and later pronouncements, and all those factors which give it power to persuade, if lacking power to control.").

The issue of deference to the EEOC has taken on considerable importance under the Americans with Disabilities Act. What judicial deference, if any, is due the regulations, Interpretive Guidances, and other materials promulgated by the agencies charged with administration and enforcement of the ADA? Congress was aware when it enacted the ADA that considerable uncertainty over the rights and obligations conferred by the statute would exist, and it charged various agencies with authority to promulgate regulations to carry out particular subchapters.

Title I of the ADA confers substantive rule-making authority on the EEOC. The statute directs that "Not later than one year after July 26, 1990, the Commission shall issue regulations in an accessible format to carry out this subchapter in accordance with [the Administrative Procedure Act.]" 42 U.S.C.S. § 12116 (2003). The EEOC carried out that mandate, issuing regulations promulgated after notice and comment. The regulations contained as an appendix an Interpretive Guidance.

The Supreme Court's decision in Bragdon v. Abbott, reproduced at page 680, suggested the Court not only was willing to adopt an expansive approach to the definition of disability but also was willing to allow agencies a leading role in interpreting the statute. However, the Court's deference to the HEW regulations in *Bragdon* was a product of Congress's directive that the ADA be interpreted in accordance with those regulations. The Court was more equivocal when it came to deferring to agency pronouncements issued under the ADA, declining to decide what level of deference such pronouncements were due.

In Sutton v. United Air Lines, Inc., the question of what deference was due the EEOC's Interpretive Guidance was presented to the Court. The EEOC's Interpretive Guidance provided that an impairment was to be assessed in its unmitigated state in determining whether a disability was present. The EEOC, backed by the Justice Department, urged the Court to defer to its interpretation. The lower courts had disagreed over whether that particular interpretation was deserving of deference. See Washington v. HCA Health Servs. of Tex., Inc., 152 F.3d 464 (5th Cir. 1998); Harris v. H & W Contracting Co., 102 F.3d 516 (11th Cir. 1996); Jonathan Bridges, Note, Mitigating Measures Under the Americans with Disabilities Act: Interpretational Deference in the Judicial Process, 74 Notre Dame L. Rev. 1061 (1999).

In Chevron U.S.A., Inc. v. Natural Resources Defense Council, Inc., 467 U.S. 837 (1984), the Supreme Court recognized that agency interpretations of silent or ambiguous statutes are due deference from the courts when Congress has delegated law-interpreting power to the agency. More recently, in United States v. Mead Corp., 533 U.S. 218 (2001), the Court explained when such an implied delegation would be found. A delegation of rule-making or adjudicative authority to an agency will support an implied delegation of interpretive authority. Other comparable indicia may also support an implied delegation of interpretive authority. *Chevron* review will attach to such an agency's statutory interpretations, if the agency was exercising that authority when it promulgated the interpretation for which deference is claimed. Even when an agency has not been delegated interpretive authority, however, its interpretations of the statutes it administers still will merit attention from the courts. Such interpretations may be given persuasive authority, depending on "the thoroughness evident in its consideration, the validity of its reasoning, its consistency with earlier and later pronouncements, and all [other] factors which give it power to persuade, if lacking power to control." Skidmore v. Swift & Co., 323 U.S. 134 (1944). This level of deference is referred to as *Skidmore* deference.

In *Sutton*, the EEOC contended its position on the mitigating measures question was deserving of heightened deference under *Chevron*. But the Supreme Court refused to defer to the agency's interpretation. It did so by finding the EEOC's interpretation was an impermissible interpretation of the statute because it was inconsistent with the statutory text. Under *Chevron*, a reviewing court will not defer to an agency's construction of a statute if it finds that Congress itself has spoken to the precise question at issue. In such cases, no implied delegation has occurred since Congress itself has made the policy choice. The *Sutton* Court, through its textualist approach, appeared to find that Congress had determined impairments are to be assessed in their mitigated state.

In rejecting the EEOC's Interpretive Guidance as an impermissible interpretation of the ADA, the Court was able to sidestep difficult, but important, questions concerning the EEOC's role in the interpretation of the ADA. Even if the *Sutton* Court had conceded ambiguity in the statutory definition, it is not clear it would have deferred to the EEOC's interpretation. That is because the Court noted that the definition of disability is not contained within Title I but instead is in the generally applicable provisions of the Act. Although the EEOC was given authority to issue regulations carrying out Title I, "no agency has been delegated authority to interpret the term 'disability.'" Thus, the Court questioned, although it did not decide, whether the EEOC's extensive regulations and Interpretive Guidance addressing what constitutes a disability were entitled to any deference at all. The suggestion of Justice Breyer's dissent that the EEOC's authority to interpret the term "qualified individual with a disability" necessarily carried with it the authority to determine what constitutes a disability was dismissed as "an imaginative interpretation of the Act's delegation provisions."

Another complicating factor in *Sutton* was that the EEOC's position on mitigating measures was found not in the text of the regulation itself, but in the Appendix accompanying the regulations. That appendix, however, had also been subject to notice and comment proceedings. The Court noted, but did not resolve, the format issue. See Christensen v. Harris County, 529 U.S. 576 (2000) (*Chevron* deference not due Labor Department opinion letter). In other words, the Court may be willing to extend *Chevron* deference to the EEOC's disability regulations but not to its Interpretive Guidance. Accordingly, *Sutton* throws up in the air the question of whether courts need pay any attention at all to the EEOC's interpretation of "disability." But *Mead* suggests that even if such interpretations are not deserving of *Chevron* deference, they should at least be entitled to deference under *Skidmore*.

It is important, however, to distinguish the interpretive issue presented in *Sutton* from interpretive questions arising from provisions of Title I itself. Issues concerning what constitutes an essential job function, a reasonable accommodation, an undue hardship, or a direct threat, for example, would implicate the terms of Title I, where a delegation of interpretive authority to the EEOC clearly exists. Even if the EEOC has not been delegated interpretive authority over the definition of disability, it has been delegated authority to interpret the provisions of Title I itself. Accordingly, its regulations, and perhaps the Appendix to those regulations, interpreting that subchapter are entitled to analysis under *Chevron*. Recognizing this point, the Supreme Court deferred, under *Chevron*, to an EEOC regulation interpreting "direct threat" in Chevron U.S.A., Inc. v. Echazabal, 536 U.S. 73 (2002), reproduced at page 760.

The EEOC also has issued various other interpretations in even more informal forms. Its Compliance Manual sets forth Enforcement Guidances, and it also has promulgated a Technical Assistance Manual. Although the failure to follow notice and comment procedures presumably deprives these interpretations of deference under *Chevron*, they still are entitled to deference under a *Skidmore* review standard.

For further discussion of the deference due the EEOC in interpreting the statutes it administers, see generally Rebecca Hanner White, Deference and Disability Discrimination, 99 Mich. L. Rev. 532 (2000); Barbara Hoffman, Reports of Its Death Were Highly Exaggerated: The EEOC Regulations that Define "Disability" Under the ADA After *Sutton v. United Air Lines*, 9 Temp. Pol. & Civ. Rts. L. Rev. 253 (2000); Rebecca Hanner White, The EEOC, the Courts, and Employment Discrimination Policy: Recognizing the Agency's Leading Role in Statutory Interpretation, 1995 Utah L. Rev. 51; Theodore W. Wern, Note, Judicial Deference to EEOC Interpretations of the Civil Rights Act, the ADA and the ADEA: Is the EEOC a Second Class Agency?, 60 Ohio St. L.J. 1533 (1999).

## PROBLEM 8.1

Sarah Smith is an assembly line worker who is diabetic and dependant on insulin injections to maintain her glucose level. She must inject up to four times a day to maintain ideal glucose levels. If her glucose level drops too low, she will become hypoglycemic and go into a coma. If her glucose level is too high, it will cause long-term physical deterioration of numerous body systems. Eating increases glucose levels, so Sarah needs to inject one half-hour before eating larger meals. Her doctor has recommended that she eat smaller and more frequent meals to help her modulate variations in her glucose levels. Outside of work, Sarah leads an active life and exercises regularly. She must be careful to time her injections depending on her exercise and eating patterns. Exercise reduces glucose levels on a short-term basis and can upset the balance of insulin and glucose in the body, possibly resulting in a hypoglycemic reaction. Because Sarah is careful about her eating, exercise, and treatment regimen, her diabetes is reasonably well controlled. She does not yet exhibit any physical damage related to excess glucose levels. She carries small amounts of sugar with her to minimize the incidence of hypoglycemic reactions. Assembly line workers operate on a very rigid schedule. Sarah wants to seek accommodations from her employer to make it easier for her to maintain her glucose levels while at work. Is Sarah an individual with a disability under the ADA? See, e.g., Nawrot v. CPC Intl., 277 F.3d 896 (7th Cir. 2002) (finding diabetic plaintiff to be a qualified individual with a disability where even with medication his ability to think and to care for himself was substantially limited and raising but not resolving whether not permitting plaintiff to take short breaks to monitor and adjust his blood sugar violated the duty of reasonable accommodation).

## PROBLEM 8.2

Serum alpha-1 antitrypsin (SAT) is a serum protein that protects the lungs from proteolytic enzymes. Approximately 80 percent of individuals who inherit an SAT deficiency from both parents develop chronic obstructive pulmonary disease (COPD). Individuals who inherit the deficiency from only one parent have an increased risk of developing COPD (1 in 10), especially if they smoke or work in dusty environments. Tuan, who inherited SAT deficiency from both of his parents, does not yet suffer from any symptoms of COPD. Is Tuan impaired? Is he substantially limited with respect to a major life activity and, therefore, protected under the ADA?

## 2. *Record of Such an Impairment*

Section 3(2) of the ADA defines disability to include having a record of an impairment that substantially limits a major life activity. A variety of records contain such information, including employment records, medical records, and education records. In light of *Sutton*, individuals with impairments that, as a result of successful treatment, are not currently substantially limiting may seek to establish that they are protected by the ADA based on a "record" of an impairment. However, "[t]he impairment indicated in the record must be an impairment that would substantially limit one or more of the individual's major life activities." 29 C.F.R. pt. 1630, app. § 1630.2(k). See Colwell v. Suffolk County Police Dept., 158 F.3d 635, 645 (2d Cir. 1998) (hospitalization for cerebral hemorrhage was too vague and too short to be record of impairment); Davidson v. Midelfort Clinic, Ltd., 133 F.3d 499, 510 n.7 (7th Cir. 1998) (no record of impairment found); Sherrod v. American Airlines, Inc., 132 F.3d 1112, 1120-21 (5th Cir. 1998) (hospitalization for back surgery did not substantially limit a major life activity).

What evidence is necessary to meet this requirement? Numerous courts have held that impairments resulting in hospitalization and subsequent extended recuperation do not constitute substantially limiting impairments (or records of such impairments) in the absence of some chronic long-term impact. See Horwitz v. L & J. G. Stickley, Inc., 2001 U.S. App. LEXIS 21866 (2d Cir. 2001) (hospitalization for bipolar disorder, followed by six weeks in psychiatric center and receipt of SSDI benefits insufficient to establish a "record of" claim); Hilburn v. Murata Elecs. No. Am., Inc., 181 F.3d 1220 (11th Cir. 1999) (absences from work of 38 days, 14 days, 13 days, and 15 days in four consecutive years for heart problems did not establish a record of a substantially limiting impairment); *Colwell*, 158 F.3d at 646 (one-month hospital stay followed by six-month home recuperation, followed by non-particularized limitations upon return to work did not establish a record of a substantially limiting impairment); Sanders v. Arneson Prods. Inc., 91 F.3d 1351, 1354 (9th Cir. 1996) (three-and-a-half-month impairment with minimal residual effects not substantially limiting); 29 C.F.R. pt. 1630, app. § 1630.2(j) ("temporary, non-chronic impairments of short duration, with little or no long term or permanent impact, are usually not disabilities").

Are these decisions consistent with *Arline*? In *Arline*, the Court stated that Arline's tuberculosis "was serious enough to require hospitalization, a fact more than sufficient to establish that one or more of her major life activities were substantially limited." Consider the following analysis from the Fifth Circuit:

> [*Arline*] cannot be construed to obviate the requirement, explicit in the ADA and its implementing regulations, that purported conditions be examined to ascertain whether a specific condition substantially limited a major life activity. The ADA requires an individualized inquiry beyond the mere existence of a hospital stay. Although the Court in *Arline* noted that the plaintiff's hospitalization established a record of impairment, the defendant had conceded that her acute tuberculosis had been substantially limiting. . . . [The contrary reading of *Arline*] would work a presumption that any condition requiring temporary hospitalization is disabling — a presumption that runs counter to the very goal of the ADA.

Burch v. Coca-Cola Co., 119 F.3d 305, 317 (5th Cir. 1997). See also Colwell v. Suffolk County Police Dept., 158 F.3d 635, 645 (2d Cir. 1998); Gutridge v. Clure, 153 F.3d 898, 901 (8th Cir. 1998) ("Unfortunately, the Court in *Arline* offered little detail regarding the teacher's actual length of hospital stay or the severity of her affliction. Thus, we find *Arline* to offer little guidance.").

The EEOC has taken the position that the ADA "protects former cancer patients from discrimination on the basis of their prior medical history." 29 C.F.R. § 1630.2. Is this regulation consistent with *Sutton's* and *Kirkingburg's* emphasis on individualized inquiry into substantial limitations? See EEOC v. R. J. Gallagher Co., 181 F.3d 645 (5th Cir. 1999) (remanding for individualized inquiry into actual effects of cancer patient's impairment). For a discussion of how the ADA's definition of "disability" treats cancer survivors, with a particular focus on breast cancer survivors, see Jane Byeff Korn, Cancer and the ADA: Rethinking Disability, 74 S. Cal. L. Rev. 399 (2001). See also Barbara Hoffman, Between a Disability and a Hard Place: The Cancer Survivors' Catch-22 of Proving Disability Status Under the Americans with Disabilities Act, 59 Md. L. Rev. 352 (2000) (arguing the ADA should be more inclusive of cancer survivors).

Following *Sutton*, will individuals with learning disabilities be able to establish ADA coverage? Establishing coverage for such individuals is particularly difficult if, through prior accommodations, treatment, and persistence, they have succeeded in compiling an adequate or even excellent educational record. The Seventh Circuit addressed this problem in Davidson v. Midelfort Clinic, Ltd., 133 F.3d 499 (7th Cir. 1998). Davidson was terminated from her position as a psychotherapist. Her employer's principal complaint was a backlog of uncompleted dictation. Davidson sued, claiming failure to accommodate her Adult Residual Attention Deficit Hyperactivity Disorder ("ADD"). Davidson had successfully completed undergraduate and graduate degrees. The Seventh Circuit remanded the case because

> we believe that she has presented enough evidence to raise a question of fact as to whether or not she has a "record" of an impairment that would qualify as a disability. It is undisputed that throughout high school, college, and graduate school, Davidson confronted impediments (later attributed to ADD) to her ability to learn — difficulties focusing in the classroom and assimilating new material, to cite two prominent examples. . . . [S]he has identified the ways in which her learning-related limitations manifested themselves, as well as the ways in which she compensated for them, with enough specificity that one can reasonably infer that her burdens were distinct from that of the average student. For example, we do not imagine that the average person in the general population finds it necessary to dictate one's school notes and then write them out again by hand, or to write out the passages she has just read in a textbook, in order to assimilate the information. A factfinder could reasonably conclude from the evidence before us that Davidson has a history of an impairment substantially limiting her ability to learn. See 2 EEOC Compliance Manual P 6887, § 902.7(b), at 5324.

Id. at 510.

Davidson's situation raises at least three additional questions concerning individuals who establish coverage under the ADA by demonstrating a record of a substantially limiting impairment. First, are such individuals entitled to reasonable accommodations relating to continuing nonsubstantial limitations associated with their impairment? The Seventh Circuit raised, but did not resolve, this question:

> The precise scope of the "record of impairment" prong of the statute is not entirely clear as it relates to the right to demand reasonable accommodations of the employer. A person with a recurring condition — a flare-up of tuberculosis, for example — might be able to show that she qualifies as disabled under the ADA based on her previous

hospitalization for that disease and is thus entitled to reasonable accommodation vis-à-vis any limitations that may result from the recurrence. E.g., *Arline*. But does the employer incur a duty to accommodate an employee based on her history of a substantially limiting impairment, even if her current limitations are not substantial? If so, the "record of impairment" provision grants the ADA a significantly broader sweep than it would otherwise have.

Id. at 509, n.6. The second question is whether, as a prerequisite to liability, the employer must be aware of the record of impairment that forms the basis of the plaintiff's claim that he or she is "disabled." Id. at 510 n.8 (yes) (citing 29 C.F.R. pt. 1630, app. § 1630.2(k)). The third question is whether the employer, in order to be liable, must discriminate based on the record of disability rather than on the basis of continuing nonsubstantial limitations. Reconsider *Arline*.

### PROBLEM 8.3

Reconsider Problems 8.1 and 8.2. Could you make a "record of impairment" argument on behalf of Sarah or Tuan?

## 3.  *Regarded As Having Such an Impairment*

### SUTTON v. UNITED AIR LINES, INC.
#### 527 U.S. 471 (1999)

[The facts of this case are found at page 699.]

#### IV

Our conclusion that petitioners have failed to state a claim that they are actually disabled under subsection (A) of the disability definition does not end our inquiry. Under subsection (C), individuals who are "regarded as" having a disability are disabled within the meaning of the ADA. See § 12102(2)(C). Subsection (C) provides that having a disability includes "being regarded as having," § 12102(2)(C), "a physical or mental impairment that substantially limits one or more of the major life activities of such individual," § 12102(2)(A). There are two apparent ways in which individuals may fall within this statutory definition: (1) a covered entity mistakenly believes that a person has a physical impairment that substantially limits one or more major life activities, or (2) a covered entity mistakenly believes that an actual, non-limiting impairment substantially limits one or more major life activities. In both cases, it is necessary that a covered entity entertain misperceptions about the individual — it must believe either that one has a substantially limiting impairment that one does not have or that one has a substantially limiting impairment when, in fact, the impairment is not so limiting. These misperceptions often "result from stereotypic assumptions not truly indicative of . . . individual ability." See 42 U.S.C. § 12101(7).

There is no dispute that petitioners are physically impaired. Petitioners do not make the obvious argument that they are regarded due to their impairments as substantially limited in the major life activity of seeing. They contend only that respondent mistakenly believes their physical impairments substantially limit them in the major life activity of working. To support this claim, petitioners allege that respondent has a vision requirement, which is allegedly based on myth and stereotype. Further, this requirement substantially limits their ability to engage in the major life activity of working by precluding them from obtaining the job of global airline pilot, which they argue is a "class of employment." In reply, respondent argues that the position of global airline pilot is not a class of jobs and therefore petitioners have not stated a claim that they are regarded as substantially limited in the major life activity of working.

Standing alone, the allegation that respondent has a vision requirement in place does not establish a claim that respondent regards petitioners as substantially limited in the major life activity of working. By its terms, the ADA allows employers to prefer some physical attributes over others and to establish physical criteria. An employer runs afoul of the ADA when it makes an employment decision based on a physical or mental impairment, real or imagined, that is regarded as substantially limiting a major life activity. Accordingly, an employer is free to decide that physical characteristics or medical conditions that do not rise to the level of an impairment — such as one's height, build, or singing voice — are preferable to others, just as it is free to decide that some limiting, but not substantially limiting, impairments make individuals less than ideally suited for a job.

Considering the allegations of the amended complaint in tandem, petitioners have not stated a claim that respondent regards their impairment as substantially limiting their ability to work. The ADA does not define "substantially limits," but "substantially" suggests "considerable" or "specified to a large degree." See Webster's Third New International Dictionary 2280 (1976) (defining "substantially" as "in a substantial manner" and "substantial" as "considerable in amount, value, or worth" and "being that specified to a large degree or in the main"). The EEOC has codified regulations interpreting the term "substantially limits" in this manner, defining the term to mean "unable to perform" or "significantly restricted." See 29 CFR §§ 1630.2(j)(1)(i),(ii) (1998).

When the major life activity under consideration is that of working, the statutory phrase "substantially limits" requires, at a minimum, that plaintiffs allege they are unable to work in a broad class of jobs. Reflecting this requirement, the EEOC uses a specialized definition of the term "substantially limits" when referring to the major life activity of working:

> significantly restricted in the ability to perform either a class of jobs or a broad range of jobs in various classes as compared to the average person having comparable training, skills and abilities. The inability to perform a single, particular job does not constitute a substantial limitation in the major life activity of working.

§ 1630.2(j)(3)(i). The EEOC further identifies several factors that courts should consider when determining whether an individual is substantially limited in the major life activity of working, including the geographical area to which the individual has reasonable access, and "the number and types of jobs utilizing similar training, knowledge, skills or abilities, within the geographical area, from which the individual is also disqualified." §§ 1630.2(j)(3)(ii)(A), (B). To be substantially limited in the major life activity of working, then, one must be precluded from more than one type of job, a specialized job, or a particular job of choice. If jobs utilizing an individual's skills (but perhaps not his or her unique talents) are available, one is not precluded from a substantial class of jobs. Similarly, if a host of different types of jobs are available, one is not precluded from a broad range of jobs.

Because the parties accept that the term "major life activities" includes working, we do not determine the validity of the cited regulations. We note, however, that there may be some conceptual difficulty in defining "major life activities" to include work, for it seems "to argue in a circle to say that if one is excluded, for instance, by reason of [an impairment, from working with others] . . . then that exclusion constitutes an impairment, when the question you're asking is, whether the exclusion itself is by reason of handicap." Tr. of Oral Argument in [*Arline*] (argument of Solicitor General). Indeed, even the EEOC has expressed reluctance to define "major life activities" to include working and has suggested that working be viewed as a residual life activity, considered, as a last resort, *only* "if an individual is not substantially limited with respect to *any other* major life activity." 29 CFR pt. 1630, App. § 1630.2(j) (1998) (emphasis added).

Assuming without deciding that working is a major life activity and that the EEOC regulations interpreting the term "substantially limits" are reasonable, petitioners have failed to allege adequately that their poor eyesight is regarded as an impairment that substantially limits them in the major life activity of working. They allege only that respondent regards their poor vision as precluding them from holding positions as a "global airline pilot." Because the position of global airline pilot is a single job, this allegation does not support the claim that respondent regards petitioners as having a substantially limiting impairment. See 29 CFR § 1630.2(j)(3)(i) ("The inability to perform a single, particular job does not constitute a substantial limitation in the major life activity of working"). Indeed, there are a number of other positions utilizing petitioners' skills, such as regional pilot and pilot instructor to name a few, that are available to them. Even under the EEOC's Interpretative Guidance, to which petitioners ask us to defer, "an individual who cannot be a commercial airline pilot because of a minor vision impairment, but who can be a commercial airline co-pilot or a pilot for a courier service, would not be substantially limited in the major life activity of working." 29 CFR pt. 1630, App. § 1630.2.

Petitioners also argue that if one were to assume that a substantial number of airline carriers have similar vision requirements, they would be substantially limited in the major life activity of working. Even assuming for the sake of argument that the adoption of similar vision requirements by other carriers would represent a substantial limitation on the major life activity of working, the argument is nevertheless flawed. It is not enough to say that if the physical criteria of a single employer were *imputed* to all similar employers one would be regarded as substantially limited in the major life activity of working *only as a result of this imputation*. An otherwise valid job requirement, such as a height requirement, does not become invalid simply because it would limit a person's employment opportunities in a substantial way if it were adopted by a substantial number of employers. Because petitioners have not alleged, and cannot demonstrate, that respondent's vision requirement reflects a belief that petitioners' vision substantially limits them, we agree with the decision of the Court of Appeals affirming the dismissal of petitioners' claim that they are regarded as disabled.

*NOTES*

1. The Court's analysis of the plaintiffs' claim that they were regarded as substantially limited with respect to working is consistent with the EEOC regulations insofar as the Court requires the plaintiffs to establish that they were regarded as excluded

from "either a class of jobs or a broad range of jobs" as compared to persons with "comparable training, skills and abilities." The opinion also rests comfortably within the EEOC's Interpretive Guidance in concluding that the plaintiffs were not substantially limited with respect to working because other airline positions were open to them.

2. How does the Court conclude that the plaintiffs were not *regarded as* substantially limited with respect to working? Reread the last paragraph of the opinion. What evidence would be necessary to satisfy the Court that an employer *regarded* an applicant as substantially limited with respect to working?

3. What is a broad class or range of jobs? In Giordano v. City of New York, 274 F.3d 740 (2d Cir. 2001), the court held plaintiff had not shown he was regarded as being substantially limited in his ability to work. His employer regarded him as unable to perform police or other investigative work that involved a risk of physical confrontation, and he thus had no evidence he was regarded as being unable to work in a broad class of jobs. Do you agree? Is fire fighting a class of jobs? See Bridges v. City of Bossier, 92 F.3d 329 (5th Cir. 1996) (no). Is law enforcement? See McKenzie v. Dovola, 242 F.3d 967 (10th Cir. 2001) (yes).

4. Location may play a role in determining whether an employee is substantially limited with respect to working. In Fjellestad v. Pizza Hut, 188 F.3d 944 (8th Cir. 1999), the court indicated that the rural nature of the area where Fjellestad lived and worked contributed to limiting her work options following injuries sustained in an automobile accident. Does it make sense to say that whether an individual is protected by the ADA depends on where she lives?

5. Note that the *Sutton* Court reserves the question whether "working" is a major life activity under the ADA, and the *Toyota* Court reserved the question as well. The Court's comments in *Sutton* suggest that the Court may not accept as "major" *all* of the activities, including working, listed in the regulations. Other activities defined as major in the EEOC's regulations include "caring for oneself, performing manual tasks, walking, seeing, hearing, speaking, breathing, [and] learning." 29 C.F.R. § 1630.2(i). Could it be argued that any of these listed activities are *not* "major life activities"? Could a holding that they are not be squared with Congress's directive that the ADA standards be no less protective that regulations adopted under the Rehabilitation Act. 42 U.S.C.S. § 12201(a) (2003). See *Bragdon*, reproduced at page 680. Those regulations include working as a major life activity. For an argument that working is a major life activity under the ADA, see Mark C. Rahdert, *Arline's* Ghost: Some Notes on Working as a Major Life Activity Under the ADA, 9 Temp. Pol. & Civ. Rts. L. Rev. 303 (2000).

6. In Murphy v. United Parcel Serv., 527 U.S. 516 (1999), the plaintiff was denied DOT certification to drive a commercial truck because of his high blood pressure. UPS dismissed Murphy from his job because he could not obtain the DOT certification. The Court held that the defendant did not regard Murphy as substantially limited in the activity of working but only regarded Murphy as unable to perform mechanics' jobs that required driving a commercial motor vehicle (defined as a vehicle weighing over 10,000 pounds, designed to carry 16 or more passengers, or used in the transportation of hazardous materials). See also EEOC v. J.B. Hunt Transport Inc., 2003 U.S. App. LEXIS 1966 (2d Cir. 2003) (employer policy precluding employment of persons taking certain prescription drugs not unlawful since employer only regarded individuals as unable to work in a very specific category of jobs — over the road truck driver).

7. Is coverage dependent on the perceived disability at least meeting the statutory definition of impairment? The First Circuit in Cook v. Rhode Island Dept. of Mental Health, 10 F.3d 17, 25 (1st Cir. 1993), suggested that an individual with turquoise eyes would be covered under the "regarded as" provision if an employer regarded

people with blue eyes as incapable of lifting heavy weights. Is this correct? Addressing allegations of discrimination on the basis of weight, both the Second and the Sixth Circuits have held that plaintiffs claiming perceived disability must establish that the defendant perceived an impairment as defined by the statute. See Andrews v. Ohio, 104 F.3d 803 (6th Cir. 1997); Francis v. City of Meriden, 129 F.3d 281 (2d Cir. 1997). The Sixth Circuit concluded, "The officers have not alleged that Ohio perceives them to have any *impairment.* That is, they have not alleged a weight or fitness status which is other than a mere, indeed possibly transitory, physical characteristic; they have not alleged a status which is the result of a physiological condition or otherwise beyond the range of "normal." *Andrews,* 104 F.3d at 810. See also Richards v. City of Topeka, 173 F.3d 1247 (10th Cir. 1999) (employer who "regarded" pregnancy as an impairment did not regard employee as disabled).

8. Reconsider ADA coverage for individuals with a genetic propensity for disease. The EEOC's Compliance Manual, § 902: Definition of the Term "Disability," states:

> Covered entities that discriminate against individuals on the basis of . . . genetic information are regarding the individuals as having impairments that substantially limit a major life activity. Those individuals, therefore, are covered by the third part of the definition of "disability." See 136 Cong. Rec. H4623 (daily ed. July 12, 1990) (statement of Rep. Owens); id. at H4624-25 (statement of Rep. Edwards); id. at H4627 (statement of Rep. Waxman).

Is the EEOC's position consistent with *Sutton?*

9. Part (2) of the ADA regulations defining "regarded as impaired" allows a plaintiff with a physical or mental impairment to argue that the impairment is substantially limiting "as a result of the attitudes of others toward such impairment." The Interpretive Guidance further explains this provision:

> For example, an individual may have a prominent facial scar or disfigurement, or may have a condition that periodically causes an involuntary jerk of the head but does not limit the individual's major life activities. If an employer discriminates against such an individual because of the negative reactions of customers, the employer would be regarding the individual as disabled and acting on the basis of that perceived disability.

29 C.F.R. pt. 1630, app. § 1630.2(*l*). Is this regulation consistent with *Sutton?* Reconsider discrimination based on obesity. Could Cook have established her case under part (2) of the "regarded as" provisions? See Jane B. Korn, Fat, 77 B.U. L. Rev. 25 (1997); Karen M. Kramer & Arlene B. Mayerson, Obesity Discrimination in the Workplace: Protection Through a Perceived Disability Claim Under the Rehabilitation Act and the Americans with Disabilities Act, 31 Cal. W. L. Rev. 41 (1994).

10. Lower courts have also given a limited reading to the ADA's "regarded as" provision. For example, Stewart v. County of Brown, 86 F.3d 107 (7th Cir. 1996), declined to find that a deputy sheriff was regarded as having a substantially limiting mental illness despite evidence that the deputy sheriff's employer referred to him as "excitable," ordered psychological evaluations for him, and told third parties that he considered him to be emotionally or psychologically imbalanced. How would you prove that an employer regarded an employee as psychologically disabled?

11. However, plaintiffs have prevailed in "regarded as" claims when there is evidence that an employer is acting on the basis of bias, prejudice, or stereotypes. For example, in Brown v. Lester E. Cox Medical Center, 286 F.3d 1040 (8th Cir. 2002), a jury verdict in favor of plaintiff on her claim that her employer regarded her as

disabled was upheld when there was evidence that the employer regarded plaintiff's multiple sclerosis as substantially limiting her ability to think. The court rejected the employer's argument that it regarded plaintiff as only below average for a surgical nurse in the face of evidence that the employer believed plaintiff's MS made her unfit for further employment in any capacity at the medical center. However, animus, in the sense of bad faith or ill will, need not be operating. A good faith, or "innocent misperception," can still result in liability under the regarded as prong. See Taylor v. Pathmark Stores, Inc., 177 F.3d 180 (3d Cir. 1999); Arline v. School Bd. of Nassau County, 480 U.S. 273 (1987).

12. In her article, Perceived Disabilities, Social Cognition, and "Innocent Mistakes," 55 Vand. L. Rev. 481 (2002), Professor Michelle A. Travis contends that "at least some perceived disabilities are likely to result not from consciously held, group-based prejudices or generalizations, but from nonmotivational cognitive processing errors." Id. at 491. She asserts that social cognition research can help in determining when such mistakes have occurred. Her "analysis concludes that . . . courts *should* apply the ADA's perceived disability prong to claims involving nonmotivational mistakes, but such mistakes should not trigger the same extent of liability as mistakes that are invidiously motivated or otherwise the product of conscious, group-based decisionmaking." Id. She advocates a "middle ground" approach to liability that would fashion the remedies awarded to the employer's conduct. Do you agree?

13. Is an employee who is "regarded as" disabled entitled to reasonable accommodation? See Buskirk v. Appollo Metals, 307 F.3d 160 (3d Cir. 2002) (reserving question but collecting cases); Weber v. Strippit, Inc., 186 F.3d 907 (8th Cir. 1999) (no); Taylor v. Phoenixville Sch. Dist., 184 F.3d 296 (3d Cir. 1999) (reserving question); Newbery v. East Tex. State Univ., 161 F. 3d 276 (5th Cir. 1998) (no). See generally Michelle A. Travis, Leveling the Playing Field or Stacking the Deck? The "Unfair Advantage" Critique of Perceived Disability Claims, 78 N.C. L. Rev. 901 (2000).

## C. THE MEANING OF "QUALIFIED INDIVIDUAL WITH A DISABILITY"

Establishing the existence of a disability is alone insufficient to bring an individual within Title I's protected class. Title I, the ADA's employment subchapter, contains the following prohibition:

> No covered entity shall discriminate against a *qualified individual with a disability* because of the disability of such individual in regard to job application procedures, the hiring, advancement, or discharge of employees, employee compensation, job training and other terms, conditions and privileges of employment.

42 U.S.C.S. § 12112(a) (2003) (emphasis added). The concept of protecting only qualified individuals from disability discrimination is borrowed from § 504 of the Rehabilitation Act of 1973, which protects only those disabled persons who are "otherwise qualified." 29 U.S.C.S. § 794(a) (2003). In Southeast Community College v. Davis, 442 U.S. 397 (1979), a case decided under § 504, the Supreme Court rejected a reading of "otherwise qualified" that would protect individuals who were qualified

apart from their disability. Instead, the Court interpreted the term to mean an individual who can meet the demands of the job or program despite the disability. The Court went on to hold, however, that an entity may be required to make changes in its program to accommodate the need of the disabled individual. As *Davis* was later described by the Court:

> *Davis* thus struck a balance between the statutory rights of the handicapped to be integrated into society and the legitimate interests of federal grantees in preserving the integrity of their programs: while a grantee need not be required to make "fundamental" or "substantial" modifications to accommodate the handicapped, it may be required to make reasonable ones.

Alexander v. Choate, 469 U.S. 287, 301 (1985).

This structure is carried over into Title I of the ADA. Title I defines a "qualified individual with a disability" as:

> an individual with a disability who, with or without reasonable accommodation, can perform the essential functions of the employment position that such individual holds or desires. For the purposes of this title, consideration shall be given to the employer's judgment as to what functions of a job are essential, and if an employer has prepared a written description before advertising or interviewing applicants for the job, this description shall be considered evidence of the essential functions of the job.

42 U.S.C.S. § 12111(8) (2003).

While Title I extends its protections to disabled individuals who can perform the essential tasks of their jobs, it will not permit employers to deny employment because a disability precludes the performance of nonessential or relatively unimportant aspects of the job. On the other hand, denying employment to someone who cannot perform the essential functions of the job with or without reasonable accommodation is not a statutory violation. Accordingly, it is necessary to distinguish the essential functions of the job from those that are not.

## 1.  Essential Job Functions

### DEANE v. POCONO MEDICAL CENTER
#### 142 F.3d 138 (3d Cir. 1998) (en banc)

BECKER, Chief Judge.

This is an appeal by Stacy L. Deane from an order of the district court granting summary judgment to her former employer, Pocono Medical Center ("PMC"), on Deane's claim under the Americans with Disabilities Act. In enacting the ADA, Congress intended that the scope of the Act would extend not only to those who are actually disabled, but also to individuals wrongly regarded by employers as being disabled. Deane, a registered nurse, sued PMC under the ADA as such a "regarded as" plaintiff to redress PMC's failure to accommodate her in a manner that would enable her to retain her position following a work-related injury that affected her ability to do heavy lifting. The case came before the en banc court to settle the question that divided the original panel — whether "regarded as" plaintiffs, in order to be considered qualified under the ADA, must show that they are able to perform all of the functions of the relevant position or just the essential functions, with or without accommodation. The panel decided that they must be able to perform all of the functions. Before the en banc court, neither party supported that position, and we now reject it, concluding that the plain language of the ADA requires proof only of a plaintiff 's ability to perform a position's essential functions.

This conclusion forces us to determine whether Deane has adduced sufficient evidence to create a genuine issue of material fact with respect to two elements of her prima facie case: (1) whether PMC misperceived Deane as being disabled; and (2) whether Deane is a "qualified individual," a decision that turns on whether lifting is an essential function of nursing at PMC. Because we conclude that Deane has adduced sufficient evidence regarding both of these matters, we hold that summary judgment was inappropriate. Accordingly, the judgment of the district court will be reversed and the case remanded for further proceedings. . . .

## I

In April 1990, PMC hired Deane as a registered nurse to work primarily on the medical/surgical floor. On June 22, 1991, while lifting a resistant patient, she sustained a cartilage tear in her right wrist causing her to miss approximately one year of work. In June 1992, Deane and Barbara Manges, a nurse assigned to Deane's workers' compensation case, telephoned PMC and advised Charlene McCool, PMC's Benefits Coordinator, that Deane intended to return to work with certain restrictions. According to Deane, she informed McCool that she was unable to lift more than 15-20 pounds or perform repetitive manual tasks such as typing, but that her physician, Dr. Osterman, had released her to return to "light duty" work. Deane further explained to McCool that, if she could not be accommodated in a light duty position on the medical/surgical floor, she was willing to move to another area of the hospital, as long as she could remain in nursing. Unfortunately, this telephone call was PMC's only meaningful interaction with Deane during which it could have assessed the severity of or possible accommodation for her injuries. PMC never requested additional information from Deane or her physicians, and, according to Deane, when she subsequently attempted to contact PMC on several occasions, she was treated rudely by McCool and told not to call again.

After speaking with Deane and Manges, McCool advised Barbara Hann, PMC's Vice President of Human Resources, of Deane's request to return to work, of her attendant work restrictions, and of her stated need for accommodation. Shortly after considering the information conveyed by McCool and after comparing it to the job description of a medical/surgical nurse at PMC, Hann determined that Deane was unable to return to her previous position. Hann then asked Carol Clarke, PMC's Vice President of Nursing, and Susan Stine, PMC's Director of Nursing Resources/Patient Care Services, to review Deane's request to return to PMC and to explore possible accommodations for her. Both Clarke and Stine concluded that Deane could not be accommodated in her previous job as a nurse on the medical/surgical floor or in any other available position at the hospital. Finally, Hann asked Marie Werkheiser, PMC's Nurse Recruiter, whether there were any current or prospective job openings for registered nurses at PMC. According to Werkheiser, there were no such openings at that time.

As a result of the collective determination that Deane could not be accommodated in her previous job or in any other available position in the hospital, PMC sent Deane an "exit interview" form on August 7, 1992. On August 10, 1992, Hann notified Deane by telephone that she could not return to work because of her "handicap," and this litigation ensued. In March 1993, Deane accepted a registered nurse position at a non-acute care facility, where she remained until May 1993. Deane has been employed by a different non-acute care facility since July 1993. Neither of these positions require heavy lifting, bathing patients, or the like. . . .

**B**

The second element of Deane's prima facie case under the ADA requires her to demonstrate that she is a "qualified individual." The ADA defines this term as an individual "who, with or without reasonable accommodation, can perform the essential functions of the employment position that such individual holds or desires." 42 U.S.C. § 12111(8). The Interpretive Guidance to the EEOC Regulations divides this inquiry into two prongs. First, a court must determine whether the individual satisfies the requisite skill, experience, education and other job-related requirements of the employment position that such individual holds or desires. See 29 C.F.R. pt. 1630, app. § 1630.2(m). Second, it must determine whether the individual, with or without reasonable accommodation, can perform the essential functions of the position held or sought. See id.; see also Bombard v. Fort Wayne Newspapers, Inc., 92 F.3d 560, 563 (7th Cir. 1996); Benson v. Northwest Airlines, Inc., 62 F.3d 1108, 1112 (8th Cir. 1995). Because PMC does not dispute Deane's general qualifications as a registered nurse, we need not dwell on the first step of the "qualified individual" analysis.

Determining whether an individual can, with or without reasonable accommodation, perform the essential functions of the position held or sought, also a two-step process, is relatively straightforward. First, a court must consider whether the individual can perform the essential functions of the job without accommodation. If so, the individual is qualified (and, a fortiori, is not entitled to accommodation). If not, then a court must look to whether the individual can perform the essential functions of the job with a reasonable accommodation. If so, the individual is qualified. If not, the individual has failed to set out a necessary element of the prima facie case.

The majority panel opinion, in deciding for PMC, reasoned that to satisfy the first step, a "regarded as" plaintiff must make a showing that he or she could perform all the functions of the job (with or without accommodation), not just its essential functions. PMC disassociated itself from the panel's position before the en banc court. As this issue is one of statutory construction, the "first step in interpreting a statute is to determine whether the language at issue has a plain and unambiguous meaning with regard to the particular dispute in the case." Robinson v. Shell Oil Co., 519 U.S. 337 (1997).

*1*

The ADA prohibits a "covered entity" from discriminating against a "qualified individual with a disability." 42 U.S.C. § 12112(a). Section 12111(8), which defines the latter term, reads:

> The term "qualified individual with a disability" means an individual with a disability who, with or without reasonable accommodation, can perform the essential functions of the employment position that such individual holds or desires. For the purposes of this subchapter, consideration shall be given to the employer's judgment as to what functions of a job are essential, and if an employer has prepared a written description before advertising or interviewing applicants for the job, this description shall be considered evidence of the essential functions of the job.

Section 12111(8) is plain and unambiguous. The first sentence of that section, makes it clear that the phrase "with or without reasonable accommodation" refers directly to "essential functions." Indeed, there is nothing in the sentence, other than "essential functions," to which "with or without reasonable accommodation" could refer. Moreover, nowhere else in the Act does it state that, to be a "qualified individual," an individual must prove his or her ability to perform all of the functions of the job, and nowhere in the Act does it distinguish between actual or perceived disabilities in terms of the threshold showing of qualifications. Therefore, if an individual can perform the essential functions of the job without accommodation as to those functions, regardless of whether the individual can perform the other functions of the job (with or without accommodation), that individual is qualified under the ADA.

The history of the ADA confirms this view. In the committee reports that accompanied the ADA, Congress spoke directly to the qualifications standard adopted in the statute. Repeatedly, Congress stated that the qualifications standard turned on the individual's ability to perform the "essential functions" of the job. See e.g., House Labor Report at 55, reprinted in 1990 U.S.C.C.A.N. at 337; House Judiciary Report at 32-33, reprinted in 1990 U.S.C.C.A.N. at 455. Congress explained that the Act focused on an individual's ability to perform "essential functions" to ensure that persons with disabilities "not be disqualified because of the inability to perform non-essential or marginal functions of the job." House Judiciary Report at 31-32, reprinted in 1990 U.S.C.C.A.N. at 454. As stated in one committee report, the purpose of the ADA's qualifications standard is to "ensure that employers can continue to require that all applicants and employees, including those with disabilities, are able to perform the *essential* functions, i.e., the non-marginal functions of the job in question." House Labor Report at 55, reprinted in 1990 U.S.C.C.A.N. at 337 (emphasis added).

## 2

Having rejected the panel's position that Deane needed to make a showing that she can perform all of the functions of her former job, we must now determine whether Deane has, in fact, adduced sufficient evidence to survive summary judgment on the question whether she can perform the essential functions of the job without accommodation as to those functions. Deane claims that the heavy lifting she is restricted from doing is not an essential job function of a nurse. Deane describes nursing as a profession that focuses primarily on skill, intellect, and knowledge. While conceding that lifting constitutes part of a nurse's duties, she submits that it is only a small part.

In support of her contentions, Deane . . . offers [vocational expert] Rappucci's affidavit and report. Rappucci opines that patient care, not heavy lifting of patients, is the essential function of registered nursing. As evidence, he references the Department of Labor's Dictionary of Occupational Titles Job Descriptions ("DOL Dictionary"), which details four critical tasks of a general duty nurse, none of which involves heavy lifting: (1) administering medications and treatments, (2) preparing equipment and aiding physicians during the treatment of patients, (3) observing patients and recording significant conditions and reactions to drugs, treatments, and significant incidents, and (4) taking temperature, pulse, blood pressure, and other vital signs to detect deviations from normal and assess the condition of the patient. Rappucci also notes that nursing is a professional occupation, and he compares it with orderly work to exemplify the differences between the two positions. For example, whereas nursing is classified by the Department of Labor as skilled, medium duty labor, orderly work is classified as semi-skilled, heavy-duty labor. Also, whereas none of a general nurse's critical tasks under the DOL Dictionary description include lifting, the description of orderly work enumerates "lifting patients onto and from bed" as critical task number five. This is because, according to Deane, the orderly position exists to assist the nurse professional in the performance of his or her job duties. Finally, Deane points out that, recognizing the difficulty of unassisted heavy lifting, PMC uses a team approach to the lifting of patients, both in routine matters and in responding to emergency situations.[10]

PMC responds that lifting is an essential function of a nurse. In support, PMC cites its job description, which details under the heading "MAJOR TASKS, DUTIES AND RESPONSIBILITIES" that one of the "WORKING CONDITIONS" for a staff registered nurse is the "frequent lifting of patients."[11] PMC also notes that Deane conceded that the PMC job description was "an accurate reflection of the tasks, duties and responsibilities as well as the qualifications, physical requirements and working conditions of a registered nurse at [PMC]," and that among her "critical job demands" at PMC were: (1) the placement of patients in water closets, tub chairs or gurneys, (2) the changing of position of patients, and (3) the lifting of laundry bags. These pieces of evidence, contends PMC, constitute multiple admissions by Deane that lifting is an essential function of a staff registered nurse at PMC. Finally, PMC asserts that the consequences of a nurse's inability to lift patients could create a dangerous situation in the hospital for Deane and her patients.

We decline to apply conclusive effect to either the job description or PMC's judgment as to whether heavy lifting is essential to Deane's job. The EEOC's Interpretive Guidance indicates that "the employer's judgment as to which functions are essential" and "written job descriptions prepared before advertising or interviewing applicants" are two *possible* types of evidence for determining the essential functions of a position, but that such evidence is not to be given greater weight simply because it is included in the non-exclusive list set out in 29 C.F.R. § 1630.2(n)(3). See 29 C.F.R. pt. 1630, app. § 1630.2(n). Thus, the job description is not, as PMC contends, incontestable evidence that unassisted patient lifting is an essential function of Deane's job. Moreover, the EEOC Regulations also provide that while "inquiry into the essential functions is not intended to second guess an employer's business judgment with regard to production standards," whether a particular function is essential "is a factual determination that must be made on a case by case basis [based upon] *all* relevant evidence." Id. (emphasis added). Finally, the import of the rest of PMC's evidence (e.g., her alleged admissions, etc.) is disputed by Deane. For all these reasons, we find that

10. Rappucci also contends that PMC misdefines the essential functions of the nurse position (e.g., by including lifting of laundry bags as a "major task duty and responsibility"). Rappucci argues that this confuses method with function in that lifting is a method of accomplishing a task, rather than a specific job function in relation to nursing.

11. Rappucci criticizes the job description for utilizing incorrect language to describe the lifting requirements. For example, according to the Department of Labor, "frequent lifting of patients" means that the task is performed 33% to 66% of the day, or approximately 3-5 hours over an eight hour work shift. Deane contends that this description is implausible (and inaccurate) and conflicts with other testimony. For example, Joan Campagna, a registered staff nurse at PMC since 1987, swore in her affidavit that a PMC nurse typically spends only minutes per day repositioning patients in their beds, transferring patients from bed to gurney or vice versa, and moving patients into and out of wheelchairs. Moreover, Campagna notes that these tasks are nearly always accomplished by two people and that PMC employs orderlies, licensed practical nurses, and nurses aides whose duties are to assist registered nurses in all patient care activities, including the lifting and transferring of patients.

there is a genuine issue of material fact on the issue of whether Deane was a qualified individual under the ADA.[12] . . .

GREENBERG, Circuit Judge, dissenting.

. . . . The majority believes that there is a genuine issue of material fact as to "whether PMC misperceived Deane as being disabled." But that dispute does not matter, for the critical issue is not how PMC viewed Deane because there is simply no escape from the fact that an essential element of Deane's case is that "PMC failed to accommodate her lifting restriction." After all, as the majority explains, "Deane maintains that she requires and is entitled to accommodation for her lifting restriction." But no matter what misconceptions PMC may have had about Deane, it was Deane who requested the accommodation. Thus, even if PMC regarded her as more substantially impaired than she actually was, this misperception does not matter for she was not entitled to any accommodation. It is critical to remember that this is not a case in which the employer perceived the employee to be disabled and then refused to make the accommodation which it believed she needed.

The majority indicates that there is a genuine dispute of material fact regarding whether heavy lifting is an essential function of her former job. I agree that there is a genuine dispute of fact as to whether heavy lifting is an essential function of the job.

12. In view of this conclusion, we need not reach the more difficult question addressed by the panel whether "regarded as" disabled plaintiffs must be accommodated by their employers if they cannot perform the essential functions of their jobs. Deane contends that, as a matter of statutory interpretation, "regarded as" plaintiffs are entitled to the same reasonable accommodations from their employers as are actually disabled plaintiffs. She reasons that, just as we found that a plain reading of the ADA only requires plaintiffs to show that they can perform the essential functions of the job, a plain reading of the definition of "qualified individual" demonstrates that a "regarded as" plaintiff is qualified so long as she can perform the essential functions with reasonable accommodation. See 42 U.S.C. § 12111(8) (defining a "qualified individual" as one "who, with or without reasonable accommodation, can perform the essential functions of the employment position that such individual holds or desires"); see also 29 C.F.R. § 1630.2(m). Moreover, Deane submits that this plain reading of the statute is buttressed by the Supreme Court's decision in Arline, (holding that, under the Rehabilitation Act, employers have an affirmative obligation to make reasonable accommodations for employees who are perceived to be handicapped). More importantly, according to Deane, failure to mandate reasonable accommodations for "regarded as" plaintiffs would undermine the role the ADA plays in ferreting out disability discrimination in employment. This is because, following Deane's logic, the "regarded as" prong of the disability definition is premised upon the reality that the perception of disability, socially constructed and reinforced, is difficult to destroy, and in most cases, merely informing the employer of its misperception will not be enough.

In countering Deane's position, PMC notes preliminarily that a "regarded as" plaintiff's only disability is the employer's irrational response to her illusory condition. Under these circumstances, reasons PMC, it simply makes no sense to talk of accommodations for any physical impairments because, by definition, the impairments are not the statutory cause of the plaintiff's disability. Adopting Deane's interpretation of the ADA would, in PMC's view: (1) permit healthy employees to, through litigation (or the threat of litigation) demand changes in their work environments under the guise of "reasonable accommodations" for disabilities based upon misperceptions; and (2) create a windfall for legitimate "regarded as" disabled employees who, after disabusing their employers of their misperceptions, would nonetheless be entitled to accommodations that their similarly situated co-workers are not, for admittedly non-disabling conditions.

While we acknowledge the considerable force of PMC's argument, especially the latter point, we express no position on the accommodation issue, and note that the [EEOC] has not taken an official position yet either. We note, however, that if it turns out that a "regarded as" plaintiff who cannot perform the essential functions of her job is not entitled to accommodation (and therefore does not have to be reinstated), he or she need not necessarily be without remedy. The plaintiff still might be entitled to injunctive relief against future discrimination, see EEOC v. Goodyear Aerospace, 813 F.2d 1539, 1544 (9th Cir. 1987) (listing benefits of injunctive relief, including: (1) instructing employers to comply with federal law, (2) subjecting employers to the contempt power of the federal courts for future violations, and (3) reducing the chilling effect of employers' alleged discrimination); King v. Trans World Airlines, Inc., 738 F.2d 255, 259 (8th Cir. 1984), to compensatory or punitive damages under 42 U.S.C. § 1981a, see Johnson v. Railway Express Agency, Inc., 421 U.S. 454, 459-60 (1975) (punitive damages); Mahone v. Waddle, 564 F.2d 1018 (3d Cir. 1977) (compensatory damages), and/or to counsel fees under 42 U.S.C. § 1988(b).

But, just as the dispute of fact regarding PMC's perception of Deane does not matter, neither does the heavy lifting dispute because it is not material. See Anderson v. Liberty Lobby, Inc., 477 U.S. 242, 248 (1986). Inasmuch as Deane is not actually disabled, she has no right to an accommodation whether or not the accommodation would impact on her ability to perform the essential functions of the job. Furthermore, an employer can determine what it believes are the essential elements for a particular job without concern that its determination might be challenged under the ADA by a person who is not actually disabled.

In my view, this case is quite straightforward but somehow has become complicated. I respectfully dissent as I would affirm the summary judgment.

## NOTES

1. Recall that § 101(8), 42 U.S.C.S. § 12111(8) (2003), states that "consideration shall be given to the employer's judgment as to what functions of a job are essential" and that written job descriptions prepared prior to advertising or interviewing applicants "shall be considered evidence of the essential functions of the job." Is *Deane* consistent with this statutory directive?

2. What makes a job function essential? The EEOC's regulations, promulgated under Title I, define the term to mean the "fundamental job duties," as opposed to the "marginal functions" of the job. Factors to consider in making that distinction are whether the position exists to perform the function, the number of employees available to perform the function, and/or whether the function is highly specialized, thus requiring special expertise. In addition to the employer's job description, other evidence to consider includes, although it is not limited to, the employer's judgment, the amount of time spent performing the function, the work experience of people previously or currently in the job or similar jobs, and the terms of any collective bargaining agreement. 29 C.F.R. § 1630.2(n).

3. Numerous courts have held that regular and timely attendance at work is an essential job function, and, therefore, a disabled individual who cannot meet that requirement is not "qualified" within the meaning of the ADA or the Rehabilitation Act. See, e.g., Spangler v. Federal Home Loan Bank, 278 F.3d 847 (8th Cir. 2002); EEOC v. Yellow Freight Sys., 253 F.3d 943 (7th Cir. 2001); Tyndall v. National Educ. Ctrs., 31 F.3d 209 (4th Cir. 1994); Jackson v. Veterans Admin., 22 F.3d 277 (11th Cir. 1994). The Sixth Circuit has cautioned, however, that a presumption that uninterrupted attendance is an essential job requirement improperly avoids the individualized assessment of accommodations required by the ADA. See Cehrs v. Northeast Ohio Alzheimer's Research Ctr., 155 F.3d 775 (6th Cir. 1998). Is there a difference between an employee whose disability results in sporadic absences and one whose disability requires a medical leave? Attendance and leave as a reasonable accommodation is discussed further in subsection C.2.

4. What are the essential functions of a job when not all incumbents in the job perform the same work? In Stone v. City of Mount Vernon, 118 F.3d 92 (2d Cir. 1997), the city argued that it could not hire a paraplegic in the fire department's fire alarm bureau because he could not engage in fire fighting or fire-suppression activities. Reversing summary judgment for the city, the Second Circuit ruled that, rather than defer to the department's judgment on essential functions, the court should have considered evidence concerning the actual job functions of fire alarm bureau employees. Id. at 99-100. The court further indicated that, even if it would be an

undue hardship to hire five or ten disabled individuals in the bureau, it might not be an undue hardship to hire one. Id. at 101.

5. *Deane* focused on the amount of time spent doing heavy lifting. However, that a job function is performed for only a small percentage of the employee's time does not mean it is not essential. For example, a group of lifeguards may work for years without ever being required to give mouth-to-mouth resuscitation. Nonetheless, isn't the ability to perform this emergency function clearly an essential function of the job? Were the courts in *Deane* and *Stone* (supra note 4) insufficiently deferential to the employer's judgment?

6. If lifting is an essential function for a nurse, then the employer need not accommodate by having another employee perform the task for her. But if the essential function is patient care, then having an orderly or aide assist the nurse in performing this task by lifting the patient may be a reasonable accommodation. Alternatively, lifting may be viewed as a nonessential job function, irrelevant to her protected class status. Will making the determination as to which of these applies usually be a question of fact?

7. As *Deane* demonstrates, an employer may not deny employment to a disabled individual because she is unable to perform functions that are not essential. In Lovejoy-Wilson v. NOCO Motor Fuel, Inc., 263 F.3d 208 (2d Cir. 2001), the plaintiff's epilepsy precluded her from obtaining a driver's license. Assistant store managers were responsible for making bank deposits at many of the employer's stores and often drove the deposits to the banks themselves. The employer refused to consider plaintiff for positions in which the managers drove to the banks. Because driving was not an essential job function, however, the court held the employer could not refuse to consider plaintiff for promotion on that basis. The essential function was making sure the money was deposited, a task plaintiff could perform by hiring a taxi or obtaining some other transportation to the bank. Nor did the employer satisfy its ADA obligations by considering plaintiff for positions at stores where managers were not responsible for making the deposits. If other employees were entitled to be considered for promotion at the stores of their choice, so was plaintiff.

8. Can the quantity or quality of work produced be an essential function of the job? The Interpretive Guidance provides:

> [T]he inquiry into essential functions is not intended to second guess an employer's business judgment with regard to production standards, whether qualitative or quantitative, nor to require employers to lower such standards. . . . If an employer requires its typists to be able to accurately type 75 words per minute, it will not be called upon to explain why an inaccurate work product, or a typing speed of 65 words per minute, would not be adequate. . . . However, if an employer does require accurate 75 word per minute typing . . . , it will have to show that it actually imposes such requirements on its employees in fact, and not simply on paper.

29 C.F.R. pt. 1630, app. § 1630.2(n). See Milton v. Scrivner, Inc., 53 F.3d 1118 (10th Cir. 1995) (employer's new production standard constituted an essential function of the selector job). What arguments would you make on the issue of essential functions on behalf of a dyslexic lawyer who produces a good product but is denied partnership on the basis of low productivity? Is she a qualified individual with a disability? Note that the statute prohibits discriminatory qualification standards unless job-related for the position in question and consistent with business necessity and the duty of reasonable accommodation. 42 U.S.C.S. § 12112(b)(6) (2003). Is the Interpretive Guidance consistent with this statutory provision?

9.  Can an employer require, as an essential job function, that employees present an attractive appearance or personality in order, for example, to represent the company to potential clients or customers? Consider the employer who is hiring a television news anchorperson, a front desk receptionist, a model, or a dancer in a nightclub. Suppose you represented an individual with a cosmetic disfigurement who was rejected for a job as a dancer in a nightclub on the basis of her appearance. Assuming all of the dancers at the club are attractive and assuming your client meets all of the other qualifications for the job, is she a qualified individual with a disability? What if an otherwise qualified cosmetically disfigured lawyer or waiter or salesperson were rejected on the same basis? What about an otherwise qualified individual with emotional problems who, as a result, is difficult to work with? Doesn't each of these situations involve some element of stereotyping and customer preference? Aren't stereotyped attitudes about disabled individuals exactly what the ADA is designed to eliminate? At the same time, is the ability to get along with co-workers and supervisors an essential job function for most positions? See Grenier v. Cyanamid Plastics, Inc., 70 F.3d 667 (1st Cir. 1995).

10.  The Third Circuit in *Deane* asserts it is *not* deciding whether the duty of reasonable accommodation applies to an individual who meets the statutory definition of disability through the "regarded as" route. But at the same time, it holds that only Deane's ability to perform essential job functions may be assessed in determining whether she is a qualified individual with a disability within the meaning of Title I. Assuming Deane meets this test, presumably the employer may not deny her employment based on her inability to perform nonessential job functions. Is excusing an individual from performing nonessential tasks a form of reasonable accommodation?

### PROBLEM 8.4

Sam is hearing impaired. He has applied for a secretarial job that includes answering phones. He asserts that he can perform all aspects of the job, except for answering the phone, without any accommodation. With respect to answering the phone, he has proposed two alternative accommodations: (1) eliminating the phone responsibilities or (2) providing a telecommunications device (TDD) that would allow him to answer the phone. Is he qualified for this job? What arguments can he make? What arguments can the employer make?

### PROBLEM 8.5

Jan works as a supervisor for Acme Products, a small manufacturing company. Jan suffers from Tourette's syndrome, a disorder that causes some individuals to uncontrollably burst out with obscene or extremely insulting remarks. Jan's outbursts usually take the form of racial epithets. Fifty percent of Acme Products' employees are African Americans. Several of these employees have complained to the EEO officer at Acme about Jan's outbursts. Acme has consulted you for advice. What advice would you give?

## 2.  The Duty of Reasonable Accommodation

A qualified individual with a disability is one who can perform the essential functions of the job she holds or desires *with or without reasonable accommodation*. The concept of reasonable accommodation distinguishes the ADA from other antidis-crimination statutes. Under the ADA, it is not enough for an employer to treat its dis-abled employees the same — no better and no worse — than it treats its nondisabled employees. In appropriate circumstances, the employer must take affirmative steps that will allow disabled employees to perform their jobs. Failing to provide reasonable accommodations constitutes one form of discrimination under the statute. Section 102(b)(5) of the ADA defines discrimination to include:

> (A)  not making reasonable accommodations to the known physical or mental limita-tions of an otherwise qualified individual with a disability who is an applicant or em-ployee, unless such covered entity can demonstrate that the accommodation would im-pose an undue hardship on the operation of the business of such covered entity; or
>
> (B)  denying employment opportunities to a job applicant or employee who is an oth-erwise qualified individual with a disability, if such denial is based on the need of such covered entity to make reasonable accommodation to the physical or mental impair-ments of the employee or applicant.

Section 102(b)(5) makes reasonable accommodation relevant both to establishing and defending against a discrimination claim based on the failure to accommodate. If a disabled individual can perform essential functions with reasonable accommoda-tion, the employer has a duty to provide those accommodations. If the disabled indi-vidual requires accommodations that are not reasonable or that impose an undue hardship, disparate treatment on the basis of disability is permitted and accommodat-ing the disability is not required.

This section considers "reasonable accommodation" in the context of proving a disability discrimination claim of "not making reasonable accommodations." Rea-sonable accommodation goes beyond providing accommodations required to per-form essential job functions. Employers also have a duty to provide accommodations that permit disabled individuals to enjoy equal access to the benefits and privileges of employment. The ADA also requires employers to make "accommodations that are required to ensure equal opportunity in the application process." See 29 C.F.R. pt. 1630, app. § 1630.2(o). Section 101(9) identifies some of the areas in which accom-modation may be required:

> The term "reasonable accommodation" may include —
>
> (A)  making existing facilities used by employees readily accessible to and usable by individuals with disabilities; and
>
> (B)  job restructuring, part-time or modified work schedules, reassignment to a vacant position, acquisition or modification of equipment or devices, appropriate ad-justment or modifications of examinations, training materials or policies, the provi-sion of qualified readers or interpreters, and other similar accommodations for indi-viduals with disabilities.

Note that the issue in a "failure to accommodate" case is not whether the employer has treated the disabled individual differently. Nor is the question whether the employer has legitimate reasons for treating a disabled individual differently. In a reasonable accommodation case, the disabled individual is *requesting* different treatment. The question is not whether the disability was considered, but rather whether the disability entitled the employee or applicant to accommodation (differ-ent treatment).

The following case illustrates that an individual may be qualified for a job if reasonable accommodations are made but unqualified if they are not, in the sense that she would be unable to perform essential job functions.

### CLEVELAND v. POLICY MANAGEMENT
### SYSTEMS CORP.
**526 U.S. 795 (1999)**

Justice BREYER delivered the opinion of the Court.

[On January 7, 1994, Carolyn Cleveland "suffered a stroke which damaged her concentration, memory, and language skills." After losing her job she "filed an SSDI application in which she stated that she was 'disabled' and 'unable to work.'" When her condition improved she returned to work at Policy Management Systems and, as a result, was denied Social Security benefits. When she was fired three months later, she asked SSA to reconsider the denial of benefits, stating in her application for reconsideration, "I was terminated [by Policy Management Systems] due to my condition and I have not been able to work since. I continue to be disabled." She later added that she had "attempted to return to work in mid April," and had "worked for three months," but that Policy Management Systems terminated her because she "could no longer do the job" in light of her "condition." At a hearing on her request for reconsideration, she again stated, "I am unable to work due to my disability." On September 29, 1995, the SSA awarded Cleveland SSDI benefits retroactive to January 7, 1994. One week before her SSDI award, Cleveland filed her ADA lawsuit, contending that Policy Management Systems "terminated" her employment without reasonably "accommodating her disability." She also alleged that she requested, but was denied, accommodations, including training and additional time to complete her work.]

The Social Security Act and the ADA both help individuals with disabilities, but in different ways. The Social Security Act provides monetary benefits to every insured individual who "is under a disability." 42 U.S.C. § 423(a)(1). The Act defines "disability" as an "inability to engage in any substantial gainful activity by reason of any . . . physical or mental impairment which can be expected to result in death or which has lasted or can be expected to last for a continuous period of not less than 12 months." § 423(d)(1)(A). The individual's impairment . . . must be "of such severity that [she] is not only unable to do [her] previous work but cannot, considering [her] age, education, and work experience, engage in any other kind of substantial gainful work which exists in the national economy." . . . § 423(d)(2)(A).

The ADA seeks to eliminate unwarranted discrimination against disabled individuals in order both to guarantee those individuals equal opportunity and to provide the Nation with the benefit of their consequently increased productivity. The Act prohibits covered employers from discriminating "against a qualified individual with a disability because of the disability of such individual." § 12112(a). The Act defines a "qualified individual with a disability" as a disabled person "who . . . can perform the essential functions" of her job, including those who can do so only "with . . . reasonable accommodation." § 12111(8).

We here consider but one of the many ways in which these two statutes might interact. This case does not involve . . . directly conflicting statements about purely factual matters, such as "The light was red/green," or "I can/cannot raise my arm above my head." An SSA representation of total disability differs from a purely factual statement in that it often implies a context-related legal conclusion, namely "I am disabled for purposes of the Social Security Act." And our consideration of this latter kind of statement consequently leaves the law related to the former, purely factual, kind of conflict where we found it.

The case before us concerns an ADA plaintiff who both applied for, and received, SSDI benefits. It requires us to review a Court of Appeals decision upholding the grant of summary judgment on the ground that an ADA plaintiff's "representation to the SSA that she was totally disabled" created a "rebuttable presumption" sufficient to "judicially estop" her later representation that, "for the time in question," with reasonable accommodation, she could perform the essential functions of her job. The Court of Appeals thought, in essence, that claims under both Acts would incorporate two directly conflicting propositions, namely "I am too disabled to work" and "I am not too disabled to work." And in an effort to prevent two claims that would embody that kind of factual conflict, the court used a special judicial presumption, which it believed would ordinarily prevent a plaintiff like Cleveland from successfully asserting an ADA claim.

In our view, however, despite the appearance of conflict that arises from the language of the two statutes, the two claims do not inherently conflict to the point where courts should apply a special negative presumption like the one applied by the Court of Appeals here. That is because there are too many situations in which an SSDI claim and an ADA claim can comfortably exist side by side.

For one thing, as we have noted, the ADA defines a "qualified individual" to include a disabled person "who . . . can perform the essential functions" of her job "with reasonable accommodation. . . ."

By way of contrast, when the SSA determines whether an individual is disabled for SSDI purposes, it does not take the possibility of "reasonable accommodation" into account, nor need an applicant refer to the possibility of reasonable accommodation when she applies for SSDI. The omission reflects the facts that the SSA receives more than 2.5 million claims for disability benefits each year; its administrative resources are limited; the matter of "reasonable accommodation" may turn on highly disputed workplace-specific matters; and an SSA misjudgment about that detailed, and often fact-specific matter would deprive a seriously disabled person of the critical financial support the statute seeks to provide. The result is that an ADA suit claiming that the plaintiff can perform her job with reasonable accommodation may well prove consistent with an SSDI claim that the plaintiff could not perform her own job (or other jobs) without it.

For another thing, in order to process the large number of SSDI claims, the SSA administers SSDI with the help of a five-step procedure that embodies a set of presumptions about disabilities, job availability, and their interrelation. The SSA asks:

> *Step One:* Are you presently working? (If so, you are ineligible.)
> *Step Two:* Do you have a "severe impairment," i.e., one that "significantly limits" your ability to do basic work activities? (If not, you are ineligible.)
> *Step Three:* Does your impairment "meet or equal" an impairment on a specific (and fairly lengthy) SSA list? (If so, you are eligible without more.)
> *Step Four:* If your impairment does not meet or equal a listed impairment, can you perform your "past relevant work?" (If so, you are ineligible.)
> *Step Five:* If your impairment does not meet or equal a listed impairment and you cannot perform your "past relevant work," then can you perform other jobs that exist in significant numbers in the national economy? (If not, you are eligible.)

[See 20 C.F.R. §§ 404.1520(b)-(f); 404.1525, 404.1526, 404.1560(c) (1998).]

The presumptions embodied in these questions — particularly those necessary to produce Step Three's list, which, the Government tells us, accounts for approximately 60 percent of all awards — grows out of the need to administer a large benefits system efficiently. But they inevitably simplify, eliminating consideration of many differences potentially relevant to an individual's ability to perform a particular job. Hence, an individual might qualify for SSDI under the SSA's administrative rules and yet, due to special individual circumstances, remain capable of "performing the essential functions" of her job.

Further, the SSA sometimes grants SSDI benefits to individuals who not only can work, but are working. For example, to facilitate a disabled person's reentry into the workforce, the SSA authorizes a 9-month trial-work period during which SSDI recipients may receive full benefits. See 42 U.S.C. § 422(c), 423(e)(1); 20 CFR § 404.1592 (1998). See also § 404.1592a (benefits available for an additional 15-month period depending upon earnings). Improvement in a totally disabled person's physical condition, while permitting that person to work, will not necessarily or immediately lead the SSA to terminate SSDI benefits. And the nature of an individual's disability may change over time, so that a statement about that disability at the time of an individual's application for SSDI benefits may not reflect an individual's capacities at the time of the relevant employment decision.

Finally, if an individual has merely applied for, but has not been awarded, SSDI benefits, any inconsistency in the theory of the claims is of the sort normally tolerated by our legal system. Our ordinary rules recognize that a person may not be sure in advance upon which legal theory she will succeed, and so permit parties to "set forth two or more statements of a claim or defense alternately or hypothetically," and to "state as many separate claims or defenses as the party has regardless of consistency." Fed. Rule Civ. Proc. 8(e)(2). We do not see why the law in respect to the assertion of SSDI and ADA claims should differ. (And, as we said, we leave the law in respect to purely factual contradictions where we found it.)

In light of these examples, we would not apply a special legal presumption permitting someone who has applied for, or received, SSDI benefits to bring an ADA suit only in "some limited and highly unusual set of circumstances."

Nonetheless, in some cases an earlier SSDI claim may turn out genuinely to conflict with an ADA claim. Summary judgment for a defendant is appropriate when the plaintiff "fails to make a showing sufficient to establish the existence of an element essential to [her] case, and on which [she] will bear the burden of proof at trial." Celotex Corp. v. Catrett, 477 U.S. 317, 322 (1986). An ADA plaintiff bears the burden of proving that she is a "qualified individual with a disability" — that is, a person "who, with or without reasonable accommodation, can perform the essential functions" of her job. 42 U.S.C. § 12111(8). And a plaintiff's sworn assertion in an application for disability benefits that she is, for example, "unable to work" will appear to negate an essential element of her ADA case — at least if she does not offer a sufficient explanation. For that reason, we hold that an ADA plaintiff cannot simply ignore the apparent contradiction that arises out of the earlier SSDI total disability claim. Rather, she must proffer a sufficient explanation.

The lower courts, in somewhat comparable circumstances, have found a similar need for explanation. They have held with virtual unanimity that a party cannot create a genuine issue of fact sufficient to survive summary judgment simply by contradicting his or her own previous sworn statement . . . without explaining the contradiction or attempting to resolve the disparity. See, e.g., Colantuoni v. Alfred Calcagni & Sons, Inc., 44 F.3d 1, 5 (CA1 1994); Rule v. Brine, Inc., 85 F.3d 1002, 1011 (CA2

1996). Although these cases for the most part involve purely factual contradictions (as to which we do not necessarily endorse these cases, but leave the law as we found it), we believe that a similar insistence upon explanation is warranted here, where the conflict involves a legal conclusion. When faced with a plaintiff's previous sworn statement asserting "total disability" or the like, the court should require an explanation of any apparent inconsistency with the necessary elements of an ADA claim. To defeat summary judgment, that explanation must be sufficient to warrant a reasonable juror's concluding that, assuming the truth of, or the plaintiff's good faith belief in, the earlier statement, the plaintiff could nonetheless "perform the essential functions" of her job, with or without "reasonable accommodation." [The case was remanded to permit the parties to present, or contest, explanations about the apparently inconsistent statements.]

## NOTES

1. As the Court indicates, the lower courts had been in substantial disagreement about the effect of disability benefits applications on ADA claims. Academics also have been troubled by this question. See Matthew Diller, Dissonant Disability Policies: The Tensions Between the Americans with Disabilities Act and Federal Disability Benefit Programs, 76 Tex. L. Rev. 1003, 1066-75 (1998) (suggesting "reconciling the two statutory programs by restructuring the disability benefit programs to harmonize them with the ADA").

2. The Court "leaves the law related to [a] . . . purely factual . . . conflict where we found it." What is a "purely factual" conflict? After *Cleveland*, what is the law with respect to purely factual conflicts?

3. After *Cleveland*, courts no longer presume that a claim for disability benefits is necessarily inconsistent with a Title I claim but instead closely examine the factual statements made in the benefits proceedings. See, e.g., Mitchell v. Washington Cent. Sch. Dist., 190 F.3d 1 (2d Cir. 1999) (statements to workers' compensation board that plaintiff could not stand or walk precluded him from showing he could perform essential functions of school custodian); Motley v. New Jersey State Police, 196 F.3d 160 (3d Cir. 1999) (factual assertions made in claim for disability retirement inconsistent with contention that plaintiff can perform essential job functions). What if an employer requires employees who seek employer-provided disability benefits to sign a statement asserting, "I cannot perform the essential functions of any job with or without reasonable accommodation." Will signing such a statement bar a subsequent ADA claim?

### VANDE ZANDE v. STATE OF WISCONSIN
### DEPARTMENT OF ADMINISTRATION
44 F.3d 538 (7th Cir. 1995)

POSNER, Chief Judge.

In 1990, Congress passed the Americans with Disabilities Act. The stated purpose is "to provide a clear and comprehensive national mandate for the elimination of discrimination against individuals with disabilities." . . . [Many] impairments are not in fact disabling but are believed to be so, and the people having them may be denied employment or otherwise shunned as a consequence. Such people, objectively capable of performing as well as the unimpaired, are analogous to capable workers discriminated against because of their skin color or some other vocationally irrelevant characteristic.

The more problematic case is that of an individual who has a vocationally relevant disability — an impairment such as blindness or paralysis that limits a major human capability, such as seeing or walking. In the common case in which such an impairment interferes with the individual's ability to perform up to the standards of the workplace, or increases the cost of employing him, hiring and firing decisions based on the impairment are not "discriminatory" in a sense closely analogous to employment discrimination on racial grounds. The draftsmen of the Act knew this. But they were unwilling to confine the concept of disability discrimination to cases in which the disability is irrelevant to the performance of the disabled person's job. Instead, they defined "discrimination" to include an employer's "not making reasonable accommodations to the known physical or mental limitations of an otherwise qualified individual with a disability who is an applicant or employee, unless . . . [the employer] can demonstrate that the accommodation would impose an undue hardship on the operation of the . . . [employer's] business."

The term "reasonable accommodations" is not a legal novelty. . . . It is one of a number of provisions in the employment subchapter that were borrowed from regulations issued by the Equal Employment Opportunity Commission in implementation of the Rehabilitation Act of 1973. Indeed, to a great extent the employment provisions of the new Act merely generalize to the economy as a whole the duties, including that of reasonable accommodation that the regulations under the Rehabilitation Act imposed on federal agencies and federal contractors. We can therefore look to the decisions interpreting those regulations for clues to the meaning of the same terms in the new law.

It is plain enough what "accommodation" means. The employer must be willing to consider making changes in its ordinary work rules, facilities, terms, and conditions in order to enable a disabled individual to work. The difficult term is "reasonable." The plaintiff in our case, a paraplegic, argues in effect that the term just means apt or efficacious. An accommodation is reasonable, she believes, when it is tailored to the particular individual's disability. A ramp or lift is thus a reasonable accommodation for a person who like this plaintiff is confined to a wheelchair. Considerations of cost do not enter into the term as the plaintiff would have us construe it. Cost is, she argues, the domain of "undue hardship" — a safe harbor for an employer that can show that it would go broke or suffer other excruciating financial distress were it compelled to make a reasonable accommodation in the sense of one effective in enabling the disabled person to overcome the vocational effects of the disability.

These are questionable interpretations both of "reasonable" and of "undue hardship." To "accommodate" a disability is to make some change that will enable the disabled person to work. An unrelated, inefficacious change would not be an accommodation of the disability at all. So "reasonable" may be intended to qualify (in the sense of weaken) "accommodation," in just the same way that if one requires a "reasonable effort" of someone this means less than the maximum possible effort, or in law that the duty of "reasonable care," the cornerstone of the law of negligence, requires something less than the maximum possible care. It is understood in that law that in deciding what care is reasonable the court considers the cost of increased care. Similar reasoning could be used to flesh out the meaning of the word "reasonable" in the term "reasonable accommodations." It would not follow that the costs and benefits of altering a workplace to enable a disabled person to work would always have to be quantified, or even that an accommodation would have to be deemed unreasonable if the cost exceeded the benefit however slightly. But, at the very least, the cost could not be disproportionate to the benefit. Even if an employer is so large or wealthy — or, like the principal defendant in this case, is a state, which can raise taxes in order to finance any accommodations that it must make to disabled employees — that it may not be able to plead "undue hardship," it would not be required to expend enormous sums in order to bring about a trivial improvement in the life of a disabled employee. . . .

[Undue hardship] is a defined term in the Americans with Disabilities Act, and the definition is "an action requiring significant difficulty or expense," 42 U.S.C. § 12111(10)(A). The financial condition of the employer is only one consideration in determining whether an accommodation otherwise reasonable would impose an undue hardship. See 42 U.S.C. §§ 12111(1)(B)(ii), (iii). The legislative history equates "undue hardship" to "unduly costly." S. Rep. No. 116, *supra*, at 35. These are terms of relation. We must ask, "undue" in relation to what? Presumably (given the statutory definition and the legislative history) in relation to the benefits of the accommodation to the disabled worker as well as to the employer's resources.

So it seems that costs enter at two points in the analysis of claims to an accommodation to a disability. The employee must show that the accommodation is reasonable in the sense both of efficacious and of proportional to costs. Even if this prima facie showing is made, the employer has an opportunity to prove that upon more careful consideration the costs are excessive in relation either to the benefits of the accommodation or to the employer's financial survival or health. In a classic negligence case, the idiosyncrasies of the particular employer are irrelevant. Having above-average costs, or being in a precarious financial situation, is not a defense to negligence. One interpretation of "undue hardship" is that it permits an employer to escape liability if he can carry the burden of proving that a disability accommodation reasonable for a normal employer would break him. Barth v. Gelb, 2 F.3d 1180, 1187 (D.C. Cir. 1993).

Lori Vande Zande, aged 35, is paralyzed from the waist down as a result of a tumor of the spinal cord. Her paralysis makes her prone to develop pressure ulcers, treatment of which often requires that she stay at home for several weeks. The defendants and the amici curiae argue that there is no duty of reasonable accommodation of pressure ulcers because they do not fit the statutory definition of a disability. Intermittent, episodic impairments are not disabilities, the standard example being a broken leg. 29 C.F.R. pt. 1630 app., § 1630.2(j). But an intermittent impairment that is a characteristic manifestation of an admitted disability is, we believe, a part of the underlying disability and hence a condition that the employer must reasonably accommodate. Often the disabling aspect of a disability is, precisely, an intermittent manifestation of the disability, rather than the underlying impairment. The AIDS virus progressively destroys the infected person's immune system. The consequence is a series of opportunistic diseases which . . . often prevent the individual from working. If they are not part of the disability, then people with AIDS do not have a disability, which seems to us a very odd interpretation of the law, and one expressly rejected in the regulations. We hold that Vande Zande's pressure ulcers are a part of her disability, and therefore a part of what the State of Wisconsin had a duty to accommodate — reasonably.

Vande Zande worked for the housing division of the state's department of administration for three years, beginning in January 1990. . . . Her job was that of a program assistant, and involved preparing public information materials, planning meetings, interpreting regulations, typing, mailing, filing, and copying. In short, her tasks were of a clerical, secretarial, and administrative assistant character. In order to enable her to do this work, the defendants, as she acknowledges, "made numerous accommodations relating to the plaintiff's disability." As examples, in her words, "they paid the landlord to have bathrooms modified and to have a step ramped; they bought special adjustable furniture for the plaintiff; they ordered and paid for one-half of the cost of a cot that the plaintiff needed for daily personal care at work; they sometimes adjusted the plaintiff's schedule to perform backup telephone duties to accommodate the plaintiff's medical appointments; they made changes to the plans for a locker room in the new state office building; and they agreed to provide some of the specific accommodations the plaintiff requested in her October 5, 1992 Reasonable Accommodation Request."

But she complains that the defendants did not go far enough in two principal respects. One concerns a period of eight weeks when a bout of pressure ulcers forced her to stay home. She wanted to work full time at home and believed that she would be able to do so if the division would provide her with a desktop computer at home (though she already had a laptop). Her supervisor refused. . . . [S]he was able to work all but 16.5 hours in the eight-week period. She took 16.5 hours of sick leave to make up the difference. As a result, she incurred no loss of income, but did lose sick leave that she could have carried forward indefinitely. She now works for another agency of the State of Wisconsin, but any unused sick leave in her employment by the housing division would have accompanied her to her new job. Restoration of the 16.5 hours of lost sick leave is one form of relief that she seeks in this suit.

She argues that a jury might have found that a reasonable accommodation required the housing division either to give her the desktop computer or to excuse her from having to dig into her sick leave to get paid for the hours in which, in the absence of the computer, she was unable to do her work at home. No jury, however, could in our view be permitted to stretch the concept of "reasonable accommodation" so far. Most jobs in organizations public or private involve team work under supervision rather than solitary unsupervised work, and team work under supervision generally cannot be performed at home without a substantial reduction in the quality of the employee's performance. This will no doubt change as communications technology advances, but is the situation today. Generally, therefore, an employer is not required to accommodate a disability by allowing the disabled worker to work, by himself, without supervision, at home. This is the majority view, illustrated by Tyndall v. National Education Centers, Inc., 31 F.3d 209, 213-14 (4th Cir. 1994), and Law v. United States Postal Service, 852 F.2d 1278 (Fed. Cir. 1988) (per curiam). The District of Columbia Circuit disagrees. Langon v. Dept. of Health & Human Services, 959 F.2d 1053, 1060-61 (D.C. Cir. 1992); Carr v. Reno, 23 F.3d 525, 530 (D.C. Cir. 1994). But we think the majority view is correct. An employer is not required to allow disabled workers to work at home, where their productivity inevitably would be greatly reduced. No doubt to this as to any generalization about so complex and varied an activity as employment there are exceptions, but it would take a very extraordinary case for the employee to be able to create a triable issue of the employer's failure to allow the employee to work at home.

And if the employer, because it is a government agency and therefore is not under intense competitive pressure to minimize its labor costs or maximize the value of its output, or for some other reason, bends over backwards to accommodate a disabled worker — goes further than the law requires — by allowing the worker to work at home, it must not be punished for its generosity by being deemed to have conceded the reasonableness of so far-reaching an accommodation. That would hurt rather than help disabled workers. Wisconsin's housing division was not required by the Americans with Disabilities Act to allow Vande Zande to work at home; even more clearly it was not required to install a computer in her home so that she could avoid using up 16.5 hours of sick leave. It is conjectural that she will ever need those 16.5 hours; the expected cost of the loss must, therefore, surely be slight. An accommodation that allows a disabled worker to work at home, at full pay, subject only to a slight loss of sick leave that may never be needed, hence never missed, is, we hold, reasonable as a matter of law.

Her second complaint has to do with the kitchenettes in the housing division's building, which are for the use of employees during lunch and coffee breaks. Both the sink and the counter in each of the kitchenettes were 36 inches high, which is too high for a person in a wheelchair. The building was under construction, and the kitchenettes not yet built, when the plaintiff complained about this feature of the design. But the defendants refused to alter the design to lower the sink and counter to 34 inches, the height convenient for a person in a wheelchair. . . . [S]he argues that once she brought the problem to the attention of her supervisors, they were obliged to lower the sink and counter, at least on the floor on which her office was located but possibly on the other floors in the building as well, since she might be moved to another floor. All that the defendants were willing to do was to install a shelf 34 inches high in the kitchenette area on Vande Zande's floor. That took care of the counter problem. As for the sink, the defendants took the position that since the plumbing was already in place it would be too costly to lower the sink and that the plaintiff could use the bathroom sink, which is 34 inches high.

Apparently it would have cost only about $150 to lower the sink on Vande Zande's floor; to lower it on all the floors might have cost as much as $2,000, though possibly less. Given the proximity of the bathroom sink, Vande Zande can hardly complain that the inaccessibility of the kitchenette sink interfered with her ability to work or with her physical comfort. Her argument rather is that forcing her to use the bathroom sink for activities (such as washing out her coffee cup) for which the other employees could use the kitchenette sink stigmatized her as different and inferior; she seeks an award of compensatory damages for the resulting emotional distress. We may assume without having to decide that emotional as well as physical barriers to the integration of disabled persons into the workforce are relevant in determining the reasonableness of an accommodation. But we do not think an employer has a duty to expend even modest amounts of money to bring about an absolute identity in working conditions between disabled and nondisabled workers. The creation of such a duty would be the inevitable consequence of deeming a failure to achieve identical conditions "stigmatizing." That is merely an epithet. We conclude that access to a particular sink, when access to an equivalent sink, conveniently located, is provided, is not a legal duty of an employer. The duty of reasonable accommodation is satisfied when the employer does what is necessary to enable the disabled worker to work in reasonable comfort. . . .

## NOTES

1. What would have been the result in *Vande Zande* if Wisconsin had argued convincingly that working at the office was an essential function of Vande Zande's job?

Would Vande Zande no longer meet the definition of a qualified individual with a disability? Remember that § 108(a) requires the individual with a disability to be able to perform the job's "essential functions" with or without reasonable accommodation in order to be "qualified." Reasonable accommodation and essential functions thus are often interrelated. Whether a function is essential or not determines whether reallocating that job function is a reasonable accommodation. An employer is not required to restructure a job by reallocating one of its essential functions to another position. See 29 C.F.R. pt. 1630, app. § 1630.2(o). Only marginal functions must be reallocated to accommodate an individual with a disability. See Lucas v. W. W. Grainger, Inc., 257 F.3d 1249, 1260 (11th Cir. 2001) ("The difference between the accommodation that is required and the transformation that is not is the difference between saddling a camel and removing its hump. Restructuring the Bins Server position by eliminating squatting, bending, lifting, or carrying bin items would have changed the nature of the beast, and that is not something the ADA requires.").

2. In U.S. Airways, Inc. v. Barnett, reproduced at page 745, the Supreme Court, like the *Vande Zande* court, refused to interpret "reasonable accommodation" to encompass any modification that would be effective. An ineffective change is not an accommodation at all, said the *Barnett* Court. By requiring employers to provide only reasonable accommodations, Congress envisioned that some changes that would be effective may not be reasonable. The *Barnett* Court also agreed that an employer's showing of undue hardship will generally focus on the employer's particular circumstances.

3. The state granted Vande Zande much of the flexibility she requested concerning working at home. Suppose another woman working at the Department in a similar position was having difficulty getting to work every day because she suffered from morning sickness. Would she have a right under the ADA to request the same flexibility with respect to working at home that was granted to Vande Zande? See Appell v. Thornburgh, No. Civ. A. 90-2112-LFO, 1991 WL 501641, at *1 (D.D.C. May 10, 1991) ("By the clear wording of the statute . . . an individual who is not handicapped is not protected under the statute from discrimination."), *aff'd mem.*, 984 F.2d 1255 (D.C. Cir. 1993).

4. Why has Congress defined unlawful "discrimination" to include failing to accommodate? Intentional discrimination ordinarily means treating similarly situated individuals differently, but the duty to accommodate *requires* employers to treat individuals with disabilities differently. The Interpretive Guidance describes reasonable accommodation in terms of according individuals with a disability with "equal employment opportunity," which means "an opportunity to attain the same level of performance, or to enjoy the same level of benefits and privileges of employment as are available to the average similarly situated employee without a disability." 29 C.F.R. pt. 1630, app. § 1630.9. Are you convinced? If Vande Zande is entitled to the accommodations she received, won't Vande Zande be able to attain a superior level of performance and superior compensation to the woman with morning sickness?

5. Improving employment opportunities for disabled individuals required Congress to devise an antidiscrimination statute for individuals who are different from other employees in job-related ways. This problem is analogous to the problem of guaranteeing equal employment opportunities for pregnant women. Recall Title VII's approach. Pregnant women must be treated like others similar in their ability or inability to work. Title VII permits different treatment of pregnant women if pregnancy alters their ability to perform job functions. Title VII does not *require* that pregnancy be accommodated to allow equal employment opportunity. In contrast, the ADA *requires* employers to accommodate individuals with disabilities to ensure equal

employment opportunity. Which approach is the better policy?

6. How does the duty to accommodate differ from Title VII's prohibition against employment criteria that have a disparate impact? Could Vande Zande have argued, for example, that requiring employees to work at the office has a disparate impact on individuals with disabilities or, more particularly, individuals suffering from pressure ulcers? Is working under a supervisor a business necessity? What would be the remedy for an impact claim? Would a successful disparate impact claim require the employer to allow *all* employees to work at home? See Christine Jolls, Commentary, Antidiscrimination and Accommodation, 115 Harv. L. Rev. 642 (2001) (analogizing Title VII's disparate impact theory to the ADA's duty to reasonably accommodate the disabled). But see Samuel Issacharoff & Justin Nelson, Discrimination with a Difference: Can Employment Discrimination Law Accommodate the Americans with Disabilities Act?, 79 N.C. L. Rev. 307 (2001) (describing the ADA as very different from Title VII because of the ADA's redistributive obligation absent any discrimination simpliciter).

7. In addition to the accommodations mentioned in the statutory definition, the ADA Interpretive Guidance suggests other accommodations that might be relevant to assisting an individual in performing essential job functions, including "making employer provided transportation accessible and providing reserved parking spaces," "permit[ting] an individual who is blind to use a guide dog at work," and permitting "an employee with a disability that inhibits the ability to write . . . to computerize records that were customarily maintained manually." 29 C.F.R. pt. 1630, app. § 1630.2(o).

8. ADA § 101(9) suggests that providing qualified readers or interpreters may be a reasonable accommodation. The Interpretive Guidance suggests additional accommodations that involve providing personal assistants such as a page turner for an employee with no hands or a travel attendant for an employee who is blind. Again, the concept of essential functions is critical: "[S]uppose a security guard position requires the individual who holds the job to inspect identification cards. An employer would not have to provide an individual who is legally blind with an assistant to look at the identification cards for the legally blind employee. In this situation the assistant would be performing the job for the individual with a disability rather than assisting the individual to perform the job." 29 C.F.R. pt. 1630, app. § 1630.2(o). These provisions do not make it clear under what circumstances providing a reader, interpreter, page turner, or travel attendant would constitute "assisting the individual [with a disability] to perform the job" rather than "performing the job for the individual."

9. Providing personal assistants raises another issue — cost. Isn't hiring a personal assistant to help an individual with a disability unreasonable unless the cost of the assistant's services is relatively low and the value of the disabled individual's qualifications and services is relatively high?

10. Was the state required to provide Vande Zande with any of the accommodations that it provided? The ADA Interpretive Guidance indicates that an employer is permitted to provide accommodations beyond those required. See 29 C.F.R. pt. 1630, app. § 1630.9 ("nothing in this part [relating to reasonable accommodation] prohibits employers or other covered entities from providing accommodations beyond those required by this part"). If an employer provides accommodations that are not required, must the employer provide the same accommodations for others? What does *Vande Zande* say about this issue? See Myers v. Hose, 50 F.3d 278, 284 (4th Cir. 1995) ("the fact that certain accommodations may have been offered . . . to some employees as a matter of good faith does not mean that they must be extended to Myers as a matter of

law"). In Holbrook v. City of Alpharetta, 112 F.3d 1522 (11th Cir. 1997), the city accommodated the plaintiff's vision impairment for several years but then stopped. The plaintiff, a police detective, sued, arguing that providing the accommodations proved they were reasonable. The court ruled that the city was free to stop providing accommodations that were not required under the statute. Moreover, in Watson v. Lithonia Lighting, 304 F.3d 749 (7th Cir. 2002), the court found that an employer's establishment of a pool of light-duty jobs for those with temporary conditions did not require that it make such assignments permanently available. Thus, there was no ADA violation when the employer refused to permit an employee to keep such a light-duty job indefinitely when her condition was diagnosed as permanent.

11.  Other courts have agreed with *Vande Zande* that working at home is not a reasonable accommodation for most employees. See, e.g., Smith v. Ameritech, 129 F.3d 857 (6th Cir. 1997). In contrast, in Humphrey v. Memorial Hosp. Assoc., 239 F.3d 1128 (9th Cir. 2001), the Ninth Circuit found that working at home can be a reasonable accommodation when the essential functions of the position can be performed at home. As *Vande Zande* predicts, in light of advances in technology, won't there be an increasing number of positions for which this will be true?

12.  Courts have ruled that timely and regular attendance is an essential job function for most jobs. See section C.1. If attending work regularly or starting work at a particular time of day or working full-time is an essential function, the employer need not offer part-time or modified work schedules as a reasonable accommodation. Employers, therefore, generally are not required to accommodate disabled individuals by allowing excessive absences or by granting long leaves of absence or leaves of absence of indefinite duration. See, e.g., EEOC v. Yellow Freight Sys., 253 F.3d 943 (7th Cir. 2001); Hudson v. MCI Telecommunications Corp., 87 F.3d 1167 (10th Cir. 1996); Rogers v. International Marine Terminals, 87 F.3d 755 (5th Cir. 1996); Myers v. Hose, 50 F.3d 278 (4th Cir. 1995). However, a short-term leave of absence often will be viewed as a reasonable accommodation, particularly when the employer's own policies provide for paid or unpaid leave as great as that requested by the disabled employee. See Nunes v. Wal-Mart Stores, Inc., 164 F.3d 1243 (9th Cir. 1999) (jury question on reasonableness when plaintiff was terminated before leave period under employer's policy expired); Rascon v. U.S. West Communications, Inc., 143 F.3d 1324 (10th Cir. 1998) (request for four- to five-month leave not unreasonable when employer's policy provided for leaves ranging from 6 to 12 months); Haschman v. Time Warner Entertainment Co., 151 F.3d 591 (7th Cir. 1998) (failure to provide two- to four-week leave supported jury verdict in favor of plaintiff). See Stephen F. Befort, The Most Difficult Reasonable Accommodation Issues: Reassignment and Leave of Absence, 37 Wake Forest L. Rev. 439 (2002).

13.  Eligible employees who are covered by the Family and Medical Leave Act are entitled to up to 12 weeks of unpaid leave per year for a serious health condition and may be permitted to take intermittent leave without pay in blocks as small as an hour at a time and without prior notice if the need for leave is unforeseeable. See Eric Paltell, Intermittent Leave Under the Family and Medical Leave Act of 1993: Job Security for the Chronically Absent Employee?, 10 Lab. Law. 1 (1994). If the employee's absences are protected by FMLA, wouldn't providing that leave under the ADA necessarily be viewed as a reasonable accommodation? In other words, how could an employer contend that doing what federal laws requires is unreasonable? See Smith v. Diffee Ford-Lincoln-Mercury, Inc., 298 F.3d 955 (10th Cir. 2002). For further discussion of FMLA, see section F.8.

14.  What evidence is relevant to whether a requested accommodation is reason-

able? On the one hand, the employer has expertise concerning the requirements of the job and the costs of accommodation. On the other hand, the employee and the employee's physician are knowledgeable regarding the needs of the employee. Clearly, not all treating physician recommendations are equally weighty, and contrary medical evidence submitted by the employer would be relevant. On what evidence did the court in *Vande Zande* rely to determine that the requested accommodation was not reasonable? Is an accommodation presumptively reasonable if it is listed in the statute, regulations, or Interpretive Guidance? See McWright v. Alexander, 982 F.2d 222, 227 (7th Cir. 1992) (fact that requested accommodation listed in regulations relevant to surviving motion for dismissal).

15. Plaintiffs who seek expensive accommodations involving removing architectural barriers should be aware that under Title III of the ADA, "public accommodations"* must remove architectural and communications barriers so that people with disabilities have equal access to the goods and services that they offer. 42 U.S.C.S. § 12182(b)(2)(A)(iv) (2003). With respect to existing facilities, if removing barriers is not "readily achievable," "alternative methods" may be used, but only if "such methods are readily achievable." See 42 U.S.C.S. § 12182(b)(2)(A)(v) (2003). Title III, however, includes additional stringent accessibility requirements that apply to new construction and alteration of public accommodations and commercial facilities (nonresidential facilities whose operations affect commerce). See 42 U.S.C.S. § 12183 (2003). These requirements are not subject to any general cost defense. Consider the following comment by the DOJ:

> Congress recognized that the employees within commercial facilities would generally be protected under title I (employment) of the Act. However, as the House Committee on Education and Labor pointed out, "[t]o the extent that new facilities are built in a manner that make[s] them accessible to all individuals, including potential employees, there will be less of a need for individual employers to engage in reasonable accommodations for particular employees." H.R. Rep. No. 485, 101st Cong., 2d Sess., pt. 2 at 117 (1990). While employers of fewer than 15 employers are not covered by title I's employment discrimination provisions, there is no such limitation with respect to new construction covered under title III.

28 C.F.R., pt. 36, app. B. Thus, accommodations that are unreasonable or an undue hardship under Title I may be required under Title III. Note that Title II imposes the new construction accessibility requirements on state and local governments. Because Vande Zande's office building was under construction, the requirements applied. Title II accessibility requirements are discussed in section G.

## NOTE ON ACCOMMODATIONS NECESSARY TO ENJOY BENEFITS AND PRIVILEGES OF EMPLOYMENT

Beyond accommodations enabling employees to perform essential functions is the question of accommodations enabling disabled employees "to enjoy equal benefits and privileges of employment as are enjoyed by employees without disabilities."

---

*Under Title III, a public accommodation is a private entity with operations that affect commerce, which falls into one of twelve exclusive categories, including, for example, places of lodging, establishments serving food, places of exhibition or entertainment, places of public gathering, sales or rental establishments, service establishments, public transportation terminals or stations, places of education, social service centers, and a variety of recreational facilities.

29 C.F.R. pt. 1630, app. § 1630.2(o). This includes, for example, accommodations designed to permit equal access to cafeterias, lounges, and restrooms. Is an individual with a disability entitled to access to all unrestricted areas of the employer's business, even areas that relate neither to essential functions nor to specific job benefits? Is it a "privilege of employment" to have access to all unrestricted areas? What if a deaf employee requests an interpreter at workplace social events? Should he be entitled to this accommodation?

*Vande Zande* discussed the degree of equality of access to benefits required by the ADA. While acknowledging that emotional barriers to equal employment of disabled individuals are relevant to determining the reasonableness of an accommodation, the court ruled that the employer need not spend "even modest amounts of money to bring about an absolute identity in working conditions." Why not?

The ADA specifically prohibits discrimination against a qualified individual with a disability with respect to job training. 42 U.S.C. § 12112(a). Thus, a failure to provide job training because of a disability is actionable, whether or not the lack of training has any adverse impact on the terms and conditions of plaintiff's employment. Hoffman v. Caterpillar, Inc., 256 F.3d 568 (7th Cir. 2001). In *Hoffman*, plaintiff, who had only one hand, had been denied training on a high-speed scanner because her employer believed the disability would prevent her from operating the machine. However, the court said *recovery* would be permitted only if plaintiff could have operated the machine with training. Because it was uncertain whether plaintiff could have operated the scanner had training been provided, she could proceed to trial on her failure-to-train claim. At the same time, however, the court held the employer was not required to provide accommodations that would enable plaintiff to run the printer if running the printer was not an essential job function.

Felde v. City of San Jose, No. 94-15272, 1995 WL 547698 (9th Cir. Sept. 14, 1995), considered what equal treatment means in the context of eligibility for retirement benefits. The employer offered two retirement options, regular service retirement or disability retirement. Regular service retirement was available to all employees, including disabled employees, and included a payment for 100 percent of unused sick leave. Disability retirement, available only to disabled employees, provided some tax benefits, but was limited by a sick leave payout capped at 80 percent of a maximum number of hours. Felde claimed that this cap was discriminatory. The Ninth Circuit disagreed because disabled employees had unlimited access to regular service retirement. What Felde wanted was a better deal than was available to other employees — all the advantages of disability retirement plus the advantages of general retirement.

Cases involving accommodations relating to the privileges and benefits of employment may also raise questions about the distinction between personal and work-related accommodations. Consider the EEOC's Interpretive Guidance:

> The obligation to make reasonable accommodation . . . does not extend to the provision of adjustments or modifications that are primarily for the personal benefit of the individual with a disability. Thus, if an adjustment or modification is job-related, e.g., specifically assists the individual in performing the duties of a particular job, it will be considered a type of reasonable accommodation. On the other hand, if an adjustment or modification assists the individual throughout his or her daily activities, on and off the job, it will be considered a personal item that the employer is not required to provide. Accordingly, an employer would generally not be required to provide an employee with a disability with a prosthetic limb, wheelchair, or eyeglasses.

29 C.F.R. pt. 1630, app. § 1630.9. See Nelson v. Ryan, 860 F. Supp. 76 (W.D.N.Y. 1994) (while an employer may be required to permit a blind employee to use a guide

dog at work, an employer is not required to provide a guide dog or paid leave to train a guide dog because guide dogs are personal items even if the employee uses the dog for work purposes).

In Lyons v. Legal Aid Socy., 68 F.3d 1512 (2d Cir. 1995), a disabled attorney sought financial assistance to park her car near her office because injuries made it difficult for her to walk, stand for extended periods of time, and climb or descend stairs. Legal Aid, in defending its refusal to pay for parking, argued that the requested accommodation was merely "a matter of personal convenience" and therefore not within Legal Aid's obligation to provide accommodation. The Second Circuit ruled that a parking place was a work-related need, not merely a personal need. Lyons could not do her job without parking near the office, reaching the office and the courts was an essential function of her job, and there was no evidence on the record that she planned to use the space for any other purpose. Id. at 1517.

Was Vande Zande's request for accessible kitchen sinks a request for a personal benefit or was it job related?

## US AIRWAYS, INC. v. BARNETT
### 535 U.S. 391 (2002)

BREYER, J., delivered the opinion of the Court, in which REHNQUIST, C. J., and STEVENS, O'CONNOR, and KENNEDY, JJ., joined. STEVENS, J., and O'CONNOR, J., filed concurring opinions. SCALIA, J., filed a dissenting opinion, in which THOMAS, J., joined. SOUTER, J., filed a dissenting opinion, in which GINSBURG, J., joined.

Justice BREYER delivered the opinion of the Court.

The Americans with Disabilities Act of 1990 prohibits an employer from discriminating against an "individual with a disability" who, with "reasonable accommodation," can perform the essential functions of the job. This case, arising in the context of summary judgment, asks us how the Act resolves a potential conflict between: (1) the interests of a disabled worker who seeks assignment to a particular position as a "reasonable accommodation," and (2) the interests of other workers with superior rights to bid for the job under an employer's seniority system. In such a case, does the accommodation demand trump the seniority system?

In our view, the seniority system will prevail in the run of cases. As we interpret the statute, to show that a requested accommodation conflicts with the rules of a seniority system is ordinarily to show that the accommodation is not "reasonable." Hence such a showing will entitle an employer/defendant to summary judgment on the question — unless there is more. The plaintiff remains free to present evidence of special circumstances that make "reasonable" a seniority rule exception in the particular case. And such a showing will defeat the employer's demand for summary judgment.

I

In 1990, Robert Barnett, the plaintiff and respondent here, injured his back while working in a cargo-handling position at petitioner US Airways, Inc. He invoked seniority rights and transferred to a less physically demanding mailroom position. Under US Airways' seniority system, that position, like others, periodically became open to seniority-based employee bidding. In 1992, Barnett learned that at least two employees senior to him intended to bid for the mailroom job. He asked US Airways to accommodate his disability-imposed limitations by making an exception that would allow him to remain in the mailroom. After permitting Barnett to continue his mailroom work for five months while it considered the matter, US Airways eventually decided not to make an exception. And Barnett lost his job.

Barnett then brought this ADA suit claiming, among other things, that he was an "individual with a disability" capable of performing the essential functions of the mailroom job, that the mailroom job amounted to a "reasonable accommodation" of his disability, and that US Airways, in refusing to assign him the job, unlawfully discriminated against him. . . .

The District Court found that the undisputed facts about seniority warranted summary judgment in US Airways' favor. The Act says that an employer who fails to make "reasonable accommodations to the known physical or mental limitations of an [employee] with a disability" discriminates "*unless*" the employer "can demonstrate that the accommodation would impose an *undue hardship* on the operation of [its] business." 42 U.S.C. § 12112(b)(5)(A) (emphasis added). The court said:

> The uncontroverted evidence shows that the USAir seniority system has been in place for "decades" and governs over 14,000 USAir Agents. Moreover, seniority policies such as the one at issue in this case are common to the airline industry. Given this context, it seems clear that the USAir employees were justified in relying upon the policy. As such, any significant alteration of that policy would result in undue hardship to both the company and its nondisabled employees.

An en banc panel of the United States Court of Appeals for the Ninth Circuit reversed. It said that the presence of a seniority system is merely "a factor in the undue hardship analysis." And it held that "[a] case-by-case fact intensive analysis is required to determine whether any particular reassignment would constitute an undue hardship to the employer."

US Airways petitioned for certiorari, asking us to decide whether "the [ADA] requires an employer to reassign a disabled employee to a position as a 'reasonable accommodation' even though another employee is entitled to hold the position under the employer's bona fide and established seniority system." . . .

## II

In answering the question presented, we must consider the following statutory provisions. First, the ADA says that an employer may not "discriminate against a qualified individual with a disability." 42 U.S.C. § 12112(a). Second, the ADA says that a "qualified" individual includes "an individual with a disability who, *with* or without *reasonable accommodation*, can perform the essential functions of" the relevant "employment position." § 12111(8) (emphasis added). Third, the ADA says that "discrimination" includes an employer's "*not making reasonable accommodations* to the known physical or mental limitations of an otherwise qualified . . . employee, *unless* [the employer] can demonstrate that the accommodation would impose an *undue hardship* on the operation of [its] business." § 12112(b)(5)(A) (emphasis added). Fourth, the ADA says that the term "'reasonable accommodation' may include . . . reassignment to a vacant position." § 12111(9)(B).

The parties interpret this statutory language as applied to seniority systems in radically different ways. In US Airways' view, the fact that an accommodation would violate the rules of a seniority system always shows that the accommodation is not a "reasonable" one. In Barnett's polar opposite view, a seniority system violation never shows that an accommodation sought is not a "reasonable" one. Barnett concedes that a violation of seniority rules might help to show that the accommodation will work "undue" employer "hardship," but that is a matter for an employer to demonstrate case by case. We shall initially consider the parties' main legal arguments in support of these conflicting positions.

A

US Airways' claim that a seniority system virtually always trumps a conflicting accommodation demand rests primarily upon its view of how the Act treats workplace "preferences." Insofar as a requested accommodation violates a disability-neutral workplace rule, such as a seniority rule, it grants the employee with a disability treatment that other workers could not receive. Yet the Act, US Airways says, seeks only "equal" treatment for those with disabilities. See, e.g., 42 U.S.C. § 12101(a)(9). It does not, it contends, require an employer to grant preferential treatment. Cf. H. R. Rep. No. 101-485, pt. 2, p. 66 (1990); S. Rep. No. 101-116, pp. 26-27 (1989) (employer has no "obligation to prefer *applicants* with disabilities over other *applicants*" (emphasis added)). Hence it does not require the employer to grant a request that, in violating a disability-neutral rule, would provide a preference.

While linguistically logical, this argument fails to recognize what the Act specifies, namely, that preferences will sometimes prove necessary to achieve the Act's basic equal opportunity goal. The Act requires preferences in the form of "reasonable accommodations" that are needed for those with disabilities to obtain the *same* workplace opportunities that those without disabilities automatically enjoy. By definition any special "accommodation" requires the employer to treat an employee with a disability differently, *i.e.*, preferentially. And the fact that the difference in treatment violates an employer's disability-neutral rule cannot by itself place the accommodation beyond the Act's potential reach.

Were that not so, the "reasonable accommodation" provision could not accomplish its intended objective. Neutral office assignment rules would automatically prevent the accommodation of an employee whose disability-imposed limitations require him to work on the ground floor. Neutral "break-from-work" rules would automatically prevent the accommodation of an individual who needs additional breaks from work, perhaps to permit medical visits. Neutral furniture budget rules would automatically prevent the accommodation of an individual who needs a different kind of chair or desk. Many employers will have neutral rules governing the kinds of actions most needed to reasonably accommodate a worker with a disability. See 42 U.S.C. § 12111(9)(b) (setting forth examples such as "job restructuring," "part-time or modified work schedules," "acquisition or modification of equipment or devices," "and other similar accommodations"). Yet Congress, while providing such examples, said nothing suggesting that the presence of such neutral rules would create an automatic exemption. Nor have the lower courts made any such suggestion. Cf. Garcia-Ayala v. Lederle Parenterals, Inc., 212 F.3d 638, 648 (CA1 2000) (requiring leave beyond that allowed under the company's own leave policy); Hendricks-Robinson v. Excel Corp., 154 F.3d 685, 699 (CA7 1998) (requiring exception to employer's neutral "physical fitness" job requirement).

In sum, the nature of the "reasonable accommodation" requirement, the statutory examples, and the Act's silence about the exempting effect of neutral rules together convince us that the Act does not create any such automatic exemption. The simple fact that an accommodation would provide a "preference" — in the sense that it would permit the worker with a disability to violate a rule that others must obey — cannot, *in and of itself,* automatically show that the accommodation is not "reasonable." As a result, we reject the position taken by US Airways and Justice Scalia to the contrary. . . .

### B

Barnett argues that the statutory words "reasonable accommodation" mean only "effective accommodation," authorizing a court to consider the requested accommodation's ability to meet an individual's disability-related needs, and nothing more. On this view, a seniority rule violation, having nothing to do with the accommodation's effectiveness, has nothing to do with its "reasonableness." It might, at most, help to prove an "undue hardship on the operation of the business." . . . Barnett adds that any other view would make the words "reasonable accommodation" and "undue hardship" virtual mirror images — creating redundancy in the statute. And he says that any such other view would create a practical burden of proof dilemma.

The practical burden of proof dilemma arises, Barnett argues, because the statute imposes the burden of demonstrating an "undue hardship" upon the employer, while the burden of proving "reasonable accommodation" remains with the plaintiff, here the employee. This allocation seems sensible in that an employer can more frequently and easily prove the presence of business hardship than an employee can prove its absence. But suppose that an employee must counter a claim of "seniority rule violation" in order to prove that an "accommodation" request is "reasonable." Would that not force the employee to prove what is in effect an absence, *i.e.,* an absence of hardship, despite the statute's insistence that the employer "demonstrate" hardship's presence?

These arguments do not persuade us that Barnett's legal interpretation of "reasonable" is correct. For one thing, in ordinary English the word "reasonable" does not mean "effective." It is the word "accommodation," not the word "reasonable," that conveys the need for effectiveness. An *ineffective* "modification" or "adjustment" will not *accommodate* a disabled individual's limitations. Nor does an ordinary English meaning of the term "reasonable accommodation" make of it a simple, redundant mirror image of the term "undue hardship." The statute refers to an "undue hardship on the operation of the business." 42 U.S.C. § 12112 (b)(5)(A). Yet a demand for an effective accommodation could prove unreasonable because of its impact, not on business operations, but on fellow employees — say because it will lead to dismissals, relocations, or modification of employee benefits to which an employer, looking at the matter from the perspective of the business itself, may be relatively indifferent.

Neither does the statute's primary purpose require Barnett's special reading. The statute seeks to diminish or to eliminate the stereotypical thought processes, the thoughtless actions, and the hostile reactions that far too often bar those with disabilities from participating fully in the Nation's life, including the workplace. See generally §§ 12101(a) and (b). These objectives demand unprejudiced thought and reasonable responsive reaction on the part of employers and fellow workers alike. They will sometimes require affirmative conduct to promote entry of disabled people into the workforce. They do not, however, demand action beyond the realm of the reasonable. . . .

Finally, an ordinary language interpretation of the word "reasonable" does not create the "burden of proof" dilemma to which Barnett points. Many of the lower courts, while rejecting both US Airways' and Barnett's more absolute views, have reconciled the phrases "reasonable accommodation" and "undue hardship" in a practical way.

They have held that a plaintiff/employee (to defeat a defendant/employer's motion for summary judgment) need only show that an "accommodation" seems reasonable on its face, *i.e.*, ordinarily or in the run of cases. See, *e.g.*, Reed v. LePage Bakeries, Inc., 244 F.3d 254, 259 (CA1 2001) (plaintiff meets burden on reasonableness by showing that, "at least on the face of things," the accommodation will be feasible for the employer); Borkowski v. Valley Central School Dist., 63 F.3d 131, 138 (CA2 1995) (plaintiff satisfies "burden of production" by showing "plausible accommodation"); Barth v. Gelb, 2 F.3d 1180, 1187 (CADC 1993) (interpreting parallel language in Rehabilitation Act, stating that plaintiff need only show he seeks a "*method of accommodation* that is reasonable in the run of cases") (emphasis in original).

Once the plaintiff has made this showing, the defendant/employer then must show special (typically case-specific) circumstances that demonstrate undue hardship in the particular circumstances. See *Reed* ("'undue hardship inquiry focuses on the hardships imposed . . . in the context of the particular [employer's] operations'") (quoting *Barth*); *Borkowski* (after plaintiff makes initial showing, burden falls on employer to show that particular accommodation "would cause it to suffer an undue hardship"); *Barth* ("undue hardship inquiry focuses on the hardships imposed . . . in the context of the particular agency's operations").

Not every court has used the same language, but their results are functionally similar. In our opinion, that practical view of the statute, applied consistently with ordinary summary judgment principles, see Fed. Rule Civ. Proc. 56, avoids Barnett's burden of proof dilemma, while reconciling the two statutory phrases ("reasonable accommodation" and "undue hardship").

### III

The question in the present case focuses on the relationship between seniority systems and the plaintiff's need to show that an "accommodation" seems reasonable on its face, *i.e.*, ordinarily or in the run of cases. We must assume that the plaintiff, an employee, is an "individual with a disability." He has requested assignment to a mailroom position as a "reasonable accommodation." We also assume that normally such a request would be reasonable within the meaning of the statute, were it not for one circumstance, namely, that the assignment would violate the rules of a seniority system. See § 12111(9) ("reasonable accommodation" may include "reassignment to a vacant position"). Does that circumstance mean that the proposed accommodation is not a "reasonable" one?

In our view, the answer to this question ordinarily is "yes." The statute does not require proof on a case-by-case basis that a seniority system should prevail. That is because it would not be reasonable in the run of cases that the assignment in question trump the rules of a seniority system. To the contrary, it will ordinarily be unreasonable for the assignment to prevail.

#### A

Several factors support our conclusion that a proposed accommodation will not be reasonable in the run of cases. Analogous case law supports this conclusion, for it has recognized the importance of seniority to employee-management relations. [The

Court cited numerous decisions issued under Title VII, the Rehabilitation Act, and the ADA holding that seniority systems found in collective bargaining agreements trump requested accommodations. The Court then noted that the advantages of and disadvantages posed by violating seniority systems did not belong to collectively bargained systems alone.]

For one thing, the typical seniority system provides important employee benefits by creating, and fulfilling, employee expectations of fair, uniform treatment. These benefits include "job security and an opportunity for steady and predictable advancement based on objective standards." They include "an element of due process," limiting "unfairness in personnel decisions." And they consequently encourage employees to invest in the employing company, accepting "less than their value to the firm early in their careers" in return for greater benefits in later years.

Most important for present purposes, to require the typical employer to show more than the existence of a seniority system might well undermine the employees' expectations of consistent, uniform treatment — expectations upon which the seniority system's benefits depend. That is because such a rule would substitute a complex case-specific "accommodation" decision made by management for the more uniform, impersonal operation of seniority rules. Such management decision making, with its inevitable discretionary elements, would involve a matter of the greatest importance to employees, namely, layoffs; it would take place outside, as well as inside, the confines of a court case; and it might well take place fairly often. Cf. ADA, 42 U.S.C. §12101(a)(1), (estimating that some 43 million Americans suffer from physical or mental disabilities). We can find nothing in the statute that suggests Congress intended to undermine seniority systems in this way. And we consequently conclude that the employer's showing of violation of the rules of a seniority system is by itself ordinarily sufficient.

### B

The plaintiff (here the employee) nonetheless remains free to show that special circumstances warrant a finding that, despite the presence of a seniority system (which the ADA may not trump in the run of cases), the requested "accommodation" is "reasonable" on the particular facts. That is because special circumstances might alter the important expectations described above. The plaintiff might show, for example, that the employer, having retained the right to change the seniority system unilaterally, exercises that right fairly frequently, reducing employee expectations that the system will be followed — to the point where one more departure, needed to accommodate an individual with a disability, will not likely make a difference. The plaintiff might show that the system already contains exceptions such that, in the circumstances, one further exception is unlikely to matter. We do not mean these examples to exhaust the kinds of showings that a plaintiff might make. But we do mean to say that the plaintiff must bear the burden of showing special circumstances that make an exception from the seniority system reasonable in the particular case. And to do so, the plaintiff must explain why, in the particular case, an exception to the employer's seniority policy can constitute a "reasonable accommodation" even though in the ordinary case it cannot.

### IV

In its question presented, US Airways asked us whether the ADA requires an employer to assign a disabled employee to a particular position even though another employee is entitled to that position under the employer's "established seniority system." We answer that *ordinarily* the ADA does not require that assignment. Hence, a showing that the assignment would violate the rules of a seniority system warrants summary judgment for the employer — unless there is more. The plaintiff must present evidence of that "more," namely, special circumstances surrounding the particular case that demonstrate the assignment is nonetheless reasonable. . . .

Justice O'CONNOR, concurring.

I agree with portions of the opinion of the Court, but I find problematic the Court's test for determining whether the fact that a job reassignment violates a seniority system makes the reassignment an unreasonable accommodation under the Americans with Disabilities Act of 1990. Although a seniority system plays an important role in the workplace, . . . I would prefer to say that the effect of a seniority system on the reasonableness of a reassignment as an accommodation for purposes of the ADA depends on whether the seniority system is legally enforceable. "Were it possible for me to adhere to [this belief] in my vote, and for the Court at the same time to [adopt a majority rule]," I would do so. Screws v. United States, 325 U.S. 91 (1945) (Rutledge, J., concurring in result). "The Court, however, is divided in opinion," and if each member voted consistently with his or her beliefs, we would not agree on a resolution of the question presented in this case. Yet "stalemate should not prevail," particularly in a case in which we are merely interpreting a statute. Accordingly, in order that the Court may adopt a rule, and because I believe the Court's rule will often lead to the same outcome as the one I would have adopted, I join the Court's opinion despite my concerns. . . .

Justice SCALIA, with whom Justice THOMAS joins, dissenting.

The principal defect of today's opinion . . . goes well beyond the uncertainty it produces regarding the relationship between the ADA and the infinite variety of seniority systems. The conclusion that any seniority system can ever be overridden is merely one consequence of a mistaken interpretation of the ADA that makes all employment rules and practices — even those which (like a seniority system) pose no *distinctive* obstacle to the disabled — subject to suspension when that is (in a court's view) a "reasonable" means of enabling a disabled employee to keep his job. That is a far cry from what I believe the accommodation provision of the ADA requires: the suspension (within reason) of those employment rules and practices *that the employee's disability prevents him from observing.*

I

The Court begins its analysis by describing the ADA as declaring that an employer may not "discriminate against a qualified individual with a disability." In fact the Act says more: an employer may not "discriminate against a qualified individual with a disability *because of the disability* of such individual." 42 U.S.C. § 12112(a) (1994 ed.) (emphasis added). It further provides that discrimination includes "not making reasonable accommodations *to the known physical or mental limitations* of an otherwise qualified individual with a disability." § 12112(b)(5)(A) (emphasis added).

Read together, these provisions order employers to modify or remove (within reason) policies and practices that burden a disabled person "because of [his] disability." In other words, the ADA eliminates workplace barriers only if a disability prevents an employee from overcoming them — those barriers that would not be barriers *but for* the employee's disability. These include, for example, work stations that cannot accept the employee's wheelchair, or an assembly-line practice that requires long periods of standing. But they do not include rules and practices that bear no more heavily upon the disabled employee than upon others — even though an exemption from such a rule or practice might in a sense "make up for" the employee's disability. It is not a required accommodation, for example, to pay a disabled employee more than others at his grade level — even if that increment is earmarked for massage or physical therapy that would enable the employee to work with as little physical discomfort as his co-workers. That would be "accommodating" the disabled employee, but it would not be "making . . . accommodation *to the known physical or mental limitations*" of the employee, § 12112(b)(5)(A), because it would not eliminate any workplace practice that constitutes an obstacle because of his disability.

So also with exemption from a seniority system, which burdens the disabled and nondisabled alike. In particular cases, seniority rules may have a harsher effect upon the disabled employee than upon his co-workers. If the disabled employee is physically capable of performing only one task in the workplace, seniority rules may be, for him, the difference between employment and unemployment. But that does not make the seniority system a disability-related obstacle, any more than harsher impact upon the more needy disabled employee renders the salary system a disability-related obstacle. When one departs from this understanding, the ADA's accommodation provision becomes a standardless grab bag — leaving it to the courts to decide which workplace preferences (higher salary, longer vacations, reassignment to positions to which others are entitled) can be deemed "reasonable" to "make up for" the particular employee's disability. . . .

## II

Although, as I have said, the uncertainty cast upon bona fide seniority systems is the least of the ill consequences produced by today's decision, a few words on that subject are nonetheless in order. . . .

One is tempted to impart some rationality to the scheme by speculating that the Court's burden-shifting rule is merely intended to give the disabled employee an opportunity to show that the employer's seniority system is in fact a sham — a system so full of exceptions that it creates no meaningful employee expectations. . . .

[But] I must conclude . . . that the Court's rebuttable presumption does not merely give disabled employees the opportunity to unmask sham seniority systems; it gives them a vague and unspecified power (whenever they can show "special circumstances") to undercut *bona fide* systems. The Court claims that its new test will not require exceptions to seniority systems "in the run of cases," but that is belied by the disposition of this case. The Court remands to give respondent an opportunity to show that an exception to petitioner's seniority system "will not likely make a difference" to employee expectations, despite the following finding by the District Court:

> The uncontroverted evidence shows that [petitioner's] seniority system has been in place for "decades" and governs over 14,000 . . . Agents. Moreover, seniority policies such as the one at issue in this case are common to the airline industry. Given this context, it seems clear that [petitioner's] employees were justified in relying upon the policy. As such, any significant alteration of that policy would result in undue hardship to both the company and its non-disabled employees. . . .

Because the Court's opinion leaves the question whether a seniority system must be disregarded in order to accommodate a disabled employee in a state of uncertainty that can be resolved only by constant litigation; and because it adopts an interpretation of the ADA that incorrectly subjects all employer rules and practices to the requirement of reasonable accommodation; I respectfully dissent.

Justice SOUTER, with whom Justice GINSBURG joins, dissenting.

"Reassignment to a vacant position," 42 U.S.C. § 12111(9) is one way an employer may "reasonably accommodate" disabled employees under the Americans with Disabilities Act of 1990.

Nothing in the ADA insulates seniority rules from the "reasonable accommodation" requirement, in marked contrast to Title VII of the Civil Rights Act of 1964 and the Age Discrimination in Employment Act of 1967, each of which has an explicit protection for seniority. See 42 U.S.C. § 2000e-2(h) ("Notwithstanding any other provision of this subchapter, it shall not be an unlawful employment practice for an employer to [provide different benefits to employees] pursuant to a bona fide seniority . . . system . . . ."); 29 U.S.C. § 623(f) ("It shall not be unlawful for an employer . . . to take any action otherwise prohibited [under previous sections] . . . to observe the terms of a bona fide seniority system [except for involuntary retirement] . . .") . . .

Because a unilaterally-imposed seniority system enjoys no special protection under the ADA, a consideration of facts peculiar to this very case is needed to gauge whether Barnett has carried the burden of showing his proposed accommodation to be a "reasonable" one despite the policy in force at US Airways. . . .

He held the mailroom job for two years before learning that employees with greater seniority planned to bid for the position, given US Airways' decision to declare the job "vacant." Thus, perhaps unlike ADA claimants who request accommodation through reassignment, Barnett was seeking not a change but a continuation of the status quo. All he asked was that US Airways refrain from declaring the position "vacant"; he did not ask to bump any other employee and no one would have lost a job on his account. There was no evidence in the District Court of any unmanageable ripple effects from Barnett's request, or showing that he would have overstepped an inordinate number of seniority levels by remaining where he was.

In fact, it is hard to see the seniority scheme here as any match for Barnett's ADA requests, since US Airways apparently took pains to ensure that its seniority rules raised no great expectations. . . .

With US Airways itself insisting that its seniority system was noncontractual and modifiable at will, there is no reason to think that Barnett's accommodation would have resulted in anything more than minimal disruption to US Airways' operations, if that. Barnett has shown his requested accommodation to be "reasonable," and the burden ought to shift to US Airways if it wishes to claim that, in spite of surface appearances, violation of the seniority scheme would have worked an undue hardship. I would therefore affirm the Ninth Circuit.

### NOTES

1. US Air contended that a position that would be allocated under a seniority system's bumping or bidding provisions was not a "vacancy" within the meaning of the statute. The majority rejected that argument out of hand.

2. A seniority system contained in a collective bargaining agreement is contractually enforceable. The lower courts, including the Ninth Circuit, had agreed that a collectively bargained for seniority system would trump a disabled employee's request for reassignment to a vacant position under the ADA. See, e.g., Willis v. Pacific Maritime Assn., 244 F.3d 675 (9th Cir. 2001) (collecting cases). But the Ninth Circuit had refused to extend the same deference to a seniority system that was not the product of collective bargaining. Was the Supreme Court correct in its assumption that a unilaterally imposed system generally confers the same advantages on workers as do those that are the result of collective bargaining?

3. Justice O'Connor was willing to accept that a unilaterally imposed system could grant such advantages *if* it were legally enforceable; thus, she would have preferred to limit the presumption in favor of seniority systems to those the employer was contractually obligated to follow. She joins the Court's opinion, however, observing that the majority's rule and her preferred one will generally reach the same result. Is she saying that if a plaintiff can demonstrate the unilaterally imposed system is not legally enforceable, then "special circumstances" will have been shown?

4. The *Barnett* Court expressly acknowledged that the ADA will sometimes require that the disabled worker receive a preference. "By definition any special 'accommodation' requires the employer to treat an employee with a disability differently, i.e., preferentially. And the fact that the difference in treatment violates an employer's disability-neutral rule cannot by itself place the accommodation beyond the Act's potential reach." 122 S. Ct. at 1521. The majority's conclusion that the duty of reasonable accommodation can require preferential treatment was foreshadowed by its opinion in Board of Trustees of Univ. of Ala. v. Garrett, 531 U.S. 356 (2001), in which the Court viewed the ADA's accommodation mandate as going beyond that demanded by the constitution. Is Justice Scalia's dissent in *Barnett* consistent with the Court's position (which he joined) in *Garrett*?

5. Although *Barnett* arose and was decided in the context of a seniority system dispute, the issue raised by the case in fact is much broader. When will a disabled employee's request for reassignment to a vacant position entitle him to the job over other qualified (or better qualified) applicants? The lower courts had sharply disagreed on their answer to this question, and that disagreement is reflected in the majority and dissenting opinions. To what extent does the ADA require employers to prefer, or to treat the disabled worker better than, his nondisabled colleagues? What is the rule advocated by the majority? The dissent? In thinking about this question, ask yourself how you think the following situations would be resolved by the majority and by the dissent:

a. Disabled employee requests reassignment to a vacant position. Employer refuses the request, pointing to a neutral rule that prohibits reassignment of employees.

b. Disabled employee requests reassignment to a vacant position. Employer refuses the request, pointing to a neutral rule that allocates job openings by employee's date of birth, with job awarded to the oldest applicant.

c. Disabled employee requests reassignment to a vacant position. Employer refuses the request, pointing to a neutral rule that awards the job to the best qualified applicant. Although the disabled employee is qualified, another applicant has better qualifications. However, but for the effects of the disability, the disabled employee would be the best qualified.

d. Same as c (above), except that the disabled employee's comparatively lower qualifications have nothing to do with the disability.

For a pre-*Barnett* discussion of reassignment under the ADA, see Stephen F. Befort, The Most Difficult Reasonable Accommodation Issues: Reassignment and Leave of

Absence, 37 Wake Forest L. Rev. 439 (2002); Stephen F. Befort & Tracey Holmes Donesky, Reassignment Under the Americans with Disabilities Act: Reasonable Accommodation, Affirmative Action, or Both? 57 Wash. & Lee L. Rev. 1045 (2000). For a post-*Barnett* discussion, see Cheryl L. Anderson, "Neutral" Employer Policies and the ADA: The Implications of *U.S. Airways Inc. v. Barnett* Beyond Seniority Systems, 51 Drake L. Rev. 1 (2002).

   6.  Shapiro v. Township of Lakewood, 292 F.3d 356 (3d Cir. 2002), in the wake of *Barnett*, overturned a district court's grant of summary judgment in favor of the employer in a failure to reassign case. The trial court reasoned that the disabled worker's failure to follow interdepartmental transfer procedures when seeking reassignment to a vacant position precluded his claim. The Third Circuit held this result could not be squared with *Barnett*.

## NOTE ON KNOWING THAT ACCOMMODATION IS NEEDED

The ADA provides that employers must make "reasonable accommodations to the *known* physical and mental limitations of an otherwise qualified individual with a disability. . . ." ADA § 102(b)(5)(A) (emphasis added). The Interpretive Guidance provides:

> Employers are obligated to make reasonable accommodation only to the physical or mental limitations resulting from the disability of a qualified individual with a disability that is known to the employer. . . . If an employee with a known disability is having difficulty performing his or her job, an employer may inquire whether the employee is in need of a reasonable accommodation. In general, however, it is the responsibility of the individual with a disability to inform the employer that an accommodation is needed.

29 C.F.R. pt. 1630, app. § 1630.9. What if the employer is aware of the disability, but not of the need for accommodation? Does the ADA require or merely *permit* an employer to ask an employee with a disability if he needs accommodation?

Courts have disagreed about whether an employee must specifically request accommodation in order to trigger the employer's obligation to engage in an interactive process. In Bultemeyer v. Fort Wayne Community Schs., 100 F.3d 1281, (7th Cir. 1996), a custodian returned to work after an extended leave for serious mental illness and then failed to report for a work assignment. He was fired hours before a letter arrived from his psychiatrist recommending that he work in a "less stressful" school. The employee himself did not ask for an accommodation. Nonetheless, the court ruled that the school system was required to engage in an interactive process about reasonable accommodations. The court noted that when an employer knows an employee has a mental disability it may have an increased responsibility to initiate the process.

Some courts, however, have taken a different approach, ruling that unless the employee suggests a concrete reasonable accommodation, the employer has no obligation to engage in an interactive process to discuss possible accommodations. See, e.g., Gaston v. Bellingrath Gardens & Home Inc., 167 F.3d 1361 (11th Cir. 1999) (employee informed employer of her disability and of her inability to perform new job functions but never requested accommodation; employer had no obligation to accommodate); Willis v. Conopco, Inc., 108 F.3d 282 (11th Cir. 1997) (employer's failure to engage in interactive process "unimportant" if employee cannot demonstrate reasonable accommodation); Miller v. National Cas. Co., 61 F.3d 629 (8th Cir. 1995) (employer had no duty to investigate reasonable accommodation even though employee's sister notified the employer that the employee "was mentally falling apart"). Which approach is more consistent with the statute? See generally EEOC Enforcement Guidance: Reasonable Accommodation and Undue Hardship Under the Americans with Disabilities Act (October 17, 2002), available at http://www. eeoc.gov/docs/accommodation.html ("To request accommodation, an individual may use 'plain English' and need not mention the ADA or use the phrase 'reasonable accommodation.'").

The Interpretive Guidance clearly contemplates that reasonable accommodation will be achieved through a process by which disabled individuals and their employers meet and negotiate accommodations that satisfy the needs of both parties. Is failing to discuss accommodation a violation of the ADA even if a court ultimately concludes that no reasonable accommodation is possible? Compare *Willis* (no obligation to engage in an interactive process independent of the obligation to reasonably accommodate) with Beck v. University of Wis. Bd. of Regents, 75 F.3d 1130 (7th Cir. 1996) (suggesting that failure to engage in interactive process may result in liability whether or not a reasonable accommodation is possible). Which approach is more consistent with the statute? Despite language in some cases suggesting otherwise, the lower courts have been unwilling to impose liability on an employer *solely* for failure to engage in the interactive process. There must be a showing that a reasonable accommodation could have been found had the process been pursued. See Lucas v. W. W. Grainger, Inc., 257 F.3d 1249, 1255 n.2 (11th Cir. 2001); Kvorjak v. Maine, 259 F.3d 48 (1st Cir. 2001). But see Lovejoy Wilson v. NOCO Motor Fuel, Inc., 263 F.3d 208, 219 (2d Cir. 2001) (raising, but not resolving, question).

An employee who fails to participate in discussions about accommodation may forfeit protection against disability discrimination. In Derbis v. U.S. Shoe Corp., No. 94-2312, 1995 WL 573036 (4th Cir. Sept. 29, 1995), the court ruled that U.S. Shoe had no obligation to employ Derbis because, although she needed an accommodation to permit her to work, she failed to provide the employer with information necessary to determine what accommodations might be appropriate. See also Templeton v. Neodata Servs., Inc., 162 F.3d 617 (10th Cir. 1998) (terminating employee for refusing to provide reasonably requested medical information does not violate the ADA); Hennenfent v. Mid Dakota Clinic, 164 F.3d 419 (8th Cir. 1998) (same). Employers cannot, however, escape liability by making unreasonable requests for medical information. See Langon v. Department of Health and Human Servs., 959 F.2d 1053 (D.C. Cir. 1992).

### 3.  *Undue Hardship*

Relatively few cases have examined closely the question of undue hardship; instead, as in *Barnett*, reproduced at page 745, they have determined the proposed accommodation is unreasonable. However, a claimed failure to make a reasonable accommodation can be defended on the ground that the plaintiff rejected a reasonable accommodation, see 29 C.F.R. § 1630.9(d), or that the necessary or proposed accommodation would pose an "undue hardship" on the operation of the employer's business, ADA § 102(b)(5)(A); 29 C.F.R. § 1630.15(d). The ADA provides in § 101(10) that an "undue hardship" is an accommodation requiring "significant difficulty or expense," which must be determined by considering all relevant factors, including the size and financial resources of the covered entity. See 29 C.F.R. § 1630.2(p). Section 102(b)(5)(A) expressly states that the covered entity must "demonstrate" the existence of an "undue hardship."

The concepts of reasonable accommodation and undue hardship, as has been observed, go somewhat "hand in hand." Riel v. Electronic Data Sys. Corp., 99 F.3d 678, 681 (5th Cir. 1996). But they are analytically distinct. Reasonable accommodation involves an assessment not only of whether the accommodation would enable the employee to do the job but also whether it is facially reasonable. If this showing is made, the employer has the opportunity to prove that under the facts and circumstances of the particular situation, the accommodation would pose as undue hardship. Reasonable accommodation is thus a more "generalized inquiry," while undue hardship focuses on the particular employer. See Barnett. Thus, while the plaintiff bears the burden of proving a reasonable accommodation exists, the burden of proving that an accommodation would pose an undue hardship is on the employer. The placement of the burdens of production and proof is explored in section E infra.

The Second Circuit in Borkowski v. Valley Cent. Sch. Dist., 63 F.3d 131 (2d Cir. 1995), discussed the elements of "undue hardship," citing ADA provisions that define "undue hardship" to mean "an action requiring significant difficulty or expense, when considered in light of" the following factors:

> (i) the nature and cost of the accommodation needed under this Act;
> (ii) the overall financial resources of the facility or facilities involved in the provision of the reasonable accommodation; the number of persons employed at such facility; the effect on expenses and resources, or the impact otherwise of such accommodation upon the operation of the facility;
> (iii) the overall financial resources of the covered entity; the overall size of the business of a covered entity with respect to the number of its employees; the number, type, and location of its facilities; and
> (iv) the type of operation or operations of the covered entity, including the composition, structure, and functions of the workforce of such entity; the geographic separateness, administrative, or fiscal relationship of the facility or facilities in question to the covered entity.

42 U.S.C.S. § 12111(10) (2003). The issue, according to Borkowski, is one of degree: "[E]ven this list of factors says little about how great a hardship an employer must bear before the hardship becomes undue." The court held that employers are not required to show that they would be driven to the brink of insolvency. The court relied on ADA legislative history rejecting a provision that would have defined an undue hardship as one that threatened the continued existence of the employer. Borkowski, 63 F.3d at 139. "Where the employer is a government entity, Congress could not have intended the only limit on the employer's duty to make reasonable accommodation to be the full extent of the tax base on which the government entity could draw." Id.

The court concluded that, in order to demonstrate both that the proposed accommodation is unreasonable and that the hardship it would impose is undue, the employer must "undertake a refined analysis" of the relative costs and benefits of the accommodation, considering both "the industry to which the employer belongs as well as the individual characteristics of the particular defendant-employer." Id. The court further noted that "mathematical precision" and "complex economic formulae" are not required. Rather "a common-sense balancing of the costs and benefits in light of the factors listed in the regulations is all that is expected." Id. at 140. But see Steven B. Epstein, In Search of a Bright Line: Determining When an Employer's Financial Hardship Becomes "Undue" Under the Americans with Disabilities Act, 48 Vand. L.

Rev. 391 (1995) (proposing a mathematical model for determining undue hardship). See also *Vande Zande* (reproduced at page 735) (adopting a cost-benefit analysis for reasonableness and undue hardship). Is a cost-benefit analysis appropriate under the ADA? The House of Representatives rejected an amendment that would have presumed undue hardship if a reasonable accommodation cost more than 10 percent of the employee's annual salary. See 136 Cong. Rec. H1475 (1990).

Is it an undue hardship if accommodations for one employee will have a negative effect on the morale of other employees? If so, how does this differ from discriminating in order to accommodate the preferences of customers or fellow employees? See Barth v. Gelb, 2 F.3d 1180 (D.C. Cir. 1993). Can undue hardship be raised as an affirmative defense if plaintiff has not requested, or does not need, an accommodation? Doesn't the statutory structure suggest the answer is no?

## D.  DISCRIMINATORY QUALIFICATION STANDARDS

ADA § 102(b) provides that "discriminate" includes

(3) utilizing standards, criteria, or methods of administration . . . that have the effect of discrimination on the basis of disability, . . .

(6) using employment tests or other selection criteria that screen out or tend to screen out an individual with a disability or a class of individuals with disabilities unless the standard, test or other selection criteria, as used by the covered entity, is shown to be job-related for the position in question and is consistent with business necessity. . . .

ADA regulations indicate that both § 102(b)(3) and § 102(b)(6) are subject to a job-relatedness and business necessity defense. See 29 C.F.R. §§ 1630.7, 1630.10. Further, § 103(a), which sets forth defenses, provides that the use of criteria with a disparate impact on the basis of disability must also be consistent with the employer's duty to provide reasonable accommodation. See 29 C.F.R. § 1630.15(b)(1), (c). Standards or selection criterion may also be defended on the basis that they are permitted or required by another federal statute or regulation. See 29 C.F.R. § 1630.15(e). Finally, ADA § 103(b) provides that "[t]he term 'qualification standards' may include a requirement that an individual shall not pose a direct threat to the health or safety of other individuals in the workplace."

In its Interpretive Guidance, the EEOC further explains that selection criteria with a disparate impact that "do not concern an essential function of the job would not be consistent with business necessity." See 29 C.F.R. pt. 1630, app. § 1630.10. The Interpretive Guidance goes on to suggest that most challenges to selection criteria can be resolved by reasonable accommodation. Finally, the EEOC interprets these provisions as "applicable to all types of selection criteria, including safety requirements, vision or hearing requirements, walking requirements, and employment tests. . . . As previously noted, however, it is not the intent of this part to second guess an employer's business judgment with regard to production standards. . . . Consequently, production standards will generally not be subject to a challenge under this provision." Id.

In short, qualification standards that are either facially discriminatory or that have a disparate impact on disabled individuals can violate the ADA, but all discriminatory qualification standards are subject to the same defenses — they may be defended on the basis that they are job related and consistent with business necessity, permitted or required by another federal statute or regulation, or necessary to prevent a direct threat to health and safety.

Most challenges to qualification standards do not raise significant issues about whether the challenged standard or criteria screens out disabled individuals. Challenged standards or selection criteria frequently are facially discriminatory, such as vision requirements for drivers. Even standards or criteria that do not expressly concern a disabling impairment generally are challenged on the ground that a disabled individual cannot meet the standard because of his or her disability. Thus, the fact that the standard or criteria screens out an individual with a disability is obvious. The primary issue in these cases, therefore, is whether the discriminatory standard or criteria can be defended.

This section first examines the direct threat defense. Second, we will consider the job-relatedness and business necessity defense as it applies to qualification standards that screen out disabled individuals, including qualification standards promulgated by the federal government. Finally, we address the application of disparate impact theory in disability discrimination cases.

## 1. Direct Threat

ADA § 103(b) provides that "[t]he term 'qualification standards' may include a requirement that an individual shall not pose a direct threat to the health or safety of other individuals in the workplace." Direct threat is defined by § 101(3) as a "significant risk to the health or safety of others" that cannot be eliminated by a reasonable accommodation. The EEOC requires the "direct threat" determination to be based on a reasonable medical judgment that considers such factors as the duration of the risk, the nature and severity of the potential harm, the likelihood of the potential harm, and the imminence of the potential harm. See 29 C.F.R. § 1630.2(r). Direct threat is simultaneously relevant to whether the individual with a disability is "qualified" to perform essential functions, whether the employer is justified in basing an employment decision on the individual's disability, and whether the employer has a duty to accommodate the individual's disability.

The ADA's "direct threat" provision is derived from the Supreme Court's decision in School Bd. of Nassau Cty. v. Arline, 480 U.S. 273 (1987). In Arline, a case decided under Section 504 of the Rehabilitation Act, the Court confronted the question of whether an individual with tuberculosis was otherwise qualified to be an elementary school teacher. The Court concluded the answer is no, if she poses a significant risk of transmitting the disease to others, and that risk cannot be eliminated through reasonable accommodation. In determining whether a significant risk exists, the Court explained that the inquiry:

> should include [findings of] facts, based on reasonable medical judgments given the state of medical knowledge, about (a) the nature of the risk (how the disease is transmitted), (b) the duration of the risk (how long is the carrier infectious), (c) the severity of the risk (what is the potential harm to third parties) and (d) the probabilities the disease will be transmitted and will cause varying degrees of harm.

Id. at 288.

760                                                    8.  Disability Discrimination

In making this determination, courts were directed to defer to the "reasonable medical judgments of public health officials," with the Court reserving judgment on whether or not courts should defer to the judgment of private physicians.

In Bragdon v. Abbott, reproduced at page 680, the defendant, a dentist, asserted that whether a risk is significant is to be assessed from the point of view of the person denying the service. The Court, however, confirmed that such assessments are to be made on the basis of medical or other objective evidence available at the time that the allegedly discriminatory action occurred. A good faith belief that a significant risk exists is not enough, nor would any special deference be afforded a defendant who is himself a medical professional.

The EEOC's regulation interpreting "direct threat" defines the term to include "a significant risk of substantial harm to the health or safety of *the individual* or others that cannot be eliminated or reduced by reasonable accommodation. 29 C.F.R. § 1630.2(r) (emphasis added). The validity of that regulation was at issue in the following case.

## CHEVRON U.S.A. INC. v. ECHAZABAL
### 536 U.S. 73 (2002)

Justice SOUTER delivered the opinion of the Court.

A regulation of the Equal Employment Opportunity Commission authorizes refusal to hire an individual because his performance on the job would endanger his own health, owing to a disability. The question in this case is whether the Americans with Disabilities Act of 1990 permits the regulation. We hold that it does.

### I

Beginning in 1972, respondent Mario Echazabal worked for independent contractors at an oil refinery owned by petitioner Chevron U.S.A. Inc. Twice he applied for a job directly with Chevron, which offered to hire him if he could pass the company's physical examination. Each time, the exam showed liver abnormality or damage, the cause eventually being identified as Hepatitis C, which Chevron's doctors said would be aggravated by continued exposure to toxins at Chevron's refinery. In each instance, the company withdrew the offer, and the second time it asked the contractor employing Echazabal either to reassign him to a job without exposure to harmful chemicals or to remove him from the refinery altogether. The contractor laid him off in early 1996.

Echazabal filed suit, ultimately removed to federal court, claiming, among other things, that Chevron violated the Americans With Disabilities Act in refusing to hire him, or even to let him continue working in the plant, because of a disability, his liver condition. Chevron defended under a regulation of the Equal Employment Opportunity Commission permitting the defense that a worker's disability on the job would pose a "direct threat" to his health, see 29 CFR § 1630.15(b)(2) (2001). Although two medical witnesses disputed Chevron's judgment that Echazabal's liver function was impaired and subject to further damage under the job conditions in the refinery, the District Court granted summary judgment for Chevron. It held that Echazabal raised no genuine issue of material fact as to whether the company acted reasonably in relying on its own doctors' medical advice, regardless of its accuracy.

On appeal, the Ninth Circuit asked for briefs on a threshold question not raised before, whether the EEOC's regulation recognizing a threat-to-self defense, exceeded the scope of permissible rulemaking under the ADA. The Circuit held that it did and reversed the summary judgment. The court rested its position on the text of the ADA itself in explicitly recognizing an employer's right to adopt an employment qualification barring anyone whose disability would place others in the workplace at risk, while saying nothing about threats to the disabled employee himself. The majority opinion reasoned that "by specifying only threats to 'other individuals in the workplace,' the statute makes it clear that threats to other persons — including the disabled individual himself — are not included within the scope of the [direct threat] defense," and it indicated that any such regulation would unreasonably conflict with congressional policy against paternalism in the workplace. The court went on to reject Chevron's further argument that Echazabal was not "'otherwise qualified'" to perform the job, holding that the ability to perform a job without risk to one's health or safety is not an "'essential function'" of the job. . . .

## II

Section 102 of the Americans with Disabilities Act of 1990 prohibits "discrimination against a qualified individual with a disability because of the disability . . . in regard to" a number of actions by an employer, including "hiring." 42 U.S.C. § 12112(a). The statutory definition of "discrimination" covers a number of things an employer might do to block a disabled person from advancing in the workplace, such as "using qualification standards . . . that screen out or tend to screen out an individual with a disability." § 12112(b)(6). By that same definition, as well as by separate provision, § 12113(a), the Act creates an affirmative defense for action under a qualification standard "shown to be job-related for the position in question and . . . consistent with business necessity." Such a standard may include "a requirement that an individual shall not pose a direct threat to the health or safety of other individuals in the workplace," § 12113(b), if the individual cannot perform the job safely with reasonable accommodation, § 12113(a). By regulation, the EEOC carries the defense one step further, in allowing an employer to screen out a potential worker with a disability not only for risks that he would pose to others in the workplace but for risks on the job to his own health or safety as well: "The term 'qualification standard' may include a requirement that an individual shall not pose a direct threat to the health or safety of the individual or others in the workplace." 29 CFR § 1630.15(b)(2) (2001).

Chevron relies on the regulation here, since it says a job in the refinery would pose a "direct threat" to Echazabal's health. In seeking deference to the agency, it argues that nothing in the statute unambiguously precludes such a defense, while the regulation was adopted under authority explicitly delegated by Congress, 42 U.S.C. § 12116, and after notice-and-comment rulemaking. See United States v. Mead Corp., 533 U.S. 218, 227 (2001); Chevron U.S.A. Inc. v. Natural Resources Defense Council, Inc., 467 U.S. 837, 842-844 (1984). Echazabal, on the contrary, argues that as a matter of law the statute precludes the regulation, which he claims would be an unreasonable interpretation even if the agency had leeway to go beyond the literal text.

## A

As for the textual bar to any agency action as a matter of law, Echazabal says that Chevron loses on the threshold question whether the statute leaves a gap for the EEOC to fill. Echazabal recognizes the generality of the language providing for a defense when a plaintiff is screened out by "qualification standards" that are "job-related and consistent with business necessity" (and reasonable accommodation would not cure the difficulty posed by employment). 42 U.S.C. § 12113(a). Without more, those provisions would allow an employer to turn away someone whose work would pose a serious risk to himself. That possibility is said to be eliminated, however, by the further specification that "'qualification standards' may include a requirement that an individual shall not pose a direct threat to the health or safety of other individuals in the workplace." § 12113(b); see also § 12111(3) (defining "direct threat" in terms of risk to others). Echazabal contrasts this provision with an EEOC regulation under the Rehabilitation Act of 1973, as amended, 29 U.S.C. § 701 *et seq.*, antedating the ADA, which recognized an employer's right to consider threats both to other workers and to the threatening employee himself. Because the ADA defense provision recognizes threats only if they extend to another, Echazabal reads the statute to imply as a matter of law that threats to the  worker himself cannot count.

The argument follows the reliance of the Ninth Circuit majority on the interpretive canon, *expressio unius exclusio alterius*, "expressing one item of [an] associated group or series excludes another left unmentioned." United States v. Vonn, 535 U.S. —, —, [122 S. Ct. 1043] (2002). The rule is fine when it applies, but this case joins some others in showing when it does not. See, *e.g.*, *id.*; United Dominion Industries, Inc. v. United States, 532 U.S. 822, 836 (2001); Pauley v. Beth Energy Mines, Inc., 501 U.S. 680, 703 (1991).

The first strike against the expression-exclusion rule here is right in the text that Echazabal quotes. Congress included the harm-to-others provision as an example of legitimate qualifications that are "job-related and consistent with business necessity." These are spacious defensive categories, which seem to give an agency (or in the absence of agency action, a court) a good deal of discretion in setting the limits of permissible qualification standards. That discretion is confirmed, if not magnified, by the provision that "qualification standards" falling within the limits of job relation and business necessity "may include" a veto on those who would directly threaten others in the workplace. Far from supporting Echazabal's position, the expansive phrasing of "may include" points directly away from the sort of exclusive specification he claims. United States v. NewYork Telephone Co., 434 U.S. 159, 169 (1977); Federal Land Bank of St. Paul v. Bismarck Lumber Co., 314 U.S. 95, 100 (1941).

Just as statutory language suggesting exclusiveness is missing, so is that essential extrastatutory ingredient of an expression-exclusion demonstration, the series of terms from which an omission bespeaks a negative implication. The canon depends on identifying a series of two or more terms or things that should be understood to go hand in hand, which are abridged in circumstances supporting a sensible inference that the term left out must have been meant to be excluded. E. Crawford, Construction of Statutes 337 (1940) (*expressio unius* "'properly applies only when in the natural association of ideas in the mind of the reader that which is expressed is so set over by way of strong contrast to that which is omitted that the contrast enforces the affirmative inference,'" *United States v. Vonn, supra.*

Strike two in this case is the failure to identify any such established series, including both threats to others and threats to self, from which Congress appears to have made a deliberate choice to omit the latter item as a signal of the affirmative defense's scope. The closest Echazabal comes is the EEOC's rule interpreting the Rehabilitation Act of 1973, a precursor of the ADA. That statute excepts from the definition of a protected "qualified individual with a handicap" anyone who would pose a "direct threat to the health or safety of other individuals," but, like the later ADA, the Rehabilitation Act says nothing about threats to self that particular employment might pose. 42 U.S.C. § 12113(b). The EEOC nonetheless extended the exception to cover threat-to-self employment, 29 CFR § 1613.702(f) (1990), and Echazabal argues that Congress's adoption only of the threat-to-others exception in the ADA must have been a deliberate omission of the Rehabilitation Act regulation's tandem term of threat-to-self, with intent to exclude it. . . .

Even if we . . . look no further than the EEOC's Rehabilitation Act regulation pairing self and others, the congressional choice to speak only of threats to others would still be equivocal. Consider what the ADA reference to threats to others might have meant on somewhat different facts. If the Rehabilitation Act had spoken only of "threats to health" and the EEOC regulation had read that to mean threats to self or others, a congressional choice to be more specific in the ADA by listing threats to others but not threats to self would have carried a message. The most probable reading would have been that Congress understood what a failure to specify could lead to and had made a choice to limit the possibilities. The statutory basis for any agency rulemaking under the ADA would have been different from its basis under the Rehabilitation Act and would have indicated a difference in the agency's rulemaking discretion. But these are not the circumstances here. Instead of making the ADA different from the Rehabilitation Act on the point at issue, Congress used identical language, knowing full well what the EEOC had made of that language under the earlier statute. Did Congress mean to imply that the agency had been wrong in reading the earlier language to allow it to recognize threats to self, or did Congress just assume that the agency was free to do under the ADA what it had already done under the earlier Act's identical language? There is no way to tell. Omitting the EEOC's reference to self-harm while using the very language that the EEOC had read as consistent with recognizing self-harm is equivocal at best. No negative inference is possible.

There is even a third strike against applying the expression-exclusion rule here. It is simply that there is no apparent stopping point to the argument that by specifying a threat-to-others defense Congress intended a negative implication about those whose safety could be considered. When Congress specified threats to others in the workplace, for example, could it possibly have meant that an employer could not defend a refusal to hire when a worker's disability would threaten others outside the workplace? If Typhoid Mary had come under the ADA, would a meat packer have been defenseless if Mary had sued after being turned away? See 42 U.S.C. § 12113(d). *Expressio unius* just fails to work here.

**B**

Since Congress has not spoken exhaustively on threats to a worker's own health, the agency regulation can claim adherence under the rule in *Chevron*, so long as it makes sense of the statutory defense for qualification standards that are "job-related and consistent with business necessity." 42 U.S.C. § 12113(a). Chevron's reasons for calling the regulation reasonable are unsurprising: moral concerns aside, it wishes to avoid time lost to sickness, excessive turnover from medical retirement or death, litigation under state tort law, and the risk of violating the national Occupational Safety and Health Act of 1970. Although Echazabal claims that none of these reasons is legitimate, focusing on the concern with OSHA will be enough to show that the regulation is entitled to survive.

Echazabal points out that there is no known instance of OSHA enforcement, or even threatened enforcement, against an employer who relied on the ADA to hire a worker willing to accept a risk to himself from his disability on the job. In Echazabal's mind, this shows that invoking OSHA policy and possible OSHA liability is just a red herring to excuse covert discrimination. But there is another side to this. The text of OSHA itself says its point is "to assure so far as possible every working man and woman in the Nation safe and healthful working conditions," § 651(b), and Congress specifically obligated an employer to "furnish to each of his employees employment and a place of employment which are free from recognized hazards that are causing or are likely to cause death or serious physical harm to his employees," § 654(a)(1). Although there may be an open question whether an employer would actually be liable under OSHA for hiring an individual who knowingly consented to the particular dangers the job would pose to him, there is no denying that the employer would be asking for trouble: his decision to hire would put Congress's policy in the ADA, a disabled individual's right to operate on equal terms within the workplace, at loggerheads with the competing policy of OSHA, to ensure the safety of "each" and "every" worker. Courts would, of course, resolve the tension if there were no agency action, but the EEOC's resolution exemplifies the substantive choices that agencies are expected to make when Congress leaves the intersection of competing objectives both imprecisely marked but subject to the administrative leeway found in 42 U.S.C. § 12113(a).

Nor can the EEOC's resolution be fairly called unreasonable as allowing the kind of workplace paternalism the ADA was meant to outlaw. It is true that Congress had paternalism in its sights when it passed the ADA, see § 12101(a)(5) (recognizing "overprotective rules and policies" as a form of discrimination). But the EEOC has taken this to mean that Congress was not aiming at an employer's refusal to place disabled workers at a specifically demonstrated risk, but was trying to get at refusals to give an even break to classes of disabled people, while claiming to act for their own good in reliance on untested and pretextual stereotypes.[5] Its regulation disallows just this sort of sham protection, through demands for a particularized enquiry into the harms the employee would probably face. The direct threat defense must be "based on a reasonable medical judgment that relies on the most current medical knowledge and/or the best available objective evidence," and upon an expressly "individualized

---

5. Echazabal's contention that the Act's legislative history is to the contrary is unpersuasive. Although some of the comments within the legislative history decry paternalism in general terms, see, *e.g.*, H. R. Rep. No. 101-485, pt. 2, p. 72 (1990) ("It is critical that paternalistic concerns for the disabled person's own safety not be used to disqualify an otherwise qualified applicant"); ADA Conf. Rep., 136 Cong. Rec. 17377 (1990) (statement of Sen. Kennedy) ("An employer could not use as an excuse for not hiring a person with HIV disease the claim that the employer was simply 'protecting the individual' from opportunistic diseases to which the individual might be exposed"), those comments that elaborate actually express the more pointed concern that such justifications are usually pretextual, rooted in generalities and misperceptions about disabilities. See, *e.g.*, H. R. Rep. No. 101-485, at 74 ("Generalized fear about risks from the employment environment, such as exacerbation of the disability caused by stress, cannot be used by an employer to disqualify a person with a disability"); S. Rep. No. 101-116, p. 28 (1989) ("It would also be a violation to deny employment to an applicant based on generalized fears about the safety of the applicant. . . . By definition, such fears are based on averages and group-based predictions. This legislation requires individualized assessments").

Similarly, Echazabal points to several of our decisions expressing concern under Title VII, which like the ADA allows employers to defend otherwise discriminatory practices that are "consistent with business necessity," 42 U.S.C. § 2000e-2(k), with employers adopting rules that exclude women from jobs that are seen as too risky. See, *e.g.*, Dothard v. Rawlinson [reproduced at page 358]; Automobile Workers v. Johnson Controls, Inc. [reproduced at page 268]. Those cases, however, are beside the point, as they, like Title VII generally, were concerned with paternalistic judgments based on the broad category of gender, while the EEOC has required that judgments based on the direct threat provision be made on the basis of individualized risk assessments.

assessment of the individual's present ability to safely perform the essential functions of the job," reached after considering, among other things, the imminence of the risk and the severity of the harm portended. 29 CFR § 1630.2(r) (2001). The EEOC was certainly acting within the reasonable zone when it saw a difference between rejecting workplace paternalism and ignoring specific and documented risks to the employee himself, even if the employee would take his chances for the sake of getting a job.[6]

Finally, our conclusions that some regulation is permissible and this one is reasonable are not open to Echazabal's objection that they reduce the direct threat provision to "surplusage," see Babbitt v. Sweet Home Chapter, Communities for Great Ore., 515 U.S. 687, 698 (1995). The mere fact that a threat-to-self defense reasonably falls within the general "job related" and "business necessity" standard does not mean that Congress accomplished nothing with its explicit provision for a defense based on threats to others. The provision made a conclusion clear that might otherwise have been fought over in litigation or administrative rulemaking. It did not lack a job to do merely because the EEOC might have adopted the same rule later in applying the general defense provisions, nor was its job any less responsible simply because the agency was left with the option to go a step further. A provision can be useful even without congressional attention being indispensable . . .

*NOTES*

1. The Court did not decide whether Chevron had made the requisite individualized inquiry into Echazabal's medical condition that the EEOC's regulation required. That issue was left for the lower court on remand.

2. The central question before the Court was whether the EEOC's regulation, which expanded the "direct threat" defense to include threats to an individual's own health and safety, was entitled to judicial deference. Is the Court's decision to defer to the EEOC in *Echazabal* consistent with its refusal to do so in *Sutton*? In *Echazabal*, the Court found the statute itself left room for agency interpretation, whereas it found no such room available in *Sutton*. Do you agree with the Court's view that the statutory language in *Sutton* was clear, while the statutory language in *Echazabal* was sufficiently ambiguous to open the door to the agency?

3. Note that in *Echazabal*, the EEOC was interpreting a provision of Title I, the chapter on which the EEOC has been expressly delegated rule-making authority. Also, the EEOC's definition in *Echazabal* was found in the regulation itself, not in an Interpretive Guidance. Thus, the *Echazabal* Court did not question whether *Chevron*'s two-step review standard applied to the EEOC's interpretation; it unquestionably did. But this question was left open in *Sutton* vis à vis EEOC regulations interpreting the statutory definition of "disability" and the agency's Interpretive Guidance generally.

---

6. Respect for this distinction does not entail the requirement, as Echazabal claims, that qualification standards be "neutral," stating what the job requires, as distinct from a worker's disqualifying characteristics. It is just as much business necessity for skyscraper contractors to have steelworkers without vertigo as to have well-balanced ones. Reasonableness does not turn on formalism. We have no occasion, however, to try to describe how acutely an employee must exhibit a disqualifying condition before an employer may exclude him from the class of the generally qualified. This is a job for the trial courts in the first instance.

4. In Koshinski v. Decatur Foundry, Inc., 177 F.3d 599 (7th Cir. 1999), the Seventh Circuit ruled in favor of an employer who removed an employee from his job in order to protect him from *future* injury. The employer's physician, after examining Koshinski, concluded that "based on his underlying degenerative osteoarthritis he will be getting to the point where he will wear out and not be able to do the heavy physical labor." Id. at 601. The court ruled that Koshinski was not qualified *now* because both his doctor and the employer's doctor recommended, based on his current condition, that he avoid the heavy physical work that he sought to do. Rather than rely on the direct threat defense, could the employer have simply argued that Koshinski was not "disabled" because his impairment did not currently prevent him from doing his job?

5. After *Arline,* the Rehabilitation Act's definition of an "individual with a disability" was amended to exclude carriers of currently contagious disease or infection who pose a "direct threat" to the health or safety of others. See 29 U.S.C.S. § 705(20)(D) (2003). ADA § 103(d)(1)-(3) provides that a food-handling position may be denied to a person who has an infectious or communicable disease that is transmittable to others through food handling if the risk to others cannot be "eliminated" by a reasonable accommodation. This defense, however, is available only for a person with a disease that the Secretary of Health and Human Services has identified as infectious and communicable and transmittable through the handling of the food. Why was it necessary to include this as a separate defense? Wouldn't a contagious individual be a "direct threat" in a food-handling job?

6. Den Hartog v. Wasatch Academy, 129 F.3d 1076 (10th Cir. 1997), held that an employee's association with a disabled individual was a direct threat and therefore provided a defense to associational discrimination. In *Hartog,* the plaintiff was a boarding school teacher whose son suffered from psychiatric disorders that caused him to engage in threatening behavior toward other boarding school personnel and their families.

7. In The ADA, The Workplace, and the Myth of the "Dangerous Mentally Ill," 34 U.C. Davis L. Rev. 849, 850-51 (2001), Professor Ann Hubbard addresses the question of the direct threat defense in the context of mental disabilities. She notes that public fears concerning persons with mental disabilities are out of proportion to the risk of violence actually posed and cautioned that a direct threat defense may not be based on erroneous risk assessments:

> The employer must assess any risks according to current objective medical or scientific information about whether and how a disability may endanger workplace health and safety. Following this assessment, the employer may exclude or restrict the individual only if the risk is "significant," rather than remote or speculative. Moreover, if that risk can be sufficiently reduced or eliminated by reasonable accommodations, including modifications to workplace practices, then the employer may not exclude the employee. In short, the direct threat inquiry is carefully structured "to ensure that employers are acting on fact rather than fear, information rather than ignorance, and medical evidence rather than mythology."

In another article, Understanding and Implementing the ADA's Direct Threat Defense, 95 Nw. U. L. Rev. 1279 (2001), Professor Hubbard elaborates on the direct threat defense more generally. She contends that lower courts and employers tend to overestimate risk that is unfamiliar or uncontrollable or more publicized over risks that are known or within our control or less in the media spotlight. For example, "[a]n employee may have more to fear from a coworker with alcoholism than one with schizophrenia, but employers and the public are more fearful of the latter." Id. at 1281. She proposes that courts adhere to five principles in evaluating a direct threat defense: (1) an individualized assessment of the applicant or employee; (2) a finding that a risk is significant, taking into account both the probabilities of occurrence and the severity of any potential harm; (3) assessment based on current medical information; (4) placement of the burden of proof on the employer; and (5) prohibition of reliance on an individual's risk to his own health or safety. Id. at 1283. The latter example, of course, has been rejected by *Echazabal.*

8. Employers have denied employment to individuals who are HIV-infected. Courts assessing the risk of hiring HIV-infected individuals have reached different results depending on the nature of the work involved. In Chalk v. United States Dist. Court, 840 F.2d 701 (9th Cir. 1988), the court held that a teacher with AIDS did not pose a "significant risk" in the workplace and that his condition could be monitored to ensure that any secondary infections he contracted would also not pose a significant risk. On the other hand, in Waddell v. Valley Forge Dental Assocs., 276 F.3d 1275 (11th Cir. 2001), *cert. denied,* 122 S. Ct. 2293 (2002), the court found that an HIV-positive dental hygienist posed a direct threat to the health and safety of others. When death could occur as a result of transmittal of a disease, the court said that a significant risk exists when two conditions are shown: that an event can occur and that the event can, according to reliable medical evidence, transmit the disease. Since a cut, prick, or patient bite could occur, and such events, were they to occur, could expose the patient to HIV, a significant risk of substantial harm was present. That the risk of transmittal was very low did not mean there was no direct threat, said the court, if there was a "sound, theoretical possibility" of transmittal. Id. at 1282. Similarly, in Estate of Mauro v. Borgess Med. Ctr., 137 F.3d 398 (6th Cir. 1998), the court held that a surgical technician with HIV was a direct threat to the health and safety of others because his job required that he place his hands in patients' body cavities in the presence of sharp instruments. See also Doe v. University of Md. Med. Sys. Corp., 50 F.3d 1261 (4th Cir. 1995) (HIV-infected individual not qualified for surgical residency); Bradley v. University of Texas M.D. Anderson Cancer Ctr., 3 F.3d 922 (5th Cir. 1993) (surgical technician infected with HIV not qualified). Have the courts correctly analyzed these cases?

9. In Altman v. New York City Health Hosps. Corp., 903 F. Supp. 503 (S.D.N.Y. 1995), *aff'd,* 100 F.3d 1054 (2d Cir. 1996), the court applied the direct threat provision when a hospital refused to reinstate, as chief of medicine, a doctor who entered an alcohol treatment program after treating patients while visibly drunk. The hospital was justified in refusing reinstatement because the doctor might suffer an undetected relapse, a danger the court deemed not insubstantial where only three months had passed since he sought treatment. The chief of medicine was responsible for final and essentially unreviewable treatment decisions whenever there was uncertainty or disagreement among physicians, interns, and residents. Even if the plaintiff removed himself from the decision-making process whenever he relapsed, his abrupt withdrawal from decisions could pose significant risks to patients. Id. at 509.

The hospital accommodated Dr. Altman's alcoholism by reinstating him as an attending physician. On the question whether Dr. Altman could be accommodated to permit him to return as chief of medicine, the court rejected as ineffective proposed methods of monitoring his condition to ensure against relapse. Problems with monitoring by colleagues included his ability to consume large quantities of alcohol without apparent effect and the awkwardness of medical staff monitoring their supervisor. External monitoring was rejected as ineffective because some of the doctor's duties were performed at odd hours and without warning. See id. at 510-12.

10. Can an accommodation that would reduce health or safety risks be unreasonable because of the burden it would place on co-workers? For example, what if co-workers can protect themselves against an individual's contagious disease by being vaccinated, wearing face masks and plastic gloves, or avoiding close contact with the person with a disability? Cf. Treadwell v. Alexander, 707 F.2d 473 (11th Cir. 1983) (a proposed accommodation that would result in substantially increased workloads for co-workers was unreasonable). See also 29 C.F.R. pt. 1630, app. § 1630.15(d) (describing accommodations that are an undue hardship).

## PROBLEM 8.6

On remand, the district court made the following findings of fact in *Arline*:

[Tuberculosis] infection begins with the inhalation by one person of "droplet nuclei" expelled by another. Droplet nuclei are tuberculosis germs suspended in moisture. . . . [W]hen droplet nuclei are expelled . . . 99.9% of the nuclei die within a second of contacting room air. The droplet nuclei that survive must reach the distal portion, which is the microscopic air space, of the lungs of the person inhaling the germs. . . . If any germ does reach the distal portion of the lungs, the body's immunological defenses are capable of rendering it harmless. . . . If a tuberculosis germ successfully implants itself into the distal portion of the lungs, and the immunological defenses of the body do not destroy it, the germ can then multiply. If this occurs, the person is infected. If the germs continue to multiply, at some point the number of tuberculosis cells becomes so great as to cause disease. . . .

The. . . test for tuberculosis is the sputum culture. A patient's sputum is placed on a laboratory dish and allowed to "grow" for a number of weeks. The organism grown on culture indicates that the person from whom the specimen came is, at present, infected with tuberculosis. . . . If growth is detected during the eight week period, the culture is allowed to continue to grow until there is a large enough culture to test. Usually growth is detected by the sixth week. . . . Communicability is determined by the actual number of colonies detected. . . . A culture can grow just one colony, but a person is not considered to be able to communicate the infection unless a vastly larger number of organisms are present. The test that will quickly determine a large number of organisms is known as the sputum smear test. This test is considered the threshold indicator of a person's communicability because the sputum smear test is not very sensitive, and thus, many organisms need to be present before the test is positive. . . .

[O]nce a person begins medical treatment for tuberculosis, the risk of communicability becomes very small. Within two weeks of drug therapy, 99% of sputum organisms are killed. In addition, the medication quickly stops the patient's cough. . . . Communicability also depends upon environmental factors. The people at the highest risk of infection are [those] in close proximity to the actively communicable person. . . .

In the summer of 1977, [Arline] suffered a relapse of tuberculosis. She was hospitalized, and treated . . . . In March of 1978 a culture tested positive with over one hundred colonies of tuberculosis. Additional drugs were added to the regimen that [Arline] was taking, and testing was continued. In November, 1978 another culture tested positive with only one colony of tuberculosis. This particular culture was grown for thirteen weeks. . . . No subsequent cultures tested positive [and Arline] did not have a positive smear test after August, 1977.

On these facts, should the court find Arline "qualified"? See Arline v. School Board of Nassau County, 692 F. Supp. 1286 (M.D. Fla. 1988). Is Arline "disabled" under current ADA law?

## 2. *Job-Related and Consistent with Business Necessity*

### ALBERTSONS, INC. v. KIRKINGBURG
#### 527 U.S. 555 (1999)

Justice SOUTER, delivered the opinion for a unanimous Court with respect to Parts I and III, and the opinion of the Court with respect to Part II, in which Chief Justice REHNQUIST, and Justices O'CONNOR, SCALIA, KENNEDY, THOMAS, and GINSBURG, joined.

The question posed is whether, under the Americans with Disabilities Act of 1990 an employer who requires as a job qualification that an employee meet an otherwise applicable federal safety regulation must justify enforcing the regulation solely because its standard may be waived in an individual case. We answer no.

### I

In August 1990, petitioner, Albertsons, Inc., a grocery-store chain with supermarkets in several States, hired respondent, Hallie Kirkingburg, as a truck driver based at its Portland, Oregon, warehouse. Kirkingburg had more than a decade's driving experience and performed well when Albertsons' transportation manager took him on a road test.

Before starting work, Kirkingburg was examined to see if he met federal vision standards for commercial truck drivers. For many decades the Department of Transportation or its predecessors has been responsible for devising these standards for individuals who drive commercial vehicles in interstate commerce. Since 1971, the basic vision regulation has required corrected distant visual acuity of at least 20/40 in each eye and distant binocular acuity of at least 20/40. See 49 CFR § 391.41(b)(10) (1998). Kirkingburg, however, suffers from amblyopia, an uncorrectable condition that leaves him with 20/200 vision in his left eye and monocular vision in effect. Despite Kirkingburg's weak left eye, the doctor erroneously certified that he met the DOT's basic vision standard, and Albertsons hired him.

In December 1991, Kirkingburg injured himself on the job and took a leave of absence. Before returning to work in November 1992, Kirkingburg went for a further physical as required by the company. This time, the examining physician correctly assessed Kirkingburg's vision and explained that his eyesight did not meet the basic DOT standards. The physician, or his nurse, told Kirkingburg that in order to be legally qualified to drive, he would have to obtain a waiver of its basic vision standards from the DOT. The doctor was alluding to a scheme begun in July 1992 for giving DOT certification to applicants with deficient vision who had three years of recent experience driving a commercial vehicle without a license suspension or revocation, involvement in a reportable accident in which the applicant was cited for a moving violation, conviction for certain driving-related offenses, citation for certain serious traffic violations, or more than two convictions for any other moving violations. A waiver applicant had to agree to have his vision checked annually for deterioration, and to report certain information about his driving experience to the Federal Highway Administration, the agency within the DOT responsible for overseeing the motor carrier safety regulations. Kirkingburg applied for a waiver, but because he could not meet the basic DOT vision standard Albertsons fired him from his job as a truck driver. In early 1993, after he had left Albertsons, Kirkingburg received a DOT waiver, but Albertsons refused to rehire him.

Kirkingburg sued Albertsons, claiming that firing him violated the ADA. [The District Court granted Albertsons' motion for summary judgment on the ground that Kirkingburg was not "qualified." The Court of Appeals reversed, holding that] Albertsons could not use compliance with a Government regulation as the justification for its vision requirement because the waiver program, which Albertsons disregarded, was "a lawful and legitimate part of the DOT regulatory scheme." The Court of Appeals conceded that Albertsons was free to set a vision standard different from that mandated by the DOT, but held that under the ADA, Albertsons would have to justify its independent standard as necessary to prevent "'a direct threat to the health or safety of other individuals in the workplace.'" Although the court suggested that Albertsons might be able to make such a showing on remand, it ultimately took the position that the company could not, interpreting Albertsons' rejection of DOT waivers as flying in the face of the judgment about safety already embodied in the DOT's decision to grant them. . . .

## III

Albertsons' primary contention is that even if Kirkingburg was disabled, he was not a "qualified" individual with a disability because Albertsons merely insisted on the minimum level of visual acuity set forth in the DOT's Motor Carrier Safety Regulations, 49 CFR § 391.41(b)(10) (1998). If Albertsons was entitled to enforce that standard as defining an "essential job function of the employment position," see 42 U.S.C. § 12111(8), that is the end of the case, for Kirkingburg concededly could not satisfy it.

Under Title I of the ADA, employers may justify their use of "qualification standards . . . that screen out or tend to screen out or otherwise deny a job or benefit to an individual with a disability," so long as such standards are "job-related and consistent with business necessity, and . . . performance cannot be accomplished by reasonable accommodation. . . ." 42 U.S.C. § 12113(a).

Kirkingburg and the Government argue that these provisions do not authorize an employer to follow even a facially applicable regulatory standard subject to waiver without making some enquiry beyond determining whether the applicant or employee meets that standard, yes or no. Before an employer may insist on compliance, they say, the employer must make a showing with reference to the particular job that the waivable regulatory standard is "job-related . . . and . . . consistent with business necessity," see § 12112(b)(6), and that after consideration of the capabilities of the individual a reasonable accommodation could not fairly resolve the competing interests when an applicant or employee cannot wholly satisfy an otherwise justifiable job qualification.

The Government extends this argument by reference to a further section of the statute, which at first blush appears to be a permissive provision for the employer's and the public's benefit. An employer may impose as a qualification standard "a requirement that an individual shall not pose a direct threat to the health or safety of other individuals in the workplace," § 12113(b), with "direct threat" being defined by the Act as "a significant risk to the health or safety of others, which cannot be eliminated by reasonable accommodation," § 12111(3). The Government urges us to read subsections (a) and (b) together to mean that when an employer would impose any safety qualification standard, however specific, tending to screen out individuals with disabilities, the application of the requirement must satisfy the ADA's "direct threat" criterion. That criterion ordinarily requires "an individualized assessment of the individual's present ability to safely perform the essential functions of the job," 29 CFR § 1630.2(r) (1998), "based on medical or other objective evidence," *Bragdon*, see 29 CFR § 1630.2(r) (1998) (assessment of direct threat "shall be based on a reasonable medical judgment that relies on the most current medical knowledge and/or on the best available objective evidence.").[15]

Albertsons answers essentially that even assuming the Government has proposed a sound reading of the statute for the general run of cases, this case is not in the general run. It is crucial to its position that Albertsons here was not insisting upon a job qualification merely of its own devising, subject to possible questions about genuine appropriateness and justifiable application to an individual for whom some accommodation may be reasonable. The job qualification it was applying was the distant visual acuity standard of the Federal Motor Carrier Safety Regulations, 49 CFR § 391.41(b)(10) (1998), which is made binding on Albertsons by § 391.11: "a motor carrier shall not . . . permit a person to drive a commercial motor vehicle unless that person is qualified to drive," by, among other things, meeting the physical qualification standards set forth in § 391.41. The validity of these regulations is unchallenged, they have the force of law, and they contain no qualifying language about individualized determinations.

If we looked no further, there would be no basis to question Albertsons' unconditional obligation to follow the regulation and its consequent right to do so. This, indeed, was the understanding of Congress when it enacted the ADA.[16] But there is more: the waiver program.

The Court of Appeals majority concluded that the waiver program "precludes [employers] from declaring that persons determined by DOT to be capable of performing the job of commercial truck driver are incapable of performing that job by virtue of their disability," and that in the face of a waiver an employer "will not be able to avoid the [ADA's] strictures by showing that its standards are necessary to prevent a direct safety threat." The Court of Appeals thus assumed that the regulatory provisions for the waiver program had to be treated as being on par with the basic visual acuity regulation, as if the general rule had been modified by some different safety standard made applicable by grant of a waiver. On this reading, an individualized determination under a different substantive safety rule was an element of the regulatory regime, which would easily fit with any requirement of 42 U.S.C. §§ 12113(a) and (b) to consider reasonable accommodation. An employer resting solely on the federal standard for its visual acuity qualification would be required to accept a waiver once obtained, and probably to provide an applicant some oppor-

---

15. This appears to be the position taken by the EEOC in the Interpretive Guidance promulgated under its authority to issue regulations to carry out Title I of the ADA, 42 U.S.C. § 12116, see 29 C.F.R. pt. 1630, App., §§ 1630.15(b) and (c) (1998) (requiring safety-related standards to be evaluated under the ADA's direct threat standard); see also App. § 1630.10 (noting that selection criteria that screen out individuals with disabilities, including "safety requirements, vision or hearing requirements," must be job-related, consistent with business necessity, and not amenable to reasonable accommodation). Although it might be questioned whether the Government's interpretation, which might impose a higher burden on employers to justify safety-related qualification standards than other job requirements, is a sound one, we have no need to confront the validity of the reading in this case.

16. The implementing regulations of Title I also recognize a defense to liability under the ADA that "a challenged action is required or necessitated by another Federal law or regulation," 29 CFR § 1630.15(e) (1998). As the parties do not invoke this specific regulation, we have no occasion to consider its effect.

tunity to obtain a waiver whenever that was reasonably possible. If this was sound analysis, the District Court's summary judgment for Albertsons was error.

But the reasoning underlying the Court of Appeal's decision was unsound, for we think it was error to read the regulations establishing the waiver program as modifying the content of the basic visual acuity standard in a way that disentitled an employer like Albertsons to insist on it. . . .

Nothing in the waiver regulation, of course, required an employer of commercial drivers to accept the hypothesis and participate in the Government's experiment. The only question, then, is whether the ADA should be read to require such an employer to defend a decision to decline the experiment. Is it reasonable, that is, to read the ADA as requiring an employer like Albertsons to shoulder the general statutory burden to justify a job qualification that would tend to exclude the disabled, whenever the employer chooses to abide by the otherwise clearly applicable, unamended substantive regulatory standard despite the Government's willingness to waive it experimentally and without any finding of its being inappropriate? If the answer were yes, an employer would in fact have an obligation of which we can think of no comparable example in our law. The employer would be required in effect to justify de novo an existing and otherwise applicable safety regulation issued by the Government itself. The employer would be required on a case-by-case basis to reinvent the Government's own wheel when the Government had merely begun an experiment to provide data to consider changing the underlying specifications. And what is even more, the employer would be required to do so when the Government had made an affirmative record indicating that contemporary empirical evidence was hard to come by. It is simply not credible that Congress enacted the ADA (before there was any waiver program) with the understanding that employers choosing to respect the Government's sole substantive visual acuity regulation in the face of an experimental waiver might be burdened with an obligation to defend the regulation's application according to its own terms.

Justice THOMAS, concurring.

As the Government reads the Americans With Disabilities Act of 1990, it requires that petitioner justify the Department of Transportation's visual acuity standards as job related, consistent with business necessity, and required to prevent employees from imposing a direct threat to the health and safety of others in the workplace. The Court assumes, for purposes of this case, that the Government's reading is, for the most part, correct. I agree with the Court's decision that, even when the case is analyzed through the Government's proposed lens, petitioner was entitled to summary judgment in this case. . . .

As the Court points out, though, DOT's visual acuity standards might also be relevant to the question whether respondent was a "qualified individual with a disability" under 42 U.S.C. § 12112(a). That section provides that no covered entity "shall discriminate against a qualified individual with a disability because of the disability of such individual." § 12112(a). Presumably, then, a plaintiff claiming a cause of action under the ADA bears the burden of proving, inter alia, that he is a qualified individual. The phrase "qualified individual with a disability" is defined to mean:

> an individual with a disability who, *with or without reasonable accommodation*, can perform the *essential functions* of the employment position that such individual holds or desires. For the purposes of this subchapter, consideration shall be given to the employer's judgment as to what functions of a job are essential, and if an employer has

prepared a written description before advertising or interviewing applicants for the job, this description shall be considered evidence of the essential functions of the job.

§ 12111(8) (emphasis added).

In this case, respondent sought a job driving trucks in interstate commerce. The quintessential function of that job, it seems to me, is to be able to drive a commercial truck in interstate commerce, and it was respondent's burden to prove that he could do so.

As the Court explains, DOT's Motor Carrier Safety Regulations have the force of law and bind petitioner — it may not, by law, "permit a person to drive a commercial motor vehicle unless that person is qualified to drive." 49 CFR § 391.11 (1999). But by the same token, DOT's regulations bind respondent who "shall not drive a commercial motor vehicle unless he/she is qualified to drive a commercial motor vehicle." Given that DOT's regulation equally binds petitioner and respondent, and that it is conceded in this case that respondent could not meet the federal requirements, respondent surely was not "qualified" to perform the essential functions of petitioner's truck driver job without a reasonable accommodation. The waiver program might be thought of as a way to reasonably accommodate respondent, but for the fact, as the Court explains, that the program did nothing to modify the regulation's unconditional requirements. For that reason, requiring petitioner to make such an accommodation most certainly would have been unreasonable.

The result of this case is the same under either view of the statute. If forced to choose between these alternatives, however, I would prefer to hold that respondent, as a matter of law, was not qualified to perform the job he sought within the meaning of the ADA. I nevertheless join the Court's opinion. . . . I join the Court's opinion, however, only on the understanding that it leaves open the argument that federal laws such as DOT's visual acuity standards might be critical in determining whether a plaintiff is a "qualified individual with a disability."

### NOTES

1. Under the ADA, evaluating qualification standards such as the DOT visual acuity standard in *Kirkingburg* that expressly screen out disabled individuals to determine whether they are justified is somewhat analogous to establishing a bona fide occupational qualification defense in a gender discrimination case under Title VII. What differences do you see? Why is disability discrimination treated differently than gender discrimination? See Morton v. United Parcel Serv., Inc., 272 F.3d 1249,1260 (9th Cir. 2001), *cert. denied*, 122 S. Ct. 1910 (2002) (business necessity defense under the ADA may apply to standards that are facially discriminatory as well as to those having a disparate impact, but "Congress must have intended to permit across-the-board exclusion of employees based upon disability-related safety criterion only on a showing somewhat similar to the one used for safety qualifications under the Title VII and the ADEA BFOQ standard.").

2. The Court notes that the regulations require an individualized determination when an employer asserts that an individual's disability constitutes a direct threat. What does an "individualized" determination mean in this context? If the employer determines that the essential functions of a specific job cannot be carried out safely by individuals with a specific disability, may the employer adopt a job qualification excluding *all* individuals with that disability? Neither the statute nor the regulations

mention individualized determinations in the context of job qualifications that are not based on the direct threat defense. Is the standard for establishing a safety qualification more stringent than the standard for establishing other qualifications that screen out those with disabilities? The Court questioned this interpretation. See footnote 15. See also Morton v. United Parcel Serv., Inc., 272 F.3d 1249, 1258 (9th Cir. 2001), *cert. denied*, 122 S. Ct. 1910 (2002) (rejecting plaintiff's argument that a safety-related qualification standard must be defended under the "direct threat" provision of the statute); Kapche v. San Antonio, 304 F.3d 493 (5th Cir. 2002) (rejecting per se rule that persons with insulin treated diabetes cannot perform essential job function of driving; individualized assessment of plaintiff required); EEOC v. Exxon Corp., 203 F.3d 871 (5th Cir. 2000) (qualification standard involving safety to be tested under business necessity, not direct threat, provision).

3. The Court holds that employers hiring drivers covered by DOT's regulations may adopt blanket rules excluding drivers who do not meet DOT's physical requirements. In other words, individualized assessments are not required in this context and the employer need not present evidence of the job-relatedness or business necessity of the qualification. See also Buck v. United States Dept. of Transp., 56 F.3d 1406 (D.C. Cir. 1995) (applicants for commercial truck driving position entitled to individualized assessments of their hearing ability, but not individualized assessments of their ability to drive a truck safely in spite of the hearing loss that made them ineligible under FHA regulations). This holding seems consistent both with the legislative history of the ADA and with the EEOC regulation providing that compliance with another federal law or regulation is a defense to liability under the ADA. See 29 C.F.R. § 1630.15(e) (1998).

4. Does the Court's reasoning extend beyond employers and drivers who are bound to follow DOT regulations? The Motor Vehicle Safety Regulations cover drivers of "commercial vehicles," generally vehicles in excess of five tons or designed to transport eight or more passengers. See 49 C.F.R. § 390.5. After *Kirkingburg*, can an employer adopt DOT standards for non-commercial drivers? Don't the DOT regulations, although not required beyond the commercial context, nonetheless establish a safety standard on which employers can rely to set standards for their drivers? Would permitting employers to rely on DOT standards in this way be consistent with the individualized determination of direct threat required by *Echazabal*?

5. Prior to *Kirkingburg*, several district courts considered the permissibility under the ADA of blanket exclusions imposed without the support of federal regulations. In Stillwell v. Kansas City, Missouri Bd. of Police Commrs., 872 F. Supp. 682 (W.D. Mo. 1995), the plaintiff, who was born without a left hand, had worked for nearly 20 years as a licensed private security guard. In 1992, his application for recertification was denied based on a recent state regulation that two hands were necessary to successfully perform defensive tactics including neck restraint, knife defense, and handcuffing. The court rejected the defendant's argument that licensing one-handed applicants would be a direct threat to health and safety. The court concluded that "[t]he determination that a person poses a direct threat to the health or safety of others may not be based on generalization or stereotypes about the effects of a particular disability; it must be based on an individual assessment. . . ." Id. at 686. See also Douglas v. California Dept. of Youth Auth., 271 F.3d 812 (9th Cir. 2001) (CYA's color vision requirement a discriminatory policy that may be challenged as a continuing violation); Bombrys v. City of Toledo, 849 F. Supp. 1210, 1216-1219 (N.D. Ohio 1993) (ADA) (striking down blanket exclusion of insulin-dependent individuals from policing positions).

6. In Cripes v. City of San Jose, 261 F.3d 877 (9th Cir. 2001), the court examined the job-relatedness test in a case involving a collective bargaining agreement covering police officers. Three types of positions were available for police officers: beat patrol, specialized assignment, and modified assignment jobs. In order to qualify for specialized assignment jobs, which were limited to three-year terms, the contract required that the officer have served in a beat patrol position the previous year. The modified assignment jobs, limited to thirty under the contract, were set aside for disabled officers. Plaintiffs acknowledged their disabilities precluded them from performing the duties of beat patrol officers, which included forcibly arresting and subduing suspects. But they challenged their exclusion from the specialized assignment jobs, which were more desirable than the modified duty assignments.

The City first argued that being able to make forcible arrests was an essential job function for the specialized assignments. The court found a question of fact on that point. But the city also contended that, even if making forcible arrests were not an essential function of all specialized assignment jobs, exempting plaintiffs from the requirement that officers serve as beat patrol officers in the year preceding their specialized assignment rotation would pose an undue hardship. The Ninth Circuit, in examining whether the qualification standard was lawful, noted that defendants' undue hardship argument was misplaced. In challenging the qualification standard, plaintiffs were not asking for a reasonable accommodation that would enable them to perform the essential job functions. Rather, they were asking for removal of a qualification standard that precluded their transfer to jobs they could perform without accommodation. Under these circumstances, said the court, the correct question was whether defendants could prove the qualification standard was job-related for the position in question and consistent with business necessity. This showing, said the Ninth Circuit, is more demanding than the undue hardship test, as a qualification standard is generally discriminatory. The court found the business necessity test not satisfied, reasoning, in part, that resentment of other workers or poor morale is insufficient to satisfy the business necessity defense.

How does the Ninth Circuit's approach differ from the EEOC guidelines? Should the fact that a qualification standard is the product of collective bargaining matter in assessing business necessity? How is this different, if at all, from a seniority system? Does *Barnett* bear on this question?

7. There is one clear difference between Title VII and the ADA with respect to the job-related and business necessity defense:

> The use of selection criteria that are related to an essential function of the job may be consistent with business necessity. However, selection criteria that are related to an essential function of the job may not be used to exclude an individual with a disability if that individual could satisfy the criteria with the provision of a reasonable accommodation. Experience under a similar provision of the regulations implementing section 504 of the Rehabilitation Act indicates that challenges to selection criteria are, in fact, most often resolved by reasonable accommodation. It is therefore anticipated that challenges to selection criteria brought under this part will generally be resolved in a like manner.

29 C.F.R. pt. 1630, app. § 1630.10. Because the business necessity defense cannot be established without consideration of reasonable accommodations and because reasonable accommodation and undue hardship determinations are based at least in part on a cost-benefit analysis, won't employers be required in most cases to produce objective evidence to meet the job-related and business necessity standard?

8. Is the ADA more or less burdensome on employers than Title VII in terms of the job-related and business necessity defense? On the one hand, under the ADA, employers may use the defense to justify facially discriminatory policies — a defense that is not available under Title VII. On the other hand, does the ADA impose a more stringent evidentiary standard to establish the defense? See Morton v. United Parcel Serv., Inc., 272 F.3d 1249 (9th Cir. 2001), *cert. denied*, 122 S. Ct. 1910 (2002) (employer rule that all applicants for "package car driver" positions have DOT certification challenged as discriminatory qualification standard as applied to driving non-DOT vehicles; court draws on both BFOQ and business necessity standards under Title VII to find that UPS was not entitled to summary judgment.).

9. Is it appropriate to refer to the proof of job relationship and business necessity as a "defense" when the statute defines covered individuals in terms of whether they are "qualified" to perform essential functions of the job? This is the point of Justice Thomas's concurrence in *Kirkingburg* — that it is the *plaintiff's* burden to prove that he is a qualified individual with a disability, which includes proof that he can perform the essential functions of driving trucks in interstate commerce, not the defendant's burden to prove he cannot. But the Court in *Echazabal*, reproduced at page 760, repeatedly refers to the showing that a qualification standard that screens out a disabled person be job related for the position in question and consistent with business necessity as an affirmative defense. Don't *Echazabal* and *Kirkingburg* clearly contemplate placing the burden of proof on this issue on the employer? For further discussion of burden of proof issues under Title I, see section E infra.

### 3.  Disparate Impact

Many disparate impact claims under the ADA can be recast as reasonable accommodation claims and vice versa. Reconsider *Deane*, reproduced at page 722, where the employer required that employees be capable of lifting a certain weight. Could Deane have attacked a hospital lifting requirement on the ground that it has a disparate impact on individuals with disabilities? What evidence would she need to prove an impact claim? What numbers would be relevant? Which approach is more advantageous to plaintiffs? Do you think inability to accommodate, undue hardship, and direct threat are harder defenses for the employer to prove than job-relatedness and business necessity? How do the remedies differ?

Some reasonable accommodation claims are not as easily transposed into a disparate impact claim. Consider, for example, the request of a covered individual for extra sick leave to deal with medical problems. Restricting sick leave may not exclude the person from work. It may just make it more difficult for her to schedule doctor's appointments or more expensive because she must take unpaid personal days to see the doctor. This policy would "impact" on individuals with disabilities because their needs differ from those of other individuals.

Is disparate impact designed to deal with claims like this? ADA § 102(b)(3) provides that "discriminate" includes "utilizing standards, criteria, or methods of administration . . . that have the effect of discrimination on the basis of disability. . . ." The EEOC Guidance relating to disparate impact defenses seems to contemplate disparate impact claims based on a variety of employer policies: "there may be uniformly applied standards, criteria and policies not relating to selection that may also screen out or tend to screen out an individual with a disability or a class of individuals with disabilities. Like selection criteria that have a disparate impact, non-selection criteria having such an impact may also have to be job-related and consistent with business necessity, subject to consideration of reasonable accommodation." 29 C.F.R. pt. 1630, app. § 1630.15(c) (1998).

Does the leave policy violate this section? In Alexander v. Choate, 469 U.S. 287 (1985), a case decided under the Rehabilitation Act, the Supreme Court rejected the claim that the Tennessee Medicaid Program's 14-day limitation on inpatient coverage would have an unlawful disparate impact on the disabled. *Choate* seems most directly relevant to a claim by an individual with a disability for more sick leave than other individuals receive. Under the ADA, can such an employee attack a sick leave policy that restricts paid leave to 14 days on the ground that the policy has a disparate impact on employees with disabilities? The EEOC suggests that such a claim is not viable but that an employee affected by such a policy may be entitled to leave as a reasonable accommodation:

> It should be noted, however, that some uniformly applied employment policies or practices, such as leave policies, are not subject to challenge under the adverse impact theory. "No-leave" policies (e.g., no leave during the first six months of employment) are likewise not subject to challenge under the adverse impact theory. However, an employer, in spite of its "no-leave" policy, may, in appropriate circumstances, have to consider the provision of leave to an employee with a disability as a reasonable accommodation, unless the provision of leave would impose an undue hardship.

29 C.F.R. pt. 1630, app. § 1630.15(c). What does this mean?

# E.   BURDENS OF PRODUCTION AND PROOF

In some respects, the concept of disability discrimination is identical to the concept of discrimination that we studied in Chapters 3, 4, and 5. Title I's basic prohibition against discrimination tracks Title VII's prohibition: "No covered entity shall discriminate against a qualified individual with a disability because of the disability of such individual in regard to job application procedures, the hiring, advancement, or discharge of employees, employee compensation, job training, and other terms, conditions, and privileges of employment." ADA § 102(a).

While § 102(b) further defines disability discrimination to include failure to accommodate and other forms of discrimination foreign to the law under Title VII, Title I of the ADA clearly contemplates an individual disparate treatment claim comparable to that available under Title VII, § 1981, and the ADEA. As with Title VII, an employer whose decision was based on a legitimate, nondiscriminatory reason will not be liable for disability discrimination unless the neutral criterion applied has a disparate impact, is not job related, and is not a business necessity.

As we have seen, however, the concept of disability discrimination differs from other discrimination for two basic reasons. First, the ADA expressly permits employers to act on the basis of an employee's disability. Thus, for example, if an individual's disability means that he cannot perform essential functions of a job or if his disability creates a direct threat to health or safety, an employer may disqualify him on the basis of his disability without incurring liability. This is true under Title VII and the ADEA only in very rare situations involving the bona fide occupational qualification defense.

Second, the ADA expressly requires employers to treat individuals differently on the basis of disability because employers are required to provide disabled employees with accommodations not available to other employees. Under Title VII and the ADEA, employers are never *required* to prefer a protected-class member, except for the very limited duty to reasonably accommodate religious practices. See Chapter 7D.

Given these differences, how do or should the burden of proof schemes devised under Title VII, the ADEA, and § 1981 apply, if at all, to ADA claims? See generally S. Elizabeth Wilborn Malloy, Something Borrowed, Something Blue: Why Disability Law Claims Are Different, 33 Conn. L. Rev. 603 (2001) (arguing that "[t]he frequent use of Title VII case law and its burden-shifting scheme suggests that the courts have often failed to understand that the ADA is fundamentally a very different type of statute than other anti-discrimination laws."). While some borrowing is perhaps inevitable and sometimes quite appropriate, other times it is less so. What proof scheme best serves the distinctive aims of the ADA?

While it is clear that the plaintiff has the burden of proving he is an individual with a disability within the meaning of the ADA, placement of the burden of proof is much more complex when considering whether the plaintiff is a *qualified* individual with a disability. In those cases, that the plaintiff's disability is causally related to the challenged decision is rarely in dispute; instead the question is who has the burden of proving that job functions are essential or that an accommodation is reasonable or is instead an undue hardship. Those issues are explored in section E2 infra. Explored below is how the burdens of production and proof have been structured when the question of impermissible motivation is at issue in a Title I claim.

## 1.  *Motive-Based Inquires*

While most disability discrimination cases under the ADA and the Rehabilitation Act have involved questions concerning the qualifications of individuals with disabilities and the reasonable accommodation obligations of employers, some cases have dealt with garden-variety disparate treatment claims.

## KIEL v. SELECT ARTIFICIALS, INC.
### 169 F.3d 1131 (8th Cir. 1998)

WOLLMAN, Circuit Judge. . . .

### I

Kiel has been deaf since birth. He was employed at Select as a billing clerk from January 1992 to February 1994. On several occasions he requested that Select purchase a telecommunications device (TDD) that would enable him to make business and personal telephone calls. Select did not provide the device because Kiel did not need it to perform his duties as a billing clerk. Although hearing employees occasionally communicated with clients by telephone, Select decided that Kiel's supervisor could make client calls for him when they were needed. Kiel was allowed to make personal calls during breaks on those occasions when he brought his TDD from home. . . .

On February 17, 1994, Kiel photocopied a letter that he had drafted to Robert Fry, co-owner of Select, again requesting that the company purchase a TDD. After observing Kiel at the photocopier, Julie Fry, the other co-owner of Select, approached him at his work station to inquire about his use of the copier. Kiel informed Ms. Fry that he was requesting that the company purchase a TDD. She told him that Select would not purchase the device. Visibly frustrated and upset, Kiel shouted at Ms. Fry, "You're selfish, you're selfish." He then slammed his desk drawer, and as Ms. Fry walked away he made a remark about her recent purchase of a new automobile. Four other employees were present when Kiel did this. According to the employee witnesses, the episode lasted "a few minutes."

Later that day, Ms. Fry asked Kiel if he realized that he had yelled at her in front of other employees. He said that he was not aware that he had raised his voice and apologized for doing so. After conferring with Mr. Fry, Ms. Fry decided to terminate Kiel for insubordination despite his apology.

Kiel raised claims of discriminatory discharge, retaliatory discharge, and failure to accommodate under the ADA. . . . The district court concluded that Kiel did not produce evidence showing that Select's non-discriminatory reason for terminating Kiel, insubordination, was pretextual. It also held that the temporal connection between Kiel's letter requesting a TDD and his termination was insufficient to demonstrate retaliatory intent and that Select had not failed to accommodate Kiel.

II

We review a grant of summary judgment de novo. . . . [W]e view the evidence and draw all justifiable inferences in favor of the nonmoving party.

In an employment discrimination case, the plaintiff must initially present a prima facie case to survive a motion for summary judgment. The employer must then rebut the presumption of discrimination by articulating a legitimate, non-discriminatory reason for the adverse employment action. If the employer does this, the burden of production shifts back to the plaintiff to demonstrate that the employer's non-discriminatory reason is pretextual.

To make out a prima facie case under the ADA, Kiel was required to show that he is disabled within the meaning of the ADA, that he is qualified to perform the essential functions of his position, and that he suffered an adverse employment action under circumstances giving rise to an inference of unlawful discrimination. Generally, evidence that a plaintiff was replaced by a similarly situated employee who is not disabled is sufficient to support an inference of discrimination. Select did not dispute that Kiel was disabled or that he was qualified to perform his duties as billing clerk, and Kiel established that he was replaced by a hearing employee. Thus, Kiel met his initial burden under *McDonnell Douglas*.

The burden of production then shifted to Select to articulate a legitimate, nondiscriminatory reason for Kiel's termination. Select stated that it terminated Kiel because he insulted Ms. Fry, slammed his desk drawer, and made a sarcastic remark about Ms. Fry in the presence of four co-workers. Our cases have repeatedly held that insubordination and violation of company policy are legitimate reasons for termination. See e.g. Ward v. Procter & Gamble Paper Prods. Co., 111 F.3d 558, 560 (8th Cir. 1997) (employee terminated for striking a co-worker).

Select having proffered a non-discriminatory reason for terminating Kiel, the burden shifted to Kiel to present evidence that Select's reason was pretextual. In essence, Kiel was required to show a genuine issue of material fact as to whether Select actually fired him because of his disability. Although it is possible for strong evidence of a prima facie case to also present a factual issue on pretext, the ultimate question is whether the plaintiff presents evidence of "conduct or statements by persons involved in [the employer's] decisionmaking process reflective of a discriminatory attitude sufficient to allow a reasonable jury to infer that that attitude was a motivating factor in [the employer's] decision to fire [the plaintiff]." Feltmann v. Sieben, 108 F.3d 970, 975 (8th Cir. 1997).

Kiel did not submit any evidence of pretext in this case. He relied entirely on his prima facie case to challenge Select's non-discriminatory reason. The bare assertion that Select hired a hearing employee to replace Kiel did not raise a genuine factual issue regarding Select's discriminatory intent, for Kiel did not point to any conduct or statements by the Frys that would permit a reasonable jury to find that insubordination was a mere pretext for his termination. Nor did he demonstrate that the Frys disciplined hearing employees less severely for insubordinate conduct. As for Kiel's assertion that he did not realize he was shouting, he himself testified that "If I want to shout, I shout," which is consistent with the co-workers' testimony that they had never heard him raise his voice. In short, there is simply no evidence that discrimination was a motivating factor in Kiel's termination.

Kiel contends that his discriminatory discharge claim falls within the mixed-motive analysis of Price Waterhouse v. Hopkins [reproduced at page 152]. To trigger *Price Waterhouse* analysis, however, a plaintiff must show that "an impermissible motive played a motivating part in an adverse employment decision." We have interpreted this to require a plaintiff to present, at a minimum, some direct evidence of discriminatory motive. Because Kiel relied entirely on circumstantial evidence to establish the existence of a discriminatory motive on Select's part, the district court was correct in reviewing Kiel's claim solely under the *McDonnell Douglas* framework. In light of Kiel's failure to establish a genuine factual issue on pretext, the district court properly granted Select summary judgment on the discriminatory discharge claim.

## III

To present a prima facie case of retaliation, a plaintiff must show that he engaged in protected conduct, that he suffered an adverse employment action, and that the adverse action was causally linked to the protected conduct. Although contesting an unlawful employment practice is protected conduct, the anti-discrimination statutes do not insulate an employee from discipline for violating the employer's rules or disrupting the workplace. Generally, more than a temporal connection between the protected conduct and the adverse employment action is required to present a genuine factual issue on retaliation.

Kiel's requests for a TDD were protected communications. Insulting Ms. Fry and indulging in an angry outburst in the presence of co-workers, however, were certainly not, for the ADA confers no right to be rude. Kiel's intervening unprotected conduct eroded any causal connection that was suggested by the temporal proximity of his protected conduct and his termination.

Kiel presented no evidence of conduct or statements that would permit a reasonable jury to find that Select actually fired him because he requested a TDD. Indeed, he had requested a TDD on numerous occasions, but he suffered no adverse employment action until he engaged in abusive, derogatory conduct towards his employer. Kiel did not allege that Select disciplined other employees less harshly for insubordinate conduct. Nor did he show a history of discrimination at Select that would present a genuine factual issue on retaliatory intent. Rather, the record showed that Select has hired a number of deaf employees, has altered job duties to accommodate deaf employees, and has maintained a satisfactory working relationship with deaf employees. In sum, there is simply no evidence from which a reasonable jury could find that Select terminated Kiel in retaliation for his exercising any rights granted to him by the ADA.

Kiel argues that summary judgment was improper because a jury should decide whether his conduct was egregious enough to warrant termination. In the absence of any evidence of discriminatory intent, however, it is not the prerogative of the courts or a jury to sit in judgment of employers' management decisions. . . .

[The court also rejected Kiel's reasonable accommodation claim on the ground that Select provided the accommodations he needed to perform his job. A TDD was not necessary to perform his job.]

## NOTES

1. Other courts have followed the *Kiel* approach in cases in which the employer denies basing its decision on the plaintiff's disability. See, e.g., Hopkins v. EDS Corp., 196 F.3d 655 (6th Cir. 1999); Lawrence v. National Westminster Bank N.J., 98 F.3d 61 (3d Cir. 1996); Daigle v. Liberty Life Ins. Co., 70 F.3d 394 (5th Cir. 1995). Just as in Title VII and ADEA cases, an ADA plaintiff may prevail by showing that the defendant's articulated reason is unworthy of credence. In Moysis v. DTG Datanet, 278 F.3d 819 (8th Cir. 2002), for example, the court characterized the defendant's argument that plaintiff was not fired because of his brain injury as "border[ing] on the frivolous" when plaintiff had had excellent evaluations prior to his disabling accident and a memo purporting to document preexisting performance problems could have been viewed as manufactured after the fact.

2. This approach to disability cases is appropriate in a variety of contexts. In *Kiel*, the employer asserted that Kiel was discharged not because of his disability but because he was insubordinate. Similarly, an employer might defend a negative employment action on the ground that the disabled individual was late, embezzled funds, or otherwise violated workplace rules. Disparate treatment analysis also is appropriate when an employer defends a promotion or hiring decision on the ground that, even aside from her disability, the plaintiff was less qualified than the preferred candidate. See, e.g., Norcross v. Sneed, 755 F.2d 113 (8th Cir. 1985). Alternatively, an employer might assert that a disabled employee was discharged not because of his disability but because of an economic layoff. Each of these assertions, if true, would provide a nondiscriminatory reason for the employer's conduct. Disparate treatment analysis is designed to determine whether the employer who denies relying on the employee's disability has, in fact, treated a qualified employee with a disability differently with respect to hiring, firing, or terms and conditions of employment because of the employee's disability.

3. Some circuits have framed the prima facie case elements differently than *Kiel*. For example in Ennis v. National Assn. of Bus. & Educ. Radio, Inc., 53 F.3d 55 (4th Cir. 1995), the court held that, to establish disparate treatment under the ADA,

> the plaintiff must prove by the preponderance of the evidence that (1) she was in the protected class; (2) she was discharged; (3) at the time of the discharge, she was performing her job at a level that met her employer's legitimate expectations; and (4) her discharge occurred under circumstances that raise a reasonable inference of unlawful discrimination.

Id. at 58. The court characterized this formulation as easing a disabled employee's burden by dispensing with any requirement that she prove that she was replaced by a person outside the protected class. Does the Fourth Circuit's approach make proving discrimination easier or more difficult? If a disabled employee is discharged for performing poorly, but other employees with similar performance are retained, should there be a prima facie case? See also Spath v. Hayes Wheels Intl.-Ind., 211 F.3d 392 (7th Cir. 2000); Hardy v. S. F. Phosphates Ltd. Co., 185 F.3d 1076 (10th Cir. 1999).

4. Is it disability discrimination to treat a disabled person less favorably than a person with a lesser or more easily accommodated disability?

5. In disability cases, employers sometimes provide, as a nondiscriminatory reason, evidence of misconduct caused by the individual's disability. Is acting on the basis of such misconduct tantamount to acting on the basis of the disability? In Borkowski v. Valley Cent. Sch. Dist., 63 F.3d 131 (2d Cir. 1995), the Second Circuit ruled that denying a teacher tenure for inadequate performance may have constituted disability discrimination because the district knew of her disabilities and had an affirmative duty to accommodate. The failure to accommodate resulted in the inadequacies on which the discharge was based. Similarly, in Teahan v. Metro-North Commuter R.R., 951 F.2d 511 (2d Cir. 1996), an employer who disciplined an employee due to excessive absenteeism resulting from her disability was deemed to have acted on the basis of her disability. Was Kiel's raised voice a product of his inability to hear? If so, was relying on his shouting a discriminatory, as opposed to a nondiscriminatory, reason? Courts, however, have tended to rule against plaintiffs whose misconduct is related to alcoholism or drug addiction. See section F.1.

6. What if an employer argues that the plaintiff, although able to perform the essential functions of the job, is less qualified than an applicant without a disability who can perform not only the essential functions but also associated marginal functions? Is this a nondiscriminatory reason, or does the ADA permit employers to evaluate applicants with disabilities only on the basis of their ability to perform essential functions? See *Deane*, reproduced at page 722. What if the employer argues that its failure to hire an individual with a disability was not discriminatory because, although the individual could perform all the essential functions of the job, she could not perform them as well as an individual without a disability? See Smith v. Midland Brake, Inc., 180 F.3d 1154, 1168 (10th Cir. 1999) (en banc) ("We have no quarrel with the proposition that an employer, when confronted with two initial job applicants for a typing position, one of whom types 50 words a minute while the other types 75 words a minute, may hire the person with the higher typing speed, notwithstanding the fact that the slower typist has a disability.").

7. *Kiel* is a case in which intent to discriminate must be inferred. Disability cases, like other discrimination cases, can also be based on direct evidence of discriminatory intent.

8. Kiel asserted that his claim should be evaluated as a "mixed motive" case. The ADA does not expressly address mixed motives, and § 703(m) of Title VIII does not expressly apply to the ADA. The ADA is, however "linked" to Title VII, in that it incorporates the "powers, remedies, and procedures set forth in sections 2000e-4, 2000e-5, 2000e-6, 2000e-8, and 2000e-9" of Title VII. 42 U.S.C.S. § 12117(a) (2003). Some courts have thus found § 703(m) applicable to claims under the ADA. See Parker v. Columbia Pictures Indus., 204 F.3d 326 (2d Cir. 2000); Pedigo v. P.A.M. Transport., Inc., 60 F.3d 1300 (8th Cir. 1999). See also John L. Flynn, Note, Mixed-Motive Causation Under the ADA: Linked Statutes, Fuzzy Thinking, and Clear Statements, 83 Geo. L.J. 2009 (1995).

9. The ADA includes another form of disparate treatment in its definitions of discrimination — "segregating" disabled individuals. 42 U.S.C.S. § 12112(b)(1) (2003). In addition, the EEOC's Interpretive Guidance states that "[r]eassignment may not be used to limit, segregate, or otherwise discriminate against employees with disabilities. . . ." 29 C.F.R. pt. 1630, app. § 1630.2(o). In Duda v. Board of Educ., 133 F.3d 1054 (7th Cir. 1998), the court found that the plaintiff stated a claim under the ADA when his employer transferred him to a new location where he worked alone and was ordered not to speak to others.

## 2. *"Qualified" Individual with a Disability*

As we have stated before, the protections of Title I, generally speaking, attach only to a qualified individual with a disability, defined as an individual with a disability who can perform the essential job functions, with or without reasonable accommodation. Although it is clear that plaintiff has the burden of proving she is an individual with a disability, the question is more complex when whether plaintiff is a "qualified" individual is at issue. Who has the burden of proving job functions are, or are not, essential? Who has the burden of proving plaintiff can perform essential job functions with or without a reasonable accommodation? Since an accommodation that poses an undue hardship is not reasonable, is it defendant's burden to prove an accommodation is unreasonable or does the burden of proving all elements of "qualified" status remain with the plaintiff at all times? These questions are explored below.

### HAMLIN v. CHARTER TOWNSHIP OF FLINT
#### 165 F.3d 426 (6th Cir. 1999)

RONALD LEE GILMAN, Circuit Judge. . . .

### I. BACKGROUND

Hamlin was employed by the Flint Township Fire Department as the Assistant Fire Chief. In September of 1992, Hamlin suffered a heart attack. Following five months of total disability, Hamlin was authorized by his cardiologist to return to work, but was advised to avoid strenuous physical activities such as front-line firefighting. For the next seventeen months, Hamlin performed his duties without complaint from his superiors.

After Hamlin declined offers to fill a vacancy in the Fire Chief position, however, newly appointed Fire Chief Greg Wright ordered Hamlin to perform the duties of a front-line firefighter, which he was unable to do because of his medical disability. On September 19, 1994, approximately three months after Wright's appointment, Flint terminated Hamlin because of his physical inability to engage in the strenuous duties of a firefighter. . . .

At trial, Hamlin contended that Flint unlawfully terminated him on the basis of his inability to fight fires, claiming that front-line firefighting was not an essential part of his duties as the Assistant Fire Chief. Based upon Hamlin's proof that he was otherwise qualified and that Flint had failed to reasonably accommodate his disability, the district court, pursuant to Monette v. Electronic Data Systems Corp., 90 F.3d 1173 (6th Cir. 1996), shifted the burden to Flint to prove that the challenged job requirement of being physically capable of fighting fires was an essential function of Hamlin's position.

[Flint appealed a $500,000 verdict in Hamlin's favor.]

## II.  ANALYSIS

### A.  THE JURY'S VERDICT

#### 1.  *Flint's Challenge to* Monette

The ADA "prohibits employers from discriminating 'against a qualified individual with a disability because of the disability of such individual in regard to application procedures, the hiring, advancement, or discharge of employees, employee compensation, job training, and other terms, conditions, and privileges of employment.'" . . .

In *Monette*, this court held that when an employer admits that it relied upon a disability in making an adverse employment decision, an employee may establish a prima facie case of employment discrimination under the ADA by showing that he or she (1) has a disability, and (2) is "otherwise qualified" for the position despite the disability either "(a) without accommodation from the employer; (b) with an alleged 'essential' job requirement eliminated; or (c) with a proposed reasonable accommodation." If the employee challenges a purported job criterion as not essential and seeks its elimination, the burden then shifts to the employer to establish that the "challenged job criterion is essential, and therefore a business necessity," or that its elimination "will impose an undue hardship upon the employer." In particular, the court stated that "if a disabled individual is challenging a particular job requirement as unessential, the employer will bear the burden of proving that the challenged criterion is necessary." Flint seeks a reversal of *Monette*.

Hamlin presented proof at trial that front-line firefighting is not an essential function of the Assistant Fire Chief position. He pointed out that the key functions of his job were supervisory and administrative in nature, as distinguished from those of a firefighter, which include 24-hour shifts, being the primary responder to emergencies, and engaging in strenuous front-line fire suppression, search, and rescue. In the event that the Assistant Fire Chief is needed at the scene of an emergency, Hamlin contended that his role at the scene would be that of an "Incident Commander," who is the one responsible for getting the right equipment to the scene, supervising front-line firefighters, and assuring that the fire department's response is safe and appropriate under the circumstances.

Hamlin argues that he would have been otherwise qualified to continue working if Flint had eliminated the nonessential firefighting functions from his position. In other words, Hamlin argues that because firefighting is not an essential function of the job, Flint could have reasonably accommodated his disability without undue hardship. Hamlin therefore claims that he presented sufficient evidence at trial to establish his prima facie case, thus shifting the burden to Flint of establishing that firefighting is an essential function of the Assistant Fire Chief position.

[T]he district court . . . properly applied *Monette* to shift the burden from Hamlin to Flint to prove that front-line firefighting was an essential element of Hamlin's job. According to *Monette*, once the disabled individual contends that a particular job requirement is unessential, the burden shifts to the employer to prove that the challenged requirement is necessary. The ADA prohibits an employer from using qualification standards to deny employment "unless the standard . . . is shown to be job-related for the position in question and is consistent with business necessity." 42 U.S.C. §12112(b)(6). *Monette* states that the "clear import" of 42 U.S.C. §12112(b)(6) of the ADA "dictates that employers bear the burden of proving that a challenged job requirement is 'job-related.'" Although an employer may establish minimum physical standards or qualifications for a position, "it will have to show that it actually imposes such requirements on its employees. . . ." 29 C.F.R. §1630.2(n), App.

. . . [W]e find that *Monette* correctly interprets the ADA to require the employer to establish that the challenged function is essential. Accordingly, if the employer cannot prove its affirmative defense, then the ADA bars the employer from terminating an employee based upon the employee's inability to perform that function.

In the present case, Flint admitted that it terminated Hamlin because of his physical inability to fight fires. Hamlin submitted proof that he could perform the duties of the Assistant Fire Chief, as long as those duties did not involve firefighting. Hamlin's evidence was sufficient to raise a genuine issue as to whether firefighting is an essential function of the position. The district court therefore properly placed the burden on Flint to prove that firefighting was in fact an essential function of Hamlin's job, thereby justifying its termination of his employment.

Flint further argues that if we decline to reverse *Monette*, we should at least limit *Monette* to disallow jury instructions that shift the burden of persuasion to defendants. . . .

The fallacy of Flint's argument is that the challenged jury instruction did not place the overall burden of persuasion on Flint. That burden always remained with Hamlin. The instruction simply placed on Flint the burden of proving that firefighting was an essential function of Hamlin's job. This is consistent with *Monette*, which properly shifts the burden of persuasion to the employer on the "essential function" issue and also with regard to an employer's assertion that a proposed accommodation will impose an undue hardship. The district court's challenged jury instruction was therefore accurate and, taken as a whole, the jury instructions more than adequately informed the jury of the law in this circuit.

*Monette* fully comports with the ADA, and the district court correctly applied *Monette* when it shifted the burden to Flint to prove what amounts to an affirmative defense. We therefore reject Flint's *Monette*-based challenges. [The court went on to reject Flint's direct threat defense.]

## NOTES

1. In Benson v. Northwest Airlines, Inc., 62 F.3d 1108, 1112 (8th Cir. 1995), the Eighth Circuit, considering burdens of proof under the ADA, allocated to the plaintiff the "ultimate burden of persuading the trier of fact that he can perform the essential functions of the job, with or without accommodation." Id. at 1113. The court, however, imposed on the employer a burden to "put on some evidence of those essential functions" because "much of the information which determines those essential functions lies uniquely with the employer." Id. How does this approach differ from the Sixth Circuit's approach in *Hamlin?* Which approach is more persuasive? See also Laurin v. Providence Hosp., 150 F.3d 52 (1st Cir. 1998) (employee's burden to prove job function is not essential, once employer proffers evidence that it is).

2. *Hamlin* dealt with the burden of proving essential functions. The legislative history of the ADA suggests that Congress intended the burdens of proof under the ADA

to be allocated as they had been in cases interpreting the Rehabilitation Act. See H.R. Rep. No. 101-484, pt. 2, at 72 (1990), *reprinted in* 1990 U.S.C.C.A.N. 303, 354. With respect to the burden of proof on the question whether the plaintiff is qualified, however, Rehabilitation Act precedent is inconsistent. Compare Doe v. New York Univ., 666 F.2d 761, 766-767 (2d Cir. 1981) (employer bears burden of producing evidence that the plaintiff's "handicap is relevant to qualifications for the position sought"; plaintiff then bears the ultimate burden of showing that he is qualified) with Pushkin v. University of Colo., 658 F.2d 1372, 1387 (10th Cir. 1981) ("Once plaintiff establishes his prima facie case, defendants have the burden of going forward and *proving* that plaintiff was not an otherwise qualified handicapped person") (emphasis added).

3. What happens when an employer contends that being able to perform a job safely is an essential job function? The EEOC has taken the position that when the health or safety of others is at issue, the employer must establish that the employee poses a "direct threat," which is an affirmative defense. The Supreme Court noted, but did not resolve, this issue in *Kirkingburg*. Does *Echazabal* resolve the question? Recall that the Ninth Circuit had rejected Chevron's alternative argument that Echazabal was not "otherwise qualified" because it concluded that performing the job without posing a risk to one's own health was not an essential job function.

The Fifth Circuit has rejected the EEOC's contention that a safety-based qualification standard must satisfy the direct threat defense, instead finding it need only be job related for the position in question and consistent with business necessity. "Direct threat" analysis applies, said that court, when the employer contends a specific individual poses a direct threat to health or safety, which is an affirmative defense. See EEOC v. Exxon Corp., 203 F.3d 871 (5th Cir. 2000). See also Lovejoy-Wilson v. NOCO Motor Fuel, Inc., 263 F.3d 208 (2d Cir. 2001) (describing "direct threat" as an affirmative defense). Other circuits hold that it is the plaintiff's burden to show that, as a qualified individual, she is not a direct threat. See Waddell v. Valley Forge Dental Assocs., 276 F.3d 1275 (11th Cir. 2001), *cert. denied*, 122 S. Ct. 2293 (2002) (plaintiff bears burden of proving he does not constitute a direct threat); EEOC v. Amego, Inc., 110 F.3d 135 (1st Cir. 1997); Moses v. American Nonwovens, Inc., 97 F.3d 446 (11th Cir. 1996). Are these latter cases still good law after *Echazabal*?

**REED v. LEPAGE BAKERIES, INC.**
244 F.3d 254 (1st Cir. 2001)

LYNCH, Circuit Judge.

Manuella Reed was fired by LePage Bakeries for insubordination and threatening her supervisor. Reed says her conduct should be forgiven because she is mentally ill, disabled within the meaning of the Americans with Disabilities Act. She sues on the claim that her termination resulted from LePage's failure to reasonably accommodate her disability and hence was discriminatory. The district court granted summary judgment against Reed. Reed appeals, and the EEOC has filed an amicus brief on her behalf on the issue of the allocation of burdens of proof in ADA reasonable accommodation cases. We reject the position of the EEOC on this issue, find that Reed neither adequately requested nor was prevented from exercising the accommodation she now claims, and affirm.

I

In 1987, Reed was hired by LePage Bakeries, a large commercial baking company, as an assembly line worker. Seven years into her employment, Reed began receiving mental health treatment. She was eventually diagnosed with bipolar disorder, a condition characterized by exaggerated mood swings and agitated emotional states. She has been on medication ever since. As a result of her disorder, Reed fares badly in stressful situations, and when involved in a personal confrontation, she is prone to lose her temper and become verbally abusive.

The first time Reed had such an episode at work was in March 1995. After a muffin-bagging machine broke down during her shift and a mechanic was unable to fix it, Reed flew into a profanity-infused rage, in which she angrily accused the mechanic of being incompetent. Shaken by the incident, Reed left work for the day, apparently with the permission of a manager. She quickly became depressed and, after having thoughts of suicide, had to be hospitalized for five days. On her release, according to Reed, her therapist advised her to ask her employer to accommodate her disability by allowing her to walk away from stressful situations in order to avoid losing control of herself.

After returning to work, Reed met with Mike Pelletier, the plant manager, to discuss her poor attendance record. Reed did not initiate a request for an accommodation at the meeting, but Pelletier on his own brought up Reed's altercation with the mechanic as an aside, and told her that in the future she should walk away from such situations before they became aggravated. Reed agreed, mentioning that she had planned to propose the idea herself, and offered to get a note from her therapist if necessary. She was told it would not be. Pelletier then took Reed to meet with her floor supervisor, Jerry Norton, about the incident. Again, all agreed that Reed should walk away from any such altercation in the future; in addition, Reed was told that after walking away she should immediately get hold of either Pelletier or Norton so that they might help settle the problem.

Reed cannot recall with certainty whether she used the term "accommodation" during either of the meetings. Nor can she unequivocally remember whether or to what extent she revealed that she needed an accommodation due to her mental illness. But she did mention during the first meeting that she had a therapist, and LePage had on earlier occasions made adjustments to Reed's work schedule upon receiving notes from her therapist indicating that she was being seen for "depression." Although Pelletier and Norton knew that Reed had left work for several days after the altercation with the mechanic, they did not know much beyond that; they thought she had left due to a heart condition or problems at home.

Reed did not have another stressful episode at work until June 1, 1996 — the incident resulting in her termination. Having been on workers' compensation leave for a week after sustaining a work-related injury to her arm, Reed met that day with Norton and a human resources director, Cindi Callahan, to discuss her return. The meeting was pursuant to standard practice at LePage; its purpose was to determine the extent of the duties Reed would be able to assume coming off of her injury.

Upon entering the meeting, Reed stated that she wished to discuss whether she could swap shifts with another employee so that she could work in the mornings, when child care was available to her. Callahan responded that they were meeting to discuss Reed's injury-related work restrictions, not her schedule. Reed insisted on discussing scheduling arrangements; Callahan repeatedly tried to steer the conversation back to the issue of restrictions; the situation grew heated. Despite Norton's pleas that Reed calm down, Reed stood up, yelled "Fuck this," and placed her hand on the door to leave.

At that point, Callahan told Reed that she would not be able to begin working if she did not stay at the meeting and discuss her work restrictions. Reed replied, "What are you going to do, fire me?", to which Callahan answered no. Reed then yelled

"Fuck you" and flew into a rage. Standing on the tips of her toes, Reed dared Callahan to fire her, telling her that if she did, Reed would sue. Callahan felt threatened by Reed's conduct.

Norton called human resources personnel to have Reed escorted from the building, but before they arrived, Reed left the room on her own volition. She then sought out Tony Nedik, head of personnel, and attempted to account for her conduct. She told Nedik that she had a mental illness that caused her to lose control of herself, that she needed an accommodation for it, and that she had tried to exercise such accommodation during the meeting but Callahan had prevented her from doing so. Reed asked if she could come back to work tomorrow; Nedik answered no. Reed was fired the next workday for insubordinate and threatening conduct.

. . . The gist of her case is that she claims to have requested and been granted a reasonable accommodation after her March 1995 altercation with the mechanic; that accommodation, she says, consisted in permission to walk away from stressful confrontations at work, whether or not those confrontations were with co-workers or supervisors. LePage discriminated against her, Reed claims, by not allowing her to exercise that accommodation at the June 1 meeting and by firing her for attempting to do so.

LePage moved for summary judgment, arguing, inter alia, that Reed was not disabled within the meaning of the ADA, that she was never prevented from exercising any accommodation, and that in any event the accommodation she claims to have been prevented from exercising was unreasonable. [The district court granted LePage's motion because] Reed had not put forward sufficient evidence that it was reasonable to demand an accommodation permitting her to walk away from supervisors when feeling stressed. The only evidence Reed had put forward, the court found, was that Reed's supervisors had advised her, as they commonly advised all employees, to walk away from conflict situations; but such evidence, in the court's view, went only toward showing the reasonableness of being permitted to walk away from conflicts with co-workers, not from conflicts with supervisors.

## II

We review the district court's order de novo, "considering the facts in the light most favorable to the nonmoving party, drawing all reasonable inferences in that party's favor." Section 102(a) of the ADA states: "No covered entity shall discriminate against a qualified individual with a disability because of the disability of such individual in regard to . . . discharge of employees. . . ." 42 U.S.C. § 12112(a). Discrimination is defined to include "not making reasonable accommodations to the known physical or mental limitations of an otherwise qualified individual with a disability . . . , unless [the] covered entity can demonstrate that the accommodation would impose an undue hardship on the operation of the business of such covered entity." 42 U.S.C. § 12112(b)(5)(A).

For purposes of summary judgment we accept that Reed has put forward sufficient evidence that she had a disability within the meaning of the ADA.[1] The case hinges instead on whether Reed was denied a reasonable accommodation of her disability. The district court entered summary judgment on the basis that Reed had not shown

---

1.  Reed offered evidence that her bipolar disorder substantially limited one or more of her "major life activities," see 42 U.S.C. § 12102(2)(A), in that it occasionally led to prolonged sleep loss, see Criado v. IBM Corp., 145 F.3d 437, 442-43 (1st Cir. 1998) (sleeping as major life activity).

her requested accommodation was reasonable. In so holding, the court raised the question of the extent of plaintiff's burden of proof on the issue. The EEOC has filed with us an amicus brief on this question, arguing that the district court effectively shifted to the plaintiff the defendant's burden of proving whether the requested accommodation would impose an undue hardship. This court has not clearly distinguished between plaintiff's and defendant's burdens in ADA reasonable accommodation cases before. We take the opportunity to do so here.

## A. REASONABLE ACCOMMODATION VIS-A-VIS UNDUE HARDSHIP

Under the ADA, the plaintiff bears the burden of proving that the defendant could provide a reasonable accommodation for her disability. At the same time, the statute places the burden on the defendant to show that the proposed accommodation would impose an undue hardship. See 42 U.S.C. § 12112(b)(5)(A). There is a well recognized tension in the statute's allocation of burdens in this fashion. The burdens might appear to be mirror images of one another: a "reasonable accommodation," it might seem, is simply one that does not impose an "undue hardship." But if this were so, the statute would effectively impose identical burdens on both parties.

Other circuit courts have dealt with this tension using linguistically different, but functionally similar, approaches. The first approach shifts the burden of persuasion from plaintiff to defendant, so that the burden of identifying a reasonable accommodation is only one of production. Under this approach, plaintiff's burden is not a heavy one. It is enough for the plaintiff to suggest the existence of a plausible accommodation, the costs of which, facially, do not clearly exceed its benefits. Once the plaintiff has done this, she has made out a prima facie showing that a reasonable accommodation is available, and the risk of nonpersuasion falls on the defendant. Borkowski v. Valley Central Sch. Dist., 63 F.3d 131, 138 (2d Cir. 1995) (citation omitted). The Third Circuit has expressly utilized this test in an ADA case, see Walton v. Mental Health Assoc., 168 F.3d 661, 670 (3d Cir. 1999), and the Eighth and Tenth Circuits use a similar approach, see Fjellestad v. Pizza Hut, 188 F.3d 944, 950 (8th Cir. 1999); Benson v. Northwest Airlines, Inc., 62 F.3d 1108, 1112 (8th Cir. 1995); White v. York Int'l Corp., 45 F.3d 357, 361 (10th Cir. 1995).

The other approach, which seems to have originated with the D.C. Circuit in a Rehabilitation Act case, Barth v. Gelb, 303 U.S. App. D.C. 211, 2 F.3d 1180 (D.C. Cir. 1993), ostensibly keeps all burdens of proving reasonable accommodation on the plaintiff. ("The burden remains with the plaintiff to prove his case by a preponderance of the evidence"). This approach is followed by the Fifth Circuit, see Riel v. Elec. Data Sys. Corp., 99 F.3d 678, 682-83 (5th Cir. 1996); the Sixth Circuit, see Hoskins v. Oakland Cty. Sheriff's Dep't, 227 F.3d 719, 728 (6th Cir. 2000); Monette v. Electronic Data Sys. Corp., 90 F.3d 1173, 1183 & n.10, 1186 n.12 (6th Cir. 1996); the Seventh Circuit, see Vande Zande v. Wisc. Dep't of Admin., 44 F.3d 538, 542-43 (7th Cir. 1995); and the Eleventh Circuit, see Willis v. Conopco, Inc., 108 F.3d 282, 285-86 (11th Cir. 1997) (also denying that "reasonable accommodation" and "undue burden" are mirror images). Nonetheless, under this approach, the plaintiff still need only make a general or facial showing of reasonableness. See, e.g., Barth (reasonable accommodation is "a *method of accommodation* that is reasonable in the run of cases, whereas undue hardship inquiry focuses on the hardships imposed by the plaintiff's preferred accommodation in the context of the particular [employer's] operations" (emphasis in original)), quoted in Willis and Riel; Vande Zande (in proving reasonable accommodation plaintiff must make facial showing of proportionality to costs, whereupon employer, in showing undue burden, has opportunity to prove upon more careful consideration that costs are excessive).

We are reluctant to talk about the problem of the relationship between "reasonable accommodation" and "undue hardship" as one of shifting burdens.[3] We prefer to discuss the burdens of showing reasonable accommodation and undue hardship as they are allocated in the statute: the plaintiff fully bears the former, and the defendant fully bears the latter. The real issue is the quantum of proof needed to show reasonable accommodation vis-a-vis the quantum of proof needed to show undue hardship.

On this issue, we reject the position urged on us by the EEOC. In contrast to the basic approach followed by our sister circuits, the EEOC argues that the only burden a plaintiff has on proving reasonable accommodation is to show that the accommodation would effectively enable her to perform her job; whether the accommodation would be too costly or difficult, on the EEOC's view, is entirely for the defendant to prove.[4] We agree that proving an accommodation's effectiveness is part of the plaintiff's burden; but it is not the whole. Indeed, simply in explaining how her proposal constitutes an "accommodation," the plaintiff must show that it would effectively enable her to perform her job. That is precisely what an accommodation does. But what plaintiff must show further under the statute is that her requested accommodation is "reasonable." And consistent with its usage throughout the law, the concept of reasonableness here constrains the plaintiff in what she can demand from the defendant. A request that the defendant relocate its operations to a warmer climate, for example, is difficult to imagine as being "reasonable." A reasonable request for an accommodation must in some way consider the difficulty or expense imposed on the one doing the accommodating. See *Vande Zande*.

Thus, we believe the best way to distinguish between the two burdens is to follow in essence the lead of our sister circuits: In order to prove "reasonable accommodation," a plaintiff needs to show not only that the proposed accommodation would enable her to perform the essential functions of her job, but also that, at least on the face of things, it is feasible for the employer under the circumstances.[5] If plaintiff succeeds in carrying this burden, the defendant then has the opportunity to show that the proposed accommodation is not as feasible as it appears but rather that there are further costs to be considered, certain devils in the details.

Under this arrangement, the difficulty of providing plaintiff's proposed accommodation will often be relevant both to the reasonableness of the accommodation and to whether it imposes an undue hardship. Cf. *Vande Zande*. Plaintiff will often need to take such difficulties into account in proving whether the accommodation is facially practicable, and defendant will of course need to provide evidence of them in

---

3. The burden-shifting model was introduced into employment law in order to allow indirect proof of the often elusive "intent" to discriminate. See Higgins v. New Balance Athletic Shoe, Inc., 194 F.3d 252, 264 (1st Cir. 1999). Thus, burden shifting allows a plaintiff to make a small showing of discrimination, whereupon the employer must articulate a non-discriminatory reason for its actions, and if that reason proves to be untrue, then an inference of discrimination may be warranted. See McDonnell Douglas Corp. v. Green; see also Texas Dep't of Cmty. Affairs v. Burdine. By contrast, whether a requested accommodation is reasonable or whether it imposes an undue hardship are questions typically proved through direct, objective evidence. Accordingly, we have already held that the *McDonnell Douglas* model does not apply to ADA discrimination claims based on failure to reasonably accommodate. *Higgins*. It would be confusing to import such a model into a subpart of the analysis of such claims.

4. The EEOC position has not been adopted by any of the circuits. . . .

5. A plaintiff may sometimes be able to establish the reasonableness of a proposed accommodation by showing it is a method of accommodation that is feasible in the run of cases. But this will not always be so. ADA cases come in an amazing variety of hues and shapes, and some jobs are sui generis, so we are reluctant to set hard and fast rules.

attempting to prove undue hardship. Indeed, where the costs of an accommodation are relatively obvious — where they really are what they appear to be on the face of things — plaintiff's burden and defendant's burden may in application be quite similar, even to the extent of being mirror images. Where the burdens will significantly differ is when the costs of an accommodation are not evident on the face of things, but rather are better known to the employer. . . . For example, an employee's proposal that her work area be modified might be facially reasonable, but the employer may still show that, given the particular limitations on its financial resources, or other hidden costs, such accommodation imposes an undue hardship. See 42 U.S.C. § 12111(10)(B).

In the end, it is difficult to propound language as to the content of the parties' burdens much more specific than the language of the statute.[6] Consequently, in many cases the dividing line between "reasonable accommodation" and "undue hardship" will be inexact — but benignly so. Given the inexactness of that dividing line, wise counsel for both parties will err on the side of offering proof beyond what their burdens require. The summary judgment decisions of this court have often turned on the surprising failure by one party or the other to proffer any significant evidence in favor of their position. See, e.g., *Garcia-Ayala; Ward.*

### B.   REQUEST FOR ACCOMMODATION

We next address whether Reed has met her burden of proving that her requested accommodation was facially reasonable. Ordinarily, this would involve an analysis of the accommodation at issue, which, in this case, would be permission to walk away from any stressful conflict, regardless of whether it was with a co-worker or a supervisor. That analysis would turn in part on the particular circumstances of the workplace. Some of the more obvious and visible circumstances, such as the general culture of the workplace, we might expect Reed to address as part of her burden. Other specifics that are more within the control or knowledge of the employer, such as its management strategy or its need to maintain a strict hierarchy, might better belong in LePage's defense. Given the factual record developed here, it would be difficult to say whether Reed's suggested accommodation is facially reasonable.

We need not concern ourselves with the reasonableness of Reed's accommodation, however, because Reed has failed to prove another essential element of her burden: that she ever sufficiently requested the accommodation in question. . . . Specifically, Reed never made LePage sufficiently aware that she had a disability marked by occasional fits of rage and consequently needed some sort of special accommodation. Moreover, even had Reed made LePage so aware, and had she subsequently been granted an accommodation permitting her to walk away not only from conflicts with co-workers but also from conflicts with supervisors, she was never prevented from invoking any such accommodation during her fateful meeting in June of 1996. These grounds suffice to dispose of her case. . . .

### *NOTES*

1. In U.S. Airways, Inc. v. Barnett, reproduced at page 745, the Supreme Court endorsed the First Circuit's approach. To defeat summary judgment, a plaintiff needs

---

6. Indeed, EEOC regulations do not offer a particularized definition of the term "reasonable accommodation." They only give examples. See 29 C.F.R. § 1630.2(o)(2).

only to show that the accommodation "seems reasonable on its face, *i.e.*, ordinarily or in the run of cases." Once this showing has been made, the defendant must show "special circumstances (typically case specific) that demonstrate undue hardship in the particular circumstances." Under this approach, the plaintiff is relieved of needing to prove the absence of undue hardship in the context of proving an accommodation is reasonable, while the defendant is not forced to shoulder the burden of proving undue hardship unless the proposed accommodation has been shown to be reasonable in the usual case or on the facts of the particular case. Id. at 749.

2. In Shapiro v. Township of Lakewood, 292 F.3d 356 (3d Cir. 2002), the Third Circuit read *Barnett* as establishing the following framework in reassignment cases:

> It therefore appears that the Court has prescribed the following two-step approach for cases in which a requested accommodation in the form of a job reassignment is claimed to violate a disability-neutral rule of the employer. The first step requires the employee to show that the accommodation is a type that is reasonable in the run of cases. The second step varies depending on the outcome of the first step. If the accommodation is shown to be a type of accommodation that is reasonable in the run of cases, the burden shifts to the employer to show that granting the accommodation would impose an undue hardship under the particular circumstances of the case. On the other hand, if the accommodation is not shown to be a type of accommodation that is reasonable in the run of cases, the employee can still prevail by showing that special circumstances warrant a finding that the accommodation is reasonable under the particular circumstances of the case.

Id. at 361. Do you agree with the *Shapiro* court's reading of *Barnett*? Even if you do not, is *Shapiro* a correct interpretation of the statute?

## F.   SPECIAL PROBLEMS OF DISABILITY DISCRIMINATION

The ADA contains detailed provisions relating to applicants and employees who use illegal drugs or alcohol and to employers who use medical examinations or inquiries. In addition, the ADA prohibits retaliation and interference and discrimination against someone who has a relationship with a person with a disability, and it has been interpreted to prohibit disability-based harassment. Also, the impact of the ADA on health and disability insurance plans and on rights under the National Labor Relations Act warrants special consideration. Finally, rights granted under the Family and Medical Leave Act may be a useful alternative to the ADA for individuals whose health problems make regular attendance at work difficult.

### 1.   Drug or Alcohol Users

Section 104(a) provides that the term "qualified individual with a disability" shall not include a person "who is currently engaging in the illegal use of drugs" when the covered entity acts on the basis of such use. Such individuals simply are not covered by the statute. The title of § 104, "Illegal Use of Drugs and Alcohol," suggests identical coverage for drug and alcohol use. However, the plain language of § 104(a) indicates that an alcoholic who is currently using alcohol may be disabled under the ADA.

Although current drug *users* are excluded from coverage, the ADA does protect alcoholics and drug addicts from discrimination on the basis of their alcoholism or drug *addiction*. Section 104(b) provides that nothing in § 104(a) shall exclude from the definition of qualified individual with a disability an individual who:

> (1) has successfully completed a supervised drug rehabilitation program and is no longer engaging in the illegal use of drugs, or has otherwise been rehabilitated successfully and is no longer engaging in such use;
> (2) is participating in a supervised rehabilitation program and is no longer engaging in such use;
> (3) is erroneously regarded as engaging in such use, but is not engaging in such use.

Section 104(c) provides employers with a number of potential defenses against a person claiming disability discrimination because of drug or alcohol addiction or use. For example, § 104(c)(1)-(2) permits a covered entity to prohibit the use of illegal drugs and alcohol, or being under the influence of alcohol, at the workplace, and § 104(c)(4) permits covered entities to "hold an employee who engages in the illegal use of drugs or who is an alcoholic to the same qualification standards for employment or job performance and behavior that such entity holds other employees, even if any unsatisfactory performance or behavior is related to the drug use or alcoholism of such employee."

## ZENOR v. EL PASO HEALTHCARE SYSTEM, LTD.
### 176 F.3d 847 (5th Cir. 1999)

GARWOOD, Circuit Judge. . . .

[El Paso Healthcare System, doing business as Columbia, hired Zenor in 1991 to work as a pharmacist in the pharmacy at its Columbia Medical Center-East hospital. In 1993, Zenor became addicted to cocaine, injecting himself four to five times a week. Despite his drug use, Zenor was a generally adequate employee. Columbia was unaware of Zenor's addiction until August 15, 1995.]

Zenor had been working the night shift at the pharmacy. When Zenor left work on August 15, 1995, at approximately 8:30 a.m., he injected himself with cocaine. As Zenor prepared to return to work that night, he became dizzy and had difficulty walking. Suspecting that he was still impaired from the morning's cocaine injection, Zenor called the pharmacy director, Joe Quintana (Quintana), and stated that he could not report to work because he was under the influence of cocaine. . . . Quintana asked whether Zenor would take advantage of Columbia's Employee Assistance Program, "ACCESS." Zenor replied that he would. . . .

. . . Zenor then called his personal physician, who arranged for Zenor to receive emergency treatment that evening. Zenor stayed overnight at R.E. Thomason General Hospital. The next morning, Zenor was transferred to the El Paso Alcohol and Drug Abuse Service Detox Center, where he remained hospitalized for nine days.

On August 23, while still at the Detox Center, Zenor became concerned about losing his job. Zenor and one of his Detox Center counselors, Pete McMillian (McMillian), contacted Yolanda Mendoza (Mendoza), Columbia's Human Resources Director. . . .

Zenor told Mendoza that he wished to enter a rehabilitation program and asked her whether his job would be secure until he returned. . . . [T]here is evidence that Mendoza assured Zenor that his job would be secure until he completed the program. Mendoza then told McMillan that Zenor was eligible for a twelve-week leave of absence under the [FMLA]. [Zenor took FMLA leave.] The next day, August 24, Zenor checked into an independent residential rehabilitation facility, Landmark Adult Intensive Residential Services Center (Landmark). . . .

After consulting with Columbia's lawyers, Mendoza and Quintana decided to terminate Zenor's employment. On September 20, 1995, Mendoza, Quintana, and ACCESS director Joe Provencio had a meeting with Zenor [and his counselors]. Zenor was told that he would remain an employee of Columbia until his medical leave expired, and then he would be terminated.

Zenor protested that Columbia could not fire him because the Policy stated that employees who completed rehabilitation would be returned to work. Zenor also argued that he had been told if he "self-reported" his addiction he would not be fired. Mendoza explained that Columbia was concerned because pharmaceutical cocaine would be readily available to Zenor in the pharmacy, and therefore Columbia would not allow Zenor to return to work.

Zenor offered to transfer to a day shift where he could be monitored, or to a satellite pharmacy where pharmaceutical cocaine would not be available. Columbia rejected these suggestions. . . .

Zenor completed the residential portion of his treatment program and was released from Landmark on October 9, 1995. On October 18, Zenor met with Mendoza and again asked to keep his job. Mendoza told Zenor that his termination stood. . . .

## DISCUSSION

### I. THE ADA . . .

At the close of Zenor's case-in-chief, the district court found insufficient evidence to support the ADA claim and granted Columbia's motion for judgment as a matter of law. On appeal, the parties raise three separate questions with respect to the ADA claim: (1) whether Zenor was disqualified from the ADA's protection because he was a "current user" of illegal drugs at the relevant time, (2) whether Zenor was an otherwise qualified individual, and (3) whether Zenor established that he suffered from a disability. . . .

The first issue is whether Zenor was "currently engaging in the illegal use of drugs" at the time the adverse employment action was taken. 42 U.S.C. § 12114 specifically exempts current illegal drug users from the definition of qualified individuals. In other words, federal law does not proscribe an employer's firing someone who currently uses illegal drugs, regardless of whether or not that drug use could otherwise be considered a disability. The issue in this case, therefore, is whether Zenor was a "current" drug user within the meaning of the statute.

As a threshold matter, this Court must determine the proper time at which to evaluate whether Zenor was "currently engaging in the illegal use of drugs." Zenor urges this Court to look to the date his employment status officially ended: November 24, 1995. The Second Circuit adopted this approach in Teahan v. Metro-North Commuter R.R. Co., 951 F.2d 511 (2d Cir. 1991). Teahan was an alcoholic who had missed an extensive amount of work due to his alcoholism. On December 28, 1987, Metro-North wrote a letter informing Teahan that his employment was terminated. That same day, before receiving the termination letter, Teahan voluntarily entered a rehabilitation program. While Teahan was in the rehabilitation program, Metro-North initiated procedures to fire Teahan pursuant to its collective bargaining agreement with . . . [IBEW]. However, the disciplinary procedures were not complete on January 28, 1988, when Teahan completed the rehabilitation program. Pursuant to its agreement with IBEW, therefore, Metro-North permitted Teahan to return to work temporarily. Metro-North finally terminated Teahan on April 11, 1989.

Teahan sued Metro-North, alleging that his dismissal violated the Rehabilitation Act. . . . The case . . . turned on whether Teahan was a current abuser of alcohol at the relevant time.

Metro-North asked the court to consider Teahan's status as a current alcohol abuser on December 28, 1987, at which time Metro-North began procedures to fire Teahan. . . . The Second Circuit disagreed, and decided instead to focus on the date on which Teahan was actually fired. The court reasoned that the word "current" within the statute prohibited an employer from firing an employee based on past substance abuse problems that the employee had overcome. That court feared that Metro-North's theory would create a loophole which would expose recovering substance abusers to retroactive punishment. Therefore, the court looked to the April 11, 1989, actual termination date to determine whether the drug use was current.

This Court has already, at least implicitly, rejected the Second Circuit's approach.[2] See McDaniel v. Mississippi Baptist Medical Center, 877 F. Supp. 321 (S.D. Miss. 1995) (interpreting current user provision under the ADA), *aff'd*, 74 F.3d 1238 (5th Cir. 1995) (table). . . . McDaniel was a recovered substance abuser who worked as an adolescent marketing representative for a substance abuse recovery program. On or around September 2, 1992, McDaniel voluntarily entered a rehabilitation program after suffering a relapse. On September 1 . . . McDaniel's supervisor notified him that he would not return to his current position. . . . The employer subsequently fired McDaniel on September 20, 1992.

McDaniel argued that he was not a current drug user on September 20, the date he was fired, and therefore he was protected by the ADA. The court disagreed, finding that the relevant adverse employment action was conveyed to McDaniel on September 1, before he entered the rehabilitation program. At that time, McDaniel was a current user of illegal drugs.

Similarly, the relevant adverse employment action in this case occurred on September 20, 1995, when Quintana and Mendoza informed Zenor that he would be terminated upon the expiration of his medical leave. We do not share the Second Circuit's fear that considering the notification date, rather than the actual termination date, creates a loophole by which employers can punish recovered addicts. There is nothing to suggest that Columbia was in any way punishing Zenor. Instead, Columbia was carrying out its rational and legally sound decision not to employ illegal cocaine users in its hospital pharmacy.

Looking to the notification of termination date provides a fair remedy both to the employer and employee. Otherwise, in this case, Columbia would effectively be penalized for allowing Zenor to take a medical leave of absence rather than terminating him right away. Such a ruling would encourage employers in Columbia's position to hasten effectuation of employment decisions, which could have adverse effects for employees who would benefit from remaining in an employee status, such as by retaining employer-provided health and insurance benefits, during their recovery programs. . . .

. . . Therefore, the question is whether Zenor, who had used cocaine on August 15, 1995, was currently engaging in the illegal use of drugs when Columbia informed him on September 20, 1995, of its decision to terminate him. We conclude, as a matter of law, that he was.

Under the ADA, "currently" means that the drug use was sufficiently recent to justify the employer's reasonable belief that the drug abuse remained an ongoing

---

2. We note that our disagreement with the *Teahan* case is only with the narrow aspect of identifying the relevant date by which to determine whether an employee is a current user of illegal drugs.

problem. See 143 Cong. Rec. H 103-01 (1997). Thus, the characterization of "currently engaging in the illegal use of drugs" is properly applied to persons who have used illegal drugs in the weeks and months preceding a negative employment action. Shafer v. Preston Memorial Hospital Corp., 107 F.3d 274, 278 (4th Cir. 1997); Collings v. Longview Fibre Co., 63 F.3d 828 (9th Cir. 1995); *McDaniel*. . . .

These holdings reflect Congress's unambiguous intent that "the [current user] provision is not intended to be limited to persons who use drugs on the day of, or within a matter of days *or weeks* before, the employment action in question." H.R. Rep. No. 101-596, at 64 (1990) (emphasis added). See also 143 Cong. Rec. H 103-01 (1997) ("Current illegal use of drugs means illegal use of drugs that occurred recently enough to justify a reasonable belief that a person's drug use is current or that continuing use is a real and ongoing problem.").

The EEOC Compliance Manual on Title I of the ADA also supports this interpretation.

> "Current" drug use means that the illegal use of drugs occurred recently enough to justify an employer's reasonable belief that involvement with drugs is an on-going problem. It is *not limited to* the day of use, or *recent weeks* or days, in terms of an employment action. It is determined on a case-by-case basis.

EEOC-M-1A Title VIII § 8.3 Illegal Use of Drugs (emphasis added).

Additionally, the Second Circuit has suggested several factors which courts should examine to determine whether a person is a current substance abuser, including "the level of responsibility entrusted to the employee; the employer's applicable job and performance requirements; the level of competence ordinarily required to adequately perform the task in question; and the employee's past performance record." See *Teahan*. Rather than focusing solely on the timing of the employee's drug use, courts should consider whether an employer could reasonably conclude that the employee's substance abuse prohibited the employee from performing the essential job duties. See *Teahan*.

Zenor admits to having used cocaine as much as five times a week for approximately two years and to having been addicted. On September 20, 1995, Zenor had refrained from using cocaine for only five weeks, all while having been hospitalized or in a residential program. Such a short period of abstinence, particularly following such a severe drug problem, does not remove from the employer's mind a reasonable belief that the drug use remains a problem. Zenor's position as a pharmacist required a great deal of care and skill, and Zenor admits that any mistakes could gravely injure Columbia's patients. Moreover, Columbia presented substantial testimony about the extremely high relapse rate of cocaine addiction. Zenor's own counselors, while supportive and speaking highly of Zenor's progress, could not say with any real assurance that Zenor wouldn't relapse. Finally, Columbia presented substantial evidence regarding the on-going nature of cocaine-addiction recovery. The fact that Zenor completed the residential portion of his treatment was only the first step in a long-term recovery program. Based on these factors, Columbia was justified in believing that the risk of harm from a potential relapse was significant, and that Zenor's drug abuse remained an ongoing threat.

Nonetheless, Zenor argues that because he voluntarily enrolled in a rehabilitation program, he is entitled to protection under the ADA's "safe harbor" provision for drug users. The safe harbor provides an exception to the current user exclusion of 42 U.S.C. § 12114(a) for individuals who are rehabilitated and no longer using drugs.

See 42 U.S.C. § 12114(b):

> (b) Rules of construction. Nothing in subsection (a) shall be construed to exclude as a qualified individual with a disability an individual who —
>   (1) has successfully completed a supervised drug rehabilitation program and is no longer engaging in the illegal use of drugs, or has otherwise been rehabilitated successfully and is no longer engaging in such use; [or]
>   (2) is participating in a supervised rehabilitation program and is no longer engaging in such use. . . .

However, the mere fact that an employee has entered a rehabilitation program does not automatically bring that employee within the safe harbor's protection. See also *Shafer.* H.R. Conf. Rep. No. 101-596, at 64 ("This provision does not permit persons to invoke the Acts [sic] protection simply by showing that they are participating in a drug treatment program."). Instead, the House Report explains that the safe harbor provision applies only to individuals who have been drug-free for a significant period of time. ("On the other hand, this provision recognizes that many people continue to participate in drug treatment programs *long after they have stopped using drugs illegally,* and that such persons should be protected under the Act.") (emphasis added).

Zenor argues that he should be protected by the safe harbor provision because he "self-reported" his addiction and voluntarily entered the rehabilitation program. At least one court has distinguished employees who voluntarily seek help for their addictions from those employees who are caught by employers using drugs. See Grimes v. U.S. Postal Serv., 872 F. Supp. 668, 675 (W.D. Mo. 1994).

However, other courts have rejected the proposition that a "chemically dependent person . . . who is currently engaging in illegal drug use[ ] can escape termination by enrolling himself in a drug treatment program before he is caught by the employer." *McDaniel; Shafer.* These holdings better align with Congress' explicit statement that a plaintiff may not evade termination merely by entering into a rehabilitation program, without first showing a significant period of recovery. Thus, to the extent that Zenor's claim of "self-reporting" is genuine, it does not propel Zenor into the safe harbor's protection simply because he had entered a rehabilitation program before the adverse employment action was taken.

For similar reasons, Columbia was free to find that Zenor was not a "qualified individual" even in the absence of the statutory exclusion for illegal drug users. A qualified individual under the ADA must be able to perform essential job requirements. . . . Columbia reasonably may have felt that having a pharmacist who had recently been treated for cocaine addiction undermined the integrity of its hospital pharmacy operation. See *McDaniel* (finding it "not unreasonable or beyond the reach of the ADA for the Defendant [addiction recovery center] to find that it was essential to the performance of the marketing job not to have a recently relapsed person holding that job"). See also Copeland v. Philadelphia Police Dept., 840 F.2d 1139, 1149 (3d Cir. 1988) (under Rehabilitation Act, illegal drug user was not qualified for position of police officer because accommodation would be substantial modification of job and cast doubt on department's integrity). Such conclusions do not violate the ADA.

Columbia was also entitled to consider the relapse rate for cocaine addiction in determining that Zenor was not qualified to work as a pharmacist. See *Teahan.* Directing courts to consider the likelihood of relapse in considering whether a recovering addict was "otherwise qualified" for a particular position. As noted, cocaine addiction has a very high relapse rate, and the risk of harm from a potential relapse was great. See D'Amico [v. City of New York, 132 F.3d 145, 151 (2d Cir. 1998)] (holding plaintiff's history of cocaine addiction coupled with risks inherent in potential relapse justified city's termination of firefighter).[7]

Finally, this evidence should be viewed in light of what was known to Columbia on the date it fired Zenor. Thus, the fact that Zenor has not thereafter relapsed does not affect the reasonableness of Columbia's decision on September 20, 1995.

As an alternate basis for our holding, we determine that Zenor was not disabled within the meaning of the ADA. . . . [Zenor sought to establish a disability by arguing that Columbia regarded him as an addict.]

However . . . the fact that a person is perceived to be a drug addict does not necessarily mean that person is perceived to be disabled under the ADA. Zenor must also show that Columbia regarded Zenor's addiction as substantially limiting one of Zenor's major life activities. See 29 C.F.R. § 1630.3 (noting that safe harbor provision "simply provides that certain individuals are not excluded from the definitions of 'disability' and 'qualified individual with a disability.' Consequently, such individuals are still required to establish that they satisfy the requirements of these definitions in order to be protected by the ADA and this part.").

In Burch v. Coca-Cola Co., 119 F.3d 305 (5th Cir. 1997), this Court held that alcoholism is not a disability per se under the ADA. The ADA requires an individualized inquiry to determine whether a particular plaintiff is disabled. Thus, even a plaintiff who suffers from a condition such as alcoholism or drug addiction — or is perceived as suffering from such a condition — must demonstrate that the condition substantially limits, or is perceived by his employer as substantially limiting, his ability to perform a major life function. . . .

Zenor argues that Columbia perceived him as substantially limited in the major life activity of working. [The Court ruled against Zenor because he presented "no evidence that Columbia regarded him as limited in his ability to work in a broad range of jobs."]

## NOTES

1. One commentator has criticized Congress's policy choice in excluding current drug users from coverage under the ADA. See Kenneth J. Vanko, Note, In Search of Common Ground: Leveling the Playing Field for Chemically Dependent Workers Under the Americans with Disabilities Act of 1990, 1996 U. Ill. L. Rev. 1257.

2. Does the Fifth Circuit or the Second Circuit have the better argument about the relevant date for determining whether an individual was "currently using" illegal drugs? If the court had focused instead on November 24, 1995, the date Zenor's employment officially ended, would Zenor have been "currently using" illegal drugs? Would he have been "qualified"?

---

7. Columbia also raises a serious question as to whether Zenor could have retained his pharmacy license. All pharmacists practicing in Texas must be licensed by the Texas State Board of Pharmacy (Board). At the time Zenor was fired, Columbia reported his cocaine addiction to the Board. The Board apparently began an investigation, but, when Zenor subsequently failed to renew his license, the investigation ceased. Clearly, one who is not licensed cannot be considered "otherwise qualified" for the position of pharmacist.

3. The court indicates that job responsibilities and past performance are part of the determination whether an individual is "currently using" illegal drugs. Is this consistent with the statutory language?

4. If Zenor had been addicted to alcohol rather than cocaine, would Columbia have been required under the ADA to grant Zenor leave to seek rehabilitation for his alcoholism? Consider the impact of § 104(c)(4), which permits employers to hold alcoholics and drug addicts to the same "job performance and behavior" as other employees, "even if any unsatisfactory performance or behavior is related to drug use or alcoholism." Consider also § 8.7 of the EEOC Technical Assistance Manual (TAM) which provides that "the ADA does not require an employer to provide an opportunity for rehabilitation in place of discipline or discharge" of an employee whose alcohol abuse adversely affects job performance.

5. Although these provisions appear to eliminate any need to make reasonable accommodations in employment policies, judicial and agency interpretations suggest that at least some level of accommodation is required under the ADA for alcoholic and drug-addicted employees. Section 8.7 of the EEOC TAM provides:

> [T]he ADA does not require an employer to provide an opportunity for rehabilitation in place of discipline or discharge to [employees with poor performance or misconduct records]. The ADA may, however, require consideration of reasonable accommodation for a drug addict who is rehabilitated or an alcoholic who remains a "qualified individual with a disability." For example, a modified work schedule, to permit an individual to attend an ongoing self-help program, might be a reasonable accommodation for such an employee.

Corbett v. National Prods. Co., No. CIV. A. 94-2652, 1995 WL 133614 (E.D. Pa. Mar. 27, 1995), concerned an alcoholic employee who needed treatment but whose job performance was not at issue. The court ruled that, absent evidence that an employee's attempt at rehabilitation would be futile, his employer should have accommodated him by allowing him to take a 28-day unpaid leave of absence to receive treatment for his alcoholism. Id. at *4. Does this approach make sense under § 104(c)(4)?

6. In Hernandez v. Hughes Aircraft Sys., Inc., 298 F.3d 1030 (9th Cir. 2002), the Ninth Circuit found a "no rehire" policy to be discriminatory as applied to a successfully rehabilitated drug addict. The company had a policy of not rehiring any employee dismissed for misconduct, and the plaintiff had been terminated for drug use. When he reapplied for employment several years later, the company denied his application based on its policy. The court reversed summary judgment in favor of the employer, stating, "Hughes's unwritten policy against rehiring former employees who were terminated for any violation of its misconduct rules, although not unlawful on its face, violates the ADA as applied to former addicts whose only offense was testing positive because of their addiction. If Hernandez is in fact no longer using drugs and has been successfully rehabilitated, he may not be denied employment simply because of his past record of drug addiction."

## DESPEARS v. MILWAUKEE COUNTY
### 63 F.3d 635 (7th Cir. 1995)

POSNER, Chief Judge. . . .

Mr. Despears worked as a maintenance worker for a public medical facility. His work involved occasional driving, to deliver parts; and a regulation of the employer required workers in his job classification to have a valid driver's license. Despears' license was revoked after he was convicted a fourth time of driving under the influence of alcohol. Upon learning of the revocation, his employer demoted Despears to custodial worker, a job classification that does not involve any driving and does not require that the worker have a driver's license — and that pays less. Despears attributes the loss of his license to his having been an alcoholic, and the defendants do not deny that alcoholism is a disability within the meaning of both statutes. In urging the reversal of the district court he argues as follows: alcoholism caused him to drive under the influence of alcohol; driving under the influence of alcohol caused him to lose his driver's license; losing his driver's license caused him to be demoted; therefore alcoholism was the cause of his being demoted; therefore he was discriminated against by his employer on account of a disability, in violation of the statutes. He acknowledges as he must that if his alcoholism prevented him from doing the work required of a maintenance worker, he would not be entitled to any relief. But he contends, and at this stage in the proceeding we must accept, that driving was not an essential part of his job as a maintenance worker.

Although something like a third of all drivers who are convicted for driving under the influence of alcohol are not alcoholics in the sense of persistent alcohol abusers, and although many alcoholics refrain from driving while under the influence of alcohol, there is no doubt (though we cannot find any statistics on the question) that an alcoholic is more likely than a nonalcoholic to lose his license because of drunk driving. The high fraction of alcoholics among persons convicted of drunk driving implies this, as does the fact that the set of nonalcoholics includes many people who do not drink at all and therefore never lose their license because of drunk driving. So alcoholics are more likely, probably much more likely, to lose their driver's license because of drunk driving than people who are not alcoholics, and this is enough to show that there is a causal relation between Despears' alcoholism and his demotion. We may assume, because he claims not implausibly and there is no contrary evidence at this stage, that he would not have been convicted four times of drunk driving had he not been an alcoholic and that his alcoholism also made it antecedently more probable that he would be convicted. A necessary condition that makes the event of which it is a condition more likely to occur is a "cause" for most purposes in law, including we may assume the ADA and the Rehabilitation Act. If someone asked Despears why he was demoted and he replied that it was because he was an alcoholic, we would not have a sense that he was using the word "cause" in an incorrect or even a nonstandard way.

But a cause is not a compulsion (or sole cause); and we think the latter is necessary to form the bridge that Despears seeks to construct between his alcoholism and his demotion. If being an alcoholic he could not have avoided becoming a drunk driver, then his alcoholism was the only cause of his being demoted, and it would be as if the employer's regulation had said not that you must have a valid driver's license to be a maintenance worker but that you must not be an alcoholic. But Despears' alcoholism was not the only cause of his being convicted of drunk driving. Another cause was his decision to drive while drunk. Some alcoholics are drunk all the time, but obviously not all — and not Despears, since if he were drunk all the time he could not function as a custodial worker, let alone as a maintenance worker. The criminal law, by refusing to recognize alcoholism as a defense to a charge of driving under the influence of alcohol, takes the not irrational position that alcoholics are capable of avoiding driving while drunk. . . .

[T]he point . . . is simply that the criminal law proceeds on the premise that even alcoholics can avoid driving while under the influence of alcohol. And if this is so, then Despears despite his alcoholism could have avoided the demotion of which he complains by avoiding driving while drunk. His disability concurred with a decision to drive while drunk to produce the loss of license and resulting demotion. The disability contributed to but did not compel the action that resulted in the demotion.

To impose liability under the Americans with Disabilities Act or the Rehabilitation Act in such circumstances would indirectly but unmistakably undermine the laws that regulate dangerous behavior. It would give alcoholics and other diseased or disabled persons a privilege to avoid some of the normal sanctions for criminal activity. It would say to an alcoholic: We know it is more difficult for you to avoid committing the crime of drunk driving than it is for healthy people, and therefore we will lighten the sanction by letting you keep your job in circumstances where anyone else who engaged in the same criminal behavior would lose it.

The refusal to excuse, or even alleviate the punishment of, the disabled person who commits a crime under the influence as it were of his disability yet not compelled by it and so not excused by it in the eyes of the criminal law is not "discrimination" against the disabled; it is a refusal to discriminate in their favor. It is true that the Americans with Disabilities Act and the Rehabilitation Act require the employer to make a reasonable accommodation of an employee's disability, but we do not think it is a reasonably required accommodation to overlook infractions of law.

We can imagine a slightly different case in which Despears would stand on firmer ground. Suppose when he was hired by the medical facility he told his employer, "I dare not drive because of my alcoholism, and therefore I ask you to excuse me from having to have a driver's license to be a maintenance worker, since driving is not an essential part of the job." That would be a request for an accommodation, rather than a request to be excused from a consequence of criminal activity. The latter request seems to us to have no status in the law of disability discrimination, save possibly in the case, if there is such a case — if the Eighth Amendment allows there to be a case — where the disability itself, or an inevitable rather than merely likely consequence of it, is the crime. . . .

## NOTES

1. Several circuits have agreed that discharging an employee for misconduct relating to alcoholism does not constitute unlawful discrimination. See, e.g., Maddox v. University of Tennessee, 62 F.3d 843 (6th Cir. 1995) (ADA); Ferby v. United States Postal Serv., No. 94-5792, 1995 WL 699618 (6th Cir. Nov. 27, 1995).

2. Remember the Seventh Circuit's treatment of symptoms of a disability in *Vande Zande*, reproduced at page 735, and the Supreme Court's treatment of the same issue in *Arline*. Does § 104(c)(4) justify treating alcoholics differently than other disabled individuals?

3. Whether Despears was "disabled" under the statute was not contested in this case. How would you demonstrate that an individual is disabled based on alcoholism?

4. Judge Posner holds that Despears is not covered by the statute because his alcoholism was not the "sole cause" of his demotion. This language is reminiscent of the Rehabilitation Act. Under the Rehabilitation Act, courts regularly used this language to defer to employers' efforts to discipline employees for poor performance related to alcohol abuse. Is this apparent reliance on Rehabilitation Act precedent appropriate under the ADA?

5. In some respects the Rehabilitation Act, prior to its amendment in 1990, provided more rights to drug addicts and alcoholics than the ADA. Prior to 1990, some courts had ruled that current substance abusers could be "individuals with disabilities" for purposes of § 504 coverage. Section 512 of the ADA amended the Rehabilitation Act to conform to the ADA's provisions relating to coverage for drug and alcohol users. See § 504 Compliance Handbook, vol. 1, ¶213 (Thompson Publishing Group, August 1999). When researching Rehabilitation Act cases relating to these issues, it is important to note which version of the Rehabilitation Act is being applied.

6. What if other employees who were not alcoholics when *they* lost their driver's licenses were not discharged? Shouldn't the court have considered whether Despears was treated the same as other similarly situated employees? Ordinary principles of individual disparate treatment theory would seem to say yes, and the specific language of § 104(c)(4) relating to alcoholics, although restrictive with respect to reasonable accommodation, is strongly supportive of the notion that alcoholics have a right to equal treatment.

7. Consider Miners v. Cargill Communications, Inc., 113 F.3d 820 (8th Cir. 1997). Cargill discovered that Miners drove a company van while intoxicated and informed her that her actions constituted grounds for termination. After suggesting to Miners that she might be an alcoholic, Cargill informed Miners that "she must either enter and complete [a chemical dependence treatment program] with no loss of pay or job position or be fired." Id. at 822. Miners rejected Cargill's offer and was fired. Miners sued under the ADA. The court described Miners' claim:

> Miners asserts that Cargill's explanation for firing her is a pretext for its discriminatory motivation: its perception that she was an alcoholic. In support, Miners contends that she was never informed of the rule she purportedly violated, that other Cargill employees who were assigned company vehicles consumed alcohol before driving the vehicles and were not fired, and that Cargill's offer of treatment demonstrates that the management thought she was an alcoholic.

Id. The Eighth Circuit found evidence to support Miners's contentions and reversed the district court's grant of summary judgment to Cargill. The court also rejected Cargill's assertion that it was merely seeking to accommodate Miners's alcoholism, stating, "[w]ithout actual knowledge that Miners was an alcoholic, Cargill cannot now argue that it attempted to accommodate Miners, and it certainly lacks a basis to claim that Miners' refusal of treatment warranted her termination." Id. at 825. Is the difference between *Despears* and *Miners* legal or factual? Which approach is more persuasive under the statute? What would you advise an employer with respect to disciplining employees for using alcohol on the job? Would Cargill have been on safer ground if it simply discharged Miners for driving under the influence? Is it good policy to structure incentives for employees in this manner?

8. In Altman v. New York City Health & Hosps. Corp., 903 F. Supp. 503 (S.D.N.Y. 1995), *aff'd*, 100 F.3d 1054 (2d Cir. 1996) (discussed at page 767), the court declined to treat a doctor returning from an alcohol rehabilitation program as successfully rehabilitated, citing the danger of relapse and ruling that the hospital was entitled to take precautions against the possibility of relapse. The court did not attempt to characterize the hospital's actions as a response to the physician's current use of alcohol. Instead, the court ruled that the hospital was justified in acting on the basis of his alcoholism, whether or not he was currently alcohol free, because the danger of

undetectable relapse posed a direct threat to patient safety. Is this approach more consistent with legislative intent than *Despears?*

## 2.   Medical Examinations and Inquiries

Section 102(c)(1)-(4) contains a number of provisions restricting the use of medical examinations and inquiries.

### a.   Pre-Employment Medical Examinations and Inquiries

An employer is prohibited from using a medical examination or inquiry to determine whether a job applicant has a disability or the nature and severity of such a disability. But the employer may inquire into the applicant's ability to do the job and may condition an offer of employment on the results of a medical examination if certain conditions are met. These conditions include subjecting all entering employees to a medical examination and keeping the results confidential. Medical examinations given *after* an offer of employment has been made but prior to the commencement of employment need not be job related or consistent with business necessity. Thus, there is no restriction on the scope of such examinations — only on the use to which they are put. Of course, if they are used to exclude an individual because of disability, then the exclusionary criteria must be job related and consistent with business necessity. See Norman-Bloodsaw v. Lawrence Berkeley Lab., 135 F.3d 1260 (9th Cir. 1998). For an argument that the ADA should eliminate the distinction between permissible examinations of employees and applicants and only permit preplacement medical examinations that are job related, see Sharona Hoffman, Preplacement Examinations and Job-Relatedness: How to Enhance Privacy and Diminish Discrimination in the Workplace, 49 U. Kan. L. Rev. 517 (2001).

In contrast to these provisions, § 104(d)(1) provides that testing for the illegal use of drugs shall not be considered a "medical examination." Further, § 104(d)(2) provides that the ADA shall not be construed to "encourage, prohibit, or authorize" testing for the illegal use of drugs or making employment decisions based on the results of such tests. As you would expect, the ADA regulations contain lengthy and detailed interpretations of these provisions. See 29 C.F.R. §§ 1630.13, 1630.14, 1630.16(c).

The EEOC has issued detailed guidance to agency personnel explaining its position on pre-employment questions. EEOC Notice 915.002 (Oct. 10, 1995). The document identifies as illegal any questions that seek information about whether the applicant is disabled including:

Do you have AIDS?
Have you ever filed for workers' compensation?
What prescription drugs are you currently taking?
Have you ever been treated for mental health problems?
How much alcohol do you drink each week?

On the other hand, the following questions are identified as lawful:

Can you perform the functions of this job with or without reasonable accommodation?
Please describe or demonstrate how you would perform these functions.
Can you meet the attendance requirements of the job?
Do you have the required licenses to perform these jobs?

Some of the distinctions drawn by the EEOC in interpreting the ADA are subtle. For example, the EEOC believes that it is permissible to ask "how many days did you take leave last year?" but not "how many days were you *sick* last year?"

The EEOC also identifies certain tests as "medical" and therefore discriminatory if used at the interview stage prior to a conditional job offer. Prohibited "medical" tests are those that seek to reveal the existence of an impairment rather than measure an individual's performance of a task. Physical fitness tests, for example, are permitted. If, however, they screen out disabled applicants, they must be job related and consistent with business necessity.

In Grenier v. Cyanamid Plastics, Inc., 70 F.3d 667 (1st Cir. 1995), an employee on disability leave due to psychological problems, including paranoia, sought reinstatement as an electrician. The employer asked whether his mental state might interfere with his ability to get along with co-workers and asked for medical documentation as to his limitations and his need for accommodation. The First Circuit ruled that the ADA does not preclude an employer, during the pre-offer stage, from asking an individual with a known disability whether he can perform the job. In addition, requests for medical documentation to confirm the existence of a disability or to determine ability to perform are permissible. The court reasoned that the ban on pre-offer inquiries is designed to ensure that a hidden disability stays hidden. Because the employer already was familiar with the former employee's disability, the employer had a right to assess his recovery and his ability to perform. See also Brumley v. Pena, 62 F.3d 277 (8th Cir. 1995) (requiring former employee disabled by severe depression to provide verification of recovery prior to restoration to duty did not violate the Rehabilitation Act).

If an employer asks an applicant questions that are *lawful* under the ADA and the applicant lies, the employer is justified in discharging the employee when the lie is discovered. See Smith v. Chrysler Corp., 155 F.3d 799 (6th Cir. 1998). But what if the employer asks questions that are *unlawful* under the ADA and the applicant lies? Should she be permitted to sue under the ADA or is she no longer qualified because she lied on the application? See Downs v. Massachusetts Bay Transp. Auth., 13 F. Supp. 2d 130 (D. Mass. 1998). Suppose an employer asks an applicant questions that are unlawful under the ADA and the applicant is not hired, allegedly because of his or her response to those questions. Must the applicant be a "qualified" disabled individual in order to sue the employer? The Ninth and Tenth Circuits have ruled that non-disabled applicants and employees can sue for medical inquiry violations of this section. See Fredenburg v. Contra Costa County Dept. of Health Servs., 172 F.3d 1176 (9th Cir. 1999) (employees) (ADA provisions governing permissible examinations refer to "employees" and "job applicants" not "qualified individual with a disability"); Griffin v. Steeltek Inc., 160 F.3d 591 (10th Cir. 1998) (applicants). What remedy is appropriate?

### b.  Medical Examinations and Inquiries of Employees

Employers are prohibited from requiring medical examinations and inquiries of employees, unless such examination or inquiry is job related and consistent with a business necessity. See, e.g., Watson v. City of Miami Beach, 177 F.3d 932 (11th Cir. 1999) (requiring police officer to submit to mandatory TB test and disclosure of HIV status permissible under the ADA because job related and consistent with business necessity). Again, however, the results of such examinations or inquiries are confidential. Would genetic testing for predisposition to cancer be permissible for a job involving exposure to carcinogenic chemicals? Should business necessity be interpreted to include protection against potential liability?

The court in Doe v. Kohn Nast & Graf, 866 F. Supp. 190 (E.D. Pa. 1994), ruled that the employer's search of a lawyer's office for the purpose of discovering whether he had AIDS was a prohibited medical inquiry. In contrast, the court in Deckert v. City of Ulysses, No. 93-1295-PFK, 1995 WL 580074 (D. Kan. Sept. 6, 1995), required a diabetic police officer to undergo a physical examination after he was suspended for not following proper procedures; this was permissible because it was consistent with business necessity. Similarly, the Ninth Circuit has held that the ADA does not prohibit an employer from requiring an employee who has missed an inordinate number of days of work to submit to a medical examination, even if the examination seeks to determine whether the individual is disabled, because such an examination is job related and consistent with business necessity. See Yin v. California, 95 F.3d 864 (9th Cir. 1996). See Enforcement Guidance on Disability-Related Inquiries and Medical Examinations of Employees under the Americans with Disabilities Act No. 915.002 (July 26, 2000), ("Enforcement Guidance on Employees.").

In Satterfield v. Tennessee, 295 F.3d 611 (6th Cir. 2002), plaintiff was terminated based on the results of a medical exam. Unable to sue his state government employer because of the Eleventh Amendment, plaintiff brought suit against the doctor and the medical services firm the state had contracted with to perform examinations. He claimed the exam was not job related and that his medical records had not been kept confidential. The court upheld summary judgment in favor of the defendants, concluding the defendants were not "covered entities" under Title I because they were not plaintiff's employer.

## 3.   Retaliation and Interference

Section 503 prohibits certain acts of retaliation and interference. Section 503(a) provides that "no person" shall discriminate against "any individual" because that person has opposed an act made unlawful by the ADA or because such person has participated in an investigation or a proceeding under the ADA. See Chapter 7, section G, dealing with similar language under Title VII and the ADEA. Similarly, § 503(b) prohibits coercion of or interference with a person who exercises or asserts ADA rights for himself or another. Violations may be redressed by the usual Title I enforcement procedures. ADA § 503(c). The Third Circuit, in Krouse v. American Sterilizer Co., 126 F.3d 494 (3d Cir. 1997), held that, because the language of the ADA retaliation provision protects "any individual," a plaintiff asserting a retaliation claim under the ADA need not establish that he or she is a qualified individual with a disability. The Second Circuit has reached the same conclusion on the ground that a plaintiff asserting a retaliation claim need not establish that the conduct he complained of actually violated the statute as long as he can establish that he had a good faith, reasonable belief that the challenged actions violated the law. Muller v. Costello, 187 F.3d 298 (2d Cir. 1999).

As noted above, the ADA's antiretaliation provision is broader than that contained in Title VII or the ADEA. While § 12203(a) parallels the antiretaliation provisions of Title VII and the ADEA, § 12203(b) has been analogized to § 8(a)(1) of the National Labor Relations Act. In Fogelman v. Mercy Hosp., Inc., 283 F.3d 561 (3d Cir. 2002), cert. denied, 123 S. Ct. 112 (2002), a son and father worked for the same employer.

The son claimed he had been fired because his father had sued the employer, alleging violations of the antiretaliation provisions of the ADA and ADEA. The Third Circuit held that the ADEA did not reach the son's claim, reasoning that it protects only persons who themselves have engaged in protected activity. But the court found a third-party retaliation claim actionable under the ADA, pointing to the broader language of § 12203(b). Moreover, the court also upheld the son's alternative claim that he had been fired because his employer believed, albeit mistakenly, that he had been assisting his father with his suit. The court found this "perception theory" viable as well. "That [plaintiff] was fired because Mercy thought he was engaged in protected activity, even if he actually was not, presents a valid legal claim." Id. at 565. It is the employer's intent, not the employee's actions, that are determinative, said the court.

In analyzing claims under § 503(a), courts, consistent with their practice under Title VII and the ADEA, have insisted that the plaintiff identify an adverse action in order to state a retaliation claim. Negative performance evaluations, for example, have been deemed insufficient to support a prima facie case of retaliation. See Lucas v. W. W. Grainger, Inc., 257 F.3d 1249 (11th Cir. 2001). Is this a correct application of the antiretaliation provisions of the statute?

### 4.  Harassment

The lower courts have either assumed or have expressly acknowledged that a claim for hostile work environment may be brought under the ADA. See Flowers v. Southern Regional Physician Servs., Inc., 247 F.3d 229 (5th Cir. 2001); Fox v. General Motors Corp., 247 F.3d 169 (4th Cir. 2001). A hostile work environment claim may arise when plaintiff can show he was targeted for harassment either because of his disability or because of his request for an accommodation. When the hostile work environment claim is based on a request for accommodation, the line between a retaliation claim and a hostile work environment claim becomes murky. Courts have sometimes divided the allegations into two separate claims, looking to see whether there is a materially adverse job action to support a retaliation claim and then looking at taunts, threats, cartoons, and jokes to see if the conduct is sufficiently severe or pervasive. See Silk v. City of Chicago, 194 F.3d 788 (7th Cir. 1999). Is this a correct approach? What about the impact of § 503(b)? For a discussion of disability-based harassment claims and criticism of courts' importation of Title VII standards, see Lisa Eichhorn, Hostile Environment Actions, Title VII, and the ADA: The Limits of the Copy-and-Paste Function, 77 Wash. L. Rev. 575 (2002).

### 5.  Protected Relationships

Section 102(b)(4) of the ADA prohibits a covered entity from discriminating against a qualified individual "because of the known disability of an individual with whom the qualified individual is known to have a relationship or association." In the Rehabilitation Act Amendments of 1992, § 504 was amended to provide the same protection. The EEOC, however, believes that this prohibition does not entitle such an individual to reasonable accommodation so that he or she can attend to the needs of his or her relative or associate. See 29 C.F.R. pt. 1630, app. § 1630.8.

The Fourth Circuit, in Tyndall v. National Educ. Ctrs., 31 F.3d 209 (4th Cir. 1994), held, consistent with the EEOC view, that a business school was not required to restructure an employee's work schedule to enable her to care for her disabled son. The court found further that the school had not discharged the plaintiff because of her association with her disabled son and unfounded fears that this would lead to increased costs or absences. Rather, the school discharged her because of her excessive absenteeism. Id. at 211. See also Pittman v. Moseley, Warren, Prichard & Parrish, 2002 U.S. Dist. LEXIS 17030 (M.D. Fla. July 29, 2002) (same).

In order to make out a case of discrimination based on association with a disabled individual, the plaintiff must show that the individual with whom she has a relationship is disabled and that the employer was aware of the third party's disability. Ennis v. National Assn. of Bus. & Educ. Radio, Inc., 53 F.3d 55 (4th Cir. 1995). Even if these minimum requirements are satisfied, the employee must be fired *because of* the relationship. In *Ennis*, the court concluded that plaintiff was discharged for inadequate performance, not because of her relationship with her disabled son. Cases of discrimination based on association are subject to ADA defenses, including the direct threat defense. See Den Hartog v. Wasatch Academy, 129 F.3d 1076 (10th Cir. 1997) (boarding school teacher lawfully discharged based on relationship with son who suffered from psychiatric disorder that caused him to engage in threatening behavior toward other boarding school personnel and their families).

## 6.   Health and Disability Insurance

### EEOC INTERIM GUIDANCE ON APPLICATION OF ADA TO HEALTH INSURANCE
EEOC Compliance Manual 915.002; ¶6902 (CCH) (June 8, 1993)

#### II.   BACKGROUND AND LEGAL FRAMEWORK

The ADA provides that it is unlawful for an employer to discriminate on the basis of disability against a qualified individual with a disability in regard to " . . . terms, conditions, and privileges of employment." . . . Section 1630.4 of the Commission's regulations implementing the employment provisions of the ADA further provides, in pertinent part, that it is unlawful for an employer to discriminate on the basis of disability against a qualified individual with a disability in regard to "[f]ringe benefits available by virtue of employment, whether or not administered by the [employer]." 29 C.F.R. § 1630.4(f). Employee benefit plans, including health insurance plans provided by an employer to its employees, are a fringe benefit available by virtue of employment. Generally speaking, therefore, the ADA prohibits employers from discriminating on the basis of disability in the provision of health insurance to their employees. . . .

Several consequences result from the application of these statutory provisions. First, disability-based insurance plan distinctions are permitted only if they are within the protective ambit of section 501(c) of the ADA. Second, decisions about the employment of an individual with a disability cannot be motivated by concerns about the impact of the individual's disability on the employer's health insurance plan. Third, employees with disabilities must be accorded "equal access" to whatever health insurance the employer provides to employees without disabilities. . . . Fourth, in view of the statute's "association provision," it would violate the ADA for an employer to make an employment decision about any person, whether or not that person has a disability, because of concerns about the impact on the health insurance plan of the disability of someone else with whom that person has a relationship. . . .

## III.  DISABILITY-BASED DISTINCTIONS

### A.  FRAMEWORK OF ANALYSIS

Whenever it is alleged that a health-related term or provision of an employer provided health insurance plan violates the ADA, the first issue is whether the challenged term or provision is, in fact, a disability-based distinction. If the Commission
determines that a challenged health insurance plan term or provision is a disability-
based distinction, the respondent will be required to prove that that disability-based
distinction is within the protective ambit of section 501(c) of the ADA.

In pertinent part, section 501(c) permits employers, insurers, and plan administrators to establish and/or observe the terms of an insured health insurance plan that is
"bona fide," based on "underwriting risks, classifying risks, or administering such risks
that are based on or not inconsistent with State law," and that is not being used as a
"subterfuge" to evade the purposes of the ADA. Section 501(c) likewise permits employers, insurers, and plan administrators to establish and/or observe the terms of a
"bona fide" self-insured plan that is not used as a "subterfuge.". . .

### B.  WHAT IS A DISABILITY-BASED DISTINCTION?

It is important to note that not all health-related plan distinctions discriminate on
the basis of disability. Insurance distinctions that are not based on disability, and that
are applied equally to all insured employees, do not discriminate on the basis of disability and so do not violate the ADA.[7]

For example, a feature of some employer provided health insurance plans is a distinction between the benefits provided for the treatment of physical conditions on the
one hand, and the benefits provided for the treatment of "mental/nervous" conditions on the other. Typically, a lower level of benefits is provided for the treatment of
mental/nervous conditions than is provided for the treatment of physical conditions.
Similarly, some health insurance plans provide fewer benefits for "eye care" than for
other physical conditions. Such broad distinctions, which apply to the treatment of a
multitude of dissimilar conditions and which constrain individuals both with and
without disabilities, are not distinctions based on disability. Consequently, although
such distinctions may have a greater impact on certain individuals with disabilities,
they do not intentionally discriminate on the basis of disability[8] and do not violate
the ADA.

Blanket pre-existing condition clauses that exclude from the coverage of a health insurance plan the treatment of conditions that pre-date an individual's eligibility for
benefits under that plan also are not distinctions based on disability, and do not violate
the ADA. Universal limits or exclusions from coverage of all experimental drugs
and/or treatments, or of all "elective surgery," are likewise not insurance distinctions
based on disability. Similarly, coverage limits on medical procedures that are not

---

7. The term "discriminates" refers only to disparate treatment. The adverse impact theory of discrimination is unavailable in this context. See Alexander v. Choate.

8. However, it would violate the ADA for an employer to selectively apply a universal or "neutral" non-
disability based insurance distinction only to individuals with disabilities. Thus, for example, it would violate the ADA for an employer to apply a "neutral" health insurance plan limitation on "eye care" only to
an employee seeking treatment for a vision disability, but not to other employees who do not have vision
disabilities. Charges alleging that a universal or "neutral" non-disability based insurance distinction has
been selectively applied to individuals with disabilities should be processed using traditional disparate
treatment theory and analysis.

exclusively, or nearly exclusively utilized for the treatment of a particular disability are not distinctions based on disability. Thus, for example, it would not violate the ADA for an employer to limit the number of blood transfusions or X-rays that it will pay for, even though this may have an adverse effect on individuals with certain disabilities. . . .

In contrast, however, health-related insurance distinctions that are based on disability may violate the ADA. A term or provision is "disability-based" if it singles out a particular disability (e.g., deafness, AIDS, schizophrenia), a discrete group of disabilities (e.g., cancers, muscular dystrophies, kidney diseases), or disability in general (e.g., non-coverage of all conditions that substantially limit a major life activity).

As previously noted, employers may establish and/or observe the terms and provisions of a bona fide benefit plan, including terms or provisions based on disability, that are not a "subterfuge to evade the purposes" of the ADA. Such terms and provisions do not violate the ADA. However, disability-based insurance distinctions that are a "subterfuge" do intentionally discriminate on the basis of disability and so violate the ADA.

Example 2. R Company's new self-insured health insurance plan caps benefits for the treatment of all physical conditions, except AIDS, at $100,000 per year. The treatment of AIDS is capped at $5,000 per year. CP, an employee with AIDS enrolled in the health insurance plan, files a charge alleging that the lower AIDS cap violates the ADA. The lower AIDS cap is a disability-based distinction. Accordingly, if R is unable to demonstrate that its health insurance plan is bona fide and that the AIDS cap is not a subterfuge, a violation of the ADA will be found. . . .

## C.   THE RESPONDENT'S BURDEN OF PROOF

Once the Commission has determined that a challenged health insurance term or provision constitutes a disability-based distinction, the respondent must prove that the health insurance plan is either a bona fide insured plan that is not inconsistent with state law, or a bona fide self-insured plan. The respondent must also prove that the challenged disability-based distinction is not being used as a subterfuge. . . . [The Commission justified this allocation of burden of proof on the ground that employers control the relevant data.]

### 1.   The Health Insurance Plan Is "Bona Fide" and Consistent with Applicable Law

. . . If the health insurance plan is an insured plan, the respondent will be able to satisfy this requirement by proving that: (1) the health insurance plan is bona fide in that it exists and pays benefits, and its terms have been accurately communicated to eligible employees; and (2) the health insurance plan's terms are not inconsistent with applicable state law as interpreted by the appropriate state authorities. If the health insurance plan is a self-insured plan, the respondent will only be required to prove that the health insurance plan is bona fide in that it exists and pays benefits, and that its terms have been accurately communicated to covered employees.

### 2.   The Disability-Based Distinction Is Not a Subterfuge

. . . "Subterfuge" refers to disability-based disparate treatment that is not justified by the risks or costs associated with the disability. Whether a particular challenged disability-based insurance distinction is being used as a subterfuge will be determined on a case by case basis, considering the totality of the circumstances.

The respondent can prove that a challenged disability-based insurance distinction is not a subterfuge in several ways. A non-exclusive list of potential business/insurance justifications follows.

a. The respondent may prove that it has not engaged in the disability-based disparate treatment alleged. For example, where a charging party has alleged that a benefit cap of a particular catastrophic disability is discriminatory, the respondent may prove that its health insurance plan actually treats all similarly catastrophic conditions in the same way.

b. The respondent may prove that the disparate treatment is justified by legitimate actuarial data, or by actual or reasonable anticipated experience, and that conditions with comparable actuarial data and/or experience are treated in the same fashion. In other words, the respondent may prove that the disability-based disparate treatment is attributable to the application of legitimate risk classification and underwriting procedures to the increased risks (and thus increased cost to the health insurance plan) of the disability, and not to the disability per se.

c. The respondent may prove that the disparate treatment is necessary (i.e., that there is no nondisability-based health insurance plan change that could be made) to ensure that the challenged health insurance plan satisfies the commonly accepted or legally required standards for the fiscal soundness of such an insurance plan. The respondent, for example, may prove that it limited coverage for the treatment of a discrete group of disabilities because continued unlimited coverage would have been so expensive as to cause the health insurance plan to become financially insolvent, and there was no nondisability-based health insurance plan alteration that would have avoided insolvency.

d. The respondent may prove that the challenged insurance practice or activity is necessary (i.e., that there is no nondisability-based change that could be made to prevent the occurrence of an unacceptable change either in the coverage of the health insurance plan, or in the premiums charged for the health insurance plan). An "unacceptable" change is a drastic increase in premium payments (or in co-payments or deductibles), or a drastic alteration to the scope of coverage or level of benefits provided, that would: (1) make the health insurance plan effectively unavailable to a significant number of other employees, (2) make the health insurance plan so unattractive as to result in significant adverse selection, or (3) make the health insurance plan so unattractive that the employer cannot compete in recruiting and maintaining qualified workers due to the superiority of health insurance plans offered by other employers in the community.

e. Where the charging party is challenging the respondent's denial of coverage for disability-specific treatment, the respondent may prove that this treatment does not provide any benefit (i.e., has no medical value). . . .

### NOTES

1. These guidelines are interim guidelines to be used until final guidelines are promulgated after publication for notice and comment. What deference should courts give them?

2. Failure to provide individuals with disabilities with equal access to benefit plans is discrimination under the ADA. Can an employer defend against such a claim by proving that to provide equal access constitutes an undue hardship?

3. If an employer excludes or caps benefits for AIDS treatment, would this violate the ADA? What arguments could you make on behalf of the employee? What arguments could you make for the employer?

4. Would it be permissible under the ADA for an employer's health plan to limit coverage for specific drugs used only to prevent the recurrence of breast cancer or used only to treat schizophrenia? Does the answer to this question depend on other circumstances?

5. A controversial insurance coverage issue concerns "experimental" treatments such as high-dose chemotherapy (HDCT) for breast cancer. In Henderson v. Bodine Aluminum, 70 F.3d 958 (8th Cir. 1995), the court ordered an insurer to certify a covered employee's wife for entry into a clinical program providing HDCT to treat an aggressive form of breast cancer. The employer provided HDCT for other forms of cancer.

6. For a general discussion of the ADA's application to insurance plans, see H. Miriam Farber, Note, Subterfuge: Do Coverage Limitations and Exclusions in Employer-Provided Health Care Plans Violate the Americans with Disabilities Act?, 69 N.Y.U. L. Rev. 850 (1994).

## FORD v. SCHERING-PLOUGH
### 145 F.3d 601 (3d Cir. 1998)

COWEN, Circuit Judge.

This appeal presents the purely legal question of whether a disparity between disability benefits for mental and physical disabilities violates the Americans with Disabilities Act. The plaintiff-appellant, Colleen Ford, sued her employer, Schering-Plough Corporation (Schering), and the carrier of Schering's group insurance policy, Metropolitan Life Insurance Company (MetLife), alleging that the two-year cap applicable to benefits for mental disabilities, but not for physical disabilities, violates the ADA. . . .

The facts concerning the plaintiff's employment and her disability are not in dispute. Ford was an employee of Schering from 1975 until May of 1992, when she became disabled by virtue of a mental disorder and was unable to continue her employment. While she served as an employee, Ford enrolled in the employee welfare benefits plan offered by Schering through MetLife. The plan provided that benefits for physical disabilities would continue until the disabled employee reached age sixty-five so long as the physical disability persisted. Regarding mental disabilities, however, the plan mandated that benefits cease after two years if the disabled employee was not hospitalized. Ford found herself in this latter category, suffering from a mental disorder yet not hospitalized and thus ineligible for a continuation of her benefits past the two-year limit. Her benefits expired on Nov. 23, 1994. . . .

III . . .

A

Ford's first claim alleges that the defendants' group insurance plan violates Title I of the ADA because of the disparity in benefits between mental and physical

disabilities. Title I of the ADA proscribes discrimination in the terms and conditions
of employment and [states that the term "discriminate" includes]

> (2) participating in a contractual or other arrangement or relationship that has the effect
> of subjecting a covered entity's qualified applicant or employee with a disability to the
> discrimination prohibited by this subchapter (such relationship includes a relationship
> with . . . an organization providing *fringe benefits* to an employee of the covered
> entity[)]. . . .

42 U.S.C. § 12112(a)-(b) (emphasis added). As the plaintiff correctly observes, the defendants' group insurance plan is a fringe benefit of employment at Schering. Ford
claims that the defendants violated Title I of the ADA because the mental-physical
disparity constitutes discrimination against her on the basis of her disability.

## I

Before addressing the merits of Ford's Title I claim, we must first ascertain whether
Ford is eligible to file suit under Title I. . . .

Title I of the ADA restricts the ability to sue under its provisions to a "qualified individual with a disability[.]" . . . Thus, an individual eligible to sue under Title I of
the ADA must be disabled but still able to perform his or her job duties with or without a reasonable accommodation by the employer. Ford, however, admits that she is
currently unable to work even with a reasonable accommodation. Indeed, her disabled status is the reason for her desire to receive the disability benefits at issue here.

The defendants-appellees argue that Ford is clearly ineligible to sue under Title I
of the ADA because she is currently disabled. . . . Ford illuminates an internal contradiction in the ADA itself, namely the disjunction between the ADA's definition of
"qualified individual with a disability" and the rights that the ADA confers. Title I of
the ADA prohibits discrimination by employers regarding the "terms, conditions, and
privileges" of employment, 42 U.S.C. § 12112(a), including "fringe benefits" such as
disability benefits. Id. § 12112(b)(2). Yet, as Ford and the EEOC as amicus argue, restricting eligibility to sue under Title I to individuals who can currently work with or
without a reasonable accommodation prevents disabled former employees from suing regarding discrimination in disability benefits. Once an individual becomes disabled and thus eligible for disability benefits, that individual loses the ability to sue
under a strict reading of Title I's definition of "qualified individual with a disability"
because that individual can no longer work with or without a reasonable accommodation. In order for the rights guaranteed by Title I to be fully effectuated, the definition of "qualified individual with a disability" would have to permit suits under Title
I by more than just individuals who are currently able to work with or without reasonable accommodations.

This disjunction between the explicit rights created by Title I of the ADA and
the ostensible eligibility standards for filing suit under Title I causes us to view the
contents of those requirements as ambiguous rather than as having an unassailable
plain meaning. "The plainness or ambiguity of statutory language is determined by
reference to the language itself, the specific context in which that language is used,
and the broader context of the statute as a whole." Robinson v. Shell Oil Co.,
519 U.S. 337 (1997). The locus of the ambiguity is whether the ADA contains a temporal qualifier of the term "qualified individual with a disability[.]" If the putative
plaintiff must, at the time of the suit, be employable with or without a reasonable accommodation, then a disabled former employee loses his ability to sue to challenge

discriminatory disability benefits. Alternatively, the term "qualified individual with a disability" may include former employees who were once employed with or without reasonable accommodations yet who, at the time of suit, are completely disabled.

The Supreme Court's recent decision in *Robinson*, which concerned the scope of Title VII, contributes to this ambiguity by lending support for interpreting Title I of the ADA to permit suits by disabled individuals against their former employers concerning their disability benefits. Cases interpreting Title VII are relevant to our analysis of the ADA because the ADA is essentially a sibling statute of Title VII. . . .

In *Robinson*, the Supreme Court analyzed whether former employees are allowed to bring suits against their previous employers under Title VII for post-termination retaliation such as negative job references. The Court found that the term "employees" as used in § 704(a) of Title VII was ambiguous regarding its temporal reach, i.e., whether it covered only current employees or encompassed former employees as well. Resolving this ambiguity, the Court held that the term encompassed former employees in order to provide former employees with a legal recourse against post-termination retaliation.

As with the term "employees" in Title VII, the ADA contains an ambiguity concerning the definition of "qualified individual with a disability" because there is no temporal qualifier for that definition. Congress could have restricted the eligibility for plaintiffs under the ADA to *current* employees or could have explicitly broadened the eligibility to include *former* employees. Since Congress did neither but still created rights regarding disability benefits, we are left with an ambiguity in the text of the statute regarding eligibility to sue under Title I.

We resolve this ambiguity by interpreting Title I of the ADA to allow disabled former employees to sue their former employers regarding their disability benefits so as to effectuate the full panoply of rights guaranteed by the ADA. This is in keeping with the ADA's rationale, namely "to provide a clear and comprehensive national mandate for the elimination of discrimination against individuals with disabilities . . . [and] to provide clear, strong, consistent, *enforceable* standards addressing [such] discrimination. . . ." 42 U.S.C. § 12101(b)(1)-(2) (emphasis added). Our decision is also in keeping with the Supreme Court's *Robinson* decision, which found that the temporal reach of Title VII encompasses former employees. . . .

By adopting this interpretation, we part ways with the Seventh and Eleventh Circuits, both of which tendered decisions prior to *Robinson*. . . .

## II

Having established Ford's eligibility to sue under Title I, we must now ascertain whether she states a claim that survives the defendants' Rule 12(b)(6) motion. Ford essentially claims that the disparity between benefits for mental and physical disabilities violates Title I of the ADA. However, Ford's argument does not support a finding of discrimination under Title I.

While the defendants' insurance plan differentiated between types of disabilities, this is a far cry from a specific disabled employee facing differential treatment due to her disability. Every Schering employee had the opportunity to join the same plan with the same schedule of coverage, meaning that every Schering employee received equal treatment. So long as every employee is offered the same plan regardless of that employee's contemporary or future disability status, then no discrimination has occurred even if the plan offers different coverage for various disabilities. The ADA does not require equal coverage for every type of disability; such a requirement, if it existed, would destabilize the insurance industry in a manner definitely not intended by Congress when passing the ADA.

This analysis is supported by Supreme Court and Third Circuit precedent concerning the Rehabilitation Act of 1973 to which we may look for guidance in interpreting the ADA. See Gaul v. Lucent Technologies, Inc., 134 F.3d 576, 580 (3d Cir. 1998). In Alexander v. Choate, plaintiffs sued in response to the Tennessee Medicaid program's reduction in the number of inpatient hospital days for which it would pay. The plaintiffs claimed that the reduction would have a disproportionate effect on handicapped individuals since they would require longer inpatient care than non-handicapped individuals. However, the Supreme Court held that the limit on inpatient hospital care was "neutral on its face[ ]" and did not "distinguish between those whose coverage will be reduced and those whose coverage will not on the basis of any test, judgment, or trait that the handicapped as a class are less capable of meeting or less likely of having." According to the Supreme Court, handicapped citizens did not suffer from discrimination because both handicapped and non-handicapped individuals were "subject to the same durational limitation."

Building on Alexander, the Supreme Court in Traynor v. Turnage, 485 U.S. 535 (1988), dismissed a challenge to a federal statute precluding the Veterans Administration from granting extensions to a ten-year delimiting period for veterans to claim their benefits if the veterans' disabilities arose from their own willful misconduct, defined by regulations as including alcoholism. The Supreme Court rejected the argument that the statute discriminated against one type of disability, namely alcoholism. "There is nothing in the Rehabilitation Act that requires that any benefit extended to one category of handicapped persons also be extended to all other categories of handicapped persons."

We have likewise held, in the context of the Rehabilitation Act, that a state's medical assistance statute need not treat every disability equally. In Doe v. Colautti, 592 F.2d 704 (3d Cir. 1979), we dismissed a challenge to a Pennsylvania statute that provided unlimited hospitalization for physical illness in a private hospital but restricted hospitalization for mental illness in private mental hospitals. We rejected the argument that the differential level of benefits violated the Rehabilitation Act by noting that, "in the treatment of their physical illnesses, the mentally ill receive the same benefits as everyone else. A mental patient with heart disease, for instance, is as entitled to benefits for treatment of the heart disease as would be a person not mentally ill." Id. at 708. Our holding in Doe is supported by the D.C. Circuit's decision in Modderno v. King, 82 F.3d 1059 (D.C. Cir. 1996), in which the D.C. Circuit rejected a challenge brought by a former spouse of a foreign service officer against the Foreign Service Benefit Plan under the Rehabilitation Act based upon the plan's lower level of benefits for mental illness as compared to physical illness.

Aside from Supreme Court and Third Circuit precedent in the Rehabilitation Act context, claims under the ADA similar to Ford's have been rejected by three courts of appeals in published opinions. While we disagree with the Seventh Circuit's reasoning in [EEOC v. CNA Ins. Co., 96 F.3d 1039 (7th Cir. 1996)] regarding the plaintiff's eligibility to sue, we agree with its discussion regarding the merits of the plaintiff's claim. In rejecting the plaintiff's challenge to the disparity between benefits for mental and physical illnesses, the Seventh Circuit stated:

> One of those terms, conditions, or privileges of employment may be a pension plan, but there is no claim here that CNA discriminated on the basis of disability in offering its pension plan to anyone. It did not charge higher prices to disabled people, on the theory

that they might require more in benefits. Nor did it vary the terms of its plan depending on whether or not the employee was disabled. All employees — the perfectly healthy, the physically disabled, and the mentally disabled — had a plan that promised them long-term benefits from the onset of disability until age 65 if their problem was physical, and long-term benefits for two years if the problem was mental or nervous. . . .

[The plaintiff] raises a different kind of discrimination claim, more grist for the ERISA mill or the national health care debate than for the ADA. She claims that the plan discriminates against employees who in the future will become disabled due to mental conditions rather than physical conditions; their present dollars (unbeknownst to them) are buying only 24 months of benefits, instead of benefits lasting much longer. However this is dressed up, it is really a claim that benefit plans themselves may not treat mental health conditions less favorably than they treat physical health conditions. Without far stronger language in the ADA supporting this result, we are loath to read into it a rule that has been the subject of vigorous, sometimes contentious, national debate for the last several years. Few, if any, mental health advocates have thought that the result they would like to see has been there all along in the ADA.

CNA. Likewise, in Krauel v. Iowa Methodist Med. Ctr., 95 F.3d 674 (8th Cir. 1996), the Eighth Circuit rejected a challenge under the ADA to an insurance plan that denied coverage for infertility. Analogizing the infertility exclusion to differential benefits for mental and physical illnesses, the Eighth Circuit stated, "Insurance distinctions that apply equally to all insured employees, that is, to individuals with disabilities and to those who are not disabled, do not discriminate on the basis of disability." Finally, the Sixth Circuit in [Parker v. Metropolitan Life Ins. Co., 121 F.3d 1006, 1009 n.2 (6th Cir. 1997) (en banc)] rejected a claim similar to Ford's made against the same defendants as in the instant case. As the Sixth Circuit held, "Because all the employees at Schering-Plough, whether disabled or not, received the same access to the long-term disability plan, neither the defendants nor the plan discriminated between the disabled and the able bodied."

The cases finding no violation of the ADA by a disparity in benefits between mental and physical disabilities are supported by the ADA's legislative history. As the Senate Labor and Human Resources Committee report states:

In addition, employers may not deny health insurance coverage completely to an individual based on the person's diagnosis or disability. For example, while it is permissible for an employer to offer insurance policies that limit coverage for certain procedures or treatments, e.g., only a specified amount per year for mental health coverage, a person who has a mental health condition may not be denied coverage for other conditions such as for a broken leg or for heart surgery because of the existence of the mental health condition. A limitation may be placed on reimbursements for a procedure or the types of drugs or procedures covered[,] e.g., a limit on the number of x-rays or non-coverage of experimental drugs or procedures; but, that limitation must apply to persons with or without disabilities. All people with disabilities must have equal access to the health insurance coverage that is provided by the employer to all employees.

S. Rep. No. 101-116, at 29 (1989).

In addition, legislative history subsequent to the ADA's passage evinces that Congress did not believe that the ADA mandated parity between mental and physical disability benefits. In 1996, the Senate defeated an amendment to the Health Insurance Portability and Accountability Act of 1996, Pub. L. No. 104-191, 110 Stat. 1936 (1996) (codified primarily in Titles 18, 26 and 42 of the U.S. Code), which would have mandated parity in insurance coverage for mental and physical illnesses.

Such an amendment would have been unnecessary altogether if the ADA already required such parity. See 142 Cong. Rec. S9477-02 (daily ed. Aug. 2, 1996) (statement of Sen. Heflin). Furthermore, Congress then passed the Mental Health Parity Act of 1996, Pub. L. No. 104-204, Title VII, 110 Stat. 2944 (1996) (codified at 29 U.S.C. § 1185a and 42 U.S.C. § 300gg-5), which mandates, *inter alia*, that a health insurance plan containing no annual or lifetime limit for medical benefits cannot have such limits on mental health benefits. Such congressional action reveals both that the ADA does not contain parity requirements and that no parity requirements for mental and physical disability benefits have been enacted subsequent to the ADA.

### III

Ford attempts to buttress her challenge to the disparity between benefits for mental and physical disabilities by pointing to section 501(c) of the ADA, which contains the "safe harbor" provision covering the insurance industry. This section, codified at 42 U.S.C. § 12201(c), reads as follows:

> (c) Insurance
> Subchapters I through III of this chapter and title IV of this Act shall not be construed to prohibit or restrict —
>
> (1) an insurer, hospital or medical service company, health maintenance organization, or any agent, or entity that administers benefit plans, or similar organizations from underwriting risks, classifying risks, or administering such risks that are based on or not inconsistent with State law; or
> (2) a person or organization covered by this chapter from establishing, sponsoring, observing or administering the terms of a bona fide benefit plan that are based on underwriting risks, classifying risks, or administering such risks that are based on or not inconsistent with State law; or
> (3) a person or organization covered by this chapter from establishing, sponsoring, observing or administering the terms of a bona fide benefit plan that is not subject to State laws that regulate insurance.
>
> Paragraphs (1), (2), and (3) shall not be used as a subterfuge to evade the purposes of subchapter [sic] I and III of this chapter.

42 U.S.C. § 12201(c). Ford essentially claims that, once she presents a *prima facie* case alleging discrimination in disability benefits, Schering and MetLife must present actuarial data demonstrating that their plan is not a "subterfuge[.]" Hence, according to Ford, the district court erred in granting the defendants' Rule 12(b)(6) motion since the defendants had not offered data justifying the actuarial basis for the disparity in benefits.

Ford's argument must fail, however, since it runs contrary to Supreme Court precedent, ignores our statutory duty regarding insurance regulation and distorts the role of this court. First, Ford's argument that Schering and MetLife must justify their insurance plan contradicts the Supreme Court's interpretation of a provision similar to section 501(c) in the context of the Age Discrimination in Employment Act (ADEA). Prior to Congress's elimination of the term "subterfuge" from the ADEA in 1990, see Older Workers Benefit Protection Act of 1990, the ADEA granted an exemption from the ADEA's prohibition of age discrimination to an employee benefit plan that was not "a subterfuge[.]" 29 U.S.C. § 623(f) (1988). In Public Employees Retirement Sys. of Ohio v. Betts, 492 U.S. 158 (1989), the Supreme Court rejected a challenge to an insurance plan that rendered covered employees ineligible for disability retirement once they reached age sixty. Relying on its decision in United Air Lines, Inc. v.

McMann, 434 U.S. 192 (1977), the Supreme Court concluded that the term "subterfuge" must be given its ordinary meaning of "'a scheme, plan, stratagem, or artifice of evasion.'" *Betts*. In addition, the Supreme Court found that requiring an insurance company to justify its coverage scheme had no basis in the statutory language.

The Supreme Court's definition and analysis of the ADEA's use of the term "subterfuge" are applicable to the ADA's use of the term "subterfuge[.]" Congress enacted section 501(c) of the ADA in 1990 while the Supreme Court decided *Betts* in 1989. Congress therefore is presumed to have adopted the Supreme Court's interpretation of "subterfuge" in the ADEA context when Congress enacted the ADA. "Where, as here, Congress adopts a new law incorporating sections of a prior law, Congress normally can be presumed to have had knowledge of the interpretation given to the incorporated law, at least insofar as it affects the new statute." Lorillard v. Pons, 434 U.S. 575, 581 (1978). Accordingly, as the Supreme Court held in the ADEA context, the term "subterfuge" does not require an insurance company to justify its policy coverage after a plaintiff's mere *prima facie* allegation.

The second reason that Ford's argument must fail is that it ignores our statutory duty under the McCarran-Ferguson Act regarding insurance cases. Pursuant to that Act, "No Act of Congress shall be construed to invalidate, impair, or supersede any law enacted by any State for the purpose of regulating the business of insurance . . . unless such Act specifically relates to the business of insurance. . . ." 15 U.S.C. § 1012(b) (1994). The ADA does not "specifically relate[ ] to the business of insurance[,]" id., and does not mention the term "insurance" in its introductory section entitled "Findings and purpose[.]" See 42 U.S.C. § 12101. Accordingly, we will not construe section 501(c) to require a seismic shift in the insurance business, namely requiring insurers to justify their coverage plans in court after a mere allegation by a plaintiff. This second reason is integrally related to the third reason Ford's argument regarding section 501(c) fails, namely that requiring insurers to justify their coverage plans elevates this court to the position of super-actuary. This court is clearly not equipped to become the watchdog of the insurance business, and it is unclear exactly what actuarial analysis the defendants would have to produce to disprove the charge of "subterfuge[.]" See *Moderno* (noting confusion as to exactly what actuarial data would be sufficient). . . .

*NOTES*

1. Is the Third Circuit's argument that the ADA covers former employees persuasive? See also Castellano v. City of New York, 142 F.3d 58 (2d Cir. 1998) (disabled former employees eligible to bring ADA claims alleging disability discrimination in retirement benefits). But see Gonzales v. Garner Food Servs., Inc., 89 F.3d 1523 (11th Cir. 1996) (denying ADA coverage under Title I to a former employee whose employer capped disability benefits after learning that he had AIDS); Weyer v. Twentieth Century Fox Film Corp., 198 F.3d 1104 (9th Cir. 2000) (disabled individuals who cannot perform essential functions of their jobs may not assert a claim under Title I against employer's benefit plan). *Weyer* was decided after *Robinson*, upon which the Third Circuit so heavily relied.

2. Courts that have not found former employees to be covered under Title I have struggled with the question whether insurance contracts and their terms are covered under Title III as public accommodations. The circuits are split on this question. *Schering-Plough*, in a portion of the opinion not reproduced, concluded that insurance contracts are not public accommodations.

Title III provides that: "No individual shall be discriminated against on the basis of disability in the full and equal enjoyment of the goods, services, facilities, privileges, advantages, or accommodations of any place of public accommodation by any person who owns, leases (or leases to), or operates a place of public accommodation." 42 U.S.C.S. § 12182(a) (2003). "Public accommodation" is defined in the statute to include an extensive list of establishments such as "auditorium," "bakery," "laundromat," "museum," "park," "nursery," "food bank," and "gymnasium[,]" 42 U.S.C.S. § 12181(7)(D)-(F), (H)-(L) (2003). The statute also lists "insurance office . . . or other service establishment." 42 U.S.C.S. § 12181(7)(F) (2003).

The courts in *Schering-Plough* and Parker v. Metropolitan Life Ins. Co., 121 F.3d 1006, 1011 (6th Cir. 1997) (en banc), found that the plain language of the statute extends coverage only to "places." Because an insurance policy is not a place and employees who receive insurance as a benefit of their employment never go to the insurance provider's office, Title III is not implicated. In Carparts Distribution Ctr., Inc. v. Automotive Wholesaler's Assn. of New England, Inc., 37 F.3d 12 (1st Cir. 1994), the First Circuit held that Title III is not limited to physical structures. With respect to the inclusion of "travel service" in the list of public accommodations it noted:

> Many travel services conduct business by telephone or correspondence without requiring their customers to enter an office in order to obtain their services. Likewise, one can easily imagine the existence of other service establishments conducting business by mail and phone without providing facilities for their customers to enter in order to utilize their services. It would be irrational to conclude that persons who enter an office to purchase services are protected by the ADA, but persons who purchase the same services over the telephone or by mail are not. Congress could not have intended such an absurd result.

Id. at 19. Is this argument persuasive? Even if the telephone services provided by establishments who maintain retail offices are covered by Title III, does that mean that businesses that conduct all of their business over the phone and maintain no retail establishment are public accommodations? The argument that Congress could not possibly have meant to leave such service providers and retailers out of the ADA is answered by pointing to the plain language of the statute.

3. Beyond the issue of whether former employees and insurance contracts are covered under the ADA is the question whether Title I or Title III of the ADA reach the substance of insurance contracts. Department of Justice regulations provide:

> The purpose of the ADA's public accommodations requirements is to ensure accessibility to the goods offered by a public accommodation, not to alter the nature or mix of goods that the public accommodation has typically provided. In other words, a bookstore, for example, must make its facilities and sales operations accessible to individuals with disabilities, but is not required to stock Brailled or large print books. Similarly, a video store must make its facilities and rental operations accessible, but is not required to stock closed-captioned video tapes.

28 C.F.R. pt. 36, app. B, at 640. But is this section properly analogized to insurance contracts? If so, why would the statute contain the "safe harbor" provisions concerning insurance? The Department of Justice Technical Assistance Manual states that Title III does cover the substance of insurance contracts; see Department of Justice, Title III Technical Assistance Manual: Covering Public Accommodations and Commercial Facilities § III-3.11000, at 19 (Nov. 1993) ("Insurance offices . . . may

not discriminate on the basis of disability in the sale of insurance contracts or in the terms or conditions of insurance contracts they offer."). Remember also that the EEOC Interim Guidance on the Application of ADA to Health Insurance also assumes that Title I of the ADA reaches the contents of insurance plans. Under *Chevron* courts must defer to agency interpretations, but only if they are consistent with the statute. Are these interpretations consistent with the ADA? Remember that these interpretations are not contained in ADA regulations. Remember also that the Supreme Court's record of deference to ADA regulations is mixed.

4. In Doe v. Mutual of Omaha Ins. Co., 179 F.3d 557 (7th Cir. 1999), Judge Posner held that Title III does not reach the contents of insurance policies. *Doe* concerned a health insurance policy that capped coverage for AIDS patients. As applied, the cap deprived AIDS patients of coverage for AIDS-related conditions such as pneumonia, even though non-AIDS infected policy holders would be covered for pneumonia. The court found no liability even though the insurer stipulated that it had no sound actuarial basis for its limitation on coverage. In reaching this conclusion, Judge Posner expressed concern that interpreting Title III to reach the contents of insurance policies would expand coverage of Title III to all goods and services offered by public accommodations and thus place a burden on the courts and on the retail sector of the economy that Congress did not intend. Assuming that *Doe* correctly interprets Title III, should it have any bearing on whether Title I's regulation of fringe benefits should reach the content of insurance policies provided by employers? Title VII's prohibition against discrimination in the terms and conditions of employment has reached the content of annuity and life insurance policies in *Manhart* (reproduced at page 200) and health insurance policies in *Newport News* (reproduced at page 471). Does the ADA's safe harbor provision or anything else in the ADA support a different result for disability discrimination cases? For criticism of *Doe*, see Sharona Hoffman, AIDS Caps, Contraceptive Coverage, and the Law: An Analysis of the Federal Anti-Discrmination Statutes' Applicability to Health Insurance, 23 Cardozo L. Rev. 1315 (2002).

5. Having concluded that Ford was covered under the ADA as a former employee, what did *Schering-Plough* say about whether the ADA reaches the content of insurance policies? Why did Ford's challenge to the distinctions drawn in her insurance contract between mental and physical disabilities fail? Most of the Third Circuit's arguments seem to be based on the notion that the ADA does not reach the content of insurance policies. If the policies, whatever their terms, are offered equally to both the disabled and the non-disabled, the statutory requirements are satisfied. Is this argument persuasive? If an employer includes a disability-based limitation in its insurance contract that is not supported by actuarial data, could it not be argued that this constitutes a subterfuge for discrimination even as defined by the Third Circuit ("a scheme, plan, stratagem, or artifice of evasion")?

6. If the court had been willing to consider the terms of the insurance policy and whether they were discriminatory on the basis of disability, what effect would these considerations have on the result? Under the approach taken by the EEOC Interim Guidance, different benefits for physical and mental conditions in a health insurance plan are not disability-based distinctions that must be supported by actuarial data because both disabled and non-disabled individuals are covered by both categories. In Krauel v. Iowa Methodist Medical Ctr., 95 F.3d 674 (8th Cir. 1996), the court took this approach to find that a restriction on benefits for the treatment of infertility did not violate the ADA because infertility affects both disabled and non-disabled individuals. Would *Krauel* come out the same way after *Bragdon?* In addition, is it

appropriate to apply this logic in the context of disability plans where all of the recipients are disabled because they have impairments that substantially limit their ability to work?

7. The Fourth Circuit, in Lewis v. Kmart, 180 F.3d 166 (4th Cir. 1999), took a different approach to determining that distinctions between mental and physical disabilities in long-term disability plans do not violate the ADA. In *Kmart*, the court concluded that it is not unlawful under the Rehabilitation Act or the ADA to give preferential treatment to one disability over another. In reaching this conclusion, the court relied on the Supreme Court's opinion in Traynor v. Turnage, 485 U.S. 535 (1988), holding that "there is nothing in the Rehabilitation Act that requires that any benefit extended to one category of handicapped persons also be extended to all other categories of handicapped persons." Id. at 549. Second, the court distinguished O'Connor v. Consolidated Coin Caterers Corp., 517 U.S. 308 (1996), discussed at pages 102-103.

> [R]eliance on *O'Connor* simply does not make intuitive sense. As recognized in *Traynor*, our federal disability statutes ensure that disabled persons are treated evenly in relation to nondisabled persons. Thus, our federal disability statutes are not designed to ensure that persons with one type of disability are treated the same as persons with another type of disability. In contrast, the ADEA, which was at issue in *O'Connor*, ensures that all persons over the age of 40 are treated evenly on account of their age in relation to all other persons, not just those persons under the age of 40. Therefore, the ADA and the Rehabilitation Act permit preferential treatment between disabilities, but the ADEA does not permit preferential treatment to any person at the expense of any other person over the age of 40 on account of age.

180 F.3d at 171-72. Is the Fourth Circuit's approach persuasive?

8. Several of these courts rely on the Mental Health Parity Act of 1996, Pub. L. No. 104-204, Title VII, 110 Stat. 2944 (1996) (codified at 29 U.S.C.S. § 1185a (2003) and 42 U.S.C.S. § 300gg-5 (2003)) as evidence that Congress does not believe that the ADA reaches distinctions between mental and physical disabilities in long-term disability plans. The Mental Health Parity Act places some restrictions on differences in coverage between mental and physical illnesses in health insurance contracts. By passing the Mental Health Parity Act, did Congress indicate (1) that it believes the ADA does not reach the content of insurance policies, or (2) that distinctions between mental and physical health problems are not covered by the ADA because such distinctions are not "disability-based," or (3) that the ADA does not reach distinctions between disabilities?

9. Although *Schering* and *Kmart* concern long-term disability plans and not health insurance plans, the logic used in these cases is not consistent with the EEOC Guidance on Health Insurance. Is the interpretation of the statute in the EEOC Guidance unreasonable?

## 7.  *National Labor Relations Act*

A number of potential conflicts between the ADA and the National Labor Relations Act, 29 U.S.C.S. §§ 151-169 (2003), have been identified. First, the ADA regulations require employers to consider whether an individual's disability can be accommodated by reallocating job functions or reassigning him to a vacant position. See 29 C.F.R. § 1630.2(o)(2). These forms of accommodation may conflict with collectively bargained seniority provisions and prohibitions against shifting bargaining-unit work.

In U.S. Airways, Inc. v. Barnett, reproduced at page 745, the Court held that an accommodation that would violate a seniority agreement will generally not be reasonable, and this reasoning likely would apply to other potential conflicts with collective bargaining agreements (CBAs) as well. Prior to *Barnett*, the lower courts had uniformly rejected an approach that would require an accommodation that would conflict with a collective bargaining agreement. In Milton v. Scrivner, 53 F.3d 1118 (10th Cir. 1995), employees who, because of their disabilities, could not meet the employer's increased production standards requested that they be accommodated with a lighter work load or by allowing them to bid for less demanding jobs. The Tenth Circuit ruled that both proposed accommodations were unreasonable and not required by the ADA because they were prohibited by the applicable CBA. Id. at 1125. See also Willis v. Pacific Maritime Assn., 236 F.3d 1160 (9th Cir. 2001) (accommodation request that directly conflicts with CBA seniority rights of other employees is unreasonable); Feliciano v. Rhode Island, 160 F.3d 780 (1st Cir. 1998) (employer did not violate the ADA by failing to reassign disabled employee in violation of the rights of an individual who received the position under a process outlined in the CBA); Kralik v. Durbin, 130 F.3d 76 (3d Cir. 1997) (ADA does not require disabled individuals to be accommodated by sacrificing CBA seniority rights of other employees); Eckles v. Consolidated Rail Corp., 94 F.3d 1041 (7th Cir. 1996) (same); Wooten v. Farmland Foods, 58 F.3d 382, 386 (8th Cir. 1995) (ADA does not require an employer to terminate other employees in violation of a CBA in order to accommodate disabled employees).

Note that the presence of a CBA does not always mean that accommodations are not possible. *Barnett* itself accepted this possibility, and the terms of some CBAs include provisions concerning accommodating disabled employees. Thus, for example, Aka v. Washington Hosp. Ctr., 156 F.3d 1284 (D.C. Cir. 1998) (en banc), held that whether accommodation is required under the ADA depends on the specific nature of the requested accommodation and of the business, including the degree to which the accommodation might upset settled expectations created by a CBA. The contract at issue in *Aka* included an exception to the seniority system permitting reassignment of disabled employees in some circumstances. See also Buckingham v. United States, 998 F.2d 735, 740 (9th Cir. 1993) (Rehabilitation Act) (employer may accommodate a disabled employee by reassigning him to a vacant position if the CBA anticipates that accommodation is a valid concern to be considered in filling vacancies).

Another possible conflict between NLRA rights and ADA rights arises when an employer negotiates with an individual employee or applicant about necessary accommodations. This process may interfere with the union's role as exclusive bargaining representative for all bargaining-unit employees. Further, even if a union representative conducts the negotiations or is involved in representing the employee, the process of negotiating reasonable accommodations may violate the union's obligations to represent all its members fairly. A further question is whether the participation of union representatives in the process of negotiating reasonable accommodations violates the ADA's requirement that medical information regarding disabled employees should be held in confidence.

## 8. *Family and Medical Leave Act*

The Family and Medical Leave Act of 1993, 29 U.S.C.S. §§ 2601 et seq. (2003) requires covered employers to provide "eligible" employees with up to 12 weeks of unpaid leave per year when the employee is unable to work because of a "serious health problem." Other aspects of the FMLA are discussed at page 485. Employers also are required to maintain pre-existing health insurance while the employee is on leave and to reinstate the employee to the same or an equivalent job when the leave period is over. An employer may require an employee to provide medical certification from a health care provider to demonstrate that the employee is suffering from a serious health condition that makes the employee unable to perform job functions and is, therefore, eligible for leave. See generally Jane Rigler, Analysis and Understanding of the Family and Medical Leave Act of 1993, 45 Case W. Res. L. Rev. 457 (1995).

Private employers must have 50 or more employees in order to be covered by the Act, and in order to be "eligible," an employee must have worked for the employer for at least 12 months and for at least 1,250 hours during the preceding year. In addition, the employee must be employed at a worksite where the employer employs at least 50 employees within a 75-mile radius.

FMLA regulations define "serious health condition":

*"[S]erious health condition"* entitling an employee to FMLA leave means an illness, injury, impairment, or physical or mental condition that involves —

    (1) Inpatient care (i.e., an overnight stay) in a hospital, hospice, or residential medical care facility, including any period of incapacity . . . or any subsequent treatment in connection with such inpatient care; or

    (2) Continuing treatment by a health care provider.

29 C.F.R. § 825.114(a).

The regulations define "incapacity" for purposes of this section to mean inability to work or perform other regular daily activities. Id. The definition of "continuing treatment by a health care provider" in the regulations provides for five different types of continuing treatment: (1) a period of incapacity of more than three consecutive calendar days; (2) a period of incapacity due to pregnancy or prenatal care; (3) a period of incapacity due to a chronic serious health condition (e.g., asthma, diabetes, epilepsy); (4) a period of incapacity that is permanent or long term due to a condition for which treatment may not be effective (e.g., Alzheimer's, stroke, terminal illness); and (5) a period of absence to receive multiple treatments for necessary restorative surgery or for conditions such as cancer, arthritis, or kidney disease which, without treatment, would result in absences of more than three days. In order to qualify for FMLA leave, each of these situations must involve specified levels of active treatment or supervision by health care professionals. See 29 C.F.R. § 825.114(a)(2)(i)-(v).

The regulations provide specific examples of conditions and treatments that are and are not eligible for FMLA leave. Routine physical, dental, or eye examinations are not covered. Cosmetic treatments not medically required do not constitute "serious health conditions," unless inpatient hospital care is required or complications arise. A variety of common short-term illnesses, such as colds and flu, do not qualify for FMLA leave, absent complications. On the other hand, restorative dental surgery following an accident; surgery to remove cancerous growths; and treatments for allergies, stress, or substance abuse are included if the other conditions of the regulation are met. Absence resulting from drug use without treatment clearly does not qualify for leave. See 29 C.F.R. § 825.114(b)-(d). Treating substance abuse as a "serious health condition" should not prevent an employer from taking employment action against an employee whose abuse interferes with job performance as long as the employer complies with the ADA and does not take action against the employee because the employee has exercised his or her right to take FMLA leave for treatment of that condition.

According to FMLA regulations, being "unable to perform the functions of the position of the employee" means: "where the health care provider finds that the employee is unable to work at all or is unable to perform any one of the essential functions of the employee's position" as defined by the ADA. See 29 C.F.R. § 825.115. The FMLA regulations expressly provide that the FMLA does not modify the ADA in any way and that employers are obligated to comply with both statutes. See 29 C.F.R. § 825.702.

With respect to the notice that employees must give in order to be eligible for FMLA leave, the statute provides that when the need for leave is foreseeable, an employee must provide her employer with no less than 30 days' advance notice. See 29 U.S.C. § 2612(e)(1) & (2)(B); see also 29 C.F.R. § 825.302. The statute does not address notice requirements when the need for leave is unforeseeable. FMLA regulations, however, provide as follows:

(a) When the approximate timing of the need for leave is not foreseeable, an employee should give notice to the employer of the need for FMLA leave as soon as practicable under the facts and circumstances of the particular case. It is expected that an employee will give notice to the employer within no more than one or two working days of learning of the need for leave, except in extraordinary circumstances where such notice is not feasible. In the case of a medical emergency requiring leave because of an employee's own serious health condition or to care for a family member with a serious health condition, written advance notice pursuant to an employer's internal rules and procedures may not be required when FMLA leave is involved.

(b) The employee should provide notice to the employer either in person or by telephone, telegraph, facsimile ("fax") machine or other electronic means. Notice may be given by the employee's spokesperson (e.g., spouse, adult family member or other responsible party) if the employee is unable to do so personally. The employee need not expressly assert rights under the FMLA or even mention the FMLA, but may only state that leave is needed. The employer will be expected to obtain any additional required information through informal means. The employee or spokesperson will be expected to provide more information when it can readily be accomplished as a practical matter, taking into consideration the exigencies of the situation.

See 29 C.F.R. § 825.303. Although these notice provisions are very generous to employees, employees will not be entitled to FMLA leave unless they provide their employer with information "sufficient to reasonably apprise it of the employee's request to take time off for a serious health condition." See Manual v. Westlake Polymers Corp., 66 F.3d 758, 764 (5th Cir. 1995). Compare Spangler v. Federal Home Loan Bank, 278 F.3d 847 (8th Cir. 2002) (requesting time off for "depression again" possibly valid request when employer knew employee suffered from depression); Collins v. NTN-Bower Corp., 272 F.3d 1006 (7th Cir. 2001) (telling employer that employee was "sick" not sufficient); Satterfield v. Wal-Mart Stores, Inc., 135 F.3d 973 (5th Cir. 1998) (note delivered by Satterfield's mother advising Wal-Mart that she "was having a lot of pain in her side" and would not be able to work that day, but would like to make it up on one of her days off, together with mother's statement to supervisor that Satterfield was "sick" were insufficient notice); Carter v. Ford Motor Co., 121 F.3d 1146 (8th Cir. 1997) (Carter informed Ford that he was sick and did not know when he could return to work but did not offer further information regarding his condition; notice insufficient); Gay v. Gilman Paper Co., 125 F.3d 1432 (11th Cir. 1997) (husband called wife's employer and stated that she was in the hospital "having some tests run," but provided additional false information about her whereabouts and condition; insufficient notice) with Price v. City of Fort Wayne, 117 F.3d 1022 (7th Cir. 1997) (employee filled out employer-provided leave request form, indicated that cause was medical need, and attached doctor's note requiring her to take the time off; notice sufficient).

The Supreme Court's first decision under FMLA concerned *employers'* notification requirements. Under regulations promulgated by the Department of Labor, an employer may not count leave against an employee's FMLA entitlement unless the employer has promptly notified the employee that the leave has been designated as FMLA leave.

In Ragsdale v. Wolverine World Wide, 535 U.S. 81 (2002), an employer's policy provided eligible employees with up to seven months of unpaid leave for illness. Tracey Ragsdale, who had cancer, requested and received the seven months of leave, although her employer did not tell Ragsdale the leave was being counted as FMLA leave. When she was unable to return to work at the leave's conclusion, Ragsdale was fired. She then asked for twelve additional weeks of leave under FMLA, but her employer refused to provide the additional leave. Although Ragsdale was entitled to the additional leave under the Labor Department regulations, the Eighth Circuit granted summary judgment to the employer. The Supreme Court affirmed. The Court viewed the regulation as inconsistent with the statutory requirements, which guarantee an employee only up to twelve weeks of leave a year. Importantly, Ragsdale could not show she had been prejudiced or harmed by the employer's failure to give notice. The Court did not decide what would happen in a case when an employee could show harm flowing from the employer's failure to provide notice.

What are the similarities and differences between the ADA and the FMLA in terms of coverage and substantive rights? Individuals who are covered by both statutes should be aware that, if they suffer from an impairment that necessitates frequent absence, they have more than one option for dealing with this issue. Even if accommodations with respect to leave are not reasonable given their employer's needs, leave without pay under the FMLA is a statutory right with no business necessity defense as long as the employer is provided with adequate notice. In addition, employees with attendance problems that are health related, but who do not meet the ADA definition of "disabled" will not be covered by the ADA. They will, however, be entitled to leave without pay if their health problem is a "serious health condition" under the FMLA.

## G.  TITLE II OF THE ADA

Although Title I contains the ADA's general employment provisions, Title II may also prohibit disability discrimination in certain public employment. Section 202, 42 U.S.C.S. § 12132 (2003), provides:

> Subject to the provisions of this title, no qualified individual with a disability shall, by reason of such disability, be excluded from participation in or be denied the benefits of the services, programs, or activities of a public entity, or be subjected to discrimination by any such entity.

Section 201, § 12131, defines a "public entity" to include any state or local government or agency. Note that Title II coverage does not have the 15-employee minimum applicable under Title I.

Section 202 has been interpreted by the Department of Justice to include employment. See 28 C.F.R. § 35.140(a). Moreover, the DOJ interprets the substantive prohibition in Title II as paralleling the substantive prohibition in Title I. In fact, the DOJ's employment regulations for Title II incorporate both the EEOC's Title I regulations and the Department's own regulations under § 504 of the Rehabilitation Act. Id. § 35.140(b).

The circuits, however, are in disagreement about whether Title II reaches employment discrimination. Compare Zimmerman v. Oregon Dept. of Justice, 170 F.3d 1169 (9th Cir. 1999) (Title II does not cover employment discrimination) with Bledsoe v. Palm Beach County Soil & Water Conservation Dist., 133 F.3d 816 (11th Cir. 1998) (Title II covers employment discrimination). The disagreement centers on the definition of discrimination under Title II. The Ninth Circuit interprets this language as prohibiting discrimination only in the provision of services, programs, and activities because the definition of a qualified individual entitled under Title II is an individual who meets the eligibility requirements of a government service, program, or activity. See 42 U.S.C.S. § 12131(2) (2003). The Eleventh Circuit reads the final clause of § 12132 — "or be subjected to discrimination by any such entity" — as encompassing employment discrimination.

Plaintiffs may wish to seek coverage under Title II because they work for an agency with fewer than 15 employees or because applicable procedures and remedies differ from Title I. Section 203, 42 U.S.C.S. § 12133 (2003), provides that § 202 shall be enforced pursuant to "the remedies, procedures, and rights set forth in section 12132 of the Rehabilitation Act. . . ." This section is the enforcement and remedies provision for § 504 of the Rehabilitation Act. Incorporation of this provision means, as recognized in the legislative history, that § 203 creates a private right of action to enforce § 202 and that, unlike Title I, a discriminatee need not invoke any administrative remedy prior to filing suit. S. Rep. No. 101-116, at 57-58 (1989). Most important, the timeliness of a Title II action will probably be determined by the most analogous state statute of limitations, see Andrews v. Consolidated Rail Corp., 831 F.2d 678 (7th Cir. 1987), rather than by the relatively short period for filing an EEOC charge under Title I. See Chapter 9.

However, in Barnes v. Gorman, 536 U.S. 181 (2002), the Supreme Court held that punitive damages are not available under Title II of the ADA. The Court asserted that the remedies for violation of § 202 of the ADA and § 504 of the Rehabilitation Act are "co-extensive." These remedies, in turn, are those available for a private cause of action under Title VI of the Civil Rights Act of 1964, which prohibits race discrimination in federally funded programs. Resolving the question of what relief is appropriate for violations of these statutes, the Court concluded that, given the contractual nature of the spending clause legislation at issue, remedies should be those traditionally available in breach of contract suits. Since punitive damages are not awardable for breach of contract, the Court held them unavailable in suits under Title VI, § 504, and Title II of the ADA.

In addition to differences relating to procedures and remedies, Title II provides an alternative claim for plaintiffs whose disabilities require removal of architectural barriers. The DOJ regulations for Title II require that, with respect to existing facilities, "[a] public entity shall operate each service, program, or activity so that the service, program, or activity, when viewed in its entirety, is readily accessible to and usable by individuals with disabilities." 28 C.F.R. § 35.150(a). This provision is subject to an "undue financial and administrative" burden exception that, together with other limitations, means that it probably does not provide additional protection beyond the reasonable accommodation requirements of Title I. See 28 C.F.R. § 35.150(a)(1)-(3). However, the accessibility requirements applicable to alterations and new construction are quite stringent. New construction must be "readily accessible to and usable by individuals with disabilities." Alterations must meet the same standard "to the maximum extent feasible." 28 C.F.R. § 35.151(b). Because these provisions are not subject to a "reasonable" requirement or an "undue hardship" defense, disabled state and local workers may be more successful in securing the removal of barriers by resorting to Title II's accessibility requirements, at least when facilities are altered or newly constructed. Consider Title II's new construction accessibility requirements applied to the request in *Vande Zande* for changes in the height of sinks. If the change is not required under Title II, should that render the requested change per se unreasonable under Title I?

## H.  THE REHABILITATION ACT OF 1973

Notwithstanding the enactment of the ADA, the Rehabilitation Act remains available and useful in certain circumstances as a remedy for disability discrimination in employment. The substantive protection accorded by the Act is now the same as in the ADA, but the Act covers some employers not covered by the ADA, most notably, the federal government. Moreover, the Act sometimes provides more favorable enforcement procedures and remedies than does the ADA. The Rehabilitation Act, however, does have two serious shortcomings. First, the Act has very narrow coverage provisions, applying only to federal employers with a specified relationship to the federal government, such as federal agencies, recipients of federal funding, and federal contractors. Second, the Act fails to provide a discriminatee with a private right of action, that is, a judicially enforceable cause of action, to redress disability discrimination by a federal contractor.

### 1.  Federal Employment

As indicated earlier, the ADA does not prohibit disability discrimination in federal employment, except with regard to employees of the House of Representatives and the instrumentalities of Congress. Therefore, nearly all federal employees must look to other sources of law for such protection. Foremost among these other sources is the Rehabilitation Act.

Section 501 of the Act, 29 U.S.C.S. § 791 (2003), requires each department, agency, and instrumentality (including the U.S. Postal Service and the Postal Rate Commission) in the executive branch to formulate and annually update an affirmative action plan for the employment of individuals with disabilities. In addition to requiring covered agencies to implement an affirmative action plan, § 501 prohibits covered agencies from discriminating against a qualified person with a disability. For purposes of determining whether such discrimination has occurred, 29 U.S.C.S. § 791(g) (2003) expressly adopts the standards contained in Title I of the ADA.

Section 505(a)(1), 29 U.S.C.S. § 794a(a)(1) (2003), makes the "remedies, procedures, and rights" accorded federal employees by § 717 of Title VII, 42 U.S.C.S. § 2000e-16 (2003), available to enforce § 501(b). Although this incorporation of Title VII procedures requires a federal employee with a § 501(b) claim to pursue his or her administrative remedy prior to suit, it also allows a federal employee who is dissatisfied with the administrative process to have his or her claim heard de novo in federal court. The procedures and remedies available to federal employees under Title VII are discussed in Chapters 9 and 10.

Section 504 of the Act might also prohibit federal executive agencies from engaging in disability discrimination in employment. This issue is important because §§ 501 and 504 have different enforcement procedures and remedies. The relationship between these provisions will be considered further in the next subsection.

The EEOC has issued regulations that prohibit employment discrimination against persons with disabilities in executive agencies, military departments, positions in the competitive service in the legislative and judicial branches, the U.S. Postal Service, and the Postal Rate Commission. See 29 C.F.R. pt. 1614. These regulations provide that the federal government shall be a "model employer" of disabled individuals and specify that the standards applied under the ADA shall govern Rehabilitation Act claims under § 501. The regulations also require each covered entity to adopt an affirmative action program for such individuals and to make a reasonable accommodation to such an individual's disability.

## 2.   Federal and Federally Assisted Programs

Section 504(a) of the Rehabilitation Act contains two coverage provisions. The first prohibits disability discrimination "under any program or activity receiving Federal financial assistance." The second prohibits disability discrimination "under any program or activity conducted by any Executive agency or by the United States Postal Service."

The first prohibition, covering programs or activities receiving federal financial assistance, presents two interpretive problems — the meaning of "program or activity" and the meaning of "receiving Federal financial assistance." Section 504(b) contains several definitions of the phrase "program or activity," the applicable definition depending on the nature and functions of the recipient of the federal funding. These definitions must be read with care: the receipt of federal funds by a particular division of a juridical entity may cause other divisions of the entity to also be covered by § 504(a), but this is frequently not the case. The meaning of the second phrase, "receiving Federal financial assistance," has been an issue in many cases. Generally, the phrase means that a direct or indirect federal monetary subsidy was intended for the entity, not merely that the entity benefited from another entity's receipt of federal funds. See, e.g., United States Dept. of Transp. v. Paralyzed Veterans of Am., 477 U.S. 597 (1986).

The first prohibition is enforced pursuant to § 505(a)(2), 29 U.S.C.S. § 794a(a)(2) (2003), which makes available the "remedies, procedures, and rights set forth in Title VI of the Civil Rights Act of 1964." Pursuant to this provision, the courts have held that a private right of action is available to a discriminatee and that federal administrative remedies do not have to be invoked prior to suit. See, e.g., Kling v. County of Los Angeles, 633 F.2d 876 (9th Cir. 1980), rev'd, 769 F.2d 532 (9th Cir.), cert. granted and judgment rev'd, 474 U.S. 936 (1985). Although the Supreme Court has held that an equitable award of backpay may be recovered, Consolidated Rail Corp. v. Darrone, 465 U.S. 624 (1984), punitive damages may not. In Barnes v. Gorman, 536 U.S. 181 (2002), the Supreme Court held that punitive damages are not available under either Title II of the ADA or § 504 of the Rehabilitation Act. The remedies are those available for a private cause of action under Title VI of the Civil Rights Act of 1964, which prohibits race discrimination in federally funded programs. The Court concluded that given the contractual nature of the spending clause legislation at issue, remedies should be those traditionally available in breach of contract suits. Since punitive damages are not awardable for breach of contract, the Court held them unavailable in suits under Title VI, § 504, and Title II of the ADA. However, § 505(b), 29 U.S.C.S. § 794a(b) (2003), does allow a prevailing plaintiff to recover reasonable attorneys' fees.

The second prohibition, covering programs and activities conducted by an executive agency or the U.S. Postal Service, has given rise to two issues: (1) Does this provision prohibit covered agencies from discriminating against their own employees or only against the public beneficiaries of agency-conducted programs? (2) Does violation of this provision give rise to a private right of action? The exclusion of agency employees from coverage is suggested by §§ 501(b) and 505(a)(1), which specifically require such agencies to take affirmative action to employ individuals with disabilities and provide a private enforcement procedure. The absence of a private right of action is suggested by the failure of § 505 to establish an enforcement procedure for this prohibition, while establishing such procedures for § 501(b) and the first prohibition in § 504(a).

Despite these considerations, several appellate courts have held that the second prohibition is applicable to agency employment and gives rise to a private right of action. See, e.g., Doe v. Garrett, 903 F.2d 1455 (11th Cir. 1990); Morgan v. United States Postal Serv., 798 F.2d 1162 (8th Cir. 1986). These same courts, however, have nullified the practical significance of this holding by also holding that a federal employee must satisfy the administrative requirements incorporated into § 505(a)(1) before bringing suit under § 504(a). Further, the Supreme Court has held that § 504(a) does not waive federal sovereign immunity in an action by a federal employee to those available in a § 501(b) action. Lane v. Pena, 518 U.S. 187 (1996). Thus there is no practical advantage to bringing suit under § 504(a). See, e.g., Johnston v. Horne, 875 F.2d 1415 (9th Cir. 1989).

The substantive protection against disability discrimination accorded by § 504(a) is the same as in Title I. Although this may have been uncertain prior to late 1992, § 504(d), 29 U.S.C.S. § 794(d) (2003), which was enacted at that time, expressly incorporates the Title I standards and certain other provisions of the ADA into § 504. However, at least one circuit has held that the 15-employee minimum for coverage under Title I of the ADA does not apply to claims under § 504. Schrader v. Ray, 296 F.3d 968 (10th Cir. 2002).

## 3.  Government Contractors

Section 503(a), 29 U.S.C.S. § 793(a) (2003), of the Rehabilitation Act provides that

> any contract in excess of $10,000 entered into by any Federal department or agency for the procurement of personal property and nonpersonal services . . . shall contain a provision requiring that the party contracting with the United States shall take affirmative action to employ and advance in employment qualified individuals with disabilities.

The affirmative action provision in the contract also prohibits the contractor from discriminating against an individual with a disability in violation of the standards established in Title I of the ADA. See § 503(d), 29 U.S.C.S. § 793(d) (2003). Section 503(b), 29 U.S.C.S. § 793(b) (2003), provides that a contractor may be charged with violating the affirmative action provision in its contract by filing a complaint with the Department of Labor and that the Department shall promptly investigate any such complaint and take such action thereon as the circumstances warrant.

Unlike §§ 501(b) and 504(a), § 503(a) does not create a private right of action for a discriminatee. See, e.g., D'Amato v. Wisconsin Gas Co., 760 F.2d 1474 (7th Cir. 1985). Thus, a victim of disability discrimination by a federal contractor cannot obtain judicial relief under § 503(a). The courts have even rejected the theory that the discriminatee has a cause of action as a third-party beneficiary of the contract between his or her employer and the federal government. Id. In short, therefore, § 503(a) imposes duties on federal contractors that are enforceable only through the administrative process.

# PART IV

---

# PROCEDURES AND REMEDIES

# Chapter 9

## Procedures for Enforcing Antidiscrimination Laws

## A.  INTRODUCTION

Each of the antidiscrimination laws we have encountered has different procedural aspects. Perhaps the simplest are the Reconstruction-era civil rights statutes, 42 U.S.C.S. §§ 1981, 1983 (2003). There is no federal agency charged with enforcing these statutes, and private suits are prosecuted in either federal or state court, much as any other civil litigation. While we have mentioned complicated questions of reach and immunity (see page 178), the major procedural issue under these statutes has been the applicable statute of limitations. Because there is no governing federal law, state laws must be borrowed. After some confusion, the rule has now emerged that all § 1983 claims, regardless of the constitutional violation alleged, are subject to the state statute applicable to "personal injury" actions. Wilson v. Garcia, 471 U.S. 261 (1985). Goodman v. Lukens Steel Co., 482 U.S. 656 (1987), extended this approach to suits under § 1981.* If the state in question has no "personal injury" statute, the

---

*There is an argument that at least some § 1981 claims are governed by 28 U.S.C.S. § 1658 (2003), the residual four-year federal statute of limitations. See Boyd A. Byers, Adventures in Topsy-Turvy Land: Are Civil Rights Claims Arising Under 42 U.S.C. § 1981 Governed by the Federal Four-Year "Catch-All" Statute of Limitations, 28 U.S.C. § 1658?, 38 Washburn L.J. 509 (1999). The first two circuits to address this question, however, held that § 1658 was not applicable to a suit under § 1981, even if the claim at issue would not have been cognizable prior to the 1991 amendment. Jones v. R.R. Donnelley & Sons Co., 305 F.3d 717 (7th Cir. 2002); Zubi v. AT&T Corp., 219 F.3d 220 (3d Cir. 2000).

most analogous statute, presumably including a general tort statute, should govern. See also Owens v. Okure, 488 U.S. 235 (1989) (§ 1983 claims are governed by general personal injury statutes even in states with a special limitations provision for "intentional" torts). The Court has recognized, however, that the state limitations statute's application may be affected by rules concerning the accrual of the cause of action, continuing violation, and tolling. These principles are generally "borrowed" from the state along with the governing statute, Johnson v. Railway Express Agency, Inc., 421 U.S. 454, 463-64 (1975); Board of Regents v. Tomanio, 446 U.S. 478 (1980), but "considerations of state law may be displaced where their application would be inconsistent with the federal policy underlying the cause of action under consideration," Johnson, 421 U.S. at 465. See Occidental Life Ins. Co. v. EEOC, 432 U.S. 355 (1977). See also Shields v. Fort James Corp., 305 F.3d 1280 (11th Cir. 2002) (remanding for a determination of whether the continuing violation doctrine of Title VII ought to be applied in a § 1981 racial harassment suit).*

More complicated procedurally are Title VII, 42 U.S.C.S. §§ 2000e et seq. (2003); the Age Discrimination in Employment Act, 29 U.S.C.S. §§ 621 et seq. (2003); and the Americans with Disabilities Act, 42 U.S.C.S. §§ 12101 et seq. (2003). The ADEA, although originally somewhat different in its provisions, has been amended several times to bring its procedures in line with those of Title VII, with only a few exceptions. As for the ADA, Title I specifically incorporates by reference the Title VII enforcement scheme. 42 U.S.C.S. § 12117(a) (2003).† Because of the substantial identity of all three statutes, the following discussion will be framed in terms of Title VII, although relevant differences between it and the ADEA will be noted where appropriate.

Essentially, Title VII creates a unique amalgam of methods — administrative and judicial — for enforcement of its substantive proscriptions. See generally Roy L. Brooks, A Roadmap Through Title VII's Procedural and Remedial Labyrinth, 24 Sw. U. L. Rev. 511 (1995). The basic Title VII procedures for enforcement of the substantive rights it creates are found in § 706, 42 U.S.C.S. § 2000e-5 (2003). A person claiming to be aggrieved by an alleged act of discrimination may file a charge with the EEOC within a specified time from the occurrence of the unfair employment practice. A charge must also be filed with any existing state antidiscrimination agency.

---

*Johnson found one federal interest insufficient to toll, holding that filing with the EEOC did not toll the statute for a § 1981 suit. Reasoning that the remedies were "separate, distinct, and independent," the Court concluded that resort to Title VII should have no effect on § 1981 rights. A grievance procedure under a collective bargaining agreement also does not toll the § 1981 statute. E.g., Intl. Union of Elec. Workers, Local 790 v. Robbins & Myers, Inc., 429 U.S. 229 (1976) (Title VII); Patterson v. Gen. Motors Corp., 631 F.2d 476 (7th Cir. 1980) (§ 1981).

†The focus of Chapter 8 was ADA Title I, which prohibits disability discrimination in employment. However, Title II of the ADA also prohibits disability discrimination by a "public entity." § 202, 42 U.S.C.S. § 12132 (2003). Section 201, 42 U.S.C.S. § 12131 (2003), defines a "public entity" to include any state or local governmental agency. Section 202 has been interpreted by the Department of Justice to include employment. 28 C.F.R. § 35.140(a) (2003).

Title II enforcement procedures and remedies, however, differ from those of Title I. Section 203, 42 U.S.C.S. § 12133 (2003), provides that § 202 shall be enforced pursuant to "the remedies, procedures, and rights set forth in § 505 of the Rehabilitation Act." Although this does not specify which subsection of § 505, 29 U.S.C.S. § 794a (2003), is applicable, the legislative history states that it is § 505(a)(2), § 794a(a)(2), the enforcement and remedial provision for § 505 of the Rehabilitation Act.

The incorporation of this provision means, as recognized in the legislative history, that § 203 creates a private right of action to enforce § 202 and that, unlike Title I, a discriminatee need not invoke an administrative remedy prior to filing suit. S. Rep. No. 116, 101st Cong., 1st Sess. 57-58 (1989). Most important, the timeliness of a Title II action will probably be determined by the most analogous state statute of limitations, see Andrews v. Consolidated Rail Corp., 831 F.2d 678 (7th Cir. 1987), rather than by the relatively short period for filing a charge with the EEOC under Title I. The differences in relief between Titles I and II of the ADA are considered in Chapter 10.

The EEOC is directed by Title VII to serve notice of the charge on the respondent within ten days and then to conduct an investigation, culminating in a determination of whether there is reasonable cause to believe that the charge is true. If the EEOC finds no reasonable cause, it must dismiss the charge and notify the charging party, who may then bring a private action within 90 days. If, however, the EEOC does find reasonable cause, it is directed first to attempt conciliation. If that fails to eliminate the alleged unlawful employment practice, the EEOC may bring a civil suit against the respondent in district court.

If the EEOC does not sue within 180 days from the filing of the charge, the charging party may request a right-to-sue letter, after receipt of which he or she has 90 days to bring an action; or the charging party may permit EEOC processes to proceed to their conclusion and bring suit within 90 days of that point. The EEOC may intervene in any private suit at the discretion of the court. If the EEOC does commence suit, the charging party loses the right to bring suit, but has a statutory right to intervene to protect his or her interests against governmental delay or inadequate representation.

## B.  PRIVATE ENFORCEMENT: THE ADMINISTRATIVE PHASE

### 1.  Introduction

Although Title VII establishes elaborate prescriptions for EEOC processing of individual charges, the only preconditions for private suit are timely resort to the EEOC and seasonable filing of a court suit thereafter. Even an EEOC finding that there is no reasonable cause to believe discrimination occurred does not bar suit. McDonnell Douglas Corp. v. Green, 411 U.S. 792, 798-99 (1972). Thus, defects in EEOC proceedings — such as failing to notify the defendant of a filed charge or failing to conduct conciliation efforts prior to private suit — do not prejudice the private plaintiff.

The following subsections undertake a more detailed examination of the two procedural prerequisites to private suit that the Supreme Court has identified: (1) timely filing of an appropriate charge with the EEOC and (2) timely filing of a court suit after receipt of an EEOC right-to-sue letter (or notice of dismissal). In looking at these two prerequisites, it is necessary to distinguish between procedures in states that have antidiscrimination agencies (deferral states) and procedures in those that do not (nondeferral states).

### 2.  Filing a Timely Charge

Every private Title VII suit must begin with a charge under oath filed with the Equal Employment Opportunity Commission. § 706(b), 42 U.S.C.S. § 20003-5(b) (2003). Title VII requires that the charge comply with EEOC requirements as to form and content, but the EEOC regulations specifically provide that, notwithstanding the absence of preferred information, "a charge is sufficient when the Commission receives from the person making the charge a written statement sufficiently precise to identify the parties and to describe generally the action or practice complained of." 29 C.F.R. § 1601.12(b) (1998).

The courts have also been very permissive as to what will be deemed a charge for purposes of satisfying this requirement. Almost any written document received by the EEOC will qualify as long as it suffices to "identify the parties and to describe generally the action or practices complained of." Waiters v. Robert Bosch Co., 683 F.2d 89, 92 (4th Cir. 1982). The absence of an oath at the time of filing can be remedied later. 29 C.F.R. § 1601.12(b) (2002). Edelman v. Lynchburg Coll., 535 U.S. 106, 115 (2002), upheld this EEOC regulation. The Court wrote: "Construing § 706 to permit the relation back of an oath omitted from an original filing ensures that the lay complainant, who may not know enough to verify on filing, will not risk forfeiting his rights inadvertently. At the same time, the Commission looks out for the employer's interest by refusing to call for any response to an otherwise sufficient complaint until the verification has been supplied." Prior to *Edelman*, the preliminary intake questionnaire used by the EEOC in its filing procedure had been held by some courts to constitute a valid charge at the time it was completed even though it was unsigned and unverified and the formal charge was not executed until later. E.g., Wilkerson v. Grinnell Corp., 270 F.3d 1314 (11th Cir. 2001). *Edelman*, however, suggested that it may be important whether the charging party and/or the EEOC treated an unverified document as a "charge." The Court remanded for determination of this issue:

> Our judgment does not, however, reach the conclusion drawn by the District Court . . . that Edelman's letter was not a charge under the statute because neither he nor the EEOC treated it as one. It is enough to say here that at the factual level their view has some support. . . . Edelman's counsel agreed with the Government that the significance of the delayed notice to the College would be open on remand.

In light of this ruling, the authority of cases such as *Wilkerson* is uncertain. On remand, the court in Edelman v. Lynchburg College, 300 F.3d 400 (4th Cir. 2002), held that the plaintiff's intent that the letter function as a charge sufficed, even if the EEOC failed in its duty to treat it as one.

This liberality as to what constitutes a charge is not, however, reflected in the law that has developed as to when a charge is deemed timely. Title VII provides two periods of limitations applicable to the filing of charges. The charge must be filed within 180 days "after the alleged unlawful employment practice occurred." § 706(e), 42 U.S.C.S. § 2000e-5(e) (2003); see also the ADEA, § 7(d)(1), 29 U.S.C.S. § 626(d)(1) (2003). However, an important exception obtains: where a state or local antidiscrimination agency exists, the charge must be filed with the state agency and also with the EEOC within 300 days of the alleged violation or "within thirty days after receiving notice that the State or local agency has terminated the proceedings under the State or local law, whichever is earlier." § 706(e), 42 U.S.C.S. § 2000e-5(e) (2003). With the spread of fair employment practices laws at the state and local levels, the 300/30-day period is more the rule than the exception. In either event, it is important to know how to determine when the alleged violation occurred and whether any factors will toll the running of the period.

### a.  Occurrence of Violation

## DELAWARE STATE COLLEGE v. RICKS
### 449 U.S. 250 (1980)

Justice POWELL delivered the opinion of the Court. . . .

Columbus Ricks is a black Liberian. In 1970, Ricks joined the faculty at Delaware State College, a state institution attended predominantly by blacks. In February 1973, the Faculty Committee on Promotions and Tenure (the tenure committee) recommended that Ricks not receive a tenured position in the education department. The tenure committee, however, agreed to reconsider its decision the following year. Upon reconsideration, in February 1974, the committee adhered to its earlier recommendation. The following month, the Faculty Senate voted to support the tenure committee's negative recommendation. On March 13, 1974, the College Board of Trustees formally voted to deny tenure to Ricks.

Dissatisfied with the decision, Ricks immediately filed a grievance with the Board's Educational Policy Committee (the grievance committee), which in May 1974 held a hearing and took the matter under submission. During the pendency of the grievance, the College administration continued to plan for Ricks' eventual termination. Like many colleges and universities, Delaware State has a policy of not discharging immediately a junior faculty member who does not receive tenure. Rather, such a person is offered a "terminal" contract to teach one additional year. When that contract expires, the employment relationship ends. Adhering to this policy, the Trustees on June 26, 1974 told Ricks that he would be offered a one-year "terminal" contract that would expire June 30, 1975.[2] Ricks signed the contract without objection or reservation on September 4, 1974. Shortly thereafter, on September 12, 1974, the Board of Trustees notified Ricks that it had denied his grievance.

[Ricks attempted to file a charge with the EEOC on April 4, 1975. The Commission initially deferred the charge to the Delaware state antidiscrimination agency, but deemed the charge filed when the state agency waived jurisdiction on April 28, 1975.]

## II

Title VII requires aggrieved persons to file a complaint with the EEOC "within one hundred and eighty days after the alleged unlawful employment practice occurred." 42 U.S.C. § 2000e-5(e). . . . The limitations periods, while guaranteeing the

---

2. The June 26 letter stated:

June 26, 1974

Dear Dr. Ricks:

On March 13, 1974, the Board of Trustees of Delaware State College officially endorsed the recommendations of the Faculty Senate at its March 11, 1974 meeting, at which time the Faculty Senate recommended that the Board not grant you tenure.

As we are both aware, the Educational Policy Committee of the Board of Trustees has heard your grievance and it is now in the process of coming to a decision. The Chairman of the Educational Policy Committee has indicated to me that a decision may not be forthcoming until sometime in July. In order to comply with the 1971 Trustee Policy Manual and AAUP requirements with regard to the amount of time needed in proper notification of non-reappointment for non-tenured faculty members, the Board has no choice but to follow actions according to its official position prior to the grievance process, and thus, notify you of its intent not to renew your contract at the end of the 1974-75 school year.

Please understand that we have no way of knowing what the outcome of the grievance process may be, and that this action is being taken at this time in order to be consistent with the present formal position of the Board and AAUP time requirements in matters of this kind. Should the Educational Policy Committee decide to recommend that you be granted tenure, and should the Board of Trustees concur with their recommendation, then of course, it will supersede any previous action taken by the Board.

Sincerely yours,

/s/ Walton H. Simpson, President
Board of Trustees of Delaware State College

protection of the civil rights laws to those who promptly assert their rights, also protect employers from the burden of defending claims arising from employment decisions that are long past. Johnson v. Railway Express Agency, Inc., 421 U.S. 454, 463-464 (1975); see United Air Lines v. Evans, 431 U.S. 553 (1977).

Determining the timeliness of Ricks' EEOC complaint, and this ensuing lawsuit, requires us to identify precisely the "unlawful employment practice" of which he complains. Ricks now insists that discrimination not only motivated the College in denying him tenure, but also in terminating his employment on June 30, 1975. In effect, he is claiming a "continuing violation" of the civil rights laws with the result that the limitations periods did not commence to run until his one-year "terminal" contract expired. This argument cannot be squared with the allegations of the complaint. Mere continuity of employment, without more, is insufficient to prolong the life of a cause of action for employment discrimination. United Air Lines v. Evans. If Ricks intended to complain of a discriminatory discharge, he should have identified the alleged discriminatory acts that continued until, or occurred at the time of, the actual termination of his employment. But the complaint alleges no such facts.

Indeed, the contrary is true. It appears that termination of employment at Delaware State is a delayed, but inevitable, consequence of the denial of tenure. In order for the limitations periods to commence with the date of discharge, Ricks would have had to allege and prove that the manner in which his employment was terminated differed discriminatorily from the manner in which the College terminated other professors who also had been denied tenure. But no suggestion has been made that Ricks was treated differently from other unsuccessful tenure aspirants. Rather, in accord with the College's practice, Ricks was offered a one-year "terminal" contract, with explicit notice that his employment would end upon its expiration.

In sum, the only alleged discrimination occurredd — and the filing limitations periods therefore commenced — at the time the tenure decision was made and communicated to Ricks.[9] That is so even though one of the *effects* of the denial of tenure — the eventual loss of a teaching positionn — did not occur until later. The Court of Appeals for the Ninth Circuit correctly held, in a similar tenure case, that "[t]he proper focus is upon the time of the *discriminatory acts*, not upon the time at which the *consequences* of the acts became most painful" (emphasis added); see United Air Lines v. Evans. It is simply insufficient for Ricks to allege that his termination "gives present effect to the past illegal act and therefore perpetuates the consequences of forbidden discrimination." The emphasis is not upon the effects of earlier employment decisions; rather, it "is [upon] whether any present *violation* exists" [*Evans*] (emphasis in original).

## III

We conclude for the foregoing reasons that the limitations periods commenced to run when the tenure decision was made and Ricks was notified. The remaining inquiry is the identification of this date.

9. Complaints that employment termination resulted from discrimination can present widely varying circumstances. In this case the only alleged discriminatory act is the denial of tenure sought by a college professor, with the termination of employment not occurring until a later date. The application of the general principles discussed herein necessarily must be made on a case-by-case basis.

A

Three dates have been advanced and argued by the parties. As indicated above, Ricks contended for June 30, 1975, the final date of his "terminal" contract, relying on a continuing violation theory. This contention fails, as we have shown, because of the absence of any allegations of facts to support it. The Court of Appeals agreed with Ricks that the relevant date was June 30, 1975, but it did so on a different theory. It found that the only alleged discriminatory act was the denial of tenure, but neverthe-less adopted the "final date of employment" rule primarily for policy reasons. Al-though this view has the virtue of simplicity, the discussion in Part II of this opinion demonstrates its fallacy as a rule of general application. Congress has decided that time limitations periods commence with the date of the "alleged unlawful employ-ment practice." Where, as here, the only challenged employment practice occurs be-fore the termination date, the limitations periods necessarily commence to run be-fore that date. It should not be forgotten that time-limitations provisions themselves promote important interests; "the period allowed for instituting suit inevitably reflects a value judgment concerning the point at which the interests in favor of protecting valid claims are outweighed by the interests in prohibiting the prosecution of stale ones." Johnson v. Railway Express Agency, Inc. See Mohasco Corp. v. Silver, 447 U.S. 807 (1980).

B

The EEOC, in its amicus brief, contends in the alternative for a different date. It was not until September 12, 1974, that the Board notified Ricks that his grievance had been denied. The EEOC therefore asserts that, for purposes of computing limi-tations periods, this was the date of the unfavorable tenure decision.[13] Two possible lines of reasoning underlie this argument. First, it could be contended that the Trustees' initial decision was only an expression of intent that did not become final until the grievance was denied. In support of this argument, the EEOC notes that the June 26 letter explicitly held out to Ricks the possibility that he would receive tenure if the Board sustained his grievance. Second, even if the Board's first decision ex-pressed its official position, it could be argued that the pendency of the grievance should toll the running of the limitations periods.

We do not find either argument to be persuasive. As to the former, we think that the Board of Trustees had made clear well before September 12 that it had formally rejected Ricks' tenure bid. The June 26 letter itself characterized that as the Board's "official position." It is apparent, of course, that the Board in the June 26 letter indi-cated a willingness to change its prior decision if Ricks' grievance were found to be meritorious. But entertaining a grievance complaining of the tenure decision does not suggest that the earlier decision was in any respect tentative. The grievance pro-cedure, by its nature, is a remedy for a prior decision, not an opportunity to influence that decision before it is made.

As to the latter argument, we already have held that the pendency of a grievance, or some other method of collateral review of an employment decision, does not toll the running of the limitations periods. International Union of Elec. Workers v. Robbins &

13. [The charge would be timely counting from September 12 if Ricks were "entitled to 300 days, rather than 180 days" to file with the EEOC because Delaware was a deferral state. The Court did not de-cide that issue: because the limitation period commenced to run no later than June 26, 1974], Ricks' filing with the EEOC was not timely even with the benefit of the 300-day period.

Myers, Inc., 429 U.S. 229 (1976). The existence of careful procedures to assure fairness in the tenure decision should not obscure the principle that limitations periods normally commence when the employer's decision is made.

### c

The District Court . . . concluded that the limitations periods had commenced to run by June 26, 1974, when the President of the Board notified Ricks that he would be offered a "terminal" contract for the 1974-1975 school year. We cannot say that this decision was erroneous. By June 26, the tenure committee had twice recommended that Ricks not receive tenure; the Faculty Senate had voted to support the tenure committee's recommendation; and the Board of Trustees formally had voted to deny Ricks tenure.[16] In light of this unbroken array of negative decisions, the District Court was justified in concluding that the College had established its official position — and made that position apparent to Ricks — no later than June 26, 1974.[17]

### NOTES

1. *Ricks* establishes a "notice of decision" rule for Title VII actions. See also Chardon v. Fernandez, 454 U.S. 6 (1981) (§ 1983); Sharp v. United Airlines, Inc., 236 F.3d 368 (7th Cir. 2000); Flaherty v. Metromail Corp., 235 F.3d 133 (2d Cir. 2000); Watson v. Eastman Kodak Co., 235 F.3d 851 (3d Cir. 2000). An extreme application of this rule is Cooper v. St. Cloud State Univ., 226 F.3d 964 (8th Cir. 2000) (denial of tenure triggered filing period, even if termination did not occur for four years). Under this rule, notice to an employee of the employer's decision to take an adverse employment action, such as a projected termination, starts the filing period running. In an ongoing relationship such as employment, however, there may be numerous adverse actions, and a charge filed too late as to one action may be timely as to another. Suppose Ricks had challenged discrimination in the consideration of his grievance separate from any discrimination in the original decision not to renew him. His charge might then have been timely. Plaintiff's remedy, however, might be limited to the harm caused him by the discrimination timely charged. We will revisit this issue in connection with the continuing violation doctrine.

2. The "notice of decision" rule may seem simple, but both "decision" and "notice" have generated difficulties.

3. With respect to the decision, the first question is, whose decision is critical? *Ricks* involved the decision-making process at Delaware State, but that process is apparently radically different elsewhere. In Lever v. Northwestern University, 979 F.2d 552 (7th Cir. 1992), the court found that a dean's decision to award a terminal contract was "self-effectuating"; the provost saw the file only if the faculty member appealed.

16. We recognize, of course, that the limitations period should not commence to run so soon that it becomes difficult for a layman to invoke the protection of the civil rights statutes. See Oscar Mayer & Co. v. Evans, 441 U.S. 750, 761 (1979); Love v. Pullman Co., 404 U.S. 522, 526-527 (1972). But, for the reasons we have stated, there can be no claim here that Ricks was not abundantly forewarned. . . .

17. We need not decide whether the District Court correctly focused on the June 26 date, rather than the date the Board communicated to Ricks its unfavorable tenure decision made at the March 13, 1974 meeting. . . .

4. *Ricks* distinguishes between a "decision" and an "appeal" or "grievance" with respect to that decision. The opinion further indicates that a decision can be final for purposes of triggering the filing periods even if it may be reversed later. How do you tell what is a "recommendation," as opposed to a "decision," or an "appeal," or a "grievance"? *Ricks* cited International Union of Elec. Workers v. Robbins & Myers, Inc., 429 U.S. 229, 234-35 (1976). There an employee filed a grievance under the governing collective bargaining agreement two days after he was terminated. After pursuing the multi-step grievance procedure, he filed a charge with the EEOC beyond the statutory period. The Court rejected the argument that the termination was "tentative" and "nonfinal" until completion of the grievance procedure. While the parties could have agreed to such a contract, the collective bargaining agreement in question was cast as a "decision," although there was a right to grieve. Cf. Currier v. Radio Free Europe/Radio Liberty, Inc., 159 F.3d 1363 (D.C. Cir. 1998) (termination letter not final when a superior informed plaintiff that decision would not be final until after an investigation).

5. The Supreme Court has rejected any formal doctrine of election of remedies in a Title VII suit, Alexander v. Gardner-Denver Co., 415 U.S. 36 (1974). Indeed, this was one factor underlying *Robbins & Myers:* because the rights under the collective bargaining agreement and under Title VII are independent, plaintiff's pursuit of the grievance procedure should not toll the time to file an EEOC charge. Nevertheless, the practical effect of *Ricks* may be to require such an election: an employee cannot safely await completion of internal procedures before filing with the EEOC. Note, however, that filing a charge could itself prejudice an employee's rights by generating antagonism by his employer. Is the statutory prohibition of retaliation for filing (see Chapter 7) sufficient to prevent this problem?

6. Another question about decision-making arises in hierarchical structures. In large organizations, decisions may effectively be made below the level at which they are formally reached even though they are cast as "recommendations" by the real decision-maker. For example, suppose a board of directors routinely rubber-stamps a president's personnel decisions. Viewed from a corporate law perspective, the board's "decision" may be critical; but viewed pragmatically, the president is the last word. For Title VII purposes, who decides? See Pearson v. Macon-Bibb County Hosp. Auth., 952 F.2d 1274 (11th Cir. 1992).

7. Assuming that the decision point is identified and distinguished from appeals or grievances, the plaintiff must also have "notice" of the employer's decision before the statute starts to run. In discharge cases, this may be relatively easy to ascertain: most workers know when they have been fired. But what about failure to hire cases? What if no rejection letter is ever sent? See Vadie v. Miss. State Univ., 218 F.3d 365 (5th Cir. 2000) (plaintiff could have held a legitimate expectation of being hired until he learned that the last vacancy was filled). Even in cases of current employees it may not be enough for the plaintiff to see the "writing on the wall": someone in authority may have to notify him. Colgan v. Fisher Scientific Co., 935 F.2d 1407 (3d Cir. 1991) (en banc) (negative performance evaluation did not start period running). See also Cada v. Baxter Healthcare Corp., 920 F.2d 446 (7th Cir. 1990).

8. Is the "notice of decision" principle applicable when the true reason for the adverse decision has not been conveyed to the plaintiff? Suppose an employee is discharged for apparently good reasons and one year later discovers facts that lead her to believe the discharge was motivated by racial animus? Does footnote 16 of the *Ricks* opinion help? Is this a question of when the violation occurs or of whether the filing period is tolled?

9. The significance of the *Ricks* Court's holding as to the "occurrence" of a violation obviously depends in large part on how strictly the courts will apply the timely filing requirement.

## b.  Continuing Violations and Tolling the Filing Period

### AMTRACK v. MORGAN
536 U.S. 101 (2002)

Justice THOMAS delivered the opinion of the Court.

Respondent Abner Morgan, Jr., sued petitioner National Railroad Passenger Corporation (Amtrak) under Title VII, alleging that he had been subjected to discrete discriminatory and retaliatory acts and had experienced a racially hostile work environment throughout his employment. Section 2000e-5(e)(1) requires that a Title VII plaintiff file a charge with the Equal Employment Opportunity Commission (EEOC) either 180 or 300 days "after the alleged unlawful employment practice occurred." We consider whether, and under what circumstances, a Title VII plaintiff may file suit on events that fall outside this statutory time period.

The United States Court of Appeals for the Ninth Circuit held that a plaintiff may sue on claims that would ordinarily be time barred so long as they either are "sufficiently related" to incidents that fall within the statutory period or are part of a systematic policy or practice of discrimination that took place, at least in part, within the limitations period. We reverse in part and affirm in part. We hold that the statute precludes recovery for discrete acts of discrimination or retaliation that occur outside the statutory time period. We also hold that consideration of the entire scope of a hostile work environment claim, including behavior alleged outside the statutory time period, is permissible for the purposes of assessing liability, so long as any act contributing to that hostile environment takes place within the statutory time period. The application of equitable doctrines, however, may either limit or toll the time period within which an employee must file a charge.

### I

On February 27, 1995, Abner J. Morgan, Jr., a black male, filed a charge of discrimination and retaliation against Amtrak with the EEOC and cross-filed with the California Department of Fair Employment and Housing. Morgan alleged that during the time period that he worked for Amtrak he was "consistently harassed and disciplined more harshly than other employees on account of his race."[1] . . . While some of the allegedly discriminatory acts about which Morgan complained occurred within 300 days of the time that he filed his charge with the EEOC, many took place prior to that time period. Amtrak filed a motion, arguing, among other things, that it was entitled to summary judgment on all incidents that occurred more than 300 days

---

1. Such discrimination, he alleges, began when the company hired him in August 1990 as an electrician helper, rather than as an electrician. Subsequent alleged racially motivated discriminatory acts included a termination for refusing to follow orders, Amtrak's refusal to allow him to participate in an apprenticeship program, numerous "written counselings" for absenteeism, as well as the use of racial epithets against him by his managers.

before the filing of Morgan's EEOC charge. The District Court granted summary judgment in part to Amtrak, holding that the company could not be liable for conduct occurring before May 3, 1994, because that conduct fell outside of the 300-day filing period. The court employed a test established by the United States Court of Appeals for the Seventh Circuit in Galloway v. General Motors Service Parts Operations, 78 F.3d 1164 (1996): A "plaintiff may not base [the] suit on conduct that occurred outside the statute of limitations unless it would have been unreasonable to expect the plaintiff to sue before the statute ran on that conduct, as in a case in which the conduct could constitute, or be recognized, as actionable harassment only in the light of events that occurred later, within the period of the statute of limitations." The District Court held that "because Morgan believed that he was being discriminated against at the time that all of these acts occurred, it would not be unreasonable to expect that Morgan should have filed an EEOC charge on these acts before the limitations period on these claims ran."

Morgan appealed. The United States Court of Appeals for the Ninth Circuit reversed, relying on its previous articulation of the continuing violation doctrine, which "allows courts to consider conduct that would ordinarily be time barred 'as long as the untimely incidents represent an ongoing unlawful employment practice.'" Contrary to both the Seventh Circuit's test, used by the District Court, and a similar test employed by the Fifth Circuit,[3] the Ninth Circuit held that its precedent "precludes such a notice limitation on the continuing violation doctrine."

In the Ninth Circuit's view, a plaintiff can establish a continuing violation that allows recovery for claims filed outside of the statutory period in one of two ways. First, a plaintiff may show "a series of related acts one or more of which are within the limitations period." Such a "serial violation is established if the evidence indicates that the alleged acts of discrimination occurring prior to the limitations period are sufficiently related to those occurring within the limitations period." The alleged incidents, however, "cannot be isolated, sporadic, or discrete." Second, a plaintiff may establish a continuing violation if he shows "a systematic policy or practice of discrimination that operated, in part, within the limitations period — a systemic violation."

To survive summary judgment under this test, Morgan had to "raise a genuine issue of disputed fact as to 1) the existence of a continuing violation — be it serial or systemic," and 2) the continuation of the violation into the limitations period. Because Morgan alleged three types of Title VII claims, namely, discrimination, hostile environment, and retaliation, the Court of Appeals considered the allegations with respect to each category of claim separately and found that the pre-limitations conduct was sufficiently related to the post-limitations conduct to invoke the continuing violation doctrine for all three. Therefore, "in light of the relatedness of the incidents, [the Court of Appeals found] that Morgan had sufficiently presented a genuine issue of disputed fact as to whether a continuing violation existed." Because the District Court should have allowed events occurring in the pre-limitations period to be "presented to the jury not merely as background information, but also for purposes of liability," the Court of Appeals reversed and remanded for a new trial.

We granted certiorari and now reverse in part and affirm in part.

---

3. The Fifth Circuit employs a multifactor test, which, among other things, takes into account: (1) whether the alleged acts involve the same type of discrimination; (2) whether the incidents are recurring or independent and isolated events; and (3) whether the earlier acts have sufficient permanency to trigger the employee's awareness of and duty to challenge the alleged violation. See Berry v. Board of Supervisors, 715 F.2d 971, 981 (1983).

## II

The Courts of Appeals have taken various approaches to the question whether acts that fall outside of the statutory time period for filing charges set forth in 42 U.S.C. § 2000e-5(e) are actionable under Title VII. While the lower courts have offered reasonable, albeit divergent solutions, none are compelled by the text of the statute. In the context of a request to alter the timely filing requirements of Title VII, this Court has stated that "strict adherence to the procedural requirements specified by the legislature is the best guarantee of evenhanded administration of the law." Mohasco Corp. v. Silver, 447 U.S. 807, 826 (1980). In *Mohasco*, the Court rejected arguments that strict adherence to a similar statutory time restriction[4] for filing a charge was "unfair" or that "a less literal reading of the Act would adequately effectuate the policy of deferring to state agencies." Instead, the Court noted that "by choosing what are obviously quite short deadlines, Congress clearly intended to encourage the prompt processing of all charges of employment discrimination." Similarly here, our most salient source for guidance is the statutory text.

Title 42 U.S.C. § 2000e-5(e)(1) is a charge filing provision that "specifies with precision" the prerequisites that a plaintiff must satisfy before filing suit. Alexander v. Gardner-Denver Co., 415 U.S. 36, 47 (1974). An individual must file a charge within the statutory time period and serve notice upon the person against whom the charge is made. In a State that has an entity with the authority to grant or seek relief with respect to the alleged unlawful practice, an employee who initially files a grievance with that agency must file the charge with the EEOC within 300 days of the employment practice; in all other States, the charge must be filed within 180 days. A claim is time barred if it is not filed within these time limits.

For our purposes, the critical sentence of the charge filing provision is: "A charge under this section shall be filed within one hundred and eighty days *after the alleged unlawful employment practice occurred.*" § 2000e-5(e)(1) (emphasis added). The operative terms are "shall," "after . . . occurred," and "unlawful employment practice." "Shall" makes the act of filing a charge within the specified time period mandatory. See, e.g., Lexecon Inc. v. Milberg Weiss Bershad Hynes & Lerach, 523 U.S. 26, 35 (1998) ("The mandatory 'shall,' . . . normally creates an obligation impervious to judicial discretion"). "Occurred" means that the practice took place or happened in the past.[5] The requirement, therefore, that the charge be filed "after" the practice "occurred" tells us that a litigant has up to 180 or 300 days after the unlawful practice happened to file a charge with the EEOC.

The critical questions, then, are: What constitutes an "unlawful employment practice" and when has that practice "occurred"? Our task is to answer these questions for both discrete discriminatory acts and hostile work environment claims. The answer varies with the practice.

---

4. The Court there considered both the 300-day time limit of 42 U.S.C. § 2000e-5(e) and the requirement of § 2000e-5(c) that, in the case of an unlawful employment practice that occurs in a State that prohibits such practices, no charge may be filed with the EEOC before the expiration of 60 days after proceedings have been commenced in the appropriate state agency unless such proceedings have been earlier terminated.

5. "In the absence of an indication to the contrary, words in a statute are assumed to bear their 'ordinary, contemporary, common meaning.'" Webster's Third New International Dictionary 1561 (1993) defines "occur" as "to present itself: come to pass: take place: HAPPEN." See also Black's Law Dictionary 1080 (6th ed. 1990) (defining "occur" as "to happen; . . . to take place; to arise").

A

We take the easier question first. A discrete retaliatory or discriminatory act "occurred" on the day that it "happened." A party, therefore, must file a charge within either 180 or 300 days of the date of the act or lose the ability to recover for it.

Morgan argues that the statute does not require the filing of a charge within 180 or 300 days of each discrete act, but that the language requires the filing of a charge within the specified number of days after an "unlawful employment practice." "Practice," Morgan contends, connotes an ongoing violation that can endure or recur over a period of time. In Morgan's view, the term "practice" therefore provides a statutory basis for the Ninth Circuit's continuing violation doctrine.[6] This argument is unavailing, however, given that 42 U.S.C. § 2000e-2 explains in great detail the sorts of actions that qualify as "unlawful employment practices" and includes among such practices numerous discrete acts. See, e.g., § 2000e-2(a) ("It shall be an unlawful employment practice for an employer — (1) to fail or refuse to hire or to discharge any individual, or otherwise to discriminate against any individual with respect to his compensation, terms, conditions, or privileges of employment, because of such individual's race, color, religion, sex, or national origin . . ."). There is simply no indication that the term "practice" converts related discrete acts into a single unlawful practice for the purposes of timely filing. Cf. § 2000e-6(a) (providing that the Attorney General may bring a civil action in "pattern or practice" cases).

We have repeatedly interpreted the term "practice" to apply to a discrete act or single "occurrence," even when it has a connection to other acts. For example, in Electrical Workers v. Robbins & Myers, Inc., 429 U.S. 229, 234 (1976), an employee asserted that his complaint was timely filed because the date "the alleged unlawful employment practice occurred" was the date after the conclusion of a grievance arbitration procedure, rather than the earlier date of his discharge. The discharge, he contended, was "tentative" and "nonfinal" until the grievance and arbitration procedure ended. Not so, the Court concluded, because the discriminatory act occurred on the date of discharge — the date that the parties understood the termination to be final. Similarly, in Bazemore v. Friday, 478 U.S. 385 (1986) (per curiam), a pattern-or-practice case, when considering a discriminatory salary structure, the Court noted that although the salary discrimination began prior to the date that the act was actionable under Title VII, "each week's paycheck that delivered less to a black than to a similarly situated white is a wrong actionable under Title VII. . . ."

This Court has also held that discrete acts that fall within the statutory time period do not make timely acts that fall outside the time period. In United Air Lines, Inc. v. Evans, 431 U.S. 553 (1977), United forced Evans to resign after she married because of its policy against married female flight attendants. Although Evans failed to file a timely charge following her initial separation, she nonetheless claimed that United was guilty of a present, continuing violation of Title VII because its seniority system failed to give her credit for her prior service once she was re-hired. The Court disagreed, concluding that "United was entitled to treat [Evans' resignation] as lawful

---

6. Morgan also argues that the EEOC's discussion of continuing violations in its Compliance Manual, which provides that certain serial violations and systemic violations constitute continuing violations that allow relief for untimely events, as well as the positions the EEOC has taken in prior briefs, warrant deference under Chevron U.S.A. Inc. v. Natural Resources Defense Council, Inc., 467 U.S. 837 (1984). But we have held that the EEOC's interpretive guidelines do not receive *Chevron* deference. See EEOC v. Arabian American Oil Co., 499 U.S. 244, 257 (1991). Such interpretations are "'entitled to respect' under our decision in Skidmore v. Swift & Co., 323 U.S. 134, 140 (1944), but only to the extent that those interpretations have the 'power to persuade.'" Christensen v. Harris County, 529 U.S. 576, 587 (2000).

after [she] failed to file a charge of discrimination within the" charge filing period then allowed by the statute. At the same time, however, the Court noted that "it may constitute relevant background evidence in a proceeding in which the status of a current practice is at issue." The emphasis, however, "should not be placed on mere continuity" but on "whether any present *violation* existed." (emphasis in original).

In Delaware State College v. Ricks [reproduced at page 836], the Court evaluated the timeliness of an EEOC complaint filed by a professor who argued that he had been denied academic tenure because of his national origin. Following the decision to deny tenure, the employer offered him a "'terminal'" contract to teach an additional year. Claiming, in effect, a "'continuing violation,'" the professor argued that the time period did not begin to run until his actual termination. The Court rejected this argument: "Mere continuity of employment, without more, is insufficient to prolong the life of a cause of action for employment discrimination." In order for the time period to commence with the discharge, "he should have identified the alleged discriminatory acts that continued until, or occurred at the time of, the actual termination of his employment." He could not use a termination that fell within the limitations period to pull in the time-barred discriminatory act. Nor could a time-barred act justify filing a charge concerning a termination that was not independently discriminatory.

We derive several principles from these cases. First, discrete discriminatory acts are not actionable if time barred, even when they are related to acts alleged in timely filed charges. Each discrete discriminatory act starts a new clock for filing charges alleging that act. The charge, therefore, must be filed within the 180- or 300-day time period after the discrete discriminatory act occurred. The existence of past acts and the employee's prior knowledge of their occurrence, however, does not bar employees from filing charges about related discrete acts so long as the acts are independently discriminatory and charges addressing those acts are themselves timely filed. Nor does the statute bar an employee from using the prior acts as background evidence in support of a timely claim.

As we have held, however, this time period for filing a charge is subject to equitable doctrines such as tolling or estoppel. See Zipes v. Trans World Airlines, Inc., 455 U.S. 385 (1982). Courts may evaluate whether it would be proper to apply such doctrines, although they are to be applied sparingly. See Baldwin County Welcome Center v. Brown, 466 U.S. 147, 152 (1984) (per curiam). ("Procedural requirements established by Congress for gaining access to the federal courts are not to be disregarded by courts out of a vague sympathy for particular litigants.")

The Court of Appeals applied the continuing violations doctrine to what it termed "serial violations," holding that so long as one act falls within the charge filing period, discriminatory and retaliatory acts that are plausibly or sufficiently related to that act may also be considered for the purposes of liability. With respect to this holding, therefore, we reverse.

Discrete acts such as termination, failure to promote, denial of transfer, or refusal to hire are easy to identify. Each incident of discrimination and each retaliatory adverse employment decision constitutes a separate actionable "unlawful employment practice." Morgan can only file a charge to cover discrete acts that "occurred" within the appropriate time period.[7] While Morgan alleged that he suffered from numerous

---

7. Because the Court of Appeals held that the "discrete acts" were actionable as part of a continuing violation, there was no need for it to further contemplate when the time period began to run for each act. The District Court noted that "Morgan believed that he was being discriminated against at the time that

discriminatory and retaliatory acts from the date that he was hired through March 3, 1995, the date that he was fired, only incidents that took place within the timely filing period are actionable. Because Morgan first filed his charge with an appropriate state agency, only those acts that occurred 300 days before February 27, 1995, the day that Morgan filed his charge, are actionable. During that time period, Morgan contends that he was wrongfully suspended and charged with a violation of Amtrak's "Rule L" for insubordination while failing to complete work assigned to him, denied training, and falsely accused of threatening a manager. All prior discrete discriminatory acts are untimely filed and no longer actionable.[9]

### B

Hostile environment claims are different in kind from discrete acts. Their very nature involves repeated conduct. See 1 B. Lindemann & P. Grossman, Employment Discrimination Law 348-349 (3d ed. 1996) (hereinafter Lindemann) ("The repeated nature of the harassment or its intensity constitutes evidence that management knew or should have known of its existence"). The " unlawful employment practice" therefore cannot be said to occur on any particular day. It occurs over a series of days or perhaps years and, in direct contrast to discrete acts, a single act of harassment may not be actionable on its own. See Harris v. Forklift Systems, Inc. [reproduced at page 507] ("As we pointed out in *Meritor* [Savings Bank, FSB v. Vinson,] [reproduced at page 487] 'mere utterance of an . . . epithet which engenders offensive feelings in a employee,' (internal quotation marks omitted) does not sufficiently affect the conditions of employment to implicate Title VII"). Such claims are based on the cumulative affect of individual acts.

"We have repeatedly made clear that although [Title VII] mentions specific employment decisions with immediate consequences, the scope of the prohibition 'is not limited to "economic" or "tangible" discrimination,'" *Harris*, (quoting *Meritor*), and that it covers more than 'terms' and 'conditions' in the narrow contractual sense." Faragher v. Boca Raton [see Burlington Industries v. Ellerth, reproduced at page 516] (quoting Oncale v. Sundowner Offshore Services, Inc. [reproduced at page 492]. As the Court stated in *Harris*, "the phrase 'terms, conditions, or privileges of employment' [of 42 U.S.C. § 2000e-2(a)(1)] evinces a congressional intent 'to strike at the entire spectrum of disparate treatment of men and women' in employment, which includes requiring people to work in a discriminatorily hostile or abusive environment."[10] "Workplace conduct is not measured in isolation. . . ." Clark County School Dist. v. Breeden [reproduced at page 638]. Thus, "when the workplace is permeated with 'discriminatory intimidation, ridicule, and insult,' that is 'sufficiently severe or pervasive to alter the conditions of the victim's employment and create an abusive working environment,' Title VII is violated." *Harris*.

In determining whether an actionable hostile work environment claim exists, we look to "all the circumstances," including "the frequency of the discriminatory

---

all of these acts occurred. . . ." There may be circumstances where it will be difficult to determine when the time period should begin to run. One issue that may arise in such circumstances is whether the time begins to run when the injury occurs as opposed to when the injury reasonably should have been discovered. But this case presents no occasion to resolve that issue.

9. We have no occasion here to consider the timely filing question with respect to "pattern-or-practice" claims brought by private litigants as none are at issue here.

10. Hostile work environment claims based on racial harassment are reviewed under the same standard as those based on sexual harassment. See Faragher v. Boca Raton; Meritor Savings Bank, FSB v. Vinson.

conduct; its severity; whether it is physically threatening or humiliating, or a mere offensive utterance; and whether it unreasonably interferes with an employee's work
performance." To assess whether a court may, for the purposes of determining liability, review all such conduct, including those acts that occur outside the filing period,
we again look to the statute. It provides that a charge must be filed within 180 or 300
days "after the alleged unlawful employment practice occurred." A hostile work environment claim is comprised of a series of separate acts that collectively constitute one
"unlawful employment practice." 42 U.S.C. § 2000e-5(e)(1). The timely filing provision only requires that a Title VII plaintiff file a charge within a certain number of
days after the unlawful practice happened. It does not matter, for purposes of the statute, that some of the component acts of the hostile work environment fall outside the
statutory time period. Provided that an act contributing to the claim occurs within
the filing period, the entire time period of the hostile environment may be considered by a court for the purposes of determining liability.[11]

That act need not, however, be the last act. As long as the employer has engaged in
enough activity to make out an actionable hostile environment claim, an unlawful
employment practice has "occurred," even if it is still occurring. Subsequent events,
however, may still be part of the one hostile work environment claim and a charge
may be filed at a later date and still encompass the whole.

It is precisely because the entire hostile work environment encompasses a single
unlawful employment practice that we do not hold, as have some of the Circuits, that
the plaintiff may not base a suit on individual acts that occurred outside the statute of
limitations unless it would have been unreasonable to expect the plaintiff to sue before the statute ran on such conduct. The statute does not separate individual acts
that are part of the hostile environment claim from the whole for the purposes of
timely filing and liability. And the statute does not contain a requirement that the employee file a charge prior to 180 or 300 days "after" the single unlawful practice "occurred." Given, therefore, that the incidents comprising a hostile work environment
are part of one unlawful employment practice, the employer may be liable for all acts
that are part of this single claim. In order for the charge to be timely, the employee
need only file a charge within 180 or 300 days of any act that is part of the hostile
work environment.

The following scenarios illustrate our point: (1) Acts on days 1-400 create a hostile
work environment. The employee files the charge on day 401. Can the employee recover for that part of the hostile work environment that occurred in the first 100 days?
(2) Acts contribute to a hostile environment on days 1-100 and on day 401, but there
are no acts between days 101-400. Can the act occurring on day 401 pull the other
acts in for the purposes of liability? In truth, all other things being equal, there is little
difference between the two scenarios as a hostile environment constitutes one "unlawful employment practice" and it does not matter whether nothing occurred within
the intervening 301 days so long as each act is part of the whole. Nor, if sufficient activity occurred by day 100 to make out a claim, does it matter that the employee
knows on that day that an actionable claim happened; on day 401 all incidents are
still part of the same claim. On the other hand, if an act on day 401 had no relation to

11. Amtrak argues that recovery for conduct taking place outside the time period for filing a timely
charge should be available only in hostile environment cases where the plaintiff reasonably did not know
such conduct was discriminatory or where the discriminatory nature of such conduct is recognized as discriminatory only in light of later events. The Court of Appeals for the Seventh Circuit adopted this approach in Galloway v. General Motors Service Parts Operations, 78 F.3d 1164 (1996). Although we reject
the test proposed by petitioner, other avenues of relief are available to employers.

the acts between days 1-100, or for some other reason, such as certain intervening action by the employer, was no longer part of the same hostile environment claim, then the employee can not recover for the previous acts, at least not by reference to the day 401 act.

Our conclusion with respect to the incidents that may be considered for the purposes of liability is reinforced by the fact that the statute in no way bars a plaintiff from recovering damages for that portion of the hostile environment that falls outside the period for filing a timely charge. Morgan correctly notes that the timeliness requirement does not dictate the amount of recoverable damages. It is but one in a series of provisions requiring that the parties take action within specified time periods, see, e.g., §§ 2000e-5(b), (c), (d), none of which function as specific limitations on damages.

Explicit limitations on damages are found elsewhere in the statute. Section 1981a(b)(3), for example, details specific limitations on compensatory and punitive damages. Likewise, § 2000e-5(g)(1) allows for recovery of backpay liability for up to two years prior to the filing of the charge. If Congress intended to limit liability to conduct occurring in the period within which the party must file the charge, it seems unlikely that Congress would have allowed recovery for two years of backpay. And the fact that Congress expressly limited the amount of recoverable damages elsewhere to a particular time period indicates that the timely filing provision was not meant to serve as a specific limitation either on damages or the conduct that may be considered for the purposes of one actionable hostile work environment claim.

It also makes little sense to limit the assessment of liability in a hostile work environment claim to the conduct that falls within the 180- or 300-day period given that this time period varies based on whether the violation occurs in a state or political subdivision that has an agency with authority to grant or seek relief. It is important to remember that the statute requires that a Title VII plaintiff must wait 60 days after proceedings have commenced under state or local law to file a charge with the EEOC, unless such proceedings have earlier terminated. § 2000e-5(c). In such circumstances, however, the charge must still be filed within 300 days of the occurrence. See *Mohasco*. The extended time period for parties who first file such charges in a State or locality ensures that employees are neither time barred from later filing their charges with the EEOC nor dissuaded from first filing with a state agency. See id. ("The history identifies only one reason for treating workers in deferral States differently from workers in other States: to give state agencies an opportunity to redress the evil at which the federal legislation was aimed, and to avoid federal intervention unless its need was demonstrated"). Surely, therefore, we cannot import such a limiting principle into the provision where its effect would be to make the reviewable time period for liability dependent upon whether an employee lives in a State that has its own remedial scheme.[12]

Simply put, § 2000e-5(e)(1) is a provision specifying when a charge is timely filed and only has the consequence of limiting liability because filing a timely charge is a prerequisite to having an actionable claim. A court's task is to determine whether the acts about which an employee complains are part of the same actionable hostile work environment practice, and if so, whether any act falls within the statutory time period.

With respect to Morgan's hostile environment claim, the Court of Appeals concluded that "the pre- and post-limitations period incidents involved the same type of employment actions, occurred relatively frequently, and were perpetrated by the

---

12. The same concern is not implicated with discrete acts given that, unlike hostile work environment claims, liability there does not depend upon proof of repeated conduct extending over a period of time.

same managers." To support his claims of a hostile environment, Morgan presented evidence from a number of other employees that managers made racial jokes, performed racially derogatory acts, made negative comments regarding the capacity of blacks to be supervisors, and used various racial epithets. Although many of the acts upon which his claim depends occurred outside the 300 day filing period, we cannot say that they are not part of the same actionable hostile environment claim. On this point, we affirm.

## c

Our holding does not leave employers defenseless against employees who bring hostile work environment claims that extend over long periods of time. Employers have recourse when a plaintiff unreasonably delays filing a charge. As noted in Zipes v. Trans World Airlines, Inc., the filing period is not a jurisdictional prerequisite to filing a Title VII suit. Rather, it is a requirement subject to waiver, estoppel, and equitable tolling "when equity so requires." These equitable doctrines allow us to honor Title VII's remedial purpose "without negating the particular purpose of the filing requirement, to give prompt notice to the employer."

This Court previously noted that despite the procedural protections of the statute "a defendant in a Title VII enforcement action might still be significantly handicapped in making his defense because of an inordinate EEOC delay in filing the action after exhausting its conciliation efforts." Occidental Life Ins. Co. of Cal. v. EEOC, 432 U.S. 355, 373 (1977).

The same is true when the delay is caused by the employee, rather than by the EEOC. Cf. Albemarle Paper Co. v. Moody, 422 U.S. 405, 424 (1975) ("[A] party may not be 'entitled' to relief if its conduct of the cause has improperly and substantially prejudiced the other party"). In such cases, the federal courts have the discretionary power to "to locate 'a just result' in light of the circumstances peculiar to the case."

In addition to other equitable defenses, therefore, an employer may raise a laches defense, which bars a plaintiff from maintaining a suit if he unreasonably delays in filing a suit and as a result harms the defendant. This defense "'requires proof of (1) lack of diligence by the party against whom the defense is asserted, and (2) prejudice to the party asserting the defense.'" Kansas v. Colorado, 514 U.S. 673, 687 (1995) (quoting Costello v. United States, 365 U.S. 265, 282, (1961)). We do not address questions here such as "how — and how much — prejudice must be shown" or "what consequences follow if laches is established." 2 Lindemann 1496-1500.[14] We observe only that employers may raise various defenses in the face of unreasonable and prejudicial delay.

## III

We conclude that a Title VII plaintiff raising claims of discrete discriminatory or retaliatory acts must file his charge within the appropriate time period — 180 or 300

---

14. Nor do we have occasion to consider whether the laches defense may be asserted against the EEOC, even though traditionally the doctrine may not be applied against the sovereign. We note, however, that in *Occidental* there seemed to be general agreement that courts can provide relief to defendants against inordinate delay by the EEOC. See Occidental Life Ins. Co. of Cal. v. EEOC, 432 U.S. 355, 373 (1977). Cf. id., at 383 (REHNQUIST, J., dissenting in part) ("Since here the suit is to recover backpay for an individual that could have brought her own suit, it is impossible to think that the EEOC was suing in the sovereign capacity of the United States").

days — set forth in 42 U.S.C. § 2000e-5(e)(1). A charge alleging a hostile work environment claim, however, will not be time barred so long as all acts which constitute the claim are part of the same unlawful employment practice and at least one act falls within the time period. Neither holding, however, precludes a court from applying equitable doctrines that may toll or limit the time period. . . .

Justice O'CONNOR, with whom The Chief Justice joins, with whom Justice SCALIA and Justice KENNEDY join as to all but Part I, and with whom Justice BREYER joins as to Part I, concurring in part and dissenting in part.

I join Part II-A of the Court's opinion because I agree that Title VII suits based on discrete discriminatory acts are time barred when the plaintiff fails to file a charge with the Equal Employment Opportunity Commission (EEOC) within the 180- or 300-day time period designated in the statute. 42 U.S.C. § 2000e-5(e)(1) (1994 ed.). I dissent from the remainder of the Court's opinion, however, because I believe a similar restriction applies to all types of Title VII suits, including those based on a claim that a plaintiff has been subjected to a hostile work environment.

I

The Court today holds that, for discrete discriminatory acts, § 2000e-5(e)(1) serves as a form of statute of limitations, barring recovery for actions that take place outside the charge-filing period. The Court acknowledges, however, that this limitation period may be adjusted by equitable doctrines. See also Zipes v. Trans World Airlines, Inc., 455 U.S. 385, 393 (1982). Like the Court, I see no need to resolve fully the application of the discovery rule to claims based on discrete discriminatory acts. I believe, however, that some version of the discovery rule applies to discrete-act claims. See 2 B. Lindemann & P. Grossman, Employment Discrimination Law 1349 (3d ed. 1996) ("Although [Supreme Court precedents] seem to establish a relatively simple 'notice' rule as to when discrimination 'occurs' (so as to start the running of the charge-filing period), courts continue to disagree on what the notice must be *of*" (emphasis in original)). In my view, therefore, the charge-filing period precludes recovery based on discrete actions that occurred more than 180 or 300 days after the employee had, or should have had, notice of the discriminatory act.

II

Unlike the Court, I would hold that § 2000e-5(e)(1) serves as a limitations period for all actions brought under Title VII, including those alleging discrimination by being subjected to a hostile working environment. Section 2000e-5(e)(1) provides that a plaintiff must file a charge with the EEOC within 180 or 300 days "after the alleged unlawful employment practice occurred."* It draws no distinction between claims based on discrete acts and claims based on hostile work environments. If a plaintiff fails to file a charge within that time period, liability may not be assessed, and damages must not be awarded, for that part of the hostile environment that occurred outside the charge-filing period.

The Court's conclusion to the contrary is based on a characterization of hostile environment discrimination as composing a single claim based on conduct potentially

---

* This case provides no occasion to determine whether the discovery rule operates in the context of hostile work environment claims.

spanning several years. I agree with this characterization. I disagree, however, with the Court's conclusion that, because of the cumulative nature of the violation, if any conduct forming part of the violation occurs within the charge-filing period, liability can be proved and damages can be collected for the entire hostile environment. Although a hostile environment claim is, by its nature, a general atmosphere of discrimination not completely reducible to particular discriminatory acts, each day the worker is exposed to the hostile environment may still be treated as a separate "occurrence," and claims based on some of those occurrences forfeited. In other words, a hostile environment is a form of discrimination that occurs every day; some of those daily occurrences may be time barred, while others are not.

The Court's treatment of hostile environment claims as constituting a single occurrence leads to results that contradict the policies behind 42 U.S.C. § 2000e-5(e)(1). Consider an employee who has been subjected to a hostile work environment for 10 years. Under the Court's approach, such an employee may, subject only to the uncertain restrictions of equity, sleep on his or her rights for a decade, bringing suit only in year 11 based in part on actions for which a charge could, and should, have been filed many years previously in accordance with the statutory mandate. § 2000e-5(e)(1) ("A charge under this section shall be filed [within 180 or 300 days] after the alleged unlawful employment practice occurred"). Allowing suits based on such remote actions raises all of the problems that statutes of limitations and other similar time limitations are designed to address. . . .

Although the statute's 2-year limitation on backpay partially addresses these concerns, § 2000e-5(g)(1), under the Court's view, liability may still be assessed and other sorts of damages (such as damages for pain and suffering) awarded based on long-past occurrences. An employer asked to defend such stale actions, when a suit challenging them could have been brought in a much more timely manner, may rightly complain of precisely this sort of unjust treatment.

The Court is correct that nothing in § 2000e-5(e)(1) can be read as imposing a cap on damages. But reading § 2000e-5(e)(1) to require that a plaintiff bring an EEOC charge within 180 or 300 days of the time individual incidents comprising a hostile work environment occur or lose the ability to bring suit based on those incidents is not equivalent to transforming it into a damages cap. The limitation is one on liability. The restriction on damages for occurrences too far in the past follows only as an obvious consequence.

Nor, as the Court claims, would reading § 2000e-5(e)(1) as limiting hostile environment claims conflict with Title VII's allowance of backpay liability for a period of up to two years prior to a charge's filing. § 2000e-5(g)(1). Because of the potential adjustments to the charge-filing period based on equitable doctrines, two years of backpay will sometimes be available even under my view. For example, two years of backpay may be available where an employee failed to file a timely charge with the EEOC because his employer deceived him in order to conceal the existence of a discrimination claim.

The Court also argues that it makes "little sense" to base relief on the charge-filing period, since that period varies depending on whether the State or political subdivision where the violation occurs has designated an agency to deal with such claims. The Court concludes that "surely . . . we cannot import such a limiting principle . . . where its effect would be to make the reviewable time period for liability dependent upon whether an employee lives in a State that has its own remedial scheme." But this is precisely the principle the Court has adopted for discrete discriminatory acts — depending on where a plaintiff lives, the time period changes as to which discrete discriminatory actions may be reviewed. The justification for the variation is the same for discrete discriminatory acts as it is for claims based on hostile work environments. The longer time period is intended to give States and other political subdivisions time to review claims themselves, if they have a mechanism for doing so. The same rationale applies to review of the daily occurrences that make up a part of a hostile environment claim.

My approach is also consistent with that taken by the Court in other contexts [citing Klehr v. A. O. Smith Corp., 521 U.S. 179, 189 (1997), involving antitrust and RICO]. I would, therefore, reverse the judgment of the Court of Appeals in its entirety.

## NOTES

1. With respect to the question of when a charge challenging a discriminatory practice must be filed, the *Morgan* Court tells us that "The answer varies with the practice," and seems to divide those practices into three kinds. The first is pattern and practice cases. The second is "discrete" violations. As to those, the violation occurs when it happens, and *Morgan* holds that the fact that there may be a series of violations is irrelevant. Any violation in the series within 180 (300) days of the filing is actionable; any violation more remote in time is not. *Morgan*, therefore, explicitly rejects the many circuit court cases that allowed suit to challenge more remote violations so long as they were part of a series, one act of which occurred within the governing period. E.g., Megwinoff v. Banco Bilbao Vizcaya, 233 F.3d 73, 74 (1st Cir. 2000). In that sense, the decision is employer-friendly.

2. However, *Morgan* carves out an exception from this rule for hostile environment harassment, both racial and sexual, which is the third category. See footnote 10. The lower courts had also recognized continuing violations in such situations, some under the now-discredited "serial violation" rule and others for other reasons. However, some of this authority, most notably the Seventh Circuit's *Galloway* decision cited by the Court, was very restrictive. The *Morgan* opinion clearly rejects that approach, see Boyer v. Cordant Techs., Inc., 2003 U.S. App. LEXIS 628 (10th Cir. Jan. 16, 2003), which permitted suits to challenge remote acts only when "it would have been unreasonable to expect the statute ran, as in a case where the conduct [was] actionable harassment only in light of events which occurred later." Galloway v. Gen. Motors Service Parts Operations, 70 F.3d 1164, 1167 (7th Cir. 1999).

3. Instead, *Morgan* treats hostile environment claims as necessarily subject to a different rule since an environment typically consists of a number of acts that "cannot be said to occur on any particular day." For such claims, the Court apparently believes that a charge is timely if filed within 180 (300) days of a series of acts that, collectively, contaminate the environment, regardless of whether "some of the component acts . . . fall outside the statutory time period." The only requirement (in addition to the collective acts being sufficient to violate the statute) is that "an act contributing to the claim occurs within the period." Thus, the Court has re-invented the "serial violation" rule but only for hostile environment claims. If one act of harassment occurs within the filing period, "the entire time period may be considered by a court for the purposes of determining liability." See also Jensen v. Henderson, 2002 U.S. App. LEXIS 25228, *12 (8th Cir. 2002) ("Only the smallest portion of that 'practice' needs to occur within the limitations period for the claim to be timely."); Shields v. Fort James Corp., 305 F.3d 1280 (11th Cir. 2002) (same).

4. This formulation may portend trouble. May a plaintiff recover damages for, say,

mental distress, for acts long outside the period? Is there a reason Justice Thomas wrote "for purposes of determining liability" rather than simply having said that all such acts are actionable?

5. Further, some of the lower court opinions preceding *Morgan* suggest other difficulties. Although Justice Thomas writes as though all harassment is part of one act, some lower courts deconstructed claims of harassment to exclude prior acts. In Garrison v. Burke, 165 F.3d 565 (7th Cir. 1999), for example, an assault two years prior to later acts of harassment which were timely charged was excluded from consideration as not sufficiently linked to the more recent acts, although the court there did rely in part on the *Galloway* rule. See also Quinn v. Green Tree Credit Corp., 159 F.3d 759, 766 (2d Cir. 1998) ("[T]he acts Quinn alleges to have occurred outside the limitations periods are not continuous in time with one another or with the timely acts that she has alleged; this discontinuity is fatal to Quinn's 'continuing violation' argument.").

6. A more serious problem is simply the *Morgan* Court's analytic scheme. Aside from pattern or practice cases, Justice Thomas's analysis requires all cases to be divided into "discrete" and "contaminated enviroment" violations. But long history has shown that the world is more complicated. One recurrent example is the negative evaluation that has no tangible effects when it is given but several years later results in a discharge. Consider Thomas v. Eastman Kodak, 183 F.3d 38 (1st Cir. 1999), which held that a discriminatory evaluation more than 300 days in the past could be challenged when it was the basis for a later layoff that was itself nondiscriminatory. The test is whether there has been some "tangible effect" from the negative evaluation. See also Colgan v. Fisher Scientific Co., 935 F.2d 1407 (3d Cir. 1991) (en banc) (discriminatory evaluation more than 180 days before discharge may still be actionable when discharge was the result of a later discretionary act relying on evaluation). Of course, under some courts' view, an unfavorable evaluation, by itself, does not constitute an actionable adverse employment action, see Note 8, pages 104-105. Under such a rule, is a nondiscriminatory adverse action based on a prior discriminatory evaluation ever actionable? See Hamilton v. Komatsu Dresser Indus., Inc., 964 F.2d 600 (7th Cir. 1992) (denial of training opportunity was discriminatory action that should have triggered charge, not later layoff that was simply a consequence of such lack of training). What effect *Morgan* will have on this recurrent problem is uncertain.

7. Similarly, in a number of cases, courts have struggled with whether establishing a hiring list (compiled on the basis of results of discriminatory tests) constitutes the violation or whether a violation occurs every time a hiring decision is made on the basis of such a list. E.g., Cox v. City of Memphis, 230 F.3d 199 (6th Cir. 2000) (the promulgation of the list is seen as the discriminatory act: since any hiring was simply *from* the list in a nondiscriminatory fashion, the creation of the list was the discriminatory act challenged, an act of which the plaintiffs had notice when the list was promulgated); Bouman v. Block, 940 F.2d 1211 (9th Cir. 1991) (EEOC charge timely as measured from the date a civil service list expired, as opposed to two years earlier when it was promulgated; because plaintiff placed highly on the list, it was by no means certain that she would not be promoted from it); Cook v. Pan American World Airways, Inc., 771 F.2d 635 (2d Cir. 1985) (continuing violation where charge filed more than 300 days after publication of an arbitration award establishing seniority rights, but less than 300 days from the point at which the employer implemented that award by making assignments from the seniority list). Again, for *Morgan* purposes, is the establishment of the list or the hiring from it the occurrence of the violation?

8. Whatever the limitations of the *Morgan* taxonomy, the opinion attempts to avoid

some of these problems by allowing an escape hatch from its rigid scheme. Citing Zipes v. Trans World Airlines, Inc., 455 U.S. 385 (1982), *Morgan* wrote, "the filing period is not a jurisdictional prerequisite to filing a Title VII suit. Rather, it is a requirement subject to waiver, estoppel, and equitable tolling 'when equity so requires.' These equitable doctrines allow us to honor Title VII's remedial purpose 'without negating the particular purpose of the filing requirement, to give prompt notice to the employer.'" Prior Supreme Court cases, however, provide little guidance.

*Zipes* itself was a class action challenging TWA's grounding of all flight cabin attendants who became mothers. The circuit court had held that most class members' claims were barred for failure to file timely EEOC charges, but the Supreme Court reversed because filing a timely charge "is not a jurisdictional prerequisite"; rather, it is a requirement "that, like a statute of limitations, is subject to waiver, estoppel, and equitable tolling." Id. at 393. But *Zipes* provided little guidance about when tolling or estoppel operated. The actual issue in the case was whether defendants had waived the timely filing requirement by failing to assert it, and the Court remanded for a decision under its new standard.

The only situation in which the Supreme Court has actually held tolling appropriate is when a class action is filed. Crown, Cork & Seal Co. v. Parker, 462 U.S. 345 (1983), held that the filing of a class action tolls the "applicable statute of limitations" for putative class members; thus, class members may use whatever still remains of the statutory time period after class certification is denied. Although *Parker* upheld tolling the 90-day period for filing suit after receipt of an EEOC finding of no reasonable cause, its logic is broad enough to encompass tolling the time period for filing a charge with the EEOC: a worker on whose behalf a class action is brought has no need to file a separate charge of discrimination because the charge can embrace the claims of even nonfiling class members as long as they are within its scope. Thus, even if the action is not certified (or is later decertified), the filing should toll the time for filing a charge with the EEOC. See Andrews v. Orr, 851 F.2d 146 (6th Cir. 1988). See also Armstrong v. Martin Marietta Corp., 93 F.3d 1505 (11th Cir. 1996) (ADEA class action claimants who intend to appeal dismissal of class suit need not file individual lawsuits while awaiting final judgment).

9. The Court has, however, rejected tolling in one situation: the time for filing with the EEOC is not tolled during the pendency of a grievance proceeding. As discussed in *Morgan*, Intl. Union of Elec. Workers v. Robbins & Myers, 429 U.S. 229 (1976), stressed that the rights involved in the two proceedings were independent ones. On that basis, *Robbins & Myers* distinguished Burnett v. New York Central R.R. Co., 380 U.S. 424 (1965), a Federal Employers' Liability Act action in which the plaintiff had asserted his claim in a state court where venue did not lie. *Burnett* held that the state filing tolled the limitations period, so the plaintiff's subsequent federal court claim was not barred. In contrast, in *Robbins & Myers*, the plaintiff's grievance proceeding "was not asserting the same statutory claim in a different forum, nor giving notice to respondent of that statutory claim, but was asserting an independent claim based on a contract right." 429 U.S. at 238. *Robbins & Myers* might also be read to bar tolling through resort not merely to grievance procedures but also to other alternative avenues of attack on employment discrimination. However, some cases hold that filing with another federal agency, such as the Department of Labor or the Office of Federal Contract Compliance Programs, is the "equitable equivalent" of an EEOC filing. E.g., Morgan v. Washington Mfg. Co., 660 F.2d 710 (6th Cir. 1981). Contra, Walker v. Novo Nordisk Pharm. Indus., No. 99-2015, 2000 U.S. App. LEXIS 17848 (4th Cir. 2000) (filing with a OFCCP did not toll period for filing with EEOC).

10. One possibility, raised in footnote 7 of *Morgan* is a "discovery" rule under Title VII, although the majority does not expressly approve it. The Supreme Court had earlier also reserved the issue in Mohasco Corp. v. Silver, 447 U.S. 807, 818 n.22 (1979). But Justices O'Connor, Rehnquist, and Breyer in *Morgan* stated that "some version of the discovery rule applies to discrete-act claims." Prior to *Morgan*, the lower courts had generally rejected such an approach, e.g., Amini v. Oberlin Coll., 259 F.3d 493 (6th Cir. 2001); Hamilton v. 1st Source Bank, 895 F.2d 159 (4th Cir. 1990) (en banc) (ADEA), but *Morgan* requires revisiting that issue. Under such an approach, notice of an adverse decision would trigger the filing period but that period would be tolled until the employee discovered, or reasonably should have discovered, that the action was discriminatory. Since much discrimination is not overt, a robust discovery rule might be far more plaintiff-friendly than many articulations of the continuing violation theory.

11. More generally, the Court's statement that "The application of equitable doctrines, however, may either limit or toll the time period within which an employee must file a charge" suggests resort to lower courts' opinions. Prior to *Morgan*, the lower courts had often mitigated the rigors of strict adherence to time limits, although they used a variety of different nomenclatures and tests. For example, employers were estopped to assert untimeliness if they engaged in certain wrongful conduct, such as "fraudulent concealment" of the discrimination. E.g., Scheerer v. Rose State Coll., 950 F.2d 661 (10th Cir. 1991); Augst v. Westinghouse Elec. Corp., 937 F.2d 1216 (7th Cir. 1991). See also Pearson v. Macon-Bibb County Hosp. Auth., 952 F.2d 1274 (11th Cir. 1992). Cf. Bishop v. Gainer, 272 F.3d 1009 (7th Cir. 2001) (plaintiffs not entitled to tolling where defendants did not fraudulently conceal information or mislead the plaintiffs); Bennett v. Quark, Inc., 258 F.3d 1220 (10th Cir. 2001) (since plaintiff failed to prove that defendant actively concealed the discrimination, tolling was not appropriate).

The filing period was also sometimes tolled when the employer failed to post antidiscrimination notices required by the statutes. Some cases toll during the entire period the notices are not posted, others toll only until the plaintiff learns of his statutory rights from any source, and still others seem to toll only when the employer intends to mislead by failing to post. See generally Jim Beall, Note, The Charge-Filing Requirement of the Age Discrimination in Employment Act: Accrual and Equitable Modification, 91 Mich. L. Rev. 798 (1993).

The time period was also tolled for reasons having nothing to do with defendant's fault, as when the EEOC refused to accept a charge, e.g., Schroeder v. Copley Newspapers, 879 F.2d 266 (7th Cir. 1989), or otherwise misled the plaintiff. Lawrence v. Cooper Communities, Inc., 132 F.3d 447 (8th Cir. 1998); Schlueter v. Anheuser-Busch, Inc., 132 F.3d 455 (8th Cir. 1998); Early v. Bankers Life & Casualty Co., 959 F.2d 75 (7th Cir. 1992); but see Ramirez v. City of San Antonio, 312 F.3d 178 (5th Cir. 2002); Conway v. Control Data Corp., 955 F.2d 358 (5th Cir. 1992). In such cases, courts tended to treat the charge as filed when it was originally presented to the Commission. Laquaglia v. Rio Hotel & Casino, Inc., 186 F.3d 1172 (9th Cir. 1999). One case even tolled the time period when the plaintiff is misled by her own attorney. Seitzinger v. Reading Hosp. & Med. Ctr., 165 F.3d 236 (3d Cir. 1999).

Equitable tolling also has been found for plaintiff's mental incapacity. Stoll v. Runyon, 165 F.3d 1238 (9th Cir. 1999) (time to file charge tolled even when plaintiff retained counsel, because wrongful conduct including severe physical abuse by defendant and extraordinary circumstances of plaintiff proven). But see Boos v. Runyon, 201 F.3d 178 (2d Cir. 2000) (equitable tolling would not apply where plaintiff's claims of paranoia, panic attacks, and depression were vague and insufficient); Santa Maria v. Pacific Bell, 202 F.3d 1170 (9th Cir. 2000) (finding that, even though plaintiff suffered from depression, no equitable tolling because the plaintiff knew or should have known that a possible disability discrimination claim existed); Hood v. Sears Roebuck & Co., 168 F.3d 231 (5th Cir. 1999) (untimely filing not excused for mental incapacity when plaintiff had retained counsel within the statute of limitations); Smith-Haynie v. District of Columbia, 155 F.3d 575 (D.C. Cir. 1998) (equitable tolling denied because plaintiff failed to produce adequate support for her "non compos mentis" claim).

But courts have rejected seemingly appealing bases for tolling. For example, the Seventh Circuit recently concluded that threatened employer retaliation for filing a charge would not be a basis for tolling. Beckel v. Wal-Mart Assocs., 301 F.3d 621, 624 (7th Cir. 2002), wrote:

> Even if there were admissible evidence that Wal-Mart had threatened the plaintiff with firing her if she sued, this would not make out a defense of equitable estoppel. Such a threat would be a form of anticipatory retaliation, actionable as retaliation under Title VII. Rather than deterring a reasonable person from suing, it would increase her incentive to sue by giving her a second claim, in this case a claim for retaliation on top of her original claim of sexual harassment. To allow the use of retaliation as a basis for extending the statute of limitations would not only distort the doctrine of equitable estoppel but circumvent the limitations that Title VII imposes on suits for retaliation, including the statute of limitations, which the plaintiff's argument implies never runs on such a suit.

12. *Morgan* took care to suggest that equitable doctrines were not one-sidedly applied. The last portion of the opinion is an invitation to the lower courts to look to laches to limit potential unfairness to employers of the extensive liability potential created for hostile environment claims. It may be that future decisions like Garrison v. Burke and Quinn v. Green Tree Credit Corp., see Note 5, can reach the same results not by finding that earlier acts were unconnected with timely-charged discrimination but rather by finding plaintiff's recovery limited by laches. That may, in fact, be the reason Justice Thomas wrote of considering older acts "for purposes of determining liability" rather than simply having said that all such acts are actionable. The Court did, however, stress the traditional elements of laches — both unreasonable delays by plaintiff and resulting prejudice.

13. Four members of the Court — O'Connor, Rehnquist, Scalia, and Kennedy — argued that there should be no distinction between discrete-act claims and hostile environment claims (although, as noted, they would apply some version of a discovery rule to all claims). Do you agree? Given the two-year limit on backpay and the possibility of laches, is potential liability of employers for old claims a serious problem?

14. Recall that, with respect to the question of when a charge challenging a discriminatory practice must be filed, *Morgan* said, "The answer varies with the practice," and divided those practices into three kinds. *Morgan*, however, analyzed only the first two — discrete violations and harassment claims. The third kind — "pattern-or-practice claims brought by private litigants" — was not addressed. See footnote 9. Prior to *Morgan*, the Court had encountered systemic claims three times. The first decision was United Air Lines, Inc. v. Evans, 431 U.S. 553 (1977), where plaintiff had been forced to resign in 1968 because she got married. United's no marriage policy was later invalidated in a suit to which Ms. Evans was not a party, and she applied and was rehired in 1972. United, however, refused to credit her with seniority she had accrued before being discharged. The plaintiff's charge was not filed until more than

a year after she was rehired as a new employee. The Court found no actionable violation. Plaintiff's original discharge had not been timely challenged, nor had United's action in rehiring her without seniority credit. As for the seniority system, there was no claim that it, as such, was discriminatory. All employees — male and female — hired between 1968 and 1972 had the same advantage over plaintiff. Nor was there any allegation "that United's seniority system treats existing female employees differently from existing male employees, or that the failure to credit prior service differentiates in any way between prior service by males and prior service by females." Id. at 558. While the seniority system did give present effect to a past act of discrimination,

> . . . United was entitled to treat that past act as lawful after respondent failed to file a charge of discrimination within the [time] allowed by § 706(d). A discriminatory act which is not made the basis for a timely charge is the legal equivalent of a discriminatory act which occurred before the statute was passed. It may constitute relevant background evidence in a proceeding in which the status of a current practice is at issue, but separately considered, it is merely an unfortunate event in history which has no present legal consequences.

In short, as to the conduct that was a violation, Evans had not filed a timely charge. As to the conduct that still affected her, there was no violation.

15. Suppose Evans had attacked the seniority system itself as intentionally discriminatory. That is, suppose she claimed that it was purposely structured to discriminate against women. Would a charge be timely so long as the system was in effect? In Lorance v. AT&T Technologies, Inc., 490 U.S. 900 (1989), plaintiffs challenged a 1979 collective bargaining agreement that altered a prior method of calculating seniority. While the change had no immediate effect on them, plaintiffs' lowered seniority later caused them to be demoted. As measured from their demotions, their charge was timely; as measured from 1979, when the seniority system was modified, it was time barred. Although plaintiffs claimed that the 1979 change resulted from an intent to discriminate against women, the Supreme Court held the charge untimely. *Ricks* had established that the violation occurs when the discriminatory decision is made, not when its effects are felt. As in *Evans*, the plaintiffs could not complain of a continuing violation. The Court struck a balance between time limitations and the "special treatment" of seniority systems under § 703(h):

> This "special treatment" strikes a balance between the interests of those protected against discrimination by Title VII and those who work — perhaps for many years — in reliance upon the validity of a facially lawful seniority system. There is no doubt, of course, that a facially discriminatory seniority system (one that treats similarly situated employees differently) can be challenged at any time. . . . But allowing a facially neutral system to be challenged, and entitlements under it to be altered, many years after its adoption would disrupt those valid reliance interests that § 703(h) was meant to protect.

Id. at 911-12. However, the Civil Rights Act of 1991 overruled *Lorance*. As amended, § 706(e)(2) of Title VII provides:

> For purposes of this section, an unlawful employment practice occurs, with respect to a seniority system that has been adopted for an intentionally discriminatory purpose in violation of this title (whether or not that discriminatory purpose is apparent on the face of the seniority provision), when the seniority system is adopted, when an individual becomes subject to the seniority system, or when a person aggrieved is injured by the application of the seniority system or provision of the system.

Neither *Lorance* nor the statutory amendment was mentioned in *Morgan*. Is that because the Court was focusing only on discrete violations, not systemic ones?

16. The law, then, is relatively clear for one kind of systemic violation — discriminatory seniority systems. *Lorance* held that systems discriminatory on their face could be challenged "at any time," and the statute basically extended that rule to systems that, while facially neutral, were the result of discriminatory motivation. Further, presumably, any systemic treatment violation that was discriminatory on its face (e.g., a mandatory retirement age or a gender requirement for a position) could also be challenged at any time under *Lorance* itself.

17. However, the statutory amendment was limited to seniority systems. Suppose an employer adopts a facially neutral policy for discriminatory reasons, for example, a residency requirement. From a systemic disparate treatment perspective, can this be challenged at any time it prevents someone from being hired? Or must a charge be filed within 180/300 days of the adoption of the policy? *Lorance* points toward the latter rule, but the Court there did stress the "special treatment" of seniority systems. Further, applying the time limitation in this way might effectively foreclose attack since many prospective plaintiffs would not even be aware of the policy until they applied for a position. Finally, while the 1991 amendment does not technically apply beyond the seniority context, Congress plainly wanted to avoid, even in the seniority area where current employees may have relied on a system, the unfairness of perpetuating discriminatory systems. In short, perhaps the new statute should prompt the Court to reconsider its entire approach. In fact, the Sponsors' Interpretive Memorandum states: "This legislation should be interpreted as disapproving the extension of [*Lorance*] to contexts outside of seniority systems." 137 Cong. Rec. S15,484 (daily ed. Oct. 30, 1991). Would Justice Scalia, who wrote *Lorance*, find such legislative history persuasive?

18. With respect to systemic discrimination, *Morgan* did cite Bazemore v. Friday, 478 U.S. 385 (1986), which it described as "a pattern-or-practice case [involving] a discriminatory salary structure." *Bazemore* had held that the North Carolina Agricultural Extension Service had a duty to eradicate salary disparities between white and black workers even though those disparities originated prior to the effective date of Title VII. Before 1965, the Service was segregated into a white branch and a "Negro branch." In 1965, the state merged the two branches, but this merger did not eliminate salary disparities resulting from the segregated branches paying black employees less than white employees. These pay disparities continued after the merger and after Title VII became applicable in 1972.

> The error of the Court of Appeals with respect to salary disparities created prior to 1972 and perpetuated thereafter is too obvious to warrant extended discussion: that the Extension Service discriminated with respect to salaries prior to the time it was covered by Title VII does not excuse perpetuating that discrimination after the Extension Service became covered by Title VII. To hold otherwise would have the effect of exempting from liability those employers who were historically the greatest offenders of the rights of blacks. A pattern or practice that would have constituted a violation of Title VII, but for the fact that the statute had not yet become effective, became a violation upon Title VII's effective date, and to the extent an employer continued to engage in that act or practice, he is liable under that statute. While recovery may not be permitted for pre-1972 acts of discrimination, to the extent that this discrimination was perpetuated after 1972, liability may be imposed.
>
> Each week's pay check that delivers less to a black than to a similarly situated white is a wrong actionable under Title VII, regardless of the fact that this pattern was begun

prior to the effective date of Title VII. The Court of Appeals plainly erred in holding that the pre-Act discriminatory difference in salaries did not have to be eliminated.

Id. at 395-96. The lower courts have read *Bazemore* to hold that, in compensation cases, each paycheck constitutes a violation rather than the initial setting of the discriminatory salary. E.g., Goodwin v. GMC, 275 F.3d 1005 (10th Cir. 2002); Cardenas v. Massey, 269 F.3d 251 (3d Cir. 2001); Anderson v. Zubieta, 180 F.3d 329 (D.C. Cir. 1999); Ashley v. Boyle's Famous Corned Beef Co., 66 F.3d 164 (8th Cir. 1995) (en banc) (Title VII and EPA); Brinkley-Obu v. Hughes Training, Inc., 36 F.3d 336 (4th Cir. 1994) (Title VII and EPA); but see Carter v. West Publg. Co., 225 F.3d 1258 (11th Cir. 2000) (payment of dividends pursuant to a discriminatory employee incentive stock program not a continuing violation); Dasgupta v. Univ. of Wisconsin Bd. of Regents, 121 F.3d 1138 (7th Cir. 1997) ("an untimely Title VII suit cannot be revived by pointing to effects within the limitations period of unlawful acts that occurred earlier").

19. But isn't a present paycheck simply the result of a past discriminatory decision to set salary on the basis of race? How can *Bazemore* be consistent with *Ricks*? The *Ricks* "notice of decision" as applied to salary discrimination would seem to require measuring the violation from when the salary was established, not when it was paid. To illustrate, suppose two employees are hired on five-year contracts in 2000; the black, though equal or superior to the white in all respects, is paid $5,000 a year less. Doesn't *Ricks* require that the statutory time limits begin running at the time that the employee is notified of the decision (although *Morgan* might toll the period if the black did not have reason to believe that she was a victim of discrimination, for example, if she did not know the white employee's salary)? The *Bazemore* Court did not mention *Ricks*, but reconciled *Evans* by describing "the present salary structure" as "illegal if it is a mere continuation of the pre-1965 discriminatory pay structure." Id. at 396-97 n.6. *Morgan* cited both *Bazemore* and *Ricks* approvingly. The most obvious synthesis, then, is that *Bazemore* involved a systemic disparate treatment violation and *Ricks* an individual disparate treatment violation. Cf. Ameritech Benefit Plan Comm. v. Communications Workers of Am., 220 F.3d 814 (7th Cir. 2000) (recognizing a very subtle difference between *Evans* and *Bazemore*, but holding that a benefit plan that did not accord service credit to those who had taken maternity leave prior to passage of the Pregnancy Discrimination Act was on the *Evans* side of the line).

20. Systemic disparate treatment is, by definition, continuing. If an employer has a practice of not hiring blacks, a charge should be timely during the entire period that this practice operates, subject to the caveat that particular plaintiffs may not be hurt by the practice, for example, if there were no openings at the time they applied. For example, Courtney v. La Salle Univ., 124 F.3d 499 (3d Cir. 1997), held that a long-established mandatory retirement policy could still be challenged by a charge filed within 300 days of the policy's application to a particular professor, although the court did stress that the policy was facially discriminatory. Similar results have been reached, however, where a pattern or practice existed without a facially discriminatory policy. Alexander v. Local 496, Laborer's Intl. Union, 177 F.3d 394 (6th Cir. 1999) (Title VII); accord EEOC v. Local 350, Plumbers and Pipefitters, 982 F.2d 1305 (9th Cir. 1992) (ADEA violation persists as long as a union continued to refuse to refer retired plumbers for employment).

21. Another possible way to explain *Bazemore* is that it was a disparate impact case. While the original low salaries for blacks were intentional, their continuation may constitute a facially neutral practice with a disparate impact, rather than intentional

discrimination. In such cases, perhaps the violation occurs whenever the impact is felt. Indeed, a passage from *Lorance* is suggestive of this view. In addressing plaintiffs' claim, the Court wrote:

> [An alternative theory] would view § 703(h) as merely providing an affirmative defense to a cause of action brought under § 703(a)(2), rather than as making intentional discrimination an element of any Title VII action challenging a seniority system. The availability of this affirmative defense would not alter the fact that the claim asserted is one of discriminatory impact under § 703(a)(2), *causing the statute of limitations to run from the time that impact is felt.* As an original matter this is a plausible, and perhaps even the most natural, reading of § 703(h). . . . But such an interpretation of § 703(h) is foreclosed by our cases, which treat the proof of discriminatory intent as a necessary element of Title VII actions challenging seniority systems. . . .

490 U.S. at 908-09 (emphasis added). Is the rule that impact cases are continuing violations and treatment cases are not?

22. Cases challenging the disparate impact of particular practices seem to call out for continuing violation analysis. Suppose a female applied for a job in 1993 and was denied it on the grounds that she was shorter than the employer's height minimum, which would not survive disparate impact attack; she then waited until 2003 and filed a charge with the EEOC upon which she now sues. At first glance, the charge is untimely; but suppose further that plaintiff can prove that during the entire ten years the defendant continued to use the same minimum. Had plaintiff applied to fill a vacancy during that period, she would have been again excluded on the basis of the continuing policy of utilizing the discriminatory requirement. She would then have been able to timely file with the Commission within 180 (300) days of the second denial. In such a context, requiring a plaintiff to apply again is an exercise in futility: what is at stake is a continuing policy that would render timely any charge filed by plaintiff no more than 180 (300) days after its discontinuance. Fielder v. UAL Corp., 218 F.3d 973 (9th Cir. 2000) (to be timely, a charge filed by plaintiff must be filed within 180 (300) days after the discontinuance of such policies); see also Phillips v. Cohen, No. 99-4057, 2001 U.S. App. LEXIS 1081 (6th Cir. 2001); Harris v. City of New York, 186 F.3d 243, 250 (2d Cir. 1999). The time of the filing should appropriately influence the relief available to the plaintiff. Certainly, it will mark the time for computing the two-year limitation on backpay and might even prevent the award of any monetary relief if, say, the absence of job openings means that the policy was not causally related to plaintiff's harm during a particular time period. Nevertheless, the time of filing ought not to affect defendant's susceptibility to suit for a persisting illegality at the instance of one who has a real interest in the employment in question. Do you agree? Can one who does nothing for ten years be said to have a "real interest" in the employment? See Douglas v. Cal. Dept. of Youth Auth., 271 F.3d 812, 824 (9th Cir. 2001).

23. It has been argued that the continuing violation concept is implicit in the statute. Title VII not only provides the 180-day (300-day) period for filing with the EEOC, but also establishes a two-year limitation on backpay liability. § 706(g), 42 U.S.C. § 2000e-5(g). By allowing plaintiffs to recover backpay prior to the filing period, Congress must have envisioned continuing remediable violations that existed prior to the running of the period. For example, if plaintiff were paid a discriminatory wage rate beginning on January 1, 1998, but did not file with the EEOC until January 1, 2000, a continuing violation theory might permit recovery of backpay for the entire period. Absent a continuing violation, the application of the two-year backpay

limitation to a private suit would be meaningless: if only discriminatory acts less than 180 days old are compensable through backpay (a proposition implicit in any argument that denies the continuing violation notion), the possibility of obtaining backpay for discriminatory acts more than six months, but less than two years, old is eliminated. See Sabree v. United Bhd. of Carpenters, Local 33, 921 F.2d 396 (1st Cir. 1990). Contra, Douglas A. Laycock, Continuing Violations, Disparate Impact in Compensation and Other Title VII Issues, 49 Law & Contemp. Probs. 53, 58 (Autumn 1986). The *Morgan* majority seems to accept this analysis, but limits its application to the harassment situation. Does this limitation make sense? It is, of course, clear that Congress did not have harassment in mind when it enacted the two-year limitation.

## C.  PRIVATE ENFORCEMENT: FILING SUIT

While Title VII suits can be filed in either federal or state court, resort to the EEOC is a prerequisite to any such action. The ADA adopts Title VII procedures, and the ADEA has been brought increasingly into line with Title VII law.* Under all three statutes, then, a timely charge of discrimination must be filed with the Commission before suit can be brought to vindicate statutory rights. Contrary to normal administrative law principles, however, exhaustion of agency remedies is not required, reflecting a congressional decision not to subject private plaintiffs to the long delays that have always plagued the Commission's charge processing. Nevertheless, it is still desirable that charging parties willing to tolerate delay be permitted to exhaust EEOC processes because a court action might be thereby avoided through the agency's conciliation efforts.

Three basic principles have evolved that give the Commission the opportunity to act while safeguarding the rights of discriminatees to prompt judicial relief. First, a charging party must usually wait a minimum of 180 days from filing with the Commission before bringing suit unless EEOC procedures are terminated earlier.† Mechanically, this is achieved by requiring a "right-to-sue" letter from the Commission as a condition for maintaining an action; the charging party may demand the suit letter from the EEOC once 180 days have passed. Upon receipt of the letter, the charging party has 90 days to file a court suit, in default of which she is barred from bringing an action based on that charge.

Second, the charging party may elect to permit the EEOC's procedures to continue after the 180-day period, but she retains the power to demand a right-to-sue

---

*One remaining exception is that a right-to-sue letter from the EEOC is not a prerequisite for an ADEA suit. Julian v. City of Houston, 314 F.3d 721 (5th Cir. 2002). While the 90-day period for suit does govern when the EEOC sends such a letter, 29 U.S.C.S. §626 (2003), the ADEA does not require an agency letter as a condition of suit.

†The EEOC has long had a policy of terminating its proceedings upon the charging party's request, 29 C.F.R. 91601.28(a)(2) (1999), thus permitting suit to be brought immediately. This practice was recently struck down by one circuit. Martini v. Fed. Natl. Mortgage Assn., 178 F.3d 1336 (D.C. Cir. 1999). Contra, Walker v. UPS, 240 F.3d 1268 (10th Cir. 2001); Sims v. Trus Joist McMillian, 22 F.3d 1059 (11th Cir. 1994); Brown v. Puget Sound Elec. Apprenticeship & Training Trust, 732 F.2d 726 (9th Cir. 1984). See generally Robert A. Kearney, Who's "In Charge" at the EEOC?, 50 Drake L. Rev. 1 (2001); Vaseem S. Hadi, Comment, Ending the 180 Day Waiting Game: An Examination of the Courts' Duty to Short-circuit the EEOC Backlog through the Power of Judicial Review, 27 U. Dayton L. Rev. 53 (2001).

letter at any time. There is no specific time limit within which the EEOC must act, and the agency sometimes takes years to finish its proceedings. The charging party can generally allow the Commission to continue to process the charge indefinitely while retaining the power to demand a right-to-sue letter at any time. There have, however, been cases holding that the charging party's decision to permit the EEOC to complete its charge processing may result in laches barring the suit or at least limiting defendant's back pay liability. E.g., Kamberos v. GTE Automatic Elec., Inc., 603 F.2d 598 (7th Cir. 1979) (deduction from the backpay award in the amount attributable to plaintiff's delay from 180 days after filing an EEOC charge to the time she requested a right-to-sue letter). In National R.R. Passenger Corp. v. Morgan, reproduced at page 842, the Court clearly indicated a role for laches in private suits. It wrote: "In addition to other equitable defenses, therefore, an employer may raise a laches defense, which bars a plaintiff from maintaining a suit if he unreasonably delays in filing a suit and as a result harms the defendant."

As traditionally applied, one element of laches is plaintiff's unreasonable delay, and permitting the EEOC to continue processing a charge after 180 days scarcely seems unreasonable as a matter of law. The better approach was taken in Rozen v. District of Columbia, 702 F.2d 1202 (D.C. Cir. 1983), where the court found no laches in a 21-month delay between a "no reasonable cause" determination by EEOC and the issuance of a right-to-sue letter: the charging party had a right to rely on the government's representation that the letter would be issued. Cf. Brown-Mitchell v. Kansas City Power & Light Co., 267 F.3d 825 (8th Cir. 2001) (a six-year delay in bringing suit is "unreasonable" and justifies dismissal); Garrett v. Gen. Motors Corp., 844 F.2d 559 (8th Cir. 1988) (more than 14 years sufficient for laches). Even assuming unreasonable delay can be established, the second element of laches is prejudice to the defendant. The *Rozen* court held that any prejudice to the defendant from loss of records was its own fault because it destroyed records in violation of EEOC regulations. Although other bases for prejudice will undoubtedly be asserted, the unavailability of witnesses has been a key factor so far in cases barring or limiting suit on laches grounds. E.g., Jeffries v. Chicago Trans. Auth., 770 F.2d 676 (7th Cir. 1985); Bernard v. Gulf Oil Co., 596 F.2d 1249 (5th Cir. 1979). See generally Ellen N. Derrig, Note, The Doctrine of Laches as a Defense to Private Plaintiff Title VII Employment Discrimination Claims, 11 W. New Eng. L. Rev. 235 (1989).

Third, if the charging party permits the agency to process the charge to conclusion, the EEOC will either (1) find no reasonable cause to believe a violation has occurred and issue a notice of dismissal; or (2) find reasonable cause, attempt conciliation, and, if that fails to resolve the matter and the Commission does not file suit itself, ultimately issue a right-to-sue letter. In either case, the charging party must file suit within 90 days of the issuance of the notice of dismissal or the suit letter, on pain of forfeiting all power to sue on the basis of the subject charge. Any action commenced without either a right-to-sue letter or a notice of charge dismissal will be dismissed by the court unless a suit letter has been issued in the interim.

Several issues have arisen under these three principles. The statute specifies that "within 90 days after the giving of such notice [by the EEOC], a civil action may be brought against the respondent named in the charge." 42 U.S.C.S. § 2000e-5 (2003).* In defining the starting point, the courts have held that "receipt" of the right-to-sue

---

* Where a state or local government is concerned, Title VII anticipates that the Attorney General will issue the right-to-sue letter. 42 U.S.C.S. § 2000e-5(f)(1) (2003). Nevertheless, a letter issued by the EEOC in such cases has been found sufficient. Stewart v. Oklahoma, 292 F.3d 1257 (10th Cir. 2002).

letter is the critical point, but what constitutes receipt has itself raised questions. See Threadgill v. Moore U.S.A. Inc., 269 F.3d 848 (7th Cir. 2001) (actual receipt of right-to-sue letter by plaintiff starts 90-day period regardless of whether attorney has notice); Jackson v. Contl. Cargo-Denver, 183 F.3d 1186 (10th Cir. 1999) (actual receipt of letter necessary); Houston v. Sidley & Austin, 185 F.3d 837 (7th Cir. 1999) (actual receipt of letter necessary); Johnson-Brown v. Wayne State Univ., No. 98-1001, 1999 U.S. App. LEXIS 4751 (6th Cir. 1999) (attempted delivery of letter sufficient to constitute receipt); Bobbitt v. Freeman Cos., 268 F.3d 535 (7th Cir. 2001) (an employee's failure to pick up certified mail from the EEOC is "patently irresponsible" and thus her claim is time-barred); Franks v. Bowman Transp. Co., 495 F.2d 398 (5th Cir. 1974) (receipt of certified letter by a nine-year-old nephew did not begin statutory period when the nephew lost the letter before it was given to the charging party), rev'd on other grounds, 424 U.S. 747 (1976). However, receipt by the charging party's attorney of record also suffices. Irwin v. Veterans Admin., 498 U.S. 89 (1990). But see Seitzinger v. Reading Hosp. & Med. Ctr., 165 F.3d 236 (3d Cir. 1999) (more than "garden variety" attorney mistakes may justify tolling). And one court indicated that oral notice by the EEOC might start the 90-day period running. Ebbert v. Daimler-Chrysler Corp., 2003 U.S. App. LEXIS 2082 (3d Cir. Feb. 4, 2003).

In Baldwin County Welcome Center v. Brown, 466 U.S. 147, 148 (1984), the Court cited Fed. R. Civ. P. 6(e) as settling the "presumed" date of receipt as being three days after the letter was mailed. That rule provides: "Whenever a party has the right or is required to do some act or take some proceedings within a prescribed period after the service of a notice or other paper upon the party and the notice or paper is served upon the party by mail, 3 days shall be added to the prescribed period." Some circuit courts have read this to add three days to the date of mailing, unless there is proof of a longer time. Nguyen v. Inova Alexandria Hosp., No. 98-2215, 1999 U.S. App. LEXIS 17978 (4th Cir. 1999); Sherlock v. Montefiore Med. Ctr., 84 F.3d 522 (2d Cir. 1996); Jarrett v. US Sprint Communications Co., 22 F.3d 256 (10th Cir. 1994). One circuit applies a five-day presumption of receipt of a right-to-sue letter sent by certified mail unless the plaintiff proves receipt occurred later. Graham-Humphreys v. Memphis Brooks Museum of Art, Inc., 209 F.3d 552 (6th Cir. 2000). Another suggests a seven-day presumption. Taylor v. Books A Million, Inc., 296 F.3d 376 (5th Cir. 2002).

Once the starting point is established, filing a complaint is normally necessary to satisfy the 90-day rule. See Baldwin County, 466 U.S. 147. However, the Federal Rules are relatively permissive, and something less than a formal complaint may satisfy them as long as the filing gives notice of the factual basis of the discrimination claim. Page v. Ark. Dept. of Corr., 222 F.3d 453 (8th Cir. 2000) (letter and attachment sufficient); Judkins v. Beech Aircraft Corp., 745 F.2d 1330 (11th Cir. 1984) (EEOC charge plus right-to-sue letter sufficed). In these cases, usually the plaintiff is seeking assistance in either filing the complaint or in appointment of counsel.

A second issue is whether satisfying the 90-day time limit is a jurisdictional prerequisite to suit. Several courts so held prior to the Supreme Court's decision in Zipes v. Trans World Airlines, 455 U.S. 147 (1984), holding that the time limitations for filing a charge with the EEOC are not jurisdictional, but "a requirement that, like a statute of limitations, is subject to waiver, estoppel, and equitable tolling." 433 U.S. at 393. Zipes has been carried over by several lower courts to the 90-day suit-filing provision, and the Supreme Court strongly suggested in Baldwin County that this was correct. In Baldwin County, however, the Court held that the mere filing of the right-to-sue letter did not constitute timely filing of suit when there were no factors justifying the failure to file a true complaint. The Court did, however, list a number of possible bases for tolling the suit-filing period, including the pendency of a motion for court appointment of counsel. In fact, without adverting to the "jurisdiction" problem, the Court had previously approved the tolling of the 90-day period by the filing of a class action for all putative class members. Crown, Cork & Seal Co. v. Parker, 462 U.S. 345 (1983).*

One final question concerning the timeliness of Title VII suits is whether state statutes of limitations have any applicability to private suits. In Occidental Life Ins. Co. v. EEOC, 432 U.S. 355 (1977), the Supreme Court held that such state laws did not apply to suits by the EEOC. The decision, however, did not consider whether such laws might govern private Title VII suits. As *Occidental Life* noted, the general rule is that, where a federal right of action is created without an applicable federal statute of limitations, the courts will look to the most analogous state statute. This principle, however, appears inapplicable to Title VII, the ADA, and the ADEA because of the elaborate timeliness provisions in those statutes. Burgh v. Borough Council of Montrose, 251 F.3d 465 (3d Cir. 2001). In National R.R. Passenger Corp. v. Morgan, 536 U.S. 101, 127 (2002), the Court clearly indicated a role for laches in private suits. It wrote: "In addition to other equitable defenses, therefore, an employer may raise a laches defense, which bars a plaintiff from maintaining a suit if he unreasonably delays in filing a suit and as a result harms the defendant." This strongly suggests that the Title VII time requirements, in the light of waiver, estoppel, and laches principles, are independent of any state law statutes of limitations.

## PROBLEM 9.1

Susan Russo, 21 years old, completed secretarial school in June 1998. Shortly after graduating and before looking for employment, she was in a serious car accident. Although she has otherwise fully recovered, she lost the effective use of her legs and now relies on a wheelchair to get around. In early January 1999, she sent a letter and resume in response to a help-wanted advertisement placed in the Gazette by Firm Bodies Health Spa. She received a phone call scheduling an interview, and on January 15, 1999, she went to the spa to meet with the personnel director. The director seemed awkward during the interview, which Russo attributed to her being in a wheelchair. The interview ended with the director telling Russo that there were "many, many applicants for this job, but we'll get back to you." Russo heard nothing further until February 15, 2000, when she received a letter thanking her for "your interest in Firm Bodies," but informing her that "your interests and ours do not coincide at this time."

Russo, however, noticed that the help-wanted ad to which she had responded was republished every Sunday in the Gazette throughout January and February, last appearing on March 13. Russo was upset about this, but did not want to be paranoid. About April 15, she discovered that one of her friends was a member of Firm Bodies and asked her to "nose around." The friend reported back to Russo on May 15 the following information: a secretary was employed who had begun work around April 4. The new secretary had found out about the position through an ad in March. Firm Bodies must know about the Americans with Disabilities Act because there is a poster in the cafeteria listing individuals' rights under the ADA. The cafeteria, however, is upstairs from the business offices (including the office of the personnel director), and there is no elevator or ramp leading to the second floor.

---

*Zipes* has also been cited to permit a suit filed before issuance of a right-to-sue letter to continue once the letter is actually issued. E.g., Portis v. State of Ohio, 141 F.3d 632 (6th Cir. 1998).

Russo had first learned about the ADA from the physical therapist who had worked with her during her convalescence in the second half of 1998. At that time, however, she had not thought much about employment discrimination against individuals with disabilities. In the wake of her turndown from Firm Bodies, and unable to find another suitable job, Russo joined a support group. Over the next few months, she became more and more upset about what had happened. On August 16, Russo visited the office of the state fair employment practices agency. The intake officer there told her she could file a charge of discrimination if she wished, but they were overworked, and it would make more sense if she filed with the federal Equal Employment Opportunity Commission. Russo did not then file a charge with the state agency. On October 17, she went to the offices of the EEOC, where an investigator completed an intake questionnaire, informed her that "you have a good case," and promised to fill out a charge form for her signature. On December 16, not having heard anything further, Russo went to the EEOC office again. The investigator she had first met had, it turned out, been transferred. The new investigator reviewed the intake questionnaire in the file and helped Russo complete a charge, which she signed and he notarized on that date.

If the EEOC does not pursue this matter, may Russo bring a private suit under the Americans with Disabilities Act? Does 42 U.S.C.S. § 12115 (2003) bear on the question? You may assume that the state fair employment practices agency in question has jurisdiction over disability claims and that it has a six-month statute of limitations for filing a state charge.

## D.  PRIVATE ENFORCEMENT: RELATIONSHIP OF THE EEOC CHARGE TO PRIVATE SUIT

Any Title VII action must be properly predicated on a charge filed with the EEOC, raising questions of the relationship between the charge and a private suit. Three aspects of the EEOC charge requirement must be considered. First, who may sue on the basis of a charge filed with the EEOC? Second, what defendants may be sued on the basis of a particular charge? And third, to what extent is the scope of the suit circumscribed by the content of the charge?

### 1.  Proper Plaintiffs

A plaintiff seeking to bring a Title VII suit must meet two interlocking requirements. First, suit may be brought only by a "person aggrieved" by the discrimination, but a person "aggrieved" under Title VII is intended to extend as far as the constitution will allow. Kyles v. J.K. Guardian Sec. Servs., 222 F.3d 289, 303 (7th Cir. 2000). This is a "standing" question that usually poses no problems: present employees, discharged employees, and unsuccessful applicants for employment unquestionably have standing to attack unlawful employment practices adversely affecting them. E.g., Hackett v. McGuire Bros., Inc., 445 F.2d 442 (3d Cir. 1971). See also Bouman v. Block, 940 F.2d 1211 (9th Cir. 1991) (plaintiff had standing to challenge a civil service examination she did not take when taking it would have been futile). Conversely, a plaintiff without a significant relationship to the employment in question will not have standing; for example, a customer or supplier of the employer would not ordinarily be permitted to sue. Cf. Fair Employment Council of Greater Washington, Inc. v. BMC Mktg. Corp., 28 F.3d 1268 (D.C. Cir. 1994) (testers had no standing to sue, although organization that employed them could have standing because of injury to its interests). See generally Michael J. Yelnosky, Filling an Enforcement Void: Using Testers to Uncover and Remedy Discrimination in Hiring for Lower-Skilled, Entry-Level Jobs, 26 U. Mich. J.L. Reform 403 (1993); Leroy D. Clark, Employment Discrimination Testing: Theories of Standing and a Reply to Professor Yelnosky, 28 U. Mich. J.L. Reform 1 (1994). Some cases have dismissed suits because the plaintiffs were not harmed by the discrimination they challenged. E.g., Smart v. Intl. Bhd. of Elec. Workers, Local 702, 2002 U.S. App. Lexis 23733 (7th Cir. 2002) (doubtful that employer had standing under Title VII to sue union for discriminating against it because it hired black employee).

This is often framed in terms of lack of constitutional standing. E.g., Aiken v. Hackett, 281 F.3d 516 (6th Cir. 2002) (equal protection challenge). However, the Supreme Court has been very generous in recognizing standing to attack racial discrimination. Thus, Northeastern Fla. Chapter of Associated Gen. Contractors of Am. v. City of Jacksonville, 508 U.S. 656 (1993), permitted an attack on a city's affirmative action program even though there was no showing that the plaintiff or any of its member contractors would have won an award even absent the alleged discrimination:

> When the government erects a barrier that makes it more difficult for members of one group to obtain a benefit than it is for members of another group, a member of the former group seeking to challenge the barrier need not allege that he would have obtained the benefit but for the barrier in order to establish standing. The "injury in fact" in an equal protection case of this variety is the denial of equal treatment resulting from the imposition of the barrier, not the ultimate inability to obtain the benefit.

Id. at 666. However, in Texas v. Lesage, 528 U.S. 18 (1999), the Court made clear that such standing existed only because of the dignitary harm inflicted by an ongoing program. Absent such a continuing violation of the law, a plaintiff must show concrete harm, such as a loss of income. If the individual would have suffered the injury without regard to the challenged policy, there is no standing. See also Donahue v. City of Boston, 304 F.3d 110 (1st Cir. 2002) (white plaintiff had no claim for damages because he would not have been hired even absent discrimination, but he did have standing to seek prospective injunctive relief because one minority candidate with a lower test score had been hired). Thus, in Aiken the court dismissed a case brought by individuals who would not have been promoted regardless of the existence of the challenged plan.

Two questions on standing have, however, recurred. The first concerns employees who are not the "object" of the charged violations, for example, whites challenging discrimination against blacks. The better authority recognizes standing, at least if the plaintiff alleges damage to herself stemming from discrimination against others. The landmark opinion in this area is not a Title VII case, but a fair housing decision. In Trafficante v. Metropolitan Life Ins. Co., 409 U.S. 205 (1972), the Supreme Court held that plaintiffs may sue if they satisfy the "case and controversy" requirement of the Constitution and that "the loss of important benefits from interracial associations" qualifies under such principles. Id. at 209-10. Thus, an employee alleging discrimination against would-be fellow workers has standing to raise the issue, at least as long as she frames the complaint in terms of harms flowing to herself as a result of the discrimination against others. However, such harm is not limited to loss of association. Plaintiffs who are victims of indirect discrimination directed against others can also sue. An example is Anjelino v. New York Times Co., 200 F.3d 73, 92 (3d Cir. 1999), where the employer's refusal to hire women from a list allegedly resulted in the male plaintiffs, who were lower down on the list, also not being hired. The court held that the plaintiffs had standing: "We hold that indirect victims of sex-based discrimination have standing to assert claims under Title VII if they allege colorable claims of injury-in-fact that are fairly traceable to acts or omissions by defendants that are unlawful under the statute. That the injury at issue is characterized as indirect is immaterial, as long as it is traceable to the defendant's unlawful acts or omissions." See also Crowley v. Prince George's County, Maryland, 890 F.2d 683 (4th Cir. 1989) (white employee had standing to sue when employer reduced his salary following black employee's complaint that he was being paid less than the white plaintiff). But see Childress v. City of Richmond, Virginia, 134 F.3d 1205, 1209 (4th Cir. 1998) (en banc court affirmed district court's decision that, to qualify as an "aggrieved person" under Title VII, the plaintiff must be a member of the class of direct victims of conduct prohibited by Title VII; thus, white male police officers did not have standing to bring a claim regarding their immediate supervisor's derogatory remarks to and about female and African-American police officers). See generally Noah Zatz, Beyond the Zero-Sum Game: Toward Title VII Protection for Intergroup Solidarity, 77 Ind. L.J. 63, 66-67 (2002); N. Morrison Torrey, Indirect Discrimination Under Title VII: Expanding Male Standing to Sue for Injuries Received as a Result of Employer Discrimination Against Females, 64 Wash. L. Rev. 365 (1989).

A second question is the standing of organizations or associations. Title VII decisions have historically been permissive with respect to unions or minority organizations, e.g., International Woodworkers of Am. v. Chesapeake Bay Plywood Corp., 659 F.2d 1259 (4th Cir. 1981), and the Supreme Court has liberalized association standing law in the discrimination context. Northeastern Florida Chapter of Assoc. Gen. Contractors v. City of Jacksonville, Florida, 508 U.S. 656 (1993), significantly broadened the definition of what constitutes the "harm" requisite for standing. The lower court had denied standing to the plaintiff association of contractors challenging a minority set-aside program because it did not demonstrate that, but for the city set-aside program, any of its members would have obtained a city contract. The Court held that the harm to the association's members lay in being foreclosed from competing for the contracts in question. See also Schurr v. Resorts Intl. Hotel, Inc., 196 F.3d 486 (3d Cir. 1999) (in order to have standing to challenge future applications of the regulations, plaintiff must show that the challenged regulations constitute an invasion of a legally protected interest which is (1) "concrete and particularized", and (2) "actual or imminent"); Fair Employment Council of Greater Washington, Inc. v. BMC Mktg. Corp., 28 F.3d 1268 (D.C. Cir. 1994) (Council suffered injury in fact in its own right even though it was pursuing the interests of third parties in being free of discrimination because of its broad goal of promoting equal employment opportunity). However, while Northeastern Florida Chapter generally liberalized standing, it did not eliminate the requirement. Where organizational standing is at issue, the plaintiff must allege either injury to the association itself (associational standing) or injury to the persons the group represents (representational standing) although apparently dignitary injury is enough. Cleveland Branch NAACP v. City of Parma, 263 F.3d 513 (6th Cir. 2001) (the organization "obtained associational standing" where one alleged victim met the requisite injury, causation, and redressability elements of standing); Maryland Minority Contrs. Assn. v. Lynch, No. 98-2655, 2000 U.S. App. LEXIS 1636 (4th Cir. 2000) (no injury to the association); see also Cotter v. Massachusetts Assn. of Minority Law, 219 F.3d 31 (1st Cir. 2000) (possibility of injury to group representatives substantial enough to satisfy representational standing).

Assuming standing, there remains the requirement of the proper relationship between the plaintiff and the charge filed with the EEOC. Title VII provides that a charge may be filed "by or on behalf of a person claiming to be aggrieved" by a violation. § 706(b), (f)(1), 42 U.S.C.S. § 2000e-5(b), (f)(1) (2003). Plainly, a charging party who properly invokes Commission processes may bring suit. But may other persons look to that charge as the basis of their own Title VII causes of action, either in the same suit with the charging party or in separate proceedings? In Title VII class actions, persons who have not filed a charge with the EEOC may nevertheless be class members. See Albemarle Paper Co. v. Moody, 422 U.S. 405 (1975). Further, because Title VII provides for charge filings "on behalf of" aggrieved persons, presumably a person on whose behalf a charge is filed (the "principal") may bring suit without regard to whether the charging party (the "agent") may also sue. But must the principal actually authorize the suit, or may everyone affected by the specified discrimination claim that the charge is on their behalf? See Wu v. Thomas, 863 F.2d 1543 (11th Cir. 1989) (husband did not have to file separate charge where wife's charge alleged that their employer had retaliated against her husband for her protected conduct).

A broad rule has been urged: any person aggrieved by an unlawful employment practice may sue so long as a charge was filed by another, without regard to whether the charge purported to be on behalf of all other aggrieved persons. This would permit persons who did not file charges (or who filed charges but did not receive a right-to-sue letter) to be named plaintiffs even in non-class suits, either by joining originally with charging parties or by intervention in actions brought by charging parties. Alexander v. Fulton County, 207 F.3d 1303 (11th Cir. 2000); Mooney v. Aramco Servs. Co., 54 F.3d 1207, 1224 n.22 (5th Cir. 1995); Howlett v. Holiday Inns, 49 F.3d 189, 195 (6th Cir. 1995); Tolliver v. Xerox Corp., 918 F.2d 1052, 1056 (2d Cir. 1990) (ADEA). But see Thomure v. Phillips Furniture Co., 30 F.3d 1020 (8th Cir. 1994) (party cannot piggyback on charge ultimately determined to be without merit); Schnellbaecher v. Baskin Clothing Co., 887 F.2d 124 (7th Cir. 1989) (charged party must have sufficient notice). Contra, Whalen v. W. R. Grace & Co., 56 F.3d 504 (3d Cir. 1995) (ADEA); Communications Workers of Am., Local 1033 v. New Jersey Dept. of Pers., 282 F.3d 213 (3d Cir. 2002) (unless asserting a claim in a class action, each individual plaintiff must file a timely charge).

## 2.  *Proper Defendants*

Even when a plaintiff's suit is based on a charge filed with the EEOC, a question may arise about what parties may be named as defendants in the complaint. Title VII authorizes the bringing of a civil action only "against the respondent named in the charge," § 706(f)(1), 42 U.S.C.S. § 2000e-5(f)(1) (2003), but the courts have been more liberal than the statutory language might suggest. E.g., Hafez v. Avis Rent-A-Car Sys., No. 99-9459, 2000 U.S. App. LEXIS 31032 (2d Cir. 2000) ("allowing a Title VII action to proceed against an unnamed party where there is a clear identity of interests between the unnamed party and the named party"). The general rule appears to be that a defendant who is sufficiently implicated by the charge on which the action is predicated may be sued under Title VII. E.g., Mickel v. South Carolina State

Employment Serv., 377 F.2d 239 (4th Cir. 1967). This formulation leaves open a number of ways persons may be made defendants, despite not being technically "named" as charge respondents. For example, the courts have been liberal in deciding what constitutes "naming" a defendant, not requiring it to be correctly identified, e.g., Tillman v. Boaz, 548 F.2d 592 (5th Cir. 1977), or to be designated as respondent if its identity is indicated in the charge papers, Kaplan v. International Alliance of Theatrical & Stage Employees (IATSE), 525 F.2d 1354 (9th Cir. 1975). Successors of charged parties have also been found proper defendants. E.g., Criswell v. Delta Air Lines, Inc., 868 F.2d 1093 (9th Cir. 1989); EEOC v. MacMillan Bloedel Containers, Inc., 503 F.2d 1086 (6th Cir. 1974). See generally Claiborne Barksdale, Successor Liability Under the National Labor Relations Act and Title VII, 54 Tex. L. Rev. 707 (1976). Further, some courts have permitted suit against non-charged defendants if no affirmative relief is sought against them, EEOC v. MacMillan Bloedel Containers, Inc., supra, or if they have a sufficient relationship to a properly charged party who is also named as a defendant, e.g., EEOC v. McLean Trucking Co., 525 F.2d 1007 (6th Cir. 1975); Evans v. Sheraton Park Hotel, 503 F.2d 177 (D.C. Cir. 1974) (international union that was an indispensable party in a suit challenging the sex segregation of two locals could be joined although only the locals were named in the charge), or if there is one "identity of interest" between a named party and an unnamed party. Johnson v. Palma, 931 F.2d 203 (2d Cir. 1991). But see Vital v. Interfaith Medical, 168 F.3d 615 (2d Cir. 1999) (no identity of interest between union local and employer). Finally, when two separate legal entities have been determined to be a "single employer" for purposes of statutory coverage, the courts hold that a charge against one is an adequate basis to sue the other. Knowlton v. Teltrust Phones, Inc., 189 F.3d 1177 (10th Cir. 1999).

The broadest rule is a functional approach that permits suit against anyone, whether or not named or even identified in the charge, so long as the purposes of filing a charge are satisfied with respect to that person. The charge requirement has been said to serve two purposes, notifying the charged party of the asserted violation and bringing it before the EEOC to secure voluntary compliance. Some courts have recognized that both these ends can be achieved as to parties who have not been technically charged. A typical example is a case in which the plaintiff wishes to sue an agent, but only the principal has been named in a charge, or vice versa. But this theory is not limited to principal-agent relationships or to any other legal categories. It is concerned only with whether the parties to be sued have notice of the charge and whether the EEOC had an opportunity to conciliate with them. E.g., Johnson v. Palma, 931 F.2d 203 (2d Cir. 1991); Eggleston v. Chicago Journeymen Plumbers' Union, 657 F.2d 890 (7th Cir. 1981). This seems to be the theory underlying those cases that allow suit against persons not named in the charge if they share "an identity of interest" with persons who are named. Alvarado v. Bd. of Trustees of Montgomery Community Coll., 848 F.2d 457 (4th Cir. 1988); Greenwood v. Ross, 778 F.2d 448 (8th Cir. 1985); Romain v. Kurek, 772 F.2d 281 (6th Cir. 1985).

The broadest version of the functional approach has emerged from the Fifth Circuit. Drawing from the cases focusing on the relationship of the charge to discrimination that may be challenged in court, the circuit has held that "[t]he reasonable limits of an investigation potentially triggered by an EEOC charge defined not only the substantive limits of a subsequent Title VII action, but also the parties potentially liable in that action." Terrell v. United States Pipe & Foundry Co., 644 F.2d 1112 (5th Cir. 1981). See also Tillman v. Milwaukee, 715 F.2d 354 (7th Cir. 1983). This principle shifts concern from questions of notice to the issue of whether a reasonable investigation of whatever facts were alleged would focus on the non-named person whose liability is at issue. It would, presumably, satisfy the requirement of giving the EEOC an opportunity to act, but would subordinate any requirement of notice to all defendants to the interest in Title VII enforcement. These broader theories frequently rely on Zipes v. Trans World Airlines, Inc., 455 U.S. 147 (1984), as a basis for relaxing any strict requirement of having to identify in the charge each party who is sued. Is this a fair interpretation of *Zipes*?

## 3.  Scope of the Suit

Because every private Title VII, ADA, and ADEA suit must be predicated on a charge properly filed with the EEOC, a significant issue is the extent to which the subsequent court complaint will be limited to the contents of the EEOC charge. In resolving this question, the courts have tried to reconcile competing considerations by giving effect to the statutory filing requirement without encroaching more than necessary on the remedial purposes of the statutes. Because many charges are filed by unsophisticated, perhaps undereducated, workers, limiting the scope of the suit to the face of the charge would be a major blow to effective statutory enforcement.

The test the courts have selected to balance these factors is that articulated by the Fifth Circuit in Sanchez v. Standard Brands, Inc., 431 F.2d 455, 466 (5th Cir. 1970). The court laid down a liberal standard to govern the proper scope of a charge-based complaint:

> [T]he allegations in a judicial complaint filed pursuant to Title VII "may encompass any kind of discrimination like or related to allegations contained in the charge and growing out of such allegations during the pendency of the case before the Commission." . . . In other words, the "scope" of the judicial complaint is limited to the "scope" of the EEOC investigation which can reasonably be expected to grow out of the charge of discrimination.

The court saw this rule as being rooted in the statutory scheme: the charge is filed not to trigger a lawsuit, but rather to invoke EEOC processes. Because suit is necessary only if the Commission fails to resolve the problems, the civil action is "much more intimately related to the EEOC investigation than to the words of the charge." Id. Further, a stricter rule would impede the EEOC's ability to obtain voluntary compliance because respondents' incentives to settle would be reduced if no issue unspecified in the charge could be sued on. *Sanchez* has generally been followed, e.g., Thomas v. Texas Dept. of Crim. Justice, 220 F.3d 389 (5th Cir. 2000); Davis v. Sodexho, 157 F.3d 460 (6th Cir. 1998); Mulhall v. Advance Security, Inc., 19 F.3d 586, 589 n.8 (11th Cir. 1994); Martin v. Nannie and the Newborns, Inc., 3 F.3d 1410, 1416 n.7 (10th Cir. 1993); Sosa v. Hiraoka, 920 F.2d 1451 (9th Cir. 1990), although the phrasing of the test has sometimes varied.

Recently, however, courts have shown more reluctance to permit suits to go beyond a plain reading of the charge. These courts tend to mechanically compare the charge to the complaint and do not look to the purposes of the charge in triggering an EEOC investigation. E.g., Dorsey v. Pinnacle Automation Co., 278 F.3d 830 (8th Cir. 2002) (claims for age discrimination based on the failure to promote at a discrete time not sufficient to encompass hostile work environment claims that occurred throughout the plaintiff's employment); Sloop v. Meml. Mission Hosp., Inc., 198

F.3d 147 (4th Cir. 1999) (age discrimination charge did not reach retaliation under Title VII); Novitsky v. American Consulting Engrs., L.L.C., 196 F.3d 699 (7th Cir. 1999) (plaintiff could not litigate an accommodation claim because the charge filed with the EEOC included only claims of age and religion discrimination); Park v. Howard Univ., 71 F.3d 904 (D.C. Cir. 1995) (charge claiming national origin discrimination but not specifically referring to a "hostile work environment" or stating specific facts of such an environment cannot support hostile environment suit); Cheek v. Western & S. Life Ins. Co., 31 F.3d 497 (7th Cir. 1994) (not all sex discrimination could be challenged in court even if the EEOC charge alleged sex discrimination). But see B.K.B. v. Maui Police Dept., 276 F.3d 1091 (9th Cir. 2002) (after comparing the charge and pre-complaint form, plaintiff's listing of "harassment" was broadly held to encompass both racial and sexual harassment).[*]

## E.  THE INTERRELATIONSHIP OF VARIOUS RIGHTS AND REMEDIES

We have encountered a number of federal remedies that address the same wrong. For example, Title VII and § 1981 overlap when race discrimination is involved. In addition, as the preceding discussion indicates, most states have state laws prohibiting race, sex, age, and disability discrimination. Finally, there are private efforts to deal with discrimination through collective bargaining agreements and private arbitration agreements. The interrelationship of all these remedies has raised difficult questions.

With respect to federal remedies, the Supreme Court has generally treated them as separate and independent, Johnson v. Railway Express Agency, 421 U.S. 454, 462 (1975), thus leaving coordination of separate suits to the normal doctrines of res judicata (or claim preclusion) and collateral estoppel (or issue preclusion). See, e.g., Clark v. Haas Group, Inc., 953 F.2d 1235 (10th Cir. 1992) (prior FLSA suit barred subsequent ADEA claims). Such principles can be applied in interesting ways. In Meredith v. Beech Aircraft Corp., 18 F.3d 890 (10th Cir. 1994), the court held that plaintiff B in the second suit could rely on a finding in the first suit that defendant's promotion decision was based on sex, but that the defendant could not rely on a finding in the first suit that plaintiff A was the best-qualified applicant. Plaintiff B, while allowed to use estoppel offensively, was not bound by the first suit because she was not a party, or in privity with a party, to that suit and thus had no opportunity to litigate the "best-qualified" issue.

A second major issue concerns the relationship between statutory remedies and arbitration. Acts of discrimination may occur in unionized settings governed by collective bargaining agreements that bar discharge except for just cause and may even prohibit discrimination. What effect does a decision under the collective bargaining agreement by an arbitrator have on rights under Title VII or other federal statutes? Similarly, outside the collective bargaining setting, suppose an employer requires as a condition of employment that non-unionized employees sign an agreement to

---

[*] Like other questions of charge-filing, a defendant may waive the requirement of properly charging discrimination by not challenging it in a timely manner. Francis v. New York, 235 F.3d 763 (2d Cir. 2000).

arbitrate any dispute involving their employment including discrimination claims. What effect does such an agreement have on federal rights?

A third major issue, the relationship between state and federal regulation of employment discrimination, has raised numerous substantive and procedural questions. The threshold question is whether federal law preempts state efforts to deal with employment discrimination. While aspects of this question have been touched on elsewhere in this book, this section summarizes some of the governing law. Because, as we will see, federal preemption is the exception and not the rule, the remaining question is the extent to which the courts will employ various procedural devices to coordinate state and federal remedies.

## 1.   Arbitrating Discrimination Claims

In an early decision involving arbitration under a collective bargaining agreement, Alexander v. Gardner-Denver Co., 415 U.S. 36 (1974), the Court viewed Title VII and collective bargaining agreement remedies as independent. Consistent with this view, the Court in Elec. Workers v. Robbins & Myers, 429 U.S. 229 (1976), held that resort to grievance arbitration does not toll Title VII precedence. *Gardner-Denver* not only held that submission of a dispute to arbitration does not preclude a subsequent Title VII suit, but also ruled improper any judicial deference to prior arbitral awards. Thus, an employee may pursue a grievance procedure established by a collective bargaining agreement without fear of prejudicing his or her Title VII rights. *Gardner-Denver* reached its result by noting that enforcing Title VII compliance was entrusted to federal courts, not to arbitrators; that the elaborate suit prerequisites did not refer to arbitration; and that Congress had evinced an intent to provide parallel or overlapping remedies. The Court stressed the inappropriateness of deference to collective bargaining arbitration because arbitrators are not selected for their knowledge and judgment concerning industrial relations, not public law concepts and arbitrators are bound to effectuate the intent of the parties as embodied in the contract, even though that intent may be in conflict with the law. Further, unions control the process, which may prejudice individual rights. But the Court also noted defects in the arbitral procedure, which are independent of the collective bargaining context, that may affect the quality of the decisions rendered:

> Moreover, the factfinding process in arbitration usually is not equivalent to judicial factfinding. The record of the arbitration proceedings is not as complete; the usual rules of evidence do not apply; and rights and procedures common to civil trials, such as discovery, compulsory process, cross-examination, and testimony under oath, are often severely limited or unavailable. And as this Court has recognized, "arbitrators have no obligation to the court to give their reasons for an award." Indeed, it is the informality of arbitral procedure that enables it to function as an efficient, inexpensive, and expeditious means for dispute resolution. This same characteristic, however, makes arbitration a less appropriate forum for final resolution of Title VII issues than the federal courts.

451 U.S. 57-58.*

*Gardner-Denver* seemed to bar enforcement of arbitration agreements, at least those agreements to arbitrate employment discrimination claims prior to a dispute arising, although it did state that courts might admit arbitral decisions as evidence,

---

*The *Gardner-Denver* Court did, however, suggest that arbitral decisions may have evidentiary weight in court decisions. 415 U.S. at 82.

415 U.S. 36, 60 n.21. See Collins v. N.Y.C. Transit Auth., 305 F.3d 113 (2d Cir. 2002). But after *Gardner-Denver* a series of Supreme Court decisions in other contexts reinvigorated the use of arbitration as part of the ADR movement that developed so strongly in the 1980s and 1990s. The Supreme Court revisited the issue of the relationship of arbitration to litigation in the discrimination context in the next case, with markedly different results.

## GILMER v. INTERSTATE/JOHNSON LANE CORP.
### 500 U.S. 20 (1991)

Justice WHITE delivered the opinion of the Court.

The question presented in this case is whether a claim under the Age Discrimination in Employment Act of 1967 can be subjected to compulsory arbitration pursuant to an arbitration agreement in a securities registration application. The Court of Appeals held that it could, and we affirm.

### I

Respondent Interstate/Johnson Lane Corporation (Interstate) hired petitioner Robert Gilmer as a Manager of Financial Services in May 1981. As required by his employment, Gilmer registered as a securities representative with several stock exchanges, including the New York Stock Exchange (NYSE). His registration application, entitled "Uniform Application for Securities Industry Registration or Transfer," provided, among other things, that Gilmer "agreed to arbitrate any dispute, claim or controversy" arising between him and Interstate "that is required to be arbitrated under the rules, constitutions or by-laws of the organizations with which I register." Of relevance to this case, NYSE Rule 347 provides for arbitration of "any controversy between a registered representative and any member or member organization arising out of the employment or termination of employment of such registered representative."

Interstate terminated Gilmer's employment in 1987, at which time Gilmer was 62 years of age. [Gilmer filed a charge with the EEOC and then sued in federal district court for age discrimination in violation of the ADEA. Interstate moved to compel arbitration, relying on the arbitration agreement in Gilmer's registration application and the Federal Arbitration Act (FAA). 9 U.S.C.S. § 1 *et seq.* (2003).]

### II

The FAA was originally enacted in 1925, and then reenacted and codified in 1947 as Title 9 of the United States Code. Its purpose was to reverse the longstanding judicial hostility to arbitration agreements that had existed at English common law and had been adopted by American courts, and to place arbitration agreements upon the same footing as other contracts. Its primary substantive provision states that "[a] written provision in any maritime transaction or a contract evidencing a transaction involving commerce to settle by arbitration a controversy thereafter arising out of such contract or transaction . . . shall be valid, irrevocable, and enforceable, save upon such grounds as exist at law or in equity for the revocation of any contract." 9 U.S.C. § 2. The FAA also provides for stays of proceedings in federal district courts when an issue in the proceeding is referable to arbitration, § 3, and for orders compelling arbitration when one party has failed, neglected, or refused to comply with an arbitration agreement, § 4. These provisions manifest a "liberal federal policy favoring arbitration agreements." Moses H. Cone Memorial Hospital v. Mercury Construction Corp., 460 U.S. 1, 24 (1983).[2]

It is by now clear that statutory claims may be the subject of an arbitration agreement, enforceable pursuant to the FAA. Indeed, in recent years we have held enforceable arbitration agreements relating to claims arising under the Sherman Act; § 10(b) of the Securities Exchange Act of 1934; the civil provisions of the Racketeer Influenced and Corrupt Organizations Act (RICO); and § 12(2) of the Securities Act of 1933. See Mitsubishi Motors Corp. v. Soler Chrysler-Plymouth, Inc., 473 U.S. 614 (1985); Shearson/American Express Inc. v. McMahon, 482 U.S. 220 (1987); Rodriguez de Quijas v. Shearson/American Express, Inc., 490 U.S. 477 (1989). In these cases we recognized that "by agreeing to arbitrate a statutory claim, a party does not forgo the substantive rights afforded by the statute; it only submits to their resolution in an arbitral, rather than a judicial, forum." *Mitsubishi*.

Although all statutory claims may not be appropriate for arbitration, "having made the bargain to arbitrate, the party should be held to it unless Congress itself has evinced an intention to preclude a waiver of judicial remedies for the statutory rights at issue." Ibid. In this regard, we note that the burden is on Gilmer to show that Congress intended to preclude a waiver of a judicial forum for ADEA claims. See *McMahon*. If such an intention exists, it will be discoverable in the text of the ADEA, its legislative history, or an "inherent conflict" between arbitration and the ADEA's underlying purposes. See ibid. Throughout such an inquiry, it should be kept in mind that "questions of arbitrability must be addressed with a healthy regard for the federal policy favoring arbitration." *Moses H. Cone*.

## III

Gilmer concedes that nothing in the text of the ADEA or its legislative history explicitly precludes arbitration. He argues, however, that compulsory arbitration of ADEA claims pursuant to arbitration agreements would be inconsistent with the statutory framework and purposes of the ADEA. Like the Court of Appeals, we disagree.

### A

Congress enacted the ADEA in 1967 "to promote employment of older persons based on their ability rather than age; to prohibit arbitrary age discrimination in

---

2. Section 1 of the FAA provides that "nothing herein contained shall apply to contracts of employment of seamen, railroad employees, or any other class of workers engaged in foreign or interstate commerce." 9 U.S.C. § 1. Several *amici curiae* in support of Gilmer argue that that section excludes from the coverage of the FAA *all* "contracts of employment." Gilmer, however, did not raise the issue in the courts below; it was not addressed there; and it was not among the questions presented in the petition for certiorari. In any event, it would be inappropriate to address the scope of the § 1 exclusion because the arbitration clause being enforced here is not contained in a contract of employment. . . . Rather, the arbitration clause at issue is in Gilmer's securities registration application, which is a contract with the securities exchanges, not with Interstate. The lower courts addressing the issue uniformly have concluded that the exclusionary clause in § 1 of the FAA is inapplicable to arbitration clauses contained in such registration applications. We implicitly assumed as much in Perry v. Thomas, 482 U.S. 483 (1987), where we held that the FAA required a former employee of a securities firm to arbitrate his statutory wage claim against his former employer, pursuant to an arbitration clause in his registration application. Unlike the dissent, we choose to follow the plain language of the FAA and the weight of authority, and we therefore hold that § 1's exclusionary clause does not apply to Gilmer's arbitration agreement. Consequently, we leave for another day the issue raised by *amici curiae*.

employment; [and] to help employers and workers find ways of meeting problems arising from the impact of age on employment." 29 U.S.C. § 621 (b). To achieve those goals, the ADEA, among other things, makes it unlawful for an employer "to fail or refuse to hire or to discharge any individual or otherwise discriminate against any individual with respect to his compensation, terms, conditions, or privileges of employment, because of such individual's age." § 623(a)(1). This proscription is enforced both by private suits and by the EEOC. In order for an aggrieved individual to bring suit under the ADEA, he or she must first file a charge with the EEOC and then wait at least 60 days. § 626(d). An individual's right to sue is extinguished, however, if the EEOC institutes an action against the employer. § 626(c)(1). Before the EEOC can bring such an action, though, it must "attempt to eliminate the discriminatory practice or practices alleged, and to effect voluntary compliance with the requirements of this chapter through informal methods of conciliation, conference, and persuasion." § 626(b); see also 29 CFR § 1626.15 (1990).

As Gilmer contends, the ADEA is designed not only to address individual grievances, but also to further important social policies. We do not perceive any inherent inconsistency between those policies, however, and enforcing agreements to arbitrate age discrimination claims. It is true that arbitration focuses on specific disputes between the parties involved. The same can be said, however, of judicial resolution of claims. Both of these dispute resolution mechanisms nevertheless also can further broader social purposes. The Sherman Act, the Securities Exchange Act of 1934, RICO, and the Securities Act of 1933 all are designed to advance important public policies, but, as noted above, claims under those statutes are appropriate for arbitration. "So long as the prospective litigant effectively may vindicate [his or her] statutory cause of action in the arbitral forum, the statute will continue to serve both its remedial and deterrent function." *Mitsubishi.*

We also are unpersuaded by the argument that arbitration will undermine the role of the EEOC in enforcing the ADEA. An individual ADEA claimant subject to an arbitration agreement will still be free to file a charge with the EEOC, even though the claimant is not able to institute a private judicial action. Indeed, Gilmer filed a charge with the EEOC in this case. In any event, the EEOC's role in combating age discrimination is not dependent on the filing of a charge; the agency may receive information concerning alleged violations of the ADEA "from any source," and it has independent authority to investigate age discrimination. See 29 CFR §§ 1626.4, 1626.13 (1990). Moreover, nothing in the ADEA indicates that Congress intended that the EEOC be involved in all employment disputes. Such disputes can be settled, for example, without any EEOC involvement.[3] Finally, the mere involvement of an administrative agency in the enforcement of a statute is not sufficient to preclude arbitration. For example, the Securities Exchange Commission is heavily involved in the enforcement of the Securities Exchange Act of 1934 and the Securities Act of 1933, but we have held that claims under both of those statutes may be subject to compulsory arbitration.

Gilmer also argues that compulsory arbitration is improper because it deprives claimants of the judicial forum provided for by the ADEA. Congress, however, did not explicitly preclude arbitration or other nonjudicial resolution of claims, even in

---

3. In the recently enacted Older Workers Benefit Protection Act, Congress amended the ADEA to provide that "an individual may not waive any right or claim under this Act unless the waiver is knowing and voluntary." See § 201. Congress also specified certain conditions that must be met in order for a waiver to be knowing and voluntary. Ibid.

its recent amendments to the ADEA. "If Congress intended the substantive protection afforded [by the ADEA] to include protection against waiver of the right to a judicial forum, that intention will be deducible from text or legislative history." *Mitsubishi.* Moreover, Gilmer's argument ignores the ADEA's flexible approach to resolution of claims. The EEOC, for example, is directed to pursue "informal methods of conciliation, conference, and persuasion," 29 U.S.C. § 626(b), which suggests that out-of-court dispute resolution, such as arbitration, is consistent with the statutory scheme established by Congress. In addition, arbitration is consistent with Congress' grant of concurrent jurisdiction over ADEA claims to state and federal courts, see 29 U.S.C. § 626 (c)(1) (allowing suits to be brought "in any court of competent jurisdiction"), because arbitration agreements, "like the provision for concurrent jurisdiction, serve to advance the objective of allowing [claimants] a broader right to select the forum for resolving disputes, whether it be judicial or otherwise." *Rodriguez de Quijas.*

B

In arguing that arbitration is inconsistent with the ADEA, Gilmer also raises a host of challenges to the adequacy of arbitration procedures. Initially, we note that in our recent arbitration cases we have already rejected most of these arguments as insufficient to preclude arbitration of statutory claims. Such generalized attacks on arbitration "rest on suspicion of arbitration as a method of weakening the protections afforded in the substantive law to would-be complainants," and as such, they are "far out of step with our current strong endorsement of the federal statutes favoring this method of resolving disputes." *Rodriguez de Quijas.* Consequently, we address these arguments only briefly.

Gilmer first speculates that arbitration panels will be biased. However, "we decline to indulge the presumption that the parties and arbitral body conducting a proceeding will be unable or unwilling to retain competent, conscientious and impartial arbitrators." *Mitsubishi.* In any event, we note that the NYSE arbitration rules, which are applicable to the dispute in this case, provide protections against biased panels. The rules require, for example, that the parties be informed of the employment histories of the arbitrators, and that they be allowed to make further inquiries into the arbitrators' backgrounds. See 2 CCH New York Stock Exchange Guide ¶2608, p. 4314 (1991) (hereinafter 2 N.Y.S.E. Guide). In addition, each party is allowed one peremptory challenge and unlimited challenges for cause. Id., ¶2609, at 4315 (Rule 609). Moreover, the arbitrators are required to disclose "any circumstances which might preclude [them] from rendering an objective and impartial determination." Id., ¶2610, at 4315 (Rule 610). The FAA also protects against bias, by providing that courts may overturn arbitration decisions "where there was evident partiality or corruption in the arbitrators." 9 U.S.C. § 10 (b). There has been no showing in this case that those provisions are inadequate to guard against potential bias.

Gilmer also complains that the discovery allowed in arbitration is more limited than in the federal courts, which he contends will make it difficult to prove discrimination. It is unlikely, however, that age discrimination claims require more extensive discovery than other claims that we have found to be arbitrable, such as RICO and antitrust claims. Moreover, there has been no showing in this case that the NYSE discovery provisions, which allow for document production, information requests, depositions, and subpoenas, see 2 N.Y.S.E. Guide ¶2619, pp. 4318 – 4320 (Rule 619); Securities and Exchange Commission Order Approving Proposed Rule Changes by New York Stock Exchange, Inc., Nat. Assn. of Securities Dealers, Inc., and the

American Stock Exchange, Inc., Relating to the Arbitration Process and the Use of Predispute Arbitration Clauses, 54 Fed. Reg. 21144, 21149-21151 (1989), will prove insufficient to allow ADEA claimants such as Gilmer a fair opportunity to present their claims. Although those procedures might not be as extensive as in the federal courts, by agreeing to arbitrate, a party "trades the procedures and opportunity for review of the courtroom for the simplicity, informality, and expedition of arbitration." *Mitsubishi.* Indeed, an important counterweight to the reduced discovery in NYSE arbitration is that arbitrators are not bound by the rules of evidence. See 2 N.Y.S.E. Guide ¶2620, p. 4320 (Rule 620).

A further alleged deficiency of arbitration is that arbitrators often will not issue written opinions, resulting, Gilmer contends, in a lack of public knowledge of employers' discriminatory policies, an inability to obtain effective appellate review, and a stifling of the development of the law. The NYSE rules, however, do require that all arbitration awards be in writing, and that the awards contain the names of the parties, a summary of the issues in controversy, and a description of the award issued. See id., ¶¶2627(a), (e), at 4321 (Rules 627(a), (e)). In addition, the award decisions are made available to the public. See id., ¶2627(f), at 4322 (Rule 627(f)). Furthermore, judicial decisions addressing ADEA claims will continue to be issued because it is unlikely that all or even most ADEA claimants will be subject to arbitration agreements. Finally, Gilmer's concerns apply equally to settlements of ADEA claims, which, as noted above, are clearly allowed.[4]

It is also argued that arbitration procedures cannot adequately further the purposes of the ADEA because they do not provide for broad equitable relief and class actions. [H]owever, arbitrators do have the power to fashion equitable relief. Indeed, the NYSE rules applicable here do not restrict the types of relief an arbitrator may award, but merely refer to "damages and/or other relief." 2 N. Y. S. E. Guide ¶2627(e), p. 4321 (Rule 627(e)). The NYSE rules also provide for collective proceedings. Id., ¶2612(d), at 4317 (Rule 612(d)). But "even if the arbitration could not go forward as a class action or class relief could not be granted by the arbitrator, the fact that the [ADEA] provides for the possibility of bringing a collective action does not mean that individual attempts at conciliation were intended to be barred." Nicholson v. CPC Int'l Inc., 877 F.2d 221, 241 (CA3 1989) (Becker, J., dissenting). Finally, it should be remembered that arbitration agreements will not preclude the *EEOC* from bringing actions seeking class-wide and equitable relief.

## C

An additional reason advanced by Gilmer for refusing to enforce arbitration agreements relating to ADEA claims is his contention that there often will be unequal bargaining power between employers and employees. Mere inequality in bargaining power, however, is not a sufficient reason to hold that arbitration agreements are never enforceable in the employment context. Relationships between securities dealers and investors, for example, may involve unequal bargaining power, but we nevertheless held in *Rodriguez de Quijas* and *McMahon* that agreements to arbitrate in that context are enforceable. As discussed above, the FAA's purpose was to place arbitration agreements on the same footing as other contracts. Thus, arbitration

---

4. Gilmer also contends that judicial review of arbitration decisions is too limited. We have stated, however, that "although judicial scrutiny of arbitration awards necessarily is limited, such review is sufficient to ensure that arbitrators comply with the requirements of the statute" at issue. Shearson/American Express Inc. v. McMahon, 482 U.S. 220, 232 (1987).

agreements are enforceable "save upon such grounds as exist at law or in equity for the revocation of any contract." 9 U.S.C. § 2. "Of course, courts should remain attuned to well-supported claims that the agreement to arbitrate resulted from the sort of fraud or overwhelming economic power that would provide grounds 'for the revocation of any contract.'" *Mitsubishi.* There is no indication in this case, however, that Gilmer, an experienced businessman, was coerced or defrauded into agreeing to the arbitration clause in his registration application. As with the claimed procedural inadequacies discussed above, this claim of unequal bargaining power is best left for resolution in specific cases.

## IV

In addition to the arguments discussed above, Gilmer vigorously asserts that our decision in Alexander v. Gardner-Denver Co. and its progeny — Barrentine v. Arkansas-Best Freight System, Inc., 450 U.S. 728 (1981), and McDonald v. West Branch, 466 U.S. 284 (1984) — preclude arbitration of employment discrimination claims. Gilmer's reliance on these cases, however, is misplaced.

In *Gardner-Denver*, the issue was whether a discharged employee whose grievance had been arbitrated pursuant to an arbitration clause in a collective-bargaining agreement was precluded from subsequently bringing a Title VII action based upon the conduct that was the subject of the grievance. In holding that the employee was not foreclosed from bringing the Title VII claim, we stressed that an employee's contractual rights under a collective-bargaining agreement are distinct from the employee's statutory Title VII rights:

> "In submitting his grievance to arbitration, an employee seeks to vindicate his contractual right under a collective-bargaining agreement. By contrast, in filing a lawsuit under Title VII, an employee asserts independent statutory rights accorded by Congress. The distinctly separate nature of these contractual and statutory rights is not vitiated merely because both were violated as a result of the same factual occurrence."

> We also noted that a labor arbitrator has authority only to resolve questions of contractual rights. The arbitrator's "task is to effectuate the intent of the parties" and he or she does not have the "general authority to invoke public laws that conflict with the bargain between the parties." By contrast, "in instituting an action under Title VII, the employee is not seeking review of the arbitrator's decision. Rather, he is asserting a statutory right independent of the arbitration process." We further expressed concern that in collective-bargaining arbitration "the interests of the individual employee may be subordinated to the collective interests of all employees in the bargaining unit."[5]

> *Barrentine* and *McDonald* similarly involved the issue whether arbitration under a collective-bargaining agreement precluded a subsequent statutory claim. In holding that the statutory claims there were not precluded, we noted, as in *Gardner-Denver*, the difference between contractual rights under a collective-bargaining agreement and individual statutory rights, the potential disparity in interests between a union and an employee, and the limited authority and power of labor arbitrators.

There are several important distinctions between the *Gardner-Denver* line of cases and the case before us. First, those cases did not involve the issue of the enforceability

---

5. The Court in Alexander v. Gardner-Denver Co. also expressed the view that arbitration was inferior to the judicial process for resolving statutory claims. That "mistrust of the arbitral process," however, has been undermined by our recent arbitration decisions. *McMahon.* "We are well past the time when judicial suspicion of the desirability of arbitration and of the competence of arbitral tribunals inhibited the development of arbitration as an alternative means of dispute resolution." Mitsubishi Motors Corp. v. Soler Chrysler-Plymouth, Inc.

of an agreement to arbitrate statutory claims. Rather, they involved the quite different issue whether arbitration of contract-based claims precluded subsequent judicial resolution of statutory claims. Since the employees there had not agreed to arbitrate their statutory claims, and the labor arbitrators were not authorized to resolve such claims, the arbitration in those cases understandably was held not to preclude subsequent statutory actions. Second, because the arbitration in those cases occurred in the context of a collective-bargaining agreement, the claimants there were represented by their unions in the arbitration proceedings. An important concern therefore was the tension between collective representation and individual statutory rights, a concern not applicable to the present case. Finally, those cases were not decided under the FAA, which, as discussed above, reflects a "liberal federal policy favoring arbitration agreements." *Mitsubishi*. Therefore, those cases provide no basis for refusing to enforce Gilmer's agreement to arbitrate his ADEA claim. . . .

Justice STEVENS, with whom Justice MARSHALL joins, dissenting.
Section 1 of the Federal Arbitration Act (FAA) states:

> [N]othing herein contained shall apply to contracts of employment of seamen, railroad employees, or any other class of workers engaged in foreign or interstate commerce. 9 U.S.C. § 1.

The Court today, in holding that the FAA compels enforcement of arbitration clauses even when claims of age discrimination are at issue, skirts the antecedent question whether the coverage of the Act even extends to arbitration clauses contained in employment contracts, regardless of the subject matter of the claim at issue. In my opinion, arbitration clauses contained in employment agreements are specifically exempt from coverage of the FAA, and for that reason respondent Interstate/Johnson Lane Corporation cannot, pursuant to the FAA, compel petitioner to submit his claims arising under the [ADEA]. . . .

Not only would I find that the FAA does not apply to employment-related disputes between employers and employees in general, but also I would hold that compulsory arbitration conflicts with the congressional purpose animating the ADEA, in particular. As this Court previously has noted, authorizing the courts to issue broad injunctive relief is the cornerstone to eliminating discrimination in society. Albemarle Paper Co. v. Moody [reproduced at page 941]. The ADEA, like Title VII of the Civil Rights Act of 1964, authorizes courts to award broad, class-based injunctive relief to achieve the purposes of the Act. Because commercial arbitration is typically limited to a specific dispute between the particular parties and because the available remedies in arbitral forums generally do not provide for class-wide injunctive relief, see Shell, ERISA and Other Federal Employment Statutes: When is Commercial Arbitration an "Adequate Substitute" for the Courts?, 68 Texas L. Rev. 509, 568 (1990), I would conclude that an essential purpose of the ADEA is frustrated by compulsory arbitration of employment discrimination claims.

. . . The Court's holding today clearly eviscerates the important role played by an independent judiciary in eradicating employment discrimination.

### NOTES

1. *Gilmer* was clearly a case with enormous potential significance. Whether that potential would be full realized depended on the answers to a series of questions that arose in the wake of the Supreme Court's opinion.

2. The first question, whether *Gilmer* overruled *Gardner-Denver* entirely or left its rejection of arbitration intact in the collective bargaining context, remains unanswered today. The *Gilmer* Court distinguished *Gardner-Denver* on three grounds. First, the arbitrator there had not purported to resolve Title VII claims but only had decided just cause under the collective bargaining agreement. Second, the plaintiff in *Gardner-Denver* had no control over prosecution of the arbitration because the union presented his grievance. Third, *Gardner-Denver* was not decided under the Federal Arbitration Act. For that reason, the overwhelming majority of circuits read *Gilmer* as not overruling *Gardner-Denver* in the unionized workplace, limiting *Gilmer* to arbitration where the employee herself, not her union, agrees to arbitrate her statutory claims. E.g., Johnson v. Bodine Elec. Co., 142 F.3d 363, 367 (7th Cir. 1998) (Title VII); Peterson v. BMI Refractories, 132 F.3d 1405 (11th Cir. 1998) (§ 1981); Harrison v. Eddy Potash, Inc., 112 F.3d 1437, 1453 (10th Cir. 1997) (Title VII); Penny v. United Parcel Serv., 128 F.3d 408, 414 (6th Cir. 1997) (ADA); Varner v. Natl. Super Markets, 94 F.3d 1209, 1213 (8th Cir. 1996) (Title VII). One circuit, however, held to the contrary: arbitration clauses, even when contained in collective bargaining agreements, may bar suit by individual employees. Austin v. Owens-Broadway Glass Container, Inc., 78 F.3d 875 (4th Cir. 1996).

The Supreme Court granted certiorari to resolve this question but ultimately decided in Wright v. Universal Maritime Serv. Corp., 525 U.S. 70 (1998), only that a collective bargaining agreement's general arbitration clause was not an express or knowing and voluntary waiver; thus, arbitration was not required. See also Safrit v. Cone Mills Corp., 248 F.3d 306 (4th Cir. 2001) (finding explicit waiver); Doyle v. Raley's Inc., 158 F.3d 1012 (9th Cir. 1998). *Wright*, therefore, left open the underlying question of whether a properly drafted collective bargaining agreement could terminate a union member's right to sue in federal court on her statutory antidiscrimination claims. See also Tice v. American Airlines, Inc., 288 F.3d 313 (7th Cir. 2002) (by virtue of the Railway Labor Act, ADEA suit had to be arbitrated to the extent it required construction of the underlying collective bargaining agreement).

3. *Gilmer* clearly swept aside the concerns *Gardner-Denver* had raised about the inherent limitations of the arbitral forums as compared to court proceedings. *Gilmer* also rejected several frontal attacks on arbitration as a means of deciding ADEA cases. It first dismissed as speculative plaintiff's claim that the arbitral process, governed by the New York Stock Exchange rules, would be biased toward the employer. It then noted that there was no showing that discovery would be inadequate for an ADEA claim under those rules. Additionally, awards would be public so that objections to hidden decisions were inapplicable. Finally, it stressed that arbitrators have the power to award broad equitable relief, and to the extent their remedial powers are deficient, the EEOC remains able to sue the employer. *Gilmer* obviously marked a sea change in the Court's attitude towards arbitration, but its actual effect depended upon several developments.

4. Before addressing more technical legal issues, however, the underlying policy implications of *Gilmer* should be traced. The opinion itself can be taken to be straightforward — the agreement to arbitrate simply means the same rights are being asserted but in a different forum. Unless there is some reason to distrust the arbitral forum, why is that problematic? Some have argued that an arbitral forum might be expected to be less sympathetic to employees, if not with respect to rights then at least with respect to remedies, than a jury. Others have questioned the ability of plaintiffs to obtain the necessary discovery to prosecute a claim outside the court context. Still others believe systemic factors will incline arbitrators toward employers, in large part

because of the "repeat player" phenomenon. The EEOC maintains that mandatory arbitration has a built-in bias favoring employers who tend to be "repeat players." This bias may be even stronger when the employer is making use of a repeat arbitrator. See generally Lisa B. Bingham, On Repeat Players, Adhesive Contracts, and the Use of Statistics in Judicial Review of Employment Arbitration Awards, 29 McGeorge L. Rev. 223 (1998).

5. There has been a lively literature on the pros and cons of mandatory arbitration. E.g., Eileen Silverstein, From Statute to Contract: The Law of the Employment Relationship Reconsidered, 18 Hofstra Lab. & Emp. L.J. 479 (2001); Martin A. Malin, Privatizing Justice — But By How Much? Questions *Gilmer* Did Not Answer, 16 Ohio St. J. on Disp. Resol. 589, 631 (2001) ("In policing mandatory arbitration systems courts should insist on certain basic due process safeguards."); see Kenneth R. Davis, A Model for Arbitration: Autonomy, Cooperation, and Curtailment of State Power, 26 Fordham Urb. L.J. 167 (1999); Stephen J. Ware, Employment Arbitration and Voluntary Consent, 25 Hofstra L. Rev. 83 (1996) (ensuring voluntary consent to arbitration agreements, even those required as a condition of employment, can be attained by employing the contract law doctrines of mutual assent and duress); Joseph R. Grodin, Arbitration of Employment Discrimination Claims: Doctrine and Policy in the Wake of *Gilmer*, 14 Hofstra Lab. L.J. 1 (1996). See also Charles B. Craver, The Use of Non-Judicial Procedures to Resolve Employment Discrimination Claims, 11 Kan. J.L. & Pub. Poly. 141, 171 (2001) (Congress might consider adopting "procedures similar to those presently used by the NLRB to resolve unfair labor practice claims. Administrative law judges could hear such cases, with ALJ determinations being subject to EEOC review. Final EEOC decisions could be reviewed by courts of appeals."). For an article arguing that mandatory arbitration presents a significant number of disadvantages for employers, see Michael Z. Green, Debunking the Myth of Employer Advantage from Using Mandatory Arbitration for Discrimination Claims, 31 Rutgers L.J. 399, 401-05 (2000).

6. *Gilmer*, of course, rejected the plaintiff's challenge to particular aspects of an arbitration system. Courts, therefore, have rejected arguments that discharge for failure to sign an agreement to arbitrate disputes is proscribed by antiretaliation provisions. Weeks v. Harden Mfg. Corp., 291 F.3d 1307 (11th Cir. 2002) (employee could not reasonably believe that arbitration system was unlawful employment practice). But *Gilmer* left open the possibility that other arbitral systems might be so deficient as to not be enforceable. Hooters of Am., Inc. v. Phillips, 173 F.3d 933, 938 (4th Cir.1999) ("The Hooters rules when taken as a whole, however, are so one-sided that their only possible purpose is to undermine the neutrality of the proceeding."). More likely than an attack on the fairness of the arbitration system, however, is the fairness of particular arbitrations. Possible bias of arbitrators is subject to review under the Federal Arbitration Act, but only in extreme cases. A court may not overturn an arbitrator's decision merely because it believes that the arbitrator is wrong on the facts or the law. The FAA provides an award may be vacated where it was procured by corruption, fraud, or undue means, there was evident partiality or corruption in the arbitrators' decision, the arbitrators were guilty of misconduct, or they exceeded their powers. 9 U.S.C.S. § 10(a) (2003). Cf. Harris v. Parker Coll. of Chiropractic, 286 F.3d 790 (5th Cir. 2002) (parties may provide in their agreement for broader judicial review). While this is a very narrow scope of review, the courts have also held that an award may be vacated when there has been a manifest disregard for the law. Wilko v. Swan, 346 U.S. 427 (1953); Halligan v. Piper Jaffray, Inc., 148 F.3d 197 (2d Cir. 1998). See also Montes v. Shearson Lehman Bros., 128

F.3d 1456 (11th Cir. 1997). One case suggested that arbitral legal determinations, as opposed to fact finding, should be fully reviewable in court, but application of that principle would require the arbitrator to write an opinion and, in doing so, to draw a distinction between his findings of fact and conclusions of law. Cole v. Burns, 105 F.3d 1465 (D.C. Cir. 1997). See generally Calvin William Sharpe, Integrity Review of Statutory Arbitration Awards, 54 Hastings L.J. — (2003); Monica J. Washington, Note, Compulsory Arbitration of Statutory Employment Disputes: Judicial Review Without Judicial Reformation, 74 N.Y.U. L. Rev. 844 (1999); Stephen L. Hayford, A New Paradigm for Commercial Arbitration: Rethinking the Relationship Between Reasoned Awards and the Judicial Standards for Vacatur, 66 Geo. Wash. L. Rev. 443 (1998); Norman S. Poser, Arbitration: Judicial Review of Arbitration Awards: Manifest Disregard of the Law, 64 Brooklyn L. Rev. 471 (1998); Martin H. Malin & Robert F. Ladenson, Privatizing Justice: A Jurisprudential Perspective on Labor and Employment Arbitration from the *Steelworkers Trilogy* to *Gilmer*, 44 Hastings L.J. 1187 (1993). See also Geraldine Szott Moohr, Arbitration and the Goals of Employment Discrimination Law, 56 Wash. & Lee 395 (1999) (arguing that the values of public forum for resolving discrimination — including deterrence, development of the law, education, and the formation of public values — suggests at a minimum that there should be "meaningful judicial review" of arbitral decisions. See also Michael J. Yelnosky, Title VII, Mediation, and Collective Action, 1999 Ill. L. Rev. 583.

7. One issue was whether *Gilmer* applied to the ADEA only or to other discrimination statutes. The lower courts uniformly applied the holding to Title VII and other antidiscrimination statutes. Seus v. Nuveen, 146 F.3d 175 (3d Cir. 1998) (Title VII); McWilliams v. Logicon, Inc., 143 F.3d 573 (10th Cir. 1998) (ADA); Paladino v. Avnet Computer Techs., Inc., 134 F.3d 1054 (11th Cir. 1998) (Title VII); Miller v. Public Storage Mgmt., Inc., 121 F.3d 215 (5th Cir. 1997) (ADA); Patterson v. Tenet Healthcare, Inc., 113 F.3d 832 (8th Cir. 1997) (Title VII).

8. A more serious question was whether the *Gilmer* rule applied only to the somewhat unusual setting in which the case arose. The arbitration agreement in that case was a part of plaintiff's registration with the New York Stock Exchange, not directly a contract with the brokerage firm that employed him. For that reason, the *Gilmer* Court did not address the argument that the Federal Arbitration Act did not apply. Section 1 of the FAA provides that "nothing herein contained shall apply to contracts of employment of seamen, railroad employees, or any other class of workers engaged in foreign or interstate commerce." If this were read to exclude coverage of all employment contracts, *Gilmer* would have had little practical effect. The dissenters in *Gilmer* had argued that the Court should have reached the question and decided that employment contracts were exempt, and a lively literature emerged on the question. However, when the Court next encountered the question in Circuit City Stores, Inc. v. Adams, 532 U.S. 105 (2001), it held that "Section 1 exempts from the FAA only contracts of employment of transportation workers." Id. at 119. The Court, therefore, concluded that the employment discrimination claims made by plaintiff must be submitted to arbitration. While *Circuit City* involved state law discrimination claims, it clearly applies to federal claims as well. *Circuit City* is also important for its holding that the adhesive nature of the agreement to arbitrate contract was irrelevant to whether § 1 applied, as were state decisions related to whether arbitration was an appropriate forum to decide matters of state law.

9. What about the policy issues involved? *Gardner-Denver* and *Gilmer* take diametrically opposed views of the adequacy of arbitration as a substitute for traditional

litigation. Which is correct? There is a consensus that employers and employees ought to be free to agree to arbitration after a dispute has arisen. In this setting, the parties can make an informed trade-off between the likely lower costs and greater speed of arbitration and the greater procedural protections of traditional court proceedings. The controversy arises, as in *Gilmer* and *Circuit City*, when arbitration agreements are required as a condition of employment, or (in the case of Mr. Gilmer) as a condition for working in a particular industry. These are often referred to as "mandatory" arbitration. But both *Gilmer* and *Circuit City* largely avoided the policy questions by finding them foreclosed by the Federal Arbitration Act. At least as a general principle, agreements to arbitrate, whether imposed as a condition of employment or after a dispute arises, are enforceable if they are valid under that statute, an issue that will be addressed after the next principal case.

10. *Gilmer* stressed that, even though private suit might be foreclosed by an arbitration agreement, the EEOC remained free to bring an action. Despite this language, there were efforts to limit EEOC suits on behalf of individual employees. In EEOC v. Waffle House, Inc., 534 U.S. 279 (2002), the Court rejected such arguments and permitted the EEOC to obtain relief in Commission lawsuits on behalf of employees even if these employees had agreed to arbitrate any claims against their employers. See also EEOC v. Circuit City, 285 F.3d 404 (6th Cir. 2002) (holding that an arbitration agreement between an employer and an employee did not bar a non-party to the agreement, such as the EEOC, from filing its own suit against the employer). While recoveries by such employees, either after litigation or by arbitration, would presumably bar duplicate recovery in the EEOC action, the Commission cannot be foreclosed from suing by virtue of an arbitration agreement to which it is not a party.

11. The controversy in *Gilmer* arose prior to both the Civil Rights Act of 1991 and the Older Workers Benefit Protection Act (although the opinion, which was handed down after OWBPA was enacted, cites that law). Opponents of mandatory predispute arbitration invoked both statutes to limit the effects of *Gilmer*, largely without success.

## ROSENBERG v. MERRILL LYNCH
### 170 F.3d 1 (1st Cir. 1999)

LYNCH, Circuit Judge.

The question raised is whether Congress intended to prohibit enforcement of predispute arbitration agreements covering employment discrimination claims under Title VII and the Age Discrimination in Employment Act as a matter of law in all cases or at least under certain facts said to be present here. Every circuit that has considered the issue save one has upheld the use of such agreements. The case here, in which the district court refused to compel a plaintiff to arbitrate such claims when the employer wished to arbitrate under a pre-dispute agreement, has also drawn much attention in the form of nine briefs amici curiae.

The plaintiff, Susan Rosenberg, signed a standard securities industry form, the "U-4 Form," agreeing to arbitrate certain claims after being hired by Merrill Lynch, Pierce, Fenner & Smith as a trainee financial consultant. The form itself did not state which claims were to be arbitrated, but rather referred to the rules of various organizations with which Rosenberg was registering. When her employment was later terminated, Rosenberg filed suit alleging age and gender discrimination and related claims. Merrill Lynch moved to enforce the agreement and compel arbitration in the arbitration system of the New York Stock Exchange.

[The district court found no actual bias in the NYSE arbitral forum, but nevertheless denied the motion to compel.]

In the end we agree that the motion to compel was properly denied on the facts of this particular case, but for reasons different than those advanced by the district court. As to the first ground relied on by the district court, we hold as a matter of law that application of pre-dispute arbitration agreements to federal claims arising under Title VII and the ADEA is not precluded by the Older Workers Benefit Protection Act ("OWBPA") amendments to the ADEA or by Title VII as amended by the 1991 CRA. As to the second ground, we disavow the district court's conclusion that the agreement is not enforceable due to "structural bias" in the NYSE arbitral forum, a conclusion that was based on errors of law and fact. We agree that there has been no showing of actual bias in the forum selected and that a refusal to grant a motion to compel arbitration therefore may not be based on that ground.

We nonetheless conclude that there is an independent ground requiring affirmance of the order denying the motion to compel arbitration. The parties have agreed that the essential material facts are undisputed and that this court should, if necessary, resolve an issue not resolved by the district court: whether the parties' agreement met the standard set forth in the 1991 CRA for enforcing arbitration clauses "where appropriate and to the extent authorized by law." We hold, on the facts presented, that this standard was not met, and thus that the motion to compel was properly denied.

I

Rosenberg, whose prior experience had been in accounting and product engineering, was hired by Merrill Lynch on January 6, 1992. She was forty-five years old and held a Bachelor of Science degree in accounting. She had no experience in the securities industry when she entered Merrill Lynch's twenty-four month training program for financial consultants.

Rosenberg was required to fill out a standardized registration form generally required of employees in the securities industry. That form, the Uniform Application for Securities Industry Registration or Transfer, commonly referred to as the U-4 Form, included the following language under the heading "THE APPLICANT MUST READ THE FOLLOWING VERY CAREFULLY":

> I agree to arbitrate any dispute, claim or controversy that may arise between me and my firm, or a customer, or any other person, that is required to be arbitrated under the rules, constitutions, or by-laws of the organizations indicated in Item 10 as may be amended from time to time and that any arbitration award rendered against me may be entered as a judgement in any court of competent jurisdiction.

Item 10 included boxes for various securities organizations and jurisdictions with which an applicant might be registered. On Rosenberg's form the boxes marked ASE, CBOE, NASD, NYSE, and MA were checked — signifying the American Stock Exchange, Chicago Board of Exchange, National Association of Securities Dealers, New York Stock Exchange, and Massachusetts. The ASE, NASD, and NYSE boxes were apparently checked on or prior to January 10, 1992. The CBOE and MA boxes were checked sometime between January 10 and January 24. Rosenberg's supervisor, John Wyllys, signed the form on January 10, but Rosenberg did not sign the form until January 24 — although the form was back-dated to January 10. Rosenberg has no memory of reading or signing the form, although she admits that the signature is hers, and she says that she did not herself check any of the boxes. Wyllys in turn certified that Rosenberg would be familiar with the applicable rules, including the NYSE rules, at the time of approval of her U-4 Form. That certification was untrue.

Rosenberg says that she was not given a copy of the rules, or any amendments to the rules, of the NYSE, the NASD, or any of the other organizations referred to in Item 10 of the U-4. Merrill Lynch does not dispute this claim.

On May 5, 1992, Rosenberg was given the title of Financial Consultant, and she worked for Merrill Lynch until May 2, 1994, when her employment was terminated by John Wyllys. The reason given for the termination was inadequate performance.

[Rosenberg brought suit in state court, asserting tort claims and alleging sex discrimination, age discrimination, and that Wyllys "sexually harassed her by activating and handing to her a phallus-shaped vibrator when she went into his office to obtain a document." The defendants removed the case to federal court and Merrill Lynch moved to compel arbitration and to stay the matter pending arbitration.]

II . . .

The NYSE rules at the time Rosenberg brought her claim required arbitration of all employment disputes. Rule 347 stated:

> Any controversy between a registered representative and any member or member organization arising out of the employment or termination of employment of such registered representative by and with such member or member organization shall be settled by arbitration, at the instance of any such party, in accordance with the arbitration procedure prescribed elsewhere in these rules.

NYSE R. 347. No one explained to Rosenberg that the U-4 Form agreement to arbitrate that she had signed encompassed employment disputes she might have with her employer. She was given a copy of Merrill Lynch's "voluminous" employment handbook, but there is no argument that the handbook states that employment disputes are to be arbitrated.

Rosenberg also said in an affidavit that if she had been informed that her agreement to arbitrate certain claims included any potential employment discrimination claims she would have raised questions and might have sought outside advice. Merrill Lynch responded that the signing of these forms is an absolute condition of employment, or at least was at that time. . . .

[The district court denied the motion to compel. After that decision, "Merrill Lynch abandoned its policy of requiring employees to agree to arbitrate employment discrimination claims; however, this change in policy applies only to claims filed after Rosenberg's.]

The NYSE has proposed a rule change [that has become final since this opinion was written, see 64 Fed. Reg. 24,437, to] exclude employment discrimination claims from the scope of cases to be arbitrated. Rosenberg argues that the NYSE's proposed rule change makes this case moot; the defendants say it is not now moot and will not become moot. Although the rule change may be approved, the proposed rules are silent as to whether the rule change would apply retroactively to existing claims. . . .

## III

### A.  CONGRESSIONAL INTENT IN TITLE VII AND THE OWBPA

#### 1.  Title VII and Arbitration Agreements

Title VII of the Civil Rights Act of 1964, as amended by the 1991 CRA, does not, as a matter of law, prohibit pre-dispute arbitration agreements, contrary to the holding of the district court. This is a legal issue which we review de novo.

Whether pre-dispute agreements are prohibited by Title VII is a question of whether Congress intended to preclude their use. It is not a question of resolving the lively current public policy debate about whether use of arbitration, rather than a court, to resolve claims of employment discrimination hinders or advances the vindication of basic civil rights. Good arguments have been made on both sides of this policy debate.[4] The EEOC has issued a policy statement discouraging the use of pre-dispute arbitration agreements. See EEOC Notice No. 915.002 (July 10, 1997), reprinted in Excerpts from Text: EEOC Rejects Mandatory Binding Employment Arbitration, 52 Disp. Resol. J. 11 (1997). Not surprisingly, supporters of arbitration have criticized the EEOC statement. See, e.g., Oppenheimer & Johnstone, Con: A Management Perspective: Mandatory Arbitration Agreements Are an Effective Alternative to Employment Litigation, 52 Disp. Resol. J. 19, 19-20 (1997).

In *Gilmer,* the Supreme Court held that the Federal Arbitration Act ("FAA") required the enforcement of the pre-dispute mandatory arbitration clause in a U-4 Form identical to the one signed by Rosenberg. *Gilmer* involved a claim of age discrimination brought under the ADEA. The Court, noting numerous other contexts in which it had held that statutory claims could be the subject of arbitration agreements, ruled that pre-dispute arbitration clauses should be enforced unless the plaintiff could show congressional intent to preclude arbitration. To determine that intent, courts were directed to look to a statute's text and legislative history and to ascertain

---

4. Controversy over mandatory arbitration has grown as the number of employers requiring employees to agree to mandatory arbitration has increased. See Bingham, Employment Arbitration: The Repeat Player Effect, 1 Employee Rts. & Employment Pol'y J. 189, 189 (1997); Covington, Employment Arbitration After *Gilmer:* Have Labor Courts Come to the United States?, 15 Hofstra Lab. & Employment L.J. 345, 345-46 (1998). Critics of the use of arbitration in employment discrimination disputes argue that arbitration procedures are inherently biased against employees, that arbitrators themselves are not neutral or are not trained, that reduced availability of discovery in arbitration favors employers, and that arbitration may limit the availability of certain remedies, especially punitive damages. See Developments in the Law — Employment Discrimination — Mandatory Arbitration of Statutory Employment Disputes, 109 Harv. L. Rev. 1670, 1674-75, 1680-82 (1996). Critics also argue that judicial review of arbitration awards is limited, due in part to the fact that many arbitration decisions are not written. See id. at 1682. Although critics of arbitration also argue that compelling arbitration denies employees claiming discrimination of the right to have their claim judged by a jury of their peers, most of the criticisms of arbitration stem from perceptions regarding how arbitration operates in practice, rather than from inherent faults in arbitration.

There are also arguments in favor of arbitration, especially where procedural safeguards are in place. Arbitration may be far less costly than litigation and resolve disputes more quickly. Indeed, the number of employment-related cases in the courts has increased dramatically in the past two decades. Moreover, arbitration may also allow parties to select arbitrators with expertise in the subject matter of the dispute. Each side may also prefer arbitration because of the confidentiality and finality that comes with arbitration. See Motley, Compulsory Arbitration Agreements in Employment Contracts from *Gardner-Denver* to *Austin:* The Legal Uncertainty and Why Employers Should Choose Not to Use Preemployment Arbitration Agreements, 51 Vand. L. Rev. 687, 714 (1998); Oppenheimer & Johnstone, Con: A Management Perspective: Mandatory Arbitration Agreements Are an Effective Alternative to Employment Litigation, 52 Disp. Resol. J. 19, 22 (1997).

Such benefits may also be attractive to employees. Statistics show that plaintiff employees appear more likely to obtain awards in arbitration than in litigation, albeit with a reduced likelihood of receiving large amounts of damages. Arbitration advocates also argue that arbitration may improve employee morale by providing an accessible and fair mechanism for resolving disputes. See Oppenheimer & Johnstone, supra, at 22.

whether there was a conflict between arbitration and the statute's goals.

We find no conflict between the language or purposes of Title VII, as amended, and arbitration. The question of congressional intent in this case is resolved primarily by looking at the language Congress chose to use in the 1991 CRA, which, at section 118, provides:

> [w]here appropriate and to the extent authorized by law, the use of alternative means of dispute resolution, including . . . arbitration, is encouraged to resolve disputes arising under the Acts or provisions of Federal law amended by this title.

Civil Rights Act of 1991, Pub. L. No. 102-166, § 118, 105 Stat. 1071, 1081 (1991).

Relying on this language, the district court found that the language and legislative history of section 118 "unambiguously reject mandatory arbitration agreements." The court focused on the language "where appropriate and to the extent authorized by law." The court acknowledged that Congress passed the 1991 amendments after the Supreme Court's decision in *Gilmer*, but noted that the specific language was drafted prior to the *Gilmer* decision. The court concluded that the legislative history of the amendments made clear that "to the extent authorized by law" referred to the law as it existed prior to *Gilmer*, and thus evidenced congressional "intent to preclude mandatory arbitration." Id. In particular, the court ruled that Congress had intended the revisions to be consistent with Alexander v. Gardner-Denver Co., in which the Supreme Court held that an arbitration clause in a collective bargaining agreement did not preclude an employee from bringing a Title VII claim in court.

In reviewing the district court's legal determination, we have the benefit of having construed identical language in the Americans with Disabilities Act ("ADA"), 42 U.S.C. § 12101 et seq. (1994). See Bercovitch [v. Baldwin Schools, Inc., 133 F.3d. 141, 150 (1st Cir. 1995)]. The district court apparently did not consider this court's opinion in *Bercovitch*, which was decided shortly before the district court issued its order refusing to compel Rosenberg to arbitrate her claims. *Bercovitch* held that a plaintiff could be compelled to arbitrate claims brought under the ADA "where the plaintiff had voluntarily signed an agreement requiring arbitration." Examining the text of the ADA, we found that the statute's language, "far from evidencing an intention to preclude arbitration, can only be interpreted as favoring it." Additionally, language in the Committee Report accompanying the 1991 CRA, cited in Rosenberg's brief as evidence of congressional intent to preclude mandatory arbitration, is identical to language in the Committee Report accompanying the ADA.[5] In *Bercovitch*, however, we found that the legislative history of the ADA did not "rebut the presumption in favor of arbitration" made manifest by the clear language of the statute. We reach the same conclusion here.

Rosenberg and her amici present additional argument that Congress intended to

---

5. . . . The House Judiciary Committee Report on the 1991 CRA similarly [to the House Judiciary Committee Report, incorporated by reference into the House Conference Report on the ADA,] states:

> The Committee emphasizes, however, that the use of alternative dispute resolution mechanisms is intended to supplement, not supplant, the remedies provided by Title VII. Thus, for example, the Committee believes that any agreement to submit disputed issues to arbitration, whether in the context of a collective bargaining agreement or in an employment contract, does not preclude the affected person from seeking relief under the enforcement provisions of Title VII. This view is consistent with the Supreme Court's interpretation of Title VII in Alexander v. Gardner-Denver Co. The Committee does not intend for the inclusion of this section be used to [sic] preclude rights and remedies that would otherwise be available.

H.R. Rep. No. 102-40(II), at 41 (1991), reprinted in 1991 U.S.C.C.A.N. 694, 735.

preclude pre-dispute arbitration agreements in the Title VII context. For example, Congress rejected a proposed amendment to the 1991 CRA that would have explicitly permitted pre-dispute mandatory arbitration agreements, and the majority report rejecting the proposed amendment stated that "under the [proposed amendment] employers could refuse to hire workers unless they signed a binding statement waiving all rights to file Title VII complaints" in court and declared that "American workers should not be forced to choose between their jobs and their civil rights." H.R.Rep. No. 102- 40(I), at 104 (1991), reprinted in 1991 U.S.C.C.A.N. 549, 642. In addition, Rosenberg and her amici point to a statement that section 118 "contemplates the use of voluntary arbitration to resolve specific disputes after they have arisen, not coercive attempts to force employees in advance to forego statutory rights." 137 Cong. Rec. H9505-01, H9530 (daily ed. Nov. 7, 1991) (statement of Rep. Edwards).

Such statements are insufficient to overcome the presumption in favor of arbitration which *Gilmer* establishes. As other amici note in support of Merrill Lynch, additional statements by members of Congress expressed the view that section 118 did not preclude binding arbitration. See 137 Cong. Rec. S15, 472-01, S15,478 (daily ed. Oct. 30, 1991) (statement of Sen. Dole) ("This provision encourages the use of alternative means of dispute resolution, including binding arbitration, where the parties knowingly and voluntarily elect to use these methods. In light of the litigation crisis facing this country and the increasing sophistication and reliability of alternatives to litigation, there is no reason to disfavor the use of such forums."). Congress has repeatedly rejected legislation that would explicitly bar mandatory agreements to arbitrate employment discrimination claims. . . .

Numerous circuit courts have held that the Supreme Court's reasoning in *Gilmer* applies to Title VII claims and that pre-dispute agreements to arbitrate Title VII claims are permissible. See, e.g., Seus v. John Nuveen & Co., 146 F.3d 175 (3d Cir. 1998); Paladino v. Avnet Computer Techs., Inc., 134 F.3d 1054 (11th Cir. 1998); Gibson v. Neighborhood Health Clinics, Inc., 121 F.3d 1126, 1130 (7th Cir. 1997); Patterson v. Tenet Healthcare, Inc., 113 F.3d 832 (8th Cir. 1997); Cole v. Burns Int'l Sec. Servs., 105 F.3d 1465 (D.C. Cir. 1997); Austin v. Owens-Brockway Glass Container, Inc., 78 F.3d 875, 882 (4th Cir. 1996). Only the Ninth Circuit has disagreed, as described below.

However, few appellate courts, it appears, have dealt with the precise issue of whether the 1991 CRA demonstrates congressional intent to ban pre-dispute agreements to arbitrate employment discrimination claims. In Duffield v. Robertson Stephens & Co., 144 F.3d 1182 (9th Cir.), the court refused to enforce the U-4 Form arbitration clause. The *Duffield* court found section 118's statement that arbitration is encouraged "[w]here appropriate and to the extent authorized by law" to be ambiguous, and thus looked to the purposes of the 1991 CRA and to legislative history to elucidate the phrase's meaning. The court concluded that the legislative history, context, and text of the 1991 CRA demonstrated "that Congress intended to preclude compulsory arbitration of Title VII claims." . . .

The Third Circuit has interpreted section 118's reference to "the extent authorized by law" to refer to the Federal Arbitration Act, not to case law as it stood at the time Congress drafted the 1991 CRA. See *Seus* (disagreeing with *Duffield*). Like this court in *Bercovitch*, the Third Circuit first looked to the plain meaning of section 118, stating that section 118's endorsement of arbitration "simply cannot be 'interpreted' to mean that the FAA is impliedly repealed with respect to agreements to arbitrate Title VII and ADEA claims that will arise in the future." We agree.

We hold that neither the language of the statute nor the legislative history demonstrates an intent in the 1991 CRA to preclude pre-dispute arbitration agreements. Under *Gilmer*, the remaining question is whether "compulsory arbitration of [Title VII] claims pursuant to arbitration agreements would be inconsistent with the statutory framework and purposes of" Title VII. The district court found that mandatory arbitration would be at odds with the "structure and purpose" of the 1991 CRA and with the 1991 CRA's creation of a right to a jury trial for Title VII plaintiffs.

Resolving this issue requires determining whether there is any meaningful distinction between Title VII, as amended, and either the ADEA, which was construed by the Supreme Court in *Gilmer*, or the ADA, which was construed by this court in *Bercovitch*. *Gilmer* found no clash between arbitration and the purposes of the ADEA, noting instead that "[s]o long as the prospective litigant effectively may vindicate [his or her] statutory cause of action in the arbitral forum, the statute will continue to serve both its remedial and deterrent function." *Gilmer* (second alteration in original). *Bercovitch* held that "[t]here is no reason to think that the ADA presents a stronger policy case against arbitration than [the] ADEA."

It is difficult to see why the purposes of Title VII present a stronger case for rejecting arbitration than do the purposes of either the ADEA or the ADA. In finding that it was "not plausible . . . that the . . . Act would have . . . undermined [a plaintiff's private attorney general] role by endorsing private mandatory pre-dispute arbitration agreements," the district court overlooked *Gilmer*'s statement that public rights may be enforced through arbitration. The district court's comment that an endorsement of arbitration would be at odds with the 1991 CRA's creation of a right to a jury trial, similarly ignores *Gilmer*'s endorsement of arbitration under the ADEA — which also provides for jury trials. It may also evince a distrust of arbitration that the Supreme Court has long since disavowed. While people may and do reasonably disagree about whether pre-dispute arbitration agreements are a wise way of resolving discrimination claims, there is no "inherent conflict" between the goals of Title VII and the goals of the FAA, as *Gilmer* used that phrase.

The Supreme Court's very recent decision in Wright v. Universal Maritime Service Corp., 119 S. Ct. 391 (1998), reinforces this conclusion. *Wright* addressed the issue of waiver of a judicial forum for ADA claims by virtue of general language in a collective bargaining agreement ("CBA"). The Court did not reach the issue of whether a "clear and unmistakable" waiver in a CBA would be enforced: nor did it take a position on waivers "in areas outside collective bargaining." But nothing in the opinion suggests that *Gilmer* is not still good law; rather, the contrary is true.

## 2.  The OWBPA and Arbitration Agreements

. . . Rosenberg and her amici argue that the OWBPA, which the district court did not analyze, provides an alternative ground for upholding the denial of Merrill Lynch's motion to compel arbitration. Congress enacted the OWBPA in 1990. Although the Supreme Court decided *Gilmer* after Congress's passage of the OWBPA, *Gilmer* involved a contract signed prior to the OWBPA, and thus did not consider the effect of the act. Rosenberg signed her U-4 Form in 1992, well after the OWBPA became effective.

As modified by the OWBPA, the ADEA provides:

> (1) An individual may not waive any right or claim under this chapter unless the waiver is knowing and voluntary. Except as provided in paragraph (2), a waiver may not be considered knowing and voluntary unless at a minimum — . . .
> (C) the individual does not waive rights or claims that may arise after the date the waiver is executed[.]

29 U.S.C. § 626(f)(1). Rosenberg and her amici argue that the reference to "waiver" should be interpreted to include the U-4 Form's arbitration clause and that the reference to "right[ ]" should be interpreted to include the right to a bench or jury trial on ADEA claims. Amici point to legislative history that suggests that Congress was particularly concerned about older workers losing the right to a jury trial for ADEA claims. However, the cited language speaks only of ensuring that older workers are able to obtain legal relief and does not mention arbitration or waiver of a judicial forum. See S. Rep. No. 101-263, at 31-36 (1990), reprinted in 1990 U.S.C.C.A.N. 1509, 1537-1541; H.R. Rep. No. 101-664 (1990).

The EEOC as amicus curiae argues that its views on the OWBPA are entitled to deference. Yet the EEOC's recently issued rules on the "Waiver of Rights and Claims Under the Age Discrimination in Employment Act" include no discussion of the definition of "right" or "claim," see 29 C.F.R. § 1625.22 (effective July 6, 1998), and do not say that "waivers" mean arbitration clauses. We do not defer to views espoused only in the context of litigation. See Massachusetts v. Blackstone Valley Elec. Co., 67 F.3d 981, 991 (1st Cir. 1995). This is particularly true where the agency has gone through rule making and has conspicuously ignored the topic in its rules.

Most courts which have considered the issue have interpreted OWBPA's reference to "any right" to apply to substantive rights, or, at any rate, not to the right to proceed in court rather than in arbitration. See, e.g., *Seus*; Williams v. Cigna Fin. Advisors, Inc., 56 F.3d 656 (5th Cir. 1995). Courts that have interpreted the OWBPA to apply to waivers of substantive rights have relied in part on dicta in *Gilmer* commenting that "Congress . . . did not explicitly preclude arbitration or other nonjudicial resolution of claims, even in its recent amendments to the ADEA." See *Seus*; *Cigna Fin. Advisors*, ("There is no indication that Congress intended the OWBPA to affect agreements to arbitrate employment disputes."). The recent *Wright* decision reaffirms what was said in *Gilmer*: that an employee's statutory right to a judicial forum for claims of employment discrimination "is not a substantive right."

Rosenberg and her amici point to the Supreme Court's decision in Oubre v. Entergy Operations, Inc. [reproduced at page 666], in which the Court commented that "[t]he OWBPA implements Congress' policy via a strict, unqualified statutory stricture on waivers, and we are bound to take Congress at its word." These comments are not particularly relevant here because they do not go to the issue of whether the term "waiver" was meant to apply to pre-dispute arbitration agreements. Indeed, while *Oubre* did not consider whether the OWBPA applies to waivers of procedural as well as substantive rights, the Court did state that the OWBPA "is clear: An employee 'may not waive' any ADEA *claim*" unless the requirements of § 626(f) are satisfied. Id. (emphasis added). To the degree that *Oubre* has any relevance here, the reference to "claim" suggests that the waiver provisions refer to substantive claims. A substantive ADEA claim may be presented in an arbitral or a judicial forum. See *Gilmer*.

Neither Rosenberg nor amicus curiae the EEOC points to any court that has held that the OWBPA evinces congressional intent to preclude pre-dispute arbitration agreements. . . .

To interpret the OWBPA's reference to "right" to include procedural rights — and the right to a judicial forum in particular — would be to ignore the Supreme Court's repeated statements that arbitral and judicial fora are both able to give effect to the policies that underlie legislation. A party who agrees to arbitrate "does not forgo the substantive rights afforded by the statute; it only submits to their resolution in an arbitral, rather than a judicial, forum." *Gilmer.* Interpreting the OWBPA to preclude pre-dispute arbitration agreements would run afoul of the presumption that arbitration provides a fair and adequate mechanism for enforcing statutory rights.

### B.  THE NEW YORK STOCK EXCHANGE'S ARBITRATION SYSTEM

In addition to finding that Congress, in enacting the 1991 CRA, had clearly precluded pre-dispute agreements to arbitrate, the district court found an additional ground for refusing to compel arbitration: what it described as "structural bias" in the NYSE's arbitration procedures. The court found that the NYSE arbitration process was "inadequate to vindicate Rosenberg's ADEA and Title VII rights." In reaching this conclusion, the district court committed two types of errors.

First, the district court misinterpreted the window available post-*Gilmer* for challenges to a specific arbitral forum. The district court found no actual bias in the NYSE's arbitration system, but nevertheless refused to compel arbitration due to alleged structural infirmities. Absent a showing of actual bias — and we agree with the district court that there was no such showing in this case — *Gilmer* required the district court to compel arbitration. Second, the district court erred in its description of the NYSE's arbitration procedures.

Rosenberg and amici argue that the arbitration agreement should not be enforced because it is unconscionable and because it is the result of a gross disparity of bargaining power. We reject these arguments, which are not frivolous, because the law has long imposed a heavy burden on those who make such arguments and Rosenberg has not met her burden of proof.

The district court found that signing the U-4 Form was a prerequisite for employment as a securities broker, and Merrill Lynch has acknowledged that it would not "employ or promote financial consultants who refuse to sign the Form U-4." Securities industry officials similarly confirmed that financial consultants were not permitted to excise the arbitration clause from the U-4 Form. Rosenberg argues that the imposition of such a requirement renders the U-4 Form arbitration clause invalid as an unenforceable contract of adhesion.

We agree with the Third Circuit that the U-4 Form arbitration clause is not unenforceable on these grounds. In *Seus,* the court found that even if the U-4 Form arbitration agreement were a contract of adhesion plaintiff would still need to show "both a lack of meaningful choice about whether to accept the provision in question, and that the disputed provisions were so onesided as to be oppressive." And section 211 of the Restatement (Second) of Contracts states that a term in a standardized agreement is enforceable unless one party "has reason to believe that the party manifesting . . . assent would not do so if he knew that the writing contained a particular term." Restatement (Second) of Contracts § 211 (1979). Rosenberg has made no such showing.

In addition, in *Gilmer,* the Court stated that inequality in bargaining power "is not a sufficient reason to hold that arbitration agreements are never enforceable in the employment context." *Gilmer,* after all, involved the same U-4 Form arbitration clause at issue here. Absent a showing of fraud or oppressive conduct — which Rosenberg does not allege occurred — the contract is not unenforceable on these grounds. . . .

### B.  WAS ROSENBERG'S AGREEMENT TO ARBITRATE APPROPRIATE AND AUTHORIZED BY LAW WITHIN THE MEANING OF THE 1991 CRA?

We repeat what Rosenberg's U-4 Form said and did not say. The U-4 Form stated that Rosenberg agreed to arbitrate "any dispute, claim or controversy that may arise . . . *that is required to be arbitrated under the rules, constitutions, or by-laws of the organizations indicated in Item 10*" (emphasis added). The agreement did not state that Rosenberg agreed to arbitrate all disputes, or even any dispute. The agreement only required Rosenberg to arbitrate any dispute that the NYSE's rules, constitution, or bylaws (or those of any of the organizations listed in item 10) required to be arbitrated. Cf. Prudential Ins. Co. of America v. Lai, 42 F.3d 1299 (9th Cir. 1994) (noting that the U-4 Form arbitration provision "does not in and of itself bind appellants to arbitrate any particular dispute"). It is undisputed that Rosenberg's execution of this provision was a condition of her employment with Merrill Lynch.

The NYSE Rules in turn required Rosenberg to arbitrate "[a]ny controversy . . . arising out of [her] employment or termination of [her] employment." NYSE R. 347. Merrill Lynch does not dispute Rosenberg's statement that she never received a copy of the NYSE rules and has provided no evidence that it gave her a copy or made one available to Rosenberg at the time of the employment, at the time of NYSE approval, or even later. Nor has Merrill Lynch provided evidence it even told Rosenberg that the clause required her to arbitrate any employment discrimination claims. Had the U-4 provided for arbitration of all disputes, or given explicit notice that employment disputes were subject to arbitration, we would have had little difficulty in finding that Rosenberg had agreed to arbitrate her employment discrimination claims within the meaning of the 1991 CRA.

For purposes of the 1991 CRA, the parties and the district court have adopted the analytical rubric of whether the agreement was "knowing and voluntary" to examine the agreement. This usage is common, and stems from a footnote in *Gardner-Denver*:

> In determining the effectiveness of any such waiver, a court would have to determine at the outset that the employee's consent . . . was voluntary and knowing.

The "knowing and voluntary" language undoubtedly comes from thinking of arbitration as "a waiver of judicial remedies." It is commonplace that waivers of certain rights, particularly substantive rights, are enforceable only if they are knowing and voluntary. Whether a standard similar to the one that applies to rights such as the right to counsel, cf. Johnson v. Zerbst, 304 U.S. 458, 465 (1938), should apply to waivers of a judicial forum is an open question. . . .

The Ninth Circuit has expressly adopted a "knowing" standard for such arbitration clauses and has described the standard as being a heightened one. See Renteria v. Prudential Ins. Co. of America, 113 F.3d 1104 (9th Cir. 1997). The Third Circuit has rejected any heightened standard. See *Seus*. The Eighth Circuit appears to have done the same in *Patterson*. . . .

We also find it unnecessary to resolve this general issue. Rather, we focus on the language of the 1991 CRA, in which the terms "knowing and voluntary" do not appear. The operative language is:

> [w]here appropriate and to the extent authorized by law, . . . arbitration . . . is encouraged to resolve disputes arising under [these laws].

1991 CRA § 118, 105 Stat. at 1081. There has been little case law on the meaning of these terms.

At a minimum the words "to the extent authorized by law" must mean that arbitration agreements that are unenforceable under the FAA are also unenforceable when applied to claims under Title VII and the ADEA. Under the FAA, arbitration agreements are enforceable "save upon such grounds as exist at law or in equity for the revocation of any contract." 9 U.S.C. §2. . . . The question under the FAA of whether an arbitration agreement is enforceable is generally determined by reference to common-law principles of general applicability. See Perry v. Thomas, 482 U.S. 483, 492 n.9 (1987); Southland Corp. v. Keating, 465 U.S. 1, 19-20 (1984). When deciding whether the parties agreed under the FAA to arbitrate a certain matter, courts "generally . . . should apply ordinary state-law principles that govern the formation of contracts." First Options of Chicago, Inc. v. Kaplan, 514 U.S. 938, 944 (1995).[14]

Similarly, the question of the scope of an arbitration agreement under the FAA is a matter not just of state law, but of general federal arbitration law. See Moses H. Cone Mem'l Hosp. v. Mercury Constr. Corp., 460 U.S. 1 (1983). There is often, as here, a predecessor question of whether there was an agreement at all to arbitrate. Reference should be made to standard principles of contract law in making such a determination. We need not resolve here whether the "to the extent authorized by law" clause has a meaning greater than a reference to the FAA.

While such principles provide background, the resolution of the case does not turn on them but on the language of the 1991 CRA; that is, whether under these facts, the arbitration clause was "appropriate." Thus, this case does not implicate any broader questions of enforceability of the arbitration clause when the 1991 CRA or ADEA are not involved.

We set the context. Rosenberg's and Merrill Lynch's arbitration agreement did not by itself define the range of claims subject to arbitration, even though Merrill Lynch expressly represented that she would be advised of the rules. It referred only to arbitration of such claims as were required to be arbitrated by the NYSE rules. But those rules were not given to Rosenberg or described to her. The question then becomes which party should bear the risk of her ignorance. Given Congress's concern that agreements to arbitrate employment discrimination claims should be enforced only where "appropriate," a concern not expressed in the FAA or at common law, Merrill Lynch should, we believe, bear that risk. As part of its employment agreement with Rosenberg, Merrill Lynch required her to agree to the terms of the U-4 Form. The U-4 Form, prepared under the NYSE Rules, requires that employees being asked to execute the U-4 Form be given a copy of the NYSE rules or information to the same effect, at least by the time of approval. The U-4 Form thus explicitly contemplated that Merrill Lynch would take the steps necessary to ensure that Rosenberg was aware of the NYSE rules. The same U-4 Form that Rosenberg signed to register with the NYSE was also signed by John Wyllys on behalf of Merrill Lynch. Under the heading, "THE FIRM MUST COMPLETE THE FOLLOWING," the U-4 Form stated:

> To the best of my knowledge and belief, the applicant is currently bonded where required, and, at the time of approval, will be familiar with the statute(s), constitutions(s), rules and by-laws of the agency, jurisdiction or self-regulatory organization with which this application is being filed, and the rules governing registered persons, and will be fully qualified for the position for which application is being made herein.

Wyllys' signature follows this statement. But Wyllys' certification was false: Merrill Lynch never provided Rosenberg with a copy of the rules and Merrill Lynch has provided no evidence it made Rosenberg familiar with the rules as to arbitration.

---

14. There is no contention here that the parties agreed that an arbitrator should decide questions of arbitrability; the parties contend that the issue is for this court. In any event, Rosenberg did not clearly agree to submit the questions of arbitrability to an arbitrator, and so the issue is indeed for the court.

Merrill Lynch's failure runs afoul of the mutual understandings. Since the arbitration requirement stems from the NYSE Rules and the U-4 Form requires that the employee be "familiar with" the rules and thus with the requirement for arbitration of employment claims, we think that Merrill Lynch's inaction undercuts the imposition of an arbitration requirement. The NYSE rules contemplated that Merrill Lynch certify to it that, at least as of the time of NYSE approval of Rosenberg's application, Rosenberg be "familiar" with the rules including the rules that all employment disputes be arbitrated. Merrill Lynch's failure, we believe, makes it inappropriate to enforce the provision. . . .

In short, under these circumstances, compelling arbitration would not be "appropriate" under the 1991 CRA. Our approach is close to that taken by the Supreme Court in *Wright*. There the court declined to mandate arbitration of an ADA claim where the waiver of a judicial forum set forth in a CBA was not "clear and unmistakable." *Wright*. To be sure, *Wright* carefully distinguished a private arbitration agreement from an agreement in the collective bargaining context. There are sound reasons to recognize such a distinction and a lesser standard than "clear and unmistakable" applies to private agreements. But *Wright* also teaches that the "appropriate" language of the 1991 CRA, which parallels that of the ADA, has some teeth:

> Our conclusion that a union waiver of employee rights to a federal judicial forum for employment discrimination claims must be clear and unmistakable means that, absent a clear waiver, it is not "appropriate" . . . to find an agreement to arbitrate.

In recognizing that "the right to a federal judicial forum is of sufficient importance to be protected," *Wright* leads to the conclusion, we think, that there be some minimal level of notice to the employee that statutory claims are subject to arbitration.[17]


## NOTES

1. Ironically, the U-4 Form in the securities industry, which resulted in *Gilmer*, *Rosenberg*, and many of the other cases involving arbitration, will cease to have much impact prospectively as a result of the changes in rules by the NYSE, NASD, and similar organizations noted by *Rosenberg*. While Merrill Lynch itself seems to have discontinued this practice prospectively, individual employers, in and outside of the securities industry, may continue to use arbitration clauses on their own initiative. Thus, the issue raised by *Rosenberg* remains very important.

2. As the changes in NYSE and NASD rules suggest, there has been considerable resistance to arbitration as a condition of employment. The EEOC has issued a Policy Statement on Mandatory Binding Arbitration of Employment Disputes as a Condition of Employment, No. 915.002 (July 10, 1997), which opposes such agreements (website visited Sept. 15, 1999), *http:www.eeoc.gov/docs/mandarb.txt*. An ADR Proto-

---

17. If Merrill Lynch had provided the rules to Rosenberg but she did not read them, that would not save her. See Tiffany v. Sturbridge Camping Club, Inc., 32 Mass. App. Ct. 173, 587 N.E.2d 238, 240 n.5 (1992) (stating the traditional rule of contract law that a party to a contract is assumed to have read and understood the terms of a contract she signs). This opinion also does not suggest utilization of a subjective standard which focuses on what the employee actually knew. But cf. Developments in the Law, supra, at 1683-84 (arguing for such a standard). Indeed, it would be an odd result if the 1991 CRA were to be interpreted based on the assumption that women and minorities, otherwise competent to enter contracts, were somehow disabled and in need of such special protections where the subject of the contract was an agreement to arbitrate.

col, endorsed by organizations such as the American Arbitration Association, suggests procedures for arbitrating workplace disputes, and urges arbitrators to refuse cases that do not provide appropriate safeguards. *http:www.naarb.org/protocol.html.* The National Employment Law Association, which represents the plaintiff's bar, has subscribed to the Protocol but urged that the profession go further and refuse to arbitrate when the arbitration agreement is a condition of employment. Leona Green, Mandatory Arbitration of Statutory Employment Disputes: A Public Policy Issue in Need of a Legislation Solution, 12 Notre Dame J.L. Ethics & Pub. Poly. 173 (1998).

3. *Rosenberg* is clearly the majority rule in rejecting both § 118 and OWBPA as limitations in FAA application to the employment context. In addition to the cases cited by the court, other decisions have held that § 118 does not bar mandatory arbitration. E.g., Haskins v. Prudential Ins. Co. of Am., 230 F.3d 231 (6th Cir. 2000); Merrill Lynch, Pierce, Fenner & Smith, Inc. v. Nixon, 210 F.3d 814 (8th Cir. 2000); Desiderio v. Natl. Assn. of Sec. Dealers, 191 F.3d 198 (2d Cir. 1999); Koveleskie v. SBC Capital Markets, Inc., 167 F.3d 361 (7th Cir. 1999).

4. The only decision holding directly that § 118 of the Civil Rights Act of 1991 bars pre-dispute arbitration was Duffield v. Robertson Stephens & Co., 144 F.3d 1182 (9th Cir. 1998), discussed in *Rosenberg. Duffield*, however, has since been overruled by the Ninth Circuit, which found it implicitly rejected by the Supreme Court. EEOC v. Luce, Forward, Hamilton & Scripps, 303 F.3d 994 (9th Cir. 2002), reasoned:

> Although Circuit City [Stores, Inc. v. Adams, 532 U.S. 105 (2001)] did not repudiate *Duffield* by name, the Supreme Court's language and reasoning decimated *Duffield's* conclusion that Congress intended to preclude compulsory arbitration of Title VII claims. In particular, *Circuit City's* unambiguous proclamation that "arbitration agreements can be enforced under the FAA without contravening the policies of congressional enactments giving employees specific protection against discrimination prohibited by federal law" cannot be reconciled with *Duffield's* holding that Congress intended Title VII, one such "congressional enactment," to preclude compulsory arbitration of discrimination claims.

5. While the Supreme Court has adopted a presumption favoring arbitrability, it has also indicated that that presumption can be overcome when "Congress has evinced an intention to preclude a waiver of judicial remedies for the statutory rights at issue." In seeking such an intent, it has indicated that "that intention will be deducible from text or legislative history." Mitsubishi Motors Corp. v. Soler Chrysler-Plymouth, Inc., 473 U.S. 614, 628 (1985). Accord, Shearson/American Express Inc. v. McMahon, 482 U.S. 220 (1987). Is this an invitation to Congress to use legislative history in order to make clear its intent? If so, does that make *Duffield* more persuasive?

6. If the *Duffield* approach to § 118 were to be taken rather than *Rosenberg's*, a question would arise as to whether § 118 applies only to Title VII or also to the ADEA. The section applies to "disputes arising under the acts or provisions of Federal law amended by this title." While most of the 1991 Civil Rights Act amends Title VII, § 115 does amend the ADEA.

7. Commentators are divided on the result reached in *Rosenberg*. See generally Karen Halverson, Arbitration and the Civil Rights Act of 1991, 67 U. Cin. L. Rev. 445 (1995) (arbitration as a condition of employment should not be upheld as within the 1991 Act or as a matter of policy); Mark L. Adams, Compulsory Arbitration of Discrimination Claims and the Civil Rights Act of 1991: Encouraged or Prescribed?,

44 Wayne L. Rev. 619 (1999) (Congress intended in the 1991 Act to encourage only voluntary, not compulsory, arbitration); Douglas E. Abrams, Arbitrability in Recent Federal Civil Rights Legislation: The Need for Amendment, 26 Conn. L. Rev. 521 (1994) (arguing that the texts of the ADA and the 1991 Civil Rights Act, "the only sources assured of judicial effectuation," favor enforcing arbitration agreements, even if the legislative histories "acknowledge qualifications on the binding effect arbitral awards would otherwise hold under the FAA").

8. As *Rosenberg* discusses, the Older Workers Benefit Protection Act (OWBPA), codified at 29 U.S.C.S. § 626 (f)(2003), while not speaking expressly of "arbitration," requires any waiver of ADEA "rights and claims" to be "knowing and voluntary." If this includes the waiver of procedural rights such as a jury trial, the OWBPA may invalidate many agreements to arbitrate that are exacted mechanically as a condition of employment. See generally Christine Godsil Cooper, Where Are We Going with *Gilmer?* — Some Ruminations on the Arbitration of Discrimination Claims, 11 St. Louis U. Pub. L. Rev. 203, 235-36 (1992). Both *Rosenberg* and Seus v. Nuveen, 146 F.3d 175 (3d Cir. 1998) rejected the claim that, since the language "any right or claim" must encompass the right to a jury trial, OWBPA prohibits the enforcement of any agreement that requires the individual to forgo her statutory right unless it complies with the requirements of the statute. See also Williams v. Cigna Fin. Advisors, Inc., 56 F.3d 656 (5th Cir. 1995) (OWBPA is inapplicable to arbitration agreements). Accord, Douglas E. Abrams, Arbitrability in Recent Federal Civil Rights Legislation: The Need for Amendment, 26 Conn. L. Rev. 521, 556 n.187 (1994) (arguing that "Congress did not intend the OWBPA's waiver provision to affect the FAA mandate's operation with respect to either post-dispute or predispute arbitration agreements"). The Supreme Court in Oubre v. Entergy Operations, Inc. (reproduced at page 666), while not addressing these issues directly, applied OWBPA literally. See also Stephen J. Ware, Arbitration Clauses, Jury Waiver Clauses and Other Contractual Waivers of Constitutional Rights, — Law & Contemp. Probs. — (2003).

9. In dealing with the 1991 Civil Rights Act, the *Rosenberg* court looked to the literal language of Title VII, and refused to resort to legislative history, which would have cut the other way. It did so because legislative history is admissible only when the statute is ambiguous. In dealing with OWBPA, however, the court refused to apply the statute literally; instead, it determined that a prohibition on waivers of "rights and claims" applied only to substantive rights. Why the different approach? Is "right" more or less ambiguous than "appropriate"?

10. The actual result in *Rosenberg* suggests that approving arbitration in general does not mean that all agreements are enforceable. In deciding whether a particular agreement is valid and whether the arbitration clause reaches the dispute in question, courts have struggled with both the appropriate standard and specific applications.

11. The first question is a procedural one — who decides whether a matter is arbitratable? The presumption is that this matter is one for the court, but that the parties may commit the question to the arbitrator. "[T]he question of arbitrability — whether a collective-bargaining agreement creates a duty for the parties to arbitrate the particular grievance — is undeniably an issue for judicial determination. Unless the parties clearly and unmistakably provide otherwise, the question of whether the parties agreed to arbitrate is to be decided by the court, not the arbitrator." AT&T Techs., Inc. v. Communications Workers of Am., 475 U.S. 643, 656 (1986). In Howsam v. Dean Witter Reynolds, Inc., 123 S. Ct. 588 (2002), the Court applied this principle outside of the collective bargaining context, but gave a narrow reading to the "the question of arbitrability" — the phrase is applicable "in the kind of narrow cir-

cumstance where contracting parties would likely have expected a court to have decided the gateway matter, where they are not likely to have thought that they had agreed that an arbitrator would do so, and, consequently, where reference of the gateway dispute to the court avoids the risk of forcing parties to arbitrate a matter that they may well not have agreed to arbitrate." Id. at 592. Applying this approach, the Court found that whether a six-year time limit on arbitration precluded arbitration of the dispute in question was one for the arbitrator, not the court: "We consequently conclude that the NASD's time limit rule falls within the class of gateway procedural disputes that do not present what our cases have called 'questions of arbitrability.' And the strong pro-court presumption as to the parties' likely intent does not apply." Id. at 593.

12. With respect to the standard applicable, the most obvious requirement is that the agreement to arbitrate be a valid contract under normal contract law principles. For example, while the Supreme Court in *Circuit City* rejected the argument that employment contracts were within the FAA exception, on remand, the Ninth Circuit invalidated the arbitration agreement as unconscionable under California contract law. 279 F.3d 889 (9th Cir. 2002) (the agreement was procedurally and substantively unconscionable; the court looked to a number of defects: (1) limitations on remedies; (2) short statute of limitations; (3) arbitral fee-splitting; and (4) one-sidedly requiring the employee to arbitrate, but not requiring the employer to do so). See also Ferguson v. Countrywide Credit Indus., 298 F.3d 778, 785 (9th Cir. Cal. 2002) ("arbitration agreement was unfairly one-sided and, therefore, substantively unconscionable because the agreement 'compels arbitration of the claims employees are most likely to bring against [the employer but] exempts from arbitration the claims [the employer] Countrywide is most likely to bring against its employees."); Murray v. United Food & Commercial Workers Intl. Union, 289 F.3d 297 (4th Cir. 2002) (arbitration agreement deemed one-sided and thus was unenforceable). Cf. Circuit City v. Ahmed, 283 F.3d 1198 (9th Cir. 2002) (opportunity to opt out of arbitration agreement saved it from unconscionability).

13. Unconscionability is, however, only one basis for invalidating a contract. Like other agreements, arbitration clauses require offer and acceptance. Compare Circuit City Stores, Inc. v. Najd, 294 F.3d 1104 (9th Cir. 2002) (employee bound when he failed to opt out of an arbitration plan distributed to workers); Tinder v. Pinkerton Sec., 305 F.3d 728 (7th Cir. 2002) (continuing work after notice from employer of arbitration requirement was sufficient assent); In re Halliburton Co. and Brown & Root Energy Serv., Relators, 80 S.W.3d 566 (Tex. 2002) (same); Hightower v. GMRI Inc., 272 F.3d 239 (4th Cir. 2001) (same); with Nelson v. Cyprus Bagdad Copper Corp., 119 F.3d 756 (9th Cir. 1997) (arbitration clause in employee handbook not enforceable even though employee read and understood the clause). They also require consideration, e.g., Floss v. Ryan's Family Steak Houses Inc., 211 F.3d 306 (6th Cir. 2000) (pre-hire arbitration agreements were found unenforceable for lack of consideration), and the absence of invalidating factors like fraud, duress, and unconscionability. While the Supreme Court's decision in *Circuit City* makes clear that conditioning employment on agreeing to arbitrate employment-related disputes is not sufficient to withhold enforcement, the Ninth Circuit's decision on remand shows that attention to normal contract analysis remains important.

14. It is clear, however, that state law cannot discriminate against arbitration agreements. That is, agreements to arbitrate must be enforced on the same basis as other contracts. The Supreme Court has reiterated that state laws requiring special treatment of arbitration clauses are preempted by the Federal Arbitration Act. Doctor's Assocs., Inc. v. Casarotto, 517 U.S. 681 (1996). See also Southland Corp. v. Keating,

465 U.S. 1 (1984) (in enacting the FAA, Congress declared "a national policy favoring arbitration" and "withdrew the power of the states to require a judicial forum for the resolution of claims which the contracting parties agreed to resolve by arbitration"). See generally Traci L. Jones, State Law of Contract Formation in the Shadow of the Federal Arbitration Act, 46 Duke L.J. 653 (1996). While state law principles applicable to contracts generally are, in effect, incorporated into the FAA on its own terms, that statute precludes states from singling out agreements to arbitrate for special treatment. E.g., Stirlen v. Supercuts, Inc., 60 Cal. Rptr. 2d 138 (Ct. App. 1997) (arbitration agreement unenforceable on the basis of unconscionability, a neutral principle applicable to contracts generally).

15. *Rosenberg*, however, seems to require more than contract validity under normal principles. Some courts apply a heightened consent requirement to enforcing employment-related arbitration agreements. For example, some hold that the employee must have "knowingly" agreed to arbitrate such claims, and this requirement is not satisfied unless the agreement clearly refers to employment discrimination claims. E.g., Paladino v. Avnet Computer, 134 F.3d 1054 (11th Cir. 1998) (to fall within the FAA, an arbitration agreement must contain terms that generally and fairly inform the signatories that it covers statutory claims although it need not list every statute); Brisintine v. Stone & Webster Engg., 117 F.3d 519 (11th Cir. 1997) (agreement must authorize arbitrator to resolve federal statutory claims rather than merely authorizing arbitrator to resolve contract claims); Renteria v. Prudential Ins. Co., 113 F.3d 1104 (9th Cir. 1997) (a U-4 form, stating that arbitrable disputes encompass those "as amended from time to time," was ineffective as a waiver since a knowing waiver of a right must be determined at the time the agreement is made); Prudential Ins. Co. v. Lai, 42 F.3d 1299 (9th Cir. 1994); Farrand v. Lutheran Bhd., 993 F.2d 1253 (7th Cir. 1993); see also Wright v. Universal Maritime Serv. Corp, 525 U.S. 70 (1998) (for a union to waive employees' rights to a federal judicial forum for statutory antidiscrimination claims, the agreement to arbitrate such claims must be clear and unmistakable; a clause providing only for arbitration of "[m]atters under dispute," without explicit incorporation of statutory antidiscrimination requirements is not sufficient.).

16. However, other courts have held that general language includes discrimination claims. Seus v. Nuveen, 146 F.3d 175 (3d Cir. 1998) (rejecting a heightened knowing and voluntary standard that considers such factors as specificity of language in agreement, plaintiff's education and experience, plaintiff's opportunity for deliberation and negotiation, and whether plaintiff was encouraged to consult counsel); Rojas v. TK Communications, Inc., 87 F.3d 745 (5th Cir. 1996); Kidd v. Equitable Life Assurance Socy., 32 F.3d 516 (11th Cir. 1994); Bender v. A.G. Edwards & Sons, Inc., 971 F.2d 698 (11th Cir. 1992). See also Patterson v. Tenet Healthcare, 113 F.3d 832 (8th Cir. 1997) (general language of arbitration clause in employee handbook encompassed federal statutory claims even though other portions of handbook disclaimed contractual obligation).

17. One recurrent issue is whether an arbitration agreement can validly impose arbitration costs on an employee. In Green Tree Fin. Corp. v. Randolph, 531 U.S. 79 (2000), the Court held an arbitration agreement valid even though it "was silent with respect to payment of filing fees, arbitrators' costs, and other arbitration expenses." Id. at 84. The plaintiff argued, and the Eleventh Circuit agreed, that the agreement was unenforceable due to the lack of such information and the risk of insurmountable arbitration costs. The Supreme Court rejected this argument, finding that the "'risk [of plaintiff being] saddled with prohibitive costs is too speculative to justify the invali-

dation of an arbitration agreement." Id. at 91. Before *Green Tree* the circuits had frequently refused to enforce arbitration agreements which allocated costs to the employee. E.g., Shankle v. B-G Maint., 163 F.3d 1230 (10th Cir. 1999) (arbitration agreement entered into as a condition of employment that requires the employee to pay a portion of the arbitrator's fees is unenforceable under the FAA; to supplant a judicial forum, arbitration must provide an effective and accessible forum, and the prohibitive cost the employee would have been required to pay meant that the arbitral forum was not accessible); Cole v. Burns Intl. Sec. Serv., 148 F.3d 197 (D.C. Cir. 1998) (valid arbitration agreement may not impose costs on employee); Hooters v. Phillips, 173 F.3d 933 (4th Cir. 1999) ("Hooters materially breached the arbitration agreement by promulgating terms so egregiously unfair as to constitute a complete default of its contractual obligation to draft arbitration rules and to do so in good faith."). See also Dumais v. American Golf Corp., 299 F.3d 1216, 1219 (10th Cir. 2002) (as construed, "an arbitration agreement allowing one party the unfettered right to alter the arbitration agreement's existence or its scope is illusory."). See generally, Michael H. LeRoy & Peter Feuille, When Is Cost an Unlawful Barrier to Alternative Dispute Resolution? The Ever Green Tree of Mandatory Employment Arbitration, 50 UCLA L. Rev. 143 (2002). Even after *Green Tree*, circuits have continued to hold that some allocations of arbitration costs invalidate the agreement to arbitrate. In McCaskill v. SCI Mgmt. Corp., 298 F.3d 677 (7th Cir. 2002), the court held that a provision in an arbitration agreement requiring each party to bear its own attorneys fees, regardless of the outcome, was unenforceable. Accord, Perez v. Globe Airport Sec. Servs., 253 F.3d 1280, 1285 (11th Cir. 2001) (a provision limiting the arbitrator's power to grant complete relief "by mandating equal sharing of fees and costs of arbitration despite the award of fees permitted a prevailing party by Title VII" made agreement unenforceable). See also Ferguson v. Countrywide Credit Indus., 298 F.3d 778, 785 (9th Cir. Cal. 2002) (applying state statute which barred requiring employees to pay more than they would have in court fees). The en banc Sixth Circuit devised a case-by-case approach looking to whether, prior to arbitration, the potential costs were great enough to deter employees from seeking to vindicate their statutory rights. Morrison v. Circuit City Stores, Inc., 2003 U.S. App. LEXIS 1456 (6th Cir. Jan. 30, 2003). Contra, Bradford v. Rockwell Semiconductor Sys., 238 F.3d 549 (4th Cir. 2001) (fee-splitting does not automatically render an arbitration agreement unenforceable). In Blair v. Scott Specialty Gases, 283 F.3d 595 (3d Cir. 2002), the Third Circuit allowed a former employee who claimed that the cost of arbitrating her employment discrimination claims would be prohibitive to conduct discovery to determine what it would cost to arbitrate her claims.

## 2.  The Relationship of Federal and State Remedies

***Preemption of State Remedies.***    In general, state remedies for employment discrimination may parallel federal prohibitions as long as the state law does not actually conflict with federal law.* An example where a potential conflict had to be considered is California Fed. Savings & Loan Assn. v. Guerra (reproduced at page 477), where the Court concluded that a state statute requiring unpaid maternity leave did not conflict with Title VII's prohibition of sex discrimination. Indeed, absent conflict,

---

* An exception is the ADEA, § 14(a), 29 U.S.C.S. § 633(a) (2003), which provides that all state proceedings are superseded upon commencement of suit. There is no comparable provision in Title VII.

state laws often may reach beyond federal proscriptions prohibiting age discrimination against a more broadly defined group and barring discrimination on grounds not addressed by federal statutes, such as marital status and political affiliation.

A possible limit on state remedies arises from the federal Employee Retirement Income Security Act of 1974 (ERISA), 29 U.S.C.S. §§ 1001 et seq. (2003), 88 Stat. 829, which was enacted to curb a variety of abuses associated with pension and other employee benefit plans. Section 514(a) of ERISA supersedes state antidiscrimination laws with certain narrow exceptions: the statute "shall supersede any and all State laws insofar as they may now or hereafter relate to any employee benefit plan described in section [4(a)] of this title and not exempt under section [4(b)] of this title." However, ERISA also establishes exemptions to this broad preemption. Section 514(d) of ERISA provides that § 514(a) shall not "be construed to . . . supersede any law of the United States" and thus exempts from preemption any state law necessary to enforce Title VII.

The question of ERISA preemption of state laws arose in Shaw v. Delta Air Lines, Inc., 463 U.S. 85 (1983). *Shaw* found that the state antidiscrimination law, which was enforced by the state deferral agency, was preempted only insofar as it prohibits practices that are lawful under Title VII. *Shaw* thus suggests that, with respect to ERISA plans, state law will have to track federal legislation in order to be valid.

State law actions can also be preempted by the Labor Management Relations Act, § 301, 29 U.S.C.S. § 185 (2003), or the Railway Labor Act, 45 U.S.C.S. §§ 151-188 (2003), when the action between an employee and an employer or union would require interpretation of a collective bargaining agreement. Hawaiian Airlines, Inc. v. Norris, 512 U.S. 246 (1994); Hirras v. National R.R. Passenger Corp., 44 F.3d 278 (5th Cir. 1995); Ramirez v. Fox Television Station, Inc., 998 F.2d 743 (9th Cir. 1993); Jackson v. Kimel, 992 F.2d 1318 (4th Cir. 1993). However, there are several exceptions to this rule. Preemption does not occur when the state law regulates activity of "a merely peripheral concern" to the statute or where the regulated conduct touches interests that are deeply rooted in local responsibility and concerns or affects public interests that transcend the employment relationship. San Diego Unions v. Garmon, 359 U.S. 236 (1959); Cook v. Lindsay Olive Growers, 911 F.2d 233 (9th Cir. 1990). Also, state claims that involve "nonnegotiable state law rights" or state law that proscribes conduct or establishes rights independent of the collective bargaining agreement is not preempted. Livadas v. Bradshaw, 512 U.S. 107 (1994); Hawaiian Airlines, Inc. v. Norris, 512 U.S. 246 (1994); Martin Marietta v. Maryland Commn. on Human Relations, 38 F.3d 1392 (4th Cir. 1994). As a result, claims under state fair employment statutes would not normally be preempted. Ramirez v. Fox Television Station, Inc., 998 F.2d 743 (9th Cir. 1993). But see Davis v. Johnson Controls, Inc., 21 F.3d 866 (8th Cir. 1994).

*Coordination of State and Federal Remedies.*   Because Title VII requires deferral to state agencies, an attack on discrimination will, in most states, set in motion two separate proceedings against discriminatory employment practices. The federal laws do not provide much express assistance in coordinating these proceedings,* but the Supreme Court has addressed the question through the use of preclusion principles.

---

* Title VII, whose procedures also apply to the ADA, provides that when a state agency has made "final findings and orders" before the EEOC's determination with respect to reasonable cause, the Commission "shall accord [them] substantial weight" in making its decision. § 706(b), 42 U.S.C.S. § 2000e-5(b) (2003). But this provision addresses only the relationship between state and federal administrative agencies. The ADEA, § 14(a), 29 U.S.C.S. § 633(a) (2003), provides that all state proceedings are superseded upon commencement of an ADEA suit.

Its first decision, Kremer v. Chemical Const. Corp., 456 U.S. 461 (1982), held simply that a state court decision rejecting an individual's employment discrimination claim under state law has preclusive effect in a subsequent Title VII suit in federal district court. In reaching this result, the Court relied on 28 U.S.C.S. §1738 (2003), which provides that state judicial proceedings "shall have the same full faith and credit in every Court within the United States . . . as they have by law or usage in the courts of such State." Finding no express or implied exception to this statute in Title VII, the Court held the plaintiff's federal suit barred by the prior state proceedings.

The *Kremer* opinion, however, suggested that neither initial resort to a state agency, as required by Title VII, the ADEA, and the ADA, nor an unfavorable agency determination would have preclusive effect. Therefore, unreviewed state administrative determinations, even those made upon a full hearing with a full panoply of procedural safeguards, are not entitled to full faith and credit with respect to a Title VII claim. Accord, Astoria Federal Sav. & Loan Assn. v. Solimino, 501 U.S. 104 (1991) (ADEA). See, e.g., Rao v. County of Fairfax, Virginia, 108 F.3d 42 (4th Cir. 1997) (unfavorable state agency decision does not preclude subsequent Title VII suit, even though agency decision was adjudicatory and would have been given binding effect in state court). This reading of *Kremer* was confirmed by University of Tennessee v. Elliott, 478 U.S. 788 (1986). In *Elliott,* however, the Supreme Court did hold that unreviewed administrative determinations could have preclusive effect with respect to employment discrimination claims brought under federal statutes that do not explicitly establish an administrative agency resort requirement. The Court, therefore, remanded for application of proper preclusion principles to a federal action asserting rights under 42 U.S.C.S. §§ 1981 and 1983 (2003), inter alia, when there has been a prior state administrative proceeding. The effect of *Kremer* and *Elliott,* then, is to create an anomaly: where a § 1981 or § 1983 claim is joined with a Title VII claim, the complainant will be able to proceed on his Title VII claim unaffected by the very state administrative adjudication precluding any § 1981 or § 1983 claims.

These cases have important practical implications. First, as Justice Blackmun observed in his dissent, the clear message of *Kremer* is that an individual who wishes to preserve his right to assert a Title VII claim in federal court should not seek state judicial review of an unfavorable agency action. See Moore v. Bonner, 695 F.2d 799 (4th Cir. 1982). But employees must be wary of at least collateral estoppel effects when they litigate other claims. E.g., Ann C. Hodges, The Preclusive Effect of Unemployment Compensation Determinations in Subsequent Litigation: A Federal Solution, 38 Wayne L. Rev. 1803 (1992). Further the circuits addressing the issue since *Kremer* have generally applied preclusion, regardless of which party sought judicial review, e.g., Trujillo v. County of Santa Clara, 775 F.2d 1359 (9th Cir. 1985); Hickman v. Electronic Keyboarding, Inc., 741 F.2d 230, 232 n.3 (8th Cir. 1984).

Second, the *Kremer* Court was not clear whether its result was founded on claim preclusion (res judicata) or issue preclusion (collateral estoppel). 456 U.S. at 481-82 n.22. Res judicata bars not only claims that were raised, but also those that could have been litigated in the earlier proceedings. Collateral estoppel, in contrast, merely precludes relitigation of issues actually decided. The distinction between the doctrines could make a difference in many discrimination contexts. For example, state and federal bases of discrimination or theories of proof might differ. Thus, depending on whether *Kremer* applies issue or claim preclusion, a plaintiff may be barred from federal suit even if the claims raised in the state suit were not the same.

Claim preclusion seems more likely since the Supreme Court held that state courts have concurrent jurisdiction with federal courts over Title VII claims. While it was long clear that ADEA suits could be tried in either state or federal court, it was not until Yellow Freight Sys., Inc. v. Donnelly, 494 U.S. 820 (1990), that the Supreme Court held that state and federal courts have concurrent jurisdiction of Title VII claims. Because a plaintiff can now prosecute both state and federal claims in a state judicial forum,* it is fair to preclude a later suit that was not raised there. Heylinger v. State Univ. & Comm. Coll. Sys. of Tennessee, 126 F.3d 849 (6th Cir. 1997) (Tennessee law of claim preclusion barred subsequent Title VII suit).

Third, *Kremer* makes clear that the state court's determination need not be made de novo in order to be preclusive. But the Court did not define what review standard will suffice. Suppose, for example, that state law requires a court to uphold a state agency if its decision is not arbitrary and capricious. Would such a decision preclude a later Title VII suit? *Kremer* did require that the due process clause of the Fourteenth Amendment be satisfied, but did not further address the effect of different standards of review.

Finally, *Kremer* makes much more important the question of federal court jurisdiction over state claims in federal court. One way to avoid the threat *Kremer* poses to a de novo federal trial is simply to bring state claims in federal court, rather than before a state court or agency (beyond any resort to a state agency required by the federal or state statutes). While in the past a number of lower courts refused to exercise jurisdiction over state claims pendent to federal discrimination causes of action, two developments have severely undercut the bases for doing so. First, the Civil Rights Act of 1991, by introducing the jury trial and compensatory and punitive damages to Title VII suits, reduced the differences between federal and state schemes relied on by courts declining to exercise pendent jurisdiction. Second, the enactment of 28 U.S.C.S. § 1367 (2003), Pub. L. No. 101-650, 104 Stat. 5113, created "supplemental jurisdiction" that clearly favors the litigation of all related claims together. Further, § 1367(d) reduces the risks of asserting a supplemental jurisdiction claim in federal court because the section tolls the relevant statute of limitations while the claim is pending. See generally Denis F. McLaughlin, The Federal Supplemental Jurisdiction Statute — A Constitutional and Statutory Analysis, 24 Ariz. St. L.J. 849 (1992).

It is true, however, that these and other developments have simultaneously reduced the need for federal courts to exercise jurisdiction over related state claims. First, the expansion of Title VII remedies and the grant of the right to jury trial undercut one of the principal incentives for a plaintiff to plead an analog state cause of action. Second, the need for federal courts to exercise jurisdiction over analog state claims has been reduced by the Supreme Court's recognition that state courts can exercise jurisdiction over Title VII claims: a plaintiff intent on trying all claims in a single proceeding normally can do so in state court.

Assuming preclusion principles are applicable, the court must pay close attention to the requirements for preclusion. E.g., Pleming v. Universal-Rundle Corp., 142 F.3d 1354 (11th Cir. 1998) (res judicata did not bar current claims based on two hiring decisions occurring after filing of prior claim, even though, in course of prior litigation, parties briefed and discussed incidents giving rise to second suit). Nor does it seem likely that claim preclusion can be avoided merely because a right to sue letter had not issued at the time of the state case. Wilkes v. Wyo. Dept. of Employ. Div. of Labor Standards, 314 F.3d 501 (10th Cir. 2002); Owens v. Kaiser Found. Health Plan, Inc., 244 F.3d 708 (9th Cir. 2001); Jang v. United Techs. Corp., 206 F.3d 1147,

---

* This may not be true when the state court decision is in the nature of a review of an agency decision. In such a case, while the issues decided will bind the parties under *Kremer,* the plaintiff may not have been permitted to raise her Title VII claims before the state agency or (given the limited nature of the court role) before the state court. Claim preclusion, therefore, seems inappropriate. Cf. Byre v. Brakbush Bros., Inc., 32 F.3d 1179 (7th Cir. 1994).

1149 (11th Cir. 2000) (plaintiffs may not split causes of action to bring an ADA claim after his state law suit proceeded to judgment on the merits, even if a right-to-sue letter had not been issued earlier.).

## F. PRIVATE CLASS ACTIONS

### 1. Introduction

Employment discrimination suits frequently pose an attorney with the threshold question of whether to proceed solely on behalf of a particular plaintiff or rather to also initiate a class action "on behalf of those similarly situated." The class action possibility is implicit in most Title VII litigation simply because a "suit for violation of Title VII is necessarily a class action as the evil sought to be ended is discrimination on the basis of a class characteristic, i.e., race, sex, religion or national origin." Bowe v. Colgate-Palmolive Co., 416 F.2d 711, 719 (7th Cir. 1969). Such statements, however, may be misleading because the fact that discrimination is necessarily a class evil does not mean that every suit attacking such discrimination qualifies as a class action. To be maintained as a class action, a Title VII, § 1981, or ADA suit must satisfy Rule 23 of the Federal Rules of Civil Procedure. While suits under the ADEA are technically not governed by Rule 23,* the courts have borrowed from Title VII decisions applying Rule 23 in deciding ADEA cases, although there remain important differences between the two approaches.†

Before considering whether Rule 23 permits a class action in a particular case, however, the plaintiff's attorney should consider whether he or she wants to bring a class action. This decision involves both strategic questions and professional respon-

---

*The Age Discrimination in Employment Act expressly incorporates the enforcement provisions of the Fair Labor Standards Act, which include 29 U.S.C.S. § 216 (2003):

> Action to recover such liability may be maintained against any employer (including a public agency) . . . by any one or more employees for and in behalf of himself or themselves and other employees similarly situated. No employee shall be a party plaintiff to any [enforcement] action unless he gives his consent in writing to become such a party and such consent is filed in the court in which such action is brought.

In view of this provision, a Rule 23 class action may not be maintained. Rather, class suits may be brought only on behalf of those persons who have provided the requisite consent. E.g., La Chapelle v. Owens-Illinois, Inc., 513 F.2d 286 (5th Cir. 1975). See generally Elizabeth K. Spahn, Resurrecting the Spurious Class: Opting-In to the Age Discrimination in Employment Act and the Equal Pay Act Through the Fair Labor Standards Act, 71 Geo. L.J. 119 (1982).

†The fundamental difference is that § 216 requires parties to "opt in" in order to be bound by a judgment, while Rule 23 either binds class members absolutely, (b)(2), or at most permits members to "opt out," (b)(3). Perhaps the most significant issue in regard to members' consent under § 216 is whether the district court may notify potential plaintiffs of the pending action in order to determine whether they wish to join it. In Hoffman-La Roche, Inc. v. Sperling, 493 U.S. 165, 169 (1989), the Court upheld a district court's notice to potential class members, stating that "district courts have discretion, in appropriate cases, to implement 29 U.S.C. § 216(b) in ADEA actions by facilitating notice to potential plaintiffs." Although not addressing the terms of the notice used, the Court also approved of discovery of the names and addresses of the class members because the ADEA's incorporation of § 216(b) expressly authorizes collective age discrimination actions, and the advantages of such actions depend on employees "receiving accurate and timely notice concerning the pendency of the collective action." Id. at 170. The Court cautioned, however, that "[i]n exercising the discretionary authority to oversee the notice-giving process, courts must be scrupulous to respect judicial neutrality. To that end, trial courts must take care to avoid even the appearance of judicial endorsement of the merits of the action." Id. at 174. See also Lusardi v. Lechner, 855 F.2d 1062 (3d Cir. 1988).

sibility issues, making the choice a complex one. On the one hand, a class action may well increase the leverage of the case because the defendant may be more likely to settle favorably as the stakes in losing rise. Escalating from an individual's suit to a class action may multiply by a factor of hundreds potential monetary liability as well as threaten radical restructuring of employment practices. On the other hand, it is possible that the class action may stiffen the defendant's resolve, thus making settlement more difficult and triggering a tougher defense. Further, the costs of litigation may soar, both in terms of the out-of-pocket costs that will have to be paid somehow and in terms of the lawyer's time, which, in most Title VII cases, is not compensated until the litigation is terminated. See generally Jonathan Harr, A Civil Action (1995). See Chapter 10 for discussion of attorneys' fee awards. Overarching these concerns are the professional responsibility questions of the lawyer's obligations to his or her client. See generally Nancy Morawetz, Bargaining, Class Representation, and Fairness, 54 Ohio St. L.J. 1 (1993); Jonathan R. Macey & Geoffrey P. Miller, The Plaintiffs' Attorney's Role in Class Action and Derivative Litigation: Economic Analysis and Recommendations for Reform, 58 U. Chi. L. Rev. 1 (1991); Lawrence Grosberg, Class Actions and Client-Centered Decisionmaking, 40 Syracuse L. Rev. 709 (1989); John C. Coffee, Jr., The Regulation of Entrepreneurial Litigation: Balancing Fairness and Efficiency in the Large Class Action, 54 U. Chi. L. Rev. 877 (1987); Mary Kay Kane, Of Carrots and Sticks: Evaluating the Role of the Class Action Lawyer, 66 Tex. L. Rev. 385 (1987).

If the plaintiff's attorney decides that strategic and professional responsibility questions favor a class suit, it is then necessary to determine whether such a suit is permissible. Although Title VII does not provide explicitly for class actions, the courts soon recognized their availability in appropriate circumstances. E.g., Albemarle Paper Co. v. Moody, 422 U.S. 405 (1975). Further, each class member need not file a charge with the EEOC in order to be a member of the class, id. at 414 n.8, because an otherwise proper Title VII class action may be brought attacking any discrimination implicated by the charge filed with the EEOC by the representative plaintiff. The purposes of the filing requirement are achieved by one charge because "[i]t would be wasteful, if not vain, for numerous employees, all with the same grievance, to have to process many identical complaints with the EEOC." Oatis v. Crown Zellerbach Corp., 398 F.2d 496, 498 (5th Cir. 1968).

One major restriction on membership in Title VII and ADA class actions is imposed by the time limitations on filing a charge with the EEOC. The charge on which the suit is predicated must be timely, just as in an individual action, but timeliness considerations are also applicable to other class members. While filing a charge tolls the time period for class members, persons whose claims are already time barred at that point are not class members. E.g., Wetzel v. Liberty Mut. Ins. Co., 508 F.2d 239 (3d Cir. 1975). These questions do not affect suits under § 1981.

## 2.  *Requirements of Rule 23(a)*

Suits under the ADA, Title VII, and § 1981 are governed by Rule 23 of the Federal Rules of Civil Procedure, which establishes two sets of requirements that class actions must meet; the party seeking to maintain the suit as a class action has the burden of persuasion with respect to them. The first set of requirements is found in Rule 23(a), which sets forth four factors, all of which must be met:

(1)  the class is so numerous that joinder of all members is impracticable,
(2)  there are questions of law or fact common to the class,
(3)  the claims or defenses of the representative parties are typical of the claims or defenses of the class, and
(4)  the representative parties will fairly and adequately protect the interests of the class.

While it is necessary to address each of these requirements, a mechanical analysis of the four categories risks overlooking the underlying concept of Rule 23(a): because class actions necessarily commit the rights of unnamed class members into the hands of the named plaintiff and her attorneys, the courts must ensure that a class action is both appropriate to the claims alleged and structured to maximize the quality of the representation of the interests of the unnamed class members.

To this end, Rule 23(a)(1), "numerosity," focuses on whether the case is appropriate for class action treatment or whether traditional multiparty litigation is preferable. E.g., Cypress v. Newport News Gen. & Nonsectarian Hosp. Assn., 375 F.2d 648 (4th Cir. 1967) (18-member class approved). The remaining three parts of paragraph (a) examine other facets of the adequacy of the named plaintiff (or her counsel) as a representative of the class. Thus, Rule 23(a)(2), "commonality," and (3), "typicality," attempt to ensure that the named plaintiff will, in the course of representing her own interests, necessarily represent the other class members because her claims are identical or very similar to theirs. However, Rule 23(a)(2) contemplates only the existence of some common questions. The existence of non-common questions does not preclude commonality. Finally, Rule 23(a)(4) again considers the adequacy of representation, but this time by focusing on the existence of conflicts of interest between the named plaintiff and other class members and on the adequacy of counsel. Rule 23(a)(4) addresses problems such as collusiveness, competence of counsel, and possible conflicts of interest ("antagonism") between the named representatives and other class members.

Although the lower courts had originally been hospitable to employment discrimination class actions, the Supreme Court was far more restrictive in two encounters with discrimination class actions. In East Texas Motor Freight Sys., Inc. v. Rodriguez, 431 U.S. 395 (1977), three Mexican Americans initiated suit, challenging the company's "no-transfer" policy to better-paid line-driver jobs. Although the named plaintiffs stipulated that they had not been discriminated against in their hiring as city drivers, the suit sought to represent all Negroes and Mexican Americans denied all employment opportunities, including hiring. The district court held against the three plaintiffs on their individual claims, finding that none of them had the qualifications for a road-driver position. The plaintiffs never moved for class certification. The Fifth Circuit, however, reversed; the court of appeals itself certified a sweeping class and simultaneously found class liability.

The Supreme Court found plain error in this certification: "[I]t was evident by the time the case reached that court that the named plaintiffs were not proper class representatives" under Rule 23(a). Id. at 403. A class representative must be part of the class and possess the same interest and suffer the same injury as the class members. Since the named plaintiffs lacked the qualifications to be line drivers, "they could have suffered no injury as a result of the alleged discriminatory [transfer] practices, and they were, therefore, simply not eligible to represent a class of persons who did allegedly suffer injury." Id. at 403-04. Since each had stipulated that he had not been discriminated against in his initial hire, "they were hardly in a position to mount a classwide attack on the no-transfer rule and seniority system on the ground that these practices perpetuated past discrimination and locked minorities into the less desirable jobs to which they had been discriminatorily assigned." Id. at 404.

The Court stressed that "a different case would be presented if the District Court had certified a class and only later had it appeared that the named plaintiffs were not class members." Id. at 406 n.12. A proper class certification would protect the claims of the class members even if "subsequent events or the proof at trial . . . undermined the named plaintiffs' individual claims." Id. See Franks v. Bowman Transp. Co., 424 U.S. 747 (1976) (after a class is properly certified, a finding that the named plaintiff had been legally discharged did not bar relief to the class members).* Because the named plaintiffs' lack of membership in the class due to deficiencies in their qualifications will not, in most cases, be decided until trial and class certification is supposed to be decided as soon as practicable, the *East Texas Motor Freight* scenario should not often arise. But see Robinson v. Sheriff, 167 F.3d 1155 (7th Cir. 1999) (27-month gap in plaintiff's employment record made him atypical class representative). Is it appropriate for the court to inquire into the merits of an individual claim before certifying a class action? Although the Supreme Court has expressly disapproved of a preliminary hearing on the merits in another context, Eisen v. Carlisle & Jacquelin, 417 U.S. 156 (1974), it is not clear whether that decision will control this question. See generally George Rutherglen, Title VII Class Actions, 47 U. Chi. L. Rev. 688 (1980).

While "the named plaintiffs' evident lack of class membership" was enough to preclude certification in *East Texas Motor Freight*, the Court noted two other strong indicators of inadequacy of representation. The first was the individual plaintiffs' failure to move for certification as a class action; that "surely bears strongly on the adequacy of the representation that those class members might expect to receive." 431 U.S. at 405. Other conduct has also been held to reveal inadequacy of representation, as when the named plaintiff voluntarily resigns her position, see Hernandez v. Gray, 530 F.2d 858 (10th Cir. 1976), or does not seek reinstatement, De Grace v. Rumsfeld, 614 F.2d 796 (1st Cir. 1980). See also Anderson v. Albuquerque, 690 F.2d 796 (10th Cir. 1982) (important consideration is whether the representative retains an interest in employment).

The second factor that *East Texas Motor Freight* found strongly indicated inadequacy of representation "was the conflict between the vote by members of the class rejecting a merger of the city- and line-driver collective-bargaining units, and the demand in the plaintiffs' complaint for just such a merger." 431 U.S. at 405. This conflict obviously implicated Rule 23(a)(4). But does it follow that such a conflict is fatal to a class action? Won't the question of remedy for a violation always divide members of the class? After all, class members will typically compete with each other generally and in terms of the benefits of the lawsuit. One example of such antagonism arose in a case involving pregnancy leave regulations. Although the class of female employees had a general interest in striking down restrictive pregnancy rules, the remedy aspect could divide class members. Present employees, for example,

---

*The possibility of a certified class being decertified after trial is considerably less likely in view of the 1998 amendments to Rule 23. New Rule 23(f) permits discretionary appeal of grants or denials of certification. It is generally anticipated that this rule will lead to more interlocutory appeals of grants of certification than of denials. See generally Michael E. Solimine & Christine Oliver Hines, Deciding to Decide: Class Action Certification and Interlocutory Review by the United States Courts of Appeals Under Rule 23(f), 41 Wm. & Mary L. Rev. 1531 (2000).

would not want former employees reinstated with retroactive seniority because that would make present employees more vulnerable to layoff. Air Line Stewards & Stewardesses Assn., Local 550 v. American Airlines, Inc., 490 F.2d 636 (7th Cir. 1973). Antagonism may sometimes be eliminated by subclasses. See Johnson v. Georgia Highway Express, Inc., 417 F.2d 1122 (5th Cir. 1969).

In the Court's next encounter with an employment discrimination class action, General Telephone Co. of the Southwest v. Falcon, 457 U.S. 147 (1982), the named plaintiff was denied a promotion. Falcon then brought suit pursuant to Rule 23(b)(2) seeking to represent a class "composed of Mexican-American persons who are employed, or who might be employed, by General Telephone Company at its place of business located in Irving, Texas, who have been and who continue to be or might be adversely affected by the practices complained of herein." The district court certified a class including Mexican-American employees and unsuccessful Mexican-American applicants for employment. It ultimately found that the employer had not discriminated against Falcon in hiring, but that it did discriminate against him in its promotion practices. "The court reached converse conclusions about the class, finding no discrimination in promotion practices, but concluding that petitioner had discriminated against Mexican-Americans at its Irving facility in its hiring practices." 457 U.S. at 152.

Stressing the efficiency of the class action device when issues involved are "common to the class as a whole" and when they "turn on a question of law applicable in the same manner to each member of the class," the Court stressed that the requirements of Rule 23 must be met even though a discrimination suit in a sense always focuses on a "class claim":

> We cannot disagree with the proposition underlying the across-the-board rule [which broadly permitted discrimination class actions] — that racial discrimination is by definition class discrimination. But the allegation that such discrimination has occurred neither determines whether a class action may be maintained in accordance with Rule 23 nor defines the class that may be certified. Conceptually, there is a wide gap between (a) an individual's claim that he has been denied a promotion on discriminatory grounds, and his otherwise unsupported allegation that the company has a policy of discrimination, and (b) the existence of a class of persons who have suffered the same injury as that individual, such that the individual's claim and the class claims will share common questions of law or fact and that the individual's claim will be typical of the class claim. For respondent to bridge that gap, he must prove much more than the validity of his own claim. Even though evidence that he was passed over for promotion when several less deserving whites were advanced may support the conclusion that respondent was denied the promotion because of his national origin, such evidence would not necessarily justify the additional inferences (1) that this discriminatory treatment is typical of petitioner's promotion practices, (2) that petitioner's promotion practices are motivated by a policy of ethnic discrimination that pervades petitioner's Irving division, or (3) that this policy of ethnic discrimination is reflected in petitioner's other employment practices, such as hiring, in the same way it is manifested in the promotion practices. . . .
>
> Without any specific presentation identifying the questions of law or fact that were common to the claims of respondent and of the members of the class he sought to represent, it was error for the District Court to presume that respondent's claim was typical of other claims against petitioner by Mexican-American employees and applicants. If one allegation of specific discriminatory treatment were sufficient to support an across-the-board attack, every Title VII case would be a potential company-wide class action. We find nothing in the statute to indicate that Congress intended to authorize such a wholesale expansion of class-action litigation.

Id. at 158-59. The Court concluded: "As the District Court's bifurcated findings on liability demonstrate, the individual and class claims might as well have been tried separately. It is clear that the maintenance of respondent's action as a class action did not advance 'the efficiency and economy of litigation which is a principal purpose of the procedure.'" Id. at 148.

*East Texas Motor Freight* did not directly reject the across-the-board theory insofar as the opinion focused on the inadequacy of representation. But *Falcon* spoke of "the error inherent" in the across-the-board rule, although it explicitly accepted "the proposition underlying the across-the-board rule — that racial discrimination is by definition class discrimination." Could one argue that *Falcon* merely requires the lower courts to apply the across-the-board theory more carefully? The Court did indicate when a class suit might be appropriate:

> If petitioner used a biased testing procedure to evaluate both applicants for employment and incumbent employees, a class action on behalf of every applicant or employee who might have been prejudiced by the test clearly would satisfy the commonality and typicality requirements of Rule 23(a). Significant proof that an employer operated under a general policy of discrimination conceivably could justify a class of both applicants and employees if the discrimination manifested itself in hiring and promotion practices in the same general fashion, such as through entirely subjective decisionmaking processes. In this regard it is noteworthy that Title VII prohibits discriminatory employment practices, not an abstract policy of discrimination. The mere fact that an aggrieved private plaintiff is a member of an identifiable class of persons of the same race or national origin is insufficient to establish his standing to litigate on their behalf all possible claims of discrimination against a common employer.

457 U.S. at 159, n.15.

The *Falcon* rule might be framed this way: the plaintiff can represent a class (assuming that the numerosity requirement is satisfied and that the plaintiff is an adequate representative in terms of competent counsel and no conflicting interests) of those persons who would have at least prima facie cases of discrimination in favor of them made out by the proof that plaintiff will offer to provide discrimination against himself. Thus, in a disparate impact case, the plaintiff can represent the class of persons that the plaintiff, in order to win, must prove suffered disproportionate adverse effects from a challenged policy. One court noted that "[b]oth the existence and the common reach of such objectively applied patterns or practices are likely to be indisputable from the outset, so that no real commonality problems for class action maintenance ever arise in this regard." Stastny v. Southern Bell Tel. & Tel. Co., 628 F.2d 267, 271 (4th Cir. 1980). Accord, Nelson v. United States Steel Corp., 709 F.2d 675 (11th Cir. 1983).

Under this approach, in a disparate treatment case the plaintiff can represent a class of persons who suffered from employment decisions made by the person(s) whose discriminatory motives the plaintiff must show to make out his case, provided that the class comprises only those persons susceptible to the motive proved (i.e., proof of antiblack bias would not support a class action on behalf of females or, perhaps, of other racial minorities). The fact that a central body has influence over the policies or practices at issue may be enough to satisfy the typicality requirement, Bazemore v. Friday, 478 U.S. 385 (1986), but in another case, a class action relating to several of an employer's facilities had to be narrowed when it became clear that the challenged practices were established locally and not centrally, Stastny v. Southern Bell Tel. & Tel. Co., 628 F.2d 267 (4th Cir. 1980).

One appellate court noted that, under the systemic theories, the class action and merit inquiries tend to coincide: to answer the procedural question of whether there is a class sufficiently homogeneous to challenge a pattern of discrimination, in effect, requires answering the substantive question of whether, under either of the available theories, there exists the requisite policy or practice of discrimination affecting an identifiable class of protected employees. Because of this, a "fair determination of the propriety of a class action may be exceedingly difficult without conducting an inquiry roughly comparable to that required to resolve the 'pattern or practice' issue on the merits." Stastny v. Southern Bell Tel. & Tel. Co., 628 F.2d 267, 274 (4th Cir. 1980). The court also noted that the heavy reliance in Title VII cases on statistical evidence — such as the appropriate statistical database for the labor market — means that the procedural question of class certification may have to follow "or at least coincide with the determination whether and to what extent there exists a set of protected employees in whose behalf a class judgment may fairly be entered." Id. at 275. See generally George Rutherglen, Notice, Scope, and Preclusion in Title VII Class Actions, 69 Va. L. Rev. 11 (1983) (surveying and criticizing court decisions on the relationship between the claims of named plaintiffs and those of the class).

To a large extent, the plaintiff under Title VII, the ADA, and § 1981 can influence the certification question by defining the class she seeks to represent. For example, an African American denied employment as a welder might seek to represent (1) the class of black applicants denied employment as welders; (2) the class of black applicants denied employment for any job by the defendant; (3) the class of blacks, both applicants and employees, within the welding category; (4) the class of blacks, applicants, and employees, within every job category of the defendant; or (5) the class of "minority" applicants (African Americans and other minorities) for the welder's job. One can confidently predict that the prospects of class action certification will vary, depending on which class is urged and that the courts will be more likely to find plaintiff an adequate representative of a narrower, rather than a broader, class.

However, while class definitions may be manipulated to some extent to satisfy Rule 23 requirements, it may be difficult to thread a way among all the requirements. For example, joinder will obviously be impracticable in an action that seeks injunctive relief to protect the rights of potential future employees simply because they are not ordinarily identifiable. E.g., Cross v. Natl. Trust Life Ins. Co., 553 F.2d 1026 (6th Cir. 1977). But such manipulation itself may cause problems under other requirements of the rule. In one case, the class claim failed because the class defined one way was too small (falling afoul of the numerosity requirement); yet defined another way, it was too large (hence unmanageable). Hill v. American Airlines, Inc., 479 F.2d 1057 (5th Cir. 1973).

Labor unions pose a special set of problems for class action suits. One problem is antagonism. Under the National Labor Relations Act, unions have a duty of fair representation to all persons in their bargaining unit. Employers have frequently argued that unions that bring class suits under Rule 23(a)(4) have a conflict of interest because, as class representative, they have to represent the interests of the class members against the interests of other employees to whom they also owe a duty of fair representation. This has led several courts to deny unions the status of class representative. Air Line Stewards & Stewardesses Assn., Local 550 v. American Airlines, Inc., 490 F.2d 636 (7th Cir. 1973). However, other appellate courts have recognized that any conflict of interest is sometimes more speculative than real. See Social Servs. Union, Local 535 v. County of Santa Clara, 609 F.2d 944 (9th Cir. 1979) (fact that union had participated in the negotiation of sex-discriminatory pay scales did not bar it as class representative because it consistently opposed such scales in negotiations). It has also been argued that unions cannot be class representatives of employee classes because, as *East Texas Motor Freight* states, the representative must be a "member" of the class. Obviously, the union is not a member of the class of discriminatees. Nevertheless, it is not clear that the Supreme Court had in mind the problem of class representatives who, like unions, are representative of their members' interests.

## 3.   Requirements of Rule 23(b)

Even if a particular suit meets all the requirements of Rule 23(a), it still may not be brought as a class action unless it meets a second set of requirements: it must fall within one of the three categories in paragraph (b) of Rule 23. Because category (b)(1) has been raised in few employment discrimination cases, the real question is whether the suit can be brought under (b)(2) or (b)(3). Rule 23(b)(2) requires that "the party opposing the class . . . act[ ] or refuse[ ] to act on grounds generally applicable to the class, thereby making appropriate final injunctive relief or corresponding declaratory relief with respect to the class as a whole." Rule 23(b)(3) requires that

> the court find that the questions of law or fact common to the members of the class predominate over any questions affecting only individual members, and that a class action [be] superior to other available methods for the fair and efficient adjudication of the controversy. The matters pertinent to the findings include: (A) the interest of members of the class in individually controlling the prosecution or defense of separate actions; (B) the extent and nature of any litigation concerning the controversy already commenced by or against members of the class; (C) the desirability or undesirability of concentrating the litigation of the claims in the particular forum; (D) the difficulties likely to be encountered in the management of a class action.

There are important procedural differences between (b)(2) and (b)(3) classes — most notably, the (b)(3) right of class members to notice and the opportunity to "opt out" of the class action. As a result, there has been some dispute about the appropriate category for Title VII class actions.

In view of its language focusing on injunctive and declaratory relief, there has been some question concerning the appropriateness of (b)(2) certification in employment discrimination suits where the relief sought includes monetary relief. When backpay was the primary monetary award available, the courts of appeals generally approved such certification. Some courts stated that the provision in Rule 23(b)(2) relating to injunctive and declaratory relief is not a limitation on the type of relief available, but a specification of the kind of conduct by a defendant that permits a class action to be brought under Rule 23(b)(2). E.g., United States Fidelity & Guar. Co. v. Lord, 585 F.2d 860, 875 (8th Cir. 1978). Other courts held that the provision does not bar suits seeking a backpay award because such relief is equitable and not legal. E.g., Franks v. Bowman Transp. Co., 495 F.2d 398 (5th Cir. 1974). A court taking either of these positions would award backpay even if it were the only relief granted. Still other courts, noting that the comments of the Advisory Committee on the Federal Rules state that Rule 23(b)(2) "does not extend to cases in which the appropriate final relief relates exclusively or predominately to money damages," Advisory Committee's Notes, 1966 F.R.D. 62, 102, seemed to require for a (b)(2) case that traditional injunctive relief be the "predominate" remedy and that the backpay award be merely incidental. E.g.,

Doninger v. Pacific Northwest Bell, Inc., 564 F.2d 1304 (9th Cir. 1977). The availability of compensatory damages in the wake of the Civil Rights Act of 1991 has sharpened this question. E.g., Lemon v. Intl. Union of Operating Engrs., Local No. 139, 216 F.3d 577 (7th Cir. 2000) (class certification under (b)(2) vacated because plaintiff's request for monetary damages was not incidental to the request for equitable relief); Allison v. Citgo Petroleum Corp., 151 F.3d 402 (5th Cir. 1998) (2-1) (suit seeking compensatory and punitive damages could not be certified under (b)(2) because such relief was not incidental to the declarative and injunctive relief sought); Jefferson v. Ingersoll Intl., Inc., 195 F.3d 894, 898 (7th Cir. 1999) (enactment of the 1991 amendments meant that (b)(2) certification of not seeking compensatory and punitive damages would be appropriate, if at all, "when any monetary relief was incidental to the equitable remedy." See also Lowery v. Circuit City Stores, Inc., 158 F.3d 742 (4th Cir. 1998). Cf. Robinson v. Metro-North Commuter R.R., 267 F.3d 147, 164 (2d Cir. 2001) ("we hold that when presented with a motion for (b)(2) class certification of a claim seeking both injunctive relief and non-incidental monetary damages, a district court may allow (b)(2) certification if it finds in its 'informed, sound judicial discretion' that (1) 'the positive weight or value [to the plaintiffs] of the injunctive or declaratory relief sought is predominant even though compensatory or punitive damages are also claimed,' and (2) class treatment would be efficient and manageable, thereby achieving an appreciable measure of judicial economy."). See Scott Shively, Resurgence of the Class Action Lawsuit in Employment Discrimination Cases: New Obstacles Presented by the 1991 Amendments to the Civil Rights Act, 23 U. Ark. Little Rock L. Rev. 925 (2001) (class actions in employment discrimination cases have increased since the passage of the Civil Rights Act of 1991 because of the availability of both damage awards and a jury trial, but those same incentives pose "additional hurdles to class certification").

Even if (b)(2) certification is not available, employment discrimination suits may typically be certified under (b)(3). Air Line Stewards & Stewardesses Assn., Local 550 v. American Airlines, Inc., 490 F.2d 636 (7th Cir. 1973). Indeed, if (b)(2) certification is appropriate, (b)(3) will normally also be satisfied. Wetzel v. Liberty Mut. Ins. Co., 508 F.2d 239 (3d Cir. 1975).

However, one court indicated that, if (b)(2) and (b)(3) certifications are both appropriate, (b)(2) is to be generally preferred because of its wider res judicata effect. Wetzel v. Liberty Mut. Ins. Co., 508 F.2d at 252. See generally George Rutherglen, Better Late Than Never: Notice and Opt-Out at the Settlement Stage of Class Actions, 71 N.Y.U. L. Rev. 258 (1996); George Rutherglen, Notice, Scope and Preclusion in Title VII Class Actions, 69 Va. L. Rev. 11 (1983). The suggestion that individual members of a proper (b)(2) class do not have a right to opt out of the class has, in fact, been held explicitly. Kyriazi v. Western Elec. Co., 647 F.2d 388 (3d Cir. 1981). See also Eubanks v. Billington, 110 F.3d 87 (D.C. Cir. 1997) (while class members do not have an unqualified right to opt out, district courts may accord such rights as part of their power to manage the class action). But see Thomas v. Albright, 139 F.3d 227 (D.C. Cir. 1998) (permitting class members to opt out was an abuse of discretion since the right to opt out of a non-(b)(3) action is not expressly provided in Rule 23(c)(2) and the district court did not adduce any tenable ground upon which opting out might be permitted). There has, however, been doubt expressed as to whether due process is satisfied insofar as judgments purport to resolve backpay claims of members where no notice is accorded. See generally Gerald E. Rosen, Title VII Classes and Due Process: To (b)(2) or (b)(3), 26 Wayne L. Rev. 919 (1980). At least one appellate court has held that res judicata is not permissible in such circumstances.

Johnson v. General Motors Corp., 598 F.2d 432 (5th Cir. 1979). See also Marshall v. Kirkland, 602 F.2d 1282 (8th Cir. 1979). However, Wetzel v. Liberty Mut. Ins. Co., 508 F.2d at 256-57, rejected this reasoning by stressing that, while notice to affected parties is ordinarily required by due process, Mullane v. Central Hanover Bank & Trust Co., 339 U.S. 306 (1950), it would not add any meaningful protection in this context.

The Supreme Court is upholding decertification of a (b)(3) "settlement only" class. Amchem Prods. v. Windsor, 521 U.S. 591 (1997), could have far-reaching effects, conceivably limiting, if not extinguishing, large discrimination class actions. While *Amchem* arose under tort law, the opinion's delineation of the problems and conflicts of the class there mirror problems that are frequently present in employment discrimination class actions. In *Amchem*, the purported class was compromised of two distinct groups of plaintiffs, those with current injuries and those with exposure-only claims. The Supreme Court found numerous conflicts of interest between these two groups as well as numerous differing issues. As a result, the requirement of Rule 23(b)(3) that common questions of law or fact predominate over any questions affecting only individual members was not satisfied. Further, Rule 23(a)(4)'s adequacy of representation requirement was not met. The Court noted several distinguishing features of the class at issue, including that it was certified as a settlement class, which may deserve heightened scrutiny. See also Ortiz v. Fireboard Corp., 527 U.S. 815 (1999) (certification of a settlement class needs at least a showing that the fund is limited by more than the agreement of the parties and that it has been allocated among class members by a process that addresses their conflicting interests). An employment discrimination class action could often pose analogous problems. For example, a class action in a disparate impact context seeking monetary as well as injunctive relief could raise most of the concerns that the Supreme Court expressed in *Amchem*. The individual claims for backpay would undercut the cohesiveness of the class, making it resemble a 23(b)(3) action, whether or not it was certified as such. Money damages could run high, which in turn would create a significant interest for the plaintiffs to individually control their case. Also, the impact of such discrimination may vary widely among these individual plaintiffs. Further, if the named plaintiffs were current employees and the class encompassed other groups (e.g., discharged employees and applicants), adequacy of representation would be questionable. Conflicts among these varied class members could also exist.

## 4.  The Preclusive Effect of a Class Action

When a proper class action is prosecuted, every member who does not opt out is bound by the judgment entered.* But the Supreme Court has made clear that the preclusive effects are more limited than might first appear. In Cooper v. Federal Reserve Bank of Richmond, 467 U.S. 867, 869 (1984), the Court held "a judgment in a class action determining that an employer did not engage in a general pattern or

---

* Of course, if the class action is not proper, class members will not be bound. These individuals can always seek to show inadequacy of representation, despite the class certification. Such a finding is, however, likely to be exceptional and require a stronger showing of inadequacy of representation than would suffice to prevent the initial certification. Otherwise, the utility of class actions in resolving broad disputes would be undermined by opening class action adjudications to subsequent attack.

practice of racial discrimination against the certified class of employees [does not preclude] a class member from maintaining a subsequent civil action alleging an individual claim of racial discrimination against the employer."

The Supreme Court stressed that the *Cooper* litigation resolved two kinds of claims in the bank's favor, the individual claims of each of the four named plaintiffs and the class claim of discriminatory "policies and practices." But that did not logically mean that the bank had never engaged in individual acts of discrimination against other employees. Just as Franks v. Bowman Transp. Co. (reproduced at page 966) had held that a successful attack on a pattern of racial discrimination in defendant's policies did not mean that every black employee was entitled to relief, so also a successful defense of an employer's policies did not show that particular individuals were not the victims of other acts of discrimination. *Cooper* reasoned:

> [t]hat judgment (1) bars the class members from bringing another class action against the Bank alleging a pattern or practice of discrimination for the relevant time period and (2) precludes the class members in any other litigation with the Bank from relitigating the question whether the Bank engaged in a pattern and practice of discrimination against black employees during the relevant time period. The judgment is not, however, dispositive of the individual claims the Baxter petitioners have alleged in their separate action.

467 U.S. at 880.

Some further considerations should be noted. First, there is a possibility that class relief, at least in the form of enjoining practices found to be discriminatory, may be appropriate even if the suit is not brought as a class action. See Meyer v. Brown & Root Constr. Co., 661 F.2d 369 (5th Cir. 1981); Gregory v. Litton Sys., Inc., 472 F.2d 631 (9th Cir. 1972); Sprogis v. United Air Lines, Inc., 444 F.2d 1194 (7th Cir. 1971). Contra, Lowery v. Circuit City Stores, Inc., 158 F.3d 742 (4th Cir. 1998).

Second, even if class relief is not to be feared from an individual suit, the defendant must consider the problem of collateral estoppel. So long as the law required mutuality of estoppel, a defendant need not have been concerned about the binding effect of any adverse decision beyond the parties (and their privies) in that case. Thus, if employee A sued the defendant and won, employee B could not take advantage of the first determination. Mutuality required that, for B to utilize the earlier decision against the defendant, B must have been in a position to have been bound by a contrary determination in A's suit. Because due process bars B from being bound by A's suit (unless it is a class action), there is no mutuality, and B could not utilize the determination in A's action to bind the defendant. See Tice v. American Airlines, 162 F.3d 966 (7th Cir. 1998) (rejecting defense argument that successive suits challenging airline policy regarding down-bidding of age disqualified pilots should be barred by prior litigation on theory of "virtual representation"). Although mutuality is not yet dead, the Supreme Court has clearly rejected it as an absolute requirement in the federal courts, at least for federal question cases. Parklane Hosiery Co. v. Shore, 439 U.S. 322 (1979); Blonder-Tongue Lab., Inc. v. Univ. of Illinois Found., 402 U.S. 313 (1971). It seems clear that a defendant faced with an individual employment discrimination suit must now consider the possibility that an adverse determination may be used against it in subsequent suits by other employees or by the EEOC. See Meredith v. Beech Aircraft Corp., 18 F.3d 890 (10th Cir. 1994) (plaintiff could rely on finding in earlier suit that defendant had discriminated on the basis of sex in a promotion decision).

## 5.  *Settling Class Actions*

While *Falcon* and *Cooper* involved class actions being prosecuted to judgment, other problems arise when the two sides consider settlement. Because a representative class member may not properly represent other members' interests in settling the action, Rule 23(e) provides: "A class action shall not be dismissed or compromised without the approval of the court, and notice of the proposed dismissal or compromise shall be given to all members of the class in such manner as the court directs." Although Rule 23(e) does not specify the procedure that follows the notice, the district court should accord a hearing to any class members making serious objections to the settlement. Assuming proper procedures are followed, the discretion accorded the district court in approving the settlement is great. There is widespread agreement on the factors to be considered, but these factors are so diverse that it is difficult to predict how they will be balanced. E.g., Mandujano v. Basic Vegetable Prods., Inc., 541 F.2d 832 (9th Cir. 1978). Recently, the courts have shown heightened concern where class counsel attorney fees negotiations may have distorted the proposed settlement. E.g. Staton v. Williams, 313 F.3d 447 (9th Cir. 2002).

# G.   FEDERAL GOVERNMENT ENFORCEMENT

Title VII and the Americans with Disabilities Act enforcement by the federal government is largely committed to the Equal Employment Opportunity Commission, although the Attorney General retains a role with respect to suits against state and local governments. § 706(f)(1), 42 U.S.C.S. § 2000e-5(f)(1) (2003); Reorganization Plan No. 1 of 1978, 43 Fed. Reg. 19,807 (1978). There is no government agency charged with enforcing § 1981, and the Age Discrimination in Employment Act has a somewhat different enforcement scheme.

In describing the procedural steps for private suits, we have already encountered the basic procedures for EEOC enforcement under § 706. Essentially, a person aggrieved by a violation of Title VII or the ADA files a charge with the EEOC. The number of charges filed with the EEOC each year has varied substantially; recently, it exceeded 90,000. Michael Selmi, The Value of the EEOC: The Agency's Role in Employment Discrimination Law, 57 Ohio St. L.J. 1, 12 (1996). See also Kathryn Moss, Scot Burris, Michael Ullman, Matthew Johnsen & Jeffrey Swanson, Unfunded Mandate: An Empirical Study of the Implementation of the Americans with Disabilities Act by the Equal Employment Opportunity Commission, 50 Kan. L. Rev. 1, 4 (2001) ("incoming [ADA] cases are given a priority categorization based on the information the complaining party provides during an initial intake interview and on his or her perceived credibility. The level of categorization effectively determines the extent to which the claim will be investigated. After categorization, the vast majority of cases that are not assigned a top priority ranking receive minimal investigative attention. . . . Aside from a chance to tell their stories, most claimants will not benefit from filing a claim, yet may assume that a federal, state, or local fair employment practices agency is actively seeking evidence to corroborate their allegations."); Michael Z. Green, Proposing a New Paradigm for EEOC Enforcement After 35 Years: Outsourcing Charge Processing by Mandatory Mediation, 105 Dick. L. Rev. 305 (2001) (documenting the improvements to EEOC charge processing resulting from mediation and advocating a statute to make it mandatory and private). See also Michael J. Yelnosky, Title VII, Mediation, and Collective Action, 1999 U. Ill. L. Rev. 583 (1999). With such a heavy caseload, mistakes in charge processing are inevitable.

Earlier sections exploring the relationship of this administrative procedure to private suits concluded that defects in EEOC charge processing do not affect such actions. The rationale for requiring only initiation of EEOC proceedings, and not exhaustion of them, as a condition to private suit lies in the Commission's perennial inability to process charges in the time intended by Congress or, often, in any reasonable time. The courts, looking to the remedial purposes of Title VII, reasoned that private plaintiffs should not be prejudiced in obtaining court relief by virtue of the Commission's deficiencies. However, a charging party has no cause of action against the EEOC for failure to properly process a charge. E.g., Baba v. Japan Travel Bureau Intl., Inc., 111 F.3d 2, 5-6 (2d Cir. 1997); Scheerer v. Rose State Coll., 950 F.2d 661 (10th Cir. 1991); McCottrell v. EEOC, 726 F.2d 350 (7th Cir. 1984). See also Jordan v. Summers, 205 F.3d 337 (7th Cir. 2000) (federal employee barred from suit against an agency for failing to properly process his internal complaint).

Title VII, however, does not envision private individuals as the only enforcers of its substantive commands. The EEOC, after the completion of its internal processes, may itself bring suit against the discrimination charged. Cf. Bell Atlantic Cash Balance Plan v. EEOC, 182 F.3d 906 (4th Cir. 1999) (court may not review EEOC reasonable cause determination before Commission files suit). It is here where agency mistakes may cause difficulties. Defendants have argued that procedural errors or omissions may limit the Commission's ability to sue. For example, § 706 requires that "notice of the charge . . . shall be served upon the person against whom such charge is made within ten days thereafter." § 706(e), 42 U.S.C.S. § 2000e-5(e) (2003). In EEOC v. Shell Oil Co., 466 U.S. 54 (1984), the defendant challenged the notice provided by the Commission, but the Court adopted a liberal approach: a general statement of the discrimination charged will suffice. See also EEOC v. Dillon Cos., 310 F.3d 1271 (10th Cir. 2002); EEOC v. Sidley, Austin, Brown & Wood, 2002 U.S. App. LEXIS 22152 (7th Cir. 2002). Cf. EEOC v. Southern Farm Bureau Casualty Ins. Co., 271 F.3d 209 (5th Cir. 2001) (EEOC could not use its subpoena power in investigating race discrimination to obtain gender information); EEOC v. United Air Lines, Inc., 287 F.3d 643 (7th Cir. 2002) (EEOC could not use its subpoena power because "in light of the tangential need for the information," the request unduly burdened UAL).

Second, Title VII requires the EEOC to conduct an investigation and find reasonable cause. Few cases have challenged an EEOC suit on the ground that the Commission entirely omitted either the investigation or the reasonable cause determination. And when the adequacy of the EEOC's investigation has been questioned, the courts have given the argument short shrift. E.g., Newsome v. EEOC, 301 F.3d 227 (5th Cir. 2002). Third, if the EEOC finds reasonable cause, Title VII directs it to "endeavor to eliminate any . . . alleged unlawful employment practice by informal methods of conference, conciliation, and persuasion." § 706(b), 42 U.S.C.S. § 2000e-5(b) (2003). Defendants have had more success in challenging alleged EEOC failures to satisfy this requirement. The courts have held that conciliation efforts are normally required, e.g., EEOC v. Great Atlantic & Pacific Tea Co., 735 F.2d 69 (3d Cir. 1984); EEOC v. Hickey-Mitchell Co., 507 F.2d 944 (8th Cir. 1974), and some cases have imposed relatively stringent requirements, see Brennan v. Ace Hardware Co., 495 F.2d 368, 375 (8th Cir. 1974) (ADEA) (government must "fulfill the affirmative burden of exhaustively employing informal methods to allow the employer the opportunity to comply voluntarily with the Act"). Other courts have been much more permissive. EEOC v. Keco Indus., 748 F.2d 1097 (6th Cir. 1984). See also EEOC v. Massey-Ferguson, Inc., 622 F.2d 271 (7th Cir. 1980).

Fourth, the requirement that Commission suits be predicated on charges filed with the EEOC has given rise to questions concerning the relationship among the charge, the EEOC's processing of it, and the complaint then filed by the EEOC. A Commission suit is not confined to the discrimination actually specified in the predicate charge or to those that the charging party had "standing" to raise. In EEOC v. General Elec. Co., 532 F.2d 359 (4th Cir. 1976), the Fourth Circuit held that the sole test for legitimacy of the suit is whether the discrimination was stated in the charge itself or disclosed in the course of a reasonable investigation of that charge. Accord, Lucky Stores, Inc. v. EEOC, 714 F.2d 911 (9th Cir. 1983). But see EEOC v. Hearst Corp., 103 F.3d 462 (5th Cir. 1997) (EEOC cannot continue to investigate charge when plaintiff employee has commenced suit); EEOC v. Harvey L. Walner & Assocs., 91 F.3d 963 (7th Cir. 1996) (EEOC could not sue for sex harassment when there were no active, timely individual charges and it did not file a Commissioner's charge); EEOC v. Bailey Co., Inc., 563 F.2d 439 (6th Cir. 1977) (Commission could not attack religious discrimination uncovered in investigation of charges of sex and race discrimination because the religious discrimination did not affect the charging party at all). *General Electric* also indicated, however, that while a "reasonable" investigation would justify a complaint broader than the basic charge, the scope of the EEOC's complaint may be limited by the agency's reasonable cause determination and conciliation efforts. But see EEOC v. Brookhaven Bank & Trust Co., 614 F.2d 1022 (5th Cir. 1980); EEOC v. McCall Printing Co., 633 F.2d 1232 (6th Cir. 1980).

There have also been efforts to limit EEOC suits on behalf of individual employees. In EEOC v. Waffle House, Inc., 534 U.S. 279 (2002), the Court permitted the EEOC to obtain relief in Commission lawsuits on behalf of employees even if these employees had agreed to arbitrate any claims against their employers. While recoveries by such employees, either after litigation or by arbitration, would presumably bar duplicate recovery in the EEOC action, the Commission cannot be foreclosed from suing by virtue of an arbitration agreement to which it is not a party.

A final question concerning EEOC suits relates to the governing time limitations. Occidental Life Ins. Co. v. EEOC, 432 U.S. 355 (1977), effectively settled most such issues, holding that there was no statute of limitations for EEOC suits. Congress's concern with limitations was restricted to the filing of a charge and the ten-day notice provision, something "wholly consistent with the Act's overall enforcement structure — a sequential series of steps beginning with the filing of a charge with the EEOC." Id. at 372. Congress did not intend any limitation period on EEOC suits other than perhaps that which resulted from the need to timely file a charge of discrimination.

While *Occidental Life* holds that no limitations period, properly so-called, controls EEOC suits, a question remained whether the doctrine of laches may limit such suits. The Court wrote:

> It is, of course, possible that despite these procedural protections a defendant in a Title VII enforcement action might still be significantly handicapped in making his defense because of an inordinate EEOC delay in filing the action after exhausting its conciliation efforts. If such cases arise the federal courts do not lack the power to provide relief.

432 U.S. at 373. While the Court never used the term, laches, (or some very similar concept) has been applied to EEOC suits by the circuits, e.g., EEOC v. Dresser

Indus., Inc., 668 F.2d 1199 (11th Cir. 1982), and the Court's recent decision in *Morgan*, reproduced at page 842, although dealing with a private plaintiff, will undoubtedly reinforce this line of authority.

The two basic elements of laches are the plaintiff's unreasonable delay and the resulting prejudice to the defendant. In most cases of agency delay, one or both will be lacking. While EEOC proceedings are frequently lengthy, the delays in bringing suit are not necessarily "unreasonable." Several courts have expressed sympathy with the problems caused by the EEOC's perennial backlog. E.g., EEOC v. Great Atl. & Pac. Tea Co., supra. But other courts have found minimum delays ranging from four to seven years sufficient to satisfy this prong of the laches doctrine. E.g., EEOC v. Dresser Indus., Inc., 668 F.2d 1199 (11th Cir. 1982); EEOC v. Alioto Fish Co., 623 F.2d 86 (9th Cir. 1980). In so doing, some courts measure delay from the date of the alleged violation; others measure from the date of the charge filing. It is not clear, however, whether the difference is important to the actual decisions.

Even assuming unreasonable Commission delay, the defendant must still suffer prejudice in order to invoke laches. Further, in assessing prejudice, the appropriate equitable response must be tailored to the harm caused by the unreasonable delay. For example, the prejudice that would warrant dismissal of the suit would have to be much more extreme than that which would suffice to justify limitations on the remedy. See EEOC v. Massey-Ferguson, Inc., supra. Dismissal would seem appropriate only when the delay prejudiced the employer's ability to defend the liability issue, for example, where witnesses have become unavailable, memories have faded, or records have been destroyed. E.g., EEOC v. Dresser Indus., Inc., supra.

## H. THE RELATIONSHIP BETWEEN PUBLIC AND PRIVATE SUIT

With the 1972 amendments, Congress probably envisioned that the typical Title VII enforcement proceeding would be a § 706 EEOC suit brought on the basis of a private charge.* In such a suit, the problems of public-private coordination would be minimal because the charging party is not authorized to bring a separate action. Similarly, the ADEA provides that the private right to sue "shall terminate upon the commencement of an action by the [EEOC] to enforce the right of such employee under this [Act]." § 7(c), 29 U.S.C.S. § 626(c) (2003). Under Title VII, the charging party is explicitly authorized to intervene in the Commission's suit. See Cooper v. Fed. Reserve Bank, 467 U.S. 867 (1984) (failure to intervene would entrust the individual's rights to the EEOC).

A problem arises, however, when it is not the EEOC, but the charging party who first brings a court suit. The courts have divided on whether the Commission may file

---

*When the EEOC prevails in a suit, it may obtain relief for individual discriminatees, an outcome identical to that of a successful Title VII class action. If, however, the Commission's suit fails, private parties may still be able to litigate the same cause against the same defendants. Because discriminatees may be benefitted, but not bound, by the EEOC suit, defendants have sought to characterize the EEOC suit as a class action: an unsuccessful action would then be res judicata and would bar class members from relitigating the same cause of action. The Supreme Court rejected this position in General Tel. Co. v. EEOC, 446 U.S. 318, 323 (1980), holding that "Rule 23 is not applicable to an enforcement action brought by the EEOC in its own name pursuant to its authority under § 706 to prevent unlawful employment practices."

its own action. Some hold that the structure of Title VII procedures bars duplicative EEOC actions, leaving the agency only the route of permissive intervention in the private suit should it wish to attack the same discrimination. EEOC v. Contl. Oil Co., 548 F.2d 884 (10th Cir. 1977); EEOC v. Missouri Pac. R.R., 493 F.2d 71 (8th Cir. 1974). Other courts have permitted duplicative Commission suits generally or when the EEOC action is broader than the private suit. EEOC v. North Hills Passavant Hosp., 544 F.2d 664 (3d Cir. 1976); EEOC v. Kimberly-Clark Corp., 511 F.2d 1352 (6th Cir. 1975); EEOC v. Huttig Sash & Door Co., 511 F.2d 453 (5th Cir. 1975).

Still another problem arises from the EEOC's role in the enforcement of Title VII. The Commission obtains much information * that may be of use to employees, and questions have arisen concerning the availability and admissibility of EEOC data. Title VII provides some guidance with several confidentiality provisions. One states that "[n]othing said or done during and as a part of [the EEOC's] informal endeavors [at conciliation] may be made public by the Commission, its officers or employees, or used as evidence in a subsequent proceeding without the written consent of the persons concerned." § 706(b), 42 U.S.C.S. § 2000e-5(b) (2003). As far as admissibility at trial, this rule basically codifies the common law rule regarding settlement negotiations. See generally Charles Tilford McCormick, Evidence § 76 (Edward W. Cleary ed., 1954).

Title VII also provides: "It shall be unlawful for any officer or employee of the Commission to make public in any manner whatever any information obtained by the Commission pursuant to its authority under this section prior to the institution of any proceeding under this title, involving such information." § 709(e), 42 U.S.C.S. § 2000e-8(e) (2003). On its face, this section prohibits disclosure only prior to filing suit, so that it has no effect on admissibility in a suit once commenced. Even with respect to the pre-suit period, the Supreme Court has limited the impact of § 709(e) by holding that the charging party is not "the public." EEOC v. Associated Dry Goods Corp., 449 U.S. 590 (1981). Accordingly, the EEOC may disclose any information to a charging party that is relevant to her charge. The Court, however, did indicate that the Commission could not provide that party with information as to other charges made against the same employer.

In short, a charging party may obtain information contained in the agency's file on his charge. The use of such information at trial, however, poses difficulties even beyond the bar on information obtained during conciliation. Consider, for example, the EEOC's reasonable cause determination. Because private suit may be brought regardless of whether or not the EEOC finds reasonable cause and Title VII suits are tried de novo, the EEOC determination of reasonable cause is arguably irrelevant to the judicial process. While a number of courts have upheld the admissibility of the Commission's determination, e.g., McClure v. Mexia Indep. Sch. Dist., 750 F.2d 396 (5th Cir. 1985), others have not. E.g., Coleman v. Home Depot, Inc., 306 F.3d 1333 (3d Cir. 2002) (while EEOC determinations are presumably trustworthy, they may be excluded under Rule 403 if their probative value is outweighed by the danger of prejudice); Beachy v. Boise Cascade Corp., 191 F.3d 1010 (9th Cir. 1999) (error made by the district judge in admitting agency documents did not require reversal because it probably would not have affected the jury's verdict); Paolito v. John Brown E. & C. Inc., 151 F.3d 60 (2d Cir. 1998) (agency findings are not required, as a matter of law, to be admitted, inasmuch as the probative value of such findings does not necessarily

---

*The EEOC may obtain data by copying the records it requires employers to keep, by using subpoenas, or by obtaining voluntary employer disclosure during the course of investigation or conciliation.

outweigh any danger of unfair prejudice). See also EEOC v. Ford Motor Co., 98 F.3d 1341 (6th Cir. 1996) (although admission is within the discretion of the district court, there was no error in a court's categorical refusal to admit EEOC cause determinations in either bench or jury trials). See generally Michael D. Moberly, Reconsidering the Impact of Reasonable Cause Determinations in the Ninth Circuit, 24 Pepp. L. Rev. 37 (1996) (criticizing the Ninth Circuit for not only establishing a rule of per se admissibility but also for holding that a reasonable cause determination is a per se basis to deny summary judgment to a defendant). Even if the EEOC's determination and findings of fact are admissible, the whole Commission investigative file may not necessarily be admitted. As to investigative reports, the admission of such records is discretionary with the trial judge Cervantes v. Wal-Mart Stores, Inc., No. 00-1058, 2001 U.S. App. LEXIS 63 (10th Cir. 2001) (summary judgment reversed in part because district court did not address evidentiary effect of EEOC determination).

# I. TITLE VII SUIT AGAINST GOVERNMENTAL EMPLOYERS

As originally enacted in 1964, Title VII did not include any government employment. The 1972 amendments broadened the statute's prohibitions to include federal, state, and local governments.

## 1. State and Local Government Employment

The 1972 extension of Title VII prohibitions to state and local governments on basically the same terms as private employers generated questions about the constitutionality of this aspect of Title VII. One question was whether the Tenth Amendment restricted federal power over state employment. See Natl. League of Cities v. Usery, 426 U.S. 833 (1976) (Tenth Amendment limits the power of the federal government under the commerce clause to control "integral governmental operations"). This question was resolved by a pair of Supreme Court decisions. EEOC v. Wyoming, 460 U.S. 226 (1983), upheld the application of the Age Discrimination in Employment Act to the states by balancing state and federal interests and finding the federal interest stronger. Then, in Garcia v. San Antonio Metro. Trans. Auth., 469 U.S. 528 (1985), the Court overruled *National League of Cities* and returned the issue of federal authority under the commerce clause from the judicial sphere to the political domain. This resolution avoided the necessity of looking to other sources of congressional power for antidiscrimination statutes, such as § 5 of the Fourteenth Amendment, which empowers Congress "to enforce, by appropriate legislation, the provisions of this article."

A second set of questions arose with respect to limitations on federal power under the Eleventh Amendment, which restricts federal court jurisdiction over the states. The Supreme Court has held that statutes that are valid exercises of Congress' power under § 5 of the Fourteenth Amendment will trump state sovereignty under the Eleventh Amendment, although the statutes must not only be valid under § 5 but also unequivocally express an intent to override the states' Eleventh Amendment immunity. Seminole Tribe of Florida v. Florida, 517 U.S. 44 (1996). That case also held that the commerce clause is not a valid basis for abrogating state Eleventh Amendment immunity. Subsequent authority has held that private suits against states are not permitted even in state court in cases in which the Eleventh Amendment immunity would bar suit in federal court. Alden v. Maine, 527 U.S. 706 (1999).

Title VII was held to trump state Eleventh Amendment immunity in Fitzpatrick v. Bitzer, 427 U.S. 445 (1976), although the court dropped a footnote indicating that there was no dispute in the case before it that Title VII was an exercise of Congress's power under §5 of the Fourteenth Amendment. More recently, however, Kimel v. Florida Bd. of Regents, 528 U.S. 62 (1999), and Board of Trustees v. Garrett, 531 U.S. 356 (2001), held, respectively, that the ADEA and Title I of the ADA were not valid exercises of Congress' power to abrogate the states' Eleventh Amendment immunity. Although *Garrett* did not reach the validity of Title II of the ADA, it seems likely to also be beyond Congress' power. Reickenbacker v. Foster, 274 F.3d 974 (5th Cir. 2001); contra, Kiman v. New Hampshire Dept. of Corr., 301 F.3d 13 (1st Cir. 2002). Cf. Garcia v. State Univ. of N.Y. Health Scis. Ctr., 280 F.3d 98, 15 (2d Cir. 2001) (Title II authorizes private suit only when a violation is "motivated by discriminatory animus or ill will based on the plaintiff's disability"). See also Raygor v. Regents of the University of Minnesota, 534 U.S. 533 (2002) (federal supplemental jurisdiction statute 28 U.S.C. §1367(d) invalid to the extent it would toll the state statute of limitations for state claims against non-consenting state defendants); Hibbs v. Dept. of Human Res., 273 F.3d 844 (9th Cir. 2001), *cert. granted*, 122 S. Ct. 2618 (2002) (FMLA application to states valid exercise of powers).

Under the *Kimel-Garrett* analysis, Congress has no commerce clause power to abrogate states' Eleventh Amendment immunity because that amendment was intended to limit federal power. While Congress may abrogate immunity when properly exercising its powers under §5 of the Fourteenth Amendment, City of Boerne v. Flores, 521 U.S. 507 (1997), applied a searching review of enactments under §5. This was confirmed by Florida Prepaid Postsecondary Educ. Expense Bd. v. College Savings Bank, 527 U.S. 627 (1999), which invalidated Congress' extension of federal patent law to the states because Congress had not sufficiently identified state "conduct transgressing the Fourteenth Amendment's substantive provisions," id. at 639, nor did it "tailor its legislative scheme to remedying or preventing such conduct," id. at 639. Under these tests, the ADA and ADEA were not a proper exercise of such powers in *Kimel* and *Garrett*. See generally, Pamela S. Karlan, Disarming the Private Attorney General, — Ill. L. Rev. —, — (2002) (*Garrett* "reveals a preference for centralized enforcement that defies the central idea behind the private attorney general — that Congress might decide that decentralized enforcement better vindicates civil rights policies."); Samuel Estreicher & Vikram D. Amar, Conduct Unbecoming a Coordinate Branch: The Supreme Court in *Garrett*, 4 Green Bag 2d 351 (2001) ("whether or not earlier cases from the Court in the 1990's construing Congress' section 5 power narrowly were correctly decided, the Court in *Garrett* makes a number of questionable analytic moves that demonstrate a disrespect for Congress' constitutional role in vindicating equal protection rights.").

The significance of *Kimel* and *Garrett* is substantial but should not be exaggerated. They do not hold that the ADA and ADEA are inapplicable to the states; rather, they hold only that *private* suits against the states are not permitted. Accordingly, federal government enforcement is still allowed. United States v. Miss. Dept. of Pub. Safety, 2003 U.S. App. LEXIS 1965 (Feb. 5, 2003); EEOC v. Bd. of Regents of the Univ. of Wis. Sys., 288 F.3d 296 (7th Cir. 2002) (even when the EEOC is proceeding on behalf of private individuals, it is not subject to Eleventh Amendment immunity in suits against the state). But see EEOC v. Kentucky Ret. Sys., No. 00-5664, 2001 U.S. App. LEXIS 17988 (6th Cir. 2001) (rejecting Eleventh Amendment restrictions on EEOC suit but finding Eleventh Amendment limitations on remedies). In that sense, *Kimel* and *Garrett* are not decisions restricting the coverage of the statutes but ones limiting who may bring suit to enforce them. Secondly, *Kimel* and *Garrett* do not bar suits against local governmental entities. They merely prohibit private suits against an employer who counts as the state, and most public sector employment will remain actionable in private suit because the employers involved are local governmental units. E.g., Mt. Healthy City Sch. Dist. Bd. of Ed. v. Doyle, 429 U.S. 274, 280 (1977) (Eleventh Amendment immunity does not reach to counties and similar municipal corporations); Eason v. Clark County Sch. Dist., 303 F.3d 1137 (9th Cir. 2002) (Nevada school districts not arms of the state).

Third, while the ADEA and the ADA may not be invoked by private suits against state employers, the Court's holding that Congress validly abrogated state immunity to Title VII suits in Fitzpatrick v. Bitzer, 427 U.S. 445 (1976), has remained intact. E.g., Maitland v. Univ. of Minn., 260 F.3d 959 (8th Cir. 2001) (Eleventh Amendment does not bar males from suing states for sex discrimination favoring women); Hundertmark v. Florida Dept. of Transp., 205 F.3d 1272 (11th Cir. 2000) (Congress sufficiently expressed its intent to subject the states to suit so the Eleventh Amendment did not bar an action against the state for violating the Equal Pay Act). See also Kovacevich v. Kent State Univ., 224 F.3d 806 (6th Cir. 2000) (Equal Pay Act validly abrogated state Eleventh Amendment immunity); Nihiser v. Ohio Envtl. Prot. Agency, 269 F.3d 626 (6th Cir. 2001) (a state can be sued by its employees under § 504 of the Rehabilitation Act because by accepting federal money the state waives immunity to suit). Cf. McCrary v. Ohio Dept. of Human Serv., No. 99-3597, 2000 U.S. App. LEXIS 19212 (6th Cir. 2000) (state immune from § 1981 suits). Therefore, private Title VII suits against even state entities should remain largely unaffected by this line of cases.

It is possible, however, that some aspects of Title VII are not within Congress' power to abrogate Eleventh Amendment immunity. Section 5 of the Fourteenth Amendment provides that "The Congress shall have power to *enforce,* by appropriate legislation, the provisions of this article." City of Boerne v. Flores, 521 U.S. 507, 517 (1997), however, held Congress can *enforce* Fourteenth Amendment rights, not define them. While Congress is not limited to parroting the provisions of the Fourteenth Amendment, to be "appropriate" under § 5 "there must be a congruence and proportionality between the injury to be prevented or remedied and the means adopted to that end." Id. at 520. In *Kimel,* the Court found no such congruence and proportionality between the ADEA and the Fourteenth Amendment's prohibitions. Under the Equal Protection Clause, age discrimination is subject to only rational basis review, whereas the ADEA applies the equivalent of a strict scrutiny analysis. The ADEA thus "prohibits substantially more state employment decisions and practices than would likely be held unconstitutional under the applicable equal protection, rational basis standard." *Kimel,* 528 U.S. at 86. While Congress might go further than the requirements of the equal protection clause if necessary to enforce that constitutional command, the Court found no evidence that Congress was in fact responding to a pattern of unconstitutional conduct when it extended the ADEA to the states. "Our examination of the ADEA's legislative record confirms that Congress' 1974 extension of the Act to the States was an unwarranted response to a perhaps inconsequential problem." Id. at 89. *Garrett* applied a similar analysis to the ADA.

As applied to Title VII, disparate treatment race and gender discrimination by states, among others, would support the extension of that statute to the states in 1972. See Nanda v. Bd. of Trs. of the Univ. of Ill., 303 F.3d 817 (7th Cir. 2002) (disparate treatment theory valid as applied to the states; no need to address disparate impact theory). While there may be more of a question with respect to religious discrimination, one court has upheld the duty to reasonably accommodate religious beliefs by a state employer against Eleventh Amendment attack. See Holmes v. Marion County Office of Family & Children, 184 F. Supp. 2d 828 (S.D. Ind. 2002). There is also a serious issue as to Title VII's prohibitions on disparate impact and pregnancy discrimination. In both cases, Title VII goes beyond what the Equal Protection Clause would require, and it is not clear that Congress developed the kind of record that the Court found wanting in *Kimel* with respect to the ADEA. See Okruhlik v. Univ. of Ark., 255 F.3d 615 (8th Cir. 2001) (Congress validly abrogated Eleventh Amendment immunity for claims of disparate treatment and impact on the basis of gender and race). It is possible, of course, that the appropriate test is not whether any particular provision of the statute is justified by § 5, but rather whether the statute as a whole is. In that event, Fitzpatrick v. Bitzer, 427 U.S. 445 (1976), would support Title VII's abrogation of state Eleventh Amendment immunity. See generally Christine Jolls, Antidiscrimination and Accommodation, 115 Harv. L. Rev. 642 (2001). Samuel Estreicher, The Section 5 Mystique, *Morrison*, and the Future of Federal Discrimination Law, 2000 Sup. Ct. Rev. 109, 173 (2001).

Fourth, even Eleventh Amendment immunity is not absolute: it may be waived by the state. Lapides v. Bd. of Regents, 535 U.S. 613 (2002) (a state can waive its Eleventh Amendment immunity by removing a state lawsuit from state court to federal court); Estes v. Wyoming DOT, 302 F.3d 1200 (10th Cir. 2002) (waiver when federal lawsuit is removed to federal court). See also, e.g., Koslow v. Pennsylvania, 302 F.3d 161 (3d Cir. 2002) (state's acceptance of federal funds waived immunity for Rehabilitation Act suit). See also Ann Carey Juliano, The More You Spend, the More You Save: Can the Spending Clause Save Federal Anti-Discrimination Laws?, 46 Villanova L. Rev. 1111 (2001) (proposing re-enacting antidiscrimination legislation under the spending clause in order to save such actions against states). However, waivers are not lightly found. See Faibisch v. Univ. of Minn., 304 F.3d 797 (8th Cir. 2002) (state statute permitting suit in "any court of competent jurisdiction" did not waive Eleventh Amendment immunity).

Fifth, injunctive relief may be available against state officials under the *Ex Parte Young* doctrine. The theory of Ex Parte Young, 209 U.S. 123 (1980), is that state officials who are violating federal law are acting ultra vires and may be enjoined to follow governing law; the official, not the state is the defendant. This theory has been employed to permit antidiscrimination suits. Gibson v. Ark. Dept. of Corr., 265 F.3d 718 (8th Cir. 2001).

Finally, the Court stressed in *Garrett* that most states had state remedies against disability discrimination that provided adequate redress for victims. However, the extent to which this is true has been questioned. Ruth Colker & Adam Milani, The Post-*Garrett* World: Insufficient State Protection Against Disability Discrimination, 53 Ala. L. Rev. 1075 (2002) (contrary to *Garrett's* reassurance about adequate state remedies, less than half the states have laws that would bar discrimination in state access and services).

Remaining federalism concerns in the antidiscrimination statutes are reflected mainly in special statutory provisions and in judicial approaches to interpreting laws such as exceptions for elected officials and their appointees found in Title VII, the ADEA, and the ADA. For example, Title VII excludes from the definition of "employee"

> any person elected to public office in any State or political subdivision of any State by the qualified voters thereof, or any person chosen by such officer to be on such officer's personal staff, or an appointee on the policy making level or an immediate adviser with respect to the exercise of the constitutional or legal power of the office.

§ 701(f), 42 U.S.C.S. § 2000e(f) (2003). The Supreme Court construed the ADEA version of this exception in Gregory v. Ashcroft, 501 U.S. 452 (1991) and held that appointed state judges are within it. While the exemption is severely limited in its own terms, Congress further undermined it with the Civil Rights Act of 1991, which provided the kind of "plain statement" that the Court had required under *Ashcroft* in order to intrude into state operations. See 5 U.S.C.S. § 1220 (2003).* See Gunaca v. State of Texas, 65 F.3d 467 (5th Cir. 1995).

## 2. *Federal Employment*

As enacted in 1964, Title VII did not authorize suit against the federal government, nor did the original Age Discrimination in Employment Act reach federal employment. Amendments, however, extended both statutes to most federal workers. Thus, in 1972, Congress added § 717 to Title VII, 42 U.S.C.S. § 2000e-16 (2003), to reach most federal employment and, in 1974, amended the ADEA to add § 15, requiring most federal personnel actions to be made "free from any discrimination based on age." 29 U.S.C.S. § 633a (2003). While the Americans with Disabilities Act does not generally reach federal employees, these employees receive comparable protection under the Rehabilitation Act, which specifically adopts the "remedies, procedures, and rights" of § 717. 29 U.S.C.S. § 794(a) (2003). See Chapter 10. Finally, the Civil Rights Act of 1991 and the Congressional Accountibility Act of 1995, Pub. L. No. 104-1 (Jan. 23, 1995), recognized antidiscrimination rights and remedies for previously unprotected workers, including employees of the House of Representatives, the Senate, and instrumentalities of Congress; many "presidential appointees" were also included.

The normal provisions of the federal laws were not, however, simply applied to federal employees. Each statute created a different scheme. For Title VII, Congress established a special procedure in § 717, 42 U.S.C.S. § 2000e-16 (2003), for the vindication of most federal employee rights. These remedies are in addition to those available under other civil service principles.† Basically, the statute requires "employees or applicants for employment" to file an administrative complaint with the agency responsible for the discrimination.‡ After final agency action on that complaint, the

---

*The statute also created a new procedure to vindicate these rights. Rather than merely subjecting appointees to the normal provisions of Title VII and the ADEA, the 1991 Act leaves the exemption technically intact, but creates a new statutory protection for appointed officials. § 321, 42 U.S.C.S. § 1220 (2003). Unlike the EEOC's role for other employees — investigation, reasonable cause determination, and conciliation — the new statute establishes an adjudicatory role for the EEOC, which is to conduct a formal agency hearing. The EEOC's decision is then subject to limited judicial review, rather than the trial de novo that exists in the private sector. There are also some other procedural differences.

†As a result, there have sometimes been questions of the interrelationship between civil service and discrimination procedures. 5 U.S.C.S. § 7702 (2003); 29 C.F.R. §§ 1614.303-.310. See, e.g., Afifi v. United States Dept. of the Interior, 924 F.2d 61 (4th Cir. 1991). Federal employees may also have rights under collective bargaining agreements, 5 U.S.C.S. § 7121 (2003), resort to which may waive Title VII rights. E.g., Vinieratos v. United States, 939 F.2d 762 (9th Cir. 1991). See generally William V. Luneburg, The Federal Personnel Complaint, Appeal, and Grievance Systems: A Structural Overview and Proposed Revisions, 78 Ky. L. Rev. 1 (1989-1990).

‡The ADEA's § 15 differs from Title VII's § 717 in that the former does not require a federal employee to resort to administrative remedies. E.g., Castro v. United States, 775 F.2d 399 (1st Cir. 1985). However, federal employees with ADEA claims may, if they so desire, resort to administrative remedies prior to suit. Thus, § 15 creates a bifurcated scheme preceding the filing of a court suit: the federal employee may avoid administrative remedies (and merely give the EEOC "notice of intent to sue"), or she may file an administrative complaint, which will trigger a formal administrative proceeding. E.g., Limongelli v. Postmaster General of the United States, 707 F.2d 368 (9th Cir. 1983); Paterson v. Weinberger, 644 F.2d 521, 523 (5th Cir. 1981).

charging party has the option of appealing to the EEOC or filing an action in district court. If appeal is taken to the EEOC, the EEOC may resolve the matter in the employee's favor and award backpay and compensatory damages against the employer-agency. West v. Gibson, 527 U.S. 212 (1999). If, however, the employee is unsatisfied with the EEOC's resolution, she may bring suit in federal court after the EEOC's final decision.

This procedure has generated a number of problems analogous to, but distinct from, those dealt with in connection with §706. Section 717 lacks an express time limitation for filing an administrative complaint comparable to the 180-day or 300-day time period under §706. The courts have, therefore, tended to follow the EEOC regulations, which contain elaborate provisions for administrative processing of a discrimination complaint. 29 C.F.R. pt. 1614 (1992). See Kevin J. Dolley, Comment, Administrative Waiver of the Untimeliness Defense in Title VII Cases Concerning Federal Employees: A Proposed Analysis, 46 St. Louis L.J. 477 (2002).

As with §706, timely resort to court after the administrative proceedings is essential. Section 717 expressly provides for filing a complaint "[w]ithin ninety days of receipt of notice of final action taken by a department, agency, or unit . . . or by the [EEOC] upon an appeal from a decision or order of such department, agency, or unit on a complaint of discrimination." While compliance with the time period is a prerequisite to suit under §717, the §717 time periods are not jurisdictional. Irwin v. Dept. of Veterans Affairs, 498 U.S. 89, 95-96 (1990) ("the same rebuttable presumption of equitable tolling applicable to suits against private defendants should also apply to suits against the United States").

After the addition of §717 to Title VII, perhaps the most pressing question was the scope of judicial review of a prior administrative decision when a civil action was brought. In Chandler v. Roudebush, 425 U.S. 840 (1976), the Supreme Court held that, like their private sector counterparts, federal employees are entitled to a trial de novo of their §717 claims. See also Rosenfeld v. Dept. of Army, 769 F.2d 237 (4th Cir. 1985) (ADEA suits tried de novo by the federal courts after resort to administrative proceedings). *Chandler*, however, does not render the administrative proceedings wholly irrelevant to the court case. In some instances, the testimony taken in the administrative proceedings may be a sufficient basis for summary judgment. E.g., Weahkee v. Perry, 587 F.2d 1256 (D.C. Cir. 1978). More generally, the administrative proceedings may be admitted into evidence in appropriate cases. See Clark v. Chasen, 619 F.2d 1330 (9th Cir. 1980).

A final question about §717 was whether that section was the exclusive avenue for redress for federal employees. In the nonfederal employment sector, Title VII is only one of several avenues for vindicating the right to be free of discrimination. Johnson v. Railway Express Agency, Inc., 421 U.S. 454 (1975). In Brown v. Gen. Servs. Admin., 425 U.S. 820 (1976), however, the Court held that §717 is the exclusive remedy for discriminations within its ambit. The Supreme Court has subsequently extended *Brown* to bar suits on grounds that were covered by the Civil Service Reform Act of 1978. Bush v. Lucas, 462 U.S. 367 (1983). See also Paterson v. Weinberger, 644 F.2d 521, 524 (5th Cir. 1981) (ADEA the exclusive route for federal employees to challenge age discrimination). There may, however, be room for constitutional suits in jobs not covered by Title VII or other comprehensive federal enactments. For example, in Davis v. Passman, 442 U.S. 228 (1979), the Court held that a damage action may be brought directly under the due process clause of the Fifth Amendment in order to attack gender discrimination in a congressman's selection of an administrative assistant. Such employment was not covered by statute at the time. See also

Kotarski v. Cooper, 799 F.2d 1342 (9th Cir. 1986) (probationary employee not protected by Civil Service Act could bring constitutional suit).

## J.  SETTLING DISCRIMINATION SUITS

Consensual resolution of discrimination disputes is common. For example, in Melanson v. Browning-Ferris Indus. Inc., 281 F.3d 272 (1st Cir. 2002), an employee's Title VII claims were barred after she "knowingly and voluntarily signed a release" of all such claims.* Indeed, one problem that has arisen is whether agreements routinely waiving discrimination claims as part of a general release connected with employment termination are valid. This question has been often litigated under the Age Discrimination in Employment Act because severance pay and other benefits are often linked to the employee's execution of a release of liability. In 1990, Congress enacted the Older Workers Benefit Protection Act (OWBPA), Pub. L. No. 101-521, 104 Stat. 978 (Oct. 16, 1990), codified at 29 U.S.C.S. § 626(f) (2003), which established principles that, though governing only ADEA cases, can be expected to have an influence in cases decided under other laws. Basically, the statute permits a "voluntary early retirement incentive plan" that includes "knowing and voluntary waiver" of ADEA claims. However, it also establishes certain minimum conditions for such waivers. These include (1) an agreement "written in a manner calculated to be understood"; (2) specific reference to ADEA claims; (3) no waiver of rights arising after execution of the document; (4) waiver only in return for consideration in addition to that to which the individual is already entitled; (5) advice in writing to the employee to consult an attorney; (6) adequate time to decide, at least 21 days; and (7) a seven-day period during which the waiver may be revoked. There are certain additional requirements when the waiver is sought as part of a program offered to a group of workers. See pages 665-666.

Discrimination claims are also settled after they have been raised in formal proceedings. Like most other civil litigation, the vast majority of antidiscrimination suits are settled before trial, although the Older Workers Benefit Protection Act also specifies requirements for an ADEA court suit. Most settlements providing for basically monetary relief pose few special problems,† but serious questions can arise

---

*There is a split in the circuits as to whether state or federal law governs the question of whether the parties have reached a settlement. Compare Makins v. District of Columbia, 277 F.3d 544 (D.C. Cir. 2002) (state law governs), with Fennell v. TLB Kent Co., 865 F.2d 498, 501 (2d Cir. 1986); Mid-South Towing Co. v. Har-Win, Inc., 733 F.2d 386 (5th Cir. 1984) (federal law). See generally Grace M. Giesel, Enforcement of Settlement Contracts: The Problem of the Attorney Agent, 12 Geo. J. Legal Ethics 543 (1999).

†There has been some question of whether settlements of federal discrimination suits could be enforced in federal court without an independent basis for federal jurisdiction. Although circuit court cases adopted a broader rule, at least for EEOC enforcement, the Supreme Court in Kokkonen v. Guardian Life Ins. Co. of Am., 511 U.S. 375 (1994), held that, after a district court has dismissed the case, it needs ancillary jurisdiction to enforce any underlying settlement agreement unless the district court specifically retained jurisdiction for that purpose or incorporated the agreement in the order for dismissal. See also Shaffer v. GTE North Inc., 284 F.3d 500 (3d Cir. 2002) (settlement agreement could not be enforced when the court did not expressly retain jurisdiction over the agreement or incorporate it into the dismissal order). Thus, for a federal court to enforce a settlement agreement where jurisdiction has not been retained for that purpose there must be an independent basis for federal jurisdiction. See also Sheng v. Starkey Lab, Inc., 53 F.3d 192 (8th Cir. 1995) (reservation of jurisdiction for the parties to reopen the action is not sufficient to assert jurisdiction to enforce a settlement agreement); Gilbert v. Mon-

when the parties wish to settle if the defendant will agree to change its conduct in some way. For example, it could promise to reinstate the plaintiff, to modify its seniority system, or to alter work rules. The basic difficulty is that such changes in conduct affect not only the parties to the suit, but also nonparties.

The form of the settlement may bear on this issue. Two basic approaches are possible, a purely contractual one and the incorporation of the settlement agreement into a court order. The resulting consent decree has aspects of both a contract and a judgment. Generally speaking, the courts do not exercise independent judgment in passing on proposed consent decrees; rather, they rubber-stamp the agreements of the parties. Consent decrees have great utility, but they also have significant drawbacks. On the positive side, they may be preferred by the EEOC and private plaintiffs because they are the "toughest" form of relief, in large part because of possible contempt sanctions. Like purely contractual settlements, such decrees achieve savings in litigation resources by avoiding complex and protracted litigation and by eliminating uncertainty of outcome. For similar reasons, employment discrimination defendants also often prefer consent decrees to litigation. Further, with a consent resolution, the defendant avoids the possible collateral estoppel effects of an adverse decision and the damaging publicity of a public trial. In light of these advantages, consent decrees are plainly useful tools for both plaintiff and defendant.

There are, however, disadvantages to consent decrees. One possibility is that consent decrees, being the outgrowth of litigation compromises, may well provide far less relief than would be awarded after full litigation. A second problem is the possibility of precisely the opposite: an employer might settle a suit that was not well based in order to avoid the costs of litigation. This may be especially troublesome if the rights of majority workers are thereby implicated. These possibilities have raised the questions of what standards government enforcement agencies should use to decide whether to consent to a decree and of the extent to which a court should second-guess the parties in determining whether to enter a proposed decree.*

Another problem is the inflexibility of consent decrees, that is, the ability of courts to alter decrees once entered. It has long been recognized that courts have the power to interpret consent decrees as well as to modify them when appropriate. The standards governing the exercise of these powers, however, are less clear. Changes in economic conditions and in the substantive law of employment discrimination have generated a number of decisions clarifying the appropriate approach to this problem. The Supreme Court addressed both the interpretation and the modification questions in Firefighters Local Union No. 1784 v. Stotts, 467 U.S. 561 (1984). The case reviewed an injunction issued by the district court, barring the city of Memphis in any layoff of workers from following a seniority system, incorporated in a "memorandum

---

santo Co., 216 F.3d 695 (8th Cir. 2000) (district court retained jurisdiction to enforce agreement settling ADEA suit).

In addition, while EEOC suits to enforce settlement agreements that involve federal questions may be brought in federal court, private suits may be held not to arise from a federal question. Thus, in the related question of the law governing such disputes, where only private parties are involved most circuits have applied state law rather than general federal common law. E.g., Resnick v. Uccello Immobilien GMBH, Inc., 227 F.3d 1347 (11th Cir. 2000).

Finally, the threshold question in suits concerning such agreements is whether the suit can be brought without resort to the charge filing procedure. Some courts have held these procedures to be irrelevant because the suit is not to enforce statutory rights but rather to enforce the conciliation agreement; a defense that the employer had not violated the statute would be irrelevant. Cisneros v. ABC Rail Corp., 217 F.3d 1299 (10th Cir. 2000).

*See generally Michael J. Zimmer & Charles A. Sullivan, Consent Decree Settlements by Administrative Agencies in Antitrust and Employment Discrimination: Optimizing Public and Private Interest, 1976 Duke L.J. 163.

of agreement" between the city and Local 1784. The lower court believed that adherence to the seniority system would violate a consent decree that the city had previously entered to settle discrimination suits brought by black firefighters.

To resolve this question, the Court had to decide (1) whether the consent decree, properly construed, barred the layoffs in question; and assuming it did not, (2) whether the entering court could modify the decree to preclude such layoffs. In approaching the first question, the Court invoked principles developed in the antitrust area, in which consent decrees had been treated as contracts for the purposes of interpretation. See United States v. Armour & Co., 402 U.S. 673 (1971). Applying that principle, *Stotts* held that the injunction did not merely implement the consent decree. The decree did not, on its face, address the question of layoffs, and as for the argument that restricting seniority-based layoffs was necessary to achieve the "purpose" of the decree, the Court stressed that the decree itself phrased its purpose as being to "remedy past hiring and promotion practices," not to address layoff rights.

Because it found the injunction not supportable as an interpretation of the consent decree, the Court had to consider whether it was justifiable as a modification of that decree. In this respect, consent decrees are somewhat schizophrenic. Although *Stotts* indicated that the courts apply relatively strict standards of contract law when they are interpreting such decrees, the judiciary seems much more prepared to modify such decrees than it would be if a mere contract were involved. The absence of defendant's consent does not bar modification of consent decrees, but the destruction of expectations based on the original consent decree imposes a heavy burden on parties seeking modification. *Stotts* ultimately took a narrow approach: because the modification in question conflicted with a seniority system that was bona fide under Title VII, the modification was inconsistent with the statute and thus invalid. Id. at 576 n.9. Since the seniority system was valid, it could not, as such, be superseded. Further, while the Court noted that it would be proper to redress discrimination against identified victims by awarding them constructive seniority, Title VII did not permit that kind of relief for the class of minorities in question. As a matter of substantive law, *Stotts* has since been limited in important respects. The opinion did not go so far as to say that a consent decree could never alter a bona fide seniority system: it merely stressed that the city had never consented to such an alteration. Subsequently, the Court held that a consent decree that reflected the true agreements of the parties could override a valid seniority system. Local No. 93, Intl. Assn. of Firefighters v. Cleveland, 478 U.S. 501 (1986). Similarly, despite the strong suggestion in *Stotts* to the contrary, the Supreme Court has since approved the power of a district court "to order race-conscious relief that may benefit individuals who are not identified victims of unlawful discrimination." See, e.g., Local 28, Sheet Metal Workers' Intl. Assn. v. EEOC, 478 U.S. 421, 426 (1986).

As a result, *Stotts* remains important as a "procedural" case. Its vitality consists largely in its reiteration of a contract-oriented approach to interpreting consent decrees and in its insistence that any judicial modification of such decrees be consistent with the governing statutes. In the wake of *Stotts*, many believed that the restrictive *Swift* standard applied, requiring "grievous wrong" to modify a decree. However, a decision in the prison reform area liberalized the judicial approach. At issue in Rufo v. Inmates of Suffolk County Jail, 502 U.S. 367 (1992), was a proposed modification of a consent decree entered to correct allegedly unconstitutional jail conditions. While portions of *Rufo* suggest that the use of institutional reform litigation to define government obligations played an important part in the result, the Court's language is broad enough to reach private employers. See Patterson v. Newspaper & Mail

Deliverers' Union, 13 F.3d 33 (2d Cir. 1993) (applying *Rufo* standard to a consent decree against private parties).

Despite the contractual aspects of consent decrees, *Rufo* found that the permissive language of Rule 60(b) of the Federal Rules of Civil Procedure, dealing with judgments in general, governed the question.* As for the appropriate test, the Court required only that "a party seeking modification of a consent decree bear[ ] the burden of establishing that a significant change in circumstances warrants revision of the decree." 502 U.S. at 383. This requires a showing of a sufficient change in either factual conditions or the law. Thus, modification may be warranted when changed facts make compliance "substantially more onerous." Similarly, modification "is also appropriate when a decree proves to be unworkable because of unforeseen obstacles or when enforcement of the decree without modification would be detrimental to the public interest." Id. at 384. Significantly, the Court rejected the argument that modification should be allowed only when the factual change was both unforeseen and unforeseeable. The Court did, however, acknowledge that ordinarily modification would be inappropriate where a party relies only on facts actually anticipated when the decree was entered.

As for a change in law, *Rufo* recognized not only that a decree must be modified where it would actually violate the law, but also that modification "may be warranted when the statutory or decisional law has changed to make legal what the decree was designed to prevent." Id. at 388. But not every legal clarification suffices. The decree does not automatically have to be altered to reflect lowered legal standards. Nevertheless, a change in the law may "constitute a change in circumstances that would support modification if the parties had based their agreement on a misunderstanding of the governing law." Id. at 390. In Title VII, the question has arisen particularly with respect to efforts to undo consent decrees modifying seniority systems. E.g., Roberts v. St. Regis Paper Co., 653 F.2d 166 (5th Cir. 1981).

*Rufo*'s relaxed standards do not necessarily mean that consent decrees will be modified to be less rigorous. In Vanguards of Cleveland v. City of Cleveland, 23 F.3d 1013, 1019 (6th Cir. 1994), the court approved an extension of a decree because

> the lower than expected pass rates by minorities on the 1984 and 1985 promotional examinations and the resulting slower than expected promotion rate for minorities, a significant change in factual circumstances, caused the consent decree to become "unworkable" as well as "detrimental to the public interest" as a vehicle for curing the previously discriminatory promotion practices in the City's Division of Fire.

Additional complications arise when a purely contractual settlement or a consent decree requires the employer to take action that affects third parties. Over the last decade, the Supreme Court has encountered this question in both contexts. The first case was W. R. Grace & Co. v. Local Union 759, Intl. Union of the United Rubber Workers, 461 U.S. 757 (1983), in which the employer entered into a conciliation agreement with the EEOC. That agreement was inconsistent with the governing collective bargaining agreement. When the company laid off certain workers in order

---

* Rule 60(b) provides:

On motion and upon such terms as are just, the court may relieve a party or a party's legal representative from a final judgment, order, or proceeding for the following reasons: . . . (5) the judgment has been satisfied, released, or discharged, or a prior judgment upon which it is based has been reversed or otherwise vacated, or it is no longer equitable that the judgment should have prospective application; or (6) any other reason justifying relief from the operation of the judgment. . . .

to comply with the conciliation agreement, which required maintaining the existing proportion of women, the union filed grievances under the controlling arbitration clause. Those workers, on the basis of the collective bargaining agreement alone, would have retained their jobs. The company went to court to bar the prosecution of such grievances, but the Fifth Circuit refused an injunction, and the arbitration was completed with an award requiring the employer to provide backpay for the workers whose rights under the collective bargaining agreement had been violated.

The Supreme Court recognized that the award was valid under normal principles governing court review of labor arbitrations, but also it recognized that the courts should not enforce an agreement that violates public policy. Accordingly, the Court had to decide whether the agreement, as interpreted by the arbitrator, violated such policy. The Court found no contrary public policy either in an interim order of the district court that the employer not violate the conciliation agreement or in the conciliation agreement itself.

As for the court order, the Court recognized the company's dilemma in being subjected to conflicting obligations regarding layoffs. But the dilemma "was of the Company's own making. The Company committed itself to two conflicting contractual obligations." Id. at 767. The existence of one contract could not exonerate the company of liability for breach of the other. Further, while the court order might have required that the actual layoffs occur pursuant to the conciliation agreement, "nothing in the collective bargaining agreement as interpreted by [the arbitrator] required the company to violate that order." Id. at 768. The award neither required layoffs nor required that any layoffs be in accordance with the collective bargaining agreement. The arbitral award merely granted backpay for layoffs that violated the labor agreement. The award, then, could not be struck down as "creat[ing] intolerable incentives to disobey a court order." Id. at 769.

Turning to the argument that the EEOC conciliation agreement itself evidenced a public policy that barred the enforcement of the arbitral award, the Court used much the same analysis. It noted that there was no showing that the collective bargaining agreement itself violated Title VII; it, therefore, explicitly refrained from addressing the issue of whether public policy would be violated by enforcing an arbitration award for breach of provisions ultimately found to violate Title VII. What was at issue, then, was whether a conciliation agreement could supersede another contract in the absence of any showing that the contract violated the law.

While recognizing the strong Title VII policy in favor of voluntary compliance, *Grace* stressed that the union had never consented to any modification of its collective bargaining agreement, and "[a]bsent a judicial determination, the Commission, not to mention the company, cannot alter the collective bargaining agreement without the Union's consent." Id. at 771. Such a result would undermine federal labor policy designed to encourage collective bargaining.

An important lesson from *Grace* is that a settlement of a discrimination claim can often coexist with other rights because the employer can comply with both sets of obligations. While it is true that the employer may be subject to double liability, that will simply be the consequence of its assuming two separate obligations. But it is certainly possible that two obligations will, in fact, conflict, and employers would naturally like to avoid double liability. *Grace* did not directly decide whether a different result would occur if one of two mutually inconsistent obligations were imposed by court order.

That issue was presented by Martin v. Wilks, 490 U.S. 755 (1989), whose outcome generally followed the *Grace* lead. *Martin* triggered an amendment to Title VII in the Civil Rights Act of 1991. In order to understand the present law, both the case and the resulting enactment must be examined.

*Martin* was a reverse discrimination suit in which white firefighters sued the City of Birmingham, alleging that they were being denied promotions in favor of less qualified black firefighters. They claimed that promotion decisions were being made on the basis of race under consent decrees. Their suit was rejected by the district court on essentially procedural grounds — the plaintiffs had failed to intervene in the prior litigation that the consent decrees had resolved. The Supreme Court, however, rejected such a "mandatory intervention" rule, concluding that "this holding contravenes the general rule that a person cannot be deprived of his legal rights in a proceeding to which he is not a party." The Court went on:

All agree that "[i]t is a principle of general application in Anglo-American jurisprudence that one is not bound by a judgment in personam in a litigation in which he is not designated as a party or to which he has not been made a party by service of process." Hansberry v. Lee, 311 U.S. 32, 40 (1940). This rule is part of our "deep-rooted historic tradition that everyone should have his own day in court." 18 C. Wright, A. Miller, & E. Cooper, Federal Practice and Procedure § 4449, p. 417 (1981) (18 Wright). A judgment or decree among parties to a lawsuit resolves issues as among them, but it does not conclude the rights of strangers to those proceedings.[2]

Petitioners argue that, because respondents failed to timely intervene in the initial proceedings, their current challenge to actions taken under the consent decree constitutes an impermissible "collateral attack." They argue that respondents were aware that the underlying suit might affect them and if they chose to pass up an opportunity to intervene, they should not be permitted to later litigate the issues in a new action. The position has sufficient appeal to have commanded the approval of the great majority of the federal courts of appeals, but we agree with the contrary view. . . .

[The Federal Rules of Civil Procedure incorporate the principle that "a party seeking a judgment binding on another cannot obligate that person to intervene; he must be joined." Rule 24, governing intervention, is cast in "permissive" terms. The drafters] determined that the concern for finality and completeness of judgments would be "better [served] by mandatory joinder procedures." 18 Wright § 4452, p. 453. Accordingly, Rule 19(a) provides for mandatory joinder in circumstances where a judgment rendered in the absence of a person may "leave . . . persons already parties subject to a substantial risk of incurring . . . inconsistent obligations. . . ." Rule 19(b) sets forth the factors to be considered by a court in deciding whether to allow an action to proceed in the absence of an interested party.

Joinder as a party, rather than knowledge of a lawsuit and an opportunity to intervene, is the method by which potential parties are subjected to the jurisdiction of the court and bound by a judgment or decree.[6] The parties to a lawsuit presumably know better than anyone else the nature and scope of relief sought in the action, and at whose ex-

---

2. We have recognized an exception to the general rule when, in certain limited circumstances, a person, although not a party, has his interests adequately represented by someone with the same interests who is a party. See Hansberry v. Lee, 311 U.S. 32 (1940) ("class" or "representative" suits); Fed. Rule Civ. Proc. 23 (same); Montana v. United States, 440 U.S. 147, 154-55 (1979) (control of litigation on behalf of one of the parties in the litigation). Additionally, where a special remedial scheme exists expressly foreclosing successive litigation by nonlitigants, as for example in bankruptcy or probate, legal proceedings may terminate preexisting rights if the scheme is otherwise consistent with due process. See NLRB v. Bildisco & Bildisco, 465 U.S. 513 (1984) ("proof of claim must be presented to the Bankruptcy Court . . . or be lost"); Tulsa Professional Collection Services, Inc. v. Pope, 485 U.S. 478 (1988) (nonclaim statute terminating unsubmitted claims against the estate). Neither of these exceptions, however, applies in this case.

6. The dissent argues on the one hand that respondents have not been "bound" by the decree but rather, that they are only suffering practical adverse affects from the consent decree. . . . Respondents in their suit have alleged that they are being racially discriminated against by their employer in violation of Title VII: either the fact that the disputed employment decisions are being made pursuant to a consent decree is a defense to respondents' Title VII claims or it is not. If it is a defense to challenges to employment practices which would otherwise violate Title VII, it is very difficult to see why respondents are not being "bound" by the decree.

pense such relief might be granted. It makes sense, therefore, to place on them a burden of bringing in additional parties where such a step is indicated, rather than placing on potential additional parties a duty to intervene when they acquire knowledge of the law-suit. The linchpin of the "impermissible collateral attack" doctrine — the attribution of preclusive effect to a failure to intervene — is therefore quite inconsistent with Rule 19 and Rule 24. . . .

Petitioners contend that a different result should be reached because the need to join affected parties will be burdensome and ultimately discouraging to civil rights litigation. Potential adverse claimants may be numerous and difficult to identify; if they are not joined, the possibility for inconsistent judgments exists. Judicial resources will be need-lessly consumed in relitigation of the same question.

Even if we were wholly persuaded by these arguments as a matter of policy, acceptance of them would require a rewriting rather than an interpretation of the relevant Rules. But we are not persuaded that their acceptance would lead to a more satisfactory method of handling cases like this one. It must be remembered that the alternatives are a duty to in-tervene based on knowledge, on the one hand, and some form of joinder, as the Rules presently provide, on the other. No one can seriously contend that an employer might successfully defend against a Title VII claim by one group of employees on the ground that its actions were required by an earlier decree entered in a suit brought against it by another, if the later group did not have adequate notice or knowledge of the earlier suit.

The difficulties petitioners foresee in identifying those who could be adversely af-fected by a decree granting broad remedial relief are undoubtedly present, but they arise from the nature of the relief sought and not because of any choice between mandatory intervention and joinder. Rule 19's provisions for joining interested parties are designed to accommodate the sort of complexities that may arise from a decree affecting numer-ous people in various ways. We doubt that a mandatory intervention rule would be any less awkward. . . .

490 U.S. at 761-67. Justice Stevens, joined by Justices Brennan, Marshall, and Black-mun, dissented, noting that "[a]s a matter of law there is a vast difference between persons who are actual parties to litigation and persons who merely have the kind of interest that may as a practical matter be impaired by the outcome of a case." Id. at 769. While the white firefighters could not be deprived of their legal rights in litiga-tion to which they were not parties, the consent decrees might change conditions of the white firefighters' employment "even though they are not bound by the decrees in any legal sense." Id. at 771.

The "procedural" dispute resolved by *Martin* had important substantive implica-tions. As our study of affirmative action in Chapter 4 reveals, racial and gender prefer-ences for minorities and women are sometimes permissible and sometimes not. Cases such as Johnson v. Transportation Agency of Santa Clara County (reproduced at page 283) and Adarand v. Pena (reproduced at page 303) presume a litigation structure in which the white male can establish the illegality of an employment decision if it is taken pursuant to an invalid affirmative action plan. If, however, such individuals are barred from suit because the plan was instituted pursuant to a court order, the right to challenge such plans will be severely undercut. Discrimination plaintiffs and employ-ers would typically seek to shelter their remedial efforts under a consent decree.

Note, however, that the issue in *Martin* was not whether white males would be barred from challenging affirmative action, but merely whether they would be re-quired to do so by intervening in the original suit, rather than filing a new action "col-laterally attacking" the consent decree. The rule of mandatory intervention, which the Supreme Court rejected in *Martin*, may appear an innocuous procedural requirement, but in practice, it was a serious barrier to "reverse discrimination" suits for two reasons. First, while some courts seemed to favor intervention, others were more hostile, frequently finding that the petition to intervene was untimely. As a result, requiring mandatory intervention sometimes meant that no avenue of relief was open at all. Second, although some courts were willing to permit suits that did not directly conflict with a decree's provisions, others held that any suit that required an interpretation of the decree constituted a collateral attack because the parties might be bound by inconsistent decisions.

The significance of *Martin* for discrimination law was immense. *Martin* involved a consent decree, but the Court speaks throughout about the law of judgments. The dissent pointed out that the decision could not be limited to consent decrees: any judgment, including one entered after full litigation, is also at risk in the sense that actions taken pursuant to it do not immunize the employer from liability to nonparties.

The mandatory intervention doctrine tried to bring all interests into one litigation. After *Martin*, this can still occur. When such parties are joined, or successfully intervene, their rights must be adjudicated, and cannot be altered by the agreement of the original parties. See United States v. City of Hialeah, 140 F.3d 968 (11th Cir. 1998) (2-1) (intervener who objects to a decree cannot have its rights modified without its consent). If plaintiff or defendant is concerned about possible third-party rights, *Martin* suggests that they can resolve all claims in one litigation merely by joining the absent parties under Rule 19. That rule is, to a large extent, the flip side of Rule 24, governing intervention. Under Rule 24, the outsider is seeking to enter the litigation; under Rule 19, an insider is seeking to bring an outsider in. Both rules speak in similar terms about the requirements for adding a party — the outsider having "an interest relating to the subject of the action" and being "so situated that the disposition of the action . . . may (i) as a practical matter impair or impede the person's ability to protect that interest." "Interests" for this purpose are much broader than legal rights. For example, although an employee at will has no "right" to continued employment, she nevertheless may have an expectation in fact that will justify intervention to protect her from the adverse consequences of a judgment. This strongly suggests that, applying the parallel language of Rule 19, either plaintiff or defendant may join those who have such an expectation.

Further, Rule 19 permits adding a party when, regardless of any threat to that outsider's interests, not joining it would leave an original party "subject to a substantial risk of incurring double, multiple, or other inconsistent obligations by reason of the claimed interest." Thus, an outsider cannot avoid joinder merely by claiming that, after *Martin*, no possible decision by the court will affect his rights. Further, under Rule 19, a party may be added to the litigation even when there is no cause of action against him. This is especially useful in employment discrimination because "reverse discriminatees" usually have not violated the statute.

*Martin* recognized certain practical problems with joinder, but saw itself bound by the Federal Rules. It also viewed the problem as more substantive than procedural: the accommodation of conflicting rights would generate difficulties regardless of whether Rule 19 or Rule 24 was the procedural mechanism used to bring all interested parties together in one action. Is this true? The *Martin* case itself arose because various self-identified individuals sought to intervene or sue. If you were attorney for either plaintiff or defendant at the outset of the suit and wanted to use Rule 19, whom would you seek to join? All present employees? What about future employees — at least individuals who will be employed during the course of the litigation? Could the practical difficulties be avoided by virtue of a "defendant class action," and if so, how does one identify the proper class representative?

Is the dissent persuasive when it argues, essentially, that nonparties could not be "bound" by a consent decree in a legal sense, but nevertheless may find their interests affected by the decree in ways they are unable to challenge? But read the Court's footnote 6. Isn't Chief Justice Rehnquist right when he says that, if the decree becomes a defense to the employer — presumably, whether an absolute defense or merely one to monetary liability — "it is very difficult to see why respondents are not being 'bound'" by it.

Or is this so strange? Perhaps the dissent is simply saying that, absent timely intervention, the judgment becomes a fact of life with which the nonparty must live. In many contexts, the law does not view individuals as "bound" to acts to which they are not parties, although they may be radically affected by them. To borrow an analogy from another area of Title VII, a disadvantaged employee is not viewed as legally "bound" by a seniority system agreed to by her union and the employer. Nevertheless, the system is a fact of life for her and in practice may substantially affect her interests.

If the dissent had prevailed, it would have upheld the district court: a motive to adhere to a court order negates the intent to discriminate requisite to a Title VII disparate treatment violation and, absent some indication of "pretext," requires dismissal of the suit of the white plaintiffs. Is this persuasive? Doesn't the employer still intend to treat persons differently because of their race?

While *Martin* rejects mandatory intervention as a way of avoiding conflicts of judgments and suggests Rule 19 joinder as a solution, it does not indicate the correct solution for such conflicts when they arise. In the case itself, the original black plaintiffs in suit 1 obtained a decree requiring the city to do certain acts. Even if the white plaintiffs in a subsequent suit 2 convince the district court that those acts are illegal, isn't the city still bound to perform them? After all, if suit 1 cannot bind nonparties (who remain free to litigate suit 2), then suit 2 cannot bind nonparties (the plaintiffs in suit 1). What's a court to do?

Consider the extent to which a judgment (whether by consent or after litigation) between A and B affects C. For example, if A sues B, obtaining relief only in the form of a money judgment, this will not be viewed as affecting C's right to a judgment against B. This is true even though C does not want a judgment in the abstract, but simply wants to collect money. A's execution on his judgment against B might, as a practical matter, prevent C from ever recovering. Nevertheless, this possibility does not undercut the first judgment: the first creditor to obtain a judgment is generally free to execute on it.

The *Martin* problem is more severe when the A-B suit requires B to perform acts that are likely or even certain to affect C. While C is not bound after *Martin*, the resulting situation creates two problems: first, B is subject to some form of additional liability to C; second, B may conceivably be subject to conflicting court orders. These problems are sometimes alternatives in that the conflict may often be avoided by double liability. This, of course, was the Court's point in *Grace*. In that case, however, the absence of a direct conflict between two mandates resulted from the arbitrator's limiting relief to back pay. Had he ordered reinstatement, the potential conflict would have been greater.*

But perhaps the arbitrator limited the relief to backpay precisely because of the prior court order that the conciliation agreement be followed. Under this view, C's rights may be affected by the prior decree even though C is not "bound" by it. This,

---

* Even here there is no logical inconsistency: the game is a zero sum one only because the employer chose to reduce its workforce. If the employer's promises require it to employ a certain number of minority workers and a certain number of white workers, it can do so by expanding its workforce.

of course, sounds like Justice Stevens's dissent in *Martin*. Another way of saying the same thing is that the prior judgment affects the remedy, not the right.

How, then, should a court address a suit by C when there is a prior decree in A's favor requiring certain conduct by B that injures C? There are several possibilities. First is decree immunization, that is, the decree somehow immunizes what would otherwise be illegal. *Martin* clearly rejected that approach. Second is to ignore the decree, that is, decide C's suit as if A's prior decree did not exist. This seems to be the majority's rule in *Martin*, but is also inappropriate. The most obvious problem is that the court in the C-B suit will order relief directly contrary to a judgment in the A-B suit. B will then be subject to inconsistent obligations. No legal system can tolerate an equitable system in which B will be damned if he does and damned if he doesn't — that is, subject to contempt no matter how he acts.

The third possibility is to reconcile the decrees, that is, either modify the prior decree or structure the second decree so that no inconsistency arises. Modification of the prior decree is at least possible when the two suits are brought before the same court, but poses an enormous conceptual problem: C is not bound in the A-B litigation because C is a nonparty. It follows that A cannot be bound in the C-B litigation, to which she is also a nonparty. The solution to possible unfairness to C is not to strip A of rights he has won through his suit. While A could be made a party to C's suit, can A be forced to relitigate rights he won against B?

The most feasible solution is to fashion the relief available in the second suit, that between C and B, to avoid a conflict with the A-B judgment. This may sound very much like "mandatory intervention," the rule rejected in *Martin*. It is, however, considerably different: there is no requirement that C intervene in the A-B litigation; she may do so (assuming she meets the requirements of Rule 24), or she may bring a separate suit challenging the employment practice required by the A-B decree, joining A in that separate suit. If she fails to do either, she may still sue B, but C's relief is limited to the extent that otherwise appropriate relief would violate the decree. This is less than mandatory intervention in that the failure to intervene leaves C free to sue, subject to the prior decree only in the sense that the court will not enter a conflicting judgment.

The most problematic aspect of this approach is the possibility that the decree is itself mandating violations of positive law. While that possibility is present for both litigated judgments and consent decrees, the absence of true adversarialness may make it more likely with consent decrees. This, of course, was the point of the white firefighters' attack in *Martin* itself: they claimed that the employer's practices would, but for the decree, violate at least the equal protection clause and that the decree could not immunize such a violation. While there is no constitutional principle giving public employees a substantive right to employment, there are certain grounds on which opportunities cannot be allocated. Most obviously, with the exception of those cases where there is a compelling state interest justifying it (such as remedying past discrimination), A cannot be preferred to C simply because A is black. Even here, however, a decree will rarely require unequal treatment: it will merely order benefits which, if they are unconstitutional, can be matched by according them to the white plaintiffs.

In some cases, the technicalities of preclusion law may minimize the impact of *Martin*. For preclusive purposes, a "party" to a proceeding includes not only named parties, but also their "privies," a notoriously amorphous concept. See Detroit Police Officers Assn. v. Young, 824 F.2d 512 (6th Cir. 1987); NAACP v. Detroit Police Officers Assn., 821 F.2d 328 (6th Cir. 1987).

What about the timing of reverse discrimination suits? From what you have learned earlier in this chapter, when would the *Martin* plaintiffs have had to file a charge with the EEOC? Within 180/300 days of the entry of the consent decree? Or does the time not begin to run until the decree is implemented by the employer? Note that this problem does not arise in intervention: the white interveners are not claiming that anyone has violated Title VII and so are not limited by charge-filing requirements. But intervention is essentially a shield, while the lawsuit authorized by *Martin* is also a sword.

Articles discussing the problem of nonparty interests in judgments include George M. Strickler, Jr., *Martin v. Wilkes*, 64 Tul. L. Rev. 1557 (1990); Samuel Issacharoff, When Substance Mandates Procedure: *Martin v. Wilks* and the Rights of Vested Incumbents in Civil Rights Consent Decrees, 77 Cornell L. Rev. 189 (1992); Joel L. Selig, Affirmative Action in Employment After *Croson* and *Martin*: The Legacy Remains Intact, 63 Temp. L.Q. 1, 22 (1990); Thomas M. Mengler, Consent Decree Paradigms: Models Without Meaning, 29 B.C. L. Rev. 291 (1988); Douglas A. Laycock, Consent Decrees Without Consent: The Rights of Nonconsenting Third Parties, 1987 U. Chi. Legal F. 103 (1987).

## NOTE ON THE CIVIL RIGHTS ACT OF 1991 AND THE PROBLEM OF BINDING NONPARTIES TO JUDGMENTS

The Civil Rights Act of 1991, Pub. L. No. 102-166, 105 Stat. 1071 (1991), attempts to strike a very different balance between the finality of judgments and the rights of nonparties than had been reached by the *Martin* Court. The Act was intended to overrule Martin v. Wilks through a carefully integrated statutory amendment designed to preserve and encourage decrees while at the same time ensuring that those affected by them have an adequate opportunity to protect their interests. Essentially, the Act provides for binding nonparties when (1) they are adequately represented by a party or (2) they have actual notice of the threat to their interest and an opportunity to protect themselves. The effectiveness of the enactment, however, remains to be seen. See generally Andrea Catania & Charles A. Sullivan, Judging Judgments: The 1991 Civil Rights Act and the Lingering Ghost of *Martin v. Wilks*, 57 Brook. L. Rev. 995 (1992); Susan Grover, The Silenced Majority: *Martin v. Wilks* and the Legislative Response, 1992 U. Ill. L. Rev. 43 (1992); Marjorie A. Silver, Fairness and Finality: Third-Party Challenges to Employment Discrimination Consent Decrees After the 1991 Civil Rights Act, 62 Fordham L. Rev. 321 (1993).

The new statute added § 703(n), 42 U.S.C.S. § 2000e-2(n) (2003), to Title VII, paragraph (1) of which begins by providing:

> (A) Notwithstanding any other provision of law, . . . an employment practice that implements and is within the scope of a litigated or consent judgment or order that resolves a claim of employment discrimination under the Constitution or Federal civil rights laws may not be challenged under the circumstances described in subparagraph (B).

The circumstances requisite for immunizing the decree from challenge are specified in subparagraph (B):

> A practice described in subparagraph (A) may not be challenged in a claim under the Constitution or Federal civil rights laws —
>    (i) by a person who, prior to the entry of the judgment or order described in subparagraph (A), had
>       (I) actual notice of the proposed judgment or order sufficient to apprize such person that such judgment or order might adversely affect the interests and legal rights of

such person and that an opportunity was available to present objections to such judgment or order by a future date certain; and

(II) a reasonable opportunity to present objections to such judgment or order; or

(ii) by a person whose interests were adequately represented by another person who had previously challenged the judgment or order on the same legal grounds and with a similar factual situation, unless there has been an intervening change in law or fact.

Since satisfying this provision immunizes implementing employment decisions from subsequent attack, they will be "legal" in the sense that they cannot be attacked. This immunity is the most radical change from prior law.* Further, the statute applies not only to federal judgments, but also to state judgments that resolve federal civil rights and constitutional claims. Thus, it immunizes employment practices more broadly than could any change in the federal joinder and intervention rules. Parties considering a settlement via consent decree can be expected to structure their agreement to maximize the prospects of immunity.

It is true that the scope or extent of the immunity is limited in that a qualifying employment practice "may not be challenged in a claim under the Constitution and the federal civil rights laws." Presumably, a challenge predicated on another federal law is not barred. Further, the terms of this provision do not, expressly at least, immunize the employment practice against suits based on state law. If this language was chosen advisedly, Congress explicitly decided to leave potential state claims unaffected by the immunity created by the statute. Under such a view, there would be no supremacy clause issue because Congress would have permitted states to challenge practices mandated by federal decrees. This reading, however, would tend to eviscerate the entire provision. Because most states have civil rights laws tracking the federal statutes, to allow state-based attacks on employment practices mandated by federal decrees would effectively deprive the vast majority of federal judgments of meaningful immunizing effect.

The requirements for immunity can be broken down in two ways. First, there are two kinds of "persons" barred from challenging employment practices, a phrasing that suggests that the ability of any subsequent plaintiff to attack an underlying practice must be assessed individually. In the first category are those who, prior to the entry of the judgment, had "actual notice" that the judgment "might adversely affect [their] interests and legal rights" and a reasonable opportunity to present objections. Actual notice clearly means that constructive notice, as by newspaper advertisements or notice to unions, will not suffice. Thus, an employer cannot safely rely on postings in the workplace. The most effective and probably least expensive method of notifying current employees would be to include notices along with the employees' paychecks; retirees whose benefits might be affected could receive notice in a similar manner. Should a potential plaintiff receive notice, even informally or by word of mouth, that person will be barred if the other requirements are satisfied.

Obviously, a remedial scheme affecting unidentifiable persons could not be completely sheltered by this provision. For example, the employer in *Martin* who agreed to a remedial hiring plan would be unable to actually notify all potential applicants. This problem is addressed by the second category of person barred, "a person whose interests were adequately represented by another person who had previously

* A lesser, but still important, change is the new statute's provision that, should a challenge be mounted, it is normally to be raised before the court that entered the decree.

challenged the judgment." This second category does not require actual notice to each person potentially affected by the decree. But while the notice burden is less, the level of protection is also reduced. The affected nonparty is barred from attacking the order only if he has been adequately represented by a party to the litigation. Assuming true adequacy of representation, there would seem to be no constitutional objection to this approach. E.g., Washington v. Washington State Commercial Passenger Fishing Vessel Assn., 443 U.S. 658 (1979).

But adequate representation is problematic where a case is resolved by consent decree. Suppose employer B vigorously litigates A's case, resisting liability to A. Should A prevail, C would presumably be barred from suit as to all issues actually litigated. Where a consent decree exists, however, B's interest dramatically diverges from C's. While B could theoretically continue to advance C's interests (either out of conviction or out of fear of liability to C for not doing so), it is no longer clear that B is an adequate representative. Indeed, determining this might well require a proceeding that would rival a trial itself. Perhaps the appropriate rule is simply to rebuttably presume no adequacy of representation where there is a showing of diverse interests. See Rutherford v. City of Cleveland, 137 F.3d 905 (6th Cir. 1998).

In any event, the nonparty is barred from relitigating only those issues actually litigated by the representative. The effect is thus one of issue, not claim, preclusion. This appears to be the intendment of the provision barring suit where the prior litigation was conducted "on the same legal grounds and with a similar factual situation." Suppose women sue an employer for pregnancy discrimination, and the employer defends vigorously, claiming that it did not discriminate on the basis of pregnancy. The resultant decree provides seniority relief to the successful plaintiffs, jumping them over male workers. The males then sue the employer, claiming discrimination in the "constructive seniority" for women. The issue of discrimination against women vel non has been litigated and cannot be relitigated. Could the males, however, claim that the discrimination was a bona fide occupational qualification, an issue not raised by the employer? Of course, the male plaintiffs might also claim that the employer's failure to raise the bona fide occupational qualification defense in the earlier suit was evidence that the employer was not an adequate representative. In fact, the adequacy of representation may tend to merge with the question of what issues, factual or legal, are raised.

Even when the common issue requirement is satisfied, there is an exception where "there has been an intervening change in law or fact." An example of a change in the law might be the Supreme Court's tightening scrutiny of affirmative action plans of public employers. Presumably, even assuming the employer was an adequate representative, its resistance to a court order under more permissive standards would not bar a white worker from challenging an affirmative action plan after the law changed.

More difficult than the change of law notion is the exception for an "intervening change in . . . fact." This is especially perplexing since the only time the immunity applies is when there is a "similar factual situation." The statute seems to suggest that C will be not barred when the facts have changed, although the factual situation is similar. Perhaps Congress meant the rule to apply to the general facts in litigation and the exception to apply when (although the general facts may stay the same) the facts relating to the particular plaintiff C are different. For example, suppose the A-B suit results in giving A remedial seniority, thereby moving C down relative to A. If the effect of this change at the time it was made would have appeared to be only to defer C's promotion, it might be fair to immunize the decree; if, however, changing economic conditions later put C's very job at risk, may that justify limiting B's immunity?

Finally, those who have actual notice of the "proposed judgment or order" are barred only if they had "a reasonable opportunity to present objections." While this provision makes sense with respect to a consent decree that can be promulgated before being actually entered by the court, its application to litigated decrees is uncertain: the judgment will not be entered until after trial, and at that point, it is too late to allow nonparties to participate. As a practical matter, perhaps litigated judgments will be immunized only if C's interests are adequately represented, while consent decrees will be immunized if there is either (1) adequate representation or (2) notice and an adequate opportunity to be heard.

As for the extent of participation by those objecting, the statute speaks of an "opportunity . . . to *present objections* to such judgment" (emphasis added). This suggests that a full trial, or even an evidentiary hearing, is not necessarily required. But, at least in some cases, anything less than an evidentiary hearing will raise constitutional questions. Suppose female plaintiffs and the employer agree that the employer has violated Title VII in its promotions. The agreed remedy is to give all current female employees a ten-point preference on the employer's rating system in future promotion decisions. Such a gender preference would undoubtedly violate Title VII were it not a remedy for past discrimination. Even as a remedy for proven discrimination, it may well go too far in favoring all women even though probably not all of them were disadvantaged by prior promotion decisions. Simply offering male workers an opportunity to air their objections would not seem to satisfy due process: the appropriateness of the decree turns on disputed questions of fact and law: was there prior discrimination against females, and if so, how pervasive was it? Presumably, due process would accord the males the right to prove that the predicates of the decree are incorrect.

While the statute speaks of a "reasonable opportunity to present objections" to the court, the reasonableness of the opportunity must be assessed in terms of the interests to be protected. Further, the statute provides that it shall not be construed to deny due process of law. $\S 703(n)(2)(D)$. These provisions can be construed together to provide for full participation where the outsider's interests require it. The statute also cautions that it is not to be construed to "alter the standards for intervention under Rule 24 of the Federal Rules of Civil Procedure or apply to the rights of parties who have successfully intervened. . . ." $\S 703(n)(2)(A)$. This would permit adequate participation by those who meet the requirements of Rule 24.

Prior to *Martin*, the timeliness requirement for intervention posed a serious obstacle. Factors the courts consider in determining whether intervention is timely include the point to which the litigation has progressed, the purpose of the intervention, the extent to which the delay in seeking intervention is excusable, and the prejudice to the original parties caused by the intervener's delay in seeking intervention. In balancing these factors, many courts, including the district court in *Martin*, denied intervention. After *Martin*, judicial economy is not served by a grudging application of the timeliness requirement. Because the outsider can commence a separate suit to challenge the remedial scheme agreed to in prior litigation, little is gained by denial of intervention on timeliness grounds. While the new statute will sometimes foreclose a subsequent attack, its stress on reasonable opportunity to object also suggests that timeliness should be viewed permissively.

In short, whether the Civil Rights Act of 1991 really overrules Martin v. Wilks is questionable. The requirements for sheltering employment practices within the immunity of a decree are so stringent as not to offer flexibility in shaping remedial schemes, whether worked by the parties through a consent decree or the courts in structuring judgments after litigation. Presumably, where the requirements of the statute are not met, *Martin* still controls. In short, *Martin* remains alive and well, if not quite as hale and hearty as when it was originally handed down in 1989.

Nevertheless, this conclusion is not as depressing for the proponents of civil rights as one might suppose. *Martin*, properly read, is not such a blow to decrees as was initially thought. Once a decree has been entered, and despite the tenor of the majority's opinion, courts should try to accommodate the decree when resolving subsequent suits. This can always be done where the interests of the plaintiffs in the subsequent suit can be fully satisfied by monetary remedies. Where that is not true, and the two interests are irreconcilable, it still does not follow that the prior judgment cannot be respected: the earlier decree may be held to limit the remedies otherwise available to a subsequent plaintiff.

The real problem with *Martin* was less that of finality, viewed after the fact, than the problem of finality as it affects parties' willingness to settle: because a decree does not protect the employer from multiple liability, or at least multiple litigation, employers will be less likely to settle suits or will at least settle them in ways that limit their risks. Short of a statutory amendment that broadens the classes of persons barred from attacking employment practices, consent decrees will not accord the immunity the drafters may have hoped.

# Chapter 10

---

# Judicial Relief

## A.  INTRODUCTION

This chapter explores the judicial relief available once a violation of Title VII, § 1981, the ADEA, or Title I or Title II of the ADA has been proved. These statutes have similar, but distinct, remedial schemes. As a result, the availability of and limitations on relief vary from statute to statute. Two examples will illustrate: (1) compensatory damages are available under Title VII, § 1981, Title I, and probably Title II, but not under the ADEA; (2) a statutory maximum is placed on compensatory damages in Title VII and Title I actions, but not in § 1981 and Title II actions. Such differences in the remedial schemes are pointed out in the text preceding and the notes following the principal cases.

This chapter begins by examining the legal remedies for discrimination, which remedies include compensatory and punitive damages, and, in lieu of punitive damages under the ADEA, liquidated damages. Following the legal remedies, the chapter turns to equitable relief, including injunctive relief, back pay, front pay and attorneys' fees.

We begin, however, with discussion of the policies that are served by the remedial schemes provided under the antidiscrimination statutes.

### ALBEMARLE PAPER CO. v. MOODY
#### 422 U.S. 405 (1975)

Justice STEWART delivered the opinion of the Court.

## I

[T]he respondents brought a class action . . . asking permanent injunctive relief against "any policy, practice, custom or usage" at the plant that violated Title VII. The respondents assured the court that the suit involved no claim for any monetary awards on a class basis, but in June 1970, after several years of discovery, the respondents moved to add a class demand for backpay. . . .

[The district court found that the employer's seniority system violated Title VII by locking black employees into low-level jobs. It ordered the employer to implement a system of "plant-wide" seniority, but refused to award backpay.]

## II

Whether a particular member of the plaintiff class should have been awarded any backpay and, if so, how much, are questions not involved in this review. The equities of individual cases were never reached. Though at least some of the members of the plaintiff class obviously suffered a loss of wage opportunities on account of Albemarle's unlawfully discriminatory system of job seniority, the District Court decided that *no* backpay should be awarded to *anyone* in the class. The court declined to make such an award on two stated grounds: the lack of "evidence of bad faith non-compliance with the Act," and the fact that "the defendants would be substantially prejudiced" by an award of backpay that was demanded contrary to an earlier representation and late in the progress of the litigation. . . . [T]he Court of Appeals reversed, holding that backpay could be denied only in "special circumstances." The petitioners argue that the Court of Appeals was in error — that a district court has virtually unfettered discretion to award or deny backpay. . . .

. . . It is true that backpay is not an automatic or mandatory remedy; like all other remedies under the Act, it is one which the courts "may" invoke. The scheme implicitly recognizes that there may be cases calling for one remedy but not another, and — owing to the structure of the federal judiciary — these choices are, of course, left in the first instance to the district courts. However, such discretionary choices are not left to a court's "inclination, but to its judgment; and its judgment is to be guided by sound legal principles." The power to award backpay was bestowed by Congress, as part of a complex legislative design directed at a historic evil of national proportions. A court must exercise this power "in light of the large objectives of the Act." That the court's discretion is equitable in nature hardly means that it is unfettered by meaningful standards or shielded from thorough appellate review. . . .

It is true that "[e]quity eschews mechanical rules . . . [and] depends on flexibility." But when Congress invokes the Chancellor's conscience to further transcendent legislative purposes, what is required is the principled application of standards consistent with those purposes and not "equity [which] varies like the Chancellor's foot." Important national goals would be frustrated by a regime of discretion that "produce[d] different results for breaches of duty in situations that cannot be differentiated in policy."

The District Court's decision must therefore be measured against the purposes which inform Title VII. As the Court observed in Griggs v. Duke Power Co. [reproduced at page 322], the primary objective was a prophylactic one: "It was to achieve equality of employment opportunities and remove barriers that have operated in the past to favor an identifiable group of white employees over other employees." Backpay has an obvious connection with this purpose. If employers faced only the prospect of an injunctive order, they would have little incentive to shun practices of dubious legality. It is the reasonably certain prospect of a backpay award that "provide[s] the spur or catalyst which causes employers and unions to self-examine and to self-evaluate their employment practices and to endeavor to eliminate, so far as possible, the last vestiges of an unfortunate and ignominious page in this country's history."

It is also the purpose of Title VII to make persons whole for injuries suffered on account of unlawful employment discrimination. This is shown by the very fact that Congress took care to arm the courts with full equitable powers. For it is the historic purpose of equity to "secur[e] complete justice." "[W]here federally protected rights have been invaded, it has been the rule from the beginning that courts will be alert to adjust their remedies so as to grant the necessary relief." Title VII deals with legal injuries of an economic character occasioned by racial or other antiminority discrimination. The terms "complete justice" and "necessary relief" have acquired a clear meaning in such circumstances. Where racial discrimination is concerned, "the [district] court has not merely the power but the duty to render a decree which will so far as possible eliminate the discriminatory effects of the past as well as bar like discrimination in the future."

And where a legal injury is of an economic character, "[t]he general rule is, that when a wrong has been done, and the law gives a remedy, the compensation shall be equal to the injury. The latter is the standard by which the former is to be measured. The injured party is to be placed, as near as may be, in the situation he would have occupied if the wrong had not been committed."

The "make-whole" purpose of Title VII is made evident by the legislative history. . . . A Section-by-Section Analysis introduced by Senator Williams to accompany the Conference Committee Report on the 1972 Act strongly reaffirmed the "make-whole" purpose of Title VII:

> The provisions of this subsection are intended to give the courts wide discretion exercising their equitable powers to fashion the most complete relief possible. In dealing with the present section 706(g) the courts have stressed that the scope of relief under that section of the Act is intended to make the victims of unlawful discrimination whole, and that the attainment of this objective rests not only upon the elimination of the particular unlawful employment practice complained of, but also requires that persons aggrieved by the consequences and effects of the unlawful employment practice be, so far as possible, restored to a position where they would have been were it not for the unlawful discrimination.

As this makes clear, Congress' purpose in vesting a variety of "discretionary" powers in the courts was not to limit appellate review of trial courts, or to invite inconsistency and caprice, but rather to make possible the "fashion[ing] [of] the most complete relief possible."

It follows that, given a finding of unlawful discrimination, backpay should be denied only for reasons which, if applied generally, would not frustrate the central statutory purposes of eradicating discrimination throughout the economy and making persons whole for injuries suffered through past discrimination. . . .

The District Court's stated grounds for denying backpay in this case must be tested against these standards. The first ground was that Albemarle's breach of Title VII had not been in "bad faith." This is not a sufficient reason for denying backpay. Where an employer *has* shown bad faith — by maintaining a practice which he knew to be illegal or of highly questionable legality — he can make no claims whatsoever on the Chancellor's conscience. But, under Title VII, the mere absence of bad faith simply opens the door to equity; it does not depress the scales in the employer's favor. If back-pay were awardable only upon a showing of bad faith, the remedy would become a punishment for moral turpitude, rather than a compensation for workers' injuries. This would read the "make whole" purpose right out of Title VII, for a worker's injury is no less real simply because his employer did not inflict it in "bad faith." Title VII is not concerned with the employer's "good intent or absence of discriminatory intent" for "Congress directed the thrust of the Act to the *consequences* of employment practices, not simply the motivation." *Griggs.* To condition the awarding of backpay on a showing of "bad faith" would be to open an enormous chasm between injunctive and backpay relief under Title VII. There is nothing on the face of the statute or in its legislative history that justifies the creation of drastic and categorical distinctions between those two remedies.

The District Court also grounded its denial of backpay on the fact that the respondents initially disclaimed any interest in backpay, first asserting their claim five years after the complaint was filed. The court concluded that the petitioners had been "prejudiced" by this conduct. . . .

. . . Title VII contains no legal bar to raising backpay claims after the complaint for injunctive relief has been filed, or indeed after a trial on that complaint has been had. Furthermore, Fed. Rule Civ. Proc. 54(c) directs that "every final judgment shall grant the relief to which the party in whose favor it is rendered is entitled, even if the party has not demanded such relief in his pleadings." But a party may not be "entitled" to relief if its conduct of the cause has improperly and substantially prejudiced the other party. The respondents here were not merely tardy, but also inconsistent, in demanding backpay. To deny backpay because a *particular* cause has been prosecuted in an eccentric fashion, prejudicial to the other party, does not offend the broad purposes of Title VII. This is not to say, however, that the District Court's ruling was necessarily correct. Whether the petitioners were in fact prejudiced, and whether the respondents' trial conduct was excusable, are questions that will be open to review by the Court of Appeals, if the District Court, on remand, decides again to decline to make any award of backpay. But the standard of review will be the familiar one of whether the District Court was "clearly erroneous" in its factual findings and whether it "abused" its traditional discretion to locate "a just result" in light of the circumstances peculiar to the case. . . .

[The concurring opinions of Justices MARSHALL and BLACKMUN have been omitted.]

Justice REHNQUIST, concurring. . . .

To the extent that an award of backpay were to be analogized to an award of damages, such an award upon proper proof would follow virtually as a matter of course from a finding that an employer had unlawfully discriminated contrary to the provisions of Title VII. . . .

But precisely to the extent that an award of backpay is thought to flow as a matter of course from a finding of wrongdoing, and thereby becomes virtually indistinguishable from an award for damages, the question (not raised by any of the parties, and therefore quite properly not discussed in the Court's opinion), of whether either side may demand a jury trial under the Seventh Amendment becomes critical. We said in Curtis v. Loether, 415 U.S. 189, 197 (1974), in explaining the difference between the provision for damages under § 812 of the Civil Rights Act of 1968 and the authorization for the award of backpay which we treat here: "In Title VII cases, also, the courts have relied on the fact that the decision whether to award backpay is committed to the discretion of the trial judge. There is no comparable discretion here: if a plaintiff proves unlawful discrimination and actual damages, he is entitled to judgment for that amount. . . . Whatever may be the merit of the 'equitable' characterization in Title VII cases, there is surely no basis for characterizing the award of compensatory and punitive damages here as equitable relief." . . .

To the extent, then, that the District Court retains substantial discretion as to whether or not to award backpay notwithstanding a finding of unlawful discrimination, the nature of the jurisdiction which the Court exercises is equitable, and under our cases neither party may demand a jury trial. To the extent that discretion is replaced by awards which follow as a matter of course from a finding of wrongdoing, the action of the Court in making such awards could not be fairly characterized as equitable in character, and would quite arguably be subject to the provisions of the Seventh Amendment. . . .

*NOTES*

1. *Albemarle Paper* was decided before Title VII had been amended to include compensatory and punitive damages as possible remedies for intentional discrimination. Based on the twin statutory objectives of Title VII, the Court created a presumption of full, make whole relief: "[G]iven a finding of unlawful discrimination, backpay should be denied only for reasons which, if applied generally, would not frustrate the central statutory purposes of eradicating discrimination throughout the economy and making persons whole for injuries suffered through past discrimination." Since the 1991 Civil Rights Act added compensatory and punitive damages to Title VII, the Supreme Court has added a further objective underpinning antidiscrimination law. In Kolstad v. American Dental Assn., 527 U.S. 526 (1999), reproduced at page 953, the Court restricted the scope of an employer's liability for punitive damages in ADA and Title VII actions and justified that restriction as consistent with a "primary objective" of antidiscrimination statutes that is a prophylactic one "not to provide redress but to avoid harm." Id. at 545. Thus, the liability of employers based on agency law was restrained so as to encourage voluntary employer policies prohibiting discrimination.

2. In Los Angeles Dept. of Water & Power v. Manhart, 435 U.S. 702, 719-21 (1978), reproduced in part at page 200, the Supreme Court held the employer had violated Title VII when, pursuant to sex-based actuarial tables, female employees were required to contribute more than male employees to its retirement program but it also held that the district court erred in ordering a refund of the excess contributions:

> The *Albemarle* presumption in favor of retroactive liability can seldom be overcome, but . . . we conclude that the District Court gave insufficient attention to the equitable nature of Title VII remedies. Although we now have no doubt about the application of the statute in this case, we must recognize that conscientious and intelligent administrators of pension funds . . . may well have assumed that a program like the Department's was entirely lawful. . . . [P]ension administrators could reasonably have thought it unfair — or even illegal — to make male employees shoulder more than their "actuarial share" of the pension burden. There is no reason to believe that the threat of a backpay award is needed to cause other administrators to amend their practices to conform to this decision.
> . . . These plans, like other forms of insurance, depend on the accumulation of large sums to cover contingencies. The amounts set aside are determined by a painstaking

assessment of the insurer's likely liability. Risks that the insurer foresees will be included in the calculation of liability, and the rates or contributions charged will reflect that calculation. The occurrence of major unforeseen contingencies, however, jeopardizes the insurer's solvency and, ultimately, the insureds' benefits. Drastic changes in the legal rules governing pension and insurance funds, like other unforeseen events, can have this effect. Consequently, the rules that apply to these funds should not be applied retroactively unless the legislature has plainly commanded that result. . . .

There can be no doubt that the prohibition against sex-differentiated employee contributions represents a marked departure from past practice. Although Title VII was enacted in 1964, this is apparently the first litigation challenging contribution differences based on valid actuarial tables. Retroactive liability could be devastating for a pension fund. The harm would fall in large part on innocent third parties. If, as the courts below apparently contemplated, the plaintiffs' contributions are recovered from the pension fund, the administrators of the fund will be forced to meet unchanged obligations with diminished assets. If the reserve proves inadequate, either the expectations of all retired employees will be disappointed or current employees will be forced to pay not only for their own future security but also for the unanticipated reduction in the contributions of past employees.

Without qualifying the force of the *Albemarle* presumption in favor of retroactive relief, we conclude that it was error to grant such relief in this case.

Is *Manhart* consistent with *Albemarle*'s emphasis on the make-whole and prophylactic purposes of Title VII? With *Albemarle*'s analysis of the role of good faith in awarding backpay? Has "the *Albemarle* presumption" been limited, or were there overriding factors that caused the *Manhart* Court to deny backpay?

3. How could Albemarle Paper Co. have been prejudiced by the plaintiffs' tardy and inconsistent backpay claims? The trial court said that, if backpay had been claimed from the start, the company "might have chosen to exercise unusual zeal" to resolve the case. Moody v. Albemarle Paper Co., 4 FEP (BNA) 561, 570 (E.D.N.C. 1971). Is this what the Supreme Court meant by "prejudice," or does "prejudice" mean being hindered in presenting a defense on the merits? See Occidental Life Ins. Co. v. EEOC, 432 U.S. 355 (1977). Even if unexcused delay had prejudiced the employer, would it follow that *all* backpay should be denied? See Kamberos v. GTE Automatic Elec., Inc., 603 F.2d 598 (7th Cir. 1979).

4. Section 706(g)(1) and *Albemarle* establish that Title VII backpay is a discretionary and thus equitable remedy. Justice Rehnquist explained the importance of this characterization for whether there is the right to a jury trial on a Title VII backpay claim. While there is now a right to jury trial on intentional discrimination claims under Title VII, the backpay remedy under that statute (and therefore under Title I of the ADA) remains equitable. However, the backpay award is considered legal in certain ADEA and other actions, which gives rise to the right to a jury trial.

5. Fitzpatrick v. Bitzer, 427 U.S. 445 (1976), held that the Eleventh Amendment does not preclude a federal court from rendering a Title VII backpay award against a state. The Court reasoned that Title VII was enacted pursuant to Congress's enforcement power under the Fourteenth Amendment, and this power permits Congress to override the states' Eleventh Amendment immunity. In contrast, such an award is precluded in a § 1983 action to enforce § 1981 by both the Eleventh Amendment and statutory interpretation. E.g., Will v. Michigan Dept. of State Police, 491 U.S. 58 (1989). For further discussion of Eleventh Amendment issues in connection with the ADA, the ADEA, and Title VII, see pages 920-923.

## B.  LEGAL REMEDIES

The availability of common-law-type legal remedies, such as compensatory and punitive damages varies from statute to statute. Both compensatory and punitive damages
awards are available under § 1981, Johnson v. Railroad Express Agency, 421 U.S. 454
(1975), but are subject to several restrictions when sought from a public official or
governmental entity. At the other extreme, the ADEA does not authorize either type
of damages for age discrimination,* although it does allow the recovery of "liquidated
damages." E.g., Mathis v. Phillips Chevrolet, Inc., 269 F.3d 771 (7th Cir. 2001).

Prior to November 1991, compensatory and punitive damages were also unavailable under Title VII and Title I. However, the Civil Rights Act of 1991 enacted 42
U.S.C.S. § 1981a (2003), which authorizes such damages in certain Title VII and
Title I actions and grants the right to a jury trial when either compensatory or punitive damages are sought.

Section 1981a(a)(1) authorizes compensatory and punitive damages for a Title VII
violation that meets two requirements. First, the claim must establish intentional disparate treatment discrimination, as opposed to disparate impact discrimination. Second, the claim must not be cognizable under § 1981. Such damages are authorized
in both federal and non-federal employee actions.

The plain statutory language of Title VII does not address the issue of whether a
plaintiff can be awarded punitive damages absent an award of actual damages, and
the courts are split on the issue. While variant positions exist as to the requirements
establishing punitive damages, the majority of circuits have generally held that punitive damages can be awarded absent an award of nominal or compensatory damages.
By contrast, the Fifth Circuit has held that punitive damages award must be vacated
absent an award of actual damages. The courts that have found actual damages as a
prerequisite to punitive damages have expressed concern over opening the door to
unreasonable jury verdicts. The counterargument is that this problem is eliminated
by the statutory caps on punitive damages. Moreover, the objectives behind compensatory and punitive damages are very different and should be addressed separately.
For a general discussion, see Cush Crawford v. Adchem Corp., 271 F.3d 352 (2d Cir.
2001); Corti v. Storage Tech. Corp., 304 F.3d 336 (4th Cir. 2002). See generally
Christy Lynn McQuality, Note, No Harm, No Foul?: An Argument for the Allowance
of Punitive Damages Without Compensatory Damage Under 42 U.S.C. 51981a, 59
Wash. & Lee L. Rev. 643 (2002).

Compensatory and punitive damages are capped based on the number of employees employed by the employer.

### 1.  Compensatory Damages

#### TURIC v. HOLLAND HOSPITALITY, INC.
**85 F.3d 1211 (6th Cir. 1996)**

KRUPANSKY, Circuit Judge.

[Holland Hospitality violated Title VII by discharging Turic, who was pregnant, for
contemplating an abortion. The district court granted various relief, including
$50,000 for emotional distress.]

---

*The ADEA does allow recovery of compensatory damages for unlawful retaliation. Moskowitz v.
Trustees of Purdue University, 5 F.3d 279 (7th Cir. 1993).

To be eligible for compensatory damages, Turic was required to prove that Holland Hospitality's unlawful actions caused her emotional distress. A plaintiff's own testimony, along with the circumstances of a particular case, can suffice to sustain the plaintiff's burden in this regard. . . .

The court . . . found that as a young, unwed mother who was walking an "economic tightrope" and who had just discovered she was pregnant for a second time, Turic was in a particularly vulnerable position and was highly dependent upon her job. Vulnerability is relevant in determining damages. See Williamson v. Handy Button Mach. Co., 817 F.2d 1290 (7th Cir. 1987) ("Perhaps [plaintiff] was unusually sensitive, but a tortfeasor takes its victims as it finds them. . . . In some cases unusual sensitivity will enhance the loss; in others unusual hardiness will reduce it; payment of the actual damage in each case will both compensate the victim and lead the injurer to take account of the full consequences of its acts"). Turic's vulnerability is particularly relevant in this case, because her supervisors had direct knowledge of her vulnerability before they discharged her. The trial judge did not err, therefore, in considering the unusual economic and emotional sensitivity of this plaintiff.

It is well settled that Title VII plaintiffs can prove emotional injury by testimony without medical support. However, damages for mental and emotional distress will not be presumed, and must be proven by "competent evidence." . . . Witnesses testified that Turic was extremely upset and frightened after being discharged, and that she ran from the meeting in tears. The Supreme Court in Carey [v. Piphus, 435 U.S. 247 (1978),] instructed that such witness testimony bolsters a finding of emotional distress: "Although essentially subjective, genuine injury in this respect may be evidenced by one's conduct and observed by others." Further, Turic testified that she continued to suffer nightmares, weight loss during her pregnancy (an undesirable occurrence often leading to low birth weight of the baby), and excessive nervousness. This testimony distinguishes the instant case from Rodgers [v. Fisher Body Div., General Motors Corp., 739 F.2d 1102 (6th Cir. 1984)], in which the plaintiff failed to testify that he suffered any manifestations of his alleged mental distress, and from Erebia v. Chrysler Plastic Prods. Corp., 772 F.2d 1250 (6th Cir. 1985), wherein the plaintiff testified merely that he was "highly upset" about racial slurs made at his workplace. See also DeNieva v. Reyes, 966 F.2d 480 (9th Cir. 1992) (plaintiff testified to suffering emotional distress manifested by insomnia, dizziness and vomiting and received $50,000 compensatory damages); Secretary of HUD v. Blackwell, 908 F.2d 864 (11th Cir. 1990) ($40,000 award upheld on basis of testimony regarding humiliation, insomnia and headaches); Moody v. Pepsi-Cola Metro. Bottling Co., 915 F.2d 201 (6th Cir. 1990) ($150,000 award upheld on basis of testimony that plaintiff was shocked and humiliated and forced to live apart from family because of termination). For the above reasons, the amount awarded as compensatory damages is not grossly excessive, and the decision of the court below as to compensatory damages is affirmed. . . .

### NOTES

1. Damages for mental distress can be recovered only when actual injury is proved; such injury cannot be presumed or inferred merely from a civil rights violation. Carey v. Piphus, 435 U.S. 247 (1978). Many decisions have upheld awards for distress, humiliation, or anxiety based on the testimony of the plaintiff and other lay persons. E.g., Migis v. Pearle Vision, Inc., 135 F.3d 1041 (5th Cir. 1998); Walz v. Town of Smithtown, 46 F.3d 162 (2d Cir. 1995); Matlock v. Barnes, 932 F.2d 658 (7th Cir. 1991). The plaintiff's uncorroborated testimony that the discrimination destroyed

him, made him physically and mentally sick, and required him to visit many doctors established actual injury but could not support more than a $10,000 award for mental distress, Vadie v. Mississippi State University, 218 F.3d 365 (5th Cir. 2000), *cert. denied*, 531 U.S. 1150 (2001). But one court seems to think that expert testimony of a medically cognizable injury is necessary. Price v. City of Charlotte, 93 F.3d 1241 (4th Cir. 1996). Is *Turic's* distinction between manifested and unmanifested emotional distress a sensible approach? In Forshee v. Waterloo Industries, Inc., 178 F.3d 527 (8th Cir. 1999), the jury found the plaintiff was terminated because she rejected her supervisor's sexual advances and awarded compensatory damages for mental distress. The appellate court reversed the award because her emotional injury was not "severe" and was due to her termination, not to her supervisor's sexual advance. Does either reason withstand scrutiny? A later Eighth Circuit decision appears inconsistent with this view. Webner v. Titan Distribution, Inc., 267 F.3d 828 (8th Cir. 2001).

2.  Should damages for mental distress be limited to the amount necessary to compensate an ordinarily sensitive person? Recall that the Supreme Court has said that an unreasonably offended person has no claim at all for a sexually hostile work environment. See Harris v. Forklift Sys., Inc., page 507. Would such a standard have produced a lower award in *Turic?*

3.  Of course, compensatory damages can be recovered for injuries other than mental distress. For example, plaintiff can recover the expenses incurred in seeking other employment. E.g., Knapp v. Whitaker, 757 F.2d 827 (7th Cir. 1985); Woods-Drake v. Lundy, 667 F.2d 1198 (5th Cir. 1982). However, plaintiff cannot recover damages merely for being deprived of a civil right. Memphis Community Sch. Dist. v. Stachura, 477 U.S. 299 (1986).

4.  What about lost earning capacity? In Williams v. Pharmacia, Inc., 137 F.3d 944 (7th Cir. 1998), the court held that a Title VII plaintiff can recover both damages for lost future earning capacity and front pay. The jury had awarded the discharged plaintiff $300,000 in compensatory damages, including $250,000 for lost future earnings. The judge then added $180,000 for lost backpay and, after denying reinstatement, another $115,530 for one year's front pay. The appellate court said that the plaintiff's discriminatory job evaluations and termination justified the damages for lost future earning capacity. The front pay award compensated a different injury — the loss plaintiff suffered from the failure to regain her old job. Is this correct? Would a different result have been reached if the front pay award had been based on losses to the date of retirement?

5.  Compensatory damages claims are subject to the usual causation rules. A familiar rule precludes liability for injuries that the plaintiff could have avoided by reasonable effort or expense. See generally 1, 2 Dan B. Dobbs, Law of Remedies §§ 3.9, 8.7(2) (2d ed. 1993). If your client has an employee who has been sexually harassed, would you advise your client to offer her professional counseling? Another rule precludes liability for pre-existing injuries. See McKinnon v. Kwong Wah Restaurant, 83 F.3d 498 (1st Cir. 1996), a sexual harassment action in which plaintiff's emotional distress was partially caused by unrelated sexual encounters. See also Buckner v. Franco, Inc., 1999 U.S. App. LEXIS 7369 (6th Cir. 1999).

6.  Section 1981a imposes liability on state and local governments for compensatory damages but not for punitive damages. In ADEA and ADA Title I actions, and perhaps in Title II suits, states have an Eleventh Amendment defense, see pages 920-923, and governmental liability for damages under § 1981 may be limited. The Supreme Court once held that § 1983 provides the exclusive damages remedy against a governmental entity for a violation of § 1981. Jett v. Dallas Indep. Sch. Dist., 491 U.S. 701 (1989). Under § 1983, a municipality has compensatory damages liability only

for an official policy or practice, as opposed to an act of an agent, and has immunity from punitive damages liability. City of Newport v. Fact Concerts, Inc., 453 U.S. 247 (1981). Moreover, § 1983 does not authorize a damages award against a state. Will v. Michigan Dept. of State Police, 491 U.S. 58 (1989). However, § 1981(c), which was enacted in 1991, can be interpreted as allowing § 1981 to be directly enforced against a governmental entity without the use of § 1983. The cases have divided on this point. One court permits suit, Federation of African American Contractors v. City of Oakland, 96 F.3d 1204 (9th Cir. 1996), while three reject it. Oden v. Oktibbeha County, 246 F.3d 458 (5th Cir.), *cert. denied,* 534 U.S. 948 (2001); Butts v. County of Volusia, 222 F.3d 891 (11th Cir. 2000); Dennis v. County of Fairfax, 55 F.3d 151 (4th Cir. 1995). But the courts that permit direct enforcement may, nevertheless, read the § 1983 limitations into § 1981. Consider *African American Contractors,* which first held that § 1981 can be directly enforced against a municipality, but then interpreted § 1981 as including the official policy or custom requirement for compensatory damages. Accord, Smith v. Chicago School Reform Bd. of Trustees, 165 F.3d 1142 (7th Cir. 1999). One would expect these courts to also follow the § 1983 analogy with regard to the unavailability of punitive damages and damages from a state. In any event, § 1981(c) may not manifest the clear congressional intent necessary to override a state's Eleventh Amendment immunity. See Chinn v. CUNY, 963 F. Supp. 218 (E.D.N.Y. 1997); Khan v. Maryland, 903 F. Supp. 881 (D. Md. 1995).

7. Many courts have reduced jury compensatory or punitive damages awards that are "grossly excessive" or "shock the conscience." E.g., Walz v. Town of Smithtown, 46 F.3d 162 (2d Cir. 1995); Sheets v. Salt Lake County, 45 F.3d 1383 (6th Cir. 1995). Can a court set aside a damages award under § 1981a as "grossly excessive or shocking" even though it is within the statutory limit? Hennessy v. Penril Datacomm Networks, Inc., 69 F.3d 1344 (7th Cir. 1995) (yes). Should courts look to the § 1981a caps to determine whether an award is excessive in a § 1981 action? Section 1981a(b)(4) provides that § 1981a does not "limit" the relief available in § 1981 actions.

8. ADA § 12112(d) contains a number of specific prohibitions regarding medical examinations and inquiries, and the maintenance of employee medical records. To date, three circuits have turned away attempts to recover compensatory or punitive damages for violations of these provisions, insisting that no actual injury had been shown. The cases are collected in Griffin v. Steeltek, Inc., 261 F.3d 1026 (10th Cir. 2001).

9. With both equitable and legal remedies available in Title VII, questions arise as to the boundary between the two types of relief. The boundary is important because the legal remedies are subject to caps that do not apply to equitable relief.

## POLLARD v. E. I. du PONT de NEMOURS & CO.
### 532 U.S. 843 (2001)

Justice THOMAS delivered the opinion of the Court.

This case presents the question whether a front pay award is an element of compensatory damages under the Civil Rights Act of 1991. We conclude that it is not.

I

Petitioner Sharon Pollard sued her former employer, alleging that she had been subjected to a hostile work environment based on her sex, in violation of Title VII. . . .

The District Court further found that the harassment resulted in a medical leave of absence from her job for psychological assistance and her eventual dismissal for refusing to return to the same hostile work environment. The court awarded Pollard $107,364 in backpay and benefits, $252,997 in attorney's fees, and, as relevant here, $300,000 in compensatory damages — the maximum permitted under the statutory cap for such damages in 42 U.S.C. § 1981a(b)(3). . . .

The issue presented for review here is whether front pay constitutes an element of "compensatory damages" under 42 U.S.C. § 1981a and thus is subject to the statutory damages cap imposed by that section. Although courts have defined "front pay" in numerous ways, front pay is simply money awarded for lost compensation during the period between judgment and reinstatement or in lieu of reinstatement. For instance, when an appropriate position for the plaintiff is not immediately available without displacing an incumbent employee, courts have ordered reinstatement upon the opening of such a position and have ordered front pay to be paid until reinstatement occurs. In cases in which reinstatement is not viable because of continuing hostility between the plaintiff and the employer or its workers, or because of psychological injuries suffered by the plaintiff as a result of the discrimination, courts have ordered front pay as a substitute for reinstatement. For the purposes of this opinion, it is not necessary for us to explain when front pay is an appropriate remedy. The question before us is only whether front pay, if found to be appropriate, is an element of compensatory damages under the Civil Rights Act of 1991 and thus subject to the Act's statutory cap on such damages. . . .

## II

Plaintiffs who allege employment discrimination on the basis of sex traditionally have been entitled to such remedies as injunctions, reinstatement, backpay, lost benefits, and attorney's fees under § 706(g). . . . In the Civil Rights Act of 1991, Congress expanded the remedies available to these plaintiffs by permitting, for the first time, the recovery of compensatory and punitive damages. The amount of compensatory damages awarded under § 1981a for "future pecuniary losses, emotional pain, suffering, inconvenience, mental anguish, loss of enjoyment of life, and other nonpecuniary losses," and the amount of punitive damages awarded under § 1981a, however, may not exceed the statutory cap set forth in § 1981a(b)(3). The statutory cap is based on the number of people employed by the respondent. In this case, the cap is $300,000 because DuPont has more than 500 employees.

. . . For the reasons discussed below, we conclude that front pay is not an element of compensatory damages within the meaning of § 1981a, and, therefore, we hold that the statutory cap of § 1981a(b)(3) is inapplicable to front pay.

### A

Under § 706(g) of the Civil Rights Act of 1964 as originally enacted, when a court found that an employer had intentionally engaged in an unlawful employment practice, the court was authorized to "enjoin the respondent from engaging in such unlawful employment practice, and order such affirmative action as may be appropriate, which may include, but is not limited to, reinstatement or hiring of employees, with or without back pay." This provision closely tracked the language of § 10(c) of the National Labor Relations Act (NLRA). The meaning of this provision of the NLRA prior to enactment of the Civil Rights Act of 1964, therefore, gives us guidance as to the proper meaning of the same language in § 706(g) of Title VII. In applying § 10(c) of the NLRA, the Board consistently had made awards of what it called "backpay" up to the date the employee was reinstated or returned to the position he should have been in had the violation of the NLRA not occurred, even if such event occurred after judgment. Consistent with the Board's interpretation of this provision of the NLRA, courts finding unlawful intentional discrimination in Title VII actions awarded this same type of backpay under § 706(g). In the Title VII context, this form of "backpay" occurring after the date of judgment is known today as "front pay."

In 1972, Congress expanded § 706(g) to specify that a court could, in addition to awarding those remedies previously listed in the provision, award "any other equitable relief as the court deems appropriate." After this amendment to § 706(g), courts endorsed a broad view of front pay. See, e.g., Patterson v. American Tobacco Co., 535 F.2d 257, 269 (CA4 1976) (stating that where reinstatement is not immediately feasible, backpay "should be supplemented by an award equal to the estimated present value of lost earnings that are reasonably likely to occur between the date of judgment and the time when the employee can assume his new position"). Courts recognized that reinstatement was not always a viable option, and that an award of front pay as a substitute for reinstatement in such cases was a necessary part of the "make whole" relief mandated by Congress and by this Court in *Albemarle* [reproduced at page 941]. . . .

In 1991, without amending § 706(g), Congress further expanded the remedies available in cases of intentional employment discrimination to include compensatory and punitive damages. At that time, § 1981 permitted the recovery of unlimited compensatory and punitive damages in cases of intentional race and ethnic discrimination, but no similar remedy existed in cases of intentional sex, religious, or disability discrimination. Thus, § 1981a brought all forms of intentional employment discrimination into alignment, at least with respect to the forms of relief available to successful plaintiffs. However, compensatory and punitive damages awarded under § 1981a may not exceed the statutory limitations set forth in § 1981a(b)(3), while such damages awarded under § 1981 are not limited by statute.

**B**

In the abstract, front pay could be considered compensation for "future pecuniary losses," in which case it would be subject to the statutory cap. § 1981a(b)(3). . . . However, we must not analyze one term of § 1981a in isolation. When § 1981a is read as a whole, the better interpretation is that front pay is not within the meaning of compensatory damages in § 1981a(b)(3), and thus front pay is excluded from the statutory cap.

In the Civil Rights Act of 1991, Congress determined that victims of employment discrimination were entitled to *additional* remedies. . . . Congress therefore made clear through the plain language of the statute that the remedies newly authorized under § 1981a were *in addition to* the relief authorized by § 706(g). Section 1981a(a)(1) provides that, in intentional discrimination cases brought under Title VII, "the complaining party may recover compensatory and punitive damages as allowed in subsection (b) of [§ 1981a], *in addition to any relief authorized by section 706(g) of the Civil Rights Act of 1964*, from the respondent." (Emphasis added.) And § 1981a(b)(2) states that "[c]ompensatory damages awarded under [§ 1981a] shall not include backpay, interest on backpay, *or any other type of relief authorized under section 706(g) of the Civil Rights Act of 1964*." (Emphasis added.) According to these statutory provisions, if front pay was a type of relief authorized under § 706(g), it is excluded from the meaning of compensatory damages under § 1981a.

As discussed above, the original language of § 706(g) authorizing backpay awards was modeled after the same language in the NLRA. This provision in the NLRA had been construed to allow awards of backpay up to the date of reinstatement, even if reinstatement occurred after judgment. Accordingly, backpay awards made for the period between the date of judgment and the date of reinstatement, which today are called front pay awards under Title VII, were authorized under § 706(g).

As to front pay awards that are made in lieu of reinstatement, we construe § 706(g) as authorizing these awards as well. We see no logical difference between front pay awards made when there eventually is reinstatement and those made when there is not. Moreover, to distinguish between the two cases would lead to the strange result that employees could receive front pay when reinstatement eventually is available but not when reinstatement is not an option — whether because of continuing hostility between the plaintiff and the employer or its workers, or because of psychological injuries that the discrimination has caused the plaintiff. Thus, the most egregious offenders could be subject to the least sanctions. . . . We conclude that front pay awards in lieu of reinstatement fit within this statutory term.

Because front pay is a remedy authorized under § 706(g), Congress did not limit the availability of such awards in § 1981a. . . .

## NOTES

1. The *Pollard* Court recognizes that front pay, like backpay, is available in Title VII and Title I actions, and is not subject to the statutory caps in § 1981a(b)(3). Does the Court imply that the award is also available in ADEA and § 1981 actions?

2. Although the *Pollard* Court regards front pay as an equitable remedy, does it also indicate that courts have little discretion to deny the award? Aren't these principles equally applicable to front pay awards in § 1981 and ADEA actions? If so, the jury in such actions should have no direct role in determining either the availability or the amount of the award.

## 2. *Punitive Damages*

### KOLSTAD v. AMERICAN DENTAL ASSOCIATION
#### 527 U.S. 526 (1999)

Justice O'CONNOR delivered the opinion of the Court.

Under the terms of the Civil Rights Act of 1991 (1991 Act) punitive damages are available in claims under Title VII [and Title I]. Punitive damages are limited, however, to cases in which the employer has engaged in intentional discrimination and has done so "with malice or with reckless indifference to the federally protected rights of an aggrieved individual." 42 U.S.C.S. § 1981a(b)(1). . . .

I

In September 1992, Jack O'Donnell announced that he would be retiring as the Director of Legislation and Legislative Policy . . . for respondent, American Dental Association (respondent or Association). Petitioner, Carole Kolstad, was . . . serving as respondent's Director of Federal Agency Relations. When she learned of O'Donnell's retirement, she expressed an interest in filling his position. Also interested in replacing O'Donnell was Tom Spangler, [who] was serving as the Association's Legislative Counsel.... Both petitioner and Spangler ... had received "distinguished" performance ratings by the acting head of the Washington office, Leonard Wheat.

... Wheat requested that Dr. William Allen, then serving as respondent's Executive Director in the Association's Chicago office, make the ultimate promotion decision. After interviewing both petitioner and Spangler, Wheat recommended that Allen select Spangler for O'Donnell's post. Allen notified petitioner in December 1992 that he had, in fact, selected Spangler....

... In petitioner's view, the entire selection process was a sham. Counsel for petitioner urged the jury to conclude that Allen's stated reasons for selecting Spangler were pretext for gender discrimination, and that Spangler had been chosen for the position before the formal selection process began. Among the evidence offered in support of this view, there was testimony to the effect that Allen modified the description of O'Donnell's post to track aspects of the job description used to hire Spangler. In petitioner's view, this "preselection" procedure suggested an intent by the Association to discriminate on the basis of sex. Petitioner also introduced testimony at trial that Wheat told sexually offensive jokes and that he had referred to certain prominent professional women in derogatory terms....

The District Court denied petitioner's request for a jury instruction on punitive damages. The jury concluded that respondent had discriminated against petitioner on the basis of sex and awarded her backpay totaling $52,718....

The Court of Appeals ... concluded that, "before the question of punitive damages can go to the jury, the evidence of the defendant's culpability must exceed what is needed to show intentional discrimination." [T]he court determined, specifically, that a defendant must be shown to have engaged in some "egregious" misconduct....

## II

### A

... The 1991 Act limits compensatory and punitive damages awards, however, to cases of "intentional discrimination" — that is, cases that do not rely on the "disparate impact" theory of discrimination. § 1981a(a)(1). Section 1981a(b)(1) further qualifies the availability of punitive awards:

> A complaining party may recover punitive damages ... if the complaining party demonstrates that the respondent engaged in a discriminatory practice or discriminatory practices *with malice or with reckless indifference to the federally protected rights of an aggrieved individual.* (Emphasis added.)

The very structure of § 1981a suggests a congressional intent to authorize punitive awards in only a subset of cases involving intentional discrimination. Section 1981a(a)(1) limits compensatory and punitive awards to instances of intentional discrimination, while § 1981a(b)(1) requires plaintiffs to make an additional "demonstrat[ion]" of their eligibility for punitive damages. Congress plainly sought to impose two standards of liability — one for establishing a right to compensatory damages and another, higher standard that a plaintiff must satisfy to qualify for a punitive award.

... The terms "malice" and "reckless" [in § 1981a(b)(1)] ultimately focus on the actor's state of mind. While egregious misconduct is evidence of the requisite mental state, § 1981a does not limit plaintiffs to this form of evidence, and the section does not require a showing of egregious or outrageous discrimination independent of the employer's state of mind. Nor does the statute's structure imply an independent role for "egregiousness" in the face of congressional silence. On the contrary, the view that § 1981a provides for punitive awards based solely on an employer's state of mind is consistent with the 1991 Act's distinction between equitable and compensatory relief. Intent determines which remedies are open to a plaintiff here as well; compensatory awards are available only where the employer has engaged in "*intentional* discrimination." (Emphasis added.)

Moreover, § 1981a's focus on the employer's state of mind gives some effect to Congress' apparent intent to narrow the class of cases for which punitive awards are available to a subset of those involving intentional discrimination. The employer must act with "malice or with reckless indifference (*to [the plaintiff's] federally protected rights.*") (Emphasis added). The terms "malice" or "reckless indifference" pertain to the employer's knowledge that it may be acting in violation of federal law, not its awareness that it is engaging in discrimination. . . .

We gain an understanding of the meaning of the terms "malice" and "reckless indifference," as used in § 1981a, from this Court's decision in Smith v. Wade, 461 U.S. 30 (1983). . . . Employing language similar to what later appeared in § 1981a, the Court concluded in *Smith* that "a jury may be permitted to assess punitive damages in an action under § 1983 when the defendant's conduct is shown to be motivated by evil motive or intent, or when it involves reckless or callous indifference to the federally protected rights of others." While the *Smith* Court determined that it was unnecessary to show actual malice to qualify for a punitive award, its intent standard, at a minimum, required recklessness in its subjective form. The Court referred to a "subjective consciousness" of a risk of injury or illegality and a "'criminal indifference to civil obligations.'" . . . Applying this standard in the context of § 1981a, an employer must at least discriminate in the face of a perceived risk that its actions will violate federal law to be liable in punitive damages.

There will be circumstances where intentional discrimination does not give rise to punitive damages liability under this standard. In some instances, the employer may simply be unaware of the relevant federal prohibition. There will be cases, moreover, in which the employer discriminates with the distinct belief that its discrimination is lawful. The underlying theory of discrimination may be novel or otherwise poorly recognized, or an employer may reasonably believe that its discrimination satisfies a bona fide occupational qualification defense or other statutory exception to liability. . . .

To be sure, egregious or outrageous acts may serve as evidence supporting an inference of the requisite "evil motive." "The allowance of exemplary damages depends upon the bad motive of the wrong-doer *as exhibited by his acts.*" Sedgwick [Measure of Damages, p. 529 (8th ed. 1891)] (emphasis added). Likewise, under § 1981a(b)(1), pointing to evidence of an employer's egregious behavior would provide one means of satisfying the plaintiff's burden to "demonstrat[e]" that the employer acted with the requisite "malice or . . . reckless indifference." Again, however, respondent has not shown that the terms "reckless indifference" and "malice," in the punitive damages context, have taken on a consistent definition including an independent, "egregiousness" requirement.

B

The inquiry does not end with a showing of the requisite "malice or . . . reckless indifference" on the part of certain individuals, however. The plaintiff must impute liability for punitive damages to respondent. The en banc dissent recognized that agency principles place limits on vicarious liability for punitive damages. . . . While we decline to engage in any definitive application of the agency standards to the facts of this case, it is important that we address the proper legal standards for imputing liability to an employer in the punitive damages context. . . .

Although jurisdictions disagree over whether and how to limit vicarious liability for punitive damages, our interpretation of Title VII is informed by "the general common law of agency, rather than . . . the law of any particular State." The common law as codified in the Restatement (Second) of Agency (1957), provides a useful starting point for defining this general common law. The Restatement of Agency places strict limits on the extent to which an agent's misconduct may be imputed to the principal for purposes of awarding punitive damages:

> Punitive damages can properly be awarded against a master or other principal because of an act by an agent if, but only if:
> (a) the principal authorized the doing and the manner of the act, or
> (b) the agent was unfit and the principal was reckless in employing him, or
> (c) the agent was employed in a managerial capacity and was acting in the scope of employment, or
> (d) the principal or a managerial agent of the principal ratified or approved the act.

See also Restatement (Second) of Torts § 909 (same).

The Restatement, for example, provides that the principal may be liable for punitive damages if it authorizes or ratifies the agent's tortious act, or if it acts recklessly in employing the malfeasing agent. The Restatement also contemplates liability for punitive awards where an employee serving in a "managerial capacity" committed the wrong while "acting in the scope of employment." "Unfortunately, no good definition of what constitutes a 'managerial capacity' has been found," and determining whether an employee meets this description requires a fact-intensive inquiry. "In making this determination, the court should review the type of authority that the employer has given to the employee, the amount of discretion that the employee has in what is done and how it is accomplished." Suffice it to say here that the examples provided in the Restatement of Torts suggest that an employee must be "important," but perhaps need not be the employer's "top management, officers, or directors," to be acting "in a managerial capacity."

Additional questions arise from the meaning of the "scope of employment" requirement. The Restatement of Agency provides that even intentional torts are within the scope of an agent's employment if the conduct is "the kind [the employee] is employed to perform," "occurs substantially within the authorized time and space limits," and "is actuated, at least in part, by a purpose to serve the" employer. According to the Restatement, so long as these rules are satisfied, an employee may be said to act within the scope of employment even if the employee engages in acts "specifically forbidden" by the employer and uses "forbidden means of accomplishing results." On this view, even an employer who makes every effort to comply with Title VII would be held liable for the discriminatory acts of agents acting in a "managerial capacity."

Holding employers liable for punitive damages when they engage in good faith efforts to comply with Title VII, however, is in some tension with the very principles underlying common law limitations on vicarious liability for punitive damage — that it is "improper ordinarily to award punitive damages against one who himself is personally innocent and therefore liable only vicariously." Where an employer has undertaken such good faith efforts at Title VII compliance, it "demonstrat[es] that it never acted in reckless disregard of federally protected rights."

Applying the Restatement of Agency's "scope of employment" rule in the Title VII punitive damages context, moreover, would reduce the incentive for employers to implement antidiscrimination programs. In fact, such a rule would likely exacerbate concerns among employers that § 1981a's "malice" and "reckless indifference" standard penalizes those employers who educate themselves and their employees on Title VII's prohibitions. Dissuading employers from implementing programs or policies to prevent discrimination in the workplace is directly contrary to the purposes underlying Title VII. The statute's "primary objective" is "a prophylactic one"; it aims, chiefly, "not to provide redress but to avoid harm." . . . The purposes underlying Title VII are similarly advanced where employers are encouraged to adopt antidiscrimination policies and to educate their personnel on Title VII's prohibitions.

In light of the perverse incentives that the Restatement's "scope of employment" rules create, we are compelled to modify these principles to avoid undermining the objectives underlying Title VII. Recognizing Title VII as an effort to promote prevention as well as remediation, and observing the very principles underlying the Restatement's strict limits on vicarious liability for punitive damages, we agree that, in the punitive damages context, an employer may not be vicariously liable for the discriminatory employment decisions of managerial agents where these decisions are contrary to the employer's "good-faith efforts to comply with Title VII." As [Judge Tatel] recognized, "[g]iving punitive damages protection to employers who make good-faith efforts to prevent discrimination in the workplace accomplishes" Title VII's objective of "motivat[ing] employers to detect and deter Title VII violations."

. . . We leave for remand the question whether petitioner can identify facts sufficient to support an inference that the requisite mental state can be imputed to respondent. The parties have not yet had an opportunity to marshal the record evidence in support of their views on the application of agency principles. . . . Although trial testimony established that Allen made the ultimate decision to promote Spangler while serving as petitioner's interim executive director, respondent's highest position, it remains to be seen whether petitioner can make a sufficient showing that Allen acted with malice or reckless indifference to petitioner's Title VII rights. Even if it could be established that Wheat effectively selected O'Donnell's replacement, moreover, several questions would remain, e.g., whether Wheat was serving in a "managerial capacity" and whether he behaved with malice or reckless indifference to petitioner's rights. It may also be necessary to determine whether the Association had been making good faith efforts to enforce an antidiscrimination policy. . . .

[Chief Justice REHNQUIST and Justice THOMAS joined concurred in Part II-B of the Court's opinion.]

Justice STEVENS, with whom Justice SOUTER, Justice GINSBURG, and Justice BREYER join, concurring in part and dissenting in part. . . .

Construing § 1981a(b)(1) to impose a purely mental standard is perfectly consistent with the structure and purpose of the 1991 Act. [T]he 1991 Act's "willful" or "reckless disregard" standard respects the Act's "two-tiered" damages scheme while deterring future intentionally unlawful discrimination. There are, for reasons the Court explains, numerous instances in which an employer might intentionally treat an individual differently because of her race, gender, religion, or disability without knowing that it is violating Title VII or the ADA. . . . [But victims] need not prove that the defendants either knew or should have known that they were violating the law. It is the additional element of willful or reckless disregard of the law that justifies . . . punitive damages. . . .

[T]here is ample evidence from which the jury could have concluded that respondent willfully violated Title VII. . . . Evidence indicated that petitioner was the more qualified of the two candidates for the job. Respondent's decisionmakers, who were senior executives of the Association, were known occasionally to tell sexually offensive jokes and referred to professional women in derogatory terms. The record further supports an inference that these executives not only deliberately refused to consider petitioner fairly and to promote her because she is a woman, but they manipulated the job requirements and conducted a "sham" selection procedure in an attempt to conceal their misconduct. . . .

In Part II-B of its opinion, the Court discusses the question "whether liability for punitive damages may be imputed to respondent" under "agency principles." . . . The absence of briefing or meaningful argument by the parties makes this Court's gratuitous decision to volunteer an opinion on this nonissue particularly ill advised. . . .

## NOTES

1. There are two hurdles to the recovery of § 1981a punitive damages — the malice or reckless indifference requirement and satisfaction of the agency principles. As to the first, how can the plaintiff show that the employer subjectively knew that it was or might be violating Title I or Title VII? Where the employer does not rely on a statutory defense or exception, is it sufficient to show that the employer knew that its action was subject to federal antidiscrimination law? If the employer relies on a statutory defense or exception, is it enough to show the employer failed to seek legal advice? Does Smith v. Wade, discussed in the Court's opinion, suggest that the malice or reckless indifference requirement also applies in § 1981 cases? See, e.g., Rowlett v. Anheuser-Busch, Inc., 832 F.2d 194 (1st Cir. 1987) (yes). The reckless indifference requirement has proved to be an especially serious obstacle in ADA cases. See, e.g., Webner v. Titan Distribution, Inc., 267 F.3d 828 (8th Cir. 2001) (employer feared employee would reinjure his back and miss work); Gile v. United Airlines, Inc., 213 F.3d 365 (7th Cir. 2000) (employer negligently failed to realize that condition was a disability under the ADA).

2. Aside from the hostile work environment cases like Ellerth, page 516, agency principles have not precluded backpay or compensatory damages for a Title I or Title VII violation. Why do agency principles have more bite in actions seeking punitive damages? Are Kolstad's agency principles also applicable when punitive damages are sought under § 1981? The Fourth Circuit has held that Kolstad's agency principles are applicable in § 1981 actions. Lowery v. Circuit City Stores, Inc., 206 F.3d 431 (4th Cir. 2000).

3. The agency determination requires two steps. First, there must be a determination of whether liability would be appropriate — whether the actor was in a managerial capacity and acting within the scope of the actor's employment. Second, did the employer use good faith efforts to comply.

4. Consider who is a "manager" and what is the meaning of "scope of employment." Is the manager of a Wal-Mart store a "manager"? EEOC v. Wal-Mart Stores, Inc., 187 F.3d 1241 (10th Cir. 1999) (yes); contra, Dudley v. Wal-Mart Stores, Inc., 166 F.3d 1317 (11th Cir. 1999). If a "manager" creates a sexually hostile environment

for which the employer is liable, might the scope of employment requirement preclude recovery of punitive damages? The Fourth Circuit has held that a supervisor who created a hostile environment and who had authority over the victimized employee acted in the scope of his employment. Anderson v. G.D.C., Inc. 281 F.3d 452 (4th Cir. 2002). The court also held that the "manager" requirement is satisfied by an employee who has the power to hire, fire, and discipline other employees. The Tenth Circuit has gone even further, holding that an employee who can make hiring and firing *recommendations* is a "manager." EEOC v. Wal-Mart Stores, Inc., 187 F.3d 1241 (10th Cir. 1999).

5. Should there be an exception for employers who have made a good faith effort to prevent discrimination? Would employers be more vigilant with or without this exception? Is good faith shown by a nondiscrimination policy? EEOC v. Wal-Mart Stores, Inc., supra (no). By an employer's efforts to educate its employees about antidiscrimination laws? Id. (yes.) Note the Supreme Court's reference to "good faith efforts to *enforce* an antidiscrimination policy" (emphasis added).

6. The First Circuit thoughtfully considered the "good faith" exception in Romano v. U-Haul International, 233 F.3d 655 (1st Cir. 2000). It viewed the exception to vicarious liability as an affirmative defense on which the employer had the burden of proof. A written nondiscrimination policy was evidence of good faith but insufficient to satisfy the employer's burden of production. "A defendant must also show that efforts have been made to implement its anti-discrimination policy, through education of its employees and actual enforcement of its mandate." Id. at 670. While the defendant's managers were instructed to comply with the policy, there was no evidence of "an active mechanism for renewing employees' awareness of the policies through either specific education programs or periodic re-dissemination" of the policies. Id. Nor was there evidence that defendant's supervisors were trained to prevent discrimination from occurring or that the defendant's policies were successfully followed. See also Cadena v. Pacesetter Corp., 224 F.3d 1203 (10th Cir. 2000).

7. Two circuits have agreed that the good faith defense is available only where the employer has derivative liability, as opposed to direct liability, for the discrimination. Accordingly, the defense is unavailable where the discriminator was by such a high level person who was acting as a proxy for the corporation. Passentino v. Johnson & Johnson Consumer Prods., Inc., 212 F.3d 493 (9th Cir. 2000). Similarly, the defense is unavailable where the employees charged with enforcing the company's antidiscrimination policies knew or should have known of the discrimination but failed to act. Deters v. Equifax Credit Information Services, Inc., 202 F.3d 1262 (10th Cir. 2000).

8. On remand, if no additional facts surface, should Kolstad's claim for punitive damages go to a jury? Did she present sufficient evidence that the Association discriminated "in the face of a perceived risk that its actions will violate federal law"? Did she present sufficient evidence that Allen and Wheat were "managers"?

9. Several circuits have added an additional threshold to the grant of punitive damages — that punitive damages may be recovered only where compensatory damages have also been awarded. Eg., Allison v. Citgo Petroleum Corp., 151 F.3d 402, 407 (5th Cir. 1998); Provencher v. CVS Pharmacy, 145 F.3d 5(1st Cir. 1998); but see, Timm v. Progressive Steel Treating, Inc., 137 F.3d 1008, 1010 (7th Cir. 1998) ("punitive damages are not inconsistent with the lack of compensatory damages"). See generally, Kristine N. Lapinski, Comment, Prerequisite or Irrelevant? Compensatory Damages in § 1981a Actions for Violation of Title VII of the Civil Rights Act of 1964, and Their Relationship to Punitive Damages, 2001 L. Rev. M.S.U.-D.C.L. 1199.

10. If the jury finds that the two *Kolstad* requirements have been satisfied, it has discretion whether to award punitive damages. This discretion is exercised in light of the need for punishment and deterrence. See Smith v. Wade, 461 U.S. 30 (1983). The jury determines the amount of the award by considering "such factors as the grievousness of the conduct, the solvency of the guilty party, and the potential for deterrence of the verdict." Rowlett v. Anheuser-Busch, Inc., 832 F.2d 194, 207 (1st Cir. 1987). See Judith J. Johnson, A Standard for Punitive Damages Under Title VII, 46 Fla. L. Rev. 521 (1995).

11. In Pacific Mut. Life Ins. Co. v. Haslip, 499 U.S. 1 (1991), the Supreme Court held that due process did permit imposing punitive damages liability under the respondeat superior doctrine and allowing a jury to assess the award. Moreover, the traditional jury instructions on punitive damages, including the preponderance of the evidence standard, do not offend due process. However, BMW of N. Am., Inc. v. Gore, 517 U.S. 559 (1996), held that a punitive damages award that is "grossly excessive" violates due process. An award is "grossly excessive" when either the amount of the award exceeds the state's legitimate interests in punishment and deterrence or the controlling legal principles fail to provide fair notice of the conduct subject to punishment and the severity of the punishment. Appellate courts must use a de novo standard when reviewing a trial court's determination of the constitutionality of a punitive damages award. Cooper Industries, Inc. v. Leatherman Tool Group, Inc., 532 U.S. 424 (2001). See also EEOC v. W & O, Inc., 213 F.3d 600 (11th Cir. 2000). *BMW* clearly has application in a § 1981 action, which has no statutory ceiling on punitive damages awards, but should it also apply in Title VII and Title I actions?

In Lansdale v. Hi-Health Supermart Corp., 314 F.3d 355 (9th Cir. 2002), the trial judge applied the caps to reduce a verdict of $100,000 compensatory and $1,000,000 punitive damages to $200,000. Affirming, the court upheld the caps against plaintiff's equal protection attack.

12. The sum of compensatory plus punitive damages available to one claimant under this provision is capped. In EEOC v. W & O, Inc. (213 F.3d 600) (11th Cir. 2000), the EEOC brought an action on behalf of three employees, and each was awarded $100,000 in punitive damages, which was the full cap for each. The employer argued that, since the EEOC brought the action, a single $100,000 cap should be imposed on the total punitive damages for the three workers. The court rejected that argument, holding that when the EEOC is the complaining party, "each aggrieved employee may receive up to the full amount permitted by the applicable statutory cap" of the statute. Id. at 613. The caps apply to the entire amount recoverable by any one claimant on all of her Title VII claims and not to each separate Title VII claim alleged by one plaintiff. See also Hagan v. Bangor & Aroostook R.R., 61 F.3d 1034, 1037 (1st Cir. 1995) (the cap is imposed on the sum of compensatory and punitive damages, not on each type of award). In Hudson v. Reno, 130 F.3d 1193 (6th Cir. 1997), the plaintiff sued for sex discrimination and retaliation, both in violation of Title VII, but the court limited the total recovery to one $300,000 amount for both the sex discrimination and retaliation counts. The court based its conclusion on the plain meaning of the statute that refers to "an action" as well as that the award shall be "for each complaining party." Baty v. Willamette Indus., 172 F.3d 1232, 1246 (10th Cir. 1999) (caps apply to each party in an action, not to each claim).

13. The size of the cap depends on the size of the employer: $50,000 for covered employers with fewer than 101 employees in each of 20 or more calendar weeks in the current or preceding calendar year; $100,000 for employers with more than 100 and fewer than 100 and fewer than 201; $200,000 for employers with more than 200

and fewer than 500; and $300,000 for employers with more than 500. To count for purposes of the cap, an employee must work during 20 different weeks within a year. 42 U.S.C.S. § 1981a(b)(3) (2003).

14. Section 1981a(c)(2) provides that "the court shall not inform the jury of the limitation. . . ." 42 U.S.C.S. § 1981a(c) (2003).

15. The statute provides for the interrelationship of Title VII claims with claims brought under § 1981. As to Title VII actions under § 1981a(a)(1) but not as to ADA actions under § 1981a(a)(2), plaintiff is eligible for compensatory damages as long as she "cannot recover under 42 U.S.C. 1981 . . ." The intent of this section was to avoid double recovery for the same harm, with the § 1981 claim taking priority because it is not capped. Where, therefore, the plaintiff alleges a single harm, such as race discrimination, but brings both a Title VII and a § 1981 cause of action, there can only be one recovery, but that recovery for compensatory damages will be under § 1981, which is not subject to the caps established for Title VII actions. The priority of uncapped § 1981 claims is further confirmed by § 1981a(c)(4), which provides that "[n]othing in this section shall be construed to limit the scope of, or the relief available under, section 1981. . . ."

One plaintiff, however, can make separate claims of, say, sex discrimination and race discrimination under Title VII that are subject to the caps. A claim of race discrimination under § 1981 is entitled to a separate recovery not limited by the caps. As long as these claims do not arise out of the same facts, the double recovery situation addressed by § 1981a(a)(1) is not implicated.

16. Suppose a jury finds the same discrimination violates both federal and state employment statutes and awards compensatory damages without apportioning the award between the two claims. If the award exceeds the § 1981a(b)(3) cap, should the court treat the amount in excess of the cap as having been awarded under state law? Martini v. Federal National Mortgage Assn., 178 F.3d 1336 (D.C. Cir. 1999) (yes). Would your answer change if the state statute contained the same cap? Giles v. GE, 245 F.3d 474 (5th Cir. 2001) (caps are coextensive, not cumulative).

17. Section 1981a(b)(2) provides that any monetary relief authorized by § 706(g) of Title VII shall *not* be considered compensatory damages. This is significant because it exempts § 706(g) awards from the § 1981a requirements. The provision clearly includes backpay, interest, and attorneys' fees, and *Pollard* holds that it also includes front pay. Thus backpay, attorneys' fees, and front pay remain forms of relief that are within the purview of the judge, not the jury. See Hennessy v. Penril Datacomm Networks, Inc., 69 F.3d 1344 (7th Cir. 1995). As important, awards of backpay, attorneys' fees, and front pay are not included when applying the cap on compensatory and punitive damages.

18. Section 1981a(a)(2) authorizes compensatory and punitive damages in Title I ADA actions for disparate treatment discrimination. This relief is in addition to the backpay, front pay, and interest permitted by § 706(g). However, compensatory and punitive damage awards are subject to the same limitations and conditions as in Title VII actions, including the immunity of governmental entities from punitive damage awards. In addition § 1981a(a)(3) provides that damages may not be awarded for the failure to make a reasonable accommodation in an ADA case where the defendant demonstrates good faith efforts, in consultation with the discriminatee, to make such an accommodation.

19. Prior to the Supreme Court's decision in Barnes v. Gorman, 536 U.S. 181 (2002), the question of the availability of compensatory and punitive damages in Title II actions against state and local governments had produced conflicting opinions in

the lower courts. The uncertainty arose because the remedies provision for Title II, 42 U.S.C.S. § 12133 (2003), incorporated the remedies provisions in two earlier statutes, but none of the three provisions expressly authorized or prohibited any particular type of relief. Barnes v. Gorman held that Title II does not permit the recovery of punitive damages. The Court reasoned that the spending clause was the constitutional basis for Title II, thus a Title II action has a contractual nature. Because traditional contract law does not allow the recovery of punitive damages, such a remedy is not available under Title II in the absence of an unambiguous statutory provision to the contrary or a reasonable basis for implying such a provision in the contract. *Barnes*, however, was a suit against a local government and, therefore, did not consider possible Eleventh Amendment limitations on suing the state.

20.  The caps have resulted in several issues concerning unions. Suppose a labor union has more than 15 *members* and so is covered by Title VII but does not have the 15 *employees* required to come under the $50,000 statutory cap. Ferroni v. Teamsters Chauffeurs & Warehousemen Local No. 222, 297 F.3d 1146 (10th Cir. 2002), holds that, without at least 15 employees, a union is not a covered employer for purposes of Title VII liability including punitive damages. If it has at least 15 employees, the union is covered as an employer and is subject to compensatory and punitive damages for its employment discrimination, and damages are "capped" by the number of employees. If a union has at least 15 members, then it is covered by Title VII as to discrimination against its members, even if it does not have 15 employees. Section 1981a(a)(1) speaks to liability of a "respondent" for compensatory and punitive damages, but § 1981a(b)(3) imposes the caps only based on numbers of employees of the respondent. Does that make a union respondent subject to uncapped liability for intentional discrimination against its members? Or should § 1981a be construed as not imposing any liability for compensatory and punitive damages on a union for discrimination against its members?

### NOTE ON PERSONAL LIABILITY OF EMPLOYEES

One issue that frequently arises is whether the person who committed the discriminatory act has personal liability to the discriminatee or whether liability is limited to the employer. In Miller v. Maxwell's Intl., Inc., 991 F.2d 583 (9th Cir. 1993), the court concluded that neither Title VII nor the ADEA imposes personal liability. The court reasoned that these statutes are addressed to "employers" and, even though this term is defined to include "agents" of the employer, this inclusion was intended to incorporate the doctrine of respondeat superior. Moreover, because both statutes exempt small employers from coverage, the court thought it "inconceivable" that Congress would have intended to impose liability on individual employees. A dissenting judge agreed as to Title VII but reasoned that the personal liability of employees was established under the Fair Labor Standards Act, and, because the ADEA adopted that statute's enforcement procedures, employees also have personal liability under the ADEA.

Other appellate decisions have agreed that employees do not have personal liability to the discriminatee under Title VII. E.g., Lissau v. Southern Food Serv., Inc., 159 F.3d 177 (4th Cir. 1998); Huckabay v. Moore, 142 F.3d 233 (5th Cir. 1998); Cross v. Alabama, 49 F.3d 1490 (11th Cir. 1995); Tomka v. Seiler Corp., 66 F.3d 1295 (2d Cir. 1995). The same result has also been reached in ADEA litigation. E.g., Stults v. Conoco, Inc., 76 F.3d 651 (5th Cir. 1996); Smith v. Lomax, 45 F.3d 402 (11th Cir.

1995). And the appellate decisions under Title I, which contains coverage provisions like those in the ADEA and Title VII, have again reached the same conclusion. Butler v. City of Prairie Village, 172 F.3d 736 (10th Cir. 1999); Mason v. Stallings, 82 F.3d 1007 (11th Cir. 1996); Williams v. Banning, 72 F.3d 552 (7th Cir. 1995). No doubt the same result will be reached under Title II. Baird v. Rose, 192 F.3d 462 (4th Cir. 1999).

In contrast to the ADA, Title VII, and ADEA, employees do have personal liability to the discriminatee under § 1981. E.g., Gierlinger v. New York State Police, 15 F.3d 32 (2d Cir. 1994); Jones v. Continental Corp., 789 F.2d 1225 (6th Cir. 1986). Contra, Oden v. Oktibbeha County, 246 F.3d 458 (5th Cir.), *cert. denied*, 534 U.S. 948 (2001). See generally Rebecca Hanner White, Vicarious and Personal Liability for Employment Discrimination, 30 Ga. L. Rev. 509 (1996). A public official may escape personal liability under § 1981, however, through the public-official immunity doctrine. The branch of this doctrine that is most likely to arise in employment discrimination litigation establishes only a qualified immunity. Such immunity can usually be overcome in a race discrimination case. The public-official immunity doctrine is discussed on pages 179-181. A remarkable Fifth Circuit decision has held that a public official does not have personal liability under § 1981 for his public employment decisions. Oden v. Oktibbeha County, 246 F.3d 458 (5th Cir.), *cert. denied*, 534 U.S. 948 (2001). The court relied on Title VII authority for the proposition that only the employer — the municipal entity — has liability. The opinion clearly indicated that the court was not basing its decision on the qualified immunity defense.

## 3.  *Liquidated Damages*

The ADEA (but not Title VII, the ADA, or § 1981) allows the recovery of "liquidated damages." Section 7(b), 29 U.S.C.S. § 626(b) (2003), incorporates the enforcement procedures and remedies contained in § 16 of the Fair Labor Standards Act (FLSA), 29 U.S.C.S. § 216 (2003). Section 16 allows the EEOC or a non-federal discriminatee to recover (1) unpaid wages and (2) liquidated damages in an amount equal to the amount of unpaid wages recovered. Section 7(b), however, imposes a condition on the recovery of liquidated damages: "*Provided*, That liquidated damages shall be payable only in cases of willful violations of this chapter."

After an initial attempt to delineate the meaning of the phrase "willful violations," the Supreme Court found it necessary to revisit the issue.

### HAZEN PAPER CO. v. BIGGINS
#### 507 U.S. 604 (1993)

Justice O'CONNOR delivered the opinion of the Court.

[The case was tried before a jury, which specifically found that the employer "willfully" violated the ADEA. Under § 7(b), a "willful" violation gives rise to liquidated damages.]

As to the issue of "willfulness" under § 7(b) of the ADEA, the Court of Appeals adopted and applied the definition set out in Trans World Airlines, Inc. v. Thurston, 469 U.S. 111 (1985). In *Thurston*, we held that the airline's facially discriminatory job-transfer policy was not a "willful" ADEA violation because the airline neither "knew [nor] showed reckless disregard for the matter of whether" the policy contravened the statute. The Court of Appeals found sufficient evidence to satisfy the *Thurston* standard, and ordered that respondent be awarded liquidated damages equal to and in addition to the underlying damages of $419,454.38.

We granted certiorari to decide [whether] the *Thurston* standard for liquidated damages appl[ies] to the case where the predicate ADEA violation is not a formal, facially discriminatory policy, as in *Thurston*, but rather an informal decision by the employer that was motivated by the employee's age. . . .

In *Thurston*, we thoroughly analyzed § 7(b) and concluded that "a violation of the Act [would be] 'willful' if the employer knew or showed reckless disregard for the matter of whether its conduct was prohibited by the ADEA." We sifted through the legislative history of § 7(b), which had derived from § 16(a) of the [FLSA], and determined that the accepted judicial interpretation of § 16(a) at the time of the passage of the ADEA supported the "knowledge or reckless disregard" standard. We found that this standard was consistent with the meaning of "willful" in other criminal and civil statutes. Finally, we observed that Congress aimed to create a "two-tiered liability scheme," under which some but not all ADEA violations would give rise to liquidated damages. We therefore rejected a broader definition of "willful" providing for liquidated damages whenever the employer knew that the ADEA was "in the picture." . . .

Surprisingly, the courts of appeals continue to be confused about the meaning of the term "willful" in § 7(b) of the ADEA. A number of circuits have declined to apply *Thurston* to what might be called an informal disparate treatment case — where age has entered into the employment decision on an ad hoc, informal basis rather than through a formal policy. At least one circuit refuses to impose liquidated damages in such a case unless the employer's conduct was "outrageous." Another requires that the underlying evidence of liability be direct rather than circumstantial. Still others have insisted that age be the "predominant" rather than simply a determinative factor. The chief concern of these circuits has been that the application of *Thurston* would defeat the two-tiered system of liability intended by Congress, because every employer that engages in informal age discrimination knows or recklessly disregards the illegality of its conduct.

We believe that this concern is misplaced. The ADEA does not provide for liquidated damages "where consistent with the principle of a two-tiered liability scheme." It provides for liquidated damages where the violation was "willful." That definition must be applied here unless we overrule *Thurston*, or unless there is some inherent difference between this case and *Thurston* to cause a shift in the meaning of the word "willful."

As for the first possibility, petitioners have not persuaded us that *Thurston* was wrongly decided, let alone that we should depart from the rule of stare decisis. The two-tiered liability principle was simply one interpretive tool among several that we used in *Thurston* to decide what Congress meant by the word "willful," and in any event we continue to believe that the "knowledge or reckless disregard" standard will create two tiers of liability across the range of ADEA cases. It is not true that an employer who knowingly relies on age in reaching its decision invariably commits a knowing or reckless violation of the ADEA. The ADEA is not an unqualified prohibition on the use of age in employment decisions, but affords the employer a "bona fide occupational qualification" defense, and exempts certain subject matters and persons, see, e.g., § 623(f)(2) (exemption for bona fide seniority systems and employee benefit plans); § 631(c) (exemption for bona fide executives and high policymakers). If an employer incorrectly but in good faith and nonrecklessly believes that the statute permits a particular age-based decision, then liquidated damages should not be imposed. Indeed, in *Thurston* itself we upheld liability but *reversed* an award of liquidated damages because the employer "acted [nonrecklessly] and in good faith in attempting to determine whether [its] plan would violate the ADEA."

Nor do we see how the instant case can be distinguished from *Thurston*, assuming that petitioners did indeed fire respondent because of his age. The only distinction between *Thurston* and the case before us is the existence of formal discrimination. Age entered into the employment decision there through a formal and publicized policy, and not as an undisclosed factor motivating the employer on an ad hoc basis, which is what respondent alleges occurred here. But surely an employer's reluctance to acknowledge its reliance on the forbidden factor should not cut against imposing a penalty. It would be a wholly circular and self-defeating interpretation of the ADEA to hold that, in cases where an employer more likely knows its conduct to be illegal, knowledge alone does not suffice for liquidated damages. We therefore reaffirm that the *Thurston* definition of "willful" — that the employer either knew or showed reckless disregard for the matter of whether its conduct was prohibited by the statute — applies to all disparate treatment cases under the ADEA. Once a "willful" violation has been shown, the employee need not additionally demonstrate that the employer's conduct was outrageous, or provide direct evidence of the employer's motivation, or prove that age was the predominant rather than a determinative factor in the employment decision. . . .

[The concurring opinion of Justice KENNEDY, with whom The Chief Justice and Justice THOMAS joined, is omitted.]

## NOTES

1. *Thurston* also clarified two other aspects of the liquidated damages award. First, liquidated damages must be awarded to a discriminatee who proves a "willful violation," but if a "willful violation" is not proved, the discriminatee cannot be awarded any amount of liquidated damages. Second, the liquidated damages award has a punitive purpose. See also Commissioner v. Schleier, 515 U.S. 323 (1995). If the liquidated damages award is punitive, can a plaintiff recover both liquidated damages and state law punitive damages for the same misconduct? See Denesha v. Farmers Insurance Exchange, 161 F.3d 491 (8th Cir. 1998).

2. After *Biggins*, has an employer who has engaged in unlawful disparate treatment discrimination acted "willfully" if it negligently (but not recklessly) relied on a defense, exemption, or coverage provision contained in the Act? See Price v. Marshall Erdman & Assocs., 966 F.2d 320 (7th Cir. 1992). What if the employer was simply ignorant of the ADEA's existence? See Brown v. M&M/Mars, 883 F.2d 505 (7th Cir. 1989). Should "willful" retaliation be found where the employer was unaware of the ADEA's antiretaliation provision? Ray v. Iuka Special Mun. Separate Dist., 51 F.3d 1246 (5th Cir. 1995); Dominic v. Consolidated Edison Co., 822 F.2d 1249 (2d Cir. 1987).

3. Compare *Biggins* with *Kolstad*. Is the Supreme Court's interpretation of "willful" in the ADEA the same as its interpretation of "malice or reckless indifference" in § 1981a? Is an employer liable for punitive damages where it has acted nonrecklessly and in good faith reliance on a statutory exception? Do the *Kolstad* agency principles limit liability for the ADEA award? Should uniform principles apply to these two awards? See generally Judith J. Johnson, A Uniform Standard for Exemplary Damages in Employment Discrimination Cases, 33 U. Rich. L. Rev. 41 (1999).

4. Can a discriminatee who recovers liquidated damages also recover pre-judgment interest on the unpaid wages award? In Kelly v. American Standard, Inc., 640 F.2d 974, 979 (9th Cir. 1981), the court thought so, remarking that "the award of liquidated damages is in effect a substitution for punitive damages." Accord, Stareaski v. Westinghouse Elec. Corp., 54 F.3d 1089 (3d Cir. 1995); Reichman v. Bonsignore, Brignati & Mazzotta, 818 F.2d 278 (2d Cir. 1987). Other courts view the liquidated damages award as partly compensatory and hold that a discriminatee cannot recover both liquidated damages and pre-judgment interest. E.g., McCann v. Texas City Ref., Inc., 984 F.2d 667 (5th Cir. 1993); Fortino v. Quasar Co., 950 F.2d 389 (7th Cir. 1991). This view seems to fly in the face of *Thurston* and *Schleier.*

5. How are liquidated damages calculated? Several courts have stated that the award should equal the amount awarded for unpaid wages and lost fringe benefits. E.g., Blim v. Western Elec. Co., 731 F.2d 1473 (10th Cir. 1984). The Tenth Circuit held that a $4.4 million award for lost gains on stock options was properly excluded from the liquidated damages calculation. Although the court acknowledged that the stock options "were a component of [the plaintiff's] compensation package" and the dates used to calculate the award were in the past, the court reasoned that the speculative nature of the award made it more like front pay than backpay. Greene v. Safeway Stores, Inc., 210 F.3d 1237 (10th Cir. 2000). Yet another court, without explanation, excluded an award for lost health insurance benefits when it calculated liquidated damages. Blackwell v. Sun Elec. Corp., 696 F.2d 1176 (6th Cir. 1983). Other courts have held that front-pay awards and state law damages awards should not be included in calculating liquidated damages. E.g., Graefenhain v. Pabst Brewing Co., 870 F.2d 1198 (7th Cir. 1989); Cassino v. Reichhold Chems., Inc., 817 F.2d 1338 (9th Cir. 1987).

6. The liquidated damages award is not available in federal employee ADEA actions. See Lehman v. Nakshian, 453 U.S. 156 (1981).

## C. EQUITABLE RELIEF

### 1. Reinstatement, Retroactive Seniority, and Injunctive Relief

The antidiscrimination statutes allow both prohibitory and compensatory equitable relief. Both types of equitable relief can take a variety of forms, but the most common form of prohibitory relief is an injunction against the discriminatory practice, and a common form of compensatory relief is an award of instatement or reinstatement. Another form of compensatory equitable relief is an award of retroactive seniority — the seniority lost due to the discrimination.

In Franks v. Bowman Transp. Co., which follows, the discriminatees sought to enjoin discriminatory practices and to recover instatement and retroactive seniority. The trial court granted the first two forms of relief but refused to award lost seniority.

### FRANKS v. BOWMAN TRANSPORTATION CO.
#### 424 U.S. 747 (1976)

Justice BRENNAN delivered the opinion of the Court. . . .
[Black applicants who had sought over-the-road (OTR) driving positions brought a Title VII class action, alleging racially discriminatory hiring and discharge policies in these positions. The trial court enjoined the discriminatory practices and ordered

that priority consideration be given to members of the class in filling OTR positions. The trial court declined, however, to award seniority relief. Certiorari was granted on this last aspect of the judgment.]

In affirming the District Court's denial of seniority relief . . ., the Court of Appeals held that the relief was barred by § 703(h) [which permits an employer to have a bona fide seniority system]. We disagree. . . .

The black applicants for OTR positions . . . are limited to those whose applications were put in evidence at the trial. The underlying legal wrong affecting them is not the alleged operation of a racially discriminatory seniority system but of a racially discriminatory hiring system. Petitioners do not ask for modification or elimination of the existing seniority system, but only for an award of the seniority status they would have individually enjoyed under the present system but for the illegal discriminatory refusal to hire. It is this context that must shape our determination as to the meaning and effect of § 703(h).

On its face, § 703(h) appears to be only a definitional provision; as with the other provisions of § 703, subsection (h) delineates which employment practices are illegal and thereby prohibited and which are not. Section 703(h) certainly does not expressly purport to qualify or proscribe relief otherwise appropriate under the remedial provisions of Title VII, § 706(g), in circumstances where an illegal discriminatory act or practice is found. Further, the legislative history of § 703(h) plainly negates its reading as limiting or qualifying the relief authorized under § 706(g). . . . [I]t is apparent that the thrust of [§ 703(h)] is directed toward defining what is and what is not an illegal discriminatory practice in instances in which the post-Act operation of a seniority system is challenged as perpetuating the effects of discrimination occurring prior to the effective date of the Act. There is no indication in the legislative materials that § 703(h) was intended to modify or restrict relief otherwise appropriate once an illegal discriminatory practice occurring after the effective date of the Act is proved — as in the instant case, a discriminatory refusal to hire. . . . We therefore hold that the Court of Appeals erred in concluding that, as a matter of law, § 703(h) barred the award of seniority relief to the [class].

## III

There remains the question whether an award of seniority relief is appropriate under the remedial provisions of Title VII, specifically, § 706(g).

. . . Last Term's Albemarle Paper Company v. Moody [reproduced at page 941], consistently with the congressional plan, held that one of the central purposes of Title VII is "to make persons whole for injuries suffered on account of unlawful employment discrimination." To effectuate this "make-whole" objective, Congress in § 706(g) vested broad equitable discretion in the federal courts to "order such affirmative action as may be appropriate, which may include, but is not limited to, reinstatement or hiring of employees, with or without backpay . . . , or any other equitable relief as the court deems appropriate." . . . This is emphatic confirmation that federal courts are empowered to fashion such relief as the particular circumstances of a case may require to effect restitution, making whole insofar as possible the victims of racial discrimination in hiring. Adequate relief may well be denied in the absence of a seniority remedy slotting the victim in that position in the seniority system that would have been his had he been hired at the time of his application. It can hardly be questioned that ordinarily such relief will be necessary to achieve the "make-whole" purposes of the Act. . . .

Seniority standing in employment with respondent Bowman, computed from the departmental date of hire, determines the order of layoff and recall of employees. Further, job assignments for OTR drivers are posted for competitive bidding and seniority is used to determine the highest bidder. As OTR drivers are paid on a per-mile basis, earnings are therefore to some extent a function of seniority. Additionally, seniority computed from the company date of hire determines the length of an employee's vacation and pension benefits. Obviously merely to require Bowman to hire the . . . victim of discrimination falls far short of a "make-whole" remedy. A concomitant award of the seniority credit he presumptively would have earned but for the wrongful treatment would also seem necessary in the absence of justification for denying that relief. Without an award of seniority dating from the time when he was discriminatorily refused employment, an individual who applies for and obtains employment as an OTR driver pursuant to the District Court's order will never obtain his rightful place in the hierarchy of seniority according to which these various employment benefits are distributed. He will perpetually remain subordinate to persons who, but for the illegal discrimination, would have been in respect to entitlement to these benefits his inferiors. . . .

## IV

We are not to be understood as holding that an award of seniority status is requisite in all circumstances. The fashioning of appropriate remedies invokes the sound equitable discretion of the district courts. . . . [But] no less than with the denial of the remedy of backpay, the denial of seniority relief to victims of illegal racial discrimination in hiring is permissible "only for reasons which, if applied generally, would not frustrate the central statutory purposes of eradicating discrimination throughout the economy and making persons whole for injuries suffered through past discrimination." . . .

Respondent Bowman raises an alternative theory of justification. Bowman argues that an award of retroactive seniority to the class of discriminatees will conflict with the economic interests of other Bowman employees. Accordingly, it is argued, the District Court acted within its discretion in denying this form of relief as an attempt to accommodate the competing interests of the various groups of employees.

We reject this argument. . . . [I]t is apparent that denial of seniority relief to identifiable victims of racial discrimination on the sole ground that such relief diminishes the expectations of other, arguably innocent, employees would if applied generally frustrate the central "make-whole" objective of Title VII. These conflicting interests of other employees will, of course, always be present in instances where some scarce employment benefit is distributed among employees on the basis of their status in the seniority hierarchy. But, as we have said, there is nothing in the language of Title VII, or in its legislative history, to show that Congress intended generally to bar this form of relief to victims of illegal discrimination, and the experience under its remedial model in the National Labor Relations Act points to the contrary. Accordingly, we find untenable the conclusion that this form of relief may be denied merely because the interests of other employees may thereby be affected. "If relief under Title VII can be denied merely because the majority group of employees, who have not suffered discrimination, will be unhappy about it, there will be little hope of correcting the wrongs to which the Act is directed."

With reference to the problems of fairness or equity respecting the conflicting interests of the various groups of employees, the relief which petitioners seek is only seniority status retroactive to the date of individual application, rather than some form of arguably more complete relief. No claim is asserted that nondiscriminatee employees holding OTR positions they would not have obtained but for the illegal discrimination should be deprived of the seniority status they have earned. It is therefore clear that even if the seniority relief petitioners seek is awarded, most if not all discriminatees who actually obtain OTR jobs under the court order will not truly be restored to the actual seniority that would have existed in the absence of the illegal discrimination. Rather, most discriminatees even under an award of retroactive seniority status will still remain subordinated in the hierarchy to a position inferior to that of a greater total number of employees than would have been the case in the absence of discrimination. Therefore, the relief which petitioners seek . . . in no sense constitutes "complete relief." Rather, the burden of the past discrimination in hiring is with respect to competitive status benefits divided among discriminatee and nondiscriminatee employees under the form of relief sought. The dissent criticizes the Court's result as not sufficiently cognizant that it will "directly implicate the rights and expectations of perfectly innocent employees." We are of the view, however, that the result which we reach today — which, standing alone, establishes that a sharing of the burden of the past discrimination is presumptively necessary — is entirely consistent with any fair characterization of equity jurisdiction. . . .

V

In holding that class-based seniority relief for identifiable victims of illegal hiring discrimination is a form of relief generally appropriate under § 706(g), we do not in any way modify our previously expressed view that the statutory scheme of Title VII "implicitly recognizes that there may be cases calling for one remedy but not another, and — owing to the structure of the federal judiciary — these choices are, of course, left in the first instance to the district courts." Circumstances peculiar to the individual case may of course justify the modification or withholding of seniority relief for reasons that would not if applied generally undermine the purposes of Title VII. . . .

Chief Justice BURGER, concurring in part and dissenting in part.

I agree generally with Justice Powell, but I would stress that although retroactive benefit-type seniority relief may sometimes be appropriate and equitable, competitive-type seniority relief at the expense of wholly innocent employees can rarely, if ever, be equitable if that term retains traditional meaning. More equitable would be a monetary award to the person suffering the discrimination. An award such as "front pay" could replace the need for competitive-type seniority relief. Such monetary relief would serve the dual purpose of deterring wrongdoing by the employer or union — or both — as well as protecting the rights of innocent employees. . . .

Justice POWELL, with whom Justice REHNQUIST joins, concurring in part and dissenting in part. . . .

. . . I cannot accept as correct [the Court's] basic interpretation of § 706(g) as virtually requiring a district court, in determining appropriate equitable relief in a case of this kind, to ignore entirely the equities that may exist in favor of innocent employees. Its holding recognizes no meaningful distinction, in terms of the equitable relief to be granted, between "benefit"-type seniority and "competitive"-type seniority. The Court reaches this result by taking an absolutist view of the "make-whole" objective of Title VII, while rendering largely meaningless the discretionary authority vested in district courts. . . .

[T]o the extent that the Court today finds a . . . presumption in favor of granting *benefit-type* seniority, it is recognizing that normally this relief . . . will be equitable. As the Court notes, this type of seniority, which determines pension rights, length of vacations, size of insurance coverage and unemployment benefits, and the like, is analogous to backpay in that its retroactive grant serves "the mutually reinforcing effect of the dual purposes of Title VII." Benefit-type seniority, like backpay, serves to work complete equity by penalizing the wrongdoer economically at the same time that it tends to make whole the one who was wronged.

But the Court fails to recognize that a retroactive grant of *competitive-type* seniority invokes wholly different considerations. This is the type of seniority that determines an employee's preferential rights to various economic advantages at the expense of other employees. These normally include the order of layoff and recall of employees, job and trip assignments, and consideration for promotion.

It is true, of course, that the retroactive grant of competitive-type seniority does go a step further in "making whole" the discrimination victim, and therefore arguably furthers one of the objectives of Title VII. But apart from extending the make-whole concept to its outer limits, there is no similarity between this drastic relief and the granting of backpay and benefit-type seniority. First, a retroactive grant of competitive-type seniority usually does not directly affect the employer at all. It causes only a rearrangement of employees along the seniority ladder without any resulting increase in cost. Thus, Title VII's "primary objective" of eradicating discrimination is not served at all, for the employer is not deterred from the practice.

The second, and in my view controlling, distinction between these types of relief is the impact on other workers. As noted above, the granting of backpay and of benefit-type seniority furthers the prophylactic and make-whole objectives of the statute without penalizing other workers. But competitive seniority benefits, as the term implies, directly implicate the rights and expectations of perfectly innocent employees. The economic benefits awarded discrimination victims would be derived not at the expense of the employer but at the expense of other workers. Putting it differently, those disadvantaged — sometimes to the extent of losing their jobs entirely — are not the wrongdoers who have no claim to the Chancellor's conscience, but rather are innocent third parties. . . .

## NOTES

1. The *Franks* trial court enjoined the discriminatory practices at issue. The Fifth Circuit has said that "absent clear and convincing proof of no reasonable probability of further noncompliance with the law a grant of injunctive relief is mandatory." James v. Stockham Valves & Fittings Co., 559 F.2d 310, 354 (5th Cir. 1977).

2. The trial court also awarded qualified discriminatees priority in filling vacant line-driver positions. If there has been disparate treatment discrimination, such relief is granted in the absence of special circumstances. Anderson v. Phillips Petroleum Co., 861 F.2d 631 (10th Cir. 1988); Cassino v. Reichhold Chems., Inc., 817 F.2d 1338 (9th Cir. 1987). Cases finding special circumstances include Ellis v. Ringgold School Dist., 832 F.2d 27 (3d Cir. 1987) (effective employment relationship now impossible), and Kamberos v. GTE Automatic Electric, Inc., 603 F.2d 598 (7th Cir. 1979) (discriminatee no longer qualified). If hiring practices have been invalidated for having a disparate impact, however, the court may not know the proper job qualifications. In such a case, the court may order the employer to develop job-related

standards and then to reconsider the discriminatee. Young v. Edgcomb Steel Co., 499 F.2d 97 (4th Cir. 1974). But if the court can determine that the discriminatee is qualified, it can order her to be hired for the next vacancy. Association Against Discrimination v. City of Bridgeport, 647 F.2d 256 (2d Cir. 1981). To compensate the discriminatee for losses while awaiting employment, the court can also award "front pay."

3. Rather than making the discriminatee wait for a vacancy, should the court require the employer to discharge the employee who wrongfully obtained the position? The courts are nearly unanimous in refusing to displace a present jobholder. E.g., Walsdorf v. Board of Commrs., 857 F.2d 1047 (5th Cir. 1988); Harper v. General Grocers Co., 590 F.2d 713 (8th Cir. 1979); but see Lander v. Lujan, 888 F.2d 153 (D.C. Cir. 1989). This policy has even been invoked to overturn a displacement order that contained a provision requiring the employer not to reduce the wages of the displaced employee. Patterson v. American Tobacco Co., 535 F.2d 257 (4th Cir. 1976). Displacement has been ordered, however, in truly exceptional cases, such as when the incumbent employee was hired in violation of the court's orders. E.g., Walters v. City of Atlanta, 803 F.2d 1135 (11th Cir. 1986); Spagnuolo v. Whirlpool Corp., 717 F.2d 114 (4th Cir. 1983). Does the burden-sharing philosophy of *Franks* support the nondisplacement rule?

4. Although *Franks* established a presumption in favor of seniority relief, its remedial philosophy differs markedly from that expressed in *Albemarle Paper Co.* The latter opinion grandly spoke of granting "complete justice" and said that courts have "the duty to render a decree which will so far as possible eliminate the discriminatory effects of the past. . . ." *Franks*, on the other hand, emphasized that the seniority relief sought in that case "in no sense constitutes 'complete relief'" because it did not grant the class members the seniority positions they would have had in the absence of discrimination. Moreover, *Franks* thought the discriminatees and the nondiscriminatee employees should share the burden of past discrimination. What caused this change in attitude? Was it recognition that granting "complete relief" would have drastically impinged on the seniority rights of innocent employees? Do you agree with this approach?

5. As a result of the burden-sharing philosophy, the discriminatees may be denied full retroactive seniority and priority in hiring. Romasanta v. United Air Lines, 717 F.2d 1140 (7th Cir. 1983), considered reinstatement and seniority relief for 1,400 flight attendants who left United because of its "no-marriage" rule. The district court had (1) denied immediate reinstatement, (2) awarded each claimant noncompetitive seniority, and (3) awarded each claimant competitive seniority equal to the period she had been employed prior to her separation. This award treated the claimants like other employees who had been furloughed and who were eligible for recall as their competitive seniority permitted. The appellate court began by detailing United's financial distress and noting that United had not hired a flight attendant since 1979. The court then analyzed *Franks* as permitting denial of full retroactive seniority when such an award would have an "unusual adverse impact" on incumbent and furloughed employees. The court found that the plaintiffs' preferred awards, including immediate reinstatement with full seniority and reinstatement as openings occur with full seniority, would result in present employees being furloughed, being transferred to other cities, being discharged, or losing their recall rights. The appellate court concluded that the trial judge had not abused his discretion.

6. Can a court award academic tenure to a discriminatee? In Kunda v. Muhlenberg College, 621 F.2d 532 (3d Cir. 1980), an instructor was denied tenure because she lacked an advanced degree. The district court, finding that she would have done

everything possible to obtain the degree if she, like the male instructors, had been counseled as to its significance, ordered the college to grant her tenure if she obtained the degree within two years. A divided appellate court affirmed, emphasizing that the lower court had not made an evaluative judgment because the college had already concluded that her teaching, scholarship, and public service were satisfactory. In a subsequent decision, Gurmankin v. Costanzo, 626 F.2d 1115 (3d Cir. 1980), the same court affirmed the denial of a tenure award to a blind applicant who was denied a teaching position in violation of § 1983 because the school district had not evaluated her qualifications and performance as a teacher. Should the courts be more hesitant to award academic tenure than retroactive seniority? See Brown v. Boston Univ., 891 F.2d 337 (1st Cir. 1989).

7. If a candidate for partnership is denied because of sex discrimination, can the candidate be granted a partnership, even though sex discrimination in partnerships is not prohibited by Title VII? See Price Waterhouse v. Hopkins, 737 F. Supp. 1202 (D.D.C. 1990).

## 2. Retroactive Seniority and Backpay

The awarding of retroactive seniority and backpay in systemic discrimination cases can pose a difficult problem. Typically, a large number of persons have experienced various acts of discrimination that have extended over a long period of time and have involved numerous employment decisions. Must the court determine the precise injuries suffered by each class member when a simpler and less burdensome alternative would provide substantial justice? What if individual determinations are highly impractical because of the factual complexities of the case?

In the following case, the circuit court approved a method for awarding constructive seniority that avoided the need for individual determinations. However, the award was overturned because it was not individualized.

### TEAMSTERS v. UNITED STATES
#### 431 U.S. 324 (1977)

Justice STEWART delivered the opinion of the Court. . . .

I

The United States brought an action in a Tennessee federal court against the petitioner, T.I.M.E.-D.C., Inc. (company), pursuant to § 707(a). . . .

The central claim . . . was that the company had engaged in a pattern or practice of discriminating against minorities in hiring so-called line drivers. Those Negroes and Spanish-surnamed persons who had been hired, the Government alleged, were given lower paying, less desirable jobs as servicemen or local city drivers, and were thereafter discriminated against with respect to promotions and transfers. . . .

The Court of Appeals [agreed] that the company had engaged in a pattern or practice of employment discrimination. . . . [T]he Court of Appeals held that all Negro and Spanish-surnamed incumbent employees were entitled to bid for future line-driver jobs on the basis of their company seniority, and that once a class member had filled a job, he could use his full company seniority — even if it predated the effective date of Title VII — for all purposes, including bidding and layoff. . . .

## III

[The Supreme Court held that the evidence established a pattern or practice of discrimination. It also held that individual post-Act discriminatees "may obtain full 'make-whole' relief, including retroactive seniority, but such seniority may not begin before the effective date of Title VII." The Court then turned to the relief awarded below.]

The petitioners argue generally that the . . . Court of Appeals' [seniority relief] sweeps with too broad a brush by granting a remedy to employees who were not shown to be actual victims of unlawful discrimination. Specifically, the petitioners assert that no employee should be entitled to relief until the Government demonstrates that he was an actual victim of the company's discriminatory practices; [and] that no employee who did not apply for a line-driver job should be granted retroactive competitive seniority. . . .

### A

The petitioners' first contention is in substance that the Government's burden of proof in a pattern or practice case must be equivalent to that outlined in McDonnell Douglas v. Green [reproduced at page 97]. Since the Government introduced specific evidence of company discrimination against only some 40 employees, they argue that the District Court properly refused to award retroactive seniority to the remainder of the class of minority incumbent employees. . . .

In Franks v. Bowman Transportation Co. [reproduced at page 966], the . . . plaintiffs proved, to the satisfaction of a district court, that Bowman Transportation Company "had engaged in a pattern of racial discrimination in various company policies, including the hiring, transfer, and discharge of employees." Despite this showing, the trial court denied seniority relief to certain members of the class of discriminatees because not every individual had shown that he was qualified for the job he sought and that a vacancy had been available. We held that the trial court had erred in placing this burden on the individual plaintiffs. By "demonstrating the existence of a discriminatory hiring pattern and practice," the plaintiffs had made out a prima facie case of discrimination against individual class members; the burden therefore shifted to the employer "to prove that individuals who reapply were not in fact victims of previous hiring discrimination." The Franks case thus illustrates another means by which a Title VII plaintiff's initial burden of proof can be met. The class there alleged a broad-based policy of employment discrimination; upon proof of that allegation there were reasonable grounds to infer that individual hiring decisions were made in pursuit of the discriminatory policy and to require the employer to come forth with evidence dispelling that inference.[45]

45. The holding in Franks that proof of a discriminatory pattern and practice creates a rebuttable presumption in favor of individual relief is consistent with the manner in which presumptions are created generally. Presumptions shifting the burden of proof are often created to reflect judicial evaluations of probabilities and to conform with a party's superior access to the proof. These factors were present in Franks. Although the prima facie case did not conclusively demonstrate that all of the employer's decisions were part of the proved discriminatory pattern and practice, it did create a greater likelihood that any single decision was a component of the overall pattern. Moreover, the finding of a pattern or practice changed the position of the employer to that of a proved wrongdoer. Finally, the employer was in the best position to show why any individual employee was denied an employment opportunity. Insofar as the reasons related to available vacancies or the employer's evaluation of the applicant's qualifications, the company's records were the most relevant items of proof. If the refusal to hire was based on other factors, the employer and its agents knew best what those factors were and the extent to which they influenced the decision making process.

Although not all class actions will necessarily follow the *Franks* model, the nature of a pattern-or-practice suit brings it squarely within our holding in *Franks.* . . .

. . . Without any further evidence from the Government, a court's finding of a pattern or practice justifies an award of prospective relief. Such relief might take the form of an injunctive order against continuation of the discriminatory practice, an order that the employer keep records of its future employment decisions and file periodic reports with the court, or any other order "necessary to ensure the full enjoyment of the rights" protected by Title VII.

When the Government seeks individual relief for the victims of the discriminatory practice, a district court must usually conduct additional proceedings after the liability phase of the trial to determine the scope of individual relief. The petitioners' contention in this case is that if the Government has not, in the course of proving a pattern or practice, already brought forth specific evidence that each individual was discriminatorily denied an employment opportunity, it must carry that burden at the second, "remedial" stage of trial. That basic contention was rejected in the *Franks* case. As was true of the particular facts in *Franks*, and as is typical of Title VII pattern-or-practice suits, the question of individual relief does not arise until it has been proved that the employer has followed an employment policy of unlawful discrimination. The force of that proof does not dissipate at the remedial stage of the trial. The employer cannot, therefore, claim that there is no reason to believe that its individual employment decisions were discriminatorily based; it has already been shown to have maintained a policy of discriminatory decisionmaking.

The proof of the pattern or practice supports an inference that any particular employment decision, during the period in which the discriminatory policy was in force, was made in pursuit of that policy. The Government need only show that an alleged individual discriminatee unsuccessfully applied for a job and therefore was a potential victim of the proved discrimination. As in *Franks*, the burden then rests on the employer to demonstrate that the individual applicant was denied an employment opportunity for lawful reasons. . . .

On remand, therefore, every post-Act minority group applicant for a line-driver position will be presumptively entitled to relief, subject to a showing by the company that its earlier refusal to place the applicant in a line-driver job was not based on its policy of discrimination.

### B

The Court of Appeals' . . . relief did not distinguish between incumbent employees who had applied for line-driver jobs and those who had not. . . . The company contends that a grant of retroactive seniority to . . . nonapplicants is inconsistent with the make-whole purpose of a Title VII remedy and impermissibly will require the company to give preferential treatment to employees solely because of their race. The thrust of the company's contention is that unless a minority-group employee actually applied for a line-driver job, either for initial hire or for transfer, he has suffered no injury from whatever discrimination might have been involved in the refusal of such jobs to those who actually applied for them. . . .

. . . We now decide that an incumbent employee's failure to apply for a job is not an inexorable bar to an award of retroactive seniority. Individual nonapplicants must be given an opportunity to undertake their difficult task of proving that they should be treated as applicants and therefore are presumptively entitled to relief accordingly.

*(1)*

[I]n Albemarle Paper Co. v. Moody [reproduced at page 941], the Court noted that a primary objective of Title VII is prophylactic: to achieve equal employment opportunity and to remove the barriers that have operated to favor white male employees over other employees. The prospect of retroactive relief for victims of discrimination serves this purpose by providing the "'spur or catalyst which causes employers and unions to self-examine and to self-evaluate their employment practices and to endeavor to eliminate, so far as possible, the last vestiges'" of their discriminatory practices. An equally important purpose of the Act is "to make persons whole for injuries suffered on account of unlawful employment discrimination." . . .

Thus, . . . the purpose of Congress in vesting broad equitable powers in Title VII courts was "to make possible the 'fashion[ing] [of] the most complete relief possible,'" and . . . the district courts have "'not merely the power but the duty to render a decree which will so far as possible eliminate the discriminatory effects of the past as well as bar like discrimination in the future.'" More specifically, in *Franks* we decided that a court must ordinarily award a seniority remedy unless there exist reasons for denying relief "'which, if applied generally, would not frustrate the central statutory purposes of eradicating discrimination . . . and making persons whole for injuries suffered.'"

Measured against these standards, the company's assertion that a person who has not actually applied for a job can never be awarded seniority relief cannot prevail. The effects of and the injuries suffered from discriminatory employment practices are not always confined to those who were expressly denied a requested employment opportunity. A consistently enforced discriminatory policy can surely deter job applications from those who are aware of it and are unwilling to subject themselves to the humiliation of explicit and certain rejection.

If an employer should announce his policy of discrimination by a sign reading "Whites Only" on the hiring-office door, his victims would not be limited to the few who ignored the sign and subjected themselves to personal rebuffs. The same message can be communicated to potential applicants more subtly but just as clearly by an employer's actual practices — by his consistent discriminatory treatment of actual applicants, by the manner in which he publicizes vacancies, his recruitment techniques, his responses to casual or tentative inquiries, and even by the racial or ethnic composition of that part of his workforce from which he has discriminatorily excluded members of minority groups. When a person's desire for a job is not translated into a formal application solely because of his unwillingness to engage in a futile gesture he is as much a victim of discrimination as is he who goes through the motions of submitting an application. . . .

The denial of Title VII relief on the ground that the claimant had not formally applied for the job could exclude from the Act's coverage the victims of the most entrenched forms of discrimination. Victims of gross and pervasive discrimination could be denied relief precisely because the unlawful practices had been so successful as totally to deter job applications from members of minority groups. A per se prohibition of relief to nonapplicants could thus put beyond the reach of equity the most invidious effects of employment discrimination — those that extend to the very hope of self-realization. . . .

*(2)*

To conclude that a person's failure to submit an application for a job does not inevitably and forever foreclose his entitlement to seniority relief under Title VII is a far cry, however, from holding that nonapplicants are always entitled to such relief. A nonapplicant must show that he was a potential victim of unlawful discrimination. Because he is necessarily claiming that he was deterred from applying for the job by the employer's discriminatory practices, his is the not always easy burden of proving that he would have applied for the job had it not been for those practices. When this burden is met, the nonapplicant is in a position analogous to that of an applicant and is entitled to the presumption discussed in Part III-A, supra.

The Government contends that the evidence it presented in this case at the liability stage of the trial identified all nonapplicants as victims of unlawful discrimination "with a fair degree of specificity." . . . It further argues that since the class of nonapplicant discriminatees is limited to incumbent employees, it is likely that every class member was aware of the futility of seeking a line-driver job and was therefore deterred from filing both an initial and a follow-up application.

We cannot agree. While the scope and duration of the company's discriminatory policy can leave little doubt that the futility of seeking line-driver jobs was communicated to the company's minority employees, that in itself is insufficient. The known prospect of discriminatory rejection shows only that employees who wanted line-driving jobs may have been deterred from applying for them. It does not show which of the nonapplicants actually wanted such jobs, or which possessed the requisite qualifications.[53] There are differences between city- and line-driving jobs, for example, but the desirability of the latter is not so self-evident as to warrant a conclusion that all employees would prefer to be line drivers if given a free choice. Indeed, a substantial number of white city drivers who were not subjected to the company's discriminatory practices were apparently content to retain their city jobs.

In order to fill this evidentiary gap, the Government argues that a nonapplicant's current willingness to transfer into a line-driver position confirms his past desire for the job. An employee's response to the court-ordered notice of his entitlement to relief demonstrates, according to this argument, that the employee would have sought a line-driver job when he first became qualified to fill one, but for his knowledge of the company's discriminatory policy.

This assumption falls short of satisfying the appropriate burden of proof. An employee who transfers into a line-driver unit is normally placed at the bottom of the seniority "board." He is thus in jeopardy of being laid off and must, at best, suffer through an initial period of bidding on only the least desirable runs. Nonapplicants who chose to accept the appellate court's post hoc invitation, however, would enter the line-driving unit with retroactive seniority dating from the time they were first qualified. A willingness to accept the job security and bidding power afforded by retroactive seniority says little about what choice an employee would have made had he previously been given the opportunity freely to choose a starting line-driver job. While it may be true that many of the nonapplicant employees desired and would have applied for line-driver jobs but for their knowledge of the company's policy of discrimination, the Government must carry its burden of proof, with respect to each

53. Inasmuch as the purpose of the nonapplicant's burden of proof will be to establish that his status is similar to that of the applicant, he must bear the burden of coming forward with the basic information about his qualifications that he would have presented in an application. As in *Franks*, and in accord with Part III-A, supra, the burden then will be on the employer to show that the nonapplicant was nonetheless not a victim of discrimination. For example, the employer might show that there were other, more qualified persons who would have been chosen for a particular vacancy, or that the nonapplicant's stated qualifications were insufficient.

specific individual, at the remedial hearings to be conducted by the District Court on remand.[58] . . .

## NOTES

1. To escape liability to a class applicant who was denied a line-driver position, does the employer have to prove that (1) discrimination was not a factor in his rejection; (2) discrimination was not the "but for" factor in his rejection; or (3) it would have rejected him in the absence of discrimination? Does the employer have to satisfy the preponderance of the evidence or the clear and convincing evidence standard? Berger v. Iron Workers, Local 201, 170 F.3d 1111 (D.C. Cir. 1999). Are these questions now answered for Title VII and Title I cases by § 706(g)(2)(B)?

2. Is the *Teamsters* burden-shifting procedure applicable in disparate impact cases? If so, suppose the class member had been denied a position because she had failed a written examination that had a disparate impact. Could the employer satisfy its burden by showing that she had later failed a written job-related test? See Cohen v. West Haven Bd., 638 F.2d 496 (2d Cir. 1980); Rodriguez v. Taylor, 569 F.2d 1231 (3d Cir. 1977). By showing that she had later refused to take a written job-related test?

3. Suppose two employees were discriminatorily denied transfer to a vacant position that was filled by a third employee, but the court cannot determine who would have received the position in the absence of discrimination. Are both claimants entitled to a constructive seniority award? What should be done regarding backpay — full, partial, or no awards? Doll v. Brown, 75 F.3d 1200 (7th Cir. 1996), considers whether each victim should receive the percentage of a backpay award that corresponds to the chance he had to obtain the position (say, 33 percent). See also Taxman v. Board of Educ., 91 F.3d 1547 (3d Cir. 1996). The courts think the employer's liability cannot exceed the amount of backpay that could have been lost, that is, "one backpay award." E.g., United States v. City of Miami, 195 F.3d 1292 (11th Cir. 1999); Dougherty v. Barry, 869 F.2d 605 (D.C. Cir. 1989). Are these cases consistent with *Teamsters?*

4. Assume a company has discriminated in hiring, job assignments, and transfers, but has a bona fide departmental seniority system. Does *Teamsters* prohibit an order allowing the victims of those practices to use their post-Act company seniority when they transfer to new jobs? Some courts think not. Pettway v. American Cast Iron Pipe Co., 576 F.2d 1157 (5th Cir. 1978); EEOC v. United Air Lines, Inc., 560 F.2d 224 (7th Cir. 1977). Do you agree?

5. *Teamsters* rejected the argument that a non-applicant's present desire to become a line driver establishes that he would have sought the position earlier, but for the discrimination. This argument was accepted in EEOC v. United Air Lines, Inc., supra, because the decree, rather than awarding transferees retroactive seniority for all purposes, awarded retroactive seniority for layoff and recall purposes, but not for purposes of shift assignments, promotions, and longevity pay. Is this a persuasive distinction?

6. Hameed v. Iron Workers, Local 396, 637 F.2d 506 (8th Cir. 1980), recognized that backpay should be awarded to a class pursuant to the *Teamsters* methodology

---

58. While the most convincing proof would be some overt act such as a pre-Act application for a line-driver job, the District Court may find evidence of an employee's informal inquiry, expression of interest, or even unexpressed desire credible and convincing. The question is a factual one for determination by the trial judge.

wherever possible, but found that factual complexities and uncertainties precluded individualized awards in the case before it. Therefore, the court concluded that a classwide backpay award could be made. It said the award should equal the difference between the class's actual earnings and the earnings the class would have had in the absence of discrimination. The amount should then be divided among the class members on an equitable basis. See also Pettway v. American Cast Iron Pipe Co., 494 F.2d 211 (5th Cir. 1974).

### 3.   Affirmative Action Relief

Affirmative action relief is a classwide remedy for systemic discrimination that requires the employer to take specified action that benefits the discriminatee class. Such relief can take a variety of forms, from requiring the employer to advertise employment openings in a newspaper to requiring the employer to have a specified percentage of minority or women employees by a certain date. The form of such relief depends on the purposes the court wishes to accomplish. Among the purposes affirmative action relief can serve are (1) preventing future discrimination by the employer; (2) dissipating the continuing effects of the employer's discrimination; (3) expanding future employment opportunities for the discriminatees; (4) providing an incentive for the employer to develop nondiscriminatory employment criteria; and (5) compensating the discriminatees for the employer's discrimination.

In the cases that follow, the Supreme Court considered the validity of affirmative action relief that established a numerical goal or quota based on race. The relief was challenged as inconsistent with Title VII and prohibited by the Constitution.

### LOCAL 28, SHEET METAL WORKERS' INTERNATIONAL ASSOCIATION v. EEOC
#### 478 U.S. 421 (1986)

Justice BRENNAN announced the judgment of the Court and delivered the opinion of the Court with respect to Parts I, II, III, and VI, and an opinion with respect to Parts IV, V, and VII in which Justice Marshall, Justice Blackmun, and Justice Stevens join.

In 1975, petitioners were found guilty of engaging in a pattern and practice of discrimination against black and Hispanic individuals (nonwhites) in violation of Title VII . . . and ordered to end their discriminatory practices, and to admit a certain percentage of nonwhites to union membership by July 1982. In 1982 and again in 1983, petitioners were found guilty of civil contempt for disobeying the District Court's earlier orders. They now challenge the District Court's contempt finding, and also the remedies the court ordered both for the Title VII violation and for contempt. . . .

[Among the district court's actions challenged by the petitioners are orders approving the affirmative action plan with the membership goal and establishing a fund for the purpose of increasing non-white union membership. The membership goal, as revised, requires the union to have a percentage of minority members (29.23 percent) equal to the minority percentage in the labor pool by August 1987. The fund is for such activities as recruiting, creating jobs, and providing tutorial, counselling, and financial support services and is financed by a contempt fine against the union and payments from the union for each hour worked by union members.]

IV

Petitioners, joined by the Solicitor General, argue that the membership goal, the Fund order, and other orders which require petitioners to grant membership preferences to nonwhites are expressly prohibited by § 706(g), which defines the remedies available under Title VII. Petitioners and the Solicitor General maintain that § 706(g) authorizes a district court to award preferential relief only to the actual victims of unlawful discrimination.

They maintain that the membership goal and the Fund violate this provision, since they require petitioners to admit to membership, and otherwise to extend benefits to black and Hispanic individuals who are not the identified victims of unlawful discrimination. We reject this argument, and hold that § 706(g) does not prohibit a court from ordering, in appropriate circumstances, affirmative race-conscious relief as a remedy for past discrimination. Specifically, we hold that such relief may be appropriate where an employer or a labor union has engaged in persistent or egregious discrimination, or where necessary to dissipate the lingering effects of pervasive discrimination.

A

[P]etitioners and the Solicitor General argue that the last sentence of § 706(g) prohibits a court from ordering an employer or labor union to take affirmative steps to eliminate discrimination which might incidentally benefit individuals who are not the actual victims of discrimination. This reading twists the plain language of the statute.

The last sentence of § 706(g) prohibits a court from ordering a union to admit an individual who was "refused admission . . . for any reason other than discrimination." It does not, as petitioners and the Solicitor General suggest, say that a court may order relief only for the actual victims of past discrimination. The sentence on its face addresses only the situation where a plaintiff demonstrates that a union (or an employer) has engaged in unlawful discrimination, but the union can show that a particular individual would have been refused admission even in the absence of discrimination, for example because that individual was unqualified. . . .

B

The availability of race-conscious affirmative relief under § 706(g) as a remedy for a violation of Title VII also furthers the broad purposes underlying the statute. Congress enacted Title VII based on its determination that racial minorities were subject to pervasive and systematic discrimination in employment. . . . In order to foster equal employment opportunities, Congress gave the lower courts broad power under § 706(g) to fashion "the most complete relief possible" to remedy past discrimination.

In most cases, the court need only order the employer or union to cease engaging in discriminatory practices, and award make-whole relief to the individuals victimized by those practices. In some instances, however, it may be necessary to require the employer or union to take affirmative steps to end discrimination effectively to enforce Title VII. Where an employer or union has engaged in particularly long-standing or egregious discrimination, an injunction simply reiterating Title VII's prohibition against discrimination will often prove useless and will only result in endless enforcement litigation. In such cases, requiring recalcitrant employers or unions to hire and to admit qualified minorities roughly in proportion to the number of qualified minorities in the work force may be the only effective way to ensure the full enjoyment of the rights protected by Title VII.

Further, even where the employer or union formally ceases to engage in discrimination, informal mechanisms may obstruct equal employment opportunities. An employer's reputation for discrimination may discourage minorities from seeking available employment. In these circumstances, affirmative race-conscious relief may be the only means available "to assure equality of employment opportunities and to eliminate those discriminatory practices and devices which have fostered racially stratified job environments to the disadvantage of minority citizens." . . .

C

Despite the fact that the plain language of § 706(g) and the purposes of Title VII suggest the opposite, petitioners and the Solicitor General maintain that the legislative history indicates that Congress intended that affirmative relief under § 706(g) benefit only the identified victims of past discrimination. To support this contention, petitioners and the Solicitor General rely principally on statements made throughout the House and Senate debates to the effect that Title VII would not require employers or labor unions to adopt quotas or preferences that would benefit racial minorities.

Our examination of the legislative history of Title VII convinces us that, when examined in context, the statements relied upon by petitioners and the Solicitor General do not indicate that Congress intended to limit relief under § 706(g) to that which benefits only the actual victims of unlawful discrimination. . . .

. . . Our task then is to determine whether Congress intended to preclude a district court from ordering affirmative action in appropriate circumstances as a remedy for past discrimination. Our examination of the legislative policy behind Title VII leads us to conclude that Congress did not intend to prohibit a court from exercising its remedial authority in that way.[37] Congress deliberately gave the district courts broad authority under Title VII to fashion the most complete relief possible to eliminate "the last vestiges of an unfortunate and ignominious page in this country's history." As we noted above, affirmative race-conscious relief may in some instances be necessary to accomplish this task. In the absence of any indication that Congress intended to limit a district court's remedial authority in a way which would frustrate the court's ability to enforce Title VII's mandate, we decline to fashion such a limitation ourselves. . . .

D

Finally, petitioners and the Solicitor General find support for their reading of § 706(g) in several of our decisions applying that provision. . . .

Petitioners claim to find their strongest support in Firefighters v. Stotts, 467 U.S. 561 (1984). In Stotts, the city of Memphis, Tennessee had entered into a consent

37. We also reject petitioners' argument that the District Court's remedies contravened § 703(j), since they require petitioners to grant preferential treatment to blacks and Hispanics based on race. Our examination of the legislative history convinces us that § 703(j) was added to Title VII to make clear that an employer or labor union does not engage in "discrimination" simply because of a racial imbalance in its workforce or membership, and would not be required to institute preferential quotas to avoid Title VII liability. . . . We reject the notion that § 703(j) somehow qualifies or proscribes a court's authority to order relief otherwise appropriate under § 706(g) in circumstances where an illegal discriminatory act or practice is established.

decree requiring affirmative steps to increase the proportion of minority employees in its Fire Department. Budgetary cuts subsequently forced the city to lay off employees; under the city's last-hired, first-fired seniority system, many of the black employees who had been hired pursuant to the consent decree would have been laid off first. These employees sought relief, and the District Court, concluding that the proposed layoffs would have a racially discriminatory effect, enjoined the city from applying its seniority policy "insofar as it will decrease the percentage of black[s] that are presently employed." We held that the District Court exceeded its authority. . . .

[W]e concluded that the District Court's order conflicted with § 703(h) of Title VII, which "permits the routine application of a seniority system absent proof of an intention to discriminate." Since the District Court had found that the proposed layoffs were not motivated by a discriminatory purpose, we held that the court erred in enjoining the city from applying its seniority system in making the layoffs.

We also rejected the Court of Appeals' suggestion that the District Court's order was justified by the fact that, had plaintiffs prevailed at trial, the court could have entered an order overriding the city's seniority system. Relying on Teamsters v. United States, 421 U.S. 324 (1977), we observed that a court may abridge a bona fide seniority system in fashioning a Title VII remedy only to make victims of intentional discrimination whole, that is, a court may award competitive seniority to individuals who show that they had been discriminated against. However, because none of the firefighters protected by the court's order was a proven victim of illegal discrimination, we reasoned that at trial the District Court would have been without authority to override the city's seniority system, and therefore the court could not enter such an order merely to effectuate the purposes of the consent decrees.

While not strictly necessary to the result, we went on to comment that "[o]ur ruling in *Teamsters* that a court can award competitive seniority only when the beneficiary of the award has actually been a victim of illegal discrimination is consistent with the policy behind § 706(g)" which, we noted, "is to provide 'make-whole' relief only to those who have been actual victims of illegal discrimination." Relying on this language, petitioners, joined by the Solicitor General, argue that both the membership goal and the Fund order contravene the policy behind § 706(g) since they extend preferential relief to individuals who were not the actual victims of illegal discrimination. We think this argument both reads *Stotts* too broadly and ignores the important differences between *Stotts* and this case.

*Stotts* discussed the "policy" behind § 706(g) in order to supplement the holding that the District Court could not have interfered with the city's seniority system in fashioning a Title VII remedy. This "policy" was read to prohibit a court from awarding make-whole relief, such as competitive seniority, back-pay, or promotion, to individuals who were denied employment opportunities for reasons unrelated to discrimination. The District Court's injunction was considered to be inconsistent with this "policy" because it was tantamount to an award of make-whole relief (in the form of competitive seniority) to individual black firefighters who had not shown that the proposed layoffs were motivated by racial discrimination. However, this limitation on *individual* make-whole relief does not affect a court's authority to order race-conscious affirmative action. The purpose of affirmative action is not to make identified victims whole, but rather to dismantle prior patterns of employment discrimination and to prevent discrimination in the future. Such relief is provided to the class as a whole rather than to individual members; no individual is entitled to relief, and beneficiaries need not show that they were themselves victims of discrimination. . . . We decline petitioners' invitation to read *Stotts* to prohibit a court from ordering any kind of race-conscious affirmative relief that might benefit nonvictims. This reading would distort the language of § 706(g), and would deprive the courts of an important means of enforcing Title VII's guarantee of equal employment opportunity.

### E

Although we conclude that § 706(g) does not foreclose a district court from instituting some sorts of racial preferences where necessary to remedy past discrimination, we do not mean to suggest that such relief is always proper. While the fashioning of "appropriate" remedies for a particular Title VII violation invokes the "equitable discretion of the district courts," we emphasize that a court's judgment should be guided by sound legal principles. In particular, the court should exercise its discretion with an eye towards Congress' concern that race-conscious affirmative measures not be invoked simply to create a racially balanced work force. In the majority of Title VII cases, the court will not have to impose affirmative action as a remedy for past discrimination, but need only order the employer or union to cease engaging in discriminatory practices and award make-whole relief to the individuals victimized by those practices. However, in some cases, affirmative action may be necessary in order effectively to enforce Title VII. As we noted before, a court may have to resort to race-conscious affirmative action when confronted with an employer or labor union that has engaged in persistent or egregious discrimination. Or, such relief may be necessary to dissipate the lingering effects of pervasive discrimination. Whether there might be other circumstances that justify the use of court-ordered affirmative action is a matter that we need not decide here. We note only that a court should consider whether affirmative action is necessary to remedy past discrimination in a particular case before imposing such measures, and that the court should also take care to tailor its orders to fit the nature of the violation it seeks to correct. In this case, several factors lead us to conclude that the relief ordered by the District Court was proper.

First, both the District Court and the Court of Appeals agreed that the membership goal and Fund order were necessary to remedy petitioners' pervasive and egregious discrimination. The District Court set the original 29% membership goal upon observing that "[t]he record in both state and federal courts against [petitioners] is replete with instances of their bad faith attempts to prevent or delay affirmative action." . . . In light of petitioners' long history of "foot-dragging resistance" to court orders, simply enjoining them from once again engaging in discriminatory practices would clearly have been futile. . . .

Both the membership goal and Fund order were similarly necessary to combat the lingering effects of past discrimination. In light of the District Court's determination that the union's reputation for discrimination operated to discourage nonwhites from even applying for membership, it is unlikely that an injunction would have been sufficient to extend to nonwhites equal opportunities for employment. Rather, because access to admission, membership, training, and employment in the industry had traditionally been obtained through informal contacts with union members, it was necessary for a substantial number of nonwhite workers to become members of the union in order for the effects of discrimination to cease. . . .

Second, the District Court's flexible application of the membership goal gives strong indication that it is not being used simply to achieve and maintain racial balance, but rather as a benchmark against which the court could gauge petitioners' efforts to remedy past discrimination. The court has twice adjusted the deadline for achieving the goal, and has continually approved of changes in the size of the apprenticeship classes to account for the fact that economic conditions prevented petitioners from meeting their membership targets; there is every reason to believe that both the court and the administrator will continue to accommodate *legitimate* explanations for the petitioners' failure to comply with the court's orders. . . . In sum, the District Court has implemented the membership goal as a means by which it can measure petitioners' compliance with its orders, rather than as a strict racial quota.

Third, both the membership goal and the Fund order are temporary measures. Under [the affirmative action plan] "[p]referential selection of union members [w]ill end as soon as the percentage of [minority union members] approximates the percentage of [minorities] in the local labor force." Similarly, the Fund is scheduled to terminate when petitioners achieve the membership goal, and the court determines that it is no longer needed to remedy past discrimination. . . .

Finally, we think it significant that neither the membership goal nor the Fund order "unnecessarily trammel the interests of white employees." Petitioners concede that the District Court's orders did not require any member of the union to be laid off, and did not discriminate against existing union members. While whites seeking admission into the union may be denied benefits extended to their nonwhite counterparts, the court's orders do not stand as an absolute bar to such individuals. . . .

## VII

To summarize our holding today, six members of the Court agree that a district court may, in appropriate circumstances, order preferential relief benefiting individuals who are not the actual victims of discrimination as a remedy for violations of Title VII, see supra, Part IV-A-D (opinion of Brennan, J., joined by Marshall, J., Blackmun, J., and Stevens, J.); (Powell, J., concurring in part and concurring in the judgment); (White, J., dissenting). . . . Five members of the Court agree that in this case . . . the membership goal and the Fund order are not violative of either Title VII or the Constitution, see supra, Parts IV-E, V (opinion of BRENNAN, J., joined by MARSHALL, J., BLACKMUN, J., and STEVENS, J.); (POWELL, J., concurring in part and concurring in the judgment). The judgment of the Court of Appeals is hereby Affirmed.

[The concurring opinion of Justice POWELL is omitted.]

Justice O'CONNOR, concurring in part and dissenting in part.

. . . I would reverse the judgment of the Court of Appeals on statutory grounds insofar as the membership "goal" and the Fund order are concerned. . . .

In Firefighters v. Stotts, the Court interpreted § 706(g) as embodying a policy against court-ordered remedies under Title VII that award racial preferences in employment to individuals who have not been subjected to unlawful discrimination. The dissenting opinion in *Stotts* urged precisely the position advanced by Justice Brennan's plurality opinion today — that any such policy extends only to awarding make-whole relief to particular non-victims of discrimination, and does not bar class-wide racial preferences in certain cases. The Court unquestionably rejected that view in *Stotts*. Although technically dicta, the discussion of § 706(g) in *Stotts* was an important part of the Court's rationale for the result it reached. . . .

. . . Even assuming that some forms of race-conscious affirmative relief, such as racial hiring goals, are permissible as remedies for egregious and pervasive violations of Title VII, in my view the membership "goal" and fund order in this case were impermissible because they operate not as goals but as racial quotas. Such quotas run counter to § 703(j) of Title VII, and are thus impermissible under § 706(g) when that section is read in light of § 703(j), as I believe it should be. . . .

. . . It is important to realize that the membership "goal" ordered by the District Court goes well beyond a requirement, such as the ones the plurality discusses approvingly, that a union "admit qualified minorities roughly in proportion to the number of qualified minorities in the work force." The "goal" here requires that the racial composition of Local 28's entire membership mirror that of the relevant labor pool by August 31, 1987, without regard to variables such as the number of qualified minority applicants available or the number of new apprentices needed. . . .

Justice WHITE, dissenting.

As the Court observes, the general policy under Title VII is to limit relief for racial discrimination in employment practices to actual victims of the discrimination. But I agree that § 706(g) does not bar relief for nonvictims in all circumstances. Hence, I generally agree with Parts I through IV-D of the Court's opinion. It may also be that this is one of those unusual cases where nonvictims of discrimination were entitled to a measure of the relief ordered by the District Court and affirmed by the Court of Appeals. But Judge Winter, in dissent below, was correct in concluding that critical parts of the remedy ordered in this case were excessive under § 706(g), absent findings that those benefiting from the relief had been victims of discriminatory practices by the union. As Judge Winter explained and contrary to the Court's views, the cumulative effect of the revised affirmative action plan and the contempt judgments against the union established not just a minority membership goal but also a strict racial quota that the union was required to attain. . . .

Justice REHNQUIST, with whom The Chief Justice joins, dissenting.

Today, in Local Number 93 v. City of Cleveland[, 478 U.S. 501 (1986)], I express my belief that § 706(g) forbids a court from ordering racial preferences that effectively displace non-minorities except to minority individuals who have been the actual victims of a particular employer's racial discrimination. [T]he legislative history of § 706(g) clearly support[s] this reading of § 706(g), and . . . this Court stated as much just two Terms ago in Firefighters v. Stotts. . . .

## NOTES

1. The justices sharply disagreed on the meaning of the *Stotts* decision. In *Stotts*, Justice White, writing for the Court, had said:

> Our ruling in *Teamsters* that a court can award competitive seniority only when the beneficiary of the award has actually been a victim of illegal discrimination is consistent with the policy behind § 706(g). . . . That policy, which is to provide make-whole relief only to those who have been actual victims of illegal discrimination, was repeatedly expressed by the sponsors of the Act. . . . Senator Humphrey explained the limits on a court's remedial powers as follows:
>
> > No court order can require hiring, reinstatement, admission to membership, or payment of back pay for anyone who was not fired, refused employment or advancement or admission to a union by an act of discrimination forbidden by this title. . . . Contrary to the allegations of some opponents of this title, there is nothing in it that will give any power to the Commission or to any court to require . . . firing . . . of employees in order to meet a racial "quota" or to achieve a certain racial balance. . . .

Similar assurances concerning the limits on a court's authority to award make-whole relief were provided by supporters of the bill throughout the legislative process. For example, following passage of the bill in the House, its Republican House sponsors published a memorandum describing the bill. . . . [T]he memorandum stated: "Upon conclusion of the trial, the federal court may enjoin an employer or labor organization from practicing further discrimination and may order the hiring or reinstatement of an employee or the acceptance or reinstatement of a union member. *But Title VII does not permit the ordering of racial quotas in business or unions . . .*" [emphasis added]. In like manner, the principal Senate sponsors . . . explained that "[u]nder title VII, not even a Court, much less the Commission, could order racial quotas or the hiring, reinstatement, admission to membership or payment of backpay for anyone who is not discriminated against in violation of this title."

467 U.S. at 579-82. Justice Blackmun's dissenting opinion, in which Justices Brennan and Marshall joined, chided the majority for not recognizing that an order requiring a proportional layoff of black to white workers constitutes "race-conscious affirmative relief," as opposed to "individual relief." Can *Sheet Metal Workers'* and *Stotts* be reconciled?

2. Justice Brennan contrasted the minority membership goal imposed by the district court with an injunction that simply prohibits discrimination. He did not discuss another possible form of affirmative action relief: an order requiring future admittees to the union to be at least 29 percent minority. How do these three types of relief compare in their effectiveness in redressing past discrimination and preventing future discrimination and in their impact on nonminority applicants? Note that the membership goal effectively required the union to admit minority applicants at a rate substantially above 29 percent of new members.

3. Justice Brennan said the membership goal served to dissipate the effects of previous discrimination and to prevent future discrimination. What do you make of his failure to point out its compensatory aspect? Is compensation not a permissible purpose? If the membership goal has to be evaluated solely on the basis of the first two purposes, why wouldn't it have been sufficient to merely require 29 percent of future admittees to be minority persons?

4. Justice Brennan implies that a minority membership goal is appropriate only when there has been "persistent," "egregious," or "pervasive" discrimination. If a minority group has experienced discrimination, shouldn't members of the group be given preference in obtaining future openings as a matter of course? Does this apparent limitation also suggest that the only purposes of goals or quotas are to prevent future discrimination and to dissipate the effects of past discrimination?

5. Should the percentage figure for the membership goal have been based on the percentage of minority members the union would have had in 1987 if the union had ceased discriminating in 1965 (the effective date of Title VII), rather than on the percentage of minority workers in the labor pool on the date the order was entered? Cf. Hazelwood Sch. Dist. v. United States (reproduced at page 218). Are there reasons to suspect the first percentage would have been smaller?

6. *Sheet Metal Workers'* indicates that a minority goal must not unduly impinge on nonminority persons. Such a remedy might also be improper because it would adversely affect the discriminatees. Consider White v. Carolina Paperboard Corp., 564 F.2d 1073 (4th Cir. 1977), in which the court found racial discrimination in promotions to positions that lead to supervisory positions, but refused to impose a goal or quota for supervisory positions. The discriminatees were presently moving through the line of progression necessary to qualify them for supervisory positions. Not only

would such a quota not benefit them because they were presently unqualified, but also it would retard their attainment of supervisory positions because the company would be forced to bring in outside supervisors.

7.  See Kenneth R. Davis, Undo Hardship: An Argument for Affirmative Action as a Mandatory Remedy in Racial Discrimination Cases, 107 Dick. L. Rev. — (2003).

## UNITED STATES v. PARADISE
### 480 U.S. 149 (1987)

Justice BRENNAN announced the judgment of the Court and delivered an opinion in which Justice MARSHALL, Justice BLACKMUN, and Justice POWELL join.

The question we must decide is whether relief awarded in this case, in the form of a one-black-for-one-white promotion requirement to be applied as an interim measure to state trooper promotions in the Alabama Department of Public Safety (Department), is permissible under the Equal Protection guarantee of the Fourteenth Amendment.

In 1972 the United States District Court . . . held that the Department had systematically excluded blacks from employment in violation of the Fourteenth Amendment. Some 11 years later, confronted with the Department's failure to develop promotion procedures that did not have an adverse impact on blacks, the District Court ordered the promotion of one black trooper for each white trooper elevated in rank, as long as qualified black candidates were available, until the Department implemented an acceptable promotion procedure. . . .

### II

The United States maintains that the race-conscious relief ordered in this case violates the Equal Protection Clause of the Fourteenth Amendment to the Constitution of the United States.

It is now well established that government bodies, including courts, may constitutionally employ racial classifications essential to remedy unlawful treatment of racial or ethnic groups subject to discrimination. . . . But although this Court has consistently held that some elevated level of scrutiny is required when a racial or ethnic distinction is made for remedial purposes, it has yet to reach consensus on the appropriate constitutional analysis. We need not do so in this case, however, because we conclude that the relief ordered survives even strict scrutiny analysis: it is "narrowly tailored" to serve a "compelling governmental purpose."

The government unquestionably has a compelling interest in remedying past and present discrimination by a state actor. In 1972 the District Court found, and the Court of Appeals affirmed, that for almost four decades the Department had excluded blacks from all positions, including jobs in the upper ranks. Such egregious discriminatory conduct was "unquestionably a violation of the Fourteenth Amendment." As the United States concedes, the pervasive, systematic, and obstinate discriminatory conduct of the Department created a profound need and a firm justification for the race-conscious relief ordered by the District Court. . . .

### III

While conceding that the District Court's order serves a compelling interest, the Government insists that it was not narrowly tailored to accomplish its purposes — to remedy past discrimination and eliminate its lingering effects, to enforce compliance with the 1979 and 1981 Decrees by bringing about the speedy implementation of a promotion procedure that would not have an adverse impact on blacks, and to eradicate the ill effects of the Department's delay in producing such a procedure. We cannot agree.

In determining whether race-conscious remedies are appropriate, we look to several factors, including the necessity for the relief and the efficacy of alternative remedies; the flexibility and duration of the relief, including the availability of waiver provisions; the relationship of the numerical goals to the relevant labor market; and the impact of the relief on the rights of third parties. When considered in light of these factors, it was amply established, and we find that the one-for-one promotion requirement was narrowly tailored to serve its several purposes, both as applied to the initial set of promotions to the rank of corporal and as a continuing contingent order with respect to the upper ranks.


A

To evaluate the District Court's determination that it was *necessary* to order the promotion of eight whites and eight blacks to the rank of corporal . . . we must examine the purposes the order was intended to serve. First, the court sought to eliminate the effects of the Department's "long term, open, and pervasive" discrimination, including the absolute exclusion of blacks from its upper ranks. Second, the judge sought to ensure expeditious compliance with the 1979 and 1981 Decrees by inducing the Department to implement a promotion procedure that would not have an adverse impact on blacks. Finally, the court needed to eliminate so far as possible the effects of the Department's delay in producing such a procedure. Confronted by the Department's urgent need to promote at least 15 troopers to corporal, the District Court determined that all of its purposes could be served only by ordering the promotion of eight blacks and eight whites, as requested by the plaintiff class.

The options proffered by the Government and the Department would not have served the court's purposes. The Department proposed, as a stop-gap measure, to promote four blacks and eleven whites and requested additional time to allow the Department of Personnel to develop and submit a nondiscriminatory promotion procedure. The United States argues that the Department's proposal would have allowed this round of promotions to be made without adverse impact on black candidates.

The Department's proposal was inadequate because it completely failed to address two of the purposes cited above. The Department's ad hoc offer to make one round of promotions without an adverse impact ignored the court's concern that an acceptable procedure be adopted with alacrity. . . .

Moreover, the Department's proposal ignored the injury to the plaintiff class that resulted from its delay in complying with the terms of the 1972 order and the 1979 and 1981 Decrees. As the Fifth Circuit pointed out, no blacks were promoted between 1972 and 1979; the four blacks promoted in 1979 were elevated pursuant to the 1979 Decree and not as a result of the voluntary action of the Department; and, finally, the whites promoted *since 1972* "were the specific beneficiaries of an official policy which systematically excluded all blacks." To permit ad hoc decisionmaking to continue and allow only four of fifteen slots to be filled by blacks would have denied relief to black troopers who had irretrievably lost promotion opportunities. Thus, adoption of the Department's proposal would have fallen far short of the remedy necessary to eliminate the effects of the Department's past discrimination, would not have ensured adoption of a procedure without adverse impact, and would not have vitiated the effects of the defendant's delay. . . .

### B

The features of the one-for-one requirement and its actual operation indicate that it is flexible in application at all ranks. The requirement may be waived if no qualified black candidates are available. . . .

Most significantly, the one-for-one requirement is ephemeral; the term of its application is contingent upon the Department's own conduct. The requirement endures only until the Department comes up with a procedure that does not have a discriminatory impact on blacks — something the Department was enjoined to do in 1972 and expressly promised to do by 1980. . . . [T]he court has taken into account the difficulty of validating a test and does not require validation as a prerequisite for suspension of the promotional requirement. . . .

### C

We must also examine the relationship between the numerical relief ordered and the percentage of nonwhites in the relevant workforce. . . . The enforcement order at issue here . . . requires the Department to promote 50% black candidates until 25% of the rank in question is black, but *only* until a promotion procedure without an adverse impact on blacks is in place. Thus, had the promotion order remained in effect for the rank of corporal, it would have survived only until 25% of the Department's corporals were black.

The Government suggests that the one-for-one requirement is arbitrary because it bears no relationship to the 25% minority labor pool relevant here. This argument ignores that the 50% figure is not itself the goal; rather it represents the speed at which the goal of 25% will be achieved. The interim requirement of one-for-one promotion (had it continued) would simply have determined how quickly the Department progressed toward this ultimate goal. . . .

To achieve the goal of 25% black representation in the upper ranks, the court was not limited to ordering the promotion of only 25% blacks at any one time. Some promptness in the administration of relief was plainly justified in this case, and use of deadlines or end-dates had proven ineffective. In these circumstances, the use of a temporary requirement of 50% minority promotions . . . was constitutionally permissible. . . .

It would have been improper for the District Judge to ignore the effects of the Department's delay and its continued default of its obligation to develop a promotion procedure, and to require only that, commencing in 1984, the Department promote one black for every three whites promoted. The figure selected to compensate for past discrimination and delay necessarily involved a delicate calibration of the rights and interests of the plaintiff class, the Department and the white troopers. The Government concedes that a one-to-three requirement would have been lawful; the District Court determined that more stringent measures were necessary. This Court should not second-guess the lower court's carefully considered choice of the figure necessary to achieve its many purposes, especially when that figure is hedged about with specific qualifying measures designed to prevent any unfair impact that might arise from rigid application.[32]

32. The dissent suggests that the percentage of minority individuals benefitted by this race-conscious remedial order should not exceed the percentage of minority group members in the relevant population

D

The one-for-one requirement did not impose an unacceptable burden on innocent third parties. As stated above, the temporary and extremely limited nature of the requirement substantially limits any potential burden on white applicants for promotion. . . .

The one-for-one requirement does not require the layoff and discharge of white employees. . . . Because the one-for-one requirement is so limited in scope and duration, it only postpones the promotions of qualified whites. . . .

IV

The remedy imposed here is an effective, temporary and flexible measure. It applies only if qualified blacks are available, only if the Department has an objective need to make promotions, and only if the Department fails to implement a promotion procedure that does not have an adverse impact on blacks. . . .

Justice STEVENS, concurring in the judgment.

. . . In this case, the record discloses an egregious violation of the Equal Protection Clause. It follows, therefore, that the District Court had broad and flexible authority to remedy the wrongs resulting from this violation — exactly the opposite of the Solicitor General's unprecedented suggestion that the judge's discretion is constricted by a "narrowly tailored to achieve a compelling governmental interest" standard. . . .

A party who has been found guilty of repeated and persistent violations of the law bears the burden of demonstrating that the chancellor's efforts to fashion effective relief exceed the bounds of "reasonableness." The burden of proof in a case like this is precisely the opposite of that in cases such as Wygant v. Jackson Board of Education, 476 U.S. 267 (1986), which did not involve any proven violations of law. In such cases the governmental decisionmaker who would make race-conscious decisions must overcome a strong presumption against them. No such burden rests on a federal district judge who has found that the governmental unit before him is guilty of racially discriminatory conduct that violates the Constitution. . . .

The District Court . . . may, and in some instances must, resort to race-conscious remedies to vindicate federal constitutional guarantees. . . .

[The concurring opinion of Justice POWELL and the dissenting opinion of Justice WHITE have been omitted.]

Justice O'CONNOR with whom The Chief Justice and Justice SCALIA join, dissenting.

. . . Because the Federal Government has a compelling interest in remedying past and present discrimination by the Department, the District Court unquestionably had the authority to fashion a remedy designed to end the Department's egregious history of discrimination. In doing so, however, the District Court was obligated to fashion a remedy that was narrowly tailored to accomplish this purpose. The Court today purports to apply strict scrutiny, and concludes that the order in this case was

or work force. We disagree. Even within the narrow confines of strict scrutiny, there remains the requirement that the district court not only *refrain* from ordering relief that violates the Constitution, but also that it *order* the relief necessary to cure past violations and to obtain compliance with its mandate. There will be cases — this is one — where some accelerated relief is plainly justified. To say that it is not overlooks the history of this litigation.

narrowly tailored for its remedial purpose. Because the Court adopts a standardless view of "narrowly tailored" far less stringent than that required by strict scrutiny, I dissent. . . .

. . . The order at issue in this case clearly had one purpose, and one purpose only — to compel the Department to develop a promotion procedure that would not have an adverse impact on blacks. . . . The order imposed the promotion quota only until the Department developed a promotion procedure that complied with the consent decrees. If the order were truly designed to eradicate the effects of the Department's delay, the District Court would certainly have continued the use of the one-for-one quota even after the Department had complied with the consent decrees. . . .

Moreover, even if the one-for-one quota had the purpose of eradicating the effects of the Department's delay, this purpose would not justify the quota imposed in this case. . . . The one-for-one promotion quota used in this case far exceeded the percentage of blacks in the trooper force, and there is no evidence in the record that such an extreme quota was necessary to eradicate the effects of the Department's delay. The Court attempts to defend this one-for-one promotion quota as merely affecting the speed by which the Department attains the goal of 25% black representation in the upper ranks. Such a justification, however, necessarily eviscerates any notion of "narrowly tailored" because it has no stopping point; even a 100% quota could be defended on the ground that it merely "determined how quickly the Department progressed toward" some ultimate goal. If strict scrutiny is to have any meaning, therefore, a promotion goal must have a closer relationship to the percentage of blacks eligible for promotions. This is not to say that the percentage of minority individuals benefited by a racial goal may never exceed the percentage of minority group members in the relevant work force. But protection of the rights of nonminority workers demands that a racial goal not substantially exceed the percentage of minority group members in the relevant population or work force absent compelling justification. . . .

. . . The District Court had available several alternatives that would have achieved full compliance with the consent decrees without trammeling on the rights of nonminority troopers. The court, for example, could have appointed a trustee to develop a promotion procedure that would satisfy the terms of the consent decrees. . . . Alternatively, the District Court could have found the recalcitrant Department in contempt of court, and imposed stiff fines or other penalties for the contempt. Surely, some combination of penalties could have been designed that would have compelled compliance with the consent decrees.

The District Court, however, did not discuss these options or *any* other alternatives to the use of a racial quota. . . . What is most disturbing about the District Court's order, therefore, is not merely that it implicitly rejected two particular options, but that the District Court imposed the promotion *without consideration of any of the available alternatives.* . . . Without any exploration of the available alternatives in the instant case, no [evaluation of the quota's necessity] is possible. Remarkably, however, the Court — purporting to apply "strict scrutiny" — concludes that the order in this case was narrowly tailored for a remedial purpose. . . .

## NOTES

1. *Paradise* involved an interim goal or quota, that is, a ratio that expires when either a nondiscriminatory employment procedure or an affirmative action plan is

judicially approved. An interim goal should be contrasted with the long-range membership goal at issue in *Sheet Metal Workers*. How do the purposes of these goals differ? Should the trial court be given more deference when interim, rather than long-range, relief is at issue?

2. Compare *Paradise* with *Sheet Metal Workers*. Does Title VII or the Equal Protection Clause impose greater limitations on affirmative action relief involving racial goals? Is this also true for affirmative action relief that redresses sex, age, or disability discrimination? Recall that strict scrutiny analysis is applicable to remedial racial classifications. Adarand Constructors v. Pena, reproduced at page 303. In omitted portions of the *Sheet Metal Workers* opinions, the Court upheld the constitutionality of the long-term membership goal. The reasoning was essentially the same as in *Paradise*.

3. *Paradise* expressly recognized that race-conscious relief may be used to compensate for past discrimination by providing the class with a greater share of promotions than it would obtain under neutral criteria. Is this equitable as between minority and nonminority employees? From a group perspective, a minority group illegally denied its rightful share of promotions should receive a preference in obtaining future promotions over the nonminority group that benefitted from the illegal action. From an individual perspective, however, discrimination should not be redressed by according an employee who was not an actual victim of that discrimination a racial preference over an employee who was not responsible for and did not benefit from that discrimination. Should the equities be viewed from either a group or an individual perspective? See generally Donald P. Judges, Light Beams and Particle Dreams: Rethinking the Individual vs. Group Rights Paradigm in Affirmative Action, 44 Ark. L. Rev. 1007 (1991).

4. Justice O'Connor's opinion questions whether a compensatory goal is ever necessary either to compensate past injuries or to prevent future discrimination. In a case like *Sheet Metal Workers*, for example, a court can award membership, backpay, front pay, and compensatory and punitive damages to actual victims; impose a minority goal on future admissions to union membership and appoint a trustee to oversee the union's compliance; and perhaps require the backpay and front pay lost by unidentified discriminatees, as well as a share of any punitive damages, to be used to promote employment opportunities for the discriminatee group. Would this solution provide adequate compensatory and prospective relief to the discriminatees with only negligible impact on nonminority applicants?

5. How much discretion does the trial court have in choosing appropriate equitable relief? Justice Brennan, in footnote 32, referred to "the requirement that the district court . . . order the relief necessary to cure past violations and to obtain compliance with its mandate." Should the *Paradise* district court have imposed long-range promotion goals in addition to requiring a nondiscriminatory promotion procedure? See Kilgo v. Bowman Transp., Inc., 789 F.2d 859 (11th Cir. 1986). Isn't it clear that Justice Brennan would not have upheld an order that simply prohibited future discrimination?

6. After *Sheet Metal Workers*, *Paradise*, and *Adarand Constructors*, constitutional challenges to affirmative action relief focus on the "narrowly tailored" requirement. In Newark Branch, NAACP v. Town of Harrison, 940 F.2d 792 (3d Cir. 1991), a town ordinance provided that only town residents were eligible for a civil service position. After finding that the ordinance had a disparate impact on blacks and the town had a marked racial imbalance in its employees, the district court ordered the town to recruit and employ qualified blacks in proportion to their availability in the labor market.

On appeal, the town argued that this relief was broader than necessary to redress the violation and the court should have simply enjoined enforcement of the ordinance. The appellate court disagreed, saying the district court's decree was properly designed to redress the racial imbalance in the town's workforce. Is this correct? If the number of blacks who were excluded by the ordinance had been known, shouldn't the decree have been limited to this number? Should the town also have argued that *Sheet Metal Workers'* does not permit such relief for a single disparate impact violation? Affirmative action relief was overturned in Carter v. Gallagher, 452 F.2d 315 (8th Cir. 1972) (en banc), where the trial court, finding pervasive discrimination, ordered a fire department to fill the next 20 vacancies with minority members. The court held that this "absolute preference" violated the constitutional rights of nonminority applicants. Is *Carter* consistent with *Paradise*?

## D.   CALCULATION OF BACKPAY

Each antidiscrimination statute permits the recovery of income lost due to the employer's discrimination. The backpay award includes all the compensation the discriminatee would have received in the absence of discrimination — lost wages, raises, overtime compensation, bonuses, vacation pay, and retirement benefits. E.g., United States v. Burke, 504 U.S. 229 (1992); Pettway v. American Cast Iron Pipe Co., 494 F.2d 211 (5th Cir. 1974). However, the award is reduced by amounts that were and reasonably could have been earned and is limited to a defined period of time.

The statutory provision governing the recovery of backpay under Title VII is § 706(g)(1), 42 U.S.C.S. § 2000e-5(g)(1) (2003):

> If the court finds that the respondent has intentionally engaged in or is intentionally engaging in an unlawful employment practice . . . the court may enjoin the respondent . . . and order such affirmative action as may be appropriate, which may include, but is not limited to, reinstatement or hiring of employees, with or without back pay (payable by the employer, employment agency, or labor organization, as the case may be, responsible for the unlawful employment practice), or any other equitable relief as the court deems appropriate. . . .

This provision also applies to Title I actions, 42 U.S.C.S. § 12117(a) (2003).

The statutes provide little guidance on how the amount of a backpay award is to be calculated. The ADEA, Title II, and § 1981 contain no relevant provision. Section 706(g)(1), 42 U.S.C.S. § 2000e-5(g)(1) (2003), however, has two provisions that govern backpay awards in Title VII and Title I actions. One provides that "[b]ack pay liability shall not accrue from a date more than two years prior to the filing of a charge with the Commission." The other states that "[i]nterim earnings or amounts earnable with reasonable diligence . . . shall operate to reduce the backpay otherwise allowable."

As suggested by these provisions, the calculation of backpay frequently presents problems concerning the beginning or ending date of the backpay period and the discriminatee's duty to mitigate damages.

## 1.  *The Backpay Period*

The beginning date of the backpay period is normally the date the discriminatee first lost wages due to the discrimination in issue. E.g., Welborn v. Reynolds Metals Co., 868 F.2d 389 (11th Cir. 1989). This may or may not be the same date the discriminatory act occurred for purposes of the EEOC filing period. In fact, the backpay period frequently begins after the date of the discriminatory act. For example, a plaintiff who was discriminatorily denied employment that would have started three months later would have a backpay period that begins three months after the date of the discriminatory act.

When there has been continuing discrimination over a period of years, however, the backpay period may not begin as early as the date the discriminatee first experienced a wage loss due to the discrimination. For example, suppose a woman was paid less than a man because of her sex for three years before she filed an EEOC charge. Under the two-year provision in § 706(g)(1), her backpay period would begin two years before the date on which she filed the charge, a year after her wage loss began.

The precise operation of the § 706(g)(1) two-year limitation is illustrated by Verzosa v. Merrill Lynch, Pierce, Fenner & Smith, Inc., 589 F.2d 974 (9th Cir. 1978). After being denied promotion to account executive in both 1970 and 1973, a clerk filed an EEOC charge in August 1973. Finding a continuing violation from 1970 through 1973, the court awarded backpay beginning in August 1971, which it calculated as the difference between the employee's salary as a clerk and the salary an average account executive would have received if he had attained the position in 1970. Note that the two-year limitation did not preclude consideration of the effect the 1970 discrimination had on the employee's losses during 1971 and later years: it simply foreclosed recovery for his losses prior to August 1971. But see White v. Carolina Paperboard Corp., 564 F.2d 1073 (4th Cir. 1977).

Although § 1981 and Title II do not contain a limitation on the beginning of the backpay period, the applicable statute of limitations provides such a limitation. As explained earlier (see pages 833-834), § 1981 is subject to the most analogous state statute of limitations, which precludes recovery of wages lost prior to the statutory period. E.g., Skinner v. Total Petroleum, Inc., 859 F.2d 1439 (10th Cir. 1988). Title II is probably also subject to the most analogous state limitation period. See Andrews v. Consolidated Rail Corp., 831 F.2d 678 (7th Cir. 1987). These limitations periods are measured from the date suit was filed in court, as opposed to the date when an EEOC charge was filed, as in Title VII and Title I actions.

A more difficult problem is presented, however, by continuing violation claims under the ADEA. Prior to the 1991 Amendments, § 7(e), 29 U.S.C.S. § 626(e) (2003), contained a provision that incorporated the statute of limitations in § 6(a) of the Portal-to-Portal Act, 29 U.S.C.S. § 255(a) (2003). The repeal of this provision leaves no obvious limitation period on ADEA lost wages claims. There are four possible solutions. The courts are most likely to apply either the two-year provision in § 706(g)(1) as the best indication of congressional intent, cf. DelCostello v. International Bhd. of Teamsters, 462 U.S. 151 (1983), or the most analogous state statute of limitations, as in § 1981 actions. The other two possible solutions — enforcing no limitations period on backpay claims and limiting such claims to the EEOC filing period — seem too extreme to be adopted.

The backpay period normally ends on the date of judgment. E.g., Walsdorf v. Board of Commrs., 857 F.2d 1047 (5th Cir. 1988). But as seen by the after-acquired evidence doctrine, the backpay period can end before this date. If, for example, the discriminatee has died or would have been permanently laid off prior to the date of judgment, the backpay period ends on the date his employment would have ceased. Berger v. Iron Workers, Local 201, 170 F.3d 1111 (D.C. Cir. 1999). More controversially, the backpay period may also end on the date the discriminatee either resigned his or her position with the defendant or rejected the defendant's offer of employment.

## FORD MOTOR CO. v. EEOC
### 458 U.S. 219 (1982)

Justice O'CONNOR delivered the opinion of the Court.

This case presents the question whether an employer charged with discrimination in hiring can toll the continuing accrual of backpay liability under § 706(g) of Title VII simply by unconditionally offering the claimant the job previously denied, or whether the employer also must offer seniority retroactive to the date of the alleged discrimination. . . .

### I

In June and July 1971, Judy Gaddis, Rebecca Starr, and Zettie Smith applied at a Ford Motor Company (Ford) parts warehouse located in Charlotte, North Carolina, for jobs as "picker-packers." . . . Gaddis and Starr recently had been laid off from equivalent jobs at a nearby General Motors (GM) warehouse, and Smith had comparable prior experience. . . . Ford, however, [discriminatorily] filled the three vacant positions with men. . . .

In January 1973, [GM] recalled Gaddis and Starr to their former positions at its warehouse. The following July, while they were still working at GM, a single vacancy opened up at Ford. Ford offered the job to Gaddis, without seniority retroactive to her 1971 application. Ford's offer, however, did not require Gaddis to abandon or compromise her Title VII claim against Ford. Gaddis did not accept the job, in part because she did not want to be the only woman working at the warehouse, and in part because she did not want to lose the seniority she had earned at [GM]. Ford then made the same unconditional offer to Starr, who declined for the same reasons. . . . [In 1974, Gaddis and Starr were again laid off by GM.]

[The Court of Appeals concluded that Ford's 1973 offer was "incomplete and unacceptable" without retroactive seniority and that Gaddis and Starr were entitled to backpay from 1971 through the 1977 trial.]

### III

[T]he legal rules fashioned to implement Title VII should be designed, consistent with other Title VII policies, to encourage Title VII defendants promptly to make curative, unconditional job offers to Title VII claimants, thereby bringing defendants into "voluntary compliance" and ending discrimination far more quickly than could litigation proceeding at its often ponderous pace. Delays in litigation unfortunately are now commonplace, forcing the victims of discrimination to suffer years of underemployment or unemployment before they can obtain a court order awarding them the jobs unlawfully denied them. . . .

The rule tolling the further accrual of backpay liability if the defendant offers the claimant the job originally sought well serves the objective of ending discrimination through voluntary compliance, for it gives an employer a strong incentive to hire the Title VII claimant. While the claimant may be no more attractive than the other job applicants, a job offer to the claimant will free the employer of the threat of liability for further backpay damages. Since paying backpay damages is like paying an extra worker who never came to work, Ford's proposed rule gives the Title VII claimant a decided edge over other competitors for the job he seeks.

The rule adopted by the court below, on the other hand, fails to provide the same incentive, because it makes hiring the Title VII claimant more costly than hiring one of the other applicants for the same job. To give the claimant retroactive seniority before an adjudication of liability, the employer must be willing to pay the additional costs of the fringe benefits that come with the seniority that newly hired workers usually do not receive. More important, the employer must also be prepared to cope with the deterioration in morale, labor unrest, and reduced productivity that may be engendered by inserting the claimant into the seniority ladder over the heads of the incumbents who have earned their places through their work on the job. In many cases, moreover, disruption of the existing seniority system will violate a collective bargaining agreement, with all that such a violation entails for the employer's labor relations. . . .

## IV

Title VII's primary goal, of course, is to end discrimination; the victims of job discrimination want jobs, not lawsuits. But when unlawful discrimination does occur, Title VII's secondary, fallback purpose is to compensate the victims for their injuries. To this end, §706(g) aims "'to make the victims of unlawful discrimination whole'" by restoring them, "'so far as possible . . . to a position where they would have been were it not for the unlawful discrimination.'" We now turn to consider whether the rule urged by Ford not only better serves the goal of ending discrimination, but also properly compensates injured Title VII claimants.

### A

If Gaddis and Starr had rejected an unconditional offer from Ford before they were recalled to their jobs at GM, tolling Ford's backpay liability from the time of Ford's offer plainly would be consistent with providing Gaddis and Starr full compensation for their injuries. An unemployed or underemployed claimant, like all other Title VII claimants, is subject to the statutory duty to minimize damages set out in §706(g). This duty, rooted in an ancient principle of law, requires the claimant to use reasonable diligence in finding other suitable employment. Although the un- or underemployed claimant need not go into another line of work, accept a demotion, or take a demeaning position, he forfeits his right to backpay if he refuses a job substantially equivalent to the one he was denied. Consequently, an employer charged with unlawful discrimination often can toll the accrual of backpay liability by unconditionally offering the claimant the job he sought, and thereby providing him with an opportunity to minimize damages.[18]

An employer's unconditional offer of the job originally sought to an un- or underemployed claimant, moreover, need not be supplemented by an offer of retroactive

18. The claimant's obligation to minimize damages in order to retain his right to compensation does not require him to settle his claim against the employer, in whole or in part. Thus, an applicant or discharged employee is not required to accept a job offered by the employer on the condition that his claims against the employer be compromised.

seniority to be effective, lest a defendant's offer be irrationally disfavored relative to other employers' offers of substantially similar jobs. The claimant, after all, plainly would be required to minimize his damages by accepting another employer's offer even though it failed to grant the benefits of seniority not yet earned.[19] Of course, if the claimant fulfills the requirement that he minimize damages by accepting the defendant's unconditional offer, he remains entitled to full compensation if he wins his case. A court may grant him backpay accrued prior to the effective date of the offer, retroactive seniority, and compensation for any losses suffered as a result of his lesser seniority before the court's judgment.

In short, the un- or underemployed claimant's statutory obligation to minimize damages requires him to accept an unconditional offer of the job originally sought, even without retroactive seniority. Acceptance of the offer preserves, rather than jeopardizes, the claimant's right to be made whole; in the case of an un- or underemployed claimant, Ford's suggested rule merely embodies the existing requirement of § 706(g) that the claimant minimize damages, without affecting his right to compensation.

### B

Ford's proposed rule also is consistent with the policy of full compensation when the claimant has had the good fortune to find a more attractive job than the defendant's, because the availability of the better job terminates the ongoing ill effects of the defendant's refusal to hire the claimant. For example, if Gaddis and Starr considered their jobs at GM to be so far superior to the jobs originally offered by Ford that, even if Ford had hired them at the outset, they would have left Ford's employ to take the new work, continuing to hold Ford responsible for backpay after Gaddis and Starr lost their GM jobs would be to require, in effect, that Ford insure them against the risks of unemployment in a new and independent undertaking. Such a rule would not merely restore Gaddis and Starr to the "'position where they would have been were it not for the unlawful discrimination,'" it would catapult them into a better position than they would have enjoyed in the absence of discrimination.

Likewise, even if Gaddis and Starr considered their GM jobs only somewhat better or even substantially equivalent to the positions they would have held at Ford had Ford hired them initially, their rejection of Ford's unconditional offer could be taken to mean that they believed that the lingering ill effects of Ford's prior refusal to hire them had been extinguished by later developments. If, for example, they thought that the Ford and GM jobs were identical in every respect, offering identical pay, identical conditions of employment, and identical risks of layoff, Gaddis and Starr would have been utterly indifferent as to which job they had — Ford's or GM's. Assuming that they could work at only one job at a time, the ongoing economic ill effects caused by Ford's prior refusal to hire them would have ceased when they found the identical jobs at GM, and they would have had no reason to accept Ford's offers. As in the case of the claimant who lands a better job, therefore, requiring a defendant to provide what amounts to a form of unemployment insurance to claimants, after they have found identical jobs and refused the defendant's unconditional job offer, would be, absent special circumstances, to grant them something more than compensation for their injuries.

---

19. For the same reasons, a defendant's job offer is effective to force minimization of damages by an un- or underemployed claimant even without a supplemental offer of backpay. . . .

In both of these situations, the claimant has the power to accept the defendant's offer and abandon the superior or substantially equivalent replacement job. As in the
case of an un- or underemployed claimant, under the rule advocated by Ford acceptance of the defendant's unconditional offer would preserve fully the ultimately victo-
rious claimant's right to full redress for the effects of discrimination. The claimant
who chooses not to follow this path does so, then, not because it provides inadequate
compensation, but because the value of the replacement job outweighs the value
of the defendant's job supplemented by the prospect of full court-ordered compensation. In other words, the victim of discrimination who finds a better or substantially equivalent job no longer suffers ongoing injury stemming from the unlawful
discrimination.

C . . .

The sole question that can be raised regarding whether the rule adequately compensates claimants arises in that narrow category of cases in which the claimant believes his replacement job to be superior to the defendant's job without seniority, but
inferior to the defendant's job with the benefits of seniority. In the present case, for example, it is possible that Gaddis and Starr considered their GM jobs more attractive
than the jobs offered by Ford, but less satisfactory than the positions they would have
held at Ford if Ford had hired them initially. If so, they were confronted with two options. They could have accepted Ford's unconditional offer, preserving their right to
full compensation if they prevailed on their Title VII claims, but forfeiting their favorable positions at GM. Alternatively, they could have kept their jobs at GM, retaining the possibility of continued employment there, but, under the operation of the
rule advocated here by Ford, losing the right to claim further backpay from Ford after
the date of Ford's offer. The court below concluded that under these circumstances
Ford's rule would present Gaddis and Starr with an "intolerable choice," depriving
them of the opportunity to receive full compensation.
    We agree that Gaddis and Starr had to choose between two alternatives. We do not
agree, however, that their opportunity to choose deprived them of compensation. After all, they had the option of accepting Ford's unconditional offer and retaining the
right to seek full compensation at trial, which would comport fully with Title VII's
goal of making discrimination victims whole. Under the rule advocated by Ford, if
Gaddis and Starr chose the option of remaining at their GM jobs rather than accept
Ford's offer, it was because they thought that the GM jobs, plus their claims to backpay accrued prior to Ford's offer, were *more* valuable to them than the jobs they originally sought from Ford, plus the right to seek full compensation from the court. It is
hard to see how Gaddis and Starr could have been deprived of adequate compensation because they chose to venture upon a path that seemed to them more attractive
than the Ford job plus the right to seek full compensation in court. . . . Ford's rule
merely requires the Title VII claimant to decide whether to take the job offered by
the defendant, retaining his rights to an award by the court of backpay accrued prior
to the effective date of the offer, and any court-ordered retroactive seniority plus compensation for any losses suffered as a result of his lesser seniority before the court's
judgment, or, instead, whether to accept a more attractive offer from another employer and the limitation of the claim for backpay to the damages that have already
accrued. The rule urged by the EEOC and adopted by the court below, by contrast,
would have the perverse result of requiring the employer in effect to insure the
claimant against the risk that the employer might win at trial.

Therefore, we conclude that, when a claimant rejects the offer of the job he originally sought, as supplemented by a right to full court-ordered compensation, his choice can be taken as establishing that he considers the ongoing injury he has suffered at the hands of the defendant to have been ended by the availability of better opportunities elsewhere. For this reason, we find that, absent special circumstances,[27] the simple rule that the ongoing accrual of backpay liability is tolled when a Title VII claimant rejects the job he originally sought comports with Title VII's policy of making discrimination victims whole. . . .

Justice BLACKMUN, with whom Justice BRENNAN and Justice MARSHALL join, dissenting. . . .

. . . The Court's approach authorizes employers to . . . terminate their backpay liability unilaterally by extending to their discrimination victims offers they cannot reasonably accept. Once an employer has refused to hire a job applicant, and that applicant has mitigated damages by obtaining and accumulating seniority in another job, the employer may offer the applicant the same job that she was denied unlawfully several years earlier. In this very case, for example, Ford offered Gaddis and Starr jobs only after they had obtained employment elsewhere and only because they had filed charges with the EEOC. If, as here, the applicant declines the offer to preserve existing job security, the employer has successfully cut off all future backpay liability to the applicant. . . .

The Court's rule also violates Title VII's second objective — making victims of discrimination whole. . . . [I]f Gaddis and Starr had accepted those offers, they would not have been made whole. . . .

### NOTES

1. Were Gaddis's and Starr's backpay periods terminated on the dates they rejected Ford's offers because they failed to mitigate damages or because such termination furthered the purposes of Title VII? Wouldn't a violation of the duty to mitigate simply have required a reduction of their backpay awards by the amounts they earned at GM and any additional amounts they could have earned with reasonable diligence?

2. The Court recognized that the termination rule does not apply when there are "special circumstances," but provided little further guidance. The Eighth Circuit interprets this as meaning only that the rejection must have been reasonable. Smith v. World Ins. Co., 38 F.3d 1456 (8th Cir. 1994). Was Gaddis reasonable in not accepting Ford's offer because "she did not want to be the only woman working in the warehouse"? Apparently, the exception is most commonly invoked when there is "excessive hostility" between the parties. See Lewis v. Federal Prison Indus., 953 F.2d 1277 (11th Cir. 1992); Thorne v. City of El Segundo, 802 F.2d 1131 (9th Cir. 1986).

3. Does *Ford* imply that a discriminatee's acceptance of a higher-paying job with another employer also terminates the accrual of backpay from the discriminator employer? Some courts think so. E.g., Stephens v. C.I.T. Group, Inc., 955 F.2d 1023 (5th

---

27. If, for example, the claimant has been forced to move a great distance to find a replacement job, a rejection of the employer's offer might reflect the costs of relocation more than a judgment that the replacement job was superior, all things considered, to the defendant's job. In exceptional circumstances, the trial court, in the exercise of its sound discretion, could give weight to such factors when deciding whether backpay damages accrued after the rejection of an employer's offer should be awarded to the claimant. . . .

Cir. 1992). Is this fair to a discriminatee who loses that job prior to trial, considering that he was required to seek and accept such other employment? One decision applied this rule at the urging of the discriminatee. If the backpay period was so terminated, her higher earnings would not retroactively offset the defendant's backpay liability. Matthews v. A-1, Inc., 748 F.2d 975 (5th Cir. 1984). Was this fair to the defendant?

4. In commenting on the duty to minimize damages, the Court said a discriminatee is not required to "go into another line of work, accept a demotion, or take a demeaning position." The question of whether two positions are "substantially equivalent" is often difficult. In Sangster v. United Air Lines, Inc., 633 F.2d 864 (9th Cir. 1980), the court held that the stewardess supervisor position from which the discriminatee had resigned, a nonflight position with (apparently) fixed working hours, was substantially equivalent to her desired position as a stewardess, a flight position that would have permitted her to tailor her schedule to that of her husband, a pilot. But in Williams v. Albemarle City Bd. of Educ., 508 F.2d 1242 (4th Cir. 1974), the court held that it was not unreasonable for a former school principal, whose position had entailed no teaching responsibilities, to refuse a position as an assistant principal, which entailed 50 percent teaching. Was either case decided correctly?

5. The *Ford* circuit court of appeals had instructed the district court to consider whether Gaddis and Starr were entitled to instatement with retroactive seniority. Does the Supreme Court's rationale preclude this relief? See Smith v. World Ins. Co., 38 F.3d 1456 (8th Cir. 1994); Stanfield v. Answering Serv., Inc., 867 F.2d 1290 (11th Cir. 1989).

**McKENNON v. NASHVILLE BANNER
PUBLISHING CO.**
**513 U.S. 352 (1995)**

Justice KENNEDY delivered the opinion of the Court.

The question before us is whether an employee discharged in violation of the [ADEA] is barred from all relief when, after her discharge, the employer discovers evidence of wrongdoing that, in any event, would have led to the employee's termination on lawful and legitimate grounds. . . .

I

For some 30 years, petitioner Christine McKennon worked for respondent Nashville Banner Publishing Company. She was discharged, the Banner claimed, as part of a work force reduction plan necessitated by cost considerations. McKennon, who was 62 years old when she lost her job, thought another reason explained her dismissal: her age. She filed suit [seeking] a variety of legal and equitable remedies available under the ADEA, including backpay.

In preparation of the case, the Banner took McKennon's deposition. She testified that, during her final year of employment, she had copied several confidential documents bearing upon the company's financial condition. . . . McKennon took the copies home and showed them to her husband. Her motivation, she averred, was an apprehension she was about to be fired because of her age. When she became concerned about her job, she removed and copied the documents for "insurance" and "protection." A few days after these deposition disclosures, the Banner sent

McKennon a letter declaring that removal and copying of the records was in violation of her job responsibilities and advising her (again) that she was terminated. . . .

## II

We shall assume, as summary judgment procedures require us to assume, that the sole reason for McKennon's initial discharge was her age, a discharge violative of the ADEA. Our further premise is that the misconduct revealed by the deposition was so grave that McKennon's immediate discharge would have followed its disclosure in any event. The District Court and the Court of Appeals found no basis for contesting that proposition, and for purposes of our review we need not question it here. We do question the legal conclusion reached by those courts that after-acquired evidence of wrongdoing which would have resulted in discharge bars employees from any relief under the ADEA. That ruling is incorrect. . . .

The ADEA and Title VII share common substantive features and also a common purpose: "the elimination of discrimination in the workplace." Congress designed the remedial measures in these statutes to serve as a "spur or catalyst" to cause employers "to self-examine and to self-evaluate their employment practices and to endeavor to eliminate, so far as possible, the last vestiges" of discrimination. Deterrence is one object of these statutes. Compensation for injuries caused by the prohibited discrimination is another. . . . The private litigant who seeks redress for his or her injuries vindicates both the deterrence and the compensation objectives of the ADEA. It would not accord with this scheme if after-acquired evidence of wrongdoing that would have resulted in termination operates, in every instance, to bar all relief for an earlier violation of the Act.

The objectives of the ADEA are furthered when even a single employee establishes that an employer has discriminated against him or her. The disclosure through litigation of incidents or practices which violate national policies respecting nondiscrimination in the work force is itself important, for the occurrence of violations may disclose patterns of noncompliance resulting from a misappreciation of the Act's operation or entrenched resistance to its commands, either of which can be of industry-wide significance. The efficacy of its enforcement mechanisms becomes one measure of the success of the Act. . . .

In Mt. Healthy [City Bd. of Ed. v. Doyle, 429 U.S. 274 (1977)] we addressed a mixed-motives case, in which two motives were said to be operative in the employer's decision to fire an employee. One was lawful, the other (an alleged constitutional violation) unlawful. We held that if the lawful reason alone would have sufficed to justify the firing, the employee could not prevail in a suit against the employer. The case was controlled by the difficulty, and what we thought was the lack of necessity, of disentangling the proper motive from the improper one where both played a part in the termination and the former motive would suffice to sustain the employer's action.

That is not the problem confronted here. As we have said, the case comes to us on the express assumption that an unlawful motive was the sole basis for the firing. McKennon's misconduct was not discovered until after she had been fired. The employer could not have been motivated by knowledge it did not have and it cannot now claim that the employee was fired for the nondiscriminatory reason. Mixed motive cases are inapposite here, except to the important extent they underscore the necessity of determining the employer's motives in ordering the discharge, an essential element in determining whether the employer violated the federal antidiscrimination law. As we have observed, "proving that the same decision would have been justified . . . is not the same as proving that the same decision would have been made."

Our inquiry is not at an end, however, for even though the employer has violated the Act, we must consider how the after-acquired evidence of the employee's wrongdoing bears on the specific remedy to be ordered. Equity's maxim that a suitor who engaged in his own reprehensible conduct in the course of the transaction at issue must be denied equitable relief because of unclean hands, a rule which in conventional formulation operated *in limine* to bar the suitor from invoking the aid of the equity court, has not been applied where Congress authorizes broad equitable relief to serve important national policies. We have rejected the unclean hands defense "where a private suit serves important public purposes." That does not mean, however, the employee's own misconduct is irrelevant to all the remedies otherwise available under the statute. . . . In giving effect to the ADEA, we must recognize the duality between the legitimate interests of the employer and the important claims of the employee who invokes the national employment policy mandated by the Act. The employee's wrongdoing must be taken into account, we conclude, lest the employer's legitimate concerns be ignored. The ADEA, like Title VII, is not a general regulation of the workplace but a law which prohibits discrimination. The statute does not constrain employers from exercising significant other prerogatives and discretion in the course of the hiring, promoting, and discharging of their employees. In determining appropriate remedial action, the employee's wrongdoing becomes relevant not to punish the employee, or out of concern "for the relative moral worth of the parties," but to take due account of the lawful prerogatives of the employer in the usual course of its business and the corresponding equities that it has arising from the employee's wrongdoing.

The proper boundaries of remedial relief in the general class of cases where, after termination, it is discovered that the employee has engaged in wrongdoing . . . will vary from case to case. We do conclude that here, and as a general rule in cases of this type, neither reinstatement nor front pay is an appropriate remedy. It would be both inequitable and pointless to order the reinstatement of someone the employer would have terminated, and will terminate, in any event and upon lawful grounds.

The proper measure of backpay presents a more difficult problem. Resolution of this question must give proper recognition to the fact that an ADEA violation has occurred which must be deterred and compensated without undue infringement upon the employer's rights and prerogatives. The object of compensation is to restore the employee to the position he or she would have been in absent the discrimination, but that principle is difficult to apply with precision where there is after-acquired evidence of wrongdoing that would have led to termination on legitimate grounds had the employer known about it. Once an employer learns about employee wrongdoing that would lead to a legitimate discharge, we cannot require the employer to ignore the information, even if it is acquired during the course of discovery in a suit against the employer and even if the information might have gone undiscovered absent the suit. The beginning point in the trial court's formulation of a remedy should be calculation of backpay from the date of the unlawful discharge to the date the new information was discovered. In determining the appropriate order for relief, the court can consider taking into further account extraordinary equitable circumstances that affect the legitimate interests of either party. An absolute rule barring any recovery of backpay, however, would undermine the ADEA's objective of forcing employers to consider and examine their motivations, and of penalizing them for employment decisions that spring from age discrimination.

Where an employer seeks to rely upon after-acquired evidence of wrongdoing, it must first establish that the wrongdoing was of such severity that the employee in fact would have been terminated on those grounds alone if the employer had known of it at the time of the discharge. The concern that employers might as a routine matter undertake extensive discovery into an employee's background or performance on the job to resist claims under the Act is not an insubstantial one, but we think the authority of the courts to award attorney's fees, mandated under the statute, and in appropriate cases to invoke the provisions of Rule 11 of the Federal Rules of Civil Procedure will deter most abuses. . . .

### NOTES

1. In a private ADEA action like *McKennon*, the unpaid wages (or backpay) award is a legal remedy. Lorillard v. Pons, 434 U.S. 575 (1978). Yet the Court seems to treat the award as equitable. For example, the Court said:

> The beginning point in the trial court's formulation of a remedy should be calculation of backpay from the date of the unlawful discharge to the date new information was discovered. In determining the appropriate order for relief, the court can consider taking into further account equitable circumstances. . . .

After *McKennon*, how should a jury in an ADEA after-acquired evidence case be instructed on the availability and amount of backpay?

2. The Court carefully distinguished between the factual situation before it and a mixed-motives case. If McKennon had been discharged because of both her age and her misconduct, but she would have been discharged even if her age had not been considered, would she have been eligible for backpay? Would there be eligibility at all under the ADEA?

3. Suppose the employer had shown that McKennon obtained her position by a fraudulent resume or job application. Should the "would have been terminated" standard or a "would not have been hired" standard be used to calculate backpay? Shatluck v. Kinetic Concepts, 49 F.3d 1106 (5th Cir. 1995) (first standard).

4. *McKennon* is also applicable to backpay awards in Title VII actions. Wallace v. Dunn Const. Co., 62 F.3d 374 (11th Cir. 1995); Wehr v. Ryan's Family Steak Houses, Inc., 49 F.3d 1150 (6th Cir. 1995). Can compensatory and punitive damages be recovered in an after-acquired evidence case or is § 706(g)(2)(B) applicable?

## 2.   *The Duty to Mitigate Damages*

Section 706(g)(1), 42 U.S.C.S. § 2000e-5(g)(1) (2003), which is applicable in Title VII and Title I actions, requires the backpay award to be reduced by amounts that were earned and could have been earned with reasonable diligence. The same principle is applied in ADEA and § 1981 actions, even without explicit statutory authorization. E.g., Hansard v. Pepsi-Cola Metro. Bottling Co., 865 F.2d 1461 (5th Cir. 1989) (ADEA); Murphy v. City of Flagler Beach, 846 F.2d 1306 (11th Cir. 1988) (§ 1981). Undoubtedly, the principle will also be applied in Title II actions. See generally Howard C. Eglit, Damages Mitigation Doctrine in the Statutory Anti-Discrimination Context: Mitigating Its Negative Impact, 69 U. Cinc. L. Rev. 71 (2000).

The courts are not entirely consistent in allocating the evidentiary burdens on these issues. Most hold that the plaintiff must establish "her damages by measuring the difference between her actual earnings and those which she would have earned absent the discrimination." E.g., Kamberos v. GTE Automatic Elec., Inc., 603 F.2d 598, 602 (7th Cir. 1979). For example, a discriminatee who was denied employment or discharged must show the amount — or lack — of any interim earnings and the amount she would have earned from the defendant. The defendant, however, must show the amount the plaintiff could have earned with reasonable diligence. E.g., Sellers v. Delgado Community College, 839 F.2d 1132 (5th Cir. 1988). Most courts hold that this requires the defendant to show the existence of a comparable employment opportunity, the amount plaintiff would have earned in such employment, and that the plaintiff's lack of reasonable diligence caused her failure to secure such employment. E.g., Hutchison v. Amateur Elec. Supply, Inc., 42 F.3d 1037 (7th Cir. 1994). But a few recent decisions hold that to satisfy the employer need only show that the plaintiff made no effort whatever to find comparable employment, thus presuming that a reasonably diligent plaintiff would have obtained comparable employment. Quint v. A. E. Staley Mfg. Co., 172 F.3d 1 (1st Cir. 1999); Greenway v. Buffalo Hilton Hotel, 143 F.3d 47 (2d Cir. 1998). See also Giles v. GE, 245 F.3d 474 (5th Cir. 2001) (court has discretion to deny backpay where plaintiff fails to produce documentation of job search). Can it be true that a qualified person can always find a suitable job? Or is it likely to be true only in a booming economy?

The following case presents two mitigation issues. First, did the discriminatee violate the duty when he retired from his position with the defendant, or was he "constructively discharged"? Second, if the discriminatee violated the duty, should his backpay period end on the date of his retirement, or should the backpay award be reduced by the salary he relinquished?

## JURGENS v. EEOC
### 903 F.2d 386 (5th Cir. 1990)

SMITH, Circuit Judge:

This appeal arises from an employment discrimination action filed by a class of white male employees of the Equal Employment Opportunity Commission (EEOC) in 1976. In 1982, the district court ruled in favor of the plaintiff class. . . . The court subsequently appointed special masters to conduct hearings and make recommendations with respect to individual class members' claims for relief. In so doing, the court clarified,

> Awards of backpay, as appropriate to eligible claimants who have left EEOC, shall run at least through the date of termination of employment. To obtain backpay or other relief for any period of time following his termination or resignation, a claimant must establish a "nexus" between his termination or resignation and the discriminatory nonselection at issue.

Jules H. Gordon, a member of the plaintiff class, . . . brought his case before a special master in order to gain relief.

I

In November 1975, the EEOC promoted an Hispanic male, instead of Gordon, from the position of Assistant Regional Attorney (ARA) at the EEOC's San Francisco Regional Litigation Center to the position of Regional Attorney (RA). . . .

As an ARA in October 1978, Gordon was a grade GS-15 employee with an annual salary of $45,792 and set the legal policies and trial strategies for the cases handled by approximately seven to twelve attorneys. At this time, the EEOC began reorganizing its field offices and reducing its forces. The EEOC abolished the position of ARA but retained that of RA, though reduced in grade from a GS-16 to a GS-15 and assigned managerial responsibilities substantially equivalent to those of the former ARA.

As a part of this reorganization, the EEOC offered Gordon the choice of accepting (i) a demotion to the position of Supervisory Trial Attorney (STA), a non-management GS-14 position with supervision over only three to five attorneys, or (ii) an early retirement. . . . Gordon felt compelled to accept the EEOC's latter option, effective January 27, 1979. . . .

[T]he special master ultimately made the following recommendations, which the district court accepted with only a few slight modifications: (1) finding that the EEOC had discriminated against Gordon in denying him the 1975 promotion to RA; (2) awarding backpay from the time of the denial of the promotion until the effective date of his retirement; and (3) . . . refusing to award any backpay to compensate him for lost wages beyond the effective date of his retirement. . . .

II . . .

B

Gordon challenges the special master's ruling that, where an employer's discriminatory denial of a promotion ultimately results in a demotion that precipitates the employee's retirement (even though that demotion occurred as part of an intervening nondiscriminatory reduction in force), the employee, in order to receive backpay compensation for any time after his retirement, must still show (i) that his retirement was the result of objectively intolerable working conditions constituting a constructive discharge and (ii) that there is a sufficient nexus or causal link between the denial and the employee's subsequent resignation — i.e., that at the time of the denial, the employer reasonably could have foreseen that the employee would face such intolerable conditions forcing him to resign. Although Gordon does not contend that the EEOC acted in a discriminatory fashion with respect to its 1978-79 reorganization, he argues that, "but for" the EEOC's discriminatory denial of his promotion to the GS-16 RA position in 1975, he would not have been compelled to retire in 1979 because, at worst, he would have been demoted to the new GS-15 RA position.

In support of his contention that the law does not require him to show constructive discharge, Gordon cites a number of cases from other jurisdictions that, according to Gordon, suggest that the relevant inquiry is whether Gordon properly mitigated his damages by accepting early retirement, not whether he was constructively discharged. However, it is well settled in this circuit that, in order for an employee to recover backpay for lost wages beyond the date of his retirement or resignation, the evidence must establish that the employer constructively discharged the employee. See Bourque v. Powell Elec. Mfg. Co., 617 F.2d 61 (5th Cir. 1980).

We find no inconsistency in determining entitlement to such backpay, in some cases, by whether the employee properly mitigated damages after his retirement or resignation, and in other cases, involving denial of promotion, by whether the employee was constructively discharged. We simply hold, as we did in *Bourque*, that where an employer discriminatorily denies promotion to an employee, that employee's duty to mitigate damages encompasses remaining on the job.

C

Thus, we now consider whether Gordon was constructively discharged. In *Bourque*, we enunciated the constructive discharge standard:

> The general rule is that if the employer deliberately makes an employee's working conditions so intolerable that the employee is forced into an involuntary resignation, then the employer has encompassed a constructive discharge and is as liable for any illegal conduct involved therein as if it had formally discharged the aggrieved employee.

We specifically endorsed a reasonable-employee test: "To find constructive discharge we believe that 'the trier of fact must be satisfied that the . . . working conditions would have been so difficult or unpleasant that a reasonable person in the employee's shoes would have felt compelled to resign.'"

Proof is not required that the employer imposed these intolerable working conditions with the specific intent to force the employee to resign. See id. (acknowledging that a number of other circuits have endorsed such a strict standard). Finally, we noted that our constructive discharge standard supports the purposes of Title VII:

> [Plaintiff] contends, however, that to require employees suffering illegal discrimination to seek legal redress while remaining in their jobs would contravene the policies served by title VII because then only "foolhardy" victims would seek relief from discrimination. We disagree. Title VII itself accords legal protection to employees who oppose unlawful discrimination. Moreover, we believe that society and the policies underlying Title VII will be best served if, wherever possible, unlawful discrimination is attacked within the context of existing employment relationships.

In cases subsequent to *Bourque*, we explicitly have placed the burden on the employee to prove constructive discharge. . . . [U]nder *Bourque* an employee who resigns in response to a discriminatory denial of promotion is presumed to have mitigated damages insufficiently. . . .

D

A review of the specific facts of the instant case leads us to conclude that our finding, on substantially similar facts, of no constructive discharge as a matter of law in Jett v. Dallas Indep. School Dist., 798 F.2d 748 (5th Cir. 1986), *modified on other grounds*, 491 U.S. 701 (1989), should control the disposition of the case now before us. In *Jett* we stated the following:

> Jett [a high school teacher] tendered his resignation on August 19, 1983, stating that, after considering his assignment to Thomas Jefferson High School, he could not accept the position and felt "forced to resign from the public education field with much sorrow and humiliation." Jett argues that his significant loss in coaching responsibilities as well as the racial discrimination and the retaliation for his protected speech that prompted his reassignment amounted to a constructive discharge.
>
> Although a demotion or transfer in some instances may constitute a constructive discharge, we find that Jett's loss of coaching responsibilities was not so intolerable that a reasonable person would have felt compelled to resign. We have noted that constructive discharge cannot be based upon the employee's subjective preference for one position over another. . . . [W]e believe that Jett's new working conditions simply were not so difficult or so unpleasant that he had no choice but to resign. Moreover, the humiliation

and embarrassment that Jett suffered are not significant enough to support a constructive termination.

. . . For example, we have held that unlawful discrimination in the form of unequal pay may be relevant to a determination of constructive discharge, but alone cannot constitute such an aggravated situation that a reasonable employee would feel forced to resign. Jett has not shown any racial discrimination or free speech violations (or likelihood or threats thereof) subsequent to March 1983 that would constitute intolerable working conditions. Significantly, Jett resigned in August 1983 after receiving his assignment for the 1983-1984 school year, but did not resign in March 1983 after the reassignment that he claims violated his equal protection and free speech rights. We conclude that Jett was not constructively terminated from his employment with the DISD.

In light of the foregoing, we examine whether the special master properly found that the facts as alleged by Gordon are insufficient to support a finding of constructive discharge. . . . Gordon felt compelled to accept early retirement in 1979 primarily because he wanted to avoid the degradation of being demoted to a non-management position after holding a management position with the EEOC for nine years. Similarly, Jett alleged that the humiliation of being transferred to another school and removed from the posts of head coach and athletic director, positions he had held for thirteen years, compelled him to resign. Just as in *Jett,* a slight decrease in pay coupled with some loss of supervisory responsibilities is insufficient to constitute a constructive discharge of Gordon. . . .

Moreover, although it may well be true that Gordon would not have been demoted to the GS-14 STA position but for the earlier discriminatory denial of promotion, most of the humiliation and embarrassment that might ordinarily accompany a demotion were necessarily absent in Gordon's case, because the demotion was part of a *non-discriminatory* reorganization. . . .

We find no support in the case law for the proposition that a simple discriminatory denial of promotion that cannot be reasonably construed as a career-ending action can alone create such embarrassment or humiliation that the denial comprises a constructive discharge. As the special master found, the STA position, though subjectively undesirable to Gordon, was not inherently demeaning, especially when it was offered as part of a comprehensive, racially neutral reorganization.

Gordon claims, though, that his compulsion to resign was aggravated by the unlikeliness of his being promoted back to a management position in light of the EEOC's pattern of discrimination against white males through July 1983. The special master recognized that the permanence of Gordon's demotion is a factor to consider under the constructive discharge analysis but found that Gordon's expectation of future discrimination in promotion involved a highly speculative forecast and, therefore, was not an aggravating factor. The master explained, "That expectation assumes that a GS-15 job would open, that Mr. Gordon would in fact be the most qualified candidate, and that EEOC would discriminate against him and select someone else."

We agree that as a matter of law such a remote possibility would not make a reasonable employee feel compelled to resign. Indeed, in virtually all cases in which there is a discriminatory denial of promotion, the reasonable employee will feel that his chances of advancement in his job are less than they would have been absent the discrimination. However, without continuing harassment or repeated discriminatory impediment to any advance, dimmed future job prospects based upon the employer's past discrimination in promotions are not alone enough to support a finding of constructive discharge. . . . In light of these facts, the special master and the district court

did not err in finding that, under the circumstances as alleged by Gordon, a reasonable employee would not have felt compelled to resign.[11]

*NOTES*

1. Gordon argued that he had been constructively discharged. In the alternative,
he argued that, even if his retirement had violated the duty to mitigate damages, the
violation should not result in the termination of his backpay period. How would
backpay have been calculated under each theory? Was it fair to terminate Gordon's
backpay upon retirement? Wouldn't he probably still have been employed on the
date of judgment but for the 1975 discrimination? Does society have an overriding
interest in having discrimination attacked in the context of existing employment relationships?

2. Would a reasonable person in Gordon's circumstances not have felt compelled
to retire? Remember, he had been denied a promotion because of his race, he had
not been promoted during the next four years, the discriminatory practices had
continued, and he had been told to accept a demotion or retire. Is *Jett* distinguishable because the discrimination had ceased before the resignation? Another line
of Fifth Circuit cases holds that "[a] plaintiff who resigns after demotion has been
constructively discharged if a reasonable employee in the plaintiff's position would
have believed that the demotion was a harbinger of dismissal." Brown v. East
Miss. Elec. Power Assn., 989 F.2d 858, 863 (5th Cir. 1993). Do these cases place too
much emphasis on attacking discrimination in the context of existing employment
relationships and not enough emphasis on relieving discriminatees from ongoing discrimination? See Mark S. Kende, Deconstructing Constructive Discharge: The
Misapplication of Constructive Discharge Standards in Employment Discrimination
Remedies, 71 Notre Dame L. Rev. 39 (1995).

3. If Gordon had met the reasonable person standard, would he have met the district court's nexus requirement i.e., a causal link between the discrmination and the
resignation? But, more important, if the constructive discharge doctrine is based on
what a reasonable person in plaintiff's position would have done, why must there be
a nexus between the resignation *and the discrimination?* Consider the result this requirement would produce if Gordon had retired because he had been publicly and
unreasonably accused by his superiors of stealing EEOC funds. See also Connors v.
Chrysler Fin. Corp., 160 F.3d 971 (3d Cir. 1998) (invoking the nexus requirement).

4. Although the Fifth Circuit holds that race discrimination in a promotion or demotion and sex discrimination in pay do not constitute a constructive discharge,
would the court think that racial or sexual harassment by a supervisor is sufficient? In
Ugalde v. W. A. McKenzie Asphalt Co., 990 F.2d 239 (5th Cir. 1993), the court
avoided the issue, saying that a victim of racial harassment cannot establish a constructive discharge unless, before resigning, he had sought assistance from a higher
company official, the union, or the EEOC. See also Lindale v. Tokheim Corp., 145
F.3d 953 (7th Cir. 1998). Is that because a reasonable employee would so act before
resigning?

---

11. As it is the law of this circuit that a finding of constructive discharge is imperative to any recovery
of backpay for the period following resignation or retirement, we need not discuss either whether the
"nexus" requirement enunciated by the district court has been met in the instant case or whether the special master properly exposited that requirement. . . .

5. Constructive discharge occurs when the employee quits but was driven to do so by the employer's harsh treatment. "When an employee involuntarily resigns in order to escape intolerable and illegal employment requirements . . . the employer has committed a constructive discharge." Young v. Southwestern Savings & Loan Assn., 509 F.2d 140 (5th Cir. 1975). As indicated in *Jurgens*, the constructive discharge cases are divided over whether the plaintiff must show both (1) that the working conditions were such that a reasonable person would have resigned and (2) that the employer intended to force his or her resignation, or whether the plaintiff must show only the first circumstance. What result would the two-pronged requirement produce if the discriminatee had resigned due to sexual harassment? After all, the harasser may strongly wish the victim to continue to work. In Wheeler v. Southland Corp., 875 F.2d 1246 (6th Cir. 1989), the plaintiff had informed the harasser's supervisor of the harassment, but resigned when the company took no action. The court found the necessary intent for a constructive discharge because a reasonable employer would have foreseen that, without corrective action, the plaintiff would have felt compelled to resign. Is predictability the same thing as intent? See Personnel Administrator v. Feeney [reproduced at page 251]. On the other hand, in Paroline v. Unisys Corp., 900 F.2d 27 (4th Cir. 1990), the court found an absence of the intent necessary for a constructive discharge when management, after being informed of the harassment, took effective steps to stop it, offered the plaintiff counseling, and encouraged her to stay.

6. The two-pronged requirement may also be problematic where an employee with a disability resigns after an employer refuses a request for a reasonable accommodation. In Johnson v. Shalala, 911 F.2d 126 (4th Cir. 1993), the court recognized that the application of the two-pronged test was complicated by the employer's affirmative duty to accommodate. But even if the working conditions were intolerable, the "plaintiff must present some evidence that the employer intentionally sought to drive her from her position." Id. at 132. The court said such a showing was not made because the employer had made some effort to accommodate the plaintiff even though the effort was less than required. However, a "complete failure to accommodate, in the face of repeated requests, might suffice as evidence to show the deliberateness necessary for constructive discharge." Id. Should an employee who faces intolerable working conditions as the result of a failure to accommodate be considered constructively discharged regardless of the employer's intent? To take an extreme case, what if the workplace lacks accessible toilet facilities? Does failure to provide such facilities undercut the employer's statutory duty?

7. The duty to mitigate has also been applied to insurance coverage. In Fariss v. Lynchburg Foundry, 769 F.2d 958 (4th Cir. 1985), a person who had been wrongfully terminated because of his age died prior to judgment. If he had not been terminated, his employer would have provided him with a $40,000 life insurance policy. The Fourth Circuit held that his widow could recover only the value of the insurance premiums the employer would have paid, not the $40,000 face value of the policy. The court emphasized that the deceased had not attempted to procure substitute coverage. But the same court allowed a woman, who was discharged because of her pregnancy and who was unsuccessful in her attempt to obtain other medical insurance, to recover the amount of the benefits she would have received in the absence of discrimination minus the amount she would have contributed toward the premiums. EEOC v. Service News Co., 898 F.2d 958 (4th Cir. 1990). If a discriminatee obtains her own insurance coverage, the cost of such coverage can be recovered from the employer. E.g., Gaworski v. ITT Comm. Fin. Corp., 17 F.3d 1104 (8th Cir. 1994).

## 3.   *Front Pay*

As the Supreme Court held in Pollard v. E. I. du Pont de Nemours & Co., reproduced at page 950, another type of compensatory equitable relief is a front-pay award,
which compensates any economic losses that will occur after the court's judgment. If
the court has ordered instatement or reinstatement, the front-pay award will redress
losses from the date of judgment until the date the discriminatee obtains the wrongfully denied position. In such circumstances, the court typically requires the employer to make weekly or monthly payments to the discriminatee, as though he or she
were already an employee. Patterson v. American Tobacco Co., 535 F.2d 257 (4th
Cir. 1976). If the court decides that instatement or reinstatement is not feasible, the
discriminatee may be awarded front pay in the form of "damages in lieu of reinstatement" — a lump sum award.

### CASSINO v. REICHHOLD CHEMICALS, INC.
**817 F.2d 1338 (9th Cir. 1987)**

SCHROEDER, Circuit Judge:
     . . . Cassino filed this suit in federal court alleging that his termination was based
on age in violation of the ADEA. . . . A jury verdict in Cassino's favor awarded him
$81,000 in backpay [and] $150,000 in front pay. . . .
     The ADEA provides that "[i]n any action brought to enforce this chapter the court
shall have jurisdiction to grant such legal or equitable relief as may be appropriate . . .
including without limitation judgments compelling employment, reinstatement or
promotion. . . ." 29 U.S.C. § 626(b). In discriminatory discharge cases, the decision
whether to order reinstatement is within the discretion of the trial court. Although reinstatement is the preferred remedy in these cases, it may not be feasible where the
relationship is hostile or no position is available due to a reduction in force. Under
such circumstances, an award of future damages or "front pay" in lieu of reinstatement furthers the remedial goals of the ADEA by returning the aggrieved party to the
economic situation he would have enjoyed but for the defendant's illegal conduct.
Thus, front pay is an award of future lost earnings to make a victim of discrimination
whole.
     The jury in this case was instructed on the measure of damages for front pay. The
district court explained that "Front pay is compensation for the loss of future salary
and benefits." Aside from this cursory definition, however, the jury was merely told
that "If you find age discrimination . . . , you may award front pay."
     It is clear that front pay awards, like backpay awards, must be reduced by the
amount plaintiff could earn using reasonable mitigation efforts. . . . [T]he plaintiff's
duty to mitigate must serve as a control on front pay damage awards. Thus, front pay
is intended to be temporary in nature. An award of front pay "does not contemplate
that a plaintiff will sit idly by and be compensated for doing nothing." The jury in this
case, in effect, without instruction on mitigation, found that Cassino was entitled to
front pay from the time of trial until the time he would have retired. Because of this
defect, the front pay award also is reversed.
     We do not find persuasive Reichhold's remaining challenges to the front pay
award. First, Reichhold contends that the district court erred in failing to instruct the
jury that a finding of hostility was a prerequisite to a front pay award. The court's failure to instruct on hostility was not error because the decision whether to order the

equitable remedy of reinstatement or, in the alternative, to award front pay, is a decision for the trial court. If the court concludes that reinstatement is not feasible, the jury then decides the amount of the front pay award. . . .

Second, Reichhold argues that Cassino failed to present competent evidence establishing future damages. Specifically, Reichhold maintains that Cassino's lay opinion testimony about future earnings and benefits, and the application of inflation and discount rates to those figures, was inadmissible because Cassino was unqualified to make such calculations.

Although the Ninth Circuit has not addressed the issue of what constitutes adequate inflation and discount rate evidence, several circuits have adopted the view that as long as the jury is properly instructed, expert testimony is not an absolute prerequisite to submitting to the jury the issue of future lost earnings and their reduction to present value. Courts that do not require expert testimony reason that the effect of inflation and interest rates on the value of money is within the common knowledge of jurors and that jurors are sufficiently intelligent to reduce an award to present value if properly instructed. Here, Reichhold does not dispute the adequacy of the jury instruction on present value. . . .

Moreover, expert testimony is not required to prove what the plaintiff would receive in future earnings and raises. Here, Cassino testified about his projected earnings based primarily on his own periodic pay increases during more than twenty years of employment at Reichhold. Therefore, Cassino's evidence was sufficient to establish the loss of future earnings and benefits. . . .

*NOTES*

1. Although a front pay award is discretionary, a strong presumption favors the award when reinstatement is inappropriate. E.g., Farber v. Massillon Bd. of Educ., 917 F.2d 1391 (6th Cir. 1990); King v. Staley, 849 F.2d 1143 (8th Cir. 1988). But where the discriminatee has received "liquidated damages" under the ADEA (see page 963), some courts say front pay may be denied as inappropriate or excessive. E.g., Walther v. Lone Star Gas Co., 952 F.2d 119 (5th Cir. 1992); Brooks v. Hilton Casinos, Inc., 959 F.2d 757 (9th Cir. 1992). Other courts think that the recovery of liquidated damages should play little or no part in the front pay decision. Price v. Marshall Erdman & Assocs., Inc., 966 F.2d 320 (7th Cir. 1992); Castle v. Sangamo Weston, Inc., 837 F.2d 1550 (11th Cir. 1988). This same division can be expected to arise under other statutes when punitive damages have been awarded. See Hadley v. VAM PTS, 44 F.3d 372 (5th Cir. 1995).

2. The *Cassino* jury was instructed that it "may" award front pay. Based on the court's discussion of allocation of functions between judge and jury, shouldn't the jury have been instructed that the judge had determined that the discriminatee was entitled to front pay, but that the jury had to determine the appropriate amount? What if the jury concludes that the plaintiff's future earnings capacity was not impaired? In McKnight v. General Motors Corp., 973 F.2d 1366 (7th Cir. 1992), the court affirmed a jury decision not to award front pay.

3. In a private suit against a non-federal employer, the ADEA unpaid wages award is a form of legal relief that gives rise to the constitutional right to a jury trial. The Ninth Circuit is among the few circuits that hold there is also the right to a jury trial on the amount of an ADEA front pay award. Most courts hold that this is for the judge to decide. Certainly, this issue is for the judge under other antidiscrimination statutes.

4. What did the court mean when it stated that "front pay is intended to be temporary in nature"? Did it mean that the front pay period should end at the time when a reasonable discriminatee would be able to obtain comparable employment? See Dominic v. Consolidated Edison Co., 822 F.2d 1249 (2d Cir. 1987). What if a reasonable discriminatee could never obtain comparable employment? In Padilla v. Metro-North Commuter R.R., 92 F.3d 117 (2d Cir. 1996), an employee demoted in violation of the ADEA was denied reinstatement, but was awarded continuing front pay for his reduced future salary (about $20,000 per year) until he either left the company or retired (in about 25 years). The appellate court upheld the award, noting that reinstatement was infeasible due to animosity and the employee had no reasonable prospect of obtaining comparable employment.

5. What factors, other than those mentioned in *Cassino*, should be considered in calculating front pay? In Price v. Marshall Erdman & Assocs., Inc., 966 F.2d 320 (7th Cir. 1992), the court said that each year's projected earnings had the plaintiff been employed by the defendant should be discounted by the probability that the discriminatee would not have lived that long. Where the discriminatee's position produced volatile earnings, the earnings should also be discounted by the reduced risk of income loss the discriminatee would have as a result of obtaining an award of damages. How can the latter amount be quantified? Can the front pay calculation be simplified by taking neither the discount rate nor the increasing cost of living into account? See Jackson v. City of Cookeville, 31 F.3d 1354 (6th Cir. 1994). But see Ramirez v. New York City Off-Track Betting Corp., 112 F.3d 38 (2d Cir. 1997).

6. Given that a judgment for front pay in lieu of reinstatement typically is paid in a lump sum, should it be reduced to present value? Plaintiff gets the money before she would have received it if she had earned it in the future as salary. Present value means that she will get a sufficient amount of money now that will, if invested, produce the same amount of money at the time she would have been paid the salary. Should the front pay award, as reduced to present value, then be increased to take account of future inflation, which reduces the purchasing power of the money she earns in the future? Maybe the front pay award should not be reduced to present value nor increased by future inflation on the assumption that the two are a wash.

7. If the court orders reinstatement with interim front pay, should the order require the employer to have good cause before removing any incumbent employee from the position awarded to the discriminatee? Otherwise, won't the employer have a strong economic incentive to "bump" an incumbent employee?

## 4. Attorneys' Fees

The provisions authorizing the awarding of attorneys' fees and costs vary from statute to statute. The ADEA, in § 7(b), 29 U.S.C.S. § 626(b) (2003), incorporates the fee provision in § 16(b) of the Fair Labor Standards Act, 29 U.S.C.S. § 216(b) (2003). This fee provision *requires* the court to award attorneys' fees and costs to a prevailing non-federal discriminatee but does not authorize the court to make such an award to either a prevailing federal discriminatee or a prevailing employer. 2 Charles A. Sullivan, Michael J. Zimmer & Rebecca Hanner White, Employment Discrimination: Law and Practice § 13.15 [B] (3d ed. 2002).

By contrast, the Title VII provision, § 706(k), 42 U.S.C.S. § 2000e-5(k) (2003), provides:

In any action or proceeding under this title the court, in its discretion, may allow the prevailing party, other than the Commission or the United States, a reasonable attorney's fee (including expert fees) as part of the costs, and the Commission and the United States shall be liable for costs the same as a private person.

This provision is also applicable in federal employee Title VII suits. Carreathers v. Alexander, 587 F.2d 1046 (10th Cir. 1978).

The fee provisions for § 1981 actions, 42 U.S.C.S. § 1988(b), (c) (2003), and ADA actions, 42 U.S.C.S. § 12205 (2003), generally follow the Title VII pattern. However, the ADA provision permits the recovery of "litigation expenses" rather than "expert fees." Most surprisingly, the ADA provision permits the EEOC, as well as a court, to make a fee award. Presumably, this agency power applies in federal employee proceedings.

The following opinion provides a tour of the Title VII provision and is undoubtedly applicable to the fee provisions for § 1981 and ADA actions.

## CHRISTIANSBURG GARMENT CO. v. EEOC
### 434 U.S. 412 (1978)

Justice STEWART delivered the opinion of the Court.

. . . The question in this case is under what circumstances an attorney's fee should be allowed when the defendant is the prevailing party in a Title VII action — a question about which the federal courts have expressed divergent views.

[In 1972, Title VII was amended to allow the EEOC to sue on behalf of complainants, including those who had a charge "pending" on the amendment's effective date. The EEOC then filed suit on behalf of a person who had received a right-to-sue letter two years earlier. The district court granted summary judgment to the employer, but refused its request for attorneys' fees.]

### II

It is the general rule in the United States that in the absence of legislation providing otherwise, litigants must pay their own attorney's fees. Congress has provided only limited exceptions to this rule "under selected statutes granting or protecting various federal rights." Some of these statutes make fee awards mandatory for prevailing plaintiffs [citing 29 U.S.C.S. § 216(b), governing awards in ADEA suits]; others make awards permissive but limit them to certain parties, usually prevailing plaintiffs. But many of the statutes are more flexible, authorizing the award of attorney's fees to either plaintiffs or defendants, and entrusting the effectuation of the statutory policy to the discretion of the district courts. Section 706(k) of Title VII of the Civil Rights Act of 1964 falls into this last category, providing as it does that a district court may in its discretion allow an attorney's fee to the prevailing party.

In Newman v. Piggie Park Enterprises, 390 U.S. 400 (1968), the Court considered a substantially identical statute authorizing the award of attorney's fees under Title II of the Civil Rights Act of 1964. In that case the plaintiffs had prevailed, and the Court of Appeals had held that they should be awarded their attorney's fees "only to the extent that the respondents' defenses had been advanced 'for purposes of delay and not in good faith.'" We ruled that this "subjective standard" did not properly effectuate the purposes of the counsel-fee provision of Title II. Relying primarily on the intent of Congress to cast a Title II plaintiff in the role of "a 'private attorney general,'" vindicating a policy that Congress considered of the highest priority," we held that a prevailing plaintiff under Title II "should ordinarily recover an attorney's fee unless special circumstances would render such an award unjust." We noted in passing that if the objective of Congress had been to permit the award of attorney's fees only against defendants who had acted in bad faith, "no new statutory provision would have been necessary," since even the American common-law rule allows the award of attorney's fees in those exceptional circumstances.

In Albemarle Paper Co. v. Moody, 422 U.S. 405 (1975), the Court made clear that the *Piggie Park* standard of awarding attorney's fees to a successful plaintiff is equally applicable in an action under Title VII of the Civil Rights Act. It can thus be taken as established, as the parties in this case both acknowledge, that under § 706(k) of Title VII a prevailing *plaintiff* ordinarily is to be awarded attorney's fees in all but special circumstances.

## III

The question in the case before us is what standard should inform a district court's discretion in deciding whether to award attorney's fees to a successful *defendant* in a Title VII action. . . .

. . . The terms of § 706(k) provide no indication whatever of the circumstances under which either a plaintiff or a defendant should be entitled to attorney's fees. And a moment's reflection reveals that there are at least two strong equitable considerations counseling an attorney's fee award to a prevailing Title VII plaintiff that are wholly absent in the case of a prevailing Title VII defendant.

First, as emphasized so forcefully in *Piggie Park*, the plaintiff is the chosen instrument of Congress to vindicate "a policy that Congress considered of the highest priority." Second, when a district court awards counsel fees to a prevailing plaintiff, it is awarding them against a violator of federal law. As the Court of Appeals clearly perceived, "these policy considerations which support the award of fees to a prevailing plaintiff are not present in the case of a prevailing defendant." A successful defendant seeking counsel fees under § 706(k) must rely on quite different equitable considerations.

But if the company's position is untenable, the Commission's argument also misses the mark. It seems clear, in short, that in enacting § 706(k) Congress did not intend to permit the award of attorney's fees to a prevailing defendant only in a situation where the plaintiff was motivated by bad faith in bringing the action. As pointed out in *Piggie Park*, if that had been the intent of Congress, no statutory provision would have been necessary, for it has long been established that even under the American common-law rule attorney's fees may be awarded against a party who has proceeded in bad faith. . . .

. . . The first federal appellate court to consider what criteria should govern the award of attorney's fees to a prevailing Title VII defendant was the Court of Appeals for the Third Circuit in United States Steel Corp. v. United States, 519 F.2d 359. There a District Court had denied a fee award to a defendant that had successfully resisted a Commission demand for documents, the court finding that the Commission's action had not been "'unfounded, meritless, frivolous or vexatiously brought.'" The Court of Appeals concluded that the District Court had not abused its discretion in denying the award. A similar standard was adopted by the Court of Appeals for the Second Circuit in Carrion v. Yeshiva University, 535 F.2d 722. In upholding an attorney's fee award to a successful defendant, that court stated that such awards should be permitted "not routinely, not simply because he succeeds, but only where the action brought is found to be unreasonable, frivolous, meritless or vexatious."

To the extent that abstract words can deal with concrete cases, we think that the concept embodied in the language adopted by these two Courts of Appeals is correct. We would qualify their words only by pointing out that the term "meritless" is to be understood as meaning groundless or without foundation, rather than simply that the plaintiff has ultimately lost his case, and that the term "vexatious" in no way implies that the plaintiff's subjective bad faith is a necessary prerequisite to a fee award against him. In sum, a district court may in its discretion award attorney's fees to a prevailing defendant in a Title VII case upon a finding that the plaintiff's action was frivolous, unreasonable, or without foundation, even though not brought in subjective bad faith.

In applying these criteria, it is important that a district court resist the understandable temptation to engage in post hoc reasoning by concluding that, because a plaintiff did not ultimately prevail, his action must have been unreasonable or without foundation. This kind of hindsight logic could discourage all but the most airtight claims, for seldom can a prospective plaintiff be sure of ultimate success. No matter how honest one's belief that he has been the victim of discrimination, no matter how meritorious one's claim may appear at the outset, the course of litigation is rarely predictable. Decisive facts may not emerge until discovery or trial. The law may change or clarify in the midst of litigation. Even when the law or the facts appear questionable or unfavorable at the outset, a party may have an entirely reasonable ground for bringing suit.

That § 706(k) allows fee awards only to *prevailing* private plaintiffs should assure that this statutory provision will not in itself operate as an incentive to the bringing of claims that have little chance of success. To take the further step of assessing attorney's fees against plaintiffs simply because they do not finally prevail would substantially add to the risks inhering in most litigation and would undercut the efforts of Congress to promote the vigorous enforcement of the provisions of Title VII. Hence, a plaintiff should not be assessed his opponent's attorney's fees unless a court finds that his claim was frivolous, unreasonable, or groundless, or that the plaintiff continued to litigate after it clearly became so. And, needless to say, if a plaintiff is found to have brought or continued such a claim in *bad faith*, there will be an even stronger basis for charging him with the attorney's fees incurred by the defense.

## IV

In denying attorney's fees to the company in this case, the District Court focused on the standards we have discussed. The court found that "the Commission's action in bringing the suit cannot be characterized as unreasonable or meritless" because "the basis upon which petitioner prevailed was an issue of first impression requiring judicial resolution" and because the "Commission's statutory interpretation of . . . the 1972 amendments was not frivolous." The court thus exercised its discretion squarely within the permissible bounds of § 706(k). . . .

### NOTES

1. Is this opinion consistent with the opinion of the Court in Fogarty v. Fantasy 510 U.S. 517 (1994), which held that "prevailing party" is to have the same meaning for plaintiffs as for defendants?

2. Under the fee provisions, only a "prevailing party" is eligible for a fee award. After the meaning of this term had produced conflicting views, the Supreme Court attempted to clarify the matter in Farrar v. Hobby, 506 U.S. 103 (1992). The precise issue was whether a plaintiff who had recovered only nominal damages in a § 1983 action was the "prevailing party." After reviewing its previous decisions, the Court said:

> [T]o qualify as a prevailing party, a civil rights plaintiff must obtain at least some relief on the merits of his claim. The plaintiff must obtain an enforceable judgment against the defendant from whom fees are sought, or comparable relief through a consent decree or settlement. Whatever relief the plaintiff secures must directly benefit him at the time of the judgment or settlement. . . . Only under these circumstances can civil rights litigation effect "the material alteration of the legal relationship of the parties" and thereby transform the plaintiff into a prevailing party. In short, a plaintiff "prevails" when actual relief on the merits of his claim materially alters the legal relationship between the parties by modifying the defendant's behavior in a way that directly benefits the plaintiff.

Id. at 111. Later in the opinion, the Court commented, "No material alteration of the legal relationship . . . occurs until the plaintiff becomes entitled to enforce a judgment, consent decree, or settlement against the defendant." Id. at 114. The Court then held that the instant plaintiff was the "prevailing party" because he could enforce the nominal damages award.

3. The courts have rejected most arguments that "special circumstances" require the denial of a fee award to a prevailing plaintiff. E.g., Saski v. Class, 92 F.3d 232 (4th Cir. 1996) (generous damages recovered); Love v. Mayor of Cheyenne, 620 F.2d 235 (10th Cir. 1980) (defendant's good faith); International Socy. for Krishna Consciousness, Inc. v. Collins, 609 F.2d 151 (5th Cir. 1980) (plaintiff's ability to pay); Northcross v. Board of Educ., 611 F.2d 624 (6th Cir. 1979) (uncertainty as to law). In New York Gaslight Club, Inc. v. Carey, 447 U.S. 54 (1980), the Supreme Court found no special circumstances where the plaintiff had been represented by a "public interest group" and was eligible for limited assistance by a state attorney. Where special circumstances have been found, several factors were usually present, such as the defendant's extraordinary good faith, the adverse effect the award would have on innocent third persons, and the questionable conduct of the plaintiff. E.g., Walker v. NationsBank of Florida, N.A., 53 F.3d 1548 (11th Cir. 1995). But in Lewis v. Kendrick, 944 F.2d 949 (1st Cir. 1991), a fee award was denied because the plaintiff had greatly exaggerated her injuries and had failed to reduce the amount of her fee request to reflect her very limited recovery ($1,000) at trial.

4. Several factors determine whether a prevailing defendant is entitled to a fee award under the frivolous, unreasonable, or groundless standard: whether the case presented an issue of first impression; whether the plaintiff established a prima facie case; whether the defendant offered to settle; whether the case was dismissed prior to trial; and whether racial, religious, or sexual slurs were involved. E.g., EEOC v. Reichhold Chems., Inc., 988 F.2d 1564 (11th Cir. 1993); Munson v. Friske, 754 F.2d 683 (7th Cir. 1985).

5. Can a party's attorney be required to pay part or all of a fee award? The Supreme Court, in Roadway Express, Inc. v. Piper, 447 U.S. 752 (1980), held that neither Title VII nor § 1988 authorizes a fee award against a party's attorney but that a court has inherent power to make such an award against an attorney who proceeded

in bad faith or willfully abused the judicial process. Another statute, 28 U.S.C.S. § 1927 (2003), permits a fee award against an attorney who "multiplies the proceedings . . . unreasonably and vexatiously." See Jones v. Continental Corp., 789 F.2d 1225 (6th Cir. 1986).

6. Innumerable cases have considered the proper calculation of a "reasonable" fee award. The basic formula was worked out in four Supreme Court decisions: Pennsylvania v. Delaware Valley Citizens' Council for Clean Air, 478 U.S. 546 (1986); City of Riverside v. Rivera, 477 U.S. 561 (1986); Blum v. Stenson, 465 U.S. 886 (1984); and Hensley v. Eckerhart, 461 U.S. 424 (1983). According to the Court, the fee calculation requires a two-step process. The first step consists of multiplying the number of hours the attorney reasonably expended on the litigation by a reasonable hourly rate. The second step is to adjust the resulting "lodestar figure" upward or downward to account for any relevant factors that were not inherent in the figures used in the first step, such as the results obtained. The Court has emphasized, however, that the lodestar figure must be presumed to be a reasonable amount and that an adjustment is appropriate only in exceptional cases. Moreover, any such adjustment must be based on specific evidence and detailed judicial findings that show that the factors relied on were not reflected in the lodestar figure. The Court, in Missouri v. Jenkins, 491 U.S. 274 (1989), upheld an upward adjustment to compensate an attorney for the delay in payment. However, an upward adjustment cannot be made to compensate attorneys retained on a contingent fee basis for assuming the risk of nonpayment. City of Burlington v. Dague, 505 U.S. 557 (1992). On the other hand, the lodestar figure should usually be adjusted down to zero where the plaintiff has recovered only nominal damages. Farrar v. Hobby, 506 U.S. 103 (1992).

7. A fee award includes the attorney's services for every stage in the enforcement scheme. In a Title VII action, for example, these stages may include arbitration, Keenan v. City of Philadelphia, 983 F.2d 459 (3d Cir. 1992); the proceeding before a state agency, New York Gaslight Club, Inc. v. Carey, 447 U.S. 54 (1980); the taking of a successful appeal, Morrow v. Dillard, 580 F.2d 1284 (5th Cir. 1978); the postjudgment monitoring of the decree, Pennsylvania v. Delaware Valley Citizens' Council for Clean Air, 478 U.S. 546 (1986); and even the hearing to establish the propriety and amount of the fee award, Davis v. City and County of San Francisco, 976 F.2d 1536 (9th Cir. 1992).

8. In Venegas v. Mitchell, 495 U.S. 82 (1990), the Supreme Court held that a fee award did not invalidate a contingent-fee contract that entitled the attorney to a larger amount. The Court found nothing in the text or legislative history of § 1988 that suggested otherwise. Moreover, "depriving plaintiffs of the option of promising to pay more than the statutory fee if that is necessary to secure counsel of their choice would not further § 1988's general purpose of enabling such plaintiffs in civil rights cases to secure competent counsel." Id. at 89.

9. Title VII contains a special fee provision that is applicable only in certain mixed-motives cases, § 706(g)(2)(B)(i), 42 U.S.C.S. § 2000e-5(g)(2)(B)(i) (2003). When the plaintiff has shown an unlawful factor entered into the decision, but the employer shows that it would have made the same decision in any event, the court "may grant" attorneys' fees to the plaintiff. A fee award under this provision turns on such factors as whether the plaintiff obtained injunctive or declaratory relief, the public interest in the litigation, and the conduct of the parties. Canup v. Chipman-Union, Inc., 123 F.3d 1440 (11th Cir. 1997); Sheppard v. Riverview Nursing Ctr., Inc., 88 F.3d 1332 (4th Cir. 1996). But see Gudenkauf v. Stauffer Communications, Inc., 158 F.3d 1074 (10th Cir. 1998). Thus, the standards for making a fee award

under § 706(k) are inapplicable, although the amount of the award should be calculated in the same way.

## BUCKHANNON BOARD & CARE HOME, INC.
## v. WEST VIRGINIA DEPARTMENT OF
## HEALTH & HUMAN RESOURCES
### 532 U.S. 598 (2001)

Chief Justice REHNQUIST delivered the opinion of the Court.

Numerous federal statutes allow courts to award attorney's fees and costs to the "prevailing party." The question presented here is whether this term includes a party that has failed to secure a judgment on the merits or a court-ordered consent decree, but has nonetheless achieved the desired result because the lawsuit brought about a voluntary change in the defendant's conduct. We hold that it does not.

Buckhannon Board and Care Home, Inc., which operates care homes that provide assisted living to their residents, failed an inspection by the West Virginia Office of the State Fire Marshal because some of the residents were incapable of "self-preservation" as defined under state law. [Buckhannon and other petitioners brought suit], seeking declaratory and injunctive relief that the "self-preservation" requirement violated the Fair Housing Amendments Act of 1988 (FHAA) and the Americans with Disabilities Act of 1990 (ADA).

. . . In 1998, the West Virginia Legislature enacted two bills eliminating the "self-preservation" requirement, and respondents moved to dismiss the case as moot. The District Court granted the motion. . . .

Petitioners requested attorney's fees as the "prevailing party" under the FHAA, 42 U.S.C. § 3613(c)(2) ("[T]he court, in its discretion, may allow the prevailing party . . . a reasonable attorney's fee and costs"), and ADA, 42 U.S.C. § 12205 ("[T]he court . . . , in its discretion, may allow the prevailing party . . . a reasonable attorney's fee, including litigation expenses, and costs"). Petitioners argued that they were entitled to attorney's fees under the "catalyst theory," which posits that a plaintiff is a "prevailing party" if it achieves the desired result because the lawsuit brought about a voluntary change in the defendant's conduct. Although most Courts of Appeals recognize the "catalyst theory," the Court of Appeals for the Fourth Circuit [has] rejected it. . . . The District Court accordingly denied the motion. . . .

In the United States, parties are ordinarily required to bear their own attorney's fees — the prevailing party is not entitled to collect from the loser. Under this "American Rule," we follow "a general practice of not awarding fees to a prevailing party absent explicit statutory authority." Congress, however, has authorized the award of attorney's fees to the "prevailing party" in numerous statutes in addition to those at issue here, such as the Civil Rights Act of 1964, the Voting Rights Act Amendments of 1975, and the Civil Rights Attorney's Fees Awards Act of 1976.[4]

In designating those parties eligible for an award of litigation costs, Congress employed the term "prevailing party," a legal term of art. Black's Law Dictionary 1145 (7th ed. 1999) defines "prevailing party" as "[a] party in whose favor a judgment is rendered, regardless of the amount of damages awarded. — Also termed successful

---

4. We have interpreted these fee-shifting provisions consistently, and so approach the nearly identical provisions at issue here.

party." This view that a "prevailing party" is one who has been awarded some relief by the court can be distilled from our prior cases.

In Hanrahan v. Hampton, 446 U.S. 754, 758 (1980) (per curiam), we reviewed the legislative history of § 1988 and found that "Congress intended to permit the interim award of counsel fees only when a party has prevailed on the merits of at least some of his claims." . . . We have held that even an award of nominal damages suffices under this test.

In addition to judgments on the merits, we have held that settlement agreements enforced through a consent decree may serve as the basis for an award of attorney's fees. Although a consent decree does not always include an admission of liability by the defendant, it nonetheless is a court-ordered "chang[e] [in] the legal relationship between [the plaintiff] and the defendant."[7]

These decisions, taken together, establish that enforceable judgments on the merits and court-ordered consent decrees create the "material alteration of the legal relationship of the parties" necessary to permit an award of attorney's fees.

We think, however, the "catalyst theory" falls on the other side of the line from these examples. It allows an award where there is no judicially sanctioned change in the legal relationship of the parties. Even under a limited form of the "catalyst theory," a plaintiff could recover attorney's fees if it established that the "complaint had sufficient merit to withstand a motion to dismiss for lack of jurisdiction or failure to state a claim on which relief may be granted." This is not the type of legal merit that our prior decisions, based upon plain language and congressional intent, have found necessary. . . . A defendant's voluntary change in conduct, although perhaps accomplishing what the plaintiff sought to achieve by the lawsuit, lacks the necessary judicial imprimatur on the change. Our precedents thus counsel against holding that the term "prevailing party" authorizes an award of attorney's fees without a corresponding alteration in the legal relationship of the parties. . . .

Petitioners finally assert that the "catalyst theory" is necessary to prevent defendants from unilaterally mooting an action before judgment in an effort to avoid an award of attorney's fees. They also claim that the rejection of the "catalyst theory" will deter plaintiffs with meritorious but expensive cases from bringing suit. We are skeptical of these assertions, which are entirely speculative and unsupported by any empirical evidence.

Petitioners discount the disincentive that the "catalyst theory" may have upon a defendant's decision to voluntarily change its conduct, conduct that may not be illegal. "The defendants' potential liability for fees in this kind of litigation can be as significant as, and sometimes even more significant than, their potential liability on the merits," and the possibility of being assessed attorney's fees may well deter a defendant from altering its conduct.

And petitioners' fear of mischievous defendants only materializes in claims for equitable relief, for so long as the plaintiff has a cause of action for damages, a defendant's change in conduct will not moot the case. Even then, it is not clear how often courts will find a case mooted: "It is well settled that a defendant's voluntary cessation of a challenged practice does not deprive a federal court of its power to determine the legality of the practice" unless it is "absolutely clear that the allegedly wrongful behavior could not reasonably be expected to recur." If a case is not found to be moot,

---

7. . . . Private settlements do not entail the judicial approval and oversight involved in consent decrees. And federal jurisdiction to enforce a private contractual settlement will often be lacking unless the terms of the agreement are incorporated into the order of dismissal.

and the plaintiff later procures an enforceable judgment, the court may of course award attorney's fees. Given this possibility, a defendant has a strong incentive to enter a settlement agreement, where it can negotiate attorney's fees and costs.

We have also stated that "[a] request for attorney's fees should not result in a second major litigation," and have accordingly avoided an interpretation of the fee-shifting statutes that would have "spawn[ed] a second litigation of significant dimension." Among other things, a "catalyst theory" hearing would require analysis of the defendant's subjective motivations in changing its conduct, an analysis that "will likely depend on a highly factbound inquiry and may turn on reasonable inferences from the nature and timing of the defendant's change in conduct." Although we do not doubt the ability of district courts to perform the nuanced "three thresholds" test required by the "catalyst theory" — whether the claim was colorable rather than groundless; whether the lawsuit was a substantial rather than an insubstantial cause of the defendant's change in conduct; whether the defendant's change in conduct was motivated by the plaintiff's threat of victory rather than threat of expense, it is clearly not a formula for "ready administrability."

Given the clear meaning of "prevailing party" in the fee-shifting statutes, we need not determine which way these various policy arguments cut. In Alyeska [Pipeline Service Co. v. Wilderness Society, 421 U.S. 240 (1975)], we said that Congress had not "extended any roving authority to the Judiciary to allow counsel fees as costs or otherwise whenever the courts might deem them warranted." To disregard the clear legislative language and the holdings of our prior cases on the basis of such policy arguments would be a similar assumption of a "roving authority." For the reasons stated above, we hold that the "catalyst theory" is not a permissible basis for the award of attorney's fees under the FHAA and ADA.

Justice SCALIA, with whom Justice THOMAS joins, concurring.
    . . . The dissent distorts the term "prevailing party" beyond its normal meaning for policy reasons, but even those seem to me misguided. They rest upon the presumption that the catalyst theory applies when "the suit's merit led the defendant to abandon the fray, to switch rather than fight on, to accord plaintiff sooner rather than later the principal redress sought in the complaint." As the dissent would have it, by giving the term its normal meaning the Court today approves the practice of denying attorney's fees to a plaintiff with a proven claim of discrimination, simply because the very merit of his claim led the defendant to capitulate before judgment. That is not the case. To the contrary, the Court approves the result in Parham v. Southwestern Bell Tel. Co., 433 F.2d 421 (8th Cir. 1970), where attorney's fees were awarded "after [a] finding that the defendant had acted unlawfully." What the dissent's stretching of the term produces is something more, and something far less reasonable: an award of attorney's fees when the merits of plaintiff's case remain unresolved — when, for all one knows, the defendant only "abandon[ed] the fray" because the cost of litigation — either financial or in terms of public relations — would be too great. . . .

It could be argued, perhaps, that insofar as abstract justice is concerned, there is little to choose between the dissent's outcome and the Court's: If the former sometimes rewards the plaintiff with a phony claim (there is no way of knowing), the latter sometimes denies fees to the plaintiff with a solid case whose adversary slinks away on the eve of judgment. But it seems to me the evil of the former far outweighs the evil of the latter. There is all the difference in the world between a rule that denies the extraordinary boon of attorney's fees to some plaintiffs who are no less "deserving" of them than others who receive them, and a rule that causes the law to be the very instrument of wrong — exacting the payment of attorney's fees to the extortionist. . . .

Justice GINSBURG, with whom Justice STEVENS, Justice SOUTER, and Justice BREYER join, dissenting.

The Court today holds that a plaintiff whose suit prompts the precise relief she seeks does not "prevail," and hence cannot obtain an award of attorney's fees, unless she also secures a court entry memorializing her victory. The entry need not be a judgment on the merits. Nor need there be any finding of wrongdoing. A court-approved settlement will do.

The Court's insistence that there be a document filed in court — a litigated judgment or court-endorsed settlement — upsets long-prevailing Circuit precedent applicable to scores of federal fee-shifting statutes. The decision allows a defendant to escape a statutory obligation to pay a plaintiff's counsel fees, even though the suit's merit led the defendant to abandon the fray, to switch rather than fight on, to accord plaintiff sooner rather than later the principal redress sought in the complaint. Concomitantly, the Court's constricted definition of "prevailing party," and consequent rejection of the "catalyst theory," impede access to court for the less well-heeled, and shrink the incentive Congress created for the enforcement of federal law by private attorneys general. . . .

A lawsuit's ultimate purpose is to achieve actual relief from an opponent. Favorable judgment may be instrumental in gaining that relief. Generally, however, "the judicial decree is not the end but the means. At the end of the rainbow lies not a judgment, but some action (or cessation of action) by the defendant. . . ." On this common understanding, if a party reaches the "sought-after destination," then the party "prevails" regardless of the "route taken."

Under a fair reading of the FHAA and ADA provisions in point, I would hold that a party "prevails" in "a true and proper sense" when she achieves, by instituting litigation, the practical relief sought in her complaint. The Court misreads Congress, as I see it, by insisting that, invariably, relief must be displayed in a judgment, and correspondingly that a defendant's voluntary action never suffices. In this case, Buckhannon's purpose in suing West Virginia officials was not narrowly to obtain a judge's approbation. The plaintiffs' objective was to stop enforcement of a rule requiring Buckhannon to evict residents like centenarian Dorsey Pierce as the price of remaining in business. If Buckhannon achieved that objective on account of the strength of its case — if it succeeded in keeping its doors open while housing and caring for Ms. Pierce and others similarly situated — then Buckhannon is properly judged a party who prevailed. . . .

Congress appears to have envisioned that very prospect. The Senate Report on the 1976 Civil Rights Attorney's Fees Awards Act states: "[F]or purposes of the award of counsel fees, parties may be considered to have prevailed when they vindicate rights through a consent judgment *or without formally obtaining relief*." S. Rep. No. 94-1011, at 5 (emphasis added). In support, the Report cites cases in which parties recovered fees in the absence of any court-conferred relief. The House Report corroborates: "[A]fter a complaint is filed, a defendant might voluntarily cease the unlawful practice. *A court should still award fees* even though it might conclude, as a matter of equity, that *no formal relief*, such as an injunction, is needed." H. R. Rep. No. 94-1558, at 7 (emphases added). . . .

## NOTES

1. The Court held that "prevailing party" status is established where a party obtains an "enforceable judgment on the merits" or a "court-ordered consent decree"

that results in a "material alteration of the legal relationship of the parties." Is one or the other required? Justices Scalia and Thomas seem to indicate that prevailing party status can be established by a finding that the defendant discriminated. Is a plaintiff who obtains a declaratory judgment a "prevailing party?" How about a plaintiff who obtains a preliminary injunction? See Watson v. County of Riverside, 300 F.3d 1092 (9th Cir. 2002) (holding that a plaintiff who wins a preliminary injunction can be qualified as a "prevailing party"). But see John T. v. Delaware County Intermediate Unit, 2003 U.S. App. LEXIS 1738 (3d Cir. Jan. 30, 2003) (IDEA suit). If the defendant then "voluntarily" ceases the challenged conduct and no further proceedings, or permanent injunction, is necessary, has the plaintiff prevailed?

2. Will rejection of the "catalyst theory" have much impact on the availability of fee awards in private employment discrimination litigation? An employer's change in conduct will not moot a case in which the plaintiff has a viable claim for injunctive relief, backpay, compensatory damages, punitive damages, or nominal damages. See generally Michael Ashton, Note, Recovering Attorneys' Fees With the Voluntary Cessation Exception to the Mootness Doctrine After *Buckhannon Board & Care Home, Inc. v. West Virginia Department of Health & Human Resources*, 2002 Wis. L. Rev. 965. Perhaps the greatest potential impact will be in those actions against a state in which the Eleventh Amendment precludes relief other than a prohibitory injunction.

# TABLE OF CASES

*Bold indicates principal cases.*

# TABLE OF SELECTED SECONDARY
# AUTHORITIES

---

Abrams, Douglas E., Arbitrability in Recent Federal Civil Rights Legislation: The Need for Amendment, 26 Conn. L. Rev. 521 (1994), 897

Abrams, Kathryn, Gender Discrimination and the Transformation of Workplace Norms, 42 Vand. L. Rev. 1183 (1989), 457, 514

Abrams, Kathryn, Social Construction, Roving Biologism, and Reasonable Women: A Response to Professor Epstein, 41 DePaul L. Rev. 1021 (1992), 53, 458

Abrams, Kathryn, Title VII and the Complex Female Subject, 92 Mich. L. Rev. 2479 (1994), 338

Abrams, Roger & Dennis Nolan, Toward a Theory of "Just Cause" in Employee Discipline Cases, 1985 Duke L.J. 594 (1985), 20, 896

Adams, Mark L., Compulsory Arbitration of Discrimination Claims and the Civil Rights Act of 1991: Encouraged or Prescribed?, 44 Wayne L. Rev. 619 (1999), 896

Adams, Michelle, The Last Wave of Affirmative Action, 1998 Wis. Rev. 1395 (1998), 318

Adler, Robert S. & Ellen R. Pierce, The Legal, Ethical, and Social Implications of the "Reasonable Woman" Standard in Sexual Harassment Cases, 61 Fordham L. Rev. 772 (1993), 515

Albert, Barbara M., Note, The Combined Effect of No-Spouse Rules and At-Will Doctrines on Career Families Where Both Spouses Are in the Same Field, 36 Brandeis J. Fam. L. 251 (1998), 365

Allred, Stephen, From Connick to Confusion: The Struggle to Define Speech on Matters of Public Concern, 64 Indiana L.J. 43 (1988), 11

Amaker, Norman C., Quittin' Time?: The Antidiscrimination Principle of Title VII vs. the Free Market, 60 U. Chi. L. Rev. 757 (1993), 42

Amar, Vikram D. & Samuel Estreicher, Conduct Unbecoming a Coordinate Branch: The Supreme Court in Garrett, 4 Greenbag 2d 351, 354 (2001), 921

Araujo, Robert John, "The Harvest Is Plentiful, But the Laborers Are Few": Hiring Practices and Religiously Affiliated Universities, 30 U. Rich. L. Rev. 713 (1996), 603

Auerbach, Judy, et al., On Gilligan's In a Different Voice, 11 Feminist Stud. 149 (1985), 258

Austin, Regina, Employer Abuse, Worker Resistance, and the Tort of Intentional Infliction of Emotional Distress, 41 Stan. L. Rev. 1 (1988), 21

Axam, Hilary S. & Deborah Zalesne, Simulated Sodomy and Other Forms of Heterosexual "Horseplay:" Same Sex Sexual Harassment, Workplace Gender Hierarchies, and the Myth of the Gender Monolith Before and After Oncale, 11 Yale J.L. & Feminism 155 (1999), 496

Ayres, Ian & Frederick E. Vars, When Does Private-Discrimination Justify Public Affirmative Action?, 98 Colum. L. Rev. 1577 (1998), 315

Ayres, Ian & Peter Siegelman, The Q-Word as Red Herring: Why Disparate Impact Liability Does Not Induce Hiring Quotas, 74 Tex. L. Rev. 1487 (1996), 339

Bagenstos, Samuel R., Subordination, Stigma and "Disability," 86 Va. L. Rev. 397 (2000), 708

Bagni, Bruce N., Discrimination in the Name of the Lord: A Critical Evaluation of Discrimination by Religious Organizations, 79 Colum. L. Rev. 1514 (1979), 603

Baker, Scott, Comment, Defining "Otherwise Qualified Applicants": Applying Antitrust Relevant-Market Analysis to Disparate Impact Cases, 2002 J. Disp. Resol. 439, 363

Baldus, David C. & James W.L. Cole, Statistical Proof of Discrimination (1989), 371

Banton, M. & J. Harwood, The Race Concept (1975), 118

Barksdale, Claiborne, Successor Liability Under the National Labor Relations Act and Title VII, 54 Tex. L. Rev. 707 (1976), 870

Barnes, David W., Statistics as Proof: Fundamentals of Quantitative Evidence (1983), 236

Bartholet, Elizabeth, Proof of Discriminatory Intent Under Title VII: United States Postal Service Board of Governors v. Aikens, 70 Cal. L. Rev. 1201 (1982), 102

Bartlett, Katharine T., Feminist Legal Methods, 103 Harv. L. Rev. 829 (1990), 217

Bartlett, Katharine T., Only Girls Wear Barrettes: Dress and Appearance Standards, Community Norms, and Workplace Equality, 92 Mich. L. Rev. 2541 (1994), 548-49

Maltby, Lewis L. & David Yamada, Beyond "Economic Realities": The Case for Amending Federal Employ-
    ment Discrimination Laws to Include Independent Contractors, 38 B.C. L. Rev. 239 (1997), 466
Maltz, Earl M., The Legacy of *Griggs v. Duke Power Co.*: A Case Study in the Impact of a Modernist Statutory
    Precedent, 1994 Utah L. Rev. 1353, 423
Manemann, Mary C., Comment, The Meaning of "Sex" in Title VII: Is Favoring an Employee Lover a Viola-
    tion of the Act?, 83 Nw. U. L. Rev. 612 (1989), 499
Marks, John H., Smoke, Mirrors, and the Disappearance of "Vicarious" Liability: The Emergence of a Dubi-
    ous Summary-Judgment Safe Harbor for Employers Whose Supervisory Personnel Commit Hostile En-
    vironment Workplace Harassment, 38 Hous. L. Rev. 1401 (2002), 534
Marshall, Edward, Excluding Participation in Internal Complaint Mechanisms from Absolute Retaliation Pro-
    tection: Why Everyone, Including the Employer, Loses, 5 Emp. Rts. & Employ. Pol'y J. 549 (2001), 641
Marshall, Edward, Title VII's Participation Clause — *Circuit City Stores v. Adams*: Making the Foxes Guard-
    ians of the Chickens, 24 Berkeley J. Emp. & Lab. L. __ (2002), 641-42
Massaro, Toni M., Significant Silences: Freedom of Speech in the Public Sector Workplace, 61 S. Cal. L. Rev.
    1 (1987), 11
Matsuda, Mari J., Public Response to Racist Speech: Considering the Victim's Story, 87 Mich. L. Rev. 2320
    (1989), 170
Matsuda, Mari J., Voices of America: Accent, Antidiscrimination Law, and a Jurisprudence for the Last Recon-
    struction, 100 Yale L.J. 1329 (1991), 170, 628
Mattzzie, Colette G., Substantive Equality and Antidiscrimination: Accommodating Pregnancy Under the
    Americans with Disabilities Act, 82 Geo. L.J. 193 (1993), 483, 687
McCarthy, Carlotta, Employers Beware: Employee's "Reasonable Reliance" on Promises Contained in Em-
    ployee Handbooks May Create Contractual Rights, 31 Suffolk U. L. Rev. 227 (1997), 17
McClusky, Martha T., Insurer Moral Hazard in the Worker's Compensation Crisis: Reforming Cost Inflation,
    Not Rate Supression, 5 Emp. Rts. & Employ. Pol'y J. 55 (2001), 7
McClusky, Martha T., The Illusion of Efficiency in Workers' Compensation "Reform," 50 Rutgers L. Rev. 657
    (1998), 7
McGinley, Ann C. Affirmative Action Awash in Confusion: Backward-Looking-Future-Oriented Justifications
    for Race-Conscious Measures, 4 Roger Williams U. L. Rev. 209 (1998), 301, 476, 481
McGinley, Ann C. & Michael J. Yelnosky, *Board of Education v. Taxman*: The Unpublished Opinions, 4 Roger
    Williams U. L. Rev. 205 (1998), 301
McGinley, Ann C. & Jeffrey W. Stempel, Condescending Contradiction: Richard Posner's Pragmatism and
    Pregnancy Discrimination, 46 Fla. L. Rev. 193 (1994), 476, 481
McGinley, Ann C., Credulous Courts and the Tortured Trilogy: The Improper Use of Summary Judgment in
    Title VII and ADEA Cases, 34 B.C. L. Rev. 203 (1993), 108
McGinley, Ann C., Rethinking Civil Rights and Employment-At-Will, 57 Ohio St. L.J. 1443 (1996), 115
McGinley, Ann C., The Emerging Cronyism Defense and Affirmative Action: A Critical Perspective on the
    Distinction Between Color-Blind and Race-Conscious Decision Making Under Title VII, 39 Ariz. L.
    Rev. 1003 (1997), 115
McGinley, Ann C., ¡Viva La Evolucion!: Recognizing Unconscious Motive In Title VII, 9 Cornell J.L. & Pub.
    Pol'y 415 (2000), 216
McLaughlin, Denis, The Federal Supplemental Jurisdiction Statute: A Constitutional and Statutory Analysis,
    24 Ariz. St. L.J. 849 (1992), 903
McMahon, Karen, The Employment-At-Will Doctrine: Can Oral Assurances of Job Security Overcome the
    At-Will Presumption?, 23 Wm. Mitchell L. Rev. 465 (1997), 16
McMorrow, Judith A., Retirement and Worker Choice: Incentives to Retire and Age Discrimination in
    Employment Act, 29 B.C. L. Rev. 347 (1988), 111, 664
McMorrow, Judith A., Retirement Incentives in the Twenty First Century: The Move Toward Employer Con-
    trol of the ADEA, 31 U. Rich. L. Rev. 795 (1997), 671
Mengler, Thomas M., Consent Decree Paradigms: Models Without Meaning, 29 B.C. L. Rev. 291 (1988), 936
Metzger, Michael B. & John F. Suhre, The Jurisdictional Reach of Title VII, 34 Sw. L.J. 817 (1980), 468
Miller, Frances H. & Philip A. Huvos, Genetic Blueprints, Employer Cost-Cutting, and the Americans with
    Disabilities Act, 46 Admin. L. Rev. 369 (1994), 689
Minda, Gary, Opportunistic Downsizing of Aging Workers: The 1990s Version of Age and Pension Discrimi-
    nation in Employment, 48 Hastings L.J. 511 (1997), 95
Minow, Martha, Making All the Difference (1990), 52
Minow, Martha, The Supreme Court, 1986 Term — Foreword: Justice Engendered, 101 Harv. L. Rev. 10
    (1987), 458
Moberly, Michael D., Bad News for Those Proclaiming the Goods News?: The Employer's Ambiguous Duty
    to Accommodate Religious Proselytizing, 42 Santa Clara L. Rev. 1 (2001), 599
Moberly, Michael D., Reconsidering the Impact of Reasonable Cause Determinations in the Ninth Circuit,
    24 Pepp. L. Rev. 37 (1996), 920
Moohr, Geraldine Szott, Arbitration and the Goals of Employment Discrimination Law, 56 Wash. & Lee 395
    (1999), 883
Moore, Michael J. & W. Kip Viscusi, Compensation Mechanisms for Job Risks: Wages, Workers' Compensa-
    tion, and Product Liability (1990), 7

Posner, Norman S., Arbitration: Judicial Review of Arbitration Awards: Manifest Disregard of the Law, 64
    Brook. L. Rev. 471 (1998), 883
Posner, Richard A., Economic Analysis of Law (2d ed. 1977), 44
Posner, Richard A., The Efficiency & the Efficacy of Title VII, 136 U. Pa. L. Rev. 513 (1987), 339
Post, Robert C., Between Governance and Management: The History and Theory of the Public Forum, 34
    UCLA L. Rev. 1713 (1987), 12
Post, Robert, Prejudicial Appearances: The Logic of American Anti-Discrimination Law, 88 Cal. L. Rev. 1
    (2000), 302
Pratt, Richard J., Unilateral Modification of Employment Handbooks: Further Encroachments on the Em-
    ployment-at-Will Doctrine, 139 U. Pa. L. Rev. 197 (1990), 17

Quigley, William P., "A Fair Day's Pay for a Fair Day's Work": Time to Raise and Index the Minimum Wage, 27
    St. Mary's L.J. 513 (1996), 9

Radford, Mary F., By Invitation Only: The Proof of Welcomeness in Sexual Harassment Cases, 72 N.C. L.
    Rev. 499 (1994), 505-06
Radford, Mary F., Sex Stereotyping and the Promotion of Women to Positions of Power, 41 Hast. L.J. 471
    (1990), 84
Rahdert, Mark C., Arline's Ghost: Some Notes on Working as a Major Life Activity Under the ADA, 9 Temp.
    Pol. & Civ. Rts. 303 (2000), 719
Ray, Douglas E., Title VII Retaliation Cases: Creating a New Protected Class, 58 U. Pitt. L. Rev. 405 (1997),
    657
Reinsmith, Laina Rose, Note, Proving an Employer's Intent: Disparate Treatment Discrimination and the
    Stray Remarks Doctrine After Reeves v. Sanderson Plumbing Products, 55 Vand. L. Rev. 219 (2002), 151
Rhode, Deborah L., Justice and Gender: Sex Discrimination and the Law (1989), 52
Rhode, Deborah L., The "No-Problem" Problem: Feminist Challenges and Cultural Change, 100 Yale L.J.
    1731 (1991), 84
Rigler, Jane, Analysis and Understanding of the Family and Medical Leave Act of 1993, 45 Case W. Res. L.
    Rev. 457 (1995), 822
Rigler, Jane, Title VII and the Applicability of Disparate Impact Analysis to Subjective Selection Criteria, 88
    W. Va. L. Rev. 25 (1995), 428
Riley, Suzanne E., Comment, Employees' Retaliation Claims Under 42 U.S.C. §1981: Ramifications of the
    Civil Rights Act of 1991, 79 Marq. L. Rev. 579 (1996), 637
Rosen, David N. & Jonathan M. Freiman, Remodeling McDonnell Douglas: Fisher v. Vassar College and the
    Structure of Employment Discrimination Law, 17 Quinnipiac L. Rev. 725 (1998), 145
Rosen, Gerald E., Title VII Classes and Due Process: To (b)(2) or (b)(3), 26 Wayne L. Rev. 919 (1980), 912
Rosenthal, Lawrence, Permissible Content Discrimination Under the First Amendment: The Strange Case of
    the Public Employee, 25 Hastings Const. L.Q. 529 (1998), 11
Rothstein, Mark A., et al., Employment Law (2d ed. 1999), 4
Rothstein, Mark A., Genetic Discrimination in Employment and the Americans with Disabilities Act, 29
    Hous. L. Rev. 23 (1992), 689
Rothstein, Mark A., Occupational Safety and Health Law (3d ed. 1990), 7
Rubenfeld, Jed, The Anti-Antidiscrimination Agenda, 111 Yale L.J. 1141 (2002), 314, 572
Rubenstein, William B., Do Gay Rights Laws Matter?: An Empirical Assessment, 75 S. Cal. L. Rev. 65 (2001),
    557
Rutherford, Jane, Equality as the Primary Constitutional Value: The Case for Applying Employment Discrim-
    ination Laws to Religion, 81 Cornell L. Rev. 1049 (1996), 603
Rutherglen, George, Abolition in a Different Voice, 78 Va. L. Rev. 1463 (1992), 71
Rutherglen, George, Better Late Than Never: Notice and Opt-Out at the Settlement Stage of Class Actions, 71
    N.Y.U. L. Rev. 1258 (1996), 912
Rutherglen, George, From Race to Age: The Expanding Scope of Employment Discrimination Laws, 24 J.
    Leg. Stud. 491 (1995), 63
Rutherglen, George, Notice, Scope and Preclusion in Title VII Class Actions, 69 Va. L. Rev. 11 (1983), 910,
    912
Rutherglen, George, Title VII Class Actions, 47 U. Chi. L. Rev. 688 (1980), 907

Samahon, Tuan N., The Religion Clauses and Political Asylum: Religious Persecution Claims and the Reli-
    gious Membership-Conversion Imposter Problem, 88 Geo. L.J. 2211 (2000), 587
Scaperlanda, Michael, Partial Membership: Aliens and the Constitutional Community, 81 Iowa L. Rev. 707
    (1996), 633
Scaperlanda, Michael, The Paradox of a Title: Discrimination Within the Antidiscrimination Provisions of the
    Immigration Reform and Control Act of 1986, 1988 Wis. L. Rev. 1043 (1988), 633, 634
Schatzki, George, United Steelworkers of America v. Weber: An Exercise in Understandable Indecision, 56
    Wash. L. Rev. 51 (1980), 70, 298
Schmedemann, Deborah A. & Judi McLean Parks, Contract Formation and Employee Handbooks: Legal,
    Psychological and Empirical Analyses, 29 Wake Forest L. Rev. 647 (1994), 17

Schmedemann, Deborah A., Of Meetings and Mailboxes: The First Amendment and Exclusive Representation in Public Sector Labor Relations, 72 Va. L. Rev. 91 (1986), 12

Schoen, Rodric B., *Pickering* Plus Thirty Years: Public Employees and Free Speech, 30 Tex. Tech L. Rev. 5 (1999), 11

Schoenheider, Krista J., A Theory of Tort Liability for Sexual Harassment in the Workplace, 134 U. Pa. L. Rev. 1461 (1986), 540

Schuck, Peter H., Affirmative Action: Past, Present, and Future, 20 Yale L. & Poly. 1 (2002), 319

Schultz, Vicki, Reconceptualizing Sexual Harassment, 107 Yale L.J. 1683 (1998), 497-98

Schultz, Vicki, Telling Stories About Women and Work: Judicial Interpretations of Sex Segregation in the Workplace in Title VII Cases Raising the Lack of Interest Argument, 103 Harv. L. Rev. 1749 (1990), 44, 64, 257, 261

Schwab, Stewart, Life-Cycle Justice: Accommodating Just Cause and Employment-At-Will, 92 Mich. L. Rev. 8 (1993), 95

Schwartz, David S., When Is Sex Because of Sex? The Causation Problem In Sexual Harassment Law, 150 U. Pa. L. Rev. 1697 (2002), 495

Scott, Joan W., Deconstructing Equality-Versus-Difference: On the Uses of Poststructural Theory for Feminism, 14 Feminist Stud. 33 (1958), 457

Seaquist, Gwen & Eileen Kelly, Faculty Dismissal Because of Enrollment Declines, 28 J.L. & Educ. 193 (1999), 10

Selig, Joel L., Affirmative Action in Employment After *Croson* and *Martin*: The Legacy Remains Intact, 63 Temp. L. Rev. 1 (1990), 936

Selmi, Michael, Discrimination as Accident: Old Whine, New Bottles, 74 Ind. L.J. 1234, (1999), 85

Selmi, Michael, Family Leave and the Gender Wage Gap, 78 N.C. L. Rev. 707 (2000), 485

Selmi, Michael, The Value of the EEOC: The Agency's Role in Employment Discrimination Law, 57 Ohio St. L.J. 1 (1996), 915

Selmi, Michael, Why Are Employment Discrimination Cases So Hard to Win?, 61 La. L. Rev. 555 (2001), 148

Shapiro, Sidney A. & Thomas O. McGarity, Reorienting OSHA: Regulatory Alternatives and Legislative Reform, 6 Yale J. on Reg. 1 (1989), 7

Sharpe, Calvin William, Integrity Review of Statutory Arbitration Awards, 54 Hastings L. Rev. ___ (2001), 883

Shell, G. Richard, ERISA and Other Federal Employment Statutes: When Is Commercial Arbitration an "Adequate Substitute" for the Courts?, 68 Tex. L. Rev. 509 (1990), 880

Sherwyn, David, Michael Heise & Zev J. Eigen, Don't Train Your Employees and Cancel Your "1-800" Harassment Hotline: An Empirical Examination of the Flaws in the Affirmative Defense to Sexual Harassment Charges, 69 Fordham L. Rev. 1265 (2001), 534

Shestowsky, Donna, Note, Where Is the Common Knowledge? Empirical Support for Requiring Expert Testimony in Sexual Harassment Trials, 51 Stan. L. Rev. 357 (1999), 511

Shively, Scott, Resurgence of the Class Action Lawsuit in Employment Discrimination Cases: New Obstacles Presented by the 1991 Amendments to the Civil Rights Act, 23 U. Ark. Little Rock L. Rev. 925 (2001), 912

Shoben, Elaine, Differential Pass-Fail Rates in Employment Testing: Statistical Proof Under Title VII, 91 Harv. L. Rev. 793 (1978), 369

Shockley, William, Dysgenics, Geneticity and Raceology: A Challenge to the Intellectual Responsibility of Educators, 72 Phi Delta Kappan 297 (1972), 458

Siegel, Reva B., Discrimination in the Eyes of the Law: How "Color Blindness" Discourse Disrupts and Rationalizes Social Stratification, 88 Cal. L. Rev. 77 (2000), 303

Silver, Isadore, Public Employee Discharge & Discipline (1989), 10

Silver, Marjorie A., The Uses and Abuses of Informal Procedures in Federal Civil Rights Enforcement, 55 Geo. Wash. L. Rev. 482 (1987), 936

Silverstein, Eileen, From Statute to Contract: The Law of the Employment Relationship Reconsidered, 18 Hofstra Lab. & Emp. L.J. 479 (2001), 671, 882

Sloan, Jacqueline H., Extending Rape Shield Protection to Sexual Harassment Actions: New Federal Rule of Evidence 412 Undermines *Meritor Savings Bank v. Vinson*, 25 Sw. U. L. Rev. 363 (1969), 491

Solove, Daniel J., Information Privacy Law (2003), 13,14

Spahn, Elizabeth K., Resurrecting the Spurious Class: Opting-In to the Age Discrimination in Employment Act and the Equal Pay Act Through the Fair Labor Standards Act, 71 Geo. L.J. 119 (1982), 904

Spieler, Emily A., Perpetuating Risk? Workers' Compensation and the Persistence of Occupational Injuries, 31 Hous. L. Rev. 119 (1994), 7

Spiropoulous, Andrew C., Defining the Business Necessity Defense to the Disparate Impact Cause of Action: Finding the Golden Mean, 74 N.C. L. Rev. 1479 (1996), 393

Sprang, Kenneth A., Beware the Toothless Tiger: A Critique of the Model Employment Termination Act, 43 Am. U. L. Rev. 849 (1994), 26

St. Antoine, Theodore J., Employment-At-Will — Is the Model Act the Answer?, 23 Stetson L. Rev. 179 (1993), 27

Steinberg, Terry Nicole, Rival Union Access to Public Employees: A New First Amendment Balancing Test, 2 Geo. Mason Ind. L. Rev. 361 (1994), 12

Storrow, Richard F., Same-Sex Sexual Harassment Claims After *Oncale*: Defining the Boundaries of Actionable Conduct, 47 Am. U. L. Rev. 677 (1998), 497

# INDEX